This book is due for return not later than the last date stamped below, unless recalled sooner.

International Territorial Administration

How Trusteeship and the Civilizing
Mission Never Went Away

RALPH WILDE

OXFORD

UNIVERSITY PRESS

OXFORD

UNIVERSITY PRESS

Great Clarendon Street, Oxford OX2 6DP

Oxford University Press is a department of the University of Oxford.
It furthers the University's objective of excellence in research, scholarship,
and education by publishing worldwide in

Oxford New York

Auckland Cape Town Dar es Salaam Hong Kong Karachi
Kuala Lumpur Madrid Melbourne Mexico City Nairobi
New Delhi Shanghai Taipei Toronto

With offices in

Argentina Austria Brazil Chile Czech Republic France Greece
Guatemala Hungary Italy Japan Poland Portugal Singapore
South Korea Switzerland Thailand Turkey Ukraine Vietnam

Oxford is a registered trade mark of Oxford University Press
in the UK and in certain other countries

Published in the United States
by Oxford University Press Inc., New York

© Ralph Wilde, 2008

British Library Cataloguing in Publication Data

Data available

Library of Congress Cataloging in Publication Data

Data available

Typeset by Newgen Imaging Systems (P) Ltd., Chennai, India
Printed in Great Britain
on acid-free paper by
Anthony Rowe Ltd, Chippenham

ISBN 978–0–19–927432–1
ISBN 978–0–19–957789–7 (pbk.)

1 3 5 7 9 10 8 6 4 2

for my parents

Preface

In 1997, I worked as a volunteer in the Dadaab refugee camps run by the United Nations High Commissioner for Refugees (UNHCR) in the north-east of Kenya. My job was to run a project monitoring the human rights of women living in the camps, write a report about this based on interviews with the women, and train women leaders in the basics of international human rights law. Two years later, in 1999, I went to Mostar in Bosnia and Herzegovina to visit my friend Jane Alexander who worked for an international entity called the 'Office of the High Representative' (OHR) which enjoyed quasi-governmental powers in the country. Nearby, in Kosovo, plans were afoot to introduce what became the United Nations Interim Administration Mission in Kosovo (UNMIK), and I was offered a job by the OSCE in that organization's mission within the new UN operation.

In the Kenyan refugee camps, I had experienced fulfilment in performing what I saw as the worthwhile enterprise of promoting the rights of refugee women using the tools of international human rights law. The OSCE job in Kosovo appealed in a similar fashion, offering the opportunity to play a part in the ambitious enterprise of inculcating standards of democracy and the rule of law through direct international intervention. The international law I had been studying up to that point could now be put into practice.

What had also struck me in Kenya and during the trip to Bosnia and Herzegovina, however, was the way the activities of UNHCR and OHR were largely unknown beyond those places, yet involved considerable authority being exercised directly over territorial units and their populations in a manner that was subject to little, if any, third-party scrutiny. My humanitarian desire to bring human rights to the women of the Kenyan refugee camps and later the Kosovar Albanians was joined by a humanitarian concern at the exercise of power over individuals in an unaccountable fashion. My first academic publication, a journal article written after the Kenya experience, encapsulated these two impulses, explaining the poor state of women's rights in the camps and advocating the application of international human rights law to the activities of UNHCR. I decided in 1999 to expand on this and commence Ph.D. studies focusing on the administration of territory by international organizations, an activity which soon spread from Kosovo to East Timor with the creation of the administration mission there.

I figured I could cast light on activities which were either largely ignored—UNHCR refugee camp administration and the activities of OHR in Bosnia and Herzegovina—or new, as was the case with the UN administrations in Kosovo and East Timor. I also thought I could use whatever understanding of international law I possessed to establish why and how the relevant areas of international law—notably international human rights law—might be applied and enforced in order to bring about greater accountability.

It soon became clear that, in many cases, commentators and people directly involved in Kosovo and East Timor regarded the missions as unique and unprecedented; the enterprise in play became known as 'post-conflict reconstruction'; and the main focus for analysis became the issue of how to make the missions more effective. I struggled to reconcile these notions with the ideas I came up with in my own research. The numerous historical instances of territorial administration by international organizations from the creation of the League of Nations onwards rendered the 'unique' position of the Kosovo and East Timor missions difficult to sustain. The fact that the East Timor mission had been conceived before the post-consultation violence that led to the destruction of infrastructure in the territory rendered the 'post-conflict reconstruction' label an explanation for the challenges faced by the mission, not an original explanation for the mission itself. The remarkably ambitious enterprise of political and economic transformation being attempted in the missions called into question the accuracy and political legitimacy of understanding the challenges raised by the missions in overwhelmingly technocratic terms.

The objective of my doctoral dissertation and, initially, that of the resulting book, was to counter the dominant representations of the Kosovo and East Timor projects, providing an alternative explanation for their purposes considered alongside the purposes of other projects involving the same activity, both contemporary, such as UNHCR refugee camp administration and OHR in Bosnia and Herzegovina, and in the past. However, at what I thought was the final stage of completing the book, I remembered the observation of one of my doctoral examiners, Dr Roger O'Keefe, that the analysis of comparisons with colonialism and the League Mandate and United Nations Trusteeship systems provided in the doctoral dissertation had been somewhat cursory. I decided to do some further work to remedy this deficiency. I thought it might take me a couple of weeks and add a few more pages to the book.

In the event, I uncovered a broader set of ideas that were of fundamental significance to understanding international territorial administration. This analysis and the conclusions I drew from it—that a general concept of 'trusteeship' exists in international law and public policy, running through colonialism, the Mandate and Trusteeship systems and 'occupation', and continuing today in the internationalized form of international territorial administration—transformed the book into a larger work now including that general concept. I had been quick to identify the limitations of others' approaches to international territorial administration, but in my own work had given only superficial treatment to what I now regard to be a fundamental feature of the historical and ideological backdrop to it.

Some of the questions raised about the legitimacy of international territorial administration when it is situated in this broader framework are of a more elemental nature that the issues of accountability that first struck me in the refugee camps. Indeed, the fundamental need to question the very idea of foreign domination places the legitimacy of my work in the camps, and the humanitarian impulses that lay behind it, into question. In 1997 I had thought that being a humanitarian meant saving African women from the oppression of African men, and that the primary humanitarian reaction to the administration of refugee camps by UNHCR should be to call for greater accountability. In failing properly to interrogate whether the relationship of domination between UNCHR and myself, on the one hand, and the people in the camps, on the other, was itself legitimate, I never considered fully whether my own actions were justified, nor did I adequately appreciate that in targeting my critical appraisal on the question of the accountability of UNHCR exclusively, I was, perhaps, missing the point.

I think this happened because I did not have the benefit of the insight that I came to after my reading on trusteeship in international law and policy: the connection between the humanitarianism of 'internationals' today and the humanitarianism of colonial administrators a century ago. That this would be the case for someone born and raised in the United Kingdom and the fortunate beneficiary of considerable educational privileges is perhaps testament to the curious lack of a general acknowledgement of, and awareness about, the significance of colonialism, both historically and in terms of its enduring legacies, in that country.

Acknowledgments

One of the privileges of working in the field of international law is the opportunity to collaborate with outstanding, gifted colleagues. I had the great fortune to begin my education in international law at LSE with Rosalyn Higgins, whose inspirational teaching led me to my vocation. Her constant and generous support and encouragement since then have been invaluable, and her example of excellence and integrity is something to which I will always aspire. As if being introduced to international law by Rosalyn Higgins was not enough, at LSE I was also lucky enough to benefit from the insightful and authoritative teaching of Daniel Bethlehem and Peter Duffy. At Yale Law School, Michael Reisman kindly took me under his wing, and the tremendously rewarding experience of being his student, research assistant, and co-author taught me a great deal. To then go on to study at Cambridge under Christine Gray, Vaughan Lowe, and Susan Marks was an immense privilege for which I will always be grateful. James Crawford was everything one could want in a doctoral supervisor; his constant provision of acutely insightful, constructive feedback was hugely beneficial, and the privilege of having a three-year-long period of regular intellectual interaction with him an educational experience of great worth.

I have benefited immeasurably from the privilege of collaborating, in various ways, with some of the most gifted scholars and practitioners of international law and international relations. In addition to the people mentioned above, the experience of working with Obi Aginam, Dapo Akande, Philip Allott, José Alvarez, Mária Aristodemou, William Bain, Asli Bali, Nathaniel Berman, Daniel Bethlehem, Pierre Bodeau, Doris Buss, Basak Çali, Simon Chesterman, Richard Caplan, Jonathan Charney, Hilary Charlesworth, Christine Chinkin, Jean-Marc Coicaud, Hans Corell, Matthew Craven, Robert Cryer, Jean d'Aspremont, Barbara Delcourt, Catriona Drew, Karen Engle, Greg Fox, Thomas Franck, Peter Galbraith, Charles Gomes, Vera Gowlland-Debbas, Christopher Greenwood, Aeyal Gross, Françoise Hampson, David Harris, James Hathaway, Erica Harper, Florian Hoffman, Agnés Hurwitz, Ian Johnstone, David Kennedy, Helen Kinsella, Dirk Klaasen, Jann Kleffner, Natalie Klein, Outi Korhonen, Karen Knop, Riika Koskenmaki, Steven Krasner, Nico Krisch, Robert McCorquodale, Fréderic Mégrét, Jonathan Morrow, Vasuki Nesiah, Roger O'Keefe, Anne Orford, Dianne Otto, Michael Pugh, Lavanya Rajamani, Lucy Reed, Eric Remacle, Julie Ringelheim, Anthea Roberts, William Schabas, Jan-Aart Scholte, Nico Schrijver, Iain Scobbie, Amr Shalakany, Gerry Simpson, Thomas Skouteris, Carsten Stahn, Chandra Sriram, Chantal Thomas, Katerina Tsotroudi, Johan van Lamoen, Nuala Mole, Guglielmo Verdirame, Paul Wapner, Colin Warbrick, Nigel White, Chanaka Wickremasinghe,

Elizabeth Wilmshurst, Michael Wood, and Dominik Zaum has been as intellectually rewarding as it has been personally enjoyable. At UCL Laws I have been lucky enough to find myself with supportive and good-humoured international law colleagues; it has been a great pleasure to work with Eileen Denza, Richard Gardiner, Douglas Guilfoyle, Catherine Redgwell, Philippe Sands, and Dan Sarooshi.

At various stages the research that has gone into this book has been financially supported by the UK Arts and Humanities Research Council, the Leverhulme Trust, the British Academy, Trinity College, Cambridge, Cambridge University Law Faculty, and the Academic Council on the United Nations System.

I am grateful to the following people working on some of the missions discussed in this book who helpfully provided me with useful information: Chris Bennett (OHR), Olivier Boonen (OHR), Merce Castells Vicente (OSCE Mission to Bosnia and Herzegovina), Myriam Dessables (UNMIK), Fidelma Donlon (OHR and the State Court of Bosnia and Herzegovina), Martin Garrod (European Union Administration in Mostar and OHR), Chris Harland (OHR), Dženana Hadžiomerović (Office of Human Rights Ombudsman in Bosnia and Herzegovina), Emma Hibling (UNMIK), Nicolas Maziau (Constitutional Court of Bosnia and Herzegovina), Javier Mier (State Court of Bosnia and Herzegovina), Gorana Mlinarević (Constitutional Court of Bosnia and Herzegovina), Bella Gjylbehare Murati (Office of the Kosovo Ombudsperson), Peter Neussl (OHR), Tanja Rakušić-Hadžić (OHR), Boris Sertć (High Judicial and Prosecutorial Council of Bosnia and Herzegovina), and several anonymous officials from the IMIE (International Mission for Iraqi Elections) team and the United Nations Reference Team. I would like to thank Jonathan Prentice and Antonia Potter for their generous hospitality in Dili, and Jane Alexander for hosting me in Mostar and for all the conversations we have had on the subject of this book.

Thanks are also due to colleagues who generously assisted me with particular enquiries: Diamond Ashiagbor, Peter Carey, Alan Dashwood, Eileen Denza, Thomas Grant, Robert McCorquodale, Sally Morphet, Roland Paris, Steven Ratner, Penelope Simons, James Sloan, Chandra Sriram, Bernard Wasserstein, Erika de Wet, Chanaka Wickremasinghe, and Michael Wood. I am grateful for the decision made by officials of the European Union to declassify the Memorandum of Understanding that formed the basis for the EU Administration of Mostar; a copy of this document is deposited in the Squire Law Library at Cambridge University.

I have benefited considerably from being given the opportunity to present the ideas contained in this book, and to obtain valuable feedback on them. My thanks are offered to the organizers of meetings and events at the Academic Council on the United Nations System (ACUNS); the American Branch of the International Law Association; the American Society of International Law; the Asian Society of International Law; the British Branch of the International Law Association; the British International Studies Association; Columbia University; the European

Society of International Law; Glasgow University; the International Association for the Study of Forced Migration; the International Studies Association; the New Approaches to International Law network; the LSE; Nottingham University; Oxford University; the Russian Association of International Law; the South African Branch of the International Law Association; Texas University; the Third World Legal Studies Association; UCL; and Westminster University. I would also like to thank the organizers of the Brussels conference on the Accountability for Human Rights Violations by International Organizations; the Brussels conference 'La guerre d'Irak: prelude d'un nouvel ordre international?'; the Hague Joint Conference on International Law; the Joint conference of the Australia/ New Zealand Association of International Law and the American Society of International Law; the Gender, Sexuality and the Law conference at the University of Keele; the State-Building conference at the University of Limerick; and the Critical Perspectives on Global Governance Conference in Monterrey.

I was fortunate to be a participant in a Summer Workshop on International Organization Studies organized by the American Society of International Law and the Academic Council on the United Nations System, and to be a member of the project on 'Faultlines of Legitimacy in International Law' convened by Hilary Charlesworth and Jean-Marc Coicaud under the auspices of the United Nations University. I am very grateful for these immensely rewarding collaborative experiences, and would like to express my thanks to the organizers for having been included and to the other participants involved for their insightful comments on my work.

As explained in the footnotes, certain parts of this book contain expanded, updated versions of ideas earlier published in journal articles and book chapters. I would like to thank the publishers for permitting this, and for those involved in the refereeing and editorial process for their helpful feedback. I am especially grateful in this regard to the American Journal of International Law and the European Journal of International Law, and the editors and reviewers from these journals who worked on my articles.

At various stages in its development, drafts of this book have been subject to sustained critical scrutiny which has been tremendously beneficial. I am grateful to Roger O'Keefe and Nigel White, my doctoral thesis examiners, who engaged very closely with the dissertation and whose insightful comments and suggestions were of great importance in terms of what has ended up here. Thanks are due to the anonymous reviewers of the book for both supporting its publication and providing helpful appraisals of it. I would also like to thank the students from my courses at UCL and the University of Texas for their helpful feedback and ideas. Catriona Drew was unbelievably generous in reading the book manuscript closely several times. Her acute insights with respect to its content, and keen eye for spotting mistakes, were invaluable, and I cannot thank her enough.

A talented team of research assistants helped me with various discrete avenues of enquiry at several stages; my thanks are offered to Daniel Geron, Edmond

Rhys Jones, Aurel Sari, and Emmanuel Voyiakis. For the main part of my work on this book after completing the doctoral dissertation, I had the good fortune to be assisted by Silvia Borelli, her work with me as a Research Fellow at UCL Laws being supported by the UK Arts and Humanities Research Council. In her talent, knowledge, industry, attention to detail, sense of humour, and willingness to offer frank commentary she provided more than I could have expected in a research assistant, and the book is much better for her involvement in it. I offer my great thanks to Silvia.

John Louth at OUP was far more tolerant of my delays in submission than I could have reasonably expected him to be, and this generosity enabled me to extend the coverage of the book to encompass a sustained treatment of the concept of trusteeship in international law and policy. I am also grateful to his colleague, Geraldine Mangley, for being very helpful during the production process, in particular in allowing me to make so many corrections and additions.

Finally, I owe the greatest debt of gratitude to my parents, Elizabeth and Raymond Wilde, to whom this book is dedicated, for raising me in a supportive and loving environment where I was always encouraged and enabled to make my own choices in life.

All of the powers exercising sovereign rights or influence in the aforesaid territories bind themselves to watch over the preservation of the native tribes, and to care for the improvement of the conditions of their moral and material well-being.

General Act of the Berlin Conference of 1884–85, Chapter I, Article VI

Inadequacy of political, economic, social or educational preparedness should never serve as a pretext for delaying independence.

United Nations General Assembly Resolution
1514 (XV) of 1960, para. 3

Decides to establish...a United Nations Transitional Administration in East Timor (UNTAET), which will be endowed with overall responsibility for the administration of East Timor and will be empowered to exercise all legislative and executive authority, including the administration of justice.

United Nations Security Council Resolution 1272 of 1999, para. 1

Contents—Summary

Contents

Principal Abbreviations and Acronyms

A.C.	Law Reports, Appeal Cases, UK
AJIL	*American Journal of International Law*
AJIL Supp.	*Supplement of the American Journal of International Law*
All E.R.	*All England Law Reports*
ASIL Proc.	*Proceedings of the American Society of International Law*
BiH	Bosnia and Herzegovina
BFSP	*British and Foreign State Papers*
BYIL	*British Yearbook of International Law*
CoE	Council of Europe
CPA	Coalition Provisional Authority
CPC	Commission on Public Corporations (Bosnia and Herzegovina)
CPNM	Commission to Preserve National Monuments (Bosnia and Herzegovina)
CPT	European Committee for the Prevention of Torture
CRPC	Commission for Real Property Claims of Displaced Persons and Refugees in Bosnia and Herzegovina
ECCC	Extraordinary Chambers in the Courts of Cambodia for the Prosecution of Crimes Committed During the Period of Democratic Kampuchea
ECHR	European Convention for the Protection of Human Rights
EHRR	*European Human Rights Reports*
EJIL	*European Journal of International Law*
EU	European Union
EUAM	European Union Administration of Mostar
EUFOR	European Union Forces in Bosnia and Herzegovina
EUSR	European Union Special Representative
ESI	European Stability Institute
ETS	European Treaty Series
FAO	Food and Agriculture Organization of the United Nations
FRY	Federal Republic of Yugoslavia
HJPC	High Judicial and Prosecutorial Council of Bosnia and Herzegovina
HRLJ	*Human Rights Law Journal*
ICC	International Criminal Court
ICCPR	International Covenant on Civil and Political Rights, 16 December 1966
ICESCR	International Covenant on Economic, Social and Cultural Rights, 16 December 1966
ICG	International Crisis Group
ICISS	International Commission on Intervention and State Sovereignty

ICJ Reports	*Reports of the International Court of Justice*
ICLQ	*International & Comparative Law Quarterly*
ICRC	International Committee of the Red Cross
ICTY	International Criminal Tribunal for the Former Yugoslavia
IECI	Independent Electoral Commission of Iraq
IFOR	NATO Implementation Force (Bosnia and Herzegovina)
IISS	International Institute for Strategic Studies
ILC	International Law Commission
ILM	*International Legal Materials*
ILO	International Labour Organization
ILR	*International Law Reports*
IMF	International Monetary Fund
IMIE	International Mission for Iraqi Elections
IPA	International Peace Academy
IRRC	*International Review of the Red Cross*
IST	Iraqi Special Tribunal
JEMB	Joint Electoral Management Body (Afghanistan)
KB	[English] Law Reports, King's Bench Division
KFOR	NATO Kosovo Force
KTA	Kosovo Trust Agency
League Covenant	Covenant of the League of Nations, Versailles, 28 June 1919
LJIL	*Leiden Journal of International Law*
LNTS	League of Nations Treaty Series
MINURSO	United Nations Mission for the Referendum in the Western Sahara
NATO	North Atlantic Treaty Organisation
OAS	Organization of American States
OAU	Organization of African Unity
OCHA	United Nations Office for the Coordination of Humanitarian Affairs
OHR	Office of the High Representative for Bosnia and Herzegovina
OJ	*Official Journal of the European Communities* (since 1 February 2003, *Official Journal of the European Union*)
ONUC	United Nations Operation in the Congo
OSCE	Organization for Security and Co-operation in Europe
OSCE P.C.J.	Organization for Security and Co-operation in Europe, Permanent Council Journal
P.	Law Reports, Probate, Divorce, and Admiralty Division, UK
PCIJ	Permanent Court of International Justice
RCS	Reports of the Canadian Supreme Court
Recueil des Cours	Collected Courses of the Hague Academy of International Law
RS	Republika Srpska
Series A	Official Publications of the European Court of Human Rights, *Series A* (Judgements and Decisions)
S.Ct.	Reports of the US Supreme Court
SCSL	Special Court for Sierra Leone
SCU	Serious Crimes Unit (East Timor)

SFOR	NATO Stabilization Force (Bosnia and Herzegovina)
SFRY	Socialist Federal Republic of Yugoslavia
TRC	Sierra Leone Truth and Reconciliation Commission
UN Charter	Charter of the United Nations, San Francisco, 26 June 1945
UN DPKO	United Nations Department of Peacekeeping Operations
UN GAOR	United Nations, General Assembly, Official Records
UN SCOR	United Nations, Security Council, Official Records
UNAMA	United Nations Assistance Mission in Afghanistan
UNAMET	United Nations Mission in East Timor
UNCC	United Nations Compensation Commission
UNDP	United Nations Development Programme
UNESCO	United Nations Educational, Scientific and Cultural Organization
UNHCHR	Office of the United Nations High Commissioner for Human Rights
UNHCR	Office of the United Nations High Commissioner for Refugees
UNIIIC	United Nations International Independent Investigation Commission for Lebanon
UNIFEM	United Nations Development Fund for Women
UNITAR	United Nations Institute for Training and Research
UNMEE	United Nations Mission in Ethiopia and Eritrea
UNMIK	United Nations Interim Administration Mission in Kosovo
UNMISET	United Nations Mission of Support in East Timor
UNMIT	United Nations Integrated Mission in Timor Leste
UNOSOM II	Second United Nations Operation in Somalia
UNOTIL	United Nations Office in Timor Leste
UNPROFOR	United Nations Protection Force (Bosnia and Herzegovina)
UNRWA	United Nations Relief and Works Agency for Palestine Refugees in the Near East
UNSF	United Nations Security Force (West Irian)
UNTAC	United Nations Transitional Authority in Cambodia
UNTAES	United Nations Transitional Administration for Eastern Slavonia, Baranja, and Western Sirmium
UNTAET	United Nations Transitional Administration in East Timor
UNTAG	United Nations Transitional Assistance Group (Namibia)
UNTEA	United Nations Temporary Executive Authority (West Irian)
UNTS	United Nations Treaty Series
Versailles Peace Treaty	Treaty of Peace between the Allied and Associated Powers and Germany, Versailles, 28 June 1919
WEU	Western European Union
WFP	World Food Programme

List of Tables

Format for Sources, Citations, and Footnotes

All the sources consulted in the preparation of this book, including those sources cited within it, are contained in the 'List of Sources' located at the back before the index. For website citations, the term 'available at' denotes a link leading directly to the source cited; the term 'obtainable from' denotes a general website within which the source can be found.

In each chapter, a full citation for each source is provided when it is first referred to. Subsequent references to the same cite are usually abbreviated, with cross references back to the note containing the original full citation. In the case of the Treaty of Versailles, the League of Nations Covenant, and the United Nations Charter, only abbreviations are used; full citations are contained in the List of Sources. Because of the complicated nature of the inter-relationship between the various agreements and side-letters adopted at the Dayton conference in 1995, full citations of these instruments are contained only in the List of Sources. An explanation of the Dayton instruments and how they will be referred to is provided when they are cited for the first time, in Chapter 1, note 38; subsequent references to one or more of these instruments in the rest of the book include cross-references back to this original explanation.

Part of the content of this book is taken up with explaining in detail the main facts of the arrangements under evaluation, since, in many cases, this has not been done comprehensively before. In order to ensure that the main text is not dominated by factual description, most of the detail is placed in the footnotes, which are used, therefore, not only to include citations for and further elaboration of ideas set out in the main text, but also, in a somewhat unorthodox fashion, to enable significant areas of factual description to be provided in a manner that does not overwhelm the analysis offered in the main text. The index includes references to key notes containing factual information on particular arrangements so that these notes can be easily located.

The content of this book was checked up to the beginning of 2007; certain discrete areas were updated over the course of 2007, and all the weblinks were verified as working in July 2007.

1

A New Field of Analysis

1.1 Introduction

At the turn of the 21st century, the United Nations was engaged in one of its most ambitious field operations ever: the administration of a territorial unit, Kosovo, by the United Nations Interim Administration Mission in Kosovo (UNMIK), operating together with the NATO-led Kosovo Force (KFOR).[1] This operation

[1] See Agreement on the Principles to Move Towards a Resolution of the Kosovo Crisis Presented to the Leadership of the Federal Republic of Yugoslavia by the President of Finland, Martti Ahtisaari, representing the European Union, and Viktor Chernomyrdin, Special Representative of the President of the Russian Federation, 3 June 1999, UN Doc. S/1999/649, Annex (hereinafter 'Kosovo Peace Plan'); SC Res. 1244, 10 June 1999. Under SC Res. 1244, UNMIK was responsible for performing, inter alia, 'basic civilian administrative functions' (ibid., para. 11(b)); '[o]rganizing and overseeing the development of provisional institutions for democratic and autonomous self-government pending a political settlement, including the holding of elections' (ibid., para.11(c)); '[t]ransferring, as these institutions are established, its administrative responsibilities while overseeing and supporting the consolidation of Kosovo's local provisional institutions and other peace-building activities' (ibid., para. 11(d)); and 'maintaining civil law and order, including establishing local police forces and meanwhile through the deployment of international police personnel to serve in Kosovo' (ibid., para. 11(i)). The functions and activities mandated to UNMIK under SC Res. 1244 (ibid.) were divided into four distinct components, referred to as 'Pillars', some of which were operated by other international organizations within the wider scheme of UNMIK and under overall UN control. The original Pillars were Pillar I on Humanitarian Assistance, Pillar II on Civil Administration, Pillar III on Democratization and Institution Building, and Pillar IV on Reconstruction and Economic Development. The original Pillar I, which was led by the Office of the United Nations High Commissioner for Refugees (UNHCR), was phased out in June 2000 and a new Pillar I on Police and Justice was established in May 2001. While the United Nations was directly responsible for the activities in Pillars I and II (at the time of writing integrated into the Office of the Special Representative of the Secretary-General as a 'Rule of Law Office' and a 'Department of Civil Administration' respectively), Pillar III was led by the Organization for Security and Co-operation in Europe (OSCE) and Pillar IV (also referred to as the 'EU Pillar') was led by the European Union. On the structure of UNMIK, see <http://www.unmikonline.org/intro.htm>; see also OSCE Permanent Council Decision No. 305, 1 July 1999, in *PC Journal No. 237*, available at <http://www.osce.org/documents/pc/1999/07/2577_en.pdf > (establishing the OSCE Mission in Kosovo); on the EU Pillar, see <http://www.euinkosovo.org/>. Certain activities were conducted by local actors under UN supervision; see, e.g., the transfer of responsibility from the UNMIK Police to the Kosovo Police Service described in UNMIK Civilian Police, *Police Report for 2002: A Year of Transition* (2002), obtainable from <http://www.unmikonline. org>. From 2001, certain public functions were exercised by the locally-composed Provisional Institutions of Self-Government (PISG) comprising an Assembly, the President of Kosovo, the Government, judicial bodies and other institutions. These responsibilities operated under the overall aegis of UNMIK and within the limits set forth by the Constitutional Framework for

began towards the end of 1999 alongside the administration of East Timor by the United Nations Transitional Administration in East Timor (UNTAET), which ran until May 2002, when the territory became an independent state, the Democratic Republic of Timor-Leste, and, unlike UNMIK, was responsible for military matters as well as civil administration.[2] Each involving the assertion of

Self-government established by UNMIK Regulation 2001/9 of 15 May 2001 (obtainable from <http://www.unmikonline.org/regulations/unmikgazette/index.htm>). For commentary on the delegation of certain functions to local actors see, e.g., S Chesterman, *You, The People: The United Nations, Transitional Administrations, and State-Building* (OUP, 2004), ch. 4; B Knoll, 'Beyond the Mission Civilisatrice: The Properties of a Normative Order within an Internationalized Territory', 19 (2006) *LJIL* 275. For an explanation of the original structures and mandate of the mission, see the Report of the Secretary-General on the United Nations Interim Administration Mission in Kosovo, UN Doc. S/1999/779, 12 July 1999 (hereinafter 'Secretary-General Report on Kosovo 1999'). On KFOR, see SC Res. 1244 (ibid.), para. 9; the KFOR website, at <http://www.nato.int/kfor/index.html>; and *Behrami and Behrami v. France & Saramati v. France, Germany and Norway*, Appl. Nos 71412/01 and 78166/01, European Court of Human Rights, Admissibility Decision, 31 May 2007 (obtainable from <http://www.echr.coe.int>). For secondary commentary on UNMIK and KFOR in Kosovo generally, see List of Sources, section 5.1.2, and the relevant parts of the relevant sources in List of Sources, section 5.1.1.

   [2] See Agreement between the Republic of Indonesia and the Portuguese Republic on the Question of East Timor, 5 May 1999, obtainable from <http://www.un.org/peace/etimor99/etimor.htm>, Art. 6 (extracted below in ch. 5, text accompanying n. 154); SC Res. 1272, 25 October 1999; SC Res. 1338, 31 January 2001; SC Res. 1392, 31 January 2002. Under SC Res. 1272 (ibid.), UNTAET was given 'overall responsibility for the administration of East Timor' and 'empowered to exercise all legislative and executive authority, including the administration of justice' (para. 1). This mandate had three components. The first component covered 'governance and public administration', and included an international police force (ibid., para. 3(a)), and the power to 'enact new laws and regulations and to amend, suspend or repeal existing ones' (ibid., para. 6). The second component covered 'humanitarian assistance and emergency rehabilitation' (ibid., para. 3(b)); the third component covered military and security matters (ibid., para. 3(c)). Soon after the commencement of UNTAET's mandate, a National Consultative Council (NCC) was created, consisting of 11 Timorese and four UNTAET members, all appointed by the Transitional Administrator, charged with making 'policy recommendation on significant executive and legislative matters'; see UNTAET Regulation 1999/2, 2 December 1999 (quotation from section 2). In summer 2000, following complaints by the local population as to the slow speed of improvements in East Timor and calls for greater involvement in decision-making, UNTAET created new structures to enhance local participation in the legislative and executive spheres (source for these reasons: author interviews with local representatives and UNTAET officials during a visit to East Timor at the time; see also the preambles to UNTAET Regulation 2000/23, 14 July 2000, and UNTAET Regulation 2000/24, 14 July 2000). The NCC was replaced by a National Council, established 'to act as a forum for all legislative matters related to the exercise of the legislative authority of the Transitional Administrator' (ibid., section 1; for its powers, see ibid., section 2). The National Council was composed of 33 representatives of East Timorese civil society organizations appointed by the Transitional Administrator after consultation with local groups (see ibid., section 3). On the executive side, a Cabinet of the 'UNTAET Transitional Government' was created (see generally UNTAET Regulation 2000/23, ibid., and, for the powers of the Cabinet, see ibid., section 4); its members were appointed by the Transitional Administrator after consulting local groups (ibid., section 2), and were accountable to the Transitional Administrator, who was also the Chair of the Cabinet (ibid., section 5.1). The Cabinet comprised four Timorese nationals and four international members (see UNTAET Daily Briefing, 17 July 2000). In August 2000, the UNTAET Transitional Government was re-named the East Timor Transitional Administration (ETTA) and

plenary administration by the United Nations,[3] and taking place after high-profile events—the NATO bombing of what was then called the Federal Republic of Yugoslavia (FRY)[4] and the violence by pro-Indonesian militias following the result of a 'popular consultation' on East Timor's future status carried out by

UNTAET's pillar of governance and public administration was dissolved (see UNTAET Daily Briefing, 8 August 2000). In August 2001, these arrangements were altered again. The National Council was replaced as the legislature by a popularly elected Constituent Assembly given the mandate to draft the constitution for an independent East Timor and to continue to serve as the legislature in the immediate post-independence period (see UNTAET Regulation 2001/2, 16 March 2001); on the arrangements for its election, see ch. 2, text accompanying n. 120 *et seq*. The Cabinet was replaced by an entirely Timorese Council of Ministers of the 'Second Transitional Government', which was appointed by the Transitional Administrator on 20 September 2001 (see UNTAET Regulation 2001/28, 19 September 2001, and UNTAET Daily Briefing, 20 September 2001). From this time, the ETTA became known as the East Timor Public Administration (ETPA) (see, e.g., UNTAET Press Office, 'Fact Sheet 3', April 2002). The text of the UNTAET documents is obtainable from <http://www.un.org/peace/etimor/untaetN.htm>. For secondary commentary on UNTAET, see the works in the List of Sources, section 5.1.3, and the relevant parts of the relevant sources, ibid., section 5.1.1. East Timor declared itself an independent state on 20 May 2002 (see 'Council endorses proposal to declare East Timor's independence 20 May 2002', UN Press release SC/7192, 31 October 2001), and was admitted as a Member State of the United Nations on 27 September 2002 (see GA Res. 57/3, 27 September 2002; SC Res. 1414, 23 May 2002). For discussion of the status of East Timor during the period 1999–2002, see ch. 5, section 5.7, below. The official name used internationally for the state comes from the Portuguese name República Democrática de Timor-Leste; the name in the other main locally-used language, Tetum, is the Repúblika Demokrátika Timor Lorosa'e. As this book concerns the territory before independence and the official adoption of a name by representatives of East Timorese, the English version of the name, 'East Timor', used at the United Nations during the UNTAET period, is adopted when the period is being discussed (this version was usually the main formulation used by UNTAET itself, although, as the stamps on the front cover of this book indicate, in some instances the versions in other languages were used).

    [3] As for the assertion of plenary authority, see, e.g., UNMIK Regulation 1999/1 (as amended), contained in UNMIK Regulation 2000/54, 27 September 2000, obtainable from <http://www.unmikonline.org/regulations/unmikgazette/index.htm>; SC Res. 1272 (above n. 2), preamble, para. 1; UNTAET Regulation 1999/1, 27 November 1999, obtainable from <http://www.un.org/peace/etimor/untaetN.htm>.
    [4] On the background to the introduction of UNMIK in Kosovo, including the NATO bombing campaign (on which the literature is voluminous), see, e.g., Independent International Commission on Kosovo, *Kosovo Report* (OUP, 2000) and sources cited therein at 364–6; M Weller (ed.), *The Crisis in Kosovo 1989–1999: From the Dissolution of Yugoslavia to Rambouillet and the Outbreak of Hostilities* (CUP, 1999); PE Auerswald and DP Auerswald (eds), *The Kosovo Conflict: A Diplomatic History Through Documents* (Kluwer Law International, 2000); International Crisis Group, *Kosovo Report: Conflict, International Response* (OUP, 2000); A Schnabel and R Thakur (eds), *Kosovo and the Challenge of Humanitarian Intervention: Selective Indignation, Collective Action, and International Citizenship* (UN University Press, 2000); H Krieger (ed.), *The Kosovo Conflict and International Law: An Analytical Documentation 1974–1999* (CUP, 2001); C Tomuschat (ed.), *Kosovo and the International Community: A Legal Assessment* (Kluwer Law International, 2002); A Orford, *Reading Humanitarian Intervention: Human Rights and the Use of Force in International Law* (CUP, 2003); M Weller, 'International Law and Chaos', 52 (1993) *Cambridge Law Journal* 6; M Guillaume, G Marhic and G Etienne, 'Le cadre juridique de l'action de la KFOR au Kosovo', 1999 *Annuaire Français de Droit International* 308; J Ringelheim, 'Considerations on the International Reaction to the Kosovo Crisis', (1999) *Revue belge de droit international* 475; M Hadzic, 'Kosovo and the Security Stabilization of South-East Europe', 7:2 (2000) *International Peacekeeping* 83;

the United Nations Mission in East Timor (UNAMET)[5]—these two missions brought to prominence an activity that had not previously been subject to sustained critical analysis in its own right.

Certain commentators had discussed particular historical administration projects (e.g., John Czerapowicz's doctoral dissertation on Leticia and West Irian).[6] Others had considered some older administration projects in general surveys of UN peace operations[7] and studies of the powers of international organizations.[8] Méir Ydit had discussed territorial administration by international organizations alongside certain other arrangements involving territorial administration by individual states (including protectorates and Mandated and Trust territories), but as a corollary to what he considered to be the vesting of sovereignty, in the sense of legal title, over these territories in the actors exercising

J Solana, 'NATO's Success in Kosovo', 78:6 (Nov/Dec 1999) *Foreign Affairs* 114; M Hadzic, 'Kosovo and the Security Stabilization of South-East Europe', 7:2 (2000) *International Peacekeeping* 83; SA Cooper, 'Air Power and the Coercive Use of Force', 24 (2001) *Washington Quarterly* 81; TW Crawford, 'Pivotal Deterrence and the Kosovo War: Why the Holbrooke Agreement Failed', 116 (2001–02) *Political Science Quarterly* 499; PC Forage, 'Bombs for Peace: A Comparative Study of the Use of Air Power in the Balkans', 28 (2002) *Armed Forces & Society* 211; K Naumann, 'NATO, Kosovo, and Military Intervention', 8 (2002) *Global Governance* 13.

    [5] On the 'popular consultation' in East Timor, see the Agreement between the Republic of Indonesia and the Portuguese Republic on the Question of East Timor (above n. 2); Agreement between the Governments of Indonesia and Portugal and the United Nations Regarding the Modalities for the Popular Consultation of the East Timorese through a Direct Ballot, 5 May 1999, and Agreement between the Governments of Indonesia and Portugal and the United Nations on Security, 5 May 1999 (both obtainable from <http://www.un.org/peace/etimor99/etimor.htm>); SC Res. 1246, 11 June 1999; Letter from the UN Secretary-General to the President of the Security Council Regarding the Result of the Popular Consultation, 3 September 1999, UN Doc. S/1999/944 (1999); Progress Report of the Secretary-General on the Question of East Timor, 13 December 1999, UN Doc. A/54/654 (1999). On UNAMET in particular, see SC Res. 1246 (ibid.) and SC Res. 1257, 3 August 1999. For academic commentary, see the contributions in 4:2 (1999) *Human Rights Law Review*, special issue on 'East Timor in Transition: Sovereignty, Self-Determination and Human Rights'; I Martin, *Self-Determination in East Timor: The United Nations, the Ballot, and International Intervention* (International Peace Academy Occasional Paper, Lynne Rienner, 2001); Orford (above n. 4), *passim*; D Emmerson, 'Moralpolitik: The Timor Test' (Winter 1999/2000) *The National Interest* 63, *passim*; C Schreuer, 'East Timor and the United Nations', 2 (2000) *International Law Forum* 18. See also below, ch. 5, text accompanying n. 145 *et seq*; on the violent aftermath in particular, see below, ch. 6, n. 62.

    [6] JV Czerapowicz, *International Territorial Authority: Leticia and West New Guinea* (1972, unpublished Ph.D. dissertation, Indiana University, on file with the author).

    [7] See, for example, D Bowett, *United Nations Forces: A Legal Study* (Stevens and Sons, 1964); R Higgins, *United Nations Peacekeeping, Vol. 2, Asia 1946–1967* (OUP, 1970); R Higgins, *United Nations Peacekeeping, Vol. 3, Africa 1946–1967* (OUP, 1980); SR Ratner, *The New UN Peacekeeping, Building Peace in Lands of Conflict after the Cold War* (St. Martin's Press, 1995).

    [8] See H Kelsen, *The Law of the United Nations* (Stevens & Sons, 1951), 195–7 n. 7 and 684–8; E Lauterpacht, 'The Contemporary Practice of the United Kingdom in the Field of International Law—Survey and Comment', 5 (1956) *ICLQ* 405, 409–13; I Sagay, *The Legal Aspects of the Namibian Dispute* (University of Ife Press, 1975), 270–1; I Brownlie, *Principles of Public International Law* (6th edn, OUP, 2003), 167; F Seyersted, 'United Nations Forces, Some Legal Problems', 37 (1962) *BYIL* 351, 451–3; JW Halderman, 'United Nations Territorial Administration and the Development of the Charter', 70 (1964) *Duke Law Journal* 95; G Marston, 'UK Materials on International Law 1982', 53 (1982) *BYIL* 391–3 (containing a government statement rather than the view of a commentator).

administrative control.[9] Only with the Kosovo and East Timor projects was the idea of international organizations (or at least the United Nations) administering territorial units other than their headquarters areas considered as a distinct focus for analysis.[10]

For the first time in UN peacekeeping reports, the Brahimi Report of 2000 on the future of UN peace operations devoted a section to what it called 'transitional civil administration'.[11] Given which missions are discussed in that section, this term would seem to be used to denote plenary UN administration projects. In the section, the Report posed but did not explore the 'larger question of whether the United Nations should be in this business [territorial administration] at all'.[12] From the context in which the remark was made—a discussion of the 'challenges and responsibilities that are unique among United Nations field operations' because of their practical scale—the concern seemed to be focused on the capacity and competence of the UN to carry out territorial administration.[13]

A technocratic focus of appraisal of the Kosovo and East Timor projects has predominated in much of the commentary on the recent administration projects by the news media, officials involved in the projects, and some in the academy.[14] As Martti Koskenniemi remarks, 'the international administration of territory is often discussed as if it involved merely problems of technical governance'.[15]

---

[9] M Ydit, *Internationalised Territories from the 'Free City of Cracow' to the 'Free City of Berlin'* (Sythoff, 1961). For other studies at that time adopting a similarly broader focus than territorial administration by international organizations exclusively, see, e.g., A Marazzi, *I territori internazionalizzati* (Giappichelli, 1959); R Beck, *Die Internationalisierung von territorien: Darstellung und rechtliche Analyse* (Kohlhammer, 1962).

[10] On the administration of headquarters areas, see, e.g., the Agreement Between the United Nations and the United States Regarding the Headquarters of the United Nations, signed 26 June 1947, approved by the General Assembly 31 October 1947, 11 UNTS 18; Seyersted (above n. 8), 451 n. 5. For recent academic commentary on territorial administration by international organizations in particular, covering the East Timor and Kosovo missions and, in some cases, other such administration missions, see the more recent entries in the List of Sources, section 5.1.1. For commentary on either the Kosovo or the East Timor mission exclusively, see the works in the List of Sources, sections 5.1.2 and 5.1.3 respectively.

[11] Panel on United Nations Peace Operations, Report to the United Nations Secretary-General, 21 August 2000, UN Doc. A/55/305-S/2000/809 (hereinafter 'Brahimi Report'), section H, from para. 76. Compare, for example, UN Secretary-General, Agenda for Peace: Preventative Diplomacy, Peacemaking and Peacekeeping, 17 June 1992, UN Doc A/47/277-S/24111; UN Secretary-General, Supplement to Agenda for Peace: Position Paper of the Secretary General on the Occasion of the Fiftieth Anniversary of the United Nations, 3 January 1995, UN Doc. A/50/60-S/1995/1.

[12] Brahimi Report (above n. 11), para. 78.

[13] Ibid., section H.

[14] See, e.g., the works in the List of Sources, section 5.2.1. On international officials' need for new skills and experience, see also Brahimi Report (above n. 11), para. 77.

[15] M Koskenniemi, 'Foreword', in O Korhonen and J Gras, *International Governance in Post-Conflict Situations* (Erik Castrén Institute Research Report 9/2001, University of Helsinki, 2001), vi (the same quotation appears in O Korhonen, J Gras, and K Creutz, *International Post-Conflict Situations: New Challenges for Co-operative Governance* (Erik Castrén Institute Research Report 18/2006, University of Helsinki, 2006), iii).

So, for example, Ruth Wedgwood questioned the ability of UN bureaucrats to administer territory;[16] one such bureaucrat, Hansjörg Strohmeyer, wrote about the formidable practical challenges involved in the two projects drawing on his first-hand involvement in them.[17]

Others have considered more normative questions, appraising, for example, the particular models of justice adopted by the international administrators,[18] the constitutional structures introduced in the territories,[19] and broader questions of legitimacy, including gender issues.[20] Experts in international law have examined some of the international legal issues raised by the projects, considering, for example, whether (where relevant) the Security Council authorization provided, and the involvement of the UN in the conduct of territorial administration, conform to United Nations law,[21] and how questions of responsibility, applicable law, and domestic jurisdiction are to be determined, impacting on the general issue of accountability.[22] UNMIK in particular, although ostensibly bound at least as a matter of its own Regulations by certain human rights standards,[23] and subject to a degree of third-party review by an independent Ombudsperson,[24] and

---

[16] R Wedgwood, Letter, 'Trouble in Timor', 79:6 (Nov/Dec 2000) *Foreign Affairs* 197 (discussing the East Timor project).

[17] H Strohmeyer, 'Collapse and Reconstruction of a Judicial System: The United Nations Missions in Kosovo and East Timor', 95 (2001) *AJIL* 46.

[18] See the works in the List of Sources, section 5.2.2.

[19] See the works in the List of Sources, section 5.2.3.

[20] See the works in the List of Sources, section 5.2.4 (on questions of legitimacy other than gender) and section 5.2.5 (on gender issues).

[21] See the works in the List of Sources, section 5.2.6.

[22] The works in section 5.2.7 of the List of Sources address differently various aspects of one or more of these issues. See also below, ch. 8, section 8.7.3 and ch. 9, text accompanying n. 36 *et seq.*

[23] See UNMIK Regulation 1999/1, 25 July 1999, section 2; UNMIK Regulation 1999/24, 12 December 1999, sections 1.3 and 1.4 and the revised version of this contained in UNMIK Regulation 2000/59, 27 October 2000 (the text of UNMIK Regulations is obtainable from <http://www.unmikonline.org/regulations/unmikgazette/index.htm>). The UN Secretary-General stated on the commencement of its mandate that UNMIK was to be '…guided by internationally recognized standards of human rights as the basis for the exercise of its authority in Kosovo'; Secretary-General Report on Kosovo 1999 (above n. 1), para. 42.

[24] The Kosovo Ombudsperson Institution was set up by UNMIK in 2000; see UNMIK Regulation No. 2000/38, 30 June 2000. Until 2006, it had 'jurisdiction to receive and investigate complaints from any person or entity in Kosovo concerning human rights violations and actions constituting an abuse of authority by the interim civil administration or any emerging central or local institution' (ibid., section 3.1), and was composed of one Ombudsperson and three Deputy Ombudspersons (ibid., section 6). The Ombudsperson could make recommendations only (ibid., section 4). The office holder, who had to be 'an eminent international figure of high moral character, impartiality and integrity', and could not be a citizen of the Federal Republic of Yugoslavia, a state that was part of the former Yugoslavia, or Albania (ibid., section 6.1), was appointed by the Special Representative of the Secretary-General (ibid., section 6.2). From 2003, at least two of the Deputy Ombudspersons, who were also appointed by the Special Representative of the Secretary-General upon recommendation of the Ombudsperson, had to be 'local' experts (ibid., section 7, as amended by UNMIK Regulation 2003/8). The Institution was 'nationalized' in 2006, with the adoption of UNMIK Regulation 2006/6, which provided that the Ombudsperson Institution be entirely composed of 'habitual residents of Kosovo' and

scrutiny by certain international mechanisms,[25] has come in for considerable criticism both on the grounds of unaccountability in general, and in

all members appointed by the Assembly of Kosovo (UNMIK Regulation 2006/6, 16 February
2006, section 6). The jurisdiction of the Ombudsperson was also limited to complaints 'concerning
violations of international human rights standards as incorporated in the applicable law and acts,
including omissions, which constitute an abuse of authority by the Kosovo Institutions' (ibid.,
section 3.1), the 'Institutions' being the locally-operated Institutions of Self-Government (see
above n. 1), thereby excluding UNMIK itself. Although, in practice, the nationalization was carried out (and was, indeed, already under way before the adoption of Regulation 2006/6), a formal
appointment of the members of the institution in accordance with the regulation had not taken
place at the time of writing. In 2003, a Human Rights Advisory Panel was created with jurisdiction over human rights violations committed by UNMIK (see UNMIK Regulation 2006/12, 23
March 2006). The Advisory Panel, which, at the time of writing, was not operative, had jurisdiction to examine complaints alleging 'a violation by UNMIK of the [sic] human rights' as set forth
in the relevant international instruments (ibid., section 1.2). This was limited *ratione temporis* to
'alleged violations of human rights that had occurred not earlier than 23 April 2005 or arising
from facts which occurred prior to this date where these facts give rise to a continuing violation
of human rights' (ibid., section 2). The four members of the Advisory Panel, who 'shall be international jurists of high moral character, impartiality and integrity with a demonstrated expertise in human rights, particularly the European system' (ibid., section 4.2), were to be appointed
by the head of UNMIK upon the proposal of the President of the European Court of Human
Rights (ibid., section 5.1). The powers of the Advisory Panel were limited to making findings and,
if appropriate, recommendations to the head of UNMIK (ibid., section 17). The Office of the
High Commissioner for Human Rights has been involved in monitoring UNMIK and KFOR;
see UNHCHR, 'Human Rights Field Presence in the Federal Republic of Yugoslavia (including
Kosovo)', available at <http://www.unhchr.ch/html/menu2/5/fryug.htm>. UNMIK regulations
are obtainable from <http://www.unmikonline.org/regulations/unmikgazette/index.htm>.

[25] Following a request formulated in 2004 by the UN Human Rights Committee, in 2006
UNMIK submitted a report on the human rights situation in Kosovo, which was considered by
the Committee in July 2006 (see Concluding Observations of the Human Rights Committee:
Serbia, UN Doc. CCPR/CO/81/SEMO, 12 August 2004, para. 3; Report Submitted by the
United Nations Interim Administration Mission in Kosovo to the Human Rights Committee
on the Human Rights Situation in Kosovo since June 1999, UN Doc. CCPR/C/UNK/1,
13 March 2006; Concluding Observations of the Human Rights Committee: Kosovo (Serbia),
UN Doc. CCPR/C/UNK/CO/1, 14 August 2006). UNMIK also entered into two agreements
with the Council of Europe enabling supervision by the European Committee for the Prevention
of Torture (CPT) and the Advisory Committee on the Framework Convention for the Protection
of National Minorities (see Agreement between the United Nations Interim Administration
Mission in Kosovo and the Council of Europe on technical arrangements related to the European
Convention for the Prevention of Torture and Inhuman or Degrading Treatment or Punishment,
Pristina, 23 August 2004 (hereinafter 'CPT Agreement'); and Agreement between the United
Nations Interim Administration Mission in Kosovo and the Council of Europe on technical
arrangements related to the Framework Convention for the Protection of National Minorities,
Pristina, 23 August 2004 (hereinafter 'Minorities Agreement')). As for the CPT, UNMIK undertook to cooperate with this body and 'permit visits...to any place in Kosovo where persons
are deprived of their liberty by an authority of UNMIK' (CPT Agreement, Art. 1), and more
generally, to co-operate with the CPT (ibid., Art. 2). The CPT Agreement was not immediately
implemented, pending the outcome of negotiations with NATO which eventually concluded with
an exchange of letters between NATO and the Council of Europe in July 2006; see 'Council of
Europe Anti-Torture Committee gains access to NATO run detention facilities in Kosovo', CoE
Press Release, 19 July 2006. The first visit was carried out in March 2007; see Council of Europe
Anti-Torture Committee visited Kosovo, CoE Press Release, 3 April 2007 (all the relevant documents are obtainable from <http://www.cpt.coe.int/en/states/srp.htm>). As for the arrangements
concerning the Minorities Convention, UNMIK agreed to 'submit to the Committee of Ministers
full information on the legislative and other measures taken to give effect to the principles set out
in the Framework Convention' (Minorities Agreement, Art. 2(2)). A first report was submitted to

relation to substantive allegations of human rights violations, notably in the area of security detentions.[26]

However, all of this analysis, clearly important in its own terms, takes the purposes served by the projects for granted, addressing second-order issues such as how the projects might be made more effective, more accountable, more gender sensitive etc. Often, insofar as the very enterprise itself is questioned, it is addressed with reference to these issues exclusively.[27]

the Advisory Committee on the Framework Convention for the Protection of National Minorities in June 2005, which adopted its opinion in November 2005 (see Report ACFC(2005)003 of 2 June 2005 submitted by the United Nations Interim Administration (UNMIK) with Annexes I–XLV; First Opinion of the Advisory Committee on Kosovo, adopted on 25 November 2005, CoE doc. CM(2005)192, 14 December 2005; UNMIK, Observations on the Opinion of the Advisory Committee on the Framework Convention for the Protection of National Minorities (adopted 25 November 2005), 18 February 2006; Council of Europe, Committee of Ministers, Resolution ResCMN(2006)9 on the implementation of the Framework Convention for the Protection of National Minorities in Kosovo (Republic of Serbia), adopted on 21 June 2006 (all documents obtainable from <http://www.coe.int>)). The Council of Europe's Commissioner for Human Rights and Venice Commission have also scrutinized UNMIK (see 'Kosovo: The Human Rights Situation and the Fate of Persons Displaced from their Homes', Report by Mr Alvaro Gil-Robles, Commissioner for Human Rights, CoE Doc. CommDH(2002)11, 16 October 2002; European Commission for Democracy through Law (Venice Commission), Opinion on Human Rights in Kosovo: Possible Establishment of Review Mechanisms (Opinion No. 280/2004, Strasbourg, 11 October 2004), obtainable from <http://www.venice.coe.int>).

[26] In 2002 the independent Ombudsperson in Kosovo stated that:

UNMIK is not structured according to democratic principles, does not function in accordance with the rule of law, and does not respect important international human rights norms. The people of Kosovo are therefore deprived of protection of their basic rights and freedoms three years after the end of the conflict by the very entity set up to guarantee them.

[…]

It is ironic that the United Nations, the self-proclaimed champion of human rights in the world, has by its own actions placed the people of Kosovo under UN control, thereby removing them from the protection of the international human rights regime that formed the justification for UN engagement in Kosovo in the first place.

Ombudsperson Institution in Kosovo, *Second Annual Report 2001–2002*, 10 July 2002, obtainable from <http://www.ombudspersonkosovo.org>, at 3 and 7. See, more generally, the first three Annual Reports and the 10 special reports of the Ombudsperson, all obtainable from <http://www.ombudspersonkosovo.org>. For criticism from the UN Human Rights Committee, see the 2006 Concluding Observations on Kosovo cited in n. 25 above. For criticism by the Council of Europe, see the report by Alvaro Gil-Robles and the Venice Commission Opinion cited in n. 25 above. In relation to the implementation of the Council of Europe Framework Convention on the Protection of National Minorities, see the First opinion on Kosovo of the Advisory Committee on the on the Framework Convention cited in n. 25 above. For NGO criticism, see, e.g., Amnesty International, 'Federal Republic of Yugoslavia (Kosovo): International officials flout international law', AI Index: EUR 70/008/2002, 1 September 2002, available at <http://web.amnesty.org/library/index/engeur700082002>, and the Kosovo NGOs cited in n. 116 below. Many of the academic commentators listed in List of Sources, section 5.2.7, are critical of UNMIK's human rights record.

[27] So for Ruth Wedgwood, for example, future administration projects are inadvisable because the UN is not up to the job; see Wedgwood (above n. 16). This is perhaps reflective of a broader tendency that can be identified within literature on international peace operations generally. Roland Paris states that:

This book addresses the deeper implications of the question posed by the Brahimi report: what is the nature of 'this business' as a matter of policy? If one wishes to consider whether or not such missions should be carried out in the future, one needs to know why they have been set up in the past. The UN has been granted the authority to act effectively as a territorial government. Why? This normative question is important not only in its own right; one cannot fully appraise the technical problems faced by the projects, nor assess normative issues such as accountability, without addressing it first. Fundamentally, one cannot appraise the legitimacy of the idea of displacing local actors in the activity of territorial administration without asking why this is taking place.[28]

Alongside the technocratic approach highlighted above, two further discursive approaches can be identified within some of the commentary on the Kosovo and East Timor projects: an exceptionalist portrayal of the projects, on the one hand, and a simplified and essentialist explanation of the purposes these particular

[o]ne of the weaknesses of the existing academic literature on peace operations is that it tends to take too much for granted. Few contributors to this literature challenge the conventional notion that peacebuilding is merely a technique for managing violence. Instead of investigating the underlying assumptions of peacebuilding, most works on the subject have sought to provide practical recommendations aimed at improving the ability of peacebuilders to control local conflicts. This is a worthy purpose…but it is also a relatively narrow focus for the scholarly study of peace operations—one that takes the purpose of peacebuilding at 'face value' rather than questioning the underlying assumptions of these operations.

R Paris, 'International Peacebuilding and the Mission Civilisatrice', 28 (2002) *Review of International Studies* 637, 655–6. See also ibid., 638.

[28] As Antony Anghie states in relation to international law, '…if we do not understand the character of this discipline, then, of course, we cannot possibly bring about any change within it'; A Anghie, *Imperialism, Sovereignty and the Making of International Law* (CUP, 2005), 320. Three research projects commenced after the creation of the Kosovo and East Timor projects, one by Richard Caplan, one by Simon Chesterman, and one by Outi Korhonen and Jutta Gras, later joined by Katja Creutz, have discussed some of the purposes served by some of the missions involving territorial administration by international organizations, as part of broad-ranging critical appraisals of this activity, sometimes together with administration performed by individual states, and sometimes limited to the more recent projects. See R Caplan, *International Governance of War-Torn Territories: Rule and Reconstruction* (OUP, 2005); Chesterman (above n. 1), especially ch. 2 part 2; Korhonen, Gras, and Creutz (above n. 15); Korhonen & Gras (above n. 15). The work by Richard Caplan is based on research conducted initially under the auspices of the International Institute for Strategic Studies, through which further analysis of this nature was produced; see R Caplan, A *New Trusteeship? The International Administration of War-Torn Territories*, Adelphi Paper No. 341 (OUP/International Institute for Strategic Studies (IISS), 2002) and the contributions in 10:1 (2004) *Global Governance* (Special issue on 'The Politics of International Administration', edited by M Berdal and R Caplan). Similarly, the work of Simon Chesterman comes from a project he headed at the International Peace Academy, from which further analysis was forthcoming. See S Chesterman, 'Virtual Trusteeship' in D Malone (ed.), *The UN Security Council: From the Cold War to the 21st Century* (Lynne Rienner, 2004), 219. A book by Dominik Zaum, *The Sovereignty Paradox: The Norms and Politics of International Statebuilding* (OUP, 2007), analyses the 'state-building' policy of the missions in Bosnia and Herzegovina, East Timor, and Kosovo, as a way of considering contemporary ideas of sovereignty. Steven Ratner's more longstanding work on complex peace operations has engaged in purposive analysis, particularly in relation to the post-Cold War projects before Kosovo and East Timor, which he characterized as a 'new' form of peacekeeping, and his ground-breaking article, co-authored with Gerald Helman in 1992, proposed a form of UN administration for 'failed states'. See SR Ratner, *The New UN Peacekeeping*,

projects, and others involving territorial administration by international organizations, serve, on the other. A brief review of some of the limitations of these approaches is useful in illustrating the nature and scope of the present enquiry.

1.2 Some Presentations of Recent Projects Involving Territorial Administration by International Organizations[29]

1.2.1 Exceptionalism

It is common to describe the administration projects in Kosovo and East Timor as unique because of the plenary administrative powers asserted, the involvement of the United Nations, and the problems caused by the supposed lack of pre-existing institutions.[30] An extreme view holds that the East Timor undertaking

Building Peace in Lands of Conflict after the Cold War (St. Martin's Press, 1995); GB Helman and SR Ratner, 'Saving Failed States', 89 (1992) *Foreign Policy* 3; SR Ratner, 'The Cambodian Settlement Agreements', 87 (1993) *AJIL* 1; SR Ratner, 'Foreign Occupation and International Territorial Administration: The Challenges of Convergence', 16 (2005) *EJIL* 695, 700. The relationship between the administration of territory by international actors and peace operations, and the 'failed states' proposals, are discussed below in ch. 7, sections 7.4 and 7.3.3 respectively; the relationship between this activity and 'occupation' is discussed below in ch. 8, section 8.2.5 *et seq*. Jarat Chopra's pioneering work on international peace operations in the early 1990s highlighted the significance of missions involving what he called 'civil governance-in-trust'; Chopra went on to work for, and become a leading critic of, UNTAET; see J Chopra, *Peace-Maintenance: The Evolution of International Political Authority* (Routledge, 1999); J Chopra, *United Nations Authority in Cambodia* (Thomas J Watson Jr. Institute for International Studies, Occasional Paper No. 15, 1994); J Chopra, 'UN Civil Governance-in-Trust', in TG Weiss (ed.), *The United Nations and Civil Wars* (Lynne Rienner, 1995), 70; J Chopra, 'The UN's Kingdom of East Timor', 42 (2000) *Survival* 27; J Chopra, 'Building State Failure in East Timor', 33 (2002) *Development & Change* 979, reprinted as 'Building State Failure in East Timor', in J Milliken (ed.), *State Failure, Collapse & Reconstruction* (Blackwell, 2003), 223 and as 'Building State Failure in East Timor', ch. 8 in A Hehir and N Robinson (eds), *State Building: Theory and Practice* (Routledge, 2007); J Chopra and T Hohe, 'Participatory Intervention', 10 (2004) *Global Governance* 289. Sally Morphet, also a scholar of peace operations, was, like Jarat Chopra, one of the first analysts to identify the significance of civil administration components in such operations: see S Morphet, 'Organizing Civil Administration', in J Chopra (ed.), *The Politics of Peace-Maintenance* (Lynne Rienner, 1998), 41; S Morphet, 'Current International Civil Administration: The Need for Political Legitimacy', 9 (2002) *International Peacekeeping* 140. Other commentators have considered the connection between certain missions involving territorial administration by international organizations and ideas of empire and trusteeship; see below, ch. 8, section 8.1. The present work aims to complement the existing literature, by offering a sustained, exclusive consideration of the purposes associated with such missions. In doing this, it expands on what was offered earlier in R Wilde, 'From Danzig to East Timor and Beyond: The Role of International Territorial Administration', 95 (2001) *AJIL* 583.

[29] Some of the ideas presented here are discussed in R Wilde, 'Representing International Territorial Administration: A Critique of Some Approaches', 15 (2004) *EJIL* 71 and ch. 11 in H Charlesworth and J-M Coicaud (eds), *Fault Lines of International Legitimacy* (United Nations University Press, forthcoming).

[30] The Brahimi Report places two post-Cold War projects (this can only refer to UNMIK and UNTAET) in a class of their own as responding to 'extreme' situations: '...United Nations operations were given executive law enforcement and administrative authority where local authority did not exist or was not able to function'; Brahimi Report (above n. 11), para. 19. Michael Matheson

was unprecedented, since nowhere else had UN administration been used to bring a new state into existence.[31] Thus, in varying ways, the projects are placed in an exceptional category, as qualitatively distinct from all the other peace operations conducted by the United Nations. This approach to describing internationalization is itself unexceptional; as Nathaniel Berman has observed, the League of Nations territorial administration missions in the Free City of Danzig and the Saar territory after the First World War, which will be discussed further below, were 'considered at the time to be extraordinary "experiments" '.[32]

refers to '[t]he novel...undertakings in Kosovo and East Timor'; MJ Matheson, 'United Nations Governance of Post-Conflict Societies', 95 (2001) *AJIL* 76, 83. He also states that, in Kosovo, 'the mission of the international civil presence...was unprecedented in scope and complexity', and that, the task of UNTAET in East Timor was 'of comparable scope and complexity' to this (ibid., 79 and 81 respectively). Michèle Griffin and Bruce Jones state that the projects take the UN into 'uncharted territory...with mandates that are broader in scope and ambition than anything that went before'; M Griffin and B Jones, 'Building Peace through Transitional Authority: New Directions, Major Challenges', 7:4 (2000) *International Peacekeeping* 75, at 75. For Hansjörg Strohmeyer, '[t]he scope of the challenges and responsibilities deriving from these mandates [UNMIK and UNTAET] was unprecedented in United Nations peacekeeping operations'; Strohmeyer (above n. 17), 46. As for working on the territory's legal and judicial system in particular, Strohmeyer states that '[n]owhere other than Kosovo and East Timor [where such a task was part of a UN mandate]...did this task require the establishment of a coherent judicial and legal system for an entire territory virtually from scratch' (ibid., 60). Boris Kondoch remarks that '[t]he scope of the responsibilities and the range of the mandate in these cases [UNMIK and UNTAET] were unprecedented in the history of UN peacekeeping missions'; B Kondoch, 'The United Nations Administration of East Timor', 6 (2001) *Journal of Conflict & Security Law* 245, 246. On the exceptional character of the two missions, see also M Ruffert, 'The Administration of Kosovo and East Timor by the International Community', 50 (2001) *ICLQ* 613, at 613; C Stahn, 'International Territorial Administration in the Former Yugoslavia: Origins, Development and Challenges Ahead', 61 (2001) *ZaöRV* 107, 134; C Stahn, 'The United Nations Transitional Administrations in Kosovo and East Timor: A First Analysis', 5 (2001) *Max Planck Yearbook of United Nations Law* 105, 107, 108. On the exceptional character of the two missions and the Eastern Slavonia mission, see, e.g., Caplan, *A New Trusteeship?* (above n. 28), 81. Michael Bothe and Thilo Marauhn argue that UNMIK and UNTAET are unique and thereby justify a new category of 'Security Council trusteeship administration'; M Bothe and T Marauhn, 'UN Administration of Kosovo and East Timor: Concept, Legality and Limitations of Security Council-Mandated Trusteeship Administration', in C Tomuschat (ed.), *Kosovo and the International Community: A Legal Assessment* (Kluwer Law International, 2002), 217. Their thesis is discussed below in ch. 7, section 7.4.2, and in ch. 8, which focuses on the significance of the concept of 'trust' for the missions (the discussion in section 8.3.3 focuses on the 'newness' aspect of their approach).

[31] Jarat Chopra, for example, proclaims that '...the UN is exercising sovereign authority within a fledgling nation for the first time in its history'; J Chopra, 'The UN's Kingdom of East Timor' (above n. 28), 27. See also J Traub, 'Inventing East Timor', 79:4 (July/Aug 2000) *Foreign Affairs* 74, at 74–5 (arguing that the East Timor mission was exceptional because of the broad mandate and lack of pre-existing institutions). John Sanderson identifies 'unprecedented boldness' in the scope of the mandate given to UNTAET, and states that '[t]he United Nations has not 'occupied' a country before, depending on all previous occasions on some other body to perform the enforcement provisions while it goes about the business of helping to build new foundations for governance'; J Sanderson, 'The Cambodian Experience: A Success Story Still?', in R Thakur and A Schnabel (eds), *United Nations Peacekeeping Operations: Ad Hoc Missions, Permanent Engagement* (UN University Press, 2001), 155, at 159.
[32] N Berman, ' "But the Alternative is Despair", European Nationalism and the Modernist Renewal of International Law', 106 (1992–93) *Harvard Law Review* 1792, at 1874. The treatment of these arrangements in this book begins in ch. 2, section 2.2.1.

The particular taxonomy used as a basis for classifying the territorial administration projects of course mediates the question of whether and to what extent they can be regarded as unique. If one is interested in considering the purposes they serve, it is necessary to consider whether the taxonomy being adopted as the basis for comparing the projects with other projects—and thereby establishing sameness or distinctiveness—is helpful in revealing these purposes and clarifying how they are served by the projects. Should the focus be on UN peace operations generally or on territorial administration in particular? Is it necessary to cover both partial and plenary administration, or only plenary administration? Is it in order to consider projects involving international organizations generally or is a focus only on the United Nations in particular appropriate? Should all administration projects be addressed, or only those with a 'state-building' purpose?

What is perhaps unhelpful about the exceptionalist approach is that the basis on which the classification rests is unexamined. Plenary administration by the United Nations with a 'state-building' objective, for example, is adopted as the relevant category, without any explanation of why this classification is more appropriate than other classifications that could have been chosen. As a result, comparison with other projects is implicitly ruled out, or at least made more difficult, even though the utility of comparison with such projects has not been disproved. Such assessments therefore risk arbitrariness.

1.2.2 Purposive simplification

A second discursive approach evident in the literature on some of the recent projects is a presentation of the purposes with which the projects are associated that is essentialized and/or drastically oversimplified. For example, some commentators have chosen to label the activity of territorial administration by international organizations in terms suggesting that it is essentially a 'post-conflict' phenomenon, using the word 'conflict' in the narrow sense of an armed conflict.[33] Such presentations imply two things about this activity: in the first place, that it is always used in the 'post-conflict' context; in the second place, that it is necessarily concerned with addressing the consequences of conflict. In particular, the suggestion is that, because of conflict, governance has broken down either partially or completely, and so administration by international actors is introduced to fill the administrative vacuum and 'reconstruct'.[34]

---

[33] See, e.g., Matheson (above n. 30); Caplan, *A New Trusteeship?* (above n. 28); Caplan, *International Governance of War-Torn Territories* (above n. 28); Korhonen & Gras (above n. 28); O Korhonen, 'International Governance in Post-Conflict Situations', 14 (2001) *LJIL* 495; Ruffert (above n. 30); Stahn, 'International Territorial Administration in the Former Yugoslavia' (above n. 30), 171; Stahn, 'The United Nations Transitional Administrations in Kosovo and East Timor' (above n. 30), 108. See also how the background to the introduction of UN administration of territory is described in P Alston, 'The "Not-a-cat" Syndrome: Can the International Human Rights Regime Accommodate Non-State Actors?', in P Alston (ed.), *Non-State Actors and Human Rights* (OUP, 2005), 3, at 8.

[34] So for Tom Parker:

The first problem with the 'post-conflict' label is that it is incorrect to state that territorial administration by international organizations has always been used after conflict. In West Irian, for example, UN administration was used in 1962–63 not because the territory was war-torn and so required external administration, but, rather, to ensure the smooth transfer of territorial control from the Netherlands to Indonesia.[35] The UN acted as a neutral 'buffer' in between control by the two states, avoiding the potential conflict feared if the transfer had been made directly between one state and the other. Rather than picking up the pieces after the end of a conflict, here UN administration was a device for preventing armed hostilities from breaking out in the first place.

Most projects involving the conduct of territorial administration by international organizations, however, have indeed taken place after conflict. That said, it is unhelpful to assume that all or any of the purposes each has served can be understood in terms of responding to the consequences of conflict—an assumption arguably implied by labelling the activity a 'post-conflict' phenomenon. When the United Nations Operation in the Congo (known by the acronym of its French title, ONUC) tried to fill the governmental vacuum in the Congo in the early 1960s, the perceived inability of local officials to perform governance was associated as much with the failure of the former colonial power, Belgium, to train them in governmental skills as with the armed conflict that ensued after independence was realized.[36] To be sure, ONUC was a 'peacekeeping' operation; it had been created to address the conflict, and its military component pursued this objective vigorously, including attempting to prevent the secession of Katanga (and so moving into what is now termed 'peace enforcement'). However, the creation of ONUC to pursue these military objectives placed it in a position to exercise certain governmental functions for a broader set of reasons than merely responding to the conflict. The fact that these functions were performed by the civilian component of a peacekeeping force perhaps led to the view that they were to be explained wholly in terms of conflict. Indeed many commentators mention these administrative activities only briefly, or ignore them altogether, focusing instead on ONUC's military role.[37]

---

[a]lthough international territorial administration has had a chequered history one common... [denominator] can be said to unite all the various disparate initiatives launched by the international community—a desire to impose order on chaos and help territories and peoples no longer in a position to help themselves.

T Parker, *The Ultimate Intervention: Revitalising the UN Trusteeship Council for the 21st Century* (Sandvika: Norwegian School of Management, 2003), at 12.

[35] See below, ch. 6, text accompanying nn. 15 and 16.

[36] See below, ch. 6, text accompanying n. 53.

[37] E.g., D Bowett, *United Nations Forces: A Legal Study* (Stevens & Sons, 1964), ch. 6 on ONUC. Bowett takes the position that '[a] detailed description of the civilian relief operations in the Congo would be out of place in this present study of United Nations Forces' (ibid., 248). A notable exception to this typical approach is Morphet, 'Organizing Civil Administration' (above n. 28), 43–5.

Similarly, in Bosnia and Herzegovina since the 1995 Dayton Peace Agreements,[38] the role of the multinational military force (from 1995 to 2004 led by NATO and first called IFOR, then SFOR; from 2004 led by the EU and called

---

[38] The term 'Dayton Peace Agreements' is used in this book to indicate a series of related but separately-binding instruments with varied participants initialled at Dayton, Ohio, on 21 November 1995, and signed in Paris on 14 December 1995 (entering into force on signature), the full citations for which are contained in the List of Sources: the General Framework Agreement for Peace in Bosnia and Herzegovina (hereinafter 'Dayton GFA'), Annex 1A, Annex 1A Appendix A, Annex 1A Appendix B(1), Annex 1A Appendix B(2), Annex 1A Appendix B(3), Annex 1B, Annex 2, Annex 3, Annex 4, Annex 5, Annex 6, Annex 7, Annex 8, Annex 9, Annex 10 and Annex 11 thereto (hereinafter referred to as 'Dayton Annex 1A, Dayton Annex 1A Appendix A, Dayton Annex 1A Appendix B(1), Dayton Annex 1A Appendix B(2), Dayton Annex 1A Appendix B(3), Dayton Annex 1B, 2, 3, 4, 5, 6, 7, 8, 9, 10 and 11'), and a series of accompanying side-letter instruments. On these agreements, including their legal status, see, e.g., P Gaeta, 'The Dayton Agreements and International Law', 7 (1996) *EJIL* 147; R Slye, 'The Dayton Peace Agreement: Constitutionalism and Ethnicity', 21 (1996) *YJIL* 459; P Szasz, 'Introductory Note' [to the Dayton Agreements], 35 (1996) *ILM* 75; P Szasz, 'The Bosnian Constitution: the Road to Dayton and Beyond', 90 (1996) *ASIL Proc.* 479; S Yee, 'The New Constitution of Bosnia-Hercegovina', 7 (1996) *EJIL* 176; P Galbraith, 'Washington, Erdut and Dayton: Negotiating and Implementing Peace in Croatia and Bosnia and Herzegovina', 30 (1997) *Cornell International Law Journal* 643; P Szasz, 'The Dayton Accord: The Balkan Peace Agreement', 30 (1997) *Cornell International Law Journal* 759; P Szasz, 'The Protection of Human Rights Through the Dayton/Paris Peace Agreement on Bosnia', 90 (1996) *AJIL* 301; Z Pajic, 'A Critical Appraisal of Human Rights Provisions of the Dayton Constitution of Bosnia and Hercegovina', 20 (1998) *Human Rights Quarterly* 125; M Cox, 'The Dayton Agreement in Bosnia and Herzegovina: A Study in Implementation Strategies', 69 (1999) *BYIL* 201; C Chinkin and K Paradine, 'Vision and Reality: Democracy and Citizenship of Women in the Dayton Peace Accords', 26 (2001) *Yale Journal of International Law* 103; F Ni Aolain, 'The Fractured Soul of the Dayton Peace Agreement: A Legal Analysis', 19 (1997–98) *Michigan Journal of International Law* 957 republished in D Sokolović and F Bieber (eds), *Reconstructing Multiethnic Societies: The Case of Bosnia and Herzegovina* (Ashgate, 2001), 63. See also European Commission for Democracy through Law (Venice Commission), *Amicus Curiae Opinion (Proceedings before the European Court of Human Rights) on the Nature of the Proceedings Before the Human Rights Chamber and the Constitutional Court of Bosnia and Herzegovina* (Opinion No. 337/2005, Venice, 10–11 June 2005), obtainable from <http://www.venice.coe.int> (hereinafter 'Venice Commission, *Amicus Curiae Opinion*'), section II; *Jeličić v Bosnia and Herzegovina*, Appl. No. 41183/02, European Court of Human Rights, Admissibility decision of 15 November 2005 (obtainable from <http://www.echr.coe.int>). A degree of cross-referencing between agreements and side letters sometimes makes it necessary to consider the parties to more than one instrument when considering who is bound by a particular provision in any given instrument. An exhaustive treatment of the interplay between these instruments insofar as they relate to particular provisions referred to in this book would take things too far away from the focus of analysis (itself explained later in this chapter). In this book, references to the Dayton instruments focus exclusively on provisions concerned directly with administrative prerogatives or related issues; to ascertain how exactly these provisions are binding, and to whom they apply, individual provisions should be situated within the broader context of all the 'Dayton Peace Agreements' listed above. Also of relevance are the Agreement pursuant to Article XIV of Annex 6 to the General Framework Agreement for Peace in Bosnia and Herzegovina, 22 and 25 September 2003, agreed to by Bosnia and Herzegovina, the Federation of Bosnia and Herzegovina and the Republika Srpska (available at <http://www.hrc.ba/ENGLISH/agreement.pdf>); the Agreed Basic Principles agreed on 8 September 1995 at Geneva by the Foreign Minister of the Republic of Bosnia and Herzegovina, the Foreign Minister of the Republic of Croatia and the Foreign Minister of the Federal Republic of Yugoslavia, and witnessed by representatives of France, Germany, the Russian Federation, the United Kingdom of Great Britain and Northern Ireland, the United States of America, and the European Union Special Negotiator for the Former Yugoslavia, UN Doc. A/50/419-S/1995/780, Annex II. See also the Further Agreed Basic Principles, agreed by

EUFOR)[39] in maintaining the cessation of armed hostilities receives more attention than the governmental activities of the Office of the High Representative in Bosnia and Herzegovina (OHR). As is explained in more detail in the next chapter, this *sui generis* entity was created as part of the Dayton process and, over time, has asserted the right, inter alia, to impose legislation and dismiss elected government officials.[40]

Attaching the 'post-conflict' tag to OHR's role implies an agenda concerned primarily or exclusively with the consequences of the conflict in the country between 1992 and 1995. If this role is then associated with the broader notion of filling an administrative vacuum, one finds the suggestion that OHR's purpose is to remedy the absence of governance caused by the previous conflict. Actually, the Dayton Peace Agreements included in Annex 4 a new Constitution for Bosnia and Herzegovina, which conceived the country as a federal-type state composed of two constituent Entities: the Federation of Bosnia and Herzegovina (hereinafter the 'Federation'), comprising the areas controlled by the wartime alliance of that name between Bosnian Muslim/Bosniak and Bosnian Croat authorities, the latter also known as 'Herzeg Bosna', and the Republika Srpska (known as the 'RS'), comprising the area controlled by the Bosnian Serb authorities.[41] New

the representatives of the Governments of the Republic of Bosnia and Herzegovina, the Federal Republic of Yugoslavia (Serbia and Montenegro), and the Republic of Croatia on 26 September 1995, UN Doc. A/50/718-S/1995/920, Annex I.

[39] Article I(1)(a) of Dayton Annex 1A (above n. 38) invited the United Nations Security Council to authorize the establishment of a multinational implementation force (IFOR), mandated to implement the military aspects of Dayton Annex 1A (ibid.); the establishment of IFOR was authorized by the Security Council with SC Res. 1031 of 15 December 1995, where the Security Council recognized that the Parties to the Peace Agreement authorized IFOR to 'take such action as required … to ensure compliance with Annex 1A of the Peace Agreement' (ibid., para. 5); see also SC Res. 1088, 12 December 1996, authorizing the establishment of a multinational stabilization force (SFOR) as 'legal successor' to IFOR, and SC Res. 1575, 22 November 2004, on the establishment of EUFOR, substituting SFOR from December 2004. On IFOR, SFOR and EUFOR generally, see the official websites, at <http://www.nato.int/ifor/ifor.htm>, <http://www.nato.int/sfor>, and <http://www.euforbih.org>; see also I Johnstone (ed.), *Annual Review of Global Peace Operations 2007* (NYU Center on International Cooperation/Lynne Rienner, 2007), section 4.2. See also the legal mandates in Dayton Annex 1A Appendix A, Dayton Annex 1A Appendix B(1), Dayton Annex 1A Appendix B(2), Dayton Annex 1A Appendix B(3) (above n. 38). On the legal basis for EUFOR within the EU framework, where it is called 'Operation Althea', see Council Joint Action 2004/570/CFSP on the European Union military Operation in Bosnia and Herzegovina, 12 July 2004, *OJ* L252 (2004), 10; Council Decision 2004/803/CFSP of 25 November 2004 on the launching of the European Union military operation in Bosnia and Herzegovina, *OJ* L353 (2004), 21. For commentary, see, e.g., DA Leurdijk, 'Before and after Dayton: the UN and NATO in the former Yugoslavia', 18 (1997) *Third World Quarterly* 457; A Sari, 'Status of Forces and Status of Mission Agreements under the ESDP: The EU's Emerging Practice' (*EJIL*, forthcoming 2007/2008).

[40] See below, ch. 2, section 2.3.3.

[41] Dayton Annex 4 (above n. 38), Art. 1, para. 1 (on the state of Bosnia and Herzegovina) and para. 3 (on the two Entities). See S Yee, 'The New Constitution of Bosnia-Hercegovina', 7 (1996) *EJIL* 176. On the wartime aspirations of these different authorities, see below, ch. 4, text accompanying n. 188. On the different groups and Entities generally, see, e.g., D Kofman, 'Self-Determination in a Multiethnic State: Bosnians, Bosniaks, Croats and Serbs', in D Sokolović and

executive, legislative, and judicial bodies were created at the state level, and the legislative activities of OHR operate alongside lawmaking by the Parliamentary Assembly.[42]

The ostensible reason for OHR's performance of administrative activities has not been the absence of institutions run by local officials, but the fact that OHR determined that such institutions and their officials were not taking the necessary action, or the action they took was inappropriate.[43] Whereas these problems may sometimes be explained in terms of war-related practicalities, they were often understood as a matter of politics: the agenda being pursued by the local institution and its officials ran counter to that promoted by OHR, or members of the legislature were deemed insufficiently rooted in the democratic tradition to perform their functions adequately.[44] Again, whereas the latter reason (whatever its merits) may be explained in part because of the conflict, one must somehow discount altogether other factors, such as the consequences of decades of totalitarian rule, in order to suggest that the conflict was its only cause. In removing government officials, OHR was clearly not attempting to fill a practical breakdown in governance; such actions actually created a governmental vacuum until the relevant position could be filled through appointment or election. Moreover, in most cases, dismissal was not because of incompetence (which sometimes may be explained as a consequence of the conflict), but because of a judgement made about the policies espoused by the official in question, such as extremist Serb nationalism in the case of the President of the Republika Srpska Nikola Poplasen, who was removed from office for this reason by OHR in 1999.[45]

In Bosnia and Herzegovina, an arrangement installed as part of a peace agreement has been engaged in promoting a liberal political and economic order. To suggest that this is essentially a 'post-conflict' agenda is to ignore how it is also addressing, for example, perceived problems arising out of a centrally planned economy and a totalitarian system of governance, both of which, of course, pre-date the conflict.

In contrast to the Congo and Bosnia and Herzegovina, the presence of UN administration in Kosovo and East Timor is rarely ignored in the discussion of these territories since 1999. At the same time, this activity is again often explained

F Bieber (eds), *Reconstructing Multiethnic Societies: The Case of Bosnia and Herzegovina* (Ashgate, 2001), 31; TD Grant, 'Internationally Guaranteed Constitutive Order: Cyprus and Bosnia as Predicates for a New Nontraditional Actor in the Society of States', 8 (1998) *Journal of Transnational Law & Policy* 1.

[42] On the domestic legislatures, see the Constitution of Bosnia and Herzegovina in Dayton Annex 4 (above n. 38), Art. IV.

[43] For examples in the context of individual officials, see below, ch. 6, text accompanying nn. 127 and 128.

[44] Ibid.

[45] OHR, 'Decision removing Mr Nikola Poplasen from the Office of President of Republika Srpska', 5 March 1999; see also OHR, Press Release, 'Removal from Office of Nikola Poplasen', 5 March 1999 (both obtainable from <http://www.ohr.int>).

wholly in terms of responding to the consequences of conflict. Ramesh Thakur and Albrecht Schnabel situate the Kosovo and East Timor projects within a class of projects 'in countries affected by civil wars' where the 'United Nations substitutes for collapsed local governments'.[46] When UNTAET is described as a 'post-conflict' mission, the implication is that the reason for the mission is that conflict—in particular, the post-'consultation' violence by pro-Indonesian militias—created a governmental vacuum and breakdown in infrastructure that rendered governance by the East Timorese impossible. Michael Matheson states that the Australian-led International Force for East Timor (INTERFET), which had been introduced to end the violence by the militias:

... quickly restored order, but the violence had already destroyed a large number of homes and other buildings, caused the collapse of the civil administration and judicial systems, and damaged or destroyed much of the waterworks and other essential public services. As a result, the Security Council ... decided to entrust the United Nations with the burden of governance of a territory shattered by conflict.[47]

What this typical presentation of UNTAET's creation ignores is that UN administration was actually envisaged before the violence, and the 'popular consultation', had taken place. In fact, it was provided for in the May Agreements that also established the terms of the 'consultation'.[48] The original reason for UN administration had nothing to do with conflict; rather, it concerned the perceived inability of the East Timorese, in the short term, to govern themselves if Indonesia withdrew. Of course, the violence that followed the 'popular consultation' made governance by any actor, Timorese or international, extremely difficult. But as an explanation for the idea of UN administration, as opposed to some of the challenges that the administration project faced once it was introduced, a focus on such violence is misplaced.

A similar problem can be seen in relation to the Kosovo project. In describing the background to UNMIK, Matheson explains the 'state of economic and social chaos' in Kosovo following the NATO bombing campaign, the military campaign by Serb forces against the Albanian population, and the withdrawal of all Serb and Yugoslav military and civilian officials.[49] He remarks that:

[c]learly, the international community had to establish a system of governance, at least for an interim period. Without such governance, the chaotic situation would present a continuing, acute threat of escalating violence and regional instability, as well as a serious humanitarian crisis.[50]

[46] R Thakur and A Schnabel, 'Cascading Generations of Peacekeeping: Across the Mogadishu Line to Kosovo and Timor', in R Thakur and A Schnabel (eds), *United Nations Peacekeeping Operations: Ad Hoc Missions, Permanent Engagement* (UN University Press, 2001), 3, at 21.

[47] Matheson (above n. 30), 82. On the military action by INTERFET, see below, ch. 6, n. 62.

[48] Agreement between the Republic of Indonesia and the Portuguese Republic on the Question of East Timor, above, n. 2, Art. 6 (extracted below in ch. 5, text accompanying n. 154).

[49] Matheson (above n. 30), 78.

[50] Ibid.

This suggests that UNMIK was conceived to respond to a pre-existing governmental vacuum. Its purpose is essentially practical: 'establishing a system of governance' where one did not exist. Such a presentation fails to acknowledge that the withdrawal of Serb and Yugoslav officials that created the governmental vacuum was actually part of the same overall settlement—the so-called 'Peace Plan' agreed to by the then FRY—that provided for UN administration.[51] The absence of the Serb and Yugoslav administrative authorities, therefore, cannot be considered separately from the presence of the UN administration project; the very purpose of the Serb and Yugoslav withdrawal was to make way for UNMIK. UNMIK was there, not to fill a governmental vacuum, but to replace an administration considered to be committed to the disenfranchisement of the Kosovar Albanians with another administration viewed as committed to the enfranchisement of that population. In other words, the reason for the UN administration was not to remedy a governmental breakdown, but to engineer a fundamental change in government policy.[52]

Adopting the term 'post-conflict' as a label to describe the administration projects holistically obscures the many other purposes that these projects have been created to serve, sometimes outside a 'post-conflict' situation and in the absence of any 'reconstruction' objective. As a means of description, therefore, it is unhelpful, and if one is seeking to understand why international organizations become involved in territorial administration, it may be misleading. For example, when Michael Matheson discusses the international approach taken with respect to Bosnia and Herzegovina at Dayton in 1995, he suggests that 'governance was left to the Bosnian political entities'.[53] The reason for this is presented as self-evident:

[c]learly, the United Nations was reluctant to assume the functions of governing the territory of a sovereign state if indigenous institutions were available for the purpose.[54]

Having conceived territorial administration by international organizations as an activity used only when 'indigenous institutions' break down after conflict, Matheson reinforces his thesis by invoking a situation that does not fit this scenario, and implying a causal relationship between the presence of indigenous institutions and the absence of this activity. Quite apart from the nature of the causal relationship, which is surely not to be assumed, what has happened in Bosnia and Herzegovina since Dayton is ignored. As already mentioned, the conduct of partial administrative prerogatives by an international organization—albeit OHR rather than the UN—has operated in that country, despite indigenous institutions being 'available for the purpose'.[55] Matheson's approach perhaps illustrates the problems

---

[51] Kosovo Peace Plan (above n. 1), paras 2 and 6 (on the withdrawal); paras 3 and 5 (on the UN administrative presence).

[52] See the discussion below in ch. 6, text accompanying n. 117 *et seq.* The significance of self-determination to this will be considered below in ch. 7, sections 7.3.2 and 7.3.3.

[53] Matheson (above n. 30), 78.

[54] Ibid.

[55] Although Matheson mentions OHR in a footnote, its status as a counter-example to the thesis he puts forward in his main text is neither acknowledged nor addressed; ibid., n. 19.

that follow from assuming that territorial administration by international organizations is only ever concerned with filling a governmental vacuum.[56]

1.3 Discipline

This book is about the history, law, and politics of a particular activity conducted by international organizations and, as will be explained, certain other international actors. As befits its subject-matter, it draws on a wide range of source material, from primary documents relating to particular administration projects, to secondary commentary from the fields of history, law, and political science. Since the focus is on an 'international' activity, much of this is drawn from work conducted under disciplinary categories of 'international relations' and 'international law'. Many have observed that these disciplinary categories are unhelpful and have sought to explain their approaches in terms of an inter- or cross-disciplinary method.[57] My own view is that the discipline of international law is best understood as part of the broader discipline of international relations, just as law is best understood within the broader framework of the social and political sciences, and international relations—encompassing international law—is best understood as the application of social and political science methodology—including legal methodology—to the 'international' (a category whose meaning is of course contested). If it is helpful for disciplinary orientations to be declared, then this book is a work within the discipline of 'international relations', concerning, within this field, legal/normative, institutional, and historical perspectives in particular.

The remainder of this chapter sets out the methodological approach to be taken in this book and explains its relationship to existing methodological approaches where relevant.

[56] The relationship between projects involving territorial administration by international organizations and the framework of international law and policy concerning peace and security is discussed further below in ch. 7, section 7.4.

[57] For work explicitly referencing the intersection between international relations and international law methodology, see, e.g., RJ Beck, AC Arend, and RD Vander Lugt (eds), *International Rules: Approaches from International Law and International Relations* (OUP, 1996); M Byers (ed.), *The Role of Law in International Politics: Essays in International Relations and International Law* (OUP, 2001); C Reus-Smit (ed.), *The Politics of International Law* (CUP, 2004); BA Ackerly, M Stern, and J True (eds), *Feminist Methodologies for International Relations* (CUP, 2006); T Biersteker, P Spiro, CL Sriram, and V Raffo (eds), *International Law and International Relations: Bridging Theory and Practice* (Routledge, 2006), in particular the introductory chapter by the editors and sources cited therein, ch. 17 by M Finnemore; D Armstrong, T Farrell, and H Lambert, *International Law and International Relations* (CUP, 2007); B Simmons and RH Steinberg (eds), *International Law and International Relations: An International Organization Reader* (OUP, 2007); KW Abbott, 'Modern International Relations Theory: A Prospectus for International Lawyers', 14 (1989) *Yale Journal of International Law* 335; A-M Slaughter Burley, 'International Law and International Relations Theory: A Dual Agenda', 87 (1993) *AJIL* 205; M Finnemore and K Sikkink, 'International Norm Dynamics and Political Change', 52 (1998) *International Organization* 887; A-M Slaughter, A Tulumello and S Wood, 'International Law and International Relations Theory: A New Generation

1.4 Determining the Subject-Matter: 'International Territorial Administration'[58]

If we want to start something, we must ignore that our starting point is, *all efforts taken*, shaky. If we want to get something done, we must ignore that, *all provisions made*, the end will be inconclusive. This ignoring is not an active forgetfulness; it is, rather, an active *marginalizing* of the marshiness, the swampiness, the lack of firm grounding in the margins, at beginning and end... These necessarily and actively marginalized margins haunt what we start and get done, as curious guardians... [We must not] forget the productive unease that what we do with the utmost care is judged in the margins.

Gayatri Chakravorty Spivak[59]

...my attempts to sketch an alternative and more inclusive history... confronts the inevitable paradox that it effects its own exclusions. In adopting a particular... method and framework I disregard the many other histories and themes that could have been explored.

Antony Anghie[60]

So far, the discussion in this chapter has concerned the merits of a sustained analysis of the purposes served by the activity of 'territorial administration by international organizations' when compared with other issues raised by this activity. But, as mentioned earlier, when discussing the exceptionalist treatment of the Kosovo and East Timor missions, more fundamental questions need to be addressed: is such activity worthy of analysis in its own right, separate from other activities that might share commonalities with it? If so, what might be the parameters of such analysis—on which individual projects should the focus be placed? These two questions implicate the choice of focus to be adopted from a wide range of options. Should one look at administration projects involving the UN, or those conducted by international organizations generally?[61] Might it be better

---

of Interdisciplinary Scholarship', 92 (1998) *AJIL* 367; KW Abbott, 'International Relations Theory, International Law, and the Regime Governing Atrocities in Internal Conflicts', 93 (1999) *AJIL* 361; KW Abbott, RO Keohane, A Moravcsik, A-M Slaughter, and D Snidal, 'The Concept of Legalization', 54 (2000) *International Organization* 401; J Goldstein, M Kahler, RO Keohane, and A-M Slaughter (eds), 'Legalization and World Politics', special issue of *International Organization* (54:3 (2000), 11–13), reprinted as JL Goldstein, M Kahler, RO Keohane, and A-M Slaughter (eds), *Legalization and World Politics* (MIT Press, 2001); A-M Slaughter, 'International law and international relations', 285 (2000) *Recueil des Cours* 9.

[58] For alternative conceptualizations of some of the activities considered here see, e.g., Caplan, *A New Trusteeship?* (above n. 28), ch. 1; Caplan, *International Governance of War-Torn Territories* (above n. 28), ch. 1 and Knoll (above n. 1), *passim* and especially 280.

[59] G Chakravorty Spivak, *A Critique of Postcolonial Reason* (Harvard University Press, 1999), 175 (emphasis in original).

[60] Anghie (above n. 28), 12.

[61] For an exclusive UN-focus, see, for example, Matheson (above n. 30). Despite being concerned with the administration of territory by the United Nations, the author's coverage is selective within this category, omitting, for example, the UN administration in Eastern Slavonia, 1996–98, which is introduced in this book below in ch. 2, n. 24 and corresponding text.

to analyse projects involving plenary administration only, or should projects where partial administrative prerogatives are exercised also be addressed? Should one look only at current and recent projects, or go further back in time?[62] And why consider situations of territorial administration by international organizations exclusively? What of occupation by foreign states, such as the allied administration of Germany, Austria, and Japan after the Second World War?

In seeking to answer these questions and determine a worthwhile focus of analysis in terms of subject-matter, the following general considerations will be influential. The activity must be in some meaningful, substantive sense 'distinctive': it must manifest certain characteristics that render treating it as *sui generis* a worthwhile enterprise. It must not have been subject to sustained purposive analysis, thereby ensuring originality to the present study. The field of study should be of a breadth that enables comparison across similar practices, but also of a depth that enables detailed, specific analysis.

1.4.1 What activity?

This study focuses on the activity of 'territorial administration', which refers to a formally-constituted, locally-based management structure operating with respect to a particular territorial unit, whether a state, a sub-state unit or a non-state territorial entity. Such an artificial definition is adopted in preference to that of 'government' or 'governance' when these terms are used to refer to, respectively, the sovereign authority in the territory concerned and the activity performed by that authority.[63] Individual instances of territorial administration as defined here

---

[62] For an example of a focus on (what were then) current projects see, for example, Strohmeyer (above n. 17).

[63] On the concept of 'government' in international law, see, e.g., S Talmon, *Recognition of Governments in International Law with Particular Reference to Governments in Exile* (OUP, 1998); BR Roth, *Governmental Illegitimacy in International Law* (OUP, 2001); MN Shaw, *International Law* (5th edn, Cambridge, 2005), 303–7; I Brownlie, *Principles of Public International Law* (6th edn, OUP, 2003), 71, 90–1. For judicial treatment of the distinction between a state and its government, see, e.g., the separate opinion of Judge Séfériadès in *Lighthouses in Crete and Samos (France v Greece)*, PCIJ, Series A/B, No. 71 (1937), at 46; *Republic of Somalia v Woodhouse Drake & Carey (Suisse) SA* [1993] QB 54, [1993] 1 All ER 371. On the 'agency' relationship between the government and the state, see below, ch. 3, n. 17 and accompanying text. Many conceptualizations of the administration of territory by international organizations generally or individual missions involving this activity in particular reference conceptions of 'government' and 'governance'. Itse Sagay stated in relation to the UN Council for South-West Africa/Namibia (the discussion of which in this book commences in ch. 2, n. 19 and corresponding text) that 'from the point of view of the extent of powers and authority, there is no difference between the position of the United Nations in South West Africa, and a sovereign authority in its own territory', (Sagay (above n. 8), 269), and therefore the Council is 'for all practical purposes equivalent to the lawful government of the Territory' (ibid., 274); see also ibid., 271. Sally Morphet's definition of 'civil administration' by the UN includes the exercise of 'executive powers of government'; see Morphet, 'Organizing Civil Administration' (above n. 28), 41. See also Fen Osler Hampson's idea of 'proxy governance' in FO Hampson, *Nurturing Peace: Why Peace Settlements Succeed or Fail* (United States Institute of Peace Press, 1996), 232–3 and FO Hampson, 'Can Peacebuilding Work?', 30 (1997) *Cornell International Law Journal* 704, 707–9, and Jarat Chopra's concept of 'governance-in-trust' in Chopra, 'UN Civil Governance-in-Trust' (above n. 28), 82–3. I invoke the role of the government in R Wilde, 'The

might constitute 'governance' in this sense, and whether they do or not might be important for how they realize their purposes in some cases. However, the present enquiry is limited to identifying what these purposes are, and given the aspirations to explore hitherto under-analysed activities and set the focus of study at the right level of specificity or generality to allow thorough examination, greater benefit is served by a focus on territorial administration generally as opposed to territorial administration operating at the level of the official 'government' in particular.

An alternative mode of analysis might treat individual instances of territorial administration by international organizations differently according to whether they manifest this extra element; such an approach would be necessary, for example, for important legal questions, such as those concerning responsibility, applicable law, and jurisdiction, to be determined. The present study is not concerned with such analysis.[64] That said, connections between territorial administration and certain meanings of 'sovereignty' and 'government' are explored when relevant for determining the status of the territories subject to administration and the purposes with which some of the projects have been associated.[65]

The meaning of the word 'administration' in 'territorial administration' is, therefore, broad. The 'administrative' activity of a state is sometimes used to denote the behaviour of the 'executive' as distinct from the 'judicial' activity of the courts and the 'legislative' activity of the legislature. By contrast, all three types of activity potentially fall within the word 'administration' as it is used here.

The purposive nature of this study also suggests that situations of partial administration (for example, a territorial programme concerned with certain matters such as food distribution) should be covered as well as plenary administration (for instance, a territorial government): as far as purposive analysis is concerned, the quantitative partial/plenary distinction is merely one of degree, and therefore arbitrary.

1.4.2 Which administering actor?

Moving from the activity conducted to the identity of the actor conducting it, a key, spatial, aspect of this identity is relevant: the actor can be

Complex Role of the Legal Adviser When International Organizations Administer Territory', 95 (2001) *ASIL Proc.* 51 and R Wilde, 'The United Nations as Government: The Tensions of an Ambivalent Role', 97 (2003) *ASIL Proc.* 212. Other such approaches can be found in many of the works contained in the List of Sources, section 5.1.

[64] On these issues see the works in the List of Sources, section 5.2.7. For discussion of the agency relationship between UNMIK and Kosovo, see Bothe & Marauhn (above n. 30), 229; B Knoll, 'From Benchmarking to Final Status? Kosovo and the Problem of an International Administration's Open-Ended Mandate', 16 (2005) *EJIL* 637, section 3. For a consideration of the capacity in which administrative acts are performed in the context of the Special Court for Sierra Leone and certain human rights bodies in Bosnia and Herzegovina, see the sources cited below, n. 81; for a consideration of it in relation to OHR in Bosnia and Herzegovina, see the sources cited below, ch. 2, n. 70.

[65] See below, chs 3–5 (on the status of the territories involved) and 6–7 (on the purposes associated with the projects).

indigenous—'local'—or exogenous—'alien'. This distinction is, of course, contested, and can be defined in various ways. It is, for example, at the heart of ideas of 'self-determination' concerning the ability of people to run their own affairs free from 'external' domination.[66]

In deciding, within the general category of 'territorial administration', to focus on the conduct of that activity by particular actors, should the focus be on territorial administration by 'international' actors in particular or 'foreign' public actors more generally?[67] Is it not in order to bring into the frame colonialism,[68] state-conducted administration of Mandate and Trust territories,[69] territorial occupation (including so-called 'belligerent occupation') by foreign states,[70] such as the allied occupation of the Rhineland after the First World War,[71] the aforementioned allied administration of Germany and Austria[72] and the US

---

[66] On self-determination, see below, ch. 5, section 5.2 and the sources cited ibid., n. 3 and in List of Sources, section 5.4. These ideas in their 'internal' manifestation are also understood to concern freedom from 'internal' domination; see below, ch. 5, n. 5.

[67] The question of whether the focus should be limited to 'public' actors is considered below, section 1.4.3, *in fine.*

[68] See the works in the List of Sources, section 5.3 and the commentary below, in ch. 5, sections 5.3, and ch. 8, section 8.2.2.

[69] See below, ch. 5, section 5.3 and ch. 8, section 8.2.3.

[70] See below, ch. 8, section 8.2.5.

[71] Agreement between the United States of America, Belgium, the British Empire, and France, of the One Part, and Germany of the Other Part, with regard to the Military Occupation of the Rhine, Versailles, 28 June 1919, reproduced in 13 (1919) *AJIL Supp.* 404. For commentary, see, e.g., E Benvenisti, *The International Law of Occupation* (paperback edn, Princeton University Press, 2004), ch. 3; A Roberts, 'What is Military Occupation?', 55 (1984) *BYIL* 249, 266.

[72] The general view is that the allied arrangements in Germany, although a special form of state collaboration, did not amount to an international organization. See Declaration Regarding the Defeat of Germany ('Berlin Declaration'), 5 June 1945, 68 UNTS 189, 145 (1953) *BFSP* 796; Statement of the Allied Governments on 'Control Machinery in Germany' of 1945 (Cmd. 6648), quoted in RY Jennings, 'Government in Commission', 23 (1946) *BYIL* 112, at 115; Exchange of Notes between the United Kingdom and Spain for the recognition of the assumption by the Allied Control Council of Powers of Disposal in regard to German Enemy Assets in Spain, with Annex, Madrid, 28 October 1946, reproduced in 147 (1947) BFSP 1059; Statement of the Allied Governments on 'Consultation with Governments of other United Nations' of 1945 (Cmd. 6648), cited in Jennings, ibid., at 118 n. 2; *R v Bottrill ex parte Kuechenmeister* [1947] 1 KB 41; *Clark v. allen,* 331 US 503, 514, 67 S.Ct. 1431 (US Supreme Court, 9 June 1947), reproduced in 14 (1951) *ILR* 171. For commentary on the legal nature of the allied arrangements in Germany, see Jennings, ibid., at 115–17. On the allies in post-war Germany, see, in general, ME Bathurst and JL Simpson, *Germany and the North Atlantic Community: A Legal Survey* (Steven & Sons, 1956), 41–5 and the sources cited therein at 21 n. 1, 25 n. 10, 44 n. 47; ID Hendry and MC Wood, *The Legal Status of Berlin* (CUP, 1987); Benvenisti (above n. 71), ch. 4; J Crawford, *The Creation of States in International Law* (2nd edn, OUP, 2006), 452–4; H Kelsen, 'The Legal Status of Germany According to the Declaration of Berlin', 39 (1945) *AJIL* 518; M Bathurst, 'Legal Aspects of the Berlin Problem', 38 (1962) *BYIL* 255; FA Mann, 'The Present Legal Status of Germany', 1 (1947) *ICLQ* 314, reproduced in FA Mann, *Studies in International Law* (OUP, 1973), 634, in particular at 645–7; JW Bishop, 'The "Contractual Agreements" with the Federal Republic of Germany', 49 (1955) *AJIL* 125; FA Mann, 'Germany's Present Legal Status Revisited', 16 (1967) *ICLQ* 760, reproduced in FA Mann, *Studies in International Law* (OUP, 1973), 660; T Schweisfurth, 'Germany, Occupation after World War II', in R Bernhardt (ed.), *Encyclopedia of Public International Law,* vol. 3 (1982), 191, at 198; Roberts (above n. 71), 268–71; AW Dulles, 'That Was Then: Allen W. Dulles on the Occupation of Germany', 82:6 (Nov/Dec 2003) *Foreign Affairs* 2; Chesterman (above n. 1),

administration of Japan[73] after the Second World War, Israel's occupation of the Golan Heights, the West Bank, the Gaza Strip and Sinai,[74] and the 2003–04 administration of Iraq by the Coalition Provisional Authority (CPA) and the foreign military presence continuing in that state thereafter?[75]

25–36 and sources cited therein. On the allied administration of Austria, see Agreement on Control Machinery in Austria, signed in the European Advisory Commission, 4 July 1945 (United States–United Kingdom–France–Soviet Union), in force 24 July 1945 available at <http://www. yale.edu/lawweb/avalon/wwii/waust01.htm>. The allied administration ended in July 1955, following the entry into force of the Austrian State Treaty; see Treaty for the Re-establishment of an Independent and Democratic Austria, Vienna, 15 May 1955, entry into force 27 July 1955, agreed to by the Allied Powers (France, United Kingdom, United States, Soviet Union) and Austria, 217 UNTS 223. For commentary, see, e.g., Benvenisti, ibid., ch. 4; Crawford, ibid., 520–1.

[73] See Japanese Instrument of Surrender (Japan–Allied Powers), Tokyo Bay, 2 September 1945, available at <http://www.yale.edu/lawweb/avalon/wwii/j4.htm>. The US occupation of Japan formally ended (except in relation to Okinawa) with the Treaty of Peace with Japan (Allied and Associated Powers – Japan), signed 8 September 1951, entry into force 28 April 1952, 136 UNTS 45. For commentary, see, e.g., EJL van Aduard, *Japan, from Surrender to Peace* (Martinus Nijhoff, 1953); Benvenisti (above n. 71), ch. 4; Roberts (above n. 71), 268–71.

[74] What constitutes primary source material on this topic is highly contested, and secondary commentary is voluminous. Examples of the latter by international law experts are: A Gerson, *Israel, the West Bank and International Law* (Frank Cass & Co., 1978); E Playfair (ed.), *International Law and the Administration of Occupied Territories* (OUP, 1992); S Bowen (ed.), *Human Rights, Self-Determination and Political Change in the Occupied Palestinian Territories* (Nijhoff, 1997); Benvenisti (above n. 71), ch. 5; D Kretzmer, *The Occupation of Justice: The Supreme Court of Israel and the Occupied Territories* (SUNY Press, 2002); A Gerson, 'Trustee Occupant: The Legal Status of Israel's Presence in the West Bank', 14 (1973) *Harvard International Law Journal* 1; A Roberts, 'Decline of Illusions: The Status of the Israeli-Occupied Territories over 21 Years', 64 (1988) *International Affairs* 345; FA Boyle, 'The Creation of the State of Palestine', 1 (1990) *EJIL* 301; J Crawford, 'The Creation of the State of Palestine: Too Much Too Soon?', 1 (1990) *EJIL* 307; A Roberts, 'Prolonged Military Occupation: The Israeli-Occupied Territories Since 1967', 84 (1990) *AJIL* 83; P Malanczuk, 'Israel: Status, Territory and Occupied Territories', in R Bernhardt (ed.), *Encyclopedia of Public International Law*, vol. II (1995), 1468; P Malanczuk, 'Some Basic Aspects of the Agreements between Israel and the PLO from the Perspective of International Law', 7 (1996) *EJIL* 485; Y Dinstein, 'The International Legal Status of the West Bank and the Gaza Strip', 28 (1998) *Israel Yearbook on Human Rights* 37; O Ben-Naftali, A Gross, and K Michaeli, 'Illegal Occupation: Framing the Occupied Palestinian Territory', 23 (2005) *Berkeley Journal of International Law* 551.

[75] For secondary commentary, see, e.g., Benvenisti (above n. 71), viii–xv; N Feldman, *What We Owe Iraq: War and the Ethics of Nation Building* (Princeton University Press, 2004); Korhonen, Gras & Creutz (above n. 15), ch. 3, section 3.1.2; S Talmon (ed.), *The Occupation of Iraq, The Official Documents of the Coalition Provisional Authority* (Hart, forthcoming, 2008); G Baldwin, 'Iraq—Managing the Peace', 3 (2003) *Conflict, Security and Development* 431; E Benvenisti, 'The Security Council and the Law on Occupation: Resolution 1483 on Iraq in Historical Perspective', 1 (2003) *Israel Defense Forces Law Review* 19; L Boisson de Chazournes, 'The United Nations on Shifting Sands: About the Rebuilding of Iraq', 5 (2003) *International Law Forum* 254; AI Dawisha and K Dawisha, 'How to Build a Democratic Iraq', 82:3 (May/June 2003) *Foreign Affairs* 32; G Day and G Freeman, 'Policekeeping is the Key: Rebuilding the Internal Security Architecture of Postwar Iraq', 79 (2003) *International Affairs* 299; T Dodge, 'A Sovereign Iraq?', 46:3 (2004) *Survival* 39; TD Grant, 'The Security Council and Iraq: An Incremental Practice', 97 (2003) *AJIL* 823; KH Kaikobad, 'Problems of Belligerent Occupation: The Scope of Powers Exercised by the Coalition Provisional Authority in Iraq, April/May 2003–June 2004', 54 (2003) *ICLQ* 253; RD Langenkamp and RJ Zedalis, 'What Happens to the Iraqi Oil?: Thoughts on Some Significant, Unexamined International Legal Questions Regarding Occupation of Oil Fields', 14 (2003) *EJIL* 417; C Lawson, 'How Best to Build Democracy: Laying a Foundation for the

If one is seeking to understand the purposes served by territorial administration conducted by international actors like the UN—for instance, rebuilding infrastructure after conflict—the identity of the administering actor may not actually be significant, even if it is relevant in other respects, for example, in terms of legitimacy, applicable law, etc. To ignore other analogous activities risks arbitrariness, setting apart an activity for a reason—the identity of the administering actor—unconnected to the enquiry at hand.

However, the performance of territorial administration by foreign states has been well-documented when compared with its performance by international actors.[76] Given this, an exclusive focus on the latter actors addresses the need to

New Iraq', 82:4 (July/Aug 2003) *Foreign Affairs* 206; L Lijnzaad, 'How Not to Be an Occupying Power: Some Reflections on UN Security Council Resolution 1483 and the Contemporary Law of Occupation', in L Lijnzaad, J van Sambeek, and B Tahzib-Lie (eds), *Making the Voice of Humanity Heard* (Martinus Nijhoff, 2003), 298; A Orakhelashvili, 'The Post-War Settlement in Iraq: The UN Security Council Resolution 1483 (2003) and General International Law', 8 (2003) *Journal of Conflict & Security Law* 307; J Richards Hope and EN Griffin, 'The New Iraq: Revising Iraq's Commercial Law is a Necessity for Foreign Direct Investment and the Reconstruction of Iraq's Decimated Economy', 11 (2003–4) *Cardozo Journal of International & Comparative Law* 876; S Chesterman, 'Occupation as Liberation: International Humanitarian Law and Regime Change', 18 (2004) *Ethics & International Affairs* 51; J Gathii, 'Foreign and Other Economic Rights upon Conquest and under Occupation: Iraq in Comparative and Historical Context', 25 (2004) *University of Pennsylvania Journal of International Economic Law* 491; TW Kassinger and DJ Williams, 'Commercial Law Reform Issues in the Reconstruction of Iraq', 33 (2004) *Georgia Journal of International & Comparative Law* 217; G Mills, 'Better with the UN? Searching for Peace and Governance in Iraq', 10 (2004) *Global Governance* 281; M Ottolenghi, 'The Stars and Stripes in Al-Fardos Square: The Implications for the International Law of Belligerent Occupation', 72 (2003–4) *Fordham Law Review* 2177; J Yoo, 'Iraqi Reconstruction and the Law of Occupation', 11 (2004) *UC Davis Journal of International Law & Policy* 7; M Zwanenburg, 'Existentialism in Iraq: Security Council Resolution 1483 and the Law of Occupation', (2004) *IRRC*, vol. 86, issue 856, 745; N Bhuta, 'The Antinomies of Transformative Occupation', 16 (2005) *EJIL* 721; D Byman, 'Five Bad Options for Iraq', 47:1 (2005) *Survival* 7; L Diamond, 'Lessons from Iraq', 16 (2005) *Journal of Democracy* 9; L Diamond, 'Building Democracy After Conflict: Lessons from Iraq', 16 (2005) *Journal of Democracy* 9; JF Dobbins, 'Iraq: Winning the Unwinnable War', 84:1 (Jan/Feb 2005) *Foreign Affairs* 16; T Dodge, 'Iraq's Future: The Aftermath of Regime Change', *Adelphi Paper No. 372* (April 2005); G Fox, 'The Occupation of Iraq', 36 (2005) *Georgetown Journal of International Law* 195; C McCarthy, 'The Paradox of the International Law of Military Occupation: Sovereignty and the Reformation of Iraq', 10 (2005) *Journal of Conflict & Security Law* 51; A Roberts, 'The End of Occupation: Iraq 2004', 54 (2005) *ICLQ* 27; M Sassòli, 'Legislation and Maintenance of Public Order and Civil Life by Occupying Powers', 16 (2005) *EJIL* 661; H Synnott, 'State-Building in Southern Iraq', 47:2 (2005) *Survival* 33; R Wilde, 'The Applicability of International Human Rights Law to the Coalition Provisional Authority (CPA) and Foreign Military Presence in Iraq', 11 (2005) *ILSA Journal of International & Comparative Law* 485; R Wolfrum, 'Iraq—From Belligerent Occupation to Iraqi Exercise of Sovereignty: Foreign Power versus International Community Interference', 9 (2005) *Max Planck Yearbook of United Nations Law* 1; A Roberts, 'Transformative Military Occupation: Applying the Laws of War and Human Rights', 100 (2006) *AJIL* 580; see also LE Halchin, 'The Coalition Provisional Authority (CPA): Origin, Characteristics, and Institutional Authorities', Congressional Research Service Report, 6 June 2005, available at <http://fpc.state.gov/documents/organization/48620.pdf>.

[76] See the sources cited above, n. 72 (on the allied occupation of Germany and Austria); n. 73 (on the allied occupation of Japan); n. 74 (on the Israeli occupations); n. 75 (on the occupation of Iraq) and below, ch. 5, section 5.3, ch. 8, section 8.2.2 and List of Sources, section 5.3 (on colonialism); ch. 5, section 5.3 and ch. 8, section 8.2.3 (on the Mandate and Trusteeship systems); and

fill a knowledge gap in the conduct of territorial administration by public actors who have an 'alien' identity when compared with the identity of the territorial unit involved.

When this has been done, it becomes possible to approach the question of linkages with territorial administration conducted by foreign states. Although the primary focus of this book is the involvement of international actors in territorial administration, the involvement by 'foreign' public actors *generally* in this activity is considered in the penultimate chapter, where a broader framework of analysis is adopted, connecting up the purposes of all the different manifestations of foreign territorial administration into a common framework. Here, then, the arbitrary distinction is dissolved; this is possible because of the foregoing analysis aiming to address the relative disparity of treatment as between territorial administration by international actors, on the one hand, and this activity performed by foreign states, on the other.

1.4.3 Linking the actor with the activity

In the previous discussion, the significance of focusing on administering actors with an 'international' identity was identified through a consideration of the relative disparity of analysis on the conduct of territorial administration by these actors, when compared with the treatment of the conduct of such activity by foreign states. Another relevant consideration when determining the focus of analysis is the nature of the connection between the international actors, on the one hand, and the activity of territorial administration, on the other. How is the conduct of the latter by the former distinctive and, indeed, how can and should such 'conduct' be defined?

As mentioned earlier, the involvement of international actors in territorial administration, like such involvement by foreign states, is distinctive because of the 'alien' identity of the administering actor when compared with the spatial identity associated with the administered territory. As Nathaniel Berman remarks in relation to the administrative involvement by the League of Nations in the Saar territory and the Free City of Danzig, such arrangements are 'local'—in that they are based in, and acting on behalf of, the territory concerned—'yet international'—because of the identity of the administering actor, a duality symbolized by the stamps issued by the UN during its administration of East Timor, reproduced on the cover of this book, where the 'local'—named Timor Lorosae—is positioned alongside the 'international'—named UNTAET.[77]

---

section 8.2.5 (on occupation). The decision not to cover the allies in Germany is a narrowing of the approach taken in Wilde, above n. 28 (text accompanying n. 3), where the allied occupation of Germany was included.

[77] Berman (above n. 32), at 1874 and 1883. (Although 'Lorosae' is used on the stamps, the more common spelling is 'Lorosa'e'—see above, n. 2.)

There is, moreover, a further aspect of the spatial identity of the administering actor which marks out an 'international' entity such as an international organization from a foreign state. This spatial identity—as 'international'—is distinct from, and opposed to, the 'local' identity of the territorial unit and population affected, even if the entity's activities are limited to that territory and some of the staff are not 'internationals' (the typical term for internationally-recruited, foreign-national staff) but drawn from the local population. This divergence between the two spatial identities is unusual; usually, territorial administration is conducted by actors—representatives of the local population or, sometimes, foreign states—who share the same spatial identity as the territory insofar as it is locally-based in character (although not necessarily a locality that matches the boundaries of the territorial unit).[78]

The distinctiveness of the international/national dichotomy is significant when determining on which 'international' actors to focus. It provides a basis for opening out the analysis to take in international organizations generally, not just the United Nations. Moreover, it becomes possible to consider another actor: what will be termed the 'international appointee'. As will be explained more fully in the next chapter, in various different places, individual officials on locally-based bodies involved in particular forms of territorial administration (as defined broadly above) are foreign-national experts who owe their position to a process of appointment involving an international actor such as an international organization or an official of an international court.[79] An example would be the foreign-nationals who sit as judges, alongside local-nationals, in a range of courts and

---

[78] Such a contrast in spatial identities distinguishes the activity under evaluation from the administrative arrangements of the European Union with respect to EU Member States (notably law-making). There, the supra-national institutions such as the Commission share the same spatial identity as the legal order in respect of which they operate (even if this legal order cuts across the distinct legal orders of Member States). On the European Union, see the Consolidated Version of the Treaty on European Union, *OJ* C325 (2002), 5. See also, e.g., D O'Keeffe and P Twomey (eds), *Legal Issues of the Maastricht Treaty* (Wiley Chancery Law, 1994); D McGoldrick, *International Relations Law of the European Union* (Longman, 1997); A Arnull, A Dashwood, M Ross, and D Wyatt, *Wyatt & Dashwood's European Union Law* (4th edn, Sweet & Maxwell, 2000); P Craig and G de Búrca, *EU Law, Text, Cases & Materials* (3rd edn, OUP, 2002); B Rudden and D Wyatt, *Basic Community Laws* (8th edn, OUP, 2002); E Denza, *The Intergovernmental Pillars of the EU* (OUP, 2002); S Douglas-Scott, *Constitutional Law of the European Union* (Pearson/Longman, 2002), especially Part I; D Chalmers, C Hadjiemmanuil, G Monti, and A Tomkins, *European Union Law: Text and Materials* (CUP, 2006), especially chs 1–5; J Steiner, L Woods, and C Twigg-Flesner, *EU Law* (9th edn, OUP, 2006), especially Part I. Similarly, although the enjoyment of privileges and immunities in state territory enables international organizations to have near-exclusive administrative competence by default, such competence usually covers only the property and personnel of the organization (the provision of consular protection is similarly limited); see, e.g., Convention on the Privileges and Immunities of the United Nations, GA Res. 22A (I), 13 February 1946, in force 17 September 1946, 1 UNTS 15, 90 UNTS 327 (corrigendum); C Wickremasinghe, 'Immunities Enjoyed by Officials of States and International Organizations', ch. 13 in MD Evans, *International Law* (2nd edn, OUP, 2006).

[79] See below, ch. 2, section 2.3.4.

tribunals operating in the territory to which their jurisdiction relates, including, but not limited to, tribunals dealing with 'serious' crimes that have come to be described as 'hybrid' tribunals mainly because of the mixed international/national composition of the bench.[80]

These appointees serve as officials on the bodies to which they are appointed, and are not usually regarded as officials of the international body involved in their appointment, even if they may have worked for it previously and/or been seconded from it. As reflected in the 'hybrid' or 'mixed' designations, the bodies on which they sit are not exclusively of an 'international' character as far as composition is concerned, although such bodies may be designated as such for particular purposes.[81] Although there may be important differences in the legal identity of such appointees when compared with that of officials working on territorial administration missions conducted by international organizations, as far as the present enquiry into purposes is concerned, such differences are less important than the common spatial identity, as 'international' in operation. This is based on foreign nationality and the involvement of an international actor in the appointments, and reflected in the popular designation 'international appointees' which will be used as shorthand in this study.[82]

Beyond considerations rooted in the distinctiveness of the 'international' identity of the administering actors, the aspiration to shed light into hitherto relatively under-explored fields of activity also supports a focus on international organizations generally, rather than the United Nations in particular. Although, as mentioned, an exclusive focus on the United Nations is a common feature across much of the literature on recent projects involving territorial administration by international organizations, the reason for excluding other international organizations—for instance, OHR in Bosnia and Herzegovina—is unexplained. If one is seeking to respond to gaps in knowledge, one would surely be drawn to cover such entities as well; indeed, even more so, given the relative lack of attention given to them. Perhaps the exclusive focus on the UN has been motivated by an understandable desire to sacrifice breadth for depth; for a study of the present length concerned exclusively with a purposive analysis, however, arguably the latter is not compromised by expanding the frame of reference from the UN to international organizations generally.

[80] See below, ch. 2, section 2.3.4.2.
[81] For example, when the question of the legal status of the tribunal for the purposes of the law of state immunity is being determined. On this, see, e.g., *Prosecutor v Charles Ghankay Taylor*, Case Number SCSL-2003-01-I, Special Court for Sierra Leone, Appeals Chamber, Decision on Immunity from Jurisdiction, 31 May 2004, obtainable from <http://www.sc-sl.org>. On a consideration of whether the Human Rights Chamber and the Constitutional Court in Bosnia and Herzegovina were 'domestic' or 'international' for the purposes of the admissibility rules of the European Court of Human Rights, see Venice Commission, *Amicus Curiae Opinion* (above n. 38), sections III and IV respectively; *Jeličić v Bosnia and Herzegovina* (above n. 38). On the Human Rights Chamber, see below, ch. 2, section 2.3.4.2; on the Constitutional Court, see below, ch. 2, section 2.3.4.1, n. 79 and accompanying text.
[82] This is discussed further in the next chapter; see below, ch. 2, section 2.3.4.

Equally, although there is now a significant amount of commentary on certain 'hybrid' processes, the range of activities studied has been mediated in many cases by an interest in responses to serious atrocities, leading to a predominant focus on processes dealing with such atrocities exclusively, such as 'hybrid' criminal tribunals.[83] What is covered here amounts to a sub-set of the actual instances of the involvement of international appointees on locally-based bodies involved in particular aspects of territorial administration, even such bodies of a 'judicial' character: for example, it leaves outside the frame the presence of internationally-appointed foreign judges on the Constitutional Court of Bosnia and Herzegovina.[84] As with the move from the UN in particular to international organizations generally, the importance of drawing attention to neglected activity thus reinforces the merits of a focus on the involvement of international appointees to nationally-based administrative institutions generally.

The issue of focusing on neglected activities suggests the question as to whether territorial administration by private entities such as corporations, militias, NGOs, and the like should also be addressed. It might be said that there is a somewhat equivalent knowledge gap to territorial administration by international organizations and some of the international appointees as far as the conduct of this activity by foreign 'private' actors is concerned.[85] However, opening out the analysis from

---

[83] See, e.g., MC Bassiouni (ed.), *Post-Conflict Justice* (Transnational Publishers, 2002); R Mani, *Beyond Retribution: Seeking Justice in the Shadows of War* (Polity Press, 2002); K Ambos and M Othman (eds), *New Approaches in International Criminal Justice: Kosovo, East Timor, Sierra Leone and Cambodia* (Max Planck Institute, 2003); CPR Romano, A Nollkaemper, and JK Kleffner (eds), *Internationalized Criminal Courts: Sierra Leone, East Timor, Kosovo, and Cambodia* (OUP, 2004) and sources cited therein; DA Mundis, 'New Mechanisms for the Enforcement of International Humanitarian Law', 95 (2001) *AJIL* 934; S Linton, 'Cambodia, East Timor and Sierra Leone: Experiments in International Justice', 12 (2001) *Criminal Law Forum* 185; S Linton, 'New Approaches to International Justice in Cambodia and East Timor', (2002) *IRRC*, vol. 84, issue 845, 93; B Pouligny, 'Building Peace in Situations of Post-Mass Crimes', 9 (2002) *International Peacekeeping* 181; C Stahn, 'United Nations Peace-Building, Amnesties and Alternative Forms of Justice: A Change in Practice?', (2002) *IRRC*, vol. 84, issue 845, 191; S de Bertodano, 'Current Developments in Internationalized Courts', 1 (2003) *Journal of International Criminal Justice* 226; LA Dickinson, 'The Promise of Hybrid Courts', 97 (2003) *AJIL* 295; J Snyder and L Vinjamuri, 'Trials and Errors: Principle and Pragmatism in Strategies of International Justice', 28 (2003) *International Security* 5; G-JA Knoops, 'International and Internationalized Criminal Courts: the New Face of International Peace and Security?', 4 (2004) *International Criminal Law Review* 527; I Simonovic, 'Dealing with the Legacy of Past War Crimes and Human Rights Abuses: Experiences and Trends', 2 (2004) *Journal of International Criminal Justice* 701; J Cockayne, 'The Fraying Shoestring: Rethinking Hybrid War Crimes Tribunals', 28 (2005) *Fordham International Law Journal* 616; F Egonda-Ntende, 'Justice after Conflict: Challenges Facing "Hybrid" Courts: National Tribunals with International Participation', 18 (2005) *Journal of International Law of Peace and Armed Conflict* 24.

[84] See below, ch. 2, n. 79 and accompanying text and section 2.3.4.1, *passim*.

[85] A brief policy proposal, Fen Osler Hampson's 1996 concept of 'proxy governance', covered the performance of administrative functions by 'international governmental and non-governmental actors'; see Hampson, *Nurturing Peace* (above n. 63), 232–3 (quotation from 232) and Hampson, 'Can Peacebuilding Work?' (above n. 63), 707–9. For a specific example of the corporate conduct of certain administrative functions, the involvement of Talisman Energy Ltd. in 'community development' activities such as building medical facilities and schools in Sudan, see G Gagnon, A Macklin, and P Simons, *Deconstructing Engagement: Corporate*

'international' actors to, essentially, all 'foreign' entities other than foreign states, apart from losing the distinctiveness of the 'international' identity of the administering actor, would also render the field too broad for a study of this length: the subject-matter of analysis must be specific enough to be able to attempt the kind of detailed analysis necessary given the paucity of existing work.

1.4.4 Defining the 'international' actor

This study concerns two 'international' actors: international organizations and international appointees who sit on locally-based bodies involved in some form of territorial administration. Which particular entities and individuals fall within these two categories?

As far as 'international organizations' are concerned, the common meaning found in international legal doctrine is adopted: 'public' organizations, viz. organizations created by states, understood as enjoying distinct identities, separate from the identities of the states that set them up.[86] In other words, entities

---

Self-Regulation in Conflict Zones—Implications for Human Rights and Canadian Public Policy, University of Toronto Public Law Research Paper No. 04-07 (2003), available at <http://ssrn. com/abstract=557002>, 46–7. On this type of corporate activity generally, and its implications for human rights law and humanitarian law in particular, see, e.g., N Jägers, *Corporate Human Rights Obligations* (Intersentia, 2002); JA Zerk, *Multinationals and Corporate Social Responsibility: Limitations and Opportunities in International Law* (CUP, 2006); S Gibson, 'Lack of Extraterritorial Jurisdiction over Civilians: A New Look at an Old Problem', 148 (1995) *Military Law Review* 114; A Clapham, 'State Responsibility, Corporate Responsibility, and Complicity in Human Rights Violations', in L Bomann-Larsen and O Wiggen (eds), *Responsibility in World Business: Managing Harmful Side-Effects of Corporate Activity* (UN University Press, 2004), 50; A McBeth, 'Privatising Human Rights: What Happens to the State's Human Rights Duties when Services are Privatised?', 5 (2004) *Melbourne Journal of International Law* 133; PW Singer, 'War, Profits, and the Vacuum of Law: Privatized Military Firms and International Law', 45 (2004) *Columbia Journal of Transnational Law* 521; M Bina, 'Private Military Contractor Liability and Accountability after Abu Ghraib', 39 (2005) *Marshall Law Review* 1237; M Schmitt, 'Humanitarian Law and Direct Participation in Hostilities by Private Contractors or Civilian Employees', 5 (2005) *Chicago Journal of International Law* 511. On non-state actors and human rights, see, e.g., the following cases: *Young, James and Webster v United Kingdom*, App. no. 7601/76, judgment of 18 October 1982, European Court of Human Rights, *Series A*, No. 55; *Lopez Ostra v Spain*, App. no. 16798/90, judgment of 9 December 1994, European Court of Human Rights, *Series A*, No. 303-A; *Guerra v Italy*, App. no. 14967/89, judgment of 19 February 1998, European Court of Human Rights, *Reports 1998-I*; *Social and Economic Rights Action Centre and Center for Economic and Social Rights v Nigeria*, Comm. No. 155/96, African Commission of Human and Peoples' Rights, 30th Ordinary Session, 13–27 October 2001, obtainable from <http://www.achpr.org>; *Yanomami Community v Brasil*, Resolution No. 12/85, Case No. 7615, 5 March 1985, in *Annual Report of the Inter-American Commission on Human Rights 1984–1985*, OEA/Ser.L/V/II.66, doc. 10 rev. 1, 1 October 1985, at 24; *Mayagna (Sumo) Awas Tingni Community v Nicaragua*, Inter-American Court of Human Rights, 31 August 2001, *Series C*, No. 79; *Hopu and Bessert v France*, Comm. No. 549/1993, Human Rights Committee, 9 July 1997, UN Doc. CCPR/C/60/D/549/1993/Rev.1 and the commentary in P Alston (ed.), *Non-State Actors and Human Rights* (OUP, 2005) and A Clapham, *Human Rights Obligations of Non-State Actors* (OUP, 2006).

[86] On international organizations generally, see, e.g., PE Corbett, 'What is the League of Nations?', 5 (1924) *BYIL* 119; C Eagleton, 'International Organization and the Law of

formed by states viewed to be more than the sum of their (state) parts. Usually, the term also denotes actors meeting the foregoing requirements and also enjoying distinct international legal personality, an extra element related to the requirement of creation by states, since for some commentators only states enjoy the competence to bring other international legal persons into existence.[87]

How has the decision been made about which entities meet this definition, and thus fall within the scope of the book? This is not a book on the law of international organizations generally or the legal status of such entities in particular; to give proper treatment of the latter issue where it is unclear would skew the focus too far from the central theme. Equally, to address the question in short order would render the explanation offered so basic as to be of little worth. The foregoing analysis proceeds from an assumption that all the entities covered as

Responsibility', 76 (1950) *Recueil des Cours* Vol. I 319; H Kelsen, *The Law of the United Nations* (Stevens & Sons, 1951); G Mangone, *A Short History of International Organization* (McGraw-Hill, 1954); P Reuter, *International Institutions* (JM Chapman transl., Allen & Unwin, 1958); F Seyersted, 'Objective International Personality of Intergovernmental Organizations; Do Their Capacities Really Depend upon the Conventions Establishing Them?', 34 (1964) *Nordisk Tidsskrift for International Ret* 3; IL Claude, *Swords into Ploughshares—The Problems and Progress of International Organization* (4th edn, Random House, 1971); TM Franck, *Nation Against Nation: What Happened to the UN Dream and What the US Can Do About It* (OUP, 1985); F Morgenstern, *Legal Problems of International Organizations* (Grotius Publications, 1986); D Mitrany, 'The Functional Approach to World Organization', in RA Falk, SS Kim, and SH Mendlovitz (eds), *The United Nations and a Just World Order* (Westview, 1991); F Kirgis, *International Organizations in their Legal Setting* (2nd edn, West Publishing Co., 1993); SD Bailey and S Daws, *The United Nations, A Concise Political Guide* (3rd edn, Macmillan, 1995); H Schermers and N Blokker, *International Institutional Law* (3rd edn, Martinus Nijhoff, 1995) and the sources cited therein in the Annex at 1199; F Knipping (ed.), *The United Nations System and its Predecessors* (2 vols, OUP, 1997); R-J Dupuy (ed.), *A Handbook on International Organizations* (2nd edn, Kluwer Law International, 1998); D Sarooshi, *The United Nations and the Development of Collective Security* (OUP, 1999); A Reinisch, *International Organizations Before National Courts* (CUP, 2000); C Archer, *International Organizations* (3rd edn, Routledge, 2001); P Sands and P Klein, *Bowett's Law of International Institutions* (5th edn, Sweet & Maxwell, 2001) and the bibliography therein at 1; J Klabbers, *An Introduction to International Institutional Law* (CUP, 2002); B Simma (ed.), *The Charter of the United Nations. A Commentary* (2nd edn, OUP, 2002); CF Amerasinghe, *Principles of the Institutional Law of International Institutions* (2nd edn, CUP, 2005); D Sarooshi, *International Organizations and Their Exercise of Sovereign Powers* (OUP, 2005); N White, *The Law of International Organizations* (2nd edn, Manchester University Press, 2005); S Daws and T Weiss (eds), *The Oxford Handbook on the United Nations* (OUP, 2007). On the international law definition of an 'international organization', see, e.g., Reuter, ibid., 214–18; Seyersted, ibid., *passim*; Schermers & Blokker, ibid., 22–31; White, ibid., ch. 1 and sources cited therein; Sands & Klein, ibid., 16–17; Klabbers, ibid., 7–13; Amerasinghe, ibid., 9–13. On theoretical ideas of international organization, see, e.g., Reuter, ibid., Part III, ch. 1; Claude, ibid.; White, ibid., ch. 1; Klabbers, ibid., ch. 2; D Kennedy, 'The Move to Institutions', 8 (1987) *Cardozo Law Review* 841. On the law of international organizations see, e.g., the works by Eagleton, Kelsen, Mangone, Reuter, Seyersted, Morgenstern, Kirgis, Schermers & Blokker (and the sources cited therein in the Annex at 1199), White, Dupuy, Sarooshi, Reinisch, Sands & Klein, Klabbers, Simma, and Amerasinghe cited above in the present footnote.

87 See the commentary by Amerasinghe (above n. 86), 10. Some commentators adopt additional criteria for international organizations status: creation through an international agreement (see Schermers & Blokker, above n. 86, 23–9; Amerasinghe, ibid.); enjoying a constitution (e.g., Amerasinghe, ibid.); and the capacity to address norms to its members (Sands & Klein, above n. 86, 16). On the enjoyment of international legal personality by international organizations,

international organizations meet the definition above, and those which are absent in this regard do not enjoy this status. [88]

As far as the 'international appointees' are concerned, as explained in the previous section, the distinctively 'international' identity of such actors is derived from their foreign nationality and the involvement of an international actor in their appointment. The present study focuses, therefore, on individuals whose identity, for the purposes of the role they perform in the locally-based institutions, has these two characteristics. The particular arrangements in this regard differ somewhat across each individual institution, and are explained in detail in the next chapter.[89]

1.4.5 Defining international territorial administration

Having considered the relationship between the administering actor and the activity of administration in determining which actors are to be covered in this study, it is now in order to focus on this relationship more directly, to determine what type of involvement in administration by international actors will be analysed.

When considering the Kosovo and East Timor UN administration projects in 2000, Louise Fréchette, the then UN Deputy Secretary-General, remarked that they:

...are qualitatively different from almost any other the Organization has ever undertaken. In each place the United Nations is the administration, responsible for fulfilling all the functions of a State—from fiscal management and judicial affairs to everyday municipal services, such as cleaning the streets and conducting customs formalities at the borders. This is a new order of magnitude for an organization that more customarily provides States with technical assistance in such areas, rather than assuming complete responsibility for them.[90]

---

see, e.g., *Reparations for Injuries Suffered in the Service of the United Nations*, *Advisory Opinion, ICJ Reports 1949*, 174 (discussing the United Nations); Eagleton (above n. 86); Reuter (above n. 86), 231; Seyersted (above n. 86); Schermers & Blokker, ibid., 975–95; White (above n. 86), ch. 2 and sources cited therein; Sands & Klein, ibid., ch. 15 and sources cited at 470; Klabbers (above n. 86), ch. 3; Amerasinghe, ibid., ch. 3 and sources cited at 66 n. 1.

   [88] However, for each entity included as an 'international organization', reference material on this status is provided in the footnote accompanying the first main reference, in ch. 2 below, to its involvement in territorial administration. Because of the obscure nature of and lack of commentary on the legal status of the Office of the High Representative in Bosnia and Herzegovina (OHR), a general explanation of this entity in particular is also provided. See below, ch. 2, nn. 11 (on the League of Nations), 16 (on the United Nations), 23 (on the Common Foreign and Security Policy (CFSP) structure of the European Union), 39 (on the OSCE); and section 2.3.3 (on OHR).

   [89] See below, ch. 2, section 2.3.4.

   [90] Statement by Louise Fréchette, Deputy Secretary-General of the United Nations, UN Press Release DSG/SM/91, 3 April 2000, cited in C Gray, *International Law and the Use of Force* (2nd edn, OUP, 2004), 210.

Also discussing the two projects, the UN 'Brahimi Report' on peace operations of the same year stated that:

[t]hese operations face challenges and responsibilities that are unique among United Nations field operations. No other operation must set and enforce the law, establish customs services and regulations, set and collect business and personal taxes, attract foreign investment, adjudicate property disputes and liabilities for war damage, reconstruct and operate all public utilities, create a banking system, run schools and pay teachers, and collect the garbage.[91]

Granting international organizations administrative prerogatives over territory is, as Fréchette remarks, 'qualitatively different' from the usual activities of international organizations within states. International organizations usually ostensibly assist state governments in their conduct of territorial administration, not take over the running of this administration directly, or exercise authority over it.[92] Although the distinction between assistance, on the one hand, and supervision or control, on the other, is contested and can be difficult to make in practice, as an idea it is key to understanding how the activity of territorial administration is compared with other activities performed by international organizations, and treated as distinctive as a result.[93]

Because of these considerations relating to distinctiveness and originality, the difference between supervision/control/conduct, on the one hand, and mere assistance/advice, on the other, is adopted as a key component in defining the nature of the involvement in territorial administration by international actors that will form the basis for this study.

Earlier, the activity of 'territorial administration' was defined as a 'formally-constituted, locally-based management structure operating with respect to a

---

[91] Brahimi Report (above n. 11), para. 77.

[92] Discussing the role of UNMIK in promoting human rights in Kosovo, Bernhard Knoll observes that '[i]nternationalization reaches beyond the conventional means of democracy assistance in less intrusive multilateral operations'; Knoll (above n. 1), 282.

[93] This is underlined by the following statement made in 2002 by the OSCE Head of Mission to Bosnia and Herzegovina, describing the shift in the OSCE's role with regard to elections in that country from direct conduct to monitoring conduct by local actors:

[o]n 5 October, Bosnia and Herzegovina will hold general elections...without the OSCE's direct involvement or funding support...On Election Day, OSCE vehicles will no longer be a common sight on the roads of Bosnia and Herzegovina. Instead, local police and national authorities will be entirely responsible for the security and transportation of election materials. From beginning to end, the responsibility for a smooth and successful election now lies with the citizens of BiH...The OSCE Mission continues, however, actively to support election preparations in discreet but useful ways. Our Elections Department...has been advising the BiH Election Commission, headed by a respected Bosnian attorney, Lidija Korac, on matters such as financial resources and interpretation of the Election Law.

Head of OSCE mission in Bosnia and Herzegovina, 'Statement to OSCE Permanent Council', Vienna, 4 July 2002, available at <http://www.oscebih.org/documents/28-eng.pdf>. On the role of OSCE in conducting the elections in Bosnia and Herzegovina before this point, see below, ch. 2, n. 39 and accompanying text. On the similar arrangement for the OSCE to shift from conduct to assistance in relation to the elections in Kosovo, see below, ch. 2, n. 38.

particular territorial unit, whether a state, a sub-state unit or a non-state territorial entity'.[94] Bearing this in mind, the present study focuses on the following
involvement in this structure by international organizations and international
appointees, which in both cases takes place directly within the territory concerned. As far as international organizations are concerned, the organization
asserts the right either to supervise and control the operation of this structure by
other (usually local) actors, or to operate the structure directly.[95] This can pertain
to the structure as a whole, or certain parts of it (e.g., the legislature). In the case
of the international appointees, the individuals in question serve as officials of
particular institutions which form part of the structure of territorial administration, such as courts, tribunals, and electoral bodies.[96]

Since not all such bodies are of a judicial character, the more general category
of 'administrative' bodies is adopted, reflecting the connection between what
they do and the general definition of 'territorial administration' adopted above,
which, as mentioned, includes judicial activity.

[94] See section 1.4.1 above.

[95] Accordingly, it includes situations where particular administrative activities are performed
by local actors, but under the overall authority of the international organization. See, for example,
the arrangements in Kosovo and East Timor during the UNMIK and UNTAET periods (above,
nn. 1 and 2 respectively).

[96] This does not, therefore, cover the provision of assistance and/or advice to such bodies. Such
involvement can sometimes be considerable and in such cases highly determinative of the activity of the institution in question, notwithstanding the lack of formal involvement in decision-
making. An example would be the Iraqi Special Tribunal (IST), later reconstituted as the Iraqi
Higher Criminal Court, created by the Coalition Provisional Authority in Iraq in 2003. As will
be mentioned below in ch. 2, section 2.3.4.2 (text accompanying nn. 109 and 110), provision was
made for internationals to be appointed as judges; although at the time of writing no such appointments had been made, the Tribunal/Higher Court was 'internationalized' in the sense that it relied
heavily on foreign assistance and advice; indeed, the degree of foreign involvement was such that its
independence was placed into question. Provisions enabling and sometimes mandating the involvement of foreign assistance and advice were included in the constituent instruments of both bodies.
Under the Statute of the IST, the President of the Tribunal was required to appoint non-Iraqis to
act in advisory capacities or as observers in proceedings before the Tribunal. See Statute of the
Iraqi Special Tribunal, 10 December 2003 (hereinafter 'IST Statute'), available at <http://www.
globalpolicy.org/intljustice/general/2003/1210iraqistatute.pdf>, Art. 6 (b), with respect to
appointments to the Trial Chambers and the Appeals Chamber; Art. 7(n) with respect to the Office
of the Investigative Judges. Similarly, the Chief Prosecutor was required to appoint non-Iraqi
advisers and observers (ibid., Art. 8(j)). The role of the appointees included monitoring respect
for due process standards in the course of investigations; see ibid., Arts 6(b); 7(n); 8(j). In making
these appointments, the IST President and Chief Prosecutor were entitled to request assistance
from the 'international community,' including the UN; see ibid., Arts 6(c); 7(o); 8(k). Under the
Law of the Higher Criminal Court, the President and the Chief Prosecutor have the discretion to
appoint international advisers and observers and, when exercising this discretion, as with the IST
are entitled to request assistance from the 'international community', including the UN. See Law
No. 10/2005 on the Iraqi Higher Criminal Court, 10 October 2005, English unofficial translation
obtainable from <http://law.case.edu/saddamtrial/documents/IST_statute_official_english.pdf>,
Arts 7(2); 8(9); 9(7)). For commentary on the 'internationalized' nature of the IST and the Higher
Court, see the remarks of Professor Michael Scharf, who was personally involved in this process, in
MP Scharf and MA Newton, 'The Iraqi High Tribunal's Dujail Trial Opinion', *ASIL Insight*, vol.
10, issue 34 (18 December 2006), obtainable from <http://www.asil.org>. For commentary on the
Special Tribunal/Higher Court generally, see List of Sources, section 5.1.4.8.

This type of involvement in territorial administration by these particular international actors will henceforth be known generically as 'international territorial administration' (ITA).[97]

As illustrated by the quotation from the then UN Deputy Secretary-General Fréchette, the activity of ITA should be contrasted with merely monitoring and/ or assisting local actors in operating the structure of territorial administration as defined in this study. For example, a distinction can be made between monitoring the conduct of elections by local authorities, and running elections directly (in the case of international organizations) or serving as an official on the locally-based body running the elections (in the case of international appointees).[98]

ITA denotes the activity under evaluation in a generic sense. How are individual manifestations of it to be determined for the purposes of analysis, and, in the light of this, how should they be understood and described?

Individual instances of territorial administration by international organizations are sometimes conceived originally and exclusively as such, as in the case of Kosovo, often leading to the name for the mission explicitly referencing this objective, as in the 'United Nations Interim Administration Mission in Kosovo', UNMIK. However, in many other cases, for example, OHR in Bosnia and Herzegovina, the performance of an administrative function is seen as only part of the organization's mandate in the territory. Given this, considerations of individual instances of territorial administration by international organizations often involve focusing on part of a particular 'mission'. It would, therefore, be misleading to talk of administration 'missions' in many cases. Moreover, as illustrated in the example of UNMIK, the word 'Mission' is an official one used in the terminology of United Nations field operations to name such operations; however, as illustrated by OHR, many individual instances of territorial administration by international organizations, including some performed by the UN, have been performed by entities that do not have the word 'Mission' in their name.

Clearly, the international appointees to locally-based institutions do not constitute 'missions'. That said, each set of such appointments constitutes a meaningful generic category as far as policy analysis is concerned. Just as one might ask why OHR has been supposedly granted administrative powers in Bosnia and Herzegovina, one might also ask why the international appointees have been placed on the Constitutional Court in that country.

---

[97] This term was first used in R Wilde, 'From Danzig to East Timor and Beyond: The Role of International Territorial Administration', 95 (2001) *AJIL* 583. The word 'international', then, relates to the identity of the administering actor; whereas the administration mission conducted by this actor may be pursuant to a mandate in international law, and/or, as is discussed below in chs 6 and 7, its purposes may reflect ideas in international policy and law, these features of the activity are not being alluded to through the use of this word.

[98] See, e.g., the Statement of the Head of OSCE Mission in Bosnia and Herzegovina cited above, n. 93.

Given the need for a term to denote a particular instantiation of international territorial administration, and the limitations of using the term 'mission', the alternative term 'project' will be used in this study, denoting a particular localized regime, in the case of administration by international organizations, classified by organization (e.g., the project involving OHR in Bosnia and Herzegovina), and in the case of the international appointees, classified by locally-based institution (e.g., the project involving international appointees on the Constitutional Court in Bosnia and Herzegovina).

1.5 Purposive Analysis: the Idea of the 'Policy Institution'

1.5.1 Policy institution

The present enquiry into the purposes served by the international territorial administration projects is pursued through the idea of a 'policy institution', a concept which draws on existing ideas but is itself new.

One particular meaning of the word 'institution' is utilized: an 'established practice'.[99] The word is, therefore, being used in its incorporeal sense and not in the more common sense of a corporeal entity; the latter meaning of 'institution' would cover one of the two 'international' entities involved in the practice, the international organization.[100] 'Institution' in the sense of an 'established practice' is sometimes used to denote practice 'established' because it has normative import: that it is itself, or is reflective of, a binding principle.[101] This is the common way in which the word is used in the term 'international institution' in international relations discourse.[102] For many international lawyers, an 'institution' used in this sense might be synonymous with customary law—indeed, international law

---

[99] Definition 6a of 'institution' in the *Oxford English Dictionary* is an '. . . established law, custom, usage, practice, organization, or other element in the political or social life of a people' (*OED Online*, at <http://www.oed.com>). For an example of a different use of the term, in the field of economics, see, e.g., DC North, *Institutions, Institutional Change, and Economic Performance* (CUP, 1990) and D Acemoglu, S Johnson, and J Robinson, 'Institutions as a Fundamental Cause of Long-Run Growth', ch. 6 in P Aghion and S Durlauf (eds), *Handbook of Economic Growth* (Elsevier, 2005).

[100] Definition 7a of 'institution' in the *Oxford English Dictionary* is an 'establishment, organization, or association . . .' (*OED Online*, at <http://www.oed.com>). International organizations are, of course, sometimes called 'international institutions': see Reuter, above n. 86.

[101] Cf. the dictionary definition 6a (above n. 99), which also includes 'a regulative principle or convention'.

[102] H Bull, *The Anarchical Society—A Study of Order in World Politics* (Macmillan, 1977), at 74 and *passim*; R Jackson and G Sørensen, *Introduction to International Relations. Theories and Approaches* (3rd edn, OUP, 2006), 117–20; B Buzan, *From International to World Society? English School Theory and the Social Structure of Globalisation* (CUP, 2004), *passim* and ch. 6; RO Keohane, 'International Institutions: Two Approaches', 32 (1988) *International Studies Quarterly* 379, at 383 and *passim*; BA Simmons and LL Martin, 'International Organizations and Institutions',

is usually given as an example of an international institution by international relations scholars.[103] The present study adopts the more general meaning of an 'institution' as an 'established practice' lacking the implication of normativity, but without prejudice to the question of whether such normativity subsists.[104]

Although not, then, being concerned with normativity in the sense of practice necessarily reflecting some sort of obligation, this study does go beyond mere practice to consider issues of policy, seeking to identify and classify the purposes with which the administration projects have been associated. The term 'policy institution' is adopted as shorthand for this teleological enquiry, combining an 'institution' as an 'established practice' with a focus on 'policy' in the sense of the ends to which the practice is put. Thus the focus is on policy *implementation* rather than, for example, policy *definition* or *formulation*.[105]

---

ch. 9 in W Carlsnaes, T Risse, and BA Simmons (eds), *Handbook of International Relations* (Sage Publications, 2002), at 194; KJ Holsti, 'The Institutions of International Politics: Continuity, Change and Transformation', paper presented at the Annual General Meeting of the International Studies Association, New Orleans, 23–27 March 2002, available at <www.leeds.ac.uk/polis/englishschool/holsti02.doc>.

[103] On customary international law, see *North Sea Continental Shelf Cases (Federal Republic of Germany v Denmark; Federal Republic of Germany v Netherlands), ICJ Reports 1969*, 3, paras 70–7; *Military and Paramilitary Activities in and Against Nicaragua (Nicaragua v United States of America), Merits, Judgment, ICJ Reports 1986*, 14, paras 174–9; A D'Amato, *The Concept of Custom in International Law* (Cornell University Press, 1971); GM Danilenko, *Law-Making in the International Community* (Martinus Nijhoff, 1993), ch. 4; M Byers, *Custom, Power and the Power of Rules* (CUP, 1999); A Cassese, *International Law* (2nd edn, OUP, 2005), ch. 8; I Brownlie, *Principles of Public International Law* (6th edn, OUP, 2003), 6–12 and sources cited therein at 6, n. 11; H Thirlway, 'The Sources of International Law', in MD Evans, *International Law* (2nd edn, OUP, 2006), 115, at 121–7; M Akehurst, 'Custom as a Source of International Law', 47 (1974–75) *BYIL* 1; P Haggenmacher, 'La doctrine des deux éléments du droit coutumier dans la pratique de la cour internationale', 90 (1986) *Revue Générale de Droit International Public* 5; R Bernhardt, 'Customary International Law', in R Bernhardt (ed.), *Encyclopedia of Public International Law*, vol. 1 (1992), 898; International Law Association, Committee on Formation of Customary (General) International Law, 'Statement of Principles Applicable to the Formation of General Customary International Law', London, 2000, obtainable from <http://www.ila-hq.org>. For a consideration of international legal rules as 'international institutions' by international relations scholars, see, e.g., Bull (above n. 102), 74; Buzan, *From International to World Society* (above n. 102), ch. 6; Jackson & Sørensen (above n. 83) 117.

[104] This use of institution echoes the idea of 'practice' utilized in theories of customary international law, viz. the practical element which together with the psychological element (*opinio juris*) reflects/constitutes law. See the sources cited above n. 103. International relations scholars usually acknowledge a more general idea of an 'international institution' not necessarily including a normative component. For example, Robert Keohane distinguishes between 'institutions that can be identified as related complexes of rules and norms' and 'institutions that are merely categories of activity'; Keohane (above n. 102), at 383.

[105] Such an enquiry echoes part of the methodology of 'policy science' as developed in the context of international law by scholars of the 'New Haven' school of international legal jurisprudence. The New Haven method is much broader than the enquiry of this study, being concerned with all aspects of the policy process (not just implementation) and, crucially, seeking to identify normativity within this process. On the New Haven school, see, e.g., MS McDougal and associates, *Studies in World Public Order* (Yale University Press, 1960); WM Reisman, *Nullity and*

The analysis in the previous section, which led to the conclusion that 'international territorial administration' is distinctive, makes the case for this activity to be regarded in some sense as a *sui generis* 'practice' when considered in the abstract.[106] The concept of the 'policy institution' builds on this foundation to ask (1) whether the historical incidence of this practice suggests that it is 'established', thus rendering the projects collectively an 'institution'; and (2) whether this common practice is being put to common ends, thus rendering the projects collectively a 'policy institution'. If it is possible to get to the second stage, identifying some kind of purposive commonality between the projects, then, as a matter of policy, the ITA projects can and should be regarded not only on an individual basis, but also as a collective phenomenon. A means is provided for appreciating the purposes served by the projects and for comparing like with like. Establishing the existence of a policy institution also assists in a consideration of how these purposes might be served by such projects in the future and provides a basis on which the legitimacy of the projects can be appraised. Indeed, it might be possible to consider whether the projects are somehow constitutive of an 'institution' in a normative sense, in having identified the practice and policy that normativity, if it operates, would relate to.

1.5.2 Certain methodological challenges

Adopting a purposive methodology potentially brings with it certain pitfalls. This book considers the 'use' of international territorial administration for particular ends, attempting to establish when particular projects have been 'aimed' at implementing particular policies. The teleological import of such language might suggest a process that is both rational and clear. International policy makers identify a particular 'problem' and decide to use the policy institution of ITA as the response. Particular projects are deployed, and the objective is achieved. Thus the use of ITA is rational, its purposes are clearly identifiable, and its effects predictable.

Revision: The Review and Enforcement of International Judgments and Awards (Yale University Press, 1971); MS McDougal and WM Reisman, *International Law Essays: A Supplement to International Law in Contemporary Perspective* (Foundation Press, 1981); WM Reisman and AR Willard (eds), *International Incidents: The Law that Counts in World Politics* (Princeton University Press, 1988); HD Lasswell and MS McDougal, *Jurisprudence for a Free Society: Studies in Law, Science, and Policy* (New Haven Press/Martinus Nijhoff, 1992); WM Reisman and JE Baker, *Regulating Covert Action: Practices, Contexts, and Policies of Covert Coercion Abroad in International and American Law* (Yale University Press, 1992); BS Chimni, *International Law and World Order: A Critique of Contemporary Approaches* (Sage Publications, 1993), 73–145; Rosalyn Higgins, *Problems and Process: International Law and How We Use It* (OUP, 1994), ch. 1; WM Reisman and AR Willard, 'The World Community: A Planetary Social Process', 21 (1988) *UC Davis Law Review* 807; M Reisman, 'The View from the New Haven School of International Law', 86 (1992) *ASIL Proc.* 118.

[106] According to the *Oxford English Dictionary*, one definition of 'practice' is: '[t]he action *of* doing something; performance, execution; working, operation; method of action or working' (definition 1a, from *OED Online*, at <http://www.oed.com>, italics in original). This implies a distinct 'something' that is being performed.

It might be said that all of this presupposes various ideas which are potentially problematic. In the first place, an assumption is made that it is possible to identify the particular actors whose views are determinative of the introduction of the administration projects, and that the position taken by these actors 'caused' the introduction of the projects. Maybe the projects were 'caused' by a whole variety of factors; indeed, perhaps they can only meaningfully be regarded as a series of accidents.

In the second place, it might be said that the language of 'using' international territorial administration to achieve certain objectives assumes that it is possible to look inside the minds of these people who 'caused' the projects to be created and say that one particular motivation was determinative of their decision to utilize the policy institution. The analysis undertaken in this study is based on the 'official purposes' put forward for the projects. But what if these purposes are pleaded in bad faith? What if they are rhetorical devices designed to conceal 'other' motivations that are less consonant with the language of generally-accepted international public policy? For example, did the Security Council authorize UNTAET to administer East Timor because its people were deemed incapable of self-administration, or to assuage the collective guilt of particular states and the United Nations at 25 years of inaction in the face of Indonesian occupation, coupled with the failure to anticipate and prevent the horrific aftermath of the UN-sponsored 'popular consultation', or a mixture of both?[107]

In the third place, a further effect of the proposed approach to the analysis of international territorial administration might be to suggest that the realization of certain objectives by this activity is inevitable. Since it is proposed to discuss the 'use' of ITA, to one end or another, the implication could be that the institution was successful in realizing these ends in each place.

These are important concerns, potentially relevant to any attempt at policy analysis. The objective of this book, however, is not to suggest the 'real' reasons for the projects, in terms of causation and rationality, and the effect that these projects necessarily have. Rather, it is to identify a justificatory framework to explain how the projects are understood in international policy discourse. Although the purposes to be considered may not have 'caused' the projects, nor have actually been the 'real' motivations for introducing the projects, nor been realized in practice, they are, nonetheless, the purposes with which the projects are associated in international policy discourse (although, as previously illustrated, not necessarily in *academic* discourse). The justificatory structure has a significance in its own right, independent of any validity it may enjoy in terms of causation, motivation, and effect.[108]

---

[107] Cf. M Ayoob, 'Third World Perspectives on Humanitarian Intervention and International Administration', 10 (2004) *Global Governance* 99, 104.

[108] For an example of a similar approach, see William Bain's study of ideas of trusteeship in international society, which he explains as an enquiry into 'interpreting human conduct' rather than 'explaining human behaviour'; W Bain, *Between Anarchy and Society. Trusteeship*

It might be said that mapping out this structure may further obscure what 'really' went on in the decision-making processes that created these projects, and the 'true' effect that the projects have. However, establishing the mainstream justificatory framework for any activity provides a benchmark for assessing this activity from within the mainstream. If international policy-makers say they are doing something for a particular reason, then this 'reason' offers one possible basis for bringing the activity to account, regardless of whether the motivation was invoked in bad faith originally, or was only part, perhaps a subsidiary part, of the picture. Moreover, far from suggesting that the projects necessarily achieve their purposes, the point of establishing a purposive framework is to provide a basis on which the projects' success can be judged. This book is about the ends to which international territorial administration projects have ostensibly been put, without prejudice to the question of whether the projects have managed to meet these ends.

That said, what of the insights from post-colonial theory, exposing the problematic nature of attempts to represent the experience of forms of domination—to tell its history—by those other than the people subjected to it?[109] Edward Said defined 'orientalism' as:

...the corporate institution for dealing with the Orient—dealing with it by making statements about it, authorizing views of it, describing it, by teaching it, settling it, ruling over it...[110]

Two critiques from post-colonial thought potentially relevant to the work in this book will be addressed here. In the first place, as Edward Said argued, the nature of the perspective of the commentator—rooted in an identity 'other' than the identity of those whose experience is being described—creates the danger that representations will be corrupted through a desire on the part of the commentator to understand him or herself through their conception of an alienated, oriental 'other'.[111] As Said revealed, narratives of the colonial encounter in Western literature are replete with representations of the colonial 'other' that reveal much more about the self-image of those crafting the representation than the reality of those being represented.[112]

---

and the Obligations of Power (OUP, 2003) (the discussion of method is at 8–13; the quotation is at 9). Bain's ideas, and the relevance of trusteeship to ITA generally, are discussed in ch. 8, below.

[109] 'Post-colonial studies' are concerned with a wide-ranging critical examination of such issues as conventional representations of colonialism within western thought, the colonial legacy, and related contemporary practices; see the List of Sources, section 5.3.3. A related academic development is 'post-colonial' and 'Third World' approaches to international law; see List of Sources, section 5.3.4.

[110] EW Said, *Orientalism. Western Conceptions of the Orient* (reissue with new afterword, Penguin Books, 1995), 3.

[111] Ibid.

[112] Ibid. For an application of this critique to the 'failed state' concept generally and the association of the concept with proposals for territorial administration by international organization in

In the second place, even if the accuracy of such representations is not considered to have been compromised because of the self-realizing nature of the act of representing the 'other', nonetheless the representational act itself is problematic because it necessarily involves 'dominating, restructuring and having authority over' that which is represented.[113] As theorists such as Gayatri Chakravorti Spivak suggest, in such circumstances, the story of those subject to domination is told through a process that is itself a form of intellectual domination, in that it is crafted by someone in a privileged position coming from outside the community being represented.[114] Regardless of whether such representations can somehow be considered to be 'accurate', they are problematic because of the nature of domination involved in having one's story told by someone else/telling someone else's story. The potentially offensive nature of this is illustrated in the following remark by the delegation from Mali during the drafting of what became General Assembly Resolution 1514 on decolonization and self-determination, in response to an attempt by certain Latin American delegations to insist on particular representations of the colonial encounter in that resolution:

[t]he delegations which speak in this Assembly of their colonial experience...can unfortunately only speak of the empire of their fathers' day; they speak of it as heritage.

If their countries were colonized at some time in history, they know it only from history books. Therein lies the fundamental difference between these delegations and ours, who have personal experience of colonial rule. Our knowledge is not based on hearsay or on what we learnt in school; we were for decades the living embodiment of that system.[115]

This book is not, however, an attempt to represent the experience of those subject to territorial administration by international actors, or indeed those 'internationals' engaged in this activity as administrators. Rather, it has a less ambitious focus: the official policy structures associated with ITA in mainstream international policy discourse. The point of this book is to appreciate how the purposes associated with ITA are understood within international public policy, not how ITA projects are experienced 'on the ground'. Equally, insofar as it is necessary to draw on the work of historians about the broader circumstances relevant to the administration projects in order to appreciate the relevance of international public policy to them, the point of this enquiry is to map out conventional historical

particular see Wilde (above n. 29), at 89–91, also set out in R Wilde, 'The Skewed Responsibility Narrative of the "Failed States" Concept', 9 (2003) *ILSA Journal of International & Comparative Law* 425. On the 'failed state' concept more generally, see below, ch. 7, section 7.3.3.

113 Said (above n. 110), 3.
114 See Chakravorty Spivak (above n. 59).
115 UN GAOR 15th Sess., 931st plenary meeting, 1 December 1960, at 1065, cited in DA Kay, 'The United Nations and Decolonization', in J Barros (ed.), *The United Nations: Past, Present and Future* (Free Press, 1972), 143, at 151 and DA Kay, 'The Politics of Decolonization: The New Nations and the United Nations Political Process', 21 (1967) *International Organizations* 786, at 792. Self-determination and decolonization, including General Assembly Resolution 1514 (XV), are discussed further in chs 5 and 8, below.

understandings implicated in international public policy, not to provide the 'true' historical account.

The present study is concerned with how mainstream discourse in international public policy and international law understands the ITA encounter; it is, therefore, an attempt to map out a particular orientalist paradigm. However, the point is not to offer this as the 'truth' of the situation, but, rather, as discussed earlier, as a way of appreciating how ITA is understood by those involved in it so as to be able to move to the stage of critical appraisal based in part on an understanding of this normative framework.

Work on the experience of foreign territorial administration by the people of the territories directly affected is clearly important but the insights from post-colonial theory outlined above offer a powerful case against this particular author's involvement in 'representing' it.[116]

1.6 An Overview of this Book

Having identified some of the limitations of the existing literature on international territorial administration above, the attempt to make a constructive contribution to the analysis of this activity begins in Chapter 2 by considering whether or not the practice of ITA can be considered an 'institution' in the sense that it is 'established'. The many instances of ITA in the past, from the League administration in the Saar between 1920 and 1935 to the UN administration in Eastern Slavonia between 1996 and 1998, are reviewed and those other projects that have more recently been under way alongside the better-known Kosovo mission, such as OHR in Bosnia and Herzegovina, are considered. From this long-standing and broad-ranging usage, it is concluded that international territorial administration constitutes an 'established practice', and, therefore, all the projects can be considered manifestations of this particular 'institution'.

But is international territorial administration a *policy* institution, i.e., an institution manifesting commonality in terms of the ends to which individual projects have ostensibly been put? The consideration of this question begins in Chapter 3 with the presentation of a thesis that attempted to conceptualize international territorial administration projects collectively, together with other projects involving territorial administration by foreign states, on a policy

---

[116] For examples of critical commentary on UNMIK in Kosovo by local groups and institutions, see the documentation of the Vetevendosje movement (<http://www.vetevendosje.org>) and the independent Ombudsperson Institution in Kosovo (<http://www.ombudspersonkosovo>); further information about the latter institution is contained in nn. 24 and 26 above. For the work of the Timor-Leste Institute for Reconstruction Monitoring and Analysis, La'o Hamutuk, which describes itself as 'a joint East Timorese-international organization that seeks to monitor and to report on the activities of the principal international institutions present in Timor Lorosa'e as they relate to the physical and social reconstruction of the country', see <http://www.laohamutuk.org>.

level: Méir Ydit's *Internationalised Territories* published in 1963. Ydit sought to explain these projects as the basis for, and/or a corollary to, what will be termed 'international territorial sovereignty', i.e. the enjoyment of sovereignty-as-title by the international actors involved. It was this formal sovereignty that was the point of the projects, a device intended to serve as a permanent solution to the status of contested territories. If Ydit is correct, then international territorial *sovereignty* is the policy institution, not international territorial administration.

Chapter 3 briefly discusses the idea of international territorial sovereignty in the abstract, setting out the two different relevant concepts, sometimes each described as 'sovereignty', that are in play here: the right of territorial ownership, on the one hand, and the right to exercise administrative prerogatives over territory, on the other. Ydit's thesis is then reviewed, and the way in which Ydit seems to assume the right of ownership from the exercise of territorial prerogatives is highlighted. The reasons why such an assumption cannot be made are explained, and it is argued that an additional characteristic needs to be included when considering the effect of ITA on the status of the territories concerned: the basis on which this administration is exercised.

Having considered the concept of 'international territorial sovereignty' in the abstract, the enquiry then turns to a detailed consideration of the status of all those territories that have been subject to international territorial administration, in an effort to establish whether this concept has ever been realized in practice.

Chapter 4 seeks to establish the legal status of those states and state territories that were made or are subject to ITA, from the Free City of Danzig to Kosovo. This analysis reveals that international territorial administration has usually bolstered rather than undermined the status quo as far as the legal position of these territories is concerned, in one or both of two ways. In the first place, international territorial administration can be authorized in legal instruments that also establish or confirm the status of the territory concerned, for example, the 'Peace Plan', and Security Council Resolution 1244 of 1999 in relation to Kosovo as part of the then FRY (later Serbia and Montenegro and now the Republic of Serbia).[117] In the second place, international territorial administration can be conducted 'on behalf of' the existing territorial sovereign, as with the League of Nations Commission in Leticia in relation to Colombia.

In Chapter 5, the enquiry turns to the legal status of those territorial units subject to ITA projects where the right of external self-determination is central to an appreciation of this status, from West Irian between 1962 and 1963 to East Timor between 1999 and 2002. The law on self-determination is reviewed and the effect that the self-determination entitlement can have on territorial status is considered. Applying these general considerations to the territories in question, it is established

---

[117] On the status of the FRY/Serbia and Montenegro, the 2006 separation of Serbia and Montenegro and the status of Kosovo, see the discussion below in ch. 4, section 4.5.3, in particular n. 220.

that the UN was never 'sovereign' in the sense of being the title-holder in such territories, since, apart from the absence of a claim to this effect by the organization, it would not have been possible for the UN to enjoy such sovereignty without the consent of the people of the territory, and such consent had not been sought in these cases.

The analysis in Chapters 4 and 5 reveals that actually none of the international territorial administration projects has involved the enjoyment of title over the territory by the relevant international actor. Consequently, it is suggested that the approach taken by Ydit is inadequate in explaining the policy role of ITA. It is necessary to consider a broader range of policies.

In Chapter 6, the historical background to all of the projects is reviewed, in an effort to establish the purposes with which they have been associated in a more complex manner than has been attempted so far, moving beyond the simplistic presentation of ITA as, for example, essentially concerned with state reconstruction after conflict in all cases. This enquiry, which partially draws on the analysis concerning territorial status in Chapters 4 and 5, reveals a wide range of purposes which are classified as falling within two headings, each denoting a perceived 'problem' associated with the conduct of territorial administration by local actors. The first heading is a perceived 'sovereignty problem', viz. a problem relating to the identity of those actors exercising territorial control; the second is a perceived 'governance problem', viz. a problem relating to the quality of governance exercised by those actors in the territory. By identifying the use of the administration projects in relation to these two types of problem, it is possible to establish how the projects can be classified collectively on a purposive level. This in turn provides a basis for understanding international territorial administration as a *policy* institution.

In order to consider the role of this policy institution fully it is necessary to engage in further analysis of how it compares with other policy institutions in international relations. In Chapter 6, the institution is analysed in isolation; in Chapters 7 and 8, it is situated within a broader context in an effort to understand better its role as an agent of international law and public policy.

Chapter 7 draws on the analysis in Chapter 6 to consider how the purposes with which ITA is associated can be understood in terms of the implementation of international law and policy. It is demonstrated how the institution has been seen as a mechanism for the prevention and settlement of disputes, the implementation of particular areas of international public policy, and the promotion of peace and security. The institution of international territorial administration is compared with other international mechanisms that purport to achieve the same ends but through different means (for example, international courts and tribunals), and it is explained how, in terms of effectiveness, the institution is sometimes considered superior to these other mechanisms because of its relatively intrusive nature.

The second area of contextualization moves outside the arena of international organizations to analogous practices conducted by states. Chapter 8 considers the similarities and differences that exist between international territorial administration and other policy institutions involving territorial administration by states or groups of states. Such institutions include so-called 'protection' (viz. the activity taking place in 'protectorates'), colonialism practised by European imperial powers, state-conducted administration of Mandated and Trust territories, and occupation, including so-called 'belligerent occupation'. It is argued that ITA and each of these institutions operate in a practical manner in a common fashion, and also manifest important purposive connections in terms of the associated policies, notably in relation to ideas of trust. Because of these commonalities, it is possible to talk of a family of policy institutions involving 'foreign territorial administration', and to understand ITA as an internationalized manifestation of 'trusteeship'. Just as considerations of individual international administration projects are usefully situated within a broader discussion of ITA, so considerations of the institution itself are usefully situated within a broader discussion of foreign territorial administration.

Given this, Chapter 8 also analyses the political and legal considerations—notably concerning the self-determination entitlement—that played a partially determinative role in the different fortunes of each manifestation of 'foreign territorial administration' over the course of the 20th century. Drawing on the analysis in Chapter 7, the enquiry then considers the normative factors that enabled the continued use of the international territorial administration institution in the so-called 'post-colonial' era when the other state-conducted institutions were no longer considered legitimate. How did trusteeship, supposedly repudiated by the self-determination entitlement, continue in its ITA manifestation?

This book aims to conceptualize the idea of international territorial administration as a policy institution, drawing on the historical background to all the projects and the relationship between the purposes with which they have been associated and areas of international law and public policy. It is neither a study of how ITA has operated in practice, nor an in-depth analysis of particular projects.[118] Moreover, it does not encompass many of the complex legal issues raised by the activity.[119]

One legal issue—the legal effect of international territorial administration on territorial status—is addressed in detail in Chapters 4 and 5, since an understanding of it is required in order to appreciate fully the purposes served by the projects.

Two further legal issues are covered more superficially. The reasons for including certain entities as 'international organizations' in cases where this status is unclear (e.g., OHR) is explained in summary form in the footnotes of Chapter 2. The nature of the legal authority provided for the projects is reviewed in Chapter 8, when considering whether 'imposition' is a key component of international trusteeship, and why international territorial administration was retained as a

[118] See List of Sources, sections 5.1 and 5.2.
[119] See List of Sources, sections 5.2.6 (commentary on the lawfulness of the UN authority provided for the administration projects) and 5.2.7 (commentary on issues of responsibility, applicable law, jurisdiction, and, more generally, accountability).

policy institution in the period after the main wave of decolonization. The superficial treatment given to these two issues is motivated by a desire to keep the focus on the issue at hand—the policy role of international territorial administration—and is not intended to imply that the issues do not merit sustained consideration.

The other legal issues that are not discussed are of vital importance to the practice of international territorial administration, but a full consideration of them can only take place once the policy objectives of the projects have been established. For example, one cannot consider fully whether Security Council authority for ITA (when such authority is forthcoming) is lawful under the UN Charter without first understanding in detail the purposes with which the administration projects have been associated.[120] Furthermore, establishing such purposes assists in comparisons with other activities such as colonialism. It is hoped that a greater understanding of such analogies will potentially be helpful in enabling the analysis of particular legal issues to be situated within a broader framework.

In establishing international territorial administration as a policy institution, therefore, this book aims to clarify the policy context in which considerations of the political, legal, and practical issues raised by the projects can be situated.

---

[120] See List of Sources, section 5.2.6.

2

The Institution of International Territorial Administration

2.1 Introduction

In the previous chapter, international territorial administration was established as a distinctive activity because of the 'international' identity of the actor involved in conducting territorial administration and the dichotomy between this identity and the identity of the administered entity.[1] Only an elemental distinctiveness has been established, however; do the ITA projects have anything else in common? This question will be pursued in this book by considering whether ITA is a 'policy institution', asking first whether the historical incidents of this practice suggest that it is 'established', thereby rendering the projects collectively an 'institution'; and second whether this common practice is being put to common ends, thereby rendering the projects collectively a 'policy institution'.[2] The present chapter addresses the first component of this enquiry: is ITA an established practice? To what extent are the projects in Kosovo and East Timor one-offs? Where has ITA been used in the past, and how often has this happened?

Necessarily, the fruits of this enquiry are largely descriptive. However, a comprehensive survey of the main factual features of many of the ITA projects has never before been put together; the provision of this information is, therefore, of significance for those who wish to know more about the specifics of each arrangement. In consequence, the factual information for each project is set out in full detail in the footnotes; detail is thereby provided for those who want it, but kept out of the main text to retain the generally analytical orientation of this study.

The activity under evaluation was defined in the previous chapter as 'international territorial administration'.[3] The activity of 'territorial administration' within this definition denotes a:

... formally-constituted, locally-based management structure operating with respect to a particular territorial unit, whether a state, a sub-state unit or a non-state territorial entity...[4]

---

[1] See above, ch. 1, section 1.4.3. [2] See above, ch. 1, section 1.5.1.
[3] See above, ch. 1, section 1.4. [4] See above, ch. 1, section 1.4.1.

...and can be partial or plenary.[5] As far as the actors associated with this activity are concerned, the focus is on 'international' actors, denoting entities meeting the conventional definition of an 'international organization' in international law,[6] or 'international appointees', viz. individuals of foreign nationality whose appointment has been made with the involvement of an international actor such as an international organization.[7] The connection between these actors and the activity of territorial administration, which takes place directly within the territory concerned, was defined thus:

[a]s far as international organizations are concerned, the organization asserts the right either to supervise and control the operation of this structure by other (usually local) actors, or to operate the structure directly. This can pertain to the structure as a whole, or certain parts of it (e.g., the legislature). In the case of the international appointees, the individuals in question serve as officials of particular institutions which form part of the structure of territorial administration, such as courts, tribunals and electoral bodies.[8]

What follows is a survey of the history of individual instances of this kind of involvement in 'territorial administration' by these two types of international actor since the start of the League of Nations. It begins with the historical precedents to the recent projects, and then turns to the projects commencing after the turn of the 21st century, many of which were ongoing at the time of writing, such as the administration of camps housing refugees and internally displaced persons by the Office of the United Nations High Commissioner for Refugees (UNHCR).[9] The survey reveals that international territorial administration has taken place throughout the 20th century and into the 21st century in a variety of territories around the world and been conducted by a range of different international actors. It is argued that the periodicity of these projects suggests that the practice they involve can be regarded as 'established', thereby rendering ITA an 'institution'.[10]

---

[5] See ch. 1, section 1.4.1.

[6] See above, ch. 1, section 1.4.1. As explained therein, in n. 88 and accompanying text, although a full treatment of the basis on which each entity covered is considered to meet the definition would not be appropriate here, reference material on this issue is provided in the footnote accompanying the first main reference to each entity's involvement in territorial administration. Because of the obscure nature of and lack of commentary on the legal status of the Office of the High Representative in Bosnia and Herzegovina (OHR), a general explanation of this particular entity is also provided. See below, nn. 11 (on the League of Nations), 16 (on the United Nations), 23 (on the Common Foreign and Security Policy (CFSP) structure of the European Union), 39 (on the OSCE); and section 2.3.3 (on OHR).

[7] See above, ch. 1, section 1.4.4.

[8] See above, ch. 1, section 1.4.5.

[9] Sections 2.2. and 2.3 below, respectively.

[10] As already explained, individual instances of this activity will be referred to as 'projects': see above, ch. 1, section 1.4.1, last paragraph.

2.2 The Historic Use of International Territorial Administration

2.2.1 Projects between the First and Second World Wars

One of the first activities of the League of Nations was to become involved in the conduct of territorial administration.[11] The League, through a High Commissioner, enjoyed certain administrative prerogatives in the Free City of Danzig from 1920 to 1939.[12] In addition, two separate League Commissions administered the German Saar Basin (the Saar) between 1920 and 1935,[13] and the Colombian town and district of Leticia from 1933 to 1934.[14] The League also appointed

[11] Whether the League enjoyed international legal personality is contested. On this issue, see, e.g., L Oppenheim, *International Law*, vol. 1 (3rd edn, Longmans, Green & Co., 1921), 269; PE Corbett, 'What is the League of Nations?', 5 (1924) *BYIL* 119; J Fischer Williams, 'The Status of the League of Nations in International Law', in J Fischer Williams (ed.), *Chapters on Current International Law and the League of Nations* (Longmans, Green & Co., 1929), 477; C Eagleton, 'International Organization and the Law of Responsibility', 76 (1950) *Recueil des Cours* Vol. I, 319, at 334.

[12] The League's administrative powers were exercised through a League High Commissioner; this position was held by the Representative of the Allied Powers in Danzig, who was appointed on 23 February 1920 (M Ydit, *Internationalised Territories from the 'Free City of Cracow' to the 'Free City of Berlin'* (Sythoff, 1961), 211). League approval was necessary before the Free City could make certain military arrangements (Art. 5, Constitution of the Free City of Danzig, 11 May 1922, text in *League of Nations Official Journal*, Spec. Suppl. 7 (July 1922), 1, as amended, 9 September 1930, text in *League of Nations Official Journal* 1794 (December 1930), hereinafter 'Danzig Constitution') or amend the Constitution (Danzig Constitution, Art. 49). The League also asserted the right to intervene if the Constitution was being applied incorrectly (see below, ch. 4, n. 84); it had power to veto certain treaties in particular circumstances (Art. 6, Convention between Poland and the Free City of Danzig, 9 November 1920, 6 LNTS 189 (hereinafter 'Poland–Danzig Treaty')) and was responsible for appointing the president of the Port and Waterways Board if the Free City and Poland failed to do so (Poland–Danzig Treaty, Art. 19). These administrative powers are discussed in more detail below in ch. 4, section 4.2.2. For commentary, see, e.g., the sources cited below in ch. 4, n. 30.

[13] On the League administration generally, see Versailles Peace Treaty, Arts 46, 49 and Annex to Part III, Section IV (after Art. 50), Arts 16–33; WR Bisschop, *The Saar Controversy* (Sweet & Maxwell, 1924), 22–31, 38–52, 87–133; FM Russell, *The International Government of the Saar* (University of California Press, 1926); F Knipping (ed.), *The United Nations System and its Predecessors* (OUP, 1997), vol. II, documents reproduced at 672–89; N Berman, '"But the Alternative is Despair", European Nationalism and the Modernist Renewal of International Law', 106 (1992–93) *Harvard Law Review* 1792, at 1874–86; J Chopra, 'UN Civil Governance-in-Trust', in TG Weiss (ed.), *The United Nations and Civil Wars* (Lynne Rienner, 1995), 70, at 73. Under Part III, Section IV, of the Versailles Peace Treaty, the Saar was administered by a Governing Commission representing the League (Arts 46, 49 and Annex Chapter II; for the rules regarding the appointment, composition and procedure of the Commission, see Annex Chapter II, Arts 17 and 18). The Commission was the 'government of the territory' (Annex Chapter II, Arts 16 and 19) and its activities in this regard covered both domestic administration (including appointing and dismissing officials, creating public institutions, running public services, raising taxation and running the judicial system), and protecting the interests of Saar inhabitants abroad (Annex Chapter II, Arts 19, 21, 25 and 26). It began its work on 26 February 1920 (Bisschop, ibid., 51) and ended on 28 February 1935, with the formal transfer of government to local representatives pending the resumption of German administration the following day (FP Walters, *A History of the League of Nations* (OUP, 1952), 597).

[14] A three-member League Commission was mandated to 'take charge of the administration' of the territory, and 'call upon military forces of its own selection, and...attach to itself any

the Chair of the Harbour Board in Memel (now called Klaipeda), Lithuania, in 1924.[15]

2.2.2 Projects since 1945

The United Nations first exercised territorial administration (outside its headquarters premises) in the 1960s.[16] The United Nations Operation in the Congo (ONUC) asserted various administrative prerogatives in the Congo between 1960 and 1964,[17] and the United Nations Temporary Executive Authority (UNTEA) administered West Irian for seven months between 1962 and 1963, operating between Dutch and Indonesian administration of the territory.[18] In 1967, the UN

other elements' as it deemed necessary (Agreement between Colombia and Peru Relating to the Procedure for Putting into Effect the Recommendations Proposed by the Council of the League of Nations, 25 May 1933, 138 LNTS 253, Arts 2 and 3 respectively). On the dates of the Commission, see below, ch. 4, nn. 112 and 113. Administration was divided into three areas, each headed by a Commissioner: order and security; public works and public health; and handling claims relating to the Peruvian attack that had preceded the Commission's administration. See Ydit (above n. 12), 61; and JV Czerapowicz, *International Territorial Authority: Leticia and West New Guinea* (1972, unpublished Ph.D. dissertation, Indiana University, on file with the author), 42–59 (public safety), 60–73 (public works and public health), 74–6 (claims); LH Woolsey, 'The Leticia Dispute Between Colombia and Peru', 29 (1935) *AJIL* 94, at 96. On the Commission generally, see, e.g., Walters (above n. 13), 540; Ydit, ibid., 61–2; Czerapowicz, ibid., 18–76; Woolsey, ibid., 96; Chopra (above n. 13), 73.

[15] Convention Concerning the Territory of Memel, 8 May 1924, 29 LNTS 87, Annex II, Art. 5. On Memel and its Harbour Board, see below, ch. 4, section 4.2.3.

[16] On the enjoyment of international legal personality by the United Nations, see, e.g., *Reparation for Injuries Suffered in the Service of the United Nations, Advisory Opinion, ICJ Reports 1949*, 174; Eagleton (above n. 11), 335–45; H Kelsen, *The Law of the United Nations* (Stevens & Sons, 1951), ch. 13; P Reuter, *International Institutions* (JM Chapman transl., Allen & Unwin, 1958), 231; H Schermers and N Blokker, *International Institutional Law* (3rd edn, Martinus Nijhoff, 1995), 975–95; P Sands and P Klein, *Bowett's Law of International Institutions* (5th edn, Sweet & Maxwell, 2001), ch. 15 and sources cited at 470; J Klabbers, *An Introduction to International Institutional Law* (CUP, 2002), ch. 3; CF Amerasinghe, *Principles of the Institutional Law of International Institutions* (2nd edn, CUP, 2005), ch. 3 and sources cited at 66 n. 1; N White, *The Law of International Organizations* (2nd edn, 2005, Manchester University Press), ch. 2 and sources cited therein; F Seyersted, 'Objective International Personality of Intergovernmental Organizations: Do Their Capacities Really Depend upon the Conventions Establishing Them?', 34 (1964) *Nordisk Tidsskrift for International Ret* 3.

[17] Based on its mandate under SC Res. 143, 14 July 1960 and subsequent instruments; see also Telegrams dated 12 and 13 July 1960 from the President and the Prime Minister of the Republic of the Congo to the UN Secretary-General, UN Doc. S/4382; UN SCOR, 15th year, Supp. (July, August and September 1960), 11. For these and the other constitutive documents of ONUC, together with associated documents, see R Higgins, *United Nations Peacekeeping, Vol. 3, Africa 1946–1967* (OUP, 1980). On ONUC, see, for example, R Simmonds, *Legal Problems Arising from the United Nations Military Operations in the Congo* (Martinus Nijhoff, 1968); G Abi-Saab, *The United Nations Operation in the Congo 1960–1964* (OUP, 1978); A House, *The UN in the Congo: The Political and Civilian Efforts* (University Press of America, 1978), *passim*; WJ Durch, 'The UN Operation in the Congo: 1960–1964', in Durch (ed.), *The Evolution of UN Peacekeeping* (St Martin's Press, 1994), 315, *passim*; SR Ratner, *The New UN Peacekeeping, Building Peace in Lands of Conflict after the Cold War* (St. Martin's Press, 1995), 102–9; Chopra (above n. 13), 77–8; S Morphet, 'Organizing Civil Administration', in J Chopra (ed.), *The Politics of Peace-Maintenance* (Lynne Rienner, 1998), 41, at 43–5.

[18] For the powers of UNTEA, see Indonesia–Netherlands, Agreement Concerning West New Guinea (West Irian), 15 August 1962, 437 UNTS 273 (hereinafter 'West Irian Agreement'),

Council for South West Africa, which, with the change in the territory's name a
year later to Namibia, was re-named the UN Council for Namibia, was established to administer the territory, but South Africa prevented the Council from
taking up this role.[19] Over twenty years later, in, 1991, the United Nations was

Arts II–III, XIII–XV; Annual Report of the Secretary-General on the Work of the Organization,
16 June 1962–15 June 1963, UN GAOR, 18th Sess., Supp. No. 1, at 35, UN Doc. A/5501 (1963)
(hereinafter 'UN Secretary-General West Irian Report'). A UN Security Force (UNSF) was
deployed alongside UNTEA, and local, Dutch, and Indonesian armed forces were placed at the
disposal of UNTEA (West Irian Agreement, Art. VII; see also Indonesia–Netherlands–United
Nations, Exchange of Letters (with Annexed Memorandum of Understanding) on Cessation
of Hostilities, 15 August 1962, 437 UNTS 294 (hereinafter 'West Irian Exchange of Letters')).
On the UNSF, see D Bowett, *United Nations Forces: A Legal Study* (1964), 257–60; R Higgins,
United Nations Peacekeeping, Vol. 2, Asia 1946–1967 (OUP, 1970), 26, 116–41; WJ Durch, 'UN
Temporary Executive Authority', in Durch (ed.), *The Evolution of UN Peacekeeping* (St Martin's
Press, 1994), 285, at 290–2. The position of UN Administrator was held initially by José Rolz-
Bennett and then by Djalal Abdoh (UN Secretary-General West Irian Report, 36). According to
the West Irian Agreement, the Administrator was given 'full authority under the direction of the
Secretary-General to administer the territory' (West Irian Agreement, Art. V). He was obliged
to replace the top 18 Dutch administrative officials with non-Dutch, non-Indonesian nationals;
for all other administrative positions, Dutch officials could stay on, with vacancies filled by people either from West Irian or provided by Indonesia (ibid., Art. IX; see UN Secretary-General
West Irian Report, 37). UNTEA was entitled to change the law (West Irian Agreement, Art.
XI) and appoint new members to local councils (West Irian Agreement, Art. XXIII); it was also
responsible for publicizing the terms of the West Irian Agreement, in particular the transfer to
Indonesia and the 'act of free choice' (ibid., Art. X; see UN Secretary-General West Irian Report,
38). On UNTEA generally, see Bowett, ibid., 255–61; Higgins, ibid., 93–149 and sources cited
therein at 149; TM Franck, *Nation Against Nation: What Happened to the UN Dream and What
the US Can Do About It* (OUP, 1985), 79–81; Durch, ibid., 285–98; J Crawford, *The Creation
of States in International Law* (2nd edn, OUP, 2006), 555–6; P van der Veur, 'The UN in West
Irian: A Critique', 18 (1963) *International Organization* 53; JW Halderman, 'United Nations
Territorial Administration and the Development of the Charter', 70 (1964) *Duke Law Journal* 95;
M Pomerance, 'Methods of Self-Determination and the Argument of "Primitiveness"', 12 (1974)
Canadian Yearbook of International Law 38; Chopra (above n. 13), 76–7; Morphet (above n. 17),
45–6; D Gruss, 'UNTEA and West New Guinea', 9 (2005) *Max Planck Yearbook of United Nations
Law* 97. The transfer to the UN took place on 1 October 1962 (UN Secretary-General West Irian
Report, 36) when, as anticipated in the West Irian Agreement, a General Assembly resolution was
passed acknowledging the role given to the Secretary-General and authorizing him to carry out
the tasks under the agreement. See West Irian Agreement, Arts I and II; West Irian Exchange of
Letters, 310–11; GA Res. 1752 (XVII), 21 September 1962 (for commentary on the resolution, see
Higgins, above, this note, 113–15). UNTEA Administration ran until 1 May 1963, when control
was handed over to Indonesia (UN Secretary-General West Irian Report, 39–40). This date marked
the end of the 'first phase' set out in the West Irian Agreement, after which the Administrator had
the discretion to transfer 'all or part' of the administration to Indonesia, and all the UN security
forces would be replaced by Indonesian armed forces (West Irian Agreement, Arts XII and XIII,
quotations taken from Art. XII).

    [19] GA Res. 2248 (S-V), 19 May 1967, section II, para 1; see also GA Res. 2372 (XXII), 12 June
1968. Under Part II of GA Res. 2248 (S-V) (ibid.), the Council was responsible to the General
Assembly and comprised 11 members elected by that body (ibid., Art. 1, preamble and Art. 2).
Its mandate was to 'administer South West Africa until independence' (ibid., Art. 1(a)), and it
was led by a United Nations Commissioner, appointed by the General Assembly on the nomination of the Secretary-General (ibid., Art. 3). The Council would establish a constituent assembly
to draft the constitution, on the basis of which elections could be held for a legislative assembly
and government (ibid., Art. 1(c)). Until the legislative assembly was established, the Council
would 'promulgate such laws, decrees and administrative regulations as are necessary for the

authorized to perform partial administrative functions in Western Sahara and Cambodia; although the Cambodia mandate was implemented by the United Nations Transitional Authority in Cambodia (UNTAC) from 1992 to 1993,[20] the Western Sahara mandate of the United Nations Mission for the Referendum in the Western Sahara (MINURSO) was, at the time of writing, yet to be fully performed.[21] In the same year when these two projects were constituted, the

administration of the Territory' (ibid., Art. 1(b)). It was also mandated to ensure that South African forces withdrew, and to maintain law and order (ibid., Art. 1(d) and Part IV, Art. 2(d)). Upon a declaration of independence, the Council would 'transfer all powers to the people of the Territory' (ibid., Art. 1(e); see also Part VI). On the role of the Council for Namibia, see J Dugard (ed.), *The South West Africa/Namibia Dispute: Documents and scholarly writings on the controversy between South Africa and the United Nations* (University of California Press, 1973), 409–13, 436–46; LCW Kaela, *The Question of Namibia* (Macmillan Press, 1996), 71–2; DA Kay, 'The United Nations and Decolonization', in J Barros (ed.), *The United Nations: Past, Present and Future* (Free Press, 1972), 143, 161–3; I Sagay, *The Legal Aspects of the Namibian Dispute* (University of Ife Press, 1975), *passim* and especially chs 12 and 13; LL Herman, 'The Legal Status of Namibia and of the United Nations Council for Namibia', 13 (1975) *Canadian Yearbook of International Law* 306, 319–22; see also the UK Government statement reported in G Marston, 'UK Materials on International Law 1982', 53 (1982) *BYIL* 391–3.

[20] UNTAC was led by a Special Representative, Yasushi Akashi, and began operation on 15 March 1992 (see United Nations, *The United Nations and Cambodia 1991–1995* (United Nations Blue Book Series, 1995), 14–15); its mandate ended on 24 September 1993 with the establishment of the new government; a phased UNTAC withdrawal was completed on 31 December 1993 (see ibid., at 50). On UNTAC's administrative functions, see Agreement on a Comprehensive Political Settlement of the Cambodia Conflict, Paris, 23 October 1991 (Cambodia Settlement Agreement), Arts 2, 6, 13, 16; Annex 1, on UNTAC's mandate; Annex 2, detailing UNTAC's role in relation to the supervision, monitoring, and verification of the ceasefire and assistance in the repatriation of refugees; and Annex 3, on elections. For the text of these instruments, see Annex to the Letter dated 30 October 1991 from the Permanent Representatives of France and Indonesia to the United Nations addressed to the Secretary-General, UN Doc. A/46/608 – S/2317730 (1991); for academic commentary on them, see below, ch. 4, n. 132. The administrative powers of UNTAC were of two types: first, to carry out elections, and, second, to supervise the government in general to ensure that the elections were fair; on the former, see below, n. 35; on the latter, see below, ch. 6, n. 110. UNTAC also had other, non-administrative functions; see Cambodia Settlement Agreement, Annex 1, section C on UNTAC's military functions and Annex 2, detailing the role of UNTAC in relation to the supervision, monitoring and verification of the ceasefire and assistance in the repatriation of refugees. On UNTAC, see also the sources cited below, n. 35.

[21] See SC Res. 690, 29 April 1991; Report of the Secretary-General, 19 April 1991, UN Doc. S/22464 (1991); Report of the Secretary-General, 18 June 1990, UN Doc. S/21360 (1990); SC Res. 907, 29 March 1994; SC Res. 973, 13 January 1995; SC Res. 997, 26 May 1995; SC Res. 1002, 30 June 1995; SC Res. 1017, 22 September 1995; SC Res. 1033, 19 December 1995; SC Res. 1042, 31 January 1996; SC Res. 1056, 29 May 1996; SC Res. 1084, 27 November 1996; SC Res. 1108, 22 May 1997; SC Res. 1131, 29 September 1997; SC Res. 1133, 20 October 1997; SC Res. 1148, 26 January 1998; SC Res. 1163, 17 April 1998; SC Res. 1185, 20 July 1998; SC Res. 1198, 18 September 1998; SC Res. 1204, 30 October 1998; SC Res. 1215, 17 December 1998; SC Res. 1224, 28 January 1999; SC Res. 1228, 11 February 1999; SC Res. 1232, 30 March 1999; SC Res. 1235, 30 April 1999; SC Res. 1238, 14 May 1999; SC Res. 1263, 13 September 1999; SC Res. 1282, 14 December 1999; SC Res. 1292, 29 February 2000; SC Res. 1301, 31 May 2000; SC Res. 1309, 25 July 2000; SC Res. 1324, 30 October 2000; SC Res. 1342, 27 February 2001; SC Res. 1349, 27 April 2001; SC Res. 1359, 29 June 2001; SC Res. 1380, 27 November 2001; SC Res. 1394, 27 February 2002; SC Res. 1406, 30 April 2002; SC Res. 1429, 30 July 2002; SC Res. 1463, 30 January 2003; SC Res. 1469, 25 March 2003; SC Res. 1485, 30 May 2003; SC Res. 1495, 31 July 2003; SC Res. 1513, 28 October 2003; SC Res. 1523, 30 January 2004; SC

Second United Nations Operation in Somalia (UNOSOM II) asserted certain administrative prerogatives in Mogadishu and the surrounding area.[22]

From 1994 to 1996, a different organization—the European Union— administered the city of Mostar in Bosnia and Herzegovina through the European Union Administration of Mostar (EUAM).[23] Then, as part of the

Res. 1541, 29 April 2004; SC Res. 1570, 28 October 2004; SC Res. 1598, 28 April 2005; SC Res. 1634, 28 October 2005; SC Res. 1675, 28 April 2006; SC Res. 1720, 31 October 2006; SC Res. 1754, 30 April 2007. On MINURSO, see also I Johnstone (ed.), *Annual Review of Global Peace Operations 2007* (NYU Center on International Cooperation/Lynne Rienner, 2007), sections 4.19 and 7.1. For commentary on these arrangements generally, see, e.g., E Milano, *Unlawful Territorial Situations in International Law: Reconciling Effectiveness, Legality and Legitimacy* (Martinus Nijhoff, 2006), 168–73; WJ Durch, 'Building on Sand: UN Peacekeeping in the Western Sahara', 17 (1993) *International Security* 151; WJ Durch (ed.), 'United Nations Mission for the Referendum in Western Sahara', in WJ Durch (ed.), *The Evolution of UN Peacekeeping* (St. Martin's Press, 1994), 406; Chopra (above n. 13), 81; Morphet (above n. 17), 49–50; JS Kreilkamp, 'UN Postconflict Reconstruction', 35 (2003) *NYU Journal of International Law & Politics* 619, 635–8. See also below, n. 32, on the prospects for the self-determination referendum in the Western Sahara, the operation of which is at the core of MINURSO's mandate.

[22] Based on its mandate in SC Res. 814, 26 March 1993, para. 4. See also Further Report of the Secretary-General on the Situation in Somalia Submitted in Pursuance of Paragraphs 18 and 19 of Resolution 794 (1992), UN Doc. S/25354, 3 March 1993. For commentary, see, e.g., J Chopra, *Peace Maintenance: The Evolution of International Political Authority* (Routledge, 1999), 49, 158; Chopra (above n. 13), 81–2; A Yannis, 'State Collapse and Prospects for Political Reconstruction and Democratic Governance in Somalia', *1998 African Yearbook of International Law* 23.

[23] This was effected through a Memorandum of Understanding between Bosnia and Herzegovina and various of its sub-state bodies, on the one hand, and EU and WEU states, on the other: see Memorandum of Understanding on the European Union Administration of Mostar (hereinafter 'Mostar MOU'), 5 July 1994 (unpublished, on file with the author). The MOU provided that the '...administration of the Mostar municipality will be assumed by the European Union' (Mostar MOU, Art. 1). It conceived an 'EU Administration' with certain 'aims and principles' (ibid., Art. 2). Mostar was to be 'governed' by this institution (ibid., Art. 4). The Council of Ministers of the European Union was responsible for appointing the EU Administrator (ibid., Art. 6) and determining the commencement of the EUAM (ibid., Art. 4). Under the MOU, the Administrator took instructions from the Council of Ministers to which the office-holder was obliged to report on a regular basis (ibid., Art. 7); the EU Administrator was supported by a team of 'EU special advisers' appointed by the Council of Ministers (ibid., Art. 9.2). Administration operated in seven Departments, each headed jointly by an EU official appointed by the Council of Ministers and one or two Mostar residents appointed by the EU Administrator (ibid., Art. 9.3). The EU Administrator and 'EU members of the administration' were given the privileges and immunities of diplomatic agents provided for in the Vienna Convention on Diplomatic Relations, *mutatis mutandis* (ibid., Art. 19.2). EUAM administration was to run for two years from the date on which the Administrator assumed her or his duties (ibid., Art. 4). It ended up operating from 23 July 1994 to 22 July 1996 (source: telephone conversation between the author and Sir Martin Garrod, Chief of Staff to the EUAM Administrator). On the background to and purposes served by the EUAM, see below, ch. 6, text corresponding to n. 26 and *passim*. Including the EUAM in this book assumes that the EU component—the Common Foreign and Security Policy structure—performing this mandate can be regarded as an international organization, an issue on which expert views differ. On the legal status of this entity in general and at the time of the EUAM, viz. under the regime of the Treaty of Maastricht, see, e.g., the sources cited above in ch. 1, n. 78 and (on the Maastricht period in particular) the original version of the Treaty on European Union, Maastricht, 7 February 1992, *OJ* C224 (1992), 1, reprinted in 31 (1992) *ILM* 247, in particular Title V on 'Common Foreign and Security Policy', and the following academic commentary: I MacLeod, ID Hendry, and S Hyett, *The External Relations of the European Communities* (OUP, 1996) and sources cited therein; D McGoldrick, *International Relations Law*

Dayton process, the territories of Eastern Slavonia, Baranja, and Western Sirmium (Eastern Slavonia) in Croatia were administered by the United Nations Transitional Administration for Eastern Slavonia (UNTAES) between 1996 and 1998.[24] In 1999, two plenary administration projects were conceived: the Kosovo

of the European Union (Longman, 1997), 28–39; A Arnull, A Dashwood, M Ross, and D Wyatt, *Wyatt & Dashwood's European Union Law* (4th edn, Sweet & Maxwell, 2000), 184–5; A Dashwood and C Hillion (eds), *General Law of EC External Relations* (Sweet & Maxwell, 2000); E Denza, *The Intergovernmental Pillars of the EU* (OUP, 2002), 121–2, 173–4 and *passim* (taking the position that the EU did not enjoy legal personality at the time the Mostar MOU was entered into); P Koutrakos, *EU International Relations Law* (Hart, 2006), 406–7; MR Eaton, 'Common Foreign and Security Policy', ch. 14 in D O'Keeffe and P Twomey (eds), *Legal Issues of the Maastricht Treaty* (Wiley Chancery Law, 1994), 224; D Curtin and I Dekker, 'The EU as a "Layered" International Organization: Institutional Unity in Disguise', in P Craig and G de Búrca, *EU Law, Text, Cases & Materials* (2nd edn, OUP, 1998), 83; A Dashwood, 'Implied External Competence of the EC', ch. 8 in M Koskenniemi (ed.), *International Law Aspects of the European Union* (Martinus Nijhoff, 1998); J Klabbers, 'Presumptive Personality: The European Union in International Law', ch. 14 in M Koskenniemi (ed.), *International Law Aspects of the European Union* (Martinus Nijhoff, 1998); M Koskenniemi, 'International Law Aspects of the Common Foreign and Security Policy', ch. 3 in Koskenniemi (ed.), *International Law Aspects of the European Union* (Martinus Nijhoff, 1998); M Cremona, 'External Relations and External Competence, the Emergence of an Integrated Policy', in P Craig and G de Búrca (eds), *The Evolution of EU Law* (OUP, 1999), 166–7; J Monar, 'Mostar: Three Lessons for the European Union', 2 (1997) *European Foreign Affairs Review* 1; A Dashwood, 'External Relations Provisions of the Amsterdam Treaty', 35 (1998) *Common Market Law Review* 1032, 1038–41.

[24] See Basic Agreement on the Region of Eastern Slavonia, Baranja and Western Sirmium, UN Doc. A/50/757–S/1995/951, 15 November 1995, Annex (hereinafter 'Eastern Slavonia Basic Agreement'); SC Res. 1037, 15 January 1996; SC Res. 1079, 15 November 1996; SC Res. 1120, 14 July 1997; Report of the Secretary-General on Eastern Slavonia, 28 August 1996, UN Doc. S/1996/705; L Silber and A Little, *The Death of Yugoslavia* (2nd edn, Penguin and BBC Books, 1996), 370–71; R Paris, *At War's End: Building Peace After Civil Conflict* (CUP, 2004), 107–8; MW Doyle and N Sambanis, *Making War and Building Peace: United Nations Peace Operations* (Princeton University Press, 2006), 223–30; M Bothe, 'The Peace Process in Eastern Slavonia', 3 (1996) *International Peacekeeping* 6; Unnamed author, 'The New UN Mission in Eastern Slavonia', 3 (1996) *International Peacekeeping* 11; P Galbraith, 'Washington, Erdut and Dayton: Negotiating and Implementing Peace in Croatia and Bosnia and Herzegovina', 30 (1997) *Cornell International Law Journal* 643; W Hanset, 'A Success Story: the United Nations Transitional Authority for Eastern Slavonia', in V-Y Ghebali and D Warner (eds), *The Operational Role of the OSCE in Southeastern Europe: Contributing to Regional Stability in the Balkans* (Ashgate, 2001), 3; JP Klein, 'The UN Transitional Administration in Eastern Slavonia (UNTAES)', 97 (2003) *ASIL Proc.* 205; D Sarooshi, 'Conferrals by States of Powers on International Organizations: The Case of Agency', 74 (2003) *BYIL* 291, 304–8; J Smoljan, 'Socio-Economic Aspects of Peacebuilding: UNTAES and the Organisation of Employment in Eastern Slavonia', 10 (2003) *International Peacekeeping* 27; D Boothby, 'The Political Challenges of Administering Eastern Slavonia', 10 (2004) *Global Governance* 37; United Nations, Department of Peacekeeping Operations, 'Eastern Slavonia, Baranja and Western Sirmium—Brief Chronology, 15 January 1996–15 January 1998', available at <http://www.un.org/Depts/DPKO/Missions/untaes_e.htm> (hereinafter 'UNTAES Chronology'). Under the Basic Agreement, the Transitional Administration was to 'govern' Eastern Slavonia during a 'transitional period' (Eastern Slavonia Basic Agreement, para. 2). As requested by the Basic Agreement, this Administration was established by the Security Council as UNTAES in SC Res. 1037 (ibid.). UNTAES had military and civilian components, both under the control of the Transitional Administrator (ibid., paras 1 and 2). The post of Transitional Administrator, appointed by the UN Secretary-General, was held first by Jacques-Paul Klein, and later by William Walker (see 'UNTAES Chronology'). UNTAES was responsible for civil and military administration during the transitional period (Eastern Slavonia Basic Agreement, paras 2 and 3; SC Res. 1037,

mission, UNMIK,[25] and UNTAET, which administered East Timor until independence in 2002.[26]

2.2.3 Projects concerning consultations

In some of the projects already mentioned, and in others, international organizations have been involved in the performance of a particular administrative function: exercising control and supervision over the conduct of 'consultations'—a wide range of different processes concerned with obtaining the view of the people of the territory on a particular issue. They can involve all the people of the territory (sometimes including non-residents, e.g., exiles) or a sub-set of them (such as certain designated 'leaders'); they can involve a formal 'vote' or some other process of ascertaining the view. The term as it is used here thus covers all processes including 'elections', 'plebiscites', and 'referendums'.[27] The consultations can be divided into two general types, as outlined in Table 1 on the following page.

The first type of consultation involves the determination of territorial status, sometimes in the context of the self-determination entitlement;[28] examples include the plebiscite run by the League of Nations Governing Commission in the

---

ibid., paras 10 and 11). The Basic Agreement envisaged that the transitional period would run for 12 months, with the possibility of an extension of a maximum further 12 months 'if so requested by one of the parties' (Eastern Slavonia Basic Agreement, para. 1). The Agreement entered into force, beginning the transitional period, on 15 January 1996 when the Security Council created UNTAES (in accordance with para. 14 of the Eastern Slavonia Basic Agreement). With the local Serb request for an extension of the transitional period for a further 12 months (see Secretary-General Report on Eastern Slavonia, 28 August 1996, UN Doc. S/1996/705, paras 11–13), the Security Council extended the mandate of UNTAES until 15 July 1997 (SC Res. 1079, ibid.); a further extension was granted until 15 January 1998 (SC Res. 1120, ibid.). After a phased draw-down of personnel, the mandate was concluded on 15 January 1998 with administrative authority transferred to Croatia and the replacement of UNTAES with a small group of police monitors (Report of the Secretary-General on Eastern Slavonia, 22 January 1998, UN Doc. S/1998/59, paras 26, 27). The establishment of the monitors was authorized in SC Res. 1145, 19 December 1997, para. 13.

[25] See the sources cited above, ch. 1, n. 1.

[26] See the sources cited above, ch. 1, n. 2.

[27] The United Nations classifies its electoral operations into eight types. The first two (A and B—conduct and supervision/control) fall within the scope of this study. The other categories cover monitoring (including verification), observation, and assistance, and have taken place in various Trust and Non-Self-Governing territories, as well as Angola, El Salvador, Eritrea, Ethiopia, Haiti, Liberia, Mexico, Malawi, Mozambique, Nicaragua, and South Africa. For the UN classification system, see Report of the Secretary-General, 17 November 1994, UN Doc. A/49/675, Annex III. For descriptions of particular missions, see Report of the Secretary-General on Enhancing the Effectiveness of the Principle of Periodic and Genuine Elections, 19 November 1991, UN Doc. A/46/609. In general, see the official website of the Electoral Assistance Division of the UN Department of Political Affairs, at <http://www.un.org/Depts/dpa/ead/index.shtml>. For commentary, see, e.g., R Ludwig, *Letting the People Decide: The Evolution of United Nations Electoral Assistance* (ACUNS, 2001); S Morphet, 'UN Peacekeeping and Election Monitoring', in A Roberts and B Kingsbury (eds), *United Nations, Divided World: The UN's Roles in International Relations* (2nd edn, Clarendon Press, 1993); B Reilly, 'Elections in Post-Conflict Scenarios: Constraints and Dangers', 9 (2002) *International Peacekeeping* 118; T Lyons, 'Post-Conflict Elections and the Process of Demilitarizing Politics: The Role of Electoral Administration', 11:3 (2004) *Democratization* 36.

[28] On this entitlement, see below, ch. 5, section 5.2.

Table 1. International administration (conduct or supervision/control) of consultations

Consultation type	Date	Location	Administering actor
Determination of territorial status	1935	The Saar	League of Nations Governing Commission
	1991	Western Sahara*	United Nations Mission for the Referendum in Western Sahara (MINURSO)
	1999	East Timor	United Nations Mission in East Timor (UNAMET)
	various	Trust and Non-Self-Governing territories	various United Nations missions
Elections of governmental officials	1989	Namibia	UN Transitional Assistance Group (UNTAG)
	1992	Cambodia	UN Transitional Authority in Cambodia (UNTAC)
	1996–2000	Bosnia and Herzegovina	Organization for Security and Co-operation in Europe (OSCE)
	1996	Mostar	European Union Administration of Mostar (EUAM)
	1997	Eastern Slavonia	UN Transitional Authority for Eastern Slavonia (UNTAES)
	from 1999	Kosovo	UN Mission in Kosovo (UNMIK), delegated to the OSCE
	various	Trust and Non-Self-Governing territories	various United Nations missions

* Administrative prerogatives authorized but not fully implemented at time of writing.

Saar in 1935,[29] and the 'popular consultation' in East Timor run by UNAMET in 1999,[30] as well as various consultations in Trust and Non-Self-Governing territories that were either administered or supervised by the United Nations.[31] The conduct of a referendum of this type was also authorized, but, at the time of writing, not implemented, in Western Sahara, to be performed by the previously mentioned MINURSO.[32]

[29] See below, ch. 4, section 4.2.1.
[30] For the consultation and UNAMET, see above, ch. 1, n. 5, and below, ch. 5, text corresponding to n. 145 *et seq.*
[31] For consultations of this type in Trust and Non-Self-Governing territories, see Report of the Secretary-General on Enhancing the Effectiveness of the Principle of Periodic and Genuine Elections, above n. 27, paras 6, 7, 12, and Annex.
[32] On MINURSO, see above n. 21. At the time of writing, the passage of Security Council Resolution 1754 in 2007 had placed a question mark over whether support at the UN for the

The second type of consultation determines the appointment of local actors to governmental positions. International supervision or conduct began in various Trust and Non-Self-Governing territories and subsequently spread to states and parts of states.[33] In some instances, international organizations supervise and control the conduct of such processes by local actors, as was the case with the United Nations Transitional Assistance Group (UNTAG) in Namibia in 1989.[34] Alternatively, they operate the consultation directly, as in the elections run by the previously mentioned UN Transitional Authority in Cambodia (UNTAC) in 1992,[35] the previously

referendum was being dropped. See SC Res. 1754, 30 April 2007, and Report of the Secretary-General on the status and progress of the negotiations on Western Sahara, UN Doc. S/2007/385, 29 June 2007. For commentary, see, e.g., the works in K Arts and P Pinto Leite (eds), *International Law and the Question of Western Sahara* (International Platform of Jurists for East Timor, 2007), in particular C Drew, 'The Meaning of Self-determination: The "Stealing of the Sahara" Redux?'.

[33] For consultations of this type held in Trust and Non-Self-Governing territories, see the report cited above, n. 31.

[34] See SC Res. 435, 29 September 1978; Contact Group, Proposal for a Settlement of the Namibian Situation, Letter to the President of the Security Council, 10 April 1978, UN Doc. S/12636 (1978); Report of the Secretary-General, 29 August 1978, UN Doc. S/12827; Secretary-General, Explanatory Statement, 29 September 1978, UN Doc. S/12869, paras 11–22; SC Res. 632, 16 February 1989; Report of the Secretary-General, 23 January 1989, UN Doc. S/20412; Report of the Secretary-General, 16 March 1989, UN Doc. S/20412/Add.1; Secretary-General, Explanatory Statement, 9 February 1989, UN Doc. S/20457. UNTAG was established in SC Res. 435, 29 September 1978, in accordance with a plan proposed by a Contact Group of countries and a report by the UN Secretary-General. This establishment was eventually implemented in 1989, through SC Res. 632 (ibid.), again in accordance with a report from the UN Secretary General. On UNTAG, see, e.g., L Cliffe, *The Transition to Independence in Namibia* (Lynne Rienner, 1994), 65–77; V Page Fortna, 'United Nations Transition Assistance Group in Namibia', in WJ Durch (ed.), *The Evolution of UN Peacekeeping* (St Martin's Press, 1994), 353; LC Kaela, *The Question of Namibia* (Macmillan Press, 1996), 96–125; Chopra (above n. 13), 78–9; Morphet (above n. 17), 47–9; LM Howard, 'UN Peace Implementation in Namibia: The Causes of Success', 9 (2002) *International Peacekeeping* 99; Kreilkamp (above n. 21), 625–6; GA Dzinesa, 'A Comparative Perspective of UN Peacekeeping in Angola and Namibia', 11 (2004) *International Peacekeeping* 644.

[35] See Cambodia Settlement Agreement (above n. 20), Arts 2, 12–14; Annex 1, para. D and Annex 3; Report of the Secretary-General on Cambodia, 19 February 1992, UN Doc. S/23613 (1992) and Addendum 1, 26 February 1992, UN Doc. S/23613/Add.1 (1992); SC Res. 745, 28 February 1992, paras 1 and 2. See also J Chopra, *United Nations Authority in Cambodia* (Thomas J Watson Jr Institute for International Studies, Occasional Paper No. 15, 1994); JE Heininger, *Peacekeeping in Transition: The United Nations in Cambodia* (Twentieth Century Fund Press, 1994), *passim*; T Findlay, *Cambodia: The Legacy and Lessons of UNTAC* (OUP, 1995), 33–74, 101–7, and bibliography at 213–22; United Nations, *The United Nations and Cambodia 1991–1995* (United Nations Blue Book Series, 1995), 15–37; FO Hampson, *Nurturing Peace: Why Peace Settlements Succeed or Fail* (United States Institute of Peace Press, 1996), ch. 6; Paris (above n. 24), 79–90; Doyle & Sambanis (above n. 24), 209–23; SR Ratner, 'The Cambodian Settlement Agreements', 87 (1993) *AJIL* 1, 9–18, 20–2; Chopra (above n. 13), 80–1; MW Doyle and A Suzuki, 'Transitional Authority in Cambodia', ch. 8 in T Weiss (ed.), *The United Nations and Civil Wars* (Lynne Rienner, 1995); JA Schear, 'Riding the Tiger: the United Nations and Cambodia's Struggle for Peace', in W Durch (ed.), *UN Peacebuilding, American Politics, and the Uncivil Wars of the 1990s* (St. Martin's Press, 1996), 135; Morphet (above n. 17), 50–2; Kreilkamp (above n. 21), 630–4; L Keller, 'UNTAC in Cambodia—From Occupation, Civil War and Genocide to Peace', 9 (2005) *Max Planck Yearbook of United Nations Law* 127; M Berdal and M Leifer, 'Cambodia', ch. 2 in M Berdal and S Economides (eds), *United Nations Interventionism, 1991–2004* (OUP, 2007).

mentioned European Union Administration of Mostar (EUAM) in 1996,[36] the UN Transitional Authority for Eastern Slavonia (UNTAES) in 1997[37] and UNMIK, delegated to the Organization for Security and Co-operation in Europe (OSCE) from 1999.[38] The OSCE was also responsible for the elections in Bosnia and Herzegovina from 1996 to 2000.[39]

[36] Mostar MOU (above n. 23), Art. 2; International Crisis Group, *Reunifying Mostar: Opportunities for Progress*, 19 April 2000, obtainable from <http://www.crisisgroup.org>, 12.

[37] Eastern Slavonia Basic Agreement (above n. 24), para. 12. Elections were held on 13–14 April 1997 (see Report of the Secretary-General on Eastern Slavonia, 23 June 1997, UN Doc. S/1997/487, paras 2 and 3).

[38] Operated by the OSCE through a Central Election Commission, with progressive delegation to a locally-staffed Central Election Commission Secretariat (CECS). See SC Res. 1244, 10 June 1999, para. 11(c); OSCE, Permanent Council, Decision No. 305, 'Decision on the OSCE Mission in Kosovo', 1 July 1999, OSCE Doc. PC.DEC/305, appended to the *Journal of the 237th Plenary Meeting of the Permanent Council* (OSCE Doc. PC.JOUR/237/Corr., 1 July 1999), obtainable from <http://www.osce.org/documents/pc/1999/07/2577_en.pdf>, para. 3. At the time of writing, the conduct of the elections had been devolved to local institutions as part of the broader devolution of authority (on which, see above, ch. 1, n. 1) but responsibility for the elections still resided ultimately with UNMIK (see the OSCE Mission in Kosovo website, at <http://www.osce.org/kosovo/13208.html>).

[39] This function was performed by the OSCE's Office for Democratic Institutions and Human Rights (ODIHR). On the creation of that Office and its mandate in relation to elections see Conference for Security and Co-operation in Europe (CSCE), Charter of Paris for a New Europe, adopted at the Paris Summit, 19–21 November 1990, obtainable from <http://www.osce.org> Supplementary Document, section I, G (creating the 'Office for Free Elections'); CSCE, Prague Document on Further Development of CSCE Institutions and Structures, adopted by the Ministerial Council, 31 January 1992, obtainable from <http://www.osce.org>, para. 9; CSCE, Helsinki Document, 'The Challenges of Change', adopted at the Helsinki Summit, 9–10 July 1992, obtainable from <http://www.osce.org>, Decision VI (The Human Dimension), para. 5a; CSCE, Budapest Document 1994, adopted at the Budapest Summit, 5–6 December 1994, Budapest Decisions, Section VIII, para. 12; OSCE Handbook, 105–15; OSCE Office for Democratic Institutions and Human Rights, *Ten Years of ODIHR: Working for Human Rights and Democracy (1991–2001)* (2001), obtainable from <http://www.osce.org>. The OSCE is covered as an 'international organization' insofar as election conduct and monitoring is concerned because the performance of this function arguably requires a distinct identity and legal personality on the part of the ODIHR. As far as missions undertaken within particular member states are concerned, the ODIHR must be more than a mere collective action of member states, since its actions presuppose separation from the particular member state whose elections it is monitoring or carrying out. For academic commentary on the OSCE generally, see, e.g., Sands & Klein (above n. 16), 119–201 and sources cited at 199; Schermers & Blokker (above n. 16), 21 and sources cited therein; White (above n. 16), 39–40. Bosnia and Herzegovina joined the OSCE on 30 April 1992, and agreed to the Helsinki Final Act on 8 July 1992 (see <http://www.osce.org>). On the mandate to conduct the elections in Bosnia and Herzegovina, see Dayton Peace Agreements (above, ch. 1, n. 38), in particular Dayton Annex 3 (ibid.). Under the Dayton Peace Agreements, the OSCE was mandated 'to supervise... the preparation and conduct of elections for the House of Representatives of Bosnia and Herzegovina; for the Presidency of Bosnia and Herzegovina; for the House of Representatives of the Federation of Bosnia and Herzegovina; for the National Assembly of the Republika Srpska; for the Presidency of the Republika Srpska; and, if feasible, for cantonal legislatures and municipal governing authorities' (Dayton Annex 3, above ch. 1, n. 38, Art. V). To this end, the OSCE set up a Provisional Electoral Commission, as the body responsible for the overall organization and running of the elections in Bosnia and Herzegovina; the Commission was responsible for the adoption of rules and regulations governing the elections, for the supervision of all aspects of the electoral process, and for the certification of the results. The Commission, in accordance with Dayton Annex 3, was chaired by the Head of the OSCE Mission, and comprised three other international members (the Deputy Head of Mission of the OSCE, the High Representative, and the Senior

2.2.4 Projects never agreed or implemented

In addition to the international territorial administration projects outlined above, other such projects (involving partial or plenary administration) were proposed but never agreed upon for Fiume in Dalmatia (in 1919),[40] Memel (between 1921 and 1923),[41] Alexandretta in Syria (in 1937),[42] Jerusalem (since 1947),[43] Antarctica (in 1956),[44] the Falklands (in 1982),[45] and Sarajevo (in 1994);[46] or authorized but never carried out in the case of the Free Territory of Trieste (in 1947).[47]

Deputy High Representative) and one 'representative' of each of the Parties to the Annex, viz. Bosnia and Herzegovina, the Federation and the Republika Srpska, with deputies. It began its work in January 1996. On the mandate and responsibilities of the Commission, see Dayton Annex 3, Art. III; see also 'Two roads lead to elections', *Slobodna Bosna*, 5 April 1996, English translation available at <http://www.oscebih.org/public/default.asp?d=6&article=show&id=1633>. See also Case U40/00 (on Articles 606 and 1212 of the Rules and Regulations of the Provisional Election Commission of the OSCE Mission to Bosnia and Herzegovina), Constitutional Court of Bosnia and Herzegovina, Decision of 2 February 2001, and Annex, Separate dissenting Opinion of Judge Prof. Dr. Vitomir Popović, obtainable from <http://www.ccbh.ba>; Case Nos CH/98/230 & 231, *Adnan Suljanović and Edita Cisić and Asim Lelić v the State of Bosnia and Herzegovina and Republika Srpska*, Human Rights Chamber for Bosnia and Herzegovina, Decision on Admissibility of 14 May 1998, obtainable from <http://www.hrc.ba>. The last general elections for which OSCE retained overall responsibility were those of 11 November 2000: see UN Press Release SC/6950, 14 November 2000, and Head of the OSCE Mission to Bosnia and Herzegovina, 'Statement to OSCE Permanent Council', Vienna, 4 July 2002, available at <http://www.oscebih.org/documents/28-eng.pdf>. The Provisional Electoral Commission was replaced in 2000 by a permanent Electoral Commission (on which, see below n. 119 and accompanying text). For commentary on the elections conducted by the OSCE, see M Ducasse-Rogier, 'The Operational Role of the OSCE in the Field of Peace-Building: The Case of Bosnia and Herzegovina', in V-Y Ghebali and D Warner (eds), *The Operational Role of the OSCE in Southeastern Europe: Contributing to Regional Stability in the Balkans* (Ashgate Publishing, 2001), 24; P Emerson, 'How a Quota Borda System of Elections may Facilitate Reconciliation', in D Sokolović and F Bieber (eds), *Reconstructing Multiethnic Societies: The Case of Bosnia and Herzegovina* (Ashgate Publishing, 2001), 147; R Belloni, 'Peacebuilding and Consociational Electoral Engineering in Bosnia and Herzegovina', 11 (2004) *International Peacekeeping* 334.

[40] Ydit (above n. 12), 51–9.   [41] Ibid., 48.
[42] SR Ratner, *The New UN Peacekeeping, Building Peace in Lands of Conflict after the Cold War* (St. Martin's Press, 1995), 97.
[43] See Report of the UN Trusteeship Council, Annex II, Statute for the City of Jerusalem, UN GAOR, 5th Sess., Supp. No. 9, at 1, 19, UN Doc. A/1286 (1950); Kelsen (above n. 16), 195–7 n. 7 and 684–8; Ydit (above n. 12), 273–314, bibliography at 315; M Hirsch, D Housen-Couriel, and R Lapidoth, *Whither Jerusalem? Proposals and Petitions Concerning the Future Status of Jerusalem* (Martinus Nijhoff, 1995), *passim*; DS Smyrek, *Internationally Administered Territories— International Protectorates? An Analysis of Sovereignty over Internationally Administered Territories with Special Reference to the Legal Status of Post-War Kosovo* (Duncker & Humblot, 2006), 92–101; F Seyersted, 'United Nations Forces, Some Legal Problems', 37 (1962) *BYIL* 351, 452; Halderman (above n. 18), *passim*.
[44] See, e.g., E Lauterpacht, 'The Contemporary Practice of the United Kingdom in the Field of International Law—Survey and Comment', 5 (1956) *ICLQ* 405, 409–13.
[45] JG Merrills, *International Dispute Settlement* (4th edn, CUP, 2005), 260 and 260 n. 52.
[46] D Owen, *Balkan Odyssey* (Victor Gollancz, 1995), 199, 210, 212, 215, 235–6, 238–40, 242–3.
[47] See Peace Treaty with Italy, Paris, 10 February 1947, 49 UNTS 126, Part II, Section III, Arts 21–22 and Annexes VI–VIII; Kelsen (above n. 16), ch. 21; Ydit (above n. 12), 231–72;

2.2.5 An activity spanning the 20th century

The foregoing survey suggests that, despite the exceptionalist suggestions made by some commentators, international organizations have been involved in the conduct of territorial administration since the start of the League of Nations. Whether the focus is on plenary or partial administration, international organizations generally or the United Nations in particular, the Kosovo and East Timor projects are not unprecedented insofar as the activity conducted and the actor performing this role are concerned. The first plenary international territorial administration projects were the Saar in 1920 (in the League era) and West Irian in 1962–63 (in the UN era); the first partial administration projects were Danzig in 1920 (in the League era) and the Congo in 1960–64 (in the UN era). Insofar as the Kosovo and East Timor projects involve plenary administration exercised by the United Nations, they are not unprecedented but follow on from the West Irian and Eastern Slavonia projects. If the focus is broadened to international organizations generally, these projects are but the latest manifestations of an activity that was first undertaken in 1920.

2.3 Into the 21st Century

Adopting a definition of international territorial administration that covers international organizations generally, situations of partial as well as plenary administration, and the involvement of international appointees on locally-based administrative bodies as defined in the previous chapter, reveals four further clusters of ITA projects that were under way at the same time as UNMIK and UNTAET were created: the administration of camps housing refugees and internally displaced persons by UNHCR and the assistance provided to Palestinian refugees by the United Nations Relief and Works Agency (UNRWA); the operation of material assistance programmes by international organizations in various territories; the conduct of certain administrative activities by the Office of the High Representative in Bosnia and Herzegovina (OHR); and various arrangements involving international appointees.

2.3.1 Administration of 'refugee' camps and provision of assistance to refugees and internally displaced people

In certain circumstances, states hand over responsibility for running camps housing refugees and/or internally displaced persons (hereinafter 'refugee camps')[48]

MD Donelan and MJ Grieve, *International Disputes: Case Histories 1945–1970* (Palgrave Macmillan, 1973), 24–7; Smyrek (above n. 43), 79–92; Seyersted (above n. 43), 451–2; Halderman (above n. 18); Morphet (above n. 17), 43.

[48] The use of the word 'refugee' in this context is misleading, since internally displaced persons are by definition not (legal) refugees. See, e.g., Convention Relating to the Status of Refugees, 28 July 1951, 189 UNTS 150, as amended by Protocol relating to the Status of Refugees, 31 January 1967, entry into force 4 October 1967, 606 UNTS 267, Art. 1; Organization of African Unity, Convention Governing the Specific Aspects of Refugee Problems in Africa, 20 June 1974, 14 UNTS 691, Art. 1; Cartagena Declaration on Refugees, adopted at the Colloquium on the International

to UNHCR.[49] One example is the Dadaab camps of Kenya.[50] These vast camps, which resemble small towns, are populated by individuals from Ethiopia,

Protection of Refugees in Central America, Mexico and Panama, 19–22 November 1984, Part III, para. 3. For academic commentary on this legal distinction, see, e.g., JC Hathaway, *The Rights of Refugees under International Law* (CUP, 2005); C Phuong, *The International Protection of Internally Displaced Persons* (CUP, 2005); G Goodwin-Gill and J McAdam, *The Refugee in International Law* (3rd edn, OUP, 2007); and sources cited therein.

[49] UNHCR was created by the UN General Assembly in 1950. On its mandate and functions, see GA Res. 428(V) of 14 December 1950, containing its Statute, and Schermers & Blokker (above n. 16), § 1695. On the UN's status as an international organization, see above, n. 16. On UNHCR generally, including its field operations and administration of refugee camps, see, e.g., G Loescher, *The UNHCR and World Politics: A Perilous Path* (OUP, 2001); MYA Zieck, *UNHCR's Worldwide Presence in the Field* (Wolf Legal Publishers, 2006). On UNHCR-run refugee camps in particular, see, e.g., J Hyndman, *Managing Displacement: Refugees and the Politics of Humanitarianism* (University of Minnesota Press, 2000); SK Lischer, *Dangerous Sanctuaries: Refugee Camps, Civil War, and the Dilemmas of Humanitarian Aid* (Cornell University Press, 2005); G Verdirame and B Harrell-Bond, *Rights in Exile: Janus-Faced Humanitarianism* (Berghahn Books, 2005); R Wilde, *Beyond the Yoke: Women's Rights in the Dadaab Refugee Camps of Kenya* (1997, report on file at UK House of Commons Library); J Hyndman and BV Nylund, 'UNHCR and the Status of Prima Facie Refugees in Kenya', 10 (1998) *International Journal of Refugee Law* 21; R Wilde, '*Quis Custodiet Ipsos Custodes?* Why and How UNHCR Governance of "Development" Refugee Camps Should Be Subject to International Human Rights Law', 1 (1998) *Yale Human Rights and Development Law Journal* 107; M Alexander, 'Refugee Status Determination Conducted by the UNHCR', 11 (1999) *International Journal of Refugee Law* 25; J Crisp, 'A State of Insecurity: The Political Economy of Violence in Refugee-Populated Areas of Kenya', *New Issues in Refugee Research*, Working Paper No. 16, December 1999, available at <http://www.unhcr.org/publ/RESEARCH/3ae6a0c44.pdf>; G Verdirame, 'Field Report, Human Rights and Refugees: the Case of Kenya', 12 (1999) *Journal of Refugees Studies* 54; M-A Perouse de Montclos and P Mwangi Kagwanja, 'Refugee Camps or Cities? The Socio-Economic Dynamics of the Dadaab and Kakuma Camps in Northern Kenya', 13 (2000) *Journal of Refugees Studies* 205; DP Forsythe, 'Humanitarian Protection: The International Committee of the Red Cross and the United Nations High Commissioner for Refugees', (2001) *IRRC*, vol. 83, issue 843, 675; B Oswald, 'The Creation and Control of Places of Protection during United Nations Peace Operations', (2001) *IRRC*, vol. 83, issue 844, 1031; K Young, 'UNHCR and ICRC in the former Yugoslavia: Bosnia-Herzegovina', (2001) *IRRC*, vol. 83, issue 843, 781; SS Chaulia, 'UNHCR's Relief, Rehabilitation and Repatriation of Rwandan Refugees in Zaire (1994–1997)', *Journal of Humanitarian Assistance* (April 2002), available at <http://www.jha.ac/articles/a086.htm>; G Verdirame, 'Compliance with Human Rights in UN Operations', 2 (2002) *Human Rights Law Review* 265, 265–7, 283–5; *UNHCR Global Report 2004*, obtainable from <http://www.unhcr.org>; G Loescher and J Milner, 'The Long Road Home: Protracted Refugee Situations in Africa', 47 (2005) *Survival* 153; M Pallis, 'The Operation of UNHCR's Accountability Mechanisms', NYU International Law and Justice Working Papers, Global Administrative Law Series, Paper 2005/12, available at <http://www.iilj.org/papers/documents/2005.12Pallis.pdf>; A Farmer, 'Refugee Responses, State-like Behavior, and Accountability for Human Rights Violations: A Case Study of Sexual Violence in Guinea's Refugee Camps', 9 (2006) *Yale Human Rights and Development Law Journal* 44, at 76–8; US Committee for Refugees, 'Statement Calling for Solutions to End the Warehousing of Refugees', undated (rolling process of endorsement), obtainable from <http://www.refugees.org/uploadedFiles/Investigate/Anti_Warehousing/statement.pdf>, and the contributions dealing with the question of 'refugee warehousing' published in US Committee for Refugees, *World Refugees Survey 2004*, available at <http://www.refugees.org/article.aspx?id=1156>.

[50] The following information is drawn from the author's personal experience working as a volunteer in the camps in 1998, and verified from more recent source material where possible. See Wilde, *Beyond the Yoke* and '*Quis Custodiet Ipsos Custodes?*' (above n. 49) and *UNHCR Global Report 2004* (above n. 49), 217. More recent verification was obtained from UNHCR, Sub-Office Dadaab, 'Dadaab Operations in Brief', 31 January 2006 (publication status verified, on file with the author) (hereinafter: UNHCR, 'Dadaab Operations in Brief'). For other commentary on these camps, see, e.g., the works by Hyndman; Verdirame & Harrell-Bond; Verdirame; Perouse de Montclos &

Somalia, the Sudan, and Uganda. Although, as the host state, Kenya is ultimately responsible for the management of the camps and for the safety of those in them, it has delegated overall administrative control to UNHCR.[51]

Most day-to-day operations are contracted out by UNHCR to various international organization, governmental, and non-governmental organization 'Implementing Partners',[52] with UNHCR retaining direct responsibility for 'protection' matters, viz. the processing of new arrivals, including determining their refugee status, and arranging resettlement and repatriation.[53] The International Partners perform a broad range of public services, being responsible for food distribution, managing water and sanitation infrastructure, education and community provision, medical services and health education, and environmental protection.[54] The only direct involvement by local governmental authorities is the provision of limited military protection, focused mainly on international agency convoys travelling between the camps, and paid for by UNHCR.[55]

Less extensive than overall refugee camp administration is the provision of certain public services for displaced people without also exercising control over the camps in which they are housed. As well as UNHCR, this role is performed by the other UN 'refugee' body, the United Nations Relief and Works Agency for Palestine Refugees in the Near East (UNRWA), which became operational before UNHCR, in 1950.[56] UNRWA provides basic education services, health

Mwangi Kagwanja cited in the previous footnote. See also M Lacey, 'Dadaab Journal—Where Showing Skin Doesn't Sell, a New Style Is a Hit', *New York Times*, 20 March 2006.

[51] On Kenya's ultimate responsibility for the camps, see UNHCR, 'Dadaab Operations in Brief' (above n. 50), 1.

[52] Ibid.

[53] Ibid.

[54] At the time of writing, UNHCR's main implementing partner in the Dadaab camps was CARE Kenya, which was responsible for camp management, food-distribution, water and sanitation, education and community services: see UNHCR, 'Dadaab Operations in Brief' (above n. 50), 1. For 11 years, until 2003, Médécins Sans Frontières Belgium (MSF–B) provided medical care, both immediate and, with immunization programmes, long-term (see Médécins Sans Frontières, 'HIV/AIDS & home-based care in western Kenya', August 2004, available at <http://www.msf.org.au/stories/twfeature/2004/053twf.shtml>). At the time of writing, medical care was provided by Deutsche Gesellschaft für Technische Zusammenarbeit (GTZ), which was also responsible for managing firewood and the environment, and for training residents of the camps in conservation skills; Handicap International (HI) organized referrals to the Garissa Provincial Hospital of complicated medical cases that could not be attended to at camp level; the National Council of Churches of Kenya (NCCK) promoted reproductive health and HIV/AIDS education; a Peace Education Programme, started in 1998, was also implemented by the NCCK; the World Food Programme (WPF) provided food supplies, and the Kenya Red Cross Society carried out tracing activities within the camps (source: UNHCR, 'Dadaab Operations in Brief', ibid., 1).

[55] On Kenya's responsibility for security, see ibid.

[56] UNRWA was created by the General Assembly in 1949. On its establishment and mandate, see GA Res. 302 (IV), 8 December 1949 and GA Res. 2252 (ES-V), 4 July 1967, para. 6. On the UN's status as an international organization see above, n. 16. For the text of General Assembly resolutions on UNRWA since 2001, see <http://www.un.org/unrwa/publications/ga_resolutions.html>. On the activities of the agency, see, in general, UNRWA website, at <http://www.un.org/unrwa/index.html>, in particular 'UNRWA Medium Term Plan 2005–2009: A Better Future for Palestine Refugees' (2005), available at <http://www.un.org/unrwa/news/mtp.pdf>.

care and relief, and social programmes (including the provision of shelter, water, basic food, and sanitation services) through a network of more than 900 installations including schools, health clinics and community centres, and development programmes for job creation and income generation, to a population of more than 4 million Palestinians, one-third of whom live in camps located in the Gaza Strip, the West Bank, Jordan, Lebanon, and Syria.[57]

2.3.2 Distribution of humanitarian supplies

Beyond assistance to forced migrants, UN bodies, notably the World Food Programme (WFP), implement programmes of material assistance in a variety of places.[58] In operating sometimes highly sophisticated arrangements of basic social provision, from food to medical supplies, these programmes involve the conduct of partial administrative prerogatives over defined territorial units in the same way as social provision by a state government constitutes an administrative function of the state. The fact that they may be unofficial, contingent on changing security and environmental factors, and operating on an ostensibly 'humanitarian', charitable basis does not alter their nature as mechanisms for managing the

---

See also W Dale, 'UNRWA—A Subsidiary Organ of the United Nations', 23 (1974) *ICLQ* 576. On the working definition of 'Palestinian refugee' adopted by UNRWA, see UNRWA, 'Who is a Palestine refugee?', undated, available at: <http://www.un.org/unrwa/refugees/whois.html>. See also L Takkenberg, 'The Protection of Palestine Refugees in the Territories Occupied by Israel', 3 (1991) *International Journal of Refugee Law* 414; MA Helwa and B Birch, 'The Demography and Housing Conditions of Palestinian Refugees in and Around the Camps in Amman, Jordan', 6 (1993) *Journal of Refugee Studies* 403; Y Besson, 'UNRWA and its Role in Lebanon', 10 (1997) *Journal of Refugee Studies* 335, at 336.

[57] At the time of writing, eight camps were located in the Gaza Strip; nineteen in the West Bank; ten in Jordan, twelve in Lebanon, and ten in Syria: see Public Information Office, UNRWA Headquarters, 'UNRWA in Figures—Figures as of 31 December 2005' (March 2006), at <http://www.un.org/unrwa/publications/pdf/uif-dec05.pdf>, and 'Map of UNRWA's Area of Operations 2005', undated, available at <http://www.un.org/unrwa/refugees/images/map.jpg>. UNRWA's asserted role in performing partial administrative activities, not involving overall responsibility for administering the camps, is illustrated by the following statement by the organization:

UNRWA does not run refugee camps. It...has never been given any mandate to administer, supervise or police the refugee camps or to have any jurisdiction or legislative power over the refugees or the areas where they lived. The Agency has no police force, no intelligence service and no mandate to report on political and military activities. This responsibility has always remained with the host countries and Israel, who maintained law and order, including within refugee camps.

UNRWA, 'Setting the Record Straight', undated, available at <http://www.un.org/unrwa/allegations/index.html>. See also 'UNRWA Response to allegations made by the Centre Simon Wiesenthal in its statement to the Commission on 31 March 2003', 9 April 2003, available at <http://www.un.org/unrwa/allegations/response.html>.

[58] As for the WFP, this body was established in 1961 by parallel resolutions of the General Assembly and the Food and Agricultural Organization (FAO), one of the UN specialized agencies, as a programme undertaken jointly between the United Nations and FAO; see the resolution adopted by the Eleventh Conference of the Food and Agricultural Organization on 24 November 1961 and GA Res. 1714 (XVI), 19 December 1961. On the UN's status as an international organization see above, n. 16. For a further example, see the discussion of the UN Office for the Coordination of Humanitarian Affairs (OCHA) in Somalia, below, ch. 6, text accompanying n. 49 *et seq.*

provision of social relief in the territory covered and in relation to the particular type of assistance provided.

To give one example, from 1996 to 2003 the UN Inter-Agency Humanitarian Programme was responsible for distributing 'humanitarian supplies' (e.g., medicine, foodstuffs) in three of the northern Governorates of Iraq—Arbil, Dihouk, and Suleimaniyeh—as part of the Oil-for-Food Programme relating to Iraq generally.[59]

2.3.3 The Office of the High Representative in Bosnia and Herzegovina (OHR)

As introduced in the previous chapter, an official called the 'High Representative' with a secretariat, together known as the 'Office of the High Representative' (OHR), began operating in Bosnia and Herzegovina after the Dayton Peace Agreements in 1995, and over time asserted the right to perform certain administrative acts in the country.[60] The title 'High Representative' comes from Annex 10 of

[59] On the UN Inter-Agency Humanitarian Programme, see SC Res. 986, 14 April 1995, para. 8 (b), and the Memorandum of Understanding between Iraq and the United Nations on the Implementation of Security Council Resolution 986 (1995) ('Iraq MOU'), 20 May 1996, UN Doc. S/1996/356 (1996), Sections II, VI and Annex I. The UN Inter-Agency Humanitarian Programme was suspended on 17 March 2003, when the UN Secretary-General, in view of warnings received from the United States and the United Kingdom in relation to the prospect of war, decided to withdraw all UN and international staff involved in implementing the Oil-for-Food Programme generally; the UN Inter-Agency Humanitarian Programme in the Northern Governorates was not resumed thereafter, although a country-wide programme of humanitarian assistance was put in place pursuant to SC Res. 1472 of 28 March 2003. On the Oil-for-Food Programme and its termination, see below, ch. 4, n. 167 and corresponding text. For background information, see the website of the UN Office for the Iraq Program, at <http://www.un.org/Depts/oip/index.html>. For a critical appraisal of a further example, UN humanitarian assistance in Afghanistan, see G Verdirame, 'Testing the Effectiveness of International Norms: The Provision of Humanitarian Assistance by the UN and Sexual Apartheid in Afghanistan', 23 (2001) *Human Rights Quarterly* 733.

[60] On the international involvement in Bosnia and Herzegovina, including OHR, and the situation in the country since the Dayton Peace Agreements more generally, see, e.g., D Chandler, *Bosnia: Faking Democracy after Dayton* (2nd edn, Pluto Press, 2000), *passim*; EM Cousens and CK Cater, *Toward Peace in Bosnia: Implementing the Dayton Accords* (IPA/Lynne Rienner, 2001), 638–42; D Sokolović and F Bieber (eds), *Reconstructing Multiethnic Societies: The Case of Bosnia and Herzegovina* (Ashgate, 2001), *passim*; M Ignatieff, *Empire Lite: Nation-building in Bosnia, Kosovo and Afghanistan* (Vintage, 2003), 27–43; A Orford, *Reading Humanitarian Intervention: Human Rights and the Use of Force in International Law* (CUP, 2003), 129–34; Paris (above n. 24), 97–107; D Chandler, *Empire in Denial: The Politics of State-building* (Pluto Press, 2006), *passim* and in particular ch. 6; P Ashdown, *Swords and Ploughshares: Bringing Peace to the 21st Century* (Weidenfeld & Nicolson, 2007); Doyle & Sambanis (above n. 24), 230–4; EM Cousens, 'Making Peace in Bosnia Work', 30 (1997) *Cornell International Law Journal* 789; P Gaeta, 'Is NATO Authorized or Obliged to Arrest Persons Indicted by the International Criminal Tribunal for the Former Yugoslavia?', 9 (1998) *EJIL* 174; TD Grant, 'Internationally Guaranteed Constitutive Order: Cyprus and Bosnia as Predicates for a New Nontraditional Actor in the Society of States', 8 (1998) *Journal of Transnational Law & Policy* 1; M Cox, 'The Dayton Agreement in Bosnia and Herzegovina: A Study in Implementation Strategies', 69 (1999) *BYIL* 201; I Daalder and M Froman, 'Dayton's Incomplete Peace', 78:6 (Nov/Dec 1999) *Foreign Affairs* 106; J Bugajski, 'Balkan In Dependence', 23:4 (2000) *Washington Quarterly* 177; D Chandler, 'Western Intervention

the Agreements,[61] but no explanation is given in that instrument or any other instruments as to who or what exactly is being 'represented'. Occasionally, an erroneous suggestion is made that the High Representative is a UN official, presumably akin to the United Nations High Commissioners for Human Rights and Refugees.[62] Over time, OHR began to use the extended designation 'the High

and the Disintegration of Yugoslavia, 1989–99', in E Herman and P Hammond (eds), *Degraded Capability: The Media and the Kosovo Crisis* (Pluto Press Ltd, 2000), 19; RL Barry, 'Bosnia and Herzegovina: Status Report', in V-Y Ghebali and D Warner (eds), *The Operational Role of the OSCE in Southeastern Europe: Contributing to Regional Stability in the Balkans* (Ashgate Publishing, 2001), 20; C Bildt, 'A Second Chance in the Balkans', 80:6 (Jan/Feb 2001) *Foreign Affairs* 148; C Chinkin and K Paradine, 'Vision and Reality: Democracy and Citizenship of Women in the Dayton Peace Accords', 26 (2001) *Yale Journal of International Law* 103; M Ducasse-Rogier, above, n. 39; PC Farrand, 'Lessons from Brcko: Necessary Components for Future Internationally Supervised Territories', 15 (2001) *Emory International Law Review* 529; AB Siegel, 'Associating Development Projects with Military Operations: Lessons from NATO's First Year in BiH', 8 (2001) *International Peacekeeping* 99; P Ashdown, 'What I Learned in Bosnia', *New York Times*, 28 October 2002, A25, column 2; D Chandler, 'Bosnia's New Colonial Governor', *The Guardian*, 9 July 2002, Comment & Analysis, 16; JS Hylton, 'Security Sector Reform: BIH Federation Ministry of the Interior', 9 (2002) *International Peacekeeping* 153; K Okuizumi, 'Peacebuilding Mission: Lessons from the UN Mission in Bosnia and Herzegovina', 24 (2002) *Human Rights Quarterly* 721; M Pugh, 'Postwar Political Economy in Bosnia and Herzegovina: The Spoils of Peace', 8 (2002) *Global Governance* 467; B Bonvin, 'Training and Non-Security Aspects of the Police Democratisation in Bosnia and Herzegovina', 3 (2003) *Conflict, Security and Development* 417; C Cordone, 'Bosnia and Herzegovina: The Creeping Protectorate', in AH Henkin (ed.), *Honoring Human Rights under International Mandates: Lessons from Bosnia, Kosovo and East Timor* (Aspen Institute, 2003), 21; G Knaus and F Martin, 'Travails of the European Raj', 14:3 (2003) *Journal of Democracy* 60; Kreilkamp (above n. 21), 638–42; C Steiner and N Ademovic, 'Kompetenzstreitigkeiten im Gefüge von Dayton', in W Vitzthum and I Winkelmann (eds), *Bosnien-Herzegowina im Horizont Europas, Demokratische und föderale Elemente der Staatswerdung in Südosteuropa* (Duncker & Humblot, 2003); R Caplan, 'International Authority and State Building: The Case of Bosnia and Herzegovina', 10 (2004) *Global Governance* 53; M Ducasse-Rogier, 'Recovering from Dayton: From "Peace-Building" to "State-Building" in Bosnia and Herzegovina', 15 (2004) *Helsinki Monitor* 76; TW Waters, 'Contemplating Failure and Creating Alternatives in the Balkans: Bosnia's Peoples, Democracy, and the Shape of Self-Determination', 29 (2004) *Yale Journal of International Law* 423; KM Osland, 'The EU Police Mission in Bosnia and Herzegovina', 11 (2004) *International Peacekeeping* 544; S Bose, 'The Bosnian State a Decade after Dayton', 12 (2005) *International Peacekeeping* 322; R Caplan, 'Who Guards the Guardians? International Accountability in Bosnia', 12 (2005) *International Peacekeeping* 463; D Chandler, 'Peace without Politics', 12 (2005) *International Peacekeeping* 307; D Chandler, 'From Dayton to Europe', 12 (2005) *International Peacekeeping* 336; G Collantes Celador, 'Police Reform: Peacebuilding through "Democratic Policing"?', 12 (2005) *International Peacekeeping* 364; K Oellers-Frahm, 'Restructuring Bosnia-Herzegovina: A Model with Pit-Falls', 9 (2005) *Max Planck Yearbook of United Nations Law* 179; MW Doyle, 'Too Little too Late? Justice and Security Reform in Bosnia and Herzegovina', ch. 7 in CT Call (ed.), *Constructing Justice and Security after War* (USIP Press, 2006); R Caplan, 'Who Guards the Guardians? International Accountability in Bosnia', ch. 6 in A Hehir and N Robinson (eds), *State Building: Theory and Practice* (Routledge, 2007); *Annual Review of Global Peace Operations 2007* (above n. 21), section 4.2; S Economides and P Taylor, 'Former Yugoslavia', ch. 3 in M Berdal and S Economides (eds), *United Nations Interventionism, 1991–2004* (OUP, 2007); see also, in general, OHR website, at <http://www.ohr.int>, and the reports on Bosnia and Herzegovina of the International Crisis Group (obtainable form <http://www.crisisgroup.org>) and the European Stability Institute (obtainable from <http://www.esiweb.org>).

[61] Dayton Annex 10 (above, ch. 1, n. 38), Art. I.
[62] See, e.g., <http://www.nato.int/docu/speech/2002/s020116a.htm>.

Representative of the International Community', but this term exists nowhere in its constituent instruments.[63] In 2002, the High Representative was appointed 'European Union Special Representative for Bosnia and Herzegovina' (EUSR) by the European Union, a process which conferred an additional competence, operating in a separate capacity, to the individual concerned.[64] The process of creating the High Representative, appointing the office holder, and conferring powers on this official is highly complex, involving the parties to the Dayton Peace Agreements, the UN Security Council, and the states who attended the 1995 Peace Implementation Conference concerning the situation in the 'former' Yugoslavia, and met frequently after then, as the 'Peace Implementation Council' (PIC), to oversee international efforts in Bosnia and Herzegovina.[65] A full treatment of this process, and clarification of the precise status of the OHR, are beyond the scope of this book.[66] However, the nature of OHR's creation and authorization

---

[63] For the use of this title, see OHR website, at <http://www.ohr.int>, *passim*.

[64] On EU Special Representatives generally, see, EU Council Secretariat, 'Factsheet—EU Special Representatives (EUSRs)', June 2005, available at <http://www.consilium.europa.ed/uedocs/cmsUpload/EUSRs.pdf>. On the role of the EUSR in Bosnia and Herzegovina, see OHR, 'Mandate of the OHR' (undated), available at <http://www.ohr.int/ohr-info/gen-info>; Council Joint Action 2002/210/CFSP on the European Police Mission, 11 March 2002, *OJ* L70 (2002), 1 (giving details of the role of the EUSR); Council Joint Action 2006/523/CFSP amending the mandate of the European Union Special Representative in Bosnia and Herzegovina, 25 July 2006, *OJ* L205 (2006), 30. On the appointment of OHR as EUSR, see Council of the European Union, 'International Police Task Force Follow-On—Council Conclusions', 2409th Council meeting, General Affairs, Brussels, 18/19 February 2002, doc. 6247/02 (Presse 30), available at <http://ue.eu.int/uedocs/cmsUpload/GENERAL%20AFFAIRS%2018.02.02.pdf>, at 16–24, para. 3; Council Joint Action 2006/49/CFSP appointing the European Union Special Representative in Bosnia and Herzegovina, 30 January 2006, *OJ* L26 (2006), 21. See also United Nations News Service, 'Bosnia and Herzegovina at the Brink of EU Membership, Security Council Told', 15 November 2005, available at <http://www.un.org>. Further source of information: e-mail correspondence with an OHR Communications Director, 22 November 2006.

[65] On this process, see the following note. On the Peace Implementation Council (PIC), see, e.g., <http://www.ohr.int/ohr-info/gen-info/#pic>; Conclusions of the Peace Implementation Conference held at Lancaster House, London, 8 and 9 December 1995, UN Doc. S/1995/1029, 12 December 1995, Annex (hereinafter 'London Peace Implementation Conference Conclusions 1995'). Preparations for the closure of OHR began in June 2006 (see Communiqué by the PIC Steering Board, 'Towards Ownership: From Peace Implementation to Euro-Atlantic Integration', 23 June 2006; Communiqué by PIC Steering Board, 7 December 2006). On 27 February 2007, the PIC decided to extend the mandate of OHR until 30 June 2008, subject to review of the situation at meetings in October 2007 and February 2008; see 'Communiqué by the PIC Steering Board', 27 February 2007, 'Schwarz-Schilling Television Address on PIC Decision', 2 March 2007. All documents are obtainable from the OHR website, at <http://www.ohr.int>.

[66] The length of the study required is such that, were it to be included, it would skew the focus of the book too far into one particular manifestation of an activity that is being considered in its generality. The key steps in the constitution of and conferral of powers on the High Representative are as follows. In Annex 10 of the Dayton Peace Agreements, the parties requested the 'designation of a High Representative, to be appointed consistent with relevant United Nations Security Council resolutions' (Dayton Annex 10 (above, ch. 1, n. 38), Art I.2); at the Peace Implementation Conference held in London on 8–9 December 1995, the states in attendance approved the designation of the first High Representative—Carl Bildt—following consultation with the government of Bosnia and Herzegovina, and invited the UN Security Council to 'agree to Mr. Bildt's designation as High Representative': see London Peace Implementation Conference Conclusions 1995

leads this author to conclude that it is a *sui generis* international organization connected to, but operating separately from, the Dayton parties, the UN Security Council, and the PIC states.[67] Although the mandate is conferred upon the High

(above n. 65). In Resolution 1031, the Security Council, acting under Chapter VII of the UN Charter, '[e]ndorses the establishment of a High Representative, following the request of the parties...and agrees to the designation of Mr. Carl Bildt as High Representative'; SC Res. 1031, 15 December 1995, para. 26. Under Dayton Annex 10, which concerns civilian matters, the High Representative is mandated inter alia 'to facilitate the Parties' own efforts' (Dayton Annex 10, Art I.2); to monitor implementation of the peace settlement and to 'promote...full compliance' by the parties 'with all civilian aspects of the peace settlement' (ibid., Art. II.1.a. and b). Both the London Peace Implementation Conference Conclusions 1995 and SC Res. 1031 (ibid.) (the latter in a provision passed under Chapter VII of the UN Charter) state that the High Representative, in accordance with Annex 10, '...will monitor the implementation of the Peace Agreement and mobilize and, as appropriate, give guidance to and coordinate the activities of the civilian organizations and agencies involved' (London Peace Implementation Conference Conclusions 1995 (ibid.), para. 17; SC Res. 1031 (ibid.), para. 26; in the Conclusions the phrase 'give guidance to' is absent). In its final clauses, Annex 10 stipulates that '[t]he High Representative is the final authority in theater regarding interpretation of this Agreement on the civilian implementation of the peace settlement' (Dayton Annex 10, Art. V). Since these arrangements were established, the PIC and its Steering Board (on which, see above n. 65) have asserted a role to supervise OHR, to make authoritative determinations the scope of OHR's powers and, possibly, unilaterally to supplement these powers, a role associated with determinations that were made at a conference in Bonn which related to OHR's removal of government officials, leading to the term 'Bonn powers'. For explicit references to the nature of the relationship between the PIC and OHR, see, e.g., London Peace Implementation Conference Conclusions 1995, ibid. para. 21 (c); Conclusions of the Peace Implementation Conference held in London, Lancaster House, 4 and 5 December 1996, 'Bosnia & Herzegovina 1997: Making Peace Work' (hereinafter 'London Peace Implementation Conference Conclusions 1996'), Section 'Co-ordinating Structures', para. 4; Conclusions of the Peace Implementation Conference held in Bonn on 10 December 1997, 'Bosnia and Herzegovina 1998: Self-sustaining Structures' (hereinafter 'Bonn Peace Implementation Conference Conclusions'), Section XI, para. 1. Important statements concerning the scope and derivation of OHR's powers, including the role of the PIC in this process, are contained in Conclusions of the Ministerial Meeting of the PIC Steering Board and of the Presidency of Bosnia-Herzegovina, 'Guiding principles of the Civilian consolidation plan', Paris, 14 November 1996; London Peace Implementation Conference Conclusions 1996 (ibid.); OHR, Decision removing Mr. Nikola Poplasen from the Office of President of Republika Srpska, 5 March 1999; OHR, Press Release, 'Removal from Office of Nikola Poplasen', 5 March 1999; Peace Implementation Council, Madrid Declaration, Annex: 'The Peace Implementation Agenda, Reinforcing Peace in Bosnia and Herzegovina—The Way Ahead', 16 December 1998; Bonn Peace Implementation Conference Conclusions (ibid.). OHR, Peace Implementation Conference and PIC documents are obtainable from the OHR website, at <http://www.ohr.int>. See also the treatment of the so-called 'Bonn powers' in the following cases: Case No. U9/00 (on the Law on State Border Service), Constitutional Court of Bosnia and Herzegovina, Decision of 3 November 2000 and Annex, Separate dissenting Opinion of Judge Snežana Savić; Case No. U25/00 (on the Decision Amending the Law on Travel Documents of Bosnia and Herzegovina), Constitutional Court of Bosnia and Herzegovina, Decision of 23 March 2001 and Annex, Separate dissenting Opinion of Judge Prof. Dr Vitomir Popović; Case U37/01 (on the Decision of the High Representative for Bosnia and Herzegovina No. 86/01 of 23 February 2001), Constitutional Court of Bosnia and Herzegovina, Decision of 2 November 2001; Case No. CH/98/1266, *Dragan Čavić v Bosnia and Herzegovina*, Human Rights Chamber of Bosnia and Herzegovina, Decision on admissibility, 18 December 1998; Cases Nos CH/97/60, CH/98/276, CH/98/362, CH/99/1766, Human Rights Chamber of Bosnia and Herzegovina, Decision on Admissibility and Merits, 7 December 2001 (Constitutional Court decisions obtainable from <http://www.ccbh.ba>; Human Rights Chamber decisions obtainable from <http://www.hrc.ba>).

[67] A conclusion based on the key steps outlined in the previous note.

Representative, once it became operationalized, an office was created and the institutional name 'Office of the High Representative' (OHR) is now most commonly used by those familiar with these arrangements, including officials of OHR itself.[68] In this book, that acronym is used as shorthand for both the individual and his (appointments have always been men) supporting organization. [69]

As previously mentioned, OHR has interpreted the mandate of the High Representative to encompass various administrative acts, including the passing of laws in a wide range of matters and the dismissal of elected officials.[70] The first

[68]   See the sources cited above n. 60.

[69]   See OHR, 'All HR's and Deputy HR's', available at <http://www.ohr.int/ohr-info/hrs-dhrs/>.

[70]   For numerous examples of the exercise of the asserted right to impose laws and dismiss public officials, see the decisions of the High Representative, obtainable from <http://www.ohr.int/decisions/removalssdec/archivc.asp>. Whether the High Representative has the authority to perform these acts, and what legal status the acts have in terms of responsibility, applicable law, and review before domestic mechanisms in Bosnia and Herzegovina such as the Constitutional Court, is beyond the scope of this book. On the authority enjoyed by OHR, see above n. 66. On the latter set of issues, see, e.g., Case No. U9/00 and the separate dissenting opinion of Judge Savić (above n. 66); Case No. U16/00 (on the Law on the Sale of Apartments with Occupancy Rights), Constitutional Court of Bosnia and Herzegovina, decision of 2 February 2001 and Annex, Separate dissenting Opinion of Judge Prof. Dr. Vitomir Popović; Case No. U25/00 and the separate dissenting opinion of Judge Popović (above n. 66); Case No. U26/01 (Request for evaluation of constitutionality of the Law on the Court of Bosnia and Herzegovina), Constitutional Court of Bosnia and Herzegovina, Decision of 28 September 2001; Case No. U37/01 (above n. 66); Case No. AP-953/05, *Milorad Bilbija and Dragan Kalinić*, Constitutional Court of Bosnia and Herzegovina, Decision on admissibility and merits, 8 July 2006; Case No. CH/98/1266 (above n. 66); Cases Nos CH/00/4027 and CH/00/4074, *Municipal Council of the Municipality of South-West Mostar v the High Representative*, Human Rights Chamber of Bosnia and Herzegovina, Decision on admissibility, 9 March 2000; Cases Nos CH/97/60, CH/98/276, CH/98/362, CH/99/1766 (above n. 66) (Constitutional Court decisions obtainable from <http://www.ccbh.ba>; Human Rights Chamber decisions obtainable from <http://www.hrc.ba>). See also OHR, Order on the Implementation of the Decision of the Constitutional Court of Bosnia and Herzegovina in the Appeal of Milorad Bilbija et al, No. AP-953/05, 23 March 2007, obtainable from <http://www.ohr.int>; European Commission for Democracy through Law (Venice Commission), *Amicus Curiae Opinion (Proceedings before the European Court of Human Rights) on the Nature of the Proceedings Before the Human Rights Chamber and the Constitutional Court of Bosnia and Herzegovina* (Opinion No. 337/2005, Venice, 10–11 June 2005), obtainable from <http://www.venice.coe.int> (hereinafter 'Venice Commission, *Amicus Curiae Opinion*'); *Jeličić v Bosnia and Herzegovina*, Appl. No. 41183/02, European Court of Human Rights, Admissibility decision of 15 November 2005, obtainable from <http://www.echr.coe.int>. For academic commentary, see, e.g., R Wilde, 'The Complex Role of the Legal Adviser When International Organizations Administer Territory', 95 (2001) *ASIL Proc.* 51; C Steiner and N Ademovic, 'Kompetenzstreitigkeiten im Gefüge von Dayton', in W Vitzthum and I Winkelmann (eds), *Bosnien-Herzegowina im Horizont Europas: Demokratische und föderale Elemente der Staatswerdung in Südosteuropa* (Duncker & Humblot, 2003), 109; E de Wet, 'The Direct Administration of Territories by the United Nations and its Member States in the Post Cold War Era: Legal Bases and Implications for National Law', 8 (2004) *Max Planck Yearbook of United Nations Law* 291, at 331; R Wilde, 'The Accountability of International Organizations and the Concept of "Functional Duality"', in WP Heere (ed.), *From Government to Governance. The Growing Impact of Non State Actors on the International and European Legal System. 2003 Hague Joint Conference on Contemporary Issues in International Law* (T.M.C. Asser Press, 2004), 164; C Stahn, 'Accountability and Legitimacy In Practice: Lawmaking by Transitional Administrations', paper presented at the 2005 *ESIL Research Forum*, Graduate Institute of International Studies (HEI), Geneva, 26–28 May 2005, obtainable from <http://www.esil-sedi.org>, at 22; J Crawford, 'Holding International Organisations and Their

dismissal came on 5 March 1999, when, as mentioned in the previous chapter, the High Representative dismissed Nikola Poplasen from the office of Republika Srpska President, for various acts considered in contravention of the Dayton Peace Agreements.[71] OHR considers the dismissals to be automatically effective in preventing the individuals concerned from holding office, without the requirement of any subsequent mechanism of implementation by the locally-controlled governmental structures in the country.[72] Similarly, it considers imposed legislation to be automatically the law of the country without the need for any kind of ratification by the legislature.[73]

In addition to OHR's state-wide activities, in the Brčko District, an area located at the intersection between the two constituent 'Entities' of Bosnia and Herzegovina, the Federation and the Republika Srpska,[74] an OHR Supervisor was given certain administrative prerogatives in 1997 by the arbitral tribunal charged by Annex 5 of the Dayton Peace Agreements with determining the District's future status.[75]

2.3.4 International appointees

A lesser known development that occurred alongside the upsurge in the ITA missions conducted by international organizations around the turn of the 21st century was the introduction of a series of regimes in different places whereby officials on certain locally-based bodies involved in particular administrative activities, from electoral institutions to courts, would be a mixture of local-nationals and foreign-nationals, the latter having been appointed through a process

Members to Account', Fifth Steinkraus-Cohen International Law Lecture, SOAS, 15 March 2007, lecture notes obtainable from <http://www.lcil.cam.ac.uk>, paras 21–25.

[71] See OHR, Decision removing Mr Nikola Poplasen from the Office of President of Republika Srpska (above n. 66). The earlier mention of this is above, ch. 1, text accompanying n. 45.

[72] See, e.g., OHR, Decision removing Mr Nikola Poplasen from the Office of President of Republika Srpska (above n. 66); OHR Press Release, 'Removal from Office of Nikola Poplasen' (above n. 66); OHR, Decision removing Edhem Bicakcic from his position as Director of Elektroprivreda for actions during his term as Prime Minister of the Federation of Bosnia and Herzegovina, 23 February 2001; OHR Press Release, 'High Representative removes Former Prime Minister Edhem Bicakcic', 23 February 2001 (both obtainable from <http://www.ohr.int>).

[73] See, e.g., Constitutional Court of Bosnia and Herzegovina, Case No. U9/00 (above n. 70).

[74] See Dayton Annex 4 (above, ch. 1, n. 38), Art. I.3 and the map in M Glenny, *The Fall of Yugoslavia: The Third Balkan War* (3rd edn, Penguin Books, 1996), xii. On the constitutional structure of Bosnia and Herzegovina, see above, ch. 1, nn. 41 and 42 and corresponding text.

[75] *Arbitration for the Brčko Area (Federation of Bosnia and Herzegovina v Republika Srpska)*, Arbitral Tribunal for Dispute over Inter-Entity Boundary in Brčko Area, Award, 14 February 1997, UN Doc. S/1997/126. On the Award and the powers of the Supervisor, see below, ch. 6, text from n. 70. For an example of the activities of the Supervisor, see Supervisory Order Prohibiting Certain Non-Salary Payments to Civil Servants, 22 March 2006; Supervisory Order Repealing the Socialist Republic of Bosnia and Herzegovina Law on Construction Land of 1986 within the Boundaries of Brčko District, 1 March 2006, both obtainable from <http://www.ohr.int>. For commentary on these activities generally, see F Bieber, 'Local Institutional Engineering: A Tale of Two Cities, Mostar and Brčko', 12 (2005) *International Peacekeeping* 420.

involving an international actor. These activities echo the role of the League of Nations-appointed Chair on the Memel Harbour Board mentioned earlier.[76] As discussed in the previous chapter, a particular set of such arrangements, concerning criminal and 'truth-telling' institutions, has been subject to academic analysis and given a popular designation as 'hybrid' or 'mixed' tribunals, but their counterparts in other areas of policy have been largely ignored.

As previously explained, this study uses the term 'international appointee' to denote an individual of foreign nationality who sits on a body concerned with some form of territorial administration and whose appointment in this regard involved an international actor such as an international organization or a member of an international court or tribunal.[77] The involvement of the international actor in this appointment covers two situations: first, where the international actor makes the decision of appointment, sometimes having consulted certain local actors; and secondly, where the appointment is made by a local authority, on the basis of individuals nominated or recommended by the international actor.

In what follows, the arrangements are set out in summary form. They are divided up into certain institutions in Bosnia and Herzegovina, where arrangements of this type were pioneered; human rights, criminal and 'truth-telling' institutions; and electoral bodies. More detailed information on each particular set of arrangements is contained in the footnotes rather than the main text, but key features, such as the nationality requirements, the identity of the international actor involved in the appointment process, the nature of this involvement, and the ratio of international to local appointees are set out in a series of tables drawing on the footnote information.

2.3.4.1 Bosnia and Herzegovina—general

The unusual and, to outsiders, largely mysterious nature of the international involvement in the governance of Bosnia and Herzegovina does not stop with OHR; the personnel of virtually all key non-elected state institutions in the country has had some sort of international appointee element.[78]

To begin with, as reflected in Table 2 on the following page, international appointees have been involved in a range of institutions other than bodies in the sphere of human rights and criminal justice (these latter bodies will be considered separately in the next section).

---

[76] See above, n. 15 and accompanying text.

[77] See further the relevant parts of the discussion in sections 1.4.3 and 1.4.4 above.

[78] For all the institutions covered in this section apart from the CPC, the Dayton Peace Agreement allowed for the presence of international appointees to end at certain dates from 2001 onwards. See Dayton Annex 4, Art. IV (Constitutional Court); Dayton Annex 7 (above, ch. 1, n. 38), Art. IX (CRPC); Dayton Annex 8 (above, ch. 1, n. 38), Arts II, IX (CPNM); Dayton Annex 4, Art. VII (Central Bank Governor). Information on the extension, revision or termination of these arrangements has been difficult to come by; where obtained, it is set out in the relevant footnotes.

Table 2. International appointees in Bosnia and Herzegovina—general*

Institution/ office	International actor involved in appointment	Obligation to consult local actors before international appointment	Number of appointments (institutions)				Position of international appointee(s)	How institutional decisions are made
			International	Federation of Bosnia and Herzegovina	Republika Srpska	Total		
Constitutional Court	President of the European Court of Human Rights	Yes—the Presidency of Bosnia and Herzegovina	3	4	2	9	ordinary members	not specified
Commission to Preserve National Monuments (CPNM)	Director-General of UNESCO	No	2	2	1	5	1 is Chair	by majority
Commission on Public Corporations (CPC)	President of the European Bank for Reconstruction and Development	No	2	2	1	5	1 is Chair	not specified
Governing Board of the Central Bank	International Monetary Fund	Yes—the Presidency of Bosnia and Herzegovina	1	2 (1 Croat, 1 Bosniak; share single vote)	1	4 (but only 3 voting)	Governor	Governor has the casting vote

* Apart from the High Judicial and Prosecutorial Council; human rights, criminal justice and 'truth-telling' bodies are covered in Table 3; electoral bodies are covered in Table 4. As a human rights mechanism, the 'Human Rights Commission within the Constitutional Court' is covered in Table 3.

Individuals, who could not be nationals of Bosnia and Herzegovina or of any neighbouring state, have been appointed by a range of international entities to sit alongside locally-appointed members on the Constitutional Court;[79] the Commission to Preserve National Monuments (CPNM), which designates properties as National Monuments;[80] the Commission on Public Corporations (CPC), which establishes joint, inter-Entity corporations to operate public services, for example energy and postal services;[81] and the High Judicial and Prosecutorial Council for Bosnia and Herzegovina, which is charged with supervising the judiciary and prosecution authorities.[82] From 1997 to December 2004, an individual

[79] Three members of the Constitutional Court are appointed by the President of the European Court of Human Rights, to sit alongside six Entity appointees (see Dayton Annex 4 (above, ch. 1, n. 38), Art. VI); the internationally-appointed members cannot be nationals of Bosnia and Herzegovina or a neighbouring state (ibid.). On this body, including a consideration of its legal status—as 'domestic' or 'international'—for the purpose of the admissibility rules of the European Court of Human Rights, see Venice Commission, *Amicus Curiae Opinion* (above n. 70), section IV and the Court's decision on admissibility in *Jeličić v Bosnia and Herzegovina* (above n. 70). For commentary on these arrangements, see, e.g., the relevant parts of A Schröder, 'Strengthening the Rule of Law in Kosovo and Bosnia and Herzegovina: The Contribution of International Judges and Prosecutors', Zentrum für Internationale Friedenseinsätze (Center for International Peace Operations), April 2005, available at <http://www.zif-berlin.org/Downloads/Almut_11.04.05.pdf>. The 'Human Rights Commission within the Constitutional Court' is covered below, n. 91 and accompanying text.

[80] Two members, including the Chair, are appointed by the Director-General of the United Nations Educational, Social and Cultural Organization (UNESCO), to sit alongside three Entity appointees (see Dayton Annex 8 (above, ch. 1, n. 38), Art. II). Despite the absence of any nationality restriction in relation to the international appointees, in practice the two internationally-appointed members were chosen among individuals who were not nationals of Bosnia and Herzegovina or a neighbouring state (source for the adoption of this approach: telephone interviews with local officials, 20 and 23 July 2001). For the composition of the Commission, see <http://www.aneks8komisija.com.ba/main.php?id_struct=74&lang=4>.

[81] Two members, including the Chair, are appointed by the President of the European Bank for Reconstruction and Development to sit alongside three Entity appointees (see Dayton Annex 9 (above, ch. 1, n. 38), Art. I). Although no limitations on the nationality of the internationally-appointed members is contained in Annex 9, in practice the international appointees have not been nationals of Bosnia and Herzegovina or a neighbouring state (source for the adoption of this approach: telephone interviews with local officials, 20 and 23 July 2001).

[82] Between 2002 and 2004, OHR was responsible for appointing the members of the three separate institutions charged with supervising the judiciary and prosecution authorities in Bosnia and Herzegovina and in the two Entities: the High Judicial and Prosecutorial Councils of Bosnia and Herzegovina, Republika Srpska and the Federation of Bosnia and Herzegovina (see Law on the High Judicial and Prosecutorial Council of Bosnia and Herzegovina, as amended, in *Official Gazette of Bosnia and Herzegovina* nos. 15/02, 26/02 and 35/02; Law on High Judicial and Prosecutorial Council of the Federation of Bosnia and Herzegovina, as amended, in *Official Gazette of the Federation of Bosnia and Herzegovina* nos. 22/02, 41/02, 42/02 and 19/03; Law on High Judicial and Prosecutorial Council of Republika Srpska, as amended, in *Official Gazette of Republika Srpska* nos. 31/02 and 55/02). The three separate Councils were abolished in May 2004 and replaced by a single High Judicial and Prosecutorial Council at the level of Bosnia and Herzegovina (hereinafter 'HJPC') which became operational on 1 June 2004 (see Law on High Judicial and Prosecutorial Council of Bosnia and Herzegovina, 21 May 2004, *Official Gazette of Bosnia and Herzegovina* no. 25/04, English translation available at <http://www.hjpc.ba/intro/?cid=1648,1,1> and, more generally, the HJPC's website at <http://www.hjpc.ba/home.aspx>). Under the relevant domestic legislation, the 15 national members of the new HJPC were elected by various authorities of Bosnia and Herzegovina and the two Entities; provision was also made for 'international experts' to be seconded to it (ibid., Arts 4 and 91(7)). In practice, however, 13 out of 15 national members were appointed

of foreign nationality was appointed Governor of the Central Bank; the appointment was made initially by the International Monetary Fund (IMF) and in 2003 reconfirmed by the Presidency of Bosnia and Herzegovina.[83]

As already mentioned, internationalization in Bosnia and Herzegovina involves further arrangements, but these are better situated within a broader discussion of similar arrangements across several different countries. In what follows, the arrangements covered are divided by subject-matter into two categories: those concerning human rights, serious crimes, and truth-telling, on the one hand, and those concerning elections, on the other. Further examples from Bosnia and Herzegovina will be given in each of these two categories.[84]

2.3.4.2 *Human rights, criminal justice, and 'truth-telling' bodies*

One innovation in the regime of international criminal justice in the 21st century has been the appointment, with international involvement, of foreign legal experts to criminal justice processes situated within the territory to which their jurisdiction relates. As set out in Table 3 overleaf, the personnel of various institutions operating or planned in Cambodia, East Timor, Bosnia and Herzegovina, Sierra Leone, and Kosovo have a mixture of international and local elements, for example, in the case of criminal tribunals, a bench comprising both local-national jurists and foreign-national experts.[85] As discussed below, the Investigation Commission and Tribunal concerning the assassination of Lebanese Prime Minister Rafik Hariri in 2004 were constituted so that the former was made up entirely of non-Lebanese nationals, and the latter involved a mixture of Lebanese and non-Lebanese judges, all appointments in both cases being made by the UN.

---

by OHR, 'taking into account that several national institutions proposed candidates' (see OHR, 'Decision on the Appointment of Members of and Advisors to the High Judicial and Prosecutorial Council of Bosnia and Herzegovina', 4 June 2004, obtainable from <http://www.ohr.int>, and 'Members of the HJPC' (as of 31 January 2006), at <http://www.hjpc.ba/intro/bios/?cid=18,1,1>). OHR also appointed international members (see ibid.; see also OHR, 'Decision on appointment of an International Member of the High Judicial and Prosecutorial Council of Bosnia and Herzegovina', 26 January 2006, obtainable from <http://www.ohr.int>. The new Members of the HJPC who took office following the expiry, in June 2006, of the mandate of some of the OHR-appointed local-national members were appointed by national authorities (source: e-mail correspondence with an official of the High Judicial and Prosecutorial Council of Bosnia and Herzegovina, 13 July 2006).

[83] The Central Bank is the 'the sole authority for issuing currency and for monetary policy throughout Bosnia and Herzegovina' (Dayton Annex 4 (above, ch. 1, n. 38), Art. VII). Under the Dayton Agreements, the Governor, who could not be a national of Bosnia and Herzegovina or a neighbouring state, was to be appointed by the IMF to sit on the Central Bank Governing Board together with three Entity appointees (ibid). After the expiry of the first six-year term of the Governor and of the Board, the Presidency re-appointed the incumbent (international) Governor; the first national of Bosnia and Herzegovina took office as Governor of the Central Bank in January 2005 (see Central Bank of Bosnia Herzegovina, *Annual Report 2003*, at 6 and *Annual Report 2004*, at 7 (both obtainable from <http://cbbh.ba/en/archive.html>)).

[84] See below, text accompanying nn. 86 and 118 *et seq.*

[85] For academic commentary on international involvement in locally-based human rights, criminal justice and 'truth-telling' processes see the List of Sources, section 5.1.4.

Table 3. International appointees on human rights, criminal justice, and 'truth-telling' institutions

This does not cover the jurisdiction of the Constitutional Court of Bosnia and Herzegovina to hear human rights complaints filed after 1 January 2004 (a separate process from the Human Rights Commission within the Constitutional Court, which is covered). On the Constitutional Court, see Table 2.

Institution		International entity/ entities involved in appointment	Nationality requirement for appointments with international involvement (whether formally stipulated or informally adopted)	Members and nature of international involvement in appointment
Bosnia and Herzegovina Human Rights Commission (1995–2003)	Human Rights Ombudsman	OSCE Chairman-in-Office	Non-national of Bosnia and Herzegovina or neighbouring states	1 appointed by international entity
	Human Rights Chamber	Committee of Ministers of the Council of Europe	Non-nationals of Bosnia and Herzegovina or neighbouring states	14 in total: 8 appointed by international entity (of which 1 was the President); 6 appointed by local actors (4 by the Federation of Bosnia and Herzegovina/2 by the Republika Srpska)
Human Rights Commission within the Constitutional Court of Bosnia and Herzegovina (2004–2006)		Committee of Ministers of the Council of Europe	5 members in total: all appointed by local actors, but chosen from among the members of the old Human Rights Chamber, who included international appointees subject to the stipulated nationality requirement (see above). In practice, 2 international members were appointed in this way	
Commission for Real Property Claims of Displaced Persons and Refugees in Bosnia and Herzegovina (CRPC) (1996–2003)		President of the European Court of Human Rights	Non-nationals of Bosnia and Herzegovina or neighbouring states	9 in total: 3 appointed by international entity (1 was the President); 6 appointed by local actors (4 by the Federation of Bosnia and Herzegovina/2 by the Republika Srpska)

State Court of Bosnia and Herzegovina, from 2003	Special Panels on Organized Crime, Economic Crime and Corruption (2003–2004)	OHR	Non-nationals of Bosnia and Herzegovina or neighbouring states	3 in total: 2 appointed by international entity; 1 appointed by local actors
	Specialized Section I, on War Crimes	OHR	Non-nationals of Bosnia and Herzegovina or neighbouring states	Members ordinarily appointed by local authorities, but OHR can also make appointments and has used this power
	Specialized Section II, on Organized Crime, Economic Crime, and Corruption	OHR	Non-nationals of Bosnia and Herzegovina or neighbouring states	Members ordinarily appointed by local authorities, but OHR can also make appointments and has used this power
	Registry for Specialized Sections I and II	OHR	Non-nationals of Bosnia and Herzegovina or neighbouring states	Chief Registrar appointed by international entity
	Prosecutor's Office (War Crimes)	OHR	All members appointed by the partly-international HJPC. 8 local-national members and 5 international members (plus one further international 'acting' member); international members cannot be nationals of Bosnia and Herzegovina or of neighbouring states	
Special Panels in the District Court of Dili, East Timor		Head of UNTAET	1 East Timorese national and 2 non-nationals	All appointed by international entity
East Timor Serious Crimes Unit		Head of UNTAET	All staff appointed by international entity; many were internationals (non-East Timorese)	
East Timor Commission on Reception, Truth and Reconciliation		Head of UNTAET	All Commissioners appointed by the international entity; provision was made for internationals to be appointed, but in practice all appointees were East Timorese	

(Continued)

Table 3. (*Contd.*)

Institution		International entity/ entities involved in appointment	Nationality requirement for appointments with international involvement (whether formally stipulated or informally adopted)	Members and nature of international involvement in appointment
Special Court for Sierra Leone (SCSL)	Trial Chambers (2)	UN Secretary-General	Not specified; in practice have always been foreign-nationals, as have some of the appointments made by the Government of Sierra Leone	3 in total: 2 appointed by international entity; 1 by the Government of Sierra Leone
	Appeals Chamber	UN Secretary-General	Not specified; in practice have always been foreign-nationals, as have some of the appointments made by the Government of Sierra Leone	5 in total: 3 appointed by international entity; 2 by the Government of Sierra Leone
	Office of the Prosecutor	UN Secretary-General	Not specified; in practice have always been foreign-nationals	Appointed by international entity
	Registry	UN Secretary-General	Not specified; in practice have always been foreign-nationals	Appointed by international entity
Sierra Leone Truth and Reconciliation Commission (2002–2004)		Special Representative of the UN Secretary-General; UNHCHR	7 members in total: 4 nationals of Sierra Leone and 3 foreign-nationals. All appointed by the Government of Sierra Leone. Special Representative of the UN Secretary General involved in the process of selecting the Sierra Leonean judges; the 3 foreign-national judges appointed on the basis of nominations by UNHCHR	7 members in total: 4 nationals of Sierra Leone and 3 foreign-nationals. All appointed by the Government of Sierra Leone. Special Representative of the UN Secretary General involved in the process of selecting the Sierra Leonean judges; the 3 foreign-national judges appointed on the basis of nominations by UNHCHR
Kosovo—Criminal proceedings under Regulation 2000/64	Investigating judge	Head of UNMIK	'International'; in practice has meant foreign-national	Appointed by international entity
	Judges and prosecutor	Head of UNMIK	3 judges, 2 'international' and 1 national; 1 'international' prosecutor; all appointed by international entity. In practice 'international' has meant foreign-national	

Extraordinary Chambers in the Courts of Cambodia (from 2006)	Trial Chamber	UN Secretary-General	Foreign-nationals	5 in total: 3 local-national and 2 foreign-national; all appointed by local actors; 2 non-national judges are nominated by international entity
	Supreme Court Chamber	UN Secretary-General	Foreign-nationals	7 in total: 4 local-national and 3 foreign-national; all appointed by local actors; 3 non-national judges are nominated by international entity
	Office of the Prosecutor	UN Secretary-General	Foreign-nationals	2 co-prosecutors: 1 local-national and 1 foreign-national; both appointed by local actors; foreign-national prosecutor nominated by international entity
Iraqi Higher Criminal Court		The 'International Community and the United Nations'	Non-Iraqi-nationals	Possibility for appointment of non-Iraqi judges by the Council of Ministers 'with the help' of the stipulated international entities in the event that a state is one of the parties in a complaint; not utilized at the time of writing
United Nations International Independent Investigation Commission (UNIIIC) for Lebanon		UN Secretary-General	All members appointed by international entity. Nationality restrictions not formally stipulated; in practice all the Head Commissioners were foreign-nationals	
Special Tribunal for Lebanon (from 2007)	Trial Chamber	UN Secretary-General	All members appointed by international entity. Composed of 1 Lebanese-national and 2 foreign-nationals	
	Appeals Chamber	UN Secretary-General	All members appointed by international entity. Composed of 2 Lebanese-nationals and 3 foreign-nationals	

These arrangements represent a new phase in international initiatives in criminal justice: after the shift from the situation-specific regime of ad hoc international tribunals to the potentially all-encompassing International Criminal Court (ICC), there was a return to the situation-specific paradigm with new initiatives in this sphere operating alongside the ICC. Key differences with the ad hoc international tribunals include the fact that, in most cases, the institutions are located in the territory to which they relate; there is a mixture of international and local elements; the scope of crimes covered is sometimes broader, including so-called 'ordinary' or 'non-international' crimes; and the institutions are more diverse in the manner in which they operate, sometimes involving alternative non-criminal processes such as truth commissions.

The criminal justice arrangements discussed so far cohabit with other arrangements either orientated towards alternative, 'truth-telling' remedies to similar violations by individuals, or concerned with complaints about human rights violations by public institutions. All are set out in Table 3 above.

In Bosnia and Herzegovina, a regime of legal human rights machinery known as the 'Human Rights Commission' was introduced through the Dayton Peace Agreements of 1995: a Human Rights Ombudsman investigated allegations of human rights violations, issuing reports and where appropriate referring cases to a tribunal, the Human Rights Chamber, which determined whether human rights law had been breached by public authorities.[86] In addition to the Human Rights Commission, a Commission for Real Property Claims of Displaced Persons and Refugees (CRPC) was created to make legally-binding determinations of property claims.[87] The Ombudsman and a proportion of the Human Rights Chamber and the CRPC were internationally-appointed and could not be nationals of Bosnia and Herzegovina or any neighbouring state.[88]

---

[86] See Dayton Annex 6 (above, ch. 1, n. 38). For academic commentary on the Human Rights Commission and the human rights monitoring system in Bosnia and Herzegovina after the adoption of the Dayton Agreements, see the List of Sources, section 5.1.4.2; for further discussion of the Human Rights Commission and the operation of human rights institutions in Bosnia Herzegovina, see also below, ch. 7, section 7.5.2.

[87] Dayton Annex 7 (above, ch. 1, n. 38). This body was originally called the Commission for Displaced Persons and Refugees. For further information, see the CRPC mirror website at <http://www.law.kuleuven.ac.be/ipr/eng/CRPC_Bosnia/CRPC/new/en/main.htm>; for commentary, see KL von Carlowitz, 'Settling Property Issues in Complex Peace Operations: the CRPC in Bosnia and Herzegovina and the HPD/DD in Kosovo', 17 (2004) *LJIL* 599.

[88] The Chairman-in-Office of the Organization for Security and Co-operation in Europe (OSCE) appointed the Human Rights Ombudsman, who could not be a national of Bosnia and Herzegovina or any neighbouring state (see Dayton Annex 6 (above, ch. 1, n. 38), Art. IV). On the powers of the Ombudsman, see ibid., Arts IV–VI and the Ombudsman website, at <http://www.ohro.ba/articles/article.php?lit_id=geninfo>. The name 'Ombudsman' is used in the Dayton Peace Agreement; however, when the position was held by Dr Gret Haller, she and her office were referred to as the 'Ombudsperson'. The Human Rights Chamber was composed of 14 members: six national members (four of whom were appointed by the Federation of Bosnia and Herzegovina, two of whom were appointed by the Republika Srpska), and eight international members (Dayton Annex 6 (above, ch. 1, n. 38), Art. VII); the international judges, who included the President of the Chamber, could not be nationals of Bosnia and Herzegovina or a neighbouring state and were

The Human Rights Commission institutions were reorientated in 2003,[89] with the termination of the Chamber's mandate[90] and the creation of a 'Human Rights Commission within the Constitutional Court of Bosnia and Herzegovina' to perform on an interim basis the role previously performed by the old Human Rights Chamber and composed of a mixture of local-national and international appointee members; new human rights cases from 2004 were also to be handled by the Constitutional Court, operating on a separate basis from its interim Commission.[91] As for the Ombudsman, from 2004 onwards, this institution was

appointed by the Committee of Ministers of the Council of Europe (ibid.). On the Human Rights Chamber, including a consideration of its legal status both nationally and internationally, see Case No. U7/98, *Decision on the Appeal of the Office of the Public Attorney of the Federation of Bosnia and Herzegovina against the Decision of the Human Rights Chamber of 11 March 1998 in Case No. CH/96/30, Sretko Damjanović v Federation of Bosnia and Herzegovina*, Constitutional Court of Bosnia and Herzegovina, Decision of 26 February 1999; Case No. U8/98, *Decision on the appeal of the Office of the Public Attorney of the Federation of Bosnia and Herzegovina against the Decision of the Human Rights Chamber for Bosnia and Herzegovina of 3 April 1998 in Case No. CH/97/41, Milorad Marčeta v the Federation of Bosnia and Herzegovina*, Constitutional Court of Bosnia and Herzegovina, Decision of 26 February 1999; Case No. U9/98, *Decision on the appeal of the Office of the Public Attorney of the Federation of Bosnia and Herzegovina against the Decision of the Human Rights Chamber for Bosnia and Herzegovina of 3 April 1998 in Case No. CH/96/21, Krstan Čegar v the Federation of Bosnia and Herzegovina*, Constitutional Court of Bosnia and Herzegovina, Decision of 26 February 1999; Venice Commission, *Amicus Curiae Opinion* (above n. 70), section III; *Jeličić v Bosnia and Herzegovina*, admissibility decision (above n. 70) (Constitutional Court decisions are obtainable from <http://www.ustavnisud.ba>). Three members of the CRPC, including the President, were appointed by the President of the European Court of Human Rights, to sit alongside six Entity appointees (see Dayton Annex 7 (above, ch. 1, n. 38), Art. IX). Dayton Annex 7 did not contain any nationality restriction for the internationally-appointed members; in practice such appointees were not nationals of Bosnia and Herzegovina or a neighbouring state (source: telephone interviews with local officials, 20 and 23 July 2001).

[89] Under Dayton Annex 6, this internationalized model of human rights machinery was to operate only for a five-year period, after which responsibility for the continued operation of the Human Rights Commission was to be transferred to the locally constituted institutions of Bosnia Herzegovina (Dayton Annex 6 (above, ch. 1, n. 38), Art. XIV). In particular, responsibility for the appointment of the Human Rights Ombudsman and the members of the Human Rights Chamber was to be transferred to the Presidency of Bosnia Herzegovina (ibid., Art. IV(2) and Art. VII(4)). In practice, the internationalized structures continued beyond 2001, remaining virtually unchanged until the end of 2003.

[90] The termination was to come into effect on 31 December 2003: see Agreement pursuant to Article XIV of Annex 6 to the General Framework Agreement for Peace in Bosnia and Herzegovina, 22 and 25 September 2003, agreed to by Bosnia and Herzegovina, the Federation of Bosnia and Herzegovina and the Republika Srpska (available at <http://www.hrc.ba/ENGLISH/agreement.pdf>), para. 2.

[91] The Human Rights Commission within the Constitutional Court was created by the Agreement pursuant to Article XIV of Annex 6 to the General Framework Agreement for Peace in Bosnia and Herzegovina (above n. 90), para. 4, as a distinct body from the Human Rights Commission established under Dayton Annex 6 (which, as noted above, comprised the Human Rights Chamber and the Ombudsman). The interim Commission comprised three national and two international members (ibid., para. 6); all were appointed by the President of the Constitutional Court from amongst the members of the old Human Rights Chamber (ibid.) Under the Agreement, the interim Commission was intended to clear through the cases received by the old Human Rights Chamber between 1 October 2003 and 31 December 2003 (ibid., paras 2 and 5); the future of the Human Rights Ombudsman was not covered (on that body, see the following note and accompanying text). The Commission, which was initially expected

'nationalized', being constituted by three locally-appointed individuals operating jointly.[92] Similarly, in 2003, the CRPC was closed down and its activities transferred to local institutions.[93]

In the field of criminal law, from 2003 to 2004, OHR appointed foreign judges to sit alongside judges of Bosnia and Herzegovinan nationality on the special criminal panels of the State Court of Bosnia and Herzegovina dealing with organized crime and corruption;[94] from 2004, OHR appointed foreign judges to

---

to terminate its work by the end of 2004 (ibid., para. 4), was operative from 1 January 2004 until 31 December 2006; the 430 cases which were still pending at the end of 2006 (see Human Rights Commission within the Constitutional Court of Bosnia and Herzegovina, 'Monthly Statistical Summaries', obtainable from <http://www.hrc.ba/commission/eng/stat_summaries_eng/index. asp>) were taken over by the Constitutional Court of Bosnia and Herzegovina. The work on the pending cases was completed at the end of June 2007 (see 'Completion of work on the cases of former Human Rights Chamber for Bosnia and Herzegovina and closure of Annex 6 to the General Framework Agreement for Peace in Bosnia and Herzegovina', Constitutional Court of Bosnia Herzegovina, Press Release, 3 July 2007, obtainable from <http://www.ccbh.ba/eng/press/ index.php?pid=2202&sta=3&pkat=507>). Meanwhile, as required by the Agreement pursuant to Art. XIV of Annex 6, the Constitutional Court has been dealing with all new applications filed from 1 January 2004 (ibid., para. 4). On the jurisdiction of the Constitutional Court with respect to human rights complaints, see Dayton Annex 4 (above, ch. 1, n. 38) Art. VI(3)(c). On the Constitutional Court, see above, n. 79.

[92] Under the OHR-imposed Law on the Human Rights Ombudsman of Bosnia and Herzegovina of 2001, the Chairman of the OSCE retained responsibility for appointing the office-holder, after consultation with the Presidency of Bosnia and Herzegovina, the Chairman of the House of Representatives of Bosnia and Herzegovina and the Chairman of the House of Peoples of Bosnia and Herzegovina, during a transitional period ending on 31 December 2003 (see Law on the Human Rights Ombudsman of Bosnia and Herzegovina, entry into force 3 January 2001, available at <http://www.ohro.ba/articles/article.php?lit_id=ombudlaw>, Art. 11). Appointees made under these arrangements could not be citizens of Bosnia and Herzegovina or any neighbouring state (ibid.). The new regime for Ombudsmen appointments introduced after the end of the transitional period on 31 December 2003 involved three citizens of Bosnia and Herzegovina sharing the office (ibid., Arts 8(1) and 11) appointed, on the basis of a proposal by the Presidency of Bosnia and Herzegovina, through a two-thirds majority affirmative vote in the two chambers of the Parliamentary Assembly of Bosnia and Herzegovina, the House of Representatives and the House of Peoples (ibid., Art. 9(1)). On the Presidency, see Dayton Annex 4 (above, ch.1, n. 38), Art. V. On the Parliamentary assembly and its two chambers, see ibid., Art. IV.

[93] Source: emails from local officials, 25 February 2007. On the modalities of the transfer of competences to the local authorities, see Migration, Asylum, Refugees Regional Initiative (MARRI) Project, *Legal and Actual Status of Refugees, Displaced Persons and Returnees to Bosnia and Herzegovina to Access Their Basic Rights* (July 2005), available at <http://www.lex-ngo.org/ dokumenti/access_to_rights_en.pdf>, in particular section 3.4.

[94] The State Court was created by OHR in 2000 and opened in January 2003 (see OHR, Decision imposing the Law on the State Court of BiH, 12 November 2000). On the structure, composition and jurisdiction of the State Court, see Law on Court of Bosnia and Herzegovina, as amended, *Official Gazette of Bosnia and Herzegovina*, Nos 29/00, 24/02, 3/03, 42/03, 37/03, 9/04, 4/04, 35/04 and 61/04; Schröder (above, n. 79). The Special Panels on Organized Crime, Economic Crime and Corruption, operating within the Criminal Division and the Appellate Division of the State Court, were created in 2002 (see Law on Amendments to the Law on Court of Bosnia and Herzegovina, 6 August 2002, Arts 6 and 7, obtainable from <http://www.ohr.int>). The inclusion of international judges on the Special Panels was authorized in an amendment to the Law on the Court of Bosnia and Herzegovina in 2003 to allow for the appointment of international judges (see Peace Implementation Council, Communiqué by the PIC Steering Board, 31 July 2002; Law re-amending the Law on Court of Bosnia and Herzegovina, 24 January 2003, Art. 12, both

the two specialized sections of the State Court covering organized crime and war crimes, including cases transferred from the International Criminal Tribunal for the Former Yugoslavia (ICTY) in The Hague.[95] Foreign experts were also

obtainable from <http://www.ohr.int>). Each Panel was composed of two international judges (who could not be citizens of Bosnia and Herzegovina or of any neighbouring state), alongside one local-national judge (ibid.).

[95] The two specialized sections of the State Court were created in 2004 (see Arts 24 and 26, Law on the Court of Bosnia and Herzegovina, as amended (above n. 94)). Section I on War Crimes had jurisdiction over three types of cases: (1) cases referred to it by the ICTY (see Law on the Transfer of Cases from the ICTY to the Prosecutor's Office of Bosnia and Herzegovina and the Use of Evidence Collected by the ICTY in Proceedings before the Courts in Bosnia and Herzegovina, *Official Gazette of Bosnia and Herzegovina*, 61/04, Art. 2(1); Rules of Procedure and Evidence of the International Criminal Tribunal for the former Yugoslavia (obtainable from <http://www. un.org/icty>), Rule 11 *bis*, allowing the ICTY to refer a case to national authorities after the indictment is confirmed but before the trial has commenced); (2) cases submitted to it by the ICTY Prosecutor where investigations by that office have not been completed (see Law on the Transfer of Cases from the ICTY to the Prosecutor's Office of Bosnia and Herzegovina (above), Art. 2(5)); and (3) certain 'highly sensitive' 'Rules of the Road' cases (see ICTY, 'Partnership and Transition between the ICTY and National Courts', undated, available at <http://www.un.org/icty/cases-e/ factsheets/partnership-e.htm>). The 'Rules of the Road' procedure was established in response to the popular fear of arbitrary arrest and detention immediately after the end of the conflict in Bosnia and Herzegovina in 1995 (see Rome Agreement, 18 February 1996 ('Rules of the Road Agreement'), President Izetbegović, President Tudman, and President Milošević, obtainable from <http://www.ohr.int>, section 5, second sentence). Under this procedure, authorities in Bosnia and Herzegovina were required to submit every war crimes case proposed for prosecution in Bosnia and Herzegovina to the Office of the Prosecutor of the ICTY, which reviewed the case file to determine whether the evidence was sufficient by international standards before proceeding to arrest; for commentary, see J Manuell and A Kontić, 'Transitional Justice: The Prosecution of War Crimes in Bosnia and Herzegovina under the "Rules of the Road" ', 5 (2002) *Yearbook of International Humanitarian Law* 331; Doyle (above n. 60), 257–9. On 1 October 2004, the ICTY ceased reviewing case files under this competence and the review process was transferred to the courts of Bosnia and Herzegovina. This was assumed by the Special Department for War Crimes within the Office of the Prosecutor of the State Court: prosecutors on the cantonal and district level in Bosnia and Herzegovina submitted cases to the Special Department, for review and assessment as to whether the sensitivity of a particular case required prosecution at state level. Where the prosecutor in the Special Department decided that the case was 'highly sensitive', the case was taken up by the Special Department for trial before Section I on War Crimes of the State Court; all other cases were returned to the competent cantonal or district court (see ICTY, 'Partnership and Transition between the ICTY and National Courts' (ibid.)). The second specialized section of the State Court dealt with 'Organized Crime, Economic Crime and Corruption' (see Arts 24 and 26, Law on the Court of Bosnia and Herzegovina, as amended (above n. 94)). OHR appointed the international judges sitting alongside local counterparts in these specialized sections (see ibid., Art. 65(4), which provides that 'a number of international judges may be appointed' by OHR to the specialized sections). As of October 2005, the State Court comprised 34 judges, of which 14 were international judges assigned to Section I or Section II (see Registry for Section I for War Crimes and Section II for Organized Crime, Economic Crimes and Corruption of the Criminal and Appellate Divisions of the Court of Bosnia and Herzegovina and the Special Department for War Crimes and the Special Department for Organized Crime, Economic Crimes and Corruption of the Prosecutor's Office of Bosnia and Herzegovina, and Ministry of Justice Prison Project, 'Project Implementation Plan Progress Report', October 2005, obtainable from <http://www.registrarbih.gov.ba>, at 14). For commentary, see, e.g., F Donlon, 'The Court of Bosnia and Herzegovina, War Crimes and Organized Crime Chambers and the Registry for War Crimes and Organized Crime', in A Fijalkowski (ed.), *International Institutional Reform, 2005 Hague Joint Conference on Contemporary Issues of International Law* (T.M.C. Asser Press, 2007), 84.

appointed by OHR to head the Registry for the two specialized sections,[96] and to serve as prosecutors for the section on war crimes.[97]

In East Timor, UNTAET initiated a Serious Crimes process to deal with the atrocities in East Timor's past, in particular those following the 'popular consultation' in 1999.[98] Special Panels of the Dili District Court were established to cover serious crimes committed in the period running up to and during the post-consultation atrocities, and genocide, war crimes and crimes against humanity whenever committed, on which two of the judges were internationals.[99] In parallel, a Serious Crimes Unit (SCU) was created to investigate and prosecute the crimes covered by the Special Panels, and was headed and largely staffed by international experts.[100] The activities of the Special Panels and the SCU

[96] OHR appoints the international Chief Registrar responsible for the separate Registry for the two specialized sections of the State Court, during a transitional period (see Art. 27, Law on Court of Bosnia and Herzegovina, as amended (above n. 94); 2004 Agreement on the Special Sections of the State Court, 1 December 2004). The 2004 Agreement, amended by an Annex signed on 23 February 2006, has been replaced by the 2006 Agreement on the Special Sections of the State Court, signed on 26 September 2006, which set out a detailed plan regarding the transition of the Registry into domestic institutions (full citations of the 2004 and 2006 Agreements are provided in the List of Sources; for the text of the instruments, see <http://www.registrarbih.gov.ba>).

[97] The Prosecutor's Office was established by the Law on the Prosecutor's Office of Bosnia and Herzegovina of 6 August 2002. A Chief Prosecutor and a Deputy Chief Prosecutor (citizens of Bosnia and Herzegovina) were appointed by the High Judicial and Prosecutorial Council of Bosnia and Herzegovina (on which, see above, n. 82 and accompanying text). The Special Department for War Crimes within the Prosecutor's Office of Bosnia and Herzegovina was established in 2004: see Law on the Amendments to the Law on the Prosecutor's Office of Bosnia Herzegovina, *Official Gazette of Bosnia and Herzegovina*, 61/04). As of November 2005, it comprised five international prosecutors, one international acting prosecutor and eight national prosecutors (see Human Rights Watch, *Looking for Justice: The War Crimes Chamber in Bosnia and Herzegovina*, Report, February 2006, available at <http://hrw.org/reports/2006/ij0206/>, 9).

[98] For commentary on this process, see List of Sources, section 5.1.4.3; see also S Linton, 'Cambodia, East Timor and Sierra Leone: Experiments in International Justice', 12 (2001) *Criminal Law Forum* 185; S Linton, 'New Approaches to International Justice in Cambodia and East Timor', (2002) *IRRC*, vol. 83, issue 845, 93; H Strohmeyer, 'Collapse and Reconstruction of a Judicial System: The United Nations Missions in Kosovo and East Timor', 95 (2001) *AJIL* 46; H Strohmeyer, 'Making Multilateral Interventions Work: The UN and the Creation of Transitional Justice Systems in Kosovo and East Timor', 25 (2001) *Fletcher Forum of World Affairs* 107; S Chesterman, 'Justice under International Administration: Kosovo, East Timor and Afghanistan', *International Peace Academy Report* (September 2002); S de Bertodano, 'Current Developments in Internationalized Courts', 1 (2003) *Journal of International Criminal Justice* 226; LA Dickinson, 'The Promise of Hybrid Courts', 97 (2003) *AJIL* 295; International Center for Transitional Justice, 'The Serious Crimes Process in Timor Leste: In Retrospect' (March 2006), available at <http://www.ictj.org/static/Prosecutions/Timor.study.pdf>.

[99] The serious crimes jurisdiction covered murder and sexual offences committed between 1 January and 25 October 1999. Appointments were made by the Transitional Administrator (the head of UNTAET) (see UNTAET Regulation 2000/11, 6 June 2000, section 10). The Special Panels were established by UNTAET (see UNTAET Regulation 2000/15, 6 June 2000). On each Panel, the two international judges sat alongside a Timorese judge (see ibid., section 22.1). UNTAET regulations are obtainable from <http://www.un.org/peace/etimor/UntaetN.htm>.

[100] The SCU was headed by the Deputy General Prosecutor for Serious Crimes appointed by the UNTAET Transitional Administrator and staffed largely by international investigators, prosecutors, and case managers. On the SCU during the UNTAET period, see UNTAET Reg. 2000/16, 6 June 2000, obtainable from <http://www.un.org/peace/etimor/UntaetN.htm>; on its composition

continued after the independence of Timor-Leste until May 2005, the internationals in the SCU being drawn from the post-UNTAET United Nations
Mission of Support in East Timor (UNMISET).[101]

During the UNTAET period, a Commission on Reception, Truth and
Reconciliation was established to address the human rights violations perpetrated in East Timor from 1974 to 1999, operating until 2005. Commissioners
were appointed by UNTAET; although provision was made for internationals to
be appointed, in fact all the Commissioners were East Timorese.[102]

In Sierra Leone, the UN Secretary-General appointed foreign-national judges
to the Special Court for Sierra Leone (SCSL), the tribunal which began operation in 2002 to try those who 'bear the greatest responsibility' for crimes against

---

and functions in particular, see International Center for Transitional Justice (above n. 98), 13–14
and 17–22.

[101] See SC Res. 1410, 17 May 2002, para. 4(a). During the post-UNTAET period the SCU
operated as part of the locally-run Office of the East Timor General Prosecutor (see Report of
the Secretary-General on the United Nations Transitional Administration in East Timor, UN
Doc. S/2002/432, 17 April 2002, para. 77). With the termination of UNMISET in May 2005,
in accordance with SC Res. 1573, 16 November 2004 (para. 1), the activities of the SCU and the
Special Panels for Serious Crimes came to an end; in particular, SCU investigations were con-
cluded in November 2004, and the SCU mandate was terminated on 20 May 2005 (see Letter
dated 24 June 2005 from the Secretary-General addressed to the President of the Security Council,
UN Doc. S/2005/458; see also SC Res. 1543, 14 May 2004; SC Res. 1573, 16 November 2004).
The post-UNMISET UN Office in Timor-Leste (UNOTIL), which operated from May 2005 to
August 2006, did not have a mandate to continue or support the serious crimes process (see SC
Res. 1599, 28 April 2005; see also Letter dated 24 June 2005 from the Secretary-General addressed
to the President of the Security Council, UN Doc. S/2005/458), but part of the mandate of its
successor, established in August 2006, the United Nations Integrated Mission in Timor-Leste
(UNMIT), was 'to assist the office of the Prosecutor-General of Timor-Leste…to resume [the]
investigative functions of the former Serious Crimes Unit, with a view to completing investigations
into outstanding cases of serious human rights violations committed in the country in 1999' (SC
Res. 1704, 25 August 2005, para. 4(i)). On UNMIT in general, see *Annual Review of Global Peace
Operations 2007* (above n. 21), sections 3.7 and 7.15.

[102] See in general, UNTAET Regulation/2001/10, 13 July 2001, obtainable from <http://
www.un.org/peace/etimor/UntaetN.htm>. The Commission was created to 'seek the truth regarding human rights violations in East Timor within the context of the political conflicts between
25 April 1974 and 25 October 1999', to 'facilitate community reconciliation by dealing with
past cases of lesser crimes' committed during that period and to report on its findings and make
recommendations for further action on reconciliation and the promotion of human rights (see
'Commission for Reception, Truth and Reconciliation in East Timor—Mandate', available at
<http://www.easttimor-reconciliation.org/mandate.htm>). On the selection procedure for, and
the nationality of, the Commissioners, see UNTAET Regulation No. 2001/10, section 4. The
Commissioners were appointed by the Transitional Administrator on the advice of a Selection
Panel comprising representatives of different community groups, political parties, and the UN
Mission's Office of Human Rights Affairs (ibid.). They were appointed on 17 January 2002 (see
transcript of the press conference held by the Transitional Administrator, Sergio Vieira de Mello
on 17 January 2002, available at <http://www.un.org/peace/etimor/DB/db170102.htm>). On the
composition of the Commission, see <http://www.easttimor-reconciliation.org/National%20
Commissioners-E htm>. The final report of the Commission, submitted to the Timorese authorities on 31 October 2005, was presented to the UN Secretary-General on 20 January 2006 (see
'Chega! Report of the Commission for Reception, Truth, and Reconciliation Timor-Leste' (2005),
available at <http://www.etan.org/news/2006/cavr.htm>). For commentary on the Commission,
see the List of Sources, section 5.1.4.4.

humanity and serious violations of international humanitarian law and Sierra Leonean law committed in the territory of Sierra Leone since 30 November 1996.[103] The Court's Chief Prosecutor and Registrar were also foreign-nationals appointed by the Secretary-General.[104]

---

[103] On the Special Court for Sierra Leone, see SC Res. 1315, 4 August 2000; Agreement between the United Nations and the Government of Sierra Leone on the Establishment of the Special Court for Sierra Leone (hereinafter 'SCSL Agreement'), signed on 16 January 2002 and the Statute of the Special Court of Sierra Leone (hereinafter 'Statute of the SCSL'), annexed thereto (the quotation comes from para. 3 of SC Res. 1315, Art. 1 of the SCSL Agreement, and Art. 1 of the Statute). These documents and further information on the SCSL are available at <http://www.sc-sl. org>. The first judges were appointed in July 2002 and took their oaths of office in December 2002; the first indictments were issued in March 2003 (see 'Appointments to Sierra Leone Special Court', UN Press Release SG/A/813-AFR/444, 26 July 2002; WA Schabas, 'The Relationship between Truth Commissions and International Courts: The Case of Sierra Leone', 25 (2003) *Human Rights Quarterly* 1035, 1037). Although it is generally agreed that the civil war began on 23 March 1991, when the Revolutionary United Front (RUF) first invaded Sierra Leone from Liberia, the starting date of the jurisdiction *ratione temporis* of the SCSL was set to coincide with the date of the signature of the Peace Agreement between the Government of Sierra Leone and the Revolutionary United Front in Abidjan, 30 November 1996. On the reasons for this limitation on the temporal jurisdiction of the SCSL see Schabas, ibid., 1041–2. On the jurisdiction *ratione materiae* of the SCSL, see, in particular, the Statute of the SCSL, Art. 2 (crimes against humanity), Art. 3 (violations of Common Article 3 of the 1949 Geneva Conventions and of Additional Protocol II), Art. 4 (other serious violations of international humanitarian law), Art. 5 (crimes under Sierra Leonean law, namely (a) offences relating to the abuse of girl-children and (b) offences relating to the wanton destruction of property). Two internationally-appointed judges sat on each of the two Trial Chambers of the SCSL, alongside one judge appointed by the Government of Sierra Leone; three judges appointed by the Secretary-General sat alongside two judges appointed by the Government of Sierra Leone on the SCSL Appeals Chamber (see Statute of the SCSL, Art. 12(1) (a) and (b)). Although the relevant provisions of the Statute do not contain any specification as to the nationality of the judges, in practice the judges appointed by the Secretary-General have always been foreign-nationals; in addition, some of the judges appointed by the local authorities were also nationals of foreign states; for the composition, see <http://www.sc-sl.org/chambers.html>. For commentary on the SCSL, see the List of Sources, section 5.1.4.5; see also DA Mundis, 'New Mechanisms for the Enforcement of International Humanitarian Law', 95 (2001) *AJIL* 934; de Bertodano (above n. 98); J Cockayne, 'The Fraying Shoestring: Rethinking Hybrid War Crimes Tribunals', 28 (2005) *Fordham International Law Journal* 616. On the legal status of the SCSL for the purposes of the international law of state immunity, see *Prosecutor v. Charles Ghankay Taylor*, Case No. SCSL-2003-01-I, Special Court for Sierra Leone, Appeals Chamber, Decision on Immunity from Jurisdiction, 31 May 2004, obtainable from <http://www.sc-sl.org>.

[104] The UN Secretary-General appointed the Chief Prosecutor and the Registrar of the Special Court, whereas the Deputy Prosecutor was appointed by the authorities of Sierra Leone in consultation with the UN (see Statute of the SCSL (above n. 103), Arts 15(3) and 16(3)). Although the Statute does not provide limitations on the nationality of the Chief Prosecutor and the Registrar, all the appointees to these posts have been non-nationals of Sierra Leone (see the information contained in the section 'Organs' of the official website of the SCSL, at <http://www.sc-sl.org>). The seat of the SCSL is in Sierra Leone, where trials are normally held (SCSL Agreement, above n. 103, Art. 10); however, following the arrest of the former Liberian President, Charles Taylor, it was decided that, since 'the continued presence of former President Taylor in the sub-region is an impediment to stability and a threat to the peace of Liberia and of Sierra Leone and to international peace and security in the region', his trial could not be conducted within the West African sub-region (SC Res. 1688, 16 June 2006, preamble). Accordingly, pursuant to a request by the President of the SCSL, arrangements were made for the trial to take place in the Netherlands, with the SCSL sitting at the premises of the International Criminal Court in The Hague (see 'Special Court President Requests Charles Taylor be Tried in The Hague', SCSL Press Release, 30 March 2006,

On the Sierra Leone Truth and Reconciliation Commission (TRC), which was created to address violations of human rights and international humanitarian law perpetrated between 1991 and 1999 and operated from 2002 to 2004, several members were non-nationals of Sierra Leone, and, although these individuals were appointed by the President of Sierra Leone, this was on the basis of names recommended by the UN High Commissioner for Human Rights.[105]

In Kosovo, UNMIK appointed foreign-nationals to the bench of local courts, including criminal courts, and to serve as prosecutors.[106]

obtainable from <http://www.sc-sl.org>). The possibility for the Special Court to sit outside Sierra Leone is expressly foreseen by Art. 10, SCSL Agreement (ibid.). The Security Council approved the measures in SC Res. 1688 (ibid.); see also the Memorandum of Understanding regarding Administrative Arrangements between the International Criminal Court and the Special Court for Sierra Leone, 14 April 2006, obtainable from <http://www.icc-cpi.int>. On the change of venue, see also *Prosecutor v Charles Ghankay Taylor*, Case No. SCSL-2003-01-AR72-104, SCSL Appeals Chamber, Decision on Urgent Defence Motion against Change of Venue, 29 May 2006, obtainable from <http://www.sc-sl.org>, and CC Jalloh, 'Special Court for Sierra Leone Dismisses Taylor Motion Against Change of Venue', *ASIL Insights*, vol. 5, issue 15 (June 2006), obtainable from <http://www.asil.org>.

[105] The TRC was established, in accordance with an undertaking in the Lomé Peace Agreement, through the Truth and Reconciliation Act 2000 (see Peace Agreement between the Government of the Republic of Sierra Leone and the Revolutionary United Front of Sierra Leone, Lomé, 7 July 1999, Art. XXVI; Truth and Reconciliation Act 2000, available at <http://www.sierra-leone.org/trcact2000.html>). The temporal jurisdiction of the TRC was different from that of the SCSL, covering the period from the beginning of the civil war (as already noted, generally recognized as having begun on 23 March 1991; see above n. 103) to the signing of the Lomé Peace Agreement. For an explanation of the differing temporal jurisdictions of the two bodies, see Schabas, 'The Relationship between Truth Commissions and International Courts', above, n. 103. The TRC consisted of seven members—four nationals of Sierra Leone and three foreign members (see Truth and Reconciliation Act 2000, section 3(1)); although all of the members were appointed by the President of Sierra Leone, a Special Representative of the UN Secretary-General played an important role in the selection process of the local members and the UN High Commissioner for Human Rights (UNHCHR) was responsible for recommending individuals to the three international member slots (see ibid., and the Schedule to the Truth and Reconciliation Act 2000, setting out the procedure for the selection of nominees for appointment to the Commission, in particular parts (a) (on the role of the Special Representative of the Secretary-General) and (b) (on the role of UNHCHR)). For commentary on the TRC see the relevant works cited in the List of Sources, section 5.1.4.5.

[106] Under UNMIK Regulation 2000/6, 15 February 2000, the Special Representative of the UN Secretary-General's power to appoint international (meaning non-local-national) judges was initially limited to courts in Mitrovica; the Regulation was subsequently amended to enable the appointment of international judges and prosecutors to any court or prosecutor's office in Kosovo (see UNMIK Regulation 2000/34, 27 May 2000). Under the then existing domestic criminal justice system, a trial panel in the district court was composed of two lay judges and one professional judge, or three lay judges and two professional judges. On the composition and jurisdiction of the criminal courts in Kosovo prior to the entry into force of the Provisional Code of Criminal Procedure in 2004, see Law on Criminal Proceedings 1986, *Official Gazette of the Socialist Federal Republic of Yugoslavia* No. 26/86, Art. 23 (unofficial English translation provided by UNMIK on file with the author). See also OSCE, 'Report 2—Development of the Kosovo Judicial System (10 June through 15 December 1999), 17 December 1999, available at <http://www.osce.org/documents/mik/1999/12/963_en.pdf>; J-C Cady and N Booth, 'Internationalized Courts in Kosovo: an UNMIK Perspective', in C Romano, A Nollkaemper and JK Kleffner (eds), *Internationalized Criminal Courts. Sierra Leone, East Timor, Kosovo, and Cambodia* (OUP, 2004), 59, 61. International appointees were to fill the 'professional' slots only (this is implicit

In Cambodia, foreign-national appointments were made to the 'Extraordinary Chambers in the Courts of Cambodia for the Prosecution of Crimes Committed During the Period of Democratic Kampuchea' (ECCC), established to try particular individuals for certain serious human rights abuses committed during the Khmer Rouge period, and to one of the two Co-Prosecutor positions for the Extraordinary Chambers.[107] As with the TRC in Sierra Leone, these individuals

in the statement by Special Representative Bernard Kouchner, 'UNMIK Marks Six Months in Kosovo', UNMIK Press Briefing, 13 December 1999, available at <http://www.un.org/peace/kosovo/pages/kouch_status.htm>; see also 'SRSG Swears in 169 Lay Judges for Kosovo Courts', UNMIK Press Release, 6 October 2004, obtainable from <http://www.unmikonline.org>). To ensure the possibility that international appointees constituted a majority on the bench, at the end of 2000 UNMIK introduced a further procedure whereby the prosecutor, the accused or the defence counsel were entitled to request the appointment of international judges or a change in venue 'where this is considered necessary to ensure the independence and impartiality of the judiciary or the proper administration of justice', and gave UNMIK the right to appoint international investigating judges and/or designate panels consisting only of three judges including at least two international judges, of which one had to be the presiding judge (see UNMIK Regulation 2000/64, 15 December 2000, section 1.1 and section 2). An international prosecutor could also be appointed in these circumstances (see ibid.). These rules were modified in 2001 to provide international prosecutors with the power to reopen prosecutions dropped by the local prosecutors (see UNMIK Regulation 2001/2 of 12 January 2001, amending UNMIK Regulation 2000/6 as amended). For the text of UNMIK regulations, see <http://www.unmikonline.org/regulations/unmikgazette/index.htm>. On 'transitional justice' in Kosovo generally, see the List of Sources, section 5.1.4.6; see also Mundis (above n. 103), and the works by Strohmeyer, Chesterman, de Bertodano, and Dickinson, cited above n. 98.

[107] The Extraordinary Chambers were established within the Trial Court and the Supreme Court of Cambodia with the mandate to 'bring to trial senior leaders of Democratic Kampuchea and those who were most responsible for the crimes and serious violations of Cambodian laws related to crimes, international humanitarian law and custom, and international conventions recognized by Cambodia, committed during the period from 17 April 1975 to 6 January 1979' (see Law on the Establishment of Extraordinary Chambers in the Courts of Cambodia for the Prosecution of Crimes Committed during the Period of Democratic Cambodia, with inclusion of amendments as promulgated on 27 October 2004 (unofficial English translation obtainable from <http://www.cambodia.gov.kh/krt/>; hereinafter 'Law on the ECCC'), Art. 2). The creation of the ECCC is based on the Agreement between the United Nations and the Royal Government of Cambodia Concerning the Prosecution under Cambodian Law of Crimes Committed during the Period of Democratic Kampuchea of 6 June 2003 (also obtainable from <http://www.cambodia.gov.kh/krt/>). The Agreement, approved by the General Assembly by GA Res. 57/228 B of 22 May 2003 and ratified by Cambodia on 19 October 2004, entered into force on 29 April 2005. Two foreign judges sit alongside the three Cambodian judges (one of whom is the president of the Extraordinary Chamber) on the Trial Chamber (see Law on the ECCC, ibid., Art. 9, first paragraph), while the Supreme Court Chamber, which serves as both appellate chamber and the court of final instance, is composed of seven judges, of whom four are Cambodian judges, with one as president, and three are foreign judges (ibid., Art. 9, second paragraph). All indictments in the ECCC are the responsibility of two 'co-prosecutors', one Cambodian and another foreign, who work together in preparing the indictments against those accused before the Extraordinary Chambers (see ibid., Art. 16). For academic commentary, see List of Sources, section 5.1.4.7; see Mundis (above n. 103), and the works by Linton and de Bertodano cited above n. 98. See also Secretariat of the Royal Government Task Force, Office of the Council of Ministers, Kingdom of Cambodia, *An Introduction to the Khmer Rouge Trials* (August 2004), available at <http://www.cambodia.gov.kh/krt/>.

were appointed by local authorities on the basis of a nomination by the UN, in this case the Secretary-General.[108]

In Iraq, provision was made for the possibility that foreign-national judges could be appointed by the Iraqi authorities to the Iraqi Special Tribunal (IST) established in 2003 to try certain individuals for genocide, crimes against humanity, war crimes, or other serious crimes under Iraqi law committed between 1968 and 2003, but no such appointments were made.[109] Similarly, the Iraqi Council of Ministers enjoyed the power to appoint international judges to sit on the bench of the Iraqi Higher Criminal Court, the judicial body which replaced the IST in June 2004 after the termination of the US and UK Coalition Provisional Authority (CPA) administration; at the time of writing, however, this power, which is limited to those cases where a state is one of the parties to a complaint, had not been used.[110]

A further innovation in the criminal law field is the International Independent Investigation Commission (UNIIIC), established by the UN Security Council with the consent of Lebanon to operate alongside local authorities in investigating the 2004 attack in Beirut which killed the former Lebanese Prime Minister Rafik Hariri and others, and later expanded to cover all 'terrorist' attacks in the

---

[108] The five international judges, who were appointed by the Supreme Council of the Magistracy of Cambodia, were nominated by the UN Secretary-General (Law on the ECCC, above n. 107, Art. 14, third and fourth paragraphs). The first local-national and international judges to sit on the ECCC were selected by the Supreme Council of the Magistracy of Cambodia on 4 May 2006 and appointed by the King of Cambodia on 7 May 2006 (see ECCC Press Release, 4 May 2006; Royal Government of Cambodia, 'Official List of National and International Judges and Prosecutors for the Extraordinary Chambers in the Courts of Cambodia as selected by the Supreme Council of the Magistracy on 4 May 2006 and appointed by Preah Reach Kret (Royal Decree) NS/RKT/0506/214 of His Majesty Norodom Sihamoni, King of Cambodia on 7 May 2006' (undated); both documents are obtainable from <http://www.cambodia.gov.kh/krt/>). The foreign co-prosecutor, who was competent to appear in both Extraordinary Chambers, was appointed by the Supreme Council of the Magistracy upon nomination by the UN Secretary-General (Law on the ECCC, ibid., Art. 18; see also 'Official List of National and International Judges and Prosecutors' (ibid.) for the first appointments made in May 2006).

[109] The Iraqi Special Tribunal was established in December 2003 by the CPA-appointed Iraqi Governing Council (see Statute of the Iraqi Special Tribunal, 10 December 2003 (hereinafter 'IST Statute'), available at <http://www.globalpolicy.org/intljustice/general/2003/1210iraqistatute. pdf>). On the jurisdiction of the Tribunal, see IST Statute, Arts 10–14. On the possibility for the Iraqi Governing Council to appoint international judges 'who have experience in the crimes encompassed in this statute, and who shall be persons of high moral character, impartiality and integrity', see IST Statute, Art. 4(d). On the involvement of foreign and international actors providing advice and support at the IST, see above, ch. 1, n. 96. For commentary on the IST generally, see List of Sources, section 5.1.4.8.

[110] See Law No. 10/2005 on the Iraqi Higher Criminal Court, 10 October 2005 (English unofficial translation obtainable from <http://law.case.edu/saddamtrial/documents/IST_statute_ official_english.pdf>, Art. 3(5)). Such appointments would be made 'with the help of the International Community and the United Nations' (ibid.). On the involvement of foreign and international actors providing advice and support at the Court, see above, ch. 1, n. 96. For commentary on the Court generally, see List of Sources, section 5.1.4.8.

country since October 2004.[111] Although there were no formal stipulations as to the nationality of the members of the Commission, in practice all those appointed were non-Lebanese nationals.[112]

In May 2007, the UN Security Council established a 'tribunal of an international character', the Special Tribunal for Lebanon, with jurisdiction over the crimes under investigation by the UNIIIC, to operate concurrently with the Lebanese court system but with primacy over Lebanese courts, and located outside Lebanon.[113] The UN Secretary-General was responsible for appointing

---

[111] The establishment of the Commission was recommended by a fact-finding mission created by the UN (see Report of the Fact-finding Mission to Lebanon inquiring into the causes, circumstances, and consequences of the assassination of former Prime Minister Rafik Hariri (25 February–24 March 2005), 24 March 2005, UN Doc. S/2005/203). It was established by SC Res. 1595, 7 April 2005; see also Letter dated 29 March 2005 from the Chargé d'affaires a.i. of the Permanent Mission of Lebanon to the United Nations addressed to the Secretary-General, UN Doc. S/2005/208, and the Memorandum of Understanding between the Government of Lebanon and the United Nations Regarding the Modalities of Cooperation for the International Independent Investigation Commission, signed on 13 June 2005, UN Doc. S/2005/393, Annex; SC Res. 1636, 31 October 2005; SC Res. 1644, 15 December 2005; SC Res. 1686, 15 June 2006. On the work of the UNIIIC, see Report of the International Independent Investigation Commission established pursuant to Security Council Resolution 1595 (2005), Beirut, 19 October 2005, UN Doc. S/2005/662; Second Report of the International Independent Investigation Commission established pursuant to Security Council Resolutions 1595 (2005) and 1636 (2005), 10 December 2005, UN Doc. S/2005/775, Annex; Third Report of the International Independent Investigation Commission established pursuant to Security Council Resolutions 1595 (2005), 1636 (2005) and 1644 (2005), 14 March 2006, UN Doc. S/2006/161; Fourth Report of the International Independent Investigation Commission established pursuant to Security Council Resolutions 1595 (2005), 1636 (2005) and 1644 (2005), 10 June 2006, UN Doc. S/2006/375, Annex. The mandate of the Commission was subsequently renewed several times at the request of the Lebanese authorities (see Letter of the Prime Minister of Lebanon to the Secretary-General, 13 October 2005, UN Doc. S/2005/651; SC Res. 1636, 31 October 2005; Letter of the Prime Minister of Lebanon to the Secretary-General, 5 December 2005, UN Doc. S/2005/762; SC Res. 1644, ibid., para. 2; SC Res. 1680, 17 May 2006; Letter of the Prime Minister of Lebanon to the Secretary-General, 5 May 2006, UN Doc S/2006/278; SC Res. 1686, ibid.). Also following a request by the Lebanese government, the scope of the investigation carried out by the Commission was expanded in December 2005 to cover 'all terrorist attacks that have occurred in Lebanon since 1 October 2004' (see the Letter of the Prime Minister of Lebanon to the Secretary-General, 13 December 2005, UN Doc. S/2005/783, Annex; SC Res. 1644, ibid., para. 7). The UNIIIC began operating on 16 June 2005 (see Spokesman for the Secretary-General, 'Statement on the UN International Independent Investigation Commission', New York, 16 June 2005, available at <http://www.un.org/apps/sg/sgstats.asp?nid=1514>). The first Head Commissioner was Detlev Mehlis, who held the position from May 2005 to January 2006 (see UN Press Release SG/A/922, 'Secretary-General Appoints Detlev Mehlis as Head of UN International Independent Investigation Commission', 13 May 2005). Mr Mehlis was followed by Serge Brammertz, on leave from his post as Deputy Prosecutor with the International Criminal Court; see UN News Service, 'Former Belgian prosecutor named as new head of UN probe into Hariri murder', 11 January 2006, available at <http://www.un.org/apps/news/story.asp?NewsID=17129&Cr=&Cr1=>. On the procedure for appointment, see SC Res. 1595 (ibid.), para. 5.

[112] SC Res. 1595 (above, n. 111) does not contain any limitation on the nationality of the members of the Commission, only requiring the Secretary-General to recruit 'impartial and experienced staff with relevant skills and expertise' (ibid., para. 5). At the time of writing, the Head Commissioners appointed by the Secretary-General were all foreign-nationals (see above, n. 111).

[113] The original intention was that the tribunal be established on the basis of an agreement between Lebanon and the UN; see the Report of the Secretary-General on the establishment of a

all the judges, the registrar, the prosecutor, the deputy prosecutor and the head of the defence.[114] Two of the three Trial Chamber judges and three of the five Appeals Chamber judges were to be non-Lebanese nationals; the remaining judges were to be of Lebanese nationality.[115]

2.3.4.3 *Electoral bodies*

The second generic subject-area covered by various arrangements involving international appointees concerns electoral bodies, as outlined in Table 4 below. Such

special tribunal for Lebanon (UN Doc. S/2006/893, 15 November 2006) and the annexed draft Agreement between the United Nations and Lebanon the Lebanese Republic on the establishment of a Special Tribunal for Lebanon (containing as an attachment the Statute of the Tribunal). The draft Agreement was signed by the Government of Lebanon and by the United Nations respectively on 23 January and 6 February 2007; however, due to what the Security Council described as 'serious obstacles' to 'the establishment of the Tribunal through the Constitutional process' (SC Res. 1757, 30 May 2007, preamble), the Agreement was not ratified by Lebanon. On 30 May 2007, the Security Council, in a resolution passed under Chapter VII of the UN Charter, decided that, in the absence of ratification by the Lebanese Government, the Lebanon Tribunal Agreement and the Statute of the Tribunal were in any case to enter into force on 10 June 2007 (see SC Res. 1757, ibid., stating that the Agreement between the United Nations and the Lebanese Republic on the establishment of a Special Tribunal for Lebanon (hereinafter 'Lebanon Tribunal Agreement') and the Statute of the Special Tribunal for Lebanon (hereinafter 'Lebanon Tribunal Statute') annexed to the resolution 'shall enter into force on 10 June 2007, unless the Government of Lebanon has provided notification [of ratification] before that date' (ibid., para. 1(a))). On the process leading to the creation of the Special Tribunal see the Letter of the Prime Minister of Lebanon to the Secretary-General, 13 December 2005 (above n. 111); SC Res. 1644 (above n. 111); Report of the Secretary-General pursuant to paragraph 6 of Resolution 1644 (2005), UN Doc. S/2006/176, 21 March 2006, in particular Part III; SC Res. 1664, 29 March 2006; Report of the Secretary-General on the establishment of a special tribunal for Lebanon (above). Under the Lebanon Tribunal Agreement and its Statute, the Special Tribunal has jurisdiction in relation to the attack of 14 February 2005 resulting in death of Mr Hariri, and also over 'other attacks that occurred in Lebanon between 1 October 2004 and 12 December 2005, or any later date decided by the Parties and with the consent of the Security Council [which] are connected in accordance with the principles of criminal justice and are of a nature and gravity similar to the attack of 14 February 2005' (Lebanon Tribunal Statute, Art. 1). On the characterization of the Special Tribunal as a 'tribunal of an international character' and its relationship to the Lebanese court system see ibid., Preamble and Art. 4 respectively. On the location of the Tribunal, see Art. 8(1), Lebanon Tribunal Agreement, and SC Res. 1757 (2007), para. 1(b). For commentary, see N Shehadi and E Wilmshurst, 'The Special Tribunal for Lebanon: The UN on Trial?' (Chatham House Middle East/International Law Briefing Paper, July 2007), obtainable from <http://www.chathamhouse.org.uk>.

114 On the responsibility of the Secretary-General for the appointment of both the international and the Lebanese judges, see Lebanon Tribunal Agreement (above n. 113), Art. 2; Lebanon Tribunal Statute (above n. 113), Art. 9(3). On the appointment of the Prosecutor and the Deputy-Prosecutor, see Lebanon Tribunal Agreement, Art. 3; Lebanon Tribunal Statute, Art. 11(3); on the appointment of the Registrar, see Lebanon Tribunal Statute, Art. 12(3); on the appointment of the Head of the Defence Office, see Lebanon Tribunal Statute, Art. 13(1).

115 On the nationality requirement for the judges, see Lebanon Tribunal Statute (above n. 113), Art. 8. The Pre-Trial judge, two of the three judges serving on the Trial Chamber, and three of the five judges sitting on the Appeals Chamber are to be 'international judges', i.e., non-Lebanese nationals (Lebanon Tribunal Statute, ibid., Art. 8). The Statute of the Tribunal also specifies that 'the Registrar shall be a staff member of the United Nations' (ibid., Art. 12(3)), which could mean non-Lebanese nationality. Similarly, although not expressly stipulated in the constituent instruments of the Tribunal, the intention that the Prosecutor will not be a Lebanese national seems to be implied by the express stipulation that the deputy prosecutor be Lebanese (see ibid., Art. 11(5)).

arrangements can be understood as a variant on the model discussed earlier of the international conduct or supervision of national elections; whereas in the earlier model, international organizations run elections, or supervise those doing so, here, foreign experts are appointed with international involvement, to national bodies charged with running elections. This was pioneered in the two sites of regime change through US-led invasion that followed the attacks of September 11, 2001—Afghanistan and Iraq.

In Afghanistan, internationally-appointed foreign experts sat alongside locally-appointed members of the Joint Electoral Management Body (JEMB), created in 2003 to run elections in the country during a transitional period after the fall of the Taliban, ending in 2005.[116]

In Iraq, reflecting the marginal role played by the UN in the 2003 US-led invasion and subsequent occupation, the only direct involvement in administration performed by the organization was the power to appoint an international electoral expert to serve as a non-voting member of the Board of Commissioners

---

[116] The JEMB was established by Presidential Decree no. 40 on the Establishment of the Joint Electoral Management Body, 26 July 2003, subsequently amended by Presidential Decree n. 110 on Arrangements for Holding Elections during the Transitional Period, 10 February 2004. It operated until 2005, and was tasked with promulgating various regulatory instruments for the election registration process and other oversight responsibilities for the October 2004 Presidential elections, the September 2005 elections to the lower house of Parliament and the Provincial Councils, and the November 2005 elections to the upper house of Parliament. On the role of the JEMB in the 2004 elections, see Presidential Decree No. 40 (above); on this role in the 2005 elections, see Presidential Decree No. 24 on Holding National Assembly, Provincial Council and District Council Elections, 6 May 2005. The JEMB originally consisted of 11 members, six being the Afghani Commissioners of the Interim Afghan Electoral Commission (on which, see Presidential Decree No. 39 on the Establishment of the Interim Electoral Commission, 26 July 2003) and five being internationals, including the UN Assistance Mission in Afghanistan (UNAMA) Chief Election Officer, appointed by the Special Representative of the Secretary-General for Afghanistan. In 2004, two non-voting members were added, the Afghani Director of the Electoral Secretariat, and the Chief Technical Adviser on Electoral Matters of UNAMA. On the original composition of the JEMB, see Presidential Decree n. 40, Art. 2; on the additional appointments in 2004, see Presidential Decree No. 110, Art. 5(2). Composition was further modified in January 2005, to comprise nine members of the Independent Election Commission (on which, see Presidential Decree No. 21 of 19 January 2005 on the Formation of the Independent Election Commission, and Presidential Decree No. 23 on the Structure and Working Procedure of the Independent Election Commission, 24 January 2005), four international members named by the Special Representative of the Secretary-General and, as a non-voting member, the UNAMA Chief Electoral Officer, also named by the Special Representative of the Secretary-General (see Presidential Decree No. 24 (above), Art. 5). Unofficial English translations of the Presidential decrees are obtainable from <http://www.elections-afghanistan.org.af/Legal%20 Framework.htm>). See also, in general, <http://www.jemb.org> and <http://www.unama-afg.org/ about/_pa/political_affairs.htm>. UNAMA was established by SC Res. 1401 of 28 March 2002, with a mandate to promote national reconciliation and fulfil the tasks and responsibilities entrusted to the UN in the 2001 Bonn Agreement (Agreement on Provisional Arrangements in Afghanistan Pending the Re-Establishment of Permanent Government Institutions, Bonn, 5 December 2001, reproduced in UN Doc. S/2001/1154, endorsed by the Security Council in SC Res. 1383, 6 December 2001). UNAMA is also responsible for managing all UN humanitarian, relief, recovery and reconstruction activities in Afghanistan in coordination with the Afghan authorities. On the mandate and structure of UNAMA see, in general, 'The situation in Afghanistan and its implications for international peace and security', Report of the Secretary-General, UN Doc. A/56/875-S/2002/278, 18 March 2002, Part V; see also <http://www.unama-afg.org>.

Table 4. International appointees on electoral bodies

Electoral body		International entity involved in appointment	Members		Total
			Internationally appointed	Locally appointed	
East Timor Independent Electoral Commission (2001)		UN Secretary-General	All appointed by international entity; 3 voting members and 1 non-voting member were internationals; 2 voting members were East Timorese		5 voting 1 non-voting
Afghanistan Joint Electoral Management Body (JEMB), 2003–2005	July 2003–December 2004	Special Representative of the UN Secretary-General	5 voting (1 non-voting added in 2004)	6 voting (1 non-voting added in 2004)	11 voting (2 non-voting from 2004)
	January–December 2005	Special Representative of the UN Secretary-General	4 voting 1 non-voting	9 voting	13 voting 1 non-voting
Board of Commissioners of the Independent Electoral Commission of Iraq (IECI) (2004–2006)		Special Representative of the UN Secretary-General	1 non-voting	7 voting 1 non-voting Appointed by the CPA with the involvement of the international entity	7 voting 2 non-voting
Election Commission of Bosnia and Herzegovina (2001–2005)		OHR	3 voting	4 voting (1 Serb, 1 Croat, 1 Bosniak, 1 representative of the group 'Others') International entity provides final approval of nominations by local authorities	7 members

of the Independent Electoral Commission of Iraq (IECI), the electoral body created by CPA.[117]

In Bosnia and Herzegovina, international involvement in national election bodies came in 2001 after the end of the period of OSCE-operated elections mentioned earlier.[118] A new Election Commission was created to run the elections, and a Complaints and Appeals Council was set up to review this activity; for a transitional period lasting until 2005, the Commission was composed of a mixture of locally-appointed local-national members and OHR-appointed foreign-national members, and the Council was composed entirely of locally-appointed local-national members; OHR also enjoyed the right of final approval of the locally-appointed members on both bodies.[119]

---

[117] The IECI was created towards the end of the one-year CPA administration period operating from 2003 to 2004, and was responsible for running the elections in Iraq during the post-CPA 'transitional period' (see Law of Administration for the State of Iraq for the Transitional Period, 8 March 2004, English translation available at <http://www.cpa-iraq.org/government/TAL.html> and <http://www.oefre.unibe.ch/law/icl/iz00000_.html>), Art. 2(a)). On the establishment of IECI, see CPA Order 92 of 31 May 2004 (obtainable from <http://www.iraqcoalition.org/>); on the Commission see, in general, the IECI website at <http://www.ieciraq.org/>. The IECI was in charge of the three electoral votes taking place during the transitional period: the elections on 30 January 2005 of members of the Transitional National Assembly responsible for drafting the new Constitution; the referendum on 15 October 2005 on the new Iraqi Constitution; and the elections for the permanent National Assembly under the new Constitution on 15 December 2005. See the website of the International Mission for Iraqi Elections (IMIE), at <http://www.imie.ca>. The IECI was responsible for the overall organization of the elections and the certification of the results (see ibid., and see also CPA Order 92 and <http://www.ieciraq.org/>). The Board of Commissioners had 7 voting and 2 non-voting members. On the UN-appointed electoral expert as one of the non-voting members, see CPA Order 92, sections 4 and 5. Although responsibility for appointing the other members of the IECI Board of Commissioners rested ultimately with the CPA Administrator, the UN was involved in providing a list of suggested candidates; see <http://www.ieciraq.org/English/aboutIEC.htm>, and CPA Order 92, sections 5 and 6. No new appointments were made following the transfer of authority from the CPA to the Iraqi authorities, and no laws were passed which modified the appointment procedures for the IECI (source: e-mail correspondence with the International Mission for Iraqi Elections, 5 June 2006). With the ratification of the Iraqi Constitution and the formation of the new Iraqi Government on 20 May 2006, the mandate of the IECI came to an end. At the time of writing, a new independent body responsible for the organization and supervision of elections was yet to be established: see IMIE, Final Report on the December 15, 2005, Iraqi Council of Representatives Elections, 12 April 2006, available at <http://www.imie.ca/pdf/final_report.pdf>, at 4–5. On the CPA generally, see the sources cited above, ch. 1, n. 75.

[118] On the OSCE conduct of the elections, see above, n. 39 and corresponding text.

[119] The Election Commission of Bosnia and Herzegovina, created in 2001 by the Election Law of Bosnia Herzegovina, in accordance with Dayton Annex 3 (above, ch. 1, n. 38), Art. V, was responsible for organizing and running elections; the 2001 Election Law also established an Election Complaints and Appeals Council. See Election Law of Bosnia and Herzegovina, 19 September 2001, as amended (*Official Gazette of Bosnia and Herzegovina* Nos 23/01, 7/02, 9/02, 20/02, 25/02, 4/04, 20/04 and 25/05); see also OHR Press Release, 'High Representative Welcomes House of Peoples' Adoption of Election Law', 23 August 2001, obtainable from <http://www.ohr.int>. These institutions were envisaged to be eventually composed entirely by local officials appointed by local institutions without the need for OHR approval; in particular, under Art. 2(5) of the 2001 Election Law, the Election Commission is composed of seven members: two Croats, two Bosnian Muslims/ Bosniaks, two Serbs, and one other member; under Art. 6(8) of the Election Law, the Election Complaints and Appeals Council consists of 'five members: one Croat member, one Bosnian

The movement from OSCE-run elections to locally-run elections through a mixed international-local process can be understood in terms of the progressive 'nationalization' of the conduct of elections.

In East Timor, during the UNTAET period, the Transitional Administrator created in 2001 an Independent Electoral Commission to run and supervise the elections to the Constituent Assembly, the body of Timorese individuals created to act under the overall aegis of UNTAET as the legislature, draft the constitution for an independent East Timor, and continue as the legislature in the immediate post-independence period.[120] All five members of the Commission were appointed by the United Nations Secretary-General, with three being internationals.[121]

2.4 Conclusion

Focusing exclusively or predominantly on the UN administration missions in Kosovo and East Timor misses a broad pattern of equivalent arrangements, whether other international organization-operated projects or the wide-ranging involvement of international appointees on locally-based institutions, from the IMF-appointed Governor of the Central Bank in Bosnia and Herzegovina to UN-appointed members of the Special Tribunal for Lebanon and the international appointees to various electoral bodies.

Muslim/Bosniak member, one Serb member, one representative of Others and a member from the Election Commission of Bosnia and Herzegovina...'. On the appointment procedures, see ibid. For a transitional period, the two bodies operated in a partially internationalized manner via OHR involvement in appointments; the Election Commission was composed of four local-national members representing each of the constituent peoples of Bosnia and Herzegovina and three members 'selected from the International Community'; OHR appointed the international members and gave final approval to the members nominated by the national authorities: see Election Law of Bosnia and Herzegovina, as amended in 2004 (*Official Gazette of Bosnia and Herzegovina* Nos 23/01, 7/02, 9/02, 20/02, 25/02, 4/04, 20/04), Art. 2.5 and Art. 20(1). Until June 2005 the Election Commission was composed one Serb, one Croat, one Bosnian Muslim/Bosniak, one representative of the group 'Others', the OSCE Head of Mission, the OSCE Deputy Head of Mission and the Senior Deputy High Representative (source: e-mail correspondence with an official at the OSCE Mission to Bosnia and Herzegovina, 6 July 2006). During the same period, all members of the Complaints and Appeals Council were appointed by the House of Representatives of the Parliament of Bosnia and Herzegovina and subject to the final approval of OHR; see 2001 Election Law, as amended in 2004, Art. 20.2.

[120] See generally UNTAET Regulation 2001/2, 16 March 2001 (obtainable from <http://www.un.org/peace/etimor/UntaetN.htm>). The various arrangements involving the Timorese in governance during the UNTAET period, including those concerning the Constituent Assembly, are mapped out in ch. 1, n. 2.

[121] The Independent Electoral Commission was created by UNTAET by Regulation 2001/2 (above n. 120), part II. The Commission, which was vested with exclusive electoral authority in East Timor (ibid., section 11.2), consisted of five voting Commissioners and a non-voting Chief Electoral Officer, all appointed by the UN Secretary-General (ibid., sections 11.3 and 17). Of the five voting Commissioners, two were East Timorese, and three had to be 'internationally recognized experts in electoral matters' (see ibid., section 13.1). On the functions of the Commission, see ibid., section 14.

As the foregoing survey and Table 5 below demonstrate, there have been numerous international territorial administration projects, distributed fairly evenly across the course of 20th century. Although there is a significant gap between 1967 and 1989 in terms of plenary administration projects, numerous election conduct/supervision projects in Trusteeship and colonial territories took place during this period.

Table 5. Chronological list of authorized ITA projects

Key   ■   Plenary administrative authority
       ◩   Partial administrative prerogatives, including the conduct or supervision/control of consultations

Date	Location	Organization/officials
1920–39	Free City of Danzig	League of Nations and a League High Commissioner ◩
1920–35	The Saar, Germany	League of Nations Governing Commission ■
1924–39	Memel, Lithuania	League of Nations–appointee on the Harbour Board ◩
1933–34	Leticia, Colombia	League of Nations Commission ■
1960–64	Congo	UN Operation in the Congo (ONUC) ◩
1962–63	West Irian	UN Temporary Executive Authority (UNTEA) ■
From 1967	South West Africa/Namibia	UN Council for South West Africa/Namibia ■
1989–90	Namibia	UN Transitional Assistance Group (UNTAG) ◩
From 1991	Western Sahara	UN Mission for the Referendum in Western Sahara (MINURSO) ◩ (authorized but not fully implemented at the time of writing)
1991–92	Cambodia	UN Transitional Authority in Cambodia (UNTAC) ◩
1993	Somalia	Second UN Operation in Somalia (UNOSOM II) ◩
1994–96	Mostar, Bosnia and Herzegovina	European Union Administration of Mostar (EUAM) ■
From 1995	Bosnia and Herzegovina in general and Brčko in particular	Office of the High Representative (OHR) (including OHR Supervisor in Brčko); Organization for Security and Co-operation in Europe (OSCE) election mission ◩
1996–2003	Governorates of Arbil, Dihouk, and Suleimaniyeh, Iraq	UN Inter-Agency Humanitarian Programme ◩

(Continued)

Table 5. (*Contd.*)

Date	Location	Organization/officials
1996–98	Eastern Slavonia, Croatia	UN Transitional Authority for Eastern Slavonia (UNTAES) ■
1999–2002	East Timor	UN Transitional Administration in East Timor (UNTAET) ■
From 1999	Kosovo	UN Interim Administration Mission in Kosovo (UNMIK) (certain functions delegated to other actors, e.g. conduct of elections delegated to the OSCE) ■
Various	'Refugee' camps	UN High Commissioner for Refugees (UNHCR) ■ or ◪
From 1950	Palestinian refugee camps	United Nations Relief and Works Agency (UNRWA) ◪
Various	Various economically under-developed countries	UN material assistance programmes ◪
Various	Cambodia, Bosnia and Herzegovina, East Timor, Kosovo, Sierra Leone, Iraq, Lebanon	Involvement of international appointees on locally-situated criminal justice/human rights/'truth-telling' tribunals and processes (some a.k.a. 'hybrid' tribunals) ◪ [possibility for such involvement not utilized in all cases]
Various	East Timor, Afghanistan, Iraq, Bosnia and Herzegovina	Involvement of international appointees on electoral bodies ◪
Various	Trust and Non-Self-Governing territories	UN consultation missions ◪

Despite such widespread practice, it cannot be said that the use of international territorial administration in general is a permanent feature of international relations. Its use is clearly contingent on a broad range of political and legal factors; whereas such factors have prevailed in the past, they may not do so in the future. That said, the frequency and distribution of ITA projects over such a long period of time and in various regions of the world do suggest that such projects may well be used again in the future. As the Brahimi Report stated in relation to plenary territorial administration by the UN:

[a]lthough the Security Council may not again direct the United Nations to do transitional civil administration, no one expected it to do so with respect to Kosovo or East Timor either. Intra-State conflicts continue and future instability is hard to predict, so that despite evident ambivalence about civil administration among United Nations Member States and within the Secretariat, other such missions may indeed be established in the future...[122]

---

[122] Panel on United Nations Peace Operations, Report to the United Nations Secretary-General ('Brahimi Report'), 21 August 2000, UN Doc. A/55/305-S/2000/809, para. 78.

Interest in this possibility is evident, for example, in the proposals current at the time of writing for some kind of international administration for the Palestinian West Bank and Gaza Strip, replacing the Israeli presence,[123] and for an international trusteeship for Haiti.[124]

The descriptive consideration of the use of ITA offered in this chapter was engaged in as a means of establishing one element of the broader framework adopted in this book to analyse the purposes of the ITA projects: the 'policy institution'. The element in question is that of an 'institution', which, as explained in Chapter 1, is a descriptive concept denoting an 'established practice'.[125]

Standard understandings of an 'established' practice require that it is 'stable and firm' or 'set up on a secure or permanent basis'.[126] Clearly ITA is not established in the sense that particular projects are constituted on a permanent basis (though 'temporary' arrangements have in some cases lasted for significant periods).[127] However, if the projects are considered collectively, it can be said that ITA is an 'established practice' because the activity has been used many times in the past, and, as a consequence of this frequency, it is reasonable to speculate that some of the political circumstances that led to the use of ITA may arise again in the future. The frequent use of this activity across the course of the 20th century means, then, that it is possible to consider the administration projects as collectively constituting an 'institution'.

Because of the distinctive nature of the activity performed, as explained in the previous chapter, an important, if limited, practical commonality exists between

---

[123] Such proposals form part of a broader set of ideas for post-Israeli foreign involvement in the Palestinian Territories, sometimes understood in terms of a 'trusteeship' or 'protectorate'. Certain proposals envisage an operation led and conducted by the US, in some cases together with Palestinian authorities. See, e.g. , TL Friedman, 'A Way Out of the Middle East Impasse' *New York Times,* 24 August 2001, A19, column 1; TL Friedman, 'How About Sending NATO Somewhere Important?', *New York Times,* 4 September 2001, A23, column 1; TL Friedman, 'Pull Up a Chair', *New York Times,* 20 March 2002, A29, column 5; M Indyk, 'A US-Led Trusteeship for Palestine', *Washington Post,* 29 June 2002, A23; M Indyk, 'A Trusteeship for Palestine?', 82:3 (May/June 2003) *Foreign Affairs* 51. More relevant for present purposes are models of a more internationalized nature, such as the proposal of Tony Klug in conjunction with the UK-based Middle East Policy Initiative Forum for a 'Transitional International Protectorate' overseen by a 'Mandate Authority' (possibly composed of the 'Quartet' of the US, EU, Russia, and the UN) and conducted by an international Protectorate administration, divided between civil and security tasks, with military personnel drawn from countries 'assented to by both the Palestinians and Israel'; see T Klug, 'An International Protectorate for the West Bank and the Gaza Strip?', May 2003, available at <http://www.opendemocracy.net/content/articles/PDF/1207.pdf>. See also the discussion in W Bain, *Between Anarchy and Society. Trusteeship and the Obligations of Power* (OUP, 2003), 4. The relationship between ITA and ideas relating to 'protectorates' and 'trusteeship' is considered in ch. 8, below.

[124] M Ward, 'The Case for International Trusteeship in Haiti', 7 (2006) *Canadian Military Journal* 25, available at <www.journal.forces.gc.ca/engraph/Vol7/no3/PDF/04-ward_e.pdf>.

[125] See above, ch. 1, section 1.5.1. In particular, as explained therein, this usage of institution is not intended necessarily to denote normativity.

[126] Definitions (1) and (3) respectively from the *Oxford English Dictionary* (OED online, at <http://www.oed.com>).

[127] This issue is discussed further below, ch. 7, section 7.6, and ch. 8, section 8.7.2.4.

what has been illustrated in this chapter to be a wide range of different projects.[128] Thus, a large group of projects is set apart from the other activities performed by international organizations and the other circumstances in which territorial administration is conducted.

At the same time, as Table 5 above demonstrates, international territorial administration projects have been conducted in many different places around the world, by different international actors, involving varying degrees of administration and for different durations, and at various times spanning the past century. Although the projects may share a certain elemental commonality by virtue of the nature of the activity performed and the identity of the actor performing this activity, are they otherwise merely a series of disconnected, *sui generis* accidents that are best understood on an individual basis?

In order to answer this question, it is necessary to consider what the purposes of the administration projects were, and are, and how they relate to each other. Is some sort of purposive commonality manifest across the projects? In the quotation from the Brahimi Report above, reference is made to '[i]ntra-State conflicts' and 'future instability' as the potential triggers for future administration projects. The analysis in the following chapters moves beyond such vague designations to consider in detail why each of the administration projects took place.

Through an examination of the historical background to all of the international administration projects, an attempt to establish purposive commonality is made. If this is possible, then, as explained in the previous chapter, ITA can be considered a 'policy institution': an established practice where important connections between the policy ends to which each individual manifestation of the practice has been put are evident.[129]

The analysis is confined to those projects that were actually implemented (including the Council for South West Africa/Namibia, which never took up its full administrative role but still purported to exercise certain administrative prerogatives, notably in the legislative sphere),[130] or merely authorized but at the time of writing still potentially to be implemented (e.g., MINURSO in Western Sahara). Thus historical projects that were authorized but never implemented— such as that for the Free Territory of Trieste[131]—are not covered.

Equally, projects that only existed as a series of proposals are not addressed. One such project, the famous 'Corpus Separatum' proposal for Jerusalem made

---

[128] See above, ch. 1, section 1.4.5.   [129] See above, ch. 1, section 1.5.

[130] See United Nations Council for Namibia, Decree No. 1 on Natural Resources of Namibia, UN Doc. A/C.131/33, in Report of the Council for Namibia, Addendum, UN Doc. A/9624/Add.1 (1974), and the commentary below, ch. 6, n. 57.

[131] See the sources cited above in n. 47. Another example falling within this category, involving partial administrative prerogatives, would be the arrangements in 1948 for the United Nations to run a plebiscite on the question of the accession of the State of Jammu and Kashmir to India or Pakistan. See SC Res. 47, 21 April 1948, in particular Section B; see also SC Res. 91, 30 March 1951; SC Res. 96, 10 November 1951; SC Res. 98, 23 December 1952; SC Res. 122, 24 January 1957; SC Res. 126, 2 December 1957.

by the UN Trusteeship Council in 1947,[132] is perhaps more well-known than many of the projects that were actually carried out. However, proposed administration projects are not covered since many different proposals were invariably made in relation to each territory. To consider all these proposals is unfeasible, and no persuasive basis for selecting one over the others could be identified. The famous 1947 Jerusalem proposal, for example, is actually one of several made by the UN Trusteeship Council that year, and was later redrafted and succeeded in the following half century by a raft of other, strikingly varied proposals made by a range of public and private bodies, and individuals.[133]

Although historical proposals are not addressed, general policy proposals, which continue to have purchase internationally—such as trusteeship proposals for so-called 'failed states'—will be considered in Chapter 7 where the purposes associated with the ITA projects are analysed within the broader context of ideas in international law and public policy.[134]

An academic thesis on the purposes of some of the early administration projects, Méir Ydit's *Internationalised Territories* of 1961, focused on the utility of these projects in terms of vesting sovereignty in the international organizations involved; what might be termed 'international territorial sovereignty'. The policy analysis in this book therefore commences with an evaluation of this particular explanation for the purposes served by international territorial administration, starting in the next chapter by considering what 'international territorial sovereignty' could mean and reviewing the legal factors on which its existence would depend.

---

[132] See the sources cited above in n. 43.

[133] For these later proposals see, for example, Hirsch, Housen-Couriel & Lapidoth (above n. 43).

[134] See below, ch. 7, section 7.3.3. Given the lack of agreement on and the specificity of the proposals for the Palestinian Territories mentioned above (n. 123 and accompanying text), a detailed treatment of them is inappropriate for a general study of this kind.

3

The Idea of International
Territorial Sovereignty

3.1 Introduction

As James Crawford remarks, '[t]he term "sovereignty" has a long and troubled
history, and a variety of meanings'.[1] As far as its meanings in international law are
concerned, Eli Lauterpacht suggests that:

...it is necessary to distinguish between the two principal meanings attributed to the
word 'sovereignty'. It is used, in one sense, to describe the right of ownership which a
State may have in any particular portion of territory. This may be called 'the legal sovereignty'... [t]his kind of sovereignty may be likened to the residual title of the owner of
freehold land which is let out on a long lease. The word 'sovereignty' is, however, more
commonly used, in its second meaning, to describe the jurisdiction and control which a
State may exercise over territory, regardless of the question of where ultimate title to the
territory may lie.[2]

---

[1] J Crawford, *The Creation of States in International Law* (2nd edn, OUP, 2006), 32. See also
WM Reisman, 'Sovereignty and Human Rights in Contemporary International Law', 84 (1990)
AJIL 866, at 866. The literature on state sovereignty is voluminous; recent works of note, which
include further references, are RH Jackson, *Quasi-states: Sovereignty, International Relations and
the Third World* (CUP, 1990); J Bartelson, *A Genealogy of Sovereignty* (CUP, 1995); A Chayes and
A Handler Chayes, *The New Sovereignty: Compliance with International Regulatory Agreements*
(Harvard University Press, 1995); TJ Biersteker and C Weber (eds), *State Sovereignty as Social
Construct* (CUP, 1996); SD Krasner, *Sovereignty: Organized Hypocrisy* (Princeton University
Press, 1999); G Kreijen (ed.), *State, Sovereignty, and International Governance* (OUP, 2002);
G Simpson, *Great Powers and Outlaw States: Unequal Sovereigns in the International Legal Order* (CUP,
2004); A Anghie, *Imperialism, Sovereignty and the Making of International Law* (CUP, 2005), *passim*;
D Sarooshi, *International Organizations and Their Exercise of Sovereign Powers* (OUP, 2005), *passim*
and especially 3–14 and sources cited therein; DS Smyrek, *Internationally Administered Territories—
International Protectorates? An Analysis of Sovereignty over Internationally Administered Territories with
Special Reference to the Legal Status of Post-War Kosovo* (Duncker & Humblot, 2006), *passim* and
especially part B; D Philpott, 'Sovereignty: An Introduction and Brief History', 48 (1995) *Journal
of International Affairs* 353; S Krasner, 'Pervasive Not Perverse: Semi-Sovereigns as the Global
Norm', 30 (1997) *Cornell International Law Journal* 651; JH Jackson, 'Sovereignty-Modern: A New
Approach to an Outdated Concept', 97 (2003) *AJIL* 782; SD Krasner, 'Problematic Sovereignty',
ch. 1 in SD Krasner (ed.), *Problematic Sovereignty: Contested Rules and Political Possibilities*
(Columbia University Press, 2001).

[2] E Lauterpacht, 'The Contemporary Practice of the United Kingdom in the Field of
International Law—Survey and Comment', 5 (1956) *ICLQ* 405, at 410.

These two ideas of 'sovereignty' reflect two potential connections between the juridical person of the state and a territorial unit: administration (what Lauterpacht terms 'jurisdiction and control'), on the one hand, and ownership, on the other.

It is sometimes assumed that the enjoyment of sovereignty in the former sense presupposes enjoyment of sovereignty in the latter sense. Thus, it is suggested that the grant of plenary territorial administrative prerogatives to an international organization necessarily constitutes and/or reflects the conferral of title over the territory to the organization involved, albeit on a temporary basis. When discussing UNTAET's administration in East Timor, for example, *Time* magazine reported that 'the UN is legally the holder of East Timor's sovereignty'.[3] This journalistic perception relating to one of the most recent administration projects reflects the approach taken by the first academic study to analyse some of the earlier administration projects collectively and explain the purposes served by these projects. In his 'internationalised territories' thesis of 1963, Méir Ydit assumed ownership from the right of administration, and considered the purposes served by a broad range of foreign territorial administration projects, including those conducted by international organizations, in terms of this enjoyment of title. As far as these purposes were concerned, the right of administration was of no consequence by itself. Territorial ownership by the international organization involved was the key feature: a device intended as a durable solution to particularly disputed territories.

One way into an enquiry of the potential policy ends to which the institution of international territorial administration has been put is to consider Ydit's thesis, since, if Ydit is correct, the idea of international territorial *administration* as a policy institution would have to be questioned—at least in some cases, it would be the vesting of *title* in the international organizations involved that is being used to achieve certain policy ends and is, therefore, the policy institution. This vesting of title might be called 'international territorial sovereignty', using the term 'sovereignty' to denote ownership/title, as in the first sense above. Is international territorial sovereignty an appropriate explanation for the purposes served by at least some of the administration projects involving international organizations as the administering actors? If so, the enjoyment of sovereignty in the other sense—the right of administration—is a corollary to the enjoyment of title as far as the purposes served by the projects are concerned. In order to answer this question, it is necessary to establish whether or not the enjoyment of title has actually ever been suggested in any of the projects in which sovereignty in the sense of administration has undoubtedly been exercised.

This brief chapter considers the concept of international territorial sovereignty, as a prelude to a detailed analysis in Chapters 4 and 5 of the legal status of each of the territories that have been made subject to administration by international

---

[3] Cited in J Chopra, 'The UN's Kingdom of East Timor', 42 (2000) *Survival* 27, 30.

organizations. What does this concept mean, and on what legal and political factors does its existence depend?

The chapter commences with Ydit's invocation of the concept in his 'internationalised territories' thesis, considering how it forms the basis for Ydit's explanation of the purposes served by some of the projects. A central methodological issue with considerations of territorial status in international law is then addressed: the importance of establishing the nature of claims made with respect to territory by those actors exercising administrative prerogatives over it. In the light of this, it is concluded that, even if the enjoyment of territorial title might be lawful according to the constitution of international organizations (an issue, like the issue of whether the enjoyment of powers of territorial administration is so lawful,[4] which is not considered in this book),[5] such enjoyment of title cannot be found merely in the exercise of administrative prerogatives over territory. It is also necessary to consider the basis on which these prerogatives are exercised, and in particular whether a claim of title by the organizations involved is evident. One cannot assume, as some do, an automatic connection between sovereignty in the sense of ownership with the exercise of sovereignty in the sense of a right of territorial administration.

3.2 Ydit's 'Internationalised Territories' Thesis

Commentators often use the term 'internationalization' to denote some kind of pronounced international involvement in a particular issue or situation. In 1961, Méir Ydit adopted the concept of an 'internationalised territory' to describe common features of various arrangements.[6] Although his definition of an 'internationalised territory' is not always clear or consistent, several broad features of the concept can be traced.

An 'internationalised territory' is a territorial unit that is neither a state itself, nor part of the territory of another state, and where 'sovereignty is vested in, and partly (or exclusively) exercised by' particular non-local actors in a certain capacity.[7] Here, Ydit is invoking the two meanings of legal sovereignty highlighted earlier: both the enjoyment of legal title ('vested in') and the

---

[4] On this question, see the List of Sources, section 5.2.6.

[5] See, e.g., Lauterpacht (above n. 2), at 411, n. 13 and sources cited therein; Dissenting Opinion of Judge Fitzmaurice in *Legal Consequences for States of the Continued Presence of South Africa in Namibia (South West Africa) Notwithstanding Security Council Resolution 276 (1970), Advisory Opinion, ICJ Reports 1971*, 16, at 220; I Brownlie, *Principles of Public International Law* (6th edn, OUP, 2003), 167.

[6] M Ydit, *Internationalised Territories from the 'Free City of Cracow' to the 'Free City of Berlin'* (Sythoff, 1961).

[7] Ibid., 320. See also ibid., 21.

right of (partial or plenary) territorial administration ('partly (or exclusively) exercised by'). The actors enjoying this sovereignty were originally a '[g]roup of states or the organized international community'[8] and later became the United Nations, as the 'supreme organization of international community'.[9] For Ydit, the *sine qua non* of internationalization is its conception as a permanent settlement of an 'unlimited duration'.[10] The idea, then, seems to be that territorial title is permanently vested in various non-local public actors (groups of foreign states and international organizations) in their capacity as representatives of a so-called international community, thereby 'internationalizing' the territory.

Appreciating Ydit's purposive approach allows the reason for his definition of internationalization to be discerned. Ydit is concerned with an activity that can be used 'as a durable solution to disputed and coveted territories'.[11] This purposive approach, which is an undercurrent throughout the analysis, provides the basis on which internationalization is defined and its role as a policy institution appraised. Ydit is concerned with solving disputes over territorial title by permanently vesting formal sovereignty 'internationally', thereby providing an outcome that does not involve any of the disputants giving up their claim in favour of another disputant.[12] The exercise of territorial administration would seem to be significant for Ydit only insofar as it is usually a corollary to the enjoyment of title by the administering actor or actors. Whether permanent international territorial *sovereignty* is in evidence is the key factor as far as he is concerned.[13] This is implied in the above quotation, where Ydit states that sovereignty-as-title needs to be 'vested' in the international entity involved, but sovereignty-as-administration need only be 'exercised' partly. As far as Ydit is concerned, then, the former is an unbending requirement, whereas the latter is merely something that usually follows if conformity to that requirement is evident. Hence the title of Ydit's monograph—*Internationalised Territories*—indicates a primary focus on 'internationalization' in terms of the effect it has on the territories involved, rather than the nature of the activity involved in it.

How could a circumstance of international territorial sovereignty arise? It would depend on the existence of a claim in this regard by the organizations involved with respect to those territories subject to their administrative control.

---

[8] Ibid., 21.

[9] Ibid., 320.

[10] Ibid., 20 (first quotation), 21 (second quotation).

[11] Ibid., 321. See also ibid., 11.

[12] A similar idea seems to be evident in Clark M Eichelberger's brief 1965 proposals to vest United Nations 'sovereignty' in 'areas where no nation has extended its own sovereign claims', identified as 'part of Antarctica; the bed of the sea beyond the continental shelf; and outer space'; CM Eichelberger, *UN: The First Twenty Years* (Harper & Row, 1965), at 133–6.

[13] For an example of the use of this term, see Ydit (above n. 6), at 16.

3.3　Claims and Territorial Status

In international law, the degree to which particular actors exercise territorial control can be a crucial factor in determining questions of both statehood and territorial title.[14] As mentioned, some suggest that when an international organization administers territory, at least when it exercises plenary administrative prerogatives, as a matter of international law it becomes a territorial sovereign; the territory 'belongs' to it as 'League' or 'United Nations' territory. In order to draw such a conclusion, however, one needs to assume that the actor asserting the right to administer territory does so in a particular capacity: as the holder of title with respect to the territory. But such an assumption cannot be made. As Eli Lauterpacht states in relation to his two models of 'sovereignty' described in the passage extracted above:

[u]sually sovereignty in this latter sense [mere jurisdiction and control] is to be found in the same hands as the legal sovereignty [i.e., ownership] but there is no reason in law why it should be and often it is not.[15]

In the absence of any positive declaration as to the status of a territory, one cannot assume that the actor exercising control over it is necessarily sovereign in the sense of being the title-holder. Rather, one must enquire as to the basis on which the actor concerned performs that role. In the words of DP O'Connell, 'a government is only recognized for what it claims to be'.[16] There is a tendency by some commentators to bypass this stage of analysis, drawing conclusions concerning the existence or non-existence of a particular territorial status without considering whether or not this status is actually claimed by the entity involved. Equally, the juridical effect of the enjoyment of administrative prerogatives in the territory by other international legal persons is often considered without reference to the basis on which these prerogatives are exercised. No doubt, the most common basis on which entities exercise territorial control is an individual claim to territory. However, it is not the only one.

There are at least two different ways in which an entity can administer territory, insofar as the status of the territory is concerned. In the first place, the entity can merely assert the right to administer the territory, without prejudice to the issue of territorial status. Of course, states may wish to pursue a claim to title over the territory, but in such circumstances an extra element—the claim—arises and (if it is recognized and justified) prevails.

In the second place, an entity may not only be exercising administrative control; it may also purport to perform this role in a particular capacity in relation to the

---

[14] Regarding statehood, see, for example, Crawford (above n. 1), 55–61; regarding territorial title, see, for example, Brownlie (above n. 5), 105–61.

[15] Lauterpacht (above n. 2), 410.

[16] DP O'Connell, 'The Status of Formosa and the Chinese Recognition Problem', 50 (1956) *AJIL* 405, 415. See also Crawford (above n. 1), 156.

status of the territory. In such circumstances, the distinction between a 'state' and a 'government' is instructive. In international law, the connection between the two is understood in terms of agency: the government is not itself a legal person, but, rather, the agent that acts on behalf of the legal person—the state—concerned. Its acts are the acts of the state.[17] This is different from the earlier scenario, where the entity does not claim to be acting on behalf of the territory as its sovereign.

Even if the administrative authority purports to perform this activity in right of a sovereign entity, however, it is still necessary to establish the identity of the entity so implicated. It may be the same as that of the authority involved, i.e., the authority purports to govern the territory as its own. On the other hand, there may be a divergence in these identities: the authority may not be acting on its own behalf insofar as its acts purport to be binding as the acts of the territorial unit concerned. An example of this is when one state requests another state to perform certain governmental acts within its territory, on its (the first state's) behalf. In such circumstances, as acts of a territorial sovereign, the acts are the acts of the former, not the latter state.[18] It follows that the presence of an actor enjoying such prerogatives does not constitute a diminution in the 'independence' of the entity in which the prerogatives are exercised as far as statehood law is concerned. As James Crawford states:

[t]he exercise of governmental competence by another international person or persons on behalf of and by delegation from a State is not inconsistent with formal independence...[t]he essential point is that the competence is exercised not adversely to but in right of the State concerned.[19]

In considering the effect of territorial administration by international organizations on status and territorial title, therefore, it is not enough merely to consider the degree of administrative prerogatives exercised. One must also establish the basis on which the prerogatives are exercised. In particular, one must consider whether or not they are exercised on behalf of the territory as a juridical unit and, if so, what assumption about the status of the unit is being made.[20]

---

[17] On the concept of 'government' in public international law, see the sources cited above, ch. 1, n. 63. On the agency relationship between the government and the state in particular, see International Law Commission, Articles on Responsibility of States for Internationally Wrongful Acts (hereinafter 'ILC's Articles on State Responsibility'), Art. 4, Commentary thereto and sources cited therein, reproduced in J Crawford, *The International Law Commission's Articles on State Responsibility. Introduction, Text and Commentaries* (CUP, 2002), 94–9, in relation to attribution to the State of acts of its organs, including the executive. As James Crawford and Simon Olleson explain, 'States are juridical abstractions. Like corporations in national law, they necessarily act through organs or agents'; J Crawford and S Olleson, 'The Nature and Forms of International Responsibility', in M Evans (ed.), *International Law* (2nd edn, OUP, 2006), 451, at 460.

[18] This is perhaps analogous to the situation envisaged under Art. 6 of the ILC's Articles on State Responsibility, where the organ of one state is placed at the disposal of another state. See ILC's Articles on State Responsibility, Art. 6, in Crawford (above n. 17), 103–5.

[19] Crawford (above n. 1), 70.

[20] Focusing on the capacity in which administrative acts are performed also has implications for questions of legal responsibility, applicable law and jurisdiction, including immunities from jurisdiction, which are beyond the scope of this study. See the sources listed above, ch. 1, n. 64.

3.4 Conclusion

The consideration of the policy role of the institution of international territorial administration commenced in this chapter with a consideration of the explanation that, in effect, this institution is merely a corollary to the vesting of sovereignty in the administering actors involved: Ydit's 'internationalised territories' thesis. According to Ydit, what has been termed 'international territorial sovereignty' constitutes a policy institution, not ITA; it is this device that serves a policy end, vesting title over contested territory in a neutral actor. ITA is merely the consequence of this arrangement, in the same way as the conduct of territorial administration by a government is viewed as a consequence of the enjoyment of title over the territory by the state concerned.

In appraising the merits of Ydit's thesis, one cannot assume, as Ydit seems to do, that the enjoyment of sovereignty in the sense of administration implies the enjoyment of sovereignty in the sense of title. Rather, one must consider the basis on which sovereignty in the former sense is exercised, in particular, whether it is exercised in the name of an actor as the title-holder.

In the following two chapters, the effect of international territorial administration on the juridical status of the territories involved is analysed.[21] Can the assumptions reflected in the approach taken by Ydit and other commentators be sustained? In the case of projects involving international organizations, have these actors actually purported to enjoy 'sovereignty', in the sense of international legal title, over the territories involved? This question is resolved by considering the juridical status of each of the territories in which international administration has taken place, bearing in mind the above considerations concerning the significance of claims in determining issues of statehood and territorial title in international law.

---

[21] For an alternative study of the legal status of some of the plenary administration projects, by way of a broader consideration of issues of sovereignty, see Smyrek (above n. 1).

4

Host Territories—States and State Territories

4.1 Introduction

Ydit's 'internationalised territories' thesis foregrounds the significance of assessing the legal status of the territories subject to ITA as part of the broader attempt to appreciate the purposes associated with this activity. Analysis of territorial status is conducted in this and the following chapter, considering how status would be viewed as a matter of international law.[1] One important development in international law and public policy in the 20th century—the self-determination entitlement—played a determinative role on this issue in some cases, and it is helpful to treat that area of international law, and the analysis of the status of those territories where it played such a role, discretely.[2] This treatment is, therefore, provided in the following chapter; the present chapter focuses on the international legal status of those territories where ITA projects operated and where the right to

---

[1] For an oft-cited definition of the test for statehood in international law, see Montevideo Convention on the Rights and Duties of States, Montevideo, 26 December 1933, 165 LNTS 19, Art. 1. For academic discussion, see, e.g., H Lauterpacht, *Recognition in International Law* (CUP, 1947); K Marek, *The Identity and Continuity of States in International Law* (2nd edn, Drodz, 1968); R Higgins, *The Development of International Law through the Political Organs of the United Nations* (OUP, 1963), 11–57; T Grant, *The Recognition of States: Law and Practice in Debate and Evolution* (Praeger, 1999); OC Okafor, *Re-Defining Legitimate Statehood: International Law and State Fragmentation in Africa* (Martinus Nijhoff, 2000); A Anghie, *Imperialism, Sovereignty and the Making of International Law* (CUP, 2005), chs 1–4; J Crawford, *The Creation of States in International Law* (2nd edn, OUP, 2006), chs 2 and 3 and sources cited therein; MG Kohen (ed.), *Secession: International Law Perspectives* (CUP, 2006); E Milano, *Unlawful Territorial Situations in International Law: Reconciling Effectiveness, Legality and Legitimacy* (Martinus Nijhoff, 2006), *passim*; TD Grant, 'Defining Statehood: The Montevideo Convention and its Discontents', 37 (1999) *Columbia Journal of Transnational Law* 403. See also *Opinion No. 1* of the Arbitration Committee of the International Conference on the Former Yugoslavia ('Badinter Committee'), reproduced in 31 (1992) *ILM* 1494. On the related treatment of 'governments' in international law, see, e.g., S Talmon, *Recognition of Governments in International Law with Particular Reference to Governments in Exile* (OUP, 1998); BR Roth, *Governmental Illegitimacy in International Law* (OUP, 2001), and sources cited therein.

[2] On self-determination see the sources cited below, ch. 5, n. 3, and in the List of Sources, section 5.4.

self-determination, even if it may have been applicable, does not appear to have played a determinative role in relation to this status during the relevant period.[3]

Despite its popular image as an activity conducted only in non-state territorial entities, international territorial administration has actually taken place in a number of states. Whereas sometimes only part of the territory of a state has been involved, as in the Colombian town and district of Leticia, in other circumstances the entire state, as in Bosnia and Herzegovina, has been covered. This chapter analyses the juridical status of most of the territories that were states or formed part of state territory for the duration of the administration project taking place in them. Did the displacement of local actors in the activity of territorial administration ever have the effect of extinguishing juridical statehood (for projects operating at the level of the state) or territorial title (for projects operating at the level of sub-state territorial units)? Where the issue of status is relatively straightforward and uncontested, it is reviewed briefly (e.g., Cambodia); where matters are more complex and contested, status is considered in depth (e.g., the Free City of Danzig).

The territories in question can be grouped according to the historical factors that partially determined their legal status. To begin, an 'inter-war quartet' is considered: the four sites of the inter-war administration projects—the Saar, Danzig, Memel, and Leticia—whose status is bound up in the Versailles settlement after the First World War and/or subsequent disputes during the inter-war period. The next territory—the Congo during the 1960s—is in a class of its own as a newly independent former colonial state at the time of the main wave of decolonization.

Attention then turns to the use of ITA outside the colonial context after the end of the Cold War. For the first three territories in this category—Somalia, Cambodia, and northern Iraq—legal status amounted to the continuation of the status quo. For the 'Balkan quartet' of Bosnia and Herzegovina, Mostar, Eastern Slavonia, and Kosovo, by contrast, the ITA projects took place when the status of the territories involved was in the process of reconstitution or had only recently been reconstituted.

Further sites involving ITA projects do not require specific treatment as to their legal status. In the first place, it is unnecessary for present purposes to clarify the legal status of those territories where ITA projects involving international organizations are of a relatively discrete nature and there is no question that this activity has any effect on territorial status: the administration of 'refugee' camps by UNHCR,[4] the provision of assistance to refugees and displaced people (e.g., by UNRWA to the Palestinian refugees)[5] and the distribution of material assistance more generally.[6]

---

[3] For one territory covered in this chapter—the Congo in the 1960s—self-determination may have been a mediating factor, but whether it was or not is uncertain. See below, n. 129.

[4] See above, ch. 2, section 2.3.1.

[5] See above, ch. 2, section 2.3.1, in particular nn. 56 and 57 and accompanying text.

[6] See above, ch. 2, section 2.3.2.

In the second place, the international appointees, sitting alongside local members on certain locally-based administrative bodies (e.g., courts), do not by themselves place the status of the territory in which they operate into question, and so for present purposes it is unnecessary to determine that status (which is in any case uncontested) in those situations where there is no further ITA activity operating in the territory, viz. Sierra Leone since 2002,[7] Afghanistan between 2003 and 2005,[8] Iraq since 2003,[9] and Lebanon and Cambodia since 2005 and 2006 respectively.[10] The status of other places where regimes of international appointees have cohabited with further forms of ITA is considered. As mentioned, Bosnia and Herzegovina and Kosovo are addressed below; East Timor will be addressed in the next chapter.

An important cross-cutting distinction can be made between the territories under analysis. Bearing in mind the foregoing analysis in Chapter 3, this chapter seeks to resolve the question of 'sovereignty' in the sense of title, taking into account, inter alia, the juridical effect of the exercise of 'sovereignty' in the sense of administration by international actors. Insofar as the potential effect on sovereignty-as-title of the exercise of international administration is concerned, two different types of enquiry are in order, differing according to the particular territorial unit under consideration. If the territory is a state, the enquiry turns on the juridical effect, if any, ITA has on the continued existence of the state. If, however, the territory is a sub-state unit, the enquiry turns on the juridical effect, if any, this arrangement has on the continued enjoyment of title over that territory by the state.

As outlined in the previous chapter, in establishing the juridical effect of international territorial administration on statehood and title to territory, it is necessary to appraise not only the degree of administrative control, but also the basis on which this control is exercised. As will be demonstrated, in most cases, the conduct of this activity has been based on the continuance of the status quo as far as title and statehood are concerned. Such a basis can be identified in either the constitutive instruments of the administrative project, or relevant statements made by the officials on the project, or both. In such circumstances, this activity supports, rather than undermines, the existing international juridical position of the territory concerned.

Although the present enquiry is concerned with the legal effect of international administration on territorial status, in seeking to resolve the status of the territories in question it is, of course, necessary to consider further relevant factors such as

---

[7] See above, ch. 2, section 2.3.4.2, nn. 103–4 and accompanying text, and n. 105 and accompanying text.

[8] See above, ch. 2, section 2.3.4.3, n. 116 and accompanying text.

[9] See above, ch. 2, section 2.3.4.2, nn. 109–10, and section 2.3.4.3, in particular n. 117 and accompanying text.

[10] See above, ch. 2, section 2.4.3.2, nn. 111–13 and accompanying text (on Lebanon) and nn. 107–8 and accompanying text (on Cambodia).

the exercise of administrative prerogatives by other foreign actors (e.g., Poland in the Free City of Danzig), and a breakdown in governmental control in the territory (e.g., in the Congo).

Before commencing the analysis of each territorial unit, it is useful to review one general consideration relevant across several different examples. As James Crawford states:

> ...there is a distinction between the creation of a new State on the one hand and the subsistence or extinction of an established State on the other. In the former situation, the criterion of effective government may be applied more strictly.[11]

As far as the latter is concerned:

> ...generally, the presumption—in practice a strong presumption—favours the continuity and disfavours the extinction of an established State.[12]

One might say that this reflects a broader presumption in favour of the status quo in relation to both statehood and territorial title: that, in general terms, the continuance of statehood and a state's title over its territory is presumed, whereas the creation of a new state and the loss of title over territory are to be proved.

In any given situation, both considerations are potentially applicable in a mutually-reinforcing manner, in that one may be seeking to resolve whether or not a particular territorial unit continues to form part of the territory of one state, or has instead become part of another state or been constituted as a new state. In such a scenario, two interlinked questions are being determined simultaneously: that of the continued title enjoyed by the original state, and that of the creation of a new state or the acquisition of a territorial unit by another state. Depending on which issue is being focused on, one approaches the status issue either in terms of a presumption in favour of the status quo (continued title by the original state) or a lack of presumption in favour of an alteration in the status quo (new statehood or alteration in title in favour of another state). The presumption and the lack of presumption are thus two sides of the same coin: each is reinforced by the other. In the following analysis, the significance of this general consideration will be illustrated in a variety of contexts.

---

[11] Crawford (above n. 1), 59 (footnote omitted).

[12] Ibid., 701, noting Marek, above, n. 1, 548; O Schachter 'State Succession: The Once and Future Law', 33 (1993) *Virginia Journal of International Law* 253, 258–60 and R Mushkat 'Hong Kong and Succession of Treaties', 46 (1997) *ICLQ* 181, 183–7. See also RY Jennings, 'Government in Commission', 23 (1946) *BYIL* 112, at 123, who states that, when one is considering 'the emergence of a new state' rather than the 'continuance of an old state with a long history of independence', then '[t]he presumption is...of...continued existence as a state'.

4.2 Inter-War Quartet: the Saar Territory, the Free City of Danzig, the Memel Territory, and Leticia

A consideration of the effect of international territorial administration on the juridical status of states and state territories begins at the very start of the era of ITA, with the four administration projects during the inter-war period in the Saar Territory (the Saar), the Free City of Danzig, the Memel Territory (Memel), and Leticia.

The legal status of the first three territories in the inter-war quartet was placed in question in different ways by the Versailles settlement. For the Saar, this question arose as a result of the administrative arrangements authorized under the Treaty of Versailles: the removal of all governmental presence by the existing sovereign, Germany, and the introduction of plenary administration by a League Commission. In the Free City of Danzig, it arose because of the provisions in the Treaty of Versailles authorizing the subsequent reconstitution of the territory as a Free City, and other provisions in that Treaty and a later agreement between the Free City and Poland providing for various administrative prerogatives exercised in the Free City by a League High Commissioner and Poland.

A different strategy was adopted for the status of the Memel territory; the Treaty of Versailles did not stipulate this status, but rather allowed for it to be determined in a subsequent agreement. The later agreement, when it was forthcoming, had the same effect as the Treaty of Versailles in relation to the Free City of Danzig, i.e., determining the status of the territory and providing for partial international administration (in this case, administrative prerogatives exercised by a League appointee to the Harbour Board). The question of the legal status of the fourth territory in the inter-war quartet, Leticia, was unconnected to the Versailles settlement, arising out of a dispute between Colombia and Peru in the 1930s.

4.2.1 The Saar territory 1920–35

Under the Treaty of Versailles, the Saar territory, hitherto forming part of Germany, was placed under the administration of a League of Nations Governing Commission, as the 'government of the territory',[13] with France given a right to exploit its mines.[14] No provision in the Treaty stipulated the status of the territory under this arrangement; in particular, neither the League Governing

---

[13] Versailles Peace Treaty, Art. 49, Annex to Part III, Section IV (after Art. 50), ch. II, Arts 16 and 19. For the League's administrative prerogatives in the territory, see above, ch. 2, n. 13.

[14] On France's powers to exploit the mines, see Versailles Peace Treaty, Arts 45, 46, 50, and Annex to Part III, Section IV (after Art. 50), ch. I. See also the discussion below, ch. 6, text from n. 19.

Commission nor the League (nor France) was granted sovereignty, in the sense of title, with respect to the territory. Did the administrative arrangements within the Saar alter the juridical status of the territory in some way?[15]

Ydit, consistent with his general approach outlined in Chapter 3, assumes from the mere enjoyment of administrative prerogatives that the League was 'sovereign' in the Saar, albeit in a special sense given that, as discussed further below, the arrangements could be (and were) terminated after 15 years.[16] However, apart from disregarding the absence of a claim to sovereignty on the part of the League, Ydit's assumption ignores the particular capacity in which the administrative prerogatives were to be enjoyed.[17] Under Article 49 of the Treaty of Versailles:

> Germany renounces in favour of the League of Nations, in the capacity of trustee, the government of the territory...[18]

This provision ruled out League enjoyment of title as a result of its administrative prerogatives; these prerogatives were enjoyed 'in the capacity of trustee', i.e., not on the League's own behalf, but on behalf of another. As Percy Corbett stated:

> [d]o the rights, duties, and powers attributed to the Governing Commission, the agent of the League, and to the League itself, amount to sovereignty? They do not. What Germany renounces is not the sovereignty, but the government of the Saar territory, and though government is indeed the chief attribute of sovereignty, there is a difference...
>
> [...]
>
> ...the League is not vested with the sovereignty of the Saar, but only with some of its attributes.[19]

Even if the Saar was not, then, 'League-territory', did the total removal of German administrative control have the effect of extinguishing German title over the territory, thereby rendering the Saar a *sui generis* entity that did not form part of the territory of any state? As far as the juridical titleholder on whose behalf the League is to exercise governmental authority is concerned, the provisions of Article 49 were ambiguous: it could be Germany generally or the people of the territory in particular. In the absence of an explicit claim or authoritative assertion in this regard, the general presumption in favour of continued title suggests

---

[15] On the legal status of the Saar during this period, see, e.g., Crawford (above n. 1), 233–4, n. 172; DS Smyrek, *Internationally Administered Territories—International Protectorates? An Analysis of Sovereignty over Internationally Administered Territories with Special Reference to the Legal Status of Post-War Kosovo* (Duncker & Humblot, 2006), 67–76; PE Corbett, 'What is the League of Nations?', 5 (1924) *BYIL* 119, 126–8; N Berman, ' "But the Alternative is Despair", European Nationalism and the Modernist Renewal of International Law', 106 (1992–3) *Harvard Law Review* 1792, at 1879, 1881–2.

[16] M Ydit, *Internationalised Territories from the 'Free City of Cracow' to the 'Free City of Berlin'* (Sythoff, 1961), 44, but see also ibid., at 45, where a different approach seems to be adopted: Germany's formal sovereignty was preserved under the arrangements.

[17] When Ydit acknowledges this, he seems to take a different view; ibid.

[18] Versailles Peace Treaty, Art. 49. The significance of the concept of 'trust' to ITA is discussed further in ch. 8, below.

[19] Corbett (above n. 15), 127 (first quote) 128 (second quote).

that the Saar continued to be German territory, and that the League was acting on behalf of Germany in exercising its governmental authority, as far as the repository of title was concerned. Writing at the time, Corbett considered that:

Germany retains, at the minimum, the *nuda proprietas* of sovereignty, as she retains the *nuda proprietas* of all her domainal property, except the mines, in the Saar.[20]

James Crawford regards Germany as having 'remained residual sovereign' over the Saar during this time, and points out that the territory was regarded by German courts as part of the Reich, convictions in the territory were convictions 'in Germany' for the purpose of a law concerning recidivism, and local inhabitants retained German nationality.[21]

This view is supported by the provisions in the Treaty of Versailles dealing with the determination of the Saar's eventual status. Fifteen years after the Treaty's entry into force, the people of the Saar '...shall be called upon to indicate the sovereignty under which they desire to be placed'.[22] The population was given three alternatives: (a) 'maintenance of the régime' established under the Treaty, i.e., maintenance of League administration, (b) 'union with France', and (c) 'union with Germany'.[23] The view of the population was to be expressed in a plebiscite,[24] and the League was to 'decide on the sovereignty under which the territory is to be placed, taking into account the wishes of the inhabitants as expressed by the voting'.[25]

Crucially, the provisions concerning the juridical consequences of options (a) and (b) assume German sovereignty at the point of the League's decision. Under option (a) Germany would 'make such renunciation of her sovereignty in favour of the League of Nations as the latter shall deem necessary' whereas under option (b) Germany would 'cede to France...all rights and title over the territory'.[26] Since the League's administrative prerogatives were still in play at this point (they were not fixed for 15 years, ending at the same time as the plebiscite, but rather were conceived of indefinite duration, but subject to the League's decision as a result of the plebiscite), the provisions surely assume that the League administration did not have a negative effect on Germany's sovereignty.[27] In other words, Germany retained title with respect to the Saar throughout the 15-year period during which it did not exercise governmental authority in the territory. So the third option, 'union with Germany' (which was overwhelmingly supported by the people of the Saar when the plebiscite was held on 13 January 1935, and

---

[20] Corbett (above n. 15), 127.
[21] Crawford (above n. 1), 233–4, n. 172.
[22] Versailles Peace Treaty, Art. 49.
[23] Ibid., Annex to Part III, Section IV (after Art. 50), Art. 34.
[24] Ibid.
[25] Ibid., Art. 35.
[26] Ibid.
[27] See Corbett (above n. 15), 127–8.

adopted by the League),[28] amounted to *administrative* union to run alongside the *juridical* union that already existed. Thus, unlike the other two options, the provisions of the Versailles Treaty dealing with the implementation of this option refer exclusively to administrative arrangements—the League enabling the 'German government to be re-established in the government of the territory'[29]—and are not also concerned with sovereign title.

In conclusion, the arrangement for League administration set out in Article 49 of the Versailles Treaty involved Germany as titleholder delegating the central prerogative of title, the right to exercise governmental control, to the League, without prejudice to its continued enjoyment of title. Thus, the Saar was German territory for the period 1920–35.

4.2.2 The Free City of Danzig 1920–39[30]

In the same overall settlement that provided for the Saar administration, a new juridical entity—the Free City of Danzig—was created. In considering the status of this territory, the enquiry turns not on the effect of plenary League administration on the continued enjoyment of title over that territory by a state, but rather on the effect on the independence of a state-like entity of a matrix of administrative prerogatives enjoyed by various foreign actors, including the League.

Under the Treaty of Versailles, Germany renounced 'all rights and title' over Danzig[31] 'in favour of the Principal Allied and Associated Powers',[32] who in turn undertook to establish the territory as a 'Free City' that was to be 'placed under the protection of the League of Nations'.[33] Thus, the Treaty of Versailles

---

[28] FP Walters, *A History of the League of Nations* (OUP, 1952), 587–98; Ydit (above n. 16), at 45, n. 1. On the later history of the territory, see, e.g., Crawford (above n. 1), 233–4, n. 172.

[29] Versailles Peace Treaty, Annex to Part III, Section IV (after Art. 50), Art. 35.

[30] On the Free City of Danzig generally, see JB Mason, *The Danzig Dilemma* (Stanford University Press, 1946), and sources in the bibliography, ibid., at 308–22; Walters (above, n. 28), 82, 90, 131, 140, 301, 453–55, 615–21, 793–97; Ydit (above n. 16), 185–228 and sources in the bibliography, ibid., at 229–30; Smyrek (above n. 15), 58–67; M Lewis, 'The Free City of Danzig', 5 (1924) *BYIL* 89; I Morrow, 'The International Status of the Free City of Danzig', 18 (1937) *BYIL* 114; JK Bleimaier, 'The Legal Status of the Free City of Danzig 1920–1939: Lessons to Be Derived from the Experience of a Non-State Entity in the International Community', 2 (1989) *Hague Yearbook of International Law* 69, and bibliography, ibid., at 93; K Skubiszewski, 'Gdansk and the Dissolution of the Free City', in E Menzel, J Delbrück, K Ipsen and D Rauschning (eds), *Recht im Dienst des Friedens: Festschrift für Eberhard Menzel zum 65 Geburtstag am 21 Jan 1976* (1975), 470; Berman (above n. 15), 1874–8, 1886–93. For a map of the location, see CM Whomersley, 'The International Legal Status of Gdansk, Klaipeda and the Former East Prussia', 42 (1993) *ICLQ* 919, at 928; J Chopra, 'UN Civil Governance-in-Trust', in TG Weiss (ed.), *The United Nations and Civil Wars* (Lynne Rienner, 1995), 70, at 72.

[31] As defined in Art. 100 of the Versailles Peace Treaty, and delimited on the spot according to the arrangements under Art. 101 of the Versailles Treaty. The territory covered the town of Danzig and an area around it. See the sources in the previous note.

[32] Versailles Peace Treaty, Art. 100. See ibid., Arts 100–108 for the Free City arrangements.

[33] Ibid., Art. 102.

transferred 'rights and title' over Danzig from Germany to the Principal Allied and Associated Powers on what was implicitly a temporary basis.

Although the Treaty of Versailles envisaged the creation of Danzig as a Free City, and provided for this through obligations borne by the Principal Allied and Associated Powers, it did not purport to effect the Free City's creation directly. Rather, an interim period prevailed, during which a special form of sovereignty (limited in duration via the obligation to bring about the 'Free City' arrangement) with respect to the territory was vested in the Principal Allied and Associated Powers.[34] During this period, a provisional Council of State made up of local actors held elections for a Constituent Assembly; members of this body then drafted the Constitution for League approval.[35] Once approval was forthcoming, the Allied representatives declared the establishment of the Free City (on 15 or 17 November 1920—sources disagree) and they and their troops then withdrew.[36] The interim period of Allied sovereignty created a space whereby local governmental structures could be up and running by the time the Free City came into being. In this way the Free City was already something of a practical reality at the time of its establishment as a juridical entity.

The details of the interim period are significant because it was during this time, before the establishment of the Free City, that the treaty between Danzig and Poland, which in part outlined the administrative prerogatives of the League in the Free City, was negotiated.[37] Drafts of this treaty were prepared separately by the local Constituent Assembly and Poland; as there were considerable divergences between the two drafts, negotiations were held in Paris under the auspices of the Conference of the Ambassadors of the Principal Allied and Associated Powers.[38] A text was finally agreed—between Poland and the 'Free City of Danzig'—on 9 November 1920.[39] Although the Free City did not exist at that point, the treaty

---

[34] The status of Danzig during this period is not discussed by academic commentators, who focus exclusively on the 'Free City' period in Danzig's history. See, however, the *Danzig Pension Case* before the High Court of Danzig in 1929, which held that, although there had been a 'cession' of the territory to the Allied and Associated Powers, the Powers were to be 'regarded merely as trustees who, from the very beginning, undertook to establish the Free City of Danzig'; *Danzig Pension Case,* High Court of Danzig, 8 May 1929, 5 (1929–30) *ILR* 66, at 68.

[35] Ydit (above n. 16), 188–9; *Free City of Danzig and International Labour Organization, Advisory Opinion,* 26 August 1930, PCIJ, *Series B,* No. 18 (1930) (hereinafter '*Danzig and ILO Case*'), 11.

[36] Ydit (above n. 16), 189. According to the Permanent Court of International Justice in the *Danzig and ILO Case,* the Allies constituted the Free City by a decision of 27 October 1920, which was accepted by the 'representatives of Danzig' on 9 November 1920 and 'was to come into force' on 15 November 1920; *Danzig and ILO Case* (above n. 35), 11. See also *Treatment of Polish Nationals and Other Persons of Polish Origin or Speech in the Danzig Territory, Advisory Opinion,* 4 February 1932, PCIJ, *Series A/B,* No. 44 (1932) (hereinafter '*Treatment of Polish Nationals Case*'), 12–13.

[37] Convention between Poland and the Free City of Danzig (hereinafter 'Poland–Danzig Treaty'), 9 November 1920, 6 LNTS 189.

[38] *Treatment of Polish Nationals Case* (above n. 36), 13–16; Ydit (above n. 16), 189.

[39] *Treatment of Polish Nationals Case* (above n. 36), 13–16; Ydit (above n. 16), 189.

was to enter into force on its establishment,[40] which, as mentioned, came several days later.

Thus the locally-constituted administrative elements of a special territorial entity under the overall administrative control and formal sovereignty of the Allies entered into an agreement on behalf not of that special territorial entity but, rather, on behalf of the 'Free City' which the special entity was to become several days later. Like the drafting of the Constitution and the creation of the Constituent Assembly, this device enabled arrangements for the Free City to be constituted by local actors before the entity formally came into existence. Whereas, before, the arrangements concerned the basic internal structures of the state, here, they addressed the central issue in the future Free City's external affairs—its relationship with Poland.

So, although the Poland–Danzig Treaty was drafted and agreed before the creation of the Free City, it was the *Free City* (rather than the earlier special territorial entity under Allied sovereignty) that was a party, and the treaty ran from the Free City's creation.[41] Given this, what was the status of the Free City?

Such an enquiry is complicated because of the existence of administrative prerogatives enjoyed by Poland and the League (separately) alongside those prerogatives enjoyed by the Free City authorities.[42] Since German sovereignty had been removed,[43] the question is usually seen as having four possible answers. The Free City must have been either (1) a state, albeit a 'protected' one; (2) under Polish sovereignty; (3) under League sovereignty; or (4) an 'international protectorate' (a non-state territorial entity that is viewed as enjoying some form of distinct legal personality—and accordingly does not form part of the territory of another juridical entity—and in relation to which other juridical entities enjoy certain administrative prerogatives).[44]

The answer turns on two related factors: first, what claims were made by the Free City, the League, and Poland in relation to the territory, and, secondly, the nature and scope of the administrative powers enjoyed by the two actors, and the effect this enjoyment had on the respective merits of each claim. Commentators, although disagreeing on the answer to the overall question of the

---

[40] Poland–Danzig Treaty (above n. 37), Art. 40.

[41] There is no need, therefore, to consider questions of succession as between the Free City and the special sovereign entity that existed in the territory before that date, since the treaty was not entered into on behalf of that entity (even though the agreement was made during its operation).

[42] For academic commentary on this question, see, e.g., Mason (above n. 30), 228–47; Walters (above n. 28), 90; Ydit (above n. 16), 224–6, and sources cited ibid., at 225, nn. 84 and 85 and at 226, n. 86; Crawford (above n. 1), 239–41, and sources cited ibid., nn. 188 and 202; Corbett (above n. 15), 138–41; Lewis (above n. 30), 100–2.

[43] 'It ceased to be German territory', *The Blonde and Other Ships* [1921] P. 155 (Prize Court) (hereinafter '*The Blonde (Prize Court)*') (reversed by the Privy Council on other grounds), per Duke P., 162; according to the Treaty of Versailles, Danzig had 'been excluded from the territory of the German *Reich* and was not subject to the authority of Germany'; *In re M (Danzig Conviction Case)*, Germany, Supreme Court, 22 June 1933, 7 (1933–34) *ILR* 59.

[44] For the distinction between 'protected states' and 'international protectorates', see, e.g., Crawford (above n. 1), 286–99. 'Protection' is discussed further below in ch. 8, section 8.2.1.

status of the Free City, are united in their disregard of the first factor when formulating their answer. In the case of Ydit, this appears to spring from the problem identified in the previous chapter: a definition of 'sovereignty' concerned solely with the enjoyment of administrative prerogatives, without considering the basis on which such prerogatives are exercised.

This elision of the two forms of sovereignty identified by Eli Lauterpacht discussed in the previous chapter is unfortunate, as in the case of both Poland and the League there is no evidence to suggest that either entity purported to exercise its administrative prerogatives in the Free City on the basis of an enjoyment of formal title over the territory (either individually or in a condominium). Certainly, Poland continued to aspire to formal sovereignty over Danzig, but this was not recognized by other states or by the League. According to the Permanent Court of International Justice (PCIJ) in 1931, 'the Port of Danzig is not Polish territory'.[45] Equally, although the Free City was under the 'protection' of the League according to the Treaty of Versailles,[46] that phrase is not a term of art in international law.[47] In this context, it is best interpreted as acknowledging both the general commitment to the Free City's survival on the part of the League of Nations, and the specific administrative powers enjoyed by the League and the League High Commissioner in the City, which (as will be discussed in Chapter 6) can be explained in terms of promoting the City's 'free' status.[48]

The Free City, as its name suggests, was constituted as an entity distinct from the surrounding states.[49] This 'freedom' was both negative (in the sense of not

---

[45] *Access to, or Anchorage in, the Port of Danzig of Polish War Vessels, Advisory Opinion,* 11 December 1931, PCIJ, *Series A/B,* No. 43 (hereinafter '*Polish War Vessels in Danzig Case*'), 142.

[46] Versailles Peace Treaty, Art. 102.

[47] In the *Nationality Decrees in Tunis and Morocco Case,* the PCIJ stated that:

[t]he extent of the powers of a protecting State in the territory of a protected State depends, first, upon the Treaties between the protecting State and the protected State establishing the Protectorate, and, secondly, upon the conditions under which the Protectorate has been recognized by third Powers as against whom there is an intention to rely on the provisions of these Treaties. *In spite of common features possessed by Protectorates under international law,* they have individual legal characteristics resulting from the special conditions under which they were created, and the stage of their development.

Nationality Decrees issued in Tunis and Morocco (French Zone) on November 8, 1921, Advisory Opinion, 7 February 1923, PCIJ, *Series B,* No. 4 (1923) (hereinafter '*Nationality Decrees in Tunis and Morocco Case*'), 27, quoted in Crawford (above n. 1), 284 (emphasis in original). Despite this, Hurst Hannum regards Danzig as a situation where 'sovereignty resided in' the League, seemingly by virtue simply of the fact that the Free City was placed under the 'protection' of the League; H Hannum, *Autonomy, Sovereignty and Self-Determination* (revised edn, University of Pennsylvania Press, 1996), 378–9.

[48] Indeed, the word 'protection' is usefully contrasted with the provisions relating to the Allies in the pre-Free City period; the Allies were assigned 'all rights and title over the territory' (Versailles Peace Treaty, Art. 100). For the purposes served by the League's powers, see below, ch. 6, text from n. 86.

[49] Under the terms of the Versailles Peace Treaty, the Allies 'would proceed to erect the community who were the occupants of that territory [Danzig] into a free and independent community, having its own international status'; *The Blonde (Prize Court)* (above n. 43) (reversed by the Privy Council on other grounds), per Duke P., 162.

being part of Germany or Poland) and positive (in the sense of being a distinct entity). It was reinforced by the notion that the Free City was being 'protected' (from assimilation into the territory of a state, in this case either Germany or Poland), and that, according to the Versailles Treaty and followed in subsequent practice, the Free City was to constitute a distinct entity both internally (in having its own Constitution) and externally (in entering into an agreement with Poland). The Free City authorities not only claimed the right to exercise certain administrative prerogatives, but also to do so in their capacity as the 'Free City' itself. Although this was not a claim to statehood in the strict sense, it was an assertion that administrative prerogatives were exercised with respect to and on behalf of a distinct juridical entity.

In determining the status of the Free City, then, the starting point is that the entity was a distinct juridical entity; it cannot be considered under some form of Polish and/or League sovereignty. As the PCIJ stated in connection with Poland's rights in the Free City, since 'Danzig is not Polish territory', any rights enjoyed by Poland were 'exercised in derogation of the rights of the Free City'.[50] The status of the Free City turns on the juridical effect that these derogations had on the conformity of the Free City to the 'independence' criterion of legal statehood.

The matrix of administrative prerogatives enjoyed by the Free City authorities, Poland and the League is best understood in terms of a basic model of self-administration, on to which were grafted limitations whereby certain powers were transferred to either Poland or the League, or where the exercise of the powers by the Free City was subject to a foreign veto. Under the Danzig Constitution, the Free City was constituted along a model of self-administration, with provisions made for a locally-run Senate, Popular Assembly, and judicial system.[51] Whether or not the Free City could be considered 'independent' turns on the quality and quantity of the restrictions placed on self-administration, and the basis on which the powers enjoyed by Poland and the League were exercised.

Poland's administrative powers in the Free City covered three areas: customs; the Port, waterways, and railways; and foreign relations.[52] Poland and the Free City formed a single customs area under Polish customs regulations;[53] customs

---

[50] *Polish War Vessels in Danzig Case* (above n. 45), 142.

[51] The Free City's powers were set out in the Constitution of Danzig, originally adopted in 1922 and subsequently amended (Constitution of the Free City of Danzig, 11 May 1922, text in *League of Nations Official Journal*, Spec. Suppl. 7 (July 1922), 1, as amended, 9 September 1930, text in *League of Nations Official Journal* 1794 (December 1930), hereinafter 'Danzig Constitution'). For the dates of the Constitution, see Danzig Constitution, note 1. For the Free City's powers, see the Danzig Constitution, *passim*. On the locally constituted administrative structures within the Free City, see Mason (above n. 30), 61–6, 89–227; Ydit (above n. 16), 191–211; Hannum (above n. 47), 376–7.

[52] There were further entitlements that Poland enjoyed in relation to the Free City that can be understood in terms of preferential trade treatment (see Poland–Danzig Treaty (above n. 37), Arts 26, 28) rather than administrative prerogatives.

[53] Ibid., Art. 13.

matters were administered by Free City officials, with the participation of some Polish customs inspectors and under the overall direction of Polish officials.[54] A Port and Waterways Board was responsible for administering the Port, waterways and railway serving the Port, and associated property;[55] control of the remaining railways was divided between the Free City and Poland.[56] The Board consisted of equal numbers of Polish and Free City representatives, with a President jointly appointed (or appointed by the Council of the League if agreement was not forthcoming),[57] and profits and losses from the administration of the Port were to be divided between Poland and the Free City.[58] Post and telecommunications between Poland and the Port, and between Poland and foreign countries via the Port, were handled by a Polish-administered service;[59] all other such communications, both within the Free City and between the Free City and foreign countries, were to be administered by the Free City.[60] Organizations engaged in immigration or immigration services from or to Poland required authorization from Poland.[61]

Most authorities on the subject do not review these prerogatives when considering the status of the Free City, preferring to focus exclusively on Poland's foreign relations power and the League's prerogatives (discussed below). For example, in its consideration the PCIJ set out all the prerogatives enjoyed by Poland and the League in Danzig (including Poland's prerogatives summarized in the paragraph above), but only concerned itself with Poland's foreign relations powers and the League's powers when it came to determining the 'special juridical status' of the Free City.[62] This might have been due to an assumption that prerogatives in the economic sphere (the Court described the prerogatives outlined in the preceding paragraph as being 'of an economic character')[63] did not 'count' as a diminution of sovereignty. James Crawford refers to the 'important rights' Poland enjoyed with respect to Danzig's territory, which, given the context in which the remark is made, refers to the administrative prerogatives within the

---

[54] Ibid., Art. 14.

[55] Ibid., ch. III and in particular Arts 19 and 20.

[56] Ibid., Art. 21. Although it is unclear from this provision how the division was to be made in practice, the provision implied that railways not falling under the jurisdiction of the Port and Waterways Board according to Art. 20 were to be further divided between Poland and the Free City.

[57] Ibid., Art. 19.

[58] Ibid., Art. 23.

[59] Ibid., Art. 29.

[60] Ibid., Art. 31.

[61] Ibid., Art. 24.

[62] *Danzig and the ILO Case* (above n. 35), 11. According to the PCIJ:

[t]he special juridical status of the Free City is seen from the above to comprise two elements: the special relation to the League of Nations, by reason of its being placed under the protection of the League and by reason of the guarantee of the constitution, and the special relation to Poland, by reason of the conduct of the foreign relations of the Free City being entrusted to the Polish Government.

Ibid., 11.

[63] Ibid.

territory, rather than the foreign relations power.[64] For Crawford, these rights should be borne in mind when assessing Danzig's status.[65] Their significance in this regard will be considered once the other areas of alien administration have been reviewed: the foreign relations power of Poland, and the administrative powers of the League.

Poland was given general responsibility for the conduct of the Free City's foreign relations.[66] Certain detailed stipulations were made in this regard, including the power to make consular arrangements for foreign authorities operating within the Free City.[67] Neither the Treaty of Versailles nor the Poland–Danzig Treaty sets out the manner in which Poland was to exercise the general foreign relations power, and many disagreements arose between Poland and the Free City which were referred to the League Commissioner. In 1930, the PCIJ found that:

[i]t is now common ground between Poland and the Free City that the rights of Poland as regards the conduct of the foreign relations of the Free City are not absolute. The Polish Government is not entitled to impose a policy on the Free City nor to take any step in connection with the foreign relations of the Free City, against its will.[68]

It continued:

On the other hand, the Free City cannot call upon Poland to take any step in connection with the foreign relations of the Free City which are opposed to her own policy. As the League High Commissioner said in his decision of December 17th, 1921, were Poland obliged to do so, she would come under the domination of the Free City, and this was certainly not contemplated by the Treaty of Versailles.

The result is that, as regards the foreign relations of the Free City, neither Poland nor the Free City are complete masters of the situation.[69]

Here, the Court seems to be adopting one of the general principles of treaty interpretation, viz., taking into account 'subsequent practice in the application of the treaty which establishes the agreement of the parties regarding its interpretation'.[70] Two treaties arguably formed the basis for Poland's foreign relations power: the Treaty of Versailles and the Poland–Danzig Treaty. Whereas Poland was a party to both, the Free City was a party only to the latter.[71] However,

---

[64] Crawford (above n. 1), 239.   [65] Ibid.

[66] Poland–Danzig Treaty (above n. 37), ch. II. These provisions were stipulated in the Versailles Peace Treaty, Art. 104. See also Danzig Constitution (above n. 51), Arts 41, 45.

[67] Poland–Danzig Treaty (above n. 37), Art. 4.

[68] *Danzig and ILO Case* (above n. 35), 13.

[69] Ibid.

[70] Vienna Convention on the Law of Treaties, 23 May 1969, 1155 UNTS 331, Art. 31(3)(b). Article 31 of the Vienna Convention is generally accepted as embodying customary international law; see, e.g., *Kasikili/Sedudu Island (Botswana v Namibia), ICJ Reports 1998*, 1045, paras 18 and 48–50.

[71] In the *Danzig and ILO Case*, the PCIJ stressed that, even where the provisions of the Versailles Peace Treaty were repeated in the Poland–Danzig Treaty, the former treaty was the 'source' of Poland's rights covered by later stipulations; *Danzig and ILO Case* (above, n. 35), 11.

in identifying practice relevant to the interpretation of rights and obligations contained in treaties, one should arguably look to the bearers of these rights and obligations.[72] In the case of Poland's foreign relations powers in the Treaty of Versailles, then, it is a question of looking at the practice of the rights-holder (Poland) and the entity which was obliged to permit the rights in question to be exercised (the Free City), rather than the parties to the Treaty of Versailles *qua* parties.

In the light of the PCIJ's finding, the situation (at least by 1930) would seem to have been that, although Poland was responsible for the conduct of Danzig's foreign affairs, it was restricted in the exercise of these powers in that it could only take decisions with the agreement of the Free City. Thus, the powers were exercised by Poland, but only with the Free City's agreement.[73]

On the conclusion of treaties in particular, Poland was already obliged to consult the Free City authorities before concluding any treaty that would affect the Free City.[74] The League High Commissioner was to be informed of the result of this consultation, and enjoyed a general right to veto such a treaty if in the opinion of the League Council it was inconsistent with the Poland–Danzig Treaty or the status of the Free City.[75] Bearing in mind the foregoing observation about the exercise of the foreign relations power generally, in the specific sub-field of treaty conclusion, it would seem that Poland was obliged, not only to consult the Free City, but also to obtain its agreement before signature. Equally, it would seem that, as far as the League Commissioner's veto was concerned, one circumstance inconsistent with the Poland–Danzig Treaty would have been if Poland had failed to obtain the agreement of the Free City before concluding an agreement on its behalf.

There was not, in any case, a wholesale delegation of foreign relations powers to Poland: foreign loans were to be contracted by the Free City authorities, in consultation with Poland (with disputes settled by the League High Commissioner);[76] the registration of ships flying the flag of Danzig was to be made by the Free City authorities, with the obligation to notify (not consult) Poland about the terms of these registrations;[77] the Free City authorities were given responsibility for the control of foreigners in the Free City, subject to Poland's rights in the

---

[72] The general approach, reflected in Art. 31 of the Vienna Convention on the Law of Treaties (above n. 70), is to look at the practice of the parties to the treaty; however, this arguably presupposes that the rights and obligations in the treaty operate reciprocally as between these parties, rather than, as was the case here, operating as between one party (among many) to the treaty and a third party.

[73] James Crawford describes these powers as 'an agency arrangement with a right of veto'; Crawford (above n. 1), 239.

[74] Poland–Danzig Treaty (above n. 37), Art. 6.

[75] Ibid., Art. 6.

[76] Ibid., Art. 7.

[77] The Free City's responsibility for flag ship registration is implicit in ibid., Art. 8.

Free City;[78] and the Free City was primarily responsible for issuing passports to Danzig nationals, with Poland enjoying the right to issue passports in certain special circumstances.[79]

What was the legal significance of the League's administrative prerogatives on the status of the Free City? Here, the relevant powers do not, despite the suggestion of most commentators, include the initial approval of the Constitution, since this took place prior to the Free City's creation.[80] The first relevant prerogative concerned military matters: League approval was necessary before the Free City could make arrangements to do the following things:

(1) serve as a military or naval base; (2) erect fortifications; (3) authorise the manufacture of munitions or war material on its territory.[81]

In the second place, the League, supported by the PCIJ, interpreted its role as guarantor of the Constitution in the Treaty of Versailles to include two powers relating to the Constitution beyond initial approval.[82] As set out in the Constitution itself, League approval was also necessary before any constitutional amendments could be made[83] and the League enjoyed the right to intervene where necessary if the Constitution was being applied incorrectly.[84] In the third place, the League

---

[78] Poland–Danzig Treaty (above n. 37), Art. 12. The meaning of this provision is unclear, but what is assumed is that there were certain rights falling outside the scope of Poland's prerogatives vis-à-vis foreigners in the Free City that were either explicit or could be inferred from Poland's powers in the Poland–Danzig Treaty.

[79] Agreement between Poland and the Free City of Danzig relative to the issue of Danzig passports to Danzig citizens abroad ('Poland–Danzig Passport Agreement'), 4 May 1924, 120 (1924) *BFSP* 227, Art. 1 (for the Free City's rights). Poland could issue or renew passports only if the applicant had a passport that had expired within the past three months (ibid., Art. 2), or in 'urgent or exceptional circumstances' such as the sudden death of a relative it could issue a Danzig passport of three months' validity (ibid., Art. 5); Poland could also hand out passports issued by the Free City (ibid., Art. 3). This regime replaced the arrangement instituted by the decision of the League Commissioner earlier that year (ibid., Art. 9). See generally D Turack, 'Passports Issued by Some Non-State Entities, 43 (1968–9) *BYIL* 209, 209–12.

[80] Another commentator who also excludes a consideration of the initial approval role when considering the Free City's status is James Crawford; see Crawford (above n. 1), 239.

[81] Danzig Constitution (above n. 51), Art. 5. For examples of the exercise of this power, see Lewis (above n. 30), 91.

[82] Versailles Peace Treaty, Art. 103.

[83] Danzig Constitution (above n. 51), Art. 49.

[84] For this interpretation of the guarantor role, see the Report of Viscount Ishii, adopted by the League Council on 17 November 1921, point (3), which stated that the guarantor role implied 'that the constitutional life of the Free City of Danzig must always be in accordance with the terms' of the Constitution (the passage is quoted in *Treatment of Polish Nationals Case* (above n. 36), at 21). Endorsing this interpretation, the PCIJ stated that '[t]he League, as guarantor of the Constitution, is therefore concerned not merely with the text of the Constitution, but also with the proper application of it'; ibid., 21. So the League, '... as guarantor of the Constitution of the Free City, has the right—which in practice, it exercises through the Council—as well as the duty, to intervene in the event of an erroneous application by Danzig of its Constitution'; ibid., 21. The Court cited the provision of Art. 42 of the Constitution, where the Free City Senate was obliged to '... furnish to the League of Nations at any time upon the request of the latter, official information regarding the public affairs of the Free City.' For the Court, the existence of this provision supported the existence of a responsibility concerning the application of the Constitution; the object of this provision

was entitled to veto treaties concluded by Poland affecting the Free City if such agreements were inconsistent with the provisions of the Poland–Danzig Treaty or the status of the Free City.[85] The fourth and final League prerogative was the power to appoint the president of Danzig's Port and Waterways Board if the Free City and Poland failed to agree on an appointment.[86]

In sum, foreign actors exercised administrative prerogatives with respect to the Free City in the following manner. In the sphere of domestic administration, Poland enjoyed the power to set the customs law and direct the customs administration, to share on an equal basis the administration of the Port and the railways, and to administer a portion of the post and telecommunications (viz., those relating to the Port) and immigration services (viz., those relating to Poland); the League enjoyed a power of veto over certain military arrangements and amendments to the Constitution, and the right to appoint a particular government official if the Free City and Poland could not agree on a candidate. In the sphere of foreign affairs, Poland was generally responsible for the conduct of the Free City's foreign relations (with the Free City enjoying certain prerogatives in this field), although it had to obtain the consent of the Free City in the exercise of this power; the League could veto any treaties concluded by Poland that fell within a certain category.

If one considers these powers as diminutions in the 'independence' of the Free City, then, taken together, they would not seem to amount to a serious intrusion into the independence of the Free City. Significant areas of administrative control were still left in the hands of the Free City authorities,[87] and some of the administrative powers of Poland and the League operated only as a reactive veto in relation to administrative prerogatives exercised by the Free City.[88] It should be noted here that the independence criterion of statehood does not contain a particularly high threshold; as James Crawford states, independence is of a 'predominantly formal' character for the purposes of statehood and 'statehood may coincide with substantial lack of actual independence'.[89]

---

was 'to enable the League to exercise its rights and fulfil its duties concerning inter alia the actual application of the Constitution' (ibid., 21).

[85] Poland–Danzig Treaty (above n. 37), Art. 6.

[86] Ibid., Art. 19. The League Council was to be requested by the High Commissioner to appoint a Swiss national to the position.

[87] On the domestic prerogatives enjoyed by Poland, Crawford remarks (without discussing the nature of these prerogatives) that 'the local administration did not cease to be independent in respect of all other matters'; Crawford (above n. 1), 239.

[88] On the League's powers relating to constitutional amendments, the PCIJ stated that 'the interpretation of the Danzig Constitution is primarily an internal question of the Free City', which 'may involve the guarantee of the League of Nations as interpreted by the Council and by the Court'; *Consistency of Certain Danzig Legislative Decrees with the Constitution of the Free City, Advisory Opinion*, PCIJ, *Series A/B*, No. 65 (1935), 13, cited in Crawford (above n. 1), 239.

[89] J Crawford, *The Creation of States in International Law* (OUP, 1979), 169 (although these remarks are not included in the second edition of the same work; see Crawford (above n. 1), 243–4).

A further factor needs to be borne in mind, moreover: the basis on which these powers enjoyed by Poland and the League were exercised. As already discussed, the enjoyment of administrative prerogatives, and its effect on issues of sovereignty and territorial title, are often considered without consideration of the basis on which the prerogatives are asserted. All other things being equal, the enjoyment of territorial prerogatives by a particular actor necessarily supports the proposition that the actor in question enjoys title over the territory, and undermines such a proposition in relation to a rival actor.

To adopt such an approach, however, it is necessary to assume two related things about the basis on which the prerogatives were being exercised by Poland and the League. In the first place, it must be assumed that the two actors were acting only on their own behalf, and not (also) on behalf of another legal entity, the Free City. In the second place, it must also be assumed that, in acting on its own behalf, the state or international organization was operating in a particular capacity: as the sovereign entity in its own territory.

The first assumption can be seen in the dicta of the PCIJ and its individual judges, who considered the basis of Poland's enjoyment of its administrative prerogatives in Danzig exclusively in terms of pursuing its own interests. In one instance, the Court stated that the consequence of Poland's enjoyment of foreign relations powers was that:

Poland is entitled to care for her own interests and to refuse to take any action which would be prejudicial to them.[90]

In a later passage, the Court stated that:

... the conduct of the foreign relations of the Free City is entrusted to the Government of Poland...in consequence the Free City is not in a position to oblige the Polish Government to take any action in the conduct of those foreign relations which is contrary to the interests of Poland herself.[91]

When the Court considered certain foreign relations activities that as such fell within the scope of Poland's powers, it stated that:

... [the] Polish Government would be entitled to refuse to take these steps on behalf of the Free City if they were prejudicial to the important interests of the Polish state.[92]

In his dissenting opinion, Judge Anzilotti reinforced the position of the majority on this issue, stating that the foreign relations rights of Poland in Danzig:

... have been conferred on her [Poland] in her own interests, the interests of the Free City being sufficiently safeguarded by the protection of the League of Nations.[93]

---

[90] *Danzig and ILO Case* (above n. 35), 13.
[91] Ibid., 15.
[92] Ibid.
[93] Ibid., dissenting opinion of Judge Anzilotti, 24. See also the dissenting opinion of Judge Huber, ibid., at 32.

It was assumed that, insofar as Poland enjoyed powers, these were to be exercised in pursuit of the state's 'own interests', and that these interests were to be understood in binary terms when compared with the interests of the Free City: each set of interests was mutually exclusive. It would appear, then, that Poland could only exercise these powers on its own behalf, and not also on behalf of the Free City.

Given what has already been said in the previous chapter about the different bases on which administration can be performed, this assumption cannot be made.[94] One can explain Poland and the League's powers as operating in two distinct senses concurrently. On the one hand, Poland and the League acted on their own behalf—the administrative acts of each actor in Danzig were, juridically, the 'acts' of Poland and the League. At the same time, the acts could also be performed in a second capacity, with the League and Poland acting also on behalf of the Free City. Thus, individual administrative acts were performed on behalf of two distinct legal persons simultaneously.

Powers exercised on behalf of the Free City should be understood differently from those exercised by Poland and the League only on their own behalf. Arguably, one difference is that powers in the former category did not derogate from the independence of the Free City. In the case of Poland's foreign relations powers in particular, just because a single entity—the government of Poland—exercised powers with respect to Poland and the Free City, it does not follow that the entity exercised those two sets of powers in the same capacity. It could just as easily have been exercising each set in a different capacity, one only on its own behalf, and the other both on its own behalf (but as agent), and on behalf of the Free City. Into which category did the Danzig-related powers fall?

Given that the enjoyment of administrative powers by Poland and the League was not predicated on an assumption that these two entities were sovereign, in the sense of enjoying title, over Danzig (because of the absence of claims to this effect), it follows that neither entity can be considered to have been exercising the powers on its own behalf in the capacity of a territorial sovereign. Given this, and bearing in mind that the Free City was a distinct juridical entity (thereby creating the possibility of a distinct, sovereign unit and an agency relationship between it and Poland and the League), Poland and the League must have been exercising the Free City powers with respect to the Free City as a separate entity, on that separate entity's behalf as the territorial sovereign.

On Poland's foreign relations power in particular, insofar as Poland did enjoy such a power, the basis on which it was exercised meant that it bolstered, rather than undermined, the Free City's independence. Although, then, in practical terms the foreign-relations power amounted to the assimilation of the Free City to Poland, on a political and a juridical level, a distinction between these two entities continued to exist. Thus, it would seem that treaties entered into by Poland would operate with respect to the territory of both Danzig and Poland because in this

---

[94] See above, ch. 3, section 3.3.

instance, agreement by 'Poland' amounted to agreement by two distinct jurid-ical entities—Poland and the Free City—rather than because Danzig was part of Poland.

It may be, therefore, that, due to the particular agency relationship involved, the administrative prerogatives of the League and Poland need not be weighed against the powers of the Free City authorities in order to determine whether or not Danzig was 'independent'. These prerogatives, although carried out by distinct legal persons, were exercised on behalf of the Free City as the territor-ial sovereign and as such were acts of that entity. But even if this approach is not adopted, the prerogatives would in any case not seem to amount to such a signifi-cant diminution in the Free City's independence as to disqualify the entity from statehood.

As James Crawford points out, the notion that the Free City was a state is supported by the fact that the Free City had its own distinct nationality,[95] and the existence of a *jurisprudence constante* in favour of statehood in the case law of the PCIJ and national courts,[96] including the High Court of Danzig in the *Danzig*

---

[95] Crawford (above n. 1), 240; this is set out in Versailles Peace Treaty, Art. 105: 'On the com-ing into force of the present Treaty German nationals ordinarily resident in the territory described in Article 100 will ipso facto lose their German nationality in order to become nationals of the Free City of Danzig'. See also Poland–Danzig Passport Agreement 1924 (above n. 79) and Turack (above n. 79), 209–12. Crawford (ibid.) asserts that 'Danzig was eligible for membership of inter-national organizations such as the League, subject to Polish rights of veto' but does not explain the basis for this assertion (nor does he discuss its relevance to the status of the Free City, with refer-ence to the membership criteria of international organizations). The PCIJ did consider whether the special status of the Free City was compatible with membership of the International Labour Organization, i.e., whether, if it were a member, the Free City would have been able to discharge its obligations fully, given the powers of Poland in the field of foreign affairs. The Court highlighted the problem of needing Polish consent if and when the requirements of membership necessitated the Free City taking steps that fell within the foreign relations power of Poland vis-à-vis the City (*Danzig and ILO Case* (above n. 35), 15–16). It considered that if an agreement were to be reached between Poland and Danzig, whereby Poland gave its consent in advance to the Free City taking such steps, then 'the fact that conduct of the foreign relations of the Free City is entrusted to the Polish Government would not constitute an obstacle' to the Free City joining the ILO (ibid., 16). This finding was without prejudice to the larger question of whether or not the Free City would satisfy the membership criteria for the ILO, an issue that the Court did not regard itself as having jurisdiction over in the case in question (ibid., 10). Whether or not the Free City would be able to discharge its responsibilities as a member would not, by itself, seem to be relevant to the question of its status.

[96] Crawford (above n. 1), 240. For the decisions of national courts in this regard, see ibid., at 240, n. 210. The Judicial Division of the Council for the Restoration of Legal Rights in the Netherlands regarded the Free City (before Nazi annexation) as '… a State within the meaning of public inter-national law'; *In re Nix et al*, The Netherlands, Council for the Restoration of Legal Rights (Judicial Division), The Hague, 14 September 1951, 18 (1951) *ILR* 260, 261. The basis for this finding is not explained. In *The Blonde* of 1922 before the Privy Council, Lord Sumner cited a proposition, form-ing part of a broader submission, that Danzig was a 'newly constituted State'; although the submis-sion itself was dismissed on another point, the particular proposition was not rejected; *The Blonde and Other Ships* [1922] 1 A.C. 313 (Privy Council) (hereinafter '*The Blonde (Privy Council)*'), 338. The judgment of the Prize Court in 1921, whose decision was reversed by the Privy Council on other grounds, described Danzig as a 'new State' having a 'Sovereign character'; *The Blonde (Prize Court)* (above n. 43), 164, per Duke P.

Pension Case.[97] According to the PCIJ, Poland was obliged to treat the Free City as if it were a state, and was therefore not entitled to assert prerogatives within the Free City that were not authorized by international law:

...the fact that the legal status of Danzig is *sui generis* does not authorize [Poland] to depart from the ordinary rules governing relations between States and to establish new rules for the relations between Poland and Danzig. The general principles of international law apply to Danzig, subject, however, to the treaty provisions binding upon the Free City and to decisions taken by the organs of the League under these provisions.[98]

As far as Poland's position in relation to the Free City is concerned, the PCIJ took the view that the Danzig Constitution 'is and remains the Constitution of a foreign State',[99] and, in discussing the relationship between Poland and Danzig, the Court applied 'generally accepted [international legal] principles' concerning the relationship between two states,[100] and remarked that:

[t]he application of the Danzig Constitution may...result in the violation of an international obligation incumbent on Danzig towards Poland, whether under treaty stipulations or under general international law...[101]

Thus international law—which for the PCIJ meant the law applicable between states—was in play as between the Free City and Poland.

It would seem, therefore, that the Free City of Danzig was a state[102] at the time that the Poland–Danzig Treaty was agreed (1920) and for the duration of the administrative powers enjoyed by the League that were partially authorized by that instrument.[103]

4.2.3 Memel 1924–39

As with Danzig, under the Treaty of Versailles, Germany renounced its 'rights and title' with respect to the Memel territory (now called Klaipeda, in present-day Lithuania) in favour of the Principal Allied and Associated Powers.[104]

---

[97] According to the High Court of Danzig, the Free City was 'an independent State'; *Danzig Pension Case*, High Court of Danzig, 5 (1929–30) *ILR* 66, at 67.

[98] *Treatment of Polish Nationals Case* (above n. 36), 23–4.

[99] Ibid., 24.

[100] Ibid.

[101] Ibid.

[102] Crawford (above n. 1), 240, *contra* I Brownlie, *Principles of Public International Law* (6th edn, OUP, 2003), 76. Turack includes the Free City within a discussion of 'non-state entities' which enjoy 'recognition as subjects of international law' but does not explain his basis for its inclusion within this classification, or what the classification means; Turack (above n. 79), 209–12, quotation from 209. On the Free City's status, see also Smyrek (above n. 15), 58–67.

[103] For the status of the Free City after this period, i.e., from 1 September 1939, see *In re Kruger*, 18 (1951) *ILR* 258; *In re Nix* (above n. 96); Skubiszewski (above n. 30), 470; Crawford (above n. 1), 241 and sources cited therein; Whomersley (above n. 30), 926–7.

[104] Versailles Peace Treaty, Art. 99. For a map of the location, see, e.g., Whomersley (above n. 30), 928.

Under the 1924 Convention of Paris, Britain, Italy, France, and Japan transferred to Lithuania, '...subject to the conditions contained in this Convention, all the rights and titles ceded to them by Germany in virtue of Article 99 of the Treaty of Versailles...'[105] over the Memel territory, which was to be 'under the sovereignty of Lithuania'.[106] Under the Statute, Memel was to be given considerable autonomy from the central Lithuanian government under the administration of a Directorate comprising local officials who were either appointed by the central government or elected by the people of the territory.[107] The Port was declared to be 'of international concern'[108] and administered by a Harbour Board comprising three persons, appointees of the Lithuanian Government, the Memel Directorate and, as mentioned in Chapter 2, a League official.[109]

Despite the suggestion of considerable internationalization made by some commentators,[110] the Memel arrangement only involved a sliver of international involvement in territorial administration, via the League appointee as one of three members on the Harbour Board. In every other respect, the administration of the territory was an arrangement of significant autonomy, not 'internationalization'. Given this, there would seem no basis to conclude that this arrangement placed the sovereignty of Lithuania over the territory under serious question.

4.2.4 Leticia 1933–34

The need for the next administration project under consideration arose, not because of the legacy of the First World War within particular European territories, as with the Saar, Danzig, and Memel, but, rather, as a consequence of a particular dispute between two Latin American states in the 1930s. In 1933, the Colombian town and district of Leticia was invaded and occupied by Peruvian irregular forces, who pledged to defend the town if Colombia attempted to drive them out.[111] Plenary administration by a League Commission, accompanied by the withdrawal of the Peruvian irregulars, was introduced for a maximum

---

[105] Lithuania–Principal Allied Powers, Convention Concerning the Territory of Memel ('Memel Convention'), 8 May 1924, 29 LNTS 87, Art. 1.

[106] Ibid., Art. 2 and Annex I, Art. 1.

[107] Ibid., Annex I.

[108] Ibid., Annex II, Art. 1.

[109] Ibid., Annex II, Art. 5 (on the composition) and 6 (on the Board generally).

[110] E.g., Ydit, who considers Memel within a general category of territories 'under the sovereignty of the League of Nations' (Ydit (above n. 16), title of ch. 3). For commentary on the status of the territory after the period that is the focus of the present analysis, see, e.g., Whomersley (above n. 30), 923–4.

[111] For background, see, e.g., Walters (above n. 28), 525–6, 536–40; Ydit (above n. 16), 59–62; JV Czerapowicz, *International Territorial Authority: Leticia and West New Guinea* (1972, unpublished Ph.D. dissertation, Indiana University, on file with the author), 6–94; LH Woolsey, 'The Leticia Dispute Between Colombia and Peru', 27 (1933) *AJIL* 317; LH Woolsey, 'The Leticia Dispute Between Colombia and Peru', 29 (1935) *AJIL* 94.

one-year period.[112] Before the end of this term, Peru and Colombia entered into a border agreement and control of the territory was transferred from the League to the Colombian authorities.[113]

What was the status of the territory for the period of League administration? Colombia exercised no governmental control in the territory, but the League Commission administered it 'in the name of the Government of Colombia'; Colombia was responsible for the Commission's expenses and the cost of administration;[114] the Colombian flag flew alongside the League flag and Colombia provided troops for the Commission.[115] According to one commentator, there was common acceptance between Peru, Colombia, and the League that Leticia was part of Colombia.[116] Given this, and the fact that the League Commission purported to act on behalf of Colombia, in administering the territory, there seems little doubt that the territory remained Colombian, for the duration of the administration project.[117] Why League administration rather than Colombian control was introduced in conjunction with the withdrawal of the Peruvian irregulars is discussed in Chapter 6.

4.3 Newly Independent Congo 1960–64

The introduction of administration arrangements in the Congo coincided with the creation of the state. Local representatives of the territory that had formed the Belgian Congo declared independence as 'The Republic of the Congo' on 30 June 1960.[118] The day after, the Congo applied for admission to the UN; membership was recommended by the Security Council on 7 July and accepted by the General Assembly on 20 September.[119] The Congo was 'widely recognized'

[112] Agreement between Colombia and Peru Relating to the Procedure for Putting into Effect the Recommendations Proposed by the Council of the League of Nations ('Colombia–Peru Agreement 1933'), 25 May 1933, 138 LNTS 253. On this agreement, see the League of Nations statement on Leticia, 14 (1933) *League of Nations Official Journal* 944–5; Walters (above n. 28), 538–40; Ydit (above n. 16), 59–61; Czerapowicz (above n. 111), 9–18; LH Woolsey, 'The Leticia Dispute Between Colombia and Peru', 29 (1935) *AJIL* 94, 95–99. On the composition and administrative powers of the Commission, see above, ch. 2, n. 14. Commission administration was introduced on 23 June 1933 (Ydit, ibid., 61; Czerapowicz, ibid., 24; Woolsey, ibid., 96).

[113] Protocol of Friendship and Co-operation between Colombia and Peru, 24 May 1934, 164 LNTS 21. The Commission withdrew from Leticia on 19 June 1934 (see Ydit, above n. 16, 62; Czerapowicz, above n. 111, 94; Woolsey, above n. 112, 96).

[114] Colombia–Peru Agreement 1933 (above n. 112), Arts 2, 7, respectively.

[115] Czerapowicz (above n. 111), 27–9 (on the flag); Ydit (above n. 16), 61 and Woolsey (above n. 112), 96 (on the troops).

[116] Czerapowicz (above n. 111), 16.

[117] See also Smyrek (above n. 15), 76–9.

[118] See M Whiteman, *Digest of International Law*, vol. 2 (US Department of State, 1963), 147–8; D Bowett, *United Nations Forces: A Legal Study* (Stevens & Sons, 1964), 153.

[119] See SC Res. 152, 23 August 1960; GA Res. 1480 (XV), 20 September 1960; Bowett (above n. 118), 153.

as a State.[120] Conflict broke out immediately on independence, following a mutiny by soldiers in the *Armée Nationale Congolaise* against their Belgian officers.[121] On 9 July, Belgium reinforced its troop garrisons that had remained in the country, and on 10 July these troops moved to exercise control in certain parts of the country, against the wishes of the new Congolese government.[122] On 11 July, Moise Tchombé, considered pro-Western (and in particular pro-Belgian), declared independence on the part of Katanga, a province where Belgium's mining interests in the Congo were primarily located.[123] Tchombé appointed Belgian nationals in charge of Katanga's civil administration, later appointing seconded Belgian officers to lead the territory's army.[124] Order broke down in the country generally,[125] and on 12 July 1960 the government made a request for assistance to the United Nations which led to the creation of the United Nations Operation in the Congo (known by its French acronym, ONUC), lasting from 1960 to 1964.[126]

Following the request to the UN, and for the duration of ONUC, the Congolese government exercised little control over the country, and no control in Katanga; indeed, the raison d'être for ONUC became the reversal of this situation, as the project attempted to assist the Congolese government in the operation of government institutions, to operate such institutions directly, and forcibly to end the Katangese attempt at secession. Since, as James Crawford remarks, 'anything less like effective government...would be hard to imagine', this situation raises the question of whether the Congo constituted a state for the period in question.[127] It can be argued that the international recognition of the Congo as a state was premature; alternatively, that this recognition was constitutive of statehood in the absence of conformity to the criterion of effective governmental control.[128] For Crawford, the better view is that the criterion applies differently in different circumstances, and that, in the case of the Congo, it can be seen as having been met because the standard required in those particular circumstances was low, bearing in mind the wide recognition of Congo's statehood, its membership of the United Nations, and the clear commitment internationally to its continued existence evidenced in the creation of ONUC.[129]

---

[120] Crawford (above n. 1), 57.
[121] WJ Durch, 'The UN Operation in the Congo: 1960–1964', in Durch (ed.), *The Evolution of UN Peacekeeping* (St. Martin's Press, 1994), 315, at 317.
[122] Ibid., 318.   [123] Ibid.
[124] Ibid.
[125] Ibid., 317–18.
[126] For the Congolese request, see SC Res. 143, 14 July 1960, second preambular sentence, and Telegrams dated 12 and 13 July 1960 from the President and the Prime Minister of the Republic of the Congo to the UN Secretary-General, UN Doc. S/4382; UN SCOR, 15th year, Supp. (July, August and September 1960), 11. For ONUC, see the sources cited above, ch. 2, n. 17.
[127] Crawford (above n. 1), 57.
[128] Ibid.
[129] Ibid., 57–8. A potentially mediating factor here is the special treatment of colonial territories within the law of self-determination, but whether it made any difference is unclear. On self-determination, see below, ch. 5, section 5.2.

4.4 States and State Territories After the End of the Cold War: Cambodia, Somalia, and Northern Iraq

Other than the consultation projects covered in the following chapter, and the administration of refugee camps in economically under-developed countries discussed below, there were no international territorial administration projects in states or state territories after the Congo until the end of the Cold War.[130] From 1991 onwards, and forming part of the broader increase in peace operations facilitated by the resurgence in UN Security Council activity, the use of international territorial administration in such territorial entities mushroomed. The entities in this category can be divided into two groups. For the three discussed in the present section—Cambodia, Somalia, and Northern Iraq—territorial status was the continuance of a situation that had prevailed for some time before the administration projects were introduced. For the Balkan quartet discussed in the next section, by contrast, this status was in the process of being established at the same time as the projects took place.

4.4.1 Cambodia 1991–93

When, in 1991, international territorial administration was introduced at the level of an entire state, as it had been in the 1960s with ONUC, the state, although a former colony like the Congo, had been legally independent for decades. Cambodia, which became a state in 1953 having formed part of French Indochina,[131] had been subject to a 20-year conflict that ended with the 1991 Paris Agreements which provided, inter alia, for partial administrative prerogatives, including the conduct of elections, exercised by the United Nations Transitional Authority in Cambodia (UNTAC) for an interim period.[132]

---

[130] The historical factors that conditioned the use of ITA over time are discussed below, ch. 8, sections 8.4–8.7.

[131] See Crawford (above n. 1), Appendix 1, at 729 and Appendix 3, at 748; SR Ratner, 'The Cambodian Settlement Agreements', 87 (1993) *AJIL* 1, 2.

[132] See the agreements adopted in Paris on 23 October 1991 (hereinafter '1991 Paris Agreements'): Final Act of the Paris Conference on Cambodia; Agreement on a Comprehensive Political Settlement of the Cambodia Conflict (hereinafter 'Cambodia Settlement Agreement'), with Annex 1, UNTAC mandate; Annex 2, 'Withdrawal, Ceasefire and Related Measures'; Annex 3 on 'Elections', Annex 4 on 'Repatriation of Cambodian Refugees and Displaced Persons' and Annex 5 on 'Principles for a New Constitution for Cambodia'; Agreement Concerning the Sovereignty, Independence, Territorial Integrity and Inviolability, Neutrality and National Unity of Cambodia; Declaration on the Rehabilitation and Reconstruction of Cambodia. The text of the 1991 Paris Agreements is contained in the Annex to the Letter dated 30 October 1991 from the Permanent Representatives of France and Indonesia to the United Nations addressed to the Secretary-General, UN doc. A/46/608-S/2317730 (1991). The Cambodia Settlement Agreement established a ceasefire, mandated the removal of foreign troops and the end of other foreign military interference, and introduced measures for arms disposal, demining, and troop demobilization (Cambodia Settlement Agreement, ibid., Arts 8–11; Annex 1, section C; Annex 2). It also allowed for the

Vietnam had invaded the country in 1979, replacing the Khmer Rouge government with a government that ruled the state as the People's Republic of Kampuchea (PRK),[133] and, from 1989, Cambodia,[134] until the Paris Agreements. In 1982 the three resistance factions—the faction around the Sihanouk royal family[135] (King Sihanouk had ruled the country from 1958 to 1970),[136] the Khmer People's National Liberation Front,[137] and the Khmer Rouge (who ruled the country as Democratic Kampuchea from 1975 until the Vietnamese invasion in 1979)[138]—joined forces to form an exile 'Coalition Government of a Democratic Kampuchea'.[139] According to Steven Ratner:

[d]uring the 1980s, approximately 30 countries...recognized and maintained diplomatic relations with the PRK. Almost 80 countries recognized Democratic Kampuchea as the government of Cambodia, although it maintained active diplomatic relations with only about 10...Other states...did not regard the PRK, Democratic Kampuchea or the Coalition Government as the government of Cambodia.[140]

The Coalition Government represented the country as Democratic Kampuchea at the United Nations until 1990.[141] The situation during the 20 years of conflict raises the question of which particular faction could legitimately claim to be the government of the state;[142] there is no doubt, however, that the state, whatever its name, continued to exist as a juridical entity for the period in question and at the signing of the Paris Agreements. At the United Nations, for example, the only issue as far as the country's membership was concerned related to the question of

release of prisoners of war (ibid., Arts 21–22; Annex 2, Art. XI), the return of displaced persons (ibid., Arts 19–20; Annex 2, Art. III; Annex 4), and the protection of human rights generally (ibid., Arts 15–17; Annex 1, section E). Finally, it initiated an international rehabilitation and reconstruction programme (ibid., Art. 24; see also Declaration on the Rehabilitation and Reconstruction of Cambodia). On the Agreements see, e.g., JE Heininger, *Peacekeeping in Transition: The United Nations in Cambodia* (Twentieth Century Fund Press, 1994), 9–30; T Findlay, *Cambodia: The Legacy and Lessons of UNTAC* (OUP, 1995), 1–20; J Sanderson, 'The Cambodian Experience: A Success Story Still?', in R Thakur and A Schnabel (eds), *United Nations Peacekeeping Operations: Ad Hoc Missions, Permanent Engagement* (UN University Press, 2001), 155; Ratner (above n. 131), 2–8 and sources cited at 2 n. 2 and 3 n. 7; United Nations Department of Public Information, *The United Nations and Cambodia* 199 1–1995 (United Nations Blue Book Series, 1995), 5–9; DPL Chong, 'UNTAC in Cambodia: A New Model for Humanitarian Aid in Failed States?', 33 (2002) *Development and Change* 957; S Peou, 'Collaborative Human Security? The UN and Other Actors in Cambodia', 12:1 (2005) *International Peacekeeping* 105. On UNTAC's responsibility for carrying out the elections, see above, ch. 2, n. 35; for its other administrative responsibilities, see below, ch. 6, n. 110.

[133] Ratner (above n. 131), 3.
[134] Ibid., 7.
[135] Known as the 'United National Front for an Independent, Neutral, Peaceful and Cooperative Cambodia', or, more commonly in French, the 'Front Uni National pour un Cambodge Indépendant, Neutre, Pacifique, et Coopératif' (FUNCINPEC).
[136] Ratner (above n. 131), 2–3.
[137] Ibid., at 4, n. 16.
[138] Ibid., at 3.
[139] Ibid., at 4, n. 16.
[140] Ibid., at 9, n. 45.
[141] Ibid., at 4, n. 16; Roth (above n. 1), 281.
[142] For a discussion of this in the 1979–90 period, see ibid., 280–3.

which faction could represent the state at the organization (and so determine its name);[143] Cambodia's membership was not itself in question.

One of the key objectives of the 1991 Paris Agreements was to attempt to resolve the rivalry between the four Cambodian factions by providing for elections to a popularly-elected government to be carried out by UNTAC.[144] An interim body called the Supreme National Council (SNC), comprising the four Cambodian factions, was conceived both to provide consent for the Agreements on behalf of Cambodia, and to be the legitimate governmental entity with respect to the country in the 'transitional period' before the elections had been carried out and the new popular government elected, during which UNTAC would exercise certain administrative prerogatives.[145] These arrangements concerned the particularities of government with respect to Cambodia, assuming continued Cambodian statehood for the interim period and beyond. Mere changes in government and/or the name of the state do not by themselves alter the juridical personality of the state[146] (provided that each actor concerned purports to be the government of the same juridical unit, and that the name changes refer to the same state, as was the case here). Thus, Cambodia was a state at the time that UNTAC's administrative prerogatives were authorized, and for the duration of its mandate in the country.

4.4.2 Somalia 1992–95

Barely a year after the Cambodia project was first conceived, international territorial administration was introduced into another former colonial state that had suffered from civil war after independence, this time in Africa. The case of Somalia during the second UN Operation in Somalia (UNOSOM II) period implicates a different aspect of the governmental criterion for statehood from the case of Cambodia: not the juridical consequence of changes in the identity of those actors exercising governmental control on the continued existence of the state but, rather, the effect on this continued existence of a lack of governmental control in the territory.[147] After the military overthrow of President Siad Barre's government in 1991, order in the country collapsed.[148] Somalia was divided into those areas under no overall control, territorial units controlled by

[143] For this issue in the 1979–90 period, see ibid., 281.

[144] On this objective for the Agreements, see the sources cited in n. 145 below on the Supreme National Council (SNC). On UNTAC's role in carrying out the elections, see above, ch. 2, n. 35.

[145] For the establishment of the transitional period, see Cambodia Settlement Agreement (above n. 132), Art. 1. On the SNC, see, e.g., Findlay (above n. 132), 57–8, and Ratner (above n. 131), 9–11. The SNC was declared to be the 'unique legitimate body and source of authority' with respect to Cambodia (Cambodia Settlement Agreement, ibid., Art. 3) and represented the country externally (ibid., Art. 5). On UNTAC's administrative responsibilities, see below, ch. 6, n. 110.

[146] Crawford (above n. 1), 678–80.

[147] For commentary, see, e.g., DJ Harris, *Cases and Materials on International Law* (6th edn, Sweet & Maxwell, 2004), 101; AA Yusuf, 'Government Collapse and State Continuity: the Case of Somalia', 13 (2003) *Italian Yearbook of International Law* 11, *passim*; see also Crawford (above n. 1), in particular the passages quoted below in n. 155.

[148] Harris (above n. 147), 101; Yusuf (above n. 147), 13–15.

militias, locally-selected authorities or clan-based governance structures, and the north-western territory of Somaliland which declared its independence in the same year.[149] It became the paradigmatic example of a state without an effective government,[150] and led to the international intervention in the country, which, in the case of UNOSOM II, involved the exercise of certain administrative prerogatives in an effort to construct basic governmental structures.[151]

Despite its manifest lack of an effective overall government, Somalia continued to be recognized as a state and as a member of the United Nations; Somaliland was not recognized as a state.[152] However, the governmental criterion for juridical statehood would not seem to have much significance by itself in terms of the continuance of an existing state, rather than the creation of a new one, bearing in mind the presumption in favour of the continuance of the status quo mentioned earlier. Writing in 1968, Krystina Marek stated that:

[c]ustomary international law does not supply any definite criterion for determining when a State ceases to exist.[153]

And that:

[t]he absence of effectiveness does not necessarily mean the extinction of a State.[154]

According to James Crawford, when the entity is a state, its status as such is, within broad limits, not lost 'by more or less prolonged anarchy within the state'; in the footnote to this assertion, Crawford states that: '[t]he strength of the presumption is demonstrated ... by the fact that scarcely any doubt has been expressed as to the continuity of States such as Somalia ...'.[155] For David Harris:

[s]tate practice suggests that the requirement of a 'stable political organization' in control of territory does not apply during a civil war or where there is a collapse of law and order in a state that already exists.[156]

---

[149] Harris (above n. 147), 101; Yusuf (above n. 147), 15–16.

[150] In 1993, it was held in the English courts that 'Somalia currently has no government'; *Republic of Somalia v Woodhouse, Drake & Carey (Suisse) SA* [1993] 1 All ER 371, [1993] QB 54.

[151] On UNOSOM II see the sources cited above, ch. 2, n. 22.

[152] On the continued recognition of Somalia as a state, including through UN membership, see the discussion in Yusuf (above n. 147), 23–5. On the non-recognition of Somaliland, see Harris (above n. 147), 101.

[153] Marek (above n. 1), 7.

[154] Ibid., 8. In their version of *Oppenheim's International Law*, Sir Robert Jennings and Sir Arthur Watts do not include governmental collapse in their various scenarios for state extinction (R Jennings and A Watts (eds), *Oppenheim's International Law, Vol. 1, Peace* (9th edn, Longman, 1992), § 59); in a separate discussion of the concept of the state in international law, they observe that '... once a state is established, temporary interruption of the effectiveness of its government, as in a civil war ... is not inconsistent with the continued existence of the state', ibid., 122. See also Yusuf (above n. 147), 19.

[155] Crawford (above n. 1), 701 n. 3. Elsewhere in the same book, James Crawford observes that '[a] State can continue to exist for example even if its government is reduced to relative impotence (e.g., ... Somalia 1991–2004 ...)'; ibid., 694, and gives Somalia as an example of the situation where 'the existence of territory and people have compensated for the virtual absence of a central government'; ibid., 223.

[156] Harris (above n. 147), 101.

For Ian Brownlie:

[o]nce a State has been established, extensive civil strife or the breakdown of order through foreign invasion or natural disasters are not considered to affect personality.[157]

As far as international law was concerned, then, the legal issues raised by the governmental breakdown were restricted to the question of which entity could lawfully represent the state, not whether or not the state continued to exist.[158] Insofar as there are limits to the principle that lack of governmental control does not by itself affect continued statehood, as suggested by Crawford, the Somalia case is evidence that they are not reached even in circumstances of total governmental collapse, although the degree of international commitment to the continued existence of the Somali state, reflected in the international efforts aimed, inter alia, at restoring some form of government in the territory, can be considered as having had a juridical effect, in the manner of recognition in certain marginal cases of new states,[159] in preventing the extinction of Somalia as a juridical entity. Concluding that, as a matter of international law, the state of Somalia continued in 'suspended animation' during and beyond the period under present evaluation, Abdulqawi Yusuf highlights as significant the fact that:

...the international community...has been constantly trying to breath (sic) new life into the comatose Somali State and keep it in suspended animation pending its effective revival,[160]

and states that:

[t]he main factor that has militated...against the death of the Somali State for lack of central government has been its maintenance as a member of the United Nations and of the Organization of African Unity (now the African Union).[161]

It is difficult to say, therefore, whether or not the limits might have been met by the Somali situation had there not been such an international commitment to Somali statehood.

4.4.3 The Governorates of Arbil, Dihouk, and Suleimaniyeh in Northern Iraq 1996–2003

At the same time that the ambitious international arrangements in Croatia and Bosnia and Herzegovina, considered below, were being introduced, a similarly intrusive mechanism was conceived in relation to northern Iraq.

---

[157] Brownlie (above n. 102), 71.
[158] See generally the discussion in Yusuf (above n. 147), 17 *et seq.*
[159] On this 'constitutive' role for recognition, see, e.g., Crawford (above n. 1), at 26–8; see also ibid., at 93: '[recognition] may also tend to consolidate a general legal status at that time precarious or in the process of being constituted'.
[160] Yusuf (above n. 147), 21.
[161] Ibid., 21 and 23. See also ibid., 23–8 and the overall conclusion at 31.

During the UN-authorized military campaign of 1991 to liberate Kuwait following the Iraqi invasion—Operation Desert Storm—the coalition states encouraged the Kurds in the north and the Shiites in the south to rebel against the Iraqi government.[162] The two UN Security Council resolutions passed at the end of Operation Desert Storm contained no provisions relating to the position of these groups in Iraq,[163] and initially no arrangements were made by the coalition forces to protect the groups once Iraqi forces had been driven out of Kuwait and a ceasefire agreement entered into by Iraq.

When the Iraqi government subsequently launched a military offensive against the two populations, the Security Council passed Resolution 688 on 4 April 1991; in provisions not adopted under Chapter VII of the UN Charter, it called for Iraq to end the repression of its civilian population and allow access by humanitarian organizations.[164] When Iraqi persecution continued, France, the US, and the UK, without a mandate from the Security Council, took forcible measures under 'Operation Restore Comfort' to drive Iraqi troops out of the Kurdish and Shiite areas and provide humanitarian aid to the affected populations;[165] they then imposed no-fly zones with respect to Iraqi aircraft above the 36th parallel (protecting the Kurdish area) and below the 33rd parallel (protecting the Shiite area).[166]

A 1996 Memorandum of Understanding between the UN and Iraq created the Oil-for-Food Programme, which allowed the Iraqi government to sell oil to pay for 'humanitarian supplies' (e.g., medicine and foodstuffs) in most of the country.[167] For the three Governorates of Arbil, Dihouk, and Suleimaniyeh, covering the main Kurdish areas in the north, the 'UN Inter-Agency Humanitarian Programme' rather than the Iraqi government would be responsible for distributing humanitarian supplies paid for by Iraqi oil revenues.[168]

---

[162] C Gray, *International Law and the Use of Force* (2nd edn, OUP, 2004), 33–4.

[163] SC Res. 686, 2 March 1991 and SC Res. 687, 3 April 1991.

[164] SC Res. 688, 5 April 1991, paras 2 and 3. For the background, see, e.g., Gray (above n. 162), 33–4.

[165] Ibid., 34.

[166] France ended its participation in patrolling the no-fly zone in 1996; see ibid., 36. On the no-fly zones, see also A Bernard, 'Lessons from Iraq and Bosnia on the Theory and Practice of No-fly Zones', 27 (2004) *Journal of Strategic Studies* 454; see also E Benvenisti, *The International Law of Occupation* (paperback edn, Princeton University Press, 2004), 181.

[167] Memorandum of Understanding between Iraq and the United Nations on the Implementation of Security Council Resolution 986 (1995) (hereinafter 'Iraq MOU'), 20 May 1996, UN Doc. S/1996/356 (1996). See also SC Res. 986, 14 April 1995. Both resolutions and other relevant UN documents are obtainable from the website of the UN Office for the Iraq Programme, at <http://www.un.org/Depts/oip/index.html>. The Oil-for-Food Programme was adjusted to meet the exigencies of the post-war situation shortly after the invasion of Iraq by US and UK forces (see SC Res. 1472, 28 March 2003 and above, ch. 2, n. 59) and terminated on 21 November 2003, pursuant to SC Res. 1483, 22 May 2003.

[168] For these arrangements, see the sources cited above, ch. 2, n. 59.

The effect of the no-fly zone above the 36th parallel, which covered Arbil, most of Dihouk and part of Suleimaniyeh, and the humanitarian supplies distribution arrangements for these Governorates, was to render the area of the Governorates, popularly known as 'Iraqi Kurdistan', *de facto* independent of Iraqi governmental control.[169] Politically, there were disagreements between different Kurdish factions; the two main factions—the Patriotic Union of Kurdistan (PUK) and the Kurdistan Democratic Party (KDP)—formed a joint administration in 1992, but this broke down with an armed confrontation between the two groups.[170] After a peace agreement between the leaders of the groups in 1998, on 4 October 2002, the elected local Parliament reconvened with both leaders present.[171] Although many Iraqi Kurds aspired to independence from Iraq, no declaration to this effect was made by their representatives or by the local Parliament during the relevant period.

The Memorandum of Understanding conceived the UN Inter-Agency Humanitarian Programme distribution in a manner that implied continued Iraqi sovereignty as-title in the area. It was stipulated that '[n]othing in the present Memorandum shall be construed as infringing upon the sovereignty or territorial integrity of Iraq'.[172] The particular arrangements dealing with distribution in the three Governorates were to be 'implemented with due regard to the sovereignty and territorial integrity of Iraq'.[173] Under these arrangements, at one stage in the distribution-process the Iraqi government had to be involved in discussions with the Programme on the most efficient method of procurement;[174] at two further stages, the Programme was under an obligation to keep the Iraqi government informed.[175] It would seem, therefore, that the three Governorates covered by the Inter-Agency Humanitarian Programme fell within Iraqi territory, albeit enjoying total autonomy from the government of Iraq, for the duration of the Programme.[176]

---

[169] On 'Iraqi Kurdistan' see, e.g., T Judah, 'In Iraqi Kurdistan', 44:4 (2002) *Survival* 39; GRV Stansfield, *Iraqi Kurdistan: Political Development and Emergent Democracy* (Routledge, 2003); N Carver, 'Is Iraq/Kurdistan a State Such That It Can Be Said to Operate State Systems and Thereby Offer Protection to its "Citizens"?', 14 (2002) *International Journal of Refugee Law* 57.

[170] 'Iraqi Kurds reconvene parliament', BBC News, 4 October 2002, available at <http://news.bbc.co.uk/1/hi/world/middle_east/2298411.stm>.

[171] Ibid.

[172] Iraq MOU, above n. 167, Art. 3.

[173] Ibid., Annex I, para. 1.

[174] Ibid., para 3.

[175] Ibid., paras 6 and 7.

[176] Cf. J Crawford, 'State Practice and International Law in Relation to Unilateral Secession', Report for the Attorney General of Canada, 19 February 1997, reproduced in A Bayefsky (ed.), *Self-determination in International Law: Quebec and Lessons Learned* (Kluwer, 2000), 31, at 53, para. 52.

The Programme was terminated after the removal of the government of Saddam Hussein in 2003; all those involved in governing Iraq from that point forward—the Coalition Provisional Authority and, subsequently, the Interim and Transitional Governments—proceeded on the basis that the three Governorates, including, in particular, the Kurdish areas in the north, had remained at all times part of Iraqi territory.[177]

4.5　Balkan Quartet: Bosnia and Herzegovina, Mostar, Eastern Slavonia, and Kosovo

In the Balkans in the mid-1990s, international territorial administration returned to the general European region of the original inter-war quartet in the first half of the 20th century, again with four projects: Mostar, Bosnia and Herzegovina generally, Eastern Slavonia, and Kosovo. The legal status of these four territories is bound up in the violent conflict within the Socialist Federal Republic of Yugoslavia (SFRY) from 1991 onwards, the claims to independent statehood made by several of its constituent entities, and, in the case of Kosovo, the NATO bombing campaign and subsequent UN administration in 1999.[178]

---

[177] For the termination, see above, ch. 2, n. 59. See, e.g., the Iraqi Interim Constitution (Law of Administration for the State of Iraq for the Transitional Period, 8 March 2004, English translation available at <http://www.cpa-iraq.org/government/TAL.html> and <http://www.oefre.unibe.ch/law/icl/iz00000_.html>, in particular Ch. 8 (Arts 52–58), making special provision for the continued autonomy of the Kurdish Governorates within the federal system. See also Chapter Five of the Constitution of 2005, approved by a referendum held on 10 October 2005 (English translation available at <http://www.msnbc.msn.com/id/9719734/>), which makes specific reference to the region of Kurdistan in Art. 113 (1) when laying out the new federal system.

[178] On the violent disintegration of the SFRY and the international response to it, see generally, e.g., S Trifunovska, *Yugoslavia Through Documents: From its Creation to its Dissolution* (Martinus Nijhoff, 1994); D Owen, *Balkan Odyssey* (Victor Gollancz, 1995); S Woodward, *Balkan Tragedy: Chaos and Dissolution after the Cold War* (Brookings Institution, 1995); M Glenny, *The Fall of Yugoslavia: The Third Balkan War* (3rd edn, 1996); L Silber and A Little, *The Death of Yugoslavia* (2nd edn, 1996); D Bethlehem and M Weller (eds), *The 'Yugoslav' Crisis in International Law: General Issues Part I* (CUP, 1997); B de Rossanet, *War and Peace in the Former Yugoslavia* (Kluwer Law International, 1997); B Ramcharan (ed.), *The International Conference on the Former Yugoslavia: Official Papers* (2 vols, Kluwer Law International, 1997); C Bildt, *Peace Journey: The Struggle for Peace in Bosnia* (Weidenfeld & Nicolson, 1998); RC Holbrooke, *To End a War* (Random House, 1998); SL Burg and PS Shoup, *The War in Bosnia-Herzegovina: Ethnic Conflict and International Intervention* (M E Sharpe, 1999); S Trifunovska, *Yugoslavia Through Documents: From its Dissolution to the Peace Settlement* (Martinus Nijhoff, 1999); M Weller (ed.), *The Crisis in Kosovo 1989–1999: From the Dissolution of Yugoslavia to Rambouillet and the Outbreak of Hostilities* (CUP, 1999); I Daalder, *Getting to Dayton: The Making of America's Bosnia Policy* (Brookings Institution Press, 2000); D Chandler, *Bosnia: Faking Democracy after Dayton* (2nd edn, Pluto Press, 2000); Crawford (above n. 1), 395–401; M Weller, 'The International Response to the Dissolution of the Socialist Federal Republic of Yugoslavia', 86 (1992) *AJIL* 569; M Weller, 'International Law and Chaos', 52 (1993) *Cambridge Law Journal* 6; S Woodward, 'Remarks' in 'Yugoslavia' Panel, 90 (1996) *ASIL Proc.* 471. On Kosovo, see the sources cited above in ch. 1, n. 4, below in section 4.5.3, and in the Sources List, section 5.1.2 and, where relevant, 5.1.1.

The responses of states to these claims, particularly those of European states, as articulated by the Arbitration Committee of the International Conference on the Former Yugoslavia (the so-called 'Badinter Committee'), was to regard this process as one of a disintegrating/dissolving state (the SFRY), rather than the equally plausible scenario of a series of purported secessions.[179] The ex federal republics were regarded as the only entities entitled to exercise what was in effect 'external' self-determination and, in accordance with the principle of *uti possidetis*, there were to be no changes to the existing internal frontiers.[180]

4.5.1 Bosnia and Herzegovina from 1994; Mostar 1994–96

Unlike the previous European arrangements, which had all been introduced after peace settlements, the European Union Administration in Mostar (EUAM) arrangement was introduced during the conflict; the Office of the High Representative in Bosnia and Herzegovina (OHR), by contrast, followed the earlier European model, being introduced in the territory once armed hostilities had largely ended with the Dayton Peace Agreements. In order to determine the juridical status of the territories subject to the administrative activities of the EUAM and OHR, it is necessary to establish the status of Bosnia and Herzegovina in general, and Mostar in particular, from 1994.

The government of Bosnia and Herzegovina, hitherto one of the six constituent Republics of the SFRY, adopted a sovereignty resolution on 14 October 1991, the validity of which was challenged by Bosnian Serb representatives in the

---

[179] On the EC recognition process and the 'Badinter Committee', see, e.g., European Community, Guidelines on the Recognition of New States in Eastern Europe and in the Soviet Union, 16 December 1991, 31 (1992) *ILM* 1486; European Community, Declaration on Yugoslavia, 16 December 1991, 31 (1992) *ILM* 1485; Arbitration Committee of the International Conference on the Former Yugoslavia ('Badinter Committee'), *Opinions on Questions Arising From the Dissolution of Yugoslavia* (hereinafter '*Badinter Committee Opinions*'), reproduced in 31 (1992) *ILM* 1494 (*Badinter Committee Opinions Nos 1–10*) and 32 (1993) *ILM* 1586 (*Badinter Committee Opinions Nos 11–13*); S Terrett, *The Dissolution of Yugoslavia and the Badinter Arbitration Commission: A Contextual Study of Peace-Making Efforts in the Post-Cold War World* (Ashgate, 2000); Crawford (above n. 1), 401; A Pellet, 'The Opinions of the Badinter Arbitration Committee: A Second Breath for the Self-Determination of Peoples', 3 (1992) *EJIL* 178; R Badinter, 'L'Europe du droit', 3 (1993) *EJIL* 15; C Warbrick, 'The Recognition of States Part 2', 42 (1993) *ICLQ* 433; M Craven, 'The European Community Arbitration Commission on Yugoslavia', 66 (1995) *BYIL* 333. On the 'dissolution' approach, see *Badinter Committee Opinions Nos 1* and *3*. For the position before the UN, see SC Res. 757, 30 May 1992; SC Res. 777, 19 September 1992; GA Res. 47/1, 22 September 1992. On the status of the FRY/Serbia and Montenegro/Serbia, see below, n. 220.

[180] *Badinter Committee Opinions Nos 2* and *3* (above n. 179). See J Crawford, 'State Practice and International Law in Relation to Secession', 69 (1998) *BYIL* 85, reprinted in J Crawford, *International Law as an Open System* (Cameron May, 2002), 199 at 214; Crawford (above n. 1), at 396–7; cf. the criticism of the approach taken by the Committee, ibid., at 401 and the comments at 418. The right to self-determination and the doctrine of *uti possidetis* are discussed below, ch. 5, section 5.2; for academic commentary on the former, see the sources cited ibid., n. 3. On the options for the exercise of the right of (external) self-determination see ibid., n. 4 and accompanying text.

territory.[181] An independence referendum, boycotted by the Bosnian Serbs, was then held on 29 February 1992; the overwhelming result was in favour of independence.[182] Fighting broke out after the result,[183] but Bosnia and Herzegovina was recognized as a state by the EC and the US on 7 April 1992,[184] and admitted as a member of the United Nations on 22 May 1992[185] following a recommendation by the Security Council.[186]

The Badinter Committee retrospectively declared Bosnia and Herzegovina to have become a state on 6 March 1992.[187] At this time, and for the duration of the conflict leading up to the Dayton Peace Agreements in 1995, the only regime in favour of the statehood of Bosnia and Herzegovina—the Bosnian Muslim/ Bosniak government of Bosnia and Herzegovina—failed to exercise control over most of the territory which it claimed constituted the state. Territory was controlled by the Bosnian Serbs, who asserted the continued existence of the old Yugoslavia with Bosnia and Herzegovina as a constituent Republic, or alternatively independence or union with the Republic of Serbia/the Federal Republic of Yugoslavia as a 'Greater Serbia', and the Bosnian Croats, who favoured independence as the state of 'Herzeg-Bosna' or union with Croatia.[188] Despite this, the process of recognition and admission to UN membership demonstrated an unequivocal international commitment to the notion that Bosnia and Herzegovina was somehow a state, albeit a commitment that did not extend to any form of effective military action to support the state from internal and external threats.

The situation in Bosnia and Herzegovina during this period demonstrates the constitutive role that recognition can sometimes play in circumstances

---

[181]   *Badinter Committee Opinion No. 1* (above n. 179), para. 2.

[182]   Weller, 'The International Response…' (above n. 178), 593 and source cited therein at n. 145; Warbrick (above n. 179), 435, and source cited therein at n. 14. Weller states the date to be 1 March; Warbrick 29 February. According to Weller (ibid.), almost 63 per cent voted for independence.

[183]   Warbrick (above n. 179), 435.

[184]   With the European Community, the decision was made on 6 April, with recognition taking place on 7 April. See European Political Cooperation (EPC) Ministerial Meeting, Declaration on Yugoslavia (Brussels, 6 April 1992), reproduced in C Hill, *European Foreign Policy: Key Documents* (Routledge, 2000), 376; EC Declaration on Recognition of Bosnia and Herzegovina, 6 April 1992, UN Doc. S/23793, Annex. For commentary, see, e.g., J Klabbers, M Koskenniemi, O Ribbelink and A Zimmerman (eds), *State Practice Regarding State Succession and Issues of Recognition* (Kluwer Law International, 1999), 61; Weller, 'The International Response…' (above n. 178), at 593. On the US recognition, see President Bush's Statement on the Recognition of Bosnia and Herzegovina, Croatia and Slovenia, 7 April 1992, reprinted in 18 (1992) *Review of International Affairs* 26. Certain EC member states recognized Bosnia and Herzegovina separately; for the UK, Austria, Belgium, and Sweden, see Klabbers, Koskenniemi, Ribbelink, & Zimmerman, ibid., 64–5, and documents cited therein. For commentary on both the EC and the US recognition, see Warbrick (above n. 179), 435 and sources cited therein at n. 16.

[185]   GA Res. 46/237, 22 May 1992.

[186]   SC Res. 755, 20 May 1992.

[187]   *Badinter Committee Opinion No. 11* (above n. 179), at 1589.

[188]   For a consideration of the legal status of the area controlled by the Bosnian Serbs before the Dayton agreements, see, e.g., *Kadic v Karadzic*, 70 F.3d 232 (2d Cir. 1995), 13 October 1995, heading 3 subheading (a).

where one or more of the criteria for statehood—in this case the existence of a government exercising effective control in the territory—are not met.[189] Arguably, Bosnia and Herzegovina became a state as a matter of law, if not as a practical reality, as a result of this process of recognition, somewhat later in 1992 than the date suggested by the Badinter Committee (which—ironically—was adhering to an absolutist position on the declaratory nature of recognition)[190] but well before there was effective governmental control in the state.[191] Certainly, by 1994, at the time of the introduction of the EUAM, and 1996, when OHR began its mandate in the country, Bosnia and Herzegovina was a generally recognized to be a state.

When the EUAM was introduced in Mostar, the city was politically and militarily split into West and East, the two halves controlled, respectively, by the Bosnian Croats and the Bosnian Muslims/Bosniaks.[192] Although the Bosnian Croat leaders in Mostar professed the same aspirations as the Bosnian Croat leaders in Bosnia and Herzegovina generally, viz. joining Croatia or achieving independent statehood as 'Herzeg-Bosna', the international commitment to the statehood of Bosnia and Herzegovina implicitly ruled these assertions out, since they necessitated the secession of part of the state territory. Thus, West Mostar, although under the control of a secessionist regime, formed part of the state of Bosnia and Herzegovina alongside East Mostar. This was bolstered by the introduction of the EUAM itself, since it purported to govern the whole of Mostar as a single entity forming part of Bosnia and Herzegovina.[193]

4.5.2 Eastern Slavonia 1996–98

The overwhelming focus on Bosnia and Herzegovina at the Dayton negotiations has perhaps led to another agreement reached as part of the same overall process to be overlooked, despite the fact that this agreement—concerning Eastern Slavonia in Croatia—marked the first ever introduction of plenary UN territorial administration.

Croatia, one of the other constituent Republics of the SFRY, held a referendum on independence in May 1991, and declared independence on 25 June 1991;

---

[189] See Crawford (above n. 1), 27–8; D Türk, 'The Dangers of Failed States and a Failed Peace in the Post Cold War Era', 27 (1995) *NYU Journal of International Law & Politics* 625, 625–6.

[190] As far as the 'existence or disappearance of the State' is concerned, 'the effects of recognition by other States are purely declaratory'; *Badinter Committee Opinion No. 1* (above n. 179), para. 1(a).

[191] See C Hillgruber, 'The Admission of New States to the International Community', 9 (1998) *EJIL* 491, text accompanying n. 8. On this question, see also Smyrek (above n. 15) ch. IX and Milano (above n. 1), 165–6.

[192] On the divisions in Mostar, see, for example, Owen (above n. 178), 239; Glenny (above n. 178), 246; International Crisis Group, *Reunifying Mostar: Opportunities for Progress*, 19 April 2000, obtainable from <http://www.crisisgroup.org>.

[193] See the discussion below, ch. 6, section 6.3.2.

this declaration of independence was initially suspended for three months, and confirmed on 8 October 1991.[194]

Croatia was recognized as a state by the member states of the European Community on 15 January 1992,[195] and admitted as a member of the United Nations by the General Assembly on 22 May 1992[196] following a recommendation by the Security Council.[197] The Badinter Committee retrospectively asserted that Croatia had become a state on 8 October 1991.[198] At this time, a significant portion of territory claimed by the regime in Zagreb as part of its state (having been within the original Republic boundary)—Eastern Slavonia and the Krajina—was occupied by Serb forces.[199] The Krajina came under Croatian government control in the summer of 1995, following a surprise military operation. Eastern Slavonia remained under the control of the local Serb militias loyal to what was then the FRY until the start of 1996,[200] and did not come under Croatian control until 1998. Under the 1995 Basic Agreement entered into at the same time as the Dayton Peace Agreements by the 'local Croatian Serb representatives', i.e., the Serb militias,[201] and Croatia, the militias gave up control of Eastern Slavonia, and the territory was administered by the United Nations Transitional Administration in Eastern Slavonia (UNTAES) for a 'transitional period', lasting from 1996 to 1998, before being transferred to the control of Croatia.[202]

The legal position of Croatia generally during the period in which Eastern Slavonia was administered by the UN is perhaps best understood in the same

---

[194] *Badinter Committee Opinion No. 1* (above n. 179), para. 2.

[195] On the recognition date in particular, see Statement of the Presidency on the Recognition of Yugoslav Republics, 15 January 1992, EPC Press Release 9/92, cited in Weller, 'The International Response...' (above n. 178), 586 n. 113; Klabbers, Koskenniemi, Ribbelink, & Zimmerman (above n. 184), 66–70, and sources cited therein (including details of individual member states' recognition of Croatia); *Keesing's Record of World Events*, vol. 38 (1992), 38703 cited in Craven (above n. 179), at 377, n. 257.

[196] GA Res. 46/238, 22 May 1992.

[197] SC Res. 753, 18 May 1992.

[198] *Badinter Committee Opinion No. 11* (above n. 179), at 1589.

[199] Craven (above n. 179), 377 at n. 257.

[200] For the Serb occupation prior to this date, see Silber and Little (above n. 178), 370–1; Holbrooke (above n. 178), 236–9.

[201] The quotation is taken from the text of the Letter dated 15 November 1995 from the Permanent Representative of Croatia to the United Nations to the Secretary-General, UN Doc. A/50/757-S/1995/951 to which was annexed the Basic Agreement on the Region of Eastern Slavonia, Baranja and Western Sirmium (hereinafter 'Eastern Slavonia Basic Agreement').

[202] For UNTAES and the duration of the transitional period, see above, ch. 2, n. 24. Under the Eastern Slavonia Basic Agreement (above n. 201), during the transitional period Eastern Slavonia was to be demilitarized (para. 3), human rights generally were to be respected (para. 6), refugees and displaced persons were to return and enjoy the same rights as current residents (paras 4, 7), certain property rights were to be enforced (paras 8, 9), and local elections were to be held (para. 12). On the elections, see above, ch. 2, n. 37. The eventual handover to Croatia was implicit in the Agreement (see M Bothe, 'The Peace Process in Eastern Slavonia', 3 (1996) *International Peacekeeping* 6, at 6), and realized in the eventual outcome. See also R Paris, *At War's End: Building Peace After Civil Conflict* (CUP, 2004), 108; R Caplan, *International Governance of War-Torn Territories: Rule and Reconstruction* (OUP, 2005), 3.

way as that of Bosnia and Herzegovina during the same period. Despite the government of Croatia failing to enjoy control over significant parts of the territory claimed as constituting the state (although controlling more than was the case in Bosnia and Herzegovina), and certain borders being disputed, the international policy of recognition had the juridical effect of constituting Croatian statehood in accordance with the claim put forward by the Croatian authorities, necessarily validating the government's claim to sovereignty with respect to Eastern Slavonia and the Krajina and, in turn, delegitimizing the basis on which the Serb forces occupied these territories.[203] The Basic Agreement itself did not stipulate the status of Eastern Slavonia, nor the juridical relationship between the two parties—Croatia and the local Serb representatives—and the territory. However, when the letter containing the Agreement was communicated to the General Assembly and the Security Council, it was recorded as a UN document under an Agenda item entitled 'The Situation in the Occupied Territories of Croatia'.[204] In its original resolution endorsing the Basic Agreement, the Security Council emphasized, in a preambular paragraph, that the territories of Eastern Slavonia 'are integral parts of the Republic of Croatia'.[205]

This situation did not change with the introduction of UN administration. As with other administration projects, the mandate of the UN was conceived exclusively in terms of exercising administration, without any explicit or implicit enjoyment of sovereignty-as-title with respect to the territory. Under the Basic Agreement, the Transitional Administration was to 'govern' Eastern Slavonia.[206] Moreover, a provision in the Basic Agreement allowing the introduction of international monitors at some point during the period of UN administration was authorized specifically by the Croatian Government; this can be seen as an implicit acknowledgment of Croatian sovereignty during this period.[207] Finally, in most of its resolutions relating to Eastern Slavonia passed once the UN administration was under way, the Security Council repeated its earlier statement on the territory forming part of Croatia.[208] Although, then, the territory was not under the control of the Croatian government from the start of Croatia's statehood

[203] See R Higgins, *Problems and Process: International Law and How We Use It* (OUP, 1994), 44–5 and Crawford (above n. 1), 50–1, 556–7.

[204] See Eastern Slavonia Basic Agreement (above n. 201).

[205] SC Res. 1023, 22 November 1995, preamble, paras 1–2.

[206] Eastern Slavonia Basic Agreement (above n. 201), para. 2. See also SC Res. 1023, above, n. 205, para. 11.

[207] The provision reads:

[d]uring the transitional period the Croatian Government authorizes the presence of international monitors along the international border of the region [the term 'region' is used in the Agreement to refer to Eastern Slavonia] . . .

Eastern Slavonia Basic Agreement (above n. 201), para. 13.

[208] SC Res. 1037, 15 January 1996, preamble, para. 2; SC Res. 1079, 15 November 1996, preamble, para. 2; SC Res. 1120, 14 July 1997, preamble, para 2; SC Res. 1145, 19 December 1997, preamble, para. 2.

until 1998, it nonetheless formed part of that state throughout the period of Serb occupation and UN administration.

4.5.3 Kosovo from 1999

The international peace negotiations during 1995 relating to the conflict in the territories of the SFRY, although not focusing exclusively on Bosnia and Herzegovina, as is sometimes suggested (cf. Eastern Slavonia), did concern themselves only with the site of the existing conflict—Bosnia and Herzegovina—and an outstanding claim made by one of the other states involved—Croatia in relation to Eastern Slavonia. The question of Kosovo did not fall into either of these categories, and was consequently ignored. However, it was in Kosovo, after the 1999 NATO bombing campaign, that the second plenary UN administration project was introduced, expanding the coverage of ITA in the Balkans from Bosnia and Herzegovina and Croatia to part of what was then called the Federal Republic of Yugoslavia, later the State Union of Serbia and Montenegro and now the Republic of Serbia.[209]

Prior to the conflict in the first half of the 1990s, Kosovo was not one of the six 'Republics' of the SFRY, but enjoyed a form of special autonomy, progressively reduced from 1989 and finally revoked in 1990, within the Serb Republic.[210] Although the Kosovar Albanians claimed a right of 'external' self-determination, this issue was not addressed directly either by the Badinter Committee or under the Dayton Peace Agreements, and the territory remained under the control of the then FRY authorities, who claimed Kosovo as an integral part of FRY territory. The introduction of UN administration and KFOR military occupation in 1999 effectively removed all of the official presence—both civilian and military—of both the federal government of the then FRY and the Republic of Serbia (the constituent state republic within which Kosovo was located).

These arrangements were authorized by instruments asserting the enjoyment of sovereignty (as title) on the part of the FRY with respect to the territory. Security Council resolution 1244 reaffirmed:

---

[209] On the background to the introduction of UNMIK in Kosovo, including the NATO bombing campaign, see above, ch. 1, n. 4. On the legal status of the larger entity within which Kosovo is located, see below, n. 220.

[210] H Poulton, *The Balkans: Minorities and States in Conflict* (2nd edn, Minority Rights Publications, 1993), 68–70; A March and R Sil, *The 'Republic of Kosova' (1989–1998) and the Resolution of Ethno-Separatist Conflict: Rethinking 'Sovereignty' in the Post-Cold War Era* (University of Pennsylvania–Browne Center for International Politics, 1999); N Malcolm, *Kosovo. A Short History* (Macmillan, 1998), 343 *et seq.*; M Vickers, *Between Serbian and Albanians: A History of Kosovo* (Hurst & Co., 1998), 241–6; C Stahn, 'Constitution Without a State? Kosovo under the United Nations Constitutional Framework for Self-Government', 14 (2001) *LJIL* 531, at 532–4; H Strohmeyer, 'Collapse and Reconstruction of a Judicial System: The United Nations Missions in Kosovo and East Timor', 95 (2001) *AJIL* 46, 80.

...the commitment of all Member States to the sovereignty and territorial integrity of the Federal Republic of Yugoslavia.[211]

Repeating the formulation that was agreed to by the FRY in a Peace Plan that preceded the resolution,[212] in a provision passed under Chapter VII of the UN Charter, the Security Council authorized:

...an interim administration for Kosovo under which the people of Kosovo can enjoy substantial autonomy within the Federal Republic of Yugoslavia...[213]

The word 'within' clearly implies an arrangement whereby the FRY enjoyed title over Kosovo; it could have no other meaning given that the FRY authorities were not to exercise any administrative control in the territory.[214] Although, then, sovereignty as control was removed, sovereignty as title was affirmed, as further reflected in the consent to the arrangements given by what was then the FRY in the preceding Peace Plan.[215]

However, the future of this arrangement was left uncertain, since the same instruments also placed Kosovo's eventual status in question, creating the possibility that there would be an alteration of this status at some point in the future depending on the outcome of negotiations.[216] The duration of the UN administration was tied to this outcome; unlike the Eastern Slavonia project, which was for a fixed period and assumed the indefinite continuation of the legal status subsisting during the project, the Kosovo project was to last until such an outcome was forthcoming, and sovereignty as control could be transferred to those representatives of whichever entity prevailed.[217]

Whether or not Kosovo enjoyed an 'external' self-determination entitlement during the period of UNMIK administration would seem to turn on the juridical consequences of the break up of the SFRY in the early 1990s, bearing in mind the 'dissolution' theory mentioned above and the question of Kosovo's status within the SFRY prior to the conflict, and the human rights situation in Kosovo prior to the introduction of UNMIK administration. A full consideration of this complex

---

[211] SC Res. 1244, 10 June 1999, preamble, para. 10.

[212] Agreement on the Principles (Peace Plan) to Move Towards a Resolution of the Kosovo Crisis Presented to the Leadership of the Federal Republic of Yugoslavia by the President of Finland, Martti Ahtisaari, representing the European Union, and Viktor Chernomyrdin, Special Representative of the President of the Russian Federation (hereinafter 'Kosovo Peace Plan'), 3 June 1999, UN Doc. S/1999/649, Annex, para. 5.

[213] SC Res. 1244 (above, n. 211), para. 10.

[214] On the meaning of 'substantial autonomy' in a situation where the Serb and FRY authorities appeared to enjoy no territorial control whatsoever, see the commentary below in ch. 6, n. 79 and accompanying text.

[215] So Steven Ratner states that the FRY as 'territorial sovereign' consented to UNMIK: see SR Ratner, 'Foreign Occupation and International Territorial Administration: The Challenges of Convergence', 16 (2005) *EJIL* 695, at 679, n. 6.

[216] See SC Res. 1244 (above, n. 211), para. 11(e) and Annex 1, para. 6; Kosovo Peace Plan (above n. 212), para. 8.

[217] See SC Res. 1244 (above, n. 211), para. 11(f). This is discussed further below in ch. 6.

issue is beyond the scope of this book,[218] although the human rights situation in Kosovo, and its potential relevance to 'external' self-determination, is addressed in Chapter 7 when considering the use of ITA to implement certain areas of international law.[219] For the present enquiry on the narrower issue of Kosovo's status during UNMIK administration, however, it is possible to arrive at an answer exclusively with reference to the foundational instruments of the project.

Arguably, the affirmation of FRY title made by the Security Council under Chapter VII in Resolution 1244 was constitutive of the subsistence of this title for a temporary period, even if this title did not exist or was in some sense defective prior to that point. This is the case even if Kosovo enjoys an 'external' self-determination entitlement, since the enjoyment of title by what was eventually called the Republic of Serbia was treated as a provisional matter allied to the commitment, also made under Chapter VII, to negotiations on the status of the territory. Although the commitment did not affirm what would amount to the exercise of 'external' self-determination as a consequence of such negotiations, it did not rule this out. Whereas the question of Kosovo's external self-determination entitlement was, therefore, to be implicated in the eventual settlement, it was not permanently affected by the formulation adopted by the Security Council concerning its status during the UNMIK period.[220]

---

[218] For commentary on this issue, and Kosovo's status more generally, see, e.g., March & Sil (above, n. 210); Independent International Commission on Kosovo, *Why Conditional Independence? The Follow-Up of the Kosovo Report* (Global Reporting, 2001); Smyrek (above n. 15), ch. D; Milano (above n. 1), 234–65; TD Grant, 'Extending Decolonization: How the United Nations Might Have Addressed Kosovo', 28 (1999) *Georgia Journal of International & Comparative Law* 9; JP Harris, 'Kosovo: An Application of the Principle of Self-Determination', 3 (1999) *Human Rights Brief* 28, available at <http://www.wcl.american.edu/hrbrief/v6i3/kosovo.htm>; J Ringelheim, 'Considerations on the International Reaction to the Kosovo Crisis', (1999) *Revue belge de droit international* 475; M Weller, 'The Rambouillet Conference on Kosovo', 75:2 (1999) *International Affairs* 211; AJ Bellamy, 'Lessons Unlearned: Why Coercive Diplomacy Failed at Rambouillet', 7:2 (2000) *International Peacekeeping* 95; H Quane, 'A Right to Self-Determination for the Kosovo Albanians?', 13 (2000) *LJIL* 219; J Ringelheim, 'Lo status giuridico del Kosovo', in F Strazzari, L Rodriguez, G Arcadu, and B Carrai (eds), *La Pace intrattabile, Kosovo 1999–2000, una radiografia del dopo bombe* (Asterios, 2000), 120 and sources cited therein; S Woodward, 'Kosovo and the Region: Consequences of the Waiting Game', (2000) *The International Spectator*, No. 1, 35; A Zimmermann and C Stahn, 'Yugoslav Territory, United Nations Trusteeship or Sovereign State? Reflections on the Current and Future Legal Status of Kosovo', 70 (2001) *Nordic Journal of International Law* 424; R Goldstone, 'Whither Kosovo, Whither Democracy', 8:2 (2002) *Global Governance* 143; C Tomuschat, 'Yugoslavia's Damaged Sovereignty over the Province of Kosovo', in G Kreijen (ed.), *State, Sovereignty, and International Governance* (OUP, 2002), 323, at 326; E Milano, 'Security Council Action in the Balkans: Reviewing the Legality of Kosovo's Territorial Status', 14 (2003) *EJIL* 999; PR Williams, 'The Road to Resolving the Conflict over Kosovo's Final Status', 31 (2003) *Denver Journal of International Law & Policy* 387; BS Brown, 'Human Rights, Sovereignty and the Final Status of Kosovo', 80 (2005) *Chicago-Kent Law Review* 235. Many of the sources cited in List of Sources, sections 5.1.1 and 5.1.2 not cited above also touch on this issue.

[219] See below, ch. 7, text accompanying n. 43 *et seq.*

[220] For the idea that Kosovo enjoyed 'limited legal personality' by virtue of, and exercised by, UNMIK, see B Knoll, 'From Benchmarking to Final Status? Kosovo and the Problem of and International Administration Open-Ended Mandate', 16 (2005) *EJIL* 637, 649–51. The legal significance of the Security Council's determination is, however, contingent on the legality of the

4.6 Conclusion

This chapter has clarified the legal status of a range of territories that were states or formed part of states when international territorial administration

determination as a matter of UN law, a matter which, like the broader question of the competence of the Council to create ITA mandates, is beyond the scope of this book. For commentary, see the works in the Sources List, section 5.2.6. The status of the FRY between 1991 and 2000, when it claimed to be the continuation of the old SFRY despite the policy of most states that such a claim was invalid, and the nature of the juridical relationship between this entity and the FRY, which in 2000 joined the UN as a new member, being renamed the 'State Union of Serbia and Montenegro' on 4 February 2003, following the adoption and promulgation of the Constitutional Charter of Serbia and Montenegro, is complex and beyond the scope of this book, having been treated in a somewhat ambiguous and contradictory fashion by states, the United Nations political organs, and the International Court of Justice. Following the split of Serbia and Montenegro in 2006, similar questions arise with respect to the nature of the juridical relationship between the FRY between 1991 and 2000 and the Republic of Serbia: having declared independence from Serbia on 3 June 2006, Montenegro was accepted as a new member of the United Nations on 28 June 2006 (see SC Res. 1691, 22 June 2006; GA Res. 60/264, 28 June 2006); in accordance with the Constitutional Charter of Serbia and Montenegro (Art. 60), the Republic of Serbia claims to be the legal successor of the State Union of Serbia and Montenegro, and therefore the continuation of the post-2000 FRY (see Communication dated 16 June 2006 from the Minister for Foreign Affairs of the Republic of Serbia to the United Nations Secretary-General, reproduced in note 1 of the 'Serbia' part of 'Status of Multilateral Treaties Deposited with the Secretary-General—Historical Information', available at <http://untreaty.un.org/ENGLISH/bible/englishinternetbible/historicalinfo.asp>). On the initial claim to continuity of the SFRY, see, e.g., Joint declaration of the President of the Republic of Serbia, Slobodan Milošević, and the President of the Presidency of Bosnia and Herzegovina, Alija Izetbegović, Paris, 3 October 1996, UN Doc. A/51/461 – S/1996/830, 7 October 1996, Annex, in particular IV, second sentence; *Badinter Committee Opinions Nos 8 and 10* (above n. 179). On the status of the FRY at the UN between 1991 and 2000, see SC Res. 757, 30 May 1992; SC Res. 777, 19 September 1992, para. 1; GA Res. 47/1, above, n. 179, para. 1; Y Blum, 'UN Membership of the "New" Yugoslavia: Continuity or Break?', 86 (1992) *AJIL* 830; MP Scharf, 'Musical Chairs: The Dissolution of States and Membership of the United Nations', 28 (1995) *Cornell ILJ* 29; L Johnson, 'Remarks' in 'Yugoslavia Panel', 90 (1996) *ASIL Proc.* 474; M Craven, 'The Genocide Case, the Law of Treaties and State Succession', 68 (1997) *BYIL* 127; M Wood, 'Participation of Former Yugoslav States in the United Nations and in Multilateral Treaties', (1997) *Max Planck Yearbook of United Nations Law* 231. On the UN membership of the post-2000 FRY/Serbia and Montenegro, see Letter dated 27 October 2000 from the President of the Federal Republic of Yugoslavia to the Secretary-General, UN Doc. A/55/528-S/2000/1043, 30 October 2000, Annex; SC Res. 1326, 31 October 2000, GA Res. 55/12, 10 November 2000; Note by the Secretary-General, 30 October 2000, UN Doc. A/55/528-S/2000/1043. On these issues generally, see also *Application of the Convention on the Prevention and Punishment of the Crime of Genocide (Bosnia and Herzegovina v Yugoslavia (Serbia and Montenegro)), Request for the Indication of Provisional Measures, Order of 8 April 1993, ICJ Reports 1993*, 3, paras 18, 21–22; *Application of the Convention on the Prevention and Punishment of the Crime of Genocide (Bosnia and Herzegovina v Yugoslavia (Serbia and Montenegro)), Preliminary Objections, ICJ Reports 1996 (II)*, 595, para. 17; *Application for Revision of the Judgment of 11 July 1996 in the Case concerning Application of the Convention on the Prevention and Punishment of the Crime of Genocide (Bosnia and Herzegovina v Yugoslavia), Preliminary Objections (Yugoslavia v Bosnia and Herzegovina), ICJ Reports 2003*, 7; *Legality of Use of Force (Serbia and Montenegro v Belgium), Preliminary Objections*, Judgment of 15 December 2004; *Application of the Convention on the Prevention and Punishment of the Crime of Genocide (Bosnia and Herzegovina v Serbia and Montenegro), Merits*, Judgment of 26 February 2007, paras 80–113 (discussing certain issues relating to the status of the SFRY/FRY) and 67–79 (on the dissolution of the State Union of Serbia and Montenegro in 2006). The ICJ decisions are obtainable from <http://www.icj-cij.org>.

was introduced in them. In none of these territories did the international actor exercising administrative control enjoy title; quite apart from any other consideration, no claim to this effect was made.

To say that the exercise of sovereignty-as-administration did not operate in conjunction with the enjoyment of sovereignty-as-title is not to say that this arrangement did not sometimes play a constitutive role in the legal status of the territory concerned. In order to appreciate this constitutive role, it is necessary to identify whether ITA was exercised on a particular basis as far as the status of the territories involved was concerned, and then place this activity within a broader consideration of the relevant issues that collectively determine status.

For all the projects in the territories covered in this chapter, with the exception of the Saar, the constituent instruments affirmed or assumed that the territories concerned were either states or state territories. The legal instruments authorizing the League Commissioner's administrative prerogatives in the Free City of Danzig, for example, also authorized the creation of the Free City as a distinct juridical person (in the case of the Treaty of Versailles) or assumed the Free City's distinct juridical personality (in the case of the Poland–Danzig Treaty, an international instrument agreed by and binding in respect of the Free City directly). Equally, the Kosovo Peace Plan and Security Council Resolution 1244 authorizing the UN administration in that territory explicitly underscored Kosovo's status as a part of what was then the FRY. In such circumstances, the exercise of administrative prerogatives cannot be understood as a diminution in the control enjoyed by the indigenous authorities over the territories concerned so as to compromise the continued enjoyment of statehood or title by the juridical person in whose name such authorities act, since the legal basis for the exercise of these prerogatives assumes and thereby bolsters this continuance.

Moreover, for some of the projects it would seem that administration was actually exercised in right of a particular territorial sovereign. So, in Leticia, the League Commission was to govern 'in the name of Colombia'. Here, the exercise of administrative prerogatives not only fails to 'count' as a negative factor in the continued enjoyment of statehood or title on the part of the juridical entity in whose name those indigenous authorities displaced by ITA had exercised control; it would actually seem to have a positive effect on the continuance of such status. In other words, the international organization becomes the agent for the territorial sovereign as far as the aspect of its claim to statehood or title based on territorial control is concerned.

Even if international territorial administration has this effect, it is necessary to review a broader range of factors before drawing a conclusion about the status of the territories concerned. In engaging in such a review, and appreciating the role that ITA can play relative to other factors in determining status, a distinction can be made between these territories according to the degree of administrative prerogatives exercised therein.

For territorial entities in which partial administrative prerogatives were exercised—Danzig, Memel, the Congo, Cambodia, Somalia, the northern Iraqi Governorates, and Bosnia and Herzegovina—the restricted nature of the prerogatives meant that they were unlikely to be the main determinant of status. In the Free City of Danzig, it was necessary to consider the administrative prerogatives alongside those other prerogatives exercised by Poland over the Free City. As was illustrated, these other prerogatives were actually of a similar nature to those enjoyed by the League High Commissioner, in that the legal authority for them was predicated on the distinct juridical status of the Free City and therefore the absence of sovereignty in the sense of ownership on the part of Poland over the Free City. Thus, arguably the prerogatives did not 'count' as diminutions of the control exercised by the Free City authorities as far as the effect of the degree of this control on the continued subsistence of Free City status was concerned. In Memel, it was necessary to consider the degree of autonomy given to the territory generally rather than the prerogatives given to the Harbour Board (and the international appointee on that body) exclusively, and the purported disposition of the territory in favour of Lithuania in the Paris Agreement of 1924.

The arrangements in the northern Iraqi Governorates bear some relation to the situation in the Free City of Danzig, in that it is necessary to consider not only the administrative prerogatives enjoyed by the UN Inter-Agency Humanitarian Programme, but also the withdrawal of Iraqi governmental authorities and the exercise of administrative control by the Kurdish authorities as a result of the imposition of the no-fly zones. Ultimately, the loss of Iraqi sovereignty is ruled out due to the absence of a rival territorial claim made by the local Kurds during the period in question.

In the Congo, Cambodia, Somalia, and Bosnia and Herzegovina, the additional factor to the presence of partial ITA is again the loss of governmental control by authorities performing this role as the territorial sovereign, but here the exercise of ITA was not partially responsible for this loss of control, as in Iraq, but rather was introduced subsequent to it (indeed, as will be discussed in Chapter 6, the purposes associated with ITA in these territories included various attempts to shore up the state).

For those territories where the plenary projects were conducted—the Saar, Leticia, Mostar, Eastern Slavonia, and Kosovo—the fact that international organizations were the exclusive administrative authorities gave this activity much greater potential in determining the status of the territories concerned. If title had been claimed by the organizations in question, then Ydit's 'internationalised territories' model of international territorial sovereignty might well have been realized. In the event, this claim was not made and the juridical significance of the exercise of plenary administrative authority was different.

Arguably, the provisions relating to territorial status in the legal instruments authorizing the projects in Leticia, Mostar, Eastern Slavonia, and Kosovo meant that the total loss of administrative control over the territory by the state concerned could not 'count' as such a loss in terms of having a negative effect on the continued enjoyment of title over the territory by that state. When administration was exercised 'on behalf of' the territorial sovereign, as in Leticia, it was as if the indigenous agents of this state were themselves performing this role as far as its effect on the continuance of title was concerned.

Of all the cases, arguably the Saar territory was the least certain in terms of the continuance of title during the period of plenary international administration, since the constituent instruments did not confirm the continuance of German title during this period, and the League Governing Commission did not exercise its administrative prerogatives in the name of the German state. However, because there was no claim made to title by the League or any other actor, the general presumption of continued territorial title suggests that the Saar remained part of Germany for the duration of the League administrative period.

In the Saar, then, the presumption in favour of the status quo in relation to statehood and territorial title was of considerable significance. What can be said of the other territories in this regard? For territories whose status had subsisted for some time before the administration projects, whether as states, as with Cambodia and Somalia, or as territories within states, as with the Saar (Germany), Leticia (Colombia), and the three northern Iraqi Governorates (Iraq), the presumption was not rebutted despite the significant (in some cases total) loss of control by indigenous authorities. In the case of Leticia, the juridical effect of this loss of control was reversed because control was exercised by an international actor in the name of the original territorial sovereign. In the other cases, however, it would seem that this loss of control was not by itself of sufficient juridical consequence to rebut the presumption of continued statehood.

For those territories the status of which was established just prior to, or at the same time as, the commencement of the administration projects, whether as states, as in the Free City of Danzig and Bosnia and Herzegovina, or as territories within states, as in Memel (Lithuania), Eastern Slavonia (Croatia), Mostar (Bosnia and Herzegovina), and Kosovo (the FRY/Serbia and Montenegro/ Republic of Serbia), it was necessary to establish a basis for statehood or territorial title. Status was usually articulated in international agreements, either providing for the enactment of this status itself, as in the Treaty of Versailles in relation to the Free City of Danzig and the 1924 Convention of Paris in relation to Memel, or at some point subsequent to this enactment, as in the Basic Agreement in relation to Eastern Slavonia, the Dayton Peace Agreements in relation to Bosnia and Herzegovina, and the 1999 Peace Plan in relation to Kosovo. In the latter two cases, Security Council resolutions adopted under Chapter VII provided additional support; in the cases of Eastern Slavonia, Bosnia and Herzegovina (including Mostar), and Kosovo, support was also forthcoming through widespread international recognition of the claims concerned (claims which included title to the territories in question). Although the authorities claiming statehood in Bosnia and Herzegovina and Croatia did not enjoy control over much of the territory forming the basis of these claims, it would seem that the claims were successful because of the broad practice of international recognition.

Displacing local actors in the activity of territorial governance always compromises the sovereignty of the state concerned, if sovereignty is understood as the capacity of those actors to exercise control within their territory. So Alexandros Yannis uses the term 'suspended sovereignty' to denote 'different situations' (including situations of plenary international administration) 'in which the internal aspect of sovereignty was perceived to be an empty legal proposition not matching the social realities'.[221] However, if one is considering sovereignty in the sense of juridical status and territorial title, then the effect of international administration is not as straightforward; it depends not only on the mere presence of administrative prerogatives, but also on the basis upon which such prerogatives are exercised. Actually, in all of the administration projects that were introduced into territories that were already states or state territories, an evaluation of this basis reveals that the projects either had no negative effect on the continuance of the territorial status, or actually bolstered this status in being conducted 'on behalf of' the particular juridical unit concerned. Sovereignty in the first sense, then, was undoubtedly diminished, but sovereignty in the second sense was at the very least left unaltered, and sometimes reinforced, by the enjoyment of administrative prerogatives by the international organizations involved.

If, then, the administration projects introduced in states or parts of state territory did not end up altering the juridical status of the territories concerned, what of those projects introduced in non-state territories where the right to self-determination was determinative of legal status, such as East Timor? This will be addressed in the following chapter.

---

[221] A Yannis, 'The Concept of Suspended Sovereignty in International Law and its Implications in International Politics', 13 (2002) *EJIL* 1037.

5

Host Territories—Self-Determination Units

5.1 Introduction

This chapter explains the legal status of those territories subject to ITA projects where the legal right to self-determination was, in varying ways, determinative of this status. In most cases, the territories concerned were neither states nor parts of state territory. As with the status of the territories discussed in the previous chapter, some commentators considering the legal status of non-state territories involving ITA projects suggest that these territories became the sovereign territory of the international organizations involved.[1] It might be thought that if a territory is neither a state nor forms part of state territory, and is administered by the UN, then it must somehow constitute 'UN territory' by virtue of the absence of a valid claim to title made by any other state (or a claim to independent statehood by the people of the territory), the existence of UN administration, and the enjoyment of international legal personality by the UN. Thus Ydit's concept, what I term 'international territorial sovereignty', is realized.[2]

This approach disregards the absence of a claim to sovereignty (as title) on the part of the United Nations. With non-state units enjoying a self-determination entitlement, an additional factor is overlooked: the possibility that such a unit can enjoy a type of legal personality by virtue of this entitlement.

Before commencing the analysis of the legal status of the territories under evaluation, a review of the law on self-determination and a consideration of the effect that the self-determination entitlement is regarded to have on juridical status are in order. The general legal framework is then applied as the status of each territory is analysed in turn, covering Mandated and Trust territories where the UN conducted consultations; West Irian in 1962–63; South West Africa/ Namibia in 1967 and 1989–90; the Western Sahara from 1991; and East Timor between 1999 and 2002. The conclusion reached is that these territories were not 'UN territories' but, rather, non-state territories with distinct legal personality derived from their self-determination entitlement.

---

[1] An example would be J Chopra, 'The UN's Kingdom of East Timor', 42 (2000) *Survival* 27.
[2] See above ch. 3, section 3.2.

5.2 The Law on Self-Determination[3]

The right of 'external' self-determination entitles a people to choose the external (i.e., international) status of their territory, whether forming part of, or enjoying some kind of free association with, another state (whether the state in which they are currently located, or another state), becoming an independent state, or some other political status.[4] This is to be distinguished from 'internal' self-determination, which concerns peoples' rights within states, and is considered further in Chapter 7.[5] In the parlance of the law on self-determination, a particular population grouping enjoying an 'external' self-determination

---

[3] On self-determination, see, e.g., UN Charter, Arts 1(2) and 55; International Covenant on Civil and Political Rights ('ICCPR'), 16 December 1966, 999 UNTS 171, Art. 1, International Covenant on Economic, Social and Cultural Rights ('ICESCR'), 16 December 1966, 993 UNTS 3, Art. 1; GA Res. 1514 (XV), 14 December 1960; GA Res. 1541 (XV), 15 December 1960, Annex; SC Res. 183, 11 December 1963, para. 4; GA Res. 2621 (XXV), 12 October 1970; Declaration on Principles of International Law Concerning Friendly Relations and Cooperation among States in Accordance with the Charter of the United Nations (hereinafter 'Friendly Relations Declaration'), GA Res. 2625 (XXV), 24 October 1970; GA Res. 3103 (XXVIII), 30 December 1973; *Legal Consequences for States of the Continued Presence of South Africa in Namibia (South West Africa) Notwithstanding Security Council Resolution 276 (1970), Advisory Opinion, ICJ Reports 1971*, 16 (hereinafter '*Namibia Advisory Opinion*'); *Western Sahara, Advisory Opinion, ICJ Reports 1975*, 12 (hereinafter '*Western Sahara Advisory Opinion*'); *East Timor (Portugal v Australia), ICJ Reports 1995*, 90 (hereinafter '*East Timor Case*'); *Legal Consequences of the Construction of a Wall in the Occupied Palestinian Territories, Advisory Opinion, ICJ Reports 2004*, 136 (hereinafter '*Wall Advisory Opinion*'); *Reference re Secession of Quebec*, Supreme Court of Canada, 28 August 1998, [1998] 2 RCS 217, 37 (1998) *ILM* 1340; and the List of Sources, section 5.4.

[4] The General Assembly Friendly Relations Declaration states the options for (external) self-determination in the following terms: '[t]he establishment of a sovereign and independent State; the free association or integration with an independent State or the emergence into any other political status freely decided by a people...'; Friendly Relations Declaration (above n. 3). In Resolution 1541 (XV), the General Assembly sets out three scenarios whereby a 'Non-Self-Governing Territory can be said to have reached a full measure of self-government':

(a)   Emergence as a sovereign independent State;
(b)   Free association with an independent State; or
(c)   Integration with an independent State.

GA Res. 1541 (XV) (above n. 3), Annex, Principle VI. See also *Western Sahara Opinion* (above n. 3), para. 57; J Crawford, *The Creation of States in International Law* (2nd edn, OUP, 2006), 128 and 621. The right to 'external' self-determination is also sometimes used to denote freedom from external interference in domestic governance (on self-determination and domestic governance, see also the right to 'internal' self-determination, covered in the next note and accompanying text).

[5] On 'internal' self-determination, see Friendly Relations Declaration; ICCPR, Art. 1, ICESCR, Art. 1 (all cited above n. 3). See also ICCPR, Art. 25 (on the right to free and fair elections). Many of the commentators cited in the List of Sources, section 5.4, address 'internal' self-determination within a broader discussion of self-determination generally; those who focus on internal self-determination specifically include Franck, Cassese, McCorquodale, Rosas, Salmon, Thornberry, and Doehring. The right to 'internal' self-determination is discussed further below, ch. 7, text accompanying n. 26 *et seq*. For the idea that a right to 'external' self-determination might arise in the case of an extreme denial of 'internal' self-determination, see the discussion below, ch. 7, text accompanying n. 30.

entitlement is sometimes referred to as a 'people' and its territory a 'self-determination unit'.[6]

As far as territories that were not already sovereign states are concerned,[7] the 'external' entitlement was first accorded, not as a result of the territory falling within a particular category, but, rather, as an ad hoc mechanism for solving a particular territorial dispute.[8] The entitlement arose, as it were, in the form of a gift by the disputants involved, one or more of which purporting to enjoy the legal competence to dispose of the juridical status of the territory. An example of this would be the plebiscites that were utilized in Europe as part of the Versailles settlement to determine the status of disputed territories, including the plebiscite held in the Saar territory in 1935.[9]

After the Second World War, the right of self-determination, which had been referred to in the UN Charter without elaboration,[10] became applicable to particular categories of territory, emerging in customary international law after the establishment of the United Nations[11] in relation to people in Mandated and Trust territories,[12] building on the Charter provision that there should be 'progressive development towards self-government or independence' in Trust territories (the League Mandate system was subsumed within the Trusteeship system).[13]

The category of Non-Self-Governing Territories was instituted within the United Nations under Chapter XI of the Charter (and defined in Article 73), covering 'territories whose peoples have not yet attained a full measure of self-government'.[14] Although this question-begging definition potentially covered both Mandated and Trust territories and colonies, it was formulated to provide a regime in relation to the latter that would complement the Trusteeship system for the former.[15] As a result, only colonial territories (and other dependent territories

---

[6] For this term, and its applicability to Non-Self-Governing Territories, see Crawford (above n. 4), 115–21.

[7] The people of a state as a whole enjoy the right of 'external' self-determination. See, e.g., ibid., 127, point (3)(b).

[8] See ibid., at 127, n. 109 and sources cited therein, and at 117, text accompanying n. 72.

[9] On the Saar plebiscite, see above, ch. 4, text corresponding to n. 22 *et seq.*, and below, ch. 6, text corresponding to n. 39 *et seq.* On the plebiscites generally, see the sources cited below, ch. 8, n. 72.

[10] UN Charter, Art. 1(2) and Art. 55. See Crawford (above n. 4), 112–14.

[11] Many of the authorities and commentators cited in List of Sources, section 5.4 affirm that self-determination forms part of customary international law; for one notable judicial affirmation of this, see, e.g., *Western Sahara Opinion* (above n. 3), para. 56.

[12] On the self-determination entitlement of Mandated and Trust territories, see *Namibia Advisory Opinion* (above n. 3), 31, paras 53 and 54; Crawford (above n. 4), 116, 127 and 567 ('mandate and trust territories…became the first distinct category of self-determination territory', ibid., 567). On the Mandate system, see the sources cited below, n. 43. On the Trusteeship system, see the sources cited below, n. 44.

[13] UN Charter, Art. 76(b).

[14] UN Charter, Art. 73.

[15] As for its applicability to colonies, the General Assembly stated that, '[t]he authors of the Charter…had in mind that Chapter XI should be applicable to territories which were then known to be of the colonial type'; GA Res. 1541 (XV) (above n. 3), Annex, Principle I. The category of

other than Mandated and Trust territories) were treated as Non-Self-Governing Territories for the purposes of Article 73.[16] At the same time, the people in colonial territories joined those in Mandated and Trust territories as enjoying the right of 'external' self-determination in the post-war period, and the category of Non-Self-Governing Territory was sometimes used to refer to both types of territory, or, put differently, territories entitled to 'external' self-determination.[17] As with Trust territories, this entitlement for colonies built on the Charter provision that 'self-government' should be developed within Non-Self-Governing Territories.[18]

An entitlement to external self-determination is also understood to arise in the context of foreign domination. This is expressly recognized by the UN General Assembly 'Friendly Relations Declaration', which, in addition to colonialism, outlines, as a further instance of a violation of the principle of self-determination, the 'subjection of peoples to alien subjugation, domination and exploitation'.[19]

In general terms, with colonial territories, the identification of a particular unit for the purposes of self-determination followed the administrative divisions adopted by the administering power, in accordance with the principle of *uti possidetis juris* (although whether this reflects a principle of international law is contested).[20]

Non-Self-Governing Territories is discussed further below, ch. 8, text accompanying n. 62 *et seq.* The United Nations exercised oversight in relation to Non-Self-Governing Territories. See below, ch. 8, n. 411.

[16] See I Sagay, *The Legal Aspects of the Namibian Dispute* (University of Ife Press, 1975), 3–6; Crawford (above n. 4), 603–10.

[17] For possible additional categories of territory enjoying a right of 'external' self-determination, see above, ch. 4, n. 180 and accompanying text, and below, ch. 7, text accompanying n. 30 *et seq.*

[18] UN Charter, Art. 73. As the International Court stated in the *Namibia Advisory Opinion* of 1971, '... the subsequent development of international law in regard to non-self-governing territories, as enshrined in the Charter of the United Nations, made the principle of self-determination applicable to all of them'; *Namibia Advisory Opinion* (above n. 3), 31, para. 52. Similarly, in the *Western Sahara Opinion*, Judge Dillard noted that '[t]he pronouncement of the Court thus indicate in my view that a norm of international law has emerged applicable to the decolonization of those non-self-governing territories which are under the aegis of the United Nations' (*Western Sahara Opinion*, above n. 3, 121 (separate opinion of Judge Dillard)). A category of peoples subject to 'alien subjugation, domination and exploitation' is sometimes used in connection with the self-determination entitlement. It has sometimes been defined in a manner suggesting it as an umbrella category for all territories enjoying an 'external' self-determination entitlement, including but not limited to Mandated/Trust territories and colonies. For example, General Assembly Resolution 1514 (XV) utilizes the 'alien subjugation' category in its first paragraph and goes on to refer to 'Trust and Non-Self-Governing Territories or all other territories which have not yet attained independence'; GA Res. 1514 (XV) (above n. 3).

[19] Friendly Relations Declaration (above n. 3). On the self-determination entitlement of people subjected to foreign domination see A Cassese, *Self-Determination of Peoples: A Legal Reappraisal* (CUP, 1995), 90–9.

[20] On the principle of *uti possidetis juris* and its legal status, see, e.g., I Brownlie, *Principles of International Law* (6th edn, OUP, 2003), 129–30 and sources cited therein; E Milano, *Unlawful Territorial Situations in International Law: Reconciling Effectiveness, Legality and Legitimacy* (Martinus Nijhoff, 2006), 108–14 and sources cited therein.

One juridical consequence of the self-determination entitlement is that the 'self-determination unit' is understood to constitute a distinct legal entity. The UN General Assembly stated that a Non-Self-Governing Territory:

...has...a status separate and distinct from the territory of the State administering it; and such separate and distinct status under the Charter shall exist until the people of the...territory have exercised their right of self-determination in accordance with the Charter.[21]

Whatever meaning of Non-Self-Governing Territory was intended here, this formulation is regarded as being applicable to all territories entitled to 'external' self-determination. Because the people of the territory enjoy the right to alter the territory's external status, they must already possess some kind of legal status; if they choose statehood, it is the connection between the self-determination unit and the state it becomes that provides the legitimacy for that state. In other words, even when self-determination has not been actualized, the people of the territory must already have some kind of juridical identity because of the prospective effect the exercise of this right will have on the legitimacy of the state (if this status is chosen).[22] All self-determination units have a distinct identity in international law, then; the precise nature and effect of this can vary, however, depending, inter alia, on whether or not a state enjoys territorial title with respect to it.

When the unit does not form part of another state, it is not *terra nullius* but enjoys legal status akin to that of a state, insofar as it is territorially-based in character.[23] When the unit forms part of the territory of a state, as was the case

---

[21] Friendly Relations Declaration (above n. 3). See Crawford (above n. 4), 617–19.

[22] As James Crawford states in relation to self-determination units, '[t]here is nothing self-contradictory in an entity having a limited status, consisting primarily in the right at some future time to opt for more permanent status'; Crawford (above n. 4), 124.

[23] Such an idea is perhaps evident in James Crawford's consideration of the status of the Palestinian territories; for Crawford, because '[t]he people of Palestine (i.e., of the remaining territories of the Mandate for Palestine) have a right of self-determination...There is thus a non-State legal entity recognized as represented by a national liberation movement. This explains the 'capacity' of the PLO to perform various acts, to enter into treaties, to bear rights and assume obligations...these are not things which in modern international law only States can do'; Crawford (above n. 4), 444. See also ibid., at 438–9 and 444–5. In the *Western Sahara Opinion* the International Court of Justice held that the Western Sahara was not *terra nullius* at the time of Spanish colonization, noting that it was 'inhabited by peoples which...were socially and politically organized' and that when Spain took control in 1884 it purported to do so on the basis not of occupation of *terra nullius* but of an agreement with the leaders of local tribes (*Western Sahara Opinion*, above n. 3, para. 81). From the Court's remarks on this issue, it is unclear whether there is a general rule that colonial territories 'inhabited by tribes or peoples having a social and political organization' are *ipso facto* not *terrae nullius* (quotation taken ibid., para. 80), since the Court underlines the 'differences of opinion' on this matter among jurists, and emphasizes the practice of colonial acquisition being based on agreements with local leaders, both generally (ibid., para. 80) and in its consideration of the Western Sahara (ibid., para. 81). It is open to question, therefore, what the position in law would be in a circumstance where an organized political structure subsisted locally but where a colonial power purported to acquire title not through agreement but on the basis of occupation of *terra nullius*.

in some colonial territories,[24] it has a dual status: it is part of the territory of that state (pending, as discussed below, the outcome of a self-determination consultation), and, because of the self-determination entitlement, it is also a distinct juridical unit. This dual status necessarily means that the nature of the state's title with respect to the unit is of a special kind. As James Crawford remarks, whereas self-determination status does not deprive the administering state of sovereignty over the unit, it does 'substantially limit' this sovereignty.[25] Sovereignty is conditional, in the sense that the continuance of title depends on the support of the people in the territory in a self-determination consultation. If the people opt for independence, the state will be obliged to implement this outcome and renounce its claim to sovereignty. The administering power enjoys the temporary form of title because of the very act of colonization that later became the basis for the self-determination entitlement. Once the entitlement formed part of international law, this title was delegitimized.

Given this, it could be argued that when the territorial control of the administering power is displaced by another administering power lacking title (e.g., through forcible occupation), the title of the first power is extinguished, not because title is transferred to the second power, but because the first power only enjoyed the title as a consequence of being in the position of exercising territorial control. That is not to say that the administering power does not continue to enjoy a special relationship with the self-determination unit, by virtue of its former status as the administering power, but rather that the power no longer enjoys title with respect to the territory. This idea will be revisited below when the cases of Spain and the Western Sahara, and Portugal and East Timor are considered.

How should the view of the people entitled to external self-determination be discerned in order for a particular territorial settlement validly to constitute the exercise of the people's right?[26] In the *Western Sahara Advisory Opinion*, the International Court of Justice stated that 'the application of the right of self-determination requires a free and genuine expression of the will of the peoples concerned'[27] and referred to taking into account the wishes of the people of the territory as a 'basic need' when choosing between the options for the realization

---

[24] See below, section 5.3, and ch. 8, section 8.2.2, below.

[25] Crawford (above n. 4), 615.

[26] In the Friendly Relations Declaration of 1970 (above n. 3), the General Assembly proclaimed that:

[e]very State has the duty to promote...the realization of the principle of...self-determination of peoples...in order:
[...]
(b) To bring a speedy end to colonialism, having due regard to the freely expressed will of the peoples concerned...

[27] *Western Sahara Opinion* (above n. 3), para. 55. See also the comment by Judge Nagendra Singh that 'the consultation of the people of a territory awaiting decolonization is an inescapable imperative...Thus even if integration of territory was demanded by an interested State, as in this case, it could not be had without ascertaining the freely expressed will of the people—the very *sine qua non* of all decolonization' (ibid., Declaration of Judge Nagendra Singh, at 81).

of 'external' self-determination.[28] James Crawford proposes that, in view of the 'close connection with fundamental human rights' of the right of a self-determination unit 'to choose its own political organization', this choice:

... is to be exercised by the people of the relevant unit without coercion and on a basis of equality.[29]

In Resolution 1541 of 1960, however, the General Assembly only mentions the requirement of taking into account the views of the people when the territory in question is not to become an independent state, stipulating the requirement in relation to the two options—free association or integration with another state—which, alongside independent statehood, it considers would amount to a 'full measure of self-government'—i.e., the realization of self-determination—on the part of a Non-Self-Governing Territory.[30] Moreover, in the *Western Sahara Advisory Opinion,* the ICJ stated that:

[t]he validity of the principle of self-determination, defined as the need to pay regard to the freely expressed will of peoples, is not affected by the fact that in certain cases the General Assembly has dispensed with the requirement of consulting the inhabitants of a given territory. Those instances were based either on the consideration that a certain population did not constitute a 'people' entitled to self-determination or on the conviction that a consultation was totally unnecessary, in view of special circumstances.[31]

The political derivation of the post-war self-determination entitlement is, of course, the repudiation of colonialism: integration as part of another state was to end, unless the people of the territory opted for some kind of continued arrangement either with the existing colonial power, or with another state.[32] The latter options would not be 'colonial' because they would be based on the consent of

---

[28] Ibid., para. 58.

[29] Crawford (above n. 4), 127–8. This is unchanged from the first edition of the same work in 1979; see J Crawford, *The Creation of States in International Law* (OUP, 1979), 101. Michael Reisman states that 'in contemporary practice, the demand for plebiscite or some other reliable consultation of popular will indicates that dispositions of territorial communities can be effected lawfully only with the free and informed consent of the members of that community'; WM Reisman, *Puerto Rico and the International Process: New Roles in Association* (American Society of International Law, West Publishing Company, 1974), at 12.

[30] For the three options, see GA Res. 1541 (XV) (above n. 3), Annex, Principle VI. As far as free association is concerned, this should be '... the result of a free and voluntary choice by the peoples of the territory concerned expressed through informed and democratic process.' Integration, on the other hand, '... should be the result of the freely expressed wishes of the territory's peoples acting with full knowledge of the change in their status, their wishes having been expressed through informed and democratic processes, impartially conducted and based on universal adult suffrage'; ibid., Annex, Principle VII, para. (a) and Principle IX, para. (b), respectively.

[31] *Western Sahara Opinion* (above n. 3), para. 59.

[32] This is discussed further below, ch. 8, sections 8.5 and 8.7.1. For commentary, see the sources cited therein.

the people forthcoming in some modality deemed to be more legitimate than the compromised notion of 'consent' on which some colonial title was based.[33]

Considering the entitlement in this negative way is perhaps helpful in appreciating the distinction made in Resolution 1541 as far as the requirement of a consultation is concerned. Colonialism is brought to an end if independence is achieved; if some other status is to be adopted, a consultation is required in order to render this arrangement legitimate and not another form of colonialism.[34] The need for the consultation is rooted in the original repudiation of colonialism as an enterprise that was understood, as previously mentioned, not to have been based on the meaningful consent of the people of the territory. According to this logic, consent is relevant only when some status other than independence is being adopted. It is only necessary to validate some kind of arrangement akin to colonialism; it is not required to reject such an arrangement via independent statehood because the arrangement was considered objectionable. Put differently, independence and some form of dependence were not normatively equal: the former came with a presumption of legitimacy, the other a presumption of illegitimacy. Consent was therefore required only for the latter, to render legitimate what would otherwise be illegitimate.

The requirement of express consent even when independence is to be chosen—thereby treating all forms of juridical status as normatively equivalent—becomes necessary when the focus is not on delegitimizing colonialism exclusively, but also on legitimizing the juridical status of the territory according to the wishes of the people of the territory: in other words, if one considers self-determination as a matter of human rights.

If one is focusing simply on the right of a people to determine its external status, no basis exists for distinguishing between independent statehood and forms of integration with other states as far as needing the consent of that people is concerned. It is notable that James Crawford cites human rights as a preface to his articulation of a seemingly absolutist position on the requirement of local agreement. Moreover, he first made his remarks in 1979.[35] Resolution 1541 was passed in 1960; it was not until 1966, with the two UN human rights Covenants, that self-determination was articulated as a 'human right' in a UN instrument, and in 1970 the General Assembly's 'Friendly Relations Declaration' underscored the general importance of 'having due regard to the freely expressed will of the

---

[33] On colonial title generally, see below, section 5.3; on the compromised notion of 'consent' in colonial treaties, see below, ch. 8, text accompanying n. 380.

[34] According to Malcolm Shaw, '[i]n a large number of colonies, neither plebiscites nor elections were held in a way directly related to the exercise of self-determination. This is because in the majority of cases no serious alternative to independence was proposed regarding the future of the territory'; MN Shaw, *Title to Territory in Africa: International Legal Issues* (OUP, 1986), 144. Note, however, the special considerations Shaw identifies to explain the reason for consultations in Trust territories (ibid.).

[35] See above, n. 29.

peoples concerned' in its affirmation of self-determination.[36] This development can perhaps be seen as the third stage in the evolution of international law's treatment of 'external' self-determination, bearing in mind its original use as an ad hoc mechanism for resolving particular disputes and its later application to a class of territories as part of the decolonization process in the post-war era. Not only does the notion of self-determination as a human right shift the emphasis so as to render all territorial outcomes of equal normative weight; it has also led to the notion of 'internal' self-determination mentioned earlier, which has come to be understood, inter alia, in terms of popular participation in public decision-making.[37] This latter element bolsters the notion that a consultation is required in all determinations of external status, since such determinations are quintessentially public decisions; moreover, it deepens the notion of 'consultation', having led to the development of certain standards—the involvement of all of the people on the basis of equality (one person one vote); the requirement that it is 'free and fair'—applicable to consultations generally.

Even if, then, it is uncertain whether or not the self-determination entitlement as formulated in the decolonization era required a consultation to validate independent statehood as the realization of the self-determination entitlement, such a requirement is arguably a corollary of the articulation of self-determination as a human right.

Having reviewed the operative legal principles in relation to self-determination units generally, a consideration of the legal status of a series of territories where, in different ways, these principles are determinative, will be carried out in the following sections.

5.3 Colonial, Mandated, and Trust Territories where the UN Conducted Consultations

It is beyond the scope of this book to determine the juridical status of each of the colonial territories, including so-called 'colonial protectorates', in which the UN conducted consultations prior to the realization of 'external' self-determination. In general terms, before the emergence of the legal self-determination entitlement, in many (but not all) cases these territories were considered to be part of the sovereign territory of the colonial power.[38]

---

[36] On the Covenants, see ICCPR (above n. 3), Art. 1 and ICESCR (above n. 3), Art. 1; R McCorquodale, 'Self-Determination: A Human Rights Approach', 43 (1994) *ICLQ* 857, at 864. The Universal Declaration of Human Rights, GA Res. 217A (III), 10 December 1948, makes no mention of self-determination. The Friendly Relations Declaration is cited above n. 3 (its paragraphs are not numbered).

[37] See above n. 5.

[38] Crawford (above n. 4), 300. Prior to the advent of the self-determination entitlement, 'colonial title' was seen as equivalent to full territorial sovereignty over the colonial territory; see, e.g., A Anghie,

The term 'colonial protectorate', reflecting the idea of a 'protectorate' more generally, was used to denote colonies where title was not regarded as residing in the colonial power; where a significant degree of administrative control was exercised over the territory by the colonial power, however, this designation is rejected by those, including international lawyers, who view its use as disingenuous, sometimes motivated by a policy of seeking to avoid the responsibilities and scrutiny that would arise were sovereignty to be considered to exist.[39]

After the advent of the external self-determination entitlement in the second half of the 20th century, the nature of colonial power's sovereignty over its

<hr />

Imperialism, Sovereignty and the Making of International Law (CUP, 2005), at 82, stating that '[o]nce colonization took place, the colonizing power assumed sovereignty over the non-European territory…'; see also ibid., 82–3; this is also implicit in Crawford's analysis of the effect of the self-determination entitlement on colonial title, ibid., at 613–15. On colonial title generally, see, e.g., WW Willoughby and CG Fenwick, *Types of Restricted Sovereignty and of Colonial Autonomy* (US Government Printing Office, 1919); MF Lindley, *The Acquisition and Government of Backward Territory in International Law: Being a Treatise on the Law and Practice Relating to Colonial Expansion* (Longmans, Green & Co., 1926); Q Wright, *Mandates Under the League of Nations* (University of Chicago Press, 1930), 14–15; DK Fieldhouse, *Colonialism 1870–1945: An Introduction* (Palgrave Macmillan, 1981), 16; R Jennings and A Watts (eds), *Oppenheim's International Law, Vol. 1, Peace* (9th edn, Longman, 1992), §§ 84–5; OC Okafor, *Re-Defining Legitimate Statehood: International Law and State Fragmentation in Africa* (Martinus Nijhoff, 2000), 20–32; Anghie, *Imperialism*, ibid., chs 1–4, *passim*; A Anghie, 'Finding the Peripheries: Sovereignty and Colonialism in Nineteenth-Century International Law', 40 (1999) *Harvard International Law Journal* 1, *passim*; Shaw (above n. 34), *passim*.

[39] For DP O'Connell, '[i]n theory the protectorate as an institution was a guarantee of 'protection' on the part of a great State given to the ruler of a small and weak one. In fact, however, it became in the nineteenth century almost a mode of acquisition of territory'; DP O'Connell, *International Law* (2nd edn, Stevens & Sons, 1970), 341–2. For James Crawford, '…the colonial protectorate was not a distinct juridical institution at all. The whole point of identifying it as colonial was that the extent of governmental authority with respect to the territory was plenary…The absence of formal annexation was not a barrier to characterizing a territory as part of a particular State, where the authority exercised was in fact plenary and permanent'; Crawford (above n. 4), 300. Note also the statement that 'colonial protectorates…were treated as equivalent to annexed territories'; ibid., 306. For Malcolm Shaw, '[t]he concept of the protectorate was founded, initially at least, upon a division made between external and internal sovereignty, with the former being delegated to the protecting power. But the concept was developed in the case of the colonial protectorate so that the institution became one more method of acquiring territory rather than the model of the classic approach'; Shaw (above n. 34), 47. For Antony Anghie, '[p]rotectorates were a common technique by which European states exercised extensive control over non-European states while not officially assuming sovereignty over those states'; Anghie, *Imperialism* (above n. 38), 87; Anghie, 'Finding the Peripheries' (above n. 38), 54. But, '[i]n the final analysis…the distinction between protectorates and colonies was gradually eroded; the protectorate was a vehicle by which the European power controlled both the internal and the external relations of the native state'; Anghie, *Imperialism*, ibid., 89–90 (footnote omitted). On the specific issue of using the 'protectorate' designation to avoid the obligations that would flow were sovereignty considered to exist, see, e.g., M Koskenniemi, *The Gentle Civilizer of Nations* (CUP, 2002), 124–5. On the legal status of 'colonial protectorates' generally see Lindley (above n. 38), 182–3; Shaw, ibid., ch. 1; SN Grovogui, *Sovereigns, Quasi Sovereigns and Africans: Race and Self-Determination in International Law* (University of Minnesota Press, 1996), *passim* and especially 86, 92; Anghie, *Imperialism*, ibid., 87–90 and sources cited therein; Crawford, ibid., 299–303 and sources cited therein; Anghie, 'Finding the Peripheries', ibid., 54–8; Koskenniemi, ibid., 124–5, 151–5; W Bain, *Between Anarchy and Society. Trusteeship and the Obligations of Power* (OUP, 2003), 67. On issues of sovereignty in relation to 'protectorates' generally, see below, ch. 8, section 8.2.1.

colonies was altered; it was obliged to allow the realization of external self-determination, potentially necessitating the termination of this sovereignty if the people of the territory chose separation from the colonial state.[40]

The first use of international territorial administration in this general class of territories came as part of the UN's role in implementing the self-determination entitlement: the conduct of consultations to determine future status. What was the juridical status of those Mandated and Trust territories in which the United Nations carried out such consultations?[41] As mentioned above, the peoples of both sets of territories were considered to enjoy a right of external self-determination and the territories were, thus, 'self-determination units'.[42] As with colonies, this status does not by itself rule out the enjoyment of title that may have subsisted before the emergence of the self-determination entitlement, even if it does alter the nature of such title. It is necessary, then, to consider the general debates about where sovereignty resided in Mandated and Trust territories.

Under Article 22 of the League Covenant, the Mandate system covered certain territories of the defeated powers after the First World War.[43] The

---

[40] See the discussion of the special nature of colonial title after the emergence of the self-determination entitlement above, in this chapter, text corresponding to n. 21 *et seq.*

[41] The broader historical background to, and purposes associated with, both systems is discussed further below, ch. 8, sections 8.2.3, 8.3 and 8.4.

[42] See above, n. 12.

[43] On the Mandates system generally, including the system of oversight exercised by the League Council and Mandates Commission under Art. 22 of the League Covenant see, e.g., S Olivier, *The League of Nations and Primitive Peoples* (OUP, 1918); F White, *Mandates* (Jonathan Cape, 1926); AM Margalith, *The International Mandates* (OUP, 1930); Wright (above n. 38); League of Nations, *The Mandates: Origins, Principles, Application* (Allen & Unwin/League of Nations, 1945); HD Hall, *Mandates, Dependencies and Trusteeship* (Stevens & Sons, 1948); RN Chowdhuri, *International Mandates and Trusteeship Systems: A Comparative Study* (Martinus Nijhoff, 1955); KE Robinson, *The Dilemmas of Trusteeship: Aspects of British Colonial Policy Between the Wars* (OUP, 1965); Sagay (above n. 16), chs 1 and 2 and sources cited therein; FS Northedge, *The League of Nations: Its Life and Times 1920–1946* (Leicester University Press, 1986), especially ch. 9; I Dore, *The International Mandate System and Namibia* (Westview Press, 1985); *Oppenheim's International Law* (above n. 38), § 86 and sources cited at 295; C Weeramantry, *Nauru: Environmental Damage under International Trusteeship* (OUP, 1992); C Redgwell, *Intergenerational Trusts and Environmental Protection* (Manchester University Press, 1999), 147–9; N Crawford, *Argument and Change in World Politics: Ethics, Decolonization, and Humanitarian Intervention* (CUP, 2002), ch. 6, Koskenniemi (above n. 39), 170–4; Bain (above n. 39), ch. 4; Anghie, *Imperialism* (above n. 38), ch. 3, *passim* and sources cited therein; Crawford (above n. 4), ch. 13; JC Hales, 'The Creation and Application of the Mandate System. (A Study in International Colonial Supervision)', 25 (1939) *Transactions of the Grotius Society* 185 and sources cited therein note (a); JC Hales, 'The Reform and Extension of the Mandate System', 26 (1940) *Transactions of the Grotius Society* 153; H Lauterpacht, 'The Mandate under International Law in the Covenant of the League of Nations', in H Lauterpacht and E Lauterpacht (eds), *International Law* (CUP, 1970), vol. III, 29; WR Louis 'The Era of the Mandates System and the Non-European World', in H Bull and A Watson (eds), *The Expansion of International Society* (Clarendon Press, 1984); WM Reisman, 'Reflections on State Responsibility for Violations of Explicit Protectorate, Mandate, and Trusteeship Obligations', 10 (1989) *Michigan Journal of International Law* 231; A Anghie, 'Colonialism and the Birth of International Institutions: Sovereignty, Economy, and the Mandate System of the League of Nations', 34 (2002) *NYU Journal of International Law & Politics* 513, *passim*; N Matz, 'Civilization and the Mandate System under the League of Nations as Origin of Trusteeship', 9 (2005) *Max Planck Yearbook of*

UN Trusteeship system covered most of the Mandated territories, together with territories detached from Germany and Italy in the Second World War.[44] In an additional mechanism not provided for under the Mandates arrangements, the Trusteeship system was also available for use in other territories (though not those with UN membership) 'voluntarily placed under the system by States responsible for their administration', but no such territories were so placed.[45] The Mandates were to be subject to the 'tutelage'

United Nations Law 47. See also *Mavrommatis Palestine Concessions (Greece v United Kingdom), Jurisdiction*, PCIJ, *Series A*, No. 2 (1924); *Mavrommatis Jerusalem Concessions, Judgment*, PCIJ, *Series A*, No. 5 (1925); *International Status of South West Africa, Advisory Opinion, ICJ Reports 1950*, 128 (hereinafter '*South West Africa Advisory Opinion*'); *South West Africa (Ethiopia v South Africa; Liberia v South Africa) (Preliminary Objections), ICJ Reports 1962*, 319; *South West Africa (Ethiopia v South Africa; Liberia v South Africa) (Second Phase), ICJ Reports 1966*, 6; *Certain Phosphate Lands in Nauru (Nauru v Australia) (Preliminary Objections), ICJ Reports 1992*, 240. For details of the territories covered, see Chowdhuri, ibid., ch. V and especially 144; Crawford (above n. 4), Appendix 2. Further discussion on the Mandates system is contained below in ch. 8, in particular sections 8.2.3, 8.3, 8.4 and 8.7.3.

[44] See UN Charter, Chapters XII and XIII, especially Art. 77. For details of the territories covered, see the relevant parts of Chowdhuri (above n. 43), ch V and especially 144; Crawford (above n. 4), Appendix 2. Several classes of Mandated territories were not transferred to the Trusteeship system. First, those territories that had become or would become independent (Iraq, Syria, Lebanon, and Palestine [what is now Israel, Jordan, and the occupied territories]; secondly, the islands in the Pacific north of the Equator [which had been Japanese Mandates], which became a 'strategic Trust area' administered by the US; thirdly, South West Africa; see DJ Harris, *Cases and Materials on International Law* (6th edn, Sweet & Maxwell, 2004), 130–1. On the Trusteeship system, see, for example, Hall (above n. 43); CLV Narayan, *United Nations' Trusteeship of Non-Self-Governing Territories* (Imprimeries populaires, 1951); Chowdhuri, ibid.; CE Toussaint, *The Trusteeship System of the United Nations* (Stevens, 1956); JN Murray Jr, *The United Nations Trusteeship System* (University of Illinois Press, 1957); E Luard, *A History of the United Nations. Vol. 2: The Age of Decolonization 1955–1965* (Macmillan, 1989), especially ch. 5; *Oppenheim's International Law* (above n. 38), §§ 89–95 and sources cited at 308; J Kent, *The Internationalization of Colonialism: Britain, France and Black Africa 1939–1956* (Clarendon Press, 1992); T Parker, *The Ultimate Intervention: Revitalising the UN Trusteeship Council for the 21st Century* (Sandvika: Norwegian School of Management, 2003); Weeramantry (above n. 43); D Rauschning, 'International Trusteeship System', in B Simma (ed.), *The Charter of the United Nations. A Commentary* (2nd edn, OUP, 2002), vol. 2, 1099; Redgwell (above n. 43), 149–54; Crawford, ibid., ch. 13; HD Hall, 'The Trusteeship System', 24 (1947) *BYIL* 33; Reisman (above n. 43); F Sayre, 'Legal Problems Arising from the United Nations Trusteeship System', 42 (1948) *AJIL* 267; A Groom, 'The Trusteeship Council: A Successful Demise', in P Taylor and A Groom (eds), *The United Nations at the Millennium: The Principal Organs* (Continuum, 2000), 142; see also <http://www.un.org/Depts/dpi/decolonization>. Further discussion on the Trusteeship system is contained below in ch. 8, in particular sections 8.2.3, 8.3, 8.4 and 8.7.3. On supervision by the UN General Assembly and the Trusteeship Council, see UN Charter, Art. 85 and Chapter XIII and, for commentary, e.g., R Geiger, 'The Trusteeship Council', in B Simma (ed.), *The Charter of the United Nations. A Commentary* (2nd edn, OUP, 2002), vol. 2, 1129; R Wilde, 'The Trusteeship Council', ch. 8 in S Daws and T Weiss (eds), *The Oxford Handbook on the United Nations* (OUP, 2007) and sources cited therein. On proposals for its reactivation generally see ibid., and, in relation to ITA projects specifically, the sources cited below, ch. 8, n. 366.

[45] UN Charter, Art. 77(1)(c) (open to further territories), Art. 78 (not open to UN members). For commentary on these provisions, see, e.g., Rauschning (above n. 44), 1114–8. For a comparison with the Mandates system, which lacked an equivalent provision, see Chowdhuri (above n. 43), 11. On the lack of any subsequent territories being placed under the Trusteeship system, see the following: the discussion in Chowdhuri, ibid., 139–43 of proposals made for placement; the list of

of an individual state 'exercised . . . on behalf of the League'; this amounted to varying degrees of administrative control exercised over the territory by the Mandatory power,[46] supervised by the League Mandates Commission and the plenary League Council.[47] Trust territories were to be subject to the 'administration' of individual states or the United Nations—in practice only states performed this role[48]—supervised by the UN General Assembly, the Trusteeship Council and the Security Council.[49]

As far as the territories detached from the defeated powers were concerned, the arrangements under both systems implied indefinite detachment, and administration was not to be conducted on behalf of these powers as the continuing title-holders or on the basis of any other relationship of title with respect to the territories.[50] This set-up presupposed the end of title to the territories on the part of the defeated powers, since it amounted to a lawful, permanent removal of any administrative control over the territory by any actor exercising such control on behalf of the defeated powers as title-holders.[51] So, the League Covenant referred to the territories concerned as having 'ceased to be under the sovereignty of the States which formerly governed them'.[52] At the same time, through the concept of 'trust', it was clear that under both systems, the territories were not being reconstituted as independent states.[53] Did, then, the administering

---

Trust Territories in Crawford (above n. 4), Appendix 2; the treatment of South West Africa/Namibia, discussed below, section 5.5; the rejection of all forms of foreign territorial administration as part of the post-Second World War self-determination entitlement, discussed below, ch. 8, section 8.5.1; and the non-utilization of the Trusteeship system in relation to East Timor, discussed below, ch.8, text accompanying n. 541.

[46] Defined as 'authority, control or administration' in the League Covenant, Art. 22. The 'tutelage' element is discussed further below, ch. 8, section 8.3.2.

[47] See above, n. 43.

[48] UN Charter, Art. 81. For commentary on this provision, see, e.g., Rauschning (above n. 44), 1121–3. Only states performed the role of the administering authority because the original Trusteeship arrangements involved states exclusively; the later UN Council for South West Africa/Namibia was never able to take up its role; and no new arrangements were created. See n. 45 above, and, below, section 5.5 (on South West Africa/Namibia); see also below, ch. 8, text accompanying n. 323 *et seq* (on the original arrangements only involving states) and text accompanying n. 541 *et seq* (on the non-reactivation of the Trusteeship Council in relation to East Timor).

[49] See above, n. 44. The nature of the supervision provided is discussed further below, ch. 8, nn. 411 and 412.

[50] See generally the sources cited above in n. 43 (on the Mandate system) and n. 44 (on the Trusteeship system).

[51] See ibid. Although, of course, nothing in each system prevented subsequent arrangements that might provide for the conferral of sovereignty with respect to the territories on the part of those states.

[52] League Covenant, Art. 22.

[53] On the debate that led up to these arrangements, during which some advocated independence, see below, ch. 8, text accompanying n. 316 *et seq*. James Crawford states that 'A' class Mandates '. . . were treated as states for the purposes of nationality, but were much less certainly states for other purposes'; Crawford (above n. 4), 31. Trusteeship is discussed further below, ch. 8, section 8.3.2.

powers and/or the international organizations involved enjoy sovereignty (in the sense of title)?[54]

Both systems conferred merely an administrative capacity on the administrative powers concerned; there was no explicit conferral of title, although the provisions for 'C' class Mandates in Article 22 of the Covenant stated that such territories:

can be best administered under the laws of the Mandatory as integral portions of its territory, subject to . . . safeguards . . . in the interests of the indigenous population.

In its Advisory Opinion of 1950 concerning South West Africa, a 'C' class Mandate, the ICJ remarked that:

. . . [t]he terms of this Mandate, as well as the provisions of Article 22 of the Covenant and the principles embodied therein, show that the creation of this new international institution did not involve any cession of territory or transfer of sovereignty to the Union of South Africa.[55]

As the Court stated in relation to the Mandate system:

. . . two principles were considered to be of paramount importance: the principle of non-annexation and the principle that the well-being and development of such peoples [not capable of self-government] form a 'sacred trust of civilization'.[56]

Not only had the administering state not been given sovereignty under the administration arrangement, then; it was also prevented from making a subsequent claim to title over the territory resting on the alternative basis of the exercise of control.[57]

Were the League and the UN 'sovereign' over the Mandated and Trust territories respectively, as was suggested (in the case of the UN and Trust territories) by Méir Ydit?[58] Again, neither organization was explicitly granted title; rather, the institutional system under which the arrangements took place operated within

---

[54] On the legal status of Mandated and Trust territories, see, e.g., *South West Africa Advisory Opinion* (above n. 43) and the separate opinion of Judge McNair (on Mandated territories); Wright (above n. 38), *passim*, especially 62–3 and Part III (on Mandated territories); Hall (above n. 43), 72–7 (on Mandated territories); Hales, 'The Reform and Extension of the Mandate System' (above n. 43), 179–80, Chowdhuri (above n. 43), 90–1 (on Trust territories) and 229–35 (on both); Sagay (above n. 16), *passim* and especially 13 (on Mandated territories); Koskenniemi (above n. 39), 172–3 (on Mandated territories); Anghie, *Imperialism* (above n. 38), ch. 3, *passim* and especially 147–9 (on Mandated territories); Crawford (above n. 4) (on both), 568–74; PE Corbett, 'What is the League of Nations?', 5 (1924) *BYIL* 119, 128–36 (on Mandated territories), and sources cited therein (on Mandated territories).

[55] *South West Africa Advisory Opinion* (above n. 43), 132.

[56] Ibid., 131.

[57] This is supported by commentary on the historical background to the Mandate system, which suggests that the arrangements were designed to be an alternative to annexation. See the discussion below, ch. 8, text accompanying n. 316 *et seq.*

[58] M Ydit, *Internationalised Territories from the 'Free City of Cracow' to the 'Free City of Berlin'* (Sythoff, 1961), 63.

the League and the UN, and, as mentioned, various organs of each organization were involved in supervising the arrangements. The purpose of these arrangements, to ensure an international guarantee, inter alia through supervision, of the relationship of trust set up between the administering states and the administered entities, did not by itself presuppose the enjoyment of title.[59]

The best view of legal status as far as Mandated and Trust territories are concerned is that such entities were not states, nor formed part of the territory of any other states (notably the administering states) nor were under the sovereignty of the supervising international organizations, but enjoyed a special international legal status as non-state territorial units placed within a special system of 'administration and supervision' (by individual states and international organizations respectively) until they were deemed sufficiently 'developed' to be able to 'stand alone' in the world as states.[60] As the ICJ stated in the 1950 *South West Africa Advisory Opinion*:

[t]he Mandate was created, in the interests of the inhabitants of the territory, and of humanity in general, as an international institution with an international object—a sacred trust of civilization.[61]

In his separate opinion in the *South West Africa Advisory Opinion*, Sir Arnold McNair remarked in a famous dictum that:

[t]he doctrine of sovereignty has no application to this new system [the Mandate system and the corresponding principles of the Trusteeship system]. Sovereignty over a Mandated Territory is in abeyance; if and when the inhabitants of the Territory obtain recognition as an independent state... sovereignty will revive and vest in the new State.[62]

Mandated and Trust territories were, therefore, not *terrae nullius* but non-state territorial units with a special status by virtue of the self-determination entitlement.[63]

In addition to Mandated and Trust territories generally, further international territorial administration projects were conceived in relation to other territories on an ad hoc basis. Whereas one such territory—South West Africa—was a Mandated territory, the other territories were colonies which, as a result of the displacement of the original colonial power with another administrative presence, no longer formed part of the sovereign territory of the colonial state. The first use of international territorial administration for a particular non-state territory was the West Irian project in 1962.

---

[59] The trust relationship is discussed further below in ch. 8, section 8.3.2.

[60] The first quotation is from UN Charter, Art. 75; the second and third quotations are from the League Covenant, Art. 22.

[61] *South West Africa Advisory Opinion* (above n. 43), 132.

[62] Ibid., Separate Opinion of Lord McNair, 150. For a consideration of this famous passage, and related issues, see, e.g., N Berman, 'Sovereignty in Abeyance: Self-Determination and International Law', 7 (1988) *Wisconsin International Law Journal* 51.

[63] On this general idea, see above, n. 23 and accompanying text.

5.4 West Irian 1962–63

West Irian formed part of the wider 'Dutch East Indies' colony.[64] With the advent of the self-determination entitlement, most of the Dutch East Indies became independent as Indonesia, with West Irian remaining under colonial administration. Whereas the Netherlands held that its colonial administration had treated what had become Indonesia separately from West Irian, thus leading to two separate units for the purpose of self-determination, Indonesia claimed that the entire Dutch East Indies was a single self-determination unit and West Irian should therefore be incorporated automatically into Indonesian territory. As far as the *uti possidetis juris* approach to determining the unit of analysis is concerned, then, there was a fundamental dispute as to the contours of the colonial administrative structures that should be followed in order to decide whether one or more 'self-determination units' were in play.[65] The compromise reached between the two states in an agreement in 1962 and series of side-letters involved the transfer of territorial control from the Netherlands to Indonesia, via a period of administration by the United Nations Temporary Executive Authority (UNTEA) from October 1962 to May 1963,[66] followed by a UN-monitored 'act of free choice' concerning 'self-determination' on the question of whether the people of West Irian should 'remain' or 'sever their ties' with Indonesia.[67] The provisions of the agreement were unclear as to what exactly the 'act of free choice' was to amount to, in particular whether it would involve a popular vote;[68] what took place was widely criticized as a sham, involving only a small number of the local elite,[69] but

[64] On this period in West Irian's history, see, for example, D Bowett, *United Nations Forces: A Legal Study* (1964), 255–6; R Higgins, *United Nations Peacekeeping, Vol. 2, Asia 1946–1967* (OUP, 1970), 93–100; MD Donelan and MJ Grieve, *International Disputes: Case Histories 1945–1970* (Palgrave Macmillan, 1973), 83–7; TM Franck, *Nation Against Nation: What Happened to the UN Dream and What the US Can Do About It* (OUP, 1985), 76–82; WJ Durch, 'UN Temporary Executive Authority', in Durch, *The Evolution of UN Peacekeeping* (St. Martin's Press, 1994), 285, at 285–7 and sources cited therein; Crawford (above n. 4), 555–6, 646 n. 201 and sources cited therein; M Pomerance, 'Methods of Self-Determination and the Argument of "Primitiveness"', 12 (1974) *Canadian Yearbook of International Law* 38.

[65] On the principle of *uti possidetis juris*, see above n. 20 and accompanying text.

[66] On UNTEA, see above, ch. 2, n. 18.

[67] See Agreement between Indonesia and the Netherlands Concerning West New Guinea (West Irian), 15 August 1962, 437 UNTS 273; Indonesia–Netherlands–United Nations, Exchange of Letters (with Annexed Memorandum of Understanding) on Cessation of Hostilities, 15 August 1962, 437 UNTS 294, approved by the General Assembly by GA Res. 1752 (XVII), 21 September 1962. The arrangements for the 'act of free choice' in the Agreement are contained in Arts XIV–XXI; the quotations are taken from Arts XVII and XVIII.

[68] In addition to using the term 'free choice', the Agreement Concerning West New Guinea (above n. 67) speaks of an 'act of' and 'arrangements for' 'self-determination' (Arts X and XVI respectively); arrangements to 'give the people of the territory the opportunity to exercise freedom of choice' (Art. XVIII) and those 'arrived at for freedom of choice' (Art. XIX); and arrangements for 'the eligibility of all adults, male and female, not foreign nationals to participate in the act of self-determination to be carried out in accordance with international practice' (ibid.).

[69] For such criticism, see the citations of Franck and Pomerance in n. 70 below.

the result, an agreement to Indonesian sovereignty, was nonetheless endorsed by the UN monitors, and the territory became part of Indonesia.[70]

Can any helpful conclusion be drawn about the self-determination entitlement of the people of West Irian from the 1962 agreement between the Netherlands and Indonesia? In explicitly associating the term 'self-determination' with the choice between two forms of 'external' status, and invoking an 'act of free choice', it was clear that at least some of the people of West Irian, rather than other actors such as the Netherlands and Indonesia, were being given the right to determine the territory's 'external' status. On the other hand, the transfer of control from the Netherlands to Indonesia via the short period of UN administration preceding the consultation treated the situation as if the people of West Irian did not enjoy a right to 'external' self-determination. As far as the agreement was concerned, the people were not to be consulted on the question of who would exercise administrative control over them. It might be said, therefore, that the agreement, which provided for both the consultation and the transfer, is of no assistance in clarifying the juridical status of West Irian for the period of UN administration (or afterwards) since it embodied two mutually contradictory positions as far as a possible self-determination entitlement was concerned.

However, such a conclusion would treat the questions of territorial status and territorial administration as being of equal significance as far as their relevance to self-determination is concerned. Whereas deciding who exercises administrative control over the territory, without prejudice to the question of territorial status, clearly impacts on the enjoyment of self-determination, in cases such as this, arguably the question of external status is considered more important. The people were denied the right to decide upon the administrative structure operating for the period leading up to the consultation. However, their right to a consultation was not only significant in terms of their eventual legal status; it also involved, as a corollary, the right to determine whether the earlier arrangement concerning administrative control would continue. It might actually be possible, therefore, to consider the agreement of 1962 as articulating a right of 'external' self-determination on the part of the West Irianese, albeit a right that would be determined in the appropriate fashion after a period when administrative arrangements clearly not based on such a right were adopted.

If this is correct, then the people of West Irian enjoyed a right of 'external' self-determination when UNTEA administered the territory, not because of separate treatment during the Dutch administration of its East Indies colony (but without prejudice to this as an alternative basis), but because the colonial power and the other state aspiring to title with respect to the territory had agreed that this would

---

[70] On the consultation, see, for example, M Pomerance, *Self-Determination in Law and Practice: The New Doctrine in the United Nations* (Martinus Nijhoff, 1982), 32–5; Franck (above n. 64), 81–2; Durch (above n. 64), 295–6 (on UNTEA); Cassese (above n. 19), 82–6; Crawford (above n. 4), 646 n. 201 and sources cited therein; Pomerance (above n. 64), 48–62. On the outcome of the 'act of free choice', see also GA Res. 2504 (XXIV), 19 November 1969.

be the case. This echoes the historical practice of external self-determination based on specific ad hoc agreements rather than the post-war entitlement arising out of the status of the territory.

If, as discussed earlier, colonial title in the era of self-determination could be extinguished if territorial control by the colonial state was brought to an end, then West Irian ceased to be Dutch territory on the transfer of administrative authority to the United Nations. Thus, for the duration of the UN administration project, the territory was a non-state territory with a special international legal status as a self-determination unit.[71]

5.5 South West Africa/Namibia 1967 and 1989–90

Four years after the end of the West Irian project, a second plenary UN administration project was conceived in relation to another non-state territorial unit, South West Africa. This time the territory was not a colonial possession but a Mandate of South Africa, having been accepted on behalf of that state by the United Kingdom under the League of Nations Mandate system.[72] As such, it was not sovereign territory of South Africa; once the post-Second World War self-determination entitlement of Mandated territories had crystallized, the legal status of South West Africa was that of a non-state territorial unit with legal personality in international law by virtue of its self-determination entitlement.

By the 1960s, when all the other states administering territories that had been Mandates had either ended these arrangements or reconstituted them under the Trusteeship system, South Africa continued to refuse to take such action with respect to South West Africa, despite repeated requests by the General Assembly,[73] claiming the territory as part of its sovereign territory.[74] On 27 October 1966, the General Assembly declared that South Africa had 'failed to fulfil its obligations

---

[71] See also DS Smyrek, *Internationally Administered Territories—International Protectorates? An Analysis of Sovereignty over Internationally Administered Territories with Special Reference to the Legal Status of Post-War Kosovo* (Duncker & Humblot, 2006), 101–10.

[72] *South West Africa Advisory Opinion* (above n. 43), 132.

[73] See the discussion in the *Namibia Advisory Opinion* (above n. 3), paras 84–6, and *South West Africa Advisory Opinion* (above n. 43), at 141–3. On the history of South West Africa/Namibia generally during this period, including treatment of its legal status, see, e.g., Hall (above n. 43), 75–7; J Dugard (ed.), *The South West Africa/Namibia Dispute: Documents and scholarly writings on the controversy between South Africa and the United Nations* (University of California Press, 1973), 409–13, 436–46; Sagay (above n. 16), *passim*; I Brownlie, *African Boundaries: A Legal and Diplomatic Encyclopedia* (University of California Press, 1979), 149–58; Shaw (above n. 34), *passim* and sources cited therein at 105–10; LCW Kaela, *The Question of Namibia* (Macmillan Press, 1996), and sources cited therein at 205–11; LL Herman, 'The Legal Status of Namibia and of the United Nations Council for Namibia', 13 (1975) *Canadian Yearbook of International Law* 306; MN Shaw, 'The Western Sahara Case', 49 (1978) *BYIL* 119; A Roberts, 'What is Military Occupation?', 55 (1984) *BYIL* 249, 291–2; J Dugard, 'The Revocation of the Mandate for Namibia Revisited', 1 (1985) *South African Journal on Human Rights* 154.

[74] On the claims of title, see, e.g., *Namibia Advisory Opinion* (above n. 3), paras 82–3.

in respect of the administration' of South West Africa,[75] and decided that the Mandate was:

> ... therefore terminated, that South Africa has no other right to administer the Territory and that henceforth South West Africa comes under the direct responsibility of the United Nations.[76]

In its *Namibia Advisory Opinion* of 1971, the ICJ held that the General Assembly enjoyed a power to terminate Mandates and that such a power had been lawfully exercised in this instance.[77]

On 19 May 1967, the General Assembly established the United Nations Council for South West Africa in order 'to administer South West Africa until independence',[78] and provided for South Africa's withdrawal.[79] In 1968, the General Assembly changed the name of South West Africa and the Council for South West Africa to Namibia and the Council for Namibia respectively.[80] Although the Council never took up its administrative role on the ground due to South Africa's continued occupation of the territory despite the Security Council calling on South Africa to withdraw in Resolution 264 of 1969,[81] what would have been the legal status of the territory had the Council plan been implemented? Did the assertion of 'direct responsibility' on the part of the United Nations suggest sovereignty?

The best way of understanding this term is as a reference to the nature of the role performed by the administering authority when compared with the UN's usual role of supervision. Arguably, the Assembly posited these two roles as, respectively, 'direct' and 'indirect' responsibilities when it came to Mandated and Trust territories. So, with the termination of South Africa's 'direct' responsibility for administration, this responsibility, in addition to the usual 'indirect' supervisory responsibility, was to be enjoyed by the United Nations, given that, as mentioned, the UN could act as the administering authority under the Trusteeship system.[82] There was no difference, then, with the situation as far

[75] GA Res. 2145 (XXI), 27 October 1966, para. 3.

[76] Ibid., para. 4.

[77] *Namibia Advisory Opinion* (above n. 3). On the termination of the Mandate, and the 1971 Advisory Opinion, see, e.g., Dugard, *The South West Africa/Namibia Dispute* (above n. 73), 51, 376–446 and sources cited at 559–60 (on the revocation of the Mandate), 447–542, and sources cited at 560–1 (on the Advisory Opinion); Sagay (above n. 16), *passim* and especially chs 8–11; *Digest on US Practice of International Law*, vol. 3 (1975), 85–90; Kaela (above n. 73), 58–60; Brownlie (above n. 20), 163–6, 491–2 and sources contained in 170, n. 14; Crawford (above n. 4), 591–6; Herman (above n. 73), 306–19.

[78] GA Res. 2248 (S-V), 19 May 1967, section II, para. 1; see also GA Res. 2372 (XXII), 12 June 1968.

[79] GA Res. 2248 (S-V) (above n. 78), section IV, para. 3.

[80] GA Res. 2372 (XXII) (above n. 78).

[81] SC Res. 264, 20 March 1969, para. 3. On South Africa's refusal, see, e.g., Dugard, *The South West Africa/Namibia Dispute* (above n. 73), 436, 440; Sagay (above n. 16), chs 15–17. On the limited role that was performed by the Council, see below, ch. 6, text accompanying nn. 54 *et seq.*

[82] Under UN Charter Art. 81. See above, n. 48.

as the administering authorities of other Mandated and Trust territories were concerned: the administrative authority of the UN was limited to administration, without also the conferral of sovereignty. The status of the territory, as far as sovereignty was concerned, would remain as it had been under South African administration, viz., a non-state territorial entity which, by this stage, enjoyed a right of 'external' self-determination.[83] Itse Sagay argued at the time that the legal status of the UN Council, as far as its relationship to South West Africa/Namibia was concerned, was:

... that of a trustee, rather than a sovereign. Its political relationship with the mandated territory is that between an administrative authority, or a *de jure* government and a territory under its rule.[84]

South Africa finally agreed to Namibian independence in 1988, implementing in 1989 a plan, originally conceived a decade earlier, whereby the United Nations supervised and controlled elections for the first government of an independent state of Namibia; once the result had been obtained, South Africa withdrew and independence was proclaimed.[85] The UN mission—the United Nations Transitional Assistance Group (UNTAG)—did not take over administrative control, then, but merely exercised particular administrative prerogatives relating to the elections with respect to South African-administered Namibia.[86] The twenty years of South African occupation had no effect as far as that country's claim to title over Namibia was concerned,[87] and the status of the territory for the duration of UNTAG's mandate remained as it had been in 1967.

5.6 Western Sahara From 1991

The two remaining international administration projects in non-state territories related to two former colonies, the Western Sahara and East Timor. Rio de Oro and Sakiet El Hamra, located in the north-east coast of Africa bordering Morocco, Mauritania, and Algeria and known as Western Sahara/Sahara Occidental at the

---

[83] See also Smyrek (above n. 71), 110–18; Shaw (above n. 34), 106–7 and sources cited therein; Roberts (above n. 73), 292.

[84] Sagay (above n. 16), 268–9. The significance of the concept of 'trust' to ITA projects generically is considered in detail below, ch. 8, section 8.3.2.

[85] Namibia became independent on 21 March 1990 and was admitted to the UN on 23 April 1990; see SC Res. 652, 17 April 1990; GA Res. S-18/1, 23 April 1990; see also Crawford (above n. 4), 596.

[86] See, above, ch. 2, n. 34.

[87] As the International Court of Justice stated in 1971 in relation to South Africa's claims to title, such claims 'are inadmissible in regard to a Mandated territory'; *Namibia Advisory Opinion* (above n. 3), para. 83.

United Nations, became a Spanish colony—the 'Spanish Sahara'—from 1884.[88] In 1974, when Spain agreed to hold a self-determination referendum in the territory, both Morocco and Mauritania made similar and overlapping claims to title that pre-dated Spanish colonization; with the end of Spanish colonial rule, they argued that as a result of their 'original title', sovereignty should revert to them automatically rather than being determined through an act of self-determination.[89] In the *Western Sahara Advisory Opinion* of 1975, the ICJ held that there had been no ties of sovereignty such as to affect the self-determination process on the part of either Morocco or Mauritania at the time immediately preceding Spanish colonization, and the self-determination principle applied to the territory.[90] This reinforced the position adopted by the General Assembly in 1966 that the people of the Western Sahara enjoyed a right of self-determination and that Spain should determine the procedures for the holding of a self-determination referendum 'under United Nations auspices'.[91] It is clear, therefore, that, once the application of the self-determination entitlement to colonial territories had crystallized as a matter of international law, it was enjoyed by the people of the Western Sahara.

In 1975, after the ICJ's Advisory Opinion, Morocco initiated the 'Green March' of unarmed civilians into Western Sahara on the mistaken basis that the Court had recognized its title over the territory.[92] Following a call by the Security Council for Morocco to withdraw the march participants from Western Sahara,[93] Spain, Morocco, and Mauritania entered into an agreement whereby the Western

---

[88] Harris (above n. 44), 114; TM Franck, 'The Stealing of the Sahara', 70 (1976) *AJIL* 694, 696–7. On the this period in the history of the Western Sahara, and the territory's legal status see, for example, Shaw (above n. 34), 123–30; E Benvenisti, *The International Law of Occupation* (paperback edn, Princeton University Press, 2004), 151–3; Crawford (above n. 4), ch. 14 *passim* and in particular at 639 *et seq.*; Franck, ibid.; RT Vance, 'Recognition as an Affirmative Step in the Decolonization Process: The Case of Western Sahara', 7 (1980) *Yale Journal of World Public Order* 45; Roberts (above n. 73); see also the summary in United Nations, 'MINURSO Background', available at <http://www.un.org/Depts/dpko/missions/minurso/background.html>, and the further sources cited in this sub-section. Many of the works cited in List of Sources, section 5.4, discuss the Western Sahara.

[89] See Harris (above n. 44), 114; Franck (above n. 88), 705.

[90] *Western Sahara Opinion* (above n. 3), conclusions at paras 162–3. For the background to the Advisory Opinion, see Franck (above n. 88), 705–7. On the decision, see the commentary in Franck, ibid., 709–11; Crawford (above n. 4), 639–40; Vance (above n. 88), 54–6; GJ Naldi, 'The Organization of African Unity and the Saharan Arab Democratic Republic', 26 (1982) *Journal of African Law* 152, 153–4.

[91] GA Res. 2229 (XXI), 20 December 1966, paras 1 (on the right of self-determination), 4 (on the referendum, where the General Assembly '*Invites* the Administering power to determine at the earliest possible date, in conformity with the aspiration of the indigenous people of Spanish Sahara and in consultation with the Governments of Mauritania and Morocco and any other interested party, the procedures for the holding of a referendum under United Nations auspices with a view to enabling the indigenous population of the Territory to exercise freely its right to self-determination...'). For commentary, see Franck (above n. 88), 702–703; Vance (above n. 88), 49–50.

[92] Harris (above n. 44), 117; Franck (above n. 88), 711–12.

[93] SC Res. 380, 6 November 1975. For the general UN reaction to the march, see Franck (above n. 88), 712–14.

Sahara would be divided between Morocco and Mauritania, with Spain enjoying a share of the phosphates industry,[94] and the 'Green March' was terminated.[95] In 1976, Spain withdrew and Morocco and Mauritania took over control as envisaged under the agreement; in the same year, the Frente Popular para la Liberación de Saguia el-Hamra y de Río de Oro (Frente POLISARIO), the Western Saharan independence movement, declared the independent state of the Saharawi Arab Democratic Republic (SADR).[96] In 1978, Mauritania withdrew its claims with respect to the territory. From that point onwards, Morocco extended its control to cover Mauritanian-administered areas, ending up in control of most of the Western Sahara.[97] At the same time, the Frente POLISARIO continued to assert its claim to statehood, which was recognized by over 50 states, and engaged in a guerrilla war with the Moroccan authorities.[98]

In 1988, the Frente POLISARIO and Morocco agreed to what are known as the 'settlement proposals' brokered by the UN Secretary-General acting in conjunction with the then Organization of African Unity (OAU).[99] These proposals provided for a ceasefire and a UN-conducted census of the people of the territory, followed by a UN-conducted self-determination referendum on the basis of that census.[100] In 1991, a ceasefire was agreed between Morocco and Frente POLISARIO; in the same year the UN Mission for the Referendum in the Western Sahara (MINURSO) was created by the Security Council, inter alia to carry out the self-determination referendum in the territory.[101] However, continuing disagreements about the prospect of an option for 'external' self-determination appearing on the ballot, and the question of who would be entitled to participate, meant that, at the time of writing, the referendum had not been held.[102]

The 1975 agreement had no legal effect insofar as it purported to transfer the title to Western Sahara from Spain to Morocco and Mauritania, since the effect

[94] The agreement itself was kept secret, but its key terms were made public. See Report of the Secretary-General, 19 November 1975, UN Doc. S/11880 (1975); Franck (above n. 88), 715. On the agreement generally, see Harris (above n. 44), 117; Franck, ibid., 714–17.

[95] Harris (above n. 44), 117; Franck (above n. 88), 716.

[96] Harris (above n. 44), 119. On the Morocco and Mauritania takeover in particular, see Franck (above n. 88). On the declaration of statehood in particular, see the sources cited in Vance (above n. 88), 59 n. 83.

[97] Harris (above n. 44), 118.

[98] Ibid., 118. Harris mentions a figure of 'over 70 states', but appears to cite Naldi (above n. 90) in support of this figure; in fact, Naldi mentions 51 states (ibid., at 157 n. 23 and accompanying text).

[99] See United Nations, 'MINURSO Background', above n. 88. For the proposals, see Report of the Secretary-General, 18 June 1990, UN Doc. S/21360 (1990).

[100] Report of the Secretary-General, 18 June 1990, UN Doc. S/21360 (1990), sections IV (the ceasefire) and V (the census and referendum).

[101] On MINURSO, see above, ch. 2, nn. 21 and 32.

[102] See, for example, Report of the Secretary-General on the Western Sahara, 19 April 2006, UN Doc. S/2006/249 and SC Res. 1675, 28 April 2006. See also above, ch. 2, n. 32.

of the self-determination entitlement was to bar Spain from disposing of its title in this manner without the option first being validated by a self-determination consultation.[103] Equally, Morocco could not validly enjoy title by virtue of the exercise of territorial control, since this status for the territory has not been validated by the Saharawis. At the same time, applying the general considerations above concerning the special nature of colonial title in the light of the self-determination entitlement, arguably Spain's title was extinguished as a result of its withdrawal and the subsequent control exercised by Morocco and Mauritania (and later just Morocco). That is not to say that Morocco (whether individually or in conjunction with Mauritania) enjoyed title, or that Spain's special relationship to the Western Sahara as the former colonial power did not continue; merely that, drawing on the idea discussed earlier, the effect of the self-determination entitlement on Spain's title was such that this title would be extinguished if effective control ceased.[104]

Did Frente POLISARIO's declaration of independent statehood render Western Sahara a state? Although Frente POLISARIO did not exercise control over much of the territory, and the state it claimed to represent did not join the United Nations, the SADR was recognized as a state by a significant number of states, becoming a member of the OAU (now the African Union),[105] an organization whose membership is restricted to any 'independent sovereign African State'.[106] Moreover, no other state enjoyed a valid claim and, as a result, the states exercising territorial control—Morocco and Mauritania, and later just Morocco—purported to exercise this control in a particular capacity as the territorial sovereign—that was unlawful. Although this exercise of control arguably extinguished Spain's title, therefore, it was irrelevant as a comparator to the degree of control exercised by the SADR authority when considering the significance of the latter's claim to statehood, since it could not itself validly form an alternative basis for title.

---

[103] After the Agreement was made, the General Assembly passed two resolutions on 10 December 1975 that were mutually contradictory as far as its status is concerned. Resolution 3458A (XXX) made no reference to the Agreement, and requested Spain to take immediately all necessary measures to enable the people of the territory to exercise their right of self-determination (GA Res. 3458A (XXX), 10 December 1975, para. 7) which is understood to entail an 'act of self-determination', viz. a consultation on external status (ibid., para. 8). Resolution 3458B (XXX) 'takes note' of the Agreement (GA Res. 3458B (XXX), 10 December 1975, para. 1) but requests the parties to the Agreement to 'ensure respect for the freely expressed aspirations of the Saharan populations' (ibid., para. 3) and that the interim administration in the territory (introduced as part of the Agreement) take steps to ensure the conduct of a self-determination consultation (ibid., para. 4). See Franck (above n. 88), 717–18.

[104] See the general discussion above, text following n. 25.

[105] For OAU Membership, see Naldi (above n. 90); for membership of the African Union (as 'Saharawi') at the time of writing, see the website of the African Union, at <http://www.africa-union.org>.

[106] Article IV, Charter of the Organization of African Unity, Addis Ababa, 25 May 1963, 479 UNTS 39.

Might the self-determination entitlement be significant here? It could be argued that, when the right of self-determination is being implemented through statehood, the new state can be regarded as a legitimate candidate by virtue of this entitlement, without necessarily conforming either fully or even at all with the criterion of effective governmental control.[107] Gino Naldi seems to be suggesting this when he argued in 1982 that the SADR 'can possibly be considered a state' given that 'the right of self-determination may compensate for the lack of certain criteria'.[108]

One potential problem here, overlooked by Naldi, is the absence of a consultation supporting independence. As mentioned above, prior to the articulation of self-determination as a human right, it is unclear whether or not a consultation was required in such circumstances for the self-determination entitlement to be realized. At what point, then, did human rights law have the effect of requiring a consultation even when independent statehood was adopted? As mentioned, in the *Western Sahara Advisory Opinion*, which was issued a year before the SADR declaration of independence, the ICJ seemed to suggest that a consultation was, in principle, an absolute requirement. Moreover, in its consideration of the applicability of General Assembly Resolution 1514 (XV) to the decolonization of the Western Sahara, the Court posited this issue of applicability 'in particular' as relating to the 'principle of self-determination through the free and genuine expression of the will of the peoples of the Territory'.[109] It would seem, therefore, that, as far as the Court was concerned, the law on self-determination at that stage required a consultation as part of the process of realizing the Saharawi entitlement.

It could also be argued that such a requirement arose out of the undertakings made by Spain prior to the declaration of independence. In 1966, in Resolution 2229, the General Assembly invited Spain, in consultation with Mauritania and Morocco, to determine the procedures 'for the holding of a referendum under United Nations auspices with a view to enabling the indigenous people of the territory to exercise freely its right to self-determination'.[110] Spain eventually agreed to hold such a referendum in 1974, prior to the claims made by Morocco and Mauritania with respect to title mentioned earlier.[111] After the 1975 agreement, the General Assembly passed two resolutions, both underscoring

---

[107] On the legal criteria for statehood generally, see the sources cited above, ch. 4, n. 1; treatment of the significance of the self-determination entitlement in the context of claims for statehood is provided by many of the works in the Sources List, section 5.4.

[108] Naldi (above n. 90), 157. Naldi discusses the conformity of the SADR to the traditional 'Montevideo' criteria for statehood ibid., at 153–7. On the practice of international recognition in relation to the SADR, see Vance (above n. 88), 63–87.

[109] *Western Sahara Opinion* (above n. 3), para. 209.

[110] GA Res. 2229 (XXI) (above n. 91), para. 4.

[111] Harris (above n. 44), 114.

the need for steps to be taken to enable the Saharawis to exercise their right of self-determination.[112]

It might be argued that Spain's undertaking and the support given to this by the General Assembly did not reflect or constitute a free-standing obligation to hold a referendum, but rather a pragmatic solution to the political situation in the territory at the time, without prejudice to the subsequent adoption of a different solution. Whatever Spain's intention, however, the undertaking can be understood to have created an entitlement by way of estoppel, since it led to an expectation of a referendum on the part of the Saharawis, which it was reasonable to assume might have been acted upon by local leaders to their detriment in some fashion. Although this approach would, of course, create an undertaking opposable to Spain in the first instance, because the self-determination entitlement is regarded as an *erga omnes* right,[113] the effect of the undertaking would be to establish an entitlement on the part of the Saharawis to participate in a self-determination referendum that was opposable to all states.

It would seem likely, then, that by virtue either of the state of the general law on self-determination at the time, or as a consequence of Spain's undertaking, or a combination of the two, the people of the Western Sahara were entitled to a self-determination referendum in 1975 before the territory could validly be constituted as a state. Following from this, it is arguable that the declaration of independence in 1976 was not capable of having juridical effect as far as statehood was concerned, and, equally, the ongoing claim to statehood on the part of Frente POLISARIO was not capable of establishing statehood in the absence of a referendum.

Resolutions by the General Assembly and the Security Council after 1975 affirmed the right to self-determination of the Saharawis.[114] The 1988 settlement proposals and the 1991 Security Council mandate for MINURSO both

---

[112] GA Res. 3458A (XXX) and GA Res. 3458B (XXX) (both cited above n. 103); see the commentary and reference in n. 103 above. The resolutions were mutually contradictory as far as the timing of a consultation were concerned, as a result of their different positions with respect to the Agreement as outlined earlier; whereas under Resolution 3458A the consultation was to take place immediately, under Resolution 3458B it was to take place once the 'interim administration' introduced as part of the Agreement was under way.

[113] On the *erga omnes* nature of the self-determination entitlement see, e.g., *East Timor Case* (above n. 3), para. 29; *Wall Advisory Opinion* (above n. 3), paras 88 and 156; see also the Dissenting Opinion of Judge Weeramantry in *East Timor Case, passim* and the commentary by M Ragazzi, *The Concept of International Obligations* Erga Omnes (OUP, 1997), 138. On the concept of *erga omnes* obligations generally see, e.g., *Barcelona Traction, Light and Power Company, Limited, Second Phase, ICJ Reports 1970*, 3, paras 33–4; *Wall Advisory Opinion*, paras 159–60; ILC, Articles on Responsibility of States for Internationally Wrongful Acts ('ILC's Articles on State Responsibility'), Part 2, Chapter III, Introductory Commentary; Art. 48(1)(b) and Commentary thereto, paras 8–10, reproduced in J Crawford, *The International Law Commission's Articles on State Responsibility. Introduction, Text and Commentaries* (CUP, 2002); Ragazzi, ibid., *passim*.

[114] In numerous instruments; see those cited on the MINURSO website, at <http://www.un.org/Depts/dpko/missions/minurso>, under separate sections for Security Council and General Assembly resolutions.

provide for a self-determination referendum in the territory, albeit one limited to two particular options—independence or integration with Morocco.[115] The combined effect of these post-1975 developments is to place beyond doubt the entitlement of the Saharawis to a self-determination referendum. If, then, in the unlikely scenario that the entitlement did not subsist in 1975, and Western Sahara was validly constituted as a state, it is a state whose people are currently denied 'internal' self-determination by virtue of the Moroccan occupation,[116] and set on course for an 'external' self-determination referendum that will revisit the question of territorial status and in its implementation lead to an alteration in this status or a continuation of statehood.[117] If, as is more likely, the entitlement did subsist in 1975, and the Western Sahara did not therefore become a (foreign occupied) state, then it is a self-determination unit that does not form part of the territory of any state.

5.7 East Timor 1999–2002

Whereas, at the time of writing, the administration arrangements in Western Sahara were yet to be fully implemented, the involvement of the UN in realizing East Timorese independence marked a dramatic reversal in the fate of a people who had suffered, like the Saharawis, from a long-standing denial of self-determination.

East Timor became populated in the broader wave of human migrations that shaped the human habitation of Australasia more generally.[118] It was colonized by Portugal in the 16th century.[119] In 1975, civil war broke out between rival local factions, leading to the withdrawal of the Portuguese administration to a nearby island.[120] Two factions made competing independence claims on 28 and

---

[115] Report of the Secretary-General, 18 June 1990, UN Doc. S/21360 (1990), para. 31; SC Res. 690, 29 April 1991.

[116] As James Crawford states, '[w]hen a self-determination unit is a State, the principle of self-determination is represented by the rule against intervention in the internal affairs of that State, and in particular in the choice of the form of government of the State'; Crawford (above n. 4), 128.

[117] Thus for Frente POLISARIO to the self-determination consultation would be a device for validating the pre-existing reality of statehood through support from a consultation and the consequent withdrawal of Morocco. On the prospects for the consultation, however, see above, ch. 2, n. 32.

[118] For a broad historical treatment of East Timor, see, e.g., GC Gunn, *Timor Loro Sae: 500 Years* (Livros do Oriente, 1999). For commentary on the position of East Timor during the period under present evaluation, including issues of legal status, see the works in the List of Sources, section 5.4, many of which address East Timor within a broader discussion of self-determination, and those cited in this section, which are more tightly focused on the issue of East Timor's legal status in particular.

[119] *East Timor Case* (above n. 3), 95.

[120] PD Elliott, 'The East Timor Dispute', 27 (1978) *ICLQ* 238, at 239, RS Clark, 'The "Decolonization" of East Timor and United Nations Norms on Self-Determination and Aggression', 7 (1980) *Yale Journal of World Public Order* 2, at 5–7.

30 November, and on 7 December Indonesia invaded and occupied the territory.[121] Indonesia claimed to be effecting East Timorese self-determination,[122]
but this claim is difficult to sustain given the continued popularity and guerrilla
activities of the East Timorese independence movement, the absence of a genuine
consultation on integration with Indonesia,[123] and the allegations of widespread
human rights violations by Indonesian forces in East Timor.[124]

The UN Security Council and General Assembly called on Indonesia to
withdraw, and on all states to respect the right of the East Timorese to self-
determination.[125] In addition, the General Assembly condemned the invasion,
explicitly linked an Indonesian withdrawal with the enabling of East Timorese
self-determination, and continued to refer to Portugal as the 'administering power'.[126] The Security Council reaffirmed its initial call relating to withdrawal and self-determination a year later, adopting no further resolutions until
1999.[127] Subsequent General Assembly resolutions reaffirmed previous General
Assembly and Security Council resolutions[128] and the right of the East Timorese
to self-determination;[129] they also rejected the integration of East Timor into
Indonesia,[130] and continued the reference to Portugal as the 'administering
power'.[131] No resolution called for non-recognition of the Indonesian annexation.[132] Support for General Assembly resolutions on East Timor diminished,
and none was passed after 1982 until 1999, but the territory remained on the UN
list of Non-Self-Governing Territories, this continuing until the independence of

---

[121] Elliott (above n. 120), 239, Clark (above n. 120), 7–9 and sources cited therein; Benvenisti (above n. 88), 153–9.

[122] See Elliott (above n. 120), 241–2; RS Clark, 'The "Decolonization" of East Timor and United Nations Norms on Self-Determination and Aggression', in *International Law and the Question of East Timor* (Catholic Institute for International Relations/International Platform of Jurists for East Timor, 1995), 65, at 74 n. 51.

[123] For this absence and its effect on self-determination, see Elliott (above n. 120), 244–6; Clark (above n. 122), 73–80; P Lawrence, 'East Timor', in R Bernhardt (ed.), *Encyclopedia of Public International Law*, 12 (1990), 3, at 4.

[124] See L Hannikainen, 'The Case of East Timor from the Perspective of *Jus Cogens*' in *International Law and the Question of East Timor* (Catholic Institute for International Relations/International Platform of Jurists for East Timor, 1995), 103, 107–9; G Nettheim, 'International Law and International Politics', in *International Law and the Question of East Timor* (Catholic Institute for International Relations/International Platform of Jurists for East Timor, 1995), 181, 188–204.

[125] SC Res. 384, 22 December 1975; GA Res. 3485 (XXX), 12 December 1975.

[126] Ibid.

[127] SC Res. 389, 22 April 1976.

[128] GA Res. 31/53, 1 December 1976; GA Res. 32/34, 28 November 1977; GA Res. 33/39, 13 December 1978.

[129] GA Res. 31/53, GA Res. 32/34, GA Res. 33/39 (all cited in n. 128 above); GA Res. 34/40, 21 November 1979; GA Res. 35/27, 11 November 1980; GA Res. 36/50, 24 November 1981.

[130] GA Res. 31/53, GA Res. 32/34 (both cited in n. 129 above).

[131] GA Res. 34/40, GA Res. 35/27, GA Res. 36/50 (all cited in n. 129 above); GA Res. 37/30, 23 November 1982.

[132] In contrast to other situations where resolutions have called for non-recognition of claims to sovereignty because of illegality in relation to the claims concerned; see C Chinkin, 'The *East Timor Case (Portugal v Australia)*', 45 (1996) *ICLQ* 712, 713 n. 11.

Timor-Leste in 2002.[133] Indonesia claimed that East Timor had become its 27th Province, and entered into an agreement with Australia to exploit the resources in the 'Timor Gap'—the sea between East Timor and Australia.[134]

Drawing on the foregoing analysis in this chapter, it may be concluded that, in 1975, Portugal enjoyed a special, conditional form of title over East Timor, in that it was obliged to allow the East Timorese to determine the future international status of the territory, an arrangement that raised the possibility of a removal of Portuguese title if the status chosen required this.[135] How, then, should the declarations of independence made in 1975 be understood in terms of the status of the territory? Setting aside the potential effect of the Indonesian annexation that came shortly afterwards, these declarations are perhaps insufficient in principle as the foundation for an alteration of title in favour of East Timorese statehood; arguably, two competing declarations by different factions, made in the absence of a self-determination consultation involving all the people of the territory, do not constitute a sufficiently certain or legitimate expression of the will of the East Timorese.[136] Moreover, as discussed above, the UN practice was to continue to treat the occupation of East Timor as that of a Non-Self-Governing Territory, not a state. It would seem, then, that the conditional form of title was not affected by the independence claims.

But was this conditional form of title affected by Indonesia's 25-year occupation of the territory? According to James Crawford, one consequence of the 'limited' enjoyment of sovereignty by a colonial power arising out of the self-determination entitlement may be that:

… sovereignty … is more readily displaced, even in the case of annexation by the use of force, provided that the principle of self-determination is not itself violated.[137]

---

[133] On the lack of resolutions after 1982, see, e.g., the discussion in Chinkin (above n. 132). On East Timor's listing as a Non-Self-Governing Territory generally and the operation of this until 2002, see, e.g., Crawford (above n. 4), Appendix III, 755; United Nations Department of Political Affairs, Decolonization Unit, 'Trust and Non-Self-Governing Territories, 1945–1999', available at <http://www.un.org/Depts/dpi/decolonization/trust2.htm>; GA Res. 56/282, 1 May 2002, and 'General Assembly decides to remove East Timor from list of Non-Self-Governing Territories upon independence, set for 20 May', UN Press Release GA/10014, 1 May 2002 <http://www.un.org/News/Press/docs/2002/GA10014.doc.htm>.

[134] Treaty between Australia and the Republic of Indonesia on the Zone of Co-operation in an Area between the Indonesian Province of East Timor and Northern Australia, Timor Sea, 11 December 1989, in force 9 February 1991, 9 *Australian Treaty Series* 1991. Portugal brought a case against Australia before the International Court of Justice, challenging the legality of this action, but the Court refused jurisdiction applying the *Monetary Gold* principle, since in order to determine the lawfulness of Australia's actions it was necessary to determine the legality of the actions of Indonesia, who had not consented to its jurisdiction. See *East Timor Case* (above n. 3), and, for commentary, Chinkin (above n. 132). See also below, n. 141 and accompanying text.

[135] See the general discussion above, in the text after n. 25.

[136] In the *Western Sahara Opinion*, the International Court defined the right of self-determination as 'the need to pay regard to the freely expressed will of peoples'. *Western Sahara Opinion* (above n. 3), para. 59.

[137] Crawford (above n. 4), 616.

When territory is annexed through the unlawful use of force, the territory is a self-determination unit and self-determination is denied, and the General Assembly and Security Council call for the annexation to be reversed and self-determination to be allowed, it is difficult to consider the annexation legally valid, notwithstanding the 25-year duration of the occupation, and the General Assembly's and Security Council's failure to call for non-recognition and adopt any resolutions after 1982.[138] As Crawford states:

[i]nvasion and annexation of territory is unlawful, and the separate status of a territory for the purposes of self-determination, if anything, aggravates the illegality.[139]

Given that the annexation denied rather than supported East Timor's right to self-determination, it can be argued that the limited form of sovereignty Portugal enjoyed with respect to East Timor was not formally extinguished during the period of occupation.[140] Portugal continued to assert its formal ties to East Timor throughout the occupation, notably by bringing a case about East Timor against Australia to the ICJ in 1991.[141] Moreover, it played a key role, both formally and informally, in establishing the arrangements for the 1999 'popular consultation' and the post-'consultation' transition to independence.[142]

Alternatively, it can be argued that the 25-year denial of territorial control extinguished Portugal's title with respect to the territory, given that this title was of a special character. This is not to say either that Indonesia's invasion and occupation were lawful, or that, because of the occupation, title was transferred to Indonesia, or that East Timor was somehow no longer a self-determination unit. As far as East Timor is concerned, in one sense there is no difference between Portuguese and Indonesian control—in either case the self-determination entitlement prevailed. Equally, because of one potential consequence of this entitlement in terms of the rights of the occupying state (if the East Timorese chose independence), both Portugal (before the invasion) and Indonesia (after it) were in the same position in terms of potentially having to give up territorial control.

The situation of East Timor raises the question of whether or not the colonial power enjoys rights with respect to a colonial territory when a second foreign

---

[138] See Hannikainen (above n. 124), 110–11. Discussing the Indonesian occupation, Antonio Cassese submits that 'effectiveness is denied any legal weight by the body of rules on self-determination'; Cassese (above n. 19), 230.

[139] Crawford (above n. 4), 137.

[140] See D Machover, 'International Humanitarian Law and the Indonesian Occupation of East Timor', in *International Law and the Question of East Timor* (Catholic Institute for International Relations/International Platform of Jurists for East Timor, 1995), 205, 208–14.

[141] *East Timor Case* (above n. 3). On Portugal's assertions and their legal significance, see Lawrence (above n. 123), *passim*. Many of the sources cited in List of Sources, section 5.4 discuss the case; see, in particular, Chinkin (above n. 132); Simpson, 'Judging the East Timor Dispute' (above n. 3); C Drew, 'The East Timor Story: International Law on Trial', 12 (2001) *EJIL* 651. Benvenisti suggests that Portugal's protests 'stood in the way of consolidation of Indonesia's title over East Timor by prescription'; Benvenisti (above n. 88), 158.

[142] On the role of Portugal in relation to the consultation, see the sources cited above, ch. 1, n. 5.

occupier takes over control unlawfully and the territory enjoys a right to 'external' self-determination. By the stage of the invasion, Portugal's rights with respect to East Timor had been altered by the self-determination entitlement: the state enjoyed title only on a temporary basis; this arrangement had no future unless it was agreed to by the East Timorese.[143] It could be argued, then, that the Indonesian occupation extinguished Portugal's title, not because title was transferred to Indonesia, but rather because, after the emergence of the self-determination entitlement, Portugal only continued to enjoy title as a consequence of exercising territorial control.

This is not to say that Portugal did not still have a special relationship with East Timor by virtue of its former status as the colonial power given that self-determination had not yet been realized. Equally, the absence of title on the part of Portugal would not make it any easier for Indonesia to claim title; Indonesia's claim depended not on the absence of title on the part of another actor, but, rather, on the views of the East Timorese. Considering the invasion and occupation as having removed Portuguese title does not allow Indonesia to gain an advantage from its unlawful acts since on this point—the removal of Portuguese title—no advantage had been obtained. It would seem, therefore, that the effect of the Indonesian occupation was to render East Timor a territory that did not form part of the territory of any state (with, of course, a self-determination entitlement).

At the point of the 'popular consultation', then, in August 1999, as a matter of law, East Timor was a self-determination unit unlawfully administered by Indonesia but forming part of the territory of no state;[144] as a matter of UN formalities, as mentioned, it was listed as a Non-Self-Governing Territory, the classification used for colonies.

Was this legal position altered by the outcome of the 'consultation'? On the basis of the 1999 'May Agreements' between Indonesia, Portugal and the UN, the 'consultation' involved asking the people of East Timor whether they accepted a proposal for 'special autonomy' within Indonesia, or rejected this proposal, 'leading to East Timor's separation from Indonesia'.[145] The result was 78.5 per cent in favour of rejection.[146] Although, as discussed above, the self-determination entitlement gave the East Timorese the right to choose any form of external

---

[143] See the general discussion above, text following n. 25.

[144] Discussing in 1984 the occupations of East Timor and the Western Sahara, Adam Roberts states that '... the international community has tended to view [each territory] not as *terra nullius*, but as territory whose sovereignty, although yet to be exercised, is vested in the inhabitants...'; Roberts (above n. 73), at 299, n. 188.

[145] Agreement between the Governments of Indonesia and Portugal and the United Nations Regarding the Modalities for the Popular Consultation of the East Timorese through a Direct Ballot, 5 May 1999 (hereinafter 'East Timor Agreement 2'), obtainable from <http://www.un.org/peace/etimor99/etimor.htm>.

[146] Secretary-General, Letter to the President of the Security Council Regarding the Result of the Popular Consultation, 3 September 1999, UN Doc. S/1999/944 (1999).

status,[147] the separation from Indonesia option was understood to entail only one such form: independence (viz. statehood). One of the May Agreements stated that, should the option of rejecting 'special autonomy' prevail in the 'consultation':

[t]he Secretary-General shall...initiate the procedure enabling East Timor to begin a process of transition towards independence.[148]

In Resolution 1236, welcoming the May Agreements, the Security Council described the 'popular consultation' options in the following terms: '...autonomy within Indonesia or transition to independence'.[149] In certain publicity materials associated with the 'popular consultation', an outcome favouring the rejection of 'substantial autonomy' was described as leading to independence. A poster by the body carrying out the 'popular consultation', the United Nations Assistance Mission in East Timor (UNAMET), explained the consequences of choosing the option to 'reject autonomy' within Indonesia as threefold:

Indonesia will end its links with East Timor
East Timor will separate from Indonesia
The United Nations will oversee East Timor's transition *towards Independence*.[150]

A UNAMET notice exhorting people to register to vote stated that:

[t]he popular consultation is your chance to decide about East Timor's future. Every eligible person, no matter whether they want autonomy or independence, has the right to vote. Your vote is your choice.[151]

The view that the East Timorese in effect voted for independence by rejecting 'substantial autonomy' is endorsed by the UN Security Council's statement that '...the East Timorese expressed their clear wish to begin a process of transition...towards independence...'.[152] Thus, UNTAET described the 'popular consultation' outcome in the following terms: '[o]ver 78 per cent of Timorese voters chose the independence option in the UN-organized ballot...'.[153]

The outcome of the 'popular consultation' modified slightly the nature of East Timor's status from that which prevailed prior to the 'popular consultation'

---

[147] See above, text accompanying n. 3.

[148] Agreement between the Republic of Indonesia and the Portuguese Republic on the Question of East Timor (hereinafter 'East Timor Agreement 1'), 5 May 1999, obtainable from <http://www.un.org/peace/etimor99/etimor.htm>, Art. 6.

[149] SC Res. 1236, 13 September 1999, para. 4.

[150] Poster entitled 'If you accept autonomy', in UNAMET Posters for the self-determination popular consultation, obtainable from <http://www.un.org/peace/etimor99/etimor.htm> (emphasis added). On UNAMET, see above, ch. 1, n. 5.

[151] UNAMET Notice, 'To vote you need to register', obtainable from <http://www.un.org/peace/etimor99/etimor.htm>.

[152] SC Res. 1272, 25 October 1999, preamble, para. 3.

[153] UNTAET, 'East Timor Update', February 2000, obtainable from <http://www.un.org/peace/etimor/etimor.htm>.

outcome, since it fixed East Timor's future destiny as a state. In other words, East Timor was no longer a self-determination unit with an entitlement to alter its external status; it was a self-determination unit with an entitlement to become an independent state. So, although it did not form part of the territory of any state, and did not constitute an independent state, it would become a state in the future. Although, as mentioned, Indonesia's claim to title had never been valid, this claim was formally withdrawn following the result of the 'popular consultation'.[154]

The question of East Timor's status after the 'consultation' in 1999 is significant because independence was not immediately enacted; rather, the territory was administered by the United Nations for a further two and a half years before independence was declared and statehood attained.[155] Did this arrangement alter the status of East Timor, notwithstanding that the territory clearly remained a self-determination unit that would become a state? In particular, did East Timor somehow constitute sovereign 'UN territory' during this period?[156]

In order to answer this question, it is necessary to appreciate how the relationship between UNTAET and East Timor was conceived. As with a consideration of questions of title and sovereignty as far as states are concerned, the appropriate starting point is the nature of the authority provided to the UN over East Timor, and the type of claim being made by the organization in respect of the territory. The May Agreement allowing the 'popular consultation' stated that, if a rejection of 'substantial autonomy' was preferred:

... the Governments of Indonesia and Portugal and the Secretary-General shall agree on arrangements for a peaceful and orderly transfer of authority in East Timor to the United Nations.[157]

Although the terms of the 'popular consultation' did not mention a role for the United Nations, the publicity associated with the 'popular consultation' did. Certain publicity repeated verbatim this provision from the agreement;[158] the 'popular consultation' poster quotation extracted above stated that the United Nations would 'oversee' East Timor's transition.[159] The UN Security Council considered the 'popular consultation' outcome as an acceptance of a 'process

---

[154] According to one of the May Agreements, if the East Timorese were to reject the autonomy option in the consultation, Indonesia was obliged to '...take the constitutional steps necessary to terminate its links with East Timor thus restoring under Indonesian law the status East Timor held prior to 17 July 1976...'; East Timor Agreement 1 (above n. 148), Art. 6. Indonesia fulfilled this obligation on 20 October 1999 when the Indonesian People's Consultative Assembly recognized the result of the consultation and revoked the law integrating East Timor within Indonesia (Progress Report of the Secretary-General on the Question of East Timor, 13 December 1999, UN Doc. A/54/654 (1999), para. 39), effectively withdrawing Indonesia's claim to the territory.

[155] See the sources cited above, ch. 1, n. 2.

[156] Cf. Chopra (above n. 1).

[157] East Timor Agreement 1 (above n. 148), Art. 6, noted by the UN Security Council acting under Chapter VII, in SC Res. 1264, 15 September 1999, para. 8.

[158] See UNAMET Posters (above n. 150).

[159] Poster entitled 'If you accept autonomy', in UNAMET Posters (above n. 150).

of transition under the authority of the United Nations'.[160] UNTAET was conceived as a 'Transitional Administration' mission:

... endowed with overall responsibility for the administration of East Timor and will be empowered to exercise all legislative and executive authority... [161]

On legislative authority in particular, the Transitional Administrator (a Special Representative of the Secretary-General) was given the:

... power to enact new laws and regulations and to amend, suspend and repeal existing ones.[162]

Thus UNTAET enjoyed the right to legislate, the laws passed (called 'Regulations') being binding on the territory of East Timor.[163] In foreign relations, UNTAET acted on behalf of East Timor, entering into agreements with Indonesia and Australia. For example, in February 2000, UNTAET entered into an agreement with the Australian Government to continue the regime exploiting the resources in the Timor Gap until independence.[164] Clearly, this agreement was intended to be binding with respect to East Timor, at least until independence. In addition to the seemingly plenary administrative powers of UNTAET in East Timor,[165] Jarat Chopra cites two further points as significant when considering the nature of the UN's relationship to East Timor. In the first place, he points out that the Portuguese Representative at the UN:

... told officials that Portugal would relinquish its legal ties to East Timor and consider UNTAET its successor with the passage of the Security Council mandate.[166]

Secondly, he points out that the World Bank's International Development Association (IDA):

... was designated as the trustee of the reconstruction Trust Fund for East Timor. According to its Articles of Agreement, the IDA can provide trust funds to sovereign governments or

---

[160] SC Res. 1272 (above n. 152), preamble, para. 3.
[161] Ibid., para. 1.
[162] Ibid., para. 6.
[163] See UNTAET Regulation 1999/1, 27 November 1999, obtainable from <http://www.un.org/peace/etimor/UntaetN.htm>, paras 1.1, 3, 4.
[164] Exchange of Notes constituting an Agreement between the Government of Australia and the United Nations Transitional Administration in East Timor (UNTAET) concerning the continued Operation of the Treaty between Australia and the Republic of Indonesia on the Zone of Cooperation in an Area between the Indonesian Province of East Timor and Northern Australia of 11 December 1989 (hereinafter 'Timor Gap Agreement 2000'), Dili, 10 February 2000, in force 10 February 2000 (with effect from 25 October 1999), *Australian Treaty Series* (2000), No. 9, obtainable from <http://www.austlii.edu.au/au/other/dfat/treaties/2000/9.html>.
[165] Chopra (above n. 1), 29.
[166] Ibid., 30.

public international organizations. But the trust fund's terms of reference specifically treat UNTAET as a separate government, rather than part of the UN as an international organization...The Bank...demanded that the Agreement be accorded the stature of an international treaty between the IDA and a sovereign government. The...Agreement defined the 'Recipient' as East Timor and UNTAET. It had to be signed by the Transitional Administrator as the head of state, and not merely as a representative of the UN.[167]

Bearing the above factors in mind, how is the legal relationship between the United Nations, on the one hand, and East Timor, on the other, to be understood?

For Chopra, the UN 'achieved a form of statehood' in East Timor.[168] 'Statehood', like 'sovereignty', is a term that can, of course, mean a variety of things.[169] It would seem (although it is not spelled out) that Chopra is suggesting that somehow East Timor had become 'UN territory' for the duration of the plenary administration period; the UN was the 'sovereign' and East Timor its 'territory' or, put a different way, a 'UN state'. Of course, it would be a special form of statehood, in that UN title would only run for a temporary period, pending a declaration of independence. Essentially it would work the same way as with Portugal before the Indonesian invasion—the United Nations enjoyed a special, conditional form of title over East Timor. Whereas Portuguese title was conditional in the sense that it would have to come to an end if the East Timorese chose separation from Portugal in a self-determination consultation, United Nations title was conditional in the sense that independence had been chosen, and would be implemented after a period during which the East Timorese would be prepared for running their own country. The UN was thus in the same position as colonial states with respect to those colonial territories over which they enjoyed title, when the territories in question had chosen some form of external status other than a continued relationship with the colonial state, but this status had not yet been implemented. The key difference would be that colonial title had been long-standing, whereas the UN's enjoyment of title began at the same time that the eventual status of the territory was fixed.

Is this interpretation of the UN's role in East Timor correct? As mentioned earlier, some commentators seem to regard the exercise of territorial control as synonymous with the enjoyment of sovereignty-as-title (or at least an assumption by the actor concerned in this regard, even if, as a matter of law, they are not the territorial sovereign). There is of course no doubt, given the evidence reviewed above, that the UN asserted the right of plenary administrative control with respect to East Timor. On its own terms, this power implies action conducted in the capacity of the territorial government. As discussed earlier in Chapter 3, in international law the term 'government' refers to the agent through which

---

[167] Chopra (above n. 1), 30.
[168] Ibid.
[169] On the different meanings of the term 'state' in international law, see the discussion in Crawford (above n. 4), 31.

the legal person of the state (or a non-state/sub-state territorial entity) acts.[170] Applying the term in this context would mean that the administrative acts of UNTAET were, legally, the acts of East Timor, at least for the duration of the United Nations' administrative powers in the territory.[171] It would have made no sense to have been able to pass laws binding on East Timor if the UN had not enjoyed legislative sovereignty; equally, agreements with foreign states entered into 'on behalf of' East Timor were predicated on the ability of UNTAET to act as agent for the territory.[172]

It is one thing to conclude that UNTAET acted as the government of East Timor; it is quite another, however, to suggest that East Timor was 'UN territory'. How can such a distinction be made? As discussed in Chapter 3, the *sine qua non* for the enjoyment of sovereignty—whether statehood, or title over a particular area of territory—is the existence of a claim in this regard, whether explicit or implicit. In the case of UNTAET, there is no suggestion from the above evidence that governmental control was being exercised in pursuance to a claim of title (albeit of a temporary nature) with respect to the territory. As for the Portuguese statement cited by Chopra, the phrase 'legal ties' need not refer to formal sovereign title: it could mean merely the right to administer the territory (the UN as a 'successor government' rather than a 'successor state').

Can a sovereignty claim not be implicit, however, in the governmental role performed, given that East Timor was not a state and did not form part of the territory of another state? Otherwise, there would have been no juridical actor on whose behalf the UN acted. Things would have been different if East Timor had formed part of a state; if it had been part of, say, Portugal or Indonesia, then the UN would have been acting as agent for the Portuguese/Indonesian territory of East Timor.

Just because East Timor neither formed part of a state, nor constituted a state itself, it does not follow that some other legal status is not possible. Actually, as previously discussed, East Timor enjoyed such status by virtue of its self-determination entitlement; its listing at the UN as a Non-Self-Governing Territory, as mentioned, continued throughout the UNTAET period until independence in 2002. It follows that East Timor between 1999 and 2002 can be considered a special form of territorial entity that was set to become a state within a finite period; in performing governmental acts in the territory, UNTAET acted on behalf of this special

---

[170] See above, ch. 3, n. 17 and accompanying text. See also above, ch. 1, n. 63.

[171] This discussion of agency is introduced for the purposes of exploring how the powers of UNTAET in East Timor might be understood in a way that does not necessarily denote the enjoyment of title; it is not concerned with establishing definitively whether an agency relationship of this kind operated, a question which is beyond the scope of this book. On this general question, see the sources cited above, ch. 1, n. 64.

[172] See UNTAET's repeated reference to 'acting on behalf of East Timor' in its note contained in the Timor Gap Agreement 2000 (above n. 164). Note also the citation of UNTAET alongside the 'Government of Australia'—i.e., the agent acting on behalf of the legal person, Australia—in the title of the Agreement.

juridical entity. There is no need, therefore, to assume UN sovereignty in order to make sense of the governmental powers UNTAET asserted in the territory.

The best way of understanding the UN role in East Timor, therefore, is that the organization acted as agent for a *sui generis* legal person—the self-determination unit of East Timor. Given this, its administrative prerogatives cannot be considered to have altered the status of East Timor. It follows that, for the period in question—running from the 1999 'popular consultation' through the period of UN administration until the declaration of independence in May 2002—East Timor constituted a non-state territorial entity with a self-determination entitlement; once the 'popular consultation' result was issued, this status was modified slightly in that East Timor was to become a state within a finite period of time.[173]

5.8 Conclusion

Although international territorial administration has sometimes been introduced in or proposed for non-state territories—Mandated and Trust territories generally, certain colonies, West Irian in 1962–63, South West Africa/Namibia in 1967 and 1989–90, Western Sahara in 1991, and East Timor between 1999 and 2002—in all cases this did not lead to the international organizations involved enjoying title over the territories concerned. As with those territories covered in the previous chapter, what I term 'international territorial sovereignty' is ruled out by the absence of a claim to sovereignty by the international organizations involved. Moreover, in the cases of both the Western Sahara and East Timor, the 'external' self-determination entitlement enjoyed by the people meant that the territory was not *terra nullius*; rather, it had an international legal status like states and state territories; the self-determination entitlement, moreover, meant that no other actor could successfully claim sovereignty on the basis of territorial control without the consent of the people.[174]

Although, then, the UN was not 'sovereign' in these territories, the presence of plenary international territorial administration did have an effect on sovereignty in particular circumstances. With certain colonial territories, the displacement of the colonial state by the UN in the activity of plenary administration arguably had the juridical effect of extinguishing the special form of title enjoyed by that state over the territory, because of the consequence of the 'external' self-determination entitlement for the nature of colonial title. In practice, plenary UN administration had this effect only with respect to Dutch title over West Irian; with East Timor, it was suggested that the previous title-holder, Portugal, had already had its title displaced as a consequence of the loss of administrative control prior to and during the Indonesian occupation.[175]

---

[173] See also Smyrek (above n. 71), 118–38.
[174] See the quotation from Adam Roberts above, n. 144.
[175] The ITA project for Western Sahara does not involve plenary administration, and by the time MINURSO was authorized, Spanish title had already been extinguished.

From the analysis above and in the previous chapter, it is evident that the popular perception of territorial control by an international legal person as being synonymous with the enjoyment of territorial title has led to the true nature of the relationship between international territorial administration and the legal status of the territory concerned being obscured. Despite the views of commentators such as Méir Ydit and Jarat Chopra, in no case have international organizations enjoyed sovereignty in the sense of legal title over territory. Whether or not international organizations are even capable of enjoying such sovereignty according to their constitutions, in practice this has never taken place; there have been no 'internationalised territories' in this sense.[176]

When the territories were states, such as the Congo, or parts of states, such as Leticia, international administration had no juridical effect in altering the status of the unit concerned, and when it was conducted in the name of a particular territorial sovereign, it actually reinforced this status. When the territories were non-state units, such as East Timor, the UN did not somehow acquire territory by virtue of administering territorial units that were *terrae nullius,* since, quite apart from the absence of a claim to title by the UN, the self-determination entitlement meant that such territorial units were not *terrae nullius* and title over them could not be enjoyed by another legal person simply by virtue of exercising administrative control.

The fact that international territorial administration has been utilized so often, and, yet, has never operated in conjunction with the enjoyment of title over territory by the international organizations involved, suggests that there is much more to the potential policy function performed by this activity than merely forming the basis of, or existing as a corollary to, 'international territorial sovereignty', as Ydit's approach might suggest.

Given this, it is necessary to look at different aspects of international territorial administration. The following chapter will evaluate a broader range of policies, analysing the role of the institution, not only in terms of its effect on territorial status (and even within this category, not only in terms of vesting the administering actor with sovereignty-as-title), but also in terms of its effect on the type of governance that takes place within the territory. Only with this broader perspective on the projects do the purposes with which they have been associated become fully apparent.

---

[176] Some of the sources cited above, ch. 1, n. 8 discuss the issue of whether such enjoyment of sovereignty would be so lawful.

6

Establishing the Policy Institution:
Purposive Analysis

6.1 Introduction[1]

The foregoing analysis on the legal status of most of the territories subject to international territorial administration projects suggests that an adequate explanation for the purposes associated with ITA cannot be found by focusing, as Méir Ydit did, exclusively on the idea of international organizations enjoying sovereignty-as-title—what I termed 'international territorial sovereignty'. Apart from any other consideration, in practice ITA has never actually subsisted in conjunction with the enjoyment of this kind of sovereignty by the administering actors involved. How, then, might the policy-role of ITA be understood?[2]

To answer this question, it is necessary to move beyond an exclusive focus on issues of sovereignty, and the effect of ITA on such issues, to consider in a broader manner the purposes with which ITA projects are, and have been, associated. In doing so, however, it is also necessary, as argued in Chapter 1, to avoid the other, more recent forms of essentialist, reductive explanation, that ITA is always, and only, concerned with post-conflict reconstruction or 'state-building'.

This chapter analyses the official explanations given for the projects, evaluating the projects on their own terms to establish what purposes they are ostensibly set up to serve. As explained in Chapter 1, the objective is not to attempt to explain the 'actual' or 'real' reasons for the projects, for example in terms of causation; nor to suggest whether the projects 'succeeded' or 'failed' in serving their stated (or unstated) goals.[3] Rather, it is to establish the justificatory framework with which the projects have been associated, as a way of conceptualizing how the projects are understood in international policy discourse. Using somewhat fragmentary

---

[1] This is an expanded and updated version of the ideas set out in R Wilde, 'From Danzig to East Timor and Beyond: The Role of International Territorial Administration', 95 (2001) *AJIL* 583. Some of the ideas in this chapter are also discussed in R Wilde, 'The Effect of Territorial Administration by International Organizations on Local Community-Building', (2003) *2000–2003 Third World Legal Studies Journal* 239.

[2] For other commentary on some of the policies associated with certain UN administration projects, see the sources cited above, ch. 1, n. 28.

[3] See above, ch. 1, section 1.5.2.

source materials, this justificatory framework is constructed by identifying the official purposes proffered in relation to each project, and conceptualizing these purposes collectively.

Although the legal status of the territories made subject to ITA addressed in detail in the previous two chapters did not provide the answer to the policy-role of ITA insofar as the idea of vesting sovereignty-as-title in the international organizations involved was concerned, this status is significant in a broader sense, and the analysis of it provided earlier will be drawn upon in what follows.

It will be demonstrated that, in addition to manifesting a common activity performed by an actor with a particular identity, thereby constituting an 'established practice' or, in my terminology, an 'institution',[4] international territorial administration projects also manifest commonality on a purposive level, since each of them has been conceived as a response to one or both of two types of perceived 'problem' associated with the conduct of administration in the territory concerned. So, as a matter of policy, it is possible to view ITA as distinctive—a 'policy institution' in my terminology.[5]

6.2 How the Policy Institution Works

In order to appreciate how its policy-role is understood, it is helpful to approach international territorial administration negatively, in terms of what it is not. ITA is seen as a substitute for what is regarded as the 'normal' conduct of territorial administration: by actors whose spatial identity, as 'local', corresponds to that of the territorial unit and its population.[6] International territorial administration is being and has been used as a substitute for the involvement of 'local' actors in the activity of territorial administration, either partially or fully, because of two perceived 'problems' associated with the 'normal' model.

In the first place, the use of international territorial administration is understood as a response to what might be termed a 'sovereignty problem' relating to the *presence* of local actors exercising administrative control over the territory. In the second place, the use of international territorial administration is understood as a response to what might be termed a 'governance problem' relating to the *conduct* of territorial administration by local actors. The first perceived 'problem' concerns the identity of the local actors being substituted in the role of carrying out administration; the second perceived 'problem' concerns the quality of governance being exercised in the territory. Whether or not conceiving

---

[4] This concept of an 'institution' is explained above, ch. 1, section 1.5.1; how ITA meets this definition is set out above, ch. 2.

[5] This concept of a 'policy institution' is explained above, ch. 1, section 1.5.1.

[6] Cf. the discussion above, ch. 1, section 1.4.3, on how the distinctiveness of the activity of international territorial administration is also rooted in part in this type of distinction in the spatial identities of the actors involved in territorial administration.

local governance in this manner is politically supportable and based on sound reasoning is not the focus of the present analysis—these issues will be raised in Chapters 8 and 9, after a sustained treatment of the significance of comparisons with colonial trusteeship. At this stage, the objective is merely to try to work out how this justificatory framework is understood by those engaged in creating and carrying out the ITA projects.

The following analysis sets out this justificatory framework, ranging across the ITA projects and foregrounding particular aspects of them where relevant. Broader contextual information for each project is contained in the general review of the projects in Chapter 2 and treatment of the legal status of the territories in which they operated in Chapters 4 and 5; such information is not repeated here in order to focus on policy analysis.

6.3 The First Purpose: Responding to a 'Sovereignty Problem'

Although, as demonstrated in the previous two chapters, international territorial administration has never been implemented in circumstances where the international actor involved enjoyed sovereignty-as-title over the territory concerned, its policy-role has often been understood in terms of some sort of effect on issues of territorial status. In Leticia, West Irian, Eastern Slavonia, the Saar, and Mostar, international territorial administration was used or proposed to solve what might be called a 'sovereignty problem' understood to have been caused by the identity of certain local actors who enjoyed or might have come to enjoy administrative control.

The key to appreciating how the policy-role of ITA is understood here is the link between administrative control and sovereignty. As discussed in Chapter 3, the question of who exercises administrative control is a crucial issue when determining issues of sovereignty-as-ownership.[7] Sometimes, international territorial administration has been understood as a means of interfering in this sovereignty process by calibrating the level of administrative control by certain local actors, or displacing such actors completely in the role of exercising such control. In such circumstances the value of its introduction is understood through the idea that the international actor involved is 'neutral' when compared with the local actors in relation to whom the particular sovereignty dispute relates.[8] In being explained in terms of a 'sovereignty problem' like this, the operation of international territorial administration is understood in several different ways. In Leticia, Kosovo, West Irian, and Eastern Slavonia, it was seen as a response to a concern stemming from a wider question about the status of the territory. In the Saar and Mostar, international territorial

---

[7] See above, ch. 3, section 3.3.

[8] Further treatment of the normative character of international actors in the context of their involvement in territorial administration is provided below, ch. 8, section 8.7.2.3.

administration was regarded as the 'response' to the status question itself. Each of these two policy-roles for ITA will be explained in turn.

6.3.1 Responding to concerns relating to a 'sovereignty problem'

The first instance where the use of international territorial administration was understood in terms of a response to a concern associated with a wider sovereignty question was in 1933, when Peruvian irregular forces invaded and occupied the Colombian town and district of Leticia and, as outlined in Chapter 4, plenary administration by the League of Nations was introduced for a maximum one-year period in conjunction with withdrawal by the Peruvian forces.[9] Why did League administration, rather than Colombian control, replace control by the Peruvian forces when there was common acceptance, as discussed in Chapter 4, that the territory formed part of Colombia?[10] For Colombia, it was a staging post between control by the Peruvian forces and control by the Colombian authorities.[11] For Peru, however, it ensured that the territory would not be transferred to Colombia until the wider border dispute between the two countries was resolved.[12]

Given this disagreement, and the absence in the terms of the administration mandate of provisions on the question of the actor to whom the League would eventually transfer control, the role of territorial administration by the League at its conception cannot be explained necessarily in terms of transferring the territory from Peru to Colombia. Rather, as John Czerapowicz suggests, League administration was intended to 'insulate the territory from further conflict while the disputants conducted comprehensive negotiations on all outstanding issues', by removing the possibility of administrative control by either disputant.[13] Only on the resolution of these outstanding issues, which, as mentioned in Chapter 4, came before the end of the maximum period mandated for League administration in the form of a border agreement, could administrative control be transferred to Colombia.[14]

This idea of ITA being introduced to 'freeze' the situation on the ground, pending a resolution of the question of the territory's status, echoes part of the role of UNMIK in Kosovo from 1999 onwards. As explained in Chapter 4, Kosovo during the UNMIK period remained legally part of the sovereign territory of the Federal Republic of Yugoslavia (FRY)/Serbia and Montenegro/

---

[9] See above, ch. 4, section 4.2.4. On the administrative arrangements, see above, Ch. 2, n. 14.

[10] On the status of Leticia during this period, see above, ch. 4, section 4.2.4.

[11] This was also the view taken by the League Commission; see JV Czerapowicz, *International Territorial Authority: Leticia and West New Guinea* (unpublished Ph.D. dissertation, Indiana University, 1972, on file with the author), 88–91.

[12] Ibid., at 83–4, 89–90.

[13] Ibid., at 226. Similarly, in a separate passage, Czerapowicz describes the objective of League administration and the withdrawal of the Peruvian irregulars as the 'temporary neutralization' of Leticia, removing the territory 'as an area of direct confrontation' (ibid., at 9).

[14] On this resolution, see above, Ch. 4, n. 113 and accompanying text.

Republic of Serbia, but under what was asserted by the UN to be plenary administrative control by UNMIK, entirely displacing such control by the administrative authorities of the sovereign entity. As will be explored further below,
since Kosovo's future status was placed into question, to be determined through
a process of negotiation, having the determination occur in the context of
UNMIK administration rather than the alternatives of a resumption of (what
was initially called) FRY administration or full control by the local people enabled the dispute over sovereignty to be addressed without either of the two main
disputants having the particular advantage of overall control.

Clearly, however, in this sense, the arrangement did not affect both disputants
equally, since the substantial autonomy granted to the people of Kosovo, albeit
under overall UNMIK authority, gave them much greater leverage when compared to the position of (what was eventually called) the Republic of Serbia.

In addition to removing what is regarded to be a sovereignty-related obstacle to
the settlement of a territorial dispute (the presence of either disputant in overall
control of the territory), the function of international territorial administration
has also been understood in terms of removing this type of obstacle to the implementation of a settlement once reached. As mentioned in Chapter 5, the relatively brief period of administration by the United Nations Temporary Executive
Authority (UNTEA) in West Irian operated in between territorial control by the
Netherlands and Indonesia, forming part of the broader settlement to a dispute
between those two countries concerning the future of the Dutch colony, whereby
Indonesia would be given control from the Netherlands, via an interim period
of UN administration, and then carry out what was in effect a consultation on
'external' self-determination, monitored by a new UN mission separate from
UNTEA.[15] So the role of UN administration here was understood as providing a
buffer between Dutch and Indonesian control.[16]

[15] See above, ch. 5, text accompanying n. 66 *et seq.*

[16] On the mandate of UNTEA, see above, ch. 2, n. 18. Several features of the mission under-
line the purpose of facilitating a territorial transfer between two states. The UN flag was hoisted
on 1 October 1962, but the Netherlands flag remained until 31 December 1962, after which the
Indonesian flag was hoisted alongside the UN flag; this lasted until the transfer to Indonesian control, when the UN flag was struck (Agreement between Indonesia and the Netherlands Concerning
West New Guinea (West Irian) 15 August 1962, 437 UNTS 273 (hereinafter 'West Irian
Agreement'), Art. VI; Indonesia–Netherlands–United Nations, Exchange of Letters (with Annexed
Memorandum of Understanding) on Cessation of Hostilities, 15 August 1962, 437 UNTS 294
(hereinafter 'West Irian Exchange of Letters'), 310–11; Annual Report of the Secretary-General on
the Work of the Organization, 16 June 1962–15 June 1963, UN GAOR, 18th Sess., Supp. No. 1,
at 35, UN Doc. A/5501 (1963) (hereinafter 'UN Secretary-General West Irian Report'), 36, 39).
UNTEA could issue travel documents that would serve as the basis for consular protection abroad
during the period of its administration; the protection itself would be provided by either Indonesia
or the Netherlands (West Irian Exchange of Letters, ibid., 304–10; UN Secretary-General West
Irian Report, ibid., 37). The two countries were responsible for UNTEA's costs, and the Secretary-
General had to take their views into account when appointing the Administrator (on the costs,
see West Irian Agreement, ibid., Art. XXIV and UN Secretary-General West Irian Report, ibid.,
40; on the appointment, see West Irian Agreement, ibid., Art. IV, and West Irian Exchange of

This use of international territorial administration resurfaced thirty years later in Eastern Slavonia, where, as mentioned in Chapter 4, on the basis of an agreement between the local Serb militias and Croatia, the United Nations Transitional Administration for Eastern Slavonia (UNTAES) took over control from the militias and administered the territory from 1995 to 1998 before handing the territory over to the administrative control of Croatia.[17]

In West Irian and Eastern Slavonia, the role of international territorial administration was understood as a bridging mechanism between, respectively, control by the Dutch, and the local Serbs, on the one hand, and control by Indonesia, and Croatia, on the other. Although agreements had been reached involving the transfer of territorial control from one party to another, the implementation of these agreements was seen as potentially problematic given the general history of dispute between the parties and the fact that one party, which had previously objected to territorial control by the other, would, absent some sort of buffer mechanism, have to facilitate such control through its own action. The United Nations, as a 'neutral' actor, was seen as offering a face-saving alternative.[18]

Comparing the cases considered so far, the policy-role of ITA in relation to 'sovereignty problems' has been limited in the sense that some other process—not ITA itself—ends up providing the resolution to the sovereignty dispute. The border agreement between Colombia and Peru and the final agreement on Kosovo's status, and the transfers of control to Indonesia and Croatia, were seen as constituting the ultimate determination of the wider sovereignty question of the eventual status of the territories concerned. The function of international territorial administration here was understood in terms of creating in some way a better climate for this determination to emerge (in the case of Leticia and Kosovo), or helping to realize it once agreed (in the case of West Irian and Eastern Slavonia). As will now be explained, in the Saar and Mostar the policy-roles associated with international territorial administration were more fundamental: either to prevent or resolve a sovereignty dispute.

6.3.2 Addressing the 'sovereignty problem' directly

One objective of the Versailles Treaty at the end of the First World War was to allow France to obtain reparations from Germany by exploiting mines in the Saar for 15 years.[19] Because French administrative control of the Saar was seen as

Letters, ibid., 300–5). On the 'buffer' role for UNTEA, see also JG Merrills, *International Dispute Settlement* (4th edn, CUP, 2005), at 260, text accompanying n. 51 *et seq.*

[17] See above, ch. 4, section 4.5.2; on the mandate of UNTAES, see above, ch. 2, n. 24.

[18] James Crawford observes that the object of UNTAES was 'to reintegrate the territory into Croatia'; J Crawford, *The Creation of States in International Law* (2nd edn, OUP, 2006), 557.

[19] On the background to, and operation of, the League administration in the Saar, see, for example, WR Bisschop, *The Saar Controversy* (Sweet & Maxwell, 1924); FP Walters, *A History of the League of Nations* (OUP, 1952), 89–90, 239–43, 337–8, 416, 586–98; M Ydit, *Internationalised*

objectionable in view of that country's perceived ambitions to annex the territory, League administration was introduced for the duration of the exploitation period.[20] The League was seen as neutral with respect to the relevant sovereignty claims, enabling the formal preservation of German title over the territory.[21]

In addition to preventing a sovereignty question from arising, the policy-role of international territorial administration has been understood, again in the Saar and also in Mostar, in terms of resolving such a question once it had arisen. After the 15-year mine exploitation period, the population of the Saar was given the choice between 'union with Germany' and 'union with France', to be expressed in a plebiscite and 'taken into account' by the League in its disposal of the territory.[22] The Versailles Treaty anticipated the problem of neither option being favoured by providing a third option in the plebiscite: the continuance of the 'régime established' in the territory.[23] Accordingly, ITA was seen as serving as part of the solution to this problem by allowing control to be given to neither Germany nor France. In fact, the problem never arose because the outcome of the plebiscite (honoured by the League) supported union with Germany.[24]

In 1993, this understanding of the role of international territorial administration resurfaced in the city of Mostar in Bosnia and Herzegovina. As discussed in Chapter 4, Mostar was politically and militarily split into West and East, the two halves controlled, respectively, by the Bosnian Croats and the Bosnian Muslims/Bosniaks.[25] Addressing the perceived inability of local actors to agree on governing the city as a unified entity, the introduction of the European Union Administration in Mostar (EUAM) from 1994 to 1996 was understood in part as a means of ensuring that the city was administered as a single entity pending the adoption of a locally-constituted structure of unified city governance.[26]

Territories from the 'Free City of Cracow' to the 'Free City of Berlin' (Sythoff, 1961), 44–8. On France's powers to exploit the mines, see above, ch. 4, n. 14. On the reason for French exploitation of the mines, see Versailles Peace Treaty, Art. 45; Bisschop, ibid., 20–2, 52–6; and Walters, ibid., 89.

[20] On the League Administration, see above, ch. 2, n. 13. In addition to its administrative powers in the Saar, the League Governing Commission was also entitled to modify the international legal regime granting French control over the mines, after consultation with France, unless the modification pertained to labour standards adopted by the League, in which case no consultation was required. See Versailles Peace Treaty, Annex to Part III, Section IV (after Art. 50), Chapter II, Art. 23.

[21] On the Saar's legal status during this period as German territory, see the discussion above, ch. 4, section 4.2.1.

[22] See above, ch. 4, text accompanying n. 22 *et seq.* The quotations come from Versailles Peace Treaty, Annex to Part III, Section IV (after Art. 50), Art. 34 (first two quotations) Art. 35 (third quotation).

[23] Versailles Peace Treaty, Annex to Part III, Section IV (after Art. 50), Art. 34.

[24] See above, ch. 4, n. 28 and accompanying text.

[25] See above, ch. 4, section 4.5.1.

[26] On the background to the EUAM, see, for example, D Owen, *Balkan Odyssey* (Victor Gollancz, 1995), 212, 238–40, 257. According to the Mostar MOU (Memorandum of Understanding on the European Union Administration of Mostar, 5 July 1994, unpublished, copy on file with the author), one of the 'aims and principles' of EUAM administration was '…to allow the parties time to find a lasting solution for the administration of the Mostar city municipality…' (Mostar MOU, ibid.,

6.3.3 Using ITA to respond to a 'sovereignty problem'

Using international territorial administration to address a 'sovereignty problem' reflects and constitutes the sovereignty matters at stake. In Eastern Slavonia and Mostar, international territorial administration was seen as addressing what was presented as an exclusively 'internal' problem. In Eastern Slavonia, it enabled the transfer of territory not from one state to another, but from separatist local forces to the state governmental authority. In Mostar, it was presented as a response to a dispute between two factions concerning city government within the state of Bosnia and Herzegovina.

Presenting sovereignty problems as exclusively 'internal' necessarily eliminates the idea that they are 'external'. In the case of Eastern Slavonia, the agreement which provided for UN administration was brokered by the United States (by the then US Ambassador to Croatia, Peter Galbraith, who was later to head the Political office of UNTAET in East Timor) in a secret pact between FRY President Milošević and Croatian President Tuđman aimed at removing an obstacle to the normalization of relations between the two countries.[27] This pact was transformed into the agreement once President Milošević supposedly obtained the support of the local Serb leaders.[28] The transfer, effected through ITA, enabled the FRY to abandon the separatist cause of the local Serbs to promote the broader interests of its relations with Croatia. Similarly, presenting the dispute in Mostar as exclusively internal denied the aspirations of the Bosnian Croats to make West Mostar part of either a new state of Herzeg-Bosna (constituting the Croatian areas of Bosnia and Herzegovina) or Croatia proper. As a matter of self-determination, the particular groups in each territory—the Serbs in Croatia, the Croats in Mostar—were to enjoy 'internal' but not 'external' self-determination.[29] The territories concerned, Eastern Slavonia and West Mostar, were therefore not to be treated as 'self-determination units', and could not unite with a Greater Serbia or Croatia/Herzeg-Bosna, respectively. In Mostar, imposing a 'united' administration in a city emblematic of the divisions between the Bosnian Muslims/Bosniaks

---

Art. 2). The European Council Joint Action adopted as part of the creation of the EUAM specified that the objective of the EUAM was 'the establishment of a single, multi-ethnic and lasting administration of the town'; Council Decision 94/790/CFSP of 12 December 1994 concerning the joint action, adopted by the Council on the basis of Article J.3 of the Treaty on European Union, on continued support for European Union administration of the town of Mostar, *OJ* L326 (1994), 2, cited in E Denza, *The Intergovernmental Pillars of the EU* (OUP, 2002), 119. On the EUAM, see also Denza, ibid., 119 and sources cited therein.

[27] L Silber and A Little, *The Death of Yugoslavia* (2nd edn, Penguin and BBC Books, 1996), 370–1; RC Holbrooke, *To End a War* (Random House, 1998), 264–5. See also P Galbraith, 'The UN Transitional Authority in East Timor (UNTAET), 97 (2003) *ASIL Proc.* 211; R Wilde, 'The United Nations as Government: The Tensions of an Ambivalent Role', 97 (2003) *ASIL Proc.* 212.

[28] Holbrooke, above n. 27, 264–5. On the agreement, see above, ch. 2, n. 24.

[29] For discussion of these two forms of self-determination, see above, ch. 5, section 5.2 and the sources cited ibid., nn. 3 and 5 respectively. For commentary, see the List of Sources, section 5.4.

and the Bosnian Croats in the country generally reflected the international commitment to a united state of Bosnia and Herzegovina.

In contrast to the use of international territorial administration in Mostar and Eastern Slavonia, the proposal or actualization of ITA in the Saar, Leticia, Kosovo, and West Irian presented the 'sovereignty problem' as 'external'—i.e., the territory's international status was in question. In the earlier cases, the options were somewhat narrow: control by one or both of two specified states: Germany and France in the Saar; Colombia and Peru in Leticia; and the Netherlands and Indonesia in West Irian. Control by any other state, or the people of the territory within the framework of independent statehood, was necessarily excluded. Moreover, only in the Saar did the general population of the territory play any direct role in the decision.[30] In Kosovo, by contrast, the options were wide open; the process of negotiation facilitated by UNMIK, discussed further below, involved the people of Kosovo but, unlike in the Saar, theirs was not the sole view to be taken into account in determining the eventual settlement.

The West Irian project took place when, as discussed in Chapter 5, 'external' self-determination was accepted as the basis for establishing the international status of colonial territories.[31] Nevertheless, the external sovereignty issue was, as with the League-era projects, narrowly conceived—control by one state or another—and decided by the two disputant states.[32] Thus, the transfer of control from the Netherlands to Indonesia treated West Irian as if its population did not enjoy the right to 'external' self-determination.[33] At the same time, the agreement between the Netherlands and Indonesia treated the population as if it did enjoy the right to some form of 'external' self-determination by providing for an 'act of free choice' concerning external status, tied to an explicit invocation of the term 'self-determination'.[34] As discussed in Chapter 5, the transfer and the 'act of free choice' were, therefore, based on opposing ideas, corresponding to the positions of Indonesia and the Netherlands.[35] Moreover, the handover transformed the situation on the ground, affecting the subsequent consultation. Indonesia could manipulate the circumstances of the consultation to ensure the outcome it desired.[36]

---

[30] On the significance of the Saar plebiscite as an exercise of self-determination, see the discussion above, ch. 5, text accompanying n. 7 *et seq.*

[31] On this entitlement, see the discussion ibid., section 5.1.

[32] See ibid., section 5.4, text accompanying nn. 66 and 67.

[33] See ibid., paragraph following n. 70.

[34] See ibid., text accompanying n. 67.

[35] See ibid., paragraph following n. 70.

[36] On the consultation, see, e.g., M Pomerance, *Self-Determination in Law and Practice: The New Doctrine in the United Nations* (Martinus Nijhoff, 1982), 32–5; TM Franck, *Nation Against Nation: What Happened to the UN Dream and What the US Can Do About It* (OUP, 1985), 81–2; WJ Durch, 'UN Temporary Executive Authority', in Durch (ed.), *The Evolution of UN Peacekeeping* (St Martin's Press, 1994), 285; Crawford (above n. 18), at 646, n. 201 and sources cited therein; M Pomerance, 'Methods of Self-Determination and the Argument of "Primitiveness"', 12 (1974) *Canadian Yearbook of International Law* 38, 48–62.

Despite the endorsement of the UN monitors, as discussed in Chapter 5, the consultation was widely criticized as a sham, involving only a small number of the local elite.[37] In being conceived to facilitate the solution to the narrow sovereignty question—the territorial transfer—exclusively, international territorial administration served not only to deny the existence of the wider sovereignty question but also partially to determine its eventual outcome. As such, it was partially constitutive of the denial of the form of self-determination that had been provided for in the agreement.

The use of international territorial administration explained in terms of a 'sovereignty problem' implies that what might be called the 'normal' sovereignty model is considered to be in some sense 'defective'. The character of this model depends on whether the sovereignty question at issue is considered internal or external. When ITA 'solves' an internal sovereignty question—who will have administrative control—as in Mostar, the perceived defect lies in the notion that the preferred model of internal sovereignty, i.e., (more or less) unified governmental structures, is absent. Equally, when ITA used for this purpose is later discontinued, as happened in Mostar in 1996 with the introduction by the EUAM of an Interim City Statute, the preferred model of internal sovereignty is considered to have been 'restored': Mostar was supposedly 'reunified'.[38] When the use of ITA is understood in terms of addressing an 'external' sovereignty question—what the international legal status of the territory should be—the perceived 'defect' it is understood to be remedying concerns the preferred model of external sovereignty not being adopted, whether this involves the territory being a state or part of a state. Here, ITA alone does not suffice, as it cannot resolve the status question by itself; the device of 'international territorial sovereignty' is also necessary.

As mentioned earlier, in the Saar plebiscite of 1935, the third (rejected) option, representing the alternative to union with Germany or union with France, involved the 'maintenance of the régime' established by the Versailles Treaty.[39] This was cited as evidence of the role of international territorial administration— here continued administration by the League Governing Commission—in solving a territorial dispute. Yet, as has been explained in Chapter 3 and illustrated in Chapters 4 and 5, the mere exercise of territorial administration does not by itself denote the enjoyment of sovereignty-as-title by the administering actor. The dispute about who would end up with this form of sovereignty over the Saar would not have been disposed of merely through the continuation of League administration. An extra step would have been necessary, conferring title with respect to the Saar upon the League.

---

[37] See above, ch. 5, text accompanying n. 68 *et seq.*

[38] See Interim Statute of the City of Mostar, 7 February 1996, published in *Official Gazette of the City of Mostar*, No. 1, 20 February 1996. On the apparent lack of unity in Mostar during and after this period, see below, text accompanying n. 93 *et seq.*

[39] Versailles Peace Treaty, Annex to Part III, Section IV (after Art. 50), Art. 34.

The Treaty of Versailles made the following provision for territorial disposition in the event that the third option in the plebiscite prevailed:

[i]f, for the whole or part of the territory, the League of Nations decides in favour of the maintenance of the régime established by the present Treaty and this Annex, Germany hereby agrees to make such renunciation of her sovereignty in favour of the League of Nations as the latter shall deem necessary. It will be the duty of the League of Nations to take appropriate steps to adapt the régime definitively adopted to the permanent welfare of the territory and the general interest.[40]

It will be recalled that the League's administrative prerogatives were conceived originally in an indefinite fashion; it follows that these prerogatives would have automatically continued under this option, subject to any modifications made to them taken under the League's powers of adaptation. Given this, the 'sovereignty' that Germany would have potentially renounced could not have consisted merely of the right to exercise administrative prerogatives, since this right was already enjoyed by the League. Rather, 'sovereignty' in that context had to refer to title.[41] Clearly, the approaches taken under this option could have varied significantly, but one possible option would have been international territorial sovereignty, viz. the Saar becoming 'League territory' either permanently or during an interim period pending the establishment of some other status, such as 'Free City' status as was the case with Danzig (discussed in Chapter 4 and further below).

As Percy Corbett remarks, although the arrangements between 1920 and 1935 did not vest the League 'with the sovereignty of the Saar, but only with some of its attributes',[42] the arrangements for the post-plebiscite regime:

...do contain an implicit recognition of the capacity of the League to exercise sovereignty properly so-called. For, not to emphasise the theoretically absolute power of disposal exercisable by the League in 1935 and limited only by the practical and moral necessity of recognizing the result of the plebiscite as the chief factor determining the decision, it is provided...that the League may in certain circumstances take over such sovereignty as remains in Germany. If this step is taken, the régime would not be the existing one shown among the options in Section 34, but something legally quite different and constituting the League of Nations a sovereign State having the Saar Basin for territory.[43]

Whatever the merits of Corbett's suggestion that international territorial sovereignty would make the League a 'state', his remarks correctly identify the key difference between these arrangements and the enjoyment of 'sovereignty' as administration only.

Here, then, Ydit's 'internationalised territories' thesis applies: as a matter of policy, international territorial *administration* is of no significance by

---

[40] Versailles Peace Treaty, Annex to Part III, Section IV (after Art. 50), Art. 35.

[41] Continuing the regime established by Versailles did not, therefore, necessarily include the aspect of the 1920–35 regime that preserved Germany's sovereignty (as title) over the territory.

[42] PE Corbett, 'What is the League of Nations?', 5 (1924) *BYIL* 119, 128.

[43] Ibid.

itself; rather, it is a corollary of the policy device—international territorial *sovereignty*—that would 'solve' the question of the status of a territory that could not be transferred to either of the claimant states. It would seem, then, that the idea of international territorial sovereignty as a potential policy device should not be discarded as fanciful. Even if this idea is inappropriately applied to the implemented projects, the third option in the Saar plebiscite in 1935 suggests that it was considered to have value.

6.3.4 Ydit's 'internationalised territories' thesis revisited

As was established in the previous two chapters, no implemented international territorial administration projects have fallen within Ydit's definition of internationalization—meaning sovereignty vested in the administering actors—despite Ydit's assertions to the contrary. The only situation where an international organization would have been granted sovereignty-as-title, rather than merely the right to exercise territorial administration, was in the third option in the 1935 plebiscite for the Saar. It is unfortunate that Ydit utilizes the idea of internationalization to cover such a narrow set of circumstances. For example, many would regard the plenary League administration in the Saar between 1920 and 1935 as internationalization. However, this arrangement does not come within Ydit's concept because it was a temporary arrangement.[44]

The example of the Saar between 1920 and 1935 not only suggests that Ydit's definition of internationalization runs counter to the broader usage of that term; it also reveals what Ydit is missing, in terms of his interest in the settlement of sovereignty disputes, by such a narrow focus. By insisting on what has been termed 'international territorial sovereignty', Ydit disregards those instances, discussed above, where international organizations' enjoyment of a right of territorial administration, rather than also title, has also been used to address sovereignty disputes, and mostly on a temporary rather than a permanent basis.

For example, in relation to Leticia, Ydit merely describes the background to the dispute and the powers of the League administration.[45] He does not attempt to explain the role this project performed—i.e., as discussed, to neutralize temporarily the territory so that all outstanding disputes between Colombia and Peru could be settled—instead dismissing its candidature for 'internationalised territory' status.[46] This is unfortunate, since in practice the relatively modest activity of international territorial administration, whether temporary or permanent—which might also be called 'internationalization'—has seen much

---

[44] Ydit (above n. 19), 45.
[45] Ibid., 59–62.
[46] '...Leticia was *not* an internationalised territory...it was surely not envisaged becoming an internationalised territory under LON [League of Nations] sovereignty'; ibid., 62 (emphasis in the original).

more use in the arena of sovereignty disputes than the permanent international sovereignty model that is Ydit's exclusive focus.

It is thus regrettable that Ydit uses the label 'internationalised territory' to denote only the circumstance of international territorial sovereignty. Territory can be internationalized in many different ways, including through the process of granting administrative prerogatives to international organizations and international appointees discussed in this book. Moreover, these other forms of internationalization may also be associated with some of the policy-roles with which Ydit is concerned when focusing on the particular modality of international territorial sovereignty.

6.3.5 Reinforcing the validity of locally-identified sovereignty

Although it involves displacing local actors in the activity of territorial administration, the idea of using international territorial administration as a response to a 'sovereignty problem' reinforces the notion that territorial administration by local actors, although unobtainable, is the ideal. When ITA is understood as a means of addressing a concern related to a wider sovereignty dispute, some form of local territorial administration is usually envisaged as the outcome to that wider dispute. Even when it is proposed as the solution to the dispute, ITA is seen as a last resort. Agreement cannot be reached on how local actors should enjoy control, so international territorial administration is used because it involves no control by any local actor.

The foregoing analysis has illustrated how the use of ITA has been understood as a means of addressing sovereignty disputes, and in a broader manner than Ydit's 'internationalised territories' thesis would suggest. But what of 'state-building' and 'post-conflict reconstruction', the dominant focus of most of the commentators writing about the projects taking place at the turn of the 21st century? Here, one must focus on the role of ITA in terms of the type of administration conducted in the territory, rather than the identity of the actor in the administrative role.

6.4 The Second Purpose: Responding to a 'Governance Problem'

International territorial administration has often been understood as a response to what might be termed a 'governance problem' relating to local territorial administration. Unlike in the 'sovereignty problem' context, the perceived 'problem' here is not the identity of local actors acting in the role of the governmental authority but, rather, the conduct of governance by such actors. This problem can have two related features. Local actors may be considered practically incapable of conducting any governance at all. The perceived 'problem', therefore, is the supposed 'lack' of governance. Alternatively, there may be a concern that local actors will exercise their governmental powers in a manner that conflicts with certain policy objectives. Here, the perceived 'problem' concerns the supposed absence of 'good governance'.[47]

6.4.1 The presence of governance

The use of international territorial administration explained as a response to the idea that local actors are incapable of exercising administrative authority is exemplified by the administration of 'refugee' camps by the Office of the High Commissioner for Refugees (UNHCR), most of which are in countries lacking the resources to administer the camps themselves.[48] Similarly, international organizations run material assistance programmes usually when the capacities of local authorities to provide social support are considered to be insufficient. An example would be the assistance coordinated by the United Nations Office for the Coordination of Humanitarian Affairs (OCHA) in Somalia, a country which, as part of its explanation for its activities there, the organization has deemed to be 'without an effective central government'.[49] Assistance activities carried out by a number of UN agencies and local and international NGOs are understood to be primarily aimed at providing basic and essential services, and also attempting to tackle underlying long-term social, economic, and technical problems.[50]

The first UN project understood in terms of filling a governmental vacuum was the United Nations Operation in the Congo (ONUC) between 1960 and

---

[47]   For other commentary highlighting some of these policies in relation to specific (usually plenary, UN-conducted) projects see, e.g., the sources cited above, ch. 1, n. 28 and M Baskin, 'Between Exit and Engagement: on the Division of Authority in Transitional Administrations', 10 (2004) *Global Governance* 119 (on the policy objective of building up local institutions); D Sokolović and F Bieber (eds), *Reconstructing Multiethnic Societies: The Case of Bosnia and Herzegovina* (Ashgate, 2001) (on the use of ITA in Bosnia and Herezegovina in promoting democracy and multi-ethnic politics); D Sokolović, 'Social Reconstruction and Moral Restoration', in Sokolović & Bieber, ibid., 95 (on the use of ITA in Kosovo to promote democratic ideas); D Chandler, *Bosnia: Faking Democracy after Dayton* (2nd edn, Pluto Press, 2000) (on the use of ITA in Bosnia and Herzegovina to promote a range of policies). Many of the works contained in the List of Sources, section 5.1., also address the role of ITA in relation to these types of policies.

[48]   See above, ch. 2, section 2.3.1 (which includes coverage of the meaning of the word 'refugee' in this context).

[49]   OCHA, 'Somalia', available at <http://ochaonline3.un.org/News/Emergencies/Complex Emergencies/Somalia/tabid/1253/Default.aspx>.

[50]   Ibid. For an example of the wide range of activities coordinated by OCHA in Somalia, see the strategy to address the chronic food insecurity in the country, detailed in OCHA Somalia, 'Livelihoods and food security' (updated March 2006), obtainable from OCHA, 'Somalia', ibid. For other examples of assistance activities carried out by UN agencies in countries or territories where the local authorities are considered incapable of providing adequate support to the population, see, in general, the OCHA website, at <http://ochaonline.un.org>.

1964.[51] ONUC interpreted a mandate to provide technical assistance flexibly, performing governmental functions directly, sometimes against the wishes of the local government.[52] Initially, the assumption of these functions was explained in terms of the failure of Belgium, the former colonial state, to train the people of the territory prior to its departure; subsequently, governmental collapse was explained in terms of the ensuing conflict, disputes between different government factions, outside interference by Belgium, and the attempted secession by Katanga province.[53]

When the United Nations set up the UN Council for South West Africa in 1967, the administrative vacuum ITA was seen as remedying was of a different kind.[54] The Council was to administer the territory, filling the gap created not by ongoing threats to the existing government, but by the anticipated withdrawal of South Africa following the termination of its power as Mandatory and the General Assembly's assumption of direct responsibility for the territory.[55] However, as discussed in Chapter 5, the Council was denied entry to Namibia by South Africa;[56] it used its administrative authority, inter alia, to issue travel documents and pass a Decree on Natural Resources.[57] When South

---

[51] On ONUC, see the sources cited above, ch. 2, n. 17. On the situation in the Congo at the time, see the discussion above, ch. 4, section 4.3, and sources cited therein.

[52] SC Res. 143, 14 July 1960; see SR Ratner, *The New UN Peacekeeping, Building Peace in Lands of Conflict after the Cold War* (St. Martin's Press, 1995), 105–9.

[53] Ibid. The military component of ONUC attempted to address this conflict, in particular by forcibly preventing the secession of Katanga province (ibid.).

[54] On the mandate of the UN Council for Namibia, see above, ch. 5, section 5.5 and below, n. 57.

[55] See Ratner, above n. 52, 105–9.

[56] See above, ch. 5, section 5.5.

[57] The General Assembly requested the Council to fulfil its mandate 'by every available means'; GA Res. 2325 (XXII), 16 December 1967, para. 2. The Council was to establish an emergency programme to render 'technical and financial assistance' to Namibia; to organize a training programme for Namibians, 'so that a *cadre* of civil servants and of technical and professional personnel may be developed' who could eventually undertake public administration and the development of the state; and to attempt to issue travel documents enabling Namibians to travel abroad (GA Res. 2372 (XXII), 12 June 1968, para. 4). On the Council's activities generally, see I Sagay, *The Legal Aspects of the Namibian Dispute* (University of Ife Press, 1975), *passim* and especially chs 12 and 13; JF Engers, 'The United Nations Travel and Identity Document for Namibians', 65 (1971) *AJIL* 571; LL Herman, 'The Legal Status of Namibia and of the United Nations Council for Namibia', 13 (1975) *Canadian Yearbook of International Law* 306, 320. A Decree on Natural Resources (United Nations Council for Namibia, Decree No. 1 on Natural Resources of Namibia, UN Doc. A/C.131/33, in Report of the Council for Namibia, Addendum, UN GAOR, 29th Sess., Supp. No. 24A, at 27, UN Doc. A/9624/Add.1 (1974)) prohibited the exploitation of Namibian natural resources without the consent of the Council and declared any exploitation concessions not granted by the Council null and void (ibid., paras 1 and 2). It also prohibited the removal of natural resources from Namibia without permission from the Council, and allowed for measures to be taken if this occurred (ibid., paras 3–5). Any persons contravening the Decree were put on notice of being held liable for damages by the future government of a Namibian state (ibid., para. 6). See GA Res. 3295 (XXIX), 13 December 1974, part IV para. 7 (requesting that member states take 'take all appropriate measures to ensure the full application of, and compliance with, the provisions' of the Decree). A member of the commissioner's office remarked in 1971 that the Council operated 'as a kind of UNTEA *in partibus,* or as the Second World War governments-in-exile'; Engers, ibid., 574.

Africa finally agreed to Namibian independence in 1988, the administrative role exercised by the United Nations Transitional Assistance Group (UNTAG) in 1989–90 was different, being limited in both scope and purpose to supervising and controlling elections.[58]

Over 30 years after the Council for Namibia was created, UNMIK and then UNTAET realized the idea of the Council's role in Kosovo and East Timor. In June 1999, as earlier mentioned, UNMIK took over the conduct of administration after the departure of the FRY governmental presence in Kosovo, following the NATO bombing campaign and the human rights abuses and mass displacement of the local Albanian population perpetrated by FRY forces.[59] It was also charged with enabling the provision of humanitarian assistance.[60] Since, as mentioned, the population of Kosovo was to enjoy 'substantial autonomy', in the short-term UNMIK provided full direct administration pending the establishment of institutions through which self-government could be exercised.[61] Later that year, international territorial administration was introduced in East Timor after the

[58] On the mandate and background to UNTAG, see above, ch. 2, n. 34.

[59] On UNMIK and the events which led to the establishment of the mission, see the sources cited above, ch. 1, nn. 1 and 4; see also above, ch. 4, section 4.5.3.

[60] In its original mandate UNMIK was charged with '[s]upporting, in coordination with international humanitarian organizations, humanitarian and disaster relief aid...'; SC Res. 1244, 10 June 1999, para. 11(h). See also Report of the Secretary-General on the United Nations Interim Administration Mission in Kosovo, 12 July 1999, UN Doc. S/1999/779 (hereinafter 'Secretary-General Report on Kosovo 1999'), 31–2, 92–8 and B Kouchner, 'The Challenge of Rebuilding Kosovo', 47:3 (1999) *NATO Review* 12, also available at <http://www.nato.int/docu/review/1999/9903-04.htm>. This came originally under the Pillar I structure in Kosovo, led by UNHCR; see above, ch. 1, n. 1.

[61] As for the departure of the FRY governmental presence, under SC Res. 1244 (1999), the FRY was mandated to '...begin and complete verifiable phased withdrawal from Kosovo of all military, police, and paramilitary forces according to a rapid timetable...'; SC Res. 1244 (above, n. 60), para. 3. The wording from 'verifiable' to 'timetable' repeats the formulation in the Agreement on the Principles (Peace Plan) to Move Towards a Resolution of the Kosovo Crisis Presented to the Leadership of the Federal Republic of Yugoslavia by the President of Finland, Martti Ahtisaari, representing the European Union, and Viktor Chernomyrdin, Special Representative of the President of the Russian Federation, 3 June 1999, UN Doc. S/1999/649, 7 June 1999, Annex (hereinafter 'Kosovo Peace Plan 1999'), para. 2. The withdrawal of civil officials from Kosovo is not mentioned in either the Kosovo Peace Plan or SC Res. 1244. As for the mandate to enable 'substantial autonomy' within the FRY, SC Res. 1244 reaffirms '...the commitment of all Member States to the sovereignty and territorial integrity of the Federal Republic of Yugoslavia' (SC Res. 1244 (ibid.), preamble, para. 10). It also authorizes UNMIK to provide '...an interim administration for Kosovo under which the people of Kosovo can enjoy substantial autonomy within the Federal Republic of Yugoslavia...'; (ibid., para. 10). This extract repeats the formulation that was agreed to by the then FRY in the Kosovo Peace Plan 1999, para. 5. UNMIK's responsibilities included:

(a) Promoting the establishment, pending a final settlement, of substantial autonomy and self-government in Kosovo...;

(b) Performing basic civilian administrative functions where and as long as required;

(c) Organizing and overseeing the development of provisional institutions for democratic and autonomous self-government pending a political settlement, including the holding of elections;

Australian-led International Force for East Timor (INTERFET) restored order in the wake of a rampage of killing and property destruction by pro-Indonesian militias.[62] The militias' actions followed the outcome of 'popular consultation' run by the UN Mission in East Timor (UNAMET), which overwhelmingly favoured separation from Indonesia.[63] After restoring order, INTERFET and a few UNAMET personnel attempted to fill the administrative vacuum created by the departure of Indonesian officials and exacerbated by the destruction.[64] UNTAET was created in part to take over this activity.

Beyond the immediate provision of humanitarian assistance, in both Kosovo and East Timor a key component of the ITA projects involved enabling the (re-) construction and operation of basic infrastructure.[65]

6.4.2 The quality of governance

In addition to filling a perceived 'vacuum' in local territorial governance, international territorial administration has been associated with broader and more ambitious purposes concerning governance. The perceived 'problems' here are concerned not with the existence of governance, but the quality of governance being performed. Four main policy objectives for governance can be identified in this use of ITA: first, the attainment of a certain status for the territorial unit concerned; secondly, a broad agenda concerning effectiveness, democracy, the rule of law, and liberal economic policy; thirdly, the furtherance of migration policy; and, fourthly, the exploitation of natural resources.

(d) Transferring, as these institutions are established, its administrative responsibilities while overseeing and supporting the consolidation of Kosovo's local provisional institutions and other peace-building activities...

Ibid., para 11. The subsequent creation of institutions involving a measure of self-government is discussed further below, text accompanying n. 80 and n. 145 and accompanying text. See also above, ch. 1, n. 1.

[62] Progress Report of the Secretary-General on the Question of East Timor, 13 December 1999, UN Doc. A/54/654 (1999), paras 32–7; SC Res. 1264, 15 September 1999, para. 3. For commentary on INTERFET, see, e.g., I Martin, *Self-Determination in East Timor: The United Nations, the Ballot, and International Intervention* (IPA/Lynne Rienner, 2001) *passim*; C de Coning, 'The UN Transitional Administration in East Timor (UNTAET): Lessons Learned from the First 100 Days', 6 (2000) *International Peacekeeping* 83, 84–5; M Dee, ' "Coalitions of the Willing" and Humanitarian Intervention: Australia's Involvement with INTERFET', 8:3 (2001) *International Peacekeeping* 1; MJ Kelly, 'Transitional Justice in Peace Operations: Shaping the Twilight Zone in Somalia and East Timor', 4 (2001) *Yearbook of International Humanitarian Law* 21.

[63] On UNAMET and the consultation, see above, ch. 1, n. 5, and ch. 5, text accompanying n. 145 *et seq.*

[64] Progress Report of the Secretary-General on the Question of East Timor, 13 December 1999 (above n. 62), paras 36, 37.

[65] For example, in Kosovo UNMIK was charged with '[s]upporting the reconstruction of key infrastructure and other economic reconstruction...'; SC Res. 1244 (above n. 60), para. 11(g). See also Secretary-General Report on Kosovo 1999 (above n. 60), 101–9; Kouchner (above n. 60).

These four policy objectives will now be set out in turn, followed by Table 6, which lists them collectively.

6.4.2.1 Governance policy—territorial status

The first type of governance policy that has been associated with international territorial administration is the promotion of a certain status for the territory concerned. Like the idea of using ITA as a response to a 'sovereignty problem' discussed earlier, ITA is used here in order to have some sort of mediating effect on issues of sovereignty. The difference between the two is that, in this instance, its significance is understood not in terms of an effect on the identity of the administering actor (e.g., introducing a 'neutral' administering authority to enhance the prospects of solving a sovereignty dispute) but, rather, in terms of an effect on how administration is carried out—i.e., which policies are promoted by it. Governance objectives associated with the use of ITA in this way include facilitating the future adoption of a particular territorial agenda; bringing a territorial settlement into being; and supporting the continuance of a territorial settlement once adopted.

ITA was first associated with the policy of promoting the adoption of a particular agenda for territorial status in the Saar territory after the First World War. As an alternative to both French and German administration, League control was seen as preventing either country from altering the Versailles plan for determining the territory's status. Moving forward to the 1960s, when the UN General Assembly terminated South Africa's Mandate and introduced Council administration in South West Africa/Namibia, it aimed to replace one administrative regime understood to be opposed to the future realization of a particular form of 'external' self-determination—independence—with another conceived to support it (though after a period of UN administration).

This use of ITA resurfaced in the 1990s, with the conflict in the southern Balkans. As mentioned earlier, the idea of EUAM administration in Mostar from 1994 to 1996 can be understood as a temporary solution to the 'sovereignty problem' caused by the perceived inability of local leaders to agree on governing the city jointly. Its use was also, moreover, understood as a response to a 'governance problem', in replacing governments in West and East Mostar opposed to unification with a (single) government supporting this policy. By promoting unification, the EUAM would aim to 'solve' the 'sovereignty problem' permanently, removing the need for its presence as the temporary solution to that problem.

The same objective lay behind the introduction of the OHR Supervisor in the Brčko District of Bosnia and Herzegovina. At the end of 1995, the city of Brčko, formerly a multi-ethnic community, was divided, together with its surrounding area, between control by the Bosnian Croat and Bosnian Muslim/Bosniak 'Federation of Bosnia and Herzegovina' (the 'Federation') and the Bosnian Serb Republika Srpska (the 'RS'), with each side claiming exclusive title over the whole district.[66] As in many areas of the country, population movements, whether voluntary or forcible, in conjunction with killing, had 'cleansed' each part of the district of members of the opposing ethnic group(s).[67] On the one hand, the Dayton Peace Agreements accepted the ethnic division of Bosnia and Herzegovina between the Federation and the Republika Srpska, conceiving the state as a federal-type arrangement consisting of two 'Entities' in the new Constitution, with their geographical boundaries determined by an Inter-Entity Boundary Line (IEBL).[68] On the other hand, Dayton promoted the return of migrants to their former homes, attempting to reverse the migratory aspect of ethnic cleansing and foster a unified, multi-ethnic politics cutting across that boundary.[69] Since agreement on the Brčko section of the boundary was not reached at Dayton, the determination of this section was placed before an arbitral tribunal.[70]

In 1997, the tribunal considered that the Republika Srpska had failed to implement its 'return' and free movement obligations, and granted an OHR Supervisor certain administrative powers—including the power to legislate—to promote the objectives of return and democratization.[71] These objectives can be explained as means

[66] On the Federation and the Republika Srpska, and the groups they represent, see above, ch. 1, text corresponding to n. 41, and above, ch. 4, section 4.5.1, in particular text corresponding to n. 188. For the situation in Brčko by 1995, see, for example, *Arbitration for the Brčko Area (Federation of Bosnia and Herzegovina v Republika Srpska)*, Arbitral Tribunal for Dispute over Inter-Entity Boundary in Brčko Area, Award, 14 February 1997, UN Doc. S/1997/126 (1997), reprinted in 36 (1997) *ILM* 396 (hereinafter 'Brčko Award 1997'), paras 42–57. By the end of 1997, the RS controlled 48 per cent and the Federation 52 per cent of the territory (ibid., para. 52). On Brčko generally, see above, ch. 2, n. 74 and accompanying text, and the relevant reports of the International Crisis Group, obtainable from <http://www.crisisgroup.org>. See also PC Farrand, 'Lessons from Brcko: Necessary Components for Future Internationally Supervised Territories', 15 (2001) *Emory International Law Review* 529; MG Karnavas, 'Creating the Legal Framework of the Brčko District of Bosnia and Herzegovina, a Model for the Region and other Postconflict Countries', 97 (2003) *AJIL* 111.

[67] Brčko Award 1997 (above n. 66), paras 50, 53.

[68] For the boundary see Dayton GFA (above, ch. 1, n. 38), especially Art. III; Dayton Annex 2 (above, ch. 1, n. 38). For the Constitution of Bosnia and Herzegovina, see Dayton GFA, Art. V; Dayton Annex 4 (above, ch. 1, n. 38).

[69] Dayton Annex 7 (above, ch. 1, n. 38).

[70] Dayton Annex 2 (above, ch. 1, n. 38), Art. V. On the Arbitral Tribunal generally, including its decisions, see OHR Brčko arbitral tribunal website, at <http://www.ohr.int/ohr-offices/brcko/arbitration/archive.asp?sa=on>.

[71] The Tribunal stated that:

[g]iven the ongoing failures to comply with the Dayton Accords in the RS area... (particularly in terms of freedom of movement and the return of former Brčko residents to their Brčko homes), and the high levels of tension resulting therefrom, there is a clear need to establish a program for implementation of the Dayton Accords in the area...

As far as administrative powers were concerned, the Supervisor was given the '...authority to promulgate binding regulations and orders in aid of the local implementation program and democratization...' and was to '...establish...a program...to govern the phased and orderly return of former residents of the relevant area to their homes of origin and for the restoration, construction and allocation of housing as necessary to accommodate old and new residents'; Brčko Award 1997 (above n. 66), para. 104, parts I A, I B (1), and I B (4) respectively. On the failure of RS to implement its return obligations, see ibid., 54. On the 'supervision' system generally (including monitoring responsibilities), see ibid., para. 104.

of promoting conditions for unified, multi-ethnic politics in the district, enabling the tribunal eventually to establish a 'unified' Brčko as the solution to the boundary dispute.[72] Whereas in Mostar, obstructions to a unified city were addressed as both a 'sovereignty' and a 'governance' 'problem', in Brčko the tribunal did not replace divided structures with an internationally-run unified structure.[73] Rather, it enabled the Supervisor to exercise governance within the divided structures to enhance the possibility that a unified structure would be supported in the future.

In Kosovo in 1999, as already mentioned, the territory's future status was placed open to question, and UNMIK was charged with '[f]acilitating a political process' to determine this status.[74] In doing so, it replaced the Serb and FRY governments, which in 1999 were seen as opposing any alteration in Kosovo's status. Like the Saar project before it, the Kosovo undertaking is distinctive within this group of projects. Whereas international territorial administration was understood to be there to promote and guarantee the eventual settlement of status, the form that this status would take was unclear when the mission started. In the Saar, the status question was to be determined according to a preset formula on a predetermined date; in Kosovo, however, UNMIK was also partially responsible for determining how the status question was to be resolved.

UNMIK's chief strategy for resolving the status question was to adopt a policy generally referred to as 'standards before status' and later 'standards for Kosovo'.[75] This posited that certain standards had to be met in Kosovo before the entity's international status would be determined.[76] As discussed further below, the standards concerned the quality of governance in Kosovo and good relations between Kosovo and Belgrade.

---

[72] *Arbitration for the Brčko Area (Federation of Bosnia and Herzegovina v Republika Srpska)*, Arbitral Tribunal for Dispute over Inter-Entity Boundary in Brčko Area, Final Award, 5 March 1999, obtainable from <http://www.ohr.int> (hereinafter 'Brčko Award 1999'). For academic commentary, see M Baros, 'The Arbitral Tribunal's Award for the Dispute over the Inter-entity Boundary in the Brčko Area', 3 (1998) *Journal of Armed Conflict Law* 233; C Schreuer, 'The Brčko Final Award of 5 March 1999', 12 (1999) *LJIL* 575.

[73] On the tribunal's consideration of this option, see, for example, Brčko Award 1997 (above n. 66), para. 68.

[74] SC Res. 1244 (above n. 60), para. 11. See also ibid., Annex 1, para. 6; Kosovo Peace Plan 1999 (above n. 61), para. 8.

[75] The broader ideas implicated by this policy, including Kantian notions of equivocal sovereignty generally, and the concept of 'earned sovereignty' in particular, are discussed in the next chapter, in section 7.3.3.

[76] The policy was originally proposed in 2002 by the then head of UNMIK, Michael Steiner, who outlined a series of standards of international expectations for Kosovo's institutions and society which had to be achieved before the issue of Kosovo's future status would be determined. See 'Highlights of the introductory remarks at a press conference by Michael Steiner, Special Representative of the Secretary-General in Kosovo', UN Press Release, 26 June 2002, obtainable from <http://www.unhchr.ch>; S Woehrel, 'Kosovo's Future Status and US Policy', Congressional Research Service Report (updated 27 January 2005), available at <http://www.fas.org/sgp/crs/row/RS21721.pdf>. The standards were promulgated by UNMIK in 2003 (UNMIK, *Standards for Kosovo*, presented on 10 December 2003, and endorsed by the Security Council in a Presidential Statement of 12 December 2003 (UN Doc. S/PRST/2003/26); see also UNMIK, Kosovo Standards Implementation Plan, 31 March 2004 (with updated actions for Standards 3 and 4 as

Besides the idea of promoting the future adoption of a particular territorial agenda, ITA has also been associated with the idea of effecting the immediate enactment of such an agenda. Here, such actualization by ITA is seen as possible in two different ways—either through performing administrative acts directly, or by transferring administrative control to certain local actors. In Mostar in 1994, and Brčko in 2000, administrative acts by the EUAM and the OHR Supervisor, respectively, were understood to bring a model of unified city government into existence. In Mostar, this was achieved through the creation of the EUAM itself. In Brčko, a new territorial settlement crafted by the arbitral tribunal in 1999 established the district as a condominium between the two Entities, run locally by a unified multi-ethnic government.[77] This new settlement was implemented through certain administrative acts by the OHR Supervisor. In the immediate period, such acts included imposing a new Statute for District Government (enacted in 2000); scheduling new elections; determining when the IEBL no longer had any effect in the district; and creating an interim regime (including an Interim District Assembly) pending the outcome of the elections.[78]

---

of 6 July 2006)). For the text of the UNMIK documents, see <http://www.unmikonline.org>. The implementation of the standards was monitored by UNMIK which conducted, in consultation with local authorities, assessments of progress and prepared reports which were submitted to the Security Council as part of the periodic Reports of the Secretary-General on UNMIK. On the monitoring and reporting procedure, see <http://www.unmikonline.org/standards/index.html>. In addition to this procedure, a comprehensive review of the implementation of the Kosovo standards was carried out by the Special Envoy of the UN Secretary-General, Kai Eide, between July and September 2006. See Report of the Special Envoy of the Secretary General, Mr. Kay Eide, 'A comprehensive review of the situation in Kosovo', UN Doc. S/2005/635, Annex, 7 October 2005; see also the Report of the Secretary-General on the United Nations Interim Administration Mission in Kosovo, UN Doc. S/2007/134, 9 March 2007. For commentary, see, e.g., PR Williams, 'The Road to Resolving the Conflict over Kosovo's Final Status', 31 (2003) *Denver Journal of International Law & Policy* 387; B Knoll, 'From Benchmarking to Final Status? Kosovo and the Problem of and International Administration Open-Ended Mandate', 16 (2005) *EJIL* 637, at 641–2.

[77] Brčko Award 1999 (above n. 72), paras 11, 34, 36. The Tribunal decided that '...the entire territory...will...be held in "condominium" by both entities simultaneously: The territory of the RS will encompass the entire Opstina, and so also will the territory of the Federation' (ibid., para. 11). The territory would exist '...under BiH sovereignty...subject to BiH control in those areas which are the responsibility of the BiH common institutions, and in other respects (subject to needed coordination by the Supervisor between the District and the two entity governments) the District government...[would] operate on a self-governing basis' (ibid., para. 34). Neither Entity would 'exercise any authority within the boundaries of the District...' (ibid., para. 11) and the District government would be '...a single, unitary, multi-ethnic democratic government to exorcise [sic], throughout the pre-war Brkco Opstina, those powers previously exercised by the two entities and the three municipal governments' (ibid., para. 36).

[78] Under the Brčko Award 1999 (above n. 72), the Supervisor was responsible for: (1) scheduling the elections to choose District Assembly (legislature) members; (2) preparing a new 'Statute for District Government' and a plan and schedule for the formation of this government; (3) determining when the IEBL 'ceases to have any legal significance in the district', at which point the IEBL will 'cease to exist within the District'; (4) making orders affecting the application of the existing governmental arrangements prior to the formation of the District government, and the obligations of the Entities in relation to these arrangements (e.g., paying salaries) if necessary; (5) determining whether Entity police can enter the area, and whether District police can take 'instruction or direction from any representative of either entity or any political party'; (6) setting the date from

Turning to Kosovo, given that the objective for the status of the territory during the UNMIK period was, as previously mentioned, 'substantial autonomy' within what was eventually called the Republic of Serbia, here the plenary (rather than 'substantial') administrative powers asserted by UNMIK during that period can be explained as a mechanism for ensuring that the people of Kosovo could practise autonomous government without having to rely for this on the central state authorities. UNMIK assumed what is effectively (though not in name) the federal-type role of the central authorities, because these authorities were seen as having failed to perform that role in the past.[79] It implemented this role by creating Provisional Institutions of Self-Government (PISG), involving local representatives in government subject to the overall authority of UNMIK.[80] UNMIK was also mandated to bring Kosovo's post-UNMIK status into being once that was resolved.[81]

ITA was conceived to implement a territorial settlement in the second way—through giving up its administrative powers to certain local actors—in the Saar, South West Africa/Namibia, Mostar, and Kosovo. In the Saar, placing the League, rather than France or Germany, in administrative control in 1935 was seen as ensuring that control would be transferred to whoever prevailed following the 1935 plebiscite. In South West Africa/Namibia, a corollary to the reason for introducing ITA—to replace one government opposed to independence with another that supported it—was the UN intention eventually to give up administrative control to local actors, enabling a declaration of independence to be made.

which all Entity armed forces must be out of the District; and (7) [with IFOR] scheduling the phased withdrawal of such forces (ibid., paras 36; 38–41). The Statute was finalized on 7 December 1999, and declared to be in force on 8 March 2000. See Statute of the Brčko District of Bosnia and Herzegovina, 7 December 1999, 39 (2000) *ILM* 879; Supervisor of Brčko, Supervisory Order on the Establishment of the Brčko District of Bosnia and Herzegovina, 8 March 2000; OHR, Decision on the Establishment of the Brčko District of Bosnia and Herzegovina, 8 March 2000 (the latter two documents obtainable from <http://www.ohr.int>). The Supervisor performed further acts designed to implement the District settlement, including establishing the interim regime. See the Orders of the Supervisor from 8 March 2000 onwards, obtainable from <http://www.ohr.int/ohr-offices/brcko>.

   [79] SC Res. 1244, creating UNMIK, affirms '...the call in previous resolutions for substantial autonomy and meaningful self-administration for Kosovo'; SC 1244 (above n. 60), preamble. The objectives of UNMIK include providing '...an interim administration for Kosovo under which the people of Kosovo can enjoy substantial autonomy within the Federal Republic of Yugoslavia...' (ibid., para. 10), and '...[p]romoting the establishment, pending a final settlement, of substantial autonomy and self-government in Kosovo...' (ibid., para. 11(a)). The word 'substantial' in the phrase 'substantial autonomy within the Federal Republic of Yugoslavia' implies that the FRY Government (later the Government of Serbia and Montenegro and then the Republic of Serbia) and possibly also the Serb Republic Government during the FRY/Serbia and Montenegro period enjoyed certain residual powers with respect to Kosovo, exercising a relationship with Kosovo akin to the relationship in a federal state between the federal government and its constituent entities (states, provinces, Länder etc.). In supposedly taking on the 'federal'-type role, UNMIK assumed these residual powers.
   [80] For information, see above, ch. 1, n. 1.
   [81] UNMIK's responsibilities included, '[i]n a final stage, overseeing the transfer of authority from Kosovo's provisional institutions to institutions established under a political settlement'; SC Res. 1244 (above n. 60), para. 11(e).

This perhaps explains the lack of a Council-type role for the United Nations in 1989–90: contrary to its behaviour in 1967, the existing administrative actor (the Government of South Africa) had agreed to enable independence by relinquishing its authority to the people of Namibia.

In Mostar in 1996, an externally-imposed settlement for unified government run by local actors was implemented through ITA. It was effected through both the creation of new local structures, as had happened in Brčko in 2000, and the transfer by the EUAM of its plenary authority to these structures. In Kosovo, insofar as the arrangements adopted pursuant to the final settlement on status did not involve an administrative role for the United Nations, UNMIK was to transfer its authority to whichever actors were to have this role.

The idea of using ITA to implement a particular territorial agenda distinguishes all these projects from the East Timor project, since in East Timor, the use of ITA was not understood in terms of replacing an existing authority opposed to the territorial agenda—independence—in that case. Although Indonesia had originally been opposed to East Timor's independence, it agreed to the idea of UN administration in the May Agreements before the 'popular consultation' in 1999,[82] and UNTAET itself began its mission after Indonesia had formally renounced its claim to sovereignty and withdrawn its governmental presence. At the same time, UNTAET was not able to continue its administration indefinitely, since, as discussed further below, it was implicitly mandated to administer itself out of existence by eventually transferring authority to local actors, which it did in May 2002.

In Danzig, Bosnia and Herzegovina, Mostar, and Kosovo, international territorial administration was conceived to promote the continuance of a territorial agenda once adopted. With Danzig, ITA formed part of the response to a territorial dispute at the end of the First World War between Germany and Poland; the Free City was part of Germany and had a majority German population, but was claimed by Poland as a means of accessing the sea.[83] The solution was to reconstitute, on a permanent basis, Danzig as a 'Free City', an arrangement which

---

[82] See Agreement between the Republic of Indonesia and the Portuguese Republic on the Question of East Timor, 5 May 1999, obtainable from <http://www.un.org/peace/etimor99/etimor.htm>, Art. 6, which states that:

[i]f the Secretary-General determines, on the basis of the result of the popular consultation and in accordance with this Agreement, that the proposed constitutional framework for special autonomy is not acceptable to the East Timorese people, the Government of Indonesia shall take the constitutional steps necessary to terminate its links with East Timor thus restoring under Indonesian law the status East Timor held prior to 17 July 1976, and the Governments of Indonesia and Portugal and the Secretary-General shall agree on arrangements for a peaceful and orderly transfer of authority in East Timor to the United Nations.

For Indonesia's renunciation of its claim to sovereignty and withdrawal from East Timor, see above, ch. 5, n. 154.

[83] On the background to the Danzig dispute, see, for example, JB Mason, *The Danzig Dilemma* (1946), 3–76; Ydit (above n. 19), 186–90, 227; JK Bleimaier, 'The Legal Status of the Free City of Danzig 1920–1939: Lessons to Be Derived from the Experience of a Non-State Entity in the International Community', 2 (1989) *Hague Yearbook of International Law* 69, 70–81.

lasted from 1920 to 1939.[84] As discussed in Chapter 4, administrative powers in Danzig were granted primarily to the Free City authorities; Poland enjoyed certain domestic authority and responsibility for the conduct of foreign policy.[85] The territory was placed under the 'protection' of the League,[86] which was to play two roles: first, to settle disputes between the Free City and Poland[87] and, secondly, to exercise, where necessary, a right to veto certain militaristic plans, constitutional amendments or incorrect applications of the Constitution and treaties.[88] Ultimately, as the Permanent Court of International Justice observed in the *Free City of Danzig and International Labour Organization Case*, these powers were aimed at ensuring the preservation of the Free City. The Court stated that:

... the duty of the League is to ensure the continued existence of the Free City on the footing on which it was established in accordance with the Treaty of Versailles, and that it was in order to enable the League to achieve this purpose that the Free City was placed under its protection and the constitution placed under its guarantee. Accordingly, the [League] Council has declared that it is bound to ensure orderly, peaceful and stable government at Danzig, to protect it from outside aggression and to see that without the consent of the League no fundamental change is made to the Treaty of Paris [outlining the rights of Poland in the Free City], nor any change in the constitution of the Free City.[89]

The Free City settlement remained an uneasy compromise; the failure of the League to protect Danzig from Nazi occupation on 1 September 1939 formed a small but significant part of the wider collapse of the League system and the resumption of war in Europe.[90]

Jumping forward to Bosnia and Herzegovina at the end of the 20th century, after the Dayton settlement OHR gradually began to assert administrative authority to take action explained in terms of ensuring the continuation of

---

[84] See above, ch. 4, section 4.2.2.

[85] On the powers of the Free City authorities and Poland, see above, ch. 4, text accompanying n. 51 (Free City authorities) and nn. 52 *et seq.* (Poland).

[86] On Danzig being under the 'protection' of the League, see Versailles Peace Treaty, Art. 102.

[87] For the dispute settlement powers, see Versailles Peace Treaty, Art. 103; Convention between Poland and the Free City of Danzig (hereinafter 'Poland–Danzig Treaty'), Paris, 9 November 1920, 6 LNTS 189, Arts 7, 8, 18, 20, 22, 25, 26, 39. The many disputes addressed by the League-appointed High Commissioner at first instance were often referred on to the League and the Permanent Court of International Justice. On these disputes, see, e.g., Walters (above n. 19), 301, 454–5; Ydit (above n. 19), 213 *et. seq.* See also *Jurisdiction of the Courts of Danzig, Advisory Opinion,* PCIJ, *Series B,* No. 15 (1928); *Free City of Danzig and International Labour Organization, Advisory Opinion,* PCIJ, *Series B,* No. 18 (1930) (hereinafter '*Danzig and ILO Case*'); *Access to, or Anchorage in, the Port of Danzig of Polish War Vessels, Advisory Opinion,* PCIJ, *Series A/B,* No. 43; *Treatment of Polish Nationals and Other persons of Polish Origin or Speech in the Danzig Territory, Advisory Opinion,* PCIJ, *Series A/B,* No. 44 (1932); *Consistency of Certain Danzig Legislative Decrees with the Constitution of the Free City, Advisory Opinion,* PCIJ, *Series A/B,* No. 65 (1935), 13. The administrative powers here were to be exercised either by the League itself, or by the High Commissioner. On these powers see, e.g., Mason (above n. 83), 77–88; Ydit, ibid., 194–7.

[88] See above, ch. 4, text from n. 82.

[89] *Danzig and ILO Case* (above n. 87), 12.

[90] On the problems in Danzig in the 1930s, and the Free City's eventual demise, see, for example, Walters (above n. 19), 453–4, 615–21, 793–7; Ydit (above n. 19), 218–21, 227.

Bosnia and Herzegovina as a state. On 7 March 2001, OHR purported to dismiss Ante Jelavić as the elected Croat representative of the state Presidency, banning him from holding public and party offices in the future, because of Jelavić's declaration of independence on the part of 'Herzeg-Bosna' covering the Bosnian Croat areas of the Federation.[91] So OHR exercised governance in an effort to prevent the Federation from unravelling. Similarly, the introduction of international appointees on various public bodies in the country (e.g., judges on the Constitutional Court) by the Dayton Peace Agreements was explained in part in terms of ensuring that the institutions involved supported the existing territorial settlement in their decisions.[92]

In Mostar, the unified settlement introduced by the EUAM in 1996 via an Interim Statute was not supported locally.[93] As a result, OHR asserted certain governmental powers within Mostar to promote the operation of unified governance structures,[94] culminating in the 2004 imposition of a new Statute for a single City of Mostar, with the aspiration of introducing a regime which 'ensures the collective rights of the constituent peoples and prevents dominance by one segment of the population of Mostar'.[95] In Kosovo, not only was UNMIK administration aimed at bringing 'substantial autonomy' into being in 1999; it was also

[91] OHR, Decision removing Ante Jelavić from his position as the Croat member of the BiH Presidency, 7 March 2001, obtainable from <http://www.ohr.int>.

[92] On these arrangements, see above, ch. 2, section 2.3.4.1.

[93] EUAM administration ended on 22 July 1996, after the formal acceptance by the local parties of an Interim Statute providing for a multi-ethnic administration in the City. See Interim Statute of the City of Mostar, 7 February 1996, published in *Official Gazette of the City of Mostar*, No. 1, 20 February 1996. An Office of the Special Envoy in Mostar was then created under the framework of the European Union, to oversee the implementation of the terms of the Interim Statute for a maximum six-month period running until 31 December 1996. See Council Joint Action 96/442/CFSP adopted on the basis of Article J3 of the Treaty on European Union on the nomination of a Special Envoy of the European Union in the city of Mostar, 15 July 1996, *OJ* L185 (1996), 2 and corrigendum *OJ* L260 (1996), 6. According to the International Crisis Group, '...a façade of power-sharing developed between the Bosniak and Croat representatives at the municipal, city and cantonal levels, barely disguising the continuation of parallel structures at all levels' (the phrase 'parallel structures' refers to the divided governance structures in West and East Mostar that the Interim Statute aimed to unite); International Crisis Group, 'Reunifying Mostar: Opportunities for Progress', *ICG Balkans Report No. 90*, 19 April 2000, obtainable from <http://www.crisisgroup.org>, quotation taken from 12.

[94] E.g., OHR, Decision Adding the Fundamental Interest Clause and the Position of Deputy Head of Municipality to the Mostar City Municipalities Statutes, 6 July 1999, obtainable from <http://www.ohr.int>.

[95] Statute of the City of Mostar, contained in OHR Decision Enacting the Statute of the City of Mostar, 28 January 2004 (quote from the Preamble of the Statute); see also Commission for Reforming the City of Mostar, 'Recommendations of the Commission—Report of the Chairman', 15 December 2003 (both documents obtainable from <http://www.ohr.int>); F Bieber, 'Local Institutional Engineering: A Tale of Two Cities, Mostar and Brčko', 12 (2005) *International Peacekeeping* 420; International Crisis Group, 'Building Bridges in Mostar', Europe Report No. 150, 20 November 2003, obtainable from <http://www.crisisgroup.org>. For some remarks on the situation in Mostar since then, see, e.g., OHR, 'Mid-Year Report to the European Parliament by the OHR and EU Special Representative for BiH, January–June 2004', 3 November 2004, obtainable from <http://www.ohr.int>.

understood as ensuring the continuance of this arrangement from that moment forward, pending the eventual resolution of the territory's status.

Thus, the first governance policy associated with the use of ITA is the promotion of a certain territorial status, whether Free City status (Danzig), unified city/district status (Mostar and Brčko), statehood (South West Africa/Namibia and Bosnia and Herzegovina), sub-state autonomy (Kosovo), or an undetermined future status (the Saar and Kosovo). ITA is seen as capable of promoting the future adoption of territorial status, bringing territorial status into being, and supporting the continuance of an existing status. In this respect, the Kosovo project is the most complex use of ITA so far, since its use has been understood in terms of performing all three functions.

6.4.2.2 Governance policy—effectiveness, democracy, the rule of law, and free market economics

The second governance policy associated with international territorial administration involves enabling the operation of governmental institutions to function in a particular way, as opposed to the earlier objective of merely seeking to ensure that there is general governance in the territory. In particular, the enterprise is concerned with fostering certain standards for governance: that it is effective, is 'democratic', is based on the 'rule of law' and follows a liberal economic model.

In the first place, ITA has been associated with the policy of ensuring that government institutions operate effectively and are not hampered in this regard by the actions of local officials.[96] This can be seen in the introduction of international appointees to locally-based bodies involved in particular aspects of territorial administration, as set out in Chapter 2, such as courts and tribunals.[97] Sometimes, the introduction of an international appointee has occurred when local actors have been considered to have failed to agree on appointing the relevant official themselves. In Danzig, for example, as mentioned in Chapter 4, the League could appoint the president of the Port and Waterways Board if the Free City and Poland were unable to agree on a candidate for this position.[98]

In other cases, the perceived problem is not so much disagreement on appointments, but the fear that, in a society perceived as 'divided', the institution will not function due to partisan disagreements between its local-national members unless 'neutral' international appointees are present. In Bosnia and Herzegovina, as outlined in Chapter 2, the international appointees to state-wide institutions (other than the human rights Ombudsman) held office alongside individuals appointed by the two Entities. In general, their use has been understood partly in

[96] On governmental effectiveness as a general ITA policy objective, see, e.g., HH Perritt, 'Structures and Standards for Political Trusteeship', 8 (2003) *UCLA Journal of International Law & Foreign Affairs* 385, 439–40.

[97] See above, ch. 2, section 2.3.4, and, for the definition of 'territorial administration' that includes judicial bodies, above, ch. 1, section 1.4.1.

[98] See above, ch. 4, n. 86 and accompanying text.

terms of avoiding deadlock caused by the adoption of opposing positions by other appointees. Introducing supposedly 'neutral' members enables the institution to function.[99]

Sometimes, it would appear that part of the explanation for the appointment of internationals is administrative convenience, enabling slots to be filled expeditiously and the institution in question to commence or resume operation quickly where there are vacancies on it. So, for example, the involvement of international appointees on the High Judicial and Prosecutorial Council (charged with scrutinizing the judiciary and prosecution authorities) in Bosnia and Herzegovina has been explained in part as a means of guaranteeing the 'continuous operation' of this body.[100]

Beyond seeking to ensure that governance is 'effective', ITA has also been concerned with fostering 'democratic' governance. As outlined in Chapter 2,[101]

---

[99] According to Paul Szasz, the role of the international appointees generally was to ensure that the government organs involved 'can continue functioning even if the rest of the government is paralyzed'; P Szasz, 'The Bosnian Constitution: the Road to Dayton and Beyond', 90 (1996) *ASIL Proc.* 479 at 483. For the composition of each institution, see above, ch. 2, section 2.3.4.1, Table 2 and the relevant parts of Table 3. In the case of Bosnia and Herzegovina, on the Central Bank Governing Board, the international appointee was only one of three voting members, but as Governor had the casting vote (Dayton Annex 4 (above, ch. 1, n. 38), Art. VII). With the other institutions, international appointees were neither in a majority nor given a special power in decision-making. Although they enjoyed certain positions—one as President in the Commission for Real Property Claims (CRPC); one was Chairman in each of the Commission to Preserve National Monuments (CPNM) and the Commission on Public Corporations (CPC)—no explicit provision granted the holders of such positions special voting powers. For the CRPC (both full Commission and smaller panels) and the CPNM, decisions were taken by a majority vote (Dayton Annex 7 (above, ch. 1, n. 38), Art. XII (CRPC), Dayton Annex 8 (above, ch. 1, n. 38), Art. V (CPNM)); for the Constitutional Court and the CPC, no specification on decision-making was made. In the Constitutional Court and CRPC (full Commission), international appointees constituted three of the nine members (note that, unlike with the original Human Rights Chamber, no express provision delineated the composition of smaller Panels for the CRPC: see Dayton Annex 7, Art. IX.3); in the CPNM and the CPC they constituted two of the five members. International appointees only held the balance of power, then; they did not constitute a majority. However, the appointment of 'local' members was split between the Federation and the RS (four and two appointees respectively on the Constitutional Court and CRPC; two and one appointees respectively on the CPNM and CPC); and the Federation appointments were potentially split between Bosnian Croat and Bosnian Muslim/Bosniak appointees. Taking these two splits into account, the international appointees were more numerous than appointees of either the Federation Bosnian Muslims/Bosniaks, the Federation Bosnian Croats, or the RS. Moreover, for the local appointees to constitute a majority would require agreement between all of them in the CPNM and the CPC, and all but one of them in the Constitutional Court and CRPC. In the absence of this, the international appointees collectively held the balance of power. The Human Rights Chamber normally sat in panels of seven, composed of two members from the Federation, one from the RS, and four international judges (Dayton Annex 6 (above, ch. 1, n. 38), Art. X(2)); decisions on the plenary Chamber and its Panels were made by majority (ibid., Art. XI) and the international appointees collectively constituted a majority on each body; the internationally-appointed President enjoyed a tie-breaking vote in the event of a tie in the plenary Chamber (ibid.).

[100] OHR, Decision on the Appointment of Members of and Advisors to the High Judicial and Prosecutorial Council of Bosnia and Herzegovina, 4 June 2004, obtainable from <http://www.ohr.int>.

[101] See above, ch. 2, section 2.2.3 and Table 1.

the use of ITA to ensure a particular feature of democratic politics—free and fair consultations—has a long history, from the conduct of what was in effect a type of self-determination referendum by the League Governing Commission in the Saar in 1935,[102] to the conduct of local elections by the OSCE in Kosovo after 1999.[103] As already mentioned, it has covered consultations on territorial status— as in the Saar—and elections to governmental office—as in Kosovo.[104] In most cases, international control or conduct is deployed because of a fear that, if left to other actors, the process would either not take place or fail to be free or fair.[105] Where the consultation in question is an 'act of self-determination', it is understood as reflecting an international commitment to the realization of some form of self-determination for the population involved.[106]

The international conduct or control of consultations is sometimes accompanied by more general ITA to furnish governmental support for the consultation process. In the Western Sahara, the UN Mission for the Referendum in the Western Sahara (MINURSO) was authorized not only to carry out the self-determination consultation, but also to exercise all necessary administrative measures, including changing laws and maintaining law and order, to ensure that the consultation operated properly and was free and fair.[107] In Cambodia, the 1991 Paris peace agreements facilitated the election of a new government via a consultation operated by the UN Transitional Authority in Cambodia (UNTAC).[108] In the transitional period before this government took office, the Supreme National Council (SNC)—comprising four Cambodian factions—enjoyed governmental authority;[109] UNTAC was granted certain powers of supervision and control over governmental institutions to ensure that the exercise of governance would not compromise the elections.[110]

---

[102] See above, ch. 4, text accompanying n. 22 *et seq.*

[103] See above, ch. 2, n. 38.

[104] See above, ch. 2, section 2.2.3.

[105] For further commentary, see the sources cited above, ch. 2, section 2.2.3; see also R Caplan, *International Governance of War-Torn Territories: Rule and Reconstruction* (OUP, 2005), ch. 5, *passim*; Perritt (above n. 96), 437–38.

[106] This is discussed further in the next chapter.

[107] See the sources cited above, ch. 2, n. 21. See also above, ch. 2, n. 32.

[108] On the peace settlement generally, see above, ch. 4, n. 132. On the UNTAC mandate to carry out the elections, see above, ch. 2, n. 35.

[109] On the transitional period and the SNC, see above, ch. 4, text from n. 144.

[110] Under the Agreement on a Comprehensive Political Settlement of the Cambodia Conflict, Paris, 23 October 1991, UN Doc. A/46/608-S/2317730 (1991) (hereinafter 'Cambodia Settlement Agreement'), UNTAC's powers included the right to supervise or control institutions that 'could directly influence the outcome of the elections' (Cambodia Settlement Agreement, Annex 1, section B, para. 2); the right to exercise control over administrative institutions 'acting in the field of foreign affairs, national defense, finance, public security and information' if this was 'necessary to ensure strict neutrality' as far as the elections were concerned (ibid., section B, para. 1); the right to issue directives and remove or install staff on all institutions (ibid., section B, paras 1 and 4); and the right to correct actions by institutions that undermined the objectives of the Settlement (ibid., section B, para. 6). Moreover, administrative institutions that 'could continue to operate in order to ensure normal day-to-day life in Cambodia' were to be placed under

Since the project in Cambodia, the scope of democratic politics associated with ITA has extended beyond consultations. However, in its application to the protection of minorities, this broader agenda echoes the League Commission's role in the Saar, which was intended, in part, to protect the German population from persecution that was feared under the alternative of French administration. This early precedent was followed much later in Eastern Slavonia, where the three-year duration of ITA was designed to reassure the local Serbs who feared the immediate resumption of Croatian control.[111] It also finds an echo in the UN programme of distributing 'humanitarian supplies' in three of the northern Iraqi Governorates between 1996 and 2003. This distribution formed part of the wider UN Oil-for-Food Programme, which used Iraqi oil revenues to pay for, inter alia, 'humanitarian supplies' for the whole country.[112] As with the US–UK-imposed no-fly zone above the 36th parallel, UN distribution in the three northern Governorates (rather than Iraqi distribution, as in the rest of the country) was explained with reference to the Iraqi government's persecution of the local Kurds.[113] The United Nations administered assistance because of the perceived unwillingness, rather than inability (as is understood to be the case in most other international assistance programmes), of the local government to do so.

In both Bosnia and Herzegovina generally, and Mostar and Brčko in particular, the use of ITA has been understood, in part, as an attempt to promote a multi-ethnic social and political culture—the other side of the coin from the territorial agenda mentioned earlier. Hence OHR's imposition of a countrywide vehicle licence-plate bearing no indication of the district in which the car is registered,

---

such UNTAC supervision as UNTAC deemed necessary (ibid., section B, para. 3), and UNTAC enjoyed the power to control civil police, and supervise 'other law enforcement and judicial processes' (ibid., section B, para. 5(b)). The SNC was entitled to offer 'advice' to UNTAC on the exercise of all components of UNTAC's mandate, and UNTAC was obliged to comply with this advice, provided that the advice was 'consistent with the objectives' of the Agreement (ibid., section A, para. 2(a) and (b)). The Special Representative had the power to decide whether the advice given met this test (ibid., section A, para. 2(e)), and he or his delegate was obliged to attend SNC meetings and provide information to the SNC on all decisions made (ibid., section A, para. 3). Advice would come from the SNC as a whole if consensus could be reached; if this was not possible, advice would come from the SNC President; if this was not possible, the Special Representative would make the decision taking into account the views of the SNC (ibid., section A, para. 2(a) and (c)). On the elections process and outcome, see, e.g., T Findlay, *Cambodia: The Legacy and Lessons of UNTAC* (OUP, 1995), 75–100; JE Heininger, *Peacekeeping in Transition: The United Nations in Cambodia* (Twentieth Century Fund Press, 1994), 100–16; NT Vu, 'The Holding of Free and Fair Elections in Cambodia: The Achievement of the United Nations' Impossible Mission', 16 (1995) *Michigan Journal of International Law* 1177; United Nations, *The United Nations and Cambodia 1991–1995*, 38–53.

[111] M Bothe, 'The Peace Process in Eastern Slavonia', 3 (1996) *International Peacekeeping* 6, at 6. Hence the 'Local Croatian Serb Authorities', as one of the parties to the Basic Agreement on the Region of Eastern Slavonia, Baranja and Western Sirmium, UN Doc. A/50/757-S/1995/951, 15 November 1995, Annex, which authorized the introduction of the UN Administration in the territory, enjoyed the right (which they exercised) to request that the duration of the mission be extended. See above, ch. 2, n. 24.

[112] See above, ch. 4, section 4.4.3.

[113] Ibid.

as was the case previously.[114] To the same effect, measures were taken to promote the return of displaced people.[115] A key strategy here was the wholesale transformation of property law in Bosnia and Herzegovina, with OHR-imposed legislation introducing individual property rights in place of socially owned property, and the internationalized Commission for Real Property Claims of Displaced Persons and Refugees (CRPC) addressing property disputes.[116]

In Kosovo, the introduction of ITA was understood as a means of ensuring that human rights abuses would no longer be perpetrated against the Kosovar Albanians. An administration that drove about 800,000 Kosovar Albanians from Kosovo and forcibly displaced a further 500,000 within the territory was replaced with another regime mandated to enable these people to return.[117] Disenfranchisement was seen as having been reversed politically via the policy of 'substantial autonomy', and, as such, the mechanisms set up to actualize this policy—the Provisional Institutions of Self-Government—can be understood in terms of promoting 'minority rights' when taken in the context of what is now called the Republic of Serbia as a whole.[118] With this new objective, UNMIK then had to address the issue of protecting the Serb minority within Kosovo.[119]

In societies perceived to be divided, and also in other cases, a related idea associated with the use of ITA is the promotion of 'impartiality' as a principle of governance. Introducing a neutral 'international' actor who, by definition, is not linked by nationality to the country in which she or he acts, is seen as one

---

[114] OHR, Decision on the deadlines for the implementation of the new uniform license plate system, 20 May 1998, obtainable from <http://www.ohr.int>.

[115] For example, in Brčko, the OHR Supervisor was charged with establishing a return programme: see Brčko Award 1997 (above n. 66), paras 54, 104. For commentary on the return programme in the country generally, see Caplan (above n. 105), ch. 3, *passim*; M Cox and C Harland, 'Internationalized Legal Structures and the Protection of Internationally Displaced Persons', in J Fitzpatrick (ed.), *Human Rights Protection for Refugees, Asylum Seekers, and Internally Displaced Persons* (Transnational Publishers, 2001), 521; E Delacić, 'Women in Between: "Where do I belong?"', in Sokolović & Bieber (above n. 47), 185; M Vandiver, 'Reclaiming Kozarac: Accompanying Returning Refugees', in Sokolović & Bieber, ibid., 167.

[116] On property legislation, see the section 'Decisions in the Field of Property Laws, Return of Displaced Persons and Refugees and Reconciliation', obtainable from <http://www.ohr.int/decisions/archive.asp>. One of many examples is OHR, Decision cancelling all permanent occupancy rights issued in the Federation during and after the war in BiH and converting them into temporary occupancy rights, 14 April 1999. On the CRPC, see above, ch. 2, n. 87 and accompanying text. For commentary on property reforms generally, see, e.g., Cox & Harland (above n. 115); H Das, 'Restoring Property Rights in the Aftermath of War', 53 (2004) *ICLQ* 429.

[117] The figures come from Secretary-General Report on Kosovo 1999 (above n. 60), paras 8–9. UNMIK's responsibilities included '[a]ssuring the safe and unimpeded return of all refugees and displaced persons to their homes in Kosovo', SC Res. 1244 (above n. 60), para. 11 (k). For commentary, see Caplan (above n. 105), ch. 3, *passim*; and Kouchner (above n. 60).

[118] On UNMIK's mandate to enable 'substantial autonomy' in Kosovo, see above, text accompanying n. 79, *et seq*. On the Provisional Institutions of Self-Government, see above, ch. 1, n. 1.

[119] On this see the general works in the List of Sources, section 5.1.2.

of the main reasons behind many of the regimes of international appointees.[120] Sometimes, the entire mechanism concerned is understood in this way; the need for neutrality arises out of the fact that the mechanism in question is intended to scrutinize public institutions in the territory. So, during its operation, the utility of having the Human Rights Ombudsman in Bosnia and Herzegovina appointed by the OSCE was explained in terms of ensuring that the office was entirely separate from the institutions of the state that the Ombudsman heard complaints against.[121] In other arrangements concerning criminal matters, the need for neutrality stems from the view that locally-run scrutiny bodies cannot be relied upon to be impartial, in relation to either such matters generally, or the particular crimes of concern to the internationalized body in particular. So the creation of the International Independent Investigation Commission (UNIIIC) to investigate the Beirut attack in 2005 was explained in terms of a concern about the lack of independence and credibility of the Lebanese investigating authorities, and similar considerations would appear to have motivated the subsequent creation of the Lebanon Special Tribunal in 2007.[122]

It will be recalled from Chapter 2 that in Kosovo, UNMIK introduced arrangements for international judges to sit on the bench of criminal trials alongside local judges; these were subsequently enhanced to ensure the possibility that the international judges were in the majority.[123] These arrangements were explained in terms of a general concern about the impartiality and expertise of local judges, something considered serious enough to require an enhanced

---

[120] See generally above, ch. 2, section 2.3.4. On the idea that the involvement of the international appointees in the judicial sphere reflect a policy of fostering impartiality by introducing people seen as not susceptible to local pressures, see, e.g., Caplan (above n. 105), 63.

[121] See above, ch. 2, section 2.3.4.2 and, below, ch. 7, section 7.5.2.

[122] The fact-finding mission which recommended the creation of the UNIIIC 'was of the opinion that, since the credibility of the Lebanese authorities conducting the investigation was questioned, an international independent investigation should be set up to establish the truth' (Report of the International Independent Investigation Commission established pursuant to Security Council Resolution 1595 (2005), para. 3). When mandating the UN Secretary-General to create the UNIIIC, the Security Council requested that 'impartial' staff be appointed (SC Res. 1595 of 7 April 2005), para. 5. As for the Lebanon Tribunal, although no mention of 'impartiality' is contained in the text of SC Res. 1757 of 30 May 2007, establishing the Tribunal, both the Agreement between the United Nations and the Lebanese Republic on the establishment of a Special Tribunal for Lebanon and the attached Statute of the Tribunal (both appended to SC Res. 1757 (ibid.)) require that the judges of the Tribunal be 'persons of...impartiality' and that '[t]hey shall be independent in the performance of their functions and shall not accept or seek instructions from any Government or any other source' (see Lebanon Tribunal Agreement, Art. 2(4) and, in identical terms, Art. 9(2) of the Statute of the Tribunal). Note also Art. 5(2) of the Statute of the Tribunal which provides: 'A person who has been tried by a national court may be subsequently tried by the Special Tribunal if the national court proceedings were not impartial or independent, were designed to shield the accused from criminal responsibility for crimes within the jurisdiction of the Tribunal or the case was not diligently prosecuted'.

[123] See above, ch. 2, text accompanying n. 106.

form of internationalization ensuring a majority of international judges on the bench.[124]

In these and other cases, the introduction of international appointees alongside local-national colleagues is also explained in terms of expertise that is considered to be lacking in local candidates for the equivalent positions.[125]

In the three main international territorial administration projects underway at the turn of the 21st century—those in Bosnia and Herzegovina, Kosovo, and East Timor—OHR and the UN adopted a broad 'democratic' agenda going beyond issues more particular to each situation like the return of refugees and internally displaced persons to their pre-war homes.[126] International administrators conceived their role as fostering a democratic political culture. So, for example, in Bosnia and Herzegovina, OHR attempted to promote a free media by appointing the Board of Governors of the Republika Srpska public broadcasting service[127] and removed public officials considered to be corrupt, as with Edhem Bičakčić,

---

[124] For example, the provision enabling UNMIK to enhance internationalization on the bench could be utilized if 'necessary to ensure the independence and impartiality of the judiciary or the proper administration of justice'; see UNMIK Regulation 2000/64, 15 December 2000, obtainable from <http://www.unmikonline.org/regulations/unmikgazette/index.htm>, section 1.1 and section 2. Jean-Christian Cady and Nicholas Booth, then head of UNMIK Pillar I and his advisor, respectively, noted that 'the key factor which has always guided UNMIK in assigning [international judges and prosecutors] to a case is the substantial risk of a miscarriage of justice'; J-C Cady and N Booth, 'Internationalized Courts in Kosovo: an UNMIK Perspective', in C Romano, A Nollkaemper, and JK Kleffner (eds), *Internationalized Criminal Courts. Sierra Leone, East Timor, Kosovo, and Cambodia* (OUP, 2004), 59, at 65. An OSCE report states that:

[a] long and continuing climate of ethnic conflict has severely impacted upon the objective impartiality of the courts and raises concerns as to actual bias on the part of certain judging panels. One response has been to appoint international judges and prosecutors to deal particularly with those serious criminal trials involving defendants from minority groups. This initiative is to be supported and should be pursued, even though, in the light of the majority voting system in the panels, the influence of the international judges over deliberations is restricted.

OSCE, 'Review 1—The Criminal Justice System in Kosovo (February–July 2000)', 10 August 2000, available at <http://www.osce.org/documents/mik/2000/08/970_en.pdf>.

[125] So the international appointees to the Independent Electoral Commission created by UNTAET in 2001 were 'internationally recognized experts in electoral matters' (see UNTAET Regulation 2001/2, 16 March 2001, obtainable from <http://www.un.org/peace/etimor/UntaetN.htm>, section 13.1). On these arrangements more generally, see above, ch. 2, n. 121 and accompanying text. The possibility (not exercised) of the Iraqi Governing Council to appoint international judges to the Iraqi Special Tribunal established in December 2003 could be used for judges 'who have experience in the crimes encompassed in this statute'; see Statute of the Iraqi Special Tribunal, 10 December 2003, available at <http://www.globalpolicy.org/intljustice/general/2003/1210iraqistatute.pdf>, Art. 4(d). On the Special Tribunal and its successor, see above, ch. 2, n. 109 *et seq.* and accompanying text. On the explanation of such arrangements in terms of expertise, see also Caplan (above n. 105), 63.

[126] See generally the works cited in the List of Sources, sections 5.1.2 and 5.1.3, and the relevant works in section 5.1.1. In particular, see, e.g., R Paris, 'International Peacebuilding and the Mission Civilisatrice', 28 (2002) *Review of International Studies* 637, 646 (on Kosovo); Perritt (above n. 96), 455 (on several missions).

[127] OHR, Decision on the appointment of the Board of Governors of Radio-Television of the RS, 27 July 2000, obtainable from <http://www.ohr.int>.

who was removed as Director of a state-run electricity company in 2001.[128] In the case of UNMIK, in 1999, the UN Secretary-General explained the objective thus:

... promoting democracy, good governance and respect for human rights... Given the recent history of the region, much work will be required to establish the foundations of a free, pluralist and multi-ethnic society.[129]

A key component of this agenda was the promotion of the 'rule of law',[130] which included initiatives for law reform and the creation and operation of transitional justice mechanisms.[131] Similarly, the introduction of governance based on 'human rights' has been seen as central to these missions,[132] as reflected, for example, in UNMIK's mandate to be engaged in 'Protecting and promoting human rights'.[133] This human rights agenda, in some cases, explicitly referenced the policy of promoting women's rights.[134]

The 'democratic' enterprise has been allied to the wide-ranging transformation of the economy along capitalistic lines, from deregulation to the removal of protectionist rules and the privatization of socially-owned property and publicly-run

[128] OHR, Decision removing Edhem Bicakcic from his position as Director of Elektroprivreda for actions during his term as Prime Minister of the Federation of Bosnia and Herzegovina, 23 February 2001; see also OHR Press Release, 'High Representative removes Former Prime Minister Edhem Bicakcic', 23 February 2001 (both documents obtainable from <http://www.ohr.int>).

[129] Secretary-General Report on Kosovo 1999 (above n. 60), para. 79, See also ibid., 80–83; Kouchner (above n. 60). This came under the Pillar III structure in Kosovo, led by the OSCE; see above, ch. 1, n. 1.

[130] On the rule of law enterprise in Kosovo and Bosnia and Herzegovina, see, e.g., M Ignatieff, *Empire Lite: Nation-building in Bosnia, Kosovo and Afghanistan* (Vintage, 2003), 113, for a sustained treatment of the rule of law and law reform initiatives in several missions, covering both substantive law and the court system, see P Bergling, *Rule of Law in the International Agenda, International Support to Legal and Judicial Reform in International Administration, Transition and Development Co-operation* (Intersentia, 2006), *passim* (examples from the following four missions are given at these places: UNTAC, 173–5; OHR, 159–64 and 175–9; UNMIK 164–70 and 179–82; UNTAET 170–2 and 182–3). To give the example of UNMIK, the mandate included responsibility for '[m]aintaining civil law and order, including establishing local police forces and meanwhile through the deployment of international police personnel to serve in Kosovo...'; SC Res. 1244 (above n. 60), para 11(i). See also Secretary-General Report on Kosovo 1999 (above n. 60), paras 40, 66–78; Kouchner (above n. 60); R Ehrenreich Brooks, 'The New Imperialism: Violence, Norms, and the "Rule of Law"', 101 (2003) *Michigan Law Review* 2275. For commentary on rule of law promotion generally, including in the context of ITA projects, see J Stromseth, D Wippman, and R Brooks, *Can Might Make Rights? Building the Rule of Law After Military Interventions* (CUP, 2006).

[131] For a discussion of law reform in several ITA projects, see SR Ratner, 'Foreign Occupation and International Territorial Administration: The Challenges of Convergence', 16 (2005) *EJIL* 695, 706–7. On the models of justice being promoted, see List of Sources, section 5.2.2.

[132] On this in relation to ITA missions generally, see, e.g., Perritt (above n. 96), 438–9.

[133] SC Res. 1244 (above n. 60), para. 11(j). See also M Brand, 'Effective Human Rights Protection When the UN "Becomes the State": Lessons from UNMIK', ch. 15 in ND White and D Klaasen (eds), *The UN, Human Rights and Post-Conflict Situations* (Manchester University Press, 2005) and Secretary-General Report on Kosovo 1999 (above n. 60), paras 33, 42, 85–90.

[134] See List of Sources, section 5.2.5; see also N Wood, 'Kosovo Leads Europe in Woman Power', BBC News Online, 29 November 2001, <http://news.bbc.co.uk/2/hi/europe/1682907.stm>.

institutions (e.g., banks) and corporations.[135] This use of international territorial administration to promote particular economic policies, as with its use to protect minorities, echoes a League-era project, in this case in Memel. The League's appointment of the Chair of the Harbour Board for that port[136] was explained as a means of ensuring that the policy of maintaining the port as an open waterway and trade centre would be implemented.[137]

Unlike in the case of the Memel arrangement, however, the promotion of free-market economics in the later projects was not pursued solely through the narrowly-defined support for a particular institution; rather, it was an ambitious enterprise that potentially had all areas of economic governance within its sights. In Kosovo, for example, one of the main 'Pillars' of UNMIK's mandate was to engage in economic reconstruction, an activity devolved to the European Union.[138] Similarly, the 'democratic' agenda in these projects was seemingly limitless in its scope.

---

[135] On privatization, in relation to Bosnia and Herzegovina, see, e.g., OHR, Decision imposing the Framework Law on Privatisation of Enterprises and Banks in BiH, 22 July 1998; OHR, Decision Enacting the Law on Banks of the Republika Srpska, 21 October 2002; OHR, Decision amending the Framework Law on Privatisation of Enterprises and Banks in BiH by introducing a clause protecting investors, 11 May 2000; OHR, Decision amending the Law on Privatisation of Enterprises, 20 December 2000; OHR, Supervisor of Brčko, Order on Privatization in the District of Brčko, 4 December 1997 (all documents obtainable from <http://www.ohr.int>). In relation to Kosovo, in an early report on UNMIK, the UN Secretary-General conceived the mandate of the head of the mission thus: '[t]he Special Representative will seek to create a viable, market-based economy and to develop a comprehensive approach to the economic and social development of Kosovo...'; Secretary-General Report on Kosovo 1999 (above n. 60), para. 103. This fell under Pillar IV of the UNMIK structure, led by the EU; see above, ch. 1, n. 1. UNMIK created the Kosovo Trust Agency (KTA) 'to preserve or enhance the value, viability, and corporate governance of socially owned and public enterprises in Kosovo' and be responsible for the process of privatizing socially owned enterprises. See UNMIK Regulation 2002/12, 13 June 2002, as amended by UNMIK Regulation 2005/18, 22 April 2005, and the website of the Agency, <http://www.kta-kosovo.org>. The powers of the KTA were vested in a Board of Directors, comprising four international Directors and four residents of Kosovo (see UNMIK Regulation 2000/12, as amended, section 12). On economic governance in Kosovo, see also UNMIK Regulation 2005/3 (on Mines and Minerals in Kosovo), 21 January 2005. On the reform of property law, for implementation in Bosnia and Herzegovina, see above n. 116; for implementation in Kosovo, see, e.g., UNMIK Regulation 2003/13, 9 May 2003; L von Carlowitz, 'Crossing the Boundary from the International to the Domestic Legal Realm: UNMIK Lawmaking and Property Rights in Kosovo', 10 (2004) *Global Governance* 307, and L von Carlowitz, 'Settling Property Issues in Complex Peace Operations: the CRPC in Bosnia and Herzegovina and the HPD/DD in Kosovo', 17 (2004) *LJIL* 599. For commentary on the economic transformation in Kosovo generally, see, e.g., Knoll (above n. 76), *passim*; Kouchner (above n. 60); for commentary on the topic across more than one project, see, e.g., Caplan (above n. 105), ch. 6, *passim*; Perritt (above n. 96), 462–5. UNMIK Regulations are obtainable from <http://www.unmikonline.org/regulations/index.htm>.

[136] See above, ch. 2, n. 15.

[137] Ydit (above n. 19), 48–9.

[138] See SC Res. 1244 (above n. 60), para. 11(g), mandating UNMIK to 'support...the reconstruction of key infrastructure and other economic reconstruction'. On the objectives and activities of the EU Pillar generally, see <http://www.euinkosovo.org>. On the Pillars arrangements, see above, ch. 1, n. 1.

The 'democratic' use of ITA is triggered when local actors are deemed to be either actively opposed to a particular political agenda or unable to govern satisfactorily because they are insufficiently rooted in a 'democratic' tradition. UNMIK's initial exercise of full administrative powers, despite being charged with effecting 'substantial autonomy', can be explained not only because institutions of self-government had not yet been created, but also because the people of the territory were deemed to be not yet capable of handling administrative authority in a democratic fashion. Equally, the continuation of UNTAET's administration after the initial period following the withdrawal of Indonesia can be understood partially on the grounds that the East Timorese were seen as unable to take over immediately. In Bosnia and Herzegovina, the involvement of the international appointees—such as the IMF-appointed governor of the Central Bank—was sometimes understood as a means of introducing individuals committed to the promotion of a particular political and economic agenda alongside local appointees perceived as lacking such commitment.

6.4.2.3 Governance policy—containment of migrants

Beyond promoting policies concerned with the return of forced migrants, ITA has also been associated with the policy of containing forced migrants in the context of the administration of 'refugee' camps. In such cases, as mentioned already, UNHCR provides material assistance to inhabitants, but in various ways—controlling where such camps are located, determining who can enter and who can leave, for example—these arrangements are also sometimes used to contain groups of migrants within particular areas, and prevent them from moving to different areas.[139]

6.4.2.4 Governance policy—exploitation of national resources

The fourth and final category of 'governance policy' associated with international territorial administration is the exploitation of natural resources. One reason for international territorial administration in the Saar was that a 15-year regime of French exploitation in the context of German administrative control was viewed as unrealistic: Germany might at some future point prevent the continuance of this regime.[140] ITA introduced an administrative authority that would support the regime throughout the entire period during which League administration was to operate. Another, more recent, example would be the role of UNTAET in East Timor in reaching an agreement with Australia on a regime to exploit the resources in the Timor Sea between East Timor and Australia during the UNTAET administration period.[141]

---

[139] For information see above, ch. 2, n. 49.
[140] See the sources cited in this chapter, n. 19 above.
[141] Exchange of Notes constituting an Agreement between the Government of Australia and the United Nations Transitional Administration in East Timor (UNTAET) concerning

6.4.2.5 Overview of governance policies

As set out in Table 6 on the following page, several governance policies have been associated with the use of ITA, including, but going beyond, the idea of reconstructing state infrastructure after conflict, the policy-objective popularly associated with ITA generally. ITA missions have been engaged in promoting particular territorial status outcomes; seeking to enable a political system that is effective, democratic, adheres to the rule of law, and follows free market economic norms; ensuring the containment of migrants; and enabling the exploitation of natural resources. These different policies having been set out, the discussion will now consider how the use of ITA to promote them is understood.

6.4.3 Using ITA to respond to a 'governance problem'

6.4.3.1 *The relationship between different 'governance problems'*

The idea of using international territorial administration to ensure that governance conforms to certain policy objectives can lie behind the idea of using it to fill a supposed administrative vacuum. The refusal of the South African authorities to allow future independence for South-West Africa/Namibia, and the refusal of the FRY and Serb authorities to allow autonomy for Kosovo and to desist from human rights violations, led to the idea of displacing these local authorities with the United Nations (unimplemented in Namibia), so that government policy would change. ITA thus filled a governmental vacuum created by its own displacement of the existing authorities.

In East Timor, as mentioned international territorial administration was understood as filling the supposed void created by Indonesia's abandonment of the territory and the militias' destruction of much of its infrastructure. However, as explained in Chapter 1, it was conceived prior to the militia violence, and, moreover, once certain basic institutions had been restored and local leaders presented themselves, it continued. The central reason for ITA in East Timor, then, was that local people were deemed to be 'not ready' for the challenge of democratic responsibility. As in Kosovo, then, ITA was actually filling a 'void' of its own making.

the continued Operation of the Treaty between Australia and the Republic of Indonesia on the Zone of Cooperation in an Area between the Indonesian Province of East Timor and Northern Australia of 11 December 1989, Dili, 10 February 2000, in force 10 February 2000 (with effect from 25 October 1999), *Australian Treaty Series* 2000, No. 9, available at <http://www.austlii.edu.au/au/other/dfat/treaties/2000/9.html>. On the earlier arrangements between Australia and Indonesia, see *East Timor (Portugal v. Australia), Preliminary Objections, ICJ Reports 1995*, 90.

Table 6. Governance policies associated with ITA

Governance policy			ITA project
Adoption of a territorial agenda	Future adoption		The Saar (process for settling status), South West Africa/Namibia (the Council), Mostar, Brčko, Kosovo (process for settling status)
	Enactment		The Saar (post-1935 settlement), South West Africa/Namibia (the Council), Mostar, Brčko, Kosovo (autonomy and outcome of status settlement)
	Continuance		Danzig (Free City status), Bosnia and Herzegovina (statehood), Mostar (unified city status), Kosovo (autonomy)
Effectiveness, democracy, the rule of law, and free market economics	Effectiveness		Danzig, various regimes involving international appointees
	Free and fair consultations	For territorial status	The Saar, various Trust and Non-Self-Governing territories, Western Sahara (authorized but not fully implemented), East Timor (UNAMET)
		For government	Namibia (UNTAG), Cambodia, Bosnia and Herzegovina, Mostar, Eastern Slavonia, Kosovo, various regimes involving international appointees
	Governmental support for free and fair consultations		Western Sahara (authorized but not fully implemented), Cambodia The Saar,
	Minority rights		Bosnia and Herzegovina, Eastern Slavonia, northern Iraq, Kosovo
	Multi-ethnic politics, including the return of forced migrants		Bosnia and Herzegovina, Mostar, Brčko, Kosovo
	Expert and impartial local institutions		Various regimes involving international appointees
	Democratization, the rule of law, human rights including women's rights		Bosnia and Herzegovina, Kosovo, East Timor
	Liberal economic policies	Open port	Memel
		Free-market economics	Bosnia and Herzegovina, Kosovo, East Timor
Containment of migrants			Various UNHCR-run 'refugee' camps
Exploitation of natural resources			The Saar, East Timor

6.4.3.2   *Reactive and proactive uses of ITA in relation to 'governance problems'*

When the use of international territorial administration is understood as a response to a perceived 'governance problem', it can operate in two ways—'reactive' and 'proactive'. Its use 'reactively' involves introducing administrative prerogatives enjoyed by international organizations and/or regimes of international appointees onto an existing governance structure operated by local actors. Power is exercised in an ad hoc fashion: when governance by local actors is seen as threatening certain policy objectives or, as in the Congo, is not regarded as operating at all. Thus, the exercise of powers by the League in Danzig, the United Nations in Cambodia (other than conducting elections), and the OHR Supervisor in Brčko between 1997 and 2000—whether negative (e.g., vetoes) or positive (e.g., appointments, passing legislation)—was understood to be aimed at stepping in to correct 'mistakes'. If mistakes were not made, the powers would not be exercised. Thus, as regards the returns policy in Brčko, the Supervisor would act only if local actors did not implement particular policies. In the Congo and Bosnia and Herzegovina (both generally and with respect to Mostar after 1996), the idea that the UN and OHR had administrative powers only became evident when such powers were used for the first time. Again, regardless of whether a power is positive or negative, it is exercised reactively when local governance is deemed to have fallen short or there is a risk of this happening in the future. For example, OHR imposed specific legislative measures when the legislature was deemed unwilling or incapable of passing such legislation itself.

In 'proactive' projects, by contrast, the need for international territorial administration is assumed from the beginning. This occurs when plenary administrative control is asserted, as in UN-run 'refugee' camps, Eastern Slavonia, Mostar (the EUAM), Kosovo, and East Timor; or when particular administrative acts are performed because local actors are assumed to be unable or intrinsically unsuitable to perform them (e.g., conducting consultations). Here, ITA does not operate alongside the existing governmental authority so as to correct perceived deficiencies when necessary. Rather, it takes over from an existing authority entirely or in part. Instead of reacting to or anticipating instances of deficient governance, ITA is understood to be initiating at the outset governance conforming to particular policy objectives.

Even in situations of ostensibly plenary administrative authority, as in UNMIK and UNTAET, on the particular issue of what law should apply within each territory, both missions initially adopted a common approach of accepting local law insofar as it was compatible with 'internationally recognized human rights standards', in the case of East Timor supplemented with the repeal of certain expressly stipulated laws.[142] Here, then, is the reactive approach to the

---

[142] In the case of UNMIK, see UNMIK Regulation 1999/1, 25 July 1999 (obtainable from <http://www.unmikonline.org/regulations/unmikgazette/index.htm>), sections 2 and 3. For

exercise of administrative authority in microcosm: only those local laws deemed to be incompatible with international standards are altered.

6.4.3.3 *The changing character of 'governance problems'*

A notable feature of ideas about the use of international territorial administration to address either type of 'governance problem' is that the nature of the problem often changes over time. One set of problems is seen as creating a need for ITA—such as the persecution of the Kosovar Albanians by the Serb-dominated FRY Government—and then another set of problems is given priority once ITA is under way. The idea that UNMIK had to address the persecution of the Serbs by the Albanians in Kosovo not only represented a direct reversal of the original problem the mission was seen as a remedy for; it was also a response to something which, in part, had been made possible by the ITA-effected solution to that original problem. A related feature of ITA is that, once an original set of objectives places an international organization in a position to exercise territorial administration, the organization sometimes chooses to adopt additional objectives which have no basis in the original concept for the project.

6.4.3.4 *Two approaches to addressing 'governance problems'—palliative and remedial*

In its association with the idea of addressing a 'governance problem', international territorial administration is understood as taking two approaches. As discussed above, in the first approach ITA directly substitutes international organizations for local actors. Some of the projects are limited to this short-term approach, which is not designed to address the causes of these perceived problems. It might be called 'palliative international territorial administration'. Thus, in the Saar, the risks associated with the alternatives of French and German administration during the mines exploitation period were accepted as a given. Similarly, UNHCR administration of 'refugee' camps can be seen as a semi-permanent means of 'burden-sharing' between economically underdeveloped host-states and the relatively prosperous states that provide most of the funding for the agency. This approach assumes the long-term incapacity of host-states, transferring responsibility elsewhere rather than enhancing local capabilities.

    In most ITA projects, however, a second approach is adopted in tandem with the first: changing the structural features of local governance to remove the

UNTAET, see UNTAET Regulation 1999/1, 27 November 1999, obtainable from <http://www.un.org/peace/etimor/UntaetN.htm>, sections 2 and 3. On UNMIK, see also Secretary-General Report on Kosovo 1999 (above n. 60), para. 36. In Kosovo these provisions were subsequently altered to accommodate the view locally that the law adopted after March 1989, when Kosovo's autonomy was revoked, should not apply at all. See UNMIK Regulation 1999/24, 12 December 1999, as amended by UNMIK Regulation 2000/59, 27 October 2000 (obtainable from <http://www.unmikonline.org/regulations/unmikgazette/index.htm>). For commentary, see, e.g., N Berman, 'Intervention in a "Divided World": Axes of Legitimacy', 17 (2006) *EJIL* 769.

supposed problem that led to the need for ITA in the first place. This approach can be termed 'remedial international territorial administration'. Here, the emphasis is not on administration for its own sake—what direct difference it makes in terms of governmental policy—but administration aimed at constructing or reconstructing institutions, broadly defined, including material infrastructure, public bodies, commercial enterprises, media and telecommunications, and civil-society organizations. When there is supposedly a governmental vacuum, these initiatives are designed to enhance the possibility that governance can be conducted by local actors. When there is a perceived absence of governance conforming to certain policy objectives, they seek to enhance the possibility that local actors will govern in a manner promoting these objectives. So the people of the territories where the projects take place are being instructed by the staff of international organizations on how to be democratic, observe the rule of law, etc.[143]

In this sense, then, ITA adopts a dual-track approach, both palliative and remedial. Within this, there are significant differences in the way arrangements are made to accommodate improvement and transfer authority to local actors, and, more fundamentally, to prepare for and actualize independence where this does not already exist.

In the case of East Timor, although the date of independence was not determined at the start of the project, it emerged quite soon into the operation of UNTAET, thereby setting the project on a fixed-time trajectory. With this backdrop, the progressive transfer of authority to local actors over the course of UNTAET's mandate had as its end point completion by the fixed date of independence.[144]

In Kosovo, by contrast, not only was there no fixed date for independence determined at the start of the project; there was no guarantee of independence at all: instead, as already mentioned, a commitment was made to the settlement of Kosovo's status, possibly, but not necessarily, involving independence. In the meantime, a progressive transfer of authority to local actors was to take place, but, at this stage, on the basis of implementing 'substantial autonomy', crucially short

---

[143] In the case of UNMIK, the UN Secretary-General stated that '[t]he tasks of the institution-building component of the UNMIK mission...include assisting the people of Kosovo in strengthening the capacity of local and central institutions and civil society organizations...'; Secretary-General Report on Kosovo 1999 (above n. 60), para. 79. On Kosovo, see also Kouchner (above n. 60). As for Bosnia and Herzegovina, the International Crisis Group stated that '...the point of the international encampment in Bosnia is to 'teach' democracy, tolerance and good governance'; International Crisis Group, 'Aid and Accountability: Dayton Implementation', ICG Bosnia Report No. 17, 24 November 1996, obtainable from <http://www.crisisgroup.org>, at 16. On the tutelage enterprise in ITA projects generally, see also Caplan (above n. 105), ch. 4, *passim*; Paris (above n. 126), 645. The paralells between this and colonial trusteeship are explained in the next chapter below.

[144] See above, ch. 1, n. 2, and, on the mandate to transfer authority, see, e.g., the provisions in SC Res. 1338, 31 January 2001, para. 3 concerning the progressive delegation of authority from UNTAET to the East Timorese.

of the end point of independence that operated in the case of devolved authority in East Timor. Autonomy was actualized through the creation of the Provisional Institutions of Self-Government, authority being transferred progressively, ostensibly on the basis of capacity, to the level of autonomy under overall UN control.[145] By itself, then, this process had no implication for the termination of UNMIK's mandate; it affected the degree to which UNMIK was involved directly in administration as opposed to exercising overall supervision of locally-run institutions.

At the same time, over the course of the mission, UNMIK adopted a strategy for governance as conducted by the Provisional Institutions tied to the resolution of the status question: the 'standards before status' policy mentioned earlier.[146] These standards included, first, the existence of effective, representative and functioning democratic institutions; secondly, respect for the rule of law; thirdly, freedom of movement; fourthly, the sustainable return of refugees and displaced persons, and respect for the rights of communities; fifthly, the creation of a sound basis for a market economy; and, sixthly, fair enforcement of property rights.[147]

Although, then, the people of Kosovo had been deemed capable of self-administration to the point of substantial autonomy, they would have to meet further tests before Kosovo's eventual status could be resolved and independence potentially realized. This implicated UNMIK's existence in the sense that if the status question were to be settled, then potentially UNMIK's mandate would come to an end.[148]

Turning from two models of plenary ITA to instances of partial ITA, by its nature, the way the regimes of international appointees operates allows multiple opportunities to alter the calibration of involvement to account for changes in the policy objectives associated with it, such as levels of expertise. Individual appointees can be replaced with 'locals' if standards are considered to have improved; for ongoing arrangements, the significance of international involvement may wax and wane, and the actions taken by those involved may alter accordingly, for example, in the practice of those 'internationals' exercising the balance of power and/or the casting vote.

In the case of 'reactive' partial ITA, such as the activities of OHR, administrative prerogatives are exercised as and when local problems are deemed evident; in a reversal of the process in East Timor and Kosovo, authority is not transferred to local actors but, rather, local actors are able to exercise the authority they already

---

[145] On these arrangements generally, see above, ch. 1, n. 1. This idea of transfer contingent on capacity is reflected in UNMIK's mandate to transfer as 'institutions are established, its administrative responsibilities' (SC Res. 1244 (above, n. 60), para. 11(d)).

[146] On the Standards Before Status Policy, see above, n. 76.

[147] UNMIK, *Standards for Kosovo* (above, n. 76).

[148] For one extended treatment of the 'temporary' nature of UNMIK in Kosovo, see, e.g., Knoll (above, n. 76), *passim*.

have, without interference from OHR. This is illustrated in the language used by the High Representative when welcoming the 2001 adoption by the local legislature of an Electoral Law he deemed acceptable, thereby obviating the need for him to exercise his professed power to legislate:

[t]he High Representative views the passage of the Election Law as a signal achievement of the elected representatives of Bosnia and Herzegovina and a very positive example of pragmatism and political maturity.[149]

6.4.3.5 *Reinforcing the validity of local territorial administration*

As with the use of international territorial administration to respond to a perceived 'sovereignty problem', ideas about the use of ITA in relation to a perceived 'governance problem' are ultimately rooted, paradoxically, in the validity of that which ITA is understood to be the opposite of: the 'normal' and 'ideal' model of territorial governance conducted by local actors. When ITA is explained in terms of filling a vacuum that it did not create, governance itself is considered to be absent. When ITA projects are explained as means of displacing local actors in the activity of territorial administration, this is because the actors being displaced are deemed to be unwilling or unable to govern in a preferred manner. According to these ideas, if such problems with the 'normal' model were not considered to exist, there would be no need for ITA.

In 'reactive' models of ITA, local territorial administration is assumed to be the norm, to be corrected only when necessary to ensure conformity to certain policy objectives. In some of these cases, and in all the 'proactive' models of ITA, the assumption that local territorial administration is the ideal is also supported by the designation of the projects as temporary (discussed further below); control is to be transferred to local actors at some future date, or, in the case of 'refugee' camps, the ostensible idea is that eventually occupants will be offered a durable solution involving repatriation or resettlement. The preference for the 'normal' model is further underscored by 'remedial' initiatives aimed at positively altering the conditions for governance by local actors.

6.5 Establishing the Policy Institution

As discussed in Chapters 1 and 2, all of the ITA projects involve a distinctive type of activity conducted by a distinctive type of actor, and, having taken place periodically since the creation of the League of Nations, can be considered collectively an 'established practice' or, in my terminology, an 'institution'. Is there anything more substantial to connect the projects? Does the League

---

[149] OHR Press Release, 'High Representative Welcomes House of Peoples' Adoption of Election Law', 23 August 2001, obtainable from <http://www.ohr.int>.

administration in the Saar have anything further in common with the UN Mission in Kosovo?

The foregoing analysis suggests that what all the projects have in common on a purposive or policy level is derived from the way in which they operate on a practical level: displacing local actors in the activity of administration, either partially or in full. In terms of the purposes associated with this displacement, the projects can be divided into two categories: the idea of displacing local actors because of the identity of such actors (a 'sovereignty problem') and the idea of displacing such actors because of the quality of governance performed by such actors (a 'governance problem').

Certain projects can be understood as operating in both senses (for example, the Saar), but most are seen to operate in only one or the other. Insofar, then, as a particular project is only introduced for one particular type of purpose, it does not enjoy a policy connection with all the ITA projects, only with those sharing its own general type. So, for example, the reason for the West Irian project was explained in terms of a 'sovereignty' issue, not also a 'governance' issue. It thus enjoys a general policy connection with the Saar, Leticia, Eastern Slavonia, Mostar, and Kosovo projects, but not with the other ITA projects.

Within the general 'sovereignty problem' and 'governance problem' categories, ITA can be associated with very different roles. So, in South West Africa/ Namibia the governance policy promoted concerned a territorial outcome (governmental support for future independence) with the Council in 1967, and the existence of free and fair elections with UNTAG in 1989. These two projects do not have anything in common in terms of the particular policies with which they are associated; the connection between them is in the promotion of administrative policy itself. Even those projects under the 'governance problem' heading associated with the same types of policy objective can each be understood to promote this policy in different ways. So, in the case of promoting a territorial outcome, in Kosovo, UNMIK was seen as promoting 'substantial autonomy' by displacing the existing governmental authority opposed to this policy, whereas in Danzig, the League was seen as promoting 'Free City' status by being able to veto the adoption of particular governmental policies by the Free City authorities if necessary to achieve this goal.

The unifying element across the projects, then, is the existence of ITA and the use of this activity to displace local actors in the activity of governance. On this elemental level, there is unity across the projects, and in this sense, they each constitute manifestations of a common policy institution. Purposive or policy commonality on a more sophisticated level—the reason for displacing local actors—is then identified by dividing up the projects; there is no commonality of this type across all of them (other than being aimed at one or both of two types of 'problem'). Understanding the administration projects as part of this common institution operating in two distinct senses as outlined in this chapter offers the opportunity both to compare like with like, and to appreciate difference. Just as it is incorrect to say that all the projects were aimed at the same objectives, so it is misleading to say that purposive commonalities of varying degrees of complexity—from solving a 'governance problem' in general to the promotion of a governance policy supporting substantial autonomy in particular—cannot be identified across many, although not all, the projects.

6.6 Conclusion

International territorial administration is a 'policy institution' as that concept was defined in Chapter 1 because in all cases it is understood to operate in a particular manner as a matter of policy or purposes, being used to displace local actors in the activity of territorial governance because of a perceived problem either with the identity of these actors, or with the quality of governance performed by them in the territory concerned. The exceptionalist appraisal of the Kosovo and East Timor projects ignores the place of these two projects as the latest manifestations of a rather well-established pattern of international involvement in a range of issues. In understanding ITA's future potential, one cannot focus only on the idea of altering the quality of governance carried out in the territory—the 'governance problem' category—since this takes in only half the picture.

Equally, focusing exclusively on situations of plenary administration and/or ITA projects involving the United Nations arbitrarily excludes other ITA projects that have been understood to serve the same purposes in the same manner.[150] Moreover, it would seem that labelling the projects holistically as 'temporary', 'interim', 'transitional', and so forth, as is done by the Brahimi Report, risks ignoring projects where the temporal duration is conceived as permanent (e.g., the League High Commissioner in Danzig) and projects which, even if they are generally understood to be a temporary, are formally constituted on an indefinite basis (e.g., OHR in Bosnia and Herzegovina).[151] ITA—irrespective of the particular international actor involved and despite different degrees of administra-

---

[150] For an example of such a focus, see MJ Matheson, 'United Nations Governance of Post-Conflict Societies, 95 (2001) *AJIL* 76, 78 n. 22 (reprinted as 'United Nations Governance of Post-Conflict Societies: East Timor and Kosovo', in MC Bassiouni (ed.), *Post-Conflict Justice* (Transnational Publishers, 2002), 523); H Strohmeyer, 'Collapse and Reconstruction of a Judicial System: The United Nations Missions in Kosovo and East Timor', 95 (2001) *AJIL* 46.

[151] For examples of the use of such labels, see the title of M Griffin and B Jones, 'Building Peace through Transitional Authority: New Directions, Major Challenges', 7:4 (2000) *International Peacekeeping* 75, concerning the UN projects, and the discussion of the Kosovo and East Timor projects in the Brahimi report under the heading of 'transitional civil administration' (Panel on United Nations Peace Operations, Report to the United Nations Secretary-General ('Brahimi Report'), 21 August 2000, UN Doc. A/55/305–S/2000/809, section H, between paras 75 and 76). The use of such labels is discussed further below, ch. 7, section 7.6, and ch. 8, section 8.7.2.4. On the mandate of OHR in Bosnia and Herzegovina, see the information contained above in the footnotes in ch.2, section 2.3.3.

tive involvement—has been used since the inception of the League as a device for certain policy ends. To understand how likely the current projects are to succeed, and for what purposes such projects might be used in the future, it is necessary to consider ITA from this historical perspective.

In the present chapter, the various purposes with which the ITA projects have been associated—from promoting particular territorial outcomes to ensuring that elections are free and fair—have been established. To what extent do these purposes reflect broader principles of international public policy and law? For example, how might the notion of 'standards before status' in Kosovo be understood in terms of liberal ideas of equivocal sovereignty and the possible relevance of human rights standards to the criteria for statehood in international law?

The next chapter will address how the association of the use of ITA with the aims of achieving particular purposes can be understood in terms of the implementation of certain areas of international law and policy.

7

Implementing International Law and Policy

7.1 Introduction[1]

International territorial administration projects are often described in terms suggestive of the particular areas of international public policy promoted by them. Labels such as 'state-building' or 'state reconstruction'—promoting state institutions and certain forms of political and economic governance—and 'peacekeeping'—promoting peace and security—are used to convey the essence of the enterprise in play.[2] More broadly, some ITA projects have been associated with prominent general concepts within international policy discourse, such as the notion of the 'failed state' and the idea of 'earned sovereignty'.[3]

To what extent are these terms and concepts relevant to ITA? This chapter considers how ITA can be understood in terms of a device for implementing certain areas of international public policy and international law. Unlike in the previous chapter, it will not be suggested here that the projects are necessarily presented in these terms, although that sometimes happens (for example, when a particular project is explained as a mechanism for settling a dispute). Rather, the purposes with which the policy institution is associated, as outlined in the previous chapter, will be recalled, with a view to identifying how the supposed use of the institution to these ends can be understood in terms of the implementation of certain areas of international public law and policy.

The point of this enquiry is to understand how the use of ITA fits within the broader structures of international law and public policy implementation. The 'policy' component in the concept of 'policy institution' explained in Chapter 1 can be understood in terms of both specific objectives and more general ideas.[4]

---

[1] Earlier versions of parts of this chapter are contained in R Wilde, 'International Territorial Administration and Human Rights', ch. 7 in ND White and D Klaasen (eds), *The UN, Human Rights and Post-conflict Situations* (Manchester University Press, 2005).

[2] On the representation of ITA as a 'state-building' and 'state reconstruction' enterprise, see the sources cited below, n. 45. For the representation of certain ITA missions as 'peacekeeping' operations, see the sources cited below, n. 98.

[3] On these two concepts, see the sources cited below, nn. 46 and 81 respectively.

[4] See above, ch. 1, section 1.5.1.

For example, as will be discussed below, UNMIK's ostensible objective to promote 'substantial autonomy' in Kosovo, explained in the previous chapter, can be understood in terms of the realization of the international legal entitlement to 'internal' self-determination; equally, UNMIK's role in implementing the 'standards before status' policy—attempting to inculcate the standards of governance deemed necessary before Kosovo's status can be determined, and playing a role in judging whether the test has been met—has been invoked by scholars of 'earned sovereignty' as evidence of the purchase of their concept within international public policy.[5]

When discussing the purposes associated with ITA in Chapter 6, it was suggested that the institution is best understood negatively, as a substitute for its 'opposite': governance by local actors. ITA is ostensibly resorted to when governance by local actors is deemed in some way objectionable. Equally, in seeking to understand how the use of ITA can be seen in terms of implementation of international law, the institution is best understood in terms of the obligations of states, which for some reason are seen as requiring the involvement of international organizations to ensure implementation. In this sense, territorial administration by international organizations is in effect concerned with the implementation of state obligations. At the same time, such activity also amounts to the fulfilment of obligations borne by international organizations, since these organizations, especially the UN, are charged with the promotion of key areas of public policy (e.g., international peace and security). Accordingly, ITA can often involve the implementation of state obligations, and the concomitant fulfilment of obligations borne by international organizations in relation to this implementation.

The use of ITA can be understood as means of implementing international law and policy in three areas: (1) the prevention and settlement of international disputes; (2) the implementation of settlements to disputes and certain areas of public policy generally, covering territorial status outcomes, 'state-building', liberal governance, and the exploitation of natural resources; and (3) the promotion of international policy in the area of peace and security. This chapter suggests how ITA can be understood as a process for the implementation of international law and policy in these areas, highlighting the relevant normative frameworks. The mechanism of ITA will then be compared with other international modalities that purport to have the same effect, but through different means (e.g., international tribunals). It will be argued that ITA amounts to one of the most intrusive forms of international implementation in this regard.

One further area of international policy—the concept of trusteeship—is treated separately in the next chapter as part of the comparison therein between ITA and state-conducted policy institutions. This separate treatment is necessitated by its central significance to the state analogues, the sustained nature of the enquiry necessary, and the fundamental significance of the concept for the legitimacy of ITA.

---

[5] On the connection with 'internal' self-determination, see below, text accompanying n. 42 *et seq.*; on the connection with 'earned sovereignty', see below, text accompanying n. 81.

7.2 Specific Role in Dispute Prevention and Settlement

According to John Collier and Vaughan Lowe, the word 'dispute' signifies:

...a specific disagreement relating to a question of rights or interests in which the parties proceed by way of claims, counter-claims, denials and so on.[6]

This is to be contrasted with the broader conflict—the 'general state of hostility between the parties'—within which a particular dispute must be understood, but which may be addressed only partially, if at all, by the settlement of the dispute.[7] As Collier & Lowe point out, there is a widespread assumption that disputes are always to be avoided.[8]

However, as Collier & Lowe state, disputes and conflict are 'by no means without benefit'.[9] Their existence 'is invariably a sign that the existing order is not satisfactorily accommodating the interests' of its members, and 'their successful resolution leads either to the confirmation and entrenchment of old rules or to the weakening and eventual replacement of old rules by new'.[10] In the international normative system a greater emphasis has been placed on the settlement rather than the prevention of disputes, notwithstanding the general prohibition of a particular type of disputative action—the use of military force—in Article 2(4) of the UN Charter. The cornerstone of this policy of settlement is Article 2(3) of

---

[6] J Collier and V Lowe, *The Settlement of Disputes in International Law* (OUP, 1999), 1. JG Merrills defines a dispute in this context as '...a specific disagreement concerning a matter of fact, law or policy in which a claim or assertion of one party is met with refusal, counter-claim or denial with another'; JG Merrills, *International Dispute Settlement* (4th edn, CUP, 2005), 1. Michael Donelan and Muriel Grieve distinguish between 'the pursuit of things wanted, which we call competition, and the demand for things considered due in justice, which we call dispute'; MD Donelan and MJ Grieve, *International Disputes: Case Histories 1945–1970* (Palgrave Macmillan, 1973), 9. On the idea of 'dispute' more generally, see, e.g., S Roberts, *Order and Dispute: An Introduction to Legal Anthropology* (Penguin, 1979).

[7] Quotation taken from Collier & Lowe (above n. 6), 1. See also S Bailey, 'Peaceful Settlement of International Disputes', in KV Raman (ed.), *Dispute Settlement through the United Nations* (Oceana Publications, 1977), 73, at 81. On the idea of 'conflict' see, e.g., A de Reuck and J Knight (eds), *Conflict in Society* (Little, Brown, 1966). A further significant definitional classification is the sub-category of a 'justiciable' dispute, viz. a dispute 'which can be resolved by the application of rules of law by judicial (including arbitral) processes'; Collier & Lowe, ibid., 10. On justiciability, see, e.g., *Mavrommatis Palestine Concessions (Greece v. United Kingdom), Jurisdiction*, PCIJ, *Series A*, No. 2 (1924),1, at 11; *Interpretation of Peace Treaties with Bulgaria, Hungary and Romania (First Phase), Advisory Opinion, ICJ Report 1950*, 65, at 74; *South West Africa (Ethiopia v. South Africa; Liberia v. South Africa), Preliminary Objections, ICJ Reports 1962*, 319, at 328; Collier & Lowe, ibid., 10–16.

[8] Collier & Lowe (above, n. 6), 1. So, for example, in 1998, the General Assembly endorsed a declaration proclaiming that '[s]tates should act so as to prevent in their international relations the emergence or aggravation of disputes'; Declaration on the Prevention and Removal of Disputes and Situations Which May Threaten International Peace and Security and on the Role of the United Nations in this Field, 5 December 1988, GA Res. 43/51, Annex, para 1.

[9] Collier & Lowe (above, n. 6), 2.

[10] Ibid.

the Charter (endorsed and elaborated by the General Assembly, inter alia, in the Friendly Relations Declaration, the Manila Declaration and Resolution 44/21), which obliges states to settle their disputes by peaceful means.[11]

A range of international (including regional) institutional mechanisms (whether permanent or ad hoc) are available for preventing and settling disputes. Whereas significant differences exist between them, they share a common element of operating within the international arena.[12] Mechanisms can be 'legal' or 'non-legal' depending on whether or not they settle disputes through the direct application of the law; they include international courts and tribunals like the International Court of Justice (ICJ), and international organizations like the UN, the African Union, and the OSCE.[13]

Under Article 33(1) of the UN Charter, dispute prevention and settlement is to include 'negotiation, enquiry, mediation, conciliation, arbitration and judicial settlement' and 'other peaceful means'.[14] Article 1(1) of the UN Charter mandates the UN:

... to bring about by peaceful means, and in conformity with the principles of justice and international law, adjustment or settlement of international disputes or situations which might lead to a breach of the peace.

The organization is understood to have pursued this function, inter alia, through its principal judicial organ, the ICJ; the good offices of the Secretary-General and special representatives and envoys; sanctions introduced by the Security Council; and peace operations.[15]

---

[11] UN Charter, Art. 2(3); Declaration on Principles of International Law Concerning Friendly Relations and Cooperation among States in Accordance with the Charter of the United Nations ('Friendly Relations Declaration'), GA Res. 2625 (XXV), 24 October 1970; Manila Declaration on the Peaceful Settlement of International Disputes, GA Res. 37/10, 15 November 1982, section I, para. 2; GA Res 44/21, 'Enhancing international peace, security and international co-operation in all its aspects in accordance with the Charter of the United Nations', 15 November 1989, para. 2.

[12] An example of a scholar who bases a classification of dispute settlement mechanisms on this element is Malcolm Shaw, who refers to the 'methods and procedures available within the international order for the peaceful resolution of disputes and conflicts'; MN Shaw, *International Law* (5th edn, CUP, 2003), 914.

[13] For the legal/non-legal distinction, see, e.g., HG Darwin in *International Disputes: The Legal Aspects* (David Davis Memorial Institute, 1972), 58–62; Collier & Lowe (above n. 6), 6; Merrills (above n. 6), ix. For a broad survey of international courts and tribunals, see P Sands, R Mackenzie and Y Shany (eds), *Manual on International Courts and Tribunals* (Butterworths, 1999). For non-legal processes, especially the OSCE and the African Union (under its previous identity as the Organization for African Unity (OAU)), see, e.g., the sources cited in Collier & Lowe, ibid., at 6, n. 2.

[14] UN Charter, Art. 33(1). See also Friendly Relations Declaration (above n. 11); Manila Declaration (above n. 11) section I, para. 5; Collier & Lowe (above n. 6), 41 and the essays by Philip Allott, HG Darwin and Hazel Fox in Part 2, section on 'Methods of Peaceful Settlement', in *International Disputes: The Legal Aspects* (David Davies Memorial Institute, 1972), from 77.

[15] On the UN and dispute settlement, see, e.g., Manila Declaration (above n. 11), Part II; *Agenda for Peace: Preventive Diplomacy, Peacemaking and Peacekeeping*, Report of the Secretary-General, 17 June 1992, UN Doc. A/47/277-S/24111 (hereinafter *'Agenda for Peace'*), paras 34–45; UNITAR, *The United Nations and the Maintenance of Peace and Security* (Kluwer, 1987), section 2; FS Northedge and MD Donelan, *International Disputes: The Political Aspects* (Europa, 1971),

The activity of ITA can be considered part of this international system of dispute prevention and settlement.[16] As such, it can be seen both in terms of the UN's obligation to settle disputes, and also in terms of enforcing states' obligations to settle disputes peaceably and in accordance with the UN Charter and international law. Similarly, insofar as the prevention of disputes by states and the involvement in dispute-prevention by the UN constitute legal obligations, the role of ITA here can be considered a mechanism for fulfilling and enforcing these obligations.[17]

The potential of ITA in relation to dispute prevention and settlement can be understood in four ways, as outlined in Table 7 below. In the first place, ITA may be seen as a means of preventing disputes from arising. So, in the Saar, League administration was understood in terms of avoiding the potential dispute that might have arisen had France been given administrative powers during the resource-exploitation period and then used these powers in an attempt to annex the territory. Equally, as mentioned in the previous chapter, the introduction of international appointees on government institutions is sometimes explained as a way of providing a neutral party amidst partisan local appointees. When the international appointees are in the majority, and/or an international appointee has the casting vote, local appointees have to avoid conflict and work together with their opponents or risk a diminished input into decisions made. In the process, the threat to the smooth operation of the institution from internal disputes is seen as reduced.

When a dispute has arisen, ITA can sometimes be used as a means of creating a more favourable climate for its resolution. In Leticia in the 1930s, the 'neutralization' of the territory through plenary ITA by the League was understood as a mechanism for creating a space whereby the wider dispute between Colombia and Peru could be resolved without either disputant enjoying control over the territory. As discussed in the previous chapter, in Kosovo at the turn of the 21st century, UNMIK was understood to be performing a similar role, although in

---

ch. 10; DW Bowett, 'The United Nations and Peaceful Settlement', in *International Disputes: The Legal Aspects* (David Davies Memorial Institute, 1972), 179; KV Raman (ed.), *Dispute Settlement through the United Nations* (Oceana Publications, 1977); C Peck, *The United Nations as a Dispute Settlement System: Improving Mechanisms for the Prevention and Resolution of Conflict* (Kluwer Law International, 1996); Merrills (above n. 6), 237–78; N White, *The Law of International Organizations* (Manchester University Press, 1996), 179–81. On the International Court of Justice, see, e.g., P Allott, 'The International Court of Justice', in *International Disputes: The Legal Aspects* (David Davies Memorial Institute, 1972), 128.

[16] Cf. the coverage of certain ITA missions in Merrills (above n. 6), 256–63. See also the discussion in M Bothe and T Marauhn, 'UN Administration of Kosovo and East Timor: Concept, Legality and Limitations of Security Council-Mandated Trusteeship Administration', in C Tomuschat (ed.), *Kosovo and the International Community: A Legal Assessment* (Kluwer Law International, 2002), 217, 218–20.

[17] For the suggestion of an obligation borne by states to prevent disputes, see the quotation from the Annex to GA Res. 43/51 (cited above n. 8), reproduced below in n. 22. The same resolution places the UN at the centre of various strategies for the enforcement of this obligation.

circumstances where the local population enjoyed significant *de facto* control through the devolution of authority by the UN to the Provisional Institutions of Self-Government.

As well as being seen as increasing the likelihood of dispute settlement, the potential of ITA is also understood in terms of providing a mechanism though which a settlement can be reached. Some of the international appointees have sat on dispute-settlement institutions, such as the Human Rights Chamber in Bosnia and Herzegovina. In being understood as preventing internal disputes, the introduction of appointees is intended to enable the institution to function and so to settle any external disputes brought before it. More generally, the international operation of dispute-settlement procedures, such as in the case of the Human Rights Ombudsman in Bosnia and Herzegovina between 1995 and 2003,[18] is seen as providing institutions that are 'neutral' as between the interests of the parties who bring their disputes to them.

Equally, the international administration of consultations on territorial status, from the Saar to East Timor (see Table 1 in Chapter 2) is seen as an internationally-provided process for settling a dispute about the future status of the territory, by reference to the view of its people. Again, international conduct is viewed as enabling the process to be settled by a 'neutral' actor who is seen as not favouring any of the states claiming the territory (cf. the criticisms of the Indonesian-conducted 'act of self-determination' in West Irian discussed in the previous chapter). In a similar manner, the international conduct or supervision/control of national election processes, from Namibia to Kosovo (again, see Table 1 in Chapter 2), can be viewed as an international process for settling contested local disputes over governmental power, sometimes involving outside states.

Finally, ITA is also viewed as having the potential to be itself the settlement to a dispute, although this potential has so far not been realized. In the Saar, permanent territorial administration by the League was available as an alternative solution to German or French sovereignty in 1935, offering to settle the sovereignty dispute by, in effect, disappointing both sides equally.[19]

Taking the foregoing analysis together, ITA has been understood to have a wide-ranging role in the prevention and settlement of disputes, as set out in Table 7 on the following page. It has been associated not only with preventing disputes from arising, but also with creating a climate conducive to the settlement of disputes, providing or enabling the functioning of a dispute settlement process, and, even, acting itself as the settlement to a dispute.

---

[18] On the Human Rights Ombudsman see above, ch. 2, text accompanying n. 86 *et seq.*

[19] This idea is also evident in some of the proposals, to 'internationalize' Jerusalem. See above, ch. 2, n. 43.

Table 7. ITA and the prevention and settlement of disputes

Role in dispute prevention or settlement	Location	Disputants	Subject-matter of dispute	Mechanism for addressing dispute
Preventing disputes from arising	The Saar (1920–35)	France and Germany	France's annexation ambitions during the exploitation period	Plenary administration of territory
	Various locally-based institutions	Opposing factions	General political disagreements	Involvement of international appointees
Creating a climate conducive to the settlement of disputes	Leticia	Colombia and Peru	Territorial control over Leticia, and wider issues	Plenary administration of territory
Providing or enabling the functioning of a dispute settlement process	Domestic dispute settlement mechanisms in Bosnia and Herzegovina, Kosovo, and East Timor	Various	Various	International conduct of or involvement of international appointees on settlement mechanism
	The Saar (1935), Western Sahara (not fully implemented at the time of writing), East Timor (1999), various Trust and Non-Self-Governing Territories (different dates)	Various states and the local population	The future status of the territory	International conduct or supervision/control of a self-determination consultation
	Namibia (1989), Cambodia (1992), Bosnia and Herzegovina (from 1996), Mostar (1996), Eastern Slavonia (1997), Kosovo (from 1999), various Trust and Non-Self-Governing territories	Local political groups, and (sometimes) their foreign state sponsors	Domestic political control	International conduct or supervision/control of national elections, and/or involvement of international appointees on electoral bodies
Acting as the settlement to a dispute (not utilized)	The Saar (1935)	France and Germany	Territorial control after 1935	Permanent plenary administration

7.3 General Role in Implementing Settlements and International Law and Policy

As well as preventing or solving disputes and the wider conflicts associated with them, ITA is understood as being capable of playing a crucial role in the implementation of settlements to conflicts and disputes once these settlements have been reached. This role can, moreover, be considered as part of the wider function of ITA as a mechanism for implementing particular areas of international public law and policy. Next, this wider function will be considered, with the dispute settlement role highlighted where appropriate.

7.3.1 Implementation of settlements

Many of the ITA projects formed part of the settlements to some of the major armed conflicts of the 20th century, addressing particular disputes arising out of these wider conflicts. The projects in Danzig, the Saar, and Memel formed part of the Versailles settlement after the Second World War; partial ITA was a central component of the agreements ending the conflict in Cambodia. The most extensive involvement of the ITA process in implementing peace agreements is in the various territories that before the 1990s had together constituted the Socialist Federal Republic of Yugoslavia (SFRY). The projects in Mostar, Brčko, Eastern Slavonia, and Bosnia and Herzegovina were introduced as part of the peace process relating to the 1991–95 conflict in the SFRY territories that led to the conclusion of the 1995 Dayton Peace Agreements, the Basic Agreement on Eastern Slavonia of the same year, and the 1999 Final Award of the Brčko Arbitral Tribunal.[20] ITA in Kosovo was the key mechanism for implementing the terms of the Peace Plan that came after the NATO bombing campaign in what was then the Federal Republic of Yugoslavia (FRY) in 1999.[21] Whereas with Dayton, the settlement purported to resolve definitively the question of the status of Bosnia and Herzegovina, in Kosovo, the settlement intended to 'freeze' the status issue pending its eventual settlement.

As well as implementing peace agreements, ITA has also been used to implement settlements to some of the most significant disputes arising out of the

---

[20] Dayton Peace Agreements (above, ch. 1, n. 38); *Arbitration for the Brčko Area (Federation of Bosnia and Herzegovina v Republika Srpska)*, Arbitral Tribunal for Dispute over Inter-Entity Boundary in Brčko Area, Final Award, 5 March 1999, 38 (1999) *ILM* 536 (also obtainable from <http://www. ohr.int>). The European Union Administration in Mostar (EUAM) was created in 1994 through the Mostar MOU (Memorandum of Understanding on the European Union Administration of Mostar, 5 July 1994 (unpublished, copy on file with the author)); the UN Transitional Authority in Eastern Slavonia (UNTAES) was created through a separate instrument adopted at the same time as the Dayton Peace Agreement (Basic Agreement on the Region of Eastern Slavonia, Baranja and Western Sirmium, UN Doc. A/50/757-S/1995/951, 15 November 1995, Annex).

[21] See Agreement on the Principles (Peace Plan) to Move Towards a Resolution of the Kosovo Crisis Presented to the Leadership of the Federal Republic of Yugoslavia by the President of Finland, Martti Ahtisaari, representing the European Union, and Viktor Chernomyrdin, Special Representative of the President of the Russian Federation, 3 June 1999, UN Doc. S/1999/649, Annex.

process of decolonization. In this regard, ITA was used in Namibia (UNTAG), West Irian, and East Timor, and authorized but not carried out fully in South West Africa/Namibia (the Council) and Western Sahara (at the time of writing).

ITA is viewed as supporting the implementation of settlements to disputes in two respects. In the first place, just as it is used to create circumstances conducive to the settlement of a dispute, so it can be used to ease the implementation of a settlement once reached, even if not implementing the settlement itself. So in West Irian and Eastern Slavonia, ITA was viewed as smoothing the transfer of territory from the Dutch to Indonesia and the local Serbs to Croatia respectively, by acting as a buffer between territorial control by the two disputants. In the second place, ITA has been used as part of the machinery created to implement settlements. In performing this role, ITA can be considered a mechanism for the implementation of international public policy. Not only is the implementation of international law often placed at the centre of any settlement to a dispute; when disputes are characterized, as they sometimes are, in terms of a failure to implement international law, mechanisms for ensuring such implementation can be considered strategies for the prevention of future disputes.[22]

The areas of policy implemented by ITA in this regard can be clustered under three headings: (1) territorial status and self-determination, (2) 'state-building', and (3) the exploitation of natural resources. Each will be addressed in turn.

7.3.2 Territorial status and self-determination outcomes

Statehood and title to territory in international law can both be understood in terms of a claim based on a right—a claim to statehood or territorial title that is legally valid.[23] As discussed in Chapter 3, a crucial factor in determining questions of statehood and title, therefore, is the presence or absence of an entity or entities claiming the rights in question.[24] ITA has been used to promote certain territorial status outcomes by controlling the political process of making claims in relation to such status. Responding to a perceived 'governance problem', international organizations exercise territorial administration to ensure that the governmental authority frames its sovereignty claim—the political unit in respect of which governance is exercised—in a particular manner.

As outlined in the previous chapter, ITA has been used in this way in the Saar, Danzig, South West Africa/Namibia, Bosnia and Herzegovina, Mostar, Brčko, and Kosovo. Settlements determine what the territorial status is to be, and then ITA is used to ensure that governance within the territory supports this status outcome. In the process, local actors are prevented from framing different

---

[22] In 1998, the General Assembly declared that '[s]tates should act so as to prevent in their international relations the emergence or aggravation of disputes... in particular by fulfilling in good faith their obligations under international law'; GA Res. 43/51 (above, n. 8), Annex, para 1.
[23] James Crawford defines statehood as 'a claim of right'; see J Crawford, *The Creation of States in International Law* (2nd edn, OUP, 2006), 156.
[24] See above, ch. 3, section 3.3.

claims that cut across the sovereignty settlement. In Bosnia and Herzegovina, for example, the fundamental objective of the Dayton Peace Agreements, beyond ensuring the permanent cessation of hostilities between the former Republics of the SFRY and within Bosnia and Herzegovina, was to promote the continued existence of Bosnia and Herzegovina as a state.[25] So those Bosnian Croats who wished to secede from Bosnia and Herzegovina and form the new state of Herzeg-Bosna were prevented from doing so through the political process by the banning of secessionist candidates from electoral office by OHR, as with Ante Jelavić in 2001 mentioned in the previous chapter.

Another way of approaching this aspect of the use of ITA is to focus on the right of self-determination, discussed earlier in Chapter 5.[26] Here, one looks at the rights of the people within the territory, in relation to their internal and external status. The emphasis thus shifts away from the territory to its people. As mentioned in Chapter 5, as a matter of law, self-determination has two manifestations, 'internal' and 'external'. Both concern the right of a 'people' or 'self-determination unit' to choose its status. 'Internal' self-determination concerns the rights of peoples within states, and is understood to include minority rights and also the right to free and fair elections, and to participate in public life.[27] 'External' self-determination, by contrast, as discussed in Chapter 5, involves the right of a people to choose its external (i.e., international) status, whether remaining within a state in which it is currently located, joining a different state, becoming an independent state, or some other status.[28]

The key controversy in relation to self-determination has been the question of which groups are entitled to which form of the right; in other words, who constitutes a 'people', or what constitutes a 'self-determination unit', for the purposes of 'internal' and 'external' self-determination. As discussed in Chapter 5, traditionally, 'external' self-determination has been regarded as limited to people in colonial and Mandated and Trust territories, and those subject to alien occupation and foreign domination.[29] All other 'peoples', such as minority groups, are considered to enjoy a right of 'internal', but not 'external', self-determination.

---

[25] For example, the Preamble to the Constitution of Bosnia and Herzegovina, which formed part of the 'civilian' aspects of the Dayton Peace Agreements which OHR was charged with promoting, stated that the parties were, '*[c]ommitted* to the sovereignty, territorial integrity, and political independence of Bosnia and Herzegovina in accordance with international law'; Dayton Annex 4 (above, ch. 1, n. 38), preamble, para. 6 (emphasis in original). Article 1 of the Constitution, entitled 'Continuation', stated that 'The Republic of Bosnia and Herzegovina...shall continue its legal existence under international law as a state, with its internal structure modified as provided herein and with its present internationally recognized borders. It shall remain a Member State of the United Nations' (ibid., Art. 1).

[26] On the law of self-determination, see the discussion and sources cited above, ch. 5, section 5.2.

[27] See above, ch. 5, n. 5.

[28] See above, ch. 5, text accompanying n. 4. As mentioned there, the term 'external' self-determination can also be used in the context of freedom from external interference in the exercise of 'internal' self-determination.

[29] See above, ch. 5, text accompanying n. 10 *et seq.*

In the final years of the 20th century, however, in addition to the traditional categories of situations which justify the invocation of an 'external' self-determination entitlement, one further possible category was suggested, which would cover peoples who are denied their right to 'internal' self-determination in some particularly extreme manner, for example through being disenfranchised and/or subject to gross violations of human rights.[30] At the time of writing,

[30] This criterion builds on understandings of the right to 'external' self-determination, generally understood as being limited to situations of colonialism or situations of 'alien subjugation, domination or exploitation' outside the colonial context. On these understandings see the discussion and sources cited above, ch. 5, section 5.2; on the right of 'internal' self-determination generally, see above, ch. 5, n. 5 and accompanying text. A possible link between the complete denial of the right to 'internal' self-determination and 'external' self-determination is suggested in the following passage from the Friendly Relations Declaration (above n. 11):

[n]othing in the foregoing paragraphs [i.e., those dealing with the principle of self-determination] shall be construed as authorizing or encouraging any action which would dismember or impair, totally or in part, the territorial integrity or political unity of sovereign and independent States conducting themselves in compliance with the principle of equal rights and self-determination of peoples as described above and thus possessed of a government representing the whole people belonging to the territory without distinction as to race, creed, or colour.

Of similar relevance is the following dictum by the African Commission of Human and Peoples' Rights in the *Katangese Peoples' Congress v Zaire* case:

[i]n the absence of concrete evidence of violations of human rights to the point that the territorial integrity of Zaire should be called to question and in the absence of evidence that the people of Katanga are denied the right to participate in Government as guaranteed by Article 13(1) of the African Charter, ... Katanga is obliged to exercise a variant of self-determination that is compatible with the sovereignty and territorial integrity of Zaire.

African Commission of Human and Peoples' Rights, *Katangese Peoples' Congress v Zaire*, Communication no. 75/92, undated, para. 6. The Advisory Opinion by the Canadian Supreme Court on the possible secession of Quebec refers to a situation when 'the ability of a people to exercise its right to self-determination internally is somehow being totally frustrated' (*Reference re Secession of Quebec*, Supreme Court of Canada, [1998] 2 RCS 217, 37 (1998) *ILM* 1340 (hereinafter '*Quebec Secession Opinion*')), para. 135 and 'where a definable group is denied meaningful access to government to pursue their political, economic, social and cultural development' (ibid., para. 138). In dismissing the idea that the situation in Quebec fell into this category, the Supreme Court quotes with approval a statement that implies a high threshold for the category: '[t]he Quebec people is not the victim of attacks on its physical existence or integrity, or of a massive violation of its fundamental rights' (ibid., para. 135). Seemingly, the *Quebec Secession Opinion* is concerned with the right to secession, rather than the right to 'external' self-determination *strictu sensu*; although the former implies the latter, the reverse may not be true. The Supreme Court sometimes uses the terms 'right to secession' and 'right to external self-determination' interchangeably. In a separate opinion in a case before the European Court of Human Rights, Judge Wildhaber, joined by Judge Ryssdal, states that:

[u]ntil recently in international practice the right to self-determination was in practical terms identical to, and indeed restricted to, a right to decolonisation. In recent years a consensus has seemed to emerge that peoples may also exercise a right to self-determination if their human rights are consistently and flagrantly violated or if they are without representation at all or are massively under-represented in an undemocratic and discriminatory way. If this description is correct, then the right to self-determination is a tool which may be used to re-establish international standards of human rights and democracy.

Loizidou v Turkey (Merits), App. No. 15318/89, European Court of Human Rights, Grand Chamber, Judgment of 28 November 1996. In what may be seen a parallel development, it has been suggested that respect for human rights, the rule of law, the rights of minorities and, in general, democratic principles constitute factors mediating recognition policy in relation to new states; see below, n. 69 and accompanying text.

whether or not this category was legally recognized was unclear.[31] What is distinctive about it for present purposes is that it is contingent on particular factual
events: denial of participation in the democratic process and/or gross violations of
human rights. Whereas in the categories of colonies, Mandated and Trust territories, this entitlement subsists by virtue of the type of territory, here it depends on
the occurrence of particular events within the territory (of course, the reason why
self-determination was granted in the traditional categories was because of the
history of foreign domination in them, and foreign domination is itself conceived
as an independent basis for the right).

ITA has been aimed at promoting the exercise of self-determination in two
ways. In the first place, it has been used to enable an 'act of self-determination',
viz. some form of consultation involving the people of the territory (not always
in their entirety) to determine the territory's external status, as in the 'popular
consultation' in East Timor in 1999.[32]

In the second place, the use of ITA to enable a particular territorial outcome has
been based on the promotion of either 'internal' or 'external' self-determination.
Apart from in the Saar, the understandings of the legal right to self-determination
underpinning these two uses of ITA have reflected and constituted the state of
the law on self-determination at the time. The territorial status promoted by the
League in Danzig—Free City status—was not rooted in the right of Danzigers
to 'external' self-determination, although, as discussed in Chapter 5, it involved
the realization of one form of this right, independent statehood.[33] In the Saar,
however, the consultation held by the League in 1935 offered a (very) limited

---

[31] The Canadian Supreme Court stated in 1998 that 'it remains unclear whether this...prop-
osition [this basis for secession] actually reflects an established international law standard' (*Quebec
Secession Opinion*, above n. 30, para. 135; see also para. 138). But cf. the more positive comment in
the 1996 dictum by Judge Wildhaber, joined by Judge Ryssdal, of the European Court of Human
Rights extracted in n. 30 above. For Antonio Cassese:

[i]nternational law tends strongly to protect the territorial integrity of sovereign States. As a consequence, the international community does not recognize the right of secession...As for peoples or
groups entitled to international self-determination, it does follow from this legal entitlement that
they have a right to secession...

A right to secession proper may only arise when a racial group is forcibly refused equal access to
government. If that is the case, the group has legal licence to use force (with the consequence that
third States are, among other things, legally authorized to grant assistance to the liberation movement that leads the racial group, while they are forbidden to assist the central government). In addition the racial group, being entitled to *external* (besides internal) self-determination is entitled to
secede, choosing to integrate, or merge with, another State or to set up an independent State.'

A Cassese, *International Law* (2nd edn, OUP, 2005), 68. James Crawford, noting the reluctance
to permit secession and the lack of any unilateral 'right to secession' for peoples within an independent state under international law, observes that, consistent with the 1970 Friendly Relations
Declaration, 'a State which is governed democratically and respects the human rights of all its
people is entitled to respect for its territorial integrity'; Crawford (above n. 23), at 417–8 (quote
from 418).

[32] On the role of the 'popular consultation' in validating an 'external' self-determination choice,
see above, ch. 5, text from n. 37.

[33] See above, ch. 4, section 4.2.2.

form of 'external' self-determination: the people of the territory could choose between three options (union with France or Germany, or some form of League sovereignty), but were not entitled to independence.[34]

In the UN-era, the use of ITA to promote self-determination was originally rooted in the 'external' self-determination entitlement of colonies and Mandated and Trust territories.[35] This can be seen in the projects for Mandated and Trust territories, the Western Sahara and East Timor, and the original 1967 plan for the UN to administer what was then South West Africa to enable the eventual realization of independent statehood. However, the people of Namibia and East Timor had to endure a quarter-century of foreign occupation before the ITA-sponsored realization of their self-determination entitlements, and the referendum in Western Sahara had, at the time of writing, yet to take place.[36] The uneven success of the use of ITA to promote self-determination in this way reflects the uncertain international commitment to the realization of 'external' self-determination, even for territories within the well-accepted colonial/Mandate/Trust category. The more fundamental question as to the compatibility of ITA itself with the right to self-determination will be considered in the following chapter.

The use of ITA in the southern Balkans can also be understood in terms of self-determination, although only after a prior issue enabling a self-determination approach to be taken was determined through recognition practice. Ultimately, self-determination norms were not determinative (hence the coverage of the status of these territories earlier in Chapter 4, rather than Chapter 5). The approach taken by the Arbitration Committee of the International Conference on the Former Yugoslavia (the so-called 'Badinter Committee') advising European states on their response to the conflict in the region was that the SFRY was in the process of dissolution; the Committee then treated the constituent components of the dissolving federation as if they enjoyed an 'external' self-determination entitlement.[37] Accordingly, on the basis of the *uti possidetis* principle, the only valid claims to 'external' self-determination were those that corresponded to the federal borders, such as the claim of independence for 'Bosnia and Herzegovina'.[38] Claims cutting across these borders, such as the claim of independence for a 'Greater Serbia' comprising the Serbs in the Republics of Serbia, Bosnia and Herzegovina, and Croatia, and the claim of independence for the Bosnian Croat 'Herzeg-Bosna', were necessarily ruled out.

Just as the recognition process that the Badinter Committee was concerned with had the effect of promoting 'external' self-determination in the context

[34] See above, ch. 4, text accompanying n. 22 *et seq.*
[35] See above, ch. 5, text accompanying n. 10 *et seq.*
[36] The significance to self-determination of the role of the UN in Namibia in 1989–1990 is illustrated in Thomas Franck's observation that the UN was 'acting as a midwife in the birth of independent Namibia'; TM Franck, 'The Emerging Right to Democratic Governance', 86 (1992) *AJIL* 46, at 71. On the prospects for the Western Sahara referendum, see above, ch. 2, n 32.
[37] See above, ch. 4, text accompanying nn. 179 and 180 and sources cited therein.
[38] On the *uti possidetis* principle, see above, ch. 5, n. 20.

of what the Committee deemed to be the dissolution of the SFRY generally, so the post-Dayton exercise of certain powers of territorial administration by the Office of the High Representative can be seen as a mechanism for promoting the continued actualization, through statehood, of the idea that the only entity entitled to external self-determination was the Republic of Bosnia and Herzegovina as a whole.[39]

For example, OHR's 1999 removal of Nikola Poplasen, a Serb regarded by the organization to be an extreme nationalist, from the Presidency of the Republika Srpska (one of the two constituent entities of Bosnia and Herzegovina, also known as the 'RS'), mentioned earlier in Chapters 1 and 2, was an attempt to prevent the dissolution of Bosnia and Herzegovina, a situation which, had the Badinter Committee's approach been adopted, would have bolstered a claim to external self-determination on the part of the Republika Srpska.[40] So, ITA exploited the contingent nature of the Badinter Committee's approach, exercising administration so as to prevent what happened to the SFRY happening to Bosnia and Herzegovina, and, from this, ensuring that the Republika Srpska is not placed into the same position that Bosnia and Herzegovina was in when, under the Badinter Committee's approach, its claim to statehood was supported.

Of course, the Badinter Committee's approach to 'dissolution' requires a position to be taken on which borders are to count for the purposes of applying the *uti possidetis* doctrine to determine which entities are to be considered entitled to 'external' self-determination, and which are not.[41] This is of particular relevance to Kosovo given that, as discussed in Chapter 4, that entity was not one of the constituent republics of the SFRY but enjoyed special autonomy, revoked in 1989, within one of the republics, Serbia.[42] If the application of the Badinter Committee's formulation to the territories of the SFRY is taken to suggest that only entities with 'Republic' status were to enjoy 'external' self-determination, then the use of ITA from 1999 to enable 'substantial autonomy' for Kosovo within the FRY/Serbia and Montenegro/Republic of Serbia can be seen as a reflection of the position that the 'dissolution' of the SFRY was itself to have no consequences for Kosovo's aspirations to external self-determination.

In the first half of 1999, the Kosovar Albanians arguably came within the final, uncertain category of 'external' self-determination mentioned earlier: the flagrant denial of 'internal' self-determination. They were denied any self-government, prevented from using their own language in all public institutions, including schools and universities, and eventually subjected to mass human

---

[39] On the people of state as a whole as a self-determination unit, see, e.g., Crawford (above n. 23), 127–8, points (3)(b) and (7).

[40] President Poplasen was removed from this office on 5 March 1999. See OHR, Decision removing Mr Nikola Poplasen from the Office of President of Republika Srpska, 5 March 1999; OHR, Press Release, 'Removal from Office of Nikola Poplasen', 5 March 1999 (both documents obtainable from <http://www.ohr.int>). The earlier references in this book to the removal are above, ch. 1, text accompanying n. 45, and ch. 2, text accompanying n. 71.

[41] See above, ch. 4, n. 180 and accompanying text.

[42] See above, ch. 4, n. 210 and accompanying text.

rights abuses.[43] The NATO bombing campaign and the subsequent introduction of ITA were both explained in terms of reversing this situation, ensuring that human rights abuses against the Kosovar Albanians ended and also (in the case of UNMIK) enabling 'substantial autonomy'. By, in effect, promoting the realization of 'internal' self-determination, therefore, ITA removed the factual basis on which a claim to 'external' self-determination based on the (uncertain) category of gross human rights violations could have been made.

As well as seeking to promote policies concerning territorial status that can be understood in terms of external self-determination, ITA has also been associated with other policies concerning the political character of territorial governance that can similarly be situated within the 'internal' dimension of self-determination. It is to policies of this nature generally that the analysis will now turn.[44]

7.3.3 'State-building'

As already mentioned in Chapter 1, it has become commonplace to use terms such as 'state-building' to label the objective of the recent ITA projects generically.[45]

---

[43] See MJ Matheson, 'United Nations Governance of Post-Conflict Societies, 95 (2001) *AJIL* 76, 78.

[44] The 'democratic' aspect of 'internal' self-determination in particular is addressed below, text accompanying n. 65 *et seq.*

[45] See above, ch. 1, section 1.2. On the representation of ITA as a 'state-building' and 'state reconstruction' enterprise, see, e.g., the inclusion of the articles by Matheson (describing some—but not all—the UN projects) and Strohmeyer (discussing the Kosovo and East Timor projects) as part of a 'Symposium on State Reconstruction after Conflict' in the *American Journal of International Law* (Matheson, above n. 43; H Strohmeyer, 'Collapse and Reconstruction of a Judicial System: The United Nations Missions in Kosovo and East Timor', 95 (2001) *AJIL* 46). A 'Transitional Administrations' project at the International Peace Academy (IPA), looking at the main UN-era ITA projects, defined these projects holistically as 'state-building' operations; see S Chesterman, 'You, The People. The United Nations, Transitional Administration, and State-Building', International Peace Academy, Final Report on the Project on Transitional Administration, November 2003, obtainable from <http://www.ipacademy.org/publications>; see also S Chesterman, *You, The People: The United Nations, Transitional Administrations, and State-Building* (OUP, 2004). For further treatments of certain ITA projects and the 'state-building' concept, and on this concept more generally, see D Chandler, *Bosnia: Faking Democracy after Dayton* (2nd edn, Pluto Press, 2000); M Pugh (ed.), *Regeneration of War-Torn Societies* (Macmillan, 2000); EM Cousens, C Kumar and K Wermester (eds), *Peacebuilding As Politics: Cultivating Peace in Fragile Societies* (Lynne Rienner, 2001); M Ignatieff, *Empire Lite: Nation-building in Bosnia, Kosovo and Afghanistan* (Vintage, 2003); F Fukuyama, *State-Building: Governance and World Order in the 21st Century* (Cornell University Press, 2004); R Paris, *At War's End: Building Peace After Civil Conflict* (CUP, 2004); MC Pugh and N Cooper (with J Goodhand), *War Economies in a Regional Context: Challenges of Transformation* (IPA/Lynne Rienner, 2004); R Caplan, *International Governance of War-Torn Territories: Rule and Reconstruction* (OUP, 2005); D Chandler, *Empire in Denial: The Politics of State-building* (Pluto Press, 2006); D Zaum, *The Sovereignty Paradox: The Norms and Politics of International Statebuilding* (OUP, 2007); A Hehir and N Robinson (eds), *State Building: Theory and Practice* (Routledge, 2007); R Paris, 'International Peacebuilding and the Mission Civilisatrice', 28 (2002) *Review of International Studies* 637; J Fearon and D Laitin, 'Neotrusteeship and the Problem of Weak States', 28 (2004) *International Security* 1; D Papadimitriou, P Petrov, and L Greiçevci, 'To Build a State: Europeanization, EU Actorness and State-Building in Kosovo', 12 (2007) *European Foreign Affairs Law Review* 219; and the *Journal of Intervention and Statebuilding*, published by Routledge since 2007.

In addition to promoting particular statehood and self-determination claims, and denying other such claims, ITA is sometimes concerned with promoting both the existence of the state itself, and a particular model for governance in that state that is considered 'democratic', with the 'rule of law' and a free-market economic system. In doing so, ITA implicates a series of general doctrines that have been conceptualized in international public policy and, to a degree, within international law, including 'state-building', the 'responsibility to protect', and the notion of equivocal or 'earned' sovereignty. This section considers how the association of ITA with policies concerned with the existence or political character of territorial governance, outlined in the previous chapter, reflects these and other general ideas.

An appropriate starting point for this analysis is the association of ITA with the objective of promoting the very existence of organized social and political institutions, especially governmental institutions, in the territory concerned. The perceived need for this is seen as arising in two main scenarios: first, when a territory has become detached from a state, and, secondly, when an existing state becomes unstable and order breaks down. The first scenario is commonly associated with the use of ITA in Kosovo and East Timor. Under such a view, these territories, when detached from the then FRY (in fact) and Indonesia (in fact and in law) respectively, with the aggravating circumstance of widespread violence and destruction, were deemed to be not viable as independent units without external assistance. The second scenario, promoting the viability of an existing state, corresponds to certain prescriptions made in the context of the 'failed state' paradigm that emerged in the early 1990s.[46] In 1992, Gerald Helman & Steven Ratner

[46] The term 'failed state' is now in popular use but is not without its critics, who include the present author. See, e.g., T Lyons and AI Samatar, *Somalia: State Collapse, Multilateral Intervention, and Strategies for Political Reconstruction* (Brookings Institution, 1995); RH Jackson, *The Global Covenant: Human Conduct in a World of States* (OUP, 2000), ch. 11; M Koskenniemi, *The Gentle Civilizer of Nations* (CUP, 2002), 176; W Bain, *Between Anarchy and Society. Trusteeship and the Obligations of Power* (OUP, 2003), 5 and ch. 6, *passim*; Ignatieff (above n. 45); T Parker, *The Ultimate Intervention: Revitalising the UN Trusteeship Council for the 21st Century* (Sandvika: Norwegian School of Management, 2003); RI Rotberg, *State Failure and State Weakness in a Time of Terror* (World Peace Foundation, 2003); Chesterman, *You, The People* (above n. 45), 83; G Kreijen, *State Failure, Sovereignty and Effectiveness: Legal Lessons from the Decolonization of Sub-Saharan Africa* (Brill, 2004); J-P Pham, *Liberia: Portrait of a Failed State* (Reed, 2004); RI Rotberg (ed.), *When States Fail: Causes and Consequences* (Princeton University Press, 2004); S Chesterman, M Ignatieff and R Thakur (eds), *Making States Work: State Failure and the Crisis of Governance* (UN University Press, 2005); Crawford (above, n. 23), 720–23; J-G Gros, 'Towards a Taxonomy of Failed States in the New World Order: Decaying Somalia, Liberia, Rwanda and Haiti', 17 (1996) *Third World Quarterly* 455; HJ Richardson, '"Failed States", Self-Determination, and Preventative Diplomacy: Colonialist Nostalgia and Democratic Expectations', 10 (1996) Temple International & Comparative Law Journal 1; J Herbst, 'Responding to State Failure in Africa', 21:3 (1996–7) *International Security* 120; A Yannis, 'State Collapse and Prospects for Political Reconstruction and Democratic Governance in Somalia', *1998 African Yearbook of International Law* 23; D Thürer, 'The "Failed State" and International Law', (1999) *IRRC*, vol. 81, issue 836, 731; N Tsagourias, 'Humanism and the Mandates System: Its Modern Revival', 13 (2000) *Hague Yearbook of International Law* 97, 100–103; S Mallaby, 'The Reluctant Imperialist: Terrorism, Failed States and the Case for American Empire', 81 (March/April 2002) *Foreign Affairs* 2; J Milliken and K Krause, 'State Failure, State Collapse, and State Reconstruction, Concepts, Lessons and Strategies', 33 (2002) *Development and Change* 753; Paris, 'International Peacebuilding' (above n. 45);

posited the 'problem' of the 'failed nation-state, utterly incapable of sustaining itself as a member of the international community' due to 'civil strife, government breakdown, and economic privation'.[47] Ruth Gordon (a critic of Helman & Ratner's thesis) later described the 'disintegrating' state in the following terms:

...the state is paralyzed and inoperative; laws are not made, order is not preserved, and societal cohesion is not enhanced. As a symbol of identity, it has lost its power of conferring a name on its people and a meaning to their social action. State territory is no longer assured security by a central sovereign organization.[48]

Helman & Ratner argued that 'something must be done' about the 'failed state' phenomenon that went beyond the 'conventional remedies' of aid programmes.[49] The solution they proposed, 'United Nations Conservatorship', envisaged three options whereby the UN 'manages the affairs' of the 'failed state'. The first option—'governance assistance'—would be used in those states where a government was struggling, but still functioning to some degree.[50] Instead of the usual prescription of advice and training, the UN would work directly with local officials, providing

RI Rotberg, 'Failed States in a World of Terror', 81:4 (July/August 2002) *Foreign Affairs* 127, reproduced in K Mingst and J Snyder (eds), *Essential Readings in World Politics* (2nd edn, Norton & Co., 2004); J Chopra, 'Building State Failure in East Timor', 33 (2002) *Development & Change* 979, reprinted as J Chopra, 'Building State Failure in East Timor', in J Milliken (ed.), *State Failure, Collapse & Reconstruction* (Blackwell, 2003), 223 and J Chopra, 'Building State Failure in East Timor', ch. 8 in A Hehir and N Robinson (eds), *State Building: Theory and Practice* (Routledge, 2007); C Crocker, 'Engaging Failing States', 82:5 (2003) *Foreign Affairs* 32; M Ignatieff, 'State Failure and Nation-Building', ch. 9 in JL Holzgrefe and R Keohane (eds), *Humanitarian Intervention* (CUP, 2003); R Wilde, 'The Skewed Responsibility Narrative of the "Failed States" Concept', 9 (2003) *ILSA Journal of International & Comparative Law* 425; HH Perritt, 'Structures and Standards for Political Trusteeship', 8 (2003) *UCLA Journal of International Law & Foreign Affairs* 385; AA Yusuf, 'Government Collapse and State Continuity: the Case of Somalia', 13 (2003) *Italian Yearbook of International Law* 11; D Carment, 'Anticipating State Failure', in D Carment and A Schnabel (eds), *Conflict Prevention from Rhetoric to Reality—Volume 2: Opportunities and Innovation* (Lexington Books, 2004), 79; CD Classen, ' "Failed States" and the Prohibition of the Use of Force', in Société française pour le droit international (ed.), *Les nouvelles menaces contre la paix et la sécurité internationales—New Threats to International Peace and Security* (Pedone, 2004), 129; Fearon & Laitin (above n. 45); A Gourevitch, 'The Unfailing of the State', 58 (2004) *Journal of International Affairs* 255; R Koskenmäki, 'Legal Implications resulting from State Failure in Light of the Case of Somalia', 73 (2004) *Nordic Journal of International Law* 1; S Krasner, 'Governance Failures and Alternatives to Sovereignty', CDDRL Working Paper No. 1 (November 2004), available at <http://iis-db.stanford.edu/pubs/20667/enhanced_sov_krasner_Aug_1_04.pdf>; R Wilde, 'Representing International Territorial Administration: A Critique of Some Approaches', 15 (2004) *EJIL* 71, 89–91; B Dunlap, 'State Failure and the Use of Force in the Age of Global Terror', 27 (2005) *Boston College International & Comparative Law Review* 453; R Geiss, 'Failed States: Legal Aspects and Security Implications', 47 (2005) *German Yearbook of International Law* 457; I Österdahl, 'Relatively Failed: Troubled Statehood and International Law', 14 (2005) *Finnish Yearbook of International Law* 49. See also the path-breaking articles by Gerald Helman and Steven Ratner, below n. 47, and Ruth Gordon, below n. 48.

[47] GB Helman and SR Ratner, 'Saving Failed States', 89 (1992) *Foreign Policy* 3, at 3.

[48] R Gordon, 'Saving Failed States: Sometimes a Neocolonialist Notion', 12 (1997) *American University Journal of International Law & Policy* 903, 915 (footnotes omitted); see also R Gordon, 'Some Legal Problems with Trusteeship', 28 (1995) *Cornell International Law Journal* 301.

[49] Helman & Ratner (above n. 47), 3 (first quote) and 6 (second quote).

[50] Ibid., at 13.

assistance but leaving final decisions to the government.[51] If, however, local officials were deemed incapable of governance even with such assistance, the authors proposed two different forms of what has been termed in this book ITA.[52] Either the state would 'delegate certain governmental functions' to the UN—partial ITA—or, 'the most radical option', the UN would 'act as the administering authority'—plenary ITA.[53] A few years later, in 1996, Fen Osler Hampson proposed a similar notion of 'proxy governance' as a device for addressing the challenge of '[r]estoring the infrastructure and administrative capacity of a war-torn state'.[54] International actors would take over 'administrative functions', serving as 'stand-ins for local authorities that are unable or unwilling to perform these activities themselves' until this willingness and ability becomes evident.[55]

Proposing ITA as a means of promoting the viability of an existing state echoes the use of ITA in the Congo in 1960–64. What was in Chapter 6 termed 'remedial ITA', involving the conduct of administration to create governmental institutions, was attempted a year after Helman & Ratner's proposals during the UNOSOM II phase of the ultimately disastrous Somalia mission. The failure of that mission is widely credited with the reluctance of states in general, and the US in particular, to pursue further administration projects in the 'failed state' context, and, indeed, there have been no such projects involving plenary ITA since then. What has continued, however, is the relatively little-noticed activity of administering aid programmes and 'refugee camps' in poor countries, mostly in Africa.

As far as this form of 'state-building'—(re)constructing state infrastructure—is concerned, in practice, plenary ITA has been reserved mainly for territories that are not yet states; for so-called 'failed states', i.e., existing states, only partial ITA has been utilized, or plenary ITA in a particular area of state territory hosting 'refugee' camps. The US–UK Coalition Provisional Authority (CPA) in Iraq in 2003–4 (not an international organization), discussed further in the next chapter, was conceived to provide governance after the removal of the government of Saddam Hussein by the coalition states, rather than as a means of responding to a pre-existing system of governmental collapse, although the actions and omissions of that body and the coalition forces then led, in part, to the breakdown of order in the state.

---

[51] Ibid.

[52] Cf. the distinction made between 'conduct' and 'assistance' in the definition of 'territorial administration' above, ch. 1, text accompanying n. 93 *et seq.*

[53] Helman & Ratner (above n. 47), at 14 (first quote) and 16 (second and third quotes). In 1993, Peter Lyon made similar proposals using the language of trusteeship; see P Lyon, 'The Rise and Fall and Possible Revival of International Trusteeship', 31 (1993) *Journal of Commonwealth & Comparative Politics* 96. As previously mentioned, the relationship between ITA and trusteeship, including Lyon's ideas in this regard, is considered in detail in the following chapter.

[54] See FO Hampson, *Nurturing Peace: Why Peace Settlements Succeed or Fail* (United States Institute of Peace Press, 1996), 232–3; FO Hampson, 'Can Peacebuilding Work?', 30 (1997) *Cornell International Law Journal* 704, at 707–9 (quotation from 707).

[55] Quotations taken from Hampson, *Nurturing Peace* (above n. 54), 232; see also Hampson, 'Can Peacebuilding Work' (above n. 54), 707.

Internationally-administered aid programmes are sometimes allied to various forms of assistance to governments, such as loans and technology transfer, which by definition do not amount to ITA. Clearly, then, plenary ITA has the potential to be used in the 'failed state' context; whether it is used in particular instances of governmental collapse is another matter.

Using ITA to promote the very existence of an organized territorial government, and thereby the viability of the state, is perhaps the most extreme form of the institution.[56] Here, ITA can be seen as a mechanism for enabling conformity with one of the legal requirements for statehood—the existence of an effective government.[57] It is 'state-building' in the most literal sense. When the entity is not yet a state—such as Kosovo and East Timor—ITA's radical alteration of the factual situation on the ground brings conformity to the legal criterion, and so statehood, closer. Equally, it makes the realization of 'external' self-determination a practical possibility. This is the other side of the coin from the use of governance to promote self-determination described earlier. Whereas, in that context, ITA was used to promote self-determination through the adoption of a particular status, here, ITA performs this role through enabling the practical realities—a functioning government, essential infrastructure—that lie behind the formal status. When East Timor became a state in May 2002, the implication was that in the year and a half of UN administration the basic structures of government had been put in place and the territory was thus independently viable.[58] In Kosovo, however, even before the final settlement, the efforts to provide 'substantial autonomy' by UNMIK created a situation of *de facto* independence in relation to (what ended up being called) the Republic of Serbia. Here, then, ITA created some of the practical capabilities for an outcome, even before the outcome itself had been agreed upon.

When the entity is a state—as in the Congo, Somalia and those states where international organizations have administered aid programmes and 'refugee' camps—ITA seeks to ensure the continued existence, rather than the creation, of the state (or the continuance of particular state activities). Since, as discussed in Chapter 4, the presumption in favour of continued statehood means that 'disintegrating' states rarely lose juridical personality as a result of the mere fact of internal disintegration (cf. Somalia since 1991),[59] the function of ITA is to make

[56] On this objective in peacebuilding missions generally, see, e.g., Paris, 'International Peacebuilding' (above n. 45).

[57] On this criterion for statehood, see, e.g., Montevideo Convention on Rights and Duties of States, 26 December 1933, 165 LNTS 19, Art. 1; Crawford (above n. 23), 55–61 and sources cited therein. Danilo Türk makes this connection when arguing that states and international organizations recognizing entities with 'deficient effectiveness' (i.e., entities lacking effective control over their territory), as in the case of Bosnia and Herzegovina in 1992, must be willing to assist the authorities in such entities to maintain order in the territory; D Türk, 'The Dangers of Failed States and a Failed Peace in the Post Cold War Era', 27 (1995) *NYU Journal of International Law & Politics* 625, at 626.

[58] For example, the Security Council described 'a process of transition under the authority of the United Nations towards independence', SC Res. 1272, 25 October 1999, Preamble, para. 3.

[59] On the presumption in favour of continued statehood in such circumstances, see above, ch. 4, text from n. 12. On Somalia, see, e.g., DJ Harris, *Cases and Materials on International Law* (6th edn, Sweet & Maxwell, 2004), 101 and the discussion above, ch. 4, section 4.4.2.

the 'state' not only a juridical notion, but also a practical reality. It ensures the existence of the agent of the state—the government—creating the possibility that the state is able to function both domestically and internationally.[60] The body that must implement the state's obligations and is able to invoke its rights in international law is established.

Thus, ITA is engaged in buttressing the institution of the state internationally as the primary unit of social union. As Roland Paris points out in relation to 'peacebuilding' generally, this enterprise reflects and constitutes the 'globalization of the very idea of what a state should look like and how it should act' and, cutting across the dominant narrative of globalization as a phenomenon that always erodes the state, 'does not undermine, but bolsters, the effective sovereignty of peacebuilding host states' and, more broadly, propagates and fortifies 'the norm that the global political space *should* be divided into Westphalian states'.[61]

From a different perspective, that of the people of the state or state territory, this enterprise can be seen as a means of implementing their rights under international human rights law, including the right to development, in the way that it aspires to secure the governmental framework necessary to protect and promote such rights. The scope of ITA then determines which rights are being implemented. So UNHCR 'refugee' camp administration, for example, purports to 'protect' occupants' rights under international human rights and refugee law.[62]

The 'failed states' commentators were concerned with situations of governmental collapse: the very existence of governance was in jeopardy. However, a much more common objective of ITA since those proposals has been the promotion of a particular model of political and economic governance in the territory concerned, also sometimes conceptualized holistically as 'state-building'. As was outlined in the previous chapter, ITA has been associated with promoting not only the existence and operation of governance, but also the objective that governance is conducted in a 'democratic' manner and on the basis of free market economic policy. Indeed, ITA has sometimes involved, as in Bosnia and Herzegovina, removing existing government officials if their behaviour was deemed to be in some way 'undemocratic'. The particular 'democratic' practices highlighted in Chapter 6 were free and fair consultations (and government support for such consultations), the protection of minorities, multi-ethnic politics, including the return of refugees and internally-displaced persons, and free-market economics.[63]

---

[60] On the relationship between the 'government' and the 'state' in international law, see the sources cited above, ch. 3, n. 17.

[61] Paris, 'International Peacebuilding' (above n. 45), 639 (first quote); 654 (second quote); 655 (third quote, emphasis in the original).

[62] See R Wilde, '*Quis Custodiet Ipsos Custodes*? Why and How UNHCR Governance of "Development" Refugee Camps Should Be Subject to International Human Rights Law', 1 (1998) *YHRDLJ* 107.

[63] See above, ch. 6, Table 6. For commentary, see, e.g., Paris, 'International Peacebuilding' (above n. 45) and Perritt (above n. 46), 438 *et seq*.

The full range of rights in international human rights law, covering civil, political, economic, social and cultural rights, and including minority rights and refugee rights, can be seen in the state context as a regime encapsulating the key aspirations of a democratic polity. The 'democratic' use of ITA, then, can be viewed alongside the earlier use to ensure the operation of governance as a mechanism for enforcing this framework of international human rights law. Whereas in the earlier context, implementation is a matter of the mere existence of governance, here it is the quality of that governance. Setting international human rights law standards as the benchmark for governance is reflected, for example, in how, as discussed in Chapter 6, the initial approach taken to the question of the applicable law by both UNMIK and UNTAET was to adopt the local law insofar as it was compatible with the mandate and 'internationally recognized human rights standards'.[64]

In addition to promoting human rights generally, certain features of the 'democratic' use of ITA can be seen as a mechanism for promoting one right in particular, the right to 'democratic governance', which Thomas Franck argued in 1992 was 'emerging' in international law.[65] Like the 'saving failed states' thesis, Franck's thesis appeared in Western scholarship during the triumphalist era at the end of the Cold War. Both theses sought to capitalize on the new opportunities that were perceived to be present with the end of the Cold War. For proponents of the 'saving failed states' thesis, these opportunities arose because the West could now act less for selfish geopolitical reasons and more for selfless humanitarian motives. Moreover, the UN, and in particular the Security Council, would no longer be deadlocked by Cold War battles, creating more opportunities for peace missions to be created and supported. For the 'right to democratic governance' thesis, these opportunities arose because of the supposed ideological 'triumph' of liberal democratic ideas over the totalitarianism of Soviet communism and the 'dictatorships of Africa and Asia'.[66]

[64] See above, ch. 6, n. 142, and, in relation to Kosovo in particular, see Report of the Secretary-General on the United Nations Interim Administration Mission in Kosovo, UN Doc. S/1999/779, 12 July 1999 (hereinafter 'Secretary-General Report on Kosovo 1999'), para 42.

[65] Franck (above n. 36). See also TM Franck, 'Democracy as a Human Right' in L Henkin and J Hargrove (eds), *Human Rights: An Agenda for the Next Century* (ASIL, 1994), 73; G Fox and B Roth (eds), *Democratic Governance and International Law* (CUP, 2000); B Roth, *Governmental Illegitimacy in International Law* (OUP, 2001), ch. 8; S Marks, *The Riddle of All Constitutions: International Law, Democracy and the Critique of Ideology* (OUP, 2000); H Steiner, 'Political Participation as a Human Right', 1 (1988) *Harvard Human Rights Yearbook* 77; WM Reisman, 'Sovereignty and Human Rights in Contemporary International Law', 84 (1990) *AJIL* 866; GH Fox, 'The Right to Political Participation in International Law', 17 (1992) *Yale Journal of International Law* 539; C Cerna, 'Universal Democracy: An International Legal Right or a Pipe Dream of the West?', 27 (1995) *NYU Journal of International Law & Politics* 289. For a discussion of the implementation of this right through peace operations, see, e.g., GH Fox, 'International Law and the Entitlement to Democracy after War', 9 (2003) *Global Governance* 179.

[66] Franck (above n. 36), 49. For Franck, '[t]he almost-complete triumph of the democratic notions of Hume, Locke, Jefferson and Madison—in Latin America, Africa, Eastern Europe and, to a lesser extent, Asia—may prove to be the most profound event of the twentieth century'; ibid.

Thomas Franck's idea of a legal right to democratic governance covers the process by which governmental structures are legitimated on a national level. It is thus largely procedural, and concerned with the existence of 'free and open elections' based on a representational model of government and articulated in Article 25 of the International Covenant on Civil and Political Rights.[67] As a legal entitlement, it builds on one understanding of the right to 'internal' self-determination, concerned not with the question of sub-state autonomy, as discussed earlier, but, rather, the entitlement of the population to choose how it is governed.[68]

ITA to secure free and fair elections, and furnish governmental support for such elections (see Table 1 in Chapter 2), can be considered as part of the broad set of practices, including election monitoring missions, that together might support the idea that a 'right' in this area is emerging. Indeed, in 1992, when Franck was writing, there had only been one such ITA project outside Mandated, Trust and Non-Self-Governing territories: Cambodia; since then, this use of ITA has been pronounced, with the projects in Bosnia and Herzegovina, Mostar, Eastern Slavonia, and Kosovo.

In the process of promoting human rights, the 'democratic' use of ITA can be seen as enforcing some of the additional criteria, concerning human rights, that have supposedly become determinative on issues of statehood during the second half of the 20th century, at least in the context of recognition: conformity to self-determination norms, the provision of minority rights guarantees, and the right to free and fair elections.[69] For example, with the independence declarations of certain SFRY Republics in 1991, the member states of the European Community purportedly attempted to use the threat of non-recognition to ensure that the entities in question adopted certain minority guarantees before attaining statehood.[70]

---

[67] Ibid., 48. Art. 25 of the Covenant extends to every citizen the right:

(a) To take part in the conduct of public affairs, directly or through freely chosen representatives;
(b) To vote and to be elected at genuine periodic elections which shall be by universal and equal suffrage and shall be held by secret ballot, guaranteeing the free expression of the will of the electors.

International Covenant on Civil and Political Rights (ICCPR), 16 December 1966, 999 UNTS 171, Art. 25.

[68] Franck (above n. 36), 57–60. In the context of Cambodia in 1991, the UN General Assembly described the UN-run elections in terms of 'self-determination for the Cambodian people', GA Res. 46/18, 20 November 1991, para. 4, cited in R McCorquodale, 'Self-Determination: A Human Rights Approach', 43 (1994) *ICLQ* 857, at 864, n. 39.

[69] See, for example, European Community, 'Guidelines on the Recognition of New States in Eastern Europe and in the Soviet Union', 16 December 1991, 31 (1992) *ILM* 1486 (hereinafter 'EC Guidelines'); Crawford (above n. 23), ch. 3, especially section 3.4. Note also the provision in the UN Charter that members should be 'able and willing to carry out the obligations in the Charter' (UN Charter, Art. 4(1)) and the significance of human rights and self-determination in the purposes and principles of the UN in the UN Charter (ibid, Art. 1).

[70] See EC Guidelines (above n. 69) and Opinions Nos 1, 2, and 4 of the Arbitration Committee of the International Conference on the Former Yugoslavia, text reproduced in 31 (1992) *ILM* 1494.

As far as Bosnia and Herzegovina is concerned, ITA can be seen as complementary to the mechanism of recognition, addressing the continuing need to promote minority rights once statehood has been attained. In promoting a state's conformity with international human rights law, ITA, like recognition, plays an important role in that state's international legitimacy.

As mentioned in the previous chapter, the human rights agenda in some of the later ITA projects has been explicitly tied to the agenda of promoting women's rights, which can be understood to reflect the broader international policy on women and international peace and security that became prominent following the adoption of Security Council Resolution 1325 in 2000.[71] In Kosovo, UNMIK adopted a quota for the elections in order to ensure that a certain proportion of those elected were women.[72] In East Timor, a Gender Affairs Unit was

---

[71] On this agenda in the context of ITA, see above, ch. 6, n. 134, sources cited therein and accompanying text. On the broader international policy on women and international peace and security, see SC Res. 1325, 31 October 2000; see also GA Res. 37/63, 3 December 1982. For an overview of the implementation of SC Res. 1325 (ibid.) in the subsequent practice of the UN (including in the context of ITA projects), see <http://www.peacewomen.org/un/sc/1325_Monitor/index.htm> and <http://www.womenwarpeace.org/toolbox/toolbox.htm>; see also S Poehlman-Doumbouya, 'Women and Peace in United Nations Documents: An Analysis', at <http://www.peacewomen.org/un/UN1325/analysis.html>. For commentary on gender and international peace and security and UN policy see, e.g., DL Wolf (ed.), *Feminist Dilemmas in Fieldwork* (Westview Press, 1996); N Yuval-Davis, *Gender & Nation* (SAGE Publications, 1997); H Charlesworth and C Chinkin, *The Boundaries of International Law: A Feminist Analysis* (Manchester University Press, 2000), chs 6, 8, and 9; UNIFEM, *Women at the Peace Table: Making a Difference* (United Nations Development Fund for Women, 2000); E Rehn and E Johnson Sirleaf, *Women, War and Peace: The Independent Experts' Assessment on the Impact of Armed Conflict on Women and Women's Role in Peace-building* (UNIFEM, 2002); H Charlesworth, C Chinkin, and S Wright, 'Feminist Approaches to International Law', 85 (1991) *AJIL* 613, *passim*; H Charlesworth, 'Women as Sherpas: Are Global Summits Useful for Women?', 22 (1996) *Feminist Studies* 537; D Otto, 'Holding Up Half the Sky, But for Whose Benefit? A Critical Analysis of the Fourth World Conference on Women', 6 (1996) *Australian Feminist Law Journal* 7; G Chakravorty Spivak, ' "Woman" as Theatre: United Nations Conference on Women, Beijing 1995', 75 (1996) *Radical Philosophy* 2; A Orford, 'Muscular Humanitarianism: Reading the Narratives of the New Interventionism', 10 (1999) *EJIL* 679; D Otto, 'A Post-Beijing Reflection on the Limitations and Potential of Human Rights Discourse for Women', in KD Askin and DM Koenig (eds), *International Human Rights Law* (Transnational Publishers, 1999), vol. 1, 115; S Kouvo, 'The United Nations and Gender Mainstreaming: Limits and Possibilities', ch. 11 in D Buss and A Manji (eds), *International Law: Modern Feminist Approaches* (Hart Publishing, 2005); J Gardam and M Jarvis, 'Women and Armed Conflict: The International Response to the Beijing PFA', 32 (2000) *Columbia Human Rights Law Review* 1; H Charlesworth and C Chinkin, 'Editorial Comment: Sex, Gender and September 11', 96 (2002) *AJIL* 600; A Orford, 'Feminism, Imperialism and the Mission of International Law', 71 (2002) *Nordic Journal of International Law* 275; S Nakaya, 'Women and Gender Equality in Peace Processes: From Women at the Negotiating Table to Postwar Structural Reforms in Guatemala and Somalia', 9 (2003) *Global Governance* 459; K Engle, 'Feminism and Its (Dis)contents: Criminalizing War-Time Rape in Bosnia', 99 (2005) *AJIL* 778; D Otto, 'A Sign of "Weakness"? Disrupting Gender certainties in the Implementation of Security Council Resolution 1325', 13 (2006) *Michigan Journal of Gender and Law* 113. For feminist commentary on international public policy generally, see the sources cited below, ch. 9, n. 54.

[72] N Wood, 'Kosovo Leads Europe in Woman Power', *BBC News Online*, 29 November 2001, at <http://news.bbc.co.uk/2/hi/europe/1682907.stm>.

established after the commencement of UNTAET and, amongst other things, acted as a focal point for the activities and development of women's NGOs.[73]

The democratic agenda understood to be part of many of the post-Cold War ITA projects goes beyond elections and human rights to encompass the entire structure of the state: the constitution, legal system, economic model, and public sector. This is also often understood as somehow reflecting a global standard for state governance. Roland Paris states that:

[o]ne way of thinking about the actions of peacebuilders is to conceive of liberal market democracy as an internationally-sanctioned model of 'legitimate' domestic governance.[74]

The economic model in particular is commonly associated with the international economic policy of the Bretton Woods institutions.[75] For Paris, the use of ITA to implement these policies amounts to a process whereby:

... peacebuilders are transmitting a set of internationally-approved norms of domestic governance into the internal affairs of war-shattered states.[76]

This process can be understood in terms of liberal notions of sovereignty, particularly cosmopolitan ideas associated with and drawn from the work of Immanuel Kant.[77] Such ideas reject notions of sovereignty that accept

---

[73] S Whittington, 'The UN Transitional Administration in East Timor: Gender Affairs', 53 (2000) *Development Bulletin* 74; H Charlesworth and M Wood, 'Mainstreaming Gender in International Peace and Security: the Case of East Timor', 26 (2001) *Yale Journal of International Law* 313; H Charlesworth and M Wood, 'Women and Human Rights in the Rebuilding of East Timor', 71 (2002) *Nordic Journal of International Law* 325; S Whittington, 'Gender and Peacekeeping: The United Nations Transitional Administration in East Timor', 28 (2003) *Signs* 1283.

[74] Paris, 'International Peacebuilding' (above n. 45), 650.

[75] Discussing UNMIK, the UN Secretary-General, explaining how '[t]he Special Representative will seek to create a viable, market-based economy and to develop a comprehensive approach to the economic and social development of Kosovo', states that:

... UNMIK will consult with representatives of Kosovo communities, the United Nations Development Programme (UNDP) and other relevant United Nations organizations, and will seek the advice and guidance of international financial institutions in order to develop a comprehensive programme for the economic and social stabilization and development of Kosovo ...

Secretary-General Report on Kosovo 1999 (above, n. 64), para 103.

[76] Paris, 'International Peacebuilding' (above n. 45), 650.

[77] I Kant, *Perpetual Peace: A Philosophical Sketch* (1795), reproduced in HS Reiss (ed.), *Kant—Political Writings* (CUP, 1970), 93. See, e.g., MW Doyle, 'Kant, Liberal Legacies and Foreign Affairs', 12 (1983) *Philosophy and Public Affairs* 205. For examples of international legal scholarship drawing on and/or discussing these ideas, see P Allott, *Eunomia: New Order for a New World* (1st edn, OUP, 1990/2nd edn, OUP, 2001); TM Franck, *The Power of Legitimacy among Nations* (OUP, 1990); TM Franck, *Fairness in International Law and Institutions* (OUP, 1995); FR Tesón, *Humanitarian Intervention: An Inquiry into Law and Morality* (2nd edn, Transnational Publishers, 1997); Roth, *Governmental Illegitimacy* (above, n. 65), *passim* and especially 419–28; TM Franck, 'Legitimacy in the International System', 82 (1988) *AJIL* 705; FR Tesón, 'The Kantian Theory of International Law', 92 (1992) *Columbia Law Review* 53; A-M Slaughter, 'International Law in a World of Liberal States', 6 (1995) *EJIL* 503; FR Tesón, 'Kantian International Liberalism', in T Nardin and D Mapel (eds), *International Society: Diverse Ethical Perspectives* (Princeton University Press, 1998), 103. For critiques, see, e.g., Marks (above n. 65); A Orford, *Reading Humanitarian Intervention: Human*

the legitimacy of the state regardless of how it is governed internally; instead, sovereignty is 'equivocal' or 'conditional': an entity should only be treated as 'sovereign' if it is, in some sense, 'liberal' as far as its internal governance is concerned.[78] Such a conception of sovereignty is implicated in the idea of the 'failed state' discussed earlier, given the way the concept suggests an entity whose statehood is fatally degraded, this situation having been caused exclusively by indigenous factors (it is the 'state'—its people, and government—that have 'failed', not also, say, other states and/or non-state actors such as corporations and international institutions).[79]

The significance of liberal ideas for the role of ITA in seeking to promote certain internal governance policies is twofold, in addition to the invocation of certain forms of ITA in cases of 'state failure'.[80] In the first place, this use of ITA in existing states like Bosnia and Herzegovina can be understood as both justified by the perceived deficiency in the state's conformity to liberal notions of the state, and also supposedly being aimed at remedying such a situation. In the second place, this use of ITA in entities that are not yet states, but wish to attain statehood, can be understood in terms of seeking to introduce the necessary 'liberal' elements of internal governance that would give rise to an entitlement to 'sovereignty'. Indeed, such an idea has come to be described by commentators on a range of situations including Kosovo and East Timor as a process of 'earned sovereignty': as the term suggests, sovereignty for aspirant states has to be 'earned' through the adoption of a certain model of liberal governmental politics.[81]

A striking illustration of the concept of 'earned sovereignty' is the policy of 'standards before status' adopted in 2002 by UNMIK in Kosovo, which, as discussed in the previous chapter, required certain governance standards, many of which concerning concepts of liberal governance such as 'effective, representative and functioning democratic institutions' and 'respect for the rule of law' to be evident before Kosovo's eventual status would be determined, although one other mediating factor outside this framework—the outcome of negotiations with the

---

Rights and the Use of Force in International Law (CUP, 2003); JE Alvarez, 'Do Liberal States Behave Better? A Critique of Slaughter's Liberal Theory', 12 (2001) *EJIL* 183.

[78] See, e.g., the works by Tesón cited in the previous footnote; see also Reisman (above n. 65).

[79] This argument is explored further in Wilde, 'The Skewed Responsibility Narrative' (above n. 46), and Wilde, 'Representing International Territorial Administration' (above n. 46).

[80] See also Paris, *At War's End* (above n. 45); Zaum (above n. 45), and sources cited therein; Paris, 'International Peacebuilding' (above n. 45), *passim* and sources cited therein. These issues are also discussed further in the next chapter, section 8.7.2.2.

[81] MP Scharf, 'Earned Sovereignty: Juridical Underpinnings', 31 (2002–03) *Denver Journal of International Law & Policy* 373; PR Williams, MP Scharf, and JR Hooper, 'Resolving Sovereignty-Based Conflicts: The Emerging Approach of Earned Sovereignty', 31 (2002–03) *Denver Journal of International Law & Policy* 349; PR Williams and JR Hooper, 'Earned Sovereignty: The Political Dimension', 31 (2002–03) *Denver Journal of International Law & Policy* 355; PR Williams and F Jannotti Pecci, 'Earned Sovereignty: Bridging the Gap between Sovereignty and Self-Determination', 40 (2004) *Stanford Journal of International Law* 347.

Republic of Serbia and the position taken by Russia on the matter—was also to be determinative.[82]

A similar approach to 'earned sovereignty' is Robert Keohane's framework of 'different categories of qualified sovereignty'.[83] Arguing that '[e]ffective solutions to the problems that arise after intervention require reconceptualizing sovereignty' as 'limited rather than unitary',[84] Keohane sets out different categories of sovereignty through which an entity made subject to international intervention should move, each reflecting a difference of degree in the type of ITA required:

[a]t first, sovereignty may not be unbundled, but actually denied... Then *nominal sovereignty* could be reintroduced, in which the country regains international legal sovereignty—and its seat at the United Nations—but domestic authority is in the hands of the United Nations or some other outside authority. As the troubled society begins to recover, it will make sense to grant its new state institutions a little bit of sovereignty at a time. The next step would be *limited sovereignty*, in which domestic governance is for the most part controlled by local people, but the UN or other external authority can override its decisions when they are seen to be abusive of human rights or to contradict agreements that have been made. The final stage could be *integrated sovereignty*, in which domestic authority is controlled by nationals of the state, and there is no continually functioning external authority, but in which there are constitutional restrictions, adjudicated by a supranational court and potentially enforceable by the country's neighbours... In this array of degrees of external sovereignty there is no opening for Westphalian sovereignty.[85]

A further, related notion is that of the 'responsibility to protect': a responsibility owed by all sovereign states to individuals in their individual jurisdictions in the first instance, but also a duty which must somehow be taken up by the 'international community' if the first tier of responsibility is abdicated, or incapable of exercise. This notion was proposed by an independent expert commission in 2001, and, although the international response to it was somewhat mixed, affirmation by the UN General Assembly was forthcoming in its *2005 World Summit Outcome* resolution.[86]

A 'responsibility to protect' references the broader cosmopolitan notion of a generalized community interest conceptualized in terms of certain fundamental principles, including the protection of human rights, reflected in Immanuel Kant's concept of what is now called international law as a normative system in which 'a violation of rights in *one* part of the world is felt *everywhere*'.[87] Such a

---

[82] See above, ch. 6, text accompanying n. 76 *et seq.* and 146 *et seq.*

[83] RO Keohane, 'Political Authority after Intervention: Gradations in Sovereignty', ch. 8 in JL Holzgrefe and RO Keohane (eds), *Humanitarian Intervention: Ethical, Legal, and Political Dilemmas* (CUP, 2003), 296.

[84] Ibid., 297.

[85] Ibid., 296–7.

[86] See International Commission on Intervention and State Sovereignty, *The Responsibility to Protect*, December 2001, available at <http://www.iciss.ca/pdf/Commission-Report.pdf>; 2005 World Summit Outcome, GA Res. 60/1, 16 September 2005.

[87] Kant, *Perpetual Peace* (above n. 77), 107–8 (emphasis in original). In international legal theory, considerations of notions of community interests are the hallmarks of both liberal and

notion is reflected in contemporary international law in the way certain obligations are conceptualized as operating *erga omnes*—against all—meaning that everyone has an interest in seeing them observed, and the way that, in relation to certain crimes by individuals, including, in an indicative term, 'crimes against humanity', all states have a right to prosecute under 'universal jurisdiction'.[88]

The significant paradigm shift in international public policy ostensibly effected by the 'responsibility to protect' is to move the invocation of a generalized interest from the arena of discretion—an entitlement—to one of obligation— a responsibility. Whether this shift has occurred or is occurring in relation to those areas of law conceived as operating *erga omnes* is contested;[89] in the case of individual criminal responsibility it is clear that, at least for certain crimes under certain treaty obligations, states are obliged to ensure that good faith attempts at prosecution take palce.[90]

The notion of a right and even a duty of all states to guarantee 'community obligations' is the conceptual basis for doctrines of military action to prevent

policy science approaches. For the former, see the sources cited in n. 78 above; for the latter, see the sources cited above, ch. 1, n. 105. See also Cassese (above n. 31), at 13–21; P Weil, 'Towards Relative Normativity in International Law?', 77 (1983) *AJIL* 413.

[88] On the concept of obligations *erga omnes*, see *Barcelona Traction, Light and Power Company Limited (Second Phase), ICJ Reports 1970*, 3, paras 33–4; *Legal Consequences of the Construction of a Wall in the Occupied Palestinian Territory, Advisory Opinion, ICJ Reports 2004* (hereinafter '*Wall Advisory Opinion*'), 136, paras 154–60; International Law Commission, Articles on Responsibility of States for Internationally Wrongful Acts (2001), Art. 48 (1)(b), reproduced in J Crawford, *The International Law Commission's Articles on State Responsibility* (CUP, 2002), and ibid., Commentary on Art. 25, para 18, Commentary on Part 2, Chapter III, and Commentary on Art. 48, paras 8–10; M Ragazzi, *The Concept of International Obligations* Erga Omnes (OUP, 1997). On universal jurisdiction for certain crimes in international law, see, e.g., Princeton Project on Universal Jurisdiction, *The Princeton Principles on Universal Jurisdiction* (Princeton, New Jersey: Program in Law and Public Affairs, 2001); L Reydams, *Universal Jurisdiction International and Municipal Legal Perspectives* (OUP, 2004); A Cassese, 'Is the Bell Tolling for Universality? A Plea for a Sensible Notion of Universal Jurisdiction', 1 (2003) *Journal of International Criminal Justice* 589; R O'Keefe, 'Universal Jurisdiction: Clarifying the Basic Concept', 2 (2004) *Journal of International Criminal Justice* 735; and the sources, including cases, cited in these works.

[89] See generally the sources cited above, n. 88, in particular the dictum of the ICJ in the *Wall Advisory Opinion*, para. 159.

[90] See, e.g., the duty to prosecute grave breaches of the four 1949 Geneva Conventions (Geneva Convention (I) for the Amelioration of the Condition of the Wounded and Sick in Armed Forces in the Field, 12 August 1949, 75 UNTS 31, Art. 49; Geneva Convention (II) for the Amelioration of the Condition of the Wounded, Sick and Shipwrecked Members of Armed Forces at Sea, Geneva, 12 August 1949, 75 UNTS 85, Art. 50; Geneva Convention (III) Relative to the Treatment of Prisoners of War, Geneva, 12 August 1949, 75 UNTS 135, Art. 129; Geneva Convention (IV) Relative to the Protection of Civilian Persons in Time of War, Geneva, 12 August 1949, 75 UNTS 287, Art. 146). See also the Convention on the Prevention and Punishment of the Crime of Genocide, New York, 9 December 1948, 78 UNTS 277, Art. I and Art. VI. A large number of international treaties providing for the criminalization of particular conduct contain obligations to prosecute or extradite suspects: see, e.g., Convention against Torture and Other Cruel, Inhuman or Degrading Treatment or Punishment, New York, 10 December 1984, 1465 UNTS 85, Arts 4, 5, and 7. On issues of prosecution by individual states and the International Criminal Court (ICC) as a matter of the ICC Statute, see Statute of the International Criminal Court, Rome, 17 July 1998, 2187 UNTS 90, preamble, para. 6; Arts 17, 90, 98 (for the crimes covered, see ibid., Arts 5–8).

human rights abuses, which draw on 'just war' theory and are commonly described as 'humanitarian intervention'.[91] For certain liberal scholars, the corollary to notions of equivocal sovereignty is that an 'illiberal' state forfeits its sovereignty and thus its entitlement to non-intervention; thus a normative basis is laid for intervention, including intervention seeking to somehow make such an entity 'liberal' through what has come to be termed 'regime change'.[92]

The relevance of this right/duty in legitimizing the use of ITA, which will be discussed further in the following chapter, is twofold.[93] In the first place, it legitimizes intervention, even, for some, military 'humanitarian intervention', to facilitate the introduction of some kind of ITA that will supposedly enable the implementation of community values such as human rights where they had previously been breached; in such cases, human rights trump sovereignty/non-intervention.[94] This idea can be seen, for example, in the introduction of UNMIK in Kosovo following the NATO bombing of what was then called the FRY: just as the bombing was justified by its proponents as guaranteeing core global values of respect for human rights in a negative sense, by preventing a feared genocide of the Kosovar Albanians, so the UN administration it enabled has also been explained in terms of guaranteeing these rights in a positive sense, by conducting governance that will supposedly emancipate the population. It is also evident in the involvement of international appointees on locally-based criminal tribunals, when such tribunals have been involved in prosecuting 'international' crimes.

In the second place, this right/duty posits a more generalized notion, applicable after any form of military intervention: that those intervening, and other states and the UN generally, can or should 'reconstruct' and transform the state, including its political and economic institutions; this is reflected, for example, in the 'responsibility to rebuild' conceived as part of the 'responsibility to protect'.[95] Such a notion can be seen both in ITA projects where the objective moves beyond the original purpose associated with the introduction of ITA—for example, in

---

[91] The literature on this topic is voluminous: examples of note, containing further references, are O Corten and P Klein, *Droit d'ingérence ou obligation de réaction?* (2nd edn, Bruylant, 1996); SD Murphy, *Humanitarian Intervention: The United Nations in an Evolving World Order* (University of Pennsylvania Press, 1996); FR Tesón, *Humanitarian Intervention* (above n. 77); NJ Wheeler, *Saving Strangers: Humanitarian Intervention in International Society* (OUP, 2000); S Chesterman, *Just War or Just Peace?: Humanitarian Intervention and International Law* (OUP, 2001); N Crawford, *Argument and Change in World Politics: Ethics, Decolonization, and Humanitarian Intervention* (CUP, 2002), ch. 9; RC DiPrizio, *Armed Humanitarians: U.S. Interventions from Northern Iraq to Kosovo* (Johns Hopkins University Press, 2002); TM Franck, *Recourse to Force, State Action against Threats and Armed Attacks* (CUP, 2002), ch. 9; JL Holzgrefe and RO Keohane (eds), *Humanitarian Intervention* (CUP, 2003); Orford (above n. 78), *passim*; C Gray, *International Law and the Use of Force* (2nd edn, OUP, 2004), 31–58; T Weiss, *Humanitarian Intervention* (Polity Press, 2007); J Welsh (ed.), *Humanitarian Intervention and International Relations* (OUP, 2007).

[92] For one example, of a thesis on 'pro-democratic' intervention, see Tesón, *Humanitarian Intervention* (above n. 77).

[93] See below, ch. 8, section 8.7.2.2.

[94] See Jackson (above n. 46), ch. 11 *passim* and especially 31.

[95] Quotation taken from the Report of the International Commission on Intervention and State Sovereignty (above n. 86), part 5.

Kosovo, where UNMIK aimed not only to enfranchise the local population, but also to transform politics and the economy more generally—and in ITA projects which come into being after an intervention that was not itself concerned with their introduction, and most of the policies with which they are associated. For example, as discussed further in the next chapter, OHR was introduced in Bosnia and Herzegovina after NATO airstrikes in that country were used to end the hostilities there. The explanation given for the military action does not cover most of the policies OHR went on to promote in the country, such as, for example, the privatization of state enterprises.

7.3.4 Exploitation of natural resources

The fourth area of policy that has been promoted by ITA is the exploitation of natural resources, as discussed in Chapter 6. ITA was used in the Saar to enable the implementation of the policy of French exploitation of the mines, which formed part of the wider programme of reparations imposed on Germany after the First World War. So ITA can be considered alongside other international mechanisms involved in implementing those aspects of peace settlements dealing with reparations for war damage, such as the UN Compensation Commission (UNCC) relating to the Iraqi invasion of Kuwait in 1990.[96] In the case of UNTAET's actions enabling the joint exploitation with Australia of the resources in the 'Timor Gap', facilitating resource exploitation was understood as a means of enhancing East Timor's prospects for independent economic viability, forming part of the mission's general objective in this regard.

7.4 Promoting International Peace and Security[97]

7.4.1 Defining peace operations

One particular area of international public policy often associated with ITA projects is the promotion of international peace and security. Indeed, projects conducted by the UN involving elements of territorial administration are commonly subsumed within the general 'peacekeeping' category both within the UN system and by academic commentators.[98] To what extent is this a helpful

[96] On the UN Compensation Commission (UNCC), see SC Res. 687, 3 April 1991; UNCC website, at <http://www2.unog.ch/uncc>; Collier & Lowe (above n. 6), 41–4 and sources cited therein at 41, n. 146.

[97] Some of the ideas below are also discussed in Wilde, 'Representing International Territorial Administration' (above n. 46), at 74–81 and R Wilde, 'Taxonomies of International Peacekeeping: An Alternative Narrative', 9 (2003) *ILSA Journal of International & Comparative Law* 39.

[98] For the representation of certain ITA missions as 'peacekeeping' operations and/or a consideration of how they involve the promotion of international peace and security, see, e.g., R Higgins, *United Nations Peacekeeping, Vol. 2, Asia 1946–1967* (OUP, 1970) (for the Congo mission); R Higgins, *United Nations Peacekeeping, Vol. 3, Africa 1946–1967* (OUP, 1980) (for the

classification for ITA? Since the concept of 'peacekeeping' is used in various, sometimes mutually contradictory, ways, it is necessary to set out a working definition for the purposes of this study.[99]

In the first place, it seems preferable to adopt the category of 'peace operations'. This category, utilized by the UN 'Brahimi Report' of 2000 about such missions, reflects the fact that the nature of multinational interventions has changed considerably, and that 'peacekeeping' is better considered as part of a broader series of UN operations 'on the ground' or 'in the field' that share the common enterprise

West Irian mission); SR Ratner, *The New UN Peacekeeping, Building Peace in Lands of Conflict after the Cold War* (St. Martin's Press, 1995); A Zacarias, *The United Nations and International Peacekeeping* (Tauris Academic Studies, 1996); Chesterman, *You, The People* (above n. 45), ch. 3 *passim*; Gray (above n. 91), 210–11; S Morphet, 'UN Peacekeeping and Election Monitoring', in A Roberts and B Kingsbury (eds), *United Nations, Divided World: The UN's Roles in International Relations* (2nd edn, Clarendon Press, 1993); Merrills (above n. 6), 256–63; Hampson, 'Can Peacebuilding Work' (above n. 54), *passim*; V Shustov, 'Transitional Civil Administration within the framework of UN Peacekeeping Operations', 7 (2001) *International Peacekeeping* 417; M Bothe, 'Peacekeeping', in B Simma (ed.), *The Charter of the United Nations. A Commentary* (2nd edn, OUP, 2002), 648, at 665–80; B Kondoch, 'The United Nations Administration of East Timor', 6 (2001) *Journal of Conflict & Security Law* 245, at 246 (on UNTAET and UNMIK); Bothe & Marauhn (above n. 16), *passim* (mainly on UNMIK and UNTAET, and discussed further in ch. 8, below); Perritt (above n. 46), 436–7. On peacekeeping/UN peace operations generally, see *Agenda for Peace* (above n. 15); *Supplement to Agenda for Peace: Position Paper of the Secretary General on the Occasion of the Fiftieth Anniversary of the United Nations*, Report of the Secretary-General, 3 January 1995, UN Doc A/50/60-S/1995/1 (hereinafter '*Agenda for Peace Supplement*'); Panel on United Nations Peace Operations, Report to the United Nations Secretary-General, 21 August 2000, UN Doc. A/55/305-S/2000/809 (hereinafter 'Brahimi Report'); UNITAR, *The United Nations and the Maintenance of Peace and Security* (Kluwer, 1987), section 3; R Higgins, *United Nations Peacekeeping, Vol. 1, The Middle East 1946–1967* (OUP, 1969); R Higgins, *United Nations Peacekeeping, Vol. 2*, ibid.; R Higgins, *United Nations Peacekeeping, Vol. 3*, ibid.; R Higgins, *United Nations Peacekeeping, Vol. 4, Europe 1946–1979* (OUP, 1981); Ratner, ibid.; Zacarias, ibid.; N White, *Keeping the Peace: The United Nations and the Maintenance of International Peace and Security* (2nd edn, Manchester University Press, 1997); O Ramsbotham and T Woodhouse (eds), *Encyclopedia of International Peacekeeping Operations* (ABC-Clio Ltd., 1999); N White, *The Law of International Organizations* (Manchester University Press, 1996), 181–5 (not covered in the second edition of the same work); AJ Bellamy, PR Williams and S Griffin, *Understanding Peacekeeping* (Polity Press, 2004); I Johnstone (ed.), *Annual Review of Global Peace Operations 2007* (NYU Center on International Cooperation/Lynne Rienner, 2007); Morphet, ibid.; C Gray, 'Peacekeeping After the Brahimi Report: Is There a Crisis of Credibility for the UN?', 6 (2001) *Journal of Conflict & Security Law* 267; Bothe, ibid.; J-M Guéhenno, 'On the Challenges and Achievements of Reforming UN Peace Operations, 9 (2002) *International Peacekeeping* 69; A Orakhelashvili, 'The Legal Basis of the United Nations Peace-Keeping Operations', 43 (2002–03) *Virginia Journal of International Law* 485; AJ Bellamy, 'The "Next Stage" in Peace Operations Theory?', 11 (2004) *International Peacekeeping* 17; AJ Bellamy and PR Williams, 'Thinking Anew about Peace Operations', 11 (2004) *International Peacekeeping* 1; AJ Bellamy and PR Williams, 'What Future for Peace Operations? Brahimi and Beyond', 11 (2004) *International Peacekeeping* 183; Fearon & Laitin (above n. 45); MW Doyle and N Sambanis, *Making War and Building Peace: United Nations Peace Operations* (Princeton University Press, 2006).

[99] For definitions of peacekeeping, see, e.g., A James, *Peacekeeping in International Politics* (Macmillan, 1990), *passim*; Morphet (above n. 98), 184; White, *Keeping the Peace* (above n. 98), 207; Ramsbotham & Woodhouse (above n. 98), xi–xii.

of the promotion of peace and security.[100] This series of peace operations was set out in the then Secretary-General Boutros Boutros-Ghali's 1992 *Agenda for Peace*.[101] Although that document is now somewhat discredited because of the ambitious nature of some of its prescriptions, notably its 'peace enforcement units' operating under the authority of the Secretary-General, the taxonomy outlined therein continues to enjoy currency.[102] Boutros-Ghali's different classifications were subsequently adopted (without attribution), in a slightly different formulation, by the Brahimi Report. They cover conflict prevention (or 'preventative diplomacy'), peacemaking, peacekeeping, and peacebuilding.[103] These classifications are based on the particular pacific enterprise being pursued, thereby offering a way of understanding field operations by international organizations in general, and ITA projects in particular, in terms of their relationship to the prevention and containment of armed conflict and the concomitant promotion of peace.[104] In using these classifications to explore this relationship, they will be applied to all ITA projects, irrespective of whether projects were classified in this manner at the time and/or have been so classified since.[105] In the following analysis, the idea of 'peace enforcement' will be side-stepped when this term is understood to mean the use of military force to end conflict directly, since the issue of the use of force is not itself part of this study.[106]

[100] However, the series of peace operations discussed below are still sometimes holistically characterized, both within and outside the UN, as 'peacekeeping' operations. For an alternative definition of peace operations, see Ramsbotham & Woodhouse (above n. 98), xix. For the Brahimi Report, see above, n. 98.

[101] *Agenda for Peace* (above n. 15). On this report, see, e.g., Ramsbotham & Woodhouse (above n. 98), 1–2.

[102] For the peace enforcement units, see *Agenda for Peace* (above n. 15), paras 44–5. See also *Agenda for Peace Supplement* (above n. 98), paras 77–80, which discusses peace enforcement without the controversial enforcement units suggestion.

[103] The Brahimi Report (above n. 98) presents the first two types of peace operation as a single category; they are presented here separately, as in *Agenda for Peace*.

[104] In *Agenda for Peace*, Boutros Boutros-Ghali remarked that the four activities taken together offered 'a coherent contribution towards securing peace in the spirit of the Charter'; *Agenda for Peace* (above n. 15), para. 22.

[105] Some commentators reserve the term 'peacekeeping' for UN operations; for example Boutros Boutros-Ghali calls it 'the invention of the United Nations' (*Agenda for Peace* (above n. 15), para. 46). However, other commentators trace peacekeeping further back. Alan James, for example, traces the origins of peacekeeping back to the delimitation commission of the 1920s; James (above n. 99), 24. See also P Diehl, *International Peacekeeping* (Johns Hopkins University Press, 1993), 17–20, on the League of Nations, and Ratner (above n. 98), 90–6, on 'peacekeeping by other names' conducted in the League era.

[106] On 'peace enforcement' see, e.g., *Agenda for Peace* (above n. 15), paras 44–5; *Agenda for Peace Supplement* (above n. 98), paras 77–80; Gray (above n. 91), 217–30; D Sarooshi, *The United Nations and the Development of Collective Security* (OUP, 1999), *passim*; White, *The Law of International Organizations* (above n. 98), 191–8 (not covered in the second edition of the same work); A James, 'The enforcement provisions of the United Nations Charter', in UNITAR, *The United Nations and the Maintenance of Peace and Security* (Kluwer, 1987), 213; Ramsbotham & Woodhouse (above n. 98), xxi, 198–9.

7.4.2 The relationship between ITA projects and the promotion of peace and security

The general role of ITA in relation to the promotion of peace and security comes out of the particular role it performs in relation to the prevention and settlement of disputes, and the implementation of settlements and international policy, outlined above. Following from Collier & Lowe's distinction, the use of ITA in relation to a specific dispute is often (although not always) aimed at addressing a broader conflict within which the dispute is situated, even though it may have a limited effect in this regard. Like the dispute-settlement and policy implementation roles, the use of ITA here can be seen to constitute the implementation and fulfilment of obligations borne by states and international organizations. In the case of states, the obligation under Article 2(4) of the UN Charter to 'refrain...from the threat or use of force' is ostensibly being implemented.[107] In the case of international organizations, notably the UN, the central obligation to promote international peace and security is ostensibly being realized. Under Article 1(1) of the UN Charter, the purpose of the organization is 'to maintain international peace and security, and to that end, to take effective collective measures for the prevention and removal of threats to the peace'.[108] It is notable in this regard that an unsuccessful Norwegian proposal made at the 1945 San Francisco Conference to include explicit authority in the Charter for the exercise of territorial administration by the United Nations conceived this authority in terms of the Security Council and in relation to '...any territory of which the continued administration by the state in possession is found to constitute a threat to the peace'.[109]

The first category of peace operation covers 'conflict prevention'. *Agenda for Peace* defines 'preventative diplomacy' as '[a]ction to prevent disputes from arising between parties, to prevent existing disputes from escalating into conflicts and to limit the spread of the latter when they occur'.[110] Those ITA projects concerned with the prevention of disputes can be seen as mechanisms for preventing conflict. For example, the dispute between France and Germany over

---

[107] UN Charter, Art. 2(4).   [108] Ibid., Art. 1(1).

[109] Quoted in F Seyersted, 'United Nations Forces, Some Legal Problems', 37 (1962) *BYIL* 351, at 453, n. 2.

[110] *Agenda for Peace* (above n. 15), para. 20. For the Brahimi Report:

[l]ong term conflict prevention addresses the structural causes of conflict in order to build a solid foundation for peace. Where those foundations are crumbling, conflict prevention attempts to reinforce them, usually in the form of a diplomatic initiative. Such preventative action is, by definition, a low-profile activity; when successful, it may even go unnoticed altogether.

Brahimi Report (above n. 98), para. 10. For an academic definition of preventative deployment/conflict prevention, see, e.g., Ramsbotham & Woodhouse (above n. 98), xxi, 47–8. On the UN and preventative diplomacy, see, e.g., *Agenda for Peace* (above n. 15), ch. III; Brahimi Report, paras 29–34; Peck (above n. 15), ch. 7.

possession of the Saar, prevented, insofar as France did not have control from which it could have claimed title, through the use of ITA during the resource exploitation period, could well have led to armed conflict. Moreover, the use of ITA to create a more favourable climate for the resolution of a dispute can be seen also as a mechanism for ensuring that the dispute does not escalate into armed conflict. The General Assembly's Manila Declaration obliges states to 'refrain from any action whatsoever which may aggravate the situation so as to endanger the maintenance of international peace and security'.[111] In *Agenda for Peace*, Boutros Boutros-Ghali emphasized the significance of preventative deployment, with a UN presence used during periods of tension to ensure that conflict does not break out.[112] This echoes the General Assembly's endorsement, in the Annex to Resolution 43/51, of the role of a 'United Nations presence' that can serve 'as a means of preventing the further deterioration of the dispute'.[113] The 'neutralization' of Leticia by the League can be seen as a prime example of the performance of this role by ITA.

Seeking to settle a particular dispute through an ITA project (with the project as either a settlement mechanism or the settlement itself) can be viewed as a means of ending something that might have escalated into war. Of course, 'conflict prevention' can be understood in a broader sense, as the enterprise of addressing 'the structural sources of conflict in order to build a solid foundation for peace'.[114] These sources of conflict are wide-ranging, but include the highly contested issues of identity, human rights, security, community, and welfare that are significantly affected by the idea of using ITA to promote the policy objectives—from territorial status to free and fair elections—outlined above. As far as seeking to neutralize conflict emanating from the territory affected, one crucial strand of thought here is the 'liberal peace' thesis, drawing on the Kantian ideas, that, put simply, 'liberal' or 'democratic' states don't go to war with each other (though they do go to war with 'non-liberal' states).[115] The 'statebuilding' use of ITA, then, can be understood in liberal terms as a matter of both the perceived value of the governance policies being promoted in and of themselves, as discussed above, and the perceived benefits this promotion can have for international order generally.[116]

---

[111] Manila Declaration (above n. 11), Part I, para. 8.
[112] *Agenda for Peace* (above n. 15), paras 28–33.
[113] GA Res. 43/51 (above n. 8), Annex, para. 12.
[114] Brahimi Report (above n. 98), para. 10.
[115] See the sources cited in n. 77 above. On international efforts to link democratic governance with international peace and security, see, e.g., Franck (above n. 36), 89. In *Agenda for Peace*, Boutros Boutros-Ghali remarked that '[t]here is an obvious connection between democratic practices—such as the rule of law and transparency in decision-making—and the achievement of true peace and security in any new and stable political order'; *Agenda for Peace* (above n. 15), para. 59.
[116] See generally Paris, *At War's End* (above n. 45).

The second category of peace operation is 'peacemaking', defined in *An Agenda for Peace* as '...action to bring hostile parties to agreement, essentially through such peaceful means as those foreseen in Chapter VI of the Charter of the United Nations'.[117] Again, the use of ITA to provide a dispute settlement mechanism or to act as the settlement to a dispute can be seen as a 'peacemaking' initiative, in that settling a particular dispute may entail an end to the broader armed conflict connected to that dispute.[118] The international administration of self-determination consultations, for example, is sometimes regarded as a mechanism for addressing the particular grievance that may lie at the heart of an armed struggle, such as the self-determination aspirations of the Frente POLISARIO in Western Sahara. Of course, using ITA in this way may prove inadequate in preventing violence. Indeed, it may precipitate further armed conflict, particularly when the 'settlement' is not accepted by one of the disputants. An example of this would be the violence by pro-Indonesian militias who objected to the result of the UNAMET-conducted 'popular consultation' in East Timor in 1999. In that situation, a military 'peace enforcement' project—the Australian-led INTERFET—was deemed necessary to respond to the consequences of an earlier 'peacemaking' mission.

These connections between the use of ITA and dispute settlement and prevention are further illustrated in the prescriptions offered by those promoting the idea of 'earned sovereignty' mentioned earlier.[119] For its advocates, earned sovereignty is a device for addressing threats to international peace and security caused by disputes over sovereignty. The endgame is 'managed devolution' from a state to a sub-state entity, via the adoption of standards concerning good governance and minority rights which the entity in question must adopt before it can 'earn' its sovereignty. Forms of ITA are seen as one of the main mechanisms for ensuring the adoption of these standards.[120]

Both 'peacekeeping' and 'peacebuilding' missions, as their names suggest, are understood as taking place when there has been some form of abatement

---

[117] Ibid., para 20. The Brahimi Report states that:

[p]eacemaking addresses conflicts in progress, attempting to bring them to a halt, using the tools of diplomacy and mediation. Peacemakers may be envoys of Governments, groups of states, regional organizations or the United Nations, or they may be unofficial and non-governmental groups, as was the case, for example, in the negotiations leading up to a peace accord for Mozambique. Peacemaking may even be the work of a prominent personality, working independently.

Brahimi Report (above, n. 98), para. 11. For an academic definition, see, e.g., Ramsbotham & Woodhouse (above n. 98), xx. On peacemaking generally, see, e.g., *Agenda for Peace* (above n. 15), ch. IV; Brahimi Report, paras 29–34.

[118] *Agenda for Peace* underlines the role of a particular dispute settlement mechanism—the International Court of Justice—as a form of peacemaking; see *Agenda for Peace* (above, n. 15), paras 38–9.

[119] See above, n. 81.

[120] For example, UNMIK in Kosovo. See the sources cited above, ch. 6, n. 76.

in armed conflict. They are, necessarily, 'post-conflict' missions.[121] As the Brahimi Report states, 'peacekeeping' was originally 'primarily a military model of observing ceasefires and force separations after inter-state wars', but became a 'complex model of many elements, military and civilian, working together to build peace in the dangerous aftermath of civil wars'.[122] The key distinction between 'peacekeeping' and 'peacebuilding' is a temporal one. For the Brahimi Report, missions in the latter category take place 'on the far side of conflict' and attempt 'to reassemble the foundations of peace and provide the tools for building on those foundations something that is more than just the absence of war'.[123] The dichotomy between the two models of peacekeeping—in terms of complexity of purpose, the involvement of civilians,

---

[121] If one adopts 'peacekeeping' as the holistic term for all UN peace operations, then it is not necessarily always a post-conflict phenomenon. In particular, so-called 'peace enforcement' is concerned with preventing conflict, not keeping the peace once conflict has abated. For example, the UN Protection Force (UNPROFOR) in Bosnia and Herzegovina operated during conflict, but was not engaged in preventing this; rather, it distributed humanitarian supplies, being able to use force only in self-defence. This interposition of a 'peacekeeping', rather than a 'peace enforcement', mission during a conflict was widely criticised as an inappropriate utilization of the peacekeeping institution. See, e.g., R Higgins, 'Second Generation Peacekeeping', 89 (1995) *ASIL Proc.* 275. On UNPROFOR, see the UNPROFOR website, at <http://www.un.org/Depts/dpko/dpko/co_mission/unprofor.htm>.

[122] Brahimi Report (above n. 98), para. 12. *Agenda for Peace* defines peacekeeping as:

...the deployment of a United Nations presence in the field, hitherto with the consent of all parties concerned, normally involving United Nations military and/or police personnel and frequently civilians as well. Peace-keeping is a technique that expands the possibilities for both the prevention of conflict and the making of peace.

Agenda for Peace (above n. 15), para. 20. As for the increased role of civilians, Boutros Boutros-Ghali remarks that, '[i]ncreasingly, peace-keeping requires that civilian political officers, human rights monitors, electoral officials, refugee and humanitarian aid specialists and police play as central a role as the military'; ibid., para. 52. In a similar vein, the UN DPKO website states that:

[i]ncreasingly...the many faces of peacekeeping include civilian police officers, electoral experts and observers, deminers, human rights monitors, and specialists in civil affairs and communications. Their responsibilities range from protecting and delivering humanitarian assistance, to helping former opponents carry out complicated peace agreements; from assisting with the demobilization of former fighters and their return to normal life, to supervising and conducting elections; from training civilian police, to monitoring respect for human rights and investigating alleged violations.

UN Department of Peacekeeping Operations, *An Introduction to United Nations Peacekeeping*, Preface, available at <http://www.un.org/Depts/dpko/dpko/intro/intro.htm>. For an academic definition of peacekeeping, see, e.g., Ramsbotham & Woodhouse (above n. 98), xx. On peacekeeping generally, see, e.g., *Agenda for Peace* (above n. 15), ch. V; *Agenda for Peace Supplement* (above n. 98), paras 33–46; Brahimi Report (above n. 98), paras 48–55.

[123] Brahimi Report (above n. 98), para. 13. *Agenda for Peace* describes peacebuilding as '...action to identify and support structures which will tend to strengthen and solidify peace in order to avoid a relapse into conflict'; *Agenda for Peace* (above n. 15), para. 21. For an academic definition of peacebuilding, see, e.g., Ramsbotham & Woodhouse (above n. 98), xx. On peacebuilding generally, see *Agenda for Peace*, ibid., ch. VI; *Agenda for Peace Supplement* (above n. 98), paras 47–65; Brahimi Report (above n. 98), paras 35–47; Peck (above n. 15), chs 5 and 6; A Schnabel, 'Post-Conflict Peacebuilding and Second-Generation Preventive Action', 9 (2002) *International Peacekeeping* 7.

and the different type of conflict—has become the frame through which 'post-conflict' peace operations generally, whether peacekeeping or peacebuilding, are understood. This dichotomy is described variously in terms of old versus new;[124] classical or traditional versus multifunctional or multidimensional;[125] and first generation versus second generation.[126] Whereas peacekeeping missions can fall into either category, peacebuilding missions, by virtue of their long-term objectives, necessarily fall into the latter category, at least in terms of complexity and the involvement of civilians.

Many of the ITA projects have been introduced in the 'post-conflict' context and the objectives of such projects can be partially explained in terms of a response to the consequences of armed conflict. In particular, most ITA projects engaged in 'state-building' are responding to the breakdown in infrastructure as a result of conflict, whether the civil war in the Congo between 1960 and 1964 or the destruction wrought by the pro-Indonesian militias in East Timor in 1999. Projects of this type are often described as 'post-conflict reconstruction'[127] operations, and the involvement of the UN in this enterprise has been characterized through the striking metaphor of 'painting a country blue'.[128] It is common to associate this use of peace missions with the consequences of 'civil' or 'internal' conflict in particular.[129] However, in some states where ITA has been used in part to address issues arising out of a conflict, for example, in Cambodia and Bosnia and Herzegovina, the conflict

[124] E.g., WJ Durch (ed.), *The Evolution of UN Peacekeeping* (St. Martin's Press, 1994), 9; Ratner (above n. 98); Ramsbotham & Woodhouse (above n. 98).

[125] E.g., Higgins (above n. 121), 275; Ramsbotham & Woodhouse (above, n. 98), xiii–xvi, 93; R Lee, 'United Nations Peacekeeping: Developments and Prospects', 28 (1995) *Cornell International Law Journal* 619, 621.

[126] E.g., 'UN Peacekeeping: An Early Reckoning of the Second Generation', 89 (1995) *ASIL Proc.* 275; J Chopra, 'Peace Maintenance: A Concept for Collective Political Authority', 89 (1995) *ASIL Proc.* 280; MW Doyle, 'Remarks', 89 (1995) *ASIL Proc.* 275, at 275; Higgins (above n. 121), 275; Ratner (above n. 98); Ramsbotham & Woodhouse (above n. 98), 93, 218–19; Gray (above n. 91), 210; Kondoch (above n. 98), 246.

[127] On 'post-conflict reconstruction', see, e.g., Ramsbotham & Woodhouse (above n. 98), 200–1.

[128] On 'painting the country blue', a phrase attributed to Douglas Hurd during his time as the UK Foreign Secretary, see, ibid., 195.

[129] So, for example, in his *Supplement* to the *Agenda for Peace*, Boutros Boutros-Ghali remarked that:

[a] feature of such ['intra-state'] conflicts is the collapse of state institutions, especially the police and judiciary, with resulting paralysis of governance, a breakdown of law and order, and general banditry and chaos. Not only are the functions of government suspended, its assets are destroyed or looted and experienced officials are killed or flee the country. This is rarely the case in inter-state wars. It means that international intervention must extend beyond military and humanitarian tasks and must include the promotion of national reconciliation and the re-establishment of effective government.

Agenda for Peace Supplement (above n. 98), para. 13.

that led to governmental collapse cannot properly be described as exclusively 'internal' or 'civil' in character.[130]

ITA projects conducted by international organizations (as distinct from the mere involvement of international appointees on locally-based administrative bodies) often involving civilian as well as military staff performing a variety of functions, fall clearly into the 'complex' model of peace operations. Plenary ITA in the post-conflict context is multifunctional 'peacekeeping' and 'peacebuilding' *par excellence*. Then UN Deputy Secretary-General Louise Fréchette remarked that plenary administration is a '…new order of magnitude for peacekeeping operations…making them extraordinarily complex and almost as dependent on civilian experts as on military personnel'.[131]

For many commentators, there was a sea-change in the nature of peacekeeping from the late 1980s onwards: a 'turning point', in the words of Jarat Chopra.[132] With the backdrop of the post-Cold War internationalist revival, and the idea that a 'different' type of conflict, both international and internal in character, was predominating, there was a dramatic growth in complex post-conflict UN peace operations, starting with UNTAG in Namibia in 1989–90.[133] Accordingly, for many, there was a paradigmatic shift from 'first generation' to 'second generation', from 'old to 'new' peacekeeping.[134] With the Kosovo and East Timor projects, it has been suggested that complexity has reached such a level that it is possible to talk about a further generation of peacekeeping.[135] As will be discussed further in the next chapter, which is concerned with the relationship between ITA and

---

[130] Steven Ratner describes the conflict in Cambodia in the following terms: '…a civil war amongst four factions, each of which had taken a turn at governing the country since its independence from France; invasion by a neighboring state seeking regional hegemony; external assistance to the factions; support of the belligerents by the major powers…'; SR Ratner, 'The Cambodian Settlement Agreements', 87 (1993) *AJIL* 1, at 1.

[131] Statement by Louise Fréchette, Deputy Secretary-General of the United Nations, Press Release DSG/SM/91, 3 April 2000, cited in Gray (above n. 91), 210.

[132] Chopra (above n. 126), 280.

[133] On the idea of a different type of conflict taking place during this period, e.g., M Kaldor, *New and Old Wars* (2nd edn, Polity Press, 2006). On UN peace operations since 1988, and the increase in them, see, e.g., Durch (above n. 124), 9–12; Ramsbotham & Woodhouse (above n. 98), xiii–xix. Many scholars assert a causal relationship between the post-1988 upsurge in peacekeeping and the end of the Cold War. See, e.g., Ratner (above n. 98), 14–16. For a critique of this thesis, see, e.g., James (above n. 99), 362–6.

[134] In a complementary development in academic discourse, Mary Kaldor described a supposed paradigmatic shift in the nature of conflict (mentioned earlier) in terms of 'old' and 'new wars'; Kaldor (above n. 133).

[135] Christine Gray observes that these two projects could be described as 'third generation' peacekeeping; Gray (above n. 91), 211. Boris Kondoch, citing W Kühn, considers 'peace enforcement' missions such as UNOSOM II in Somalia 'third generation' peacekeeping and UNTAET and UNMIK—because of their complexity—examples of 'fourth generation' peacekeeping; Kondoch (above n. 98), 246. Most scholars consider 'peace enforcement' missions as a special type of 'second generation' peacekeeping, rather than a separate 'generation' of the peacekeeping paradigm. See, e.g., 'UN Peacekeeping: An Early Reckoning of the Second Generation', above, n. 126.

one particular area of international public policy—trusteeship and the civilizing mission—Michael Bothe and Thilo Marauhn argue that UNTAET and UNMIK are, because of their complexity, 'new', and, as such, warrant separate treatment from all other peace operations under a new category they call 'Security Council trusteeship administration'.[136]

Whereas missions can be classified meaningfully in terms of the level of complexity and degree of involvement by civilians, it is more difficult to present the history of international peace operations in terms of a progressive evolution through successive generations of ever-increasing complexity, as the language of 'generations' and the 'old'/'new' dichotomy suggest. If one is focusing on the complexity of the tasks performed by such missions, and the presence of civilian officials, then, as suggested earlier, one is surely going to be concerned, inter alia, with missions involving the exercise of administrative prerogatives. If so, complex peace operations have had a long history. Whether one is focusing on plenary administration or partial administration, international organizations generally or the United Nations in particular, the history of international territorial administration suggests that the complex international peace operations from 1988 onwards are, in terms of their complexity, nothing new.

The first complex peace operations involving plenary administration were the Saar in 1920 (in the League era) and West Irian in 1962–63 (in the UN era); the first such missions involving partial administration were Danzig in 1920 (in the League era) and the Congo in 1960–64 (in the UN era). Perhaps some commentators are only concerned with the 'state-building' aspect of 'post-conflict' peace operations—that exercising territorial prerogatives is one thing, but the use of such prerogatives with a 'state-building' purpose is a relatively new phenomenon. Whereas ONUC in the 1960s is widely regarded as the first UN operation to engage in 'peace enforcement',[137] the equally pioneering 'state-building' administrative activities of that same mission are rarely acknowledged.[138] Yet, once the full scope of ONUC's operation is borne in mind, it becomes just as difficult to see a clear distinction between post-and pre-1998 operations on 'state-building' grounds as it is on 'enforcement' grounds.[139] Certainly, the next operations of these types did not take place until the post-1988 era (Namibia in 1989–90 for 'state-building' and UNOSOM II in 1991 for 'peace enforcement'). The point is that the enterprise that lay behind these later operations was not unprecedented.

'State-building' is not, then, an exclusively post-1998 phenomenon. But a qualitative difference is perhaps in evidence as between UNMIK and UNTAET, on the one hand, and the 'state-building' projects that came before them, on

[136] Bothe & Marauhn (above n. 16). See the discussion in the next chapter, section 8.3.3.
[137] E.g., Durch (above n. 124), 8; Lee (above, n. 125), 624.
[138] A notable exception is Steven Ratner; see Ratner (above, n. 98), 105–09.
[139] Like 'state-building', 'peace enforcement' is often presented as a 'new' phenomenon through reference to 'generations', whether second or third.

the other. Arguably, the degree to which these two projects have engaged in the reconstruction of infrastructure and governmental institutions is unprecedented as far as ITA is concerned.[140] A question remains, however, as to whether the scope of a 'state-building' mandate should be the exclusive standard by which complexity is measured. For example, what of plenary administration concerned with territorial disposition? Is the three-year UN administration in Eastern Slavonia, for example, which necessitated the eventual transfer of a territory and its people to the control of authorities from whom local militias had hitherto sought independence, necessarily less complex than the three-year East Timor project, where, infrastructural problems notwithstanding, the eventual outcome for the territory was overwhelmingly supported? Similarly, what of administration aimed at facilitating a particularly controversial policy? Stepping back to the League era, can it really be said that the three-year long project in East Timor is more complex than the 15-year project in the Saar? The League was involved in administering a territory bitterly contested between France and Germany, enabling a key component of Germany's much resented reparations programme, before organizing a limited form of self-determination plebiscite (full independence was not an option) and then implementing the result of that plebiscite.

Actually, neither *Agenda for Peace,* nor its *Supplement,* nor the Brahimi Report were particularly concerned with a progressivist presentation of the complexity of international peace operations, even though, by virtue of their remit, these reports were able to discount the League era projects that so obviously undermine such a presentation. In *Agenda for Peace,* the terms 'new' and 'second-generation' peacekeeping are absent.[141] Only one, passing reference (in a table) is made to 'classical' and 'multifunctional' peacekeeping in the *Supplement* to *Agenda for Peace*;[142] similarly, the Brahimi Report makes the odd reference to 'new generation' or 'newer generations' of peacekeeping without defining these terms.[143] Nonetheless, the language of 'generations' has come to play a central role in academic discourse on peace operations since the early 1990s. So one has, on the one hand, a set of historical circumstances placing into question the notion that complex international peace operations are an exclusively late-20th-century phenomenon and, on the other hand, an established academic discourse predicated on this notion.

---

[140] But not if one broadens the focus, as will be done in ch. 8, below, to foreign territorial administration generally, which would bring in, for example, the allied administrations of postwar Germany, Austria, and Japan. Writing in 1999, before the Kosovo and East Timor projects, Ramsbotham & Woodhouse remarked that, '[t]he most extensive peace-building effort in history took place in Europe and Asia in the post-World War II era when the US and its allies assisted nations in those continents devastated by a decade of war'; Ramsbotham & Woodhouse (above n. 98), xx.

[141] As are the terms 'old' and 'first generation' peacekeeping.

[142] *Agenda for Peace Supplement* (above n. 98), Table.

[143] Brahimi Report (above n. 98), paras 102, 128, 140.

One of the few scholars writing in the 'new' era to acknowledge the long-standing existence of complex international peace operations is Steven Ratner's 1995 book *The New UN Peacekeeping*.[144] However, as his title suggests, Ratner adopts the language of 'generations' and the 'new'/'old' dichotomy in his study of such operations, perhaps because of the widespread currency this approach enjoyed at the time. One quarter of his book concerns operations—the League projects and ONUC, for example—that took place before the 'new' era, in some cases 70 years before.[145] These projects are described as examples of the 'new' peacekeeping; in order to accommodate the problem this raises with the 'new'/'old' dichotomy, the presence of these projects in the 'old' era is explained in terms of 'earlier efforts' at the 'new' paradigm.[146] For example, the League administration in the Saar is 'second generation peacekeeping before its time'.[147] When there are so many earlier efforts, stretching back over such a long period, of a supposedly 'new' phenomenon, are the dichotomies of 'new'/'old' and 'first generation'/'second generation' helpful? Why was 1989 in particular the 'time' of complex peace operations, and not also 1919?[148]

Clearly, some peace operations are more complex than others. Moreover, some projects have a 'state-building' purpose, others do not. The point is that the complexity of peace operations has waxed and waned since the start of the League; similarly, the involvement of such operations in 'state-building' has been present since the 1960s. The 'time' of complexity and civilian involvement in international peace operations has been the entire 20th century and into the 21st century. To be sure, with the ITA projects in Cambodia, Mostar, Eastern Slavonia, Bosnia and Herzegovina, Kosovo, East Timor, and certain 'refugee' camps, and the other complex peace missions without an administration component, the final decade of the 20th century witnessed a marked upsurge in the use of peace operations that were both complex and engaged in a 'state-building' enterprise. However, an upsurge in, and intensification of, an activity with a long-standing pedigree (with the possible exception of the ambitious scope of state-building in Kosovo and East Timor) do not necessarily denote

---

[144] Ratner (above, n. 98).

[145] Ibid., Part II.

[146] Ibid., ch. 4.

[147] Ibid., 91. The League mandate in Danzig is 'a variation on a theme' (ibid., 94) and internationalization experiments in Leticia and Memel are described as 'forgotten forays here and there' (ibid., 95).

[148] Nathaniel Berman's work has highlighted the commonalities between contemporary interventions and certain arrangements during the post-Versailles period in Europe. See N Berman, ' "But the Alternative is Despair", European Nationalism and the Modernist Renewal of International Law', 106 (1992–93) *Harvard Law Review* 1792; N Berman, 'In the Wake of Empire', 14 (1998–99) *American University International Law Review* 1521, at 1531; N Berman, 'Imperial Rivalry and the Genealogy of Human Rights: the Nationality Decrees Case', 94 (2000) *ASIL Proceedings* 53; N Berman, 'Les Ambivalences Impériales', in E Jouannet (ed.), *Impérialisme et Droit International en Europe et en Amérique* (2007); N Berman, 'Intervention in a "Divided World": Axes of Legitimacy', 17 (2006) *EJIL* 769.

the emergence of a 'new' type of peace operation. 1989, then, marks a particular moment of renewal, not a qualitative 'turning point'.

Furthermore, the dramatic increase in peace operations since 1989 has covered both 'complex' and relatively simple (in terms of the range of tasks involved) operations, an example of the latter being the UN ceasefire verification mission on the Ethiopia/Eritrea border, created in 2000.[149] Just as the 'old' era contains many examples of the 'new' peacekeeping, so the 'new' era is replete with 'old' style peacekeeping operations.[150]

The history of international territorial administration suggests that describing the relative complexity of peace operations in terms that suggest a progressive increase over time is mistaken. The language of 'generations' and 'old' versus 'new' peace operations (or peacekeeping) should perhaps be substituted with a taxonomy that does not connote a linear process of historical evolution: for example, 'basic' versus 'complex' or 'multifunctional'. Certainly, this alternative lacks the elegance of 'first generation' versus 'second generation', but, in avoiding the misleading impression such terms can give, it is preferable.

7.4.3 Using the 'peace' and 'post-conflict' labels

No doubt because of the introduction of many ITA projects (and, in particular, the projects in Kosovo and East Timor) after conflict, certain commentators have chosen to label territorial administration by the UN or international organizations generally a 'post-conflict' phenomenon, using the word 'conflict' in the narrow sense of an armed conflict.[151] The involvement of the Security Council in providing legal authority for the missions in resolutions passed under Chapter VII of the UN Charter similarly leads to an essentialized emphasis on the 'peace and security' aspects of the missions, no doubt reflecting the fact that, under Article 39 of the UN Charter, such authority can only be provided if the Council has determined that the situation to which it relates constitutes a 'threat to international peace and security'.[152] In naming UNMIK and UNTAET as 'Security

---

[149] The UN Mission in Ethiopia and Eritrea (UNMEE); see SC Res. 1312, 31 July 2000; see also SC Res. 1320, 15 September 2000; SC Res. 1344, 15 March 2001; SC Res. 1369, 14 September 2001; and SC Res. 1741, 30 January 2007; see also UNMEE website, at <http://www.un.org/Depts/dpko/unmee/body_unmee.htm>, and *Annual Review of Global Peace Operations 2007* (above n. 98), section 4.8.

[150] Most scholars accept that in the 'new' era, 'old' and 'new' peacekeeping coexists. Ratner, for example, states that '[t]oday we witness both the continuation of older first-generation missions as well as the establishment of new ones. Moreover, a given operation can evolve from one [first generation] to the other [second generation] over time...'; Ratner (above n. 98), 17.

[151] See the sources cited above, ch. 1, section 1.2.2.

[152] The authority provided for the missions is not discussed in detail in this book. See, however, the coverage below, ch. 8, section 8.7.2.1. For commentary on the Security Council's general authority under Chapter VII of the UN Charter, and the threshold test of Art. 39, see, e.g., J Frowein and N Krisch, 'Introduction to Chapter VII' and 'Art. 39', in B Simma (ed.), *The Charter of the United Nations. A Commentary* (2nd edn, OUP, 2002) at 701 and 717 respectively, and sources cited therein.

Council trusteeship administration', Michael Bothe and Thilo Marauhn adopt the involvement of the Security Council in providing such authority as a primary characteristic of the missions.[153] They then conceptualize the purposes of the missions exclusively in terms of peace and security; the extended title they give the missions is 'Security Council trusteeship administration for the maintenance or restoration of international peace and security'.[154]

As the foregoing discussion has demonstrated, the relationship between ITA and conflict is complex, not only addressing the consequences of conflict but also trying to prevent conflict from breaking out to begin with (as opposed to preventing its resumption in a 'post-conflict' situation). ITA does not always take place after armed conflict (cf. West Irian), and, even when it does, it is misleading to suggest that all the policy objectives pursued will be connected to that conflict. In Bosnia and Herzegovina, for example, the use of ITA to foster liberal democratic politics and economics in the country has been an attempt to address the consequences of decades of totalitarian rule and centrally planned economics, as well as four years of armed conflict. So the OHR-imposition of property laws, which created individual property rights in a society hitherto operating a socialized form of property ownership, was concerned as much with creating a liberal economic system as with enabling refugees and displaced persons to return to their pre-war homes.

When ITA projects are labelled 'peace operations', 'peacekeeping missions', or 'Security Council trusteeship administrations', the implication is that ITA is an enterprise essentially concerned with the promotion of peace and the end of conflict. Adopting a narrow, literal understanding of conflict, this implication is invariably incorrect—promoting a liberal form of governance, for example, does not keep the peace; armed forces observing a ceasefire may do. Of course, few would adopt such a narrow understanding of the causes of armed conflict. So, as has been assumed in the foregoing analysis, the broad range of policy objectives can perhaps be understood in terms of a causal relationship with peace (cf. the 'liberal peace' thesis discussed earlier). What is objectionable, however, is that, in presenting ITA as a 'peace' operation, these other policy objectives are all reduced to the pursuit of peace. One cannot escape the normative implication that the other policy objectives are being pursued solely because they lead to peace and an end to conflict, and not also because they are of independent value. No doubt, one can argue about whether or not the pursuit of peace is the fundamental objective of any political system.[155] The problem with the 'peace operation' classification is that it implies that this debate is closed.[156]

    [153] Bothe & Marauhn (above n. 16).

    [154] Ibid., quote from 242.

    [155] On this idea in relation to the UN, see, e.g., the comments of the ICJ in *Certain Expenses of the United Nations (Art. 17, paragraph 2, of the Charter), Advisory Opinion, ICJ Reports 1962*, 151, at 167–8.

    [156] One of the problems with essentializing the projects in this way is that fruitful avenues of comparative analysis with analogous activities can be closed off. This is discussed in the context

7.5 Comparing ITA with other Equivalent International Enforcement Modalities

7.5.1 Intrusiveness

The foregoing analysis has explained how ITA can be seen as a mechanism for implementing settlements, enforcing certain areas of international public policy, and promoting peace and security. To what extent does it compare, in terms of the manner in which it operates, with other international mechanisms that aim to have the same effects? One point of comparison is what might be called the 'level of intrusiveness'. This is distinct from the question of consent or imposition (the latter sometimes termed 'intervention'), which will be considered in the next chapter. Rather, the focus is on the relationship between the international mechanism, on the one hand, and the domestic government it attempts to influence, on the other, whether or not this relationship is agreed to by, or imposed upon, the territory concerned. How does ITA compare with other international mechanisms in terms of the intrusive way in which it ensures the implementation of international law? Here, a general distinction can be made between mechanisms that operate at one step removed from the territorial government, and mechanisms that operate at the level of that government.

A significant number of international mechanisms, from international tribunals to particular peace missions, are engaged in promoting the implementation of international law in general, including in the areas of the law set out above. In the main, these mechanisms depend on the state itself to act. Some assist governments in ways that make them better able to implement their legal obligations, such as aid programmes that support government initiatives, and missions involved in training the local police and members of the judiciary.[157] International scrutiny bodies, including judicial tribunals, determine the conformity of a state's conduct with its legal obligations; if unlawful action is found, the state has a moral and sometimes a legal obligation to take whatever steps are required, if any, to remedy the situation and/or compensate those affected.[158] It is left to the state to take these steps.

Similarly, all forms of sanctions regimes, from the threat of non-recognition of statehood to the suspension of trade privileges and arms blockades, are aimed at putting pressure on the state (or aspirant state) to change its behaviour;

---

of colonial trusteeship in the next chapter; see in particular, the discussion of the ideas of Michael Bothe and Thilo Marauhn in section 8.3.3 therein.

[157] Cf. the distinction between 'assistance' and 'conduct/supervision' discussed above, ch. 1, text accompanying n. 93 *et seq.*

[158] On remedies in international law, see, e.g., C Gray, *Judicial Remedies in International Law* (OUP, 1987) and the bibliography in D Shelton, *Remedies in International Human Rights Law* (2nd edn, OUP, 2005), 478.

necessarily, they rely on the state itself to act. Monitoring or verification missions, whether concerned with disarmament, the implementation of peace agreements or the conduct of consultations, are concerned with ensuring that state authorities are complying with particular policy prescriptions, whether destroying weapons, allowing refugees to return, or carrying out consultations in a free and fair manner.[159] Thus, their role is to monitor and influence state behaviour.

ITA does not operate in this way. It aims to achieve implementation by taking over directly those areas of government determinative of the conduct by the state of behaviour in conformity with particular areas of international policy and law. Norms are supposedly implemented because the relevant national administrative process is operated by international officials. International actors are not trying to influence a state's behaviour; they are acting as that state.

This argument about intrusiveness presupposes, then, that ITA is equivalent to other international mechanisms, sharing a common aim of implementing international law and policy. What can also be postulated is that ITA, because of its comparative intrusiveness, is regarded in one sense as superior to other international mechanisms. As a means of enforcement, it is more effective—it does not suffer from being dependent on the state to act, since it operates as part of the state.[160] The comparative effectiveness of ITA in implementing international law and policy can be illustrated in more detail through the example of human rights institutions operating with respect to Bosnia and Herzegovina.

7.5.2 Case study—human rights institutions in Bosnia and Herzegovina

In addition to their role of settling disputes, human rights institutions can be regarded as mechanisms for ensuring the implementation of states' obligations under international human rights law. One obvious way of explaining the role of international human rights machinery, such as the European Court of Human Rights, is in terms of the provision of a remedy to individuals for a breach of their rights under the relevant human rights instrument.

Under the European Convention of Human Rights (ECHR), states are obliged to provide a remedy for breaches of the Convention in national law; when no such remedy is forthcoming, individuals can initiate proceedings in Strasbourg.[161] This

---

[159] For example, the role of the OSCE in elections outside the ITA projects is monitoring or verification rather than conduct or supervision. On this distinction, see also above, ch. 1, n. 93.

[160] See, e.g., Collier & Lowe's commentary on the limited options available if a state is unwilling to implement a decision of the International Court of Justice; Collier & Lowe (above n. 6), 178–9.

[161] European Convention for the Protection of Human Rights and Fundamental Freedoms (hereinafter 'European Convention on Human Rights' or 'ECHR'), Strasbourg, 4 November 1959, ETS, No. 5, Art. 13 (right to an effective remedy); Art. 35(1) (applicants to the Court must exhaust

reserve role for Strasbourg reflects the idea that, as the European Court stated in the *Handyside* case, 'the machinery of protection established by the Convention is subsidiary to the national systems safeguarding human rights'.[162] The Court steps in to provide a remedy only if the national process has been given the 'opportunity of preventing or putting right the violations alleged' and nonetheless failed to provide an adequate and effective remedy.[163] So, the objective of securing effective remedies is mediated by the 'subsidiarity' policy that the national legal order is the 'ideal' in terms of the actual provision of these remedies.

Whatever the merits of this set-up, it necessarily requires the cumbersome, expensive and time-consuming process of pursuing a case through the procedures of two separate legal systems. A further consequence is the 'margin of appreciation' approach adopted by the European Court, a comparatively attenuated level of review justified by the Court on the basis that the national legal order is, in most cases, in a better position to judge the necessity or otherwise of a particular restriction on the rights under the Convention.[164] Moreover, determinations by the Court usually only establish whether or not there has been a violation.[165] Operating at one step removed from the national process, the Court does not normally also stipulate what changes to national law and governmental practice, if any, are consequently required.[166] As the Court said in the *Marckx* case, a decision 'leaves to the state the choice of the means to be utilized in its domestic system for the performance of its obligations' of implementation.[167] *A fortiori*, the

domestic remedies); Art. 34 (right of individual application). There are other admissibility requirements in addition to exhausting remedies; see ibid., Art. 35.

[162] *Handyside v United Kingdom*, Appl. no. 5493/72, judgment of 7 December 1976, European Court of Human Rights, *Series A*, No. 24, para. 48.

[163] Quotation taken from *Cardot v France*, Appl. no. 11069/84, judgment of 19 March 1991, European Court of Human Rights, *Series A*, No. 200, para. 36. On the requirement that the remedy be 'adequate and effective', see ECHR (above n. 161), Art. 13 ('effective') and, e.g., *De Jong, Baljet and van den Brink v Netherlands*, Appl. nos 8805/79; 8806/79; 9242/81, judgment of 24 May 1984, European Court of Human Rights, *Series A*, No. 77, para. 39.

[164] On the doctrine of the margin of appreciation, see, e.g., *Handyside v United Kingdom* (above n. 162), paras 48–9; DJ Harris, M O'Boyle, and C Warbrick, *Law of the European Convention of Human Rights* (Butterworths, 1995), 12–15, cases cited therein and sources cited at 12, n. 18; R Higgins, 'Derogations under Human Rights Treaties', 48 (1976–77) *BYIL* 281, 296–315; S Marks, 'Civil Liberties at the Margin: the UK Derogation and the European Court of Human Rights', 15 (1995) *Oxford Journal of Legal Studies* 69.

[165] Harris, O'Boyle & Warbrick (above n. 164), 700.

[166] Ibid. There have been exceptions to this; see, e.g., *Assanidze v Georgia*, Appl. no. 71503/01, Judgment of 8 April 2004, *Reports 2004-II*); *Broniowski v Poland* (Grand Chamber), Appl. no. 31443/96, Judgment of 22 June 2004, *Reports 2004-V*; *Sejdovic v Italy* (Grand Chamber), Appl. no. 56581/00, Judgment of 1 March 2006; *Scordino v. Italy* (No. 1) (Grand Chamber), Appl. No. 36813/97, Judgment of 29 March 2006; all obtainable from <www.echr.coe.int>.

[167] *Marckx v Belgium*, Appl. no. 6833/74, judgment of 13 June 1979, European Court of Human Rights, *Series A*, No. 31, para. 58. The Human Rights Committee under the International Covenant on Civil and Political Rights has been willing to indicate the measures necessary in order to implement a particular finding on the question of a violation, and to conceive these measures as 'obligations'. See, e.g., D McGoldrick, *The Human Rights Committee* (Clarendon Press, 1994), 152–3.

Court has no authority to make such changes itself (e.g., changing a particular provision of the law), as some national judicial institutions can do: '[i]t is for the respondent State, and the respondent State alone, to take the measures it considers appropriate to ensure that domestic law is coherent and consistent'.[168] The only supra-national role here is that of the Committee of Ministers in supervising the execution of judgments.[169]

Taking all these factors together, the machinery of supra-national judicial human rights review is, on its own terms, limited in its capacity to secure a remedy for human rights violations when compared with the national 'ideal', reflecting the general policy of subsidiarity.

All the former constituent republics of the SFRY are members of the Council of Europe.[170] As such, they are also parties to the ECHR and subject to the compulsory jurisdiction of the Strasbourg Court in relation to cases brought by individuals.[171] Three of the then five separate legal entities originating in the SFRY joined the Council of Europe in the 1990s: Slovenia joined soon after attaining statehood in 1993, the Former Yugoslav Republic of Macedonia (FYROM) and Croatia joined after the conclusion of the Dayton Peace Agreements, in 1995 and 1996 respectively.[172] Bosnia and Herzegovina did not join until 2002, 10 years after declaring independence and seven years after the conclusion of the Dayton Peace Agreements;[173] Serbia and Montenegro did not join until April 2003 and, following its departure from the union with Serbia, Montenegro joined in May 2007.[174]

---

[168] *Marckx v Belgium* (above n. 167), para. 42.

[169] ECHR (above n. 161), Art. 46(2).

[170] See Council of Europe, 'Member States of the Council of Europe', at <http://www.coe.int/T/E/Com/About_Coe/Member_states/default.asp>.

[171] Convention ratification dates: Bosnia and Herzegovina, 12 July 2002; Croatia, 5 November 1997; Slovenia, 28 June 1994; the Former Yugoslav Republic of Macedonia, 10 April 1997. The State Union of Serbia and Montenegro ratified the convention on 3 March 2004. This is regarded to be the date at which it was ratified and entered into force for the Republic of Serbia (which is treated as the continuation of Serbia and Montenegro—see below, n. 174). Montenegro is treated as having ratified the Convention on this date, but with the Convention not entering into force until 6 June 2006 (Montenegro declared independence on 3 June 2006—see below, n. 174). Source: Council of Europe, Treaty Office, at <http://conventions.coe.int/Treaty/Commun/ChercheSig.asp?NT=005&CM=8&DF=08/01/2006&CL=ENG>). On the compulsory jurisdiction of the Court with respect to individual applications, see ECHR (above n. 161), Art. 34.

[172] Dates of joining: Croatia, 6 November 1996; Slovenia, 14 May 1993; the former Yugoslav Republic of Macedonia, 9 November 1995 (source: Council of Europe, 'Member States of the Council of Europe', above n. 170).

[173] 24 April 2002 (ibid.).

[174] The State Union of Serbia and Montenegro joined the Council of Europe on 3 April 2003 (ibid.). Following the declaration of independence of the Republic of Montenegro, on 3 June 2006, the Republic of Serbia was considered to be continuing the membership of Serbia and Montenegro (see Declaration by the Committee of Ministers of the Council of Europe, Declaration on the Continuation by the Republic of Serbia of membership of the State Union of Serbia and Montenegro in the Council of Europe', CoE Press release no. 343 (2006), 14 June 2006, available at <https://wcd.coe.int/ViewDoc.jsp?id=1010125&BackColorInternet=F5CA75&BackColorIntranet=F5CA75&BackColorLogged=A9BACE>). Montenegro applied for membership soon after the dissolution of the State Union (see 'Request by the Republic of Montenegro for accession to the Council of Europe: Statement by the Committee of Ministers

Whereas the non-membership and non-ratification of the then joint entity called FRY/Serbia and Montenegro can be attributed to the policies of the government of President Slobodan Milošević up to 2001, and the subsequent negotiations on the interim confederal structure for the union of Serbia and Montenegro between 2001 and 2003, the absence of Bosnia and Herzegovina until 2002 appears, at first glance, inexplicable. Why did the former Yugoslav Republic committed by virtue of Annex 6 of the Dayton Peace Agreements to securing to all persons within its jurisdiction 'the highest level of internationally recognized human rights' not join the Council of Europe at the same time as the FYROM and Croatia?[175]

One potential factor here is that, in Bosnia and Herzegovina, international machinery aimed at securing remedies for human rights violations already existed, albeit operating in the national, rather than the international, legal order. Far from overlooking what Strasbourg could offer Bosnia and Herzegovina, Annex 6 of the Dayton Agreements arguably took the model of international human rights review epitomized by Strasbourg and refashioned it into a unique, internationally-run, municipal process, obviating the need for the relatively cumbersome model of Strasbourg review operating elsewhere in the region.

As outlined earlier,[176] under Annex 6 of the Dayton Agreements, two domestic institutions, the Human Rights Ombudsman and the Human Rights Chamber, which collectively constituted the 'Commission on Human Rights', were charged with enforcing the human rights obligations of the state and Entity governments under the Dayton Peace Agreements (which include, inter alia, the provisions of the European Convention on Human Rights).[177] The Human Rights Ombudsman was appointed by the Chairman-in-Office of the Organization for Security and Co-operation in Europe (OSCE); the Chamber contained several members appointed by the Committee of Ministers of the Council of Europe

---

of the Council of Europe', CoE Press release no. 344 (2006), 14 June 2006, obtainable from <http://www.coe.int/press>) and acceded to the Council of Europe on 11 May 2007 (see <http://www.coe.int/T/E/Com/About_Coe/Member_states/default.asp>). For general commentary on Montenegro's legal position leading up to the independence declaration, see, e.g., S Darmanović, 'Montenegro: Dilemmas of a Small Republic', 14 (2003) *Journal of Democracy* 145; S Cross and P Komnenich, 'Ethnonational Identity, Security and the Implosion of Yugoslavia: The Case of Montenegro and the Relationship with Serbia', 33 (2005) *Nationality Papers* 1; T Gallagher, 'Identity in Flux, Destination Uncertain: Montenegro During and After the Yugoslav Wars', 17 (2003) *International Journal of Politics, Culture and Society* 53; J Kim, 'Serbia and Montenegro Union: Prospects and Policy Implications', CRS Report for Congress, updated 2 February 2005; R Wilde, 'Self-Determination in International Law and the Position of Montenegro', in S Elezovic (ed.), *Legal Aspects for Referendum in Montenegro in the Context of International Law and Practice* (Foundation Open Society Institute, Representative Office Montenegro, 2005), 25, obtainable from <http://www.osim.cg.yu>.

[175] Quotation from Dayton Annex 6 (above, ch. 1, n. 38), Art. 1.

[176] See above, ch. 2, section 2.3.4.2.

[177] For the obligations, see Dayton Annex 6 (above, ch. 1, n. 38), Art. 1. On the Commission, see ibid. There were also locally-run Ombudsmen at the Entity level. See OHR Fact Sheet, 'Support for Human Rights Institutions', 15 April 2001, obtainable from <http://www.ohr.int>.

(see Table 3 in Chapter 2). These appointees could not be nationals of Bosnia and Herzegovina or of a neighbouring state.[178]

As discussed earlier, the original, internationalized Human Rights Commission provided for in Annex 6 was intended to operate until 2001, and functioned until 2003.[179] The Office of the Ombudsman was an independent agency and the Entities and the central government were prohibited from interfering with its functions.[180] It considered cases of human rights violations by the state or Entity authorities, either on its own motion or in response to individual complaints. Such cases could be addressed by the Ombudsman (who would issue a non-binding report with a finding on the question of violations and recommendations to the relevant authorities), and/or referred to the Human Rights Chamber.[181] The Chamber determined cases referred to it by the Ombudsman or any other party; like the European Court of Human Rights, it attempted a friendly settlement, and, if this was not possible, it proceeded to a decision that was binding on the relevant authorities.[182] Unlike the European Court of Human Rights, this decision determined not only whether there had been a breach of human rights obligations, but also:

... what steps shall be taken by the Party to remedy such breach, including orders to cease and desist, monetary relief (including pecuniary and non-pecuniary injuries), and provisional measures.[183]

Annex 6 of the Dayton Peace Agreements contained no provisions concerning supervision of the implementation of the steps set out in Chamber decisions, but, in practice, OHR took an active role in monitoring compliance. Although it did not seem to use the executive powers asserted elsewhere to effect the implementation of decisions made by the Chamber, this perhaps had more to do with a lack of necessity rather than of willingness, since in fact, there was a high level of compliance with Chamber decisions.[184] The regime of international appointees to domestic institutions can be explained in part through an assumption that local actors were deemed lacking in the skills necessary to perform the task adequately, and that institutions would become deadlocked because of disagreements between 'factions' in each institution (the local members of the Human Rights Chamber were appointed by the two Entities) or, in the case of the Ombudsman, that a local appointee would not manifest the necessary impartiality to be able to discharge the responsibilities of the institution appropriately. To use the terminology adopted in the previous chapter, there would have been

[178] See above, ch. 2, section 2.3.4.1.
[179] See above, ch. 2, section 2.3.4.2, text accompanying n. 86 *et seq.*
[180] Dayton Annex 6 (above, ch. 1, n. 38), Art. 4.3.
[181] Ibid., Art. 5.
[182] Ibid., Arts 9 (friendly settlement) and 11 (decisions).
[183] Ibid., Art. 11.1.b.
[184] See OHR, 'Support for Human Rights Institutions' (above n. 177).

a potential 'governance problem' if the Ombudsman and all the members of the Human Rights Chamber had been locally-appointed local nationals. This problem was supposedly remedied by the introduction of international appointees, considered to have both the expertise and the impartiality that the local actors were seen to lack. The question, however, is why this system was not complemented in the usual way by a supra-national enforcement mechanism.

Why were the checks and balances provided by the European Court of Human Rights not introduced in Bosnia and Herzegovina until 2002? One can appreciate that, immediately after the Dayton Peace Agreements, when the new institutions of the state of Bosnia and Herzegovina were being created, there was perhaps no role for the European Court of Human Rights until the domestic human rights institutions were up and running. However, these institutions were soon operational, not least because of the provision for partial ITA via the international appointees to fill the supposed gaps in expertise. Yet, even at this stage—where its human rights institutions, at least arguably, compared favourably with many of the Council of Europe's more recent members at the time of their entry—Bosnia and Herzegovina did not become a member of the organization.

Clearly, the political context surrounding membership of the Council of Europe is complex, and the factors that determine the fate of individual candidates for membership are various. That said, one way of explaining Bosnia and Herzegovina's late entry into the Council of Europe is to view the domestic human rights institutions—because of the international involvement in them—as equivalent to the international mechanism of the European Court of Human Rights, and, indeed, a superior means of implementation because of their relatively intrusive nature. Unlike the supra-national model, the domestic model does not operate at one step removed from the national authorities; it forms part of those authorities. It ensures that individuals obtain an effective remedy nationally, not by scrutinizing a state's obligation to provide this remedy, and stepping in if necessary to provide a limited equivalent supra-nationally, but by operating within the municipal system as part of the national human rights machinery.[185] Individuals in Bosnia and Herzegovina did not have to go to Strasbourg because, in effect, Strasbourg, or at least an altered version of it, had come to Bosnia and Herzegovina. Moreover, unlike in Strasbourg, the principle of subsidiarity did not apply; the human rights institutions formed part of the national legal order. So, for example, the Chamber could make binding determinations of the particular steps deemed necessary to remedy a violation.[186]

---

[185] However, officials in Bosnia and Herzegovina sometimes refer to the human rights institutions as 'international' institutions, because of the international involvement in them (source: author interviews with these officials).

[186] A counter-indication here is that, despite forming part of the national legal order, the Chamber has nonetheless adopted the 'margin of appreciation' doctrine in some of its judgments. See, e.g., Human Rights Chamber for Bosnia and Herzegovina, Cases Nos CH/97/60, CH/98/276,

When the human rights institutions are considered in this light, Bosnia and Herzegovina's anomalous position up to 2002 (when compared with the other former Yugoslav Republics over this period other than the then FRY/Serbia and Montenegro) as a non-member of the Council of Europe is explicable: an equivalent and more effective form of international enforcement was already in operation through the internationalized domestic institutions. Such an idea is also perhaps evidenced in the general overlap between the initial period of internationalization, which was intended to end after 2001 but continued until 2003, and the period of non-membership of the Council of Europe, which operated until 2002, and also the overlap between the later period of more localized structures, functioning from 2003, and Council of Europe membership, operating from 2002.[187]

Although ITA can be regarded as more 'effective' as a means of implementation because of its intrusive nature, such an approach is predicated on the formal distinction between placing pressure on a government to take action, and actually taking over the machinery of government so as to perform such action directly. In practice, it may well be just as easy to achieve a policy outcome through a particularly extreme version of the second modality as through the first. The use of near-overwhelming coercion—for example the imposition of comprehensive economic sanctions—may make the probability of a change in policy so high as to be a near-certainty. The value of the formal distinction, then, must not be overstated. Ultimately, however, extreme versions of the second option always contain an element of uncertainty—governments may choose, even in the face of considerable hardship, not to give in to pressure. As the history of the use of sanctions demonstrates, severe regimes of external coercion can still fail to deliver the desired results, at least in the short term. What marks out ITA, relatively speaking, is the removal of this element of doubt. Assuming, of course, that this activity is actually capable of having the intended effect (discussed further in Chapter 9), its use makes policy implementation a given, not a highly probable outcome. Equally, it becomes certain that this implementation will occur at a particular moment in time.

7.6 Conclusion

This chapter has outlined the broad areas of international law and policy, from the settlement of disputes to the protection of human rights and the promotion of international peace and security, that international territorial administration can, in different circumstances, be used to implement. The breadth of international policy promoted by ITA suggests that the adoption of labels based on particular policies—whether 'state-building' or 'peace and security'—to describe the ITA

CH/98/362, CH/99/1766, Decision on Admissibility and Merits, 7 December 2001, para. 152. See in general the website of the Human Rights Chamber, at <http://www.hrc.ba/ENGLISH/DEFAULT.HTM>.

[187] On the new structures operating from 2003, see above, ch. 2, section 2.3.4.2, text accompanying n. 89 *et seq.*

enterprise holistically is unhelpful. The popular adoption of such labels reflects the way in which some commentary on the administration projects has tended to take a somewhat superficial view of the purposes associated with them. In general, analysis has proceeded from the recent projects, simplifying the objectives of these projects, and then universalizing to all the historical projects on the basis of the recent projects. This approach risks ignoring the complex nature of the projects under consideration, and failing to appreciate the full potential of ITA based on recent and previous uses of the institution.

In Chapter 6, it was suggested that the use of the label 'temporary', 'interim', 'transitional', etc., in relation to the ITA projects collectively was incorrect as far as how the duration of some of the projects was conceived (e.g., Danzig). What can be seen now, in the light of the foregoing discussion of the policies associated with ITA, is that ITA projects can sometimes be concerned with a highly ambitious transformative enterprise, from seeking to alter identity politics to the inculcation of a democratic and pacific culture. Whereas certain projects may be set at a short duration—such as the 'state-building' project in East Timor—there is nothing inherent in the nature of the enterprise to suggest that it is achievable in a brief period of time. Considering these ambitious goals alongside the intrusive manner in which ITA pursues them, ITA may have a much greater effect on the local population than decades of being subjected to many of the other forms of international policy implementation that operate more at arm's length.[188]

This chapter also considered how the use of ITA as an implementation mechanism for international law and policy compares with other international mechanisms that purport to have the same effect: how other international mechanisms seek to achieve the same ends but through different means. To appreciate fully the role of ITA as a policy institution, however, another type of comparator also needs to be considered, viz. other policy institutions that purport to achieve the same aims through the same means, but involving a different administering actor: states or groups of state representatives. To what extent does ITA compare with the administration of separate territorial units by individual states, as under colonialism and the Mandate and Trusteeship systems? Is ITA 'trusteeship' and, if so, how did it survive as an ostensibly legitimate feature of international public policy after the repudiation of colonial trusteeship with the post-Second World War self-determination entitlement?

The following chapter situates the ITA institution within a wider conceptual framework by considering it in relation to state-conducted analogues. It then appraises the legal and political factors, notably concerning self-determination, which conditioned the historical evolution in the use of different manifestations of what might be called 'foreign territorial administration' over the course of the 20th century.

---

[188] The use of the designation 'temporary' in relation to the projects is addressed again in the next chapter: see below, ch. 8, section 8.7.2.4.

8

Colonialism and Trusteeship Redux? Imperial Connections, Historical Evolution, and Legitimation in the 'Post-Colonial' Era

8.1 Introduction[1]

[i]n our time, direct colonialism has largely ended

Edward Said[2]

[m]ost Bosnians view their country as an international protectorate

International Crisis Group[3]

Over the course of the unipolar period since the end of the Cold War, the term 'empire' returned to vogue amongst mainstream commentators.[4] It was only

---

[1] Earlier versions of parts of this chapter are contained in Parts I and II of R Wilde and B Delcourt, 'Le retour des "protectorats": L'irrésistible attrait de l'administration des territoires étrangers', in B Delcourt, D Duez, and E Remacle (eds), *La guerre d'Irak: Prélude d'un nouvel ordre international?* (PIE—Peter Lang, 2004), 219. Some of the ideas in this introduction and section 8.7 below are discussed in R Wilde, 'The Post-Colonial Use of International Territorial Administration and Issues of Legitimacy', 99 (2005) *ASIL Proc.* 38 and R Wilde, 'Colonialism Redux? Territorial Administration by International Organizations, Colonial Echoes, and the Legitimacy of the "International"', ch. 2 in N Robinson and A Hehir (eds), *State Building: Theory and Practice* (Routledge, 2007).

[2] EW Said, *Culture and Imperialism* (Vintage, 1993), 8. According to Shashi Tharoor, '[i]nternationally, the subject of colonialism is...passé...[t]here is little room for controversy, since the need for decolonization is no longer much debated, and what little remains of colonialism itself no longer generates much conflict'; S Tharoor, 'The Messy Afterlife of Colonialism', 8 (2002) *Global Governance* 1, at 1. For Antony Anghie, 'the period following the establishment of the United Nations...witnessed the end of formal colonialism...This is the period in which we now live'; A Anghie, *Imperialism, Sovereignty and the Making of International Law* (CUP, 2005), 11–12; but see below, n. 31.

[3] International Crisis Group, 'Is Dayton Failing? Bosnia Four Years after the Peace Agreement', ICG Europe Report No. 80, 28 October 1999, obtainable from <http://www.crisisgroup.org>, at 133. See also D Chandler, 'Bosnia's new colonial governor', *The Guardian*, 9 July 2002, Comment & Analysis, 16.

[4] E.g., F Füredi, *The New Ideology of Imperialism: Renewing the Moral Imperative* (Pluto Press, 1994); M Hardt and A Negri, *Empire* (Harvard University Press, 2000); M Ignatieff, *Empire Lite: Nation-building in Bosnia, Kosovo and Afghanistan* (Vintage, 2003); N Ferguson, *Colossus: The Price of America's Empire* (Penguin, 2004); Anghie (above n. 2), 273–4; D Harvey, *The New Imperialism*

with the fall of Saddam Hussein in 2003 and the introduction of the Coalition Provisional Authority (CPA) administration in Iraq led by US Ambassador Paul Bremer, however, that the cognate term 'colonialism' resurfaced in mainstream discourse.[5] To be sure, colonialism had never gone away in some places, and the Palestinians and the Saharawi continued to be denied self-determination,[6] but Iraq perhaps marked the first time in the unipolar era that something *new* was criticized in mainstream commentary via direct colonial comparisons: the imperial hyperpower had shifted into an activity with echoes of post-Renaissance European colonialism, not only toppling a local government, but also administering the territory and attempting to reorientate profoundly its economic, political and cultural system.[7] In this narrative, as a 'new' form of colonialism, Iraq was aberrant, a sole exception to the view, as reflected in the 1993 statement by Edward Said above, that as options on the palette of national and international policy, colonies and protectorates are the stuff of history.[8]

Yet, away from Iraq and other longstanding instances of foreign state occupation, people in other parts of the world have for some time used the colonial tag to question the legitimacy of their own forms of government: those subject to what has been discussed in this book, international territorial administration. As has been explained previously, the use of ITA increased significantly towards the end of the 20th century with the plenary UN administration projects in Eastern Slavonia, Kosovo, and East Timor, the partial administration conducted by the Office of the High Representative in Bosnia and Herzegovina (OHR), and the introduction of a range of international appointees to locally-based judicial and quasi-judicial bodies. Such widespread and frequent use suggests that

(OUP, 2005); D Chandler, *Empire in Denial: The Politics of State-building* (Pluto Press, 2006); B Porter, *Empire and Superempire: Britain, America and the World* (Yale University Press, 2006); J Fearon and D Laitin, 'Neotrusteeship and the Problem of Weak States', 28 (2004) *International Security* 1.

[5] See, e.g., D Gregory, *The Colonial Present: Afghanistan, Palestine, Iraq* (Blackwell, 2004); S Kurtz, 'Democratic Imperialism: A Blueprint', *Policy Review* No. 118 (2003), obtainable from <http://www.policyreview.org>; J Steele, 'Read the small print', *The Guardian*, 31 March 2003, 18; A Murray, 'Hostages of the empire', *The Guardian*, 1 July 2003, 19; H Juma'a Awad, 'Leave our country now', *The Guardian*, 18 February 2005, 26; 'Tony Blair cannot really want to invade Africa', *Sunday Telegraph*, 10 October 2004, 27; S Jenkins, 'To say we must stay in Iraq to save it from chaos is a lie', *The Guardian*, 21 September 2005, 33. On the CPA, see the sources cited above, ch. 1, n. 75.

[6] On the Western Sahara, see above, ch. 5, section 5.6.

[7] The category of 'post-Renaissance' colonialism is discussed further below, section 8.2.2.

[8] Thus Edward Said focused his critical attention on other manifestations of what he considered to be 'imperialism'. In the full version of the sentence from which the above quotation is taken, Said observes that, '[i]n our time direct colonialism has largely ended; imperialism...lingers where it has always been, in a kind of general cultural sphere as well as in specific political, ideological, economic and social practices'; Said (above n. 2), 8. More broadly, many commentators focus on the *legacy* of colonialism in former colonies, and/or other practices that are described as 'neo-colonial' because they share certain commonalities with colonialism. Such studies, along with re-interpretations of colonial history, have been conducted within the discipline of 'post-colonial studies'. See below, n. 44, and sources cited therein.

this particular activity *was* somehow considered internationally legitimate in the unipolar phase of the 'post-colonial' era.

Language echoing the colonial paradigm—terms such as 'trusteeship' and 'protectorate'—is often used to describe the current and recent ITA projects.[9] In many cases, such designations are made only provocatively, without much examination; alternatively, they are used axiomatically, assuming a connection between ITA and colonialism by way of a prelude to a detailed analysis of the nature of the powers being exercised in a particular project, without having first engaged in a detailed consideration of how and to what extent the colonial analogy holds water.[10]

---

[9] As with the quote above relating to Bosnia and Herzegovina, Kosovo is frequently described as a 'protectorate' (see, e.g., 'Kosovo and Macedonia—Better and Worse', *The Economist*, 17 November 2001, 46; W O'Neill, 'Kosovo: Unexpected Barriers to Building Peace and Security', in AH Henkin (ed.), *Honoring Human Rights under International Mandates: Lessons from Bosnia, Kosovo and East Timor* (Aspen Institute, 2003), 75); the High Representative in Bosnia and Herzegovina is often described as a 'colonial governor' (see, e.g., Chandler, above n. 3); the UN Administrator in Kosovo is often described as a 'Proconsul' (see, again, the Economist's article on Kosovo and Macedonia cited above). For further examples of the use of this and similar language, see EM Cousens and CK Cater, *Toward Peace in Bosnia: Implementing the Dayton Accords* (IPA/Lynne Rienner, 2001); E Benvenisti, *The International Law of Occupation* (paperback edn, Princeton University Press, 2004), xvi; S Chesterman, *You, The People: The United Nations, Transitional Administrations, and State-Building* (OUP, 2004), 6–7, 11–12; TD Grant, 'Internationally Guaranteed Constitutive Order: Cyprus and Bosnia as Predicates for a New Nontraditional Actor in the Society of States, 8 (1998) *Journal of Transnational Law & Policy* 1; TD Grant, 'Extending Decolonization: How The United Nations Might Have Addressed Kosovo', 28 (1999) *Georgia Journal of International & Comparative Law* 9, at 50–1; M Bothe and T Marauhn, 'The United Nations in Kosovo and East Timor. Problems of a Trusteeship Administration', 6 (2000) *International Peacekeeping* 152; E Remacle, 'The Co-operation between International Organizations in the Management of the Third Yugoslav War', in V-Y Ghebali and D Warner (eds), *The Operational Role of the OSCE in Southeastern Europe: Contributing to Regional Stability in the Balkans* (Ashgate, 2001), 69; M Ruffert, 'The Administration of Kosovo and East Timor by the International Community', 50 (2001) *ICLQ* 613, 628–9; A Zimmermann and C Stahn, 'Yugoslav Territory, United Nations Trusteeship or Sovereign State? Reflections on the Current and Future Legal Status of Kosovo', 70 (2001) *Nordic Journal of International Law* 424, 448; R Cooper, 'Why we still need empires', *The Observer*, 7 April 2002, available at <http://observer.guardian.co.uk/worldview/story/0,,680117,00.html>; S Vieira de Mello, 'How Not to Run a Country: Lessons for the UN from Kosovo and East Timor', June 2002, obtainable from <http://www.jsmp.minihub.org/Resources/2000/INTERFET%20DETAINEE%20MANAGEMENT%20UNIT%20(e).pdf>; JS Kreilkamp, 'UN Postconflict Reconstruction', 35 (2003) *NYU Journal of International Law & Politics* 619; S Chesterman, 'Virtual Trusteeship' in D Malone (ed.), *The UN Security Council: From the Cold War to the 21st Century* (Lynne Rienner, 2004), 219; Y Hysa, 'Kosovo: A Permanent International Protectorate?', ch. 12 in E Newman and R Rich (eds), *The UN Role in Promoting Democracy: Between Ideals and Reality* (UN University Press, 2004); SR Ratner, 'Foreign Occupation and International Territorial Administration: The Challenges of Convergence', 16 (2005) *EJIL* 695, 696; R Wolfrum, 'International Administration of Post-Conflict Situations by the United Nations and Other International Actors', 9 (2005) *Max Planck Yearbook of United Nations Law* 649, 672–3; B Knoll, 'Beyond the Mission Civilisatrice: The Properties of a Normative Order within an Internationalized Territory', 19 (2006) *LJIL* 275. See also the sources cited below, nn. 11–17.

[10] One example of this approach is a report of the European Stability Initiative (ESI), which invoked the colonial analogy of the British Raj before considering in detail the nature of the High Representative's powers in Bosnia and Herzegovina. See G Knaus and F Martin, 'Lessons from

Some have offered more sustained considerations of the relevance of the colonial analogy to ITA. The path-breaking 'failed states' commentators mentioned in the previous chapter, Gerald Helman and Steven Ratner, and others, to be discussed below, who have made similar remedial proposals, Charles Krauthammer, Gerhard Kreijen, Peter Lyon, Ali Mazrui, Tom Parker, Henry Perritt, William Pfaff, and Helman and Ratner's original critics, Ruth Gordon and Henry Richardson, have all, in different ways, touched on certain connections between particular forms of UN territorial administration, on the one hand, and colonialism and trusteeship, on the other.[11] Beyond the realm of policy advocacy (but no less normative in their orientation), William Bain, Michael Bothe and Thilo Marauhn, Richard Caplan, Jarat Chopra, Robert Jackson, Roland Paris, Nicholas Tsagourias, and Alexandros Yannis have variously considered how ideas of protection, trusteeship and the civilizing mission are reflected in contemporary peace missions and/or proposals for such missions.[12] In 2003, Michael Ignatieff

Bosnia and Herzegovina—Travails of the European Raj', ESI Report, 3 July 2003, obtainable from <http://www.esiweb.org>, reprinted in 14 (2003) *Journal of Democracy* 60.

[11] G Kreijen, *State Failure, Sovereignty and Effectiveness: Legal Lessons from the Decolonization of Sub-Saharan Africa* (Brill, 2004), ch. 6, section 3; GB Helman and SR Ratner, 'Saving Failed States', 89 (1992) *Foreign Policy* 3; C Krauthammer, 'Trusteeship for Somalia; an old colonial idea whose time has come again', *Washington Post*, 9 October 1992; P Lyon, 'The Rise and Fall and Possible Revival of International Trusteeship', 31 (1993) *Journal of Commonwealth & Comparative Politics* 96; T Parker, *The Ultimate Intervention: Revitalising the UN Trusteeship Council for the 21st Century* (Sandvika: Norwegian School of Management, 2003); AA Mazrui, 'Decaying Parts of Africa Need Benign Colonization', *International Herald Tribune*, 4 August 1994; R Gordon, 'Some Legal Problems with Trusteeship', 28 (1995) *Cornell International Law Journal* 301; W Pfaff, 'A New Colonialism? Europe Must Go Back Into Africa', 74:1 (Jan/Feb 1995) *Foreign Affairs* 2; HJ Richardson, '"Failed States", Self-Determination, and Preventative Diplomacy: Colonialist Nostalgia and Democratic Expectations', 10 (1996) *Temple International & Comparative Law Journal* 1; R Gordon, 'Saving Failed States: Sometimes a Neocolonialist Notion', 12 (1997) *American University Journal of International Law & Policy* 903; HH Perritt, 'Structures and Standards for Political Trusteeship', 8 (2003) *UCLA Journal of International Law & Foreign Affairs* 385; HH Perritt, 'Providing Judicial Review for Decisions by Political Trustees', 15 (2004) *Duke Journal of Comparative & International Law* 1. On the 'failed states' proposals, see further above, ch. 7, section 7.3.3. The present author has also previously offered critical commentary on the 'failed state' concept, inter alia by asking whether colonial comparisons can be made; see R Wilde, 'Representing International Territorial Administration: A Critique of Some Approaches', 15 (2004) *EJIL* 71, 94.

[12] For William Bain and Robert Jackson, as part of more general studies of concepts of trusteeship in international relations: see W Bain, *Between Anarchy and Society. Trusteeship and the Obligations of Power* (OUP, 2003); W Bain, 'The Political Theory of Trusteeship and the Twilight of International Equality', 16 (2003) *International Relations* 59; W Bain, 'The Idea of Trusteeship in International Society', 386 (2003) *The Round Table* 67; W Bain, 'In Praise of Folly: International Administration and the Corruption of Humanity', 82 (2006) *International Affairs* 532 reprinted as W Bain, 'In Praise of Folly: International Administration and the Moral Breakdown of International Society', ch. 9 in A Hehir and N Robinson (eds), *State Building: Theory and Practice* (Routledge, 2007); RH Jackson, *The Global Covenant: Human Conduct in a World of States* (OUP, 2000), ch. 11. Michael Bothe and Thilo Marauhn argue that UNMIK and UNTAET constitute 'Security Council trusteeship administrations', a new paradigm in international peace operations; M Bothe and T Marauhn, 'UN Administration of Kosovo and East Timor: Concept, Legality and Limitations of Security Council-Mandated Trusteeship Administration', in C Tomuschat (ed.), *Kosovo and the International Community: A Legal Assessment* (Kluwer Law International, 2002), 217. In the title of his original work on ITA, Richard Caplan questioned

defined the 'state-building' aspects of internationally-run projects in Bosnia and Herzegovina and Kosovo, alongside the US-run operation in Afghanistan, as manifestations of a new 'Empire Lite';[13] in 2004, James Fearon and David Laitin described a broader set of ITA projects and state-conducted interventions as 'a form of international governance that may be described as neotrusteeship, or, more provocatively, postmodern imperialism';[14] in 2006, David Chandler labelled, by way of criticism, contemporary 'state building' projects, notably in Bosnia and Herzegovina, as 'Empire in Denial', expanding on his earlier work along the same lines focusing exclusively on Bosnia and Herzegovina.[15] Rosa Ehrenreich Brooks characterized the promotion of the rule of law across various interventions as a 'fundamentally imperialist enterprise' and, together with Jane Stromseth and David Wippman, asked whether this constituted a 'New Imperialism'.[16] Nathaniel Berman has for some time explored the linkages between certain forms of internationalized and state-conducted experiments, through a consideration of the 'Modernist' tradition of thought.[17]

---

the relevance of the concept of trusteeship; see R Caplan, *A New Trusteeship? The International Administration of War-Torn Territories*, Adelphi Paper No. 341 (OUP/IISS, 2002). In his subsequent book on the topic, Caplan discusses the relevance of 'trust' to the issue of accountability; R Caplan, *International Governance of War-Torn Territories: Rule and Reconstruction* (OUP, 2005), ch. 9. Jarat Chopra conceptualizes certain international peace operations as 'Civil Governance-in-Trust'; see J Chopra, 'UN Civil Governance-in-Trust', in TG Weiss (ed.), *The United Nations and Civil Wars* (Lynne Rienner, 1995), 70. Roland Paris considers the possible existence of the 'civilizing mission' in contemporary 'peacebuilding' missions generally; see R Paris, 'International Peacebuilding and the Mission Civilisatrice', 28 (2002) *Review of International Studies* 637; see also R Paris, *At War's End: Building Peace After Civil Conflict* (CUP, 2004), *passim*. Nicholas Tsagourias discusses the connections between the trusteeship of the League Mandate system and UNMIK in particular; N Tsagourias, 'Humanism and the Mandates System: Its Modern Revival', 13 (2000) *Hague Yearbook of International Law* 97. Alexandros Yannis discusses the similarities and differences between protectorates and trusteeship, on the one hand, and certain peace operations, on the other; A Yannis, 'The Creation and Politics of International Protectorates in the Balkans: Bridges Over Troubled Waters', 5 (2003) *Journal of International Relations & Development* 258.

13 Ignatieff (above n. 4).
14 Fearon & Laitin (above n. 4), 7.
15 Chandler (above n. 4); D Chandler, *Bosnia: Faking Democracy after Dayton* (2nd edn, Pluto Press, 2000); D Chandler, 'Western Intervention and the Disintegration of Yugoslavia, 1989–99', in E Herman and P Hammond (eds), *Degraded Capability: The Media and the Kosovo Crisis* (Pluto Press Ltd, 2000), 19, at 27; D Chandler, 'Imperialism may be out, but aggressive wars and colonial protectorates are back', *The Observer*, 14 April 2002, available at <http://observer.guardian.co.uk/worldview/story/0,,684308,00.html>; Chandler (above n. 3). For other commentary on 'state-building' see the sources cited above, ch. 7, n. 45.
16 R Ehrenreich Brooks, 'The New Imperialism: Violence, Norms, and the "Rule of Law"', 101 (2003) *Michigan Law Review* 2275, *passim* and especially 2280; J Stromseth, D Wippman and R Brooks, *Can Might Make Rights? Building the Rule of Law After Military Interventions* (CUP, 2006), ch. 1.
17 N Berman, '"But the Alternative is Despair", European Nationalism and the Modernist Renewal of International Law', 106 (1992–3) *Harvard Law Review* 1792; N Berman, 'In the Wake of Empire', 14 (1998–99) *American University International Law Review* 1521, at 1531; N Berman, 'Imperial Rivalry and the Genealogy of Human Rights: the Nationality Decrees Case', 94 (2000) *ASIL Proceedings* 53; N Berman, 'Les Ambivalences Impériales', in E Jouannet (ed.), *Impérialisme*

Turning from specialist commentators, the potential relevance of the colonial analogy to contemporary ITA projects has rarely been picked up in a mainstream discourse that, by contrast, frequently described the CPA in Iraq as 'colonial'.[18] More typical is analysis taking the ITA projects for granted, addressing second-order issues concerned with how international territorial administrators could better do their jobs. Alternatively, the projects are invisible when the activities in which they are involved are discussed generically. On economic matters, for example, one would think from mainstream commentary that foreign actors exercising direct administrative power to transform the economic system in a state was, in recent times, particular to Iraq, yet of course it was a central pillar of the administrative set up in certain parts of the southern Balkans which predated Iraq and continued after the end of the CPA.[19]

Even when ITA is considered, there is often partial coverage—considering the international presence in the Balkans, for example, exclusively in terms of military forces generally and UNMIK in particular, ignoring OHR—and for many there is a lack of interest in, or strong resistance to, drawing analogies with colonialism generally and the CPA in Iraq in particular.[20]

Indeed, as Simon Chesterman suggests in the following comment about both ITA and the US actions in Afghanistan and Iraq after 9/11, the exceptionalist narrative associated with the recent ITA projects discussed earlier in Chapter 1— that the Kosovo and East Timor projects are in a class of their own—may be explained in part because of the desire to avoid a broader historical viewpoint

---

et Droit International en Europe et en Amérique (2007); N Berman, 'Intervention in a "Divided World": Axes of Legitimacy', 17 (2006) *EJIL* 769.

[18] On this description of the CPA, see above, n. 5. One exception to the lack of coverage of the ITA projects would be a story in the UK *Guardian* newspaper on the ESI report describing the set-up in Bosnia and Herzegovina as the European 'Raj' (on which, see above, n.10) which made a brief splash but was soon forgotten; see I Traynor, 'Ashdown "running Bosnia like a Raj"', *The Guardian*, 5 July 2003.

[19] For examples of these policies in Bosnia and Herzegovina and Kosovo see above, ch. 6, nn. 116 and 135.

[20] An example of strong resistance from a prominent national politician would be the UK Cabinet member responsible for overseas development assistance, Claire Short, who resigned soon after the commencement of the Iraq war in 2003 alleging that she had been let down by the Prime Minister in relation to post-war arrangements, including the role of the UN. Ms Short set out the reasons for her resignation in a speech delivered in the House of Commons on 12 May 2003 (Hansard, HC Deb 12 May 2003 cc 36–9, and available at <http://www.publications.parliament.uk/pa/cm200203/cmhansrd/vo030512/debtext/30512-09.htm#30512-09_spnew8>; see also the Briefing from the Prime Minister's Official Spokesman, 12 May 2003, available at <http://www.pm.gov.uk/output/Page3648.asp>). When at the time the present author put to Ms Short that the UN representative in Kosovo was, in terms of the nature of the role being performed, 'Kosovo's Paul Bremer', Ms Short angrily denied any such connection between the two situations. This exchange took place at the opening panel of a conference on 'Post-War Iraq' held by the British Institute for International and Comparative Law (BIICL) at the University of London Senate House, 26 February 2004. The powerful role played by the sharp normative distinction made between individual states and the UN as administering actors in legitimizing the ITA projects is discussed below, section 8.7.2.3.

which would make any resistance to drawing colonial analogies more difficult to sustain:

[o]ne of the many ironies in the recent history of transitional administration of territory by international actors is that the practice is regarded as novel. Attempts to draw analogies either with trusteeships and decolonization on the one hand, or the post-war occupation of Germany and Japan on the other, are seen as invitations to charges that the United Nations or the United States are engaging in neo-colonialism or imperialism respectively. Within the United Nations in particular, such comparisons are politically impossible.[21]

Michael Bothe and Thilo Marauhn's idea that UNMIK and UNTAET constitute a new form of peace operation, which they term 'Security Council trusteeship administration', was mentioned in the previous chapter. For present purposes, their use of the term 'trusteeship' is significant. However, although one might think that this would lead to a consideration of comparisons with colonialism, such a consideration is strongly resisted. The authors comment that:

[t]he concepts of occupation, protectorate and trusteeship as [sic] such are ideologically still linked to particular political and historical situations, related to traditional armed conflict or to colonialism. Simply referring to or relying upon these concepts may give rise to fears that the UN provides a forum for a new form of 'benevolent colonialism.'[22]

But what if one were not simply to refer to or rely upon such concepts, but, rather, to consider their potential significance in detail? Should this not be done? And even if it isn't, and a simple reliance on such concepts led to the fears outlined, would the fears necessarily be wrong, as opposed to being unproved? The passage continues:

[i]n order to avoid such misconceptions it is necessary to take a closer look at the context of the UN Security Council mandated interim administrations in Kosovo and East Timor.[23]

The authors move to a consideration of the two missions within the taxonomy of peace operations exclusively (as was done in the previous chapter), and conclude that, if one thinks about the two missions 'from the perspective of peacekeeping and peace-building', then 'the concept, legality and limitations of such operations can be more easily discussed without giving rise to concerns about neo-colonialism'.[24] So the authors identify the potential relevance of the colonial analogy, but pull back from it immediately, choosing to try to find a way of thinking about the missions *other* than through the colonial comparator, via the

---

[21] Chesterman, *You, The People* (above n. 9), 11. Alexandros Yannis speculates that the term 'protectorate' is not used in relation to ITA because of the 'inevitable association with the imperialist past of the Western World'; Yannis (above n. 12), 262–3.
[22] Bothe & Marauhn (above n. 12), 218, footnote omitted.
[23] Ibid.
[24] Ibid., 219.

'context' of the missions and the 'perspective' of peace operations. Why the classi-fication of the missions as peace operations somehow takes them out of the arena of any meaningful comparisons with colonialism is unexplained. More funda-mentally, the authors seem to take as their premise a need not to 'give rise to con-cerns about neo-colonialism'. But one cannot avoid such concerns by failing to face up to them. Such an approach is as limited as the approach they highlight of 'simply referring to or relying upon' colonial comparisons: it may be right, it may be wrong, but its advocates have not provided any substantive argumentation to explain why they have adopted it.

Are colonialism and trusteeship 'back', albeit in some modified, ostensibly temporary form? To what extent do current operations mirror their colonial pre-cursors? What normative distinction, if any, subsists between an administration project conducted by an international organization—as in Kosovo—and one conducted by a military coalition of states—as in Iraq? Does the existence of the ITA projects in the unipolar era require the 'bygone' story of colonialism to be revised? This enquiry is important if we are to understand fully how the legitimacy of the ITA projects is understood and is to be appraised. As Roland Paris states in relation to his own comparison between peace-building and the civilizing mission:

[t]hinking this way about peace operations—as compared with the prevailing tendency to conceive of these operations as technical (or non-ideological) exercises in conflict management—helps to situate the study of peacebuilding in a broader historical and analytical context.[25]

This enquiry is also significant for understanding the history of colonialism gen-erally and ideas of international trusteeship in particular, and appreciating how this history and these ideas occupy the present. Scholars who identify themselves with post-colonial or Third World approaches to international law, for example, have challenged the bygone story of colonialism, demonstrating how colonial ideas live on today in practices that echo the underlying premises of colonialism even if they operate differently as a matter of practicality, such as the disciplining role of the international financial institutions like the International Monetary Fund (IMF) on matters of economic governance, development and trade.[26] ITA, however, involves the same direct administrative activity as colonial trusteeship.

---

[25] Paris, 'International Peacebuilding' (above n. 12), 638.
[26] For example, in explaining the coverage of his book on imperialism and international law, Antony Anghie states that:

[c]olonialism is a thing of the past. This is the broad understanding that informs the conventional narrative of international law. The principal concerns of this book are to question this assump-tion and to examine how this narrative sustains itself and how international law seeks to suppress its relationship with colonialism—a relationship that was, and continues to be, central to inter-national law's very identity. An examination of the Mandate System makes it clear how colonialism continues. The colonial practices and management techniques formulated by Lugard were adopted and refined by the Mandate System, and these same practices continue today through the BWI.

So, whereas in the case of most states the IMF influences decisions taken by local officials, in Bosnia and Herzegovina, as discussed in previous chapters, the head of the Central Bank was appointed by the organization directly. The existence of the ITA missions raises the possibility, then, that colonial ideas live on today in practices that operate in *exactly the same manner* as colonial trusteeship, the only difference being in the identity of the administering actor.

As a complement to the existing literature mentioned already, and drawing on it where relevant, this chapter conceptualizes collectively a series of different practices—ITA, 'protection', colonialism, state-conducted administration under the Mandate and Trusteeship systems, occupation conducted by foreign states—as 'foreign territorial administration'; considers the differences and similarities in conventional representations of each activity; and identifies the political and legal factors that mediated their differential treatment in international law and policy across the 20th century, notably the self-determination entitlement and ideas of legitimacy associated with the 'international'.[27]

In Chapter 1, ideas concerning the problematic nature of having relations of domination 'represented' by people other than those subject to such relations were highlighted.[28] Such ideas were formulated in large part in response to attempts to 'tell' the story of colonialism. As with the approach to ITA in this book so far, the following approach in relation to various state practices is an attempt to understand how these practices were understood as a matter of international law and policy at the time. The objective, then, is not to tell the story of colonialism, but to identify and conceptualize strands of colonial thought. The focus of attention is on both how colonialism was explained by those involved in it, and also what ideas were formulated to resist it. In both cases, the scope of the enquiry is mediated by the objective of seeking to identify ideas that are relevant in appreciating how ITA is understood. So, for example, the survey of critiques of colonialism in this chapter is aimed at identifying those ideas that are relevant to the question of how ITA is distinguished normatively from colonial trusteeship.[29] It is not an attempt to 'represent' the colonial critique in some sort of authentic, authoritative and comprehensive manner.[30]

The chapter begins by establishing the contours of each of the practices under evaluation, other than ITA, and comparing these features with ITA. The policy

---

Anghie (above n. 2), 193 (BWI refers to the Bretton Woods Institutions—the World Bank and the International Monetary Fund). Lord Frederick Lugard was a British colonialist whose ideas are discussed further in this chapter. On post-colonial/third world approaches to international law, see List of Sources, section 5.3.4.

[27] For the work of others on contemporary colonial forms generally, including in relation to international law, see the sources cited in List of Sources, sections 5.3.3 and 5.3.4. See also below, n. 44, and accompanying text.

[28] See above, ch. 1, section 1.5.2.

[29] For broader frames of reference, see, e.g., the works in List of Sources, sections 5.3.1 and 5.3.3.

[30] Cf. the quotation reproduced above, ch. 1, text accompanying n. 115.

connections between these different activities are then considered. Policies are divided into two main categories: territorial status outcomes and strategic advantage, on the one hand, and trusteeship, the civilizing mission and other administrative policies, on the other. It is argued that the nature of these policy connections suggests that ITA should be considered as part of a broader 'family' of policy institutions, each involving what has been termed above 'foreign territorial administration'.[31]

The historical evolution of the use of these different manifestations of foreign territorial administration in the era of international territorial administration, viz. the 20th century, is then mapped out, considering the effect that the self-determination entitlement that emerged after the Second World War had on the use of foreign territorial administration generally, and how the ITA manifestation came to be used again in the 'post-colonial' era. Explanation is provided as to how international territorial administration survived as a seemingly appropriate and legitimate policy institution.

8.2 Analogous Institutions

When have states been involved in a similar type of activity to that performed by international actors in the international territorial administration projects? Adopting the concept of an 'institution' as an 'established practice' defined in Chapter 1 and discussed in Chapter 2, this section reviews five different (but sometimes overlapping) institutions involving states in the administration of distinct territorial units, and considers how the manner in which these institutions operated compares with the activity performed in the ITA institution. The

---

[31] This line of argument builds on the comparative analysis of ITA with protectorates (including colonial protectorates), the Mandate and Trusteeship arrangements, and representative bodies first offered briefly in R Wilde, 'From Danzig to East Timor and Beyond: The Role of International Territorial Administration', 95 (2001) *AJIL* 583, 602–5. A similar position has also been adopted by Antony Anghie, who remarks that, '[a]ttempts by the United Nations to administer Somalia, Cambodia, Timor and Kosovo are contemporary manifestations of a project that began with the Mandate system and continued in a more refined comprehensive form with its successor, the Trusteeship system'; Anghie (above n. 2), 190–1, footnote omitted. Citing the analysis of the purposes of ITA presented in Wilde, ibid. (for an expanded version of such purposive analysis, see ch. 6, above), Anghie observes that these purposes:

... are precisely the problems the Mandate System attempted to address. The assumptions inherent in these projects—about the people and territories to be administered, the character of 'progress', and the actual legal techniques and instruments used by institutions to effect the transformation of these societies—all derive in important ways from that earlier, formative experiment.

Anghie, ibid., 191. See also A Anghie, 'Colonialism and the Birth of International Institutions: Sovereignty, Economy, and the Mandate System of the League of Nations', 34 (2002) *NYU Journal of International Law & Politics* 513, 622–3. For an earlier suggestion of the same parallels, see Wilde, ibid., in particular at 604. See also Jackson (above n. 12), 307, who states that 'the role and responsibilities' of UNMIK 'are identical to those of a colonial administration, a League of Nations mandate administration, or a UN trusteeship administration'.

institutions concerned are protection, colonialism, state-conducted adminis-tration under the Mandate and Trusteeship systems, territorial administration by bodies made up of foreign state representatives, and occupation, including so-called 'belligerent occupation'. At this stage, the analysis is concerned merely with the activity performed in each institution; the purposes/policies with which the institutions were associated are considered later.

8.2.1 Protection

As James Crawford remarks, '[p]rotection of one State by another is one of the oldest features of international relations'.[32] The arrangement is understood to involve the exercise of some form of influence by one or more states over a sep-arate territorial entity, without formal incorporation. Necessarily, it involves a diminution in the 'independence' of the unit affected. Since 'independence' is a criterion for legal statehood, and the protectorate concept is predicated on the territorial unit not being considered part of the territory of the administering state, this unit is regarded legally as either a 'protected state' (a state despite pro-tection) or an 'international protectorate' (a territorial entity not qualifying for statehood, in some cases wholly or partly due to the diminution in independ-ence caused by the protection arrangement).[33] For both types of protectorate, the territorial unit involved is considered to be a distinct juridical entity from the 'protecting' state, despite the exercise of control by the latter over it. In many protectorate arrangements, the control exercised concerned the conduct of exter-nal relations; in some, however, it involved the conduct of certain administra-tive prerogatives, notably an asserted competence to change domestic law. The

---

[32] J Crawford, *The Creation of States in International Law* (2nd edn, OUP, 2006), 286. On protectorates generally, see Q Wright, *Mandates Under the League of Nations* (University of Chicago Press, 1930), 14–15; DK Fieldhouse, *Colonialism 1870–1945: An Introduction* (Palgrave Macmillan, 1981), 17; AWB Simpson, *Human Rights and the End of Empire: Britain and the Genesis of the European Convention* (OUP, 2001), 279; Crawford, ibid., 286–320 and sources cited therein; Anghie (above n. 2), 87–90; WM Reisman, 'Reflections on State Responsibility for Violations of Explicit Protectorate, Mandate, and Trusteeship Obligations', 10 (1989) *Michigan Journal of International Law* 231; R Higgins, 'Colonial law and the clarity of drafting: the International Court of Justice and William Dale's two abiding interests', Inaugural Sir William Dale Memorial Lecture, Chancellor Hall, Senate House, University of London, 2 July 2001, reprinted in *Amicus Curiae*, issue 37 (Sept./Oct. 2001), 16, at 18. On 'colonial protectorates' see above, ch. 4, section 5.3 and below, text accompanying n. 34.

[33] Crawford (above n. 32), 286–7. See also Fieldhouse, *Colonialism* (above n. 32), 17; MN Shaw, *Title to Territory in Africa. International Legal Issues* (OUP, 1986), 47 *et seq.*; R Jennings and A Watts (eds), *Oppenheim's International Law, Vol. 1, Peace* (9th edn, Longman, 1992), 275; Anghie (above n. 2), 87; and the dictum of Kennedy LJ in *R. v Earl of Crewe, ex parte Sekgome* [1910] 2 KB 576, at 620:

[w]hat the idea of a Protectorate excludes, and the idea of annexation on the other hand would include, is that absolute ownership which was signified by the word 'dominium' in Roman law, and which, though perhaps not quite satisfactorily, is sometimes described as territorial sovereignty. The protected country remains in regard to the protecting State a foreign country...

term 'protectorate' was sometimes invoked in certain forms of colonialism, but its association with arrangements involving significant administrative control—the 'colonial protectorate'—is dismissed by international lawyers on the grounds that title did subsist, and the term 'protectorate' was being used to obscure this so as to avoid the responsibilities that would flow from the enjoyment of sovereignty.[34]

One example of an entity regarded by international lawyers to be a 'true' protectorate, viz. a protectorate where the 'protecting' actors did not enjoy title, is the Free City of Danzig. As discussed in Chapter 4, in the Free City certain administrative prerogatives were exercised by both a foreign state (Poland) and the League of Nations.[35] Under the Versailles Treaty, Danzig was placed under the 'protection' of the League.[36] Academic discussions about the status of the Free City treat territorial administration by the League and the powers exercised by Poland as essentially the same type of activity.[37] Collectively they constitute a form of protection,[38] thereby raising a question about the level of independence enjoyed by the Free City, potentially affecting its international legal status.

As established earlier in Chapters 4 and 5, in all the international organization-conducted ITA projects—even those involving plenary administration—the international organization involved is not the sovereign entity in the sense that it claims title over the territory involved. Thus the same juridical distinction is made between the administering entity and the administered territory as with 'protectorate' arrangements. Given this, international territorial administration can properly be understood as an internationalized form of protection.[39] Protection is internationalized in the sense that the actor in the 'protector' role is an international organization rather than a state.[40]

---

[34] The legal status of colonial territories, including colonial protectorates, is discussed above, ch. 5 section 5.3.

[35] See above, ch. 4, section 4.2.2.

[36] Versailles Peace Treaty, Art. 102.

[37] E.g., Crawford (above n. 32), at 239

[38] Although, as Percy Corbett points out, they are 'several and distinct' rather than 'joint'; PE Corbett, 'What is the League of Nations?', 5 (1924) *BYIL* 119, 141.

[39] Alexandros Yannis states that:

[p]rotectorates historically refer to a form of relationship in which a state surrenders part of its sovereignty to another. Whereas there have been several forms of protectorates, they all share two major characteristics. First, the protectorate nominally retains its sovereignty and, second, its territory remains distinct from that of the protector. The direct analogy of these two features with those of most of the experiments in the 1990s, particularly in the Balkans, may explain why the term protectorates tends to be preferred by many commentators even though it is not used officially.

Yannis (above n. 12), 262. Not all protectorates enjoy 'sovereignty' in the sense of statehood (cf. the concept of the 'international protectorate'); however, they are all 'sovereign' in the sense that they do not form part of the 'protecting' entity. For Yannis' view as to why the term 'protectorate' is not used officially, see above, n. 21.

[40] As Alexandros Yannis states, '[a] major new feature in the 1990s is that the protector tends to be multilateral organizations'; Yannis (above n. 12), 263. Internationalization can be understood differently, of course; some protectorate arrangements conducted by states were described in this way because they operated on the basis of a multilateral rather than a bilateral treaty. For an example of such a use of 'internationalization', see Crawford (above n. 32), 285.

The history of ITA in the 20th century (see Table 5 in Chapter 2) suggests that the usual definitions of 'protection', which cover administration by foreign states, need to be expanded to take into account the involvement of international organizations in the same type of activity. Whereas protection practised by states became less pronounced over the course of the 20th century (but by no means died out), the institution of protection itself continued through its internationalized manifestation. It has become commonplace to describe Kosovo during the UNMIK period and sometimes also, as in the quotation at the start of this chapter, post-Dayton Bosnia and Herzegovina as 'international protectorates' because of the involvement of international organizations in the performance of administrative prerogatives in each place.[41] Given the meanings of and distinction between an 'international protectorate' and a 'protected state' explained earlier, and bearing in mind the conclusions drawn in Chapter 4 on the status of these two territories,[42] during the relevant periods Kosovo is better described as a 'protected state territory' and Bosnia and Herzegovina a 'protected state'.

These distinctions notwithstanding, the popular use of the language of protection in relation to the ITA projects does fit with general understandings of this activity in international relations, as far as the nature of the activity and the relationship between the administering actor and the administered entity are concerned.

8.2.2 Colonialism

The term colonialism is, of course, a site of contestation and used in various different ways beyond the simple meaning of 'implanting... settlements on distant territory'.[43] Many use the language of colonialism to represent forms of domination generally, and in particular such forms operating globally on the North/South or developed/developing state axis.[44] As Robert Young states, the:

---

[41] This is done by many of the commentators listed above in n. 9.

[42] See above, ch. 4, sections 4.5.3 (for Kosovo) and 4.5.1 (for Bosnia and Herzegovina).

[43] Said (above n. 2), 8. On this meaning of colonialism, see also A Loomba, *Colonialism/Postcolonialism* (Routledge, 1998), 1–2; Fieldhouse, *Colonialism* (above n. 32), 4; M Ferro, *Colonization: A Global History* (Routledge, 1997), 1 and *passim*. See below, n. 89 and corresponding text, for a discussion of 'colonization'. On colonialism, see the works in List of Sources, section 5.3, which are divided into anti-colonial critiques (section 5.3.1); commentary on the practices of colonialism that are the focus of this study by those from the colonial states involved writing contemporaneously, and from others from the West writing subsequently (section 5.3.2); work on 'post-colonial studies' (section 5.3.3); and work on 'third world approaches to international law' (section 5.3.4).

[44] For Fieldhouse, at some stage after the Berlin Conference of 1884–85, the term colonialism '...emerged as a general description of the state of subjection—political, economic and intellectual— of a non-European society which was the product of imperialism.... [c]olonialism, therefore, now means the condition of a subject people and is used exclusively of a non-European society when under the political control of a European state or the USA...'; Fieldhouse, *Colonialism* (above n. 32), 6. See also M Koskenniemi, *The Gentle Civilizer of Nations* (CUP, 2002), 175. Sometimes the term 'neo-colonialism' is used to cover, in the words of Antony Anghie, 'the enduring character of what in essence are colonial relations even after Third World states acquired

... extraordinary diversity, both historically and geographically, even within the practices of a single colonial power, or with respect to different historical epochs and successive colonial powers in the history of a single colony... troubles the possibility of any general theory.[45]

The present study is not concerned with somehow articulating a 'general theory' but, rather, identifying those representations of particular manifestations of colonialism that compare with ITA as it has been defined here.[46] A narrower frame of reference is, therefore, adopted.

One main way the term colonialism is used is to stand for the practice and ideology of a particular historical manifestation of colonialism practised by the European powers after the Renaissance, often represented as 'imperial', 'modern', or 'capitalist' colonialism because of its operation during, and its relationship to, the distinctive phase in the broader trends these terms connote, an association which, indeed, is partly the basis for treating this period of colonialism as distinctive.[47]

The varied character of 'colonialism' includes, of course, the nature of the activity performed; during this period the activity is usually represented as having ranged from staking a claim over territory without introducing any substantive

independence'; Anghie (above n. 2), 118; see also N Crawford, *Argument and Change in World Politics: Ethics, Decolonization, and Humanitarian Intervention* (CUP, 2002), 131–2. One influential definition of neo-colonialism is provided by Kwame Nkrumah: '... the State which is subject to it is, in theory, independent and has all the outward trappings of international sovereignty. In reality its economic and thus political policy is directed from outside'; K Nkrumah, *Neo-Colonialism: The Last Stage of Imperialism* (Panaf, 1965), ix. On this broader use of 'colonialism', and 'post-colonialism', see List of Sources, section 5.3.3.

[45] RJC Young, *Postcolonialism—An Historical Introduction* (Blackwell, 2001), 18. See also ibid., at 17–19; Higgins (above n. 32), 19; Ferro (above n. 43), *passim*. But *contra* J-P Sartre, *Colonialism and Neocolonialism* (1956) (Haddour, Brewer, and McWilliams, transl.) (Routledge, 2001); F Fanon, 'Reciprocal Bases of National Culture and the Fight for Freedom—Speech to Congress of Black African Writers (1959)', reproduced in F Fanon, *The Wretched of the Earth* (1961) (R Philcox transl., Grove Press, 2004); F Fanon, *Toward the African Revolution: Political Essays* (1964) (transl. H Chevalier, Monthly Review Press, 1967); Said (above n. 2), 8; B Ashcroft, G Griffiths, and H Tiffin, *Post-Colonial Studies: The Key Concepts* (Routledge, 2000), 46. For a useful overview of the different conventional understandings of historical colonialism, see Fieldhouse, *Colonialism* (above n. 32), 1–13.

[46] See above, ch. 1, section 1.4.5.

[47] See, e.g., Fieldhouse, *Colonialism* (above n. 32), 6, 11; Ashcroft, Griffiths & Tiffin (above n. 45), 46; Loomba (above n. 43), 2–4; JC Hales, 'The Creation and Application of the Mandate System (A Study in International Colonial Supervision)', 25 (1939) *Transactions of the Grotius Society* 185, at 185. As for the distinctiveness of modern colonial 'ideology' in particular, for Bill Ashcroft, Gareth Griffiths, and Helen Tiffin, post-Renaissance colonialism by European powers constitutes '... a sufficiently specialized and historically specific form of imperial expansion to justify its current general usage as a distinctive kind of political ideology'; Ashcroft, Griffiths & Tiffin, ibid., 46. Others contest the utility of treating post-Renaissance colonialism as distinctive; see, e.g., Ferro (above n. 43), 1–3. On the relationship between this form of colonialism and imperial ideology, see below, n. 58. One important aspect of the idea of ideological distinctiveness concerns notions of trust associated with certain forms of colonialism during this period, which reflected broader trends in political thought generally and imperial ideology in particular. See below, text from n. 104.

presence, to informal control exercised by corporate entities such as the East India Companies, to direct administrative presence by European states exercised on top of local structures of governance, to more intrusive and extensive administrative conduct.[48] Differences of degree in this regard are commonly understood to have subsisted across and within individual manifestations of colonialism over time.

As with, and because of, the definition of ITA in Chapter 1,[49] the present study will focus on forms of colonialism understood to involve some kind of direct administrative control exercised over the colonial territory by the imperial state, even if power was exercised through local representatives and officials to a significant degree: the key point in such cases is that the officials in question are themselves understood to be under the direct control of the colonial authority, for example through appointment and removal and/or being subject to overall imperial law and policy.[50]

Plenary administration was the hallmark of the primarily African 'colonial protectorate' that emerged during this time in relation to which, as mentioned previously, commentators challenge the use of the 'protectorate' label on the grounds that in many cases the territories involved were considered to form part of the sovereign territory of the colonial states.[51]

The nature of the relationship between the metropolitan state and the colony is relevant for present purposes, because of the way, as discussed in Chapter 1, the activity of ITA understood in terms of a distinction as between the spatial identities of the administering actor, on the one hand, and the administered entity, on the other.[52] The significance of this distinction in relation to ITA was deepened

---

[48] Treatment of the nature of the activity performed in colonialism runs through most of the commentary in List of Sources, section 5.3. See further below, nn. 50, 54, and 55 and accompanying text.

[49] Above, ch. 1, section 1.4.5.

[50] Examples of a focus on some form of administrative control include Bipan Chandra, who defines colonialism as a situation where the foreign power 'controls state power in the colony'; B Chandra, *Essays on Colonialism* (Sangam Books, 1999), 12; and Jürgen Osterhammel, who defines colonial rule as a situation where 'indigenous rulers are replaced by foreign rulers'; J Osterhammel, *Colonialism: A Theoretical Overview* (1995) (SL Frisch, transl., Markus Wiener Publishers, 1997), 20. Fieldhouse states that:

[u]nder colonialism a dependent society was totally controlled by the imperial power. Its government was in the hands of officials of the imperial state, its social, legal, educational, cultural and even religious life was moulded by alien hands and its economy was structured to meet the needs of European capitalism... The distinctive and most important single feature of modern colonialism was the fact that the colonial powers took full control over the government of the dependent societies with their empires.

Fieldhouse, *Colonialism* (above n. 32), 11. Fieldhouse reports that, in the 'tropical colonies' in particular, '... government consisted of officials, appointed and removable by the metropolitan authorities and thus in no sense responsible to those they ruled'; (ibid., 12). For a discussion of the varying degrees of administrative control exercised in colonies, see, e.g., Koskenniemi (above n. 44), 120, 142; Anghie (above n. 2), 168–71.

[51] On the legal status of colonial territories, including 'colonial protectorates', see above, ch. 5, section 5.3.

[52] See above, ch. 1, section 1.4.3.

when it was established, through the analysis in Chapters 3–5, that in no ITA project has the international organization involved enjoyed sovereignty in the sense of title over the territory concerned.

Given what has been said already about the legal status of 'colonial protectorates', and the broader observations about colonial title in Chapter 5, such a juridical distinction was not in evidence in all colonies.[53] Moreover, a further point of potential dissonance with ITA as far as the relationship between the administering actor and the administered territory concerns those forms of colonialism associated with an aspiration to assimilate the territory and its people politically and culturally into the 'metropolitan' state. Such an association was not in play in all cases, of course; the operation of many British colonies, for example, was understood in terms of a model of supervision exercised over government institutions operated by local officials, on the basis of a distinct 'legal personality, constitution, laws'.[54] It was, though, the case in, for example, certain French and Portuguese colonies, which are understood to have operated through a more direct form of administration and a much greater administrative integration into the 'metropolis' as provinces, with the people of the colonies being granted citizenship in certain cases.[55]

However, even when sovereignty-as-title would appear to have resided in the colonial power, and where an assimilationist goal was evident, further, more subtle distinctions, including those of a legal and administrative nature, operated between the metropolis and the colony,[56] and in practice the assimilationist 'ideal' was considerably modified for a variety of reasons.[57]

The ideology of 'imperialism' that underpinned these forms of colonialism was itself rooted in the paradoxical linkage of dominance and control with difference and separation.[58] So Edward Said defines imperialism as 'the practice, the theory and the attitudes of a dominating metropolitan centre ruling a distant territory',[59]

---

[53] See above, ch. 5, section 5.2.

[54] Fieldhouse, *Colonialism* (above n. 32), 30. See also FD Lugard, *The Dual Mandate in British Tropical Africa* (3rd edn, Blackwood, 1926), *passim*, and Bain, *Between Anarchy and Society* (above n. 12), 59 *et seq*. Rosalyn Higgins defines 'full British colonialism' as the as 'the full exercise of the authority of the Crown...whether directly or with a significant degree of delegation, as in the case of the Dominions'; Higgins (above n. 32), 17.

[55] Fieldhouse, *Colonialism* (above n. 32), 30 and 35; RH Jackson, *Quasi-States: Sovereignty, International Relations and the Third World* (CUP, 1990), 99. For comparisons of the French and British models, see, e.g., V Dimier, *Le gouvernement des colonies, regards croisés franco-britanniques* (Editions de l'Université de Bruxelles, 2004); V Dimier, 'On Good Colonial Government: Lessons from the League of Nations', 18 (2004) *Global Society* 279.

[56] See, e.g., the discussion in *Oppenheim's International Law* (above n. 33), 276–82.

[57] Accordingly, many commentators on colonialism conceive the metropolis/colony distinction in a generic fashion; see, e.g., Osterhammel (above n. 50), 15. On the modified application of the assimilationist ideal, see, e.g., Dimier (above n. 55), 36.

[58] Much of the commentary in List of Sources, section 5.3, discusses the relationship between colonialism and imperialism. On this relationship, see, for example, the treatment by Wright (above n. 32), ch. 1; Fieldhouse, *Colonialism* (above n. 32), 1–13; MW Doyle, *Empires* (Cornell University Press, 1986), 25; Said (above n. 2), 8; Anghie (above n. 2), *passim*.

[59] Said (above n. 2), 8.

and Michael Doyle defines it as a process of establishing 'a relationship, formal or informal, in which one state controls the effective political sovereignty of another political society'.[60] This distinction was further constituted in the ideological and legal conceptualization and treatment of colonial peoples, discussed below, based on differences in the 'level of civilization' and embedded in the concept of 'trust' predicated on a separation between the colonial 'guardian' and the native 'ward' and reflected, for example, in discriminatory treatment in the extension of rights as between citizens of the colonial state, on the one hand, and the 'native' population of the colonial territory, on the other (even, sometimes, when members of the latter were granted citizenship).[61]

The formulation in UN Charter Chapter XI of a category of territory to cover colonies defines such territories, as discussed earlier in Chapter 5, as 'Non-Self-Governing' (in the title of Chapter XI) and 'whose peoples have not yet attained a full measure of self-government' (in Article 73).[62] This negative formulation suggests that the 'governing' authority, such as it exists, and the colonial state more generally, is understood to be something other than the 'self' of the territory and its people.

Just as colonial peoples were conceived as civilizationally distinct from the people of the colonizing powers, so too the concept of geographical distinctiveness formed part of colonial ideology.[63] Such a concept became the basis for defining 'Non-Self-Governing' territories within the United Nations. Article 74 of the UN Charter conceives such territories as something other than the 'metropolitan areas' of the administering states, and for the purpose of the reporting obligations under Article 73 paragraph (e), the General Assembly stated in 1960 that coverage included '*prima facie*...a territory which is geographically separate and is distinct ethnically and/or culturally from the country administering it'.[64]

[60] Doyle (above n. 58), 45.

[61] On ideas of colonial trusteeship generally, see below, section 8.3.2. On their relationship to ideas of empire in particular, see below, text accompanying n. 112 *et seq*. Martti Koskenniemi describes the cohabitation of 'distinction' with 'connection' in the civilizing mission as understood by international lawyers thus:

[i]t was a discourse of exclusion-inclusion; exclusion in terms of colonial argument about the otherness of the non-European that made it impossible to extend European rights to the native, inclusion in terms of the native's similarity with the European, the native's otherness having been erased by a universal humanitarianism under which international lawyers sought to replace native institutions by European sovereignty.

Koskenniemi (above n. 44), 130. On discriminatory treatment as between colonial settlers and the 'native' population, see below, n. 404.

[62] On Non-Self-Governing Territories see also above, ch. 5, text accompanying n. 14 *et seq*.

[63] For examples, Quincy Wright defines a colony as 'not territorially continuous with the motherland'; Wright (above n. 32), 4 and Neta Crawford states that '[i]n most cases, occupied land was distant from the center, or metropole, of the people from the occupying state'; Crawford (above n. 44), 131–2.

[64] GA Res. 1541 (XV), 15 December 1960, Annex, Principle IV. The reporting obligations are discussed further below, n. 411.

Arguments challenging and repudiating colonialism also often involved restating the geographical distinction and/or the notion that the people of the metropolis and their settlers were something 'other' than the indigenous population in articulating the reasons for, and the people entitled to, self-determination. So, in an example of the latter approach, as mentioned earlier in Chapter 5, a right of self-determination was articulated in the context of the 'subjection of peoples to *alien* subjugation, domination and exploitation'.[65]

As far as the activity conducted is concerned, then, the conventional representations of the particular set of colonial forms discussed in this section can be considered analogous to such representations of international territorial administration, because of the various distinctions that operated between the administering entity and the administered territory.

8.2.3 The Mandate and Trusteeship systems[66]

The Mandate and Trusteeship systems, as outlined in Chapter 5, involved the administration of separate territories by foreign states 'on trust', subject to the overall supervision of the respective international organizations.

Neither the administering powers nor the supervising international organizations enjoyed sovereignty-as-title over the territories,[67] which subsisted as non-state territorial units with international legal personality by virtue of the special arrangements under which they were placed, and whose people came to enjoy a right of 'external' self-determination in the second half of the 20th century.[68] The Mandate and Trusteeship institutions can be understood as a modification of an existing set of colonial arrangements, in that they provided for territorial administration of the former colonies of the defeated powers by the victorious powers at the end of the two world wars, but, as will be discussed further below, reconstituting them on the basis of an internationally-guaranteed notion of trust.[69] The juridical distinction between the administering entity and the

---

[65] In the Declaration on Principles of International Law Concerning Friendly Relations and Cooperation among States in Accordance with the Charter of the United Nations (hereinafter 'Friendly Relations Declaration'), GA Res. 2625 (XXV), 24 October 1970 (emphasis added). This is discussed above, in ch. 5, n. 19, and below, text accompanying n. 334.

[66] See the sources cited above, ch. 5, nn. 43 (the Mandate system) and 44 (the Trusteeship system).

[67] See the discussion above, ch. 5, section 5.3.

[68] See ibid., and, on the right of self-determination, the discussion above, ch. 5, section 5.2.

[69] The Trusteeship system also covered former mandated territories, and allowed for further territories to be placed under it. No further placements were made. On the territories covered, see above, ch. 5, nn. 43 (on the Mandate system) and 44 (on the Trusteeship system). On the Trusteeship system being open to other territories (UN Charter Art. 77) but not being used in this regard, see above, ch. 5, n. 45 and accompanying text; the non-use is illustrated by the case of South West Africa/Namibia (see above, ch. 5, section 5.5), the rejection of all forms of foreign territorial administration as part of the post-Second World War self-determination entitlement (see below, section 8.5.1), and fact that the Trusteeship system was not reactivated in relation to East Timor in

administered territory means that, unlike the misnamed 'colonial protectorate' (at least before the self-determination entitlement), they were understood to operate as a matter of law as two sets of internationally-institutionalized protectorates. Equally, this distinction coupled with the activity involved means that they operated in the same fashion as the plenary ITA projects, the only difference being the identity of the administering actor.

8.2.4 Representative bodies

The next set of relevant arrangements concerns comparatively under-explored projects involving territorial administration by bodies made up of representatives of certain states, acting in a representative capacity ('representative bodies'). These bodies were used from the early 19th century, and fall into four broad categories.

The first category covers the exercise of plenary or partial administrative prerogatives in various disputed territories, including Cracow (1815–46), Shanghai (1854–1943), Crete (1897–1909), Tangier (1923–57), and Albania (1913–14).[70] The second category comprises the various waterway commissions (e.g., the Central Rhine Commission, begun in 1804, and the International Danube Commission, begun in 1856), which exercised various administrative powers over their respective waterways.[71] The third category covers the international commissions created by the Treaty of Versailles to hold plebiscites in certain territories.[72] The fourth category covers mixed commissions, including that created in 1923 to 'supervise and facilitate' the compulsory exchange of Turkish and Greek minority populations between Greece and Turkey.[73] Taken together, these projects involved

---

1999 (see below, text accompanying n. 541). This non-use is discussed further below, text accompanying nn. 118, 327, 345.

[70] M Ydit, *Internationalised Territories from the 'Free City of Cracow' to the 'Free City of Berlin'* (Sythoff, 1961), 32, 95–108 (Cracow), 23–4, 127–53 (Shanghai), 28–9, 109–26 (Crete), 27–8, 154–84 (Tangier), 29–33 (Albania). According to Ydit, proposals were made, but never realized, for similar experiments in Istanbul (1821 and 1896), Mount Athos (1913), and Spitzbergen (1914); see, ibid., at 32–3 (Istanbul), 33–4 (Mount Athos), 34–9 (Spitzbergen).

[71] On the waterway commissions, see, e.g., N Hill, *International Organization* (Harper, 1952), 507–510; P Reuter, *International Institutions* (JM Chapman transl., Allen & Unwin, 1958), 206–209; DG LeMarquand, *International Rivers: The Politics of Cooperation* (Westwater Research Centre, University of British Columbia, 1977); F Knipping (ed.), *The United Nations System and its Predecessors* (OUP, 1997), vol. II, 153–80; CF Amerasinghe, *Principles of the Institutional Law of International Institutions* (2nd edn, CUP, 2005), 4 and source cited therein at n. 4, 66–7; DH Miller, 'The International Regime of Ports, Railways and Waterways', 13 (1919) *AJIL* 669. On the International Congo River Commission proposed in 1885, see Ydit (above n. 70), 25–7.

[72] For the plebiscite commissions generally, see S Wambaugh, *Plebiscites Since the World War* (2 vols, Carnegie Endowment for International Peace, 1933); Ydit (above n. 70), at 505–6; N Berman, '"But the Alternative is Despair"' (above n. 17), *passim* and especially section III.

[73] On the 1923 Commission, see the Convention between Greece and Turkey Concerning the Exchange of Greek and Turkish Populations, Lausanne, 30 January 1923, 32 LNTS 75, in particular Arts 11 and 12 (quotation from Art. 11), and the Treaty of Peace with Turkey (between the British Empire, France, Italy, Japan, Greece, Roumania, the Serb-Croat-Slovene State, of the one part, and Turkey, of the other part), Lausanne, 24 July 1923, 28 LNTS 11, Art. 142 (incorporating

varying degrees of territorial administration exercised in discrete territorial units not considered the sovereign territories of the states whose representatives sat on the bodies concerned.

8.2.5 Occupation[74]

The final type of state-conducted activity potentially relevant by analogy to ITA is 'occupation', when this term is used, as in the international law of occupation, to denote territorial control by a state or group of states over territory the title to which is not vested in the state or states concerned; in occupation law, claiming or altering this title through the occupation is legally prohibited.[75]

by reference the early bilateral treaty). See also, e.g., Hill (above n. 71), 505. On the population transfer more generally, see C Drew, 'Population Transfer: The Untold Story of the International Law of Self-determination', unpublished doctoral thesis, LSE 2006 (on file at Senate House Library, University of London), ch. 2, at 93 *et seq.*, and sources cited therein.

[74] For conventional representations of the forms of 'occupation' considered here, see generally Benvenisti (above n. 9), *passim*; A Roberts, 'What is Military Occupation?', 55 (1984) *BYIL* 249. On the international law of belligerent occupation, see Hague Regulations Respecting the Laws and Customs of War on Land, annex to the Convention (IV) Respecting the Laws and Customs of War on Land, The Hague, 18 October 1907, *Martens Nouveau* (Series 3), vol. 3, 461 ('Hague Regulations'), Arts 42–56; Geneva Convention (I) for the Amelioration of the Condition of the Wounded and Sick in Armed Forces in the Field, 12 August 1949, 75 UNTS 31, Art. 2; Geneva Convention (II) for the Amelioration of the Condition of the Wounded, Sick and Shipwrecked Members of Armed Forces at Sea, Geneva, 12 August 1949, 75 UNTS 85, Art. 2; Geneva Convention (III) Relative to the Treatment of Prisoners of War, Geneva, 12 August 1949, 75 UNTS 135, Art. 2; Geneva Convention (IV) Relative to the Protection of Civilian Persons in Time of War, Geneva, 12 August 1949, 75 UNTS 287 (hereinafter Geneva Convention (IV)) Arts. 2, 27–34 and 47–78; JS Pictet (ed.), *The Geneva Conventions of 12 August 1949, Commentary to the IV Geneva Convention Relative to the Protection of Civilian Persons in Time of War* (International Committee of the Red Cross, 1958), Commentary to Article 2 (2), 21–2; G von Glahn, *Law Among Nations: An Introduction to Public International Law* (7th edn, Allyn & Bacon, 1995), ch. 25; A Gerson, *Israel, the West Bank and International Law* (Frank Cass & Co., 1978); Benvenisti, ibid.; D Kretzmer, *The Occupation of Justice: The Supreme Court of Israel and the Occupied Territories* (SUNY Press, 2002); UK Ministry of Defence, *The Manual of the Law of Armed Conflict* (OUP, 2004); A Wilson, 'The Laws of War in Occupied Territory', 18 (1932) *Transactions of the Grotius Society* 17; A Gerson, 'Trustee Occupant: The Legal Status of Israel's Presence in the West Bank', 14 (1973) *Harvard International Law Journal* 1; D Thürer, 'Current challenges to the law of occupation', speech delivered at the 6th Bruges Colloquium, 20–21 October 2005, obtainable from <http://www.icrc.org>; Roberts, 'What is Military Occupation?', ibid.; H-P Gasser, 'Protection of the Civilian Population', ch. 5 in D Fleck (ed.), *The Handbook of Humanitarian Law in Armed Conflicts* (OUP, 1995), 240–79 and sources cited therein; D Scheffer, 'Beyond Occupation Law', 97 (2003) *AJIL* 842; S Vité, 'L'applicabilité du droit international de l'occupation militaire aux activités des organisations internationales', (2004) *IRRC*, vol. 86, issue 853, 9; N Bhuta, 'The Antinomies of Transformative Occupation', 16 (2005) *EJIL* 721; Ratner (above n. 9); A Roberts, 'Transformative Military Occupation: Applying the Laws of War and Human Rights', 100 (2006) *AJIL* 580. Commentators considering the link between occupation and ITA include Ratner, ibid.; Roberts, 'Transformative Military Occupation', ibid.; Benvenisti, ibid., xv – xvii and, more briefly, Caplan, *International Governance* (above n. 12), 3–4; Chesterman, *You, The People* (above n. 9), 6–7, 11–12, 145. See also the discussion below, section 8.3.3 and ch. 9, n. 11.

[75] Under Art. 42 of the Hague Regulations (above n.74): '[t]erritory is considered occupied when it is actually placed under the authority of the hostile army. The occupation extends only to

Examples include the allied occupations of the Rhineland in the First World War,[76] the allied occupations of Germany, Austria, and Japan after the Second World War, including the Allied Control Council administration of Berlin,[77] and the US and UK Coalition Provisional Authority (CPA) occupation of Iraq after their military action in that country in 2003.[78] Many instances of occupation involve the conduct of administration; as a matter of international law, administration is treated separately from the mere exercise of control, in that the latter triggers substantive obligations (discussed further below) which themselves presuppose the exercise of the former.[79]

the territory where such authority has been established and can be exercised'. Art. 43 of the Hague Regulations refers to '[t]he authority of the legitimate power having in fact passed into the hands of the occupant'. According to Adam Roberts, the test in Art. 42 'consists of direct control' by the 'armed forces' of the occupying state (Roberts, 'What is Military Occupation?', above n. 74, 251) and has an 'implicit assumption that an occupant exercises authority directly, through its armed forces, rather than indirectly, through local agents' (ibid., 252), a position that 'is also evident' in Art. 43 and 'also seems to be taken for granted' in Arts 48, 49, 51–3 and 55 (ibid.). Roberts concludes that '[a]n open and identifiable command structure is thus a central feature of the Hague definition of military occupation' (ibid.). On the Hague test for applicability, see also *Prosecutor v Naletilic and Martinovic*, Case No. IT-98-34-T, ICTY, Trial Chamber Judgment, 31 March 2003, para. 217. Common Article 2 to the Geneva Conventions of 1949 makes the conventions applicable to 'all cases of partial or total occupation of the territory of a High Contracting Party, even if the said occupation meets with no armed resistance'; see Article 2 in each of the Geneva Conventions (I)–(IV), above n. 74, partially extracted below, n. 80. More generally, see Geneva Convention (IV), ibid., Arts. 27–34 and 47–78. On the test in occupation law generally, Adam Roberts states that, '[a]t the heart of treaty provisions, court decisions and legal writings about occupations is the image of the armed forces of a state exercising some kind of domination or authority over inhabited territory outside the accepted international frontiers of their State and its dependencies'; Roberts, 'What is Military Occupation?', ibid., 300. Eyal Benvenisti defines occupation as 'effective control of a power (be it one or more states or an international organization, such as the United Nations) over a territory to which that power has no sovereign title, without the volition of the sovereign of that territory'; Benvenisti (above n. 9), 4. The previous two quotes illustrate the idea that occupation denotes situations where the occupier lacks title. Not only is this the case as a matter of the factual definition of occupation; the law of occupation also prohibits annexation by the occupying state or states, reflecting an underlying policy objective that changes in territorial status cannot be brought about through the use of military force. Eyal Benvenisti states that '[t]he foundation upon which the entire law of occupation is based is the principle of inalienability of sovereignty through the actual or threatened use of force. Effective control by foreign military force can never bring about by itself a valid transfer of sovereignty'; ibid., 5. See also ibid., xi and Roberts, 'Transformative Military Occupation' (above n. 74), 582–5. This idea is implicated in the notion that the relationship between the occupier and the occupied territory is one of 'trust', discussed further below in section 8.3.2. Of course, states have in practice used occupation as a device for altering the status of the territory concerned; this is discussed below in section 8.3.1.

[76] On the allied occupation of the Rhineland after the First World War, see generally the sources cited above, ch. 1, n. 71.

[77] On the allied occupation of Germany and Austria after the Second World War, see the sources cited above, ch. 1, n. 72; on the allied occupation of Japan, see the sources cited above, ch. 1, n. 73.

[78] On the CPA see the sources cited above, ch. 1, n. 75.

[79] The 1956 version of the *US Army Field Manual* states that '[m]ilitary government is the form of administration by which an occupying power exercises governmental authority over occupied territory'; United States Department of the Army, *The Law of Land Warfare*, US Army Field Manual, FM 27–10 (US Government Printing Office, 1956), para. 362, quoted in Benvenisti (above n. 9), at 4–5, n. 8. Eyal Benvenisti states that Art. 43 of the Hague Regulations, by defining occupation

As the above examples illustrate, many occupations result from military conflict. As a matter of international law, the formulation in one body of regulatory norms—the Hague Regulations of 1907—seems to presuppose a belligerent context, whereas that in the other body of such norms—the Geneva Conventions of 1949—does not require this context as an essential part of the trigger of applicability.[80]

as a situation where '...the authority of the legitimate power ha[s] in fact passed *into the hands of the occupant*' assumes that an occupant will introduce a system of administration, and obliges it to do so (ibid., 4 n. 8 and accompanying text). Explaining the nature of and rationale for an administrative structure, Benvenisti states that '...it is of little significance whether the occupant chooses to establish a system of military administration or a civil one, or a mixture of both. What is important is the establishment of a separate system by the occupant to execute the powers and duties allotted to it by the law of occupation'; ibid., 5, citing British War Office, *The Law of War on Land, Being Part III of the Manual of Military Law* (HMSO, 1958), at 145, para. 518. It might also be said that, if the substantive obligations give rise to a need to conduct administration, so the factual trigger for their operation—the exercise of control—must include a capacity to exercise such administration. In *Prosecutor v Naletilic and Martinovic*, the Trial Chamber of the International Criminal Tribunal for the Former Yugoslavia stated that '[t]o determine whether the authority of the occupying power has been actually established' one guideline that provides 'some assistance' is that 'the occupying power must be in a position to substitute its own authority for that of the occupied authorities, which must have been rendered incapable of functioning publicly'; *Prosecutor v Naletilic and Martinovic* (above n. 75), para. 217. However, this dictum is articulated in the context of what might indicate the existence of occupation rather than what is necessary for a situation to constitute occupation; so, for example, another guideline cited by the Trial Chamber is that 'the occupying power has issued and enforced directions to the civilian population', an activity which, although indicating the existence of an occupation, and fulfilling the obligations of occupation law, is not required for occupation *per se* to exist. A further approach to defining 'occupation' legally is instrumental in character: the definition should be set so as to encompass those situations to which the regulations of occupation law relate. This is discussed further below, n. 134.

[80] Art. 42 of the Hague Regulations states that '[t]erritory is considered occupied when it is actually placed under the authority of the hostile army'; Hague Regulations (above n. 74), Art. 42. Adam Roberts states that this provision 'appears to be based on an assumption that a military occupation occurs in the context of a war'; Roberts, 'What is Military Occupation?' (above n. 74), 251. See also the British *Manual of the Law of Armed Conflict* (above n. 74), 274, ch. 11, para. 11.1.1 and 11.2. Common Art. 2 to the Geneva Conventions (on scope of application) provides that:

[i]n addition to the provisions which shall be implemented in peacetime, the present Convention shall apply to all cases of declared war or of any other armed conflict which may arise between two or more of the High Contracting Parties, even if the state of war is not recognized by one of them.

The Convention shall also apply to all cases of partial or total occupation of the territory of a High Contracting Party, even if the said occupation meets with no armed resistance.

Geneva Conventions (I)–(IV), (above n. 74), Art. 2, paras 1 and 2. The Commentary on the second paragraph by the International Committee of the Red Cross states that:

...the wording adopted was based on the experience of the Second World War, which saw territories occupied without hostilities, the Government of the occupied country considering that armed resistance was useless. In such cases the interests of protected persons are, of course, just as deserving of protection as when the occupation is carried out by force.

...[the paragraph] does not refer to cases in which territory is occupied during hostilities; in such cases the Convention will have been in force since the outbreak of hostilities or since the time war was declared. The paragraph only refers to cases where the occupation has taken place without a declaration of war and without hostilities, and makes provision for the entry into force of the Convention in those particular circumstances.

ICRC, *Commentary to the IV Geneva Convention* (above n. 74), 59–60.

Commentators now prefer to use the generic term 'occupation' to cover both belligerent and non-belligerent occupations, even if in some respects the legal regime may differ in each case. In the words of Eyal Benvenisti:

[t]he law of occupation developed as part of the law of war. Initially, occupation was viewed as a possible by-product of military actions during war, and therefore it was referred to in legal literature as 'belligerent occupation'. But the history of the twentieth century has shown that occupation is not necessarily the outcome of actual fighting: it could be the result of a threat to use force that prompted the threatened government to concede effective control over its territory to a foreign power; occupation could be established through an armistice agreement between the enemies; and it could also be the product of a peace agreement. Moreover, because of many occupants' reluctance to admit the existence of a state of 'war' or of an international armed conflict, or their failure to acknowledge the true nature of their activities on foreign soil, the utility of retaining the adjectives 'belligerent' or 'wartime' has become rather limited. Today the more inclusive term, 'occupations,' is generally used. The emphasis is thus put not on the course through which the territory came under the foreign state's control, whether through actual fighting or otherwise, but rather on the phenomenon of occupation.[81]

An additional point of difference between occupier and occupied territory is suggested by the conceptualization of occupation in terms of 'trusteeship'; this conceptualization is discussed further below.[82]

8.2.6 Commonalities

In all of the above institutions, a discrete territorial unit is administered, either partially or in full, by a state, a group of states, or a collectivity of state representatives. The nature of the separation between the administering entity and the administered territory is different as between protection, administration by the representative bodies and foreign state administration under the Mandate and Trusteeship systems, and most if not all instances of occupation, on the one hand, and colonialism, on the other. Whereas in the former category the administering entity is not understood to enjoy sovereignty-as-title (and, as mentioned, in the case of occupation is prohibited from claiming such a privilege), in the latter this form of sovereignty is sometimes considered to subsist, but the territory and its people are, nonetheless, considered in a variety of ways to be something 'other' than the metropolitan state, a distinction that in many cases was later reinforced by the self-determination entitlement.

When considering the nature of the activity performed in the ITA projects, it was observed in Chapter 1 that the spatial identity of the administering actor, as 'international', is understood to be distinct from and opposed to the 'local'

---

[81] Benvenisti (above n. 9), 3–4 (footnotes omitted).
[82] See below, text accompanying n. 122, *et seq*, and sources cited therein.

identity of the territorial unit.[83] Albeit in different ways (and with different legal outcomes), the institutions considered presently are also predicated on an important distinction operating between the identity of the administering entity or entities and that of the administered territorial unit. This distinction marks the institutions out from a state's administration of its own territory in other circumstances. As with international territorial administration, the distinction is of a spatial nature. However, rather than a distinction between an 'international' actor and the 'local' territory (e.g., 'The High Representative of the International Community', and 'Bosnia and Herzegovina'), it is a distinction in terms of two different 'local' identities (e.g., 'Great Britain' and 'India').

It might be said, therefore, that the state-conducted institutions and ITA are of a piece in that they involve the same type of activity—territorial administration—predicated on the same type of distinction between the administering actor and the territory concerned.[84]

Collectively they might be referred to as 'foreign territorial administration', with a difference prevailing in the identity of the administering actor: a state/ group of states, a collection of state representatives, or an international organization. It is also possible to distinguish between them in terms of the degree to which they were 'internationalized', from protection and colonialism, with no international involvement, to the representative bodies, where the actors performing administration could be considered early forms of international organization, to the Mandate and Trusteeship systems, with individual state administrators but supervision by international organizations, and then international territorial administration, where the activity of administration is performed by an international organization. These differences will be discussed further below.

In an elemental sense, then, the policy institutions discussed above, and ITA, operated in the same fashion. To what extent can they be considered analogous in terms of the ends to which the activity they involved was put? In other words, to what extent are they analogous *policy* institutions?

8.3 Analogous Policy Institutions

... neither imperialism nor colonialism is a simple act of accumulation and acquisition. Both are supported and perhaps even impelled by impressive ideological formations that

---

[83] See above, ch. 1, section 1.4.3.

[84] Discussing both unilateral and multilateral interventions, the latter including ITA, Fearon & Laitin state that, '[s]imilar to classical imperialism, these efforts involve a remarkable degree of control over domestic political authority and basic economic functions by foreign countries'; Fearon & Laitin (above n. 4), 7. Michael Ignatieff regards the projects in Bosnia and Herzegovina and Kosovo as 'imperial' because of the existence of '...imperial means: garrisons of troops and foreign civilian administrators...'; Ignatieff (above n. 4), 59. The other feature Ignatieff regards as 'imperial'—the way the projects serve the political objectives of Europe and the US—is discussed below, ch. 9, text accompanying n. 24 *et seq.*

include notions that certain territories and people *require* and beseech domination, as well as forms of knowledge affiliated with domination.

Edward Said[85]

This section considers whether parallels can be identified between particular forms of protection, colonialism, administration by representative bodies, state-conducted administration under the Mandate and Trusteeship systems, and occupation as far as the purposes invoked in relation to these practices are concerned.[86] Based on the concept of a 'policy institution' defined in Chapter 1, the following analysis maps out the general contours of the policy framework. It will be suggested that important parallels with the general areas of international public policy highlighted in Chapter 7 in relation to international territorial administration are evident. As with the analysis on ITA, the focus is on purposes associated with the original reasons for the arrangements and which came to be associated with them over the course of their operation.[87]

Of course, not all of the practices under evaluation were associated with all the policies considered below. Moreover, to varying degrees each practice was heterogeneous across its individual manifestations in terms of the purposes with which it was associated.[88] The exception to this, as will become apparent, is state administration under the Mandate and Trusteeship institution, which was associated with a particular objective, although, even here, the nature of the perceived problem being addressed, and the way state administration was understood to address it varied considerably as between the different classes of Mandated territories and between these territories and Trust territories.

Only policies that bear comparison with the purposes associated with ITA are considered. One notable area of divergence here concerns the 'colonization' policy associated with certain forms of colonialism. Conventional representations of colonialism commonly distinguish betweens forms associated with the objective of settlement, whether forcible or non-forcible (e.g., the settlers in North America) and forms associated with other objectives (e.g., opening markets). Both forms were sometimes understood as cohabiting in a single colony,

---

[85] Said (above n. 2), 8, emphasis in original. See also the quote from Conrad, below, text accompanying n. 372.

[86] For work by others, see the sources cited in List of Sources, section 5.3 (regarding colonialism); in ch. 5 above, nn. 43 (on the Mandate system) and 44 (on the Trusteeship system); above in this chapter, nn. 70–73 (regarding the representative bodies) and n. 74 (on occupation in general); in ch. 1 above, nn. 72 (on the allied occupation of Germany and Austria), 73 (on the allied occupation of Japan), 74 (on occupation by Israel), 75 (on Iraq).

[87] This echoes the approach taken by Adam Roberts in his discussion of the policies associated with occupations, which covers why they were 'initiated, or later maintained'; see Roberts, 'What is Military Occupation?' (above n. 74), 300.

[88] On occupation, for example, Adam Roberts states that it is necessary to '...get away from the *idée fixe* that all occupations are essentially the same in their character and purpose'; ibid., 251. Roberts insists that '...there are extreme variations. Even within one single type of occupation...there could be any of several completely different motives'; ibid., 300.

and those colonies in relation to which settlement was not associated as a direct objective often involved settlers from the metropolitan state, for example people who served as colonial administrators. The distinction between the two forms is sometimes represented in terms of 'colonization' versus 'colonialism', or 'settlement' versus 'exploitation'/'dependency' colonialism.[89] For present purposes, colonization, or colonialism as settlement, is excluded from consideration when it was the exclusive or primary purpose associated with a particular case.

This study, then, is concerned with what is commonly called 'exploitation' or 'domination' as opposed to 'settlement' colonialism. The term 'exploitation' is used to suggest that the purposes associated with colonialism were either directly exploitative (e.g., the plunder of natural resources) or smokescreens for exploitation (e.g., the civilizing mission). These and other critiques of colonialism will be discussed further below;[90] prior to that discussion, the purposes themselves will be considered.

8.3.1 Territorial status outcomes and strategic advantage

Foreign state administration under protection, colonialism, occupation and a certain class of the representative bodies was sometimes associated with the objective of promoting a particular status for the territories affected. Often, European protectorates (using this term to denote both protected states and international protectorates) were considered 'weak' political entities brought under the influence of the 'stronger', 'protecting' state.[91] Certain administrative prerogatives were exercised by the latter to ensure that the protectorate did not fall under the sway of its rivals. So, for example, a state would control the foreign policy of a protectorate to prevent the protectorate from forming an alliance with, or consenting to assimilation into, another state.

Strategic concerns similarly lay behind the introduction of plenary or partial administration by representative bodies (rather than single states) in the class of 'disputed territories' mentioned above. Certain powerful states vied with each

---

[89] As Robert Young states, imperial ideas of colonialism took two major forms: 'French colonial theorists typically distinguished between colonization and domination, the British between dominions and dependencies; modern historians between settlement and exploitation colonies'; Young (above n. 45), 17. See also ibid., 19. So Jean-Paul Sartre discusses particular instances of colonialism in terms of settlement (giving the example of Australia), exploitation (giving the example of India) or mixture of both (giving the example of Algeria); Sartre (above n. 45), 30. See also the discussion in Ferro (above n. 43), *passim*, especially 1–3 and Crawford (above n. 44), 131. On settlements, see also Fieldhouse, *Colonialism* (above n. 32), 4, 20; D Ribeiro, *The Brazilian People: The Formation and Meaning of Brazil* G Rabassa transl., University Press of Florida, 2000), ch. 3, in particular 40–3; Ashcroft, Griffiths & Tiffin (above n. 45), 211–12; Bain, *Between Anarchy and Society* (above n. 12), 16–17; N Ferguson, *Empire, How Britain Made the Modern World* (Allen Lane, 2003), *passim*.

[90] Section 8.7.1.

[91] See the sources cited above, n. 32.

other and, sometimes, local actors for control over the territories concerned.[92] The attempted solution established various representative bodies to exercise either plenary administration or certain administrative prerogatives.[93] Plenary administration denied the possibility that any individual state could enjoy control, and plenary or partial administration ensured that governance policies in the territory supported a particular status for the territory.

Similarly, and reflecting their relationship to imperial policy, the forms of colonialism considered in this study (including so-called 'colonial protectorates') were usually associated with the aim of ensuring that the colonial territories became part of the sphere of influence of the metropolitan state.[94] The introduction and enhancement of colonial administration was often associated with this objective, whether at the commencement of a new colonial arrangement or in an existing dominion where indirect rule through private companies and/or a general claim to precedence was deemed insufficient to maintain exclusive authority in the face of challenges from both the indigenous population and imperial rivals.[95] More formally, this process was also sometimes associated with the establishment of legal title, via the international legal criterion of 'effective control'.[96]

The Mandate and Trusteeship arrangements were also associated with security considerations. As discussed further below, after the First World War some of the victorious states had wanted to annex the colonies of the defeated states; although annexation was rejected, the policy of allowing the retention of administrative control enabled these states to benefit in terms of prestige and national security, as it did also for the victorious states in the Second World War under the Trusteeship system.[97]

More generally, outward-facing security-related policy objectives, later conceptualized in terms of 'international peace and security', were associated with colonialism and the Mandate and Trusteeship systems, with specific provisions to this effect in the main international treaties relating to these arrangements,

---

[92] See, e.g., the citations from Ydit, above n. 70.

[93] See ibid.

[94] For example, Neta Crawford states that '...great powers seek colonies to balance against rivals, or to protect the geopolitical assets they already hold, such as trade routes...'; Crawford (above n. 44), 136. See also HD Hall, *Mandates, Dependencies and Trusteeship* (Stevens & Sons, 1948), *passim*.

[95] See generally A Anghie, 'Finding the Peripheries: Sovereignty and Colonialism in Nineteenth-Century International Law', 40 (1999) *Harvard International Law Journal* 1, *passim*; Anghie (above n. 2), 89, and Koskenniemi (above n. 44), 118, 121, 145–6, 148.

[96] Although the extent of administrative control deemed necessary for this varied considerably; see the discussion ibid., 116–78. On colonial title generally, see above, ch. 5, section 5.3.

[97] On the annexation ambitions of the victorious powers, see the discussion below, text accompanying n. 316 *et seq*. On the legal status of Mandated and Trust territories, see above, ch. 5, section 5.3. The value of exercising control over these territories to the national security of the administering states is discussed in Wright (above n. 32), *passim*; RN Chowdhuri, *International Mandates and Trusteeship Systems: A Comparative Study* (Martinus Nijhoff, 1955), *passim*; Bain, *Between Anarchy and Society* (above n. 12), ch. 4, *passim*, especially 78.

often including, for example, specific policies of non-militarization such as the prohibition on armaments.[98]

Although the Mandate and Trusteeship arrangements were considered beneficial to the administering powers in security and imperial prestige, the failure to provide for the kind of annexation possible under colonialism meant that, conversely, they were understood by some, notably the USA, to have an anti-imperial potential.[99] This was pronounced in the case of the Trusteeship arrangements because of the clear provision, discussed further in the next section, made for progressive development towards self-administration, a situation that would necessitate the end of foreign rule and thus the end of imperial control.[100] In this sense, then, the Trusteeship arrangements served the strategic objective of providing a temporary concession to furthering the imperial power of some of the administering powers, but set up on a basis ostensibly designed ultimately to diminish this power.

Other forms of territorial occupation beyond colonialism and the Mandate and Trusteeship systems have also been used by states to mediate questions as to the status of the territories involved and to obtain strategic advantage even though, as mentioned, the international law of occupation prohibits the occupying state or states from altering the status of the territory involved.[101] For example, in post-Second

---

[98] The administering authorities in 'B' class Mandated territories were obliged to guarantee 'the prohibition of abuses, such as...the arms traffic' and obliged to ensure '...the prevention of the establishment of fortifications or military and naval bases and of military training of the natives for other than police purposes and the defence of territory...'; League Covenant, Art. 22. On the different classes of Mandated territory, see below, n. 200 and accompanying text. For commentary on non-militarization policies generally in relation to Mandated territories, see, e.g., Hall (above n. 94), 66–72; Hales (above n. 47), 236–42. Trust territories were divided up on the basis of security considerations into those that were 'strategic' and 'non-strategic'; see UN Charter, Arts. 82–3, 85. For commentary on this, see, e.g., Chowdhuri (above n. 97), 11 and, by way of a comparison with the Mandate arrangements, Hall, ibid., 279–80. The main set of obligations imposed on the administering authorities of both Non-Self-Governing and Trust territories includes the objective to 'further international peace and security': see UN Charter, Art. 73 (c) (on Non-Self-Governing Territories) and ibid., Art. 76 (a) (on Trust territories). The Administering authorities in Trust territories were also subject to a specific obligation to:

...ensure that the trust territory shall play its part in the maintenance of international peace and security. To this end the administering authority may make use of volunteer forces, facilities, and assistance from the trust territory in carrying out the obligations towards the Security Council undertaken in this regard by the administering authority, as well as for local defense and the maintenance of law and order within the trust territory.

UN Charter, Art. 84.

[99] Hall (above n. 94), 13; Bain, *Between Anarchy and Society* (above n. 12), 21.

[100] See the discussion ibid., 108–14.

[101] For Adam Roberts, occupation has been used, inter alia, '...to implement territorial claims...to prevent the use of the occupied territory as a military base, including for guerrilla or other attacks against the occupying state...to enable the occupant himself to establish military bases...'; Roberts, 'What is Military Occupation?' (above n. 74), 300. Eyal Benvenisti discusses how the occupation of the Rhineland by the allies after the First World War was 'orientated first and foremost toward the future allocation of military powers and economic resources within postwar Europe'; Benvenisti (above n. 9), 49. France, for example, '...conceived its zone as a buffer between Germany and its eastern border, the only meaningful protection from a renewed German offensive'

World War Germany, the emergence of East–West splits led the Allies to use their administrative authority to support the particular territorial agenda of carving up Germany into two separate entities, the German Democratic Republic and the Federal Republic of Germany, and dividing Berlin into two entities.[102]

8.3.2 Trusteeship, the civilizing mission, and other administrative policies

I remember Cecil Rhodes used to say that the proper relation between Whites and Blacks in this country [South Africa] was the relation between guardian and ward. This is the basis of trusteeship. Much later, the principle of trusteeship was put in the Covenant of the League of Nations.

Jan Smuts, reported by HG Wells[103]

An overall concept evident at the heart of many instances of foreign territorial administration is that of 'trusteeship'. This concept is significant in explaining how the internal governance of the territories has been understood—the basis on which foreign rule was to operate. International trusteeship can be understood in terms of a response to two distinct ideas relating to the pre-existing governance structure in the territory. In the first place, the racialized concept of a 'standard of civilization' was deployed to determine that certain peoples in the world were 'uncivilized', lacking organized societies, a position reflected and constituted in the notion that their 'sovereignty' was either completely lacking or at least of an inferior character when compared to that of 'civilized' peoples.[104] The development of this notion in the period under evaluation drew in large measure from

---

(ibid., 50, footnote omitted). For the association of annexation policies with the occupations by Italy and Germany in the Second World War, see the commentary by Benvenisti, ibid., 63–4 and 64–6 respectively. On the legal prohibition on altering territorial status, see above, n. 75.

[102] See, e.g., Crawford (above n. 32), 454–9.

[103] HG Wells, '42 to '44: A Contemporary Memoir upon Human Behaviour During the Crisis of the World Revolution* (Secker & Warburg, 1944), 71.

[104] Ideas concerning a 'standard of civilization' can be found in the works contained in List of Sources, section 5.3. On such ideas, see, in particular, F de Vitoria, 'On the American Indians' (1539), in *Vitoria—Political Writings* (A Pagden and J Lawrance eds and transl., CUP, 1991), 231; AH Snow, *The Question of Aborigines in the Law and Practice of Nations* (US Government Printing Office, 1919); Wright (above n. 32), ch. 1; GW Gong, *The Standard of 'Civilization' in International Society* (Clarendon Press, 1984), *passim* and especially 14–21; Jackson (above n. 55), 143; Bain, *Between Anarchy and Society* (above n. 12), 74–7 and sources cited therein; Anghie (above n. 2), 52–65, 150; B Ibhawoh, *Imperialism and Human Rights: Colonial Discourses of Rights and Liberties in African History* (SUNY Press, 2006); G Schwarzenberger, 'The Standard of Civilization in International Law', 17 (1955) *Current Legal Problems* 212; Anghie (above n. 95), 25–34 and 52–4; H Owada, 'Inaugural Address of the President of the Society, Inaugural Conference of the Asian Society of International Law', delivered in Singapore, 7 April 2007 (to be published in Asian Society of International Law, *Conference Papers of the Singapore Inaugural Meeting*, forthcoming, copy of delivered text on file with the author). See also the quotation from Edward Said, above, text accompanying n. 85.

Enlightenment ideas. As William Bain relates, for those advocating cosmopolitan notions of a single human family, the only way to:

> ... make sense of the great differences that separated the European and non-European worlds, and yet sustain this claim of unity, was to make distinctions within the human family and to express those differences in terms of degrees of improvement, development, advancement or maturity.[105]

In the second place, the idea of trusteeship has been associated with the introduction of foreign rule after conflict, often in circumstances where governance in the territory has been degraded in some way by that conflict, for example, through the collapse of a defeated government and the destruction of infrastructure.[106]

Understanding the exercise of administrative prerogatives over territory in these two circumstances as 'trusteeship' conceptualizes the relationship between the foreign actor and the territory and its people in a particular manner: the trustee/guardian state is controlling the beneficiary/ward territory, acting on behalf of the latter entity—the 'sacred trust of civilization' or the 'civilizing mission'.[107]

---

[105] Bain, *Between Anarchy and Society* (above n. 12), 19. See also Gong (above n. 104), 45–53.

[106] For a discussion of 'armistice' and 'post-surrender' occupations, see Roberts, 'What is Military Occupation?' (above n. 74), 265–7 and 267–71 respectively.

[107] For commentary on the concept of international trusteeship conducted by individual states, mostly concerned with colonialism and/or the Mandate and Trusteeship systems, see, e.g., CG Fenwick, *Wardship in International Law* (US Government Printing Office, 1919); Snow (above n. 104); MF Lindley, *The Acquisition and Government of Backward Territory in International Law: Being a Treatise on the Law and Practice Relating to Colonial Expansion* (Longmans, Green & Co., 1926); Lugard (above n. 54), *passim*; Wright (above n. 32), ch. 1; Hall (above n. 94), 97–100; KE Robinson, *The Dilemmas of Trusteeship: Aspects of British Colonial Policy Between the Wars* (OUP, 1965); Chowdhuri (above n. 97), 13–16, 20–4, 35–6; Jackson (above n. 55), 71–4; Ashcroft, Griffiths & Tiffin (above n. 45), 47; Simpson (above n. 32), 291–5; Jackson (above n. 12), ch. 11; S Schama, *A History of Britain, Volume 3: The Fate of Empire 1776–2000* (Miramax Books, 2002), 269–70; Bain, *Between Anarchy and Society* (above n. 12), *passim*; PH Kerr, 'Political Relations between Advanced and Backward Peoples', in AJ Grant, A Greenwood, JDI Hughes, PH Kerr, and FF Urquhart, *An Introduction to the Study of International Relations* (Macmillan, 1916), 141; JC Hales, 'The Reform and Extension of the Mandate System', 26 (1940) *Transactions of the Grotius Society* 153, at 155, 174–7; CH Alexandrowicz, 'The Juridical Expression of the Sacred Trust of Civilization', 65 (1971) *AJIL* 149; Lyon (above n. 11); Gordon, 'Saving Failed States' (above n. 11), 926; Anghie (above n. 95), 62–5 and sources cited therein; Tsagourias (above n. 12), *passim*. See also the separate opinion of Judge (Sir) Arnold McNair in *International Status of South West Africa, Advisory Opinion, ICJ Reports 1950*, 128, *passim* and in particular at 149. For an example of the link between the standard of civilization and the civilizing mission, Neta Crawford states that '...colonialism was justified and good because the inhabitants of the colonized lands were less-than-human savages who lacked the attributes Europeans believed were marks of civilization'; Crawford (above n. 44), 140. See further, ibid., 140 *et seq.* and Gong (above n. 104), *passim*. The legal basis for international trusteeship is discussed further below, text accompanying n. 434 *et seq.* Trusteeship is of course related to the concept of paternalism. On the latter concept see, e.g., G Dworkin, 'Paternalism', in RA Wasserstrom (ed.), *Morality and the Law* (Wadsworth Publishing Company, 1971), 107. The notion of relative capacities for reason between individuals as a basis for inclusion or exclusion from the arena of politics and the exercise of or subjugation to rule goes back to ideas from antiquity. See, for example, the following statement by Aristotle:

[t]hus it becomes clear that both ruler and ruled must have a share in virtue, but that there are differences in virtue in each case, as there are also among those who by nature rule. An immediate

The concept of trusteeship became associated with certain (but by no means all) forms of colonialism in the period under evaluation, as illustrated in Edmund Burke's influential recitation of the concept in relation to British rule in India in 1783:

all political power which is set over men and . . . all privilege claimed or exercised in exclusion of them, being wholly artificial, and for so much a derogation from the natural equality of mankind at large, ought to be some way or other exercised ultimately for their benefit. If this is true with regard to every species of political dominion, and every description of commercial privilege, none of which can be original, self-derived rights, or grants for mere private benefit of the holders, then such rights, or privileges, or whatever you choose to call them, are all, in the strictest sense, a *trust*.[108]

indication of this is afforded by the soul, where we find natural ruler and natural subject, whose virtues we regard as different—one being the rational element, the other the non-rational. It is therefore clear that the same feature will be found in the other cases too, so that most instances of ruling and being ruled are natural. For rule of free over slave, male over female, man over boy, are all different, because, while parts of the soul are present in each case, the distribution is different. Thus the deliberative faculty in the soul is not present at all in the slave; in a female it is present but ineffective, in a child present but undeveloped.

Aristotle, *The Politics* (TA Sinclair transl., revised by TJ Saunders, Penguin Books, 1992), 95. On the civilizing mission in particular and the link therein between trusteeship and the 'standard of civilization', see, e.g., Gong (above n. 104), 51–3.

[108] E Burke, 'Speech on Mr Fox's East India Bill, 1 December 1783', reproduced in E Burke, *The Speeches of the Right Honorable Edmund Burke in the House of Commons, and in Westminster-Hall* (Longman & Ridgeway, 1816), vol. II, 406, at 411 (emphasis in original). In its 1923 parliamentary White Paper on Kenya, the British Government stated that they 'regard themselves as exercising a trust on behalf of the African population'; 'Indians in Kenya', *Parliamentary Papers* Cmd. 1922 (1923), 10 quoted in Bain, *Between Anarchy and Society* (above n. 12), 62. On this statement see, e.g., R Hyam, *Britain's Imperial Century, 1815–1914* (3rd edn, Palgrave Macmillan, 2002), 265 and Simpson (above n. 32), 291. So for Brian Simpson, in the case of British colonial ideology, '. . . the basic justifying conception, derived from the common law tradition, was trusteeship; colonial peoples were the beneficiaries, the colonial power the trustee' (ibid.). The increased significance of trusteeship ideas to colonialism over time is reflected in the comment by James Hales that '. . . despite the diversity of colonial aims in the nineteenth century, it is clear that since the institution of the Mandate System, the governing principle behind all colonial administration is trusteeship'; Hales (above n. 107), 155. One of the definitions of 'trusteeship' in the *Oxford English Dictionary* is '[t]he function of a colonial power or other dominant people as protectors of a subject people'; (definition 2a, *OED Online*, at <http://www.oed.com>). On the association of trusteeship with colonialism generally, see the sources above, n. 107. This association was taken up by the international lawyers of the time, as reflected in the following statement by Joseph Hornung in 1885: '[w]e accept the hegemony and trusteeship of the strong but only in the interests of the weak and in view of their full future emancipation'; J Hornung, 'Civilisés et barbares' (Part 3), 17 (1885) *Revue de Droit International* 559, quoted in Koskenniemi (above n. 44), 130. On the relationship between trusteeship and international law generally, see, e.g., the discussion in Anghie (above n. 2), ch. 2 and Koskenniemi, ibid., ch. 2. As for the notion reflected in the quote from Edmund Burke that colonial trusteeship denotes the colonial power acting on behalf of the colonial peoples, this of course references the general idea of a legal trust whereby the trustee acts on behalf of the beneficiary, not on its own behalf. The *Oxford English Dictionary* defines 'trust' in the law of property as '[t]he confidence reposed in a person in whom the legal ownership of property is vested *to hold or use for the benefit of another*' (definition 6, *OED Online*, at <http://www.oed.com> emphasis added). Applying this to international trusteeship, bearing in mind what was said in section 8.2 above about the legal status of certain colonies, all Mandate and Trusteeship territories, and occupied territories under to the

A concept of trust was implicit in Article VI of Chapter I of the General Act of the Berlin Conference of 1884–85, under which the colonial powers in Africa were bound to:

> ...watch over the preservation of the native tribes, and to care for the improvement of the conditions of their moral and material well-being.[109]

In the UN Charter, the Declaration Regarding Non-Self-Governing Territories (i.e., as previously discussed, colonies) states that:

> Members of the United Nations which have or assume responsibilities for the administration of territories whose peoples have not yet attained a full measure of self-government recognize the principle that the interests of the inhabitants of these territories are paramount, and accept as a sacred trust the obligation to promote to the utmost, within the system of international peace and security established by the present Charter, the well-being of the inhabitants of these territories.[110]

As these quotes suggest, the concept of trust was understood by its proponents as a way of placing colonial rule on an ethical, humanitarian footing.[111] As with the origins of the standard of civilization on which it was based, this enterprise of humanizing colonialism is understood to reflect the changes in imperial thought wrought by the Enlightenment in general and the experience of the American and French revolutions in particular: to be justified, empire now had to be conceived

---

law of occupation, 'ownership' is best understood in terms of the right to administer the territory, as opposed to the enjoyment of territorial title (although title may sometimes subsist). On the idea that international trusteeship denotes selfless rule, James Hales states that 'in perfect trusteeship, the guardian of colonial peoples...cannot seek any advantage for himself'; Hales (above n. 107), 176–7. See, however, the idea of the 'dual mandate', discussed below, text accompanying n.139 *et seq.* Edmund Burke is popularly regarded as the original theorist of colonial trusteeship, but the concept is evident in the ideas of Francisco de Vitoria and Bartolomé de Las Casas in relation to Spanish colonialism in the 16th century. See de Vitoria (above n. 104) and, for commentary, the discussion in Chowdhuri (above n. 97), 20–4, Anghie (above n. 2), ch. 1; A Anghie, 'Francisco de Vitoria and the Colonial Origins of International Law', 5 (1996) *Social & Legal Studies* 321; Bain, *Between Anarchy and Society* (above n. 12), 15 *et seq.*

[109] General Act of the Conference respecting (1) Freedom of Trade in the Basin of the Congo; (2) the Slave Trade; (3) Neutrality of the Territories in the Basin of the Congo; (4) Navigation of the Congo; (5) Navigation of the Niger; and (6) Rules for Future Occupation on the Coast of the African Continent, signed at Berlin, 26 February 1885, 165 CTS 485 (hereinafter 'Berlin Conference General Act'), Chapter I, Art. VI. On the idea that these provisions reflected ideas of trusteeship see, e.g., Hall (above n. 94), 104.

[110] UN Charter, Art. 73. For commentary, see, e.g., U Fastenrath, 'Article 73', in B Simma (ed.), *The Charter of the United Nations. A Commentary* (2nd edn, OUP, 2002), vol. 2, 1089 and sources cited therein. In the words of H Duncan Hall: '[t]he Declaration fully recognizes national trusteeship in dependent areas. It defines the principles upon which national trusteeship should operate, thus giving international recognition to the long-established national principle of the 'sacred trust''; Hall (above n. 94), 285.

[111] See, e.g., Hall (above n. 94), 98–9 and sources cited therein; Bain, *Between Anarchy and Society* (above n. 12), *passim*, especially 1, 53 *et seq*, and ch. 2. This in turn reflected one of the reasons for the idea of the standard of civilization as explained by Gerrit Gong: 'Europe's need to explain and justify its overlordship of non-European countries in other than merely military terms'; Gong (above n. 104), 42.

in terms of the 'benefit it conferred on the governed'.[112] These cosmopolitan ideas also provided a normative basis for the notion that there was an obligation to engage in imperial rule over those less civilized—that, as William Bain states, 'the strong should rule on behalf of the weak'.[113] In the words of one proponent of colonial trusteeship in 1916, Philip Kerr, there was a duty on the part of European states to engage in imperial rule, arising:

...not from any pride of dominion, or because they wish to exploit the resources, but in order to protect them alike from oppression and corruption, by strict laws and strict administration, which shall bind the foreigner as well as the native...[114]

The political notion of obligation is reflected in the legalization of trusteeship, notably in the Berlin General Act and the UN Charter, as illustrated in the extracted provisions above, and the League of Nations Covenant, as will be illustrated below in this section and discussed further in a later section.[115]

The move to humanize colonial rule arose in part from concerns related to that which 'trusteeship' administration was called upon to replace: earlier forms of state colonialism and/or control by corporate entities like trading companies understood in terms of neglect, exploitation, profit, and general irresponsibility.[116]

As reflected in the quote from HG Wells above, the concept of trust was formally adopted as the basis for the Mandate and Trusteeship systems after the two world wars, which, as mentioned, were conceived in relation to the

---

[112] Bain, *Between Anarchy and Society* (above n. 12), 17–21, quotation taken from 17. See also Gong (above n. 104), *passim*.

[113] Ibid., 51. See further the discussion ibid., at 17–21, 23. Cf. the quotation from Edward Said above, text accompanying n. 85.

[114] Kerr (above n. 107), 149, quoted in Bain, *Between Anarchy and Society* (above n. 12), 1.

[115] The later discussion can be found in the text accompanying n. 434 *et seq.*

[116] Indeed, in the case of British colonialism, ideas of trusteeship originated in attempts to regulate the activities of the British East India Company, the perceived failure of which leading to calls for rule by the Crown and the eventual dissolution of the company. See generally the discussion in Bain, *Between Anarchy and Society* (above n. 12), ch. 2, and Anghie (above n. 2), 69, and sources cited therein at n. 104. Antony Anghie reports that '[b]y the end of the nineteenth century... [the] direct involvement of European States in the whole process of governing resulted in a shift in the ideology justifying Empire from the vulgar language of profit to that of order, proper governance and humanitarianism'; Anghie (above n. 95), 37. See also Anghie (above n. 2), 69. In 1945, the international lawyer Philip Marshall Brown stated that:

[a]rbitrary rule and selfish exploitation has gradually given way to the recognition of the right of such [colonial] peoples to attain self-government and enjoy their own material resources. The present war has given a great impetus to the acceptance of the principle that colonial administration must be considered as a trusteeship in behalf of the subject peoples.

PM Brown, 'Editorial Comment: Imperialism', 39 (1945) *AJIL* 84, 85. On the notion that trusteeship administration would replace control by 'private companies that pursue no other objective than immediate personal enrichment' (C Salomon, *L'Occupation des territoires sans maître* (A Giard, 1889), at 186), see, e.g., the discussion in Koskenniemi (above n. 44), 118, 144. On the general idea of the civilizing mission as a shift towards a humanitarian ethic for colonialism, see also Fieldhouse, *Colonialism* (above n. 32), 173; Koskenniemi (above n. 44), 151, 129–30.

detached colonies of the defeated powers.[117] The Trusteeship system also covered former Mandated territories, and was open to these territories 'voluntarily placed under the system by States responsible for their administration', but no placements in the latter category were made.[118] The twin notions of incapacity for self-administration, and foreign state administration on a trusteeship basis, were the hallmarks of both systems. According to Article 22 of the Covenant, the people of Mandated territories were deemed 'not yet able to stand by themselves' and the administration of Mandated territories was to be a 'sacred trust of civilization'.[119] In the UN Charter, the concept of trust is reflected in the name given to the arrangements; the designation of incapacity, by contrast, is made by implication, in the provision for trusteeship itself, and the objectives for trusteeship administration such as the promotion of development.[120] The imperial concept of colonial trusteeship was, thus, refashioned as the explicit basis for a set of modified colonial arrangements.[121]

As far as occupation is concerned, (Sir) Arnold Wilson stated in 1932 that:

... enemy territories in the occupation of the armed forces of another country constitute (in the language of Art. 22 of the League of Nations Covenant) a sacred trust, which must be administered as a whole in the interests of both the inhabitants and of the legitimate sovereign or the duly constituted successor in title.[122]

---

[117] On the particular territories covered, see above, ch. 5, nn. 43 and 44.

[118] See above, n. 69.

[119] On the origins of the Mandate system, see Wright (above n. 32), ch. I. On the origins of the Trusteeship system, see Chowdhuri (above n. 97), 27–35. On the provisions for trusteeship and development for Trust Territories, see UN Charter, Art. 76. On the trusteeship basis for the Mandate arrangements, see, e.g., Hales (above n. 107), 177–87. Reflecting the connection between these arrangements and colonial trusteeship, and the influence of Edmund Burke in that earlier paradigm, Peter Lyon states that Article 22 of the League Covenant was the '... ripe fruit or late blossom of Burkean ideas'; Lyon (above n. 11), 99. In its definition of 'trusteeship' the *Oxford English Dictionary* covers colonial trusteeship and the UN Trusteeship systems (see above, n. 108, and below, n. 120) but not also the Mandate arrangements, although in one of the examples given of the use of the word to refer to UN Trusteeship, the previous status of the UK Trust Territory of the Cameroons as a British Mandate is mentioned (see the definition cited below in n. 120).

[120] One of the definitions of 'trusteeship' in the *Oxford English Dictionary* is '[t]he administration of a territory by a nation acting on behalf of the United Nations Organization' (definition 2b, *OED Online*, at <http://www.oed.com>).

[121] On the common origins and bases for both systems, see, e.g., Chowdhuri (above n. 97), *passim* and especially 8–12 and ch III; *Oppenheim's International Law* (above n. 33), § 89; DJ Harris, *Cases and Materials on International Law* (6th edn, Sweet & Maxwell, 2004), 130. The notion that Mandated territories were a class of colonies is illustrated, for example, in the sub-title of James Hales' study of the Mandate arrangements: 'A Study in International Colonial Supervision'; see Hales (above n. 47).

[122] Wilson (above n. 74), 38. Gerhard von Glahn defines occupation as '... a temporary right of administration on a sort of trusteeship basis...'; von Glahn (above n. 74), 668. Adam Roberts states that, '... the idea of "trusteeship" is implicit in all occupation law... all occupants are in some vague and general sense trustees'; Roberts, 'What is Military Occupation?' (above n. 74), 295, citing Wilson (above) and von Glahn (above, the same quote contained in an earlier edition). For Roberts, the law of occupation in both the Hague Regulations and the Geneva Conventions 'can be interpreted as putting the occupant in a quasi-trustee role' (Roberts, ibid., 295). See also

Gerhard von Glahn considers occupation to operate on a trusteeship basis denoting a 'temporary right of administration' operating 'until the occupation ceases'.[123] Eyal Benvenisti states that the 'occupant's status is conceived to be that of a trustee'.[124]

As with ideas of colonial trusteeship, those who advocate understanding occupation as trusteeship explain this in terms of its reflection of an underlying objective to humanize the basis for and the conduct of occupations. Occupation as trusteeship reflects the policy objective that, as mentioned earlier, occupying powers do not enjoy sovereignty over the territories concerned and are to be prevented from claiming such sovereignty through an obligation to this effect in occupation law.[125] This objective is promoted by conceiving the relationship between the occupant and the occupied territory as one of trusteeship; the notion of acting on behalf of the beneficiary obliges the occupier to protect, not alter (or claim for itself) the sovereignty of the occupant.[126]

Gerhard von Glahn conceives occupation on a trusteeship basis on the grounds that 'the legitimate government of an occupied territory retains its sovereignty' which is only 'suspended in the area for the duration of the belligerent occupation'.[127] Elaborating on this theme, Eyal Benvenisti states that:

[t]he foundation upon which the entire law of occupation is based is the principle of inalienability of sovereignty through the actual or threatened use of force. Effective control by foreign military force can never bring about by itself a valid transfer of sovereignty. From the principle of inalienable sovereignty over a territory spring[s] the constraints that international

the discussion by Perritt, who describes the occupations of post-Second World War Germany and Japan, and the CPA occupation of Iraq, as instances of the exercise of trust; see Perritt, 'Structures and Standards' (above n. 11), 410–16, 422 (general discussion of trusteeship and occupation) 393–5 (on Germany); 395–6 (on Japan); 407–10 (on Iraq). In 1973, Allan Gerson proposed a concept of 'trustee occupation' to be applied to Israel's presence in the Palestinian Territories; the idea was that this would enable the situation under evaluation to be distinguished from occupation generally and, in consequence, certain obligations in the law of occupation; see Gerson, 'Trustee Occupant' (above n. 74); Gerson, *Israel, the West Bank and International Law* (above n. 74), *passim* and in particular 78–82. This notion that 'trusteeship occupation' is somehow a distinct category of occupation is not reflected in the generalized notions of trusteeship adopted by the commentators above in the present footnote. Adam Roberts in particular makes the comments reproduced above in the context of dismissing Gerson's notion, and concludes by expressing scepticism that 'trusteeship occupation' is a 'separate category of occupation'; Roberts, ibid., 295.

123 von Glahn (above n. 74), 668.
124 Benvenisti (above n. 9), 6, footnote omitted which cites the works by Wilson, von Glahn, and Roberts cited herein above in n. 122 (in the case of von Glahn, Benvenisti cites the same quote cited above contained in an earlier edition of the same work).
125 On this, see text accompanying n. 75 above.
126 On the notion of acting on behalf of the beneficiary, see the discussion above, n. 108. The significance of the trusteeship concept for issues of title in occupation law discussed here underlines the observations therein about how the notion of 'trust' from domestic property law relates to the concept of international trusteeship.
127 von Glahn (above n. 74), 668.

law imposes upon the occupant. The power exercising effective control within another sovereign's territory has only temporary managerial powers, for the period until a peaceful solution is reached. During that limited period, the occupant administers the territory on behalf of the sovereign. Thus the occupant's status is conceived to be that of a trustee.[128]

The central 'humanizing' element of the occupation law conception of trusteeship, then, is the objective of preventing occupations from enabling occupiers to obtain title through force, echoing the reason why rule over the Mandated and Trust territories was also conceived in this way.

The substantive obligations of occupation law are sometimes also explained through their association with this underlying objective. The occupation of Iraq by the CPA in 2003 brought to prominence the long-standing question as to the extent to which occupation law prevents occupants from transforming the political and economic structures of occupied territory.[129] Clearly, the notion that the territory is not to be considered part of the sovereign territory of the occupant

---

[128] Benvenisti (above n. 9), 5–6, footnote omitted (on the contents of the omitted footnote, see above, n. 124).

[129] See the sources cited above, ch. 8, n. 75. The norm of occupation law most often cited to illustrate a status quo orientation is the obligation in the Hague Regulations that occupying states are obliged to respect, 'unless absolutely prevented, the laws in force in the country'; Hague Regulations (above n. 74). Art. 43. For commentary, see, e.g., Benvenisti (above n. 9), 7, n. 1. In his survey of occupations published in 1984, Adam Roberts describes how many, in their transformatory activities, 'went beyond the letter of the Hague regulations, yet fell short of annexation or assumption of sovereignty'; Roberts, 'What is Military Occupation?' (above n. 74), 269. In both that survey and a later piece written in the context of the occupation of Iraq by the Coalition Provisional Authority (CPA), Roberts takes a fairly expansive view of what is possible under occupation law, but also, in the latter article, accepts that this normative framework can be supplemented from other sources in the case of so-called 'transformatory' occupations; see Roberts, 'Transformative Military Occupation' (above n. 74). Eyal Benvenisti states that '[t]he occupant's powers have expanded through time to cover almost all the areas in which modern governments assert legitimacy to police, a far cry from the turn of the century laissez-faire conception of minimal governmental intervention'; Benvenisti, ibid., 6. Discussing SC Res. 1483 of 22 May 2003, which, it is claimed, authorized the political and economic transformation of Iraq by the CPA, Benvenisti states that the resolution:

[e]nvisions the role of the modern occupant as the role of the heavily involved regulator, when it calls upon the occupants to pursue an 'effective administration' of Iraq. This call stands in contrast to the initial orientation of the Hague Regulations, which envisioned the disinterested occupant who does not intervene in the lives of the occupied population.

Ibid., x. David Scheffer's broad thesis about the inadequacies of occupation law alone to govern the conduct of transformative occupations includes the argument that the law is sometimes at odds with the transformation agenda; Scheffer (above n. 74). In general, Scheffer argues that transformation 'requires strained interpretations of occupation law', ibid., 843. The law of occupation in Geneva Convention (IV) (above, n.74) is 'far more relevant to a belligerent occupation than to an occupation designed to liberate a society from its repressive governance and transform it as a nation guided by international norms and the self-determination of its liberated populace'; ibid., 849. Discussing peacekeeping in particular, he argues that the full operation of occupation law may be 'inappropriate and even undesirable in many situations'; ibid., 848. Discussing Adam Roberts' broad conception in his 1984 article of what is possible under occupation law, Scheffer argues that the attempt to square occupation law with the realities of modern occupations is 'increasingly artificial and begs for an alternative legal framework that more accurately reflects the development of key areas of international law and that recognizes . . . the political realities of modern practice'; Scheffer, ibid., 848–9, footnote omitted. See also Chesterman, *You, The People* (above n. 9), 6–7.

is tied to the notion that the occupier should not be in the business of altering the economic and political status quo. Comparing annexation with political and economic transformation, Adam Roberts states that although they are:

conceptually and legally very different, they do have one thing in common—they tend to involve extending to the occupied territory the type of political system adhered to by the occupying power.[130]

Insofar as the substantive norms of occupation law are concerned with maintaining the status quo, they can be understood as a consequence of the underlying policy that the territory in question is not, and should not become, part of the territory of the occupying state.[131] More broadly, conceiving occupation as 'trust' is an attempt to rein in the impulse of occupying states to use the occupation to pursue self-serving objectives.[132]

Beyond this, the 'humanitarian' norms of occupation law concerned with protecting individuals and maintaining order can similarly be understood as a means of humanizing the conduct of occupations, seeking to rule out, for example, abusive practices such as sexual assault and rape, retributional attacks on civilians, pillage, and the failure to restore order historically associated with occupations.[133]

The general humanizing explanation for the norms of occupation law is further reinforced by the instrumental approach of those who seek to define the factual test of 'occupation' which, if met, triggers the substantive obligations, in terms of activity that they consider to require regulation by the obligations that would be so triggered.[134]

---

[130] Roberts, 'Transformative Military Occupation' (above n. 74), 582–3.

[131] On this, see Ratner (above n. 9), 700.

[132] Discussing the rationale for occupation law, Eyal Benvenisti states that '. . . in the heart of all occupations exists a potential—if not an inherent—conflict of interest between occupant and occupied'; Benvenisti (above n. 9), 4.

[133] On obligations to protect individuals, see the instruments and sources cited above, n. 74; on the obligation to restore and preserve order, see below, text accompanying n. 177 *et seq.*

[134] The factual definition of occupation in law is discussed above, section 8.2.5. Discussing 'specific cases differing in some respect from the most classic forms of occupation', Adam Roberts states that there are nonetheless 'some markers which may help to indicate the existence of an occupation, or may suggest the need for the law on occupations to be applied'; Roberts, 'What is Military Occupation?' (above n. 74), 300. In setting out these markers without explaining whether they are indicative in relation to occupation as fact or occupation as the need for regulation—or both—the issues of how occupation is defined factually so as to trigger occupation law, and what circumstances require the norms of occupation law as a matter of principle, are elided. All the factors set out can be understood to implicate the latter issue:

(i) there is a military force whose presence in a territory is not sanctioned or regulated by a valid agreement, or whose activities there involve an extensive range of contacts with the host society not adequately covered by the original agreement under which it intervened; (ii) the military force has either displaced the territory's ordinary system of public order and government, replacing it with its own command structure, or else has shown the clear physical ability to displace it; (iii) there is a difference of nationality and interest between the inhabitants on the one hand and the forces intervening and exercising power over them on the other, with the former not owing allegiance to

As will be discussed further, the conception of occupation as trusteeship aimed at safeguarding the status quo is at odds with how many occupations have been conducted and, more broadly, how trusteeship as it developed in the context of colonialism sometimes operated, where transformation of the political and economic system of the territories concerned was evident.

The concept of colonial trusteeship was often, but not always, understood to have a two-part character in terms of the role of the trustee: first, to care for the ward and, secondly, tutelage of the ward in order that it can mature and eventually care for itself. The colonial idea of the 'civilizing mission', then, was understood in terms of governing so as to address the perceived incapacity for self-government itself, or at least governance that meets the standard of civilization, and also building up local capacities, sometimes with the aim that self-administration, meeting the standard, would eventually be possible.[135] The general contours of this idea are evident in the earlier quotation from the General Act of the Berlin Conference, with its obligation to 'watch over' and 'care for...improvement'.[136]

In the same way, Article 22 of the League Covenant articulates the 'sacred trust of civilization' forming the basis for the Mandate arrangements in terms of the 'well-being and development' of the people in Mandated territories.[137] The provisions of the UN Charter concerning non-self-governing territories and Trust territories are similarly concerned with ideas of both care and advancement.[138]

For many, colonial rule had a further dual nature: it was to be mutually beneficial to both the native population and European states generally, including, notably, the administering state involved in each case. Perhaps the most

the latter; (iv) within an overall framework of a breach of important parts of the national or international legal order, administration and the life of society have to continue on some legal basis, and there is a practical need for an emergency set of rules to reduce the dangers which can result from clashes between the military force and the inhabitants.

Ibid., 300–301. In what appears to be a similarly instrumental approach, Steven Ratner adopts a broad definition of occupation, discussed further below (see text accompanying n. 268) as 'occupation in a functional sense to describe control of territory by outside entities'; Ratner (above n. 9), 697.

[135] See generally the sources cited above n. 107. For Bill Ashcroft, Gareth Griffiths, and Helen Tiffin, through the civilizing mission, '...colonialism could be (re)presented as a virtuous and necessary civilizing task involving education and paternalistic nurture'; Ashcroft, Griffiths & Tiffin (above n. 45), 47. Antony Anghie describes the civilizing mission as the idea of 'extending Empire for the higher purpose of educating and rescuing the barbarian'; Anghie (above n. 2), 96; see also ibid., 96 *et seq*; Koskenniemi (above n. 44), 145, 147, 168.

[136] Berlin Conference General Act (above n. 109), ch. I, Art. VI. In its 1923 parliamentary White Paper on colonial rule in Kenya, the British Government stated that the 'object' of the trust exercised by the Crown in Kenya was the 'protection and advancement of the native races'; 'Indians in Kenya' (above n. 108), 10.

[137] On this, see further the dictum of the International Court of Justice in the *International Status of South West Africa, Advisory Opinion, ICJ Reports 1950*, 128, at 131.

[138] For Non-Self-Governing Territories, see UN Charter, Art 73; for Trust territories, see ibid., Art. 76.

prominent theorist of this approach was the British colonialist (Lord) Frederick Lugard in his idea of the 'dual mandate' for colonial rule.[139] In the words of Lugard:

[l]et it be admitted at the outset that European brains, capital, and energy have not been, and never will be, expended in developing the resources of Africa from motives of pure philanthropy; that Europe is in Africa for the mutual benefit of her own industrial classes, and of the native races in their progress to a higher plane; that the benefit can be made reciprocal, and that it is the aim and desire of civilised administration to fulfil this dual mandate.[140]

Humanizing colonialism, then, did not mean removing the original focus on the benefits to the colonizing state and its traders, but, rather, supplementing it with a focus on native welfare that was considered to have been absent, notably during the period of control by the trading companies.[141]

As with trusteeship generally, aspects of this concept of mutual benefit can be identified in certain Enlightenment ideas.[142] In the first place, as William Bain points out, the concept echoes the Kantian cosmopolitan notion that 'the wealth of the earth is by natural right the common inheritance of all'.[143] In the second place, the need for colonialism to benefit the economies of colonial states was also sometimes explained in terms of the democratic obligations of the governments of those states to serve the needs of their citizens.[144]

The dual mandate objective can be seen, for example, in the Berlin General Act, where provisions on care and improvement mentioned above co-existed with other provisions concerning free trade.[145] As for how choices were to be made when the 'dual' objectives were at odds with each other, it was sometimes

---

[139] Lugard (above n. 54); for commentary, see, e.g., Crawford (above n. 44), 131; Bain, *Between Anarchy and Society* (above n. 12), 58–63; Anghie (above n. 2), 157–8.

[140] Lugard (above n. 54), 617. In a similar vein, Lugard articulated the objective as '...bringing to the dark places of the earth...the torch of culture and progress, while ministering to the material needs of our own civilization' (ibid., 618, cited by Anghie (above n. 2), 158, n. 169).

[141] Antony Anghie states that '[t]he dual mandate...marked a different approach to colonialism from the colonialism practised up to the latter half of the nineteenth century. It succeeded the colonialism promoted by chartered companies and adventurers, who were unredeemable in their exploitation'; Anghie (above n. 2), 158, n. 169.

[142] See above, text following n. 104.

[143] Bain, *Between Anarchy and Society* (above n. 12), 61–2 (quote from 61). See also Anghie (above n. 2), at 160.

[144] Frederick Lugard claimed in 1926 that '[t]he democracies of to-day claim the right to work, and the satisfaction of that claim is impossible without the raw materials of the tropics on the one hand and their markets on the other'; Lugard (above n. 54), 61, cited by Anghie (above n. 2) in 158 n. 169.

[145] Berlin Conference General Act (above n. 109), Ch I, Arts. I–V. Antony Anghie states that, at the Berlin Conference, '...humanitarianism and profit-seeking were presented in proper and judicious balance as the European Powers carved up Africa'; Anghie (above n. 2), 69.

suggested that the interests of the local population would come first. For example, the British Government stated in relation to Kenya in 1923 that:

...the interests of the African natives must be paramount, and that if, and when, those interests and the interests of the immigrant races should conflict, the former should prevail.[146]

Colonial trusteeship was often understood to mean an obligation to provide a system of government where one was considered to be lacking. In the law of occupation, as mentioned earlier, occupying states are obliged to provide an administrative structure in occupied territory.[147] Examples of this being done in practice include the allied occupations of Germany, Austria, and Japan after the Second World War.[148] So the Berlin Declaration of 1945, through which the Allies assumed administrative control, stated that:

[t]here is no central Government or authority in Germany capable of accepting responsibility for the maintenance of order, the administration of the country and compliance with the requirements of the victorious Powers.

It is in these circumstances necessary, without prejudice to any subsequent decisions that may be taken respecting Germany, to make provision for the cessation of any further hostilities on the part of the German armed forces, for the maintenance of order in Germany and for the administration of the country....[149]

The civilizing mission of colonial trusteeship often went beyond the mere provision of governance, of course: it was also associated with enabling a certain *quality* of 'civilized' governance.[150] As far as occupations are concerned, whether or not such an enterprise is permissible under the law of occupation, given what has been said earlier, many occupations, including, of course, those after the Second World War and the occupation of Iraq from 2003, have similarly been

---

[146] 'Indians in Kenya' (above n. 108), 10.

[147] On the requirement to provide an administrative structure, see the discussion above, n. 79, and accompanying text. Eyal Benvenisti describes occupation generally as 'temporary measure for re-establishing order and civil life after the end of active hostilities...'; Benvenisti (above n. 9), xi.

[148] See the sources cited above, ch. 1, nn. 72 and 73.

[149] The Declaration then states that, for the 'purposes stated above', the Allies assert supreme authority in the territory; (Declaration Regarding the Defeat of Germany ('Berlin Declaration'), 5 June 1945, 68 UNTS 189, 145 (1953) *BFSP* 796, preambular paragraph).

[150] In general, see Ashcroft, Griffiths & Tiffin (above n. 45), 47; Simpson (above n. 32), 291–5; Schama (above n. 107), 269–70; Bain, *Between Anarchy and Society* (above n. 12), *passim*; Anghie (above n. 95), 62–5 and sources cited therein. The policies to be promoted in Mandated and Trust territories can be found in the provisions in the League Covenant and the UN Charter, the individual agreements set up for each particular arrangement, broader treaties applicable to the subject-matter, and the practice of each administration. See, for example, the discussion about the Mandate arrangements in Wright (above n. 32), 226–7; Hales (above n. 47), 197–202; Bain, ibid., 102–105 and the text of the Mandate treaties contained in the appendices in Wright, ibid. On the governance policies promoted in Mandated territories, see the commentary by Wright (above n. 32), ch. VIII; on policies in both Mandated and Trust territories, see Chowdhuri (above n. 97), ch. IX. In 1833, Thomas Babington Macaulay, a member of the British 'Board of Control' in India, set out his vision of British rule thus: '[t]o have found a great people sunk in the lowest depths of slavery and superstition, to have so ruled them as to have made them desirous and capable of all the privileges of citizens...' (statement quoted in Schama, above n. 107, 270).

engaged not only in filling an administrative vacuum but also in transforming the political and economic systems in the territories concerned.[151]

A key governance objective associated with colonial trusteeship was the restructuring of the economies of the colonies in order to bring about, in the words of Bipan Chandra, the 'complete...integration and enmeshing of' their 'economy and society...with world capitalism'.[152] In particular, the markets of the colonies were to be open to European traders, a policy represented as being beneficial to the economies of both the metropolitan states and the colonies, the justification in relation to the latter drawing on, and reinforcing, the civilizing mission.[153] This 'open door' policy was the 'external' feature of the dual mandate, enabling all states, not just the colonial states, to benefit from the colonies.[154] It was set out in various provisions contained in the Berlin General Act, the League Covenant, and the UN Charter (the latter concerning both Trust and Non-Self-Governing territories).[155]

[151] On the allied occupation of Germany and Austria after the Second World War, see the sources cited above in ch. 1, n. 72; on the allied occupation of Japan, see the sources cited ibid., n. 73; on the occupation of Iraq, see the sources cited ibid., n. 75. Discussing Germany and Japan, Adam Roberts states that 'the victors decided to exercise their power freely...in particular to make drastic political and other changes in the defeated States'; Roberts, 'What is Military Occupation?' (above n. 74), 268. On the issue of whether such a transformatory objective is compatible with occupation law, see above, n. 129.

[152] Chandra (above n. 50), 15. See also VI Lenin, *Imperialism: The Highest Stage of Capitalism* (International Publishers, 1939); Loomba (above n. 43), 20.

[153] Ashcroft, Griffiths & Tiffin (above n. 45), 46–7; Schama (above n. 107), 318 and ch. 6, *passim*; Ferguson (above n. 89), *passim*; Anghie (above n. 2), 90; Anghie (above n. 95), 62, text accompanying n. 230 and sources cited therein. As for the benefits to the European states, for Ania Loomba the motivation was 'to fuel European capitalism', 'so that there was a flow of human and natural resources between colonised and colonial countries'; Loomba (above n. 43), 20 and 3 respectively. See also L Woolf, *Empire and Commerce in Africa: A Study in Economic Imperialism* (Allen & Unwin, 1920); Crawford (above n. 44), 135; Anghie (above n. 2), 90, 97, 141–4. As for the benefits to the colonial economies, Antony Anghie reports that a shift had occurred at the time of the Berlin Conference of 1884–85: '[t]rade was not what it had been earlier, a means of simply maximizing profit and increasing national power. Rather, trade was an indispensable part of the civilizing mission itself; the expansion of commerce was the means by which the backwards nations could be civilized'; Anghie (above n. 95), 97. Thus, 'the native was no longer merely to be conquered and dispossessed; rather, he was to be made more productive'; Anghie (above n. 2), 163. See also ibid., 156–78 and Anghie (above n. 95), 63, and sources cited therein.

[154] On the link to the dual mandate, see, e.g., Anghie (above n. 2), 143 and sources cited therein. On the 'open door' policy in specific arrangements, see the next note.

[155] Berlin Conference General Act (above n. 109), Ch I, Arts I–V. On the 'open door' policy in relation to colonialism see, e.g., Hall (above n. 94), 57–8, 104. 'Open door' stipulations were only included explicitly in the League Covenant for 'B' class Mandated territories, where the administering authorities were obliged to 'secure equal opportunities for the trade and commerce of other Members of the League' (League Covenant, Art. 22). However, according to James Hales, the specific Mandate agreements provided for the 'open door' in the case of 'A' and 'B' class Mandated territories, but not 'C' class Mandated territories; Hales (above n. 47), 197–202, 245–6. Where these provisions existed, the general idea was that '...the Mandatories should not reap any commercial advantages from their trust which other States Members of the League did not obtain'; ibid., 245. According to Antony Anghie, the failure to provide explicitly for the 'open door' policy across all Mandated territories in the League Covenant was one of the main reasons for the US decision not to join the League of Nations, the US then pursuing this policy itself through bilateral

Especially in those cases where imperial state administration replaced rule by trading companies, trusteeship to enable the 'open door' was often explained, reflecting one limb of the normative case for trusteeship discussed above, as a remedy to the problem that the companies had breached their charters by introducing protectionist policies.[156] More generally, an 'open door' to all would supposedly reduce the potential for rivalry over colonial possessions.[157]

An aspect of the free trade regime concerned the securing of key trade routes, notably through the policy of securing the free navigation of waterways as in the Congo.[158] The waterways commissions responded to the concern that, without joint administration, individual riparian states might hinder free navigation through active restriction or neglect.[159]

Moving beyond free trade, the second main area of policy for the conduct of governance promoted through trusteeship was understood in terms of caring for the people of the territories involved.[160] In some instances the civilizing mission was associated with the enterprise of introducing 'good governance' and the 'rule of law' in the administered territories.[161] As Adam Roberts identifies, occupations

treaties regarding individual Mandated territories; see Anghie (above n. 2), 163 n. 186 and source cited therein and accompanying text. On the 'open door' policy and the Mandate arrangements generally, see also Hall, ibid., 57–8, 247–9; Hales, ibid., 245–54; Hales (above n. 107), 184–5. On the different classes of Mandated territory, see below, n. 200 and accompanying text. On the 'open door' policy in relation to Trust territories, see UN Charter, Art. 76(d) (extracted below, n. 173). The Declaration Regarding Non-Self-Governing Territories in the UN Charter states that:

Members of the United Nations...agree that their policy in respect of the territories to which this Chapter applies, no less than in respect of their metropolitan areas, must be based on the general principle of good-neighborliness, due account being taken of the interests and well-being of the rest of the world, in social, economic, and commercial matters.

UN Charter, Art. 74. For commentary see, e.g., Fastenrath, 'Article 74', in B Simma (ed.), *The Charter of the United Nations. A Commentary* (2nd edn, OUP, 2002), vol. 2, 1097.

[156] See, e.g., the discussion in Koskenniemi (above n. 44), 118; see also Anghie (above n. 2), 162.

[157] Hall (above n. 94), 14.

[158] Wright (above n. 32), 18.

[159] See Hill (above n. 71), 507–10.

[160] Under the General Act of the Berlin Conference, states were obliged to 'watch over the preservation of the native tribes': see Berlin Conference General Act (above n. 109), ch. I, Art. VI. Under Art. 23 of the League of Nations Covenant, states were obliged to 'secure the just treatment of the native inhabitants of territories under their control', a formulation broad enough to cover both colonies and the Mandated territories addressed in Art. 22. Under Art. 73 of the UN Charter, states are obliged to ensure 'just treatment, and protection against abuses' in Non-Self-Governing territories. There is no equivalent generalized obligation in the UN Charter relating to Trust territories, but, rather, more specific provisions on human rights, reproduced below, n. 168.

[161] On 'good governance' generally, see, e.g., Fieldhouse, *Colonialism* (above n. 32), 173; Anghie (above n. 2), 88; Anghie (above n. 95), 37. H Duncan Hall asserts that promoting the 'democratic way of life' was a goal in all Mandated territories; see Hall (above n. 94), 128–9. The pursuit of this objective and the extent to which direct administrative control was exercised in place of 'native' institutions were interrelated. On the varying nature of the administrative activity conducted, see above, nn. 50, 54, and 55. An example of 'good governance' as an objective can be found in the provisions of the 'B' Class Mandate agreements. See I Sagay, *The Legal Aspects of the Namibian Dispute*

have also been aimed at preventing 'political or economic developments which cause concern to the intervening power'.[162]

The provision of good governance was sometimes associated with infrastructure projects, such as the construction of railways and public buildings.[163] An example of rule of law promotion in the colonial context would be the doctrine that native laws were applicable insofar as they were compatible with 'civilized' standards.[164] More generally, the idea of promoting particular welfare issues concerning the native population was evident in colonial trusteeship, and understood to reflect a concern with eradicating human suffering and enabling social provision such as education.[165] Health promotion was often a focus for attention, including clamping down on alcohol consumption.[166] Along similar lines, occupation law contains obligations concerning health provision and sanitation.[167]

The objectives of promoting individual rights and freedoms (notably freedom of conscience and religion and non-discrimination) were associated with various trusteeship arrangements; the protection of individual rights forms part of occupation law.[168] One area of policy in the general field of individual rights

(University of Ife Press, 1975), 13, who speculates that the absence of such provisions in the agreements for 'C' class Mandated territories:

... is because the mandatory is given full power of administration and legislation over the territory subject to the mandate, as an integral portion of its own territory. Under the circumstances, responsibility for peace, order and good government would be automatic.

On the 'rule of law', see, e.g., Bain, *Between Anarchy and Society* (above n. 12), 1; Anghie (above n. 2), 157, 169.

[162] Roberts, 'What is Military Occupation?' (above n. 74), 300.

[163] On such infrastructure projects, see, e.g., Crawford (above n. 44), 135; Anghie (above n. 2), 163.

[164] Antony Anghie reports that the practice under the Mandate arrangements was that 'native laws that were not incompatible with civilization were allowed to remain in force at least for the moment', Anghie (above n. 2), 169, text accompanying n. 208.

[165] On the invocation of this generalized concern in relation to colonialism, see, e.g., ibid., 1 and ch. 2, *passim*; on the promotion of educational standards in particular, see, e.g., Crawford (above n. 44), 135. For illustrations of policies of this type in the Mandate arrangements, see the discussion in Wright (above n. 32), ch. VIII and Hall (above n. 94), 65; Hales (above n. 107), 155. In relation to 'B' class Mandated territories in particular, see, e.g., Sagay (above n. 161), 13. On the different classes of Mandated territory, see below, n. 200 and accompanying text.

[166] On the objective of health promotion generally in the Mandate arrangements, see Hales (above n. 47), 232–3; Anghie (above n. 2), 166. On alcohol consumption in particular, under Art. 22 of the League Covenant, the administering authorities in 'B' class Mandated territories were responsible for 'the prohibition of abuses, such as ... the liquor traffic ...'. According to James Hales, this responsibility was explained in terms of health concerns, rooted in the view that '[n]atives in undeveloped countries have always been only too keen to trade their wares for spirits, and this has been the cause of frequent illnesses and death among them'; Hales, ibid., 233. See generally ibid., 233–6 and Hall (above n. 94), 424–7. On the different classes of Mandated territory, see below, n. 200 and accompanying text.

[167] See, e.g., Geneva Convention (IV) (above n. 74), Art. 56.

[168] See, for example, Berlin Conference General Act (above n. 109), ch. I, Art. VI (on freedom of conscience and religion) and the obligation in Art. 22 of the League Covenant that in 'B' class Mandated territories, '... the Mandatory must be responsible for the administration of the territory under conditions which will guarantee freedom of conscience and religion, subject only to

associated with later forms of colonial trusteeship was the prohibition of the slave trade.[169] Initiatives were also adopted to prohibit forced labour and promote labour standards generally.[170]

the maintenance of public order and morals...'. On the different classes of Mandated territory, see below, n. 200 and accompanying text. The administering authorities in Trust territories were obliged 'to encourage respect for human rights and for fundamental freedoms for all without distinction as to race, sex, language, or religion' (UN Charter, Art. 76(c)). Many of the human rights treaties agreed over the course of the second half of the 20th century, overlapping with the period of decolonization, were applicable to the overseas territories of their contracting states, through the general concept of 'jurisdiction' and/or specific 'colonial clauses'; see, e.g., European Convention for the Protection of Human Rights and Fundamental Freedoms (Rome, 4 November 1950), ETS, No. 5, in force 3 September 1953 (hereinafter 'ECHR' or 'European Convention on Human Rights'), Art. 1 and Art. 56; International Covenant on Civil and Political Rights (New York, 16 December 1966), 999 UNTS 171, in force 23 March 1976 ('ICCPR'), Art. 2. See also the instruments aiming at abolishing slavery and similar practices listed below, n. 169, and the instruments on the abolition of forced labour cited below, n. 170. On the protections of the individual in the law of occupation, see the instruments and the sources cited above, n. 74.

    [169] Under the Berlin Conference General Act (above n. 109), ch. I, Art VI, parties agreed to 'help in suppressing slavery, and especially the slave trade'. In Art. IX, each of the parties '...binds itself to employ all the means at its disposal for putting an end to...' the slave trade '...and for punishing those who engage in it'. In Art. 22 of the League Covenant, the administering authorities in 'B' class Mandated territories were responsible for 'the prohibition of abuses, such as the slave trade...'. On the different classes of Mandated territory, see below, n. 200 and accompanying text. Provisions regarding slavery were also included in the specific Mandate agreements; see Anghie (above n. 2), at 167, n. 203 and sources cited therein; Hales (above n. 47), 230. Also relevant is the general obligation concerning the just treatment of 'natives' in all dependencies in Art. 23 of the League Covenant (mentioned in n. 160 above). On the role of the League in supervising the implementation of obligations relating to slavery in Mandated territories, see, e.g., Hales, ibid., 230–1. The Convention to Suppress the Slave Trade and Slavery, adopted under the auspices of the League in 1926, imposed upon the states parties an obligation to suppress the slave trade and to 'bring about, progressively and as soon as possible, the complete abolition of slavery in all its forms' in 'the territories placed under [their] sovereignty, jurisdiction, protection, suzerainty or tutelage' (Art. 2, Convention to Suppress the Slave Trade and Slavery, 25 September 1926, 60 LNTS 253, as amended by the Protocol Amending the Slavery Convention, New York, 7 December 1953, 182 UNTS 51). See also the Supplementary Convention on the Abolition of Slavery, the Slave Trade, and Institutions and Practices Similar to Slavery, 7 September 1956, 226 UNTS 3. For commentary on the association of this policy with colonial trusteeship and the Mandate arrangements generally, see, e.g., Hall (above n. 94), 99–101, 238–42; Bain, *Between Anarchy and Society* (above n. 12), 53 *et seq*. On the turn against slavery and its relationship to colonial policy, see, e.g. Crawford (above n. 44), ch. 4 and sources cited therein.

    [170] In the case of the Mandate arrangements, provisions on labour standards were included not in Art. 22 of the League Covenant but in the text of the Mandate agreements. See Hall (above n. 94), 249–55. More generally, under Art. 421 of Part XIII of the Versailles Peace Treaty (establishing a 'Labour Organization'), contracting states were obliged to apply the international labour conventions 'to their colonies, protectorates and possessions which are not fully self-governing'. Under the Constitution of the International Labour Organization (ILO) of 1946, member states agreed 'that Conventions which they have ratified in accordance with the provisions of this Constitution shall be applied to the non-metropolitan territories for whose international relations they are responsible, including any trust territories for which they are the administering authority'; see Constitution of the International Labour Organization, 9 October 1946, 15 UNTS 35, Art. 35. For commentary on these arrangements, see, e.g., Hall, ibid., 250. On the prohibition on forced labour in particular, see ILO Convention (No. 29) Concerning Forced or Compulsory Labour (Geneva, 28 June 1930), 39 UNTS 55, in force 1 May 1932; ILO Convention (No. 105) on the Abolition of Forced Labour (Geneva, 25 June 1957), 320 UNTS 291, in force 17 January 1959.

A prominent aspect of the 'welfare' agenda was the objective of ensuring that certain cultural, religious, and social norms were followed and that other such norms considered objectionable, including social practices deemed to be uncivilized, often on the basis of ideas from Christian theology, were stamped out, sometimes through the means of religious conversion.[171]

Sometimes, the policy of promoting standards concerning the conduct of popular consultations was evident, for example in the case of the plebiscite commissions provided for in the Treaty of Versailles aimed at ensuring that the plebiscites would take place and be carried out fairly.[172]

The process of structuring the relationship between and the treatment of individuals in colonial trusteeship also covered protecting the welfare of settlers and other foreign actors such as missionaries, traders, and adventurers, including, as part of promoting the 'open door' policy, the economic interests of such actors.[173] It also involved actualizing various population transfers.[174] An example of such a transfer was the 1923 Mixed Commission created to facilitate the compulsory

---

[171] An example of the focus on social practices is illustrated in the following identification by Ruth Vanita and Saleem Kidwai of 'overgeneralizations...intended to justify the imperial enterprise' in India:

British educators and missionaries often denounced Indian marital, familial, and sexual arrangements as primitive—demeaning to women and permissive for men. Arranged marriage, child marriage, dowry, polygamy, polyandry and matriliny were treated as evidence of Indian culture's degeneracy. Hindu gods were seen as licentious, and Indian monarchs, both Hindu and Muslim, as decadent hedonists, equally given to heterosexual and homosexual behaviour but indifferent to their subjects' welfare. Brahmans came in for similar stereotyping as greedy sensualists.

R Vanita and S Kidwai (eds.), *Same-Sex Love in India: Readings from Literature and History* (Palgrave, 2001), 196. One classic example of a work taking such an approach is K Mayo, *Mother India* (Harcourt, Brace & Co., 1927), discussed in Vanita & Kidwai, ibid., 197 and M Sinha, *Specters of Mother India—The Global Restructuring of an Empire* (Duke University Press, 2006). James Hales reports that the influence of the cinema on the population of Mandated territories became a concern of the League of Nations, on the grounds that '[n]atives are powerfully attracted by the cinema. It is an important influence in their education and if uncontrolled can be of the utmost harm in their development'; Hales (above n. 47), 236. Hales reports that the League Council asked the Permanent Mandates Commission to ensure that the Mandatories took active steps on the issue. 'Cinema displays' were '... of the right kind and prepared by persons with a personal knowledge of the mentalities and aptitudes of the various races, might have a very useful educative influence. If such displays were unsuitable, however, they might constitute an international menace' (ibid., 236). On the link with Christianity and the specific policy of religious conversion, see, e.g., Wright (above n. 32), 7–8; Young (above n. 45), 21; Crawford (above n. 44), 133–5; Bain, *Between Anarchy and Society* (above n. 12), 43 *et seq*.

[172] On these commissions, see the sources cited above, n. 72.

[173] See, e.g., Berlin Conference General Act (above n. 109), ch. I, Art. VI. The Administering authorities in Trust territories were obliged '... to ensure equal treatment in social, economic, and commercial matters for all Members of the United Nations and their nationals and also equal treatment for the latter in the administration of justice...'; UN Charter, Art. 76(d). On the protection of settlers, see, e.g., Crawford (above n. 44), 135; Koskenniemi (above n. 44), 145; and the sources cited below, n. 404.

[174] On population transfer in the context of 'self-determination' in particular, see, e.g., Drew (above n. 73), *passim*.

exchange of Turkish and Greek minorities between Greece and Turkey, which enjoyed certain powers to adjudicate property rights in each territory.[175]

Colonial policy was often concerned with the preservation of security and order, prompted by perceived threats, including those aimed at the structure of colonial rule itself, from both the local population and rival colonial powers.[176] In occupation law, the promotion of order is obligatory.[177] In the words of Adam Roberts, two of the main policies associated with occupation law are 'to re-establish order and stability in a case where government has collapsed or is in danger of so doing' and 'to protect a given area or section of the population against internal disturbances...'.[178]

Beyond objectives concerned with the nature of political and economic policy, the treatment of individuals and the promotion of security, colonialism was also sometimes utilized in many cases to 'exploit raw materials' and extract 'tribute, goods and wealth', in the words of Antony Anghie and Ania Loomba respectively.[179] It introduced an administrative structure to enable exploitation to take place unhindered, whether conducted by the colonial state itself or commercial enterprises operating with its sanction. This was evident also in the Mandate and Trusteeship arrangements, for example with the extraction of the phosphate deposits by Australia from the island of Nauru.[180]

---

[175] See Convention between Greece and Turkey Concerning the Exchange of Greek and Turkish Populations (above n. 73), in particular Arts 12 and 13 and the commentary cited above, n. 73.

[176] See Fieldhouse, *Colonialism* (above n. 32), 171; Anghie (above n. 95), 37; Bain, *Between Anarchy and Society* (above n. 12), 1. An entitlement to preserve order in the face of other objectives that might prevent this is reflected in the provisions of 'B' class Mandated territories, for example, under which the administering authorities, as discussed above, were obliged to guarantee freedom of conscience and religion 'subject only to the maintenance of public order and morals' (League Covenant, Art. 22). The preservation of order was, in part, tied to the need to quell resistance to colonial rule generally and particular colonial practices such as forced labour and, in certain cases, slavery. Neta Crawford remarks that '...as long as colonialism involved slavery and forced labor, large police forces were required to make those systems work in the face of slaves' and forced labourers' resistance and rebellion'; Crawford (above n. 44), 160. On the different classes of Mandated territory, see below, n. 200 and accompanying text.

[177] See the sources cited above, n. 74.

[178] Roberts, 'What is Military Occupation?' (above n. 74), 300. On the law of occupation, see the sources listed above, n. 74. Art. 43 of the Hague Regulations obliges the occupying state to 'take all the measures in his power to restore, and ensure, as far as possible, public order and safety'; Hague Regulations (above n. 74), Art. 43. On the restoration of order, see also Benvenisti (above n. 9), xi.

[179] Anghie (above n. 2), 90 (first quote); Loomba (above n. 43), 3 (second quote). See also Anghie, ibid., 142 n. 116 sources cited therein and accompanying text; Ashcroft, Griffiths & Tiffin (above n. 45), 46–7; Young (above n. 45), 21, 23; Schama (above n. 107), ch. 6, *passim*; Crawford (above n. 44), 135; Koskenniemi (above n. 44), 145, 157.

[180] Nauru was both a Mandated and a Trust territory. See, generally, *Report of the Commission of Inquiry into the Rehabilitation of the Worked-Out Phosphate Lands of Nauru* (Government of Nauru, 1988), Vols I–X; C Weeramantry, *Nauru: Environmental Damage under International Trusteeship* (OUP, 1992); see also the Trusteeship Agreement for the Territory of Nauru, UN Doc. A/402/Rev. 1, approved by GA Res. 140 (II), 1 November 1947; *Certain Phosphate Lands in Nauru (Nauru v. Australia) (Preliminary Objections), ICJ Reports 1992*, 240; A Anghie, 'The Heart of My Home: Colonialism,

So far the analysis of the policy of trusteeship has focused on how states involved in this activity understood the policies promoted through their own governance. Insofar as this was explained in terms of addressing perceived local incapacities for governance, it amounts to a remedy of direct substitution. But trusteeship was also sometimes associated with the idea that local conditions could improve, and that part of the role of the trustee was to bring about improvement, through tutelage.

Before considering how tutelage was understood, it is necessary to set out the different ways in which the prospects for improvement on which tutelage was based were understood across the different arrangements.

In some instances of colonialism, the introduction of foreign administration was viewed originally as being of indefinite duration.[181] As a result, the people of the territories involved were to be displaced from the role of territorial administration indefinitely. As far as the status of the colonial territory was concerned, there was no suggestion, whether implicit or explicit, that the people would attain independence at some future date. The civilizing mission, then, was conceived to be exclusively palliative, not also remedial. The colonial authorities would step in to provide a functioning administrative system; they were not, in the main, concerned with increasing the capacity of the people of the territory to govern in a particular manner so that they would eventually be able to take over territorial administration directly.[182]

In some cases, in the latter stages of colonial rule ideas concerning the possibility for progressive improvement in local capacities entered the discourse of colonial ideology.[183] Allied to such ideas was the notion that one of the objectives of colonial administration was to foster improvement through 'tutelage'.[184] This

---

Environmental Damage, and the Nauru Case', 34 (1993) *Harvard International Law Journal* 445 and sources cited therein. For commentary on the discussions on the issue in the League Mandates Commission, see Wright (above n. 32), 261.

[181] See, e.g., Ignatieff (above n. 4), 113. More generally, see the works in List of Sources, sections 5.3.1–5.3.3.

[182] These ideas are discussed further in below, section 8.7.1, the context of analysis on critiques of colonialism.

[183] This is illustrated in the inscription on Herbert Baker and Edwin Lutyens's Viceroy's Palace in New Delhi:

LIBERTY DOES NOT DESCEND TO A PEOPLE
A PEOPLE MUST RAISE THEMSELVES TO LIBERTY
IT IS A BLESSING THAT MUST BE EARNED
BEFORE IT CAN BE ENJOYED

(inscription quoted in Ferguson (above n. 89), 215). As Bill Ashcroft, Gareth Griffiths, and Helen Tiffin observe: '[t]he colonialist system permitted a notional idea of improvement for the colonized, via such metaphors as parent/child, tree/branch etc., which in theory allowed that at some future time the inferior colonials might be raised to the status of the colonizer'; Ashcroft, Griffiths, & Tiffin (above n. 45), 49. See generally Bain, *Between Anarchy and Society* (above n. 12), *passim*; Anghie (above n. 2), 114; Hales (above n. 107), 155.

[184] In the words of Philip Kerr in 1916, colonial authorities 'must gradually develop, by education and example, the capacity in the natives to manage their own affairs'; Kerr (above

is evident in Article VI of Chapter I of the General Act of the Berlin Conference of 1884–85 mentioned above, with its reference to an obligation to 'care for the improvement of the conditions of their [the natives] moral and material well-being'.[185] Similarly, Article 73 of the UN Charter obliges colonial states to 'promote ... the well-being of the inhabitants' and:

... to ensure ... their political, economic, social, and educational advancement ...
[...]
[and] to develop self-government, to take due account of the political aspirations of the peoples, and to assist them in the progressive development of their free political institutions ...[186]

From these understandings of capacity for self-administration came the idea that within overall colonial control, the level of self-administration would be calibrated according to such capacity. According to Frederick Lugard's dual mandate for British colonialism in Africa:

[t]he British Empire ... has only one mission—for liberty and self-development ... [which] can be best secured to the native population by leaving them free to manage their own affairs through their own rulers, proportionately to their degree of advancement, under the guidance of the British staff, and subject to the law and policy of the administration.[187]

Along the same lines, under Article 73 of the UN Charter the 'progressive development' of 'free political institutions' in Non-Self-Governing Territories is to be 'according to the particular circumstances of each territory and its peoples and their varying stages of advancement'.[188]

The next potential stage in this process is the idea that the people would become capable of the level of self-administration that would justify independence.

---

n. 107), 149, quoted in Bain, *Between Anarchy and Society* (above n. 12), 1. In its 1923 parliamentary White Paper on rule in Kenya, the British Government stated that the object of such rule was '... the advancement of the native races ...' and that:

... there can be no room for doubt that it is the mission of Great Britain to work continuously for the training and education of the Africans towards a higher intellectual, moral, and economic level than that which they had reached when the Crown assumed the responsibility for the administration of this territory.

'Indians in Kenya' (above n. 108), 10. Hilton Poynton, Permanent Under-Secretary at the British Colonial office in 1947, stated before the UN General Assembly Fourth Committee that '[t]he colonial system was a practical illustration of democracy under tuition' (quoted in Simpson, above n. 32, 294).

[185] Berlin Conference General Act (above n. 109), ch. I, Art. VI.
[186] UN Charter, Art. 73(a) and (b); see also ibid., para. (d).
[187] Lugard (above n. 54), 94, quoted in Jackson (above n. 12), 302. Fieldhouse reports that one important British colonial policy was that 'government should be influenced by the governed and that the ultimate objective should be representative self-government'; Fieldhouse, *Colonialism* (above n. 32), 32.
[188] UN Charter, Art. 73 (b). Brian Simpson reports that this provision in the UN Charter was based on a draft put forward by the British and thus in effect 'wrote into the Charter the theory of colonialism developed by the British Colonial Office'; Simpson (above n. 32), 303.

In other words, that they would attain a measure of progress that would bring the notion of foreign administration conceived on the basis of incapacity into question. If this led to independence, the overall process would amount to what Robert Jackson terms 'evolutionary decolonization'.[189]

However, in the colonial context, states were divided as to whether full independence, or self-administration within the framework of overall imperial rule, should be the end stage.[190] Notably, the relevant provision of the UN Charter concerning Non-Self-Governing Territories uses the phrase 'self-government or independence'.[191] William Bain reports that these differences in policy mapped onto general trends in attitudes towards colonial rule as between the USA, who took the former position, and the British, who took the latter.[192] Bain states that:

American scepticism of empire transformed trusteeship from a justification of empire, as it was in the British tradition, into an alternative to empire that was expressed concretely in the form of the League of Nations mandates system and the United Nations trusteeship system...[193]

As far as the Mandate and Trusteeship systems were concerned, provisions implicating the issues of progressive improvement, the role of the administering authority in fostering improvement, and the prospects for eventual independence, were explicitly included in the Covenant and the Charter respectively. Moreover, as will be discussed below, the provisions conceived these issues in a variated fashion, both as between the two systems and within the Mandate system through the adoption of different classes of territory. However, the leading scholars on these two systems, Quincy Wright and Ramendra Nath Chowdhuri, argue that, despite this differential treatment within the Covenant and between the Covenant and the Charter, the two systems were generally understood at the time to operate on the basis that in all cases the developmental level was expected to improve, the administering authorities had a role in fostering this, and once improvements occurred independence would be actualized.[194]

---

[189] Jackson (above n. 55), 86–91. On the goal of independence, see also Hales (above n. 107), 155.

[190] On the idea of self-government, see, e.g., Hall (above n. 94), 95–7.

[191] UN Charter, Art. 73(b).

[192] See Bain, *Between Anarchy and Society* (above n. 12), ch. 5, *passim*, and especially 117. On the British view, see also Simpson (above n. 32), 303.

[193] Bain, *Between Anarchy and Society* (above n. 12), 21. See also ibid., 108.

[194] On these arguments in relation to the Mandate arrangements, see generally Wright (above n. 32), 232 *et seq.*; see also Hall (above n. 94), 31, 94; Sagay (above n. 161), 13. Ramendra Nath Chowdhuri reports that '[t]he Mandates Commission considered the Mandates System as temporary and had formulated certain conditions for the termination of a Mandated regime'; Chowdhuri (above n. 97), 246. For a discussion of these conditions, see ibid., 246–7; for a discussion of the practice around their meaning and implementation, see ibid., 246–53. Commenting on the arrangements for each system in the League Covenant and the UN Charter, Chowdhuri considers that it was 'implied that the tutelage is provisional in character, and there can be no indefinite postponement of the right to self-determination' (ibid., 9–10). On the notion that eventual independence was the objective in relation to Trust territories in particular, see ibid., 246–52. At the opening session of the Trusteeship Council, then UN Secretary-General

The differentiated treatment of these issues within the Covenant and the Charter is still worth considering, however, because the arrangements represent two important and influential attempts to conceptualize tutelage and progress. Since the present focus is on how trusteeship was understood as a matter of international policy and law, a consideration of the Covenant and Charter provisions is appropriate.[195]

For the League Mandate arrangements, although there were no provisions on termination, the use of the word 'yet' in the phrase 'not yet able to stand by themselves' at the beginning of Article 22 of the Covenant suggests a possibility, indeed an expectation, that capacity for self-administration may arise in the future; thus the inability to 'stand by themselves' is not fixed, and may be remedied.[196]

The conception of this capacity to 'stand by themselves' in terms of the 'strenuous conditions of the modern world' implies a notion of external freedom, something beyond internal self-administration within the overall framework of a colonial authority.[197] This suggests that foreign administration is not to last indefinitely, but, rather, will operate until the people of the territory are deemed 'able to stand by themselves', an ability that might include the capacity to exist as an independent entity.[198]

However, the provisions of Article 22 arrange things in a fashion running counter to the idea that the suggestion made in the first paragraph applies to all Mandated territories equally. Paragraph 3 states that:

Trygve Lie stated that '[the] ultimate goal is to give the Trust Territories full statehood', Trusteeship Council, Official Records: First Year, First Session, 1st Meeting, 26 March 1947, at 5, quoted in B Rivlin, 'Self-Determination and Dependent Areas', 30 (1953–55) *International Conciliation*, no. 501 (January 1955), 195, at 221.

[195] For other commentary on the relevant provisions of the League Covenant and the UN Charter, see, e.g., Wright (above n. 32), *passim* and Sagay (above n. 161), 13 *et seq* (on the Covenant only); Chowdhuri (above n. 97), *passim*. Due to constraints of space, it is not possible also to consider the numerous individual agreements that formed the basis for the arrangements for each territory. See the commentary in Wright and Sagay (on the Mandate arrangements), *passim*, and Chowdhuri (on the Mandate and Trusteeship arrangements), *passim* and especially 95–9. For an illustrative collection of agreements, see the following Annexes in Hall (above n. 94): Annex III containing an 'A' class Mandate agreement (Palestine); Annex IV, a 'B' class Mandate agreement (Tanganyika); Annex V, a 'C' class Mandate agreement (Japanese Mandated Islands); Annex XIII, the Trusteeship agreements of 1946 and 1947; Annex XIV, the Trusteeship agreement for former Japanese Mandated Islands. On the different classes of Mandated territory, see below, n. 200 and accompanying text.

[196] James Hales observes that Art. 22 'refers to peoples not yet capable of standing alone, thus implying that it is hoped that some day they will be able to stand alone'; Hales (above n. 107),185. See also Anghie (above n. 2), 121. On the lack of a termination provision, see the discussion in Chowdhuri (above n. 97), 9, 62–3, 246. Whether termination was possible by the United Nations, acting as a successor to the League of Nations, was at issue when the General Assembly terminated South Africa's Mandate over South West Africa. See above, ch. 5, text accompanying n. 75.

[197] On these origins, see above, text accompanying n. 317 *et seq*.

[198] According to H Duncan Hall, Art. 22 conceived an arrangement of 'trusteeship with independence' as the 'goal of the trust'; Hall (above n. 94), 94. See also Hales (above n. 47), 191 and Sagay (above n. 161), 8–9.

[t]he character of the mandate must differ according to the stage of the development of the people, the geographical situation of the territory, its economic conditions and other similar circumstances.[199]

So the developmental level, hitherto the sole principle governing the introduction of foreign administration, is now but one of several factors in operation. Placing a varied emphasis on these factors, the Covenant divided up the Mandated territories into three classes, later designated as classes 'A', 'B', and 'C'.[200] For classes 'A' and 'B', the 'stage of development' is seemingly determinative of the character of the Mandate. The people of 'A' class Mandated territories are deemed to have:

... reached a stage of development where their existence as independent nations can be provisionally recognized subject to the rendering of administrative advice and assistance by the Mandatory until such time as they are able to stand alone.[201]

Thus the people of the territory are judged to be almost capable of self-administration, requiring only an attenuated form of administrative involvement ('advice and assistance') of a finite duration, the end point being contingent on improvements in local capacity ('until such time as they are able to stand alone'). By contrast, 'B' class territories are deemed to be 'at such a stage' that the Mandatory power must be responsible for plenary administration, and without any cut-off point.[202] Unlike 'A' and 'B' class Mandated territories, 'C' class Mandated territories are arranged according to factors other than the level of development:

... the sparseness of their population, or their small size, or their remoteness from the centers of civilization, or their geographical contiguity to the territory of the Mandatory, and other circumstances...[203]

For these Mandated territories, plenary administration 'under the laws of the Mandatory as integral portions of its territory' was in order, again without any suggestion of subsequent alteration.[204]

Taken together, these arrangements built on the trusteeship concept developed in the earlier colonial context, adopting the developmental level as the ostensible reason for the need for foreign administration and the ostensible grounds for ending it. As far as the end of foreign administration was concerned, this factor would also determine a possible change in territorial status, with the possibility,

---

[199] League Covenant, Art. 22.

[200] Ibid., Art. 22, fourth, fifth and sixth paragraphs (corresponding to classes 'A', 'B', and 'C' respectively). The letters A, B, and C are not found in the Covenant but were adopted by the League to denote the different classes of territory set out therein. For more detail on the particular territories covered, see, e.g., Wright (above n. 32), *passim*; Chowdhuri (above n. 97), *passim*. Although all the territories in each class of Mandate were deemed to be at a particular, common developmental level, other considerations also mediated the conceptualization of each class. See the discussion in Wright, ibid., 34 *et seq*.

[201] League Covenant, Art. 22.

[202] League Covenant, Art. 22.

[203] Ibid.

[204] Ibid. On this, see also Sagay (above n. 161).

for example, of independent statehood. However, despite the suggestion made in the 'not yet able to stand by themselves' phrase of Article 22's opening paragraph, which is seemingly applicable to all territories, the Mandate system actually adopted a differentiated policy for the three classes of territory.[205]

For 'C' class territories, external administration is set at an indefinite duration, as in certain forms of colonialism. The reasons for introducing external administration suggest somewhat unchangeable factors (e.g., small size) and do not concern the level of development; this appears to rule out the possibility that the need for administration may change in the future. By contrast, although trusteeship in 'B' class Mandated territories is similarly set at an indefinite duration, by making the reason for external administration the level of development, the contingent factor from the earlier phrase is picked up. However, this factor is only set as the basis for introducing external administration, not also for withdrawing it, and there is no explicit anticipation that, in fact, the level of development may improve in the future. This only suggests that they are 'not able' to stand by themselves, rather than 'not yet' being able.[206]

Only 'A' class Mandated territories are conceived so that the duration is contingent on the same factor—the level of development—as the basis for the introduction of foreign administration; moreover, an express statement is made that the situation is expected to improve in the future.[207] Only with respect to this class of Mandated territories is there an implicit reference to a change in status—becoming recognized as 'independent nations' on a non-provisional basis—if and when such improvement came about.[208]

---

[205] On this, see generally the discussion in Wright (above n. 32), 232 *et seq.*

[206] For James Hales:

...one of the cardinal features of trusteeship as applied to peoples is lacking: there is no precise indication...that when the territories can be governed by their own peoples, the latter will secure their independence. It is obviously impossible to fix a precise time for this operation, but it could at least be indicated as a certainty, and not merely to be left to be implied from the general text of Article 22. If such a provision had been indicated, the temporary character of the trust would have been emphasized.

Hales (above n. 107), 185.

[207] For James Hales, '[i]t is unfortunate that the distinction between the A. Mandates and the B. and C. Mandates tends to indicate the temporary nature of the former but not of the latter' (ibid., 185).

[208] On the clear intention of eventual independence for 'A' class Mandated territories, see the discussion in Wright (above n. 32), 231–2; Chowdhuri (above n. 97), 11; Sagay (above n. 161), 9–10. With the emergence of the self-determination entitlement and its invocation in relation to the people of Mandated territories generally, the distinctions between the different classes on the issue of eventual independence dissolved. So in 1970 the International Court of Justice, having taken into account changes in international law subsequent to the creation of the League of Nations, stated in relation to the Mandate arrangements that '[t]hese developments leave little doubt that the ultimate objective of the sacred trust was the self-determination and independence of the peoples concerned'; *Legal Consequences for States of the Continued Presence of South Africa in Namibia (South West Africa) Notwithstanding Security Council Resolution 276 (1970), Advisory Opinion, ICJ Reports 1971*, 16 (hereinafter '*Namibia Advisory Opinion*'), para. 53. Because of this, 'C' class Mandated territories were to be treated no differently from 'A' or 'B' class Mandated territories; ibid., para. 54.

Like the Mandate system, the Trusteeship system contained no explicit provisions on the termination of Trusteeship arrangements.[209] In contrast to the variations of the Mandate system, however, it adopted a simple, uniform approach for evolutionary developmental improvement echoing certain aspects of the formula adopted for 'A' class Mandated territories.[210] Administration in Trust territories was to:

... promote the political, economic, social and educational advancement of the inhabitants... and their progressive development towards self-government or independence.[211]

The end goal, then—'self-government or independence'—is clearer than the vague notion of being able to 'stand by themselves' applied to Mandated territories generally, but, conversely, is more equivocal, with its option of self-government without independence, than the provisions for 'A' class Mandated territories.[212]

It will be recalled that with the Mandate arrangements the level of development was explicitly invoked as the basis for introducing external administration (classes 'A' and 'B'), and the reason for removing it (class 'A'). By contrast, in the Trusteeship arrangements it is invoked in a third sense: a positive alteration in the developmental level becomes one of the objectives for administration. Not only, then, is administration introduced because of the idea of a poor developmental level; it should also be aimed at somehow improving this situation. Whereas an increase in development is seen as likely in 'A' class Mandated territories, and not ruled out in 'B' class Mandated territories, in neither class is the administering authority explicitly obliged to support such improvement, beyond the vague objective applicable to all Mandated territories that 'improvement' is part of the 'sacred trust'. Recalling the general policy objectives operating with respect to both the Mandate and Trusteeship arrangements, this difference between them in terms of a responsibility for enabling improvement indicates that, in the words of Ramendra Nath Chowdhuri:

... the emphasis has shifted from the mere prohibition of abuses under the Mandate regime to the more positive aspect of constructive development in political, social, and educational spheres.[213]

As with 'A' class Mandated territories, the end of foreign administration in Trust territories is conceived to be contingent on an increase in the

---

[209] See the discussion in Chowdhuri (above n. 97), 9, 62–3, 246.

[210] The territories were, however, divided in to 'strategic' and 'non-strategic' Trust territories; see above n. 98. As Michael Reisman points out, '[a]rticle 77 established three categories of trusteeship, based on their provenance, but avoided the invidious developmental distinctions of the Covenant'; Reisman (above n. 32), 237.

[211] UN Charter, Art. 76(b). For commentary see D Rauschning, 'International Trusteeship System', in B Simma (ed.), *The Charter of the United Nations. A Commentary* (2nd edn, OUP, 2002), vol. 2, 1099, 1107.

[212] Cf. the debate about self-administration versus independence mentioned above, text accompanying n. 190 *et seq*. On the equivocal nature of this formulation for Trust territories in the Charter see, e.g., Hall (above n. 94), 280.

[213] Chowdhuri (above n. 97), 11.

developmental level. Whereas this is explicit for 'A' class Mandated territories ('until such time as they are able to stand alone'), for Trust territories it is implicit as the negative outcome of the end point—'self-government or independence'—towards which the progressive increase in development through external administration is aimed. Whereas the Mandate system only adopted this formula for territories understood to be the most highly developed, the Trusteeship system applied it across the board, to territories conceived as being at varying levels of development. It would be expected, then, that these territories would attain the enhanced developmental level at different stages.

Arguably, this difference between the Mandate and Trusteeship systems mediated the different formulae these two systems adopted in terms of changes in territorial status. For 'A' class Mandated territories, the level of development was such that independent statehood could be already 'provisionally recognized'; implicitly, this status was to operate on a provisional basis until the level of development increased to a level where the people of the territory were 'able to stand alone'. For Trust territories, however, the starting point was merely the negative sovereignty outcome of detachment from the belligerent powers, as in 'B' and 'C' class Mandated territories. A change in status—'self-government or independence'—depended on developmental improvements. Given that such improvements would take place at different stages in different territories, the adoption of a formula for territorial status change that assumed a particular level of development, as was done in the case of 'A' class Mandated territories, was not followed.

Moving from Mandated and Trust territories to the final relevant category of trusteeship under evaluation—occupation—here it will be recalled that there is a general idea that the arrangements are temporary; the specific outcome of title vesting in the occupying state by virtue of its exercise of control is legally prohibited.[214] The obligation to preserve order and provide a system of administration creates a possiblity for improving local conditions for governance, and such improvement and an increase in development become clear objectives when occupations pursue a broader 'transformatory' agenda of economic and political reconstruction and transformation, often explicitly referencing some sort of aim at improvement to a level that will enable self-administration and the end of occupation.

Comparing these different arrangements concerning improvement and/or termination, one can see a progressive refinement of a common enterprise. In many instances of colonial trusteeship, external administration is introduced on a seemingly indefinite basis, vague notions of eventual self-improvement notwithstanding. Foreign administration is associated exclusively with the provision of governance. With no assumption that the people of the territories involved may become more capable of self-administration, there is no suggestion of future independence and thus a change in territorial status. As a matter of the provisions of the Covenant, this model continues in the case of 'C' class Mandated territories;

---

[214] On the idea that occupation is a 'temporary' measure, see, e.g., Benvenisti (above n. 9), xi.

with 'A' and 'B' class Mandated territories under the Covenant, Trust territories in the Charter, later forms of colonialism, and occupation trusteeship, it is modified.

In the case of 'A' and 'B' class Mandated territories under the Covenant, invoking the level of development as the basis for foreign administration, and, with later ideas of colonialism, explaining the role for colonial administration in terms of local incapacities, the possibility of an end to administration, and so potentially a change in territorial status, is suggested.

A contingent developmental level and the idea of eventual independence are explicitly referenced by the Covenant in the case of 'A' class Mandated territories; the Trusteeship model in the Charter supplements this formula, introducing the missing element in terms of actualizing improvement (other than the vague objective of 'improvement' articulated in relation to all Mandated territories): the administering power should not only provide governance until local capacities for self-government improve, but also attempt to effect such improvements itself. The later forms of colonial trusteeship lack the clear commitment to independence as the eventual outcome (the phrase 'self-government or independence' is used in the UN Charter) but do share the general notion of seeking to improve local conditions. The temporary conception of occupation trusteeship presupposes eventual independence; whereas this is not necessarily tied to developmental improvement and initiatives are not always taken to promote improvement, when such initiatives are attempted—'transformatory' occupations—the end of occupation may be tied to some sort of benchmark of improvement.

As far as a suggestion that self-administration may arise eventually, and, where applicable, the territorial status may be altered in favour of the people of the territory (e.g. through statehood) there are two models: (1), no such suggestion (certain forms of colonial trusteeship, 'C' class Mandated territories); and (2), the suggestion, either contingent on developmental improvements ('B' class Mandated territories by implication, 'A' class Mandated territories, all Trust territories and colonies under the UN Charter explicitly, 'transformatory' occupations) or not necessarily contingent in this way (non-'transformatory' occupations).

8.3.3 Family of policy institutions

Quincy Wright states that the League's activities in Danzig and the Saar were 'analogous' to the Mandate system.[215] Discussing the League administration in the Saar and the Mandate arrangements, H Duncan Hall asserts that:

[w]hat matters is the substance and not the form. The Saar Territory was under the Saar Governing Commission and not the Permanent Mandates Commission...such differences are largely a matter of the internal economy of the League...[216]

[215] Wright (above n. 32), 101.
[216] Hall (above n. 94), 11. Indeed, as mentioned above in Chapter 4, the provisions in the Treaty of Versailles creating the Saar arrangements utilize the trust concept: 'Germany renounces in favour of the League of Nations, in the capacity of trustee, the government of the territory'; Treaty of Versailles, Art. 49, extracted and discussed above, ch. 4, text accompanying n.18, *et seq.*

To what extent do the purposes of the ITA projects discussed in the previous two chapters fit within the general constellation of policies associated with the state-conducted practices discussed above? Is ITA another form of 'trusteeship'?

Discussing in 1975 the character of the administrative mandate given to the UN Council for South West Africa/Namibia, Itse Sagay stated that:

...the legal status of the United Nations is that of a trustee, rather than a sovereign. Its political relationship with the mandated territory is that between an administrative authority, or a *de jure* government and a territory under its rule. From the point of view of the extent of powers and authority, there is no difference between the position of the United Nations in South West Africa, and a sovereign authority in its own territory. However, fundamental and decisive differences exist with regard to the aims and the goal of the United Nations in the Territory, and its corresponding obligations, and the aims and goal of a sovereign authority in its own territory.

In the first place, the United Nations' administration is carried out primarily in the interest and for the benefits of the inhabitants of the Territory; an indispensable element of a trust regime. A sovereign authority in its own territory, on the other hand, rules primarily for its own benefit, or could do so lawfully, while the United Nations cannot. Moreover one of the specific and fundamental obligations of the United Nations is to prepare the mandated territory for immediate independence. In the case of a sovereign authority, the position is the same where a colony is concerned. If, however, the territory concerned is its home territory the question of independence would not even arise.[217]

In foregrounding the idea that administration is performed by an external actor 'primarily in the interest and for the benefits of the inhabitants of the Territory', Sagay reflects the general way in which ITA is understood by those involved in it. In describing this in terms of trusteeship, Sagay's approach suggests a common link between the colonial trusteeship of Burke and Lugard, the Mandate and Trusteeship arrangements, the concept of occupation trusteeship, and ITA. All of the practices can be regarded as species of a common institution, 'international trusteeship'. The reasons that give rise to these arrangements, the way the arrangements operate and seek to alter the political and economic regime in the territories concerned, and the extent to which attempts are made to improve local capacities may differ radically, but the central conception of alien actors exercising administrative control ostensibly on behalf of the people of the territories is the same.

As previously mentioned, Michael Bothe's and Thilo Marauhn's attempt to situate UNMIK and UNTAET within a broader policy framework does not take in—indeed, seeks to avoid—the colonial comparator; the 'trusteeship' in their notion of 'Security Council trusteeship administration' is based on an analogy from domestic law concepts of trust in the area of property, from which they assert that 'the establishment of a foreign presence in a territory... may be termed

---

[217] Sagay (above n. 161), 268–9. See also ibid., 271. Indeed, as mentioned above in Chapter 4, the provisions in the Treaty of Versailles creating the Saar arrangements utilize the trust concept: 'Germany renounces in favour of the League of Nations, in the capacity of trustee, the government of the territory'; Treaty of Versailles, Art. 49, extracted and discussed above, ch. 4, text accompanying n. 18, *et seq.*

a trusteeship administration'.[218] Addressing ITA in the case of UNMIK and UNTAET, they conclude that:

[t]he concept of trusteeship seems applicable because such an administration is exercised in the interest or on behalf of another corporate body, the 'old' or 'new' sovereign and/ or the population of the territory. This other corporate body, in the technical sense, can be considered to be the 'cestui que trust' or the 'trustor' [beneficiary]. While there may be cases in which it is difficult to identify the trustor and while there may even be cases involving several trustors, this does not affect the underlying concept as such.[219]

Bearing in mind these observations in the light of the broader contextual analysis provided in the present chapter, one might conclude that, in acting in the way described, UNMIK and UNTAET are nothing new and fit within the general idea of international trusteeship as articulated, for example, by Edmund Burke. However, Bothe and Marauhn take a different approach. Echoing the exceptionalist commentators highlighted in the first chapter, they argue that the two missions are merely 'first steps' towards 'Security Council mandated trusteeship administration'.[220] UNMIK and UNTAET constitute 'modern trusteeship' and 'demonstrate the need to re-conceptualize the trust in public international law'.[221] The authors acknowledge the existence of earlier ITA projects such as UNTEA, UNTAC, and UNTAES, but insist that:

[n]one of these cases have, however, been extensively discussed as an example for a modern trust under public international law. Obviously, the simple fact that an international organization assumes governmental powers does not seem to be the decisive criterion for distinguishing such a modern trust [i.e., UNMIK and UNTAET] from other forms of second-generation peacekeeping...[222]

For Bothe and Marauhn, then, the mere fact that the potential significance of trusteeship to these earlier projects hasn't been 'extensively discussed' means that it cannot be significant. The authors do not explain why this particular conclusion is chosen over, say, the explanation that commentators missed the significance of trusteeship. As with their earlier denial of the relevance of colonialism by seeking to avoid an exploration of its potential relevance, here the authors find evidence for the idea that UNMIK and UNTAET, as 'trusteeships', are 'new' simply from the absence of much discussion about the relevance of trusteeship to the earlier ITA projects.

---

[218] Bothe & Marauhn (above n. 12), 219. For the earlier discussion of the authors' orientation towards comparisons with colonialism, see text from n. 22, above. On the significance of the domestic law analogy, see the discussion above, in n. 108.

[219] Bothe & Marauhn (above n. 12), 220 (footnote omitted).

[220] Ibid., 222. For the earlier discussion see above, ch. 1, section 1.2.1.

[221] Bothe & Marauhn (above n. 12), 222.

[222] Bothe & Marauhn (above n. 12), 223. For the discussion of the earlier projects see ibid., 220–221.

Bothe and Marauhn do offer substantive reasons for newness: the projects are 'unique' within UN territorial administration missions because of their long-term objectives, the fact that they are acting 'fully as interim governments' (this means 'their tasks go far beyond the scope of past UN peacekeeping operations'), they have plenary competence, and they cover territories which 'form part of another State and whose future status is not quite certain'.[223] Taking all this together, 'the characteristic criterion' distinguishing UNMIK and UNTAET '...from other, more traditional forms of peacekeeping, is that the UN in Kosovo and East Timor has replaced the government of the State to which the territory in question belongs *in toto*'.[224]

Given the discussion about the scope of the ITA projects generally in Chapters 1, 2, 6, and 7, this presentation of the extreme nature of the projects in Kosovo and East Timor is perhaps exaggerated, but, as was said in Chapters 1 and 7, even if in some senses the two missions can be considered unique, what is served by treating them entirely separately from other ITA missions bearing in mind what is lost in terms of being able to appreciate commonalities?[225] As the previous exploration of state-conducted forms of international trusteeship reveals, a situation can be regarded as one of trust—some sort of control by an outside actor exercised ostensibly on behalf of the local population—even if it does not manifest the scale and ambition of the Kosovo and East Timor projects.

One further feature of the overall 'trusteeship' concept that might exclude certain arrangements is the question of whether or not the arrangements were 'imposed' on the territories concerned. Many commentators who use the 'trusteeship' label for the ITA projects in Bosnia and Herzegovina, Kosovo, and East Timor gloss over this issue and the significance, if any, it has to the question of whether 'trust' is evident. However, one of the leading scholars of international trusteeship, William Bain, sees it as crucial to the general concept. The significance of consent/imposition for international trusteeship generally is also implicated by a debate within the law of occupation as to whether this law only regulates situations that have been imposed on the territories concerned, or whether it also covers arrangements involving some kind of consent.

Before turning to Bain's ideas and the debates on 'occupation', it is perhaps helpful to set out in overview the main relevant features of the international legal authority claimed by OHR in Bosnia and Herzegovina, UNMIK in Kosovo, and UNTAET in East Timor, the three projects explicitly referenced by Bain in his treatment of the consent/imposition issue.[226] In the case of OHR, authority comes from both the Dayton Peace Agreements and Security Council resolutions passed

---

[223] Ibid., 224. Whereas Kosovo during the UNMIK period did indeed form part of a state (what was, when the mission commenced, called the Federal Republic of Yugoslavia), East Timor did not form part of any state in the sense that another state enjoyed sovereignty, meaning title, over it. See the discussion above, ch. 4, section 4.5.3 (on Kosovo) and ch. 5, section 5.7 (on East Timor).

[224] Bothe & Marauhn (above n. 12), 224.

[225] See above, ch. 1, section 1.2.1.

[226] This is discussed further below, section 8.7.2.1.

under Chapter VII of the UN Charter.[227] In the case of UNMIK, legal authority comes from both Security Council Resolution 1244 passed under Chapter VII of the UN Charter, and the 'Peace Plan' agreed to by the then FRY.[228] In the case of UNTAET, authority comes from both the May Agreements between Portugal and Indonesia, and Security Council Resolution 1272, passed under Chapter VII of the UN Charter.[229]

William Bain argues that a central feature of the trusteeship paradigm is that the 'ward' entity is not a sovereign state and legal consent from it for the trusteeship arrangements has not been forthcoming.[230] Bain's conception of trustee/fiduciary and beneficiary, then, is rooted in ideas of an international community of equal sovereign states; international trusteeship has to be understood in terms of whether or not the entities in question are or are not members of this community. If they are, they can act as the trustee but cannot be the 'ward', a position which can only be occupied by a non-sovereign entity.

For Bain, a situation where the capacity for self-administration within a state is compromised by the existence of ITA is not one of trusteeship but, rather, should be understood in terms of the social contract: the sovereign state has agreed to the arrangement, something which reinforces its sovereignty and distinguishes the situation fundamentally from one of trusteeship where the 'ward' is, by virtue of its non-sovereign nature, incapable of giving consent.[231] Elements of these ideas can be identified in the view of Alexandros Yannis that international trusteeship cannot be introduced in states because of the self-determination entitlement—the other side of the coin, as it were, from Bain's focus on sovereign equality as a bar.[232]

By contrast, other scholars assume that a relationship of dependency can be 'agreed' to by the ward. Henry Perritt, for example, asserts that international trusteeship '...may be either voluntary or imposed...' and that '...acquiescence to an intervention can be construed as consent to a trust'.[233] For him, the agreement of the then FRY to UNMIK was 'akin to placing Kosovo in trust voluntarily' and in relation to the projects in Bosnia and Herzegovina, Kosovo and East Timor, all of which he regards as trusteeship, there was 'acquiescence by the original sovereign'.[234] Moving further back, elements of 'consent' were forthcoming in both the Mandate

---

[227] See below nn. 461 and 467 and accompanying text.
[228] See below nn. 466 and 467 and accompanying text.
[229] See below nn. 469 and 476 and accompanying text.
[230] Bain, *Between Anarchy and Society* (above n. 12), 149–154.
[231] Ibid., 150.
[232] Yannis (above n. 12), 263. However, Yannis is equivocal on whether or not this is the reason why the term 'protectorate' is absent from official descriptions of the ITA projects: '[i]n any case, political correctness and the fact that the international administrations of the 1990s form part of different historical experiences do not encourage official use of the term 'trusteeship'' (ibid). Why it might not be 'politically correct' to use the term 'trusteeship' is discussed further below, section 8.7. The potential bar to trusteeship created by the self-determination entitlement is discussed below, from section 8.5.1 onwards.
[233] Perritt, 'Structures and Standards' (above n. 11), at 390, text accompanying n. 6.
[234] Ibid., 390, n. 6 (first quote) and 398 (second quote).

and Trusteeship arrangements; in some instances the views of the people in the territories involved were taken into account when responsibilities to act as administrative authorities were allocated.[235] More broadly, some of the seminal articulations of 'trust' like those of Edmund Burke cited above are framed in terms of dominion generally, rather than dominion actualized through a foundational moment of imposition exclusively. Indeed, certain articulations explicitly associate trust with ostensibly consensual arrangements, even those of a 'social contract' nature.[236]

These ideas notwithstanding, William Bain argues that the activities of OHR in Bosnia and Herzegovina do not constitute 'trusteeship' because the actor that would be the 'ward' if this were so is a sovereign state which consented to OHR through the Dayton Peace Agreements (Security Council authority is not mentioned).[237] The role of UNTAET in East Timor, by contrast, is trusteeship because of East Timor's non-sovereign nature during the period in question, and the lack of consent from its people to the arrangements.[238] As far as UNMIK in Kosovo is concerned, Bain states that it is not:

...like UNTAET, legitimized by the obligations of trusteeship that apply to non-self-governing territories and which are laid down in Chapter XI [of the UN Charter]; nor is it legitimized by an international treaty, sanctioned by the consent of the contracting parties, as is the case [regarding OHR] in Bosnia and Herzegovina. Rather, international administration in Kosovo is the result of a controversial, if not dubious, use of force that obtained retroactive assent from the Security Council in the form of resolution 1244.
[...]
...the international administration of Kosovo stands outside the normative framework of international society because it is an arrangement of power rather than one of law.[239]

---

[235] As far as 'A' class Mandated territories were concerned, Art. 22 of the League Covenant stated that '[t]he wishes of these communities must be a principal consideration in the selection of the Mandatory.' Although an equivalent provision was not included in the UN Charter for any of the Trust Territories, Peter Lyon states that in practice it was 'applied on a number of occasions'; Lyon (above n. 11), 102–3.

[236] So John Locke states that:

...the legislative being only a fiduciary power to act for certain ends, there remains still in the people a supreme power to remove or alter the legislative when they find the legislative act contrary to the *trust* reposed in them; for all power given with trust for the attaining an end, being limited by that end, whenever that end is manifestly neglected or opposed, the *trust* must necessarily be forfeited, and the power devolve into the hands of those that gave it, who may place it anew where they shall think best for their safety or security.

J Locke, *The Second Treatise of Civil Government and a Letter Concerning Toleration* (JW Gough ed., Blackwell, 1946), 74, para. 149 (emphasis added), cited by Lyon (above n. 11), 97.

[237] Bain, *Between Anarchy and Society* (above n. 12), 3, 149–50. On the status of Bosnia and Herzegovina, see above, ch. 4, section 4.5.1. On this legal authority, see below, n. 461 and accompanying text.

[238] Bain, *Between Anarchy and Society* (above n. 12), 152. On the status of East Timor during the period in question, see above, ch. 5, section 5.7. On the legal authority for UNTAET, including the issue of consent by the East Timorese, see below, n. 469 *et seq* and accompanying text.

[239] Bain, *Between Anarchy and Society* (above n. 12), 153. On the legality of the NATO bombing campaign, including whether or not it was somehow retroactively assented to in Security Council Resolution 1244, see the sources cited above, ch. 1, n. 4.

What is meant by the assertion, which lacks further elaboration, that UNMIK is an arrangement of 'power rather than one of law'? Two explanations seem possible, bearing in mind the overall focus on the dichotomy between consent and imposition as the key determinant of trusteeship.

On the one hand, if one views Security Council authority validly passed under Chapter VII of the UN Charter as essentially 'imposed', then it does not 'count' as law as far as preserving the sovereignty of the state is concerned – the only authoritative basis that matters is consent to the specific arrangement through a treaty. If the 'consent' of the FRY is overlooked—it is not mentioned by Bain in the relevant passage—then as far as this approach is concerned, specific consent would be regarded as absent, and UNMIK would constitute trusteeship.

On the other hand, if one views Security Council Chapter VII authority as 'consensual', on the basis that member states have agreed to it indirectly through being parties to the UN Charter, then it is capable of 'counting' as law in terms of preserving state sovereignty, but in the particular case of UNMIK, this has been somehow tainted by association with the 'dubious legality' of the preceding NATO bombing campaign which created the conditions for its introduction.[240] So, again, there is no consent, and UNMIK is trusteeship. Of course, this argument presupposes the illegality of the NATO bombing campaign, and more broadly rests on a particular contention about the transferable effect such illegality can have on the legitimacy of subsequent Security Council authority.[241] Moreover, in invoking the bombing campaign to distinguish the Kosovo case from that in Bosnia and Herzegovina, the significance of another NATO bombing campaign needs to be discounted. In 1995 NATO bombed mostly Serb forces in Bosnia and Herzegovina, an action generally regarded to have influenced a decision by their representatives to reach a peace settlement; the parties to the Dayton Peace Agreements include not only Bosnia and Herzegovina but also— and this is the case for Annex 10 in particular, the supposed treaty basis for OHR's powers—its two constituent entities, one of which being made up of the Bosnian Serb authorities.[242]

---

[240] For an example of the 'indirect consent' approach to Security Council authority in the context of ITA missions, see the discussion about UNMIK and UNTAET in Bothe & Marauhn (above n. 12).

[241] On the legality of the bombing campaign, see the sources cited above, ch. 1, n. 4. On the general question of whether agreements are invalidated if procured through the use of force, see, e.g., Vienna Convention on the Law of Treaties, 23 May 1969, 1155 UNTS 331, Art. 52; *Fisheries Jurisdiction Case (United Kingdom v Iceland), ICJ Reports 1973*, 3 at 14; AD McNair, *The Law of Treaties* (OUP, 1961), 206–11; P Malanczuk (ed.), *Akehurst's Modern Introduction to International Law* (7th rev. edn, Routledge, 1997), 139–40. Further mediating factors are of course the question of the FRY's legal status and UN membership at the time (on which, see above, ch. 4, n. 220); and the question as to whether the Security Council was acting within its powers under the UN Charter (on which, see, e.g., the works in List of Sources, section 5.2.6).

[242] The NATO campaign was called 'Operation Deliberate Force' and occurred between 29 August and 14 September 1995. See, e.g., Ignatieff (above n. 4), 59; see also the NATO Fact Sheet on the operation, available at <http://www.afsouth.nato.int/factsheets/DeliberateForceFactSheet.htm>; DA Leurdijk, 'Before and after Dayton: the UN and NATO in the former Yugoslavia', 18 (1997) *Third*

Bain's thesis must also discount as a potential counter-indicator the question of whether OHR's powers to impose legislation and dismiss elected officials can actually be found in Annex 10, given that they are not explicitly mentioned therein and have somehow been read into vague provisions through supposedly authoritative determinations made by the states of the Peace Implementation Council.[243] This stands in contrast to the relatively clear mandate for territorial administration contained in the Kosovo Peace Plan and Resolution 1244.[244]

Assuming for the sake of argument that these issues can be resolved successfully in favour of Bain's thesis, more fundamentally it must also be asked why the particular notion of degraded legal authority and therefore imposition is being adopted over the alternatives. As discussed earlier in Chapter 4, Bosnia and Herzegovina's 'statehood' in 1995 was almost exclusively juridical.[245] It could be said, then, that this entity's 'consent' to OHR, both directly in the case of the Dayton Peace Agreements, and indirectly in the case of the Security Council authority, was not 'meaningful'. Dismissing such an argument but accepting the thesis that the authority for the establishment of UNMIK was tainted necessarily involves a selective formalism.

This selectivity is perhaps explicable when the particular assertions about UNMIK and OHR are considered within the broader context of Bain's general thesis on international trusteeship. Bain's overall interest is in the relationship between the concept and formal notions of state sovereignty. He concludes, in an approach which echoes that of Robert Jackson, by expressing concerns about the degrading effect of UNMIK in particular, and contemporary calls for international trusteeship generally, on state sovereignty and sovereign equality.[246] If the concept of trusteeship is approached in this way, then the selective formalism of Bain's definition of degraded legality can be seen as rooted in a commitment to the sovereignty of the entity in question. Legal authority should be dismissed as somehow compromised if this is necessary to protect the sovereignty of the state (the case of the FRY); on the other hand, such authority is acceptable if it doesn't undermine this sovereignty (the case of Bosnia and Herzegovina). The normative commitment to sovereign equality leads to a definition of trusteeship incorporating conceptions of valid or invalid legal authority determined according to their significance for this broader commitment.

World Quarterly 457, *passim*; T Ripley, *Operation Deliberate Force: The UN and NATO Campaign in Bosnia* (Centre for Defence and International Security Studies (CDISS), 1999); SA Cooper, 'Air Power and the Coercive Use of Force', 24 (2001) *Washington Quarterly* 81, 85–6; PC Forage, 'Bombs for Peace: A Comparative Study of the Use of Air Power in the Balkans', 28 (2002) *Armed Forces & Society* 211, *passim*. On the Dayton Peace Agreements generally and Annex 10 in particular, see above ch. 1, n. 38. On OHR's authority in Annex 10, see above, ch. 2, n. 66 and below, n. 461.

[243] See above, ch. 2, n. 66.
[244] See the extracts of the provisions above, ch. 1, n. 1.
[245] See above, ch. 4, section 4.5.1.
[246] See Jackson (above n. 12), ch. 11; Bain, *Between Anarchy and Society* (above n. 12), ch. 7.

The present study, however, is not rooted in the same normative commitment; the objective here is to consider parallels between ITA and the state-conducted analogues in their broadest sense, including, but not limited to, parallels rooted in a particular effect on formal notions of state sovereignty and equality. Clearly the issues of the presence or absence of sovereign statehood and consent in international law were often implicated in colonial-era ideas of trusteeship, and vice versa. In many cases, the standard of civilization according to which entities were regarded as 'advanced' and capable of acting as trustees, or 'backward' and thereby requiring tutelage as 'wards', was also a determinant of whether or not entities were regarded as states: lacking an organized governmental structure along European lines, for example, was sometimes invoked as evidence both of a lack of civilization and a need for guardianship, and of non-conformity to a juridical criterion for statehood.[247]

Characterizing relations of domination as trusteeship only if they implicate issues of state sovereignty and consent/imposition in the particular manner emphasized by Bain is helpful in enabling a sophisticated comparison between colonial trusteeship and the modern ITA projects. Thus Bain offers acute insights into the nature of UNTAET and UNMIK in this regard. He argues that the creation of UNTAET did not herald a new era of trusteeship because it did not involve imposing foreign rule in a sovereign state territory; this, together with the objective of UNTAET to bring a new state into existence, rendered that mission compatible with the idea of state sovereignty, fitting exactly with its colonial precursors and, in consequence, belonging to a category 'that is for the most part historically exhausted'.[248] UNMIK, by contrast, is the 'only contemporary example of international administration that sustains the claim of innovation' because of the way it is rooted, as Bain sees things, in a violation of the sovereignty of what was, when the project started, called the FRY.[249]

As Bain's own study demonstrates, however, international trusteeship was and is a much broader paradigm. However illuminating analysis of the institution defined in terms of imposition as conceptualized by Bain can be, there are other, cross-cutting insights to be found if one moves beyond such an exclusive focus. Given the objective of the present study, it is more helpful to view the colonial-era conceptions of statehood and consent as particular, historically-specific features of broader notions of dominance based on ideas of advancement and backwardness, notions which may continue to have purchase even if these particular features have changed.

---

[247] See, for example, the discussion in Anghie (above n. 2), chs 1 and 2. On the legal status of colonial territories, see above, ch. 5, section 5.3, and sources cited therein.

[248] Bain, *Between Anarchy and Society* (above n. 12), 152. In a similar way, Alexandros Yannis states that UNTAET in East Timor fits within the older paradigm of international trusteeship in a former colony prior to independence, and, as such, the project should be understood as a 'delayed case of decolonization'; Yannis (above n. 12), 263.

[249] Bain, *Between Anarchy and Society* (above n. 12), 152.

Instead of seeing colonial-era notions of trusteeship as international trustee-ship in its totality, one could, alternatively, see them as the manifestation of a phenomenon that interacted in a particular manner with issues of statehood and consent during that period—specifically, that differences between trustee and ward usually mapped onto differences in conformity to the criteria for juridical statehood, and trusteeship was usually not rooted on the basis of legal consent by the ward—but in its later manifestation had a more complex interaction with these issues. Freed of an exclusive preoccupation with formal state sovereignty, one need not require that the normative distinction in the stage of development between peoples be reflected in the formal concept of sovereign statehood, nor require a lack of consent in legal terms, before the situation can be regarded as one of 'trusteeship'.

Can a concept of imposition be understood in a broader manner than in the terms of positive law exclusively? Here it is worth recalling that the present focus is on the political character of these arrangements. The objective is not to adopt a definite conclusion as to the nature of the legal authority provided for them. Indeed, it may be more illuminating for an exploration of how the projects are understood politically to consider whether, in any given situation, the invocation of multiple, mutually-incompatible positions on the issue of legal authority in particular and trusteeship in general are possible. From the foregoing analysis, it is evident that one can focus on particular features of each arrangement in order to arrive at different, contradictory conclusions on the issue of consent and imposition, regardless of what the 'true' legal position is and whether or not it is even possible to arrive at such a position. Focusing on Bosnia and Herzegovina's legal statehood and membership of the UN, one can insist, as Bain does, that valid sovereign consent for OHR was forthcoming; focusing on Bosnia and Herzegovina's lack of a coherent and effective political identity at the time the Dayton Agreements were stipulated, and the questionable fit between OHR's legal entitlements in Dayton Annex 10 and the powers being exercised, one can suggest that the arrangements there have been imposed. In one way, then, OHR operates on the basis of the social contract; in another, it is a situation of imposed trusteeship.

Whether or not these arguments are of equal weight is, in one important sense, irrelevant; the fact that they can both be made has significance in its own right, if it helps in explaining how the political character of the projects is understood by those involved in them. Nathaniel Berman's work in this regard, particularly on Kosovo, suggests that when one looks at such understandings, one sees that, indeed, it is helpful in this way.[250] To give an example of my own from Bosnia and Herzegovina, when OHR attempts to ground its purported powers to legis-late and dismiss government officials on a legitimate basis, it seeks to have things

---

[250] See Berman, 'Les Ambivalences Impériales' (above n. 17); Berman, 'Intervention in a "Divided World"' (above n. 17).

both ways: it emphasizes both the supposed consent to this that was forthcoming in Annex 10, implicitly referencing the social contract idea, and also the authority provided by the Security Council passed under Chapter VII of the UN Charter, implicitly referencing, whatever one might think about indirect consent forthcoming through UN membership, a capacity for imposition and so one understanding of trusteeship. Each of these characterizations of the missions is deemed politically useful, sometimes at different times, and in other cases even at the same time.[251] One might dismiss this as confused at best, disingenuous at worst, but to do so is to miss the point: this ambivalence is highly significant to how the projects are understood and explained.

Understanding international trusteeship generally, rather than trusteeship operating on the sovereign/non-sovereign axis exclusively, requires a broader conception of imposition than can necessarily be provided by international law.[252] More fundamentally, it must be asked whether imposition should even be part of the definition of trusteeship at all. As mentioned earlier, some of the canonical ideas of trusteeship (e.g. Edmund Burke) do not include imposition as an essential requirement. If one is not focusing exclusively on a class of activities that have the particular effect on issues of sovereignty that is the concern of William Bain, then the issue of imposition or consent is irrelevant. To be sure, most trusteeships have been imposed, but the idea of trust itself concerns only the structure of relations of domination, not also, necessarily, how such a structure is introduced.

The second area of debate where the issue of consent and imposition has been raised concerns the definition of 'occupation' for the purposes of the international law regulating the conduct of occupation. Given that the imposition of occupation is usually arrived at through the use of military force, the debate here intersects with the question discussed earlier of whether the definition of 'occupation' only covers those situations that have their origins in warfare.[253]

Certain scholars, including Eyal Benvenisti, incorporate the absence of consent by the host sovereign entity as a key element of their definitions of occupation.[254]

---

[251] An example of the general recitation of both forms of authority would be the preamble to an Order by OHR purporting to be binding within Bosnia and Herzegovina, where a series of clauses explaining the authority to be so binding invoke both Annex 10 of the Dayton Peace Agreements and provisions of Security Council resolutions passed under Chapter VII of the UN Charter. See OHR, Order on the Implementation of the Decision of the Constitutional Court of Bosnia and Herzegovina in the Appeal of Milorad Bilbija et al, No. AP-953/05, 23 March 2007, obtainable from <http://www.ohr.int>.

[252] Michael Ignatieff, discussing OHR in Bosnia and Herzegovina and the US presence in Afghanistan in 2003, states that: 'Bosnia and Afghanistan are supposed to be independent states, and Kosovo is being prepared for an independent future. Yet all three are on life support, dependent for their survival on foreign troops, international aid and diplomatic protection from the great powers'; Ignatieff (above n. 4), 109.

[253] See above, text accompanying n. 80 *et seq*.

[254] Benvenisti's definition includes the requirement that the control is exercised 'without the volition of the sovereign of the territory'; Benvenisti (above n. 9), 4. See also Vité (above n. 74), 14 and the UK *Manual of the Law of Armed Conflict* (above n. 74), 274, ch. 11, paras 11.1.1 and 11.2.

Others, including Adam Roberts, include both consensual and non-consensual occupations within their treatment of the topic.[255] If occupation is understood to be limited to arrangements understood to have been 'imposed', then it cannot be seen to map across the concept of trusteeship generally.[256] Steven Ratner argues that occupation should be viewed as covering both consensual and imposed arrangements.[257] Adam Roberts appears to endorse this view; whereas he speculates that the tendency of characterizations of many of the peace operations since the end of the Cold War, including certain ITA missions, not to use the term 'occupation' might be explained in part because of the degree of consent that was forthcoming in relation to them, he nonetheless affirms the applicability of occupation law to consensual arrangements.[258] For present purposes, this broader definition of occupation speaks to the essential commonality concerning the structure of domination that exists as between occupation and all the other forms of trusteeship reviewed above.

Steven Ratner's argument that the category of 'occupation' should be broad enough to cover both imposed and consensual arrangements is made as part of a broader thesis advocating the conceptualization of ITA within the occupation paradigm.[259] One approach to defining 'occupation' that might seem to prevent this is the idea that the term only covers activities by states, not also international organizations. Clearly the law of occupation traditionally understood is so limited.[260] Perhaps because of this, some commentators have defined

---

[255] See generally Roberts, 'What is Military Occupation?' (above n. 74), *passim*, and the view expressed in Roberts, 'Transformative Military Occupation' (above n. 74), 603, that the existence of formal consent does not render impossible the applicability of the law of occupation.

[256] So, for example, in setting out a definition of occupation that appears to exclude arrangements involving consent, the UK *Manual of the Law of Armed Conflict* invokes certain ITA projects as examples of situations that would be excluded; see *Manual of the Law of Armed Conflict* (above n. 74), 274, ch. 11, paras 11.1.1 and 11.2.

[257] Ratner (above n. 9), 697–8.

[258] In his 1984 article, Roberts states that, if missions are operating on the basis of a Status of Forces Agreement with the host state, then:

. . . they would not be in occupation of the territory as the term has been traditionally used in international law. It is just conceivable, however, that in different circumstances a peacekeeping force could find itself organizing some kind of 'occupation by consent'.

Roberts, 'What is Military Occupation?' (above n. 74), 291, footnote omitted. Discussing when such different circumstances might prevail, Roberts covers the scenario of state collapse, and cites ONUC in the Congo (one of the early UN projects involving ITA) as an example. Roberts' consideration of these issues in his later article 'Transformative Military Occupation' (above n. 74) is at 603.

[259] Ratner (above n. 9).

[260] On the law of occupation generally, see the sources cited above, n. 74. On the question of the applicability of the laws of war to UN peace operations, see Legal Opinions of the Secretariat of the United Nations, 'Question of the possible accession of intergovernmental organizations to the Geneva Conventions for the protection of war victims', 15 June 1972, (1972) *United Nations Juridical Yearbook* 153; UN Secretary-General, 'Observance by United Nations Forces of international humanitarian law' Secretary-General's Bulletin, 6 August 1999, UN Doc. ST/SGB/1999/13; for academic commentary, see D Bowett, *United Nations Forces: A Legal Study of United Nations Practice* (Stevens, 1964), ch. 15; F Seyersted, *United Nations Forces in the Law of Peace and War* (Sijthoff,

occupation itself as being limited to the actions of states.[261] In the same way, some commentators seem to understand occupation as always something following armed conflict, perhaps reflecting the traditional legal conception of occupation discussed earlier.[262] From this, it is sometimes suggested that the main commonality between occupation and ITA relates only to those ITA missions that come after conflict.[263] More broadly, for many, the term 'occupation' is pejorative, and is therefore resisted as inappropriate for the ITA missions.[264]

However, for present purposes, where the focus is on activities, purposes, and policies generally, not being limited to matters regulated by occupation law or those concerned only with particular policies, and where the objective is to foreground, not avoid, normative implications, whether or not they are perjorative, the activity of state-conducted occupation does bear important similarities with ITA; it is more helpful to emphasize the similarities, rather than the differences,

---

1966), ch. 3; R Kolb, G Porretto, and S Vité, *L'Articulation des règles de droit international humanitaire et de droits de l'homme applicables aux forces internationales et aux administrations civiles internationales transitoires* (CUDIH, 2003); Y Sandoz, 'The Application of Humanitarian Law by the Armed Forces of the United Nations Organization', (1978) *IRRC*, vol. 18, issue 206, 274; D Schindler, 'United Nations Forces and International Humanitarian Law', in C Swinarski (ed.), *Studies and Essays on International Humanitarian Law and Red Cross Principles in Honour of Jean Pictet* (ICRC/ Martinus Nijhoff, 1984), 521; U Palwankar, 'Applicability of International Humanitarian Law to United Nations Peace-Keeping Forces', (1993) *IRRC*, vol. 33, issue 294, 227.

[261] Adam Roberts' general definition of occupation in his 1984 article is an activity involving 'the armed forces of a state exercising some kind of domination or authority over inhabited territory'; Roberts, 'What is Military Occupation?' (above n. 74), 300. See, however, the comments on peacekeeping extracted in n. 265 below. In his later article, Roberts states that the tendency in characterizations of post-Cold War interventions including the ITA projects for the occupation label not to be used might be explained in part because 'the foreign presence had a multinational character'; Roberts, 'Transformative Military Occupation' (above n. 74), 603. On the potential causal relationship between the restriction of the legal definition and the formulation adopted in more general definitions as far as the state/international organization issue is concerned, see, e.g., Ratner (above n. 9), 697. For a discussion of the fit between the norms of occupation law and ITA, see below, ch. 9, text accompanying n. 10 *et seq*.

[262] See above, section 8.2.5.

[263] For example, when discussing occupation and ITA, Richard Caplan states that 'insofar as the two... are initiated and sustained by force, they can... be said to exhibit a strong family resemblance'; Caplan, *International Governance* (above n. 12), 3 (footnote omitted).

[264] Such resistance exists in the case of state occupations as well. Adam Roberts identifies one...

...reason for reluctance to use the word 'occupation': the adverse connotations of the word itself. To many, 'occupation' is almost synonymous with aggression and oppression.

Thus there has been widespread use of terms with a supposedly better ring: protectorate, fraternal aid, rescue mission, technical incursion, peacekeeping operation, military operation, civil administration, liberation and so on. Sometimes these terms are used in addition to the term 'occupation', in order to qualify it, to highlight the special features of a situation, and to clarify the purpose of the military action in question. Sometimes, and perhaps more often, these terms are used in total substitution for 'occupation'. Occasionally there may be some merit in not classifying a situation as an occupation: the maintenance of a fiction that a country retains its independence may act as a lever for gradually reasserting independence as a fact.

Roberts, 'What is Military Occupation?' (above n. 74), 301. Steven Ratner makes this point in relation to ITA missions in particular; see Ratner (above n. 9), 697.

between the two.[265] As Steven Ratner states, 'both missions can resemble each other in the eyes of those living in the occupied or administered territory' and, as Richard Caplan states, 'many of the challenges between the two may be similar...'.[266] Ratner argues that:

...the disconnect between the ways international law and organizations have conceptualized occupations and territorial administrations and the ways these missions are actually carried out...is no longer tenable. In fact, the two sorts of operations share a great deal, and lines separating them, adopted by international elites and reflected in international law, are disappearing. Although numerous works have examined state occupations *or* international administrations separately, my claim here is that only an understanding of them together will enable both lawyers and policy-makers to develop optimal doctrine and operating procedures...[267]

So Ratner chooses to define occupation broadly, as 'control of territory by outside entities'.[268] As the final part of the longer quotation above indicates, the objective is to develop a taxonomy of interventions in order to be able to compare like with like on two normative/operational issues: the legal framework and the legitimacy of coercion used during such missions.[269] The analysis offered in the present chapter suggests that such a taxonomy also has broader utility in emphasizing the commonality that exists in terms of the nature of the activity performed and the policies with which it is associated.

To bring together the foregoing analysis on the relationship between occupation, colonial trusteeship, the Mandate and Trusteeship arrangements and ITA, it might be said that there is a general institution in international public policy that can be termed 'international trusteeship' and covers a relationship of administrative control by an international actor or a group of such actors—whether states or international organizations—over a territorial unit whose identity is understood as something 'other' than that of the administering actor or actors, in most cases

---

[265] For examples of commentators who define occupation to include the actions of international organizations, see Benvenisti (above n. 9); Vité (above n. 74), Ratner (above n. 9). Although, as mentioned, Adam Roberts's general definition of occupation in 1984 was exclusive to state occupations, his discussion of peacekeeping generally, and the role of ONUC in the Congo in particular, suggests an acknowledgement of the connections between state-conducted occupations and what was the first UN-conducted ITA project:

...if central authority in the host State were to collapse, a peacekeeping force might find itself extending its authority and taking full charge of such matters as public order and safety.

The situation in the Congo during the United Nations operation 1960–4 affords one example illustrating the possibility of a United Nations peacekeeping force finding itself in a role closely analogous to that of an occupant...Congolese political developments made it unclear for a time who was the constitutional government, and there was United Nations intervention in administrative activities and in internal conflict beyond what had originally been envisaged.

Roberts, 'What is Military Occupation?' (above n. 74), 291, footnote omitted.
[266] Ratner (above n. 9), 696 and Caplan, *International Governance* (above n. 12), 3.
[267] Ratner (above n. 9), 697 (emphasis in original).
[268] Ibid.
[269] See ibid., *passim*.

because of the lack of title, and which is conceptualized in terms of the administering actor or actors performing this role on behalf of the administered territory.

As discussed earlier, colonial-era trusteeship conducted by states was commonly understood in terms of a 'dual mandate'—the colonial power acted on behalf of both the people of the territory and also itself and states more generally.[270] Is this concept relevant to the ITA projects? In conceptualizing a broad set of practices, including ITA, as 'UN Governance-in-Trust', Jarat Chopra addresses activity conducted 'in the interests of the territory in question and by the international community as a whole'.[271] Similarly, Michael Bothe and Thilo Marauhn state that in the case of UNMIK and UNTAET:

[t]he administration is exercised both in the interest and on behalf of the international community but above all in the interest of the inhabitants of the territory.[272]

These ideas suggest that one way of understanding international trusteeship as conducted through ITA is on the basis of a revised version of the colonial-era 'dual mandate', where the 'other' beneficiary is now the 'international community' as a whole. The significance of this in terms of both changes in the internationalization of trusteeship, and the legitimacy of ITA, will be explored later in this chapter and also in the next chapter.

If, then, ITA fits within a broader set of practices that constitute 'international trusteeship' in terms of the nature of the activity performed, how should the question of possible similarities between the policies with which it has been associated, and those associated with other forms of international trusteeship, be approached? As mentioned in Chapter 7, Michael Bothe and Thilo Marauhn essentialize the purpose of 'Security Council trusteeship administration', as 'the maintenance or restoration of international peace and security'.[273] In that earlier discussion, it was argued that such an essentialist approach is problematic because it raises one aspect of the missions to a primary characteristic without having considered the merits of representing the purposes of the missions in this way: the decision to do this appears to have been made chiefly because of the Security Council's involvement in providing legal authority for the missions.[274] When such an approach is considered in the present context of analysis, a further problem is evident: an essentialized characterization also has the effect of obscuring aspects of the missions which, if focused on, would give rise to a connection with colonial trusteeship. The authors conclude that the activity as they have characterized it:

...should not be discussed within the context of the traditional Trusteeship System...Security Council mandated trusteeship administration is no more and no less

---

[270] The original colonial conception of the dual mandate is discussed above, text accompanying n. 139 *et seq.*
[271] Chopra (above n. 12), 85.
[272] Bothe & Marauhn (above n. 12), 236.
[273] Ibid., 242.
[274] See the discussion above, ch. 7, section 7.4.3.

than a tool for refined peacekeeping which means that the established trust should not really be considered as a 'new' political entity in public international law.[275]

The argument here would seem to be that whereas UNMIK and UNTAET are 'new' as far as the activity normally performed in peace operations is concerned, nonetheless because these missions are species of peacekeeping, and peacekeeping and the UN Trusteeship arrangements are entirely different from one another, then although the two ITA missions involve 'trusteeship', this is not the trusteeship of the Trusteeship system. UNMIK and UNTAET are not, then, 'new' in being somehow a revival of the paradigm that was evident in the Trusteeship system; rather, they are part of the 'existing' framework of peacekeeping, albeit 'new' within this framework because of their complexity.

As already mentioned, the authors do not explain why the association of an activity with the promotion of international peace and security thereby rules it out from bearing any relation to trusteeship as practised under colonialism and the Mandate and Trusteeship arrangements. Given what has been said above about the role of strategic considerations in relation to all these arrangements, the association of peace and security objectives with UNMIK and UNTAET marks a continuance with, not a break from, earlier forms of trusteeship. With respect to the Trusteeship system in particular, as mentioned, such objectives were associated with all the arrangements; indeed, 'strategic' Trust territories were placed under the special authority of the Security Council in certain respects.[276] More fundamentally, the insistence on an essentialized depiction of the policies of UNMIK and UNTAET in terms of peace and security cannot be sustained if it leads to policies like democratization and 'state-building' to be concealed and, because of this, an understanding of the links between these policies and the civilizing mission of colonial trusteeship to be undermined.

It is submitted, therefore, that a broader approach to understanding the policies associated with ITA, as provided in the previous two chapters of this book, is a more solid foundation for considering the question of parallels with state-conducted international trusteeship.

When such an approach is adopted, it is evident that the main contours of the policy framework outlined above map onto what has been set out in relation to ITA in Chapters 6 and 7. The significance of strategic outcomes and issues of territorial status to the state analogues echoes the association of ITA with a 'sovereignty problem' generally and the particular 'governance problem' relating to policy concerning territorial status. Broad contrasts in the strategic policies pursued—between the balance of power in colonialism and the perceived destabilizing effects on regional security of state collapse in the case of certain forms

---

[275] Bothe & Marauhn (above n. 12), 242.
[276] On this competence of the UN Security Council, see UN Charter, Arts 76, 83–5. On the general policy of promoting international peace and security, see above, n. 98 and accompanying text.

of ITA—do not undermine the commonality that exists in terms of the nature of the overall enterprise.[277]

Many of the general areas of policy promoted under state-conducted trusteeship set out above are reflected in the purposes and policies of ITA. Colonial-era policies of population transfers[278] resonate with the use of ITA to enable migration policy, such as the work of OHR in Bosnia and Herzegovina in using property legislation as a way of enabling the transfer of displaced persons to their pre-war homes.[279] The colonial model of law reform outlined above, whereby local laws were altered if they were incompatible with the 'standard of civilization',[280] was adopted by UNMIK and UNTAET who, as discussed in Chapter 6, determined the applicable law in Kosovo and East Timor at the commencement of the administration missions by accepting the existing law insofar as it was compatible with the standards of international human rights law.[281] Obviously in some ways ITA does not replicate the colonial paradigm, for example in facilitating the direct extraction of human resources (the exploitation of material resources, however, has sometimes been a feature of ITA).[282] In the general mode of operation, however—the use of territorial control to pursue certain polices concerning the nature of governance—there is a clear link, and in many of the substantive policies the same ideas are in play.

One significant comparision to be drawn between ITA and the other forms of international trusteeship is in how the level of administrative control has been calibrated. In colonialism, as previously discussed, the idea of trusteeship was often grafted onto existing arrangements, often to 'humanize' them, often explained in terms of a greater sense of concern for the people in the territories and the need for better governance than had been provided by the trading companies. In the Mandate and Trusteeship systems, by contrast, plenary trusteeship administration was in operation from the start. To an extent, these differences map onto the model of 'reactive' ITA conducted by OHR in Bosnia and Herzegovina, where administrative prerogatives were conceived and utilized over time when the need for them was considered to be evident (because of problems associated with governance by local actors, rather than, as in certain cases of colonial trusteeship, earlier forms of foreign rule), compared with the alternative of full administration in Kosovo and East Timor. The connection between OHR and the more

---

[277] For a comparison of such differences, see, e.g., Fearon & Laitin (above n. 4), 13–14.

[278] See above, n. 174 and accompanying text.

[279] See below, ch. 6, text accompanying n. 115 *et seq.*

[280] See above, n. 164.

[281] See below, ch. 6, n. 142 and accompanying text.

[282] Roland Paris similarly affirms a general connection with peacebuilding missions, while acknowledging certain differences; see Paris, 'International Peacebuilding' (above n. 12), 652. On the exploitation of natural resources in the context of ITA missions, see above, ch. 6., section 6.4.2.4. One key idea of distinction is, of course, the notion that ITA is not 'exploitative' but 'humanitarian'; this is discussed further below, section 8.7.

rudimentary forms of colonial trusteeship is evident in the statement by Henry Perritt that:

...the events in Bosnia and Herzegovina reveal an international community only vaguely embracing the political trusteeship concept at the outset of its intervention. As a result, it had to gradually strengthen the powers of the trustee as stronger oversight of local institutions proved necessary to achieve the goals of intervention.[283]

The quote about South West Africa/Namibia from Ise Sagay at the start of this section mentioned the responsibility of the UN to prepare the territory for independence. How does the role of ITA in seeking to improve local conditions for self-administration in the context of 'governance problems' echo the civilizing mission in other forms of international trusteeship?

Some commentators argue that the term 'trusteeship' denotes a clear commitment to eventual independence for the territory concerned. Tom Parker defines international trusteeship in this manner, and on such a basis argues that UNMIK in Kosovo does not constitute a trusteeship because of the absence in UNMIK's mandate, as discussed earlier, of a clear commitment to independence as the eventual outcome.[284] UNTAET, by contrast, did constitute trusteeship because there was 'no limit to [the eventual goal of] self-administration and the clear goal' was to 'prepare for independence'.[285] Parker's definition of trusteeship, like that of William Bain, is rooted in an underlying normative commitment: whereas for Bain a concern with the inroads trusteeship has on sovereignty leads to a definition that always includes 'imposition' of a particular kind, for Parker what amounts to a commitment to self-determination leads to a definition of that always includes a clear commitment to eventual independence.[286]

Whereas this reflects, as will be discussed further below, one vision of what trusteeship *ought* to be in the era of external self-determination, for present purposes it is too narrow as a definition of international trusteeship in its totality. As mentioned above, international trusteeship has encompassed varying commitments to independence across its different manifestations. How do these compare with Kosovo and East Timor?

In Kosovo, as discussed in Chapter 6 the goal of UNMIK was to both provide administration itself and build up local capacities for self-administration. Under Security Council Resolution 1244, UNMIK was to:

...provide transitional administration while establishing and overseeing the development of provisional democratic self-governing institutions.[287]

UNMIK's mandate did not have an explicit sunset-clause; its duration was, thus, open-ended. The end point of its general objective for governance was

[283] Perritt, 'Structures and Standards' (above n. 11), 401.
[284] Parker (above n. 11), 36.
[285] Ibid., 36–7 (quotation from 37).
[286] Ibid., *passim*.
[287] SC Res. 1244, 10 June 1999, para. 10.

the occurrence of a particular event: a 'final settlement' on future status.[288] Until then, the general objective involved promoting 'substantial autonomy and self-government'.[289] When the settlement was forthcoming, UNMIK was mandated to oversee the transfer of authority from provisional institutions of self-government to the institutions established under it.[290]

The Kosovo model echoes other forms of international trusteeship with the twin objectives of acting as a direct remedy for perceived incapacities for governance and building up local capacities for self-administration. Being committed from the outset to an end point of self-administration pending an eventual settlement on status echoes the later forms of colonial trusteeship, notably the conception for Non-Self-Governing Territories in the UN Charter, in failing to guarantee independence if local capacities are deemed to have improved sufficiently (although not ruling it out). With Non-Self-Governing Territories, a guarantee of sorts arose through the self-determination entitlement (discussed further below); in Kosovo, by contrast, whether independence was to be a possibility was conceived as contingent on the outcome of the political settlement.

In East Timor, UNTAET's original mandate was fixed until the end of January 2001; at the expiry of that initial period, the mandate was renewed for a further year until the end of January 2002 and then again until 20 May 2002.[291] This temporal arrangement reflected the underlying commitment to eventual independence; the only issue was when the East Timorese would be judged ready for independence to be actualized, not also, as with Kosovo, whether independence was necessarily the end goal. Although the East Timorese commitment was not spelled out in UNTAET's original mandate under Security Council Resolution 1272, it is implicit in the preambular statement of that resolution, which takes note of the outcome of the 'popular consultation':

... through which the East Timorese people expressed their clear wish to begin a process of transition under the authority of the United Nations towards independence, which it regards as an accurate reflection of the views of the East Timorese people.[292]

Subsequent resolutions made explicit references to the eventual outcome of independence, and tied this directly to the duration of the mission.[293]

---

[288] Ibid., para 11(a); see also para 11(e).

[289] Ibid., para 11(a); see also para 11(e).

[290] Ibid., para 11(f).

[291] See SC Res. 1272, 25 October 1999, para. 17 (establishing UNTAET for an initial period until 31 January 2001); SC Res. 1338, 31 January 2001 (extending the mandate until 31 January 2002); SC Res. 1392, 31 January 2002 (extending the mandate until 20 May 2002).

[292] SC Res. 1272 (above n. 291), preamble. Whether or not the consultation result can be regarded as the expression of a 'clear wish' in favour of the interim period of UN administration is discussed further below, text accompanying nn. 472 *et seq.*

[293] For example, in the preamble to Resolution 1338 of January 2001, the Security Council prefaces its main provisions by '*Encouraging* efforts to achieve the goal of independence for East

The Kosovo and East Timor models echo the model of trusteeship articulated in the League Covenant and the UN Charter for 'A' class Mandated territories and all Trust territories respectively: foreign administration due to incapacity and the eventual goal of self-government. In being mandated to improve local conditions for governance and capacities for self-administration, the missions also manifest the additional element of effecting improvement vaguely articulated in the Covenant in relation to all Mandated territories and made a clear objective in relation to Trust territories. [294]

Reviewing the treatment of the connections between ITA and the state-conducted analogues conducted so far, the analysis from section 8.2. above suggests that all the forms of foreign state territorial administration reviewed echo the general idea in ITA of an important distinction operating with respect to the identity of the administering actors when compared to that of the administered territories. The discussion of policy objectives in the present section suggests that the state-conducted models were also understood to serve particular objectives in the same manner as ITA.

From this, it is possible to conceive a general category of 'foreign territorial administration' including both states and international organizations as the foreign actor, denoting one international legal person, or collection of international legal

---

Timor by the end of 2001 ...' (emphasis in original); in the operative paragraphs of the resolution, the Council:

2. Decides to extend the current mandate of UNTAET until 31 January 2002, bearing in mind the possible need for adjustments related to the independence timetable;
3. Requests the Special Representative of the Secretary-General to continue to take steps to delegate progressively further authority within the East Timor Transitional Administration (ETTA) to the East Timorese people until authority is fully transferred to the government of an independent State of East Timor...
4. Encourages UNTAET, bearing in mind the need to support capacity building for self-government, to continue to support fully the transition to independence, including through development and training for the East Timorese people.

SC Res. 1338 (above n. 291). A Presidential statement in October 2001 states that '[t]he Security Council welcomes the political progress achieved to date towards establishing an independent East Timorese state and endorses the recommendation by the Constituent Assembly that independence be declared on 20 May 2002 ...'; Statement of the President of the Security Council, 31 October 2001, UN Doc. S/PRST/2001/32. In the preamble to Resolution 1392 of January 2002, the Council prefaces its main provisions by:

Commending the work of the United Nations Transitional Administration in East Timor (UNTAET) and the leadership of the Special Representative of the Secretary-General in assisting the people of East Timor in laying the foundations for the transition to independence,
Recalling the Security Council's endorsement in its statement of the President (S/PRST/2001/32) of the proposal of the Constituent Assembly of East Timor of 19 October 2001 that independence be declared on 20 May 2002, and welcoming the strenuous efforts of the Second Transitional Government and the people of East Timor to achieve independence by that date...

SC Res. 1392 (above n. 291), (emphasis in original).

[294] For an alternative analysis of UNMIK and UNTAET's mandates in relation to the realization of external self-determination, see Bothe & Marauhn (above n. 12), 239; the conclusions of this are discussed below, text accompanying n. 528.

persons, displacing local actors in the administration of a territorial unit conceptualized in some way to be 'other' than that of the administering actors (usually through
the lack of title), in order to serve a particular policy objective or series of objectives.
When this arrangement is understood in terms of the foreign actor acting 'on behalf
of' the territory and its people, as is the case in all forms of ITA, certain, later forms
of colonialism, state administration under the Mandate and Trusteeship systems,
and 'occupation' as it is conceptualized in occupation law, it is 'trusteeship'. Such
arrangements might be termed generically 'international trusteeship'.

The policies associated with these different forms of foreign territorial administration vary significantly. Apart from the Mandate and Trusteeship arrangements, each institution was used in different places at different times to pursue
very different policies. In seeking to establish commonality in terms of the policies
promoted, therefore, one has to disaggregate each model, considering particular
manifestations of it and purposive connections that can be made with particular manifestations of the other models. When this is done, however, meaningful
connections can be made.

If, for example, one is considering the use of international territorial administration
to remedy perceived local incapacities for governance, it would seem appropriate to
review how this particular policy was pursued not only in previous ITA projects, but
also under certain forms of colonialism, the Mandate and Trusteeship arrangements,
and occupations. To appreciate the role of international territorial administration,
then, it is necessary to situate this institution within a broader 'family' of policy institutions operating in the same manner. Although the rest of the policy institutions in
this family have, as Edward Said remarked, largely come to an end, they are not only
of historical interest (or of current interest merely in terms of the continued effects
that they have on today's world);[295] they are also of purchase in understanding how a
related contemporary policy institution continues to operate.

In this book, a chronological analysis of ITA in particular and foreign territorial administration in general has been avoided in favour of a cross-project focus
on policies.[296] Now that the purposive bases for and links between all the different manifestations of foreign territorial administration have been established, it is
possible to consider how the use of foreign territorial administration evolved historically, and on what basis choices were made as between different models and
the particular policies that each model was used to implement.

The forthcoming historical analysis will consider two interrelated questions:
first, how did ideas about the utility of foreign territorial administration—
whether it should be used at all, and, if so, for what purpose—alter over time; and,
secondly, how did views on the identity of the foreign actors performing the role
of administering authorities shift during this period? The historical evolution of
foreign territorial administration in the 20th century can be divided into three

---

[295] See List of Sources, section 5.3.3.
[296] Although the treatment, above, in chs 4 and 5, of the legal status of the territories involved
proceeded on a chronological basis within each chapter.

phases; during each, the choices that were made about the utility of this institution were mediated by a discrete set of ideas. The phases will be addressed in the following three sections.

The first phase, considered in section 8.4, runs from the Treaty of Versailles to the immediate post-Second World War period, where the 'improvement' aspect of certain later forms of colonial trusteeship became formalized in the Mandate and Trusteeship arrangements. ITA was used, alongside the representative bodies, for other purposes.

The second phase, covered in section 8.5, begins with the emergence of the self-determination entitlement after the Second World War. This right can be understood in terms of a fundamental rejection of any form of foreign territorial administration, including such administration on a trusteeship basis. It led to the dismantlement of existing foreign territorial administration projects, in particular colonialism and the Trusteeship system, and the use of ITA, somewhat paradoxically, as a mechanism for realizing self-determination (for example, the UN Council in South West Africa/Namibia being introduced to provide an administrative authority in the territory that would implement the right of self-determination).

The third phase, addressed in section 8.6, covers those projects outside the context of effecting decolonization, where the institution again became used for purposes—notably filling a perceived vacuum in governance and/or addressing supposed deficiencies in the quality of governance—echoing the earlier models of state-conducted trusteeship that had seemingly been rejected by the self-determination entitlement.

8.4 From the Berlin Conference to the Allied Control Council in Berlin—Foreign Territorial Administration in the First Half of the 20th Century and the Internationalization of Trusteeship

The conduct of territorial administration by the League of Nations took place within the broader period between the Berlin General Act of 1885 and the Allied Control Council administration of Berlin after the Second World War, during which the concept of international trusteeship moved through several different models of internationalization.

In the Berlin General Act, trusteeship was internationalized in the sense that it was implicitly referenced in the objectives set out for colonial rule. Here, then, internationalization amounted to legalization internationally. So, for William Bain, the Berlin Conference 'internationalized the idea of trusteeship' by enshrining it as an obligation in international law.[297]

---

[297] Bain, *Between Anarchy and Society* (above n. 12), *passim*, especially ch. 3 and in particular at 53. On the question of whether there was a broader obligation in international law concerning a trust basis for colonial administration, see the discussion below, text accompanying n. 434 *et seq.*, and in particular n. 435.

As well as ushering in the introduction of international territorial administration with the Danzig and Saar arrangements, the Treaty of Versailles also marked a paradigmatic shift in the use of foreign territorial administration generally, with the creation of the Mandate system. The colonial institution was revised as between the colonies and protectorates of the victorious and the defeated powers: whereas in broad terms the former actors retained their dominions, the latter actors were forced to renounce their colonial possessions. This did not lead to independence, however, but the substitution of one form of foreign territorial administration with another. The trusteeship notion associated with certain forms of colonialism was explicitly articulated at the commencement of administration arrangements, rather than, as under Berlin, being introduced as a means of reorienting existing arrangements. So the notion of trust that had already been invoked in relation to certain forms of colonialism was again legalized internationally.[298]

Given that Article 22 of the League Covenant conceives the 'tutelage' role of the Mandatories as being 'exercised by them as Mandatories on behalf of the League', James Hales suggests that under this system the League itself was the 'trustee', the states charged with administration performing their role as agents for the League.[299] Under this view, trusteeship under the Mandate system marked a break from that under Berlin, since, although the administering entities were individual states in both arrangements, in Berlin these entities were also the 'trustees', whereas under the Mandate system they were mere agents of a separate body, the League, who acted as 'trustee'. As far as internationalization is concerned, then, the Mandate arrangements built on internationalization in terms of the obligation of trusteeship with internationalization in terms of the actor in the role of trustee, even if the arrangements were to be conducted on that actor's behalf by state agents.

More broadly, for many commentators the more systematic and comprehensive nature of the substantive obligations in Article 22, their broader field of operation geographically, and what turned out to be a general repudiation of annexation, render the nature of the 'trust' relatively sophisticated when compared with the Berlin arrangements, so much so that some regard the passage of the Treaty of Versailles, rather than the Berlin General Act, as the seminal

---

[298] Michael Reisman describes the Mandate arrangements as a '...modified form of internationally lawful superordination'; Reisman (above n. 32), 234.

[299] In 1939, James Hales stated that '...it may be argued that the League is the trustee of the development of the territories and that the Mandatories are merely the agents exercising certain powers on behalf of the trustee'; Hales (above n. 47), 193. In 1940, he stated that the League was the trustee, and that '...the actual tutelage...[is] exercised on behalf of the League by agents, namely Mandatories, who...account to the League of their stewardship'; Hales (above n. 107), 179. The consequence of this idea for the regime of accountability is addressed below, text accompanying n. 308 *et seq.*

moment in terms of internationalized efforts to humanize colonialism via the concept of trust.[300]

However one characterizes the trusteeship of Versailles when compared with that of Berlin, a clear difference existed as far as the provision of an overall structural guarantee of international supervision was concerned. James Hales states that:

[t]he essential difference between the old colonial system..., and the mandate system, is that in the former, the colony is administered under the guidance of the Mother Country without appeal against any abuse existing in the administration other than remedies provided by the colony's constitution. The native is restricted to vindicating his rights in the local Courts and legislation may be passed depriving him of all such rights, while foreigners whose rights may also be violated may only have a remedy by diplomatic means.

In the Mandate System, the idea overshadowing the whole administration is the idea of international supervision by certain institutions, in the working of which the Mandatory Power will only have one vote among many. As a result, the natives' interests are more fully protected, white settlers are prevented from exploiting the natural resources of the territory to their sole advantage, and all States members of the League of Nations are given an equal voice in this supervision, with a view to maintaining the trust undertaken by the League on behalf of civilization.[301]

On the ability of individuals to bring petitions to the Permanent Mandates Commission in particular, Hales states that:

[f]or the first time in colonial history, the administrators are made to answer challenges from those whom they administer, before an independent Commission.[302]

This extra element marked a further stage in the efforts to 'humanize' colonial rule through trusteeship.[303] As far as internationalization is concerned, the idea

---

[300] For James Hales, the conditions set for administration in 'B' and 'C' class Mandated territories were 'with a view to removing many of the abuses existing under the old Colonial System, when natives were in some cases exploited in favour of the owner of the territory'; Hales (above n. 107), 192. Antony Anghie states that '...the mandate was not a departure from colonialism as such; rather, it was a system of progressive, enlightened colonialism, as opposed to the bad, exploitative colonialism of the nineteenth century'; Anghie (above n. 2), 157. In a similar vein, he states that '[t]he Mandates System, by adopting the concept of trusteeship, justified the management of colonized peoples by presenting it as directed by concern for native interests and a desire to promote their self-government rather than by the selfish desires of the colonial power' (ibid., 140). On the significance of this in its international context, Anghie states that the Mandate system '...represented the international community's aspiration, through the League, to address colonial problems in general in a systematic, coordinated and ethical manner'; Ibid., 137. On the issue of non-annexation of Mandated territories, see the discussion of legal status above, ch. 5, section 5.3.

[301] Hales (above n. 47), 204. In the words of William Bain, '[t]he mandates system reaffirmed the principle of trusteeship enshrined in the Berlin Act; but it went further than the arrangements of Berlin in specifying procedures of international supervision'; Bain, *Between Anarchy and Society* (above n. 12), 79. See also ibid., 102 and, more generally, the discussion in Wright (above n. 32), chs 1 and 2.

[302] Hales (above n. 47), 224.

[303] On these efforts generally, see above, n. 111 and accompanying text *et seq*. James Hales describes the general objective of the Mandate arrangements as '...furthering the ideal of better colonial administration'; Hales (above n. 47), 283.

of internationalizing a trust basis for colonial administration from Berlin was supplemented by an internationalized mechanism of accountability.[304] For Hales:

[t]he methods of administration . . . are open to the world for inspection and are subject to the supervision of certain League Organs and of the Permanent Court of International Justice, which have a restraining influence over the exercise of the administrator's powers.[305]

As will be discussed further below, one essential component of trusteeship is the existence of external guarantees to ensure the trustee does not abuse this trust.[306] For those who insist that this component is an essential prerequisite for an arrangement to be regarded as one of trust, its absence in the Berlin regime and existence in the Mandate system leads to an assertion that only the latter can be regarded as the 'internationalization' of trust. For example, Ramendra Nath Chowdhuri states that there is a 'common misconception' that the internationalized trusteeship of the Mandate and the Trusteeship systems 'grew out' of ideas of trusteeship associated with colonialism; for Chowdhuri, this is a misconception because the colonial arrangements lacked an 'independent and impartial judge to hold the Trustee liable for damages in case of breach of Trust'.[307]

As with the earlier discussion about whether trusteeship presupposes 'imposition' (cf. William Bain's ideas) and eventual self-determination (cf. Tom Parker's ideas), this approach is helpful in identifying the features of certain manifestations of trusteeship. To adopt it as the definition of trusteeship in its totality, however, prevents the identification of common features across activities in terms of how they have been conceptualized, even if in some cases there may be important deficiencies in terms of how the conception is realized, such as the lack of accountability. For present purposes, it is more illuminating to focus at the more elemental level of the idea of trusteeship, and then within this distinguish between different forms according to whether or not they meet the requirement of accountability, than to exclude models lacking accountability from the outset.

The earlier question of who exactly was the 'trustee' in the Mandate system has implications for the nature of the accountability regime. If the League was 'trustee', the administering states merely its agents, where was the 'external' guarantee? James Hales argues that the agency relationship between the League and the administering entities is 'itself a trust', which means that:

. . . the Trustee or Guardian—the League—has been placed in the curious position of owing a duty to the civilised world of seeing to the welfare of the territories, and at the

---

[304] The distinction between the two in this regard is reflected in the sub-title to James Hales' treatment of the Mandate system: 'A Study in International Colonial Supervision'; Hales (above n. 47).

[305] Hales (above n. 47), 282.

[306] See below, text accompanying n. 409 *et seq.*

[307] Chowdhuri (above n. 97), 36. See also the discussion ibid., 21–3.

same time is the judge of whether its agents have faithfully carried out their own trust towards the League, whilst exercising the League's trust towards the Natives. The League, being an international person, sui generis, composed of other international persons, it follows that the latter in their individual capacity represent civilization and are in a position to see that the League carries out its trust.[308]

So it is League member states generally, acting through League bodies in their individual capacities, rather than as the 'League' as a distinct actor, who serve as the third party scrutiny body of the 'League' in its performance of a 'trust' carried out by its agents (who were certain League member states). If right as an explanation (how is the involvement of the Permanent Court of International Justice explained?) this suggests that the internationalization in accountability provided by the Mandate arrangements amounted to a process of scrutiny by a collection of states acting in their individual capacities of the actions of an international organization conducted through a sub-set of the same collection of states.[309]

As already discussed, the Mandate model was repeated after the Second World War with the colonial territories of the defeated powers in that conflict being administered by the victorious states under the Trusteeship system. With the lack of an equivalent provision in the UN Charter stating that the administering authorities act 'on behalf of' the UN, and the idea of distinct legal personality for the United Nations, it is possible to think of the individual states acting as 'trustees' and the UN, through various Organs, the body providing third party scrutiny.[310] If this is correct, and Hales's explanation of the Mandate arrangements is correct, then the Trusteeship arrangements marked a shift from the earlier arrangements: the trustee, previously internationalized, was again nationalized—in this sense, a step back to the trusteeship of Berlin; the actor carrying out the trusteeship was, as before, nationalized; the entity providing third party guarantees was internationalized in a different way from the Mandate arrangements, being the plenary international organization of the day acting in a distinct capacity, rather than its member states acting together in their individual capacities.

In any case, a further development marks the UN regime out from the League regime: all other colonial territories were, like the colonies covered by the Berlin regime, subject to an overall legal regime of trusteeship via the

---

[308] Hales (above n. 107), 179.

[309] This is considered further below, n. 412.

[310] On the legal personality of the UN, see above, ch. 2, n. 16. On the idea that under the Trusteeship system it is the individual states who act as the trustees, see, e.g., the commentary on Art. 75 of the UN Charter by Dietrich Rauschning in B Simma (ed.), *The Charter of the United Nations. A Commentary* (2nd edn, OUP, 2002), vol. 2, 1099, at 1099, who describes the administering authorities as 'States acting as trustees'. Of course, if the organization took on the role of administering authority, the scrutiny exercized would not be of a 'third party' kind in the same way. The possibility of the UN taking on this role is discussed further below, text accompanying n. 323. This consequence for the accountability mechanism is discussed further below, text following n. 553.

Declaration Regarding Non-Self-Governing Territories of the UN Charter.[311] An idea that had been partially legalized for certain colonies was now extended to colonies generally.[312] Moreover, unlike the Berlin regime, trusteeship for Non-Self-Governing Territories was made subject to a dedicated mechanism of oversight via the reporting obligations of Article 73(e), a relatively modest equivalent to the mechanism operating through the same treaty for Trust territories. By this stage, then, what Peter Lyon describes as the 20th-century efforts to 'institutionalize trusteeship as a system of international surveillance and accountability' were complete in the sense that, to varying extents, the two main components of colonial trusteeship—a trust obligation, and a mechanism for review of the performance of this trust—existed internationally, viz. as a matter of international law and under the auspices of the plenary international organization.[313]

At the end of the Second World War the association of foreign territorial administration with the idea of remedying local incapacities for governance shifted into a different category of territory. Occupation trusteeship conducted by the allies in Germany, Austria, and Japan, including the Allied Control Council in Berlin, was associated with both filling an administrative vacuum and engaging in the 'transformatory' project of what would now be called 'state-building', not in colonial territories, but in the territories of the two main defeated powers in the Second World War. Local governance was deemed deficient not because of the general 'stage' of development in the territory, but, rather, the devastating consequences of an armed conflict on states that were understood to be hitherto 'developed' and the particular political orientation of these states during the war.

With the exception of the allied-conducted operations after the Second World War, the other manifestations of foreign territorial administration introduced in the first half of the 20th century—ITA and the representative bodies, both in the inter-war period—were not used to fill a governmental vacuum and 'reconstruct' but, like some forms of colonialism before them, to ensure that particular

---

[311] UN Charter, Chapter XI. Reflecting the general link between the Trusteeship and Non-Self-Governing territory arrangements, Michael Reisman states that '[t]he innovation of the League was carried over to the United Nations system in both an optional "Trusteeship" arrangement and an automatic non-self-governing arrangement'; Reisman (above n. 32), 236.

[312] Michael Reisman states that Art. 73 of the UN Charter:

...represented a radical departure from prior international law: administration of non-self-governing territories *automatically* imposed on the superordinated party specific obligations for the welfare of the inhabitants of the territory.
[...]
In most general terms, the Charter established a contingent regime of obligations for the welfare of subordinated states that came into operation for any state controlling non-self-governing territory, without regard to any explicit undertaking of such an obligation.

Reisman (above n. 32), 236–7 (emphasis in the original). The question of whether there was a general international law obligation of trusteeship even before this time is discussed further below, text accompanying n. 434 *et seq.*, and in particular n. 435.

[313] Lyon (above n. 11), 98.

government policies were pursued in the territories in question (for example the exploitation of the resources of the Saar by France) and/or to address a sovereignty problem (for example the dispute between Colombia and Peru relating to Leticia).

Given the use of plenary ITA in this period, which lasted for 15 years in the Saar, how is the choice between this form of foreign territorial administration with respect to these territories, and the alternative option of state-conducted administration in Mandate and Trust territories, explained? In relation to the Trusteeship system in particular, whereas in the case of the allied administrations of Germany, Austria, and Japan there was no functioning organization in place to perform the role of administering authority in 1945, the Trusteeship arrangements formed part of the same instrument that created the United Nations as such an organization (with the name the allies had used for themselves during the war).[314]

In the first place, the policy basis for the use of foreign territorial administration in the Saar, Leticia, and Danzig was predicated on particular identity of the administering entity as an international organization. For example, the assumption that the League of Nations, as an international organization, would not claim sovereignty over the Saar led to the utilization of League administration in that territory in preference to administration by France. In these projects, then, the choice of administering actor is directly significant to the ostensible purpose being served by the foreign administration project.

With the Mandate and Trusteeship systems, by contrast, the choice of administering actor was determined by factors other than the ostensible purpose for introducing foreign administration. That purpose—the idea that local people were in some way deficient in exercising territorial governance—by itself did not require an administering actor with a particular identity. Why, then, did the Mandate and Trusteeship systems involve states as the administering authorities rather than the League and the UN?

As mentioned in relation to the Trusteeship arrangements, both systems were conceived at the same time that the relevant international organization was created, being set out in the foundational instruments of that organization. Whereas the Treaty of Versailles did provide for League administration in the Saar at the same moment that its related instrument, the Covenant, was creating the League itself, this was only one project and in a relatively small area of territory. It would have been quite another matter for the two post-war settlements

---

[314] The term 'United Nations' was used during the Second World War in the Declaration by United Nations, signed at Washington on 1 January 1942, reproduced in 36 (1942) *AJIL Suppl.*, 192, in which 26 allied governments committed themselves to employ their full resources, military or economic, against the Axis powers and pledged not to seek a separate peace with those powers. On the origins of the term, see also <http://www.un.org/Overview/origin.html>.

to assign the administration of numerous territories of varying sizes around the world to organizations that were themselves being created.[315]

That said, Quincy Wright reports that after the First World War, the options of 'annexation, internationalization, independence, and restoration' each had their advocates amongst representatives of the victorious powers crafting the post-war settlement.[316] Those in favour of independence, including the US, did not prevail over the view that the populations of the territories involved were not ready for self-administration, leading to the explicit articulation of this perceived incapacity in Article 22 of the Covenant.[317] The main contest was between annexation, which, as mentioned earlier, was an aspiration of some of the victorious states, and internationalization, meaning direct administration by the League, which was advocated on self-determination grounds, notably by Woodrow Wilson of the US.[318] The compromise model adopted—administration by the victorious states, 'on trust', subject to international supervision—enabled states who, by way of resisting internationalization had complained of their sacrifice of 'blood and treasure', to retain control, but without an explicit provision for annexation being made.[319]

At the end of the Second World War, internationalization again had its advocates, building on arguments formulated in relation to colonies generally over the course of the inter-war period.[320] As Ramendra Nath Chowdhuri relates, it was argued that internationalization would better enable the administration of colonies to be conducted in the interest of all states, and offered greater humanitarian potential in terms of the treatment of the local population.[321] Furthermore, it was also argued that, in the words of Chowdhuri:

...the League experiment in direct administration in...the Saar (1920–34), and in the Leticia (1933–34) revealed the immense possibility of the success of international administration of the colonial areas.[322]

Unlike the provision in Article 22 of the League Covenant, that the administering authorities in Mandated territories would be 'advanced nations' only,

---

[315] On the perceived incapacity of the League in this regard, see, e.g., Jackson (above n. 12), 309.

[316] Wright (above n. 32), 29. On the aspirations to annexation in particular, see also Hales (above n. 47), 187.

[317] Wright (above n. 32), 27. On the US position, see, e.g., Hales (above n. 47), 187 and the quotation from Woodrow Wilson in Anghie (above n. 2), 120, n. 6.

[318] Wright (above n. 32), 24 *et seq*; on internationalization in particular, see Chowdhuri (above n. 97), 56–7.

[319] Wright (above n. 32), 24 *et seq* (quotation from 27), see also Hall (above n. 94), 13, 31. On the legal status of Mandated territories, see the discussion above, ch. 5, section 5.3. On the broader strategic value to the states concerned of being able to retain control, see the discussion above, section 8.3.1. James Hales reports that, although in general the victorious powers were prevented from annexing the colonies of the defeated powers, some annexations did occur as a result of the war; Hales (above n. 47), 186–7.

[320] Chowdhuri (above n. 97), 25–7.

[321] See the quotations from Chowdhuri below, text corresponding to nn. 512 and 514.

[322] Chowdhuri (above n. 97), 25 (note omitted).

Article 81 of the UN Charter provided that, as mentioned earlier in Chapter 5, the administering authority in the Trusteeship system could be 'one or more states or the Organization [the United Nations] itself'.[323]

However, again the advocates of administration by individual states prevailed, successfully arguing that internationalization would be prohibitively expensive, that the staff of international organizations would be incapable of conducting it because of the multiplicity of languages used in the organization, and, as (Lord) Frederick Lugard of Britain insisted, because it would be 'heart-breaking' for the colonial administrators who had been involved so far to be removed from this role.[324] In consequence, all the Trusteeship arrangements created involved administration by individual states.[325]

As mentioned previously, the UN Charter provided (in Article 77) that new territories could be 'voluntarily placed under the system by States responsible for their administration'; the possibility for direct UN administration under the system according to Article 81, then, could have been actualized.[326] However, as no new placements were made, the provisions of Article 81 remained a dead letter.[327]

In those instances where territorial administration by international organizations has taken place, the set-up constitutes the ultimate form of internationalized trusteeship: the actor conducting administration is internationalized. Whereas under James Hales's explanation of the Mandate arrangements, the League was 'trustee' but acted through state agents in the conduct of administration, here the trustee itself acts as the administering authority. Furthermore, recalling the idea mentioned above, that ITA can be seen as a modified version of the 'dual mandate' with the 'other' beneficiary now the 'international community' as a whole, here too there is an additional development in internationalization.[328]

At the start of the post-war United Nations era, all the different manifestations of foreign territorial administration were in operation around the world apart from ITA. Although the UN Charter introduced a new version of the League-based Mandate arrangements, the Trusteeship system, it also enshrined (albeit vaguely) a general principle—self-determination—that was to develop into an entitlement placing all the foreign territorial administration projects, including those conducted under its own Trusteeship system, into question.[329]

---

[323] Quotation taken from UN Charter, Art. 81. See also above, ch. 5, n. 48. For commentary on the provision, see, e.g., Rauschning (above n. 211), 1121–1122; on the point of distinction with the League Mandate arrangements, see, e.g., Hall (above n. 94), 133.

[324] Ibid., 26–7. See also *Oppenheim's International Law* (above n. 33), § 89. On the perceived incapacity of the UN in particular, see, e.g., Jackson (above n. 12), 309.

[325] For information on the territories covered, see the sources cited above, ch. 5, n. 44.

[326] See the discussion in Chowdhuri (above n. 97), 57–8.

[327] On the lack of new placements, see above, n. 69 and text accompanying n.118.

[328] See above, text accompanying nn. 271 *et seq.*

[329] UN Charter, Arts 1(2) and 55.

8.5 The Post-War Self-Determination Entitlement and the Repudiation of Foreign Territorial Administration

It has been suggested above that colonialism, protection, territorial administration by representative bodies, the Mandate and Trusteeship systems, occupation, and ITA are comparable because of the nature of the activity performed, the relationship between the administering actors and the administered territories, and the way these arrangements were associated with the pursuit of certain policies. In what follows, it will be argued that a further commonality is evident when nature of the self-determination entitlement that emerged after the Second World War is considered. This entitlement reflected and constituted the notion that foreign territorial administration itself was to be challenged; the existence of such activity in a territory formed the basis for a self-determination entitlement on the part of the people of the territory. The effect of the entitlement was to reject automatically the continued conduct of existing arrangements, unless they were agreed to by the people. New projects introduced in this era were restricted to those circumstances when it was deemed necessary to alter the identity of the actor exercising administrative control so as to implement the right of self-determination.

8.5.1 Rejection of foreign territorial administration

The call for self-determination amounted to a repudiation of the system of foreign territorial administration that existed in the forms of protection, colonialism, international territorial administration, the Mandate and Trusteeship systems, and occupation.[330] Administration by an outside actor, necessarily preventing self-administration, was considered *ipso facto* objectionable.[331]

---

[330] On self-determination, see the sources cited above, ch. 5, n. 3 and those contained in the List of Sources, section 5.4. The critiques of colonialism are considered in more detail below in section 8.7.1.

[331] On this absolutist rejection of foreign territorial administration, see the sources cited below, n. 377. In the words of Robert Jackson:

...for several centuries prior to the middle of the twentieth century, an activist doctrine of military intervention and foreign rule was a norm that was imposed by the West on most of the world. By 1960 that old doctrine had been completely repudiated by international society. That was not because trusteeship could not produce peace, order, and good governance in some places. It was because it was generally held to be wrong for people from some countries to appoint themselves and install themselves as rulers for people in other countries...Self-government was seen to be morally superior to foreign government, even if self-government was less effective and less civil and foreign government was more benevolent. Political *laissez-faire* was adopted as the universal norm of international society.

Jackson (above n. 12), 314. In the words of William Bain, 'the idea of trusteeship...was relegated to the dustbin of history along with the legitimacy of empire' because of a 'normative shift whereby

As discussed in Chapter 5, the original roots of the legal 'external' self-determination entitlement applicable to a particular class of territories (before its articulation as a 'human right') were in a negative rejection of foreign administration.[332] It followed, then, that in general terms independence was considered automatically valid, regardless of the views of the people of the territory, whereas, conversely, the existing foreign administration arrangements, or other such arrangements, would be valid only if they were agreed to by the people in a consultation. So the normative tenor of the institution shifted; it was now presumed to be invalid, unless a particular type of consent for it was forthcoming from the people.

This transformation is strikingly illustrated in proclamations such as those in General Assembly Resolution 2621 of 1970, that the continuation of colonialism 'in all its forms and manifestations' was a 'crime' and that colonial peoples had the right to 'struggle by all necessary means ... against colonial powers which suppress their aspiration for freedom and independence', and General Assembly Resolution 3103 of 1973, that attempts to suppress struggles against 'alien and colonial domination' were a breach of the UN Charter and, specifically, constituted a 'threat to international peace and security'.[333]

All the existing foreign territorial administration arrangements were treated together for the purposes of self-determination: as previously mentioned in the context of the distinction between the metropolis and the colony that was at the heart of colonial arrangements, they were all manifestations of 'alien subjugation, domination and exploitation'.[334] The effect of the self-determination entitlement was to render the continued duration of existing arrangements contingent on the views of the people of the territories concerned (though not necessarily all these people), rather than, as before, on the policy objectives that had led to the

---

independence became an unqualified right and colonialism an absolute wrong'; Bain, *Between Anarchy and Society* (above n. 12), 4 and 134 respectively.

[332] See above, ch. 5, section 5.2.

[333] See GA Res. 2621 (XXV), 12 October 1970, paras 1 and 2; GA Res. 3103 (XXVIII), 30 December 1973, para. 2. See Jackson (above n. 55), 107. Art. 19(3)(b) of the UN International Law Commission's draft Articles on State Responsibility in 1996 provided that an international crime could result from 'a serious breach of an international obligation of essential importance for safeguarding the right of self-determination of peoples, such as that prohibiting the establishment or maintenance by force of colonial domination ...'; for the text and commentary see *Yearbook of the International Law Commission* 1976, vol. II (2), 95 and 106–107. The concept of a state crime did not survive to the eventual formulation adopted on second reading by the ILC in 2001 (see International Law Commission, Articles on Responsibility of States for Internationally Wrongful Acts, reproduced in J Crawford, *The International Law Commission's Articles on State Responsibility. Introduction, Text and Commentaries* (CUP, 2002)) and noted and commended to the attention of states by the General Assembly in GA Res. 56/83, 12 December 2001. On the idea of state crimes generally, see, e.g., A Pellet, 'Can a State Commit a Crime? Definitely, Yes!', 10 (1999) *EJIL* 425.

[334] The quote is taken from GA Res. 1514 (XV), 14 December 1960, para. 1. The significance of the general distinction in the colonial context is discussed above, text accompanying n. 52 *et seq.*; the quote itself is mentioned above, text accompanying n. 65.

introduction of foreign administration to begin with, and the determination of such objectives by the administering authorities.

For example, with those arrangements introduced because of the perceived incapacity for self-administration, independence was no longer to be granted if and when the stage of development had reached a certain level; it was an automatic entitlement. So it made no difference whether the administration arrangement envisaged a contingent form of future independence (as the treaty conceptions for 'A' class Mandated and Trust territories) or was indefinitely constituted (as in certain colonial arrangements); the arrangement was to end unless it was given the support of the people (as some arrangements were). Thus even if there was not much local capacity for governance, self-administration would be actualized unless the people of the territory decided otherwise.[335]

This idea is articulated in paragraph 3 of General Assembly Resolution 1514 of 1960, which states:

[i]nadequacy of political, economic, social or educational preparedness should never serve as a pretext for delaying independence.[336]

As Robert Jackson observes, 'independence was a matter of political choice and not empirical condition.'[337] In the words of William Bain:

... decolonization abolished the distinction upon which the idea of trusteeship depended. There were no more 'child-like' peoples that required guidance in becoming 'adult' peoples: everyone was entitled by right to the independence that came with adulthood. Thus it no longer made any sense to speak of a hierarchical world order in which a measure of development or a test of fitness determined membership in the society of states.[338]

Concerns by Western states about 'underdevelopment' in the global south, and activities by them to try to 'improve' this situation shifted into the arena of what is called 'aid' and 'development assistance'.[339] Jackson, adopting a forward-looking perspective from the era of decolonization, remarks that:

[d]evelopment would later become an international doctrine, except that independence would no longer depend on it and the international community—in particular the rich countries—would then be responsible for the development of poor countries.[340]

---

[335] For Robert Jackson, decolonization thus shifted from being 'evolutionary', i.e., depending on improvements in and capacity for self-administration (as mentioned above, text accompanying n. 189) to being 'accelerated' and 'precipitous'; Jackson (above n. 55), 95–102.

[336] GA Res. 1514 (XV) (above, n. 334), para. 3.

[337] See Jackson (above n. 55), 95. Of course, which particular associations of people could claim or, put differently, which territorial units would form the basis for, independence was in a different sense a matter of 'empirical condition', cf. the doctrine of *uti possidetis* discussed above, ch. 5, text accompanying n. 20.

[338] Bain, *Between Anarchy and Society* (above n. 12), 135.

[339] For an example of commentary on this link between contemporary notions of development assistance and the activities of colonial trusteeship, see Bain, *Between Anarchy and Society* (above n. 12), 7.

[340] Jackson (above n. 55), 91.

The manner in which the original presumption against foreign territorial administration operated meant that the future use of this institution was limited to existing arrangements whose continuance was understood as being in accordance with the wishes of the people of the territory. This amounted to an invalid situation supposedly rendered valid; since the starting point was invalidity, no new foreign territorial administration projects were conceived during this period. However, in some cases it was deemed necessary, as an exceptional measure, to introduce foreign administration so as to implement the self-determination entitlement.

8.5.2 Remaining role for foreign territorial administration—realizing self-determination

Before foreign territorial administration could be brought to an end (unless it was consented to) by the self-determination entitlement, it was to be utilized for one final purpose. The a priori rejection of foreign territorial administration had the effect of transforming the policy objective of the existing administration arrangements. Regardless of their original policy bases, their role now was to prosecute the decolonization agenda: to address the various aspects of this agenda that required certain administrative arrangements.[341] As a result, the administering authority was obliged to promote a new territorial status for the territory, both in terms of (what were called in Chapter 6) a 'sovereignty problem' (giving up territorial control, if appropriate) and a 'governance problem' (for example performing certain constitutional measures to implement the new status). Since this status, if it were not to be independence, was to be validated by the people, the administering authority was also obliged to implement a particular governance policy: the conduct of a consultation. Overall, then, the decolonization agenda not only brought the colonial and Mandate and Trusteeship arrangements to an end; it also effected a temporary, uniform reorientation of the purposive framework of these institutions in order to achieve their demise.

At the time the push towards decolonization occurred, there were no inherited ITA projects that could be challenged, like colonialism and the Trusteeship arrangements, by the call for self-determination. The Saar was assimilated into Germany in 1935, and the League involvement in the Free City of Danzig ended with the German invasion of Poland in 1939. The Free Territory of Trieste arrangement for an administrative role for the new United Nations was never implemented.[342] So ITA was not targeted, like colonialism and the Trusteeship

---

[341] Steven Ratner also identifies the connection between the objectives of the projects in Namibia, Cambodia, and East Timor and the process of decolonization and self-determination; see Ratner (above n. 9), 696.

[342] See Crawford (above n. 32), 454–8. Because the Trieste arrangements were not actualized, they are not covered in this book. See above, ch. 2, n. 47 and accompanying text.

system, as an existing phenomenon which, in the light of changing political circumstances, should be brought to an end. That said, new ITA projects were conceived during this time in order to support the decolonization agenda.[343]

In all but one case, the new ITA projects introduced in this era—what might be called the 'decolonization projects'—involved performing the administrative activities incumbent on the existing administering authorities, in circumstances where those authorities were understood to be either unwilling or unable to do so, either at all, or in an acceptable fashion. The two projects in South West Africa/Namibia epitomize the two different roles that ITA performed in this regard. Originally, the perceived problem concerned the administering authority's unwillingness to accept the policy of self-determination. Had the Council's mandate been implemented, it would have created an administrative structure willing to give up administrative control to whatever authority was agreed to under a self-determination consultation. South Africa's long-standing refusal to accept 'external' self-determination was unusual, and recourse to ITA in this context was unique. However, when South Africa belatedly changed its position, the different problem its administration manifested, concerning the conduct of a consultation (in this case elections for government office), was common.

The UN began its involvement in the conduct of consultations before the Council's creation, ensuring that when they took place in Non-Self-Governing and Trust territories they were seen to be free and fair.[344] Although the organization's activity in this regard was pronounced in the main 'wave' of decolonization in the 1960s and 1970s, enduring disputes about certain territories meant that it was used as late as 1989–1990 (in Namibia) and 1999 (in East Timor). Given the unimplemented mandate in Western Sahara at the time this book was completed, it may yet be used again in this regard.

In these missions, ITA was understood to be supporting the implementation of the self-determination agenda through the adoption of particular policies in the self-determination unit. Although this replicated the underlying activity that had been repudiated by the agenda of self-determination, it was not inconsistent with this agenda for that reason.

ITA responded to a paradoxical problem arising out of the decolonization process. Because of the historical denial of self-administration, peoples were entitled to decide how their internal administrative arrangements, and external status, were to operate in the future. However, the legacy of foreign administration also meant that they were not in a position to carry out the process through which their entitlement would be realized—they were not in control—and, moreover, the actors who had imposed external administration to begin with were in control. Thus, as an exceptional measure, a new phase of external administration was

---

[343] According to Robert Jackson, '[f]rom 1945 until the end of the cold war, legitimate and lawful international trusteeship was confined to [the] UN supervised transition of a small number of territories from quasi-colonial territories to independence'; Jackson (above n. 12), 305.

[344] See above, ch. 2, n. 31 and accompanying text.

introduced, limited to the particular administrative activity necessary to bring an end to, or legitimize through some form of consent from the people, the externally-imposed plenary arrangements that had operated hitherto, and/or to enable elections for the governments of the newly independent states.

In the case of self-determination consultations in particular, with the continuance of existing arrangements one possible option for the realization of 'external' self-determination, the administering state had a clear interest in the outcome of the consultation (although not necessarily an outcome favouring maintenance of the status quo). Given that, as will be discussed further below, one of the bases for the self-determination agenda was that foreign administration had originally been imposed on the people concerned, having the administering authority carry out the process that would determine whether this arrangement continued was not considered appropriate in many cases.

In general, the use of ITA to implement the obligations of the administering authority, enable the 'act of self-determination', and enable government elections, is ultimately not inconsistent with the self-determination agenda of preventing a repeat of the colonial activity in the future. Involving, paradoxically, a form of this activity, ITA was necessary to bring the activity to a permanent end, and set up an essential component of its replacement, a locally-constituted government.

It might have been thought in the 1960s that the self-determination entitlement of the post-Second World War era, an idea based on the rejection of foreign territorial administration itself, meant a permanent end to this activity and its family of policy institutions, from colonialism to ITA. So although, as mentioned above and in Chapter 5, under Article 77 of the UN Charter the Trusteeship system remained open to new territories to be placed under it, were this to be utilized it would undermine the new norm against trusteeship.[345] More narrowly, since its utilization for territories that were UN members was already explicitly ruled out under Article 78 of the Charter, the effect of decolonization rendered most people in the world residents in state territory and thereby excluded from this form of trusteeship.[346] Robert Jackson states that:

[t]he UN Trusteeship Council was expected to go out of business when all trust territories became independent... UN trusteeship was not intended to reverse the process and transfer already independent states back to quasi-colonial status... the UN charter does not provide for trusteeship for sovereign states: independence is a one-way street with no return to dependency status (article 78). A basic norm of post-1945 world politics forbids the institution of trusteeship, colonial status, or any other form of international dependency where independence previously existed. Article 78 should be read as a confirmation and reinforcement of the *Grundnorm* of non-intervention.[347]

---

[345] On this possibility and its non-actualization, see above, n. 69, text accompanying nn. 118 and 327.

[346] On this restriction see also above, ch. 5, n. 45 and accompanying text.

[347] Jackson (above n. 12), 305 (emphasis in the original).

However, whereas the other manifestations of foreign territorial administration did fall away in the sense that, in the main, no new arrangements in these categories, including UN Trusteeship arrangements, were subsequently created (although various existing arrangements continued), and those that were created (e.g., the CPA in Iraq) were treated as *sui generis* at best and illegitimate at worst, the practice of ITA continued, and not only to bring colonialism to an end but for some of the other purposes with which foreign territorial administration had traditionally been associated.[348] In East Timor, for example, the UN not only conducted the 'popular consultation'—the paradigmatic international territorial administration decolonization activity—it also took over control of the territory for almost two years, not, as in South West Africa/Namibia, to replace an existing authority refusing to implement self-determination (Indonesia had withdrawn), but because the East Timorese, although having opted already in the consultation for what was in effect independence, were considered to be not immediately capable of running their own affairs.[349]

8.6 The Revival of Foreign Territorial Administration: The Use of ITA in the 'Post-colonial' Context

Those who imagine a world beyond empire imagine rightly, but they have not seen how prostrate societies actually are when nation-building fails, when civil war has torn them apart. Then and only then is there a case for temporary imperial rule, to provide the force and will necessary to bring order out of chaos.

Michael Ignatieff[350]

International trusteeship conducted by foreign actors did not end with the post-Second World War call for self-determination and the subsequent creation of many new states. Rather, a particular strand of this phenomenon—trusteeship through ITA—continued while the other state-based models were dismantled or, at least, rendered illegitimate. This period is also distinctive at the level of policy discourse, since it is during this time that a series of proposals was made, beginning with the 'saving failed states' proposals mentioned in the previous chapter and more recently reflected in Michael Ignatieff's 'Empire Lite' thesis quoted above, advocating the introduction of international territorial administration in particular situations.

---

[348] On the lack of any new Trusteeship arrangements, see above, ch. 5, n. 45.

[349] How this project was normatively distinguished from the colonial paradigm generally, and why East Timor was not placed under the Trusteeship system in particular, is discussed further below in section 8.7.3 (on being normatively distinguished generally) and text accompanying nn. 541 *et seq* (on the non-reactivation of the Trusteeship system).

[350] Ignatieff (above n. 4), 125.

The 'post-colonial' use of ITA saw the revival of the trusteeship aspect of the colonial paradigm that had been institutionalized in the Mandate and Trusteeship institutions earlier in the 20th century.[351] This use of ITA began at the very time that decolonization was brought about: ONUC in the Congo in the 1960s attempted to provide an administration because of the perceived lack of local capacity at the start of that country's existence as an independent state. It was used in this way later on in Somalia, East Timor, internationally-conducted aid programmes, and UN-administered 'refugee' camps.

David Helman and Steven Ratner's 'failed states' proposal for 'UN conservatorship' and Fen Osler Hampson's notion of 'proxy governance' discussed in the previous chapter reflect both enduring international concerns about local incapacities for territorial governance in the 'post-colonial' era, and the continued invocation of foreign territorial administration as a potential remedy.[352] Moreover, a commonality between ITA and some of the other manifestations of foreign territorial administration outlined in this chapter, insofar as the perceived utility of these institutions in this particular context, is suggested by Helman & Ratner's proposal, since they consider the Mandate and Trusteeship arrangements alongside the ITA projects in West Irian, Namibia (the Council), and Western Sahara, implying equivalence between them.[353]

In the period between the Helman & Ratner and Hampson proposals, from 1992 to 1996, other commentators made similar proposals; these are significant not for their originality but because they make more direct links to colonialism and trusteeship in how they characterize the prescriptions they offer. Also, the different role they envisage for the UN reflects the fluctuation in the fortunes of the organization as the atmosphere of post-Cold War internationalist optimism reflected in the Helman & Ratner proposal was replaced with disillusionment and retrenchment following the humiliating failure of the intervention in Somalia in 1993 and the unwillingness to prevent genocide in Rwanda in 1994 and Bosnia and Herzegovina between 1992 and 1995.

In 1992, Charles Krauthammer argued in the context of Somalia that 'trusteeship' was an 'old colonial idea whose time has come again'; the country:

... desperately needs to be taken over and run by some outside power so that its suffering people can be afforded the minimal human decencies of food, medicine and personal safety.[354]

In 1993, Peter Lyon surveyed the concept of international trusteeship and concluded that 'UN trusteeship would almost certainly be an improvement

---

[351] Discussing 'peacebuilding' generally, Roland Paris states that the connection he identifies between this activity and the civilizing mission means that '... peace operations can be viewed as a new chapter in the history of relations between the developed and the developing worlds'; Paris, 'International Peacebuilding' (above n. 12), 638.

[352] The earlier discussion is located in ch. 7, section 7.3.3.

[353] Helman & Ratner (above n. 11), 6.

[354] Krauthammer (above n. 11).

on the anarchical condition of the several quasi-states the world has now'.[355] In August 1994, Ali Mazrui argued for the revival of colonialism in an article entitled 'Decaying Parts of Africa Need Benign Colonialism'.[356] Perhaps reflecting the fall in the UN's fortunes the year after the Somalia intervention and a month after the end of the Rwanda genocide, the solution now being proposed involved not the UN directly but a broad range of foreign states, including those from Africa and Asia, supervised by a council of African states acting on behalf of the UN.[357]

In 1995, William Pfaff argued in 'A New Colonialism?' that 'Europe must go back to Africa' to respond to the destabilization and lack of democracy in certain African countries.[358] Confusingly, Pfaff dismisses Mazrui's proposal on the grounds that the UN does not have the capacity to administer territory, even though (as Pfaff's own description of the proposal demonstrates) Mazrui actually advocated administration by foreign states within a UN supervisory framework.[359] For Pfaff, European states should take over territorial administration where necessary, in the same states that they administered as colonies.[360] Implicit in Pfaff's dismissal of ITA is the positioning of this institution as equivalent to his proposal for administration by European states, the only important difference being in the identity of the administering actors involved.

A common feature of many of these proposals is the idea that decolonization came too quickly. For Pfaff:

[c]olonialism lasted long enough to destroy the preexisting social and political institutions, but not long enough to put anything solid and lasting in its place.[361]

Helman & Ratner argued that the collapse of the state in Africa had its roots in decolonization, where 'self-determination, in fact, was given more attention than long-term survivability'.[362] Roland Paris, in his conceptualization of 'state-building' generally inter alia in terms of promoting the institution of the Westphalian state (mentioned in the previous chapter), suggests that this enterprise of modern state-building can be explained as addressing the missing component in an agenda of decolonization understood in terms of creating new states regardless of vibility.[363] In seeking to prop up '... the institutional form of the Westphalian state in parts of the periphery where the state lacks firm roots', state-building is aimed at preventing '... a reversal in the historic expansion of the modern state

---

[355] Lyon (above n. 11), *passim* and in particular 106–8, quotation taken from 107.
[356] Mazrui (above n. 11).
[357] Ibid.
[358] Pfaff (above n. 11).
[359] Ibid., 4.
[360] Ibid., 5–6.
[361] Ibid., 4.
[362] Helman & Ratner (above n. 11), 4. See also the discussion in Jackson (above n. 12), 304–5.
[363] See above, ch. 7, text accompanying n. 61; see also Paris, 'International Peacekeeping' (above n. 12), 655.

from Europe to the rest of the world' as part of the 'ongoing reproduction of the Westphalian state model'.[364]

As reflected in the quote at the start of this section, in his 2003 thesis 'Empire Lite', justifying the general enterprise being engaged in through the interventions and administrations in Bosnia and Herzegovina, Kosovo, and Afghanistan, Michael Ignatieff called for what is in essence trusteeship to be re-embraced as a legitimate feature of international policy, to address 'problems' in existing states more than those in non-sovereign entities.[365] This cohabits with the most recent advocate of trusteeship for 'failed states' at the time of writing, Gerhard Kreijen.[366]

The articulation of these policy prescriptions coincided with the development or re-emergence of certain broader ideas concerning limited sovereignty discussed in Chapter 7, which provided important underpinnings to the idea of reviving trusteeship. Along with the 'failed states' paradigm were Kantian notions of 'equivocal' and 'earned' sovereignty.[367] These will be discussed further, together with other general policies that legitimize trusteeship such as the 'responsibility to protect', below.[368]

The ideas underlying the academic revival of international trusteeship are perhaps partially explanatory of why international territorial administration was introduced in East Timor. As with many other colonial territories, when independence was agreed it was felt that the people of the territory might not actually be ready to take over the reins of administration. In the first wave of decolonization, however, the absolutist rejection of foreign territorial administration meant that independence was to be realized (unless rejected by the people of the territory), regardless of practical capacities. A period of international administration would have amounted to the reintroduction of colonialism. Thus independence had to be granted, even if, as in the Congo, some form of foreign administrative presence was soon considered necessary. Several decades on, the absolutist rejection of foreign territorial administration was perhaps not so keenly felt, and so it became conscionable to consider a period of ITA after the removal of Indonesian administration, rather than rushing straight to independence. It was unusual, however, to have a situation of decolonization at this time, hence Pfaff and Helman & Ratner's focus on the breakdown of governance in existing states

---

[364] See also Paris, 'International Peacekeeping' (above n. 12), 655.

[365] Ignatieff (above n. 4), *passim*. Ignatieff's thesis is discussed further below, text accompanying n. 525.

[366] Kreijen (above n. 11). On the 'failed states' ideas generally, see above, ch 7, text accompanying n. 46 *et seq*. Tom Parker's work (above n. 11), published in 2003, advocates reviving the UN Trusteeship system on the grounds that this is a more suitable institutional umbrella for present and future ITA projects than the UN Security Council (this is discussed further below, text accompanying n. 537 *et seq*.); however, unlike Kreijen, he is not concerned with justifying the creation of new trusteeships.

[367] See above, ch. 7, text accompanying nn. 77 *et seq* (on 'equivocal sovereignty') and 81 *et seq* (on 'earned sovereignty').

[368] See below, section 8.7.2.

that had been colonies, rather than the potential lack of local capacities for governance in the remaining colonies set for decolonization.

The critiques that were made of the Helman & Ratner and Pfaff proposals similarly considered colonialism, the Mandate and Trusteeships systems and ITA as essentially the same enterprise. Ruth Gordon and Henry Richardson dismissed the proposals made by the first wave of 'failed states' scholars as amounting to the reintroduction of colonialism, the only relevant difference being (in the case of Helman & Ratner's proposal) the identity of the administering actor.[369] In the process, Ruth Gordon also equated state administration under the Mandate and Trusteeship systems with colonialism.[370]

Gordon and Richardson were critiquing mere proposals; by the time their commentary was published—the mid 1990s—what they regarded as a return to colonialism had actually been realized in practice. The original 'failed states' scholars and their critics envisaged international territorial administration projects taking place primarily in Africa. In fact the only relevant project in this regard was the Somalia mission, which was only concerned with institution-building. ITA projects in Africa have otherwise amounted to low-key activities specific to particular administrative competences—the distribution of humanitarian supplies and the administration of 'refugee' camps—the one-off self-determination project (not implemented at the time of writing) in the Western Sahara, and the international judges on the Special Court for Sierra Leone.

It is outside Africa that international territorial administration took off as a policy institution in the 1990s: initially in Asia, with the partial administrative activities in the Cambodia project at the start of the 1990s, then in the southern Balkans from the mid 1990s with the plenary projects in Mostar, Eastern Slavonia, and Kosovo, and the partial project in Bosnia and Herzegovina, then again in Asia with the East Timor plenary project at the turn of the century, and more broadly with the various arrangements involving international appointees on locally-based bodies such as courts and tribunals.

In 1948, a scholar analysing the new Trusteeship system alongside its precursor, the Mandate system, H Duncan Hall, stated that 'Mandates are finished but trusteeship goes on'.[371] In other words, a particular manifestation of trusteeship had ended, but not trusteeship itself. What is striking about the ITA projects in the final quarter of the 20th century and into the 21st century is that they have taken place in an era when trusteeship *itself* had supposedly ended. To borrow from Hall's language, trusteeship is finished, but trusteeship goes on. How did this happen?

If the ITA projects that have taken place since the emergence of the self-determination entitlement operate in the same manner as the old state-conducted

---

[369] Richardson (above n. 11); Gordon, 'Saving Failed States' (above n. 11).
[370] Gordon, 'Saving Failed States' (above n. 11).
[371] Hall (above n. 94), 277.

models, how have they been allowed to take place with the broad support, or at least lack of concerted opposition, of most of the world's states, including former colonial states? Why did many commentators, as mentioned earlier, view the CPA in Iraq, but not also UNMIK in Kosovo, as 'colonial'? What follows is an attempt to explore how an activity operating in the same manner as colonialism and state administration under the Mandate and Trusteeship systems is popularly distinguished from these activities on a normative level. In other words, how has international trusteeship somehow survived in the 'post-colonial' era, the self-determination entitlement notwithstanding?

8.7 From Lord Lugard to Lord Ashdown: Normative Disassociation from the Earlier Models

The conquest of the earth, which mostly means the taking it away from those who have a different complexion or flatter noses than ourselves, is not a pretty thing when you look into it too much. What redeems it is the idea only. An idea at the back of it; not a sentimental pretence but an idea; and an unselfish belief in the idea—something you can set up, and bow down before, and offer a sacrifice to . . .

Marlow, in *Heart of Darkness* [372]

Despite provocative statements made in relation to the recent projects, the reactions to the first-wave 'failed states' proposals by critics such as Ruth Gordon and Henry Richardson, and the parallels that were identified earlier in the present study, the equation of the 'post-colonial' ITA projects with the earlier state-conducted manifestations of foreign territorial administration has in practice been resisted at the United Nations and in commentary on the administration projects generally. So, as already mentioned, Michael Bothe and Thilo Marauhn use the language of 'trusteeship' to describe UNMIK and UNTAET, but resist engaging in an enquiry as to the similarities between this enterprise and colonialism.[373] Steven Ratner, although as mentioned above arguing that the term 'occupation' should be used in relation to the ITA projects, nonetheless rejects the 'colonial' tag; for Ratner, occupation has 'traction', but colonialism does not.[374]

   Two general approaches can be identified in these and other arguments: sometimes, any colonial parallel is fiercely rejected; in other cases, certain commonalities are accepted, but important distinctions are emphasized by way of mitigation. The following analysis considers how such positions are adopted, by identifying how certain features of the 'post-colonial' international territorial administration projects are distinguished normatively from the corresponding

---

[372] J Conrad, *Heart of Darkness* (1902) (Penguin Books, 1995 edn), 20.
[373] See above, text accompanying nn. 22 *et seq.*
[374] Ratner (above n. 9), 696. Steven Ratner's thesis about using the term 'occupation' in relation to ITA is discussed above, text following n. 266.

features of colonialism that led to the repudiation of state-conducted foreign territorial administration.[375]

8.7.1 Critiques of colonialism, trusteeship, and occupation

In appreciating how attempts are made to portray ITA as legitimate when compared with colonial trusteeship, it is necessary to understand first some of the main critiques that were made of colonialism, since in part the legitimating strategies associated with ITA are conceived as inverted versions of these critiques.[376]

Fundamentally, colonialism was critiqued on the grounds that alien domination itself, whether or not on the basis of trust, was unjust; people who were subject to such domination were entitled to self-determination.[377] In the words of Mr Alemayehou, the representative of Ethiopia at the UN in 1960:

... if, in spite of all, the question would be to choose between freedom with all its attendant economic difficulties and internal conflicts on the one hand, and the maintenance of colonial rule with all its attendant subjugation, exploitation, degradation and humiliation, and so on, on the other, I would right away and unequivocally say that the peoples, all peoples, under colonial rule prefer poverty in freedom to wealth in slavery, and they will definitely prefer fighting in freedom to peace in slavery.[378]

---

[375] A discussion of how the merit of these presentations might be appraised, as well as what further considerations might also form the basis for appraising the legitimacy of ITA, is provided in the next chapter. For commentary by others on issues of legitimacy, see the works in List of Sources, section 5.2.4 (on questions of legitimacy other than gender) and section 5.2.5 (on gender issues).

[376] On the different forms of anti-colonial argument, see List of Sources, sections 5.3.1 and 5.3.3. For an attempt to map these out, see Young (above n. 45), 165. For one recent discussion of the relationship between anti-colonial argumentation and human rights discourse, see Simpson (above n. 32), 300–305.

[377] See generally the sources cited in the previous note. For examples of an absolutist rejection of colonialism based simply on a rejection of domination, see Sartre (above n. 45), 81; Fanon, *Toward the African Revolution* (above n. 45), 81, 83. The final document adopted by the 1955 Bandung Conference stated that 'colonialism in all its forms is an evil which should be speedily brought to an end'. See Final Communiqué of the Bandung Conference, 24 April 1955, Section G, 'Declaration on the promotion of world peace and co-operation', reproduced in P Braillard and M-R Djalili (eds), *The Third World and International Relations* (Pinter, 1986), 60, Section D, para. 1, part (a). See also ibid., Section D, para. 1, parts (b)–(d). On the legal right to self-determination, see above, section 8.5 and ch. 5, section 5.2; for a discussion of the significance of self-determination in repudiating trusteeship in particular, see, e.g., Bain, *Between Anarchy and Society* (above n. 12), 129–39. The rejection of foreign rule can be found in some of the canonical works of liberal political thought, such as those of Immanuel Kant and John Stuart Mill. For Mill:

[i]t is always under great difficulties, and very imperfectly, that a country can be governed by foreigners; even when there is no extreme disparity, in habits and ideas, between the rulers and the ruled. Foreigners do not feel with the people . . . The government of a people by itself has a meaning, and a reality; but such a thing as government of one people by another, does not and cannot exist.

JS Mill, *Considerations on Representative Government* (Parker, Son and Bourn, 1861), 331; I Kant, 'On the Relationship of Theory to Practice in Political Right' (1792), reproduced in HS Reiss (ed.), *Kant – Political Writings* (CUP, 1970), 73. See also the equivocal comments by Koskenniemi (above n. 44), 177–8.

[378] UN General Assembly, 928th Plenary Meeting, 30 November 1960, UN Doc. A/PV928, 1021, cited in Bain, *Between Anarchy and Society* (above n. 12), 136.

This idea is illustrated in the formulation of the right to self-determination discussed earlier when it is conceptualized generally as freedom from alien 'subjugation' and 'domination'[379] An aspect of this critique was that foreign domination had been imposed: the people subjected to it had not consented to the presence of foreign administration, either at all (the Mandate and Trust territories, certain colonies, and most occupied territories) or in a just and meaningful manner (those colonies based on agreements with local tribes). In the words of Antony Anghie, agreements, where they were forthcoming, were the 'product of unequal power'.[380] For those like the commentators discussed earlier who see imposition as an intrinsic feature of trusteeship, this critique of imposition formed part of the concept of trust itself.[381]

Many have remarked that one strategy for opposing colonization was, in the words of Robert Young, the 'appropriation and subversion of forms borrowed from the institutions of the colonizer and turned back against them'.[382] Critiques of trusteeship in particular were formulated in this way, positing that notions of tutelage and improvement through domination were intrinsically flawed[383] or, at any rate, would take a very long time to bring about meaningful change.[384] More radically, it was argued that the basis for the civilizing mission was intellectually incoherent; its indeterminacy meant that the notion that colonial rulers could

---

[379] See above, ch. 5, n. 19 and accompanying text and above, text accompanying n. 65.

[380] Anghie (above n. 2), 65–82 (quotation taken from 72). On this argument, see also Crawford (above n. 44), 131–2; Gordon, 'Saving Failed States' (above n. 11), *passim*; Anghie (above n. 95), 36–49. On colonial title generally, see above, ch. 5, section 5.3 and sources cited therein.

[381] See above, text accompanying nn. 230 *et seq.*

[382] Young (above n. 45), 14–15.

[383] One prominent proponent of this idea in Western thought is John Stuart Mill, who argued that:

[w]hen a people has had the misfortune to be ruled by a government under which the feelings and the virtues needful for maintaining freedom could not develop themselves, it is during an arduous struggle to become free by their own efforts that these feelings and virtues have the best chance of springing up.
[...]
It can seldom, therefore—I will not go so far as to say never—be either judicious or right, in a country which has a free government, to assist, otherwise than by the moral support of its opinion, the endeavours of another to extort the same blessing from its native rulers.

JS Mill, 'A Few Words on Non-Intervention' (1859) reproduced in JS Mill, *Dissertations and Discussions* (Longmans, Green, Reader, and Dyer, 1867), vol. III, 153, at 175. On these ideas in the context of international trusteeship, see, e.g., the discussion in Bain, *Between Anarchy and Society* (above n. 12), *passim*. For Fanon:

[c]olonial domination, because it is total and tends to over-simplify, very soon manages to disrupt in spectacular fashion the cultural life of a conquered people. This cultural obliteration is made possible by the negation of national reality, by new legal relations introduced by the occupying power, by the banishment of the natives and their customs to outlying districts by colonial society, by expropriation, and by the systematic enslaving of men and women.

Fanon, 'Reciprocal Bases of National Culture' (above n. 45).

[384] See generally the literature in List of Sources, sections 5.3.1, 5.3.2, and 5.3.3. For one example of the treatment of these ideas, see Jackson (above n. 55), 90.

actually judge how to run the colonies, and work out when they had reached the stage of progress to become independent, was a fallacy.[385]

It was argued that the concepts forming the basis for the supposed need for and objectives of foreign rule, such as the 'standard of civilization', were not universally legitimate, reflecting the particular interests and traditions of the administering authorities but not necessarily those of the people of the administered territories.[386] Given their racialized origins, such policies were condemned as racist.[387] In some

---

[385] See generally the work of 'post-colonial' scholars listed in List of Sources, section 5.3.3. Discussing concepts of sovereignty invoked by international lawyers engaged in the colonial project, Martti Koskenniemi observes that:

...sovereignty *had no determined meaning*. It could be associated with liberality and with tyranny, it could justify a limited state that delegated its power to private actors, or an interventionist State—just as it could carry out a politics of assimilation or association...As abstract status it did not dictate any specific colonial policy—after all, it had not replaced the need for domestic politics in the metropolitan territories either. It merely created a right of exclusivity in its European holder.

Koskenniemi (above n. 44), 169 (emphasis in original). Similarly, Gerrit Gong makes the following remark about the 'standard of civilization': '[p]rogress toward 'civilized' status was necessary and possible for the less 'civilized' to achieve, but complete and perfect equality was not. Like Sisyphus, the less 'civilized' were doomed to work toward an equality which an elastic standard of 'civilization' put forever beyond their reach'; Gong (above n. 104), 63.

[386] See, e.g., Ashcroft, Griffiths, & Tiffin (above n. 45), 46–8; Koskenniemi (above n. 44), 174–5; D Otto, 'Subalternity and International Law: the Problems of Global Community and the Incommensurability of Difference', 5 (1996) *Social and Legal Studies* 337, *passim*; Gordon, 'Saving Failed States' (above n. 11), 907, 925–7, 946, and *passim*. For Antony Anghie, these polices 'amounted, essentially, to idealized European standards in both their external and ... internal relations'; Anghie (above n. 2), 52. Gerrit Gong states that '[i]n general, the standard of "civilization" reflected the norms of the liberal European civilization', Gong (above n. 104), 15. On the standard of civilization generally, see the sources cited above, n. 104 and corresponding text. Tracing the connection between Vitoria's ideas and the Mandate system, Antony Anghie identifies an '...idea that a single process of development—that which was followed by the European states—was to be imitated and reproduced in non-European societies, which had to strive to conform to this model'; Anghie (above n. 2), 145. According to this approach, the Mandate model assumed that 'every society could be placed on...[a] continuum, based on its approximation to the ideal of the European nation-state', and 'implicitly repudiated the idea that different societies had devised different forms of political organization that should command some degree of respect and validity in international law'; Anghie, ibid., both quotes from 148. Similarly, H Duncan Hall states that '...the political and social system that had to be fostered in the mandated territories...was the democratic way of life as it had developed historically in the English-speaking world and in France'; Hall (above n. 94), 128.

[387] In the words of Bill Ashcroft, Gareth Griffiths, and Helen Tiffin:

...the idea of the colonial world became one of a people intrinsically inferior, not just outside history and civilization, but genetically pre-determined to inferiority. Their subjection was not just a matter of profit and convenience but also could be constructed as a natural state. The idea of the 'evolution of mankind' and the survival of the fittest 'race', in the crude application of Social Darwinism, went hand in hand with the doctrines of imperialism that evolved at the end of the nineteenth century.

Ashcroft, Griffiths, & Tiffin (above n. 45), 46–7. So for Siba N'Zatioula Grovogui, '[t]he sole rational basis of the protectorate was the unwavering belief in African inferiority'; SN Grovogui, *Sovereigns, Quasi Sovereigns and Africans: Race and Self-Determination in International Law* (University of Minnesota Press, 1996), 87. For Fanon, '[e]very effort is made to bring the colonised person to admit the inferiority of his culture which has been transformed into instinctive patterns of behaviour, to

cases, anti-colonial resistance responded to this by repudiating notions of racial difference. So in the words of Jomo Kenyatta in relation to Kenya, independence would cause:

> ...the implementation in this country of that which the European calls democracy. True democracy has no colour distinction. It does not choose between black and white.[388]

In other cases, racism was resisted through affirming racial and cultural difference and particularity, ideas of distinctiveness such as negritude, and the platform of racial liberation.[389] As a consequence of the racial and cultural chauvinism associated with the policies of colonialism, the practices conducted in furtherance to these policies were delegitimized as unfair, and as unsuitable and destructive in terms of their effect on the local culture.[390] Because of the flawed and unjust conception of the nature of the native 'ward', colonial authorities had failed in their duty of trust to care adequately for its wellbeing.[391] More fundamentally, because the civilizational difference was flawed, there was no basis for a trust relationship: colonial peoples were, therefore, not in need of the colonial guardian—they were entitled to freedom as 'adults'.[392]

Related to this critique of the culturally-specific nature of the standards being promoted, is the notion that the colonial states were acting in their own interest.[393] The connection between the two is evident in the following remark by John Westlake in 1894, who references a racialized notion of the civilizational difference as the basis for the adoption of particular governmental policies in the colonies aimed at securing the interests of the Europeans there:

recognise the unreality of his 'nation', and, in the last extreme, the confused and imperfect character of his own biological structure'; Fanon, 'Reciprocal Bases of National Culture' (above n. 45). See also Ignatieff (above n. 4), 122; Anghie (above n. 2), 189; Paris, 'International Peacebuilding' (above n. 12), 651 and sources cited therein.

[388] J Kenyatta, 'Speech at the Kenya African Union Meeting' (Nyeri, 26 July 1952), reproduced in FD Corfield, *Historical Survey of the Origins and Growth of Mau Mau* (Great Britain Colonial Office, 1960), 301, at 301; also available online at <http://www.africawithin.com/kenyatta/speech_at_kau.htm>.

[389] Young (above n. 45), 15–16, 161, 240.

[390] J Nehru, *The Discovery of India* (John Day, 1946), 294, 486.

[391] Bain, *Between Anarchy and Society* (above n. 12), 130.

[392] In making this argument, colonial peoples were able to turn ideas of liberty in Western liberal thought, such as those of John Stuart Mill, back on the colonial powers. In the words of Mill: '...neither one person, nor any number of persons, is warranted in saying to another human creature of ripe years that he shall not do with his life for his own benefit what he chooses to do with it'; JS Mill, *On Liberty* (1859) (E Rapaport ed., Hackett, 1978), 74.

[393] See generally K Nkrumah, *Towards Colonial Freedom: Africa in the Struggle Against World Imperialism* (Heinemann, 1962), *passim* and especially 1–6 and 35. Antony Anghie defines colonialism as '[t]he conquest of non-European peoples for economic and political advantage...'; Anghie (above n. 2), 32. For Bipan Chandra, '...the fundamental aspects of the colony's economy and society are determined...by the needs and interests of the metropolitan economy and its capitalist class...subordination of the colony's economy and society is the crucial or determining aspect...'; Chandra (above n. 50), 10. For Jürgen Osterhammel, colonial territories were 'transformed according to the needs and interests of the colonial rulers'; Osterhammel (above n. 50), 15.

[w]hen people of European race come into contact with American or African tribes, the prime necessity is a government under the protection of which the former may carry on the complex life to which they have been accustomed in their homes...[394]

It will be recalled from the earlier analysis that colonial trusteeship and administration under the Mandate and Trusteeship arrangements were often associated explicitly with policies concerning the interests of the administering state, its settlers, and corporate interests, from wealth extraction to opening markets and protecting traders.[395] Certain colonial ideology conceived this as a mutually-beneficial enterprise: as mentioned, (Lord) Frederick Lugard's 'dual mandate' theory of colonial rule set forth a programme seen as benefiting both the colonial state and the 'native' population.[396]

One critique of this idea held it to be a perversion of the concept of trust, under which the trustee is supposed to be acting selflessly, in the interests of the beneficiary only and not also for its own sake.[397] Either it was flawed in its general theory—the dual mandate—or it was flawed in that what claimed to be selfless was in fact not adhered to.

From a different perspective, the underlying assumption that both interests could be harmoniously promoted was questioned: a zero-sum situation often prevailed, and in such cases a choice had to be made between competing interests. It was argued that statements such as the one issued by the British Government about Kenya extracted earlier, that in cases of conflict the interests of the 'African natives' would prevail, were not implemented in practice.[398] And even when the interests of the local population were being promoted, it was argued that the manner in which such interests were defined was itself mediated by the needs of the administering state.[399]

[394] J Westlake, *Chapters on the Principles of International Law* (CUP, 1894), 141. On these ideas, see also Koskenniemi (above n. 44), 145 and Anghie (above n. 95), 52.

[395] Anthony Anghie identifies the 'central importance of colonial possessions for the economic wellbeing of the metropolitan power'; Anghie (above n. 2), 142. Bill Ashcroft, Gareth Griffiths, and Helen Tiffin report the 'perception of colonies as primarily established to provide raw materials for the burgeoning economies of the colonial powers'; Ashcroft, Griffiths & Tiffin (above n. 45), 46.

[396] See above, text accompanying n. 139 *et seq.*

[397] The idea of international trusteeship denoting action on behalf of the beneficiary is reflected in the quotation from Edmund Burke extracted above, text accompanying n. 108, in which Burke states that colonial rule 'ought to be some way or other exercised ultimately for their [colonial peoples'] benefit'. On this idea, and the notion that colonial trusteeship denotes acting *exclusively* in the interests of colonial peoples, see further the other cites in n. 108. For the idea that the self-orientation of colonial trusteeship constituted a fundamental contravention of the idea of trusteeship, see generally the discussion in Bain, *Between Anarchy and Society* (above n. 12), 130. In his study of imperialism, John Atkinson Hobson states that the 'self-assertive' aspect of colonial trusteeship 'lacks the first essentials of a trust, viz. security that the "trustee" represents fairly all the interested parties'; JA Hobson, *Imperialism: A Study* (2nd edn, Constable, 1905), 209.

[398] See the statement reported above, text accompanying n. 146. For Antony Anghie, 'the fact that the terms of the exploitation were set by the colonial powers or the mandatory powers inevitably led to the sacrifice of native interests'; Anghie (above n. 2), 161–2, footnote omitted.

[399] For example, it is suggested that the motivations for having standards of welfare promotion in Mandated territories had more to do with the need for labour than with the interests

More generally, it was argued that the humanitarian civilizing policies associated with colonialism were in any case often (or even, as some argued, always) invoked in bad faith: there was, thus, little (or even nothing) else being done other than the promotion of the state's interests; the actuality of trusteeship was, therefore, largely a fiction.[400] In this view, Philip Kerr's idea, mentioned earlier, of colonial trusteeship as something other than 'pride of dominion' was an illusion.[401]

Critiques focusing on the self-serving nature of colonialism went beyond accusations of bad faith: for many, as far as its effect on the local population was concerned, colonialism was exploitation, and being subjected to alien exploitation was posited as a basis for the right to self-determination.[402] In the words of Kwame Nkrumah:

of the local population. See, e.g., Wright (above n. 32), 10. Because of this, the nature of the welfare agenda was determined by labour considerations. Antony Anghie states that 'the preoccupation with productivity and labour...was the prism through which questions of welfare in general were approached'; Anghie (above n. 2), 166. So a humanist agenda of trusteeship was invoked to explain and legitimize policies that were being understood in instrumental terms. Anghie states that '[t]he new form of colonialism, based on preserving and developing the native and her territories as productive assets rather than exploiting and exhausting these assets, presented itself as the exemplification of humanist and liberal principles;' Anghie (above n. 2), 166–7. In a similar vein, Neta Crawford asserts that the agenda of improving infrastructure, where it was evident, was orientated 'to facilitate settlement and resource extraction'; Crawford (above n. 44), 135.

[400] So, for example, it was argued that the 'open door' policy was in fact one-sided, in that the markets in the colonies were opened to goods from the metropolis, but not vice versa. In relation to the Mandate provisions in the League Covenant, for example, James Hales argued that:

[i]n perfect trusteeship, the ward's rights ought to be the main consideration of all parties...and less consideration ought to be given to the rights of other parties.... [T]his view is not put forward in Article 22 where in paragraph 5 it is stated that the 'Mandatory...will also secure equal opportunity for the trade and commerce of other Members of the League.' This sentence is of a negative nature for it aims at preventing the Mandatory from seizing advantages denied to other Members of the League; it does not aim at preventing the exploitation of the Mandate by all nations...there is no provision to the effect that the Mandates will have the same advantages in the territories of...other States; consequently it is possible for these states to dump goods in the Mandates while scarcely taking anything in return from the latter.

Hales (above n. 107), 184–5. See also ibid., 177.

[401] See above, text accompanying n. 114. For John Atkinson Hobson, writing in 1905 on colonial trusteeship, it would be better for colonial states to 'avow commercial necessity or political ambition as the real determinant of their protection of lower races' rather 'than to feign a "trust"'; Hobson (above n. 397), 210. For Bill Ashcroft, Gareth Griffiths, and Helen Tiffin: '...colonialism developed an ideology rooted in obfuscatory justification, and its violent and essentially unjust processes became increasingly difficult to perceive behind a liberal smokescreen of civilizing 'task'...'; Ashcroft, Griffiths & Tiffin (above n. 45), 47. Thus terms such as 'protectorate' and 'Trust territory' merely masked selfish motivations, serving '...to justify the continuing process of colonialism as well as to hide the fact that these territories were the displaced sites of the increasingly violent struggles for markets and raw materials by the industrial nations of the West'; ibid. In the words of Simon Schama: '[t]he annexations were more often than not driven by British strategic and financial interests, rather than by any high-minded commitment to 'improved' government'; Schama (above n. 107), 318. For Martti Koskenniemi, the civilizing mission was 'more an instrument for inter-European struggle than a program to reorganize non-European society'; Koskenniemi (above n. 44), 168–9.

[402] On the conceptualization of a right to self-determination arising in the context of alien exploitation, see the Friendly Relations Declaration (above n. 65) discussed above, ch. 5, text

[b]eneath the 'humanitarian' and 'appeasement' shibboleths of colonial governments, a proper scrutiny leads one to discover nothing but deception, hypocrisy, oppression, and exploitation.[403]

In many instances the people of colonial territories were treated in a discriminatory, oppressive, and sometimes violently brutal manner, from structural arrangements that privileged settlers over 'natives' to specific atrocities such as the suppression of the Mau Mau rebellion in Kenya and generalized systems of oppression such as the introduction of bonded labour, or slavery, in the Belgian Congo.[404] Antony Anghie reports that whereas provision was made to ban slavery in Mandated territories, forced labour with remuneration for essential public works and services was also sanctioned by the League Council and provided for in various mandate agreements.[405] For Anghie, the implementation of these provisions:

... took an enormous toll on native populations to the point that it became unclear as to which of these two practices—the primitive practice of slavery or the modern practice of development—had more devastating consequences.[406]

accompanying n. 19 and above, this chapter, text accompanying n. 65. On the presentation of colonialism as exploitative, see generally List of Sources, sections 5.3.1 and 5.3.3; for some examples, see Said (above n. 2), *passim*; Ashcroft, Griffiths & Tiffin (above n. 45), 45–7; Schama (above n. 107), ch. 6; Paris, 'International Peacebuilding' (above n. 12), 651 and sources cited therein; Crawford (above n. 44), *passim* and especially 137. The exploitation narrative is often associated particularly with the economic aspects of colonialism. Bipan Chandra characterizes certain key features of colonialism as 'unequal exchange' and the 'drain of wealth or unilateral transfer of social surplus to the metropolis through unrequited exports'; Chandra (above n. 50), 10. For Jean-Paul Sartre:

[t]he concomitant of ... colonial imperialism is that spending power has to be created in the colonies ... The colonist is above all an artificial consumer, created overseas from nothing by a capitalism which is seeking new markets ...

Because tribal property was usually collective and we wanted to fragment it to allow land speculators to buy it back bit by bit ... The long and confusing French procedure ruined all the co-owners; the traders in European goods then bought the whole lot for peanuts.

Sartre (above n. 45), 34–5. See also Woolf (above n. 153) and W Rodney, *How Europe Underdeveloped Africa* (Bogle-L'Ouverture Publications, 1972). For Marxist theorists, the critique of colonial economic restructuring formed part of the broader critique of capitalism. See the discussion in Young (above n. 45), 101.

[403] Nkrumah, *Towards Colonial Freedom* (above n. 393), xvi, cited in Bain, *Between Anarchy and Society* (above n. 12), 130. See also the quotation reproduced in Young (above n. 45), 240.

[404] On settler privileges, see, e.g., Simpson (above n. 32), 318 and Anghie (above n. 2), 176. For a discussion of the use of security detentions, restrictions on freedom of expression and collective punishments in British colonies, see Simpson, ibid., 317–21. On the Mau Mau rebellion, see, e.g., D Anderson, *Histories of the Hanged: Britain's Dirty War in Kenya and the End of Empire* (Weidenfeld & Nicolson, 2005); C Elkins, *Imperial Reckoning. The Untold Story of Britain's Gulag in Kenya* (Henry Holt, 2005). On the Congo, see, e.g., F Cattier, *Etude sur la situation de l'Etat indépendant du Congo* (2nd edn, Larcier and Pedone, 1906); R Anstey, *King Leopold's Legacy: The Congo under Belgian Rule, 1908–1960* (OUP, 1966); A Hochschild, *King Leopold's Ghost* (Houghton Mifflin, 1999); see also Koskenniemi (above n. 44), 158.

[405] Anghie (above n. 2), at 167, n. 203 and accompanying text.

[406] Anghie (above n. 2), 167 (footnote omitted). On forced labour, see also Simpson (above n. 32), 318.

So anti-colonialism and independence were articulated in terms of the removal of inequality and exploitation. In the words of Jomo Kenyatta:

[w]e want our cattle to get fat on our land so that our children grow up in prosperity; we do not want that fat removed to feed others... We want to prosper as a nation, and as a nation we demand equality, that is equal pay for equal work... Those who profess to be just must realize that this is the foundation of justice.[407]

As is evident in the above quotes, this critique was often formulated to turn colonial justifications back on the colonizers ('those who profess to be just'); in those cases where the introduction of colonial rule had been explained in terms of ending exploitation (by the trading companies), this explanation was invoked as a promise that had not been delivered upon.[408]

A related criticism drew on a further aspect of the trust concept: the requirement of accountability, which in the formulation of Edmund Burke 'is of the very essence of every trust'.[409] Provision for accountability can be seen in the twin features outlined earlier whereby trusteeship was legalized as an obligation, and specific institutional mechanisms were created to enforce these obligations and provide, in the words of Article 22 of the League Covenant in relation to the Mandate arrangements, 'securities for the performance of this trust'.[410] Various such mechanisms existed internationally with respect to colonies and Mandate and Trust territories, notably the Permanent Mandates Commission and the Trusteeship Council.[411] However, in general it was argued that these mechanisms

---

[407] Kenyatta (above n. 388), 301.

[408] See above, n. 116.

[409] Burke (above n. 108). James Hales, writing about what he regards as the 'perfect' form of colonial trusteeship, states that the colonial guardian 'must render accounts of his stewardship to a superior authority which will have the power to remove him if need be and which will be able to guide him if necessary in his administration'; Hales (above n. 107), 177.

[410] On the significance of the existence of international accountability mechanisms for arrangements to be properly regarded as 'internationalized trusteeship', see above, n. 307, accompanying text *et seq.*

[411] With the League Mandate system, oversight of different kinds was provided by League of Nations Assembly, the Council, the Permanent Mandates Commission (to whom individuals in Mandated territories could bring petitions), the Mandate section of the Secretariat, other League bodies, the possibility that issues relating to Mandated territories could be brought before the Permanent Court of International Justice and, finally, the ILO. See generally the sources cited above, ch. 5, n. 43 and in particular Hall (above n. 94), *passim*, especially 32, 48–52, Part III, Annexes VII, VIII, IX and, on the ILO in particular, 249–55; Hales (above n. 47), 204–63; Anghie (above n. 2), 151 *et seq.* (on the Permanent Mandates Commission in particular); Crawford (above n. 44), 265–73 (also on the Mandates Commission in particular). Oversight was exercised in relation to Trust territories by the UN General Assembly, the Trusteeship Council and the Security Council and through the possibility that issues relating to Trust territories could be brought before the International Court of Justice. See the sources cited above, ch. 5, n. 44. Oversight was exercised in relation to Non-Self-Governing Territories through the reporting obligations under Art. 73(e) of the UN Charter. See Hall, ibid., 285–90; U Sud, *United Nations and the Non-Self-Governing Territories* (University Publishers, 1965); Y El-Ayouty, *The United Nations and Decolonization: The Role of Afro-Asia* (Martinus Nijhoff, 1971); M Barbier, *Le Comité de décolonisation des Nations Unies* (Librairie générale de droit et de jurisprudence, 1974); SH Ahmad, *The United Nations and the Colonies* (Asia Publishing House, 1974); *Oppenheim's International Law* (above n. 33), 291–5 and

only covered certain arrangements and on their own terms were inadequate.[412] The concept of trust was corrupted, then, because there was an inadequate mechanism to address problems raised by the self-serving policies of the trustees. For those who considered the existence of an effective accountability mechanism an essential requirement for something to be considered trust, these were not even proper trusteeship arrangements at all.

Holding to the view that trust was at best compromised by the dual mandate and inadequate provision of accountability, at worst an overwhelmingly or entirely self-serving sham, led to the concern that notions of eventual improvement and thus independence were a fallacy, because the benchmark adopted was determined by a trustee acting other than in the interests of the beneficiary, without any external body capable of remedying this problem effectively.[413]

sources cited therein; Crawford (above n. 32), ch. 14, *passim*; Fastenrath (above n. 110), at 1091–3. See also <http://www.un.org/Depts/dpi/decolonization> (covering both Non-Self-Governing and Trust territories). For a characteristically insightful cross-cutting analysis of the issue of legal responsibility, see Reisman (above n. 32).

[412] Commenting on colonial trusteeship in 1905, John Atkinson Hobson observes that one of the 'first essentials' of a trust is lacking: '...security that the 'trustee'...is responsible to some judicial body for the faithful fulfilment of the terms of the trust. Otherwise what safeguard exists against the abuse of the powers of the trustee?'; Hobson (above n. 397), 209. As for the League mechanisms operating in relation to Mandate administration, James Hales states that:

...the powers given to the Assembly, the Council and the Permanent Mandates Commission, although wide in theory, are restricted in practice. The resolutions of the Assembly are merely expressions of desire and pious hopes on the part of that Institution, and the resolutions of the Council are in most cases only reached after the Mandatories have had occasion to make their influence felt, whereas the Commission has merely the power of advising the Council. These Organs have no actual power to enforce their resolutions, apart from the Covenant, and content themselves in most cases with reminding the Mandatories of their duties.

Hales (above n. 47), 282. See also Hales (above n. 107), 177, 182–3, 186–7. It will be recalled that Hales argued that the League was the 'trustee' in the Mandate arrangements, the administering states merely its 'agents', and that the system of accountability operating through League organs had to be understood in terms of member states acting together on an individual basis rather than the League operating as a distinct actor; see the discussion above, text accompanying n. 308 *et seq*. Whereas such a conception preserves the notion of third-party review, this hinges mostly (the PCIJ excepted) on the abstract notion of the League as the trustee; administration was conducted by the individual member states, and accountability was exercised by groups of states, including the administering authorities. It is notable that Hales begins his explanation of these ideas with the remark that the Mandate system 'does not reproduce entirely the principles of trusteeship'; Hales (above n. 107), 178. On accountability problems with regard to the Mandate arrangements, see also Hall (above n. 94), 104–5; Chopra (above n. 12), 74; Lyon (above n. 11), 99–100. On accountability problems in relation to colonialism generally, see, e.g., Crawford (above n. 44), 137. On accountability problems in relation to the Trusteeship system, see, e.g., Lyon, ibid., 102–3.

[413] Discussing the difficulties international lawyers had trying to capture a coherent notion of the civilizing mission, Martti Koskenniemi observes that, '...no single civilization spoke in their voice. The sovereignty which they offered to the colonies was more an instrument for inter-European struggle than a program to reorganize non-European society'; Koskenniemi (above n. 44), 168–9. Equally, the 'sacred trust could be emptied of meaning by becoming whatever the administrator wanted it to mean'; Koskenniemi, ibid., 174.

Little, if any, faith could be placed, therefore, in the promise of eventual independence through improvements in local capacities,[414] and in many places little was done to effect 'improvements', and/or the relatively modest nature of the colonial presence meant that efforts in this regard were practically impossible.[415]

One overarching critique pulling many of these strands together was that international trusteeship as carried out by individual states was part of the problem, not the solution, as far as the moral and material conditions of those it was ostensibly aimed at 'saving'. In the words of Antony Anghie in the context of the Mandate arrangements:

...in seeking to liberate the mandate peoples from the 'strenuous conditions of the modern world', the system instead entraps the mandate peoples within these conditions. The peculiar cycle thus creates a situation whereby international institutions present themselves as a solution to a problem of which they are an integral part.[416]

Put differently, the critiques amounted to a proposition that there was a fundamental breach of trust. When this occurs, the trustee is divested of its entitlements. In the words of Edmund Burke: 'it is of the very essence of every trust... totally to *cease*, when it substantially varies from the purposes for which alone it could have lawful existence'.[417]

---

[414] According to Bill Ashcroft, Gareth Griffiths, and Helen Tiffin, although vague suggestions of eventual independence were made, '...in practice this future was endlessly deferred...' and, in fact, '...no society ever attained full freedom from the colonial system by the involuntary, active disengagement of the colonial power until it was provoked by a considerable internal struggle for self-determination or, most usually, by extended and active violent opposition by the colonized'; Ashcroft, Griffiths & Tiffin (above n. 45), 49. Similar points are made by Simpson (above n. 32), 291–5 and Schama (above n. 107), 269. Niall Ferguson argues that, in the case of the British, decolonization was effected solely because of the prohibitive economic costs of continued colonial rule following the Second World War; whatever the merits of this as totalizing explanation, it is notable that the idea that colonial people were 'ready' for freedom is implicitly ruled out as a causal factor; see Ferguson (above n. 89), 346–55 and *passim*. An example of how the concept of self-improvement was understood in a manner that would not lead to separation from the colonial power is given by Brian Simpson, who, when discussing the concept of British colonial tutelage, reports the idea that:

...as the colonies...achieved adulthood, and became able to stand on their own feet, they would voluntarily remain part of the family, as children ideally do. So Lord Cranborne, as Colonial Secretary, said in 1942:
'We are pledged to guide Colonial people along the road to self-government *within the framework of the British Empire.*'

Simpson (above n. 32), 291 (emphasis in original) (quoting a speech by Lord Cranborne delivered in the House of Lords on 21 July 1942). See also the further statement cited by Simpson, ibid., at 291, n. 55.

[415] For Martti Koskenniemi, 'the African colonial entity remained an abstraction' because of the relatively light colonial presence in terms of administration, and that '[p]olitical emancipation could hardly be achieved under such conditions'; Koskenniemi (above n. 44), 169. See also Hobson (above n. 397), 100.

[416] Anghie (above n. 2), 178.

[417] Burke, above n. 108 (emphasis in original). When, as a result of these developments in ideas, people in colonial, Mandated, and Trust territories were considered to enjoy a right of self-determination, a failure to implement this right on the part of the administering authority was

A further feature of the self-serving limb of anti-colonial critique related to the effect state-conducted international trusteeship had not on the people of the territory, but in international politics. Earlier, the strategic importance of colonies was highlighted; for some anti-colonialists, this and the other benefits to the colonial state were precisely the problem, not in and of themselves, but because of the destabilizing effects on world order caused by wars over the acquisition and retention of colonies. States as colonial powers were a problem not only because they exploited the people of the territories involved, but also because they fought each other for the privilege of doing so, harming global order generally. Deepening colonial commitments through the replacement of indirect rule with direct administration on a trust basis that would guarantee the 'open door' had not prevented this, as some had hoped.[418] Indeed, for many, the fact that imperial rivalry over colonies was so strong placed the ostensibly humanitarian nature of the enterprise into question. For example, the British theorist of imperialism, John Atkinson Hobson, stated in 1905 that:

[t]he notorious fact that half the friction between European nations arises from conflicting claims to undertake the office of 'trustee for civilization' over lower races and their possessions augurs ill alike for the sincerity of the profession and the moral capacity to fulfil it. It is surely no mark of cynicism to question closely the extreme anxiety to bear one another's burdens among the nations.[419]

More broadly, the rivals of administering authorities often objected to colonial rule for self-serving motives, wishing to see their rivals disempowered.[420] In the particular context of occupations, the idea of occupation as trusteeship promoted by the law of occupation was seen as having failed to prevent rivalry between states acting together in multinational occupations, with each state promoting national objectives within their particular sphere of control.[421]

8.7.2 Structures of legitimation

The 'post-colonial' use of ITA suggests that the original absolutist rejection of foreign territorial administration was altered so that this activity could again be introduced if it were considered legitimate, as colonialism and state administration in Mandate and Trust territories were not, as far as the needs of the people

regarded as a breach of trust. See the discussion of the case of South West Africa/Namibia, and sources cited therein, above, ch. 5, section 5.5.

[418] See the discussion in Koskenniemi (above n. 44), 145, 169.

[419] Hobson (above n. 397), 209.

[420] Young cites 'rivalry between imperial powers' as one form of resistance to colonialism: Young (above n. 45), 165. For a discussion of the example of Stalin's critique of exploitation under the Mandate arrangements, see Wright (above n. 32), 72.

[421] See generally the discussion in Benvenisti (above n. 9), *passim*. For example, Benvenisti chronicles the major disputes between the allied powers occupying the Rhineland after the Second World War, notably on the issue of trade policy; ibid., 51.

of the territory involved were concerned. In 2003, Henry Perritt proposed that 'political trusteeship' should be adopted 'as the legal guiding force for continuing and future interventions'.[422] Echoing the sentiments of those who advocated trusteeship as a basis for humanizing colonial rule, Perritt argued that this would serve 'to shape and limit...interventions...to assure both the international and internal legitimacy that is demanded of intervention in today's world', by underscoring an obligation that they operated 'for the betterment of the host territory population'.[423] Writing in 2005, Richard Caplan stated that:

[i]nternational administrations...derive their legitimacy...from the notion of a 'trust'...The idea of international governance of a foreign territory...can be legitimate only if that governance is perceived—locally and internationally—to be exercised on behalf of, and for the benefit of, the foreign population. To establish international administration on any other basis...would constitute exploitation.[424]

The legitimacy of ITA must involve something in addition to a 'trust' basis, however, if ITA is to distinguish itself from 'colonial' (i.e., state-conducted) trusteeship. This section considers what ideas are invoked to resist the purchase of the critiques outlined above as far as ITA is concerned.[425]

When considering the charge that international trusteeship is reminiscent of colonialism, the most recent academic standard-bearer for the 'failed states' paradigm, Gerhard Kreijen, states that '[t]his is both true and beside the point. When legitimately established, trusteeship...*is paternalism legitimized*.'[426] The tendency for certain forms of anti-colonial argument to invoke, and invert, the original justificatory structure, particularly in relation to trust, to oppose colonialism was discussed in the previous section. What will become clear from the following analysis is that strategies aimed at distinguishing 'post-colonial' ITA missions from colonialism take this process of inversion one stage further, recasting forms associated with anti-colonial discourse in order to justify internationally-conducted trusteeship.

The ideas of legitimacy that are invoked to 'redeem' ITA from the colonial tag are drawn in large part from broader normative ideas associated with international politics, law and institutions. As Anne Orford states in relation to the views of those in one particular discipline:

...international lawyers who support the new interventionism of the post-Cold War era have tended not to discuss the potential imperial character of multilateral intervention. Instead, they present an image of international institutions and international law as agents of democracy and human rights. The UN and other post-World War II institutions have

---

[422] Perritt, 'Structures and Standards' (above n. 11), 387.
[423] Ibid., 471 and 387 respectively.
[424] Caplan, *International Governance* (above n. 12), 195.
[425] Richard Caplan does identify a further legitimating factor in addition to the 'trust' idea; see below, n. 454.
[426] Kreijen (above n. 11), 309, emphasis in the original.

embodied the faith of many people in the ability of international institutions to protect ideals of universalism, humanitarianism, peace, security and human rights. Multilateralism has seemed to offer an escape from unrestrained self-interest and power politics.[427]

For humanitarianism in particular, this process marks yet another turn in the meaning and significance of the concept. Neta Crawford observes that those who argued against colonialism:

... were a new set of 'humanitarians,' distinct from the old-fashioned humanitarians who thought colonialism was good for the colonized ... [428]

Now, it would seem, humanitarianism has been reclaimed by those who would use it to argue for that which it was used earlier to resist, building on the earlier tradition in which it was used to justify trusteeship.

A key plank in this structure of legitimation is international law. Gerhard Kreijen, for example, asserts that international trusteeship can be legitimized if it is 'legitimately established' and 'carries the blessings of the law'.[429] One meaning of legitimacy is, of course, the notion that something is lawful; indeed, 'legitimacy' is sometimes used as a synonym for 'lawfulness' and vice versa.[430] Within international law generally, the ideas discussed in Chapter 7 that certain rules of international law reflect 'community interests' and operate *erga omnes*, i.e., confer on all a legitimate interest in ensuring compliance, are particularly relevant here.[431]

As illuminated in particular by the work of international legal scholars engaged in 'post-colonial' or 'Third World' approaches to international law, and as already indicated in the foregoing discussion of colonial trusteeship, international law was (and is) integral to imperialism and colonialism.[432] In 1894, John Westlake set out the case for the civilizational difference as the basis for both a positive legal entitlement to engage in colonial rule and a negative absence of legal restrictions

---

[427] A Orford, *Reading Humanitarian Intervention: Human Rights and the Use of Force in International Law* (CUP, 2003), 20.

[428] Crawford (above n. 44), 133.

[429] Kreijen (above n. 11), 309. See also the discussion in Perritt, 'Structures and Standards' (above n. 11), 424–36.

[430] On 'legitimacy' understood as lawfulness, see definition 3 of the word in the *Oxford English Dictionary, OED Online*, at <http://www.oed.com>. On this idea in the context of international law, see, e.g., TM Franck, *The Power of Legitimacy among Nations* (OUP, 1990) and sources cited therein.

[431] See above ch. 7, nn. 87 (on community interests) and 88 (on *erga omnes* obligations).

[432] See List of Sources, section 5.3.4. See also Koskenniemi (above n. 44), 116–78 generally, especially at 121; Reisman (above n. 32), 233–4; Owada (above n. 104). As one such scholar, Antony Anghie, argues, colonialism and imperialism were integral to the foundational moments of international law, and this influence continues to be present in the way international law is structured. Anghie argues that:

... the 'civilizing mission', the maintenance of this dichotomy—variously understood in different phases of the history of international law—combined with the task of bridging this gap, provided international law with a dynamic that shaped the character of sovereignty—and, more broadly, of international law and institutions.

Anghie (above n. 2), 11. See more generally, ibid., *passim*.

governing the conduct of such rule as far as the treatment of the local population was concerned:

[i]nternational law has to treat such natives as uncivilised. It regulates, for the mutual benefit of the civilised states, the claims which they make to sovereignty over the region, and leaves the treatment of the natives to the conscience of the state to which sovereignty is awarded.[433]

This negative freedom was challenged by moves to legalize the concept of trustee-ship as the basis for colonial rule, through both the provisions in agreements such as the Berlin Conference General Act, the League Covenant and the UN Charter discussed above, and more general concepts of obligation modifying the freedom of action of colonial states, reflecting the idea of trusteeship as a means to human-ize colonial rule.[434] Quincy Wright reported the development over the turn of the 20th century of a:

... growing conviction that imperial responsibilities of trusteeship and tutelage toward dependencies is not merely a moral responsibility but is a responsibility under inter-national law which can properly be sanctioned by legal guaranties.[435]

Defending the inroads made into the freedom of colonial states by this responsi-bility, Philip Marshall Brown argued in 1945 that:

---

[433] Westlake (above n. 394), 143. John Westlake was Whewell Professor of International Law at Cambridge University.

[434] For commentary on the international law underpinnings of international trusteeship, see the sources cited above, n. 107. See also below, n. 435. William Bain, discussing the Berlin Conference, talks of how '... members of European international society ... [established] in inter-national law obligations that explicitly repudiated relations based on domination and exploitation; and, in doing so ... accorded international legitimacy to the principle that the strong should rule on behalf of the weak'; Bain, *Between Anarchy and Society* (above n. 12), 3. Neta Crawford, discussing the Mandate and Trusteeship systems, invokes them as arrangements 'where, by international law, certain colonies were to be administered in a more humane way'; Crawford (above n. 44), 133.

[435] Wright (above n. 32), 15–16. The existence of a general rule imposing the concept of trust on colonial administration in customary international law, in addition, when it was forthcoming, to the treaty obligation to this effect under Art. 73 of the UN Charter, was a matter of dispute when it was raised in relation to the South West Africa/Namibia situation. In its controversial decision of 1966 adopted by a divided bench on the casting vote of the President, the International Court of Justice asserted that 'the principle of the sacred trust has as its sole juridical expression the mandates system'; *South West Africa (Ethiopia v South Africa; Liberia v South Africa) (Second Phase), ICJ Reports 1966*, 6, para 52. From the context of the determination, which concerned the standing of third-party states to raise the allegation of a breach of trust, it would appear that the Court was concerned with one aspect of the 'sacred trust' articulated in relation to the League Mandate arrangements—that it was 'of civilization', and 'hence all civilized nations have an inter-est in seeing that it is carried out' (see ibid., para. 51)—rather than, necessarily, the general idea of trusteeship as an obligation applicable to colonialism. For commentary on the Court's determin-ation and more broadly the idea of a trusteeship obligation in general international law, see, e.g., GW Gong, *The Standard of 'Civilization' in International Society* (Clarendon Press, 1984), 79–81 and Alexandrowicz (above n. 107), *passim* and sources cited therein. On the South West Africa/ Namibia situation, including references to its extensive treatment by the ICJ, see above, ch. 5, section 5.5 and sources cited therein.

[t]he obligation of trusteeship... is in no way a derogation from the right of independence [of the colonial authority]. It is the acknowledgment that the highest exercise of sovereign power lies in the willingness to submit to restrictions and onerous responsibilities for the sake of international security and the general welfare.[436]

As reflected in the quote from Philip Kerr reproduced earlier, for some, this obligation not only operated to modify the conduct of imperial rule; it also more fundamentally legitimized the existence of this rule.[437] In other words, it was invoked to justify the constitution, as well as regulate the operation, of colonial administration.

The general repudiation of colonial trusteeship was also itself conducted in part through the international legal process, which, in the words of Antony Anghie, formulated 'doctrines of self-determination where once it formulated doctrines of annexation and *terra nullius*'.[438] So, as Anghie states, the:

... civilized–non-civilized distinction which had featured in the doctrines and treaties of the nineteenth century was generally expunged from the vocabulary of international law.[439]

At the same time, however, the general rules of international law were delegitimized by this ideological shift: as non-sovereign states, colonial territories had not been part of the process of norm-formation, and international law was thus of questionable legitimacy as a normative framework to apply to newly-independent former colonial states, even if its applicability was accepted in many cases.[440] That said, looking to the future, the act of decolonization created the possibility of a truly universal international law as these states now participated in the international legal system as formal equals.[441] In the words of Anghie, this offered the promise of 'separating international law from its colonial past and reconstructing an anti-colonial international law that would serve the interests of the entire community'.[442]

Rooted in this 'new' law, the international trusteeship of the 'post-colonial' era can invoke universal validity in a way that its earlier manifestations could not;

---

[436] Brown (above n. 116), 86. Philip Marshall Brown was a professor of international law at Princeton University.

[437] The quotation accompanies n. 114, above.

[438] Anghie (above n. 2), 109.

[439] Ibid., 110.

[440] Ibid., 108.

[441] As Antony Anghie states, '[t]he transformation of colonial territories into sovereign states is central to the claim that international law is now truly universal because all societies, whether European or non-European, participate as equal and sovereign states in the international system'; (ibid.), 117. Thus: '...international law became 'universal' in the...profound sense that Asian and African societies that had been excluded from the realm of sovereignty even while being subjected to the operation of international law, could now participate in that system as equal and sovereign states. Thus a true 'community of states' had come into being'; ibid., 197 (footnote omitted). See also the discussion ibid., 196–8.

[442] Ibid., 198.

ironically, the universalizing effect of decolonization paves the way for the continuation of trusteeship in its internationalized form.

Four main legitimating arguments are commonly invoked in relation to the ITA projects: first, that the projects have been lawfully authorized; secondly, that the policies they are used to implement reflect principles of international law and are therefore universally valid; thirdly, that the projects are conducted by international organizations created through international law rather than individual states and are therefore humanitarian rather than exploitative; and fourth, in a final, non-legal strand of argumentation which, however, gains purchase when taken together with the earlier arguments, that the projects are 'temporary'.[443]

The following analysis addresses each limb of legitimacy in turn; the objective is to consider how international territorial administration has become normatively acceptable according to international policy, rather than to consider whether this claim to legitimacy is sustainable.[444]

8.7.2.1 'Legitimate' authority[445]

The first way that the legitimacy of the projects has been distinguished normatively from that of their colonial antecedents is in the way certain ideas in international law and policy are invoked to provide a legitimate basis for their introduction (the role of such ideas as the basis for the policies being conducted once introduced will be treated separately). This legitimation has two aspects: first, the invocation of concepts operating in a generalized sense in relation to the idea of ITA and, secondly, the invocation of concepts implicated in the way ITA is legally authorized.

---

[443] The significance of the normative character of the purposes of, and legal authority for, the ITA projects as far as their legitimacy is concerned would appear to be evident in James Crawford's remark that '[t]he older dependent States have now disappeared: modern practice has developed its own categories of shared governmental practice' which include 'international administration of territory' and are 'mostly different both in their purpose and in the modalities through which they have been established, and which can operate without the stigma of dependence, colonial or otherwise'; Crawford (above n. 32), 283.

[444] The latter issue is discussed further in ch. 9, below. For other commentary on issues of legitimacy raised when ITA is compared with colonialism, see, e.g., Berman, 'Les Ambivalences Impériales' (above n. 17).

[445] This issue is discussed further in R Wilde, 'From Bosnia to Kosovo and East Timor: The Changing Role of the United Nations in the Administration of Territory', 6 (2000) *ILSA Journal of International & Comparative Law* 467 and R Wilde, 'Recent Developments in the Security Council: Authorizing International Administration in Kosovo and East Timor', *International Organizations Bulletin: Newsletter of the International Organizations Interest Group of the American Society of International Law* (Spring 2001), 12, obtainable from <http://www.nesl.edu/center/asilnews/spr01.pdf>. On issue of legal authority and consent, see also Chesterman, *You, The People* (above n. 9), 143 and 152; Ratner (above n. 9), 698 and the relevant parts of MJ Matheson, *Council Unbound: The Growth of UN Decision Making on Conflict and Postconflict Issues After the Cold War* (USIP Press, 2006) and, in relation to UNHCR administration of 'refugee' camps in particular, MYA Zieck, *UNHCR's Worldwide Presence in the Field* (Wolf Legal Publishers, 2006). For commentary on the legality in United Nations law of authority provided by the UN, see the List of Sources, section 5.2.6. On issues of consent and imposition more broadly, including legal authority, see, e.g., Kreilkamp (above n. 9).

The legitimating concepts operating in a generalized sense were outlined in the discussion of ITA's association with the 'state-building' enterprise in the previous chapter: notions of saving 'failed states', liberal ideas of equivocal sovereignty, the 'responsibility to protect', and the right/duty to engage in 'humanitarian' military action. In different ways, each of these devices legitimizes the idea of introducing ITA to engage in the transformation of the politics and economy in a particular territory.

Conceiving a state as having 'failed' or being 'illiberal' paves the way for a loss of sovereignty and thereby the entitlement to non-intervention, just as colonial-era notions of sovereignty enabled the introduction of colonial rule.[446] Gerhard Kreijen suggests that states can, through recognition, extinguish the statehood of 'failed states' and advocates this in order to enable the introduction of trusteeship without requiring the consent of the target entity.[447] In a complementary move, the intervening actor is given an entitlement to introduce ITA through the 'responsibility to protect' and doctrines of 'just war' and 'humanitarian intervention.'[448] Gerhard Kreijen appears to reference these ideas when he suggests, by way of distinguishing colonialism from contemporary trusteeship, that:

…the present state of human rights and humanitarian law leaves little room for the stronger members of the international legal order to turn their backs on those members that are not 'able to stand by themselves'.[449]

As well as these generalized legal concepts, each ITA mission claims a specific international legal mandate for its own particular existence.[450] Discussing his concept of 'UN Civil Governance-in-trust', Jarat Chopra states that:

[t]he mandate is a critical feature of governance-in-trust because in the field it is regarded as the source of authority for exercising one set of powers or another. It sets standards against which to measure whether the operation is conducted 'in trust'.…[451]

As discussed earlier in this chapter, such an international legal benchmark was, of course, evident in many instances of state-conducted trusteeship. However, certain aspects of the particular modes of authority through which this benchmark

---

[446] On the notion of 'failed states' and liberal ideas of sovereignty, see above, ch. 7, nn. 46 and 77 respectively. Robert Jackson (a critic) describes the general idea thus: '…failed states should lose their sovereign rights and privileges and be made wards of international society'; Jackson (above n. 12), 289.

[447] Kreijen (above n. 11), 328–9 *et seq.*

[448] See above, ch. 7, n. 86 and accompanying text (on the responsibility to protect) and n. 91 and accompanying text (on just war theory and humanitarian intervention).

[449] Kreijen (above n. 11), 301.

[450] The following analysis concerns the legal authority for many, but not all, of the ITA projects involving international organizations and not also those involving international appointees other than in Bosnia and Herzegovina. For commentary on the legal authority for refugee camp arrangements (not discussed in the following analysis), see, e.g., Zieck (above n. 445).

[451] Chopra (above n. 12), 85. Chopra questions the legitimacy of this, however; see below, ch. 9, n. 35.

has been forthcoming with the ITA projects are invoked to distinguish this authority from its colonial equivalent.

The views of Gerhard Kreijen on the loss of sovereignty notwithstanding, most commentators accept that introducing ITA lawfully requires the consent of the host state, but emphasize that this consent has been, or could be, forthcoming, and/or that the one legitimate means of bypassing such consent has been, or could be, utilized: authority from the United Nations Security Council acting under Chapter VII of the UN Charter. The latter form of authority became possible as the activity of the Security Council after the end of the Cold War expanded into areas that were hitherto regarded as the exclusive domain of states.[452] So legitimacy in terms of legal authority has covered not only consensual authority but also Security Council authority passed under Chapter VII.

Projects with a legal mandate enshrined in an authoritative instrument resting on 'consent' distinguish themselves from the 'imposed' nature of colonialism by claiming to be its opposite; projects with a mandate based on Security Council authority assert such a distinction through the legal entitlement of the Security Council, within the bounds of the UN Charter, to render legitimate that which would otherwise be illegitimate in the field of intervention.[453] So the projects are again imposed, but this time their normative character is not considered to be degraded because an actor now exists, as was not the case previously, which enjoys the authority to make such impositions by virtue of its identity as an institution of the organized international community. As Henry Richardson stated in relation to the proposals for international administration in the 'failed state' context in particular:

[t]he proponents of 'failed states' rely heavily on the assumed legitimacy of United Nations organs, such as the Security Council, to mediate such conflicts, and to legitimate actions of intervention that otherwise would be illegal colonialism.[454]

---

[452] Cf. the general lack of authority under the UN Charter for UN intervention in matters 'essentially within the domestic jurisdiction' of states set out in Art. 2(7), and the requirement in Art. 39 of a 'threat to international peace and security' in order for Chapter VII enforcement action not subject to this restriction (according to Art. 2(7)) to be lawful. On the expansion in Security Council activities generally, see, e.g., D Sarooshi, *The United Nations and the Development of Collective Security* (OUP, 1999); Matheson (above n. 445).

[453] See in particular Arts 2(4), 2(7) and 25, Chapter VII, Art. 103 of the UN Charter. Doctrinal treatment of this issue is voluminous; see, for example, the relevant parts of the commentaries to the previously-cited articles, and supporting references thereto, in B Simma (ed.), *The Charter of the United Nations. A Commentary* (2nd edn, OUP, 2002). For this aspect of legitimation in relation to some of the UN administration projects, see also S Morphet, 'Organizing Civil Administration', in J Chopra (ed.), *The Politics of Peace-Maintenance* (Lynne Rienner, 1998), 41, *passim*.

[454] Richardson (above n. 11), 53. For Richard Caplan, '[i]nternational administrations...derive their legitimacy...from the international legislation that establishes them'; Caplan, *International Governance* (above n. 12), 195. Elaborating on this theme, Caplan states that ITA projects '...are institutions created and sustained by international processes, which, though themselves democratically deficient in certain respects, establish a legitimate basis and the parameters for the exercise of international authority...' (ibid., 246, footnote omitted).

For some, then, the projects can be distinguished from the 'imposed' nature of colonialism by invoking 'consent' and/or ideas of legitimacy associated with Security Council Chapter VII authority.[455] Not only, then, have the projects been legally conceived to operate on the basis of trust, as happened with certain state-conducted arrangements, but this has been done through legal processes that claim legitimacy in ways distinguishing them from the legal processes through which colonial trusteeship was authorized.

The invocation of these two types of legal authority has differed as between the various 'post-colonial' administration projects; one set of projects has rested on consent from the territorial sovereign, in conjunction (with two exceptions) with Security Council authority; a second set has been based solely on Security Council authority. The following analysis is limited to what has been claimed by the international organization supposedly authorized to carry out territorial administration. Whether or not the powers exercised actually fall within the scope of this claim is beyond the scope of the present evaluation. Before turning to the two models for legal authority, it is necessary to review briefly what is understood to be valid legal authority in the case of ITA introduced in a self-determination unit.

What is 'legitimate' sovereign authority when the territory concerned is considered to be entitled to an 'external' self-determination entitlement? If the territory forms part of another state, then consent from that state is not by itself seen as sufficient; the arrangement has to be validated by the population of the territory. If the territory does not form part of any state, then the unit itself should be treated as the 'sovereign authority' for the purpose of providing consent, given that, as discussed in Chapter 5, it is understood to enjoy distinct legal personality akin to the personality of a state in that it is territorially-based in character; thus consent from the sovereign authority should be understood in terms of the agreement of the people of the territory.

One special case here is West Irian. As discussed in Chapter 5, whether or not West Irian enjoyed a self-determination entitlement by virtue of having been treated as a discrete administrative unit by the Netherlands is unclear.[456] However, it was suggested that in any case the people of the territory can be seen as having enjoyed a self-determination entitlement by virtue of having been promised this right in the same agreement that provided for the transfer of territorial control to Indonesia from the Netherlands via UN administration. Although, then, the territory was a self-determination unit at the time UN administration was introduced, this was a special form of such status, in that it was only to be realized

---

[455] When discussing the distinction between contemporary 'peacebuilding' and colonialism, Roland Paris mentions that 'peacebuilding missions have normally been deployed...at the request of local parties, with the approval of international organizations'; Paris, 'International Peacebuilding' (above n. 12), 652. See also the discussion in Perritt, 'Structures and Standards' (above n. 11), 434.

[456] See the discussion above, ch. 5, section 5.4.

after the introduction of UN and then Indonesian-conducted administration. It follows, then, that as far as providing consent for foreign administration, such an entitlement did not subsist on the part of the people at the time when UN administration was to be introduced. At this stage, the Dutch consent to UNTEA validly amounted to consent from the sovereign authority, notwithstanding that it was given without consulting the West Irianese. This is different from a colonial territory enjoying self-determination as an automatic entitlement; in such cases, the requirement for consent for any form of foreign administration subsisted as soon as the self-determination entitlement became applicable.

For most of the 'post-colonial' projects, the sovereign authority in the territories concerned provided agreement to the administrative arrangements: the Congo agreed to ONUC;[457] the Netherlands agreed to UNTEA;[458] Cambodia agreed to UNTAC;[459] Bosnia and Herzegovina and/or the relevant sub-state Entities agreed to the European Union Administration in Mostar[460] and OHR,[461] the international appointees,[462] and the OSCE's role in running elections[463];

---

[457] In its request to the United Nations for assistance. See SC. Res. 143, 14 July 1960, second preambular sentence, and Telegrams dated 12 and 13 July 1960 from the President and the Prime Minister of the Republic of the Congo to the UN Secretary-General, UN Doc. S/4382; UN SCOR, 15th year, Supp. (July, August, and September 1960), 11.

[458] In the Agreement between Indonesia and the Netherlands Concerning West New Guinea (West Irian), 15 August 1962, 437 UNTS 273, signed by the Netherlands.

[459] In the instruments agreed to by Cambodia in 1991 (Final Act of the Paris Conference on Cambodia; Agreement on a Comprehensive Political Settlement of the Cambodia Conflict; Agreement Concerning the Sovereignty, Independence, Territorial Integrity and Inviolability, Neutrality and National Unity of Cambodia; Declaration on the Rehabilitation and Reconstruction of Cambodia, Paris, 23 October 1991, UN Doc. A/46/608-S/2317730 (1991), Annex).

[460] In the Memorandum of Understanding on the European Union Administration of Mostar ('Mostar MOU') of 5 July 1994, signed by 'the Republic of Bosnia and Herzegovina, as well as the Federation of Bosnia and Herzegovina, the Local Administration of Mostar East, the Local Administration of Mostar West and the Bosnian Croats'.

[461] In Dayton Annex 10 (above, ch. 1, n. 38), agreed to by Bosnia and Herzegovina, Croatia, the Federal Republic of Yugoslavia, the Federation of Bosnia and Herzegovina and the Republika Srpska. Dayton Annex 5 (above, ch. 1, n. 38), agreed to by Bosnia and Herzegovina, the Federation of Bosnia and Herzegovina, and the Republika Srpska, authorized the arbitral tribunal that provided the authority for the OHR Supervisor in Brčko in the Brčko Award 1997 (*Arbitration for the Brčko Area (Federation of Bosnia and Herzegovina v Republika Srpska)*, Arbitral Tribunal for Dispute over Inter-Entity Boundary in Brčko Area, Award, 14 February 1997, UN Doc. S/1997/126 (1997)).

[462] In Dayton Annex 4 (above, ch. 1, n. 38), approved by Bosnia and Herzegovina, the Federation of Bosnia and Herzegovina and the Republika Srpska (for the Constitutional Court and the Central Bank), Dayton Annex 6 (ibid.), agreed to by Bosnia and Herzegovina, the Federation of Bosnia and Herzegovina, and the Republika Srpska (for the Human Rights Chamber and the Human Rights Ombudsman), Dayton Annex 7 (ibid.) agreed to by Bosnia and Herzegovina, the Federation of Bosnia and Herzegovina, and the Republika Srpska (for the Commission for Real Property Claims), Annex 8 (ibid.) agreed to by Bosnia and Herzegovina, the Federation of Bosnia and Herzegovina, and the Republika Srpska (for the Commission to Preserve National Monuments), Dayton Annex 9 (ibid.), agreed to by the Federation of Bosnia and Herzegovina and the Republika Srpska (for the Commission on Public Corporations).

[463] In Dayton Annex 3 (above, ch. 1, n. 38), agreed to by Bosnia and Herzegovina, the Federation of Bosnia, and Herzegovina, and the Republika Srpska.

Croatia agreed to UNTAES;[464] Iraq agreed to the UN Inter-Agency Humanitarian Programme;[465] and the then Federal Republic of Yugoslavia agreed to UNMIK.[466]

In all these cases apart from West Irian, the states providing consent were in a particularly vulnerable position, through internal conflict—for example, Bosnia and Herzegovina—and/or as a result of external coercion—as with the then FRY in 1999 following the NATO bombing campaign. It might be said, therefore, that, as discussed earlier, although the administration agreements were based on the consent of the local sovereign, this was consent of a largely formal character; due to weakness and/or external pressure, the significance of consent was compromised and the projects might better be regarded as imposed. It is notable in this regard that in all these cases except the EUAM, authority for the projects was also derived from Security Council resolutions.[467]

A detailed exploration of the interplay between the legal authority provided by the consensual instruments, on the one hand, and the Security Council resolutions, on the other, is beyond the scope of this book, but in general terms, as mentioned earlier, this dual authority had the normative effect of conceiving projects whose legal bases combined elements of both consent and imposition. Since the latter is a particular form of imposed authority—Security Council resolutions passed under Chapter VII of the UN Charter—considered politically legitimate, the effect is to provide legitimacy in cases where the nature of the consent provided by the sovereign authorities is placed into question.

In the second class of projects, covering UNOSOM II in Somalia and UNAMET and UNTAET in East Timor, the arrangements did not enjoy any legitimate consensual authority from the territorial sovereign. The Somalia mission was based not on the consent of the state, but, rather, on Security Council authority exclusively.[468] East Timor, as previously discussed, was part neither of Portugal nor of Indonesia at the time of the conclusion of the May Agreements between these two

---

[464] In the Basic Agreement on the Region of Eastern Slavonia, Baranja and Western Sirmium, UN Doc. A/50/757-S/1995/951, 15 November 1995, Annex.

[465] In the Memorandum of Understanding between Iraq and the United Nations on the Implementation of Security Council Resolution 986 (1995), 20 May 1996, UN Doc. S/1996/356 (1996).

[466] In the Agreement on the Principles (Peace Plan) to Move Towards a Resolution of the Kosovo Crisis Presented to the Leadership of the Federal Republic of Yugoslavia by the President of Finland, Martti Ahtisaari, representing the European Union, and Viktor Chernomyrdin, Special Representative of the President of the Russian Federation, 3 June 1999, UN Doc. S/1999/649, Annex. So Steven Ratner notes that consent was provided for UNMIK by the FRY as the 'territorial sovereign'; Ratner (above n. 9), 697 n. 6. On this, see also, E Milano, *Unlawful Territorial Situations in International Law: Reconciling Effectiveness, Legality and Legitimacy* (Martinus Nijhoff, 2006), 234–65.

[467] See SC Res. 143 (above n. 457) (for the Congo); SC Res. 717, 16 October 1991 (for Cambodia); SC Res. 1031, 15 December 1995 (for Bosnia and Herzegovina); SC Res. 1037, 15 January 1996, SC Res. 1079, 15 November 1996 and SC Res. 1120, 14 July 1997 (for Eastern Slavonia); SC Res. 986, 14 April 1995 (for northern Iraq); SC Res. 1244 (above n. 287) (for Kosovo).

[468] See the sources cited above, ch. 2, n. 22.

states which provided for the 'popular consultation' and subsequent UN administration arrangements.[469] Although the plenary UN administration arrangements
were authorized by these agreements, this cannot be considered authority derived
from the sovereign authority with respect to the territory. Rather, the agreements
reflected the political need to obtain consent from Indonesia, as the occupying
power, and acknowledge the legal interest that Portugal had in East Timor as the
former administering power, notwithstanding its lack of sovereignty over the territory.[470] In other words, they reflected the need to involve other interested states,
rather than states enjoying sovereignty with respect to the territory.[471]

Since UN administration was to follow the 'popular consultation', there was a
ready-made opportunity to derive consent from the East Timorese for the administration arrangements. When the Security Council welcomed the outcome of
the consultation, it suggested that such consent had in fact been forthcoming in
this; as mentioned above, it described the outcome as the East Timorese expressing a '…clear wish to begin a process of transition under the authority of the
United Nations…'.[472] Similarly, during his time as the head of UNTAET, Sergio
Vieira de Mello, stated that his mission 'draws its legitimacy from the 30 August
referendum, where the population overwhelmingly opted for independence after
a transition under UN administration'.[473]

However, the ballot was concerned exclusively with East Timor's future status: it failed to mention either a process of transition or any role for the United
Nations.[474] It might be said that the East Timorese knew about the content of
the May Agreements, and in particular were aware that choosing independence
would involve a temporary period of UN administration. Although this was
probably the case as far as the leadership and the elite generally were concerned,
it is far from clear how many involved in the consultation, given the high rates of
illiteracy and isolation of much of the population from Dili, knew of this arrangement. That said, some of the publicity materials issued by UNAMET referred to
some kind of UN role if special autonomy within Indonesia was rejected. For
example, a UNAMET poster stated that in such circumstances '[t]he United
Nations will oversee East Timor's transition'.[475]

Even for those people who were aware that rejecting special autonomy within
Indonesia would lead to UN administration, it is not possible, however, to

---

[469] Agreement between the Republic of Indonesia and the Portuguese Republic on the
Question of East Timor, 5 May 1999; Agreement between the Governments of Indonesia and
Portugal and the United Nations Regarding the Modalities for the Popular Consultation of the
East Timorese through a Direct Ballot (hereinafter 'East Timor Agreement 2'), 5 May 1999;
Agreement between the Governments of Indonesia and Portugal and the United Nations on
Security, 5 May 1999 (the text of the Agreements is obtainable from <http://www.un.org/peace/
etimor99/etimor.htm>). On the issue of status, see the discussion above, section 5.7.
[470] On this, see the discussion above, ch. 5, text accompanying nn. 126 *et seq.*
[471] Steven Ratner notes that although it provided its consent, Indonesia, 'was not clearly the
lawful sovereign'; Ratner (above n. 9), at 697, n. 6.
[472] SC Res. 1272 (above n. 292), preamble, para. 3.
[473] Vieira de Mello (above n. 9).
[474] See East Timor Agreement 2 (above n. 469).
[475] See <http://www.un.org/peace/etimor99/POSTERS/p3ee.jpg>.

assume that taking the former position necessarily meant accepting the latter set-up. The East Timorese were not given the opportunity to express their view on each arrangement separately; if they favoured independence, they had to 'agree' to UN administration into the bargain. One imagines that for most people, if a choice had to be made between the two, the eventual status of the territory was of more importance than the question of an interim-period of UN administration. If this is the case, then in most instances those who may have not wished for the latter would have nonetheless voted in favour of separation from Indonesia if they supported eventual independence. One cannot, therefore, draw any conclusion either way about local support for UNTAET from the popular consultation. Far from expressing a 'clear wish', the East Timorese were not given the opportunity to express their view as to whether or not they agreed to a temporary period of UN administration before independence.

It follows that UNTAET in East Timor, like UNAMET in the same territory and UNOSOM II in Somalia, enjoyed no legal authority from either the territorial sovereign or the people of the territory, but claimed legitimacy exclusively through its Security Council mandate passed under Chapter VII.[476]

Legal authority for ITA provided by the UN Security Council, in addition to the idea that it constitutes 'legitimate' imposition, is also significant to the legitimacy of the projects in that it can be invoked to suggest that the organized international community as a whole has decided where trusteeship will take place, and how it will be conducted. This responds to one aspect of the critique of state-conducted trusteeship as self-serving: that individual states have decided where arrangements will take place.

As discussed earlier, the internationalization of colonial trusteeship was in most cases a matter of grafting a trusteeship obligation onto existing arrangements, rather than a global process of allocating new trusteeships to colonial states, and where such allocation did happen, it was, of course, through agreements between imperial states only. Writing in 1905, John Atkinson Hobson argued that:

[t]his claim to justify aggression, annexation and forcible government by talk of duty, trust or mission can only be made good by providing that the claimant is accredited by a body genuinely representative of civilization, to which it acknowledges a real responsibility...

[...]

...until some genuine international council exists, which shall accredit a civilized nation with the duty of educating a lower race, the claim of a 'trust' is nothing else than an impudent act of self-assertion.[477]

Hobson hoped for a:

...permanent authoritative body, representative of all the Powers, to which might be referred not only the quarrels between nations, but the entire partition of this 'civilizing' work...[478]

---

[476] SC Res. 1272 (above n. 212).   [477] Hobson (above n. 397), 209–10.
[478] Ibid., 210.

Although the League of Nations and the United Nations played a role in the allocation of Mandate and Trust territories, these arrangements were, in large part, intended to ratify what had already taken place by way of territorial occupation by the victorious powers after the two world wars.[479] Had things been different, the arrangements would not have worked as a compromise between annexation and internationalization.[480]

The 'post-colonial' ITA projects claim legitimacy, by contrast, in part through the idea that, as 'new' arrangements whose existence has been in part determined by the UN, usually through the Security Council, their very existence—the choice of territory, the determination that its people 'require' trusteeship—has been authoritatively determined in the sense that the decision was made by a body acting on behalf of the 'international community' rather than the state that would be involved in the administration arrangement.

8.7.2.2 'Legitimate' policies

In 1990, Robert Jackson stated that the standard of civilization embedded in colonialism was:

> ...of historical interest only. It has been categorically rejected by the Third World as a form of Western imperialism: an expression of contempt for their cultures and a pretext for denying self-government. The expressions 'sacred trust of civilization' and 'civilized state' have been erased from current international law and the dialogue between states carefully avoids these terms.[481]

Beyond ideas of legitimacy concerned with the introduction of ITA, further legitimating structures are evident as far as the particular policies promoted through it are concerned, just as the 'standard of civilization', as discussed earlier, underpinned not only why colonial trusteeship was introduced, but also what it sought to achieve. What ideas perform an equivalent role for ITA to that performed by the standard of civilization in relation to colonial trusteeship?

It may no longer be politically correct in international public policy to describe people as 'uncivilized', but descriptions of states as having 'failed' is commonplace. Just as characterizing colonial trusteeship as a 'civilizing mission' imbued it with normative significance, so understanding ITA as a response to state 'failure' legitimates the activity—who could dispute that 'failure' must be addressed, or that an enterprise implicitly aimed at a 'succeeful' state is invalid?[482] In a similar fashion, notions that sovereignty is the entitlement only of 'liberal' states and

---

[479] See the discussion above, text accompanying n. 316. Although John Atkinson Hobson revised his book in a new edition published in 1938, the comments extracted above were retained (see JA Hobson, *Imperialism: A Study* (3rd edn, Allen & Unwin, 1938), at 238–9 and 239 respectively), although in a section that does not appear to be updated from the 1905 edition (see in particular ibid., n. 1).

[480] On this compromise, see above, text accompanying n. 316 *et seq.*

[481] Jackson (above n. 55), 143.

[482] See above, ch. 7, n. 46.

must be 'earned' legitimizes those ITA projects associated with objectives such as promoting democracy, the rule of law, and free-market economics that are seen as epitomizing the essential features of the liberal state.[483]

Ideas concerning the universality of human rights are clearly relevant here, given the significance of human rights promotion to many of the 'post-colonial' ITA projects. Robert Jackson's statement above continues with the observation that the old 'standard of civilization still exists, but is expressed differently'.[484] Jackson invokes the earlier work of Gerrit Gong, who in 1984 discussed the potential for benchmarks of human rights, together with other norms, to serve as the new standard of civilization.[485] Actually, Gong's analysis, completed during the Cold War and only a few years after the entry into force of the two global human rights Covenants, seemed to conclude that human rights norms had not yet achieved the level of universal consensus to constitute a new equivalent to the old standard of civilization.[486]

---

[483] See above, ch. 7, nn. 77 (on liberal notions of sovereignty) and 81 (on 'earned sovereignty').

[484] Jackson (above n. 55), 143. Roland Paris states that '...although modern peacebuilders have largely abandoned the archaic language of civilized versus uncivilized, they nevertheless appear to act upon the belief that one model of domestic governance—liberal market economy—is superior to all others'; Paris, 'International Peacebuilding' (above n. 12), 638.

[485] Gong (above n. 104), *passim* (mentioned by Robert Jackson in *Quasi-States* (above n. 55), 143). See also J Vincent, 'The Factor of Culture in the Global International Order', in *Yearbook of World Affairs 1980*, 34; J Vincent, 'Race in International Relations', 58 (1982) *International Affairs* 658; J Vincent, 'Racial Equality', in H Bull and A Watson (eds), *The Expansion of International Society* (Clarendon Press, 1984), 239; J Donnelly, 'Human Rights: A New Standard of Civilization?', 74:1 (1998) *International Affairs* 1.

[486] Early in his study, Gong asserts that '[h]uman rights [and other norms] have all vied for acceptance as international norms, but so far none has attained universal consensus'; Gong (above n. 104), 13. Later, Gong begins a discussion of whether a 'standard of human rights' might be a 'possible successor' to the standard of civilization, but does not conclude with a definite answer (see ibid., 90–2), which one must therefore find from his earlier statement. The later discussion mentions the references to human rights in the UN Charter, the Universal Declaration of Human Rights, the two global human rights Covenants, and the idea that there might be a global standard on non-discrimination (ibid., 91), but what seems to be most significant for Gong is the requirement of 'compulsory jurisdiction' to enforce such norms, and Gong observes that it is 'internationally recognized that only the European Human Rights Conventions [sic] require compulsory jurisdiction' (ibid., 91). Of course, under the ICCPR jurisdiction is possible over inter-state complaints through acceptance under Art. 41, and over individual complaints under the (First) Optional Protocol, although the Views of the Human Rights Committee in relation to such complaints are not legally binding, unlike the decisions of the European Court and Commission (as was) of Human Rights; at the time Gong was writing, before the reforms introduced by Protocol No. 11, the European Commission of Human Rights had compulsory jurisdiction over inter-state cases but such cases could only go before the Court with the consent of the state or states they were being brought against; jurisdiction over individual cases by both the Commission and the Court depended on a separate, general acceptance of this by contracting states. For the relevant instruments, see Universal Declaration of Human Rights, GA Res. 217 A (III), 10 December 1948; ECHR (above n. 168); ICCPR (above n. 168); First Optional Protocol to the International Covenant on Civil and Political Rights (New York, 16 December 1966), 999 UNTS 302, in force 23 March 1976; International Covenant on Economic, Social and Cultural Rights, 16 December 1966, 993 UNTS 3, in force 3 January 1976. On the supervisory mechanism within the European system before the entry into force of Protocol No. 11 to the European Convention, see European Convention for the Protection of Human Rights and Fundamental Freedoms as amended by Protocols Nos 3, 5, 8

After Gong's book was published, the mushrooming of human rights treaties and their widespread ratification by states, including former colonial states added greater credence to the notion that the human rights standards in international law are of universal purchase.[487] With the end of the Cold War, this notion of universality was deepened for many, with, as mentioned in the previous chapter, the idea of the triumph of liberal values of human rights and democracy.[488]

(text reprinted in MD Evans (ed.), *Blackstone's International Law Documents* (3rd edn, Blackstone, 1996), 43), Art. 24 (in relation to inter-state complaints before the Commission); Art. 25 (on the individual petition procedure before the Commission); Art. 48 (in relation to the consensual jurisdiction of the Court); Art. 53 (on the binding nature of the Court's decisions).

[487] The main international legal documents on human rights are replete with references to the universal character of the rights they contain, from the Universal Declaration of Human Rights (above, n. 486) onwards. Commentary on this issue is voluminous; see, e.g., J Donnelly, *The Concept of Human Rights* (Croom Helm, 1985); I Shivji, *The Concept of Human Rights in Africa* (Codesria, 1989); AA An-Na'im and FM Deng (eds), *Human Rights in Africa: Cross-Cultural Perspectives* (Brookings Institution, 1990); AD Rentein, *International Human Rights: Universalism Versus Relativism* (Sage, 1990); H Steiner and P Alston (eds), *International Human Rights in Context: Law, Politics, Morals* (2nd edn, OUP, 2000), ch. 6; W Kymlicka and M Opalski (eds), *Can Liberal Pluralism Be Exported? Western Political Theory and Ethnic Relations in Eastern Europe* (OUP, 2002); Anghie (above n. 2), 254–8 and sources cited therein; A Clapham and S Marks, *International Human Rights Lexicon* (OUP, 2005), 385–98; A Pollis and P Schwab, 'Human Rights: A Western Construct With Limited Applicability', in A Pollis and P Schwab (eds), *Human Rights: Cultural and Ideological Perspectives* (Praeger, 1979); J Donnelly, 'Human Rights and Human Dignity: An Analytic Critique of Non-Western Conceptions of Human Rights', 76 (1982) *American Political Science Review* 303; AD Rentein, 'The Unanswered Challenge of Relativism and the Consequences for Human Rights', 7 (1985) *Human Rights Quarterly* 514; R Falk, 'Cultural Foundations for the International Protection of Human Rights', in AA An-Na'im (ed.), *Human Rights in Cross-Cultural Perspectives: Quest for Consensus* (University of Philadelphia Press, 1992), 44; RE Howard, 'Dignity, Community and Human Rights', in AA An-Na'im (ed.), *Human Rights in Cross-Cultural Perspectives: Quest for Consensus* (University of Philadelphia Press, 1992), 81; B Tibi, 'Islamic Law/ Shari'a Human Rights, Universal Morality and International Relations', 16 (1994) *Human Rights Quarterly* 277; C Christie, 'Regime Security and Human Rights in South East Asia', 43 (1995) *Political Studies* 204; F Halliday, 'Relativism and Universalism in Human Rights: the Case of the Islamic Middle East', 43 (1995) *Political Studies* 152; AE Mayer, 'Cultural Particularism as a Bar to Women's Rights: Reflections on the Middle Eastern Experience' in J Peters and A Wolper (eds), *Women's Rights, Human Rights: International Feminist Perspectives* (Routledge, 1994); A Rao, 'The Politics of Gender and Culture in International Human Rights Discourse', in J Peters and A Wolper (eds), *Women's Rights, Human Rights: International Feminist Perspectives* (Routledge, 1994); MJ Perry, 'Are Human Rights Universal? The Relativist Challenge and Related Matters', 19 (1997) *Human Rights Quarterly* 461; T Weiming, 'Joining East and West: A Confucian Perspective on Human Rights', 20 (1998) *Harvard International Review* 44; A Sen, 'Universal Truths: Human Rights and the Westernizing Illusion', 20 (1998) *Harvard International Review* 40; TM Franck, 'Are Human Rights Universal?', 80 (Jan–Feb 2001) *Foreign Affairs* 191.

[488] See F Fukuyama, *The End of History and the Last Man* (Free Press, 1992); F Fukuyama, 'The End of History?', 16 (1989) *National Interest* 3, and, for critical treatment of this thesis in the context of democracy, S Marks, *The Riddle of All Constitutions: International Law, Democracy and the Critique of Ideology* (OUP, 2000) and S Marks, 'The End of History? Reflections on Some International Legal Theses', 8 (1997) *EJIL* 449. The relevance of this thesis to ideas of legitimacy associated with international trusteeship is discussed by Bain, *Between Anarchy and Society* (above n. 12), 155–6. For the earlier discussion of ideas concerning liberalism after the end of the Cold War, see above, ch. 7, text accompanying n. 65 *et seq.*

In the immediate period of decolonization, by contrast, the only universal human rights instrument was the non-binding UN Universal Declaration of Human Rights. This normative climate is evident in Robert Jackson's remark that:

[i]ndependence freed colonies not only from imperial direction but also from metropolitan protection under the rule of law. Decolonization multiplied the number of independent governments with responsibility to safeguard civil standards but also with power to violate them. These governments had the sovereign right to abandon the rule of law or do almost anything else in their jurisdictions.[489]

The shift in the fortunes of international trusteeship with the increase in the use of ITA towards the end of the 20th century corresponds to the alteration in the position of states in relation to human rights when compared with the period of decolonization. To paraphrase Jackson, states—whether or not former colonies—no longer had the sovereign right to violate human rights, and so ITA might be legitimate as a remedy for such violations in a way that it could not have been before the global norms had been accepted.

The idea of international human rights as universal is not simply a matter of the existence of widely accepted treaties; it is also rooted in the notion that the ideas of rights contained in these treaties are of universal validity, in contrast to the racist standards associated with colonialism. Brian Simpson states that:

[i]n so far as colonialism was associated with ideas of innate and therefore permanent racial superiority, it plainly impinged upon the conceptions of human equality and human dignity which underlie the belief in human rights.[490]

In general terms, intervention to promote human rights in the 'post-colonial' era, including the use of ITA in this regard, claims legitimacy because what it is understood to be promoting can be portrayed as universally valid, not culturally specific and based on the superiority of one race over another.[491] Thus even if such activities involve, in the words of the General Act of the Berlin Conference, 'bringing home' to the people affected 'the blessings of civilization', the civilization in question is now a universal, not a culturally-specific, Europeanized model, and so the 'bringing' of it is not the same process as Berlin sought to facilitate.[492]

These ideas are also implicated in the debates on the question of the legality of 'transformative' occupation.[493] The objective behind the traditional notion of occupation law preserving the status quo—preventing the occupying state

[489] Jackson (above n. 55), 146.
[490] Simpson (above n. 32), 300.
[491] Much of the literature on so-called 'humanitarian intervention' discusses this general issue in relation to military action in particular: see the sources cited above, ch. 7, n. 91. In the context of ITA, Steven Ratner finds that the 'tar of colonialism is not sticking' and speculates that one possible reason for this is the 'delegitimization of racial superiority'; Ratner (above n. 9), 696. For a discussion of this issue in the context of 'peacebuilding' generally, see Paris, 'International Peacebuilding' (above n. 12), 652.
[492] Berlin Conference General Act (above n. 109), Ch. I, Art. VI.
[493] On this debate, see above, n. 129 and accompanying text *et seq.*

from imposing its particular political and economic system upon the occupied territory—falls away if universal conceptions of political and economic governance exist, through the standards of international law, which can then form the basis for non-culturally-specific transformations.

One important feature of the justificatory structure of universalism is the idea that the values being promoted, as 'universal', necessarily exclude the interests of powerful states. This is evident in the comment by (Lord) Paddy Ashdown, then High Representative in Bosnia Herzegovina, that:

Bosnia [and Herzegovina] will be seen as a new model for international intervention— one designed not to pursue narrow national interests but to prevent conflict, to promote human rights and to rebuild war-torn societies.[494]

The idea of universalism also implicates notions of a generalized, community interest mentioned above and in the previous chapter.[495] The standards being implemented are not only understood to have universal validity; there is also a universal interest in seeing them adhered to. In other words, not only are they valid everywhere; also, everyone has an interest in their implementation everywhere. This in turn creates legitimacy for intervention like ITA to bring about such implementation, which is, because of the 'international interest', no longer the exclusive domain of the state and people affected. Put differently, the target state is no longer entitled to 'independence' from international involvement in it, because of the supposed international public interest.[496] Jarat Chopra states that:

[s]overeignty and the barriers it raises cannot withstand inevitable intervention in issues that are legitimately deemed international. The scope of 'international' is widening to the point that UN administration is becoming a necessity rather than an intrusion.[497]

As the latter sentence illustrates, some commentators suggest that intervention on humanitarian grounds is shifting from the terrain of discretion to that of obligation, through concepts of the 'responsibility to protect' and 'humanitarian intervention'.[498] Not only, then, is the idea of ITA conceived as generally legitimate in those cases where it is used; in the context of pursuing humanitarian objectives, the use of ITA is rendered obligatory.

As discussed in the previous chapter, the purposes with which all the administration projects have been associated can be understood in terms of implementing certain norms of international law. The 'lawfulness' of the 'post-colonial' projects in particular is significant in terms of legitimacy when it is allied to more general ideas of legitimacy associated with international law formulated in the

---

[494] P Ashdown, 'What I Learned in Bosnia', *New York Times* 28 October 2002, quoted in Bain, *Between Anarchy and Society* (above n. 12), 5
[495] See above, ch. 7, nn. 87 (on community interest) and 88 (on *erga omnes* obligations).
[496] Cf. UN Charter, Art. 2(7).
[497] Chopra (above n. 12), 87.
[498] The 'responsibility to protect' is discussed above, ch. 7, text accompanying n. 86 *et seq*; 'humanitarian intervention' is discussed above, ch. 7, text accompanying n. 91 *et seq.*

'post-colonial' era with the participation of former colonial states. The significance of ideas of universality associated with international human rights law, for example, is underscored by the designation as 'universally recognized human rights' the standards of law that, as discussed earlier, UNMIK and UNTAET proclaimed they would use as the benchmark for determining whether local laws should apply during the course of their authority over Kosovo and East Timor.[499]

Apart from providing an entitlement to be in administrative control, then, international law also provides an underpinning to the ostensible reasons for such control in terms of policies carried out. Through this, policies are associated with international law's claim to universality, which can then be invoked in response to a colonial critique that one particular, culturally-specific set of values is being imposed on a population that does not share them. Whereas colonialism was delegitimized on the grounds that the 'standard of civilization' was not universally valid but Eurocentric and racist, so, it is claimed, ITA is legitimized on the grounds that the civilizing policies it is sometimes associated with, such as improved respect for human rights, are now 'universal'.

8.7.2.3 'Legitimate' administering actors

When advocating in 1905 a permanent international authoritative body that would allocate international trusteeships between states, thereby improving the colonial model where imperial states themselves determined where they would engage in the civilizing mission, John Atkinson Hobson cautioned that:

...the issue would still remain precarious.
[...]
...there would exist the peril of the establishment of a self-chosen oligarchy among the nations which, under the cloak of the civilizing process, might learn to live parasitically upon the lower races, imposing upon them 'for their own good' all the harder or more servile work of industry, and arrogating to themselves the honours and emoluments of government and supervision.[500]

Even if, then, trusteeships were legitimately imposed by a universal process of allocation and operated on the basis of policies that were of universal purchase, a central problem from the experience of colonial trusteeship would remain: the administering authorities would still be individual states, who would act 'parasitically'.

The final way in which international territorial administration is distinguished normatively from the state-conducted precursors is in the identity of the administering actors involved. The normative character of international organizations,

---

[499] See above, ch. 6, n. 142 and accompanying text; in relation to Kosovo in particular, see the Report of the Secretary-General on the United Nations Interim Administration Mission in Kosovo, UN Doc. S/1999/779, 12 July 1999, para. 42.
[500] Hobson (above n. 397), 210.

especially the United Nations, is often presented through the positioning of such organizations in contradistinction to states.[501] In this Manichean, two-legs-bad four-legs-good vision, whereas states are considered 'imperial', self-interested and exploitative, international organizations are presented as selfless and humanitarian. Such relational positioning is a powerful aid in distinguishing international territorial administration from colonialism in that it enables the activity of territorial administration when conducted by international organizations to be disassociated, normatively, from the same activity when performed by states, which would always be vulnerable to suspicions of bad faith and self-serving motivations.

There are two interrelated aspects to this idea. In the first place, on a political level the reification of the 'international' in the form of international organizations permits the notion of a distinct actor, created by, but separate from, states. This enables international organizations to be presented as independent from states, as impartial manifestations of the global community.[502] Actions conducted by such actors are 'public' in the sense that they are not conducted by an individual member of the international 'polity' (a particular state) but, rather, the 'polity' as a whole.

In the second place, states and international organizations are set up as binary opposites in terms of their respective moral characters. Whereas states are suspected of acting for self-serving motives, international organizations are considered selfless, neither representing the interests of particular states,[503] nor

---

[501] For an early invocation of a sharp distinction between the identity of the UN and that of states, see the observation by the International Court of Justice that its conclusion that the United Nations enjoys legal personality, 'is not the same thing as saying that it is State, which it certainly is not'; *Reparations for Injuries Suffered in the Service of the United Nations*, Advisory Opinion, *ICJ Reports 1949*, 174, at 179.

[502] See S Vohra, 'Impartiality in United Nations Peace-Keeping', 9 (1996) *LJIL* 63; M Von Grunigen, 'Neutrality and Peace Keeping', in A Cassese, *United Nations Peace-Keeping: Legal Essays* (Sijthoff & Noordhoff, 1978), 125.

[503] As for independence vis-à-vis member states, Art. 100 of the UN Charter states that:

1. In the performance of their duties the Secretary-General and the staff shall not seek or receive instructions from any government or from any other authority external to the Organization. They shall refrain from any action which might reflect on their position as international officials responsible only to the Organization.

2. Each Member of the United Nations undertakes to respect the exclusively international character of the responsibilities of the Secretary-General and the staff and not to seek to influence them in the discharge of their responsibilities.

The UN Staff Regulations state that the responsibilities of UN staff 'are not national but exclusively international', and staff must declare that they will regulate their conduct 'with the interests of the United Nations only in view'; 'Staff Regulations of the United Nations', Secretary-General's bulletin ST/SGB/2000/7, 23 February 2000, Regulation 1.1. See also ibid., Regulation 1.2. For commentary, see, e.g., C Schreuer and C Ebner, 'Article 100', in B Simma (ed.), *The Charter of the United Nations. A Commentary* (2nd edn, OUP, 2002), vol. 2, 1230, at 1232–51 and sources cited therein. On the 'impartiality' of UN peace operations, see, e.g., Vohra (above n. 502) and sources cited therein.

pursuing any self-interested objectives other than what is for the benefit of the so-called 'international community' as a whole.[504]

This is demonstrated, for example, in the understanding of ITA's role in responding to a perceived 'sovereignty problem', where the normative identity of the international organization as 'neutral' in relation to the interests of disputing states forms the basis for its involvement in an attempt to address a territorial dispute. Equally, the suspicion of self-interest on the part of states leads to a fear that states' actions outside their territory will be exploitative of the population affected. International organizations, by contrast, are presented as humanitarian and benign. ITA projects, therefore, are not acts of 'conquest', as in Marlow's description of colonialism, but, rather, acts of charity.[505]

The evolution of this idea from the start of the post-Second World War movement away from colonialism to the time of writing can be seen in the following three quotations. In 1945, the international lawyer Philip Marshall Brown stated that:

... the exploitation of peoples not yet prepared for self-government, nor ready to assume all of their obligations in the family of nations, is definitely proscribed. Their best interests are to be subserved through consortiums of nations, or by an international organization seeking the safety and welfare of all.[506]

When proposing the revival of international trusteeship in 1993, Peter Lyon stated that:

... it has to be admitted that a mandatory system, so reminiscent of colonialism in the days of the overseas ascendancies of the west Europeans, will almost certainly not prove generally acceptable nowadays and therefore be practicable. Thus the best that might be practicable is a second best: trusteeship by the UN itself.[507]

One of Lyon's post-millennium successors as advocate for international trusteeship, Gerhard Kreijen, complained in 2004, that:

... those who criticise the notion of an international trusteeship [because of colonial echoes] focus too much on the wrongs that accompanied Western Imperialism and consequently fail to appreciate the essence of a trust.[508]

---

[504] See, for example, the award of the Nobel peace prize to the UN and its Secretary-General in 2001, 'for their work for a better organized and more peaceful world'; see Norwegian Nobel Committee, Press Release, 'The Nobel Peace Prize 2001', 12 October 2001, available at <http://www.nobel.se/peace/laureates/2001/press.html>.

[505] Roland Paris states that '[o]f course, the old and new versions of *mission civilisatrice* differ in many respects, not least of which is the fact that European colonialism was practiced primarily to benefit the imperial states themselves, whereas the motivation behind recent peacebuilding operations is less mercenary'; Paris, 'International Peacebuilding' (above n. 12), 638.

[506] Brown (above n. 116), 86.

[507] Lyon (above n. 11), 105.

[508] Kreijen (above n. 11), 309–10.

For some observers, if actors can be found who will not abuse the trust placed in them, as states were seen to have done with colonialism, then the colonial critique falls away. If such actors exist in the form of international organizations, trusteeship can be legitimately re-introduced into international public policy. From this standpoint, ITA projects are 'true' trusteeship because an actor is present who can be relied upon to act in the selfless and humanitarian manner required by the position of trustee.[509]

This portrayal of the normative difference between international organizations and individual states, however simplistic and potentially problematic, is of significant purchase when understanding ideas of legitimacy associated with the international organization-conducted administration projects.[510] Just as territorial administration by foreign states was presented as unjust in the era of decolonization, so this activity performed by international organizations is sometimes considered essentially legitimate because it is conducted by international organizations. At the very least, the presumption is reversed; what was presumed to be illegitimate is now presumed to be legitimate. Mathias Ruffert, for example, essentializes the normative tenor of 'international administration' in terms of an assumed 'benevolent character'.[511]

These ideas echo the arguments made in the period between the two world wars by advocates of internationalization; as Ramendra Nath Chowdhuri relates, they emphasized:

... the numerous advantages of the Mandated status in comparison to the colonies such as the provisions for the guarantee of native rights, of restrictions on alienation of native lands and of economic equality of all members of the League.[512]

---

[509] James Hales, discussing the compromise in the Mandate arrangements between 'annexation' (by individual states) or 'internationalization' (i.e., ITA), represents this as a 'compromise between the application of perfect trusteeship and the ordinary annexation of territories'; Hales (above n. 107), 177. This implies that state-conducted trusteeship is less than perfect compared with ITA, presumably because of the normative character of the administering actors as far as their suitability to act as trustees is concerned. The question of accountability for ITA is picked up below, text accompanying nn. 554 *et seq.*

[510] As already mentioned (above n. 491), Steven Ratner finds that the 'tar of colonialism is not sticking' to ITA and speculates that one possible reason for this, in addition to the reason mentioned already, is the 'absence of an exploitative economic motive'; Ratner (above n. 9), 696. Considering ideas of impartiality associated with the United Nations and their significance for the use of the 'occupation' label in relation to ITA projects, he states that:

... from this perspective, state occupiers, even so-called 'coalitions of the willing,' lack the broad multinationality of the UN; they are in a confrontational relationship with the population, self-interested, and in need of reining in. In contrast, the UN, thanks to its multinationality, can only be working for loftier goals to benefit the population: thus its operations cannot be termed occupations.

Ratner (above n. 9), 711–12. See also WJ Durch, 'Building on Sand: UN Peacekeeping in the Western Sahara', 17 (1993) *International Security* 151; Caplan, *International Governance* (above n. 12), 4 and 34; Tsagourias (above n. 12), *passim.*

[511] Ruffert (above n. 9), 629. See the discussion in Orford (above n. 427), 142.

[512] Chowdhuri (above n. 97), 25 (note omitted).

It will be recalled that one of the critiques of colonialism was that it created international tension as states fought each other for the right to have colonies. This did not necessarily mean, then, that trusteeship per se needed to come to an end—it could be conducted if a way to reduce inter-state tensions could be conceived. An early model with this aspiration was the internationalized structures of supervision created for the Mandate and Trusteeship systems. ITA takes this process of internationalization one step further by removing states entirely from the conduct of administration.[513]

One aspect of the inter-state rivalry problem concerned the interests promoted within colonies. As discussed, the 'open door' policy sought to guarantee that international trusteeship in each territory benefited all states, not just the particular administering authority involved; its significance as a means of reducing colonial rivalry depended, however, on effective enforcement. Again, Chowdhuri relates that in the inter-war debates leading up to the decision on the fate of the colonies of the defeated states in the Second World War:

> ...the advocates of internationalization of colonial administration considered the sharing of the economic and political responsibilities, and even prestige, as the *sine qua non* for permanent peace and appeasement of the 'have-nots'. They point out the numerous advantages of the Mandated status in comparison to the colonies such as the provisions for...economic equality of all members of the League.[514]

If, as discussed earlier, under ITA the 'other' beneficiary in the 'dual mandate' is the international community as a whole, then ITA acts as a means of ensuring the policy of equality across all states when compared to individual state administration.[515]

An alternative, contrasting approach to the ITA version of the 'dual mandate' is to view it as a response to the critique that the colonial-era dual mandate, in conceiving interests in addition to those of the local population as a legitimate focus for administration, was incompatible with the notion of trusteeship, which should operate exclusively in the interests of the local population. If the 'international community' is viewed as a generalized community interest rather than the interests of all of the world's states individually, then this limb of critique falls away.[516]

---

[513] On this policy in relation to the creation of the Mandate system, see Chowdhuri (above n. 97), 22–4, and sources cited therein. As David Kay relates:

...the competitive struggle of states for colonies [was identified] as a principal cause of war as well as being destructive of the interest of the native population. Unless this policy of war was brought to a halt and colonies put under some form of international supervision...colonies would serve as a perpetual source of international conflict.

DA Kay, 'The United Nations and Decolonization', in J Barros (ed.), *The United Nations: Past, Present and Future* (Free Press, 1972), 143, at 143, citing Chowdhuri.

[514] Chowdhuri (above n. 97), 25 (note omitted).

[515] On the 'dual mandate' in the colonial context, see above, text accompanying nn. 139 *et seq.* On the equivalent ideas in the context of ITA, see above, text accompanying nn. 271 *et seq.*

[516] On the critique of the dual mandate as a perversion of trust, see above, text accompanying n. 397 *et seq.*

8.7.2.4 *Temporary nature and the commitment to independence*

Many commentators appear to take the view that the purchase of the colonial paradigm is successfully resisted by one or more of the legitimating strategies outlined above. Because ITA is supposedly conducted on a legitimate basis, for legitimate policies, by legitimate actors, it is not colonialism. Whatever the merits of such an argument, understanding the legitimacy of ITA exclusively in its terms ignores the more fundamental critique of colonialism addressed earlier: the rejection of all foreign rule, including such rule on the basis of trusteeship, in and of itself, regardless of second-order criticisms such as exploitation.[517] As William Bain states:

[t]he charge that European colonial rulers failed to fulfil their obligations as trustees of civilization provided a powerful argument in support of their claim of independence. But this argument did not discredit the idea of trusteeship itself; it merely undermined the justification of the means by which colonial powers attempted to carry out their obligations. The argument of self-determination achieved something quite different: self-determination rendered trusteeship an unsustainable practice by definition.[518]

So, as Robert Jackson reminds us:

[t]he fundamental question that should be asked of those who advocate a social work relationship between successful states and failed states is this: are they prepared to accept the moral implications of their argument which may be indistinguishable from paternalism? [. . .]
Whatever we may prefer to call it, trusteeship is sharply at odds with the doctrine of international freedom based on self-determination and self-government.[519]

Gerhard Kreijen, who, as mentioned previously, seems to view the colonial critique exclusively in terms of illegitimate authority and exploitative administering actors, and not also as a rejection of trusteeship itself, struggles to explain why the UN Trusteeship Council was not revived after the Cold War to put trusteeship on a more formal and institutionalized footing:

---

[517] For this absolutist rejection of foreign rule see the sources cited above, n. 377. So in 1945 the international lawyer Philip Marshall Brown noted that '[t]he arguments now generally used in criticism of the colonial powers...are not based do much on charges of unjust exploitation as on the abstract right of all peoples to attain self-government...'; Brown (above n. 116), 85. Brian Simpson observes that '...the main thrust of the anti-colonialist movement...was simply to bring an end foreign domination of government. It was about the legitimacy of the structures of government, about who should govern colonial peoples, not about how they should be governed'; Simpson (above n. 32), 300. Equally, the oppressive forms of government within colonial administration, and the anti-colonial resistance to this oppression '...did not affect the fact that the anti-colonial movement had as its principal aim simply the ending of foreign rule, not the imposition of restraints on the powers of government'; ibid., 301. See also Gordon, 'Some Legal Problems with Trusteeship' (above n. 11).

[518] Bain, *Between Anarchy and Society* (above n. 12), 132–3.

[519] Jackson (above n. 12), 311 and 314. See also, along similar lines, Gordon, 'Saving Failed States' (above n. 11); Gordon, 'Some Legal Problems with Trusteeship' (above n. 11).

[g]iven the many similarities between international territorial administration and international trusteeship, the prominent position of the former in modern state practice—in particular its increased use over the last decade—seems to add to the relevance and weight of the latter. In this light it is somewhat surprising that the UN Trusteeship System was mothballed...[520]

The continued inactivity of the Trusteeship system during the era of the Kosovo and East Timor administration projects is perhaps less of a surprise, however, if one bears in mind the absolutist rejection of direct foreign territorial domination, a political doctrine reflected in the legal entitlement to self-determination.[521]

Kreijen does identify the legal right to self-determination as one of the 'main legal obstacles' to trusteeship, but argues that trusteeship can be seen as compatible with self-determination in the context of 'failed states', because the territories concerned lack sovereignty by virtue of their 'failure', and are therefore in the same position as Mandated territories, in relation to which the concept of trust was applied.[522] This argument rests on Kreijen's broader thesis concerning 'failed states' and their supposed lack of legal sovereignty.[523] On its own terms, it lacks an acknowledgement that, as previously discussed, self-determination was articulated in part to repudiate the notion of trust—Mandated territories were, along with Trust territories and colonies, the paradigmatic class of entities in relation to which the 'external' right was conceived. Put differently, the idea of self-determination rejected the notion that peoples deemed incapable of self-administration were thereby not entitled to freedom from external control. The self-determination entitlement applies, of course, not only to the people of a certain class of non-state territories (e.g., Western Sahara), but also to the people of existing states.[524] Actually, then, Kreijen's thesis is opposed to and incompatible with self-determination.

Kreijen's ideological counterpart, Michael Ignatieff, is more aware of this problem with the idea of introducing trusteeship into existing states, a phenomenon he characterizes as 'Empire Lite'. Ignatieff states that:

[t]he moral premises of anti-imperialist struggles in this century—all peoples should be equal, and all peoples should rule themselves—are not wrong. But history is not a morality tale. The age of empire ought to have been succeeded by an age of independent, equal and self-governing nation states. In reality, it has been succeeded by an age of ethnic cleansing and state failure. This is the context in which empire has made its return. Empire is an attempted solution to the crisis of state order that has followed two botched decolonizations: the Soviet exit from Europe, and the European exit from Africa and Asia.[525]

---

[520] Kreijen (above n. 11), 322.

[521] On the right to self-determination see the sources cited above, ch. 5, n. 3 and in List of Sources, section 5.4. On this particular legal impediment to trusteeship, see also the discussion in Gordon, 'Some Legal Problems with Trusteeship' (above n. 11), *passim*.

[522] Kreijen (above n. 11), 326 *et seq.*   [523] Ibid., *passim*.

[524] See generally the sources cited above, ch. 5, n. 3 and in List of Sources, section 5.4; see also the remarks by Jackson quoted above, n. 331.

[525] Ignatieff (above n. 4), 123. (Ignatieff makes these remarks in a book published in 2003, but presumably his reference to 'this century' concerns the 20th century [the book itself is partly based

Ignatieff acknowledges and justifies the inroads this 'attempted solution' has on the right to self-determination thus:

[i]t is at least ironic that liberal believers in [ideas of self-determination]...can end up supporting the creation of a new humanitarian empire, a new form of colonial tutelage...The reason simply is that, however right these principles [of self-determination] may be, the political form in which they are realized—the nationalist nation-building project—so often fails to deliver them. For every nationalist struggle that succeeds in giving its people self-determination and dignity, there are more that only deliver their people up to a self-immolating slaughter, terror, enforced partition and failure.[526]

Self-determination, then, should not always mean automatic independence; to revise the language of General Assembly Resolution 1514 quoted earlier, inadequacy of preparedness *should* be a pretext for delaying self-administration. Similarly, certain serious governance problems in existing states should be a pretext for suspending the rights of non-intervention and self-administration of those states.

Indeed, some commentators even advocate arrangements that not only in their nature cut against self-determination during their operation, but also lack a clear commitment to future self-determination. When considering the limitations that might fetter the conduct of ITA in Kosovo and East Timor, Michael Bothe and Thilo Marauhn consider the potential relevance of the self-determination entitlement.[527] Having reviewed the relevant Security Council resolutions relating to UNMIK and UNTAET, they conclude that:

...neither case can be said to constitute a step forward in the recognition of a right to external self-determination. Whether this is regrettable is another question. If each ethnic conflict became an issue about the right to external self-determination, this might enhance the divisive character of these conflicts and, eventually, international law might contribute to the deepening of the ditches between parts of the populations who would then live better together rather than separately. The Security Council is to be commended for having treated both conflicts as a matter of human rights, the populations concerned can live in an atmosphere of internal and external security, and of peace maintenance in the area. For these purposes, trusteeship administration seems to be a useful tool.

It is thus recognition of the internal rather than the external dimension of self-determination which opens up a proper perspective of the democratic limitations on trusteeship administration.[528]

Because of this:

[n]otwithstanding political claims to self-determination, the power of final decision remains with the UN.[529]

on previously-published articles].)

[526] Ibid., 122.
[527] Bothe & Marauhn (above n. 12), 238–9.
[528] Ibid., 239.
[529] Ibid., 240.

Whatever the merits of Bothe & Marauhn's conclusions about what the Security Council resolutions say about self-determination (notably in relation to East Timor), their failure to account for the potential significance to the scope of the mandates of the broader legal position in this regard (rendering claims to self-determination merely 'political' and not also 'legal' in character), and their descriptions of the purposes of both missions as essentially responses to 'ethnic conflict', what is significant about these remarks, given the commendation offered to the Security Council, is that the authors appear to find justified that external self-determination as an eventual entitlement should be sidelined if this is necessary to deal with the consequences of ethnic conflict.[530]

Even within the context of 'failed states' scholarship and contemporary advocates of trusteeship, this is an extreme view; most argue that, to be legitimate, trusteeship should be based on a commitment to eventual independence. Key to such an idea is the notion that the projects will be temporary. Earlier, the use of labels like 'temporary', interim', 'transitional' etc. in relation to ITA generically was discussed; in Chapter 6 it was suggested that this use ignores those (albeit all historical) projects conceived to be permanent, and other projects set indefinitely, and in Chapter 7 it was suggested that the remarkably ambitious enterprise associated with many ITA projects, notably 'state-building', does not in and of itself suggest a short duration.[531]

The prominent conception of the projects as temporary (e.g., as mentioned in Chapter 6, the 'transitional administrations' of the Brahimi Report), whether descriptively correct or not, raises the temporal duration of the projects to the level of a primary characteristic.[532] This, in turn, can have the effect of downgrading the importance of ITA as a focus for critical attention. If individual projects are not going to last long, why focus on them? Indeed, many commentators invoke the temporary nature of the ITA projects as a reason for distinguishing them from colonialism, or, put differently, to address the challenge they seem to pose to the idea of self-determination and independence.[533]

What lies behind these approaches are ideas as to the normative significance of a limited duration. For some, the temporal restriction is a mitigating factor: international trusteeship may be objectionable, for example on self-determination grounds, but it will not last long. For others, it is significant in reflecting the true

---

[530] The significance of the resolutions for external self-determination is discussed earlier in this chapter, text from n. 291. The purposes of the missions are discussed above, in ch. 6, *passim*. See also above, ch. 1, section 1.2.2.

[531] See above, ch. 7, section 7.6.

[532] See above, ch. 6, n. 151 and corresponding text.

[533] Jarat Chopra, for example, posits the 'purposefully temporary manner' of his concept of UN Civil Governance in Trust as the opposite of 'exploitation' in terms of the objective for territorial administration; see Chopra (above n. 12), 71. Fearon & Laitin, discussing both unilateral and multilateral interventions, state that: '...whereas classical imperialists conceived of their empires as indefinite in time, the agents of neotrusteeship want to exit as quickly as possible'; Fearon & Laitin (above n. 4), 7; see also ibid., 12. See also Ignatieff (above n. 4), 113– 15; Paris, 'International Peacebuilding' (above n. 12), 652; Knoll (above n. 9), *passim*.

nature of a trusteeship arrangement as something that should operate only until the people of the territory are deemed capable of self-administration; indeed, one of the core objectives of the mission should be to bring this situation about.[534] Trusteeship can then be presented as compatible with the right to self-determination, because it is aimed at achieving it as an end-point.[535]

As previously mentioned, Tom Parker defines 'trusteeship' as foreign administration bound to ensure eventual self-determination understood as independence.[536] On the basis that this obligation would exist were ITA projects placed under the UN Trusteeship system, but not necessarily if they operated under the aegis of the Security Council, Parker argues that the Trusteeship system should be revived for future such projects.[537] As the original theorists of colonial trusteeship sought to humanize existing and future arrangements through the idea of selfless administration and a general aspiration to improving local conditions, so commentators such as Parker seek to humanize the ITA projects of the 21st century through a clear commitment to improvement leading to eventual independence.[538]

Although the foregoing analysis in this chapter indicates that a commitment to independence was not evident in all instances of international trusteeship, even, it could be argued, the UN Trusteeship system prior to the advent of the post-Second World War self-determination entitlement, Parker's argument is illustrative of how some view the legitimacy of trusteeship and its relationship to the self-determination entitlement now. Interventionists such as Michael Ignatieff and Gerhard Kreijen advocate new arrangements assuming an eventual reversion to independence, necessarily involving a revision of the non-intervention aspect of the self-determination entitlement, but only on a temporary basis; others, such as Parker, who wish to humanize existing and future projects without going into the question as to whether the projects themselves are legitimate, seek to affirm the position that existed in relation to colonial trusteeship on the emergence of the self-determination entitlement: preparation should be made for self-government meaning independence. In both cases—creating new arrange-

---

[534] So, for example, Henry Perritt, discussing both plenary ITA projects and the interventions in Afghanistan and Iraq, states that 'the intervening parties and sanctioning authorities justified the trusteeship explicitly in terms of governing for...the purpose of preparing the...territory for eventual self-rule'; Perritt, 'Structures and Standards' (above n. 11), 399. Roland Paris distinguishes 'peacebuilding' missions generally from colonial rule on the grounds that the former are established 'with the goal of establishing conditions for war-shattered states to govern themselves'; Paris, 'International Peacebuilding' (above n. 12), 652.

[535] Richard Caplan states that '[t]he contradiction between executive international authority and local self-determination can only be overcome with the progressive transfer of responsibility to local authorities'; Caplan, *International Governance* (above n. 12), 194.

[536] See above, text accompanying nn. 284 *et seq.*

[537] Parker (above n. 11), *passim* and especially 12, 50.

[538] The original idea that trusteeship would humanize colonialism is discussed above, text accompanying n. 111 *et seq.*

ments and reconstituting existing arrangements—trusteeship is legitimized and even reconciled with self-determination because of the clear commitment to eventual independence.

Whereas, as mapped out above, the notion of international trusteeship as temporary was articulated implicitly and explicitly in the different ways non-ITA international trusteeship arrangements were conceived, with the post-Cold War plenary ITA missions it is invoked explicitly in the name given to the missions. For many commentators this reflects the idea that it is now beyond doubt, as was not the case with previous forms of international trusteeship, that the notion of progressive improvement leading to self-administration is both realizable and will be implemented in good faith by international administrators. The arrangements, then, are portrayed as not 'colonial' because the promise of eventual self-administration is seen as a genuine one; there will not be endless deferrals of independence.

This has purchase—temporary is seen as *really* meaning temporary—when it is coupled with the other legitimating ideas discussed in this section. Because the notion of governmental capacity seen as having created the need for ITA in some cases is supposedly based on a universal, universally-realizable standard, not the racialized, culturally-specific standard of civilization posited as the basis for earlier forms of trusteeship, the underlying reason for conceiving the arrangements as temporary—that the people's capacities will improve—is now rooted in a standard represented as meaningful to and realizable by them.

Since the standard according to which improvement is judged is now seen as legitimate, so the prospects for meeting this standard, and the likelihood that the temporary projects will indeed be temporary, are enhanced. Equally, because the actor involved in both fostering improvement and judging whether development has occurred is now conceived as selfless and humanitarian, critiques of colonial trusteeship based on the failure of the administering authorities to prepare people adequately for self-administration and the corrupted nature of these authorities' judgments on whether local capacity for self-administration existed can be dismissed. The 'international' in the form of both a universal normative framework that can serve as the legitimate basis for trusteeship, and a responsible actor to act as trustee, has created the conditions for 'true' or, in the words of James Hales, 'perfect' temporary trusteeship to exist.[539]

---

[539] In 1940 James Hales, discussing the 'perfect' model of colonial trusteeship, stated that the colonial guardian:

... cannot stay on any longer in the territory than he is required, but must cause sovereignty to be recognized as existing in the government of the territory, as soon as the latter is suitably trained to take over control. The essence of a perfect trusteeship is the gradual training of backward peoples towards nationhood and sovereignty. It implies the faithful application of this principle by the guardian, and its strict respect by all other existing nations.

Hales (above n. 107), 177.

8.7.3 Disassociation from the state-conducted models

The four features of the 'post-colonial' international territorial administration projects identified above—legal authority, the connection between the policies promoted and norms of international law, the identity of the administering actors, and the 'temporary' nature are all invoked as the basis for distinguishing these projects on a normative level from earlier administration arrangements involving individual states. The first three justifications can be seen as direct challenges to certain key objectional features of colonialism: ITA projects are not 'colonial', because they rest on international legal authority regarded to be in some way more legitimate than the legal authority, when it was evident, on which colonial arrangements were based; because the policies they are promoting are supposedly more legitimately 'universal' than the policies associated with colonialism; and because they are conducted by 'humanitarian' international organizations rather than individual states whose motives and actions are always to be questioned. The fourth justification—that the projects are temporary—is similarly invoked to distinguish ITA projects from open-ended colonial arrangements; further-more, it is sometimes invoked when the purchase of the colonial comparator is accepted, by way of a mitigating factor.[540]

The desire to disassociate international territorial administration from the UN Trusteeship system in particular can be seen, for example, in the reluctance to revive the Trusteeship Council as a mechanism for supervising the conduct of administration in East Timor.[541] As mentioned earlier, the Trusteeship system covered not only the former colonies of the defeated powers and the remaining Mandated territories; it was also open to any other territories 'voluntarily placed

---

[540] The interlinking significance of these different strands of justification can be seen in Robert Keohane's remark that:

> ...intervention creates a situation in which external authorities control the politics of a formerly independent state...a quasi-imperial situation in which outsiders rule by virtue of force, legitimated by their supposed good intentions and the pronouncement of international organizations...Such a situation is uncomfortable for post-colonial sensitivities, especially when it is prolonged.

RO Keohane, 'Political Authority after Intervention: Gradations in Sovereignty', ch. 8 in JL Holzgrefe and RO Keohane (eds), *Humanitarian Intervention: Ethical, Legal, and Political Dilemmas* (CUP, 2003), 296.

[541] On the Trusteeship Council, see the sources cited above, ch. 5, n. 44. For proposals for the reactivation of the Trusteeship system in regard to future territorial administration projects, see above n. 366. As for the issue of placing Kosovo under the system, as already mentioned, under Art. 78 of the UN Charter, the system was not open to the territories of member states. Kosovo was part of what was in 1999 called the Federal Republic of Yugoslavia, which claimed to be a member of the UN as the renamed continuation of the old Socialist Federal Republic of Yugoslavia, although this was disputed in a somewhat confused fashion within the UN; the state joined the UN in 2000, continuing this membership under the new name of Serbia and Montenegro from 2003 and as the Republic of Serbia on the independence of Montenegro in 2006. See above, ch. 4, n. 220 and sources cited therein. For a consideration of the alternative of designating Kosovo a 'Non-Self-Governing Territory', see Grant, 'Extending Decolonization' (above n. 9).

under the system by States responsible for their administration'.[542] Moreover, under the system the administering authority could be individual states or the UN itself.[543] East Timor fitted into the category of a Trust territory: it had been detached from what was in effect a colonial power; its people enjoyed a right of self-determination; it was not under the sovereignty of any other actor but rather had distinct legal personality by virtue of the self-determination entitlement; and the East Timorese were deemed incapable of self-administration in the short term following Indonesian withdrawal. The state 'responsible' for its administration could have been considered to be Portugal, as the former colonial power which, as discussed earlier in Chapter 5, although no longer enjoying territorial title because of the Indonesian occupation, still manifested certain residual prerogatives in relation to the territory before independence because of its original relationship, evidenced in its activity of raising East Timor's situation during this period, including bringing the *East Timor Case* to the International Court of Justice, and the continued UN references to it as the 'administering power'.[544]

More generally, commentators have proposed that the Trusteeship Council should be revived to provide oversight in relation to ITA missions.[545] However, at the time of writing there seemed to be a general international consensus that the Council should be abolished, as proposed by then UN Secretary-General Kofi Annan and endorsed by the General Assembly in 2005.[546] Attention has shifted towards the Peacebuilding Commission, but at the time of writing there was no mandate given to that body to exercise the kind of oversight in relation to ITA that was the case with the Trusteeship Council.[547] The Brahimi Report on UN

[542] UN Charter, Art. 77. See above ch. 5, n. 45 and accompanying text and the discussion above, in this chapter, text accompanying n. 118.

[543] UN Charter, Art. 81. See the discussion above, ch. 5, section 5.3., text accompanying n. 48 and above, section 8.4, text accompanying n. 323.

[544] On Portugal's activity in raising the situation of East Timor, including bringing the *East Timor Case*, see above, ch. 5, n. 141 and accompanying text. On the continued references to Portugal as the 'administering power', see above, ch. 5, text accompanying n. 126 *et seq.*

[545] Ruffert (above n. 9), 631; Parker (above n. 11), 43–50. On the question of reviving the Council, see also International Commission on Intervention and State Sovereignty, *The Responsibility to Protect*, December 2001, available at <http://www.iciss.ca/pdf/Commission-Report.pdf> (hereinafter 'ICISS Report'), at 43, paras 5.22–5.23 (on the principles of Chapter XII generally, rather than the Trusteeship Council in particular); Caplan, *International Governance* (above n. 12), 249; Chesterman, *You, The People* (above n. 9), 55 and 152; Chesterman, 'Virtual Trusteeship' (above n. 9), 222; Fearon & Laitin (above n. 4), 34–35. See also the quotation by Michael Bothe and Thilo Marauhn, above, text accompanying n. 275. On accountability issues generally, see List of Sources, section 5.2.7 and the discussion below, ch. 9, text accompanying nn. 36 *et seq.*

[546] See 'In Larger Freedom, Towards Development, Security and Human Rights for All', Report of the Secretary-General, 21 March 2005, UN Doc. A/59/2005, Chapter V, Section B, paras 165–6 and section F, para. 218; *2005 World Summit Outcome*, GA Res. 60/1, 16 September 2005, para. 176.

[547] The creation of the Peacebuilding Commission was recommended by the General Assembly in 2005: see *2005 World Summit Outcome* (above n. 546), paras 97–105; on the establishment of the Commission, see SC Res. 1645, 20 December 2005; SC Res. 1646, 20 December 2005; GA Res. 60/180, 30 December 2005. More generally, see <http://www.un.org/peace/peacebuilding>.

peace operations of 2000, when considering what might be needed at the UN if steps should be taken to anticipate future 'transitional administrations', focused on the Secretariat exclusively.[548] No attention was given to the need for oversight mechanisms.

Why was the Trusteeship Council not revived to supervise the East Timor project, and why, in the light of that project and the other projects in Bosnia and Herzegovina and Kosovo, which continued after the independence of Timor-Leste, did states wish to see the Trusteeship Council scrapped? Was it because of a view that the Peacebuilding Commission would necessarily perform an equivalent supervisory role?

In the case of the non-revival for East Timor, clearly several potentially mediating factors were in play, including the fact that, as discussed in Chapter 5, East Timor had already been officially classified within the UN as a 'Non-Self-Governing Territory', as a former colony, a classification that continued until independence in 2002.[549] More generally, there appears to be a resistance at the UN to formalizing UN-conducted trusteeship as a general option within the range of international peace operations because of issues of resources and practicality.[550]

As mentioned above, the Trusteeship Council, like the Permanent Mandates Commission before it, was seen as a mechanism of accountability to provide third-party guarantees for trust; to ensure that the administration served the interests of the people of the territories.[551] To revive the Trusteeship Council or explicitly to provide for oversight of ITA by the Peacebuilding Commission would be to accept that the self-determination paradigm has somehow become qualified—that trusteeship is back as a legitimate feature of international public policy. Formalizing an accountability mechanism would inevitably represent the formalizing and legitimizing of trusteeship itself.

Yet for many states, particularly, obviously, G77 states, international trusteeship is not a legitimate international policy institution. Perhaps reflecting this, in discussing what might come after 'humanitarian' intervention in the context of

---

[548] In particular, creating a 'dedicated and distinct responsibility centre' for 'transitional administrations' rather than such missions operating through DPKO; see Panel on United Nations Peace Operations, Report to the United Nations Secretary-General, 21 August 2000, UN Doc. A/55/305-S/2000/809 (hereinafter 'Brahimi Report'), at 14, para 78.

[549] See the discussion above, ch. 5, n. 133 and accompanying text.

[550] The International Commission on Intervention and State Sovereignty stated in 2001 that:

[t]he strongest argument against the proposal [to resurrect trusteeship] is probably practical: the cost of such an operation for the necessarily long time it would take to recreate civil society and rehabilitate the infrastructure in such a state. There must be real doubts about the willingness of governments to provide those kinds of resources, other than on a very infrequent and ad hoc basis.

ICISS Report (above n. 545), at 43, para. 5.2.4. On the resistance to ITA on the grounds of practicality, see also the Brahimi Report (above n. 548), at 13–14, para. 78.

[551] On these mechanisms, see above, n. 411 and accompanying text.

its 'responsibility to protect', the International Commission on Intervention and State Sovereignty stated in 2001 that:

[t]here is always likely in the UN to be a generalized resistance to any resurrection of the 'trusteeship' concept, on the ground that it represents just another kind of intrusion into internal affairs.[552]

It might be speculated, then, that states might be prepared to turn a blind eye to international trusteeship on an ad hoc basis, but formally to acknowledge its existence generally would be a step too far.[553]

As far as the Trusteeship Council is concerned, if there is no general acknowledgement that trusteeship is back, then one cannot invoke this as the basis for reactivating mechanisms for guaranteeing the performance of trusteeship missions. Thus, ironically, the denial of a dedicated body concerned with accountability for trusteeship in particular places is the price paid for a rejection of trusteeship generally. In an unfortunate coupling, unaccountability in certain instances is tied to the affirmation of self-determination in general.

Another potentially significant explanation for the non-revival of the Trusteeship Council is the normative portrayal of international organizations mentioned earlier. Whereas colonial trusteeship was seen as requiring international oversight because of concerns that, without such checks and balances, states would act in a self-interested and exploitative manner, the normative portrayal of international organizations as essentially humanitarian and selfless has the effect of downgrading the significance of, and even extinguishing completely, the issue of accountability.[554]

---

[552] ICISS Report (above n. 545), at 43, para. 5.2.4.

[553] Matthias Ruffert, although himself advocating the revival of the Trusteeship Council (see above n. 545), speculates that it was not revived to supervise the projects in Kosovo and East Timor 'because of its link to colonialism'; Ruffert (above n. 9), 631. When considering the fact that the Trusteeship Council was not revived, Simon Chesterman states that 'direct associations with colonialism would be politically prohibitive'; Chesterman, *You, The People* (above n. 9), 33 and Chesterman, 'Virtual Trusteeship' (above n. 9), 222 and S Chesterman, 'Occupation as Liberation: International Humanitarian Law and Regime Change', 18:3 (2004) *Ethics & International Affairs* 51, 58.

[554] In the context of occupation, Steven Ratner observes that:

...the equation between the multinational nature of the occupying force and perceptions of impartiality seems to translate into limited need for accountability as well—as if multinationality were itself a form of or a substitute for accountability.

This dynamic suggests the somewhat subversive possibility that democratic occupiers face greater accountability regarding their occupying forces than do international institutions [...]

...the closer scrutiny of occupying troops by individual democratic governments compared to that of transitional administrators is a response to the increased likelihood of abuse when only one state is in charge of an occupation...while transitional administrations receive less scrutiny than occupations, they probably need it less.

Ratner (above n. 9), 716–17. Richard Caplan, however, states that '[a]n international administration is...subject to constraints that an occupying power can more easily elude—with respect to the transfer of authority to local officials, for example, or the award of reconstruction contracts

The underlying objective of ensuring that trusteeship is conducted in good faith is pursued through the choice of the administering actor, rather than the operation of a dedicated international oversight mechanism. Now that the administering actor *is* the United Nations—the actor that would safeguard the interests of the people through supervising the conduct of administration by individual states—the need for a supervisory mechanism is obviated. Whereas with states, good faith and selflessness are questioned, with the United Nations they are assumed.

This outcome also avoids the contradictory situation of the United Nations supervising itself; in monitoring the administering authorities in Trust territories, the various Organs involved acted on behalf of the UN as a whole. In this sense, there was a distinction between the two and, thus, the accountability mechanism could be understood to be of a third-party nature. By contrast, had the UN 'itself' ever been utilized as an administering authority, this particular notion of a formal separation between the scrutineer and the scrutinized would have dissolved.

The present section has illustrated how the 'post-colonial' administration projects have been distinguished normatively from their colonial forebears, in the sense that they have become acceptable in practice within the mainstream international policy framework despite operating in many respects like those predecessors. Whether this normative distinction is supportable, however, is, of course, another question, and one which will be addressed in the following chapter.[555]

8.8 Conclusion

When discussing the nature of the activity performed by OHR in Bosnia and Herzegovina, the (partly internationalized) Constitutional Court in that country made the following observation:

the...role of the High Representative, as agent for the international community, is not unprecedented...similar functions are known from other countries in special political circumstances. Pertinent examples are the Mandates under the regime of the League of Nations and, in some respects, Germany and Austria after the Second World War. Though recognized as sovereign, the States concerned were placed under international supervision, and foreign authorities acted in these States, on behalf of the international community, substituting themselves for the domestic authorities. Acts by such...authorities were often passed in the name of the States under supervision.[556]

to foreign firms and other aspects of post-war reconstruction'; Caplan, *International Governance* (above n. 12), 4.

[555] Some of the works in sections 5.2.4 and 5.2.5 of the List of Sources also discuss this question.
[556] *Case No. U 9/00* (evaluating the Law on State Border Service), Constitutional Court of Bosnia and Herzegovina, 3 November 2000, para. 5. For commentary, see the sources cited above, ch. 2, n. 70.

In this passage, the Court captures the essence of the commonality operating as between international territorial administration and the other state-conducted manifestations of foreign territorial administration discussed in this chapter, insofar as the activity performed is concerned: 'foreign authorities...acted in these States' performing administrative functions—'substituting themselves for the domestic authorities'. Although the Court is incorrect in referring to Mandate and Trust territories as 'states', the suggestion of entities that are juridically distinct from the territory of the administering authority does fit with a key feature of the arrangements.[557]

The Court is concerned with a particular sub-group of arrangements manifesting the commonality it identifies in the activity involved: institutions where the administering authority is acting 'on behalf of the international community' in a particular way. The Court discusses commonality in terms of the activity performed; the purposes served by this activity—the 'special political circumstances' that led to the projects' creation—are not explored. How commonality in this second, purposive sense can also be identified has been the task of the previous two chapters, in the case of ITA, and the present chapter, in the case of other forms of foreign territorial administration.

The present enquiry adopts a broader focus of analysis than the Court, identifying the common enterprise of 'foreign territorial administration' in which the different policy institutions are best situated. In terms of the status of the territorial unit affected, situations where the unit is regarded as a 'distinct' entity are considered. Whereas distinctiveness may subsist because the entity is regarded legally to be not part of the territory of the administering state, it may subsist for other reasons, in circumstances where the territory is legally part of that state, as was the case with certain forms of colonialism.

Considering a broader category of territorial administration of entities regarded as distinct from the administering actors does not, by itself, add anything to the scope of projects that fall within the Court's view, since the Court focuses on two particular internationalized versions of this activity. As discussed, in all of the ITA projects and the Mandate and Trusteeship systems, the administering authorities did not enjoy title over the territories concerned. When one drops the Court's particular internationalized focus, however, the view is broadened significantly. It takes in protection, colonialism, occupation trusteeship, and the projects involving administration by representative bodies. The analysis presented in this chapter suggests that, despite key differences between these institutions in terms of the type of 'internationalization' involved, the way the arrangements operated and the purposes with which they were associated manifest commonalities in many areas.

---

[557] On the legal status of Mandated and Trust territories, see above, ch. 5, section 5.3. In discussing the different meanings of the word 'state' in international law, as already mentioned (see above, ch. 5, n. 53), James Crawford observes that 'A' class Mandated territories were treated as 'states' for the purposes of nationality, but not more generally.

Focusing exclusively on international territorial administration and the Mandate and Trust arrangements excludes other activities which, in terms of the purposes involved, operate in a similar fashion, even if they are internationalized in a different sense, or not internationalized at all. In this chapter, it has been argued that the institution of international territorial administration forms part of a wider family of policy institutions covering, in addition, colonialism, protection, administration by the representative bodies, the Mandate and Trusteeship systems, and occupation. These institutions constitute a 'family' because they involve a common activity performed in pursuance to a common range of purposes, although these purposes vary significantly both within and between the different institutions. In most cases, the arrangements are understood in terms of 'trust', and the analysis in this chapter has argued that a concept of 'international trusteeship' is a meaningful umbrella term to cover most forms of foreign territorial administration, including ITA.

The use of particular forms of international trusteeship altered significantly over the course of the 20th century, with changes mediated by the radical shift in the fortunes of the colonial and Mandate/Trusteeship institutions in particular brought about by the self-determination entitlement. With the end of the First World War, the existing arrangements involving protection, colonialism, occupation, and administration by representative bodies were joined by two new models: first, the partially-internationalized model of state administration with international organization-supervision of the Mandate system and, secondly, the fully-internationalized, but comparatively under-utilized, model of international territorial administration. The state-conducted models continued (the Mandate model under a new guise) in the immediate aftermath of the Second World War, but then the entire notion of foreign territorial administration came under threat with the call for self-determination. All the existing state-conducted models were either terminated, converted into 'legitimate' arrangements via self-determination consultations, or perpetuated by the states concerned in spite of the delegitimizing effect of the self-determination entitlement. By contrast, new forms of the internationally-conducted model—ITA—continued to be introduced, not only to perform a special decolonization role, but also for a broader range of purposes.

By the turn of the 21st century, the model of international territorial administration was going through something of a resurgence, with the plenary Kosovo and East Timor projects, the partial projects in Bosnia and Herzegovina, Northern Iraq, 'refugee' camps and aid distribution programmes, and the various regimes of international appointees on locally-based institutions. Proposals for 'saving failed states' via some form of international trusteeship made originally after the end of the Cold War continued to have purchase internationally.

International territorial administration remains on the international policy agenda, and in understanding whether projects of this nature may take place in the future, it is necessary to take into account not only the purposes with which the institution has been associated in the past, as outlined in the previous two chapters, but also how the institution relates to its colonial precursors, as outlined above.[558]

[558] For examples of proposals made for new forms of international trusteeship at the time this book was completed, see above, ch. 2, nn. 123 and 124.

9

Analysing International Territorial Administration

9.1 Introducing a Policy Institution

9.1.1 International territorial administration as an 'institution'

With the two high-profile UN administration projects beginning in 1999 in East Timor and Kosovo, the idea of handing over the administration of territory to international actors either partially or completely began to be considered in academic and policy circles as a distinctive activity, worthy of consideration in its own right. This idea of international territorial administration (ITA) as distinctive is supportable because international actors do not normally administer territory or, putting the emphasis in reverse, territory and its people are not normally administered directly by international actors. Since it involves a particular activity ('territorial administration') performed by a particular actor (an 'international actor'), and because a direct opposition operates between the spatial identities of international actors and those 'local' actors who normally carry out the activity, as suggested in Chapter 1, international territorial administration can be regarded as a distinctive 'practice'. Moreover, if, as in Chapter 2, one considers the number of times projects involving this type of arrangement have been deployed at periodic intervals since the founding of the League of Nations, it is possible to regard this 'practice' as 'established', viz., regularly used over a long period of time, and thus conforming to one meaning of the term 'institution'.

Conceptualizing the activity of ITA as an 'institution' takes the idea of ITA as a distinctive activity to its logical conclusion, establishing what is implied when commentators present the administration projects as *sui generis*, in a class apart from, say, other UN peace operations. However, it does not take things very far; specifically, it leaves unresolved the issue of whether the commonality operating across the projects in the activity performed is matched by commonality in the reasons why this activity is being introduced. In consequence, the basis for bundling the projects together is somewhat superficial.

As explained in Chapter 1, certain commentators have made some reference to some of the purposes served by some of the projects, but oversimplification is commonplace, for example, when territorial administration by international organizations is presented as essentially a 'state-building' enterprise in a 'post-conflict' context. A brief consideration of some of the other purposes associated with the projects in that chapter revealed the misleading nature of these representations.

This book has sought to provide an alternative explanation of the purposes associated with the ITA projects based on a sustained evaluation of the projects' history. The point of the enterprise was not merely to narrate the history of international territorial administration projects; it was also to analyse the institution of international territorial administration—the projects in a collective sense—as a matter of policy and consider whether it can be regarded as a 'policy institution', viz. an established practice that operates in a common way on a purposive level. In other words, the objective was to see whether projects can be understood collectively in terms of the uses to which they have been and are being put. This would then enable a sustained consideration of the extent to which the projects compare with state-conducted activities such as colonial trusteeship, and, in turn, a re-evaluation of the history of 'international trusteeship', its progressive internationalization, and how it is legitimated in the 'post-colonial' era.

This final chapter reviews what has been established in the foregoing analysis, and then considers how ITA might be appraised in the light of what has been said about it so far.

9.1.2 International territorial administration as a 'policy institution'

9.1.2.1 *International territorial sovereignty?*

The enquiry into the policy role of ITA began in Chapter 3 with a consideration of Méir Ydit's thesis that sought to establish purposive commonality across some of the earlier, mostly League-era ITA projects (and other state-conducted projects during the same period), not in terms of the conduct of administration but, rather, in the vesting of sovereignty (as ownership) in the administering actors involved. The question of whether this concept—termed 'international territorial sovereignty'—might assist in explaining the purposes associated with some or all of the ITA projects led to a detailed consideration in Chapters 4 and 5 of the legal status of most of the territories in which the projects have taken place.

As a result of this analysis, it was suggested that Ydit's explanation was based on a false premise; in practice, international organizations have never enjoyed title over the territories they have administered. It was necessary, therefore, to consider alternative explanations for the projects that do not necessarily entail 'international territorial sovereignty'. However, the quest to establish the legal status of the territories subject to international administration was not in vain; appreciating this status, alongside a range of other considerations, would be necessary for an understanding of the purposes associated with the projects.

9.1.2.2 *Purposive analysis and the policy institution*

Broad-ranging purposive analysis was conducted in Chapter 6. Having moved beyond Ydit's approach to international territorial administration as a mere corollary to international territorial sovereignty, the focus returned to where it had started off, on ITA itself. The history of each of the administration projects set out in the earlier chapters was drawn upon to identify the purposes with which the projects were associated. Although it was not possible to explain all the projects in terms of a single purpose (e.g., reconstruction after conflict), the case was made for situating the projects within a single, albeit variated, purposive framework.

It was argued that each project can be understood as a response to one or both of two perceived 'problems' invoked in relation to the conduct of territorial administration by local actors. In the first place, the identity of those local actors is deemed problematic in terms of the relationship between it and a claim to the territory concerned: what was termed a 'sovereignty problem'. In the second place, the nature of administration performed by those actors is deemed to be problematic: what was termed a 'governance problem'.

It was suggested that all the administration projects can be explained on a purposive level in terms of a response to one or both of the two perceived 'problems' identified. Since not all projects cater to both, as far as focusing on the two problems is concerned, a single explanation for all the projects is not provided. However, a common feature is evident in the manner in which the institution responds to the problems, since this response is essentially the same in relation to both. As already mentioned, the distinctive nature of the activity of ITA is rooted in the spatial identity of the administering actor: as 'international', it is opposed to the 'local' identity of the actors who usually perform the role of territorial administration. When the purposes associated with ITA are considered, it becomes evident that this spatial opposition is also central to the way the institution is understood to perform its policy role.

As far as a perceived 'sovereignty problem' is concerned, the 'international' identity of the administering actor lies at the heart of the use of ITA; by virtue of this identity, the actor is considered 'neutral' as concerns the interests of the actors in relation to whom the sovereignty problem is considered to subsist (for example when rival states claim title to the territory placed under international administration). In consequence, ITA is understood to act as the temporary or permanent solution to the problem.

As far as a perceived 'governance problem' is concerned, the 'international' identity of the administering actor is relevant in a more limited sense. Here, the spatial opposition is not between 'international' and 'national' in general, but between 'international' and the particular local actors who are being displaced in the activity of governance. It reflects the fact that ITA is being used because it is administration by someone 'other' than the local actors who are deemed incapable and/or unwilling to perform governance either at all, or in a particular manner. Here, 'international' denotes expertise and conformity to the policy objectives that are deemed worthy of implementation in the territory concerned (e.g., free and fair elections).

So, the distinctive nature of the activity, which formed the basis for establishing international territorial administration as an 'institution' in Chapter 1, is also central to understanding ITA's policy role. Because of this connection between the institution and all the purposes with which it is associated, the institution can be understood to be a 'policy institution', meaning an established practice that manifests certain elements of commonality as a matter of purpose or policy. By situating current and recent ITA projects in their proper historical context and establishing the broad range of policies with which they have been associated, the book reveals the existence of a policy institution that has hitherto not been conceptualized. In doing so, it counters the ahistorical and technocratic presentations of the recent administration projects and enables a greater appreciation of the potential and normative implications of these and future projects.

9.1.3 Hidden projects and the proper framework for analysis

In exploring the possibility of a policy institution based on the administration of territory by international actors, this book uncovered a number of projects, notably the EU Administration of Mostar, the UN administration of Eastern Slavonia, the role of OHR in Bosnia and Herzegovina, and the role of UNHCR in administering 'refugee' camps, which were largely invisible within general commentaries on international organizations and even, in some cases, in the studies that have been made of the recent administration projects.[1]

If the impetus for such studies comes from the distinctiveness of the activity conducted, there would seem to be no grounds for focusing exclusively on particular international organizations or situations of plenary administration. Given this, how might the adoption by some of a partial focus be explained? It was suggested above that the distinctiveness of the activity conducted is a somewhat elemental basis for analysing ITA projects collectively. In every other respect, there is no commonality; thus bundling the projects together might seem somewhat arbitrary. Perhaps because of this, a focus on the United Nations and/or situations of plenary administration was adopted, to achieve a more meaningful commonality across the projects under evaluation by reducing the differences between them.

---

[1] To give an example: in one 2001 survey of the UN-conducted administration projects, mention of the two-year Eastern Slavonia project is absent; see MJ Matheson, 'United Nations Governance of Post-Conflict Societies', 95 (2001) *AJIL* 76, reprinted as 'United Nations Governance of Post-Conflict Societies: East Timor and Kosovo', in MC Bassiouni (ed.), *Post-Conflict Justice* (Transnational Publishers, 2002), 523.

Yet such an approach, however more focused, is still operating at the superficial level of the nature of the activity performed and the identity of the actors performing it. When one turns to the relatively complex matter of the purposes associated with the projects, and considers this in conjunction with the nature of the activity performed and the identity of the administering actors, there is a relatively sophisticated basis for deciding which projects to include and exclude, provided that purposive simplification has been avoided.[2]

When a proper purposive approach is taken, it becomes possible to see more clearly where the boundaries of analysis might be set if the objective is to compare like with like. For example, in understanding the commonality between the purposes associated with the use of League administration in Leticia and UN administration in West Irian and Eastern Slavonia—the attempted 'neutralization' of a contested territory—it becomes apparent that the exclusion of League-era projects from consideration is unhelpful. In sum, it is suggested that the boundaries might be more usefully set at all administration projects, partial and plenary, involving any international organization, not just the United Nations, and also covering the involvement of international appointees on locally-based bodies such as courts and tribunals.

9.1.4 Crossing the boundaries—situating the policy institution within a broader context

Even if, as argued, the institution of international territorial administration offers a more helpful framework within which to consider the legal and policy issues raised by the projects when compared to a narrower frame of reference, conceptual links exist between the projects and other activities outside the boundaries of the institution that are illuminating for such legal and policy analysis. Hence, the study in this book did not stop with the establishment of the policy institution in Chapter 6, but went on to consider the links operating between the policy institution and two further classes of policy institution: first, other policy institutions conducted by international organizations that seek to achieve the same ends but through different means (e.g., international tribunals and the implementation of international law); and, secondly, other policy institutions conducted by individual states that operate in the same manner as ITA (e.g., the Trusteeship system arrangements).

Only with an awareness of these links is it possible to appreciate fully the role played by ITA generally and individual ITA projects in particular. More fundamentally, establishing these links enables an understanding of how ITA fits within broader trends in international law and public policy, both generally and in relation to the concept of 'international trusteeship' in particular.

---

[2] See the discussion above, ch. 1, section 1.2.2.

9.1.4.1 *Implementing international law and policy*

Understanding how the purposes with which ITA has been associated reflect certain areas of international law and public policy assists in understanding what it is that the administration projects are trying to achieve. Moreover, understanding ITA as one of several international mechanisms that exist to implement international law and policy, and appreciating how the institution compares with these other mechanisms in the way it performs this role, assists in seeking to explain why ITA is used in particular situations, and what consequence this has for the involvement of other mechanisms in relation to the same territory.

9.1.4.2 *Foreign territorial administration*

Appreciating how ITA relates to the colonial paradigm, and considering it as part of a broader family of policy institutions involving 'foreign territorial administration' and constituting 'international trusteeship' enables one to know where to look, and where not to look, in seeking to draw lessons from the state analogues for current and future administration projects.

Looking to instances of foreign territorial administration generally also assists in appreciating the historical origins of the ITA institution, as an internationalized version of policy institutions conducted by individual states. This in turn provides a new narrative strand to the histories of colonialism generally and colonial trusteeship in particular, revealing new linkages between these histories and the history of international organizations and demonstrating what Nathaniel Berman has characterized as the 'ability of the colonial imagination to reinvent itself under changing conditions'.[3] From one perspective, the United Nations is seen as the international mechanism through which the decolonization process was engineered, via important General Assembly resolutions on self-determination, such as Resolutions 1514 and 1541,[4] and the transformation of UN membership with the admission of newly-independent states.[5] What can now be appreciated is that in a different arena of UN activity—field operations—in certain respects the colonial paradigm survived in a form where the organization itself took on the role previously performed by the 'metropolitan' state.

---

[3] N Berman, 'In the Wake of Empire', 14 (1998–99) *American University International Law Review* 1521.

[4] GA Res. 1514 (XV), 14 December 1960 and GA Res. 1541 (XV), 15 December 1960. See the commentary above, ch. 5, section 5.2, *passim*.

[5] On the UN and decolonization, see, e.g., DA Kay, 'The United Nations and Decolonization', in J Barros (ed.), *The United Nations: Past, Present and Future* (Free Press, 1972), 143, *passim*; DA Kay, 'The Politics of Decolonization: The New Nations and the United Nations Political Process', 21 (1967) *International Organizations* 786. This topic is covered by much of the general self-determination literature; see List of Sources, section 5.4.

9.2 Analysing the Policy Institution

The conceptualization of international territorial administration as a policy institution facilitates analysis of the complex legal and policy issues relating to the administration projects by providing an understanding of the broader historical and political context within which the projects operate. This context becomes apparent when individual projects are considered as particular manifestations of the policy institution, the relationship between the institution and other policy institutions conducted by international organizations is appreciated, and the institution is understood as part of a broader family of policy institutions involving foreign territorial administration.

Although such analysis is beyond the scope of this book, it is perhaps in order to consider what the conclusions drawn above suggest about how it might proceed.[6]

9.2.1 Legal issues

Although this book was not aimed at resolving all the legal issues raised by international territorial administration, it was necessary to address some of these issues as part of the process of purposive and policy analysis.

The legal status of most of the territories in which ITA projects have been implemented was established in Chapters 4 and 5 as part of the enquiry into the possible policy role of 'international territorial sovereignty'—the vesting of sovereignty as title in the international organizations involved. This analysis demonstrated that title cannot be assumed from the mere enjoyment of territorial control, and that it is necessary to identify the basis on which such control is exercised when seeking to appreciate the juridical effect of such control on the status of the territory affected.

As far as the legal authority provided for the administration projects is concerned, in Chapter 8 this was reviewed in relation to UNMIK and UNTAET in particular, when the question of whether 'trusteeship' presupposes an 'imposed' rather than 'consensual' arrangement was addressed, and in relation to all of the projects as part of the discussion of the role of legal authority in legitimizing the 'post-colonial' administration projects.

---

[6] I discuss this topic further in R Wilde, 'Representing International Territorial Administration: A Critique of Some Approaches', 15 (2004) *EJIL* 71 and ch. 11 in H Charlesworth and J-M Coicaud (eds), *Fault Lines of International Legitimacy* (United Nations University Press, forthcoming); R Wilde, 'Legitimacy and Accountability of International Administrations: A Commentary on Four Papers', paper presented at the 2005 *ESIL Research Forum*, Graduate Institute of International Studies (HEI), Geneva, 26–28 May 2005, obtainable from <http://www.esil-sedi.org>. For the work of others, see List of Sources, sections 5.1 and 5.2.

Now that the contours of the ITA policy institution have been delineated, it is possible to proceed with a thorough analysis of the legal issues raised by it. Being aware of the purposes associated with the projects will assist in explaining the choices that were made in terms of the legal authority provided. For example, the authorization of UNTEA in a treaty between the Netherlands and Indonesia[7] is explained when the objective of that project—providing a buffer between territorial control by the two states as a means of resolving a dispute between them—is appreciated.

Understanding the policy background will also assist in assessing whether the authority provided is lawful as a matter of general international law and, when this authority comes from the United Nations, the law of that organization. Equally, it is crucial for understanding whether the exercise of territorial administration is lawful according to the law of international organizations. In either case, considering the nature of the activity being authorized or conducted is only part of the picture: it is also necessary to know the purposes associated with this activity. So one would identify these purposes (Chapter 6), consider how they can be understood in terms of the implementation of international legal obligations on the part of the host territorial unit and the international organization involved (Chapter 7), and then analyse the compatibility of this arrangement with the role of the United Nations (in terms of providing legal authority where relevant), and the role of international organizations generally, including the UN where relevant (in terms of carrying out the mandate).[8]

An appreciation of the purposes associated with the projects also assists in addressing the question of the appropriate standards governing the conduct of the projects.[9] For example, in seeking to determine the suitability of occupation law, it is possible to enter the debate discussed in Chapter 8, about whether this law is problematic in the context of 'transformatory' situations, with a greater appreciation of the implications for the nature of the enterprise engaged in during the ITA missions.[10] A regulatory regime concerned with maintaining the status quo would seem to fit with those ITA projects

---

[7] Agreement between Indonesia and the Netherlands Concerning West New Guinea (West Irian), 15 August 1962, 437 UNTS 273.

[8] For commentary on the competence of the UN to authorize territorial administration, see List of Sources, section 5.2.6.

[9] For commentary touching on issues of applicable law, see List of Sources, section 5.2.7. Further source material relevant to this enquiry in particular contexts is contained above, ch. 1, n. 64. On Kosovo in particular, see also Ombudsperson Institution in Kosovo, 'Special report no. 1 on the compatibility with recognized international standards of UNMIK Regulation No. 2000/47 on the Status, Privileges and Immunities of KFOR and UNMIK and Their Personnel in Kosovo (18 August 2000) and on the implementation of the above regulation', 26 April 2001, available at <http://www.ombudspersonkosovo.org>, para. 23; European Commission for Democracy through Law (Venice Commission), Opinion on Human Rights in Kosovo: Possible Establishment of Review Mechanisms (Opinion No. 280/2004, Strasbourg, 11 October 2004), available at <http://www.venice.coe.int>.

[10] On this debate, see above, ch. 8, n. 129 and accompanying text *et seq*.

concerned exclusively with a 'sovereignty problem'—i.e., the reason for the mission is the identity of the administering actor—whereas such a regime would be at odds with some of the more ambitious ITA projects concerned with 'governance problems'. Bundling all the projects together under an essentialized and simplified category concerning legal and political transformation misses this distinction.[11]

9.2.2 Legitimacy

Situating international territorial administration within a broader 'family' category of 'foreign territorial administration' is helpful not only in terms of establishing its analogous relationship to other, relatively familiar, international policy institutions; it is also crucial in appraising questions of legitimacy. Identifying the close resemblance between ITA and the other state-conducted policy institutions in the family, and considering the fact that these other institutions were ostensibly repudiated in the decolonization era, calls the legitimacy of ITA into question. What was it about ITA that enabled it to avoid the 'colonial' label in the second half of the 20th century?

In seeking to answer this question in Chapter 8, it was illustrated that the two 'international' elements of ITA—the identity of the administering actors discussed in Chapter 1, on the one hand, and the use of international territorial

---

[11] On the applicability of the laws of war to peace operations generally, see above, ch. 8, n. 260. On the fit between occupation law and the ITA projects, Eyal Benvenisti states that UNTAET and UNMIK are 'trusteeship of the kind the law of occupation is designed to address'; E Benvenisti, *The International Law of Occupation* (paperback edn, Princeton University Press, 2004), xvi. See also the discussion in A Roberts, 'Transformative Military Occupation: Applying the Laws of War and Human Rights', 100 (2006) *AJIL* 580. Others are more sceptical; Simon Chesterman states that '[a]s the purpose of transitional administration is precisely to change the laws and institutions, further legal authority is therefore required'; S Chesterman, *You, The People: The United Nations, Transitional Administrations, and State-Building* (OUP, 2004), 7. The principles of occupation law are 'at odds' with those ITA projects '... where the entire purpose of temporary occupation was to change the political structures in the occupied territory'; ibid., 145. Discussing this issue, Steven Ratner states that 'for international organization missions, the status quo is an obstacle to be overcome, not a situation to maintain'; SR Ratner, 'Foreign Occupation and International Territorial Administration: The Challenges of Convergence', 16 (2005) *EJIL* 695, 700. As part of his more general thesis about the problems of applying occupation law to transformational interventions, David Scheffer considers peacekeeping in particular, and argues that in this context the full operation of occupation law may be 'inappropriate and even undesirable in many situations'; D Scheffer, 'Beyond Occupation Law', 97 (2003) *AJIL* 842, 848. Scheffer's argument covers not only the question of occupation law prohibiting certain aspects of transformatory projects, but also, more broadly, whether by itself occupation law is sufficient as a general regime of regulation, given the wide-ranging activities engaged in during such occupations. He argues that '... the dominant premise of occupation law has been that regulation is required for the military occupation of foreign territory, but not necessarily for its transformation' ibid., 848, footnote omitted. For Scheffer, a wider normative regime is necessary, taking in 'principles of modern international law pertaining, for example, to human rights, self-determination, the environment, and economic development...'; ibid., 843.

administration to implement international law and policy discussed in Chapter 7, on the other—are vital. As explained in Chapter 8, these two elements, together with the legal authority often provided for the projects by the UN Security Council, form a triptych of 'international' mirror opposites to the three 'statist' aspects of the colonial paradigm—individual states pursuing individual policy objectives in arrangements 'imposed' in an unjustified manner by them on the territories concerned—that are key as far as the delegitimized nature of that paradigm is concerned.

So, the identity of the administering actors is not only important in terms of the purposes associated with the projects, and thereby integral to an understanding of ITA as a policy institution; it is also important when the analysis shifts to a consideration of the legitimacy of this policy institution. Equally, exploring how the purposes associated with ITA relate to areas of international law and policy not only provides a greater appreciation of the policy role of ITA; it also helps to explain how this policy role is appraised normatively. In other words, it tells us not only what ITA seeks to achieve, but also why ITA is considered legitimate in performing such a function.

Considering the genesis of international territorial administration as an internationalized version of a state-conducted paradigm, the institution is part of the broader move towards international law and institutions that took place in the 20th century, particularly in its second half.[12] Traditional conceptions of international organizations and international law saw things in terms of an institutional and normative framework to constrain and regulate the relations between states.[13] Now, of course, the subject-matter of international law and the activities of international organizations also concern what happens within states, notably in relation to human rights. The history of ITA underscores a key institutional counterpart to such developments; this particular move is inward-facing, towards the direct governance of particular territories.

In performing the role of administering district territories, and being considered legitimate in doing so, international organizations have displaced states. The CPA in Iraq is regarded as aberrant, 'colonial'; UNMIK in Kosovo is regarded as part of a species of legitimate international peace operations, and 'humanitarian'. Explaining how international territorial administration has been, and is, normatively distinguished from colonialism within international public policy, as was done in Chapter 8, is not, of course, the same as holding that such a normative distinction has merit. Rather, it provides the starting point for a critical evaluation of the legitimacy of the policy institution, by mapping out some of the sites in which the current structures of its legitimation are located: the nature of international organizations, the substantive content of international law and

---

[12] For a critical treatment of this, see, e.g., D Kennedy, 'The Move to Institutions', 8 (1986–87) *Cardozo Law Review* 841.
[13] On international organizations, see the sources listed above, ch. 1, n. 86.

public policy, and the authority of the UN Security Council to impose binding obligations on states in certain areas.

As scholars within the tradition of 'ideology critique' applying the methodology of 'immanent critique' assert, taking the conventional structure of legitimation seriously—even if it is pleaded in bad faith—provides a powerful tool for critique.[14] The point is not to validate the rhetorical structure, but to explore its logical conclusions, potentially revealing limitations and internal contradictions. The analysis carried out in this book is intended to lay the groundwork for such 'immanent critique', by identifying the contours of the policy institution that is to be appraised. For example, to say that part of the reason for the UN administration in East Timor was to engage in 'state-building' is not to say that this project was, *ipso facto*, legitimate; rather, it enables legitimacy to be appraised by establishing how the project was understood by those carrying it out. Unlike in other areas of international policy, it was necessary to reveal the very existence of this policy institution before critical evaluation could begin.[15]

Although a comprehensive critical evaluation is beyond the scope of this book, how might it proceed?[16] In Chapter 8, ITA was established as part of a broader family of institutions involving foreign territorial administration; in particular, connections with colonial trusteeship were explored. In the light of this analysis, one way of appraising the legitimacy of ITA is to compare its operation with colonialism, and to seek to learn lessons for its operation from the practice of colonial trusteeship.[17] More importantly, however, the connection with colonialism

---

[14] On ideology critique generally, see, e.g., JB Thompson, *Ideology and Modern Culture: Critical Social Theory in the Era of Mass Communication* (Stanford University Press, 1990); T Eagleton, *Ideology: An Introduction* (Verso, 1991); S Žižek (ed.), *Mapping Ideology* (Verso, 1994). For the application of 'immanent critique' to international legal texts, see S Marks, *The Riddle of All Constitutions: International Law, Democracy and the Critique of Ideology* (OUP, 2000); S Marks, 'Big Brother is Bleeping Us—With the Message that Ideology Doesn't Matter', 12 (2001) *EJIL* 109.

[15] For example, in considering democratic ideas in international law, Susan Marks was able to begin at the stage of critique, since an established body of work on this topic was already in existence. See Marks, *The Riddle of All Constitutions* (above n. 14).

[16] For discussions of various legitimacy issues by academic commentators, see, e.g., the works in List of Sources, section 5.2.4 (on questions of legitimacy other than gender) and section 5.2.5 (on gender issues).

[17] Jarat Chopra states that:

[h]owever unpalatable the experience of colonial administration, its origins and motivations including the experience of the mandates and trusteeships, it nevertheless developed many mechanisms for administering large populations and geographic areas. If truly international administration is to be effective, UN planners may have to revisit the lessons of this experience.

J Chopra, 'UN Civil Governance-in-Trust', in TG Weiss (ed.) *The United Nations and Civil Wars* (Lynne Rienner, 1995), 70, at 74. When setting out the contours of the 'responsibility to rebuild' that forms part of its 'responsibility to protect,' the International Commission on Intervention and State Sovereignty implicitly references the utility of drawing lessons from colonial practice when it discusses the provisions in the UN Charter concerning Trust Territories:

[u]seful guidelines for the behaviour of intervening authorities during a military intervention in failed states, and in the follow-up period, might be found in a constructive adaptation of Chapter XII of the UN Charter. This would enable reconstruction and rehabilitation to take place in an

underscores the need to question the legitimacy of the idea of ITA itself. Earlier, some of the 'legal issues' raised by ITA were reviewed, such as the questions of legal authority and applicable law. These topics tend to be the exclusive focus of analysis by international lawyers. But the articulation of self-determination that formed the basis for decolonization, denoting freedom from external control, is also an area of law. If ITA breaches this either generally or in certain instances, then focusing on the other 'legal issues' first is to come at things in the wrong order.

To be justified, ITA must be able to resist the fundamental critique of trusteeship itself discussed in the previous chapter: that exercising control over people from outside is inherently unjust. Discussing those international lawyers who, as discussed in Chapter 8, sought to explain and justify the civilizing mission within international law, Martti Koskenniemi states that:

[t]he men of 1873 felt that the introduction of Western institutions in the Orient would be to do history's work, in that it would gradually transform backward societies into the European state form. The historical and the normative assumption coalesced in their image of themselves as the juridical conscience-consciousness of the civilized world. None of this language, or this self-image, is available today.[18]

If Koskenniemi is right, then there is no international normative basis for the ITA projects. The status of ITA as the latest manifestation of international trusteeship established in the previous chapter requires a fundamental question to be faced up to: is ITA part of the solution, or part of the problem, of global inequality?

On its own terms, the idea of trusteeship implicates the general dilemma as to how a choice should be made between, as William Bain states, the 'good of assisting persons in need and the good of respecting human autonomy.'[19] Even if this can somehow been resolved in favour of intervention as far as the introduction of trusteeship is concerned, it resurfaces when attention turns to the conduct of trusteeship and its ability to realize its purpose. Is trusteeship capable of delivering what it promises? Will what it is seeking to foster locally have purchase when associated with imposition and alien rule, and will the history of domination and

---

orderly way across the full spectrum, with the support and assistance of the international community. The most relevant provision in this regard is Article 76 which notes that the aim of the system is to promote the political, economic, social and educational advancement of the people of the territory in question; to encourage respect for human rights; to ensure the equal treatment of all peoples in the UN in social, economic and commercial matters; and also to ensure equal treatment in the administration of justice.

International Commission on Intervention and State Sovereignty, *The Responsibility to Protect*, December 2001, available at <http://www.iciss.ca/pdf/Commission-Report.pdf>, at 43, para. 5.22. See also ibid., para. 5.23.

[18] M Koskenniemi, *The Gentle Civilizer of Nations* (CUP, 2002), 177. See also R Gordon, 'Some Legal Problems with Trusteeship', 28 (1995) *Cornell International Law Journal* 301.

[19] W Bain, *Between Anarchy and Society. Trusteeship and the Obligations of Power* (OUP, 2003), 2. On the general anti-colonial rejection of domination per se, see above, ch. 8, n. 377 and accompanying text *et seq.*

local disempowerment breed dependence and thereby undermine the prospects for independent viability?[20]

Stepping outwards from a focus on the particular 'beneficiaries' of trusteeship in each case, what of the effect of the existence of trusteeship on global politics? Antony Anghie characterizes ideas concerning relations between non-European and European peoples in 19th century positivist international legal discourse as a system that:

> ...establishes a hierarchy...suggesting that one is advanced, just and authoritative while the other is backward, violent and barbaric; it asserts that the only history which may be written of the backward is in terms of its progress towards the advanced; it silences the backward and denies it any subjectivity or autonomy; it assumes and promotes the centrality of the civilized...[21]

Anghie argues that colonial ideas of 'an essential difference...between Europeans and non-Europeans...the civilized and the uncivilized' have been 'reproduced, in a supposedly non-imperial world, in the distinctions that play such a decisive role in contemporary international relations'.[22] Is ITA part of this? Whereas the language of 'civilization' is not used, as discussed in Chapter 8, ITA is often based on the same underlying notion of backwardness requiring and justifying control by an international organization: the people who are subject to the ITA projects are conceived as subaltern; they are a 'failure' and must 'earn' sovereignty. Can an institution predicated on hierarchies between peoples in the world—those who are subjected to trusteeship, those who are not—be tolerated when it further entrenches inequality on the global axis?[23] Or is ITA justified as a means of bridging such inequality when it is aimed at development and 'state-building'? Part of the answer to this question depends on whether the legitimating strategies set out in Chapter 8 are sustainable.

Is ITA actually 'perfect' trusteeship, in providing administration that seeks to serve the interests of the inhabitants of the territory only? As discussed in Chapter 8, a key legitimizing feature of the ITA projects is the normative identity of the administering actors. How sustainable is this? In his conception of the

---

[20] For this critique in relation to colonial trusteeship, see the sources cited above, ch. 8, n. 383. This issue is discussed in the context of ITA by D Chandler, *Bosnia: Faking Democracy after Dayton* (2nd edn, Pluto Press, 2000); M Ignatieff, *Empire Lite: Nation-building in Bosnia, Kosovo and Afghanistan* (Vintage, 2003), 113–14, D Chandler, *Empire in Denial: The Politics of State-building* (Pluto Press, 2006), *passim*; D Zaum, *The Sovereignty Paradox: The Norms and Politics of International Statebuilding* (OUP, 2007) and R Wilde, 'The Ambivalent Mandates of International Organizations in Bosnia-Herzegovina, Kosovo and East Timor', (2000) *Proceedings of the Joint Meeting of the Australian & New Zealand Society of International Law and the American Society of International Law* 319.

[21] A Anghie, *Imperialism, Sovereignty and the Making of International Law* (CUP, 2005), 113.

[22] Ibid., 310–11.

[23] For a discussion of the degrading effects of trusteeship on the idea of sovereign equality, see the discussion in Bain (above n. 19), ch. 7 and especially 163–72. See also Chandler, *Empire in Denial* (above n. 20), *passim*.

'state-building' projects in Kosovo and Bosnia and Herzegovina as 'Empire Lite', Michael Ignatieff uses the term 'Empire' not only to denote echoes of imperial colonialism that resonate in how these practices are conducted; for Ignatieff, state-building is also 'imperial', '...because its essential purpose is to create order in border zones essential to the security of great powers.'[24] This focus on self-serving motives is used to explain the selective deployment of interventions: humanitarian concerns are only determinative when they map on to self-serving interests; there is 'humanitarian' intervention and then ITA in Kosovo, but relatively little, and sometimes nothing, is done in the many other places where human rights atrocities also take place.[25] For Ignatieff, the best way of understanding the normative character of interventions when they happen is in how self-serving objectives have been allied to humanitarianism.[26]

Necessarily, this undermines the normative significance of having the UN, rather than individual states, in the role of conducting operations as far as making distinctions with colonialism is concerned. Indeed, Ignatieff's 'Empire

---

[24] Ignatieff (above n. 20), 109. Ignatieff states that the state-building enterprise in the Balkans:

...has not been an exercise in humanitarian social work. It has always been an imperial project, driven by a clear, if reluctantly grasped imperative to replace the collapsed Communist imperium of Tito's era with a new architecture of states that would bring stability to a combustible corner of Europe. Why else would there be 12,000 troops in Bosnia and thousands more in Kosovo under the command of American generals, together with experts from many nations investing billions in an otherwise marginal part of the continent? The aim is to integrate the Balkan peninsula— eventually—into the architecture of Europe, and, in the meantime, to reduce the flow of its major exports: crime, refugees, and drugs.
[...]
It is imperial because...it serves imperial interests: the creation of long-term political stability in the south Balkans, the containment of refugee flows into Western Europe, and the control of crime, drugs and human trafficking...

Ibid., 32 and 70. See also ibid., 125, and the approach of J Fearon and D Laitin, 'Neotrusteeship and the Problem of Weak States', 28 (2004) *International Security* 1, *passim*.
[25] Discussing Bosnia and Herzegovina, Kosovo, and Afghanistan, Ignatieff states that:

[n]one of the three would have been chosen for humanitarian treatment had they not also been a practical venue for the exercise of military force by the United States.
...
To the extent that human rights justify the humanitarian use of military forces, the new empire can claim that it serves the cause of moral universalism. Yet its service to the cause is equivocal....Empires that are successful learn to ration their service to moral principle to the few strategic zones where the defence of principle is simultaneously the defence of a vital interest, and where the risks do not outweigh the benefits. This is why modern imperial ethics can only be hypocritical. The new imperium has been exposed in the Balkans but it is never going to be extended to Chechnya.

Ignatieff (above n. 20), 110–11. See also ibid., 652–3.
[26] Ignatieff states that:

[n]ation-building would lack all soulfulness if it were just about creating stability in zones important to Western interests. The idea that redeems nation-building is the spiritual component, assisting former enemies to reconcile, to bind up their wounds and transcend a painful past. This is what gives the imperial project its moral allure.

Ibid., 32. See also ibid., 69–70.

Lite' is explicated through three case studies: two ITA projects and the US-led intervention in Afghanistan.[27] Ignatieff argues that:

[t]he imperial design needs to be stressed, because the usual way of describing Bosnia, Kosovo and Afghanistan, as wards of the 'international community', obscures the imperial interests that brought them under the administration of the United Nations in the first place.[28]

From this perspective, ITA is the trusteeship of (Lord) Frederick Lugard, not 'perfect', selfless trusteeship. Even if, then, the new 'dual mandate' for the ITA projects involves, as discussed in Chapter 8, a cohabitation of the interests of the local population and the interests of the international community, the latter brings in, rather than transcends, the interests of powerful states.[29] So, the notion that the ITA projects are legitimate because the 'other' interests being promoted in the new dual mandate are those of states as a whole, not powerful states in particular, is questioned.[30]

   Moving beyond the view of those described at the start of Chapter 8 who see a sharp normative distinction between the CPA in Iraq and UNMIK in Kosovo, Ignatieff's more pragmatic conception of state-building for imperial ends foregrounds the way in which the UN can entrench and promote, not constrain and transcend, the business of global power politics, with fundamental consequences for the idea that association with the UN somehow takes the ITA projects into the arena of 'perfect' trusteeship and thereby into a different class from colonial trusteeship. Normative portrayals of the UN as essentially selfless and humanitarian tend to focus on the Secretariat exclusively, but a full appreciation of the politics of UN involvement also needs to account for the role of the Security Council, rather than the General Assembly, in deciding where the ITA projects will take place and what form their mandates will take, and the way in which the Secretariat itself is politicized, both generally in relation to permanent staff members, and in particular in terms of the use of ad hoc, seconded staff members from national governments, whose involvement in the ITA missions has been pronounced.[31]

---

[27] See also the slightly later studies by Henry Perritt, which also take in Iraq: HH Perritt, 'Structures and Standards for Political Trusteeship', 8 (2003) *UCLA Journal of International Law & Foreign Affairs* 385; HH Perritt 'Providing Judicial Review for Decisions by Political Trustees', 15 (2004) *Duke Journal of Comparative & International Law* 1.

[28] Ignatieff (above n. 20), 110.

[29] On this new 'dual mandate', see above, ch. 8, text accompanying n. 271 *et seq.*

[30] On this idea of legitimacy, see above, ch. 8, text accompanying n. 515.

[31] On the issue of Secretariat 'impartiality' and the involvement of states in Secretariat matters, see the sources cited above, ch. 8, n. 503, in particular the commentary on Article 100 of the UN Charter by Christoph Schreuer and Christian Ebner. On the use of secondees in the ITA missions, see, e.g., the discussion in R Wilde, 'The Complex Role of the Legal Adviser When International Organizations Administer Territory', 95 (2001) *ASIL Proc.* 51. On the legitimacy of international organizations, see, e.g., the essays and sources cited in J-M Coicaud and V Heiskanen (eds), *The Legitimacy of International Organizations* (UN University Press, 2001) and sources cited therein.

Considering the normative character of this particular internationalized manifestation of the 'dual mandate' is only possible, however, if the underlying connection with colonial trusteeship is acknowledged. So Michael Bothe and Thilo Marauhn, who resist considering such a connection, are thereby able to think about UNMIK and UNTAET only as types of peace operations, and their dismissal of the relevance of the Trusteeship Council and affirmation of the exclusive competence of the Security Council can be made solely on the grounds that, in their view, colonial trusteeship was concerned with something 'other' than the promotion of international peace and security.[32] An acknowledgment of the relevance of the trusteeship concept (and the way it was used to serve objectives concerning peace and security), however, changes the nature of the enquiry considerably. Bearing in mind the critiques of colonial trusteeship, the association with the Security Council appears problematic because of the way that it enables ITA trusteeship to be conducted in pursuance to the interests of Council members.[33]

Acknowledging the role of power politics within the UN is only the start of the enquiry. It needs to be asked whether replacing the essentialism of the projects as inherently beneficial and humanitarian with the essentialism of those such as Michael Ignatieff who see them as always compromised by power politics is helpful. Significantly, Ignatieff's thesis omits a consideration of one case study taking place at the same time as the projects he does consider, which is not so easily explained primarily in terms of power politics: UNTAET in East Timor. More fundamentally, whereas for some, the nature of the contemporary 'dual mandate' rendering most, if not all, the projects deficient as species of 'perfect', selfless, trusteeship might be fatal to the legitimacy of the projects, others who might not take this view—for example on the grounds that even if power politics leads to selectivity, this does not by itself delegitimize the projects that do take place—still need to account for the effect on the objectives associated with the missions of the intersection between self-serving and selfless motivations.

Some of the policies associated with the projects do not make sense on their own terms unless their implementation has somehow been conceived outside the arena of state politics. The role of ITA as a 'neutral' buffer facilitating the handover of territory between two states presupposes a particular normative idea of the international organization involved, as independent and impartial as between the interests of states generally and the two states involved in particular. It might be said that the notion of international public policy taking place outside the

---

[32] See above, ch. 8, text accompanying n. 22 *et seq.*
[33] Tom Parker states that:

[i]f trusteeship means anything it means ensuring a brighter future for those placed under its auspices and an expectation that the Trustees will act in the best interests of their charges not in the best interests of the global *status quo*. The great drawback of using the Security Council to create and administer *ersatz* trusteeships is that in this respect at least it can often find itself conflicted.

T Parker, *The Ultimate Intervention: Revitalising the UN Trusteeship Council for the 21st Century* (Sandvika: Norwegian School of Management, 2003), 36. See also ibid., 50.

arena of state politics is a fantasy, but if so, the idea of ITA realizing policies such as these needs to be questioned.

Other policies concerning 'governance problems' can only be considered legitimate if they are implemented in good faith. So, for example, the notion that ITA will take over governance of people deemed incapable of this, either at all, or in a manner that conforms to certain important policy objectives, and will restore local control when such capacity improves, is on its own terms only legitimate if a fair assessment of capacity is actually being used by those in charge of the projects to determine the duration of their missions. This is undermined if other considerations unrelated to 'capacity' are actually partially determinative; such considerations might lead to an outcome that would have been arrived at had capacity been the sole determinant, but equally they might not. If not, then even if one accepts the legitimacy of trusteeship on the grounds of incapacity in principle, the legitimacy of its implementation in practice is potentially compromised. Michael Ignatieff argues that in understanding why the projects are temporary:

> ...the central factor has to be the democratic character of the Western powers... Democratic empire is short-term. The political timetables imposed on Bosnia, Kosovo and Afghanistan are dependent on the electoral cycle back home.[34]

Beyond questions of selflessness and good faith, as discussed in Chapter 8, ITA is also regarded as legitimate because the policies with which it is associated are understood to be universally valid, not culturally-specific. Any justification of the legitimacy of the projects needs to take into account whether this argument is sustainable.[35] The significance of asking this question is acute in relation to those ITA missions concerned with a profound transformation in the political and economic models in the territories under their charge, whose legitimacy in conducting this enterprise hinges in part on the universal purchase of the models of economics and politics they are promoting. Certainly as a matter of international law, as discussed in Chapter 7, it is difficult to move beyond a rudimentary standard of periodic free and fair elections when seeking to establish the substantive contours of an agreed normative framework of democratic governance, yet democracy means much more than this, and indeed some of the ITA projects attempt to make a more profound change in domestic politics. If such a model does not

---

[34] Ignatieff (above n. 20), 115.

[35] Jarat Chopra states that:

[t]he mandate is a critical feature of governance-in-trust because in the field it is regarded as the source of authority for exercising one set of powers or another. It sets standards against which to measure whether the operation is conducted 'in trust,' that is, in the interests of the territory in question and by the international community as a whole. A criticism of this category of mandate is that is implies the imposition of the UN Charter and international law, instruments developed essentially by Western Judeo-Christian culture in areas with different values and cultures. However, an unfortunate aspect of the international system is that it has been based on these concepts and that nations that are not part of this single tradition have had to accept much from it.

Chopra (above n. 17), 85.

in reality command universal consensus, then is its promotion through ITA any different from the civilizing mission in terms of the legitimacy of the policies being implemented?

In Chapter 8, the notion of accountability being integral to the concept of trust was discussed. As Michael Reisman observes in his discussion of the law applicable to trusteeship arrangements, the requirement of accountability is rooted in the fact that 'the power relationship between the parties concerned is manifestly asymmetrical'.[36] By understanding the ITA projects as trusteeship, this general idea is foregrounded in discussions of them.[37] Given what was said in Chapter 8 about the critiques of colonial trusteeship and the Mandate and Trusteeship systems as far as the quality of accountability provided was concerned, clearly one way in which ITA could claim to be different from colonial trusteeship is in being rooted in an adequate regime of accountability.[38]

Despite this, the accountability mechanisms operating in relation to the ITA projects were not invoked in the discussion of how the projects are legitimized in the previous chapter. As was mentioned in Chapter 1, there has been considerable criticism of UNMIK in Kosovo on accountability grounds; in general, those who justify the legitimacy of the ITA projects do not tend to invoke the quality of accountability provided for them as part of this justification. How should questions of accountability be understood in the light of what has been said about the purposes of the projects, the connection with international trusteeship generally, and how ITA is distinguished normatively from colonial trusteeship in particular?

In Chapter 8, it was speculated that one reason for the non-revival of the UN Trusteeship Council to scrutinize the project in East Timor was the notion that one of the arguments for greater external accountability for international trusteeship—concerns about the self-serving and exploitative actions of states—was no longer relevant now that the administering actor was an international organization. Even if the questions raised earlier about the normative portrayal of international organizations as 'selfless' and 'humanitarian' can somehow be resisted, the question of whether or not there should be accountability cannot be determined solely on the basis of the normative character of the administering actor. The introduction of unjustified restrictions on human rights, for example, cannot

---

[36] WM Reisman, 'Reflections on State Responsibility for Violations of Explicit Protectorate, Mandate, and Trusteeship Obligations', 10 (1989) *Michigan Journal of International Law* 231, at 233.

[37] Richard Caplan states that the concept of trust evident in the ITA projects 'is ensured in part through the principle of accountability: the idea is that the administering authority can and should be held responsible for its actions'; R Caplan, *International Governance of War-Torn Territories: Rule and Reconstruction* (OUP, 2005), 195. See also Perritt, 'Structures and Standards' (above n. 27), *passim*.

[38] Richard Caplan's statement extracted in the previous note is made by way of explaining what trust means and how it would render ITA legitimate. Similarly, Jarat Chopra states that '... governance-in-trust must be distinguished from colonial or imperial acts by its mechanisms of accountability to the interests of the international community as a whole'; Chopra (above n. 17), 84.

somehow be rendered legitimate simply because there is a general idea that the organization involved is acting selflessly and on a humanitarian basis.

Even if accountability is necessary, should the same regime of accountability that would apply to an indigenous government operate with respect to the ITA missions? Specifically, even if the concept of trust suggests that the ITA missions should be acting in the interests of the people in the administered territories, should the missions be brought within a framework that enables these people directly to bring the missions to account? On the question of who should exercise oversight in relation to the missions, Richard Caplan asks:

[w]hose opinion should count...? International transitional authorities cannot function as governments answerable *primarily* to the people whose territories they administer. International trusteeships are not representative democracies...[39]

Even if the international administrators have not been elected by the people they govern, does this necessarily mean that they should not be answerable to them? Simon Chesterman argues that:

...final authority remains with the international presence and it is misleading to suggest otherwise. If the local population had the military and economic wherewithal to provide for their security and economic development then a transitional administration would not have been created. Where a transitional administration is created, its role is—or should be—precisely to undertake military, economic, and political tasks that are beyond existing capacities.[40]

Here, then, it is suggested that direct accountability is at odds with the underlying enterprise: international organizations have taken over control of governance precisely because of a judgment concerning the inability or unwillingness of the local population to perform this role themselves, either at all, or in a manner that conforms to certain policy objectives. To render the projects directly accountable to the local population in any meaningful way—i.e., in a way that meant policies were altered to take into account the views of the population—would be to miss the point of the enterprise. In Bosnia and Herzegovina, for example, as discussed, the High Representative sometimes removes elected officials from office, inter alia because the policies espoused by the officials in question, such as what is deemed to be extremist nationalism, run counter to the political agenda OHR has for Bosnia and Herzegovina. Necessarily, this goes against the popular will insofar as it was meaningfully exercised in the vote that brought the official in question to office in the first place.

Even on its own terms such an argument only goes so far. It only applies to those ITA policies concerned with remedying problems associated directly with the local population. For a mission associated with a 'sovereignty problem'

---

[39] Caplan (above n. 37), 246, emphasis added, footnote omitted.
[40] Chesterman (above n. 11), 143.

exclusively, like UNTAES in Eastern Slavonia, there is nothing contradictory to the mission's objective in making the policies it promotes during the period of administration—as opposed to the policy of eventual transfer to Croatia—accountable directly to the local population. The fact that a mission is intended to hand the territory over to another sovereign after an interim period does not by itself necessitate, for example, an ability to make decisions about the economy of the territory during that period without having to account to the local population in doing so.

Even in ITA projects addressing a perceived 'governance problem', the mandate itself should not be taken for more than it is. A mandate to foster economic development and reconstruction, for example, does not by itself presuppose that the economic model being implemented in the territory should not be determined by the local population. In East Timor, for example, development was needed because the East Timorese had been denied self-determination, not because they were deemed incapable of making decisions on economic matters. Part of the answer to the accountability issue, then, concerns the scope of the mandate and what this means in terms of decision-making.[41]

More fundamentally, however, accountability issues run much wider than the particular policies being promoted: corruption, mismanagement, and human rights abuses are not part of the mandate of the projects, and to exercise scrutiny over them is not to undermine the policy objectives of the missions. Effective accountability mechanisms concerning such matters are not incompatible with the idea of ITA itself; indeed, for those projects concerned with transforming the politics of the territories concerned along the lines of the rule of law and the promotion of human rights, a key component of 'tutelage' is leading by example.

Returning to the question of the legitimacy of the ITA version of trusteeship—not the more fundamental question of the legitimacy of trusteeship itself—how would the normative character be understood if it failed to withstand the questions set out so far? What if the model of trusteeship is not 'selfless' as far as global power politics is concerned; what if the policies being implemented are not universally valid but culturally-specific; what if the missions are being conducted in an unaccountable manner, thereby breaching a fundamental requirement of trusteeship? It would follow that ITA fits with the colonial paradigm even more closely than was established in the previous chapter, since the legitimating strategies set out therein are, in the final analysis, unsustainable.

If the policies being promoted do not have universal purchase and/or reflect the priorities of powerful states, then they echo the way in which, as related by Antony Anghie, international law and public policy in the colonial era contemplated

---

[41] In both Kosovo and East Timor, the UN set up bodies to whom certain prerogatives were devolved, but final authority on decision-making always resided in the head of the UN mission. See above, ch. 1, nn. 1 and 2.

'...no other approaches to the problems of society than those which have been formulated by the civilized.'[42] The bias and lack of universal purchase of these policies would render them alibis for domination, as such echoing the concepts of international law and public policy in the colonial era whose 'universal' identity concealed biases that enabled uni-directional domination on the European–non-European axis. Colonial-era notions of sovereignty were, as Anghie states:

...formulated in such a way as to exclude the non-European; following which, sovereignty [could]...then be deployed to identify, locate and sanction and transform the uncivilized.[43]

Connecting up these ideas with contemporary international law and public policy, Anghie argues that:

...the only thing unique about the nineteenth century is that it explicitly adopted the civilizing mission and reflected its goals in its very vocabulary. The more alarming and likely possibility is that the civilizing mission is inherent in one form or another in the principal concepts and categories which govern our existence: ideas of modernity, progress, development, emancipation and rights.
[...]
...the essential structure of the civilizing mission may be reconstructed in the very contemporary vocabulary of human rights, governance and economic liberalization.[44]

If notions of 'failure' and equivocal/earned sovereignty similarly manifest biases along the axes of global power, then the legitimacy of ITA's use as a 'remedy' for them is compromised. ITA would amount to a repeat of the colonial civilizing mission, where an attempt was made to transmit the norms of the powerful 'core' to the subaltern 'periphery'. Discussing the standards promoted in 'peacebuilding' generally, Roland Paris states that:

[t]o the extent that these standards reflect the ideological predilections of the most powerful states in the world—the core of the international system—peacebuilding is not merely a tool of conflict management, but a new phase in the ongoing and evolving relationship between the core and the periphery of the international system, with the core continuing to define the standards of acceptable behaviour and international peacebuilding agencies serving as 'transmission belts' that convey these standards to the periphery.[45]

'Transmission' through ITA may not actually effect improvement and development, therefore; indeed, it may actually cause more harm than good. Instead of bridging the divide between the powerful and the subaltern, it may actually be making the gap wider. As such, it would repeat a process associated with

---

[42] Anghie (above n. 21), 113.
[43] Ibid., 311.
[44] Ibid., 114.
[45] R Paris, 'International Peacebuilding and the Mission Civilisatrice', 28 (2002) *Review of International Studies* 637, 653–4. See also ibid., 637, 650 *et seq.*

state-conducted trusteeship. Discussing the Mandate arrangements, Antony Anghie states that:

[t]he Mandate System had devised a set of technologies that would compromise...independence and maintain—indeed, entrench—the division between advanced and backward states. Having in this way ensured the existence of the division, international law and institutions nevertheless proclaimed themselves intent on bridging that division, on promoting global equality and justice. This project and the many initiatives that are part of it are inherently problematic because it is sometimes precisely the international system and institutions that exacerbate, if not create, the problem that they ostensibly seek to resolve.[46]

Scholars such as Anghie argue that, in the context of decolonization, the biased, imperial structures of international law and public policy into which colonial peoples had to fit on 'independence' set the conditions for the perpetuation of their subordination.[47] If the standards being implemented through the ITA projects are similarly compromised, then the troubling conclusion is that these projects are setting up their beneficiaries to fail as independently viable, prosperous, and just societies.

What would this mean for international law and public policy? It would suggest that, as some have argued, the imperial structures of domination and subordination that formed the origins of the system of international law and institutions are still important features of it today.[48] It would indicate the way in which concepts of universality are used to promote policies that privilege the powerful and seek to eradicate meaningful differences between the powerful and the powerless, providing a further example of how international law has, in the words of Antony Anghie, '...endlessly reached out towards universality, expanding, confronting, including and suppressing the different societies and peoples it encountered.'[49] It would underscore the need to interrogate how concepts and practices in international law and public policy that are articulated in terms of

---

[46] Anghie (above n. 21), 192.

[47] As Antony Anghie states:

...the processes and mechanisms that transformed colonies into sovereign states had an enduring importance for the non-European state. As such, it is misleading to focus simply on the outcome, on the achievement of sovereign statehood, rather than on the unique character of non-European statehood that stems in part from the mechanisms that created it.
[...]
...the tragedy for the Third World is that the mechanisms used by international law to achieve decolonization were also the mechanisms that created neo-colonialism.

Ibid., 191 and 192. See generally the sources in sections 5.3.3 and 5.3.4 of the List of Sources.

[48] See generally the works in List of Sources, section 5.3.4 and especially Anghie (above n. 21), chs 4–6, in particular 112–13, 117–18.

[49] Ibid., 314.

emancipation and humanitarianism can be deployed to achieve their opposite. As Anghie states:

[t]he point is not to condemn the ideals of 'the rule of law' 'good governance' and 'democracy' as being inherently imperial constructs, but rather, to question how it is that these ideas have become used as a means of furthering imperialism and why it is that international law and institutions seem so often to fail to make these ideals a reality.[50]

Moving from the general back to the specific, although this book has attempted to foreground the normative character of ITA in part to counter a technocratic, managerial approach to the ITA projects, this is not to say, of course, that the projects do not also raise formidable practical challenges. Even if ITA generally and specific ITA missions in particular somehow retain merit in the face of the foregoing issues, legitimacy can still be fundamentally compromised if the projects do not operate effectively.

Adequate and effective modes of delivery and competence are not only important in their own right; many of the policies associated with ITA, or the way it operates, assume them. Taking over control of administration from local people in order to ensure democratic governance presupposes that the officials of international organizations are able to govern in a better manner in this regard than the people they have displaced. Equally, arrangements that follow from such central assumptions—for example, the notion discussed in Chapter 7 that the use of ITA to promote particular human rights norms within a territory obviates the need for the usual supra-national scrutiny mechanisms—similarly presuppose that international organizations and their officials are willing and able to provide an effective protection system domestically.

There is a tendency to argue for the legitimacy of 'state-building' generally as a matter of principle in complete isolation from how it is and has been conducted in practice; for its proponents, it is a good idea, even if, when one looks at how it is implemented, there are often considerable problems. An extreme example of this would be the occupation of Iraq, where those who insist that the overall enterprise was justified tend to treat the egregious incompetence of the occupation as entirely severable from the legitimacy of the operation itself; if only decisions about the conduct of the occupation had been different, then it would have succeeded. Michael Ignatieff's thesis justifying the idea of 'Empire Lite' on a normative level, written in the context of Bosnia and Herzegovina, Kosovo, and Afghanistan before the 2003 invasion and occupation of Iraq, ends up criticizing all the instances of its actualization on a practical level: lack of adequate funding, incompetence, unwillingness or inability to stay the course, and the like.[51]

---

[50] Ibid., 320.   [51] Ignatieff (above n. 20), *passim*.

It must be asked, however, whether in some ways practical problems of implementation are not linked to conceptual problems with the enterprise itself. Fundamentally, if trusteeship itself is a flawed concept, for example, because democracy that is 'imposed' will not take root, then it is hardly a surprise that those involved in it come up against formidable 'practical' challenges. If the policies being promoted in the projects reflect, in part, objectives that have little to do with the interests of the local population, the possibility that such policies fail to resonate locally forms part of the enterprise itself—success or failure will not depend exclusively on how well international administrators do their job on the ground.[52]

So far, the legitimacy of ITA has been understood with reference to issues raised by the connection established in Chapter 8 with international trusteeship. In one sense, this marks a step away from a dominant discourse on legitimacy that foregrounds second-order issues such as the question of the applicable law. In another sense, however, it replicates a dominant approach to understandings of international legitimacy in its focus on self-determination. It is important to ask whether the sites of legitimation raised by a comparison with the colonial institution are themselves sufficient in approaching questions of legitimacy. In one sense, this is a matter of considering the adequacy of what is raised on its terms—for example, considering the critiques that have been made of the emancipatory potential of the self-determination entitlement given the predominant focus on formal independence within conventional self-determination discourse.[53] In another sense, it is a matter of asking what further normative issues are raised by ITA other than those concerning the legitimacy of intervention.

One methodological approach that encompasses both these 'departures' from an exclusive focus on the colonial comparator is feminist analysis.[54] As discussed

[52] For further analysis on the tension on the part of officials between their duties to the people in the territory and their loyalties to the organization, see, e.g., Wilde (above n. 31) and R Wilde, 'The United Nations as Government: The Tensions of an Ambivalent Role', 97 (2003) *ASIL Proc.* 212.

[53] On the limited nature of what self-determination can deliver, see the discussion in A Orford, *Reading Humanitarian Intervention: Human Rights and the Use of Force in International Law* (CUP, 2003), 143–57. On self-determination generally, including further critiques of this kind, see List of Sources, section 5.4.

[54] On such analysis in relation to international law and public policy generally, see CT Mohanty, A Russo, and L Torres (eds), *Third World Women and the Politics of Feminism* (Indiana University Press, 1991); N Chaudhuri and M Strobel (eds), *Western Women and Imperialism: Complicity and Resistance* (Indiana University Press, 1992); DG Dallmeyer (ed.), *Reconceiving Reality: Women and International Law* (ASIL, 1993); M Cook and A Woollacott (eds), *Gendering War Talk* (Princeton University Press, 1993); R Cook (ed.), *Human Rights of Women: National and International Perspectives* (University of Pennsylvania Press, 1994); JJ Pettman, *Worlding Women: A Feminist International Politics* (Routledge, 1996); LA Lorentzen and J Turpin (eds), *The Women and War Reader* (NYU Press, 1998); H Charlesworth and C Chinkin, *The Boundaries of International Law: A Feminist Analysis* (Manchester University Press, 2000); U Narayan and S Harding (eds), *Decentering the Center: Philosophy for a Multicultural, Postcolonial and Feminist World* (Indiana University Press, 2000); K-K Bhavnani, *Feminism and 'Race'* (OUP, 2001); C Saunders and K LeRoy (eds), *The Rule of Law* (Federation Press, 2003); BA Ackerly, M Stern, and J True (eds), *Feminist Methodologies for International Relations* (CUP, 2006); V Amos and

in Chapter 6, ITA at least in its later manifestations has sought in some cases to promote the rights of women; as mentioned in Chapter 7, this can be understood to reflect the idea of incorporating gender-based analysis of and strategies within international law and public policy concerning peace and security. One important site of critical appraisal of the ITA projects, then, is to evaluate their merit along gender lines.[55] Do they promote the interests of women and men equally in their specific policies, the way policies are implemented, the manner in which the 'problems' associated with ITA are understood, how the missions are staffed, which local people are involved in decision-making, what effects the missions have more generally, and so on?

More fundamentally, what insights from feminist theory can be brought to bear on the nature and legitimacy of the act of control and domination generally—trusteeship—and its association with the promotion of policy objectives in particular? In part this implicates conceptual issues concerning the intersection between feminism and anti-colonialism. A long-standing critique of certain feminist activism concerned complicity with forms of domination operating on axes other than gender, such as race. Clearly such arguments—such as Valerie Amos's and Pratibha Parmar's influential notion of 'Imperial Feminism'—are significant in highlighting the need to approach critique in a multifaceted manner, and to face up to the tensions this may produce.[56] It is not enough, for example, to ask whether UNMIK in Kosovo is ensuring that its policies for governance in Kosovo are gender-sensitive; one also needs to ask whether the use of ITA as a means of promoting these policies is itself legitimate. In one sense, however, this

P Parmar, 'Challenging Imperial Feminism', 17 (July 1984) *Feminist Review* 3; C Chinkin, 'A Gendered Perspective to the Use of Force', 12 (1988–89) *Australian Yearbook of International Law* 279; K Engle, 'International Human Rights and Feminism: When Discourses Meet', 13 (1992) *Michigan Journal of International Law* 517; J Mertus and P Goldberg, 'A Perspective on Women and International Human Rights After the Vienna Declaration: The Inside/Outside Construct', 26 (1994) *International Law and Politics* 201; V Nesiah, 'Towards a Feminist Internationality: A Critique of US Feminist Legal Scholarship', 16 (1993) *Harvard Women's Law Journal* 189; D Buss, 'Robes, Relics and Rights: The Vatican and the Beijing Conference on Women', 7 (1998) *Social and Legal Studies* 339; H Charlesworth, 'Feminist Methods in International Law', 93 (1999) *AJIL* 379; A Orford, 'Contesting Globalization: A Feminist Perspective on the Future of Human Rights', in BH Weston and SP Marks (eds), *The Future of International Human Rights* (Transnational Publishers, 1999); H Charlesworth, 'International Law: A Discipline of Crisis', 65 (2002) *Modern Law Review* 377; R Kapur, 'The Tragedy of Victimization Rhetoric: Resurrecting the "Native" Subject in International/Post-Colonial Feminist Legal Politics', 15 (2002) *Harvard Human Rights Journal* 1; A Orford, 'Feminism, Imperialism and the Mission of International Law,' 71 (2002) *Nordic Journal of International Law* 275; V Nesiah, 'The Ground Beneath Her Feet: TWAIL Feminisms', in A Anghie, BS Chimni, K Mickelson, and OC Okafor (eds), *The Third World and International Order: Law, Politics and Globalization* (Brill, 2003), 133.

[55] For work by commentators who have appraised one or more of the ITA projects on the basis of a gender-based/feminist analysis, see List of Sources, section 5.2.5. For an NGO report on gender and UNMIK, see Kvinna till Kvinna Foundation, *Getting it Right? A Gender Approach to UNMIK Administration in Kosovo* (2001), obtainable from <http://www.iktk.se/publikationer/rapporter/pdf/Kosovorapport.pdf>. For feminist/gender-based analysis in relation to women and international peace and security generally, see the sources cited above, ch. 7, n. 71.

[56] Amos & Parmar (above n. 54). See also Orford, 'Feminism, Imperialism...' (above n. 54).

is not a matter of 'departing' from feminism; feminist critique is itself, of course, concerned with understanding relations of domination. The entry-level question of whether trusteeship is normatively supportable, then, should be approached through feminist analysis; understanding the gender of international trusteeship can enrich how this fundamental aspect of ITA is appraised.[57]

Moving away from a consideration of the legitimacy of ITA, one final avenue of enquiry raised by the activity as it has been explained in this book is offered by Edward Said's concept of *orientalism*.[58] As discussed in Chapter 1, one of the insights of Said's work is that representations of the 'other' conceived in the context of relations of domination, although of questionable merit for an enquiry as to the nature of the 'other' itself, can be illuminating as indications of the self-image of those engaged in crafting such representations. Whatever the merits of ITA as far as its ability to capture, understand, and discipline the interests of the populations in relation to which it operates, an appreciation of how this process is understood by those engaged in the projects and in international law and public policy generally may open up insights into how these people, how those who work for international organizations, and how experts in international law and public policy, view themselves. Martti Koskenniemi states that the humanitarianism of colonial trusteeship can be understood in part in:

... the connection liberals have made between progress and civilization on the one hand, and a particular political form, Western statehood, on the other. The men of 1873 saw great danger in Africa and elsewhere in terms of a continued anarchy inside 'primitive' communities and an unrestricted scramble driven by private economic interests between the European powers. They hoped to deal with these dangers by introducing European public administration into the colonies. When that attempt failed, they moved to support the internationalization of colonial administration, again with the view to replacing indigenous political forms with European ones... When in more recent years those forms of government have nonetheless failed, international lawyers have been left uneasily poised between exhaustion and arrogance in the face of the endemic political, social and economic crises in the third world: either leaving the colonies a playground of 'tribal' policies and Western private economic domination, or suggesting ever more streamlined versions of civilized guardianship over 'failed states.' Both are reaction formations to an unarticulated—yet pervasive—liberal unease about the virtues of Western political institutions.[59]

How does the use of ITA to engage in 'state-building' in 'failed states' reflect anxieties about the nature of the state and democracy for those living in states that would never be subjected to these forms of intervention? Put differently,

---

[57] Cf. the example of the relations between men and women given by Aristotle in the passage quoted above (ch. 8, n. 107), when discussing relative capacities for rationality as the basis for distinctions between ruler and ruled.
[58] EW Said, *Orientalism. Western Conceptions of the Orient* (reissue with new afterword, Penguin Books, 1995).
[59] Koskenniemi (above n. 18), 176.

what does the 'failed state' say about concerns felt in relation to its 'successful' 'other'? For the international organizations concerned, especially the UN, what does involvement in the activity of ITA in a few places say about their contrasting relationship with the majority of the world's states? How does the ability to discipline people in the global periphery relate to such ability as far as powerful states are concerned? The legitimacy of ITA in general and specific ITA projects in particular is, of course, vitally important, but the existence of the policy institution revealed in this book also raises questions as to what is at stake for both the actors in control in the ITA projects—the international organizations—and for those states and their populations who are not made subject to the projects. The colonial legacy is of enduring significance for both those who were colonialists and those who were colonized; what will direct involvement in the conduct of international trusteeship mean for the future identities and roles of international organizations?

Now that the policy role of international territorial administration and its place in the history of international trusteeship have been established, normative appraisal becomes possible. Regarding individual administration projects as manifestations of the policy institution of ITA is not only helpful in seeking to identify commonalities and differences between these projects; it also provides the broader context that is necessary for the politics of ITA, both on its own terms and in its relationship to international law and public policy generally, to be contested.

List of Sources

The following lists contain all the sources consulted in the preparation of this book, including the sources cited in the footnotes. All the weblinks worked as of July 2007. The term 'available at' denotes a link leading directly to the source cited; the term 'obtainable from' denotes a general website within which the source can be found. The primary sources in the lists within sections 1–4 are ordered chronologically. Further explanation of the lists of secondary commentary in section 5 is provided at the start of that section.

1   Cases and Related Documents

In chronological order

1.1   African Commission on Human and Peoples' Rights

Social and Economic Rights Action Centre and Center for Economic and Social Rights v Nigeria, Comm. No. 155/96, African Commission of Human and Peoples' Rights, 30th Ordinary Session, 13–27 October 2001, obtainable from <http://www.achpr.org>

1.2   Bosnia and Herzegovina

1.2.1   Human Rights Chamber

Website: <http://www.hrc.ba/ENGLISH/DEFAULT.HTM>
Archive of decisions: <http://www.hrc.ba/database/searchForm.asp>
Case Nos CH/98/230 and 231, *Adnan Suljanović and Edita Cisić and Asim Lelić v the State of Bosnia and Herzegovina and Republika Srpska*, Decision on Admissibility, 14 May 1998
Case No. CH/98/1266, *Dragan Čavić v Bosnia and Herzegovina*, decision on admissibility, 18 December 1998
Cases Nos CH/00/4027 and CH/00/4074, *Municipal Council of the Municipality of South-West Mostar v the High Representative*, decision on admissibility, 9 March 2000
Cases Nos CH/97/60, CH/98/276, CH/98/362, CH/99/1766, decision on admissibility and merits, 7 December 2001

1.2.2   Constitutional Court

Website: <http://www.ustavnisud.ba>
Archive of judgments and decisions: <http://www.ustavnisud.ba/eng/odluke>
Case No. U7/98, *Decision on the Appeal of the Office of the Public Attorney of the Federation of Bosnia and Herzegovina against the Decision of the Human Rights Chamber of 11 March 1998 in Case No. CH/96/30, Sretko Damjanović v Federation of Bosnia and Herzegovina*, 26 February 1999
Case No. U8/98, *Decision on the appeal of the Office of the Public Attorney of the Federation of Bosnia and Herzegovina against the Decision of the Human Rights Chamber for Bosnia and Herzegovina of 3 April 1998 in Case No. CH/97/41, Milorad Marčeta v the Federation of Bosnia and Herzegovina*, 26 February 1999
Case No. U9/98, *Decision on the appeal of the Office of the Public Attorney of the Federation of Bosnia and Herzegovina against the Decision of the Human Rights Chamber for Bosnia and Herzegovina of 3 April 1998 in Case No. CH/96/21, Krstan Čegar v the Federation of Bosnia and Herzegovina*, 26 February 1999

Case No. U 9/00 (on the Law on State Border Service), decision of 3 November 2000 and Annex, Separate dissenting opinion of Judge Snežana Savić

Case No. U16/00 (on the Law on the Sale of Apartments with Occupancy Rights), decision of 2 February 2001 and Annex, Separate dissenting opinion of Judge Prof. Dr Vitomir Popović

Case No. U 25/00 (on the Decision Amending the Law on Travel Documents of Bosnia and Herzegovina), decision of 23 March 2001 and Annex, Separate dissenting Opinion of Judge Prof. Dr Vitomir Popović

Case No. U26/01 (Request for evaluation of constitutionality of the Law on the Court of Bosnia and Herzegovina), decision of 28 September 2001

Case U37/01 (on the Decision of the High Representative for Bosnia and Herzegovina No. 86/01 of 23 February 2001), decision of 2 November 2001

Case No. AP-953/05, *Milorad Bilbija and Dragan Kalinić*, Decision on admissibility and merits, 8 July 2006

1.3 Brčko Arbitral Tribunal

Brčko Arbitration webpage and archive of decisions: <http://www.ohr.int/ohr-offices/ brcko/arbitration/archive.asp?sa=on>

Arbitration for the Brčko Area (Federation of Bosnia and Herzegovina v Republika Srpska), Arbitral Tribunal for Dispute over Inter-Entity Boundary in Brčko Area, Award of 14 February 1997, UN Doc. S/1997/126 (1997), reproduced in 36 (1997) *ILM* 396

Arbitration for the Brčko Area (Federation of Bosnia and Herzegovina v Republika Srpska), Arbitral Tribunal for Dispute over Inter-Entity Boundary in Brčko Area, Final Award of 5 March 1999, obtainable from <http:// www.ohr.int/ohr-offices/brcko/arbitration/ archive.asp?sa=on>

1.4 Canada

Reference re Secession of Quebec, Supreme Court of Canada, Advisory Opinion [1998] 2 RCS 217, 37 (1998) *ILM* 1340

1.5 European Court of Human Rights

Handyside v United Kingdom, Appl. no. 5493/72, Judgment of 7 December 1976, *Series A*, No. 24

Cardot v France, Appl. no. 11069/84, Judgment of 19 March 1991, *Series A*, No. 200

De Jong, Baljet and van den Brink v Netherlands, Appl. nos 8805/79; 8806/79; 9242/81, Judgment of 24 May 1984, *Series A*, No. 77

Marckx v Belgium, Appl. no. 6833/74, Judgment of 13 June 1979, *Series A*, No. 31

Young, James, and Webster v United Kingdom, Appl. no. 7601/76, Judgment of 18 October 1982, *Series A*, No. 55

Lopez Ostra v Spain, Appl. no. 16798/90, Judgment of 9 December 1994, *Series A*, No. 303-A

Guerra v Italy, Appl. no. 14967/89, Judgment of 19 February 1998, *Reports* 1998-I

Assanidze v Georgia, Appl. no. 71503/01, Judgment of 8 April 2004, *Reports* 2004-II *Broniowski v Poland* (Grand Chamber), Appl. no. 31443/96, Judgment of 22 June 2004, *Reports 2004-V*

Jeličić v Bosnia and Herzegovina, Appl. no. 41183/02, Admissibility Decision, 15 November 2005, obtainable from <http://www.echr.coe.int>

Sejdovic v Italy (Grand Chamber), Appl. no. 56581/00, Judgment of 1 March 2006, obtainable from <www.echr.coe.int>

Scordino v Italy (No. 1) (Grand Chamber), Appl. no. 36813/97, Judgment of 29 March 2006, obtainable from <www.echr.coe.int>

Behrami and Behrami v France & Saramati v France, Germany and Norway, Appl. nos 71412/01 and 78166/01, European Court of Human Rights, Admissibility Decision, 31 May 2007, obtainable from <http://www.echr.coe.int>

1.6 Free City of Danzig

Danzig Pension Case, High Court of Danzig (Obergericht), 8 May 1929, 5 (1929–30) *ILR* 66

1.7 Germany

In re M (Danzig Conviction Case), Germany, Supreme Court, 22 June 1933, 7 (1933–34) *ILR* 59

Re Lachinger, German Federal Republic, Federal Supreme Court, 23 February 1954, 21 (1957) *ILR* 43

1.8 Inter-American Commission of Human Rights/Inter-American Court of Human Rights

Yanomami Community v Brasil, Resolution No. 12/85, Case No. 7615, 5 March 1985, in *Annual Report of the Inter-American Commission on Human Rights 1984–1985*, OEA/ Ser.L/V/II.66, doc. 10 rev. 1, 1 October 1985, at 24

Mayagna (Sumo) Awas Tingni Community v Nicaragua, Inter-American Court of Human Rights, 31 August 2001, *Series C*, No. 79

1.9 International Court of Justice

1.9.1 Decisions

Reparations for Injuries Suffered in the Service of the United Nations, Advisory Opinion, ICJ Reports 1949, 174

Interpretation of Peace Treaties with Bulgaria, Hungary and Romania, Advisory Opinion, ICJ Report 1950, 65 (First Phase), 221 (Second Phase)

International Status of South West Africa, Advisory Opinion, ICJ Reports 1950, 128

Voting Procedure on Questions Relating to Reports and Petitions concerning the Territory of South-West Africa, Advisory Opinion, ICJ Reports 1955, 67

Admissibility of Hearings of Petitioners by the Committee on South West Africa, Advisory Opinion, ICJ Reports 1956, 23

Interhandel (Switzerland v United States of America), Preliminary Objections, ICJ Reports 1959, 6

South West Africa (Ethiopia v South Africa; Liberia v. South Africa), Preliminary Objections, ICJ Reports 1962, 319

South West Africa (Ethiopia v South Africa; Liberia v South Africa), Second Phase, ICJ Reports 1966, 6

North Sea Continental Shelf Cases (Federal Republic of Germany v Denmark; Federal Republic of Germany v Netherlands), ICJ Reports 1969, 3

Barcelona Traction, Light and Power Company, Limited (Belgium v Spain), Second Phase, ICJ Reports 1970, 3

Legal Consequences for States of the Continued Presence of South Africa in Namibia (South West Africa) Notwithstanding Security Council Resolution 276 (1970), Advisory Opinion, ICJ Reports 1971, 16

Fisheries Jurisdiction Case (United Kingdom v Iceland), ICJ Reports 1973, 3

Western Sahara, Advisory Opinion, ICJ Reports 1975, 12

Military and Paramilitary Activities in and Against Nicaragua (Nicaragua v United States of America), Merits, Judgment, ICJ Reports 1986, 14

East Timor (Portugal v Australia), Preliminary Objections, ICJ Reports 1995, 90

Application of the Convention on the Prevention and Punishment of the Crime of Genocide (Bosnia and Herzegovina v Yugoslavia (Serbia and Montenegro)), Request for the Indication of Provisional Measures, Order of 8 April 1993, ICJ Reports 1993, 3

Application of the Convention on the Prevention and Punishment of the Crime of Genocide (Bosnia and Herzegovina v Yugoslavia (Serbia and Montenegro)), Preliminary Objections, ICJ Reports 1996 (II), 595

Kasikili/Sedudu Island (Botswana v Namibia), ICJ Reports 1998, 1045

LaGrand (Germany v United States of America), ICJ Reports 2001, 466

Application for Revision of the Judgment of 11 July 1996 in the Case concerning Application of the Convention on the Prevention and Punishment of the Crime of Genocide (Bosnia and Herzegovina v Yugoslavia), Preliminary Objections (Yugoslavia v Bosnia and Herzegovina), ICJ Reports 2003, 7

Application of the Convention on the Prevention and Punishment of the Crime of Genocide (Bosnia and Herzegovina v Serbia and Montenegro), Merits, Judgment of 26 February 2007, obtainable from <http://www.icj-cij.org>

1.9.2 Applications

Application of Yugoslavia for Revision of the Judgment of 11 July 1996 in the Case Concerning Application of the Convention on the Prevention and Punishment of the Crime of Genocide (Bosnia and Herzegovina v Yugoslavia), Preliminary Objections (Yugoslavia v Bosnia and Herzegovina), 23 April 2001, obtainable from <http://www.icj-cij.org>

1.10 International Criminal Tribunal for the Former Yugoslavia

Prosecutor v Naletilic and Martinovic, Case No. IT-98–34-T, Trial Chamber, Judgment, 31 March 2003

1.11 The Netherlands

In re Krüger, Council for the Restoration of Legal Rights (Judicial Division), The Hague, 13 September 1951, 18 (1951) *ILR* 258

In re Nix et al, Council for the Restoration of Legal Rights (Judicial Division), The Hague, 14 September 1951, 18 (1951) *ILR* 260

1.12 Permanent Court of International Justice

Nationality Decrees issued in Tunis and Morocco (French Zone) on November 8, 1921, Advisory Opinion, PCIJ, *Series B*, No. 4 (1923)

Mavrommatis Palestine Concessions (Greece v United Kingdom), Jurisdiction, PCIJ, *Series A*, No. 2 (1924)

Polish Postal Service in Danzig, Advisory Opinion, PCIJ, *Series B*, No. 11 (1925)

Jurisdiction of the Courts of Danzig, Advisory Opinion, PCIJ, *Series B*, No. 15 (1928)

Free City of Danzig and International Labour Organization, Advisory Opinion, PCIJ, *Series B*, No. 18 (1930)

Access to, or Anchorage in, the Port of Danzig of Polish War Vessels, Advisory Opinion, PCIJ, *Series A/B*, No. 43 1931

Treatment of Polish Nationals and Other persons of Polish Origin or Speech in the Danzig Territory, Advisory Opinion, PCIJ, *Series A/B*, No, 44 (1932)

Consistency of Certain Danzig Legislative Decrees with the Constitution of the Free City, Advisory Opinion, PCIJ, *Series A/B*, No. 65 (1935), 13

Lighthouses in Crete and Samos (France v Greece), PCIJ, *Series A/B*, No. 71 (1937)

1.13 Special Court for Sierra Leone (SCSL)

Website: <http://www.sc-sl.org>

Prosecutor v Charles Ghankay Taylor, Case No. SCSL-2003–01-I, SCSL Appeals Chamber, Decision on Immunity from Jurisdiction, 31 May 2004, obtainable from <http://www.sc-sl.org>

Prosecutor v Charles Ghankay Taylor, Case No. SCSL-2003–01-AR72–104, SCSL Appeals Chamber, Decision on Urgent Defence Motion against Change of Venue, 29 May 2006, available at <http://www.sc-sl.org/Documents/SCSL-03–01-AR72–104.pdf>

'Special Court President Requests Charles Taylor be Tried in The Hague', SCSL Press Release, 30 March 2006, available at <http://www.sc-sl.org/Press/pressrelease-033006.pdf>

1.14 United Kingdom

The Blonde and Other Ships [1921] P. 155 (Prize Court)

The Blonde and Other Ships [1922] 1 A.C. 313 (Privy Council)

R v Bottrill ex parte Kuechenmeister [1947] 1 K.B. 41

Republic of Somalia v Woodhouse, Drake & Carey (Suisse) SA [1993] 1 All ER 371, [1993] QB 54

1.15 United Nations Human Rights Committee

Hopu and Bessert v France, Comm. No. 549/1993, Views of 9 July 1997, UN Doc. CCPR/C/60/D/549/1993/Rev.1

Concluding Observations of the Human Rights Committee: Serbia, UN Doc. CCPR/
CO/81/SEMO, 12 August 2004

Concluding Observations of the Human Rights Committee: Kosovo (Serbia), UN Doc.
CCPR/C/UNK/CO/1, 14 August 2006

1.16 United States of America

Clark v Allen, 331 US 503, 514, 67 SCt 1431 (US Supreme Court, 9 June 1947), reproduced in 14 (1951) *ILR* 171

2 International Agreements, Unilateral Undertakings, and Associated Documents

In chronological order

2.1 Bilateral/multilateral

General Act of the Conference respecting (1) Freedom of Trade in the Basin of the Congo; (2)
the Slave Trade; (3) Neutrality of the Territories in the Basin of the Congo; (4) Navigation
of the Congo; (5) Navigation of the Niger; and (6) Rules for Future Occupation on the
Coast of the African Continent, signed at Berlin, 26 February 1885, 165 CTS 485

Hague Regulations Respecting the Laws and Customs of War on Land, annex to the
Convention (IV) Respecting the Laws and Customs of War on Land, The Hague,
18 October 1907, *Martens Nouveau (Series 3)*, vol. 3, 461

Treaty of Peace between the Allied and Associated Powers and Germany, Versailles,
28 June 1919, 112 BFSP 1, reprinted in 13 (1919) *AJIL Supp.* 151

Covenant of the League of Nations, Versailles, 28 June 1919 (Part I of the Versailles
Treaty), reprinted in 13 (1919) *AJIL Supp.* 128

Agreement between the United States of America, Belgium, the British Empire, and France,
of the One Part, and Germany of the Other Part, with regard to the Military Occupation
of the Rhine, Versailles, 28 June 1919, reprinted in 13 (1919) *AJIL Supp.* 404

Convention between Poland and the Free City of Danzig, Paris, 9 November 1920,
6 LNTS 189

Agreement between Poland and the Free City of Danzig relative to the issue of Danzig
passports to Danzig citizens abroad, 4 May 1924, 120 (1924) BFSP 227

Convention Concerning the Territory of Memel, 8 May 1924 (Lithuania–Principal
Allied Powers), 29 LNTS 85

Convention to Suppress the Slave Trade and Slavery, 25 September 1926, 60 LNTS 253

Montevideo Convention on Rights and Duties of States, 26 December 1933, 165 LNTS
19, reproduced in 28 (1934) *AJIL Supp.* 75

Agreement between Colombia and Peru Relating to the Procedure for Putting into Effect
the Recommendations Proposed by the Council of the League of Nations, 25 May
1933, 138 LNTS 253

Protocol of Friendship and Co-operation between Colombia and Peru, 24 May 1934,
164 LNTS 21

Declaration by United Nations, signed at Washington on 1 January 1942, reproduced in
36 (1942) *AJIL Suppl.*, 192

Declaration Regarding the Defeat of Germany, Berlin, 5 June 1945 (United Kingdom–United
States of America–USSR–France), 68 UNTS 189, TIAS No. 1520, 145 (1953) BFSP 796

Agreement on Control Machinery in Austria, signed in the European Advisory Commission, 4 July 1945 (United States–United Kingdom–France–Soviet Union), in force 24 July 1945, available at <http://www.yale.edu/lawweb/avalon/wwii/waust01. htm>

Japanese Instrument of Surrender, Tokyo Bay, 2 September 1945 (Japan–Allied Powers), available at <http://www.yale.edu/lawweb/avalon/wwii/j4.htm>

Charter of the United Nations, San Francisco, 26 June 1945, (1946–47) *United Nations Yearbook* 831

Convention on the Privileges and Immunities of the United Nations, GA Res. 22A (I), 13 February 1946, in force 17 September 1946, 1 UNTS 15, 90 UNTS 327 (corrigendum)

Treaty of Peace with Italy, Paris, 10 February 1947 (Allied and Associated Powers–Italy), 49 UNTS 126

Agreement Between the United Nations and the United States Regarding the Headquarters of the United Nations, signed 26 June 1947, approved by the General Assembly on 31 October 1947, 11 UNTS 18

Geneva Convention (I) for the Amelioration of the Condition of the Wounded and Sick in Armed Forces in the Field, 12 August 1949, 75 UNTS 31

Geneva Convention (II) for the Amelioration of the Condition of the Wounded, Sick and Shipwrecked Members of Armed Forces at Sea, Geneva, 12 August 1949, 75 UNTS 85

Geneva Convention (III) Relative to the Treatment of Prisoners of War, Geneva, 12 August 1949, 75 UNTS 135

Geneva Convention (IV) Relative to the Protection of Civilian Persons in Time of War, Geneva, 12 August 1949, 75 UNTS 287

European Convention for the Protection of Human Rights and Fundamental Freedoms, Rome, 4 November 1950, ETS No. 5

Treaty of Peace with Japan, San Francisco, 8 September 1951 (Allied and Associated Powers–Japan), 136 UNTS 45

Convention Relating to the Status of Refugees, 28 July 1951, 189 UNTS 150, as amended by Protocol relating to the Status of Refugees, 31 January 1967, 606 UNTS 267

Treaty for the Re-establishment of an Independent and Democratic Austria, Vienna, 15 May 1955, agreed to by the Allied and Associated Powers (France, United Kingdom, United States, Soviet Union) and Austria, 217 UNTS 223

Supplementary Convention on the Abolition of Slavery, the Slave Trade, and Institutions and Practices Similar to Slavery, 7 September 1956, 226 UNTS 3

Agreement between Indonesia and the Netherlands Concerning West New Guinea (West Irian), 15 August 1962, 437 UNTS 273

Exchange of Letters (with Annexed Memorandum of Understanding) on Cessation of Hostilities, 15 August 1962 (Indonesia–Netherlands–United Nations), 437 UNTS 294

Charter of the Organization of African Unity, Addis Ababa, 25 May 1963, 479 UNTS 39 (abrogated in 2001)

International Covenant on Economic, Social and Cultural Rights, 16 December 1966, 993 UNTS 3

International Covenant on Civil and Political Rights, 16 December 1966, 999 UNTS 171

Vienna Convention on the Law of Treaties, Vienna, 23 May 1969, 1155 UNTS 331

American Convention on Human Rights, San José, 22 November 1969, OAS Treaty Series No. 36, 1144 UNTS 123

Organization of African Unity, Convention Governing the Specific Aspects of Refugee Problems in Africa 20 June 1974, 14 UNTS 691

Contact Group, Proposal for a Settlement of the Namibian Situation, Letter to the President of the Security Council, 10 April 1978, UN Doc. S/12636

Cartagena Declaration on Refugees, Colloquium on the International Protection of Refugees in Central America, Mexico and Panama, 19–22 November 1984, *Annual Report of the Inter-American Commission on Human Rights*, OAS Doc. OEA/Ser.L/V/II.66/Doc.10, rev. 1 (1984–85), at 190–3

Treaty between Australia and the Republic of Indonesia on the Zone of Co-operation in an Area between the Indonesian Province of East Timor and Northern Australia, Timor Sea, 11 December 1989, in force 9 February 1991, 9 *Australian Treaty Series* 1991

1991 Paris Agreements:

> Final Act of the Paris Conference on Cambodia, Paris, 23 October 1991, UN Doc. A/46/608 – S/2317730 (1991), Annex
>
> Agreement on a Comprehensive Political Settlement of the Cambodia Conflict, Paris, 23 October 1991, UN Doc. A/46/608 – S/2317730 (1991), Annex
>
> Agreement Concerning the Sovereignty, Independence, Territorial Integrity and Inviolability, Neutrality and National Unity of Cambodia, Paris, 23 October 1991, UN Doc. A/46/608 – S/2317730 (1991), Annex
>
> Declaration on the Rehabilitation and Reconstruction of Cambodia, Paris, 23 October 1991, UN Doc. A/46/608 – S/2317730 (1991), Annex

Treaty on European Union, Maastricht, 7 February 1992, in force 1 November 1993, *OJ* C24 (1992), 1

Memorandum of Understanding on the European Union Administration of Mostar, 5 July 1994 (Member States of the European Union – Member States of the Western European Union – Republic of Bosnia and Herzegovina – Federation of Bosnia and Herzegovina – Local Administration of Mostar East – Local Administration of Mostar West – Bosnian Croats) (unpublished, on file with the author)

Dayton Peace Agreements:

Dayton GFA:	General Framework Agreement for Peace in Bosnia and Herzegovina, 14 December 1995, agreed to by Bosnia Herzegovina, Croatia and Federal Republic of Yugoslavia, 35 (1996) *ILM* 89
Dayton Annex 1A:	Agreement on the Military Aspects of the Peace Settlement, Annex 1A to the General Framework Agreement for Peace in Bosnia and Herzegovina, 14 December 1995, agreed to by Bosnia and Herzegovina, Federation of Bosnia and Herzegovina and Republika Srpska and endorsed by Croatia and Federal Republic of Yugoslavia, 35 (1996) *ILM* 91
Dayton Annex 1A, Appendix A:	Appendix A (with maps) to Annex 1A to the General Framework Agreement for Peace in Bosnia and Herzegovina, 14 December 1995, agreed to by Bosnia and Herzegovina, Federation of Bosnia and Herzegovina and Republika Srpska and endorsed by Croatia and Federal Republic of Yugoslavia, 14 December 1995, 35 (1996) *ILM* 101

Dayton Annex 1A, Appendix B (1): Agreement Between the Republic of Bosnia and Herzegovina and the North Atlantic Treaty Organisation (NATO) Concerning the Status of NATO and its Personnel, Appendix B to Annex 1A to the General Framework Agreement for Peace in Bosnia and Herzegovina, 14 December 1995, 35 (1996) *ILM* 102

Dayton Annex 1A, Appendix B (2): Agreement Between the Republic of Croatia and the North Atlantic Treaty Organisation (NATO) Concerning the Status of NATO and its Personnel; Appendix B to Annex 1A to the General Framework Agreement for Peace in Bosnia and Herzegovina, 14 December 1995, 35 (1996) *ILM* 104

Dayton Annex 1A, Appendix B (3): Agreement Between the Federal Republic of Yugoslavia and the North Atlantic Treaty Organisation (NATO) Concerning Transit Arrangements for Peace Plan Operations; Appendix B to Annex 1A to the General Framework Agreement for Peace in Bosnia and Herzegovina, 14 December 1995, 35 (1996) *ILM* 106

Dayton Annex 1B: Agreement on Regional Stabilization, Annex 1B to the General Framework Agreement for Peace in Bosnia and Herzegovina, 14 December 1995, agreed to by Bosnia and Herzegovina, Republika Srpska, Federation of Bosnia and Herzegovina, Croatia and Federal Republic of Yugoslavia, 35 (1996) *ILM* 108

Dayton Annex 2: Agreement on Inter-Entity Boundary Line and Related Issues, Annex 2 (with Appendix) to the General Framework Agreement for Peace in Bosnia and Herzegovina, 14 December 1995, agreed to by Bosnia and Herzegovina, Republika Srpska and Federation of Bosnia and Herzegovina and endorsed by Croatia and Federal Republic of Yugoslavia, 35 (1996) *ILM* 111

Dayton Annex 3: Agreement on Elections, Annex 3 (with Attachment) to the General Framework Agreement for Peace in Bosnia and Herzegovina, 14 December 1995, agreed to by Bosnia and Herzegovina, Republika Srpska and Federation of Bosnia and Herzegovina, 35 (1996) *ILM* 114

Dayton Annex 4: Constitution of Bosnia and Herzegovina, Annex 4 (with Annexes I and II) to the General Framework Agreement for Peace in Bosnia and Herzegovina, 14 December 1995, approved by

Bosnia and Herzegovina, Republika Srpska and Federation of Bosnia and Herzegovina, 35 (1996) *ILM* 117

Dayton Annex 5:   Agreement on Arbitration, Annex 5 to the General Framework Agreement for Peace in Bosnia and Herzegovina, 14 December 1995, agreed to by Federation of Bosnia and Herzegovina and Republika Srpska on 14 December 1995, 35 (1996) *ILM* 129

Dayton Annex 6:   Agreement on Human Rights, Annex 6 (and Appendix thereto) to the General Framework Agreement for Peace in Bosnia and Herzegovina, 14 December 1995, agreed to by Bosnia and Herzegovina, Republika Srpska and Federation of Bosnia and Herzegovina, 35 (1996) *ILM* 130

Dayton Annex 7:   Agreement on Refugees and Displaced Persons, Annex 7 to the General Framework Agreement for Peace in Bosnia and Herzegovina, 14 December 1995, agreed to by Bosnia and Herzegovina, Republika Srpska and Federation of Bosnia and Herzegovina, 35 (1996) *ILM* 136

Dayton Annex 8:   Agreement on Commission to Preserve National Monuments, Annex 8 to the General Framework Agreement for Peace in Bosnia and Herzegovina, 14 December 1995, agreed to by Bosnia and Herzegovina, Republika Srpska and Federation of Bosnia and Herzegovina, 35 (1996) *ILM* 141

Dayton Annex 9:   Agreement on Establishment of Bosnia and Herzegovina Public Corporations, Annex 9 to the General Framework Agreement for Peace in Bosnia and Herzegovina, 14 December 1995, agreed to by Republika Srpska and Federation of Bosnia and Herzegovina, 35 (1996) *ILM* 144

Dayton Annex 10:   Agreement on Civilian Implementation of the Peace Settlement, Annex 10 to the General Framework Agreement for Peace in Bosnia and Herzegovina, 14 December 1995, agreed to by Bosnia and Herzegovina, Republika Srpska, Federation of Bosnia and Herzegovina, Croatia, Federal Republic of Yugoslavia, 35 (1996) *ILM* 146

Dayton Annex 11:   Agreement on International Police Task Force, Annex 11 to the General Framework Agreement for Peace in Bosnia and Herzegovina, 14 December 1995, agreed to by Bosnia and Herzegovina, Republika Srpska and Federation of Bosnia and Herzegovina, 35 (1996) *ILM* 149

Dayton Side-Letters:
>   Federation of Bosnia and Herzegovina, Deputy Prime Minister, to Acting Secretary-General, NATO, 21 November 1995, 35 (1996) *ILM* 103
>
>   Republika Srpksa, President, to Acting Secretary-General, NATO, 21 November 1995, 35 (1996) *ILM* 108
>
>   Croatia, Minister of Foreign Affairs, to NATO Assistant Secretary-General, 21 November 1995, 35 (1996) *ILM* 105
>
>   Federal Republic of Yugoslavia, President, to NATO Assistant Secretary-General, 21 November 1995, 35 (1996) *ILM* 107
>
>   Croatia, Minister of Foreign Affairs, to Germany, Minister of Foreign Affairs, 21 November 1995, 35 (1996) *ILM* 154
>
>   Croatia, Minister of Foreign Affairs, to France, Minister for Foreign Affairs, 21 November 1995, 35 (1996) *ILM* 154
>
>   Croatia, Minister of Foreign Affairs, to Russia, Minister for Foreign Affairs, 21 November 1995, 35 (1996) *ILM* 155
>
>   Croatia, Minister of Foreign Affairs, to United Kingdom, Foreign Secretary, 21 November 1995, 35 (1996) *ILM* 155
>
>   Croatia, Minister of Foreign Affairs, to USA, Secretary of State, 21 November 1995, 35 (1996) *ILM* 156
>
>   Federal Republic of Yugoslavia, Minister of Foreign Affairs, to Germany, Minister of Foreign Affairs, 21 November 1995, 35 (1996) *ILM* 158
>
>   Federal Republic of Yugoslavia, Minister of Foreign Affairs, to France, Minister for Foreign Affairs, 21 November 1995, (1996) 35 *ILM* 159
>
>   Federal Republic of Yugoslavia, Minister of Foreign Affairs, to Russia, Minister for Foreign Affairs, 21 November 1995, 35 (1996) *ILM* 159
>
>   Federal Republic of Yugoslavia, Minister of Foreign Affairs, to UK, Foreign Secretary, 21 November 1995, 35 (1996) *ILM* 160
>
>   Federal Republic of Yugoslavia, Minister of Foreign Affairs, to USA, Secretary of State, 21 November 1995, 35 (1996) *ILM* 160
>
>   Croatia, Minister of Foreign Affairs, to United Nations Secretary-General, 21 November 1995, 35 (1996) *ILM* 156
>
>   Croatia, Minister of Foreign Affairs, to NATO Assistant Secretary-General, 21 November 1995, 35 (1996) *ILM* 157
>
>   Federal Republic of Yugoslavia, Minister of Foreign Affairs, to United Nations Secretary-General, 21 November 1995, 35 (1996) *ILM* 158
>
>   Federal Republic of Yugoslavia, Minister of Foreign Affairs, to NATO Assistant Secretary-General, 21 November 1995, 35 (1996) *ILM* 157
>
>   Bosnia and Herzegovina, President, to USA, Secretary of State, 21 November 1995, 35 (1996) *ILM* 161
>
>   Federal Republic of Yugoslavia, President, to USA, Secretary of State, 21 November 1995, 35 (1996) *ILM* 162

Agreement on Implementing the Federation of Bosnia and Hercegovina, with Attached Agreed Principles for the Interim Statute for the City of Mostar, Dayton, 10 November 1995 (Republic of Bosnia and Hercegovina – Federation of Bosnia and Hercegovina), UN Doc. A/50/810 – S/1995/1021

Basic Agreement on the Region of Eastern Slavonia, Baranja and Western Sirmium, contained in Annex to the Letter dated 15 November 1995 from the Permanent Representative of Croatia to the United Nations to the Secretary-General, UN Doc. A/50/757 – S/1995/951

Rome Agreement, 18 February 1996, President Izetbegović, President Tuđman and President Milošević, available at <http://www.ohr.int/ohr-dept/hr-rol/thedept/war-crime-tr/default.asp?content_id=6093>

Communiqué and Agreement on the Regulation of Relations and Promotion of Co-operation, Belgrade, 8 April 1996 (Macedonia – Federal Republic of Yugoslavia), UN Doc. S/1996/291, Annex

Memorandum of understanding between the Secretariat of the United Nations and the Government of Iraq on the implementation of Security Council resolution 986 (1995), 20 May 1996, UN Doc. S/1996/356

Agreement on Normalization of Relations between the Federal Republic of Yugoslavia and the Republic of Croatia, 23 August 1996, UN Doc. A/51/318 – S/1996/706, Annex

Joint declaration of the President of the Republic of Serbia, Slobodan Milošević, and the President of the Presidency of Bosnia and Herzegovina, Alija Izetbegović, Paris, 3 October 1996, reproduced in the letter dated 7 October 1996 from the Chargé d'affaires a.i. of the Permanent Mission of Yugoslavia to the United Nations addressed to the Secretary-General, UN Doc. A/51/461 – S/1996/830, Annex

Statute of the International Criminal Court, Rome, 17 July 1998, 2187 UNTS 90

East Timor Agreements 1999:

Agreement between the Republic of Indonesia and the Portuguese Republic on the Question of East Timor, 5 May 1999, available at <http://www.un.org/peace/etimor99/agreement/agreeFrame_Eng01.html> and Appendix, 'A Constitutional Framework for a Special Autonomy for East Timor', available at <http://www.un.org/peace/etimor99/agreement/agreeFrame_Eng02.html>

Agreement between the Governments of Indonesia and Portugal and the United Nations Regarding the Modalities for the Popular Consultation of the East Timorese through a Direct Ballot, 5 May 1999, available at <http://www.un.org/peace/etimor99/agreement/agreeFrame_Eng03.html>

Agreement between the Governments of Indonesia and Portugal and the United Nations on Security, 5 May 1999, available at <http://www.un.org/peace/etimor99/agreement/agreeFrame_Eng04.html>

Exchange of Notes constituting an Agreement between the Government of Australia and the United Nations Transitional Administration in East Timor (UNTAET) concerning the continued Operation of the Treaty between Australia and the Republic of Indonesia on the Zone of Cooperation in an Area between the Indonesian Province of East Timor and Northern Australia of 11 December 1989, Dili, 10 February 2000, in force 10 February 2000 (with effect from 25 October 1999), Australian Treaty Series 2000 No. 9, available at <http://www.austlii.edu.au/au/other/dfat/treaties/2000/9.html>

Agreement on Provisional Arrangements in Afghanistan Pending the Re-Establishment of Permanent Government Institutions, Bonn, 5 December 2001, reproduced in UN Doc. S/2001/1154, endorsed by the Security Council in SC Res. 1383 (2001), 6 December 2001

Agreement on Succession Issues and Annexes A to G, Vienna, 29 June 2001 (Bosnia and Herzegovina – Croatia – Macedonia – Slovenia – Federal Republic of Yugoslavia), reproduced in 41 (2002) *ILM* 3

Treaty on European Union (consolidated text), *OJ* C325 (2002), 5

Agreement between the United Nations and the Government of Sierra Leone on the Establishment of the Special Court for Sierra Leone, including Annex, Statute of the Special Court of Sierra Leone, signed on 16 January 2002, obtainable from <http://www.sc-sl.org>

Agreement pursuant to Article XIV of Annex 6 to the General Framework Agreement for Peace in Bosnia and Herzegovina, 22 and 25 September 2003, agreed to by Bosnia and Herzegovina, the Federation of Bosnia and Herzegovina and the Republika Srpska, available at <http://www.hrc.ba/ENGLISH/agreement.pdf>

Agreement between the United Nations Interim Administration Mission in Kosovo and the Council of Europe on technical arrangements related to the Framework Convention for the Protection of National Minorities, Pristina, 23 August 2004, obtainable from <http://www.coe.int>

Agreement between the United Nations Interim Administration Mission in Kosovo and the Council of Europe on technical arrangements related to the European Convention for the Prevention of Torture and Inhuman or Degrading Treatment or Punishment, Pristina, 23 August 2004, available at <http://www.cpt.coe.int/en/states/srp.htm>

Agreement between the High Representative for Bosnia and Herzegovina and Bosnia and Herzegovina on the Establishment of a Registry for Section I on War Crimes and Section II on Organized Crime, Economic Crime and Corruption of the Criminal and Appellate Divisions of the Court of Bosnia and Herzegovina and the Special Department for War Crimes and the Special Department for Organized Crime, Economic Crime and Corruption of the Prosecutor's Office of Bosnia and Herzegovina, 1 December 2004, available at <http://www.registrarbih.gov.ba/files/docs/New_Registry_Agreement_-_eng.pdf>

Memorandum of Understanding between the Government of Lebanon and the United Nations Regarding the Modalities of Cooperation for the International Independent Investigation Commission, signed on 13 June 2005, UN Doc. S/2005/393, Annex

Agreement between the High Representative for Bosnia and Herzegovina and Bosnia and Herzegovina on the Registry for Section I for War Crimes and Section II for Organised crime, Economic Crime and Corruption of the Criminal and Appellate Divisions of the Court of Bosnia and Herzegovina and for the Special Department for War Crimes and the Special Department for Organised Crime, Economic Crime and Corruption of the Prosecutor's Office of Bosnia and Herzegovina, as well as on the Creation of the transition Council, replacing the Registry Agreement of 1 December 2004 and the Annex thereto, 26 September 2006, available at <http://www.registrarbih.gov.ba/files/docs/New_Registry_Agreement_-_eng.pdf>

2.2 Unilateral undertakings

Telegrams dated 12 and 13 July 1960 from the President and the Prime Minister of the Republic of the Congo to the UN Secretary-General, UN Doc. S/4382, UN SCOR, 15th year, Supp. (July, August and September 1960), 11

Letter from the Permanent Representative of Croatia to the United Nations Addressed to the Secretary-General, 15 November 1995, UN Doc. A/50/757 – S/1995/951

Agreement on the Principles (Peace Plan) to Move Towards a Resolution of the Kosovo Crisis Presented to the Leadership of the Federal Republic of Yugoslavia by the President of Finland, Martti Ahtisaari, representing the European Union, and Viktor Chernomyrdin, Special Representative of the President of the Russian Federation, 3 June 1999, UN Doc. S/1999/649, Annex

Letter dated 27 October 2000 from the President of the Federal Republic of Yugoslavia to the Secretary-General, UN Doc. A/55/528 – S/2000/1043, Annex

Letter dated 8 May 2003 from the Permanent Representatives of the United Kingdom of Great Britain and Northern Ireland and the United States of America to the United Nations addressed to the President of the Security Council, UN Doc. S/2003/538

3 Documents of International/Intergovernmental Organizations

3.1 African Union

African Union website: <www.africa-union.org>

3.2 Council of Europe

Council of Europe, Treaty Office, 'Chart of signatures and ratifications for the Convention for the Protection of Human Rights and Fundamental Freedoms', available at <http://conventions.coe.int/Treaty/Commun/ChercheSig.asp?NT=005&CM=8&DF=08/01/2006&CL=ENG>

Council of Europe, 'Member States of the Council of Europe', available at <http://www.coe.int/T/E/Com/About_Coe/Member_states/default.asp>

'Kosovo: The Human Rights Situation and the Fate of Persons Displaced from their Homes', Report by Mr Alvaro Gil-Robles, Commissioner for Human Rights, CoE Doc. CommDH(2002)11, 16 October 2002, obtainable from <http://www.coe.int>

European Commission for Democracy through Law (Venice Commission), Opinion on Human Rights in Kosovo: Possible Establishment of Review Mechanisms (Opinion No. 280/2004, Strasbourg, 11 October 2004), obtainable from <http://www.venice.coe.int>

Advisory Committee on the Framework Convention for the Protection of National Minorities, First opinion of the Advisory Committee on Kosovo, adopted on 25 November 2005, CoE Doc. CM(2005)192, 14 December 2005, obtainable from <http://www.coe.int>

'Request by the Republic of Montenegro for accession to the Council of Europe: Statement by the Committee of Ministers of the Council of Europe', Council of Europe Press Release No. 344 (2006), 14 June 2006, obtainable from <http://www.coe.int/press>

'Committee of Ministers of the Council of Europe, Declaration on the Continuation by the Republic of Serbia of membership of the State Union of Serbia and Montenegro in the Council of Europe', Council of Europe Press Release no. 343 (2006), 14 June 2006, obtainable from <http://www.coe.int/press>

Council of Europe, Committee of Ministers, Resolution ResCMN(2006)9 on the implementation of the Framework Convention for the Protection of National Minorities in Kosovo (Republic of Serbia), adopted on 21 June 2006, obtainable from <http://www.coe.int>

'Council of Europe Anti-Torture Committee gains access to NATO run detention facilities in Kosovo', CoE Press Release, 19 July 2006, obtainable from <http://www.cpt.coe.int/en/states/srp.htm>

'Council of Europe Anti-Torture Committee visited Kosovo', CoE Press Release, 3 April 2007, obtainable from <http://www.cpt.coe.int/en/states/srp.htm>

3.3 European Community/European Union

3.3.1 General

European Community, Guidelines on the Recognition of New States in Eastern Europe and in the Soviet Union, 16 December 1991, reproduced in 31 (1992) *ILM* 1486

European Community, Declaration on Yugoslavia, 16 December 1991, reproduced in 31 (1992) *ILM* 1485

European Political Cooperation (EPC) Ministerial Meeting, Declaration on Yugoslavia (Brussels, 6 April 1992), reproduced in C Hill, *European Foreign Policy: Key Documents* (Routledge, 2000), 376

European Community, Declaration on Recognition of Bosnia and Herzegovina, 6 April 1992, UN Doc. S/23793, Annex

International Conference on the Former Yugoslavia Arbitration Committee, *Opinions on Questions Arising From the Dissolution of Yugoslavia*, reproduced in 92 *ILR* 162; 31 (1992) *ILM* 1494 (*Opinions Nos 1–10*) and 32 (1993) *ILM* 1586 (*Opinions Nos 11–13*)

3.3.2 EU Council

Council Joint Action 96/442/CFSP adopted on the basis of Article J.3 of the Treaty on European Union on the nomination of a Special Envoy of the European Union in the city of Mostar, 15 July 1996, *OJ* L185 (1996), 2 and corrigendum *OJ* L260 (1996), 6

Council Decision 94/790/CFSP concerning the joint action, adopted by the Council on the basis of Article J.3 of the Treaty on European Union, on continued support for European Union administration of the town of Mostar, 12 December 1994, *OJ* L326 (1994), 2

Council Joint Action 2002/210/CFSP on the European Police Mission, 11 March 2002, *OJ* L70 (2002), 1

Council Joint Action 2004/570/CFSP on the European Union military Operation in Bosnia and Herzegovina, 12 July 2004, *OJ* L252 (2004), 10

Council Decision 2004/803/CFSP of 25 November 2004 on the launching of the European Union military operation in Bosnia and Herzegovina, *OJ* L353 (2004), 21

Council Joint Action 2006/49/CFSP appointing the European Union Special Representative in Bosnia and Herzegovina, 30 January 2006, *OJ* L26 (2006), 21

Council Joint Action 2006/523/CFSP amending the mandate of the European Union Special Representative in Bosnia and Herzegovina, 25 July 2006, *OJ* L205 (2006), 30

'International Police Task Force Follow-On – Council Conclusions', 2409th Council meeting, General Affairs, Brussels, 18/19 February 2002, Doc. 6247/02 (Presse 30), available at <http://ue.eu.int/uedocs/cmsUpload/GENERAL%20AFFAIRS%2018. 02.02.pdf>, at 16–24

EU Council Secretariat, 'Factsheet – EU Special Representatives (EUSRs)', June 2005, available at <http://www.consilium.europa.eu/uedocs/cmsUpload/EUSRs.pdf>

3.3.3 European Union Administration of Mostar (EUAM)

Interim Statute of the City of Mostar, 7 February 1996, *Official Gazette of the City of Mostar*, No. 1, 20 February 1996

3.3.4 European Union in Kosovo

Website: <http://www.euinkosovo.org>

3.3.5 European Union Force in Bosnia and Herzegovina (EUFOR)

Website: <http://www.euforbih.org>

3.4 League of Nations

Constitution of the Free City of Danzig, 11 May 1922, text in *League of Nations Official Journal, Spec. Suppl.* 7 (July 1922), 1, as amended, 9 September 1930, text in *League of Nations Official Journal* 1794 (December 1930)

League of Nations, Statement on Leticia, 14 (1933) *League of Nations Official Journal* 944–5

3.5 Office of the High Representative in Bosnia and Herzegovina (OHR) (including Brčko Supervisor), Peace Implementation Council, and Peace Implementation Conference

3.5.1 Statements/Reports

OHR Fact Sheet, 'Support for Human Rights Institutions', 15 April 2001, available at <http://www.ohr.int/ohr-dept/hr-rol/thedept/sup-ohr-inst/default.asp?content_id=5570>

OHR Press Release, 'Removal from Office of Nikola Poplasen', 5 March 1999, available at <http://www.ohr.int/ohr-dept/presso/pressr/default.asp?content_id=4706>

OHR Press Release, 'High Representative removes Former Prime Minister Edhem Bicakcic', 23 February 2001, available at <http://www.ohr.int/ohr-dept/presso/pressr/default.asp?content_id=4241>

Wolfgang Petrisch, quoted in 'Petrisch upbeat on Bosnia future', BBC News, 6 February 2002, obtainable from <http://www.news.bbc.co.uk>

OHR Press Release, 'High Representative Welcomes House of Peoples' Adoption of Election Law', 23 August 2001, available at <http://www.ohr.int/ohr-dept/presso/pressr/default.asp?content_id=5501>

OHR, 'Mid-Year Report to the European Parliament by the OHR and EU Special Representative for BiH, January–June 2004', 3 November 2004, available at <http://www.ohr.int/other-doc/hr-reports/default.asp?content_id=33446>

OHR, 'All HR's and Deputy HR's', available at <http://www.ohr.int/ohr-info/hrs-dhrs>

OHR General Information, 'Mandate of the OHR' (undated), available at <http://www.ohr.int/ohr-info/gen-info>

OHR General Information, 'The Peace Implementation Council and its Steering Board' (undated), available at <http://www.ohr.int/ohr-info/gen-info/#pic>

OHR Press Office, 'Schwarz-Schilling Television Address on PIC Decision', 2 March 2007, available at <http://www.ohr.int/ohr-dept/presso/presssp/default.asp?content_id=39267>

3.5.2 Decisions, Orders, and legislation

OHR – archive of Decisions: <http://www.ohr.int/decisions/archive.asp>

OHR, Decision on the deadlines for the implementation of the new uniform license plate system, 20 May 1998

OHR, Decision imposing the Framework Law on Privatisation of Enterprises and Banks in BiH, 22 July 1998

OHR, Decision removing Mr Nikola Poplasen from the Office of President of Republika Srpska, 5 March 1999

OHR, Decision canceling all permanent occupancy rights issued in the Federation during and after the war in BiH and converting them into temporary occupancy rights, 14 April 1999

OHR, Decision adding the fundamental interest clause and the position of Deputy Head of Municipality to the Mostar City Municipalities Statutes, 6 July 1999

OHR, Law on Implementation of the Decisions of the Commission for Real Property Claims of Displaced Persons and Refugees, Federation of Bosnia and Herzegovina, entry into force on 28 October 1999 in accordance with the OHR Decision on the Recognition and Implementation of CRPC Decisions in the Federation, 27 October 1999

OHR, Decision on the Establishment of the Brčko District of Bosnia and Herzegovina, 8 March 2000

OHR, Decision amending the Framework Law on Privatisation of Enterprises and Banks in BiH by introducing a clause protecting investors, 11 May 2000

OHR, Decision on the appointment of the Board of Governors of Radio-Television of the RS, 27 July 2000

OHR, Decision imposing the Law on the State Court of BiH, 12 November 2000

OHR, Decision amending the Law on Privatisation of Enterprises, 20 December 2000

OHR, Decision removing Edhem Bicakcic from his position as Director of Elektroprivreda for actions during his term as Prime Minister of the Federation of Bosnia and Herzegovina, 23 February 2001

OHR, Decision removing Ante Jelavić from his position as the Croat Member of the BiH Presidency and further banning Jelavić from holding public and Party offices, 7 March 2001

OHR, Decision amending the Law on Sale of Apartments with Occupancy Rights, 17 July 2001

OHR, Decision further amending the Law on the Privatization of State Owned Apartments, 17 July 2001

OHR, Decision on a Temporary Freeze of Apartment Privatisations (RS), 4 December 2001

OHR, Decision enacting the Law on Amendments to the Law on Court of Bosnia and Herzegovina, 6 August 2002

OHR, Decision enacting the Law on Banks of the Republika Srpska, 21 October 2002

OHR, Decision on the appointment of members of and advisors to the High Judicial and Prosecutorial Council of Bosnia and Herzegovina, 4 June 2004

OHR, Decision enacting the Law on the Temporary Prohibition of Disposal of State Property of Bosnia and Herzegovina, 20 January 2005

OHR, Decision enacting the Law on Amendments of the Election Law of Bosnia and Herzegovina, 4 April 2005

OHR, Decision extending the mandate of Mr Sven Marius Urke as an International Member of the High Judicial and Prosecutorial Council of Bosnia and Herzegovina, 3 June 2005

OHR, Decision on appointment of an International Member of the High Judicial and Prosecutorial Council of Bosnia and Herzegovina, 26 January 2006

OHR, Order on the Implementation of the Decision of the Constitutional Court of Bosnia and Herzegovina in the Appeal of Milorad Bilbija et al, No. AP-953/05, 23 March 2007

OHR, Decisions in the Field of Property Laws, Return of Displaced Persons and Refugees and Reconciliation, obtainable from <http://www.ohr.int/decisions/archive.asp>

OHR Supervisor of Brčko orders obtainable from: <http://ohr.int/ohr-offices/brcko>

OHR Supervisor of Brčko, Order on Privatization in the District of Brčko, 4 December 1997

OHR Supervisor of Brčko, Supervisory Order on the Establishment of the Brčko District of Bosnia and Herzegovina, 8 March 2000

OHR Supervisor of Brčko, Supervisory Order Repealing the Socialist Republic of Bosnia and Herzegovina Law on Construction Land of 1986 within the Boundaries of Brčko District, 1 March 2006

OHR Supervisor of Brčko, Supervisory Order Prohibiting Certain Non-Salary Payments to Civil Servants, 22 March 2006

3.5.3 *Peace Implementation Conference and Peace Implementation Council*

Conclusions of the Peace Implementation Conference held at Lancaster House, London, 8 and 9 December 1995, UN Doc. S/1995/1029, 12 December 1995, Annex, reprinted in 35 (1996) *ILM* 223

Conclusions of the Ministerial Meeting of the PIC Steering Board and of the Presidency of Bosnia-Herzegovina, 'Guiding principles of the Civilian consolidation plan', Paris, 14 November 1996, available at <http://www.ohr.int/pic/default.asp?content_id=5173>

Conclusions of the Peace Implementation Conference held in London, Lancaster House, 4 and 5 December 1996, 'Bosnia & Herzegovina 1997: Making Peace Work', available at <http://www.ohr.int/pic/default.asp?content_id=5175>

Conclusions of the Peace Implementation Conference held in Bonn on 10 December 1997, 'Bosnia and Herzegovina 1998: Self-sustaining Structures', available at <http://www.ohr.int/pic/default.asp?content_id=5182>

Peace Implementation Council, Madrid Declaration, Annex: 'The Peace Implementation Agenda, Reinforcing Peace in Bosnia and Herzegovina – The Way Ahead', 16 December 1998, available at <http://www.ohr.int/pic/default.asp?content_id=5191>

Peace Implementation Council, Communiqué by the PIC Steering Board, 31 July 2002, available at <http://www.ohr.int/pic/default.asp?content_id=27575>

Communiqué by the PIC Steering Board, 'Towards Ownership: From Peace Implementation to Euro-Atlantic Integration', 23 June 2006, available at <http://www.ohr.int/pic/default.asp?content_id=37503>

Communiqué by PIC Steering Board, 7 December 2006, available at <http://www.ohr.int/pic/default.asp?content_id=38641>

Communiqué by the PIC Steering Board, 27 February 2007, available at <http://www.ohr.int/pic/default.asp?content_id=39236>

3.5.4 *Other*

OHR website: <http://www.ohr.int>

Statute of the Brčko District of Bosnia and Herzegovina (Brčko Statute), 7 December 1999, 39 (2000) *ILM* 879

Statute of the City of Mostar, enacted by OHR Decision enacting the Statute of the City of Mostar, 28 January 2004, obtainable from <http://www.ohr.int/decisions/mo-hncantdec/archive.asp>

Commission for Reforming the City of Mostar, 'Recommendations of the Commission – Report of the Chairman', 15 December 2003, available at <http://www.ohr.int/archive/report-mostar/pdf/Reforming%20Mostar-Report%20(EN).pdf>

3.6 Conference for Security and Co-operation in Europe (CSCE)/ Organization for Security and Co-operation in Europe (OSCE)

OSCE website: <http://www.osce.org>

3.6.1 *International documents*

CSCE, *Helsinki Final Act 1975*, adopted at the Helsinki Summit, 1 August 1975, obtainable from OSCE website

CSCE, *Charter of Paris for a New Europe*, adopted at the Paris Summit, 19–21 November 1990, obtainable from OSCE website

CSCE, *Helsinki Document: The Challenges of Change*, adopted at the Helsinki Summit, 9–10 July 1992, obtainable from OSCE website

CSCE, *Budapest Document* (containing several Declarations and Decisions), adopted at the CSCE Budapest Summit, 5–6 December 1994, obtainable from OSCE website

CSCE, *Prague Document on Further Development of CSCE Institutions and Structures*, adopted by the Ministerial Council, 31 January 1992, obtainable from OSCE website

OSCE, Permanent Council, Decision No. 305, 'Decision on the OSCE Mission in Kosovo', 1 July 1999, OSCE Doc. PC.DEC/305, appended to the Journal of the

237th Plenary Meeting of the Permanent Council (OSCE Doc. PC.JOUR/237/Corr., 1 July 1999), available at <http://www.osce.org/documents/pc/1999/07/2577_en.pdf>

OSCE Office for Democratic Institutions and Human Rights, *Ten Years of ODIHR: Working for Human Rights and Democracy (1991–2001)* (2001), obtainable from OSCE website

OSCE Office for Democratic Institutions and Human Rights, Elections reports, obtainable from <http://www.osce.org/odihr/documents/reports/election_reports>

3.6.2 OSCE Mission in Bosnia and Herzegovina

Head of OSCE Mission in Bosnia Herzegovina, 'Statement to OSCE Permanent Council', Vienna, 4 July 2002, available at <http://www.oscebih.org/documents/28-eng.pdf>

OSCE Mission in Bosnia and Herzegovina, Press Release, 'Bosnia and Herzegovina Election Commission fully nationalized', undated (from 2005), available at <http://www.oscebih.org/public/print_news.asp?id=971>

3.6.3 OSCE Mission in Kosovo

OSCE Mission in Kosovo website, 'Elections' page: <http://www.osce.org/kosovo/13208.html>

OSCE, 'Review 1 – The Criminal Justice System in Kosovo (February–July 2000)', 10 August 2000, available at <http://www.osce.org/documents/mik/2000/08/970_en.pdf>

OSCE, 'Report 2 – Development of the Kosovo Judicial System (10 June through 15 December 1999), 17 December 1999, available at <http://www.osce.org/documents/mik/1999/12/963_en.pdf>

3.7 North Atlantic Treaty Organization (NATO)

NATO, 'Operation Deliberate Force', Fact sheet (undated), available at <http://www.afsouth.nato.int/factsheets/DeliberateForceFactSheet.htm>

Transcript of the Press point by NATO Secretary General, Lord Robertson and Wolfgang Petritsch, High Representative of the International Community for Bosnia and Herzegovina, 16 January 2002, available at <http://www.nato.int/docu/speech/2002/s020116a.htm>

Implementation Force in Bosnia and Herzegovina (IFOR) website: <http://www.nato.int/ifor/ifor.htm>

Kosovo Force (KFOR) website:< http://www.nato.int/kfor/index.html>

Stabilisation Force in Bosnia and Herzegovina (SFOR) website: <http://www.nato.int/sfor>

3.8 United Nations

UN Documentation Centre: <http://www.un.org/documents/index.html>
Official Documents System of the United Nations (ODS): <http://documents.un.org>

3.8.1 United Nations – General Assembly

3.8.1.1 Resolutions

General Assembly Resolutions: <http://www.un.org/documents/resga.htm>
GA Res. 217A (III), 10 December 1948 (Universal Declaration of Human Rights)

GA Res. 302 (IV), 8 December 1949

GA Res. 428 (V), 14 December 1950 (Statute of the United Nations Office of the High Commissioner for Refugees)

GA Res. 1480 (XV), 20 September 1960

GA Res. 1514 (XV), 14 December 1960

GA Res. 1541 (XV), 15 December 1960

GA Res. 1714 (XVI), 19 December 1961

GA Res. 1752 (XVII), 21 September 1962

GA Res. 2145 (XXI), 27 October 1966

GA Res. 2229 (XXI), 20 December 1966

GA Res. 2248 (S-V), 19 May 1967

GA Res. 2252 (ES-V), 4 July 1967

GA Res. 2325 (XXII), 16 December 1967

GA Res. 2372 (XXII), 12 June 1968

GA Res. 2504 (XXIV), 19 November 1969

GA Res. 2621 (XXV), 12 October 1970

GA Res. 2625 (XXV), 24 October 1970 (Declaration on Principles of International Law Concerning Friendly Relations and Cooperation among States in Accordance with the Charter of the United Nations)

GA Res. 3103 (XXVIII), 30 December 1973

GA Res. 3295 (XXIX), 13 December 1974

GA Res. 3458A (XX), 10 December 1975

GA Res. 3458B (XX), 10 December 1975

GA Res. 3485 (XXX), 12 December 1975

GA Res. 31/53, 1 December 1976

GA Res. 32/34, 28 November 1977

GA Res. 33/39, 13 December 1978

GA Res. 34/40, 21 November 1979

GA Res. 35/27, 11 November 1980

GA Res. 36/50, 24 November 1981

GA Res. 37/10, 15 November 1982 (Manila Declaration on the Peaceful Settlement of International Disputes)

GA Res. 37/30, 23 November 1982

GA Res. 37/63, 3 December 1982

GA Res. 43/51, 5 December 1988 (Declaration on the Prevention and Removal of Disputes and Situations Which May Threaten International Peace and Security and on the Role of the United Nations in this Field)

GA Res. 44/21, 15 November 1989 (Enhancing international peace, security and international co-operation in all its aspects in accordance with the Charter of the United Nations)

GA Res. 46/18, 20 November 1991

GA Res. 46/237, 22 May 1992

GA Res. 46/238, 22 May 1992

GA Res. 47/1, 22 September 1992

GA Res. 55/12, 10 November 2000

GA Res. 57/3, 27 September 2002

GA Res. 57/228 B, 22 May 2003

GA Res. 60/1, 16 September 2005 (2005 World Summit Outcome)

GA Res. 60/264, 28 June 2006

3.8.1.2 Debates

UN GAOR, 15th Sess., 931st plenary meeting, 1 December 1960, 1065

3.8.2 United Nations – Secretariat

3.8.2.1 Secretary-General

Reports

Annual Report of the Secretary-General on the Work of the Organization, 16 June
     1962–15 June 1963, UN GAOR, 18th Sess., Supp. No. 1, at 35, UN Doc. A/5501
Report of the Secretary-General, 19 November 1975, UN Doc. S/11880
Report of the Secretary-General, 29 August 1978, UN Doc. S/12827
Report of the Secretary-General, 23 January 1989, UN Doc. S/20412
Report of the Secretary-General, 16 March 1989, UN Doc. S/20412/Add.1
Report of the Secretary-General, 18 June 1990, UN Doc. S/21360
Report of the Secretary-General, 19 April 1991, UN Doc. S/22464
Report of the Secretary-General on Enhancing the Effectiveness of the Principle of
     Periodic and Genuine Elections, 19 November 1991, UN Doc. A/46/609
Report of the Secretary-General on Cambodia, 19 February 1992, UN Doc. S/23613
     and Addendum 1, 26 February 1992, UN Doc. S/23613/Add.1
Agenda for Peace: Preventive Diplomacy, Peacemaking and Peacekeeping, Report of the
     Secretary-General, 17 June 1992, UN Doc. A/47/277 – S/24111
Report of the Secretary-General, 11 November 1992, UN Doc. S/24795
Further Report of the Secretary-General on the Situation in Somalia Submitted in Pursuance
     of Paragraphs 18 and 19 of Resolution 794, 3 March 1993, UN Doc. S/25354
Report of the Secretary-General, 7 January 1994, UN Doc. A/48/847
Report of the Secretary-General, 17 November 1994, UN Doc. A/49/675, Annex III
*Supplement to Agenda for Peace: Position Paper of the Secretary General on the Occasion
     of the Fiftieth Anniversary of the United Nations*, Report of the Secretary-General,
     3 January 1995, UN Doc A/50/60 – S/1995/1
Report of the Secretary-General on Eastern Slavonia, 28 August 1996, UN Doc.
     S/1996/705
Report of the Secretary-General on Eastern Slavonia, 23 June 1997, UN Doc.
     S/1997/487
Report of the Secretary-General on Eastern Slavonia, 22 January 1998, UN Doc.
     S/1998/59
Report of the Secretary-General on the United Nations Interim Administration Mission
     in Kosovo, 12 July 1999, UN Doc. S/1999/779
'Observance by United Nations Forces of international humanitarian law', Secretary-
     General's Bulletin, 6 August 1999, UN Doc. ST/SGB/1999/13
Report of the Secretary-General pursuant to General Assembly Resolution 53/35, 'The
     fall of Srebrenica', 15 November 1999, UN Doc. A/54/549
Progress Report of the Secretary-General on the Question of East Timor, 13 December
     1999, UN Doc. A/54/654 (1999)
Report of the Secretary-General on the Situation Concerning Western Sahara, 20 June
     2001, UN Doc. S/2001/613

Report of the Secretary-General on the situation in Afghanistan and its implications for international peace and security, 18 March 2002, UN Doc. A/56/875–S/2002/278

Report of the Secretary-General on the United Nations Transitional Administration in East Timor, 17 April 2002, UN Doc. S/2002/432

Report of the Secretary-General on the Western Sahara, 16 January 2003, UN Doc. S/2003/59

Report of the Secretary-General pursuant to paragraph 6 of resolution 1644 (2005), 21 March 2006, UN Doc. S/2006/176

Report of the Secretary-General on the establishment of a special tribunal for Lebanon, UN Doc. S/2006/893, 15 November 2006, with Annex, draft Agreement between the United Nations and the Lebanese Republic on the establishment of a Special Tribunal for Lebanon and Statute of the Special Tribunal for Lebanon

Report of the Secretary-General on the United Nations Interim Administration Mission in Kosovo, 9 March 2007, UN Doc. S/2007/134

Report of the Secretary-General on the status and progress of the negotiations on Western Sahara, 29 June 2007, UN Doc. S/2007/385

Statements

Explanatory Statement, 9 February 1989, UN Doc. S/20457

Explanatory Statement, 29 September 1978, UN Doc. S/12869

Statement on UN Operations in the Congo before the General Assembly, 17 October 1960, UN Doc. A/PV.906, UN GAOR, 15th Sess., Plenary Meetings, vol. I, 741

Letters

Letter to the President of the Security Council Regarding the Result of the Popular Consultation, 3 September 1999, UN Doc. S/1999/944

Letter dated 15 December 1999 from the Secretary General addressed to the President of the Security Council (containing the 'Report of the independent inquiry into the actions of the United Nations during the 1994 genocide in Rwanda'), UN Doc. S/1999/1257

Letter dated 24 June 2005 from the Secretary-General addressed to the President of the Security Council, UN Doc. S/2005/458

Notes

Application of the Federal Republic of Yugoslavia for admission to membership in the United Nations, Note by the Secretary-General, 30 October 2000, UN Doc. A/55/528 – S/2000/1043

Miscellaneous

UN Press Release SG/A/922, 'Secretary-General Appoints Detlev Mehlis as Head of UN International Independent Investigation Commission', 13 May 2005

Spokesman for the Secretary-General, 'Statement on the UN International Independent Investigation Commission', New York, 16 June 2005, available at <http://www.un.org/apps/sg/sgstats.asp?nid=1514>

UN News Service, 'Former Belgian prosecutor named as new head of UN probe into Hariri murder', 11 January 2006, available at <http://www.un.org/apps/news/story.asp?NewsID=17129&Cr=&Crl=>

3.8.2.2 Deputy Secretary-General

Statement by Louise Fréchette, Deputy Secretary-General of the United Nations, Press Release DSG/SM/91, 3 April 2000

3.8.2.3 United Nations Department of Peacekeeping Operations (DPKO)

United Nations Department of Peacekeeping Operations, *An Introduction to United Nations Peacekeeping*, 'Preface', obtainable from <http://www.un.org/Depts/dpko/dpko/intro/intro.htm>

United Nations Department of Peacekeeping Operations, 'Eastern Slavonia, Baranja and Western Sirmium – Brief Chronology, 15 January 1996 – 15 January 1998', available at <http://www.un.org/Depts/DPKO/Missions/untaes_e.htm>

3.8.2.4 United Nations Department of Political Affairs (DPA)

United Nations Department of Political Affairs, Decolonization Unit, 'Trust and Non-Self-Governing Territories, 1945–1999', available at <http://www.un.org/Depts/dpi/decolonization/trust2.htm>

United Nations Department of Political Affairs, Decolonization Unit, 'The United Nations and Decolonization' website, at <http://www.un.org/Depts/dpi/decolonization>

3.8.2.5 Miscellaneous

Legal Opinions of the Secretariat of the United Nations, Question of the possible accession of intergovernmental organizations to the Geneva Conventions for the protection of war victims, 15 June 1972, (1972) *United Nations Juridical Yearbook* 153

Panel on United Nations Peace Operations, Report to the United Nations Secretary-General (Brahimi Report), 21 August 2000, UN Doc. A/55/305 – S/2000/809

'General Assembly decides to remove East Timor from list of Non-Self-Governing Territories upon independence, set for 20 May', UN Press Release GA/10014, 1 May 2002, available at <http://www.un.org/News/Press/docs/2002/GA10014.doc.htm>

'Appointments to Sierra Leone Special Court', UN Press Release SG/A/813 – AFR/444, 26 July 2002

Report of the Fact-finding Mission to Lebanon inquiring into the causes, circumstances and consequences of the assassination of former Prime Minister Rafik Hariri (25 February–24 March 2005), 24 March 2005, UN Doc. S/2005/203

Report of the Special Envoy of the Secretary General, Mr. Kay Eide, 'A comprehensive review of the situation in Kosovo', UN Doc. S/2005/635, Annex, 7 October 2005

'Bosnia and Herzegovina at the Brink of EU Membership, Security Council Told', 15 November 2005, United Nations News Service, available at <http://www.un.org/apps/news/story.asp?NewsID=16573&Cr=bosnia&Cr1=herzegovina>

3.8.3 United Nations – Security Council

3.8.3.1 Presidential statements

Statement of the President of the Security Council, 31 October 2001, UN Doc. S/PRST/2001/32

Statement by the President of the Security Council, 3 September 1999, UN Doc. S/PRST/1999/27

Statement by the President of the Security Council, 12 December 2003, UN Doc. S/PRST/2003/26

3.8.3.2 Resolutions

Security Council Resolutions: <http://www.un.org/documents/scres.htm>

SC Res. 47, 21 April 1948
SC Res. 91, 30 March 1951
SC Res. 96, 10 November 1951
SC Res. 98, 23 December 1952
SC Res. 122, 24 January 1957
SC Res. 126, 2 December 1957
SC Res. 143, 14 July 1960
SC Res. 152, 23 August 1960
SC Res. 264, 20 March 1969
SC Res. 380, 6 November 1975
SC Res. 384, 22 December 1975
SC Res. 389, 22 April 1976
SC Res. 435, 29 September 1978
SC Res. 632, 16 February 1989
SC Res. 686, 2 March 1991
SC Res. 687, 3 April 1991
SC Res. 688, 5 April 1991
SC Res. 690, 29 April 1991
SC Res. 717, 16 October 1991
SC Res. 745, 28 February 1992
SC Res. 753, 18 May 1992
SC Res. 755, 20 May 1992
SC Res. 757, 30 May 1992
SC Res. 777, 19 September 1992
SC Res. 814, 26 March 1993
SC Res. 907, 29 March 1994
SC Res. 973, 13 January 1995
SC Res. 986, 14 April 1995
SC Res. 997, 26 May 1995
SC Res. 1002, 30 June 1995
SC Res. 1017, 22 September 1995
SC Res. 1023, 22 November 1995
SC Res. 1031, 15 December 1995
SC Res. 1033, 22 December 1995
SC Res. 1037, 15 January 1996
SC Res. 1042, 31 January 1996
SC Res. 1056, 29 May 1996
SC Res. 1079, 15 November 1996
SC Res. 1084, 27 November 1996
SC Res. 1108, 22 May 1997

SC Res. 1120, 14 July 1997
SC Res. 1131, 29 September 1997
SC Res. 1133, 20 October 1997
SC Res. 1145, 19 December 1997
SC Res. 1148, 26 January 1998
SC Res. 1163, 17 April 1998
SC Res. 1185, 20 July 1998
SC Res. 1198, 18 September 1998
SC Res. 1204, 30 October 1998
SC Res. 1215, 17 December 1998
SC Res. 1224, 28 January 1999
SC Res. 1228, 11 February 1999
SC Res. 1232, 30 March 1999
SC Res. 1235, 30 April 1999
SC Res. 1238, 14 May 1999
SC Res. 1244, 10 June 1999
SC Res. 1246, 11 June 1999
SC Res. 1236, 13 September 1999
SC Res. 1264, 15 September 1999
SC Res. 1272, 25 October 1999
SC Res. 1282, 14 December 1999
SC Res. 1292, 29 February 2000
SC Res. 1301, 31 May 2000
SC Res. 1309, 25 July 2000
SC Res. 1312, 31 July 2000
SC Res. 1315, 4 August 2000
SC Res. 1320, 15 September 2000
SC Res. 1324, 30 October 2000
SC Res. 1325, 31 October 2000
SC Res. 1326, 31 October 2000
SC Res. 1338, 31 January 2001
SC Res. 1342, 27 February 2001
SC Res. 1344, 15 March 2001
SC Res. 1349, 27 April 2001
SC Res. 1359, 29 June 2001
SC Res. 1362, 11 July 2001
SC Res. 1369, 14 September 2001
SC Res. 1380, 27 November 2001
SC Res. 1383, 6 December 2001
SC Res. 1392, 31 January 2002
SC Res. 1394, 27 February 2002
SC Res. 1401, 28 March 2002
SC Res. 1406, 30 April 2002
SC Res. 1410, 17 May 2002
SC Res. 1414, 23 May 2002
SC Res. 1429, 30 July 2002
SC Res. 1463, 30 January 2003

SC Res. 1469, 25 March 2003
SC Res. 1472, 28 March 2003
SC Res. 1483, 22 May 2003
SC Res. 1485, 30 May 2003
SC Res. 1495, 31 July 2003
SC Res. 1513, 28 October 2003
SC Res. 1523, 30 January 2004
SC Res. 1541, 29 April 2004
SC Res. 1543, 14 May 2004
SC Res. 1570, 28 October 2004
SC Res. 1573, 16 November 2004
SC Res. 1575, 22 November 2004
SC Res. 1595, 7 April 2005
SC Res. 1598, 28 April 2005
SC Res. 1599, 28 April 2005
SC Res. 1634, 28 October 2005
SC Res. 1636, 31 October 2005
SC Res. 1644, 15 December 2005
SC Res. 1664, 29 March 2006
SC Res. 1675, 28 April 2006
SC Res. 1680, 17 May 2006
SC Res. 1681, 31 May 2006
SC Res. 1686, 15 June 2006
SC Res. 1688, 16 June 2006
SC Res. 1691, 22 June 2006
SC Res. 1704, 25 August 2006
SC Res. 1710, 29 September 2006
SC Res. 1720, 31 October 2006
SC Res. 1741, 30 January 2007
SC Res. 1754, 30 April 2007
SC Res. 1757, 30 May 2007

3.8.4 United Nations – Trusteeship Council

Report of the UN Trusteeship Council, Annex II, Statute for the City of Jerusalem, UN
GAOR, 5th Sess., Suppl. No. 9, at 1, 19, UN Doc. A/1286 (1950)

3.8.5 United Nations – Peacebuilding Commission

Website: <http://www.un.org/peace/peacebuilding>

3.8.6 United Nations – Office of the High Commissioner for Refugees (UNHCR)

UNHCR Global Report 2004, available at <http://www.unhcr.ch/static/publ/gr2004toc.
htm>
UNHCR, Sub-Office Dadaab, 'Dadaab Operations in Brief', 31 January 2006 (publication status unverified, on file with the author)

3.8.7 United Nations – Office of the High Commissioner for Human Rights (UNHCHR)

UNHCHR, 'Human Rights Field Presence in the Federal Republic of Yugoslavia (including Kosovo)', available at <http://www.unhchr.ch/html/menu2/5/fryug.htm>

3.8.8 United Nations Office for the Coordination of Humanitarian Affairs (OCHA)

Website: <http://ochaonline.un.org>
OCHA, 'Somalia', available at <http://ochaonline3.un.org/News/Emergencies/ComplexEmergencies/Somalia/tabid/1253/Default.aspx>
OCHA Somalia, 'Livelihoods and food security' (updated March 2006), obtainable from <http://ochaonline3.un.org/News/Emergencies/ComplexEmergencies/Somalia/tabid/1253/Default.aspx>

3.8.9 United Nations – International Criminal Tribunal for the Former Yugoslavia (ICTY)

Rules of Procedure and Evidence of the International Criminal Tribunal for the former Yugoslavia, obtainable from <http://www.un.org/icty>
ICTY, 'Partnership and Transition between the ICTY and National Courts', undated, available at <http://www.un.org/icty/cases-e/factsheets/partnership-e.htm>

3.8.10 United Nations – Peace Operations

3.8.10.1 United Nations Council for Namibia

United Nations Council for Namibia, Decree No. 1 on Natural Resources of Namibia, UN Doc. A/C.131/33, in Report of the Council for Namibia, Addendum, UN GAOR, 29th Sess., Supp. No. 24A, at 27, UN Doc. A/9624/Add.1 (1974)

3.8.10.2 United Nations Office of the Iraq Programme

Website: <http://www.un.org/Depts/oip/index.html>

3.8.10.3 United Nations Mission in East Timor (UNAMET)

UNAMET Notice, 'To vote you need to register' (1999), obtainable from <http://www.un.org/peace/etimor99/civic/vote-e.htm>
UNAMET, Posters (1999), obtainable from <http://www.un.org/peace/etimor99/POSTERS/posters_frame.htm>
UNAMET, Posters 'If you accept autonomy...' and 'If you reject autonomy...' (1999), available at <http://www.un.org/peace/etimor99/POSTERS/p3ee.jpg>

3.8.10.4 United Nations Transitional Administration in East Timor (UNTAET)

Regulations
UNTAET Regulations obtainable from <http://www.un.org/peace/etimor/untaetN.htm>
UNTAET Regulation 1999/1 27 November 1999

UNTAET Regulation 1999/2, 2 December 1999
UNTAET Regulation 2000/11, 6 June 2000
UNTAET Regulation 2000/15, 6 June 2000
UNTAET Regulation 2000/16, 6 June 2000
UNTAET Regulation 2000/23, 14 July 2000
UNTAET Regulation 2000/24, 14 July 2000
UNTAET Regulation 2001/2, 16 March 2001
UNTAET Regulation 2001/10, 13 July 2001
UNTAET Regulation 2001/28, 19 September 2001

Statements, press releases, and other documents
UNTAET, 'East Timor Update', February 2000, obtainable from <http://www.un.org/peace/etimor/untaetPU/ETupdateFE.pdf>
UNTAET, Daily Briefing, 17 July 2000, available at <http://www.un.org/peace/etimor/DB/DB170700.HTM>
UNTAET Daily Briefing, 8 August 2000, available at <http://www.un.org/peace/etimor/DB/DB080800.HTM>
UNTAET Daily Briefing, 'Twenty Cases Examined by Ombudsperson', Dili, 1 June 2001, available at <http://www.un.org/peace/etimor/DB/Db010601.htm>
UNTAET, Daily Briefing, 20 September 2001, available at <http://www.un.org/peace/etimor/DB/db200901.htm>
Transcript of the press conference held by the Transitional Administrator, Sergio Vieira de Mello on 17 January 2002, available at <http://www.un.org/peace/etimor/DB/db170102.htm>
UNTAET Press Office, 'Fact Sheet 3' (April 2002), available at <http://www.un.org/peace/etimor/fact/fs3.PDF>

3.8.10.5 United Nations Assistance Mission in Afghanistan (UNAMA)
Website: <http://www.unama-afg.org>

3.8.10.6 United Nations Interim Administration Mission in Kosovo (UNMIK)

Website: <http://www.unmikonline.org>
UNMIK 'Standards for Kosovo' webpage: <http://www.unmikonline.org/standards/index.html>

Regulations
UNMIK regulations obtainable from: <http://www.unmikonline.org/regulations/unmikgazette/index.htm>
UNMIK Regulation No. 1999/1 (as amended), contained in UNMIK Regulation 2000/54, 27 September 2000
UNMIK Regulation 2000/6, 15 February 2000, amended by UNMIK Regulation 2000/34, 27 May 2000 and UNMIK Regulation 2001/2, 12 January 2001
UNMIK Regulation No. 2000/38, 30 June 2000
UNMIK Regulation 2000/64, 15 December 2000
UNMIK Regulation 2001/9, 15 May 2001
UNMIK Regulation No. 2002/12, 13 June 2002, as amended by UNMIK Regulation No. 2005/18, 22 April 2005

UNMIK Regulation No. 2003/13, 9 May 2003
UNMIK Regulation No. 2005/3, 21 January 2005
UNMIK Regulation No. 2006/6, 16 February 2006
UNMIK Regulation No. 2006/12, 23 March 2006

Press releases
'UNMIK Marks Six Months in Kosovo', UNMIK Press Briefing, 13 December 1999,
    available at <http://www.un.org/peace/kosovo/pages/kouch_status.htm>
'Highlights of the introductory remarks at a press conference by Michael Steiner, Special
    Representative of the Secretary-General in Kosovo', UN Press Release, 26 June 2002,
    available at <http://www.unhchr.ch/huricane/huricane.nsf/view01/6BEC09E5B4BE
    EBCBC1256BE60025221E?opendocument>
'SRSG Swears in 169 Lay Judges for Kosovo Courts', UNMIK Press Release,
    6 October 2004, available at <http://www.unmikonline.org/press/2004/pressr/
    pr1238.pdf>

Miscellaneous
UNMIK Civilian Police, *Police Report for 2002: A Year of Transition* (2002), available at
    <http://www.unmikonline.org/civpol/reports/Police%20Report%202002%20-%20
    Book.pdf>
UNMIK, *Standards for Kosovo*, presented on 10 December 2003, available at <http://
    www.unmikonline.org/standards/docs/leaflet_stand_eng.pdf>
UNMIK, Kosovo Standards Implementation Plan, 31 March 2004 (with updated actions
    for Standards 3 and 4 as of 6 July 2006), available at <http://www.unmikonline.org/
    pub/misc/ksip_eng.pdf>
Report ACFC(2005)003 of 2 June 2005 submitted to the Advisory Committee on the
    Framework Convention for the Protection of National Minorities by the United
    Nations Interim Administration (UNMIK) with Annexes I–XLV, obtainable from
    <http://www.coe.int/
UNMIK, Observations on the Opinion of the Advisory Committee on the Framework
    Convention for the Protection of National Minorities (adopted 25 November 2005),
    18 February 2006, obtainable from <http://www.coe.int/>
Report Submitted by the United Nations Interim Administration Mission in Kosovo to
    the Human Rights Committee on the Human Rights Situation in Kosovo since June
    1999, 13 March 2006, UN Doc. CCPR/C/UNK/1

3.8.10.7 United Nations Mission in Ethiopia and Eritrea (UNMEE)

Website: <http://www.un.org/Depts/dpko/unmee/body_unmee.htm>

3.8.10.8 United Nations Mission for the Referendum in Western Sahara (MINURSO)

Website: <http://www.un.org/Depts/dpko/missions/minurso>
United Nations, 'MINURSO Background', available at <http://www.un.org/Depts/
    dpko/missions/minurso/background.html>

3.8.10.9 United Nations Relief and Works Agency for Palestine Refugees in the Near East (UNRWA)

Website: <http://www.un.org/unrwa>

Archive of General Assembly Resolutions on UNRWA since 2001: <http://www.un.org/unrwa/publications/ga_resolutions.html>

UNRWA, 'UNRWA Response to allegations made by the Centre Simon Wiesenthal in its statement to the Commission on 31 March 2003', 9 April 2003, available at <http://www.un.org/unrwa/allegations/response.html>

UNRWA, 'UNRWA Medium Term Plan 2005–2009, A Better Future for Palestine Refugees' (2005), available at <http://www.un.org/unrwa/news/mtp.pdf>

Public Information Office, UNRWA Headquarters, 'UNRWA in Figures – Figures as of 31 December 2005', March 2006, available at <http://www.un.org/unrwa/publications/pdf/uif-dec05.pdf>

'Map of UNRWA's Area of Operations 2005', undated, available at <http://www.un.org/unrwa/refugees/images/map.jpg>

UNRWA, 'Who is a Palestine refugee?', undated, available at: <http://www.un.org/unrwa/refugees/whois.html>

UNRWA, 'Setting the Record Straight', undated, available at <http://www.un.org/unrwa/allegations/index.html>

3.8.10.10 United Nations International Independent Investigation Commission for Lebanon (UNIIIC)

Report of the International Independent Investigation Commission established pursuant to Security Council Resolution 1595 (2005), UN Doc. S/2005/662, 19 October 2005

Second report of the International Independent Investigation Commission established pursuant to Security Council resolutions 1595 (2005) and 1636 (2005), 10 December 2005, UN Doc. S/2005/775, Annex

Third Report of the International Independent Investigation Commission established pursuant to Security Council resolutions 1595 (2005), 1636 (2005) and 1644 (2005), 14 March 2006, UN Doc. S/2006/161, Annex

Fourth Report of the International Independent Investigation Commission established pursuant to Security Council resolutions 1595 (2005), 1636 (2005) and 1644 (2005), 10 June 2006, UN Doc. S/2006/375, Annex

3.8.10.11 United Nations Protection Force (UNPROFOR)

Website: <http://www.un.org/Depts/dpko/dpko/co_mission/unprofor.htm>

4 Documents of National/Locally-Based Institutions and Organizations

4.1 Afghanistan

Presidential Decree No. 39 on the Establishment of the Interim Electoral Commission, 26 July 2003 (English translation obtainable from <http://www.elections-afghanistan.org.af/Legal%20Framework.htm>)

Presidential Decree No. 40 on the establishment of the Joint Electoral Management Body, 26 July 2003, subsequently amended by Presidential Decree n. 110 on arrangements for holding elections during the transitional period, 10 February 2004 (unofficial English translations obtainable from <http://www.elections-afghanistan.org.af/Legal%20Framework.htm>)

Presidential Decree No. 21 of 19 January 2005 on the Formation of the Independent Election Commission, available at <http://www.jemb.org/eng/Legal%20Framework/Decree%20on%20the%20Establishment%20of%20the%20IAEC%20(English)2005.pdf>

Presidential Decree No. 23 on the Structure and Working Procedure of the Independent Election Commission, 24 January 2005, available at <http://www.jemb.org/eng/Legal%20Framework/Decree%20on%20the%20Establishment%20of%20the%20IAEC%20(English)2005.pdf>

Presidential Decree No. 24 on Holding National Assembly, Provincial Council and District Council Elections, 6 May 2005 (English translation obtainable from <http://www.elections-afghanistan.org.af/Legal%20Framework.htm>)

4.2 Bosnia and Herzegovina

4.2.1 Official Gazette

Law on High Judicial and Prosecutorial Council of Bosnia and Herzegovina, 21 May 2004, *Official Gazette of Bosnia and Herzegovina* No. 25/04, English translation available at <http://www.hjpc.ba/intro/?cid=1648,1,1>

Law on the Prosecutor's Office of Bosnia and Herzegovina, as amended in 2004, *Official Gazette of Bosnia and Herzegovina* Nos 24/02, 3/03, 37/03, 42/03, 9/04, 35/04, and 61/04

Law on the Amendments to the Law on the Prosecutor's Office of Bosnia Herzegovina, *Official Gazette of Bosnia and Herzegovina* No. 61/04

Law on Court of Bosnia and Herzegovina, as amended in 2004, *Official Gazette of Bosnia and Herzegovina*, Nos 29/00, 24/02, 3/03, 42/03, 37/03, 9/04, 4/04, 35/04, and 61/04

Law on the Transfer of Cases from the ICTY to the Prosecutor's Office of Bosnia and Herzegovina and the Use of Evidence Collected by the ICTY in Proceedings before the Courts in Bosnia and Herzegovina, *Official Gazette of Bosnia and Herzegovina* No. 61/04

Election Law of Bosnia and Herzegovina, as amended in 2004, *Official Gazette of Bosnia and Herzegovina* Nos 23/01, 7/02, 9/02, 20/02, 25/02, 4/04, and 20/04

Election Law of Bosnia and Herzegovina, 19 September 2001, as amended in 2005, *Official Gazette of Bosnia and Herzegovina* Nos 23/01, 7/02, 9/02, 20/02, 25/02, 4/04, 20/04, and 25/05

4.2.2 Human Rights Ombudsperson

Human Rights Ombudsperson website: <http://www.ohro.ba>

Law on the Human Rights Ombudsman of Bosnia and Herzegovina, entry into force 3 January 2001, available at <http://www.ohro.ba/articles/article.php?lit_id=ombudlaw>

4.2.3 Constitutional Court

Constitutional Court of Bosnia Herzegovina, Press Release, Completion of work on the cases of former Human Rights Chamber for Bosnia and Herzegovina and closure of Annex 6 to the General Framework Agreement for Peace in Bosnia and Herzegovina', 3 July 2007, obtainable from <http://www.ccbh.ba/eng/press/index.php?pid=2202&sta=3&pkat=507>

4.2.4 Human Rights Commission within the Constitutional Court of Bosnia and Herzegovina

Human Rights Commission within the Constitutional Court of Bosnia and Herzegovina, 'Monthly Statistical Summaries', obtainable from <http://www.hrc.ba/commission/eng/stat_summaries_eng/index.asp>

4.2.5 Central Bank

Central Bank of Bosnia Herzegovina, *Annual Report 2003*, obtainable from <http://cbbh.ba/en/archive.html>

Central Bank of Bosnia Herzegovina, *Annual Report 2004*, obtainable from <http://cbbh.ba/en/archive.html>

4.2.6 Commission for Real Property Claims of Displaced Persons and Refugees (CRPC)

Mirror website:
<http://www.law.kuleuven.ac.be/ipr/eng/CRPC_Bosnia/CRPC/new/en/main.htm>

4.2.7 High Judicial and Prosecutorial Council (HJPC)

Website: <http://www.hjpc.ba/home.aspx>
'Members of the HJPC' (as of 31 January 2006), available at <http://www.hjpc.ba/intro/bios/?cid=18,1,1>

4.2.8 Commission to Preserve National Monuments (CPNM)

Bosnia and Herzegovina Commission to Preserve National Monuments, 'Commissioners' CV's', available at <http://www.aneks8komisija.com.ba/main.php?id_struct=74&lang=4>

4.2.9 Registry for Section I for War Crimes & Section II for Organized Crime, Economic Crimes and Corruption of the Court of Bosnia and Herzegovina

Registry for Section I for War Crimes & Section II for Organized Crime, Economic Crimes and Corruption of the Criminal and Appellate Divisions of the Court of Bosnia and Herzegovina and the Special Department for War Crimes and the Special Department for Organized Crime, Economic Crimes and Corruption of the Prosecutor's Office of Bosnia and Herzegovina, and Ministry of Justice Prison Project, 'Project Implementation Plan Progress Report', October 2005, obtainable from <http://www.registrarbih.gov.ba>

4.3 Cambodia

Secretariat of the Royal Government Task Force, Office of the Council of Ministers, Kingdom of Cambodia, *An Introduction to the Khmer Rouge Trials* (August 2004), available at <http://www.cambodia.gov.kh/krt/english/introduction_eng/Khmer% 20Rouge%20Trials_English.pdf>

Law on the Establishment of Extraordinary Chambers in the Courts of Cambodia for the Prosecution of Crimes Committed during the Period of Democratic Cambodia, with inclusion of amendments as promulgated on 27 October 2004, unofficial English translation available at <http://www.cambodia.gov.kh/krt/pdfs/KR%20Law%20 as%20amended%2027%20Oct%202004%20Eng.pdf>

Extraordinary Chambers in the Courts of Cambodia Press Release, 4 May 2006, available at <http://www.cambodia.gov.kh/krt/pdfs/ECCC%20Press%20Release%20 04%20May%202006.pdf>

Royal Government of Cambodia, 'Official List of National and International Judges and Prosecutors for the Extraordinary Chambers in the Courts of Cambodia as selected by the Supreme Council of the Magistracy on 4 May 2006 and appointed by Preah Reach Kret (Royal Decree) NS/RKT/0506/214 of His Majesty Norodom Sihamoni, King of Cambodia on 7 May 2006', undated, available at <http://www.cambodia.gov.kh/krt/ english/judicial_officer.htm>

4.4 Coalition Provisional Authority (CPA) in Iraq

CPA Order 92, 31 May 2004, available at <http://www.iraqcoalition.org/regulations/ 20040531_CPAORD_92_Independent_Electoral_commission_of_Iraq.pdf>

4.5 East Timor

Commission for Reception, Truth, and Reconciliation Timor-Leste, 'Chega! Report of the Commission for Reception, Truth, and Reconciliation Timor-Leste' (2005), available at <http://www.etan.org/news/2006/cavr.htm>

Commission for Reception, Truth, and Reconciliation Timor-Leste, 'Profiles of the National Commissioners', available at <http://www.easttimor-reconciliation.org/ National%20Commissioners-E.htm>

Commission for Reception, Truth and Reconciliation in East Timor, 'Mandate', available at <http://www.easttimor-reconciliation.org/mandate.htm>

4.6 Iraq

Independent Electoral Commission of Iraq (IECI) website: <http://www.ieciraq.org/ English/Frameset_english.htm>

Statute of the Iraqi Special Tribunal, 10 December 2003, available at <http://www. globalpolicy.org/intljustice/general/2003/1210iraqistatute.pdf>

Law of Administration for the State of Iraq for the Transitional Period, 8 March 2004 (English translation available at <http://www.cpa-iraq.org/government/TAL.html> and <http://www.oefre.unibe.ch/law/icl/iz00000_.html>)

Constitution of Iraq, approved by a referendum held on 10 October 2005 (English translation available at <http://www.msnbc.msn.com/id/9719734/>)

Law of the Iraqi Higher Criminal Court (Law No. (10) 2005), 10 October 2005 (English translation available at <http://law.case.edu/saddamtrial/documents/IST_statute_official_english.pdf>)

4.7 Kosovo

Ombudsperson Institution in Kosovo website: <http://www.ombudspersonkosovo>

Ombudsperson Institution in Kosovo, 'Special report no. 1 on the compatibility with recognized international standards of UNMIK Regulation No. 2000/47 on the Status, Privileges and Immunities of KFOR and UNMIK and Their Personnel in Kosovo (18 August 2000) and on the implementation of the above regulation', 26 April 2001, obtainable from Ombudsperson website

Ombudsperson Institution in Kosovo, *Second Annual Report 2001–2002*, 10 July 2002, obtainable from Ombudsperson website

Kosovo Trust Agency (KTA) website: <http://www.kta-kosovo.org>

4.8 Lebanon

Letter dated 29 March 2005 from the Chargé d'affaires a.i. of the Permanent Mission of Lebanon to the United Nations addressed to the Secretary-General, UN Doc. S/2005/208

Letter of the Prime Minister of Lebanon to the United Nations Secretary-General, 13 October 2005, UN Doc. S/2005/651

Letter of the Prime Minister of Lebanon to the United Nations Secretary-General, 5 December 2005, UN Doc. S/2005/762

Letter of the Prime Minister of Lebanon to the United Nations Secretary-General, 13 December 2005, UN Doc. S/2005/783, Annex

Letter of the Prime Minister of Lebanon to the United Nations Secretary-General, 5 May 2006, UN Doc. S/2006/278

4.9 Nauru

Report of the Commission of Inquiry into the Rehabilitation of the Worked-Out Phosphate Lands of Nauru (Government of Nauru, 1988)

4.10 Serbia

Communication dated 16 June 2006 from the Minister for Foreign Affairs of the Republic of Serbia to the United Nations Secretary-General, reproduced in note 1 of the 'Serbia' part of 'Status of Multilateral Treaties Deposited with the Secretary-General – Historical Information', available at <http://untreaty.un.org/ENGLISH/bible/englishinternetbible/historicalinfo.asp>

4.11 Sierra Leone

Truth and Reconciliation Act 2000 (Sierra Leone), available at <http://www.sierra-leone.org/trcact2000.html>

4.12 United Kingdom

Briefing from the Prime Minister's Official Spokesman, 12 May 2003, available at
<http://www.pm.gov.uk/output/Page3648.asp>
Clare Short MP, Speech delivered in the House of Commons on 12 May 2003, Hansard,
HC Deb 12 May 2003 cc 36–39, available at <http://www.publications.parliament.
uk/pa/cm200203/cmhansrd/vo030512/debtext/30512–09.htm#30512–09_spnew8>

4.13 United States of America

President Bush's Statement on the Recognition of Bosnia and Herzegovina, Croatia and
Slovenia, 7 April 1992, reprinted in 18 (1992) *Review of International Affairs* 26

5 Secondary Commentary

Sections 5.1 to 5.4 contain lists of secondary commentary divided according to subject-
matter for reference purposes. Some sources are included in more than one list. Within
each of the lists in these sections, commentary is ordered according to publication type,
and, within this, year of publication.

Sections 5.1 and 5.2 contain commentary on ITA. Section 5.1 contains lists of commentary on ITA according to project, whereas section 5.2 contains lists of commentary
on ITA according to topic. Sections 5.3 and 5.4 contain commentary on the two main
areas of international law and public policy related to the analysis of ITA in this book:
colonialism and self-determination. The coverage of the particular topic under which any
given source in listed is *passim* unless a specific page or set of pages is referred to.

Section 5.5 contains all the commentary not included in one or more of the earlier lists,
ordered alphabetically by author.

5.1 ITA according to project

5.1.1 *ITA generally and/or more than one ITA project, including general works on international organizations and peace operations which include such coverage*

European Stability Institute (ESI) website: <http://www.esiweb.org>
International Crisis Group (ICG) website: <http://www.crisisgroup.org>
Walters, FP, *A History of the League of Nations* (2 vols, OUP, 1952)
Marazzi, A, *I territori internazionalizzati* (Giappichelli, 1959)
Ydit, M, *Internationalised Territories from the 'Free City of Cracow' to the 'Free City of
Berlin'* (Sythoff, 1961)
Beck, R, *Die Internationalisierung von territorien: Darstellung und rechtliche Analyse*
(Kohlhammer, 1962)
Czerapowicz, JV, 'International Territorial Authority: Leticia and West New Guinea'
(1972) (unpublished Ph D dissertation, Indiana University, on file with the author)
James, A, *Peacekeeping in International Politics* (Palgrave Macmillan, 1990)

Durch, WJ (ed.), *The Evolution of UN Peacekeeping* (St Martin's Press, 1994)

Ratner, SR, *The New UN Peacekeeping: Building Peace in Lands of Conflict after the Cold War* (St. Martin's Press, 1995)

Chopra, J (ed.), *The Politics of Peace-Maintenance* (Lynne Rienner, 1998)

Oakley, R, Dziedzic, M, and Goldberg, E (eds), *Policing the New World Disorder: Peace Operations and the Public Security Function* (National Defense University Press, 1998)

Chopra, J, *Peace-Maintenance: The Evolution of International Political Authority* (Routledge, 1999)

Ramsbotham, O/Woodhouse, T (eds), *Encyclopedia of International Peacekeeping Operations* (ABC-Clio Ltd, 1999)

Holm, TT/Eide, EB (eds), *Peacebuilding and Police Reform* (Frank Cass, 2000)

Chomsky, N, *A New Generation Draws the Line: Kosovo, East Timor and the Standards of the West* (Verso, 2000)

Pugh, M (ed.), *Regeneration of War-Torn Societies* (Macmillan, 2000)

Shawcross, W, *Deliver Us from Evil: Peacekeepers, Warlords, and a World of Endless Conflict* (Simon and Schuster, 2000)

Cousens, EM/Kumar, C/Wermester, K (eds), *Peacebuilding as Politics: Cultivating Peace in Fragile Societies* (Lynne Rienner, 2001)

Korhonen, O/Gras, J, *International Governance in Post-Conflict Situations* (Erik Castrén Institute Research Report 9/2001, University of Helsinki, 2001)

Thakur, R/Schnabel, A (eds), *United Nations Peacekeeping Operations: Ad Hoc Missions, Permanent Engagement* (UN University Press, 2001)

Caplan, R, *A New Trusteeship? The International Administration of War-Torn Territories*, Adelphi Paper No. 341 (OUP/IISS, 2002)

Hansen, AS, *From Congo to Kosovo: Civilian Police in Peace Operations*, Adelphi Paper No. 343 (May 2002)

Perito, R, *The American Experience with Police in Peace Operations* (Canadian Peacekeeping Press, 2002)

Rothchild, DS/Stedman, SJ/Cousens, EM (eds), *Ending Civil Wars: The Implementation of Peace Agreements* (IPA/Lynne Rienner, 2002)

Bain, W, *Between Anarchy and Society. Trusteeship and the Obligations of Power* (OUP, 2003)

Durch, WJ/Holt, VK/Earle, CR/Shanahan, MK, *The Brahimi Report and the Future of UN Peace Operations* (The Henry L Stimson Center, 2003)

Henkin, AH (ed.), *Honoring Human Rights under International Mandates: Lessons from Bosnia, Kosovo and East Timor* (Aspen Institute, 2003)

Holzgrefe, JL/Keohane, RO (eds), *Humanitarian Intervention: Ethical, Legal, and Political Dilemmas* (CUP, 2003)

Ignatieff, M, *Empire Lite: Nation-building in Bosnia, Kosovo and Afghanistan* (Vintage, 2003)

Kolb, R/Porretto, G/Vité, S, *L'Articulation des règles de droit international humanitaire et de droits de l'homme applicables aux forces internationales et aux administrations civiles internationales transitoires* (CUDIH, 2003)

Lindholt, L/De Mesquita Neto, P/Titus, D/Alemika, EE (eds), *Human Rights and the Police in Transitional Countries* (Martinus Nijhoff & Danish Institute for Human Rights, 2003)

Maley, E/Sampford, C/Thakur, R (eds), *From Civil Strife to Civil Society: Civil and Military Responsibilities in Disrupted States* (UN University Press, 2003)

Orford, A, *Reading Humanitarian Intervention: Human Rights and the Use of Force in International Law* (CUP, 2003)

Chesterman, S, *You, The People: The United Nations, Transitional Administration, and State-Building* (OUP, 2004)

Fukuyama, F, *State-Building: Governance and World Order in the 21st Century* (Cornell University Press, 2004)

Newman, E/Rich, R (eds), *The UN Role in Promoting Democracy: Between Ideals and Reality* (UN University Press, 2004)

Paris, R, *At War's End: Building Peace After Civil Conflict* (CUP, 2004)

Zisk Marten, K, *Enforcing the Peace: Learning from the Imperial Past* (Columbia University Press, 2004)

Azimi, N/Chang, LL (eds), *United Nations as Peacekeeper and Nation-Builder: Continuity and Change – What Lies Ahead?* (Martinus Nijhoff for UNITAR, 2005)

Caplan, R, *International Governance of War-Torn Territories: Rule and Reconstruction* (OUP, 2005)

Chesterman, S/Ignatieff, M/Thakur, R (eds), *Making States Work: State Failure and the Crisis of Governance* (UN University Press, 2005)

White, ND/Klaasen, D (eds), *The UN, Human Rights and Post-Conflict Situations* (Manchester University Press, 2005)

Bergling, P, *Rule of Law in the International Agenda, International Support to Legal and Judicial Reform in International Administration, Transition and Development Co-operation* (Intersentia, 2006)

Chandler, D, *Empire in Denial: The Politics of State-building* (Pluto Press, 2006)

Clapham, A, *Human Rights Obligations of Non-State Actors* (OUP, 2006), 128–32

Doyle, MW/Sambanis, N, *Making War and Building Peace: United Nations Peace Operations* (Princeton University Press, 2006)

Korhonen, O/Gras, J/Creutz, K, *International Post-Conflict Situations: New Challenges for Co-Operative Governance* (Erik Castrén Institute Research Reports 18/2006, University of Helsinki, 2006)

Matheson, MJ, *Council Unbound: The Growth of UN Decision Making on Conflict and Postconflict Issues after the Cold War* (USIP Press, 2006)

Smyrek, DS, *Internationally Administered Territories – International Protectorates? An Analysis of Sovereignty over Internationally Administered Territories with Special Reference to the Legal Status of Post-War Kosovo* (Duncker & Humblot, 2006)

Stromseth, J/Wippman, D/Brooks, R, *Can Might Make Rights? Building the Rule of Law After Military Interventions* (CUP, 2006)

Ashdown, P, *Swords and Ploughshares: Bringing Peace to the 21st Century* (Weidenfeld & Nicolson, 2007)

Hehir, A/Robinson, N (eds), *State Building: Theory and Practice* (Routledge, 2007)

Korhonen, O (ed.), *Characteristics of International Administration of Crisis Areas: Nine National Approaches* (KDG Research & Publications, 2007)

Zaum, D, *The Sovereignty Paradox: The Norms and Politics of International Statebuilding* (OUP, 2007)

National Institute of Justice, *Civilian Police and Multinational Peacekeeping – A Workshop Series: A Role for Democratic Policing*, Washington, D.C., January 1999, available at <http://www.ncjrs.org/pdffiles/172842.pdf>

International Crisis Group, 'Kosovo: Let's Learn from Bosnia: Models and Methods of International Administration', ICG Balkans Report No. 66, 17 May 1999, available at <http://www.crisisgroup.org>

Chesterman, S, 'You, The People. The United Nations, Transitional Administration, and State-Building', International Peace Academy, Final Report on the Project on Transitional Administration, November 2003, obtainable from <http://www.ipacademy.org/publications>

International Peace Academy/Crisis Management Initiative, 'State-Building and Strengthening of Civilian Administration in Post-Conflict Societies and Failed States', Report of the High-level Workshop, New York, 21 June 2004, available at <http://www.cmi.fi/files/GooB_report_2004.pdf>

Krasner, S, 'Governance Failures and Alternatives to Sovereignty', CDDRL Working Paper No. 1, November 2004, available at <http://iis-db.stanford.edu/pubs/20667/enhanced_sov_krasner_Aug_1_04.pdf>

O'Neill, W, 'Police Reform In Post-Conflict Societies – What We Know and What We Still Need To Know', International Peace Academy Policy Report, April 2005, available at <http://www.ipacademy.org/publications>

Halderman, JW, 'United Nations Territorial Administration and the Development of the Charter', 70 (1964) *Duke Law Journal* 95

Helman, GB/Ratner, SR, 'Saving Failed States', 89 (1992) *Foreign Policy* 3

Berman, N, ' "But the Alternative is Despair", European Nationalism and the Modernist Renewal of International Law', 106 (1992–93) *Harvard Law Review* 1792

Whomersley, CM, 'The International Legal Status of Gdansk, Klaipeda and the Former East Prussia', 42 (1993) *ICLQ* 919

Chopra, J, 'UN Civil Governance-in-Trust', in TG Weiss (ed.), *The United Nations and Civil Wars* (Lynne Rienner, 1995), 70

Gordon, RE, 'Some Legal Problems with Trusteeship', 28 (1995) *Cornell International Law Journal* 301

Wedgwood, R, 'The Evolution of United Nations Peacekeeping', 28 (1995) *Cornell International Law Journal* 631

Richardson, HJ, ' "Failed States", Self-Determination, and Preventative Diplomacy: Colonialist Nostalgia and Democratic Expectations', 10 (1996) *Temple International & Comparative Law Journal* 1

Vohra, S, 'Impartiality in United Nations Peace-Keeping', 9 (1996) *LJIL* 63

Gordon, RE, 'Saving Failed States: Sometimes a Neocolonialist Notion', 12 (1997) *American University Journal of International Law & Policy* 903

Hampson, FO, 'Can Peacebuilding Work?', 30 (1997) *Cornell International Law Journal* 704

Krasner, S, 'Pervasive Not Perverse: Semi-Sovereigns as the Global Norm', 30 (1997) *Cornell International Law Journal* 651

Morphet, S, 'Organizing Civil Administration', in J Chopra (ed.), *The Politics of Peace-Maintenance* (Lynne Rienner, 1998), 41

Wilde, R, '*Quis Custodiet Ipsos Custodes*? Why and How UNHCR Governance of "Development" Refugee Camps Should Be Subject to International Human Rights Law', 1 (1998) *Yale Human Rights and Development Law Journal* 107

Boot, M, 'Paving the Road to Hell: The Failure of UN Peacekeeping', 79:2 (March/April 2000) *Foreign Affairs* 143

Bothe, M/Marauhn, T, 'The United Nations in Kosovo and East Timor – Problems of a Trusteeship Administration', 6 (2000) *International Peacekeeping* 152

Bugajski, J, 'Balkan In Dependence', 23:4 (2000) *Washington Quarterly* 177

Chandler, D, 'Western Intervention and the Disintegration of Yugoslavia, 1989–99', in E Herman, and P Hammond (eds), *Degraded Capability: The Media and the Kosovo Crisis* (Pluto Press Ltd, 2000), 19

Downie, S, 'The United Nations in East Timor: Comparisons with Cambodia', in D Kingsbury (ed.), *Guns and Ballot Boxes: East Timor's Vote for Independence* (Monash Asia Institute, 2000), 117

Doyle, MW/Sambanis, N, 'International Peacebuilding: A Theoretical and Quantitative Analysis', 94 (2000) *American Political Science Review* 779

Griffin, M/Jones, B, 'Building Peace through Transitional Authority: New Directions, Major Challenges', 7:4 (2000) *International Peacekeeping* 75

Hirsh, M, 'Calling All Regio-Cops: Peacekeeping's Hybrid Future', 79:6 (Nov/Dec 2000) *Foreign Affairs* 2

Ramsbotham, O, 'Reflections on UN Post-Settlement Peace-Building', 7 (2000) *International Peacekeeping* 169

Szasz, P, 'Bosnia Herzegovina and Kosovo', 94 (2000) *ASIL Proc.* 298

Schrijver, N, 'Some Aspects of UN Involvement with Indonesia, West Irian and East Timor', 2 (2000) *International Law Forum* 26

Tsagourias, N, 'Humanism and the Mandates System: Its Modern Revival', 13 (2000) *Hague Yearbook of International Law* 97

Wilde, R, 'The Ambivalent Mandates of International Organizations in Bosnia-Herzegovina, Kosovo and East Timor', (2000) *Proceedings of the Joint Meeting of the Australian & New Zealand Society of International Law and the American Society of International Law* 319, available at <http://www.law.usyd.edu.au/scigl/anzsil/Conferences/2000ASILProceedings.pdf>

Wilde, R, 'From Bosnia to Kosovo and East Timor: The Changing Role of the United Nations in the Administration of Territory', 6 (2000) *ILSA Journal of International & Comparative Law* 467

Akashi, Y, 'The Politics of UN Peacekeeping from Cambodia to Yugoslavia', in R Thakur and A Schnabel (eds), *United Nations Peacekeeping Operations: Ad Hoc Missions, Permanent Engagement* (UN University Press, 2001), 149

Bolton, JR, 'United States Policy on United Nations Peacekeeping: Case Studies in the Congo, Sierra Leone, Ethiopia – Eritrea, Kosovo, and East Timor', 163 (Winter 2001) *World Affairs* 139

Charney, JI, 'Self-Determination: Chechnya, Kosovo and East Timor', 34 (2001) *Vanderbilt Journal of International Law* 455

Chinkin, C/Paradine, K, 'Vision and Reality: Democracy and Citizenship of Women in the Dayton Peace Accords', 26 (2001) *Yale Journal of International Law* 103

Hills, A, 'The Inherent Limits of Military Forces in Policing Peace Operations', 8:3 (2001) *International Peacekeeping* 79

Kiehl, WP, 'Peacekeeper or Occupier? US Experience with Information Operations in the Balkans', 8:4 (2001) *International Peacekeeping* 136

Kirgis, FL, 'Security Council Governance of Post Conflict Societies: A Plea for Good Faith and Informed Decision Making', 95 (2001) *AJIL* 583

Korhonen, O, 'International Governance in Post-Conflict Situations', 14 (2001) *LJIL* 495

Matheson, MJ, 'United Nations Governance of Post-Conflict Societies', 95 (2001) *AJIL* 76, reprinted as 'United Nations Governance of Post-Conflict Societies: East Timor and Kosovo', in MC Bassiouni (ed.), *Post-Conflict Justice* (Transnational Publishers, 2002), 523

Reinisch, A, 'Governance without Accountability?', 44 (2001) *German Yearbook of International Law* 270

Ruffert, M, 'The Administration of Kosovo and East Timor by the International Community', 50 (2001) *ICLQ* 613

Schrijver, N, 'Lecture Commentary: The Complex Role of the Legal Adviser When International Organizations Administer Territory', 95 (2001) *ASIL Proc.* 259

Several authors, 10:1 (2004) *Global Governance,* special issue on 'The Politics of International Administration' (edited by M Berdal and R Caplan)

Shustov, V, 'Transitional Civil Administration within the framework of UN Peacekeeping Operations', 7 (2001) *International Peacekeeping* 417

Stahn, C, 'International Territorial Administration in the Former Yugoslavia: Origins, Development and Challenges Ahead', 61 (2001) *ZaöRV* 107

Stahn, C, 'The United Nations Transitional Administrations in Kosovo and East Timor: A First Analysis', 5 (2001) *Max Planck Yearbook of United Nations Law* 105

Stahn, C, 'NGOs and International Peacekeeping. Issues, Prospects and Lessons Learned', 61 (2001) *ZaöRV* 379

Strohmeyer, H, 'Collapse and Reconstruction of a Judicial System: The United Nations Missions in Kosovo and East Timor', 95 (2001) *AJIL* 46

Thakur, R/Schnabel, A, 'Cascading Generations of Peacekeeping: Across the Mogadishu Line to Kosovo and Timor', in R Thakur, and A Schnabel (eds), *United Nations Peacekeeping Operations: Ad Hoc Missions, Permanent Engagement* (UN University Press, 2001), 3

Thakur, R, 'Research Note: Cambodia, East Timor and the Brahimi Report', 8:3 (2001) *International Peacekeeping* 115

Wilde, R, 'From Danzig to East Timor and Beyond: the Role of International Territorial Administration', 95 (2001) *AJIL* 583

Wilde, R, 'The Complex Role of the Legal Adviser When International Organizations Administer Territory', 95 (2001) *ASIL Proc.* 51

Wilde, R, 'Accountability and International Actors in Bosnia and Herzegovina, Kosovo and East Timor', 7 (2001) *ILSA Journal of International & Comparative Law* 455

Wilde, R, 'Recent Developments in the Security Council: Authorizing International Administration in Kosovo & East Timor', *International Organizations Bulletin: Newsletter of the International Organizations Interest Group of the American Society of International Law* (Spring 2001), 12, obtainable from <http://www.nesl.edu/center/asilnews/spr01.pdf>

Wouters, J/Naert, F, 'How Effective is the European Security Architecture? Lessons from Bosnia and Kosovo', 50 (2001) *ICLQ* 540

Bothe, M/Marauhn, T, 'UN Administration of Kosovo and East Timor: Concept, Legality and Limitations of Security Council-Mandated Trusteeship Administration', in C Tomuschat (ed.), *Kosovo and the International Community: A Legal Assessment* (Kluwer Law International, 2002), 217

Chesterman, S, 'The United Nations as Government: Accountability Mechanisms for Territories under UN Administration', Paper delivered at the conference *Fighting Corruption in Kosovo: Lessons from the Region*, Pristina, Kosovo, 4–5 March 2002

Milliken, J/Krause, K, 'State Failure, State Collapse, and State Reconstruction, Concepts, Lessons and Strategies', 33 (2002) *Development & Change* 753

Paris, R, 'International Peacebuilding and the Mission Civilisatrice', 28 (2002) *Review of International Studies* 637

Rawski, F, 'To Waive or Not to Waive? Immunity and Accountability in UN Peacekeeping Operations', 18 (2002) *Connecticut Journal of International Law* 103

Sörensen, JS, 'Balkanism and the New Radical Interventionism: A Structural Critique', 9 (2002) *International Peacekeeping* 1

Vieira de Mello, S, 'How Not to Run a Country: Lessons for the UN from Kosovo and East Timor', unpublished paper, June 2002, obtainable from <http://www.jsmp.minihub. org/Resources/2000/INTERFET%20DETAINEE%20MANAGEMENT%20 UNIT%20(e).pdf>

Yannis, A, 'State Collapse and its Implications for Peace-Building and Reconstruction', 33 (2002) *Development & Change* 817

Yannis, A, 'The Concept of Suspended Sovereignty in International Law and Its Implications in International Politics', 13 (2002) *EJIL* 1037

Williams, PR/Scharf, MP/Hooper, JR, 'Resolving Sovereignty-Based Conflicts: The Emerging Approach of Earned Sovereignty', 31 (2002–3) *Denver Journal of International Law & Policy* 349

Bain, W, 'The Political Theory of Trusteeship and the Twilight of International Equality', 16 (2003) *International Relations* 59

Dobbins, JF, 'America's Role in Nation-building: From Germany to Iraq', 45:4 (2003) *Survival* 47

Korhonen, O, ' "Post" As Justification: International Law and Democracy-Building after Iraq', 2:7 (2003) *German Law Journal*, available at <http://www.germanlawjournal. com/article.php?id=292>

Kreilkamp, JS, 'UN Postconflict Reconstruction', 35 (2003) *NYU Journal of International Law & Politics* 619

Mégret, F, and Hoffmann, T, 'The UN as a Human Rights Violator? Some Reflections on the United Nations Changing Human Rights Responsibilities', 25 (2003) *Human Rights Quarterly* 314

Paris, R, 'Peacekeeping and the Constraints of Global Culture', 9 (2003) *European Journal of International Relations* 441

Perritt, HH, 'Structures and Standards for Political Trusteeship', 8 (2003) *UCLA Journal of International Law & Foreign Affairs* 385

Steffek, J, 'The Legitimation of International Governance: A Discourse Approach', 9 (2003) *European Journal of International Relations* 249

Thakur, R, 'Cascading Generations of Peacekeeping: Across the Mogadishu Line to Kosovo and East Timor', in N Azimi and LL Chang (eds), *The United Nations Transitional Administration In East Timor (UNTAET): Debriefing and Lessons, Report of the 2002 Tokyo Conference* (Martinus Nijhoff for UNITAR, 2003), ch. 6.1.2

Wilde, R, 'Taxonomies of International Peacekeeping: an Alternative Narrative', 9 (2003) *ILSA Journal of International & Comparative Law* 391

Wilde, R, 'The Effect of Territorial Administration by International Organizations on Local Community-Building', (2003) 2000 – 2003 *Third World Legal Studies Journal* 239

Wilde, R, 'The United Nations as Government: The Tensions of an Ambivalent Role', 97 (2003) *ASIL Proc.* 212

Williams, PR/Hooper, JR, 'Earned Sovereignty: The Political Dimension', 31 (2002–03) *Denver Journal of International Law & Policy* 355

Yannis, A, 'The Creation and Politics of International Protectorates in the Balkans: Bridges Over Troubled Waters', 5 (2003) *Journal of International Relations & Development* 3

Ayoob, M, 'Third World Perspectives on Humanitarian Intervention and International Administration', 10 (2004) *Global Governance* 99

Baskin, M, 'Between Exit and Engagement: on the Division of Authority in Transitional Administrations', 10 (2004) *Global Governance* 119

Berdal, M/Caplan, R, 'The Politics of International Administration', 10 (2004) *Global Governance* 1

Caplan, R, 'Partner or Patron? International Civil Administration and Local Capacity-Building', 11 (2004) *International Peacekeeping* 229

Chandler, D, 'Imposing the "Rule of Law": The Lessons of BiH for Peacebuilding in Iraq', 11 (2004) *International Peacekeeping* 1

Chandler, D, 'The Problems of "Nation-Building": Imposing Bureaucratic "Rule from Above"', 17 (2004) *Cambridge Review of International Affairs* 577

Chandler, D, 'The Responsibility to Protect? Imposing the "Liberal Peace"', 11 (2004) *International Peacekeeping* 59

Chesterman, S, 'Building Democracy through benevolent autocracy: Consultation and accountability in UN transitional administrations', ch. 4 in E Newman and R Rich (eds), *The UN Role in Promoting Democracy: Between Ideals and Reality* (UN University Press, 2004)

Chesterman, S, 'Bush, the United Nations and Nation-building', 46:1 (2004) *Survival* 101

Chesterman, S, 'Virtual Trusteeship' in D Malone (ed.), *The UN Security Council: From the Cold War to the 21st Century* (Lynne Rienner, 2004), 219

Chopra, J/Hohe, T, 'Participatory Intervention', 10 (2004) *Global Governance* 289

Das, H, 'Restoring Property Rights in the Aftermath of War', 53 (2004) *ICLQ* 429

de Wet, E, 'The Direct Administration of Territories by the United Nations and its Member States in the Post Cold War Era: Legal Bases and Implications for National Law', 8 (2004) *Max Planck Yearbook of United Nations Law* 291

Dobbins, JF, 'The UN's Role in Nation-building: from the Belgian Congo to Iraq', 46:4 (2004) *Survival* 81

Fearon, J/Laitin, D, 'Neotrusteeship and the Problem of Weak States', 28 (2004) *International Security* 1

Harland, D, 'Legitimacy and Effectiveness in International Administration', 10 (2004) *Global Governance* 15

Jackson, RH, 'International Engagement in War-Torn Countries', 10 (2004) *Global Governance* 21

Koenig-Archibugi, M, 'International Governance as New Raison d'État? The Case of the EU Common Foreign and Security Policy', 10 (2004) *European Journal of International Relations* 147

Krasner, S, 'Sharing Sovereignty: New Institutions for Collapsed and Failing States', 29:2 (2004) *International Security* 85

Krasner, S, 'The Hole in the Whole: Sovereignty, Shared Sovereignty, and International Law', 25 (2004) *Michigan Journal of International Law* 1075

Mortimer, E, 'International Administration of War-Torn Societies', 10 (2004) *Global Governance* 7

Oswald, B, 'Model Codes for Criminal Justice and Peace Operations: Some Legal Issues', 9 (2004) *Journal of Conflict & Security Law* 253

Richmond, OP, 'UN Peace Operations and the Dilemmas of the Peacebuilding Consensus', 11 (2004) *International Peacekeeping* 83

von Carlowitz, L, 'Settling Property Issues in Complex Peace Operations: the CRPC in Bosnia and Herzegovina and the HPD/DD in Kosovo', 17 (2004) *LJIL* 599

Wilde, R, 'Representing International Territorial Administration: A Critique of Some Approaches', 15 (2004) *EJIL* 71 and ch. 11 in H Charlesworth and J-M Coicaud (eds), *Fault Lines of International Legitimacy* (United Nations University Press, forthcoming)

Wilde, R, 'The Accountability of International Organizations and the Concept of "Functional Duality"', in WP Heere (ed.), *From Government to Governance: The Growing Impact of Non State Actors on the International and European Legal System. 2003 Hague Joint Conference on Contemporary Issues in International Law* (T.M.C. Asser Press, 2004), 164

Wilde, R/Delcourt, B, 'Le retour des "protectorats". L'irrésistible attrait de l'administration des territoires étrangers', in B Delcourt, D Duez, and E Remacle (eds), *La guerre d'Irak: Prélude d'un nouvel ordre international?* (PIE – Peter Lang 2004), 219

Williams, PR/Jannotti Pecci, F, 'Earned Sovereignty: Bridging the Gap between Sovereignty and Self-Determination', 40 (2004) *Stanford Journal of International Law* 347

Bieber, F, 'Local Institutional Engineering: A Tale of Two Cities, Mostar and Brčko', 12 (2005) *International Peacekeeping* 420

Boulden, J, 'Mandates Matter: An Exploration of Impartiality in the United Nations Operations', 11:2 (2005) *Global Governance* 147

Caplan, R, 'Who Guards the Guardians? International Accountability in Bosnia', 12 (2005) *International Peacekeeping* 463, reprinted as R Caplan, 'Who Guards the Guardians? International Accountability in Bosnia', ch. 6 in A Hehir and N Robinson (eds), *State Building: Theory and Practice* (Routledge, 2007)

d'Aspremont, J, 'Les administrations internationales de territoire et la création internationale d'Etats démocratiques', paper presented at the *ESIL Research Forum 2005*, Graduate Institute of International Studies (HEI), Geneva, 26–28 May 2005, obtainable from <http://www.esil-sedi.org>

Eizenstat, S/Porter, JE/Weinstein, J, 'Rebuilding Weak States', 84:1 (Jan/Feb 2005) *Foreign Affairs* 134

Fukuyama, F, '"Stateness" First', 16 (2005) *Journal of Democracy* 84

Joseph, EP, 'Back to the Balkans', 84:1 (Jan/Feb 2005) *Foreign Affairs* 111

Hurwitz, A, 'Towards Enhanced Legitimacy of Rule of Law Programs in Multidimensional Peace Operations', paper presented at the *ESIL Research Forum 2005*, Graduate Institute of International Studies (HEI), Geneva, 26–28 May 2005, obtainable from <http://www.esil-sedi.org>

Koskenmäki, R, 'Workshop on Legitimacy and Accountability of International Administrations, Introductory Remarks', paper presented at the *ESIL Research Forum 2005*, Graduate Institute of International Studies (HEI), Geneva, 26–28 May 2005, obtainable from <http://www.esil-sedi.org>

Krasner, S, 'The Case for Shared Sovereignty', 16:1 (2005) *Journal of Democracy* 69

Mersiades, M, 'Peacekeeping and Legitimacy: Lessons from Cambodia and Somalia', 12 (2005) *International Peacekeeping* 205

Mohamed, S, 'From Keeping Peace to Building Peace: a Proposal for a Revitalized United Nations Trusteeship Council', 105 (2005) *Columbia Law Review* 809

Ratner, SR, 'Foreign Occupation and International Territorial Administration: The Challenges of Convergence', 16 (2005) *EJIL* 695

Sassòli, M, 'Legislation and Maintenance of Public Order and Civil Life by Occupying Powers', 16 (2005) *EJIL* 661

Schröder, A, 'Strengthening the Rule of Law in Kosovo and Bosnia and Herzegovina: The Contribution of International Judges and Prosecutors', Zentrum für Internationale Friedenseinsätze (Center for International Peace Operations), April 2005, available at <http://www.zif-berlin.org/Downloads/Almut_11.04.05.pdf>

Stahn, C, 'Governance beyond the State: Issues of Legitimacy in International Territorial Administration', 2 (2005) *International Organizations Law Review* 9

Stahn, C, 'Accountability and Legitimacy in Practice: Lawmaking by Transitional Administrations', paper presented at the *ESIL Research Forum 2005*, Graduate Institute of International Studies (HEI), Geneva, 26–28 May 2005, obtainable from <http://www.esil-sedi.org>

Utz, R, 'Nations, Nation-Building, and Cultural Intervention: A Social Science Perspective', 9 (2005) *Max Planck Yearbook of United Nations Law* 615

von Bogdandy, A/Häußler, S/Hanschmann, F/Utz, R, 'State-Building, Nation-Building, and Constitutional Politics in Post-Conflict Situations: Conceptual Clarifications and an Appraisal of Different Approaches', 9 (2005) *Max Planck Yearbook of United Nations Law* 579

Wilde, R, 'The Post-Colonial Use of International Territorial Administration and Issues of Legitimacy', 99 (2005) *ASIL Proc.* 38

Wilde, R, 'International Territorial Administration and Human Rights', ch. 7 in ND White and D Klaasen (eds), *The UN, Human Rights and Post-Conflict Situations* (Manchester University Press, 2005), 149

Wilde, R, 'Legitimacy and Accountability of International Administrations: A Commentary on Four Papers', paper presented at the *ESIL Research Forum 2005*, Graduate Institute of International Studies (HEI), Geneva, 26–28 May 2005, obtainable from <http://www.esil-sedi.org>

Wolfrum, R, 'International Administration of Post-Conflict Situations by the United Nations and Other International Actors', 9 (2005) *Max Planck Yearbook of United Nations Law* 649

Berman, N, 'Intervention in a "Divided World": Axes of Legitimacy', 17 (2006) *EJIL* 769

Dickerson, HK, 'Assumptions of Legitimacy and the Foundations of International Territorial Administration', 20 (2006) *Denver Journal of International Law & Policy* 161

Knoll, B, 'Beyond the Mission Civilisatrice: The Properties of a Normative Order within an Internationalized Territory', 19 (2006) *LJIL* 275

Bain, W, 'In Praise of Folly: International Administration and the Moral Breakdown of International Society', ch. 9 in A Hehir and N Robinson (eds), *State Building: Theory and Practice* (Routledge, 2007)

Berman, N, 'Les Ambivalences Impériales', in E Jouannet (ed.), *Impéralisme et droit international en Europe et en Amérique* (2007)

Chandler, D, 'The State-Building Dilemma: Good Governance or Democratic Government?', ch. 4 in A Hehir and N Robinson (eds), *State Building: Theory and Practice* (Routledge, 2007)

Quénivet, N, 'The United Nations' Legal Obligations in Terms of Rule of Law in Peacebuilding Operations,' 11 (2007) *International Peacekeeping: Yearbook of International Peace Operations* 203, section 3.2.1

Stahn, C, 'Lawmaking by International Territorial Administrations', 11 (2007) International Peacekeeping: Yearbook of International Peace Operations 81

Wilde, R, 'Colonialism Redux? Territorial Administration by International Organizations, Colonial Echoes, and the Legitimacy of the "International"', ch. 2 in N Robinson and A Hehir (eds), *State Building: Theory and Practice* (Routledge, 2007)

Wilde, R, 'Report on the United Kingdom', in O Korhonen (ed.), *Characteristics of International Administration of Crisis Areas: Nine National Approaches* (KDG Research & Publications, 2007), 169–97, available online as R Wilde, 'Characteristics of International Administration in Crisis Areas: Aspects of UK Government Policy', 10.3 (2006) *Electronic Journal of Comparative Law*, available at <http://www.ejcl.org/103/art103–15.pdf>

Williams, PD/Bellamy, AD, 'Contemporary Peace Operations: Four Challenges for the Brahimi Paradigm' in 11 (2007) *International Peacekeeping: Yearbook of International Peace Operations* 1

Journal of Intervention and Statebuilding, published by Routledge from 2007

5.1.2 UNMIK period in Kosovo predominantly or exclusively

Vetevendosje movement website: <http://www.vetevendosje.org>

International Crisis Group, *The Kosovo Report: Conflict, International Response, Lessons Learned* (OUP, 2000)

Independent International Commission on Kosovo, *Why Conditional Independence? The Follow-Up of the Kosovo Report* (Global Reporting, 2001)

Yannis, A, *Kosovo under International Administration: An Unfinished Conflict* (Hellenic Foundation for European and Foreign Policy, 2001)

Tomuschat, C, *Kosovo and the International Community. A Legal Assessment* (Kluwer Law International, 2001)

O'Neill, W, *Kosovo: An Unfinished Peace* (Lynne Rienner, 2002)

Milano, E, *Unlawful Territorial Situations in International Law: Reconciling Effectiveness, Legality and Legitimacy* (Martinus Nijhoff, 2006), ch. 6

Murphy, R, *UN Peacekeeping in Lebanon, Somalia and Kosovo: Operational Legal Issues in Practice* (OUP, 2007)

Johnstone, I (ed.), *Annual Review of Global Peace Operations 2007* (NYU Center on International Cooperation/Lynne Rienner, 2007), sections 4.11 and 7.12

Kvinna till Kvinna Foundation, *Getting it Right? A Gender Approach to UNMIK Administration in Kosovo* (2001), available at <http://www.iktk.se/publikationer/rapporter/pdf/Kosovorapport.pdf>

International Crisis Group, 'The New Kosovo Protectorate', ICG Balkans Report No. 69, 20 June 1999, obtainable from <http://www.crisisgroup.org>

International Crisis Group, 'The Policing Gap: Law and Order in the New Kosovo', ICG Balkans Report No. 74, 6 August 1999, obtainable from <http://www.crisisgroup.org>

International Crisis Group, 'Waiting for UNMIK: Local Administration in Kosovo', ICG Europe Report No. 79, 18 October 1999, obtainable from <http://www.crisisgroup.org>

International Crisis Group, 'Starting from Scratch in Kosovo: The Honeymoon is Over', ICG Balkans Report No. 83, 10 December 1999, obtainable from <http://www.crisisgroup.org>

International Crisis Group, 'Elections in Kosovo: Moving toward Democracy?', ICG Balkans Report No. 97, 7 July 2000, obtainable from <http://www.crisisgroup.org>

International Crisis Group, 'Kosovo Report Card', ICG Balkans Report No. 100, 28 August 2000, obtainable from <http://www.crisisgroup.org>

Perritt, HH/Scheib, JM, 'Rebuilding Kosovo – UNMIK as a Trustee Occupant', paper delivered at the *Southern European Business Conference* (2000), available at <http://pbosnia.kentlaw.edu/projects/kosovo/econ_development/HHPgersonAPP.htm>

Chesterman, S, 'Kosovo in Limbo: State-Building and "Substantial Autonomy"', International Peace Academy Report, August 2001, obtainable from <http://www.ipacademy.org/publications>

International Crisis Group, 'A Kosovo Roadmap (I): Addressing Final Status', ICG Balkans Report No. 124, 1 March 2002, obtainable from <http://www.crisisgroup.org>

International Crisis Group, 'A Kosovo Roadmap (II): Internal Benchmarks', ICG Balkans Report No. 125, 1 March 2002, obtainable from <http://www.crisisgroup.org>

International Crisis Group, 'UNMIK's Kosovo Albatross: Tackling Division in Mitrovica', ICG Balkans Report No. 131, 3 June 2002, obtainable from <http://www.crisisgroup.org>

International Crisis Group, 'Kosovo's Internally Displaced and the Return Process', ICG Balkans Report No. 139, 13 December 2002, obtainable from <http://www.crisisgroup.org>

Pckmez, J, 'The Intervention by the International Community and the Rehabilitation of Kosovo' (Centre for Applied Studies in International Negotiations (CASIN), 2001), available at <http://www.casin.ch/web/pdf/pekmez.pdf>

International Crisis Group, 'Kosovo: Toward Final Status', ICG Europe Report No. 161, 24 January 2005, obtainable from <http://www.crisisgroup.org>

Muharremi, R/Peci, L/Malazogu, L/Knaus, V/Murati, T, *Administration and Governance in Kosovo: Lessons Learned and Lessons to be Learned* (KIPRED Occasional Paper, 2nd edn, June 2005), available at <http://akm.logincee.org/store/training/20060822_%7B119FAAD1–90B1–494B-B021–3149E4FC2B4B%7D.pdf>

Brand, M, *The Development of Kosovo Institutions and the Transition of Authority from UNMIK to Local Self-Government* (Centre for Applied Studies in International Negotiations (CASIN), 2006), available at <http://www.isn.ethz.ch/5isf/5/Papers/Brand.pdf>

Grant, TD, 'Extending Decolonization: How the United Nations Might Have Addressed Kosovo', 28 (1999) *Georgia Journal of International & Comparative Law* 9

Holm, TT/Eide, EB, 'Postscript: Towards Executive Authority Policing? The Lessons of Kosovo', 6 (1999) *International Peacekeeping* 210

Kouchner, B, 'The Challenge of Rebuilding Kosovo', 47:3 (1999) *NATO Review* 12, also available at <http://www.nato.int/docu/review/1999/9903–04.htm>

Lagrange, E, 'La mission intérimaire des Nations Unies au Kosovo, nouvel essai d'administration directe d'un territorie', (1999) *Annuaire Français de Droit International* 335

Perritt, HH, 'Conflict of Laws in Judicial Administration of Kosovo' (University of Chicago, 1999), available at <http://pbosnia.kentlaw.edu/projects/kosovo/police/conflict_law.htm>

García, T, 'La Mission d'administration intermaire des Nations Unies au Kosovo', 104 (2000) *RGDIP* 61

Gjorgjievski, B, 'A Year of Failure: KFOR and UNMIK's unsuccessful missions in Kosovo', 2:23 (2000) *Central Europe Review* 5, also available at <http://www.ce-review.org/00/23/gjeorgjievski23.html>

Layne, C/Schwarz, B, 'Dubious anniversary – Kosovo one year later', *Policy Analysis No. 373* (June 2000), 1, available at <http://www.cato.org/pubs/pas/pa373.pdf>

Pouligny, B, 'Promoting Democratic Institutions in Post-Conflict Societies: Giving Diversity a chance', 7 (2000) *International Peacekeeping* 17

Rohde, D, 'Kosovo Seething', 79:3 (May/June 2000) *Foreign Affairs* 65

Rupnik, J, 'Kosovo: Dilemmas of the Protectorate', 9 (2000) *East European Constitutional Review* 48

Betts, WS/Carlson, SN/Gisvold, G, 'The Post-Conflict Transitional Administration of Kosovo and the Lessons-Learned in Efforts to Establish a Judiciary and Rule of Law', 22 (2001) *Michigan Journal of International Law* 371

Bieber, F, 'The Challenge of Democracy in Democratic Societies: Lessons from Bosnia – challenges for Kosovo', in D Sokolović and F Bieber (eds), *Reconstructing Multiethnic Societies: The Case of Bosnia and Herzegovina* (Ashgate, 2001), 109

Brand, M, 'Institution-Building and Human Rights Protection in Kosovo in the Light of UNMIK Legislation', 70 (2001) *Nordic Journal of International Law* 461

Cerone, J, 'The Human Rights Legal Framework Applicable to Trafficking in Persons and Its Incorporation into UNMIK Regulation 2001/4', 7 (2001) *International Peacekeeping: Yearbook of International Peace Operations* 43

Cerone, J, 'Minding the Gap: Outlining KFOR Accountability in Post-Conflict Kosovo', 12 (2001) *EJIL* 469

Everts, D, 'Kosovo: Status Report', in V-Y Ghebali and D Warner (eds), *The Operational Role of the OSCE in Southeastern Europe: Contributing to Regional Stability in the Balkans* (Ashgate, 2001), 37

Fleck, D, 'Civil and Military Administrations in International Peacekeeping Operations: Focus on Kosovo', 7 (2001) *International Peacekeeping* 409

Herrero, JL, 'The United Nations in Kosovo: Finding the Path through the Maze', *Favorita Papers No. 4/2001* (Diplomatische Akademie, 2001)

Irmscher, T, 'The Legal Framework for the Activities of the United Nations Interim Administration in Kosovo: The Charter, Human Rights and the Law of Occupation', 44 (2001) *German Yearbook of International Law* 353

Månsson, K, 'Cooperation in Human Rights: Experience from the Peace Operation in Kosovo', 8:4 (2001) *International Peacekeeping* 111

Stahn, C, 'Constitution without a State? Kosovo under the United Nations Constitutional Framework for Self-Government', 14 (2001) *LJIL* 531

Yannis, A, 'Kosovo under International Administration', 43:2 (2001) *Survival* 31

Amnesty International, 'Federal Republic of Yugoslavia (Kosovo): International officials flout international law', AI Index: EUR 70/008/2002, 1 September 2002, available at <http://web.amnesty.org/library/index/engeur700082002>

Chevallier, E, 'L'ONU au Kosovo: leçons de la premiere MINUK', Chaillot Occasional Papers No. 35 (Western European Union, Institute of Security Studies, May 2002)

Cockell, JG, 'Civil-Military Responses to Security Challenges in Peace Operations: Ten Lessons from Kosovo', 8 (2002) *Global Governance* 483

Goldstone, R, 'Whither Kosovo, Whither Democracy', 8:2 (2002) *Global Governance* 143

Tomuschat, C, 'Yugoslavia's Damaged Sovereignty over the Province of Kosovo', in G Kreijen (ed.), *State, Sovereignty, and International Governance* (OUP, 2002), 323

Abraham, E, 'The Sins of the Savior: Holding the United Nations Accountable to International Human Rights Standards for Executive Order Detentions in its Mission in Kosovo', 52 (2003) *American University Law Review* 1291

Ehrenreich Brooks, R, 'The New Imperialism: Violence, Norms, and the "Rule of Law"', 101 (2003) *Michigan Law Review* 2275

Kreilkamp, JS, 'UN Postconflict Reconstruction', 35 (2003) *NYU Journal of International Law & Politics* 619, 642–52

O'Neill, W, 'Kosovo: Unexpected Barriers to Building Peace and Security', in AH Henkin (ed.), *Honoring Human Rights under International Mandates: Lessons from Bosnia, Kosovo and East Timor* (Aspen Institute, 2003), 75

Pandolfi, M, 'Contract of Mutual (In)Difference: Governance and the Humanitarian Apparatus in Contemporary Albania and Kosovo', 10 (2003) *Indiana Journal of Global Legal Studies* 369

Reka, B, 'UNMIK as an International Governance within Post-Conflict Society', *New Balkan Politics*, issue 7/8 (2003), available at <http://www.newbalkanpolitics.org.mk/default.asp?issue=8>

Williams, PR, 'The Road to Resolving the Conflict over Kosovo's Final Status', 31 (2003) *Denver Journal of International Law & Policy* 387

Hysa, Y, 'Kosovo: A Permanent International Protectorate?', ch. 12 in E Newman and R Rich (eds), *The UN Role in Promoting Democracy: Between Ideals and Reality* (UN University Press, 2004)

Mertus, J, 'Improving Post-Agreement Intervention: The Role of Human Rights Culture in Kosovo', 10 (2004) *Global Governance* 333

Nilsson, J, 'UNMIK and the Ombudsperson Institution in Kosovo: Human Rights Protection in a United Nations "Surrogate State"', 22 (2004) *Netherlands Human Rights Quarterly* 389

Perritt, HH, 'Providing Judicial Review for Decisions by Political Trustees', 15 (2004) *Duke Journal of Comparative & International Law* 1

von Carlowitz, L, 'Crossing the Boundary from the International to the Domestic Legal Realm: UNMIK Lawmaking and Property Rights in Kosovo', 10 (2004) *Global Governance* 307

Yannis, A, 'The UN as Government in Kosovo', 10 (2004) *Global Governance* 67

Brand, M, 'Effective Human Rights Protection when the UN "Becomes the State": Lessons from UNMIK', ch. 15 in ND White and D Klaasen (eds), *The UN, Human Rights and Post-Conflict Situations* (Manchester University Press, 2005)

Friedrich, J, 'UNMIK in Kosovo: Struggling with Uncertainty', 9 (2005) *Max Planck Yearbook of United Nations Law* 225

Knoll, B, 'From Benchmarking to Final Status? Kosovo and the Problem of an International Administration's Open-Ended Mandate', 16 (2005) *EJIL* 637

Rausch, C, 'From Elation to Disappointment: Justice and Security Reform in Kosovo', ch. 8 in CT Call (ed.), *Constructing Justice and Security after War* (USIP Press, 2006)

Economides, S, 'Kosovo', ch. 8 in M Berdal and S Economides (eds), *United Nations Interventionism, 1991–2004* (OUP, 2007)

Hehir, A, 'UNMIK – Facilitating Kosovo's Final Status or its Future Status? Reconceptualising the Problem, Changing the Solution', ch. 7 in A Hehir and N Robinson (eds), *State Building: Theory and Practice* (Routledge, 2007)

Papadimitriou, D/Petrov, P/Greiçevci, L, 'To Build a State: Europeanization, EU Actorness and State-Building in Kosovo', 12 (2007) *European Foreign Affairs Law Review* 219

5.1.3 UNAMET and UNTAET periods in East Timor predominantly or exclusively

La'o Hamutuk (Timor-Leste Institute for Reconstruction Monitoring and Analysis) website: <http://www.laohamutuk.org>

Fox, JJ/Soares, DB (eds), *Out of the Ashes: Destruction and Reconstruction of East Timor* (Hurst & Co., 2000)

Kingsbury, D (ed.), *Guns and Ballot Boxes: East Timor's Vote for Independence* (Monash Asia Institute, 2000)

Martin, I, *Self-Determination in East Timor: The United Nations, the Ballot, and International Intervention* (IPA/Lynne Rienner, 2001)

Soesastro, H/Subianto, LH (eds), *Peace Building and State Building in East Timor* (Centre for Strategic and International Studies, 2001)

Azimi, N/Chang, LL (eds), *The United Nations Transitional Administration In East Timor (UNTAET): Debriefing and Lessons, Report of the 2002 Tokyo Conference* (Martinus Nijhoff for UNITAR, 2003)

Orford, A, *Reading Humanitarian Intervention: Human Rights and the Use of Force in International Law* (CUP, 2003), 134–40

Smith, MG (with M Dee), *Peacekeeping in East Timor: The Path to Independence* (Lynne Rienner for IPA, 2003)

Cotton, J, *East Timor, Australia and Regional Order: Intervention and Its Aftermath in Southeast Asia* (Routledge, 2004)

Doyle, MW/Sambanis, N, *Making War and Building Peace: United Nations Peace Operations* (Princeton University Press, 2006), 243–57

Chesterman, S, 'East Timor in Transition: From Conflict Prevention to State-Building', International Peace Academy Report, May 2001, obtainable from <http://www.ipacademy.org/publications>

Nettheim, G, 'International Law and International Politics', in *International Law and the Question of East Timor* (Catholic Institute for International Relations/International Platform of Jurists for East Timor, 1995), 181

Chinkin, C, 'East Timor: A Failure of Decolonization', 20 (1999) *Australian Yearbook of International Law* 35

Several authors, 4:2 (1999) *Human Rights Law Review*, special issue, 'East Timor in Transition: Sovereignty, Self-Determination and Human Rights'

Chopra, J, 'The UN's Kingdom of East Timor', 42 (2000) *Survival* 27

Emmerson, E, 'Moralpolitik: The Timor Test', (Winter 1999/2000) *The National Interest* 63

de Coning, C, 'The UN Transitional Administration in East Timor (UNTAET): Lessons Learned from the First 100 Days', 6 (2000) *International Peacekeeping: Yearbook of International Peace Operations* 83

Maley, W, 'The UN and East Timor', 12 (2000) *Pacifica Review* 63

Mathew, P, 'A Clean Slate? Timor Lorosa'e during and after UNTAET'S Administration', in (2000) *Proceedings of the Joint Meeting of the Australian & New Zealand Society of International Law and the American Society of International Law* 305

Schreuer, C, 'East Timor and the United Nations', 2 (2000) *International Law Forum* 18

Tool, J, 'False Sense of Security: Lessons Learned from the United Nations Organization and Conduct Mission in East Timor', 16 (2000) *American University International Law Review* 199

Traub, J, 'Inventing East Timor', 79:4 (July/Aug 2000) *Foreign Affairs* 74

Wedgwood, R, 'Letter: Trouble in Timor', 79:6 (Nov/Dec 2000) *Foreign Affairs* 197

Whittington, S, 'The UN Transitional Administration in East Timor: Gender Affairs', 53 (2000) *Development Bulletin* 74

Beauvais, JC, 'Benevolent Despotism: A Critique of UN State-Building in East Timor', 33 (2001) *NYU Journal of International Law & Politics* 1101

Charlesworth, H/Wood, M, 'Mainstreaming Gender in International Peace and Security: the Case of East Timor', 26 (2001) *Yale Journal of International Law* 313

Cotton, J, 'Against the Grain: the East Timor Intervention', 43:1 (2001) *Survival* 127

Dee, M, '"Coalitions of the Willing" and Humanitarian Intervention: Australia's Involvement with INTERFET', 8:3 (2001) *International Peacekeeping* 1

de Hoogh, AJJ, 'Attribution or Delegation of (Legislative) Power by the Security Council? The Case of the United Nations Transitional Administration in East Timor (UNTAET)', 7 (2001) *International Peacekeeping: Yearbook of International Peace Operations* 1

Drew, C, 'The East Timor Story: International Law on Trial', 12 (2001) *EJIL* 651

Kelly, MJ/McCormack, T/Muggleton, P/Oswald, B, 'Legal Aspects of Australia's Involvement in the International Force for East Timor', (2001) *IRRC* vol. 83, issue 841, 101

Kondoch, B, 'The United Nations Administration of East Timor', 6 (2001) *Journal of Conflict & Security Law* 245

Mobekk, E, *Policing Peace Operations: United Nations Civilian Police in East Timor* (Department of War Studies, Kings College London, October 2001)

Othman, M, 'Peacekeeping Operations in Asia: Justice and UNTAET', 3 (2001) *International Law Forum* 114

Plunkett, M, 'Re-Establishing the Rule of Law in Peace Operation: The East Timor Experience', paper delivered at the 15th International Conference of the International Society for the Reform of the Criminal Law, Canberra, 26–30 August 2001, available at <http://www.jsmp.minihub.org/Reports/Re-Establishing-Plunkett10203.pdf>

Pritchard, S, 'United Nations Involvement in Post-Conflict Reconstruction Efforts: New and Continuing Challenges in the Case of East Timor', 24 (2001) *University of New South Wales Law Journal* 183

Rothert, M, 'UN Intervention in East Timor', 39 (2000–2001) *Columbia Journal of Transnational Law* 257

Suhrke, A, 'Peacekeepers as Nation-builders: Dilemmas of the UN in East Timor', 8:4 (2001) *International Peacekeeping* 1

Bongiorno, C, 'A Culture of Impunity: Applying International Human Rights Law to the United Nations in East Timor', 33 (2002) *Columbia Human Rights Law Review* 623

Charlesworth, H/Wood, M, 'Women and Human Rights in the Rebuilding of East Timor', 71 (2002) *Nordic Journal of International Law* 325

Chesterman, S, 'East Timor in Transition: Self-Determination, State-Building and the United Nations', 9 (2002) *International Peacekeeping* 45

Chopra, J, 'Building State Failure in East Timor', 33 (2002) *Development & Change* 979, reprinted as J Chopra, 'Building State Failure in East Timor', in J Milliken (ed.), *State Failure, Collapse & Reconstruction* (Blackwell, 2003), 223 and as J Chopra, 'Building State Failure in East Timor', ch. 8 in A Hehir and N Robinson (eds), *State Building: Theory and Practice* (Routledge, 2007)

Fox, JJ, 'Assessing UNTAET's role in building local capacities for the future', in H Soesastro and LH Subianto (eds), *Peace Building and State Building in East Timor* (Jakarta: Centre for Strategic and International Studies, 2002)

Gorjao, P, 'The Legacy and Lessons of the United Nations Transitional Administration in East Timor', 24:2 (2002) *Contemporary Southeast Asia* 313

Hohe, T, ' "Totem Polls": Indigenous Concepts and "Free and Fair" Elections in East Timor', 9 (2002) *International Peacekeeping* 69

Hohe, T, 'The Clash of Paradigms: International Administration and Local Political Legitimacy in East Timor', 24:3 (2002) *Contemporary Southeast Asia* 569

Morrow, J/White, R, 'The United Nations in Transitional East Timor: International Standards and the Reality of Governance', 22 (2002) *Australian Yearbook of International Law* 1

Ryan, A, 'The Strong Lead-Nation Model in an Ad-hoc Coalition of the Willing: Operation Stabilize in East Timor', 9 (2002) *International Peacekeeping* 23

Steele, J, 'Nation Building in East Timor', 19:2 (2002) *World Policy Journal* 76

Galbraith, P, 'The UN Transitional Authority in East Timor (UNTAET)', 97 (2003) *ASIL Proc.* 211

Jones, S, 'East Timor: The Troubled Path to Independence', in AH Henkin (ed.), *Honoring Human Rights under International Mandates: Lessons from Bosnia, Kosovo and East Timor* (Aspen Institute, 2003), 115

Kreilkamp, JS, 'UN Postconflict Reconstruction', 35 (2003) *NYU Journal of International Law & Politics* 619, 652–7

McLaughlin, R, 'East Timor, Transitional Administration and the Status of the Territorial Sea', 4 (2003) *Melbourne Journal of International Law* 323

Smith, AL, 'Peacekeeping in East Timor: The Path to Independence', 25 (2003) *Contemporary Southeast Asia* 163

Whittington, S, 'Gender and Peacekeeping: The United Nations Transitional Administration in East Timor', 28 (2003) *Signs* 1283

Eldon, S, 'East Timor', in D Malone (ed.), *The UN Security Council: From the Cold War to the 21st Century* (Lynne Rienner, 2004), 551

Goldstone, A, 'UNTAET with Hindsight: The Peculiarities of Politics in an Incomplete State', 10 (2004) *Global Governance* 83

Hayde, W, 'Ideals and Realities of the Rule of Law and Administration of Justice in Post Conflict East Timor', 8 (2004) *International Peacekeeping* 65

Harris Rimmer, S, 'East Timorese Women and Transitional Justice', in S Pickering and C Lambert (eds), *Global Issues: Women and Justice* (Sydney Institute of Criminology, University of Sydney Faculty of Law, 2004), 335

Hohe, T, 'Delivering Feudal Democracy in East Timor', ch. 13 in E Newman and R Rich (eds), *The UN Role in Promoting Democracy: Between Ideals and Reality* (UN University Press, 2004)

Benzing, M, 'Midwifing a New State: The United Nations in East Timor', 9 (2005) *Max Planck Yearbook of United Nations Law* 295

Devereux, A, 'Searching for Clarity: A Case-Study of UNTAET's Application of International Human Rights Norms', ch. 13 in ND White and D Klaasen (eds), *The UN, Human Rights and Post-Conflict Situations* (Manchester University Press, 2005)

Martin, I/Mayer-Rieckh, A, 'The United Nations and East Timor: From Self-determination to State-Building', 12 (2005) *International Peacekeeping* 125

Woehrel, S, 'Kosovo's Future Status and US Policy', Congressional Research Service Report (updated 27 January 2005), available at <http://www.fas.org/sgp/crs/row/RS21721.pdf>

West, RA, 'Lawyers, Guns and Money: Justice and Security Reform in East Timor', ch. 9 in CT Call (ed.), *Constructing Justice and Security after War* (USIP Press, 2006)

Chesterman, S, 'East Timor', ch. 7 in M Berdal and S Economides (eds), *United Nations Interventionism, 1991–2004* (OUP, 2007)

5.1.4 *International appointees on human rights, criminal justice and 'truth-telling' bodies*

5.1.4.1 More than one situation and/or ideas of transitional/ post-conflict justice generally

Teitel, RG, *Transitional Justice* (OUP, 2000)

Bassiouni, MC (ed.), *Post-Conflict Justice* (Transnational Publishers, 2002)

Mani, R, *Beyond Retribution: Seeking Justice in the Shadows of War* (Polity Press, 2002)

Ambos, K/Othman, M (eds), *New Approaches in International Criminal Justice: Kosovo, East Timor, Sierra Leone and Cambodia* (Max Planck Institute, 2003)

Romano, CPR/Nollkaemper, A/Kleffner, JK (eds), *Internationalized Criminal Courts: Sierra Leone, East Timor, Kosovo, and Cambodia* (OUP, 2004)

Schröder, A, 'Strengthening the Rule of Law in Kosovo and Bosnia and Herzegovina: The Contribution of International Judges and Prosecutors', Zentrum für Internationale Friedenseinsätze (Center for International Peace Operations), April 2005, available at <http://www.zif-berlin.org/Downloads/Almut_11.04.05.pdf>

Roht-Arriaza, N/Mariezcurrena, J (eds), *Transitional Justice in the Twenty- First Century: Beyond Truth Versus Justice* (CUP, 2006)

Roper, SD/Barria, LA, *Designing Criminal Tribunals: Sovereignty and International Concerns in the Protection of Human Rights* (Ashgate, 2006)

Stromseth, J/Wippman, D/Brooks, R, *Can Might Make Rights? Building the Rule of Law After Military Interventions* (CUP, 2006)

Chesterman, S, 'Justice under International Administration: Kosovo, East Timor and Afghanistan', International Peace Academy Report (September 2002), available at <http://www.globalpolicy.org/intljustice/general/2002/0902justice.pdf>

Linton, S, 'Cambodia, East Timor and Sierra Leone: Experiments in International Justice', 12 (2001) *Criminal Law Forum* 185

Mundis, DA, 'New Mechanisms for the Enforcement of International Humanitarian Law', 95 (2001) *AJIL* 934

Strohmeyer, H, 'Collapse and Reconstruction of a Judicial System: The United Nations Missions in Kosovo and East Timor', 95 (2001) *AJIL* 46

Strohmeyer, H, 'Making Multilateral Interventions Work: The UN and the Creation of Transitional Justice Systems in Kosovo and East Timor', 25 (2001) *Fletcher Forum of World Affairs* 107

Dickinson, LA, 'Transitional Justice in Afghanistan: The Promise of Mixed Tribunals', 31 (2002) *Denver Journal of International Law & Policy* 23

Kritz, N, 'Progress and Humility: The Ongoing Search for Post Conflict Justice', in MC Bassiouni (ed.), *Post-Conflict Justice* (Transnational Publishers, 2002), 55

Linton, S, 'New Approaches to International Justice in Cambodia and East Timor', (2002) *IRRC*, vol. 83, issue 845, 93

Newman, E, ' "Transitional Justice": The Impact of Transnational Norms and the UN', 9 (2002) *International Peacekeeping* 31

Pouligny, B, 'Building Peace in Situations of Post-Mass Crimes', 9 (2002) *International Peacekeeping* 181

Stahn, C, 'United Nations Peace-Building, Amnesties and Alternative Forms of Justice: A Change in Practice?', (2002) *IRRC*, vol. 84, issue 845, 191

de Bertodano, S, 'Current Developments in Internationalized Courts', 1 (2003) *Journal of International Criminal Justice* 226

Dickinson, LA, 'The Promise of Hybrid Courts', 97 (2003) *AJIL* 295

Snyder, J/Vinjamuri, L, 'Trials and Errors: Principle and Pragmatism in Strategies of International Justice', 28 (2003) *International Security* 5

Knoops, G-JA, 'International and Internationalized Criminal Courts: the New Face of International Peace and Security?', 4 (2004) *International Criminal Law Review* 527

Simonovic, I, 'Dealing with the Legacy of Past War Crimes and Human Rights Abuses: Experiences and Trends', 2 (2004) *Journal of International Criminal Justice* 701

Boraine, A, 'Transitional Justice', in S Chesterman, M Ignatieff, and R Thakur (eds), *Making States Work: State Failure and the Crisis of Governance* (UN University Press, 2005), 318

Cockayne, J, 'The Fraying Shoestring: Rethinking Hybrid War Crimes Tribunals', 28 (2005) *Fordham International Law Journal* 616

Egonda-Ntende, F, 'Justice after Conflict: Challenges Facing "Hybrid" Courts: National Tribunals with International Participation', 18 (2005) *Journal of International Law of Peace and Armed Conflict* 24

Stahn, C, 'Justice under Transitional Administration: Contours and Critique of a Paradigm', 27 (2005) *Houston Journal of International Law* 311

Harper, E, 'The Challenge of Judicial Rehabilitation under UN Auspices: Reconciling Legal-Cultural Incompatibilities', in A Fijalkowski (ed.), *International Institutional Reform, 2005 Hague Joint Conference on Contemporary Issues of International Law* (T.M.C. Asser Press, 2007), 91

Wilde, R, 'The Role of International Institutions in Territorial Administration and Post-Conflict Justice – Introductory Remarks', in A Fijalkowski (ed.), *International Institutional Reform, 2005 Hague Joint Conference on Contemporary Issues of International Law* (T.M.C. Asser Press, 2007), 83

Various authors, 'Panel Discussion on the Role of International Institutions in Territorial Administration and Post-Conflict Justice', in A Fijalkowski (ed.), *International*

Institutional Reform, 2005 Hague Joint Conference on Contemporary Issues of International Law (TMC Asser Press, 2007), 107
International Journal of Transitional Justice (published by OUP – since 2007)

5.1.4.2 Human rights mechanisms in Bosnia and Herzegovina

O'Flaherty, M, 'International Human Rights Operations in Bosnia and Herzegovina', in G Gisvold and M O'Flaherty (eds), *Post-War Protection of Human Rights in Bosnia and Herzegovina* (Brill, 1998), ch. 4

Pajic, Z, 'A Critical Appraisal of Human Rights Provisions of the Dayton Constitution of Bosnia and Hercegovina', 20 (1998) *Human Rights Quarterly* 125

Szasz, P, 'The Protection of Human Rights Through the Dayton/Paris Peace Agreement on Bosnia', 90 (1996) *AJIL* 301

Aybay, R, 'A New Institution in the Field: The Human Rights Chamber of Bosnia and Herzegovina', 15 (1997) *Netherlands Human Rights Quarterly* 529

Cox, M/Harland, C, 'Internationalized Legal Structures and the Protection of Internationally Displaced Persons', in J Fitzpatrick (ed.), *Human Rights Protection for Refugees, Asylum Seekers, and Internally Displaced Persons* (Transnational Publishers, 2001), 521

Schröder, A, 'Strengthening the Rule of Law in Kosovo and Bosnia and Herzegovina: The Contribution of International Judges and Prosecutors', Zentrum für Internationale Friedenseinsätze (Center for International Peace Operations), April 2005, available at <http://www.zif-berlin.org/Downloads/Almut_11.04.05.pdf>

5.1.4.3 East Timor: Serious Crimes process

Cryer, R, *Prosecuting International Crimes: Selectivity and the International Criminal Law Regime* (CUP, 2005), 70–1

Plunkett, M, 'Re-Establishing the Rule of Law in Peace Operation – the East Timor Experience', paper delivered at the 15th International Conference of the International Society for the Reform of the Criminal Law, Canberra, 26–30 August 2001

Amnesty International, 'East Timor: Justice past, present and future', 27 July 2001, AI Index: ASA 57/001/2001, available at <http://web.amnesty.org/library/pdf/ASA570012001ENGLISH/$File/ASA5700101.pdf>

Hirst, M/Varney, H, 'Justice Abandoned? An Assessment of the Serious Crimes Process in East Timor', International Centre for Transitional Justice Occasional Paper (June 2005)

International Center for Transitional Justice, 'The Serious Crimes Process in Timor Leste: In Retrospect' (March 2006), available at <http://www.ictj.org/static/Prosecutions/Timor.study.pdf>

Linton, S, 'Prosecuting Atrocities at the District Court of Dili', 2 (2001) *Melbourne Journal of International Law* 414

Linton, S, 'Rising from the Ashes: The Creation of a Viable Criminal Justice System in East Timor', 25 (2001) *Melbourne University Law Review* 122

Linton, S/Reiger, C, 'The Evolving Jurisprudence and Practice of East Timor's Special Panels for Serious Crimes on Admissions of Guilt, Duress, and Superior Orders', 4 (2001) *Yearbook of International Humanitarian Law* 167

Strohmeyer, H, 'Policing the Peace: Post-Conflict Judicial System Reconstruction in East Timor', 24 (2001) *University of New South Wales Law Journal* 171

Cohen, D, 'Seeking Justice on the Cheap: Is the East Timor Tribunal Really a Model for the Future?', Asia Pacific Issues No. 61 (August 2002)

Fairlie, MA, 'Affirming Brahimi: East Timor Makes the Case for a Model Criminal Code', 18 (2003) *American University International Law Review* 1059

Hohe, T, 'Justice without Judiciary in East Timor', 3 (2003) *Conflict, Security and Development* 335

Katzenstein, S, 'Hybrid Tribunals: Searching for Justice in East Timor', 16 (2003) *Harvard Human Rights Journal* 245

Ohlsen, OH, 'Investigation of Serious Crimes in East Timor', ch. 2.3 in K Ambos and M Othman (eds), *New Approaches in International Criminal Justice: Kosovo, East Timor, Sierra Leone and Cambodia* (Max Planck Institute, 2003)

Othman, M, 'The Framework of Prosecutions and the Court System in East Timor', in K Ambos and M Othman (eds), *New Approaches in International Criminal Justice: Kosovo, East Timor, Sierra Leone and Cambodia* (Max Planck Institute, 2003), 102

Harris Rimmer, S, 'East Timorese Women and Transitional Justice', in S Pickering and C Lambert (eds), *Global Issues: Women and Justice* (Sydney Institute of Criminology, University of Sydney Faculty of Law, 2004), 335

Stromseth, J/Wippman, D/Brooks, R, *Can Might Make Rights? Building the Rule of Law after Military Interventions* (CUP, 2006), 278–85

5.1.4.4 East Timor: Commission for Reception, Truth and Reconciliation

Stromseth, J/Wippman, D/Brooks, R, *Can Might Make Rights? Building the Rule of Law after Military Interventions* (CUP, 2006), 285–6

Stahn, C, 'Accommodating Individual Criminal Responsibility and National Reconciliation: The UN Truth Commission for East Timor', 95 (2001) *AJIL* 952

Jenkins, C, 'A Truth Commission for East Timor: Lessons from South Africa?', 7 (2002) *Journal of Conflict & Security Law* 233

Lyons, BS, 'Getting Untrapped, Struggling for Truths: The Commission for Reception, Truth and Reconciliation (CAVER) in East Timor', in CPR Romano, A Nollkaemper and JK Kleffner (eds), *Internationalized Criminal Courts: Sierra Leone, East Timor, Kosovo, and Cambodia* (OUP, 2004), 99

5.1.4.5 Sierra Leone: Special Court for Sierra Leone and Truth and Reconciliation Commission

Cryer, R, *Prosecuting International Crimes: Selectivity and the International Criminal Law Regime* (CUP, 2005), 61–5

Stromseth, J/Wippman, D/Brooks, R, *Can Might Make Rights? Building the Rule of Law after Military Interventions* (CUP, 2006), 289–301

Frulli, M, 'The Special Court for Sierra Leone: Some Preliminary Comments', 11 (2000) *EJIL* 859

Gallagher, K, 'No Justice, No Peace: The Legalities and Realities of Amnesty in Sierra Leone', 23 (2000) *Thomas Jefferson Law Review* 149

McDonald, A, 'Sierra Leone's Uneasy Peace: the Amnesties Granted in the Lomé Peace Agreement and the United Nations' Dilemma', 1 (2000) *Humanitäres Völkerrecht – Informationsschriften* 11

Parlevliet, M, 'Truth Commissions in Africa: The Non-Case of Namibia and the Emerging Case of Sierra Leone', 2 (2000) *International Law Forum* 98

Scharf, MP, 'The Special Court of Sierra Leone', *ASIL Insight No. 53*, October 2000, available at <http://www.asil.org/insights/insigh53.htm>

Beresford, S, 'The Special Court for Sierra Leone: An Initial Comment', 14 (2001) *LJIL* 635

Cryer, R, 'A "Special Court" for Sierra Leone?', 50 (2001) *ICLQ* 435

De Sanctis, F, 'Il processo di istituzione di una Special Court per i crimini della guerra civile in Sierra Leone', 56 (2001) *La Comunità Internazionale* 475

Fritz, N/Smith, A, 'Current Apathy for Coming Anarchy: Building the Special Court for Sierra Leone', 25 (2001) *Fordham International Law Journal* 391

Magliveras, KD, 'The Special Court for Sierra Leone: A New Type of Regional Criminal Court for the International Community?', 17 (2001) *International Enforcement Law Report* 81

Webster, J, 'Sierra Leone: Responding to the Crisis, Planning for the Future: The Role of International Justice in the Quest for National and Global Security', 11 (2001) *Indiana International & Comparative Law Review* 731

Cerone, J, 'The Special Court for Sierra Leone: Establishing a New Approach to International Criminal Justice', 8 (2002) *ILSA Journal of International & Comparative Law* 379

Cissé, C, 'Le Tribunal spécial pour la Sierra Leone', 4 (2002) *International Law Forum* 7

McDonald, A, 'Sierra Leone's Shoestring Special Court', (2002) *IRRC*, vol. 84, issue 845, 121

Poole, JL, 'Post-Conflict Justice in Sierra Leone', in MC Bassiouni (ed.), *Post-Conflict Justice* (Transnational Publishers, 2002), 563

Tejan-Cole, A, 'The Complementary and Conflicting Relationship between the Special Court for Sierra Leone and the Truth and Reconciliation Commission', 5 (2002) *Yearbook of International Humanitarian Law* 313

Hall, LR/Kazemi, N, 'Recent Development: Prospects for Justice and Reconciliation in Sierra Leone', 44 (2003) *Harvard International Law Journal* 287

Kah-Jallow, H, 'The Legal Framework of the Special Court for Sierra Leone', ch. 3.2 in K Ambos and M Othman (eds), *New Approaches in International Criminal Justice: Kosovo, East Timor, Sierra Leone and Cambodia* (Max Planck Institute, 2003)

Romano, CPR/Nollkaemper, A, 'The Arrest Warrant against the Liberian President, Charles Taylor', *ASIL Insights No. 110* (June 2003), available at <http://www.asil.org/insights/insigh110.htm>

Schabas, WA, 'The Relationship Between Truth Commissions and International Courts: The Case of Sierra Leone', 25 (2003) *Human Rights Quarterly* 1035

Jones, J/Carlton-Hanciles, C/Kah-Jallow, H/Scratch, S/Yillah, I, 'The Special Court for Sierra Leone', 2 (2004) *Journal of International Criminal Justice* 211

Schabas, WA, 'A Synergistic Relationship: The Sierra Leone Truth and Reconciliation Commission and the Special Court for Sierra Leone', 15 (2004) *Criminal Law Forum* 3 reprinted in WA Schabas and S Darcy (eds), *Truth Commissions and Courts, The Tension Between Criminal Justice and the Search for Truth* (Dordrecht, 2004), 3

Schabas, WA, 'Addressing Impunity in Developing Countries: Lessons from Rwanda and Sierra Leone', in H Dumont and A-M Boisvert (eds), *La Voie vers la Cour pénale internationale: Tous les chemins mènent à Rome* (Thémis, 2004), 159

Schabas, WA, 'Internationalised Courts and their Relationship with Alternative Accountability Mechanisms: The Case of Sierra Leone', in C Romano/A Nollkaemper/

JK Kleffner (eds), *Internationalized Criminal Courts: Sierra Leone, East Timor, Kosovo, and Cambodia* (OUP, 2004), 157

Schabas, WA, ' "Internationalised" Courts and their Relationship with Alternative Accountability Mechanisms: The Case of Sierra Leone', in *Proceedings of the 31st Annual Conference of the Canadian Council on International Law* (2004), 322

Schabas, WA, 'Amnesty, the Sierra Leone Truth and Reconciliation Commission and the Special Court for Sierra Leone', 11 (2004) *UC Davis Journal of International Law & Policy* 145

Schabas, WA, 'Conjoined Twins of Transitional Justice? The Sierra Leone Truth and Reconciliation Commission and the Special Court', 2 (2004) *Journal of International Criminal Justice* 1082

Schabas, WA, 'Truth Commissions and Courts Working in Parallel: The Sierra Leone Experience', 98 (2004) *ASIL Proc.* 189

Smith, A, 'Sierra Leone: The Intersection of Law, Policy and Practice', in C Romano, A Nollkaemper and JK Kleffner (eds), *Internationalized Criminal Courts: Sierra Leone, East Timor, Kosovo, and Cambodia* (OUP, 2004), 125

Shaw, R, 'Rethinking Truth and Reconciliation Commissions: Lessons from Sierra Leone', US Institute for Peace Special Report No. 130, February 2005, available <http://www.usip.org/pubs/specialreports/sr130.pdf>

Schabas, WA, 'The Sierra Leone Truth and Reconciliation Commission', in E Skaar, S Gloppen and A Suhrke (eds), *Roads to Reconciliation* (Lanham, 2005), 129

Jalloh, CC, 'Special Court for Sierra Leone Dismisses Taylor Motion against Change of Venue,' *ASIL Insights*, vol. 5, issue 15 (June 2006), available at <http://www.asil.org/insights/2006/06/insights060615.html>

Lekha Sriram, C/Mahmoud, Y, 'Bringing Security Back In: International Relations Theories and Moving Beyond the "Justice versus Peace" Dilemma in Transitional Societies', ch. 14 in T Biersteker, P Spiro, C Lekha Sriram, and V Raffo (eds), *International Law and International Relations: Bridging Theory and Practice* (Routledge, 2006)

Schabas, WA, 'The Sierra Leone Truth and Reconciliation Commission and the Special Court for Sierra Leone', in A Fijalkowski (ed.), *International Institutional Reform, 2005 Hague Joint Conference on Contemporary Issues of International Law* (T.M.C. Asser Press, 2007), 100

5.1.4.6 Kosovo

Cryer, R, *Prosecuting International Crimes: Selectivity and the International Criminal Law Regime* (CUP, 2005), 69–70

Stromseth, J/Wippman, D/Brooks, R, *Can Might Make Rights? Building the Rule of Law after Military Interventions* (CUP, 2006), 275–8

Villmoare, E, 'Ethnic Crimes and UN Justice in Kosovo: The Trial of Igor Simic', 37 (2000) *Texas International Law Journal* 373

Bohlander, M, 'Kosovo: The Legal Framework of the Prosecution and the Courts', in K Ambos and M Othman (eds), *New Approaches in International Criminal Justice: Kosovo, East Timor, Sierra Leone and Cambodia* (Max Planck Institute, 2003), 21

Risch, I, 'Some Practical Issues Concerning the Development of the Judicial System in Kosovo', ch. 1.3 in K Ambos and M Othman (eds), *New Approaches in International Criminal Justice: Kosovo, East Timor, Sierra Leone and Cambodia* (Max Planck Institute, 2003)

Cady, J-C/Booth, N, 'Internationalized Courts in Kosovo: an UNMIK Perspective', in C Romano, A Nollkaemper and JK Kleffner (eds), *Internationalized Criminal Courts: Sierra Leone, East Timor, Kosovo, and Cambodia* (OUP, 2004), 59

Cerone, J/Baldwin, C, 'Explaining and Evaluating the UNMIK Court System', in C Romano, A Nollkaemper and JK Kleffner (eds), *Internationalized Criminal Courts: Sierra Leone, East Timor, Kosovo, and Cambodia* (OUP, 2004), 41

Marshall, D/Inglis, S, 'The Disempowerment of Human Rights-Based Justice in the United Nations Mission in Kosovo', 16 (2003) *Harvard Human Rights Journal* 95

Naarden, GL/Locke, JB, 'Peacekeeping and Prosecutorial Policy: Lessons from Kosovo', 98 (2004) *AJIL* 727

Schröder, A, 'Strengthening the Rule of Law in Kosovo and Bosnia and Herzegovina: The Contribution of International Judges and Prosecutors', Zentrum für Internationale Friedenseinsätze (Center for International Peace Operations), April 2005, available at <http://www.zif-berlin.org/Downloads/Almut_11.04.05.pdf>

Rausch, C, 'From Elation to Disappointment: Justice and Security Reform in Kosovo', ch. 8 in CT Call (ed.), *Constructing Justice and Security after War* (USIP Press, 2006)

5.1.4.7 Cambodia: Extraordinary Chambers

Cryer, R, *Prosecuting International Crimes: Selectivity and the International Criminal Law Regime* (CUP, 2005), 65–9

Boyle, D, 'Establishing the Responsibility of the Khmer Rouge Leadership for International Crimes', 5 (2002) *Yearbook of International Humanitarian Law* 167

Buckley, AA, 'The Conflict in Cambodia and Post-Conflict Justice' in MC Bassiouni (ed.), *Post-Conflict Justice* (Transnational Publishers, 2002), 635

Ratner, SR, 'Accountability for the Khmer Rouge: A (Lack of) Progress Report', in MC Bassiouni (ed.), *Post-Conflict Justice* (Transnational Publishers, 2002), 613

Kashyap, S, 'The Framework of the Prosecutions in Cambodia', ch. 4.2 in K Ambos and M Othman (eds), *New Approaches in International Criminal Justice: Kosovo, East Timor, Sierra Leone and Cambodia* (Max Planck Institute, 2003)

Etcheson, C, 'The Politics of Genocide in Cambodia', in C Romano, A Nollkaemper and JK Kleffner (eds), *Internationalized Criminal Courts: Sierra Leone, East Timor, Kosovo, and Cambodia* (OUP, 2004), 181

Meijer, EE, 'The Extraordinary Chambers in the Courts of Cambodia for Prosecuting Crimes Committed by the Khmer Rouge: Jurisdiction, Organization, and Procedure of an Internationalized National Tribunal', in C Romano, A Nollkaemper and JK Kleffner (eds), *Internationalized Criminal Courts: Sierra Leone, East Timor, Kosovo, and Cambodia* (OUP, 2004), 208

Williams, S, 'The Cambodian Extraordinary Chambers – A Dangerous Precedent for International Justice?', 53 (2004) *ICLQ* 227

5.1.4.8 Iraq: Iraqi Special Tribunal and Iraqi Higher Criminal Court

Cryer, R, *Prosecuting International Crimes: Selectivity and the International Criminal Law Regime* (CUP, 2005), 71–2

Stromseth, J/Wippman, D/Brooks, R, *Can Might Make Rights? Building the Rule of Law after Military Interventions* (CUP, 2006), 302–4

Bantekas, I, 'The Iraqi Special Tribunal for Crimes against Humanity', 54 (2003) *ICLQ* 237

Orentlicher, DF, 'Venues for Prosecuting Saddam Hussein: The Legal Framework', *ASIL Insights No. 124*, December 2003, available at <http://www.asil.org/insights/insigh124.htm>

Alvarez, JE, 'Trying Hussein: Between Hubris and Hegemony', 2 (2004) *Journal of International Criminal Justice* 319

Shany, Y, 'Does One Size Fit All?: Reading the Jurisdictional Provisions of the New Iraqi Special Tribunal Statute in the Light of the Statutes of International Criminal Tribunals', 2 (2004) *Journal of International Criminal Justice* 338

Scharf, MP, 'Is It International Enough? – A Critique of the Iraqi Special Tribunal in Light of the Goals of International Justice', 2 (2004) *Journal of International Criminal Justice* 330

United States Institute of Peace, 'Special Report: Building the Iraqi Special Tribunal', USIP Special Report No. 122, June 2004, available at <http://www.usip.org/pubs/specialreports/sr122.pdf>

Scharf, MP/Newton, MA, 'The Iraqi High Tribunal's Dujail Trial Opinion', *ASIL Insight*, vol. 10, issue 34 (18 December 2006), available at <http://www.asil.org/insights/2006/12/insights061218.html>

5.2 Particular issues raised by ITA

5.2.1 Practical challenges

Strohmeyer, H, 'Collapse and Reconstruction of a Judicial System: The United Nations Missions in Kosovo and East Timor', 95 (2001) *AJIL* 46

Chandler, D, *Bosnia: Faking Democracy after Dayton* (2nd edn, Pluto Press, 2000)

Korhonen, O/Gras, J, *International Governance in Post-Conflict Situations* (Erik Castrén Institute Research Report 9/2001, University of Helsinki, 2001), chs 2 and 4

Sokolović, D/Bieber, F (eds), *Reconstructing Multiethnic Societies: The Case of Bosnia and Herzegovina* (Ashgate, 2001)

Caplan, R, *A New Trusteeship? The International Administration of War-Torn Territories*, Adelphi Paper No. 341 (OUP/IISS, 2002)

Chesterman, S, *You, The People: The United Nations, Transitional Administration, and State-Building* (OUP, 2004)

Caplan, R, *International Governance of War-Torn Territories: Rule and Reconstruction* (OUP, 2005)

Korhonen, O/Gras, J/Creutz, K, *International Post-Conflict Situations: New Challenges for Co-Operative Governance* (Erik Castrén Institute Research Reports 18/2006, University of Helsinki, 2006)

Ashdown, P, *Swords and Ploughshares: Bringing Peace to the 21st Century* (Weidenfeld & Nicolson, 2007)

Chopra, J, 'The UN's Kingdom of East Timor', 42 (2000) *Survival* 27

Rohde, D, 'Kosovo Seething', 79:3 (May/June 2000) *Foreign Affairs* 65

Traub, J, 'Inventing East Timor', 79:4 (July/Aug 2000) *Foreign Affairs* 74

Wedgwood, R, 'Letter: Trouble in Timor', 79:6 (Nov/Dec 2000) *Foreign Affairs* 197

Wilde, R, 'The Complex Role of the Legal Adviser When International Organizations Administer Territory', 95 (2001) *ASIL Proc.* 51

Cockell, JG, 'Civil-Military Responses to Security Challenges in Peace Operations: Ten Lessons from Kosovo', 8 (2002) *Global Governance* 483

Vieira de Mello, S, 'How Not to Run a Country: Lessons for the UN from Kosovo and East Timor', unpublished paper, June 2002 obtainable from <http://www.jsmp.minihub. org/Resources/2000/INTERFET%20DETAINEE%20MANAGEMENT%20 UNIT%20(e).pdf>

Perritt, HH, 'Structures and Standards for Political Trusteeship', 8 (2003) *UCLA Journal of International Law & Foreign Affairs* 385, 418–24

Yannis, A, 'The Creation and Politics of International Protectorates in the Balkans: Bridges Over Troubled Waters', 5 (2003) *Journal of International Relations & Development* 258, 270–2

Fearon, J/Laitin, D, 'Neotrusteeship and the Problem of Weak States', 28 (2004) *International Security* 1

Harland, D, 'Legitimacy and Effectiveness in International Administration', 10 (2004) *Global Governance* 15

Schröder, A, 'Strengthening the Rule of Law in Kosovo and Bosnia and Herzegovina: The Contribution of International Judges and Prosecutors', Zentrum für Internationale Friedenseinsätze (Center for International Peace Operations), April 2005, available at <http://www.zif-berlin.org/Downloads/Almut_11.04.05.pdf>

5.2.2 Models of justice being promoted

(See also the sources contained in section 5.1.4 above)

Call, CT (ed.), *Constructing Justice and Security after War* (USIP Press, 2006)

Stromseth, J/Wippman, D/Brooks, R, *Can Might Make Rights? Building the Rule of Law after Military Interventions* (CUP, 2006)

Mathew, P, 'A Clean Slate? Timor Lorosa'e during and after UNTAET'S Administration', in (2000) *Proceedings of the Joint Meeting of the Australian & New Zealand Society of International Law and the American Society of International Law* 305

Beauvais, JC, 'Benevolent Despotism: A Critique of UN State-Building in East Timor', 33 (2001) *NYU Journal of International Law & Politics* 1101

Betts, WS/Carlson, SN/Gisvold, G, 'The Post-Conflict Transitional Administration of Kosovo and the Lessons-Learned in Efforts to Establish a Judiciary and Rule of Law', 22 (2001) *Michigan Journal of International Law* 371

Strohmeyer, H, 'Collapse and Reconstruction of a Judicial System: The United Nations Missions in Kosovo and East Timor', 95 (2001) *AJIL* 46

Ehrenreich Brooks, R, 'The New Imperialism: Violence, Norms, and the "Rule of Law"', 101 (2003) *Michigan Law Review* 2275

Marshall, D/Inglis, S, 'The Disempowerment of Human Rights-Based Justice in the United Nations Mission in Kosovo', 16 (2003) *Harvard Human Rights Journal* 95

Oswald, B, 'Model Codes for Criminal Justice and Peace Operations: Some Legal Issues', 9 (2004) *Journal of Conflict & Security Law* 253

5.2.3 Constitutional structures introduced in the territories

Chandler, D, *Bosnia: Faking Democracy after Dayton* (2nd edn, Pluto Press, 2000)

Caplan, R, *A New Trusteeship? The International Administration of War-Torn Territories*, Adelphi Paper No. 341 (OUP/International Institute for Strategic Studies (IISS), 2002)

Korhonen, O/Gras, J, *International Governance in Post-Conflict Situations* (Erik Castrén Institute Research Report 9/2001, University of Helsinki, 2001)

Sokolović, D/Bieber, F (eds), *Reconstructing Multiethnic Societies: The Case of Bosnia and Herzegovina* (Ashgate, 2001)

Chesterman, S, *You, The People: The United Nations, Transitional Administration, and State-Building* (OUP, 2004)

Caplan, R, *International Governance of War-Torn Territories: Rule and Reconstruction* (OUP, 2005)

Korhonen, O/Gras, J/Creutz, K, *International Post-Conflict Situations: New Challenges for Co-Operative Governance* (Erik Castrén Institute Research Reports 18/2006, University of Helsinki, 2006)

Beauvais, JC, 'Benevolent Despotism: A Critique of UN State-Building in East Timor', 33 (2001) *NYU Journal of International Law & Politics* 1101

Stahn, C, 'Constitution without a State? Kosovo under the United Nations Constitutional Framework for Self-Government', 14 (2001) *LJIL* 531

5.2.4 *Questions of legitimacy (gender issues covered under a separate heading)*

Hampson, FO, *Nurturing Peace: Why Peace Settlements Succeed or Fail* (United States Institute of Peace Press, 1996), 232–3

Chandler, D, *Bosnia: Faking Democracy after Dayton* (2nd edn, Pluto Press, 2000)

Cousens, EM/Cater, CK, *Toward Peace in Bosnia: Implementing the Dayton Accords* (IPA/ Lynne Rienner, 2001)

Korhonen, O/Gras, J, *International Governance in Post-Conflict Situations* (Erik Castrén Institute Research Report 9/2001, University of Helsinki, 2001)

Martin, I, *Self-Determination in East Timor: The United Nations, the Ballot, and International Intervention* (IPA/Lynne Rienner, 2001)

Sokolović, D/Bieber, F (eds), *Reconstructing Multiethnic Societies: The Case of Bosnia and Herzegovina* (Ashgate, 2001)

Caplan, R, *A New Trusteeship? The International Administration of War-Torn Territories*, Adelphi Paper No. 341 (OUP/International Institute for Strategic Studies (IISS), 2002)

Bain, W, *Between Anarchy and Society. Trusteeship and the Obligations of Power* (OUP, 2003), ch. 6

Orford, A, *Reading Humanitarian Intervention: Human Rights and the Use of Force in International Law* (CUP, 2003), 131–4

Chesterman, S, *You, The People: The United Nations, Transitional Administration, and State-Building* (OUP, 2004)

Caplan, R, *International Governance of War-Torn Territories: Rule and Reconstruction* (OUP, 2005)

Chandler, D, *Empire in Denial: The Politics of State-building* (Pluto Press, 2006)

Korhonen, O/Gras, J/Creutz, K, *International Post-Conflict Situations: New Challenges for Co-Operative Governance* (Erik Castrén Institute Research Reports 18/2006, University of Helsinki, 2006)

Milano, E, *Unlawful Territorial Situations in International Law: Reconciling Effectiveness, Legality and Legitimacy* (Martinus Nijhoff, 2006), 234–65

Smyrek, DS, *Internationally Administered Territories – International Protectorates? An Analysis of Sovereignty over Internationally Administered Territories with Special Reference to the Legal Status of Post-War Kosovo* (Duncker & Humblot, 2006), ch. E

Stromseth, J/Wippman, D/Brooks, R, *Can Might Make Rights? Building the Rule of Law After Military Interventions* (CUP, 2006)

Ashdown, P, *Swords and Ploughshares: Bringing Peace to the 21st Century* (Weidenfeld & Nicolson, 2007)

Zaum, D, *The Sovereignty Paradox: The Norms and Politics of International Statebuilding* (OUP, 2007)

Chesterman, S, 'You, The People: The United Nations, Transitional Administration, and State-Building', International Peace Academy, Final Report on the Project on Transitional Administration, November 2003, available at <http://www.ipacademy. org/publications>

Gordon, RE, 'Some Legal Problems with Trusteeship', 28 (1995) *Cornell International Law Journal* 301

Richardson, HJ, '"Failed States", Self-Determination, and Preventative Diplomacy: Colonialist Nostalgia and Democratic Expectations', 10 (1996) *Temple International & Comparative Law Journal* 1

Gordon, RE, 'Saving Failed States: Sometimes a Neocolonialist Notion', 12 (1997) *American University Journal of International Law & Policy* 903

Hampson, FO, 'Can Peacebuilding Work?', 30 (1997) *Cornell International Law Journal* 704, 707–9

Morphet, S, 'Organizing Civil Administration', in J Chopra (ed.), *The Politics of Peace-Maintenance* (Lynne Rienner, 1998), 41

Drew, C, 'The East Timor Popular Consultation: Self-Determination Denied', 4:2 (1999) *Human Rights Law Review* 3

Gathii, J, 'Good Governance as a Counter Insurgency Agenda to Oppositional and Transformative Social Projects in International Law', 5 (1999) *Buffalo Human Rights Law Review* 107

Berman, N, 'Imperial Rivalry and the Genealogy of Human Rights: The Nationality Decrees Case', 94 (2000) *ASIL Proc.* 53

Wilde, R, 'The Ambivalent Mandates of International Organizations in Bosnia-Herzegovina, Kosovo and East Timor', in (2000) *Proceedings of the Joint Meeting of the Australian & New Zealand Society of International Law and the American Society of International Law* 319, also available at <http://www.law.usyd.edu.au/scigl/anzsil/ Conferences/2000ASILProceedings.pdf>

Beauvais, JC, 'Benevolent Despotism: A Critique of UN State-Building in East Timor', 33 (2001) *NYU Journal of International Law & Politics* 1101

Korhonen, O, 'International Governance in Post-Conflict Situations', 14 (2001) *LJIL* 495, 524–8

Pekmez, J, 'The Intervention by the International Community and the Rehabilitation of Kosovo' (Centre for Applied Studies in International Negotiations (CASIN), 2001), available at <http://www.casin.ch/web/pdf/pekmez.pdf>

Several authors, 10:1 (2004) *Global Governance*, special issue on 'The Politics of International Administration' (edited by M Berdal/R Caplan)

Hohe, T, '"Totem Polls": Indigenous Concepts and "Free and Fair" Elections in East Timor', 9 (2002) *International Peacekeeping* 69

Hohe, T, 'The Clash of Paradigms: International Administration and Local Political Legitimacy in East Timor', 24 (2002) *Contemporary Southeast Asia* 569

Morphet, S, 'Current International Civil Administration: The Need for Political Legitimacy', 9 (2002) *International Peacekeeping* 140

Paris, R, 'International Peacebuilding and the Mission Civilisatrice', 28 (2002) *Review of International Studies* 637

Sörensen, JS, 'Balkanism and the New Radical Interventionism: A Structural Critique', 9 (2002) *International Peacekeeping* 1

Yannis, A, 'State Collapse and its Implications for Peace-Building and Reconstruction', 33 (2002) *Development & Change* 817

Bain, W, 'The Political Theory of Trusteeship and the Twilight of International Equality', 16 (2003) *International Relations* 59

Korhonen, O, ' "Post" As Justification: International Law and Democracy-Building after Iraq', 2:7 *German Law Journal* (1 July 2003), available at <http://www.germanlawjournal.com/article.php?id=292>

Marshall, D/Inglis, S, 'The Disempowerment of Human Rights-Based Justice in the United Nations Mission in Kosovo', 16 (2003) *Harvard Human Rights Journal* 95

Perritt, HH, 'Structures and Standards for Political Trusteeship', 8 (2003) *UCLA Journal of International Law & Foreign Affairs* 385, 424

Yannis, A, 'The Creation and Politics of International Protectorates in the Balkans: Bridges Over Troubled Waters', 5 (2003) *Journal of International Relations & Development* 258, 267–9

Ayoob, M, 'Third World Perspectives on Humanitarian Intervention and International Administration', 10 (2004) *Global Governance* 99

Berdal, M/Caplan, R, 'The Politics of International Administration', 10 (2004) *Global Governance* 1

Chandler, D, 'Imposing the "Rule of Law": The Lessons of BiH for Peacebuilding in Iraq', 11 (2004) *International Peacekeeping* 1

Chandler, D, 'The Problems of "Nation-Building": Imposing Bureaucratic "Rule from Above" ', 17 (2004) *Cambridge Review of International Affairs* 577

Chandler, D, 'The Responsibility to Protect? Imposing the "Liberal Peace" ', 11 (2004) *International Peacekeeping* 59

Fearon, J/Laitin, D, 'Neotrusteeship and the Problem of Weak States', 28 (2004) *International Security* 1

Harland, D, 'Legitimacy and Effectiveness in International Administration', 10 (2004) *Global Governance* 15

Hohe, T, 'Delivering Feudal Democracy in East Timor', ch. 13 in E Newman and R Rich (eds), *The UN Role in Promoting Democracy: Between Ideals and Reality* (UN University Press, 2004)

Mertus, J, 'Improving Post-Agreement Intervention: The Role of Human Rights Culture in Kosovo', 10 (2004) *Global Governance* 333

Wilde, R/Delcourt, B, 'Le retour des "protectorats". L'irrésistible attrait de l'administration des territoires étrangers', in B Delcourt, D Duez, and E Remacle (eds), *La guerre d'Irak: Prélude d'un nouvel ordre international?* (PIE – Peter Lang 2004), 219

Chandler, D, 'Peace without Politics', 12 (2005) *International Peacekeeping* 307

d'Aspremont, J, 'Les administrations internationales de territoire et la création internationale d'Etats démocratiques', paper presented at the 'Workshop on Legitimacy and Accountability of International Administrations', *ESIL Research Forum 2005*, Geneva, 26–28 May 2005, obtainable from <http://www.esil-sedi.org>

Hurwitz, A, 'Towards Enhanced Legitimacy of Rule of Law Programs in Multidimensional Peace Operations', paper presented at the 'Workshop on Legitimacy and Accountability of International Administrations', *ESIL Research Forum 2005*, Geneva, 26–28 May 2005, obtainable from <http://www.esil-sedi.org>

Koskenmäki, R, 'Introductory Remarks', paper presented at the 'Workshop on Legitimacy and Accountability of International Administrations', *ESIL Research Forum 2005*, Geneva, 26–28 May 2005, obtainable from <http://www.esil-sedi.org>

Mersiades, M, 'Peacekeeping and Legitimacy: Lessons from Cambodia and Somalia', 12 (2005) *International Peacekeeping* 205

Ratner, SR, 'Foreign Occupation and International Territorial Administration: The Challenges of Convergence', 16 (2005) *EJIL* 695

Stahn, C, 'Accountability and Legitimacy in Practice: Lawmaking by Transitional Administrations', paper presented at the 'Workshop on Legitimacy and Accountability of International Administrations', *ESIL Research Forum 2005*, Geneva, 26–28 May 2005, obtainable from <http://www.esil-sedi.org>

Stahn, C, 'Governance Beyond the State: Issues of Legitimacy in International Territorial Administration', 1 (2005) *International Organizations Law Review* 9

Wilde, R, 'Legitimacy and Accountability of International Administrations: A Commentary on Four Papers', paper presented at the 'Workshop on Legitimacy and Accountability of International Administrations', *ESIL Research Forum 2005*, Geneva, 26–28 May 2005, obtainable from <http://www.esil-sedi.org>

Wilde, R, 'The Post-Colonial Use of International Territorial Administration and Issues of Legitimacy', 99 (2005) *ASIL Proc.* 38

Wolfrum, R, 'International Administration of Post-Conflict Situations by the United Nations and Other International Actors', 9 (2005) *Max Planck Yearbook of United Nations Law* 649, 678–80

Bain, W, 'In Praise of Folly: International Administration and the Corruption of Humanity', 82 (2006) *International Affairs* 532, reprinted as W Bain, 'In Praise of Folly: International Administration and the Moral Breakdown of International Society', ch. 9 in A Hehir and N Robinson (eds), *State Building: Theory and Practice* (Routledge, 2007)

Berman, N, 'Intervention in a "Divided World": Axes of Legitimacy', 17 (2006) *EJIL* 769

Dickerson, HK, 'Assumptions of Legitimacy and the Foundations of International Territorial Administration', 20 (2006) *Denver Journal of International Law & Politics* 161

Knoll, B, 'Beyond the Mission Civilisatrice: The Properties of a Normative Order within an Internationalized Territory', 19 (2006) *LJIL* 275

Berman, N, 'Les Ambivalences Impériales', in E Jouannet (ed.), *Impérialisme et Droit International en Europe et en Amérique* (2007)

Chandler, D, 'The State-Building Dilemma: Good Governance or Democratic Government?', ch. 4 in A Hehir and N Robinson (eds), *State Building: Theory and Practice* (Routledge, 2007)

Harper, E, 'The Challenge of Judicial Rehabilitation under UN Auspices: Reconciling Legal–Cultural Incompatibilities', in A Fijalkowski (ed.), *International Institutional Reform, 2005 Hague Joint Conference on Contemporary Issues of International Law* (T.M.C. Asser Press, 2007), 91

Wilde, R, 'Colonialism Redux? Territorial Administration by International Organizations, Colonial Echoes, and the Legitimacy of the "International"', ch. 2 in N Robinson and A Hehir (eds), *State Building: Theory and Practice* (Routledge, 2007)

5.2.5 Gender issues

Wilde, R, *Beyond the Yoke: Women's Rights in the Dadaab Refugee Camps of Kenya* (1997, report on file at UK House of Commons Library)

Wilde, R, '*Quis Custodiet Ipsos Custodes*? Why and How UNHCR Governance of "Development" Refugee Camps Should Be Subject to International Human Rights Law', 1 (1998) *Yale Human Rights and Development Law Journal* 107

Whittington, S, 'The UN Transitional Administration in East Timor: Gender Affairs', 53 (2000) *Development Bulletin* 74

Charlesworth, H/Wood, M, 'Mainstreaming Gender in International Peace and Security: the Case of East Timor', 26 (2001) *Yale Journal of International Law* 313

Chinkin, C/Paradine, K, 'Vision and Reality: Democracy and Citizenship of Women in the Dayton Peace Accords', 26 (2001) *Yale Journal of International Law* 103

Delacić, E, 'Women in Between: "Where do I belong?"', in D Sokolović and F Bieber (eds), *Reconstructing Multiethnic Societies: The Case of Bosnia and Herzegovina* (Ashgate, 2001), 185

Kvinna till Kvinna Foundation, *Getting it Right? A Gender Approach to UNMIK Administration in Kosovo* (2001), available at <http://www.iktk.se/publikationer/rapporter/pdf/Kosovorapport.pdf>

Verdirame, G, 'Testing the Effectiveness of International Norms: The Provision of Humanitarian Assistance by the UN and Sexual Apartheid in Afghanistan', 23 (2001) *Human Rights Quarterly* 733

Wood, N, 'Kosovo Leads Europe in Woman Power', *BBC News Online*, 29 November 2001, <http://news.bbc.co.uk/2/hi/europe/1682907.stm>

Charlesworth, H/Wood, M, 'Women and Human Rights in the Rebuilding of East Timor', 71 (2002) *Nordic Journal of International Law* 325

Whittington, S, 'Gender and Peacekeeping: The United Nations Transitional Administration in East Timor', 28 (2003) *Signs* 1283

Harris Rimmer, S, 'East Timorese Women and Transitional Justice', in S Pickering and C Lambert (eds), *Global Issues: Women and Justice* (Sydney Institute of Criminology, University of Sydney Faculty of Law, 2004), 335

Handrahan, L, 'Rhetoric and Reality: Post-conflict Recovery and Development – The UN and Gender Reform', ch. 17 in ND White and D Klaasen (eds), *The UN, Human Rights and Post-Conflict Situations* (Manchester University Press, 2005)

Fitzsimmons, T, 'Engendering Justice and Security after War', ch. 10 in CT Call (ed.), *Constructing Justice and Security after War* (USIP Press, 2006)

5.2.6 Legality under the UN Charter

Kelsen, H, *The Law of the United Nations* (Stevens & Sons, 1951), 195–7 n. 7 and 684–8

Sagay, I, *The Legal Aspects of the Namibian Dispute* (University of Ife Press, 1975), 270–1

Sarooshi, D, *The United Nations and the Development of Collective Security* (OUP, 1999), 59–63

Brownlie, I, *Principles of Public International Law* (6th edn, OUP, 2003), 167

Chesterman, S, *You, The People: The United Nations, Transitional Administration, and State-Building* (OUP, 2004), 50–6

Matheson, MJ, *Council Unbound: The Growth of UN Decision Making on Conflict and Postconflict Issues After the Cold War* (USIP Press, 2006), ch. 4

Smyrek, DS, *Internationally Administered Territories – International Protectorates? An Analysis of Sovereignty over Internationally Administered Territories with Special Reference to the Legal Status of Post-War Kosovo* (Duncker & Humblot, 2006), 89–92

Lauterpacht, E, 'The Contemporary Practice of the United Kingdom in the Field of International Law – Survey and Comment', 5 (1956) *ICLQ* 405, 409–13

Seyersted, F, 'United Nations Forces, Some Legal Problems', 37 (1962) *BYIL* 351, 451–3

Halderman, JW, 'United Nations Territorial Administration and the Development of the Charter', 70 (1964) *Duke Law Journal* 95

de Hoogh, AJJ, 'Attribution or Delegation of (Legislative) Power by the Security Council? The Case of the United Nations Transitional Administration in East Timor (UNTAET)', 7 (2001) *International Peacekeeping: Yearbook of International Peace Operations* 1

Irmscher, T, 'The Legal Framework for the Activities of the United Nations Interim Administration Mission in Kosovo: The Charter, Human Rights, and the Law of Occupation', 44 (2001) *German Yearbook of International Law* 353, 362–6

Kondoch, B, 'The United Nations Administration of East Timor', 6 (2001) *Journal of Conflict & Security Law* 245

Matheson, MJ, 'United Nations Governance of Post-Conflict Societies', 95 (2001) *AJIL* 76, at 83–5, also published as 'United Nations Governance of Post-Conflict Societies: East Timor and Kosovo', in MC Bassiouni (ed.), *Post-Conflict Justice* (Transnational Publishers, 2002), 523

Ruffert, M, 'The Administration of Kosovo and East Timor by the International Community', 50 (2001) *ICLQ* 613, 616–22

Stahn, C, 'International Territorial Administration in the Former Yugoslavia: Origins, Development and Challenges Ahead', 61 (2001) *ZaöRV* 107, 129–33

Stahn, C, 'The United Nations Transitional Administrations in Kosovo and East Timor: A First Analysis', 5 (2001) *Max Planck Yearbook of United Nations Law* 105, 134–40

Zimmermann, A/Stahn, C, 'Yugoslav Territory, United Nations Trusteeship or Sovereign State? Reflections on the Current and Future Legal Status of Kosovo', 70 (2001) *Nordic Journal of International Law* 424, section 3.2

Bothe, M/Marauhn, T, 'UN Administration of Kosovo and East Timor: Concept, Legality and Limitations of Security Council-Mandated Trusteeship Administration', in C Tomuschat (ed.), *Kosovo and the International Community: A Legal Assessment* (Kluwer Law International, 2002), 217, 230–5

Frowein, J/Krisch, N, 'Article 41', in B Simma (ed.), *The Charter of the United Nations. A Commentary* (2nd edn, OUP, 2002), 735, section IV

Tomuschat, C, 'Yugoslavia's Damaged Sovereignty over the Province of Kosovo', in G Kreijen (ed.), *State, Sovereignty, and International Governance* (OUP, 2002), 323, 333–45

Orakhelashvili, A, 'The Legal Basis of the United Nations Peace-Keeping Operations', 43 (2002–2003) *Virginia Journal of International Law* 485

de Wet, E, 'The Direct Administration of Territories by the United Nations and its Member States in the Post Cold War Era: Legal Bases and Implications for National Law', 8 (2004) *Max Planck Yearbook of United Nations Law* 291

Nilsson, J, 'UNMIK and the Ombudsperson Institution in Kosovo: Human Rights Protection in a United Nations "Surrogate State"', 22 (2004) *Netherlands Human Rights Quarterly* 389, 391 n. 1

Ratner, SR, 'Foreign Occupation and International Territorial Administration: The Challenges of Convergence', 16 (2005) *EJIL* 695, text accompanying n. 10

Wolfrum, R, 'International Administration of Post-Conflict Situations by the United Nations and Other International Actors', 9 (2005) *Max Planck Yearbook of United Nations Law* 649, 667–72

5.2.7 Legal issues of responsibility, applicable law, and jurisdiction, and/or accountability generally

Sagay, I, *The Legal Aspects of the Namibian Dispute* (University of Ife Press, 1975), 271–4

Chandler, D, *Bosnia: Faking Democracy after Dayton* (2nd edn, Pluto Press, 2000)

Korhonen, O/Gras, J, *International Governance in Post-Conflict Situations* (Erik Castrén Institute Research Report 9/2001, University of Helsinki, 2001), 150–2

Sokolović, D/Bieber, F (eds), *Reconstructing Multiethnic Societies: The Case of Bosnia and Herzegovina* (Ashgate, 2001)

Kolb, R/Porretto, G/Vité, S, *L'Articulation des règles de droit international humanitaire et de droits de l'homme applicables aux forces internationales et aux administrations civiles internationales transitoires* (CUDIH, 2003)

Chesterman, S, *You, The People: The United Nations, Transitional Administration, and State-Building* (OUP, 2004), ch. 4

Caplan, R, *International Governance of War-Torn Territories: Rule and Reconstruction* (OUP, 2005), chs 9 and 11

Verdirame, G/Harrell-Bond, B, *Rights in Exile: Janus-Faced Humanitarianism* (Berghahn Books, 2005)

Clapham, A, *Human Rights Obligations of Non-State Actors* (OUP, 2006), 128–32

Korhonen, O/Gras, J/Creutz, K, *International Post-Conflict Situations: New Challenges for Co-Operative Governance* (Erik Castrén Institute Research Reports 18/2006, University of Helsinki, 2006)

Verdirame, G, *UN Accountability: Compliance with Human Rights* (CUP, forthcoming 2008)

Amnesty International, 'Federal Republic of Yugoslavia (Kosovo): International officials flout international law', AI Index: EUR 70/008/2002, 1 September 2002, available at <http://web.amnesty.org/library/index/engeur700082002>

Wilde, R, '*Quis Custodiet Ipsos Custodes*? Why and How UNHCR Governance of "Development" Refugee Camps Should Be Subject to International Human Rights Law', 1 (1998) *Yale Human Rights and Development Law Journal* 107

Chopra, J, 'The UN's Kingdom of East Timor', 42 (2000) *Survival* 27

Beauvais, JC, 'Benevolent Despotism: A Critique of UN State-Building in East Timor', 33 (2001) *NYU Journal of International Law & Politics* 1101

Cerone, J, 'Minding the Gap: Outlining KFOR Accountability in Post-Conflict Kosovo', 12 (2001) *EJIL* 469

de Hoogh, AJJ, 'Attribution or Delegation of (Legislative) Power by the Security Council? The Case of the United Nations Transitional Administration in East Timor (UNTAET)', 7 (2001) *International Peacekeeping: Yearbook of International Peace Operations* 1

Irmscher, T, 'The Legal Framework for the Activities of the United Nations Interim Administration Mission in Kosovo: The Charter, Human Rights, and the Law of Occupation', 44 (2001) *German Yearbook of International Law* 353, 366–95

Kondoch, B, 'The United Nations Administration of East Timor', 6 (2001) *Journal of Conflict & Security Law* 245, 257–65

Korhonen, O, 'International Governance in Post-Conflict Situations', 14 (2001) *LJIL* 495, 526–7

Reinisch, A, 'Governance Without Accountability', 44 (2001) *German Yearbook of International Law* 270

Ruffert, M, 'The Administration of Kosovo and East Timor by the International Community', 50 (2001) *ICLQ* 613, 622–7

Stahn, C, 'International Territorial Administration in the Former Yugoslavia: Origins, Development and Challenges Ahead', 61 (2001) *ZaöRV* 107, 137–71

Stahn, C, 'The United Nations Transitional Administrations in Kosovo and East Timor: A First Analysis', 5 (2001) *Max Planck Yearbook of United Nations Law* 105, 140–8, 148–79

Verdirame, G, 'Testing the Effectiveness of International Norms: The Provision of Humanitarian Assistance by the UN and Sexual Apartheid in Afghanistan', 23 (2001) *Human Rights Quarterly* 733

Wickremasinghe, C/Verdirame, G, 'Responsibility and Liability for Violations of Human Rights in the Course of UN Field Operations', in C Scott (ed.), *Torture as Tort: Comparative Perspectives on the Development of Transnational Human Rights Litigation* (Hart Publishing, 2001), 465

Wilde, R, 'The Complex Role of the Legal Adviser When International Organizations Administer Territory', 95 (2001) *ASIL Proc.* 51

Wilde, R, 'Accountability and International Actors in Bosnia and Herzegovina, Kosovo and East Timor', 7 (2001) *ILSA Journal of International & Comparative Law* 455

Bongiorno, C, 'A Culture of Impunity: Applying International Human Rights Law to the United Nations in East Timor', 33 (2002) *Columbia Human Rights Law Review* 623

Bothe, M/Marauhn, T, 'UN Administration of Kosovo and East Timor: Concept, Legality and Limitations of Security Council-Mandated Trusteeship Administration', in C Tomuschat (ed.), *Kosovo and the International Community: A Legal Assessment* (Kluwer Law International, 2002), 217, 228–9, 237–9

Chesterman, S, 'The United Nations as Government: Accountability Mechanisms for Territories under UN Administration', Paper delivered at the conference *Fighting Corruption in Kosovo: Lessons from the Region*, Pristina, Kosovo, 4–5 March 2002

Morrow, J/White, R, 'The United Nations in Transitional East Timor: International Standards and the Reality of Governance', 22 (2002) *Australian Yearbook of International Law* 1

Rawski, F, 'To Waive or Not to Waive? Immunity and Accountability in UN Peacekeeping Operations', 18 (2002) *Connecticut Journal of International Law* 103

Verdirame, G, 'Compliance with Human Rights in UN Operations', 2 (2002) *Human Rights Law Review* 265

Abraham, E, 'The Sins of the Savior: Holding the United Nations Accountable to International Human Rights Standards for Executive Order Detentions in its Mission in Kosovo', 52 (2003) *American University Law Review* 1291

Keohane, RO, 'Political Authority after Intervention: Gradations in Sovereignty', ch. 8 in JL Holzgrefe and RO Keohane (eds), *Humanitarian Intervention: Ethical, Legal, and Political Dilemmas* (CUP, 2003)

Mégret, F/Hoffmann, T, 'The UN as a Human Rights Violator? Some Reflections on the United Nations Changing Human Rights Responsibilities', 25 (2003) *Human Rights Quarterly* 314

Yannis, A, 'The Creation and Politics of International Protectorates in the Balkans: Bridges Over Troubled Waters', 5 (2003) *Journal of International Relations & Development* 258, 267– 9

Chesterman, S, 'Building Democracy through Benevolent Autocracy: Consultation and Accountability in UN Transitional Administrations', ch. 4 in E Newman and R Rich (eds), *The UN Role in Promoting Democracy: Between Ideals and Reality* (UN University Press, 2004)

de Wet, E, 'The Direct Administration of Territories by the United Nations and its Member States in the Post Cold War Era: Legal Bases and Implications for National Law', 8 (2004) *Max Planck Yearbook of United Nations Law* 291

Fearon, J/Laitin, D, 'Neotrusteeship and the Problem of Weak States', 28 (2004) *International Security* 1, 33–6

Nilsson, J, 'UNMIK and the Ombudsperson Institution in Kosovo: Human Rights Protection in a United Nations "Surrogate State"', 22 (2004) *Netherlands Human Rights Quarterly* 389

Perritt, HH, 'Providing Judicial Review for Decisions by Political Trustees', 15 (2004) *Duke Journal of Comparative & International Law* 1

Wilde, R, 'The Accountability of International Organizations and the Concept of "Functional Duality"', in WP Heere (ed.), *From Government to Governance. The Growing Impact of Non State Actors on the International and European Legal System. Proceedings of the Sixth Hague Joint Conference held in The Hague, The Netherlands* (T.M.C. Asser Press, 2004), 164

Alston, P, 'The "Not-a-cat" Syndrome: Can the International Human Rights Regime Accommodate Non-State Actors?', in P Alston (ed.), *Non-State Actors and Human Rights* (OUP, 2005), 3, at 8–9

Brand, M, 'Effective Human Rights Protection When the UN "Becomes the State": Lessons from UNMIK', ch. 15 in ND White and D Klaasen (eds), *The UN, Human Rights and Post-Conflict Situations* (Manchester University Press, 2005)

Caplan, R, 'Who Guards the Guardians? International Accountability in Bosnia', 12 (2005) *International Peacekeeping* 463, reprinted as R Caplan, 'Who Guards the Guardians? International Accountability in Bosnia', ch. 6 in A Hehir and N Robinson (eds), *State Building: Theory and Practice* (Routledge, 2007)

Cerone, J, 'Reasonable Measures in Unreasonable Circumstances: A Legal Responsibility Framework for Human Rights Violations in Post-Conflict territories under UN Administration', ch. 3 in ND White and D Klaasen (eds), *The UN, Human Rights and Post-Conflict Situations* (Manchester University Press, 2005)

Hurwitz, A, 'Towards Enhanced Legitimacy of Rule of Law Programs in Multidimensional Peace Operations', paper presented at the 'Workshop on Legitimacy and Accountability of International Administrations', *ESIL Research Forum 2005*, Graduate Institute of International Studies (HEI), Geneva, 26–28 May 2005, obtainable from <http://www.esil-sedi.org>

Mersiades, M, 'Peacekeeping and Legitimacy: Lessons from Cambodia and Somalia', 12 (2005) *International Peacekeeping* 205

Pallis, M, 'The Operation of UNHCR's Accountability Mechanisms', NYU International Law and Justice Working Papers, Global Administrative Law Series, Paper 2005/12 (2005), available at <http://www.iilj.org/papers/documents/2005.12Pallis.pdf>

Ratner, SR, 'Foreign Occupation and International Territorial Administration: The Challenges of Convergence', 16 (2005) *EJIL* 695

Sassòli, M, 'Legislation and Maintenance of Public Order and Civil Life by Occupying Powers', 16 (2005) *EJIL* 661

Seibert-Fohr, A, 'Reconstruction through Accountability', 9 (2005) *Max Planck Yearbook of United Nations Law* 555

Stahn, C, 'Accountability and Legitimacy in Practice: Lawmaking by Transitional Administrations', paper presented at the 'Workshop on Legitimacy and Accountability of International Administrations', *ESIL Research Forum 2005*, Graduate Institute of International Studies (HEI), Geneva, 26–28 May 2005, obtainable from <http://www.esil-sedi.org>

Stahn, C, 'Governance Beyond the State: Issues of Legitimacy in International Territorial Administration', 1 (2005) *International Organizations Law Review* 9

Verdirame, G, 'UN Accountability for Human Rights Violations in Post-Conflict Situations', ch. 4 in ND White and D Klaasen (eds), *The UN, Human Rights and Post-Conflict Situations* (Manchester University Press, 2005)

Wilde, R, 'Legitimacy and Accountability of International Administrations: A Commentary on Four Papers', paper presented at the 'Workshop on Legitimacy and Accountability of International Administrations', *ESIL Research Forum 2005*, Graduate Institute of International Studies (HEI), Geneva, 26–28 May 2005, obtainable from <http://www.esil-sedi.org>

Wilde, R, 'International Territorial Administration and Human Rights', ch. 7 in ND White and D Klaasen (eds), *The UN, Human Rights and Post-Conflict Situations* (Manchester University Press, 2005), at 167–73

Wolfrum, R, 'International Administration of Post-Conflict Situations by the United Nations and Other International Actors', 9 (2005) *Max Planck Yearbook of United Nations Law* 649, 685 7 and 688–91

Farmer, A, 'Refugee Responses, State-like Behavior, and Accountability for Human Rights Violations: A Case Study of Sexual Violence in Guinea's Refugee Camps', 9 (2006) *Yale Human Rights and Development Law Journal* 44

Knoll, B, 'Beyond the Mission Civilisatrice: The Properties of a Normative Order within an Internationalized Territory', 19 (2006) *LJIL* 275

Roberts, A, 'Transformative Military Occupation: Applying the Laws of War and Human Rights', 100 (2006) *AJIL* 580

Quénivet, N, 'The United Nations' Legal Obligations in Terms of Rule of Law in Peacebuilding Operations', 11 (2007) *International Peacekeeping: Yearbook of International Peace Operations* 203, section 3.2.1

Stahn, C, 'Lawmaking by International Territorial Administrations', 11 (2007) *International Peacekeeping: Yearbook of International Peace Operations* 81

5.3 Colonialism

5.3.1 Selected anti-colonial texts

Nehru, J, *The Discovery of India* (John Day, 1946)

Gandhi, MK, *The Collected Works of Mahatma Gandhi* [1888–1948], vols 1–90 (Publications Division of the Ministry of Information and Broadcasting, Government of India, 1958–1984); supplementary vols 91–97 (Publications Division of the Ministry of Information and Broadcasting, Government of India, 1994) (the entire collection also available online at <http://www.gandhiserve.org/cwmg/cwmg.html>)

Kenyatta, J, 'Speech at the Kenya African Union Meeting' (Nyeri, 26 July 1952), reproduced in Corfield, FD, *Historical Survey of the Origins and Growth of Mau Mau* (Great Britain Colonial Office, 1960), 301, also available at <http://www.africawithin.com/kenyatta/speech_at_kau.htm>

Nkrumah, K, *Towards Colonial Freedom: Africa in the Struggle Against World Imperialism* (Heinemann, 1962)

Nkrumah, K, *Consciencism: Philosophy and Ideology for Decolonization and Development* (Heinemann, 1964)

Nyerere, J, *Freedom and Development: A Selection from Writings and Speeches, 1968–1973* (OUP, 1973)

Nehru, J, 'Economic Development and Nonalignment', speech in Washington, D.C., 18 December 1956, reproduced in *US Department of State Bulletin*, 14 January 1957, 49–50

5.3.2 Texts by those from colonial states writing contemporaneously, and others from the West writing at the time and subsequently (writers within the discipline of 'post-colonial studies' are listed separately)

de Vitoria, F, 'On the American Indians' (1539), in *Vitoria – Political Writings* (A Pagden and J Lawrance eds and transl.), (CUP, 1991), 231

Smith, A, *An Inquiry into the Nature and Causes of the Wealth of Nations* (1776) (Nelsons and Sons, 1852), Book IV, ch. VII, 'Of Colonies'

Wilberforce, W, *An Appeal to the Religion, Justice and Humanity of the Inhabitants of the British Empire, in Behalf of the Negro Slaves in the West Indies* (Hatchard & Son, 1823)

Smith Bell, S, *Colonial Administration of Great Britain* (1859) (AM Kelley, 1970 edn)

Salomon, C, *L'Occupation des territoires sans maître* (A Giard, 1889)

Kipling, R, 'The White Man's Burden', *McClure's Magazine* (February 1899), reproduced in R Kipling, *The Collected Poems of Rudyard Kipling* (Wordsworth Editions, 2001), 334

Conrad, J, *Heart of Darkness* (1902) (Penguin Books, 1995 edn)

Cattier, F, *Etude sur la situation de l'Etat indépendant du Congo* (2nd edn, Larcier and Pedone, 1906)

Fenwick, CG, *Wardship in International Law* (US Government Printing Office, 1919)

Snow, AH, *The Question of Aborigines in the Law and Practice of Nations* (US Government Printing Office, 1919)

Willoughby, WW/Fenwick, CG, *Types of Restricted Sovereignty and of Colonial Autonomy* (US Government Printing Office, 1919)

Woolf, L, *Empire and Commerce in Africa: A Study in Economic Imperialism* (Allen & Unwin, 1920)

Lindley, MF, *The Acquisition and Government of Backward Territory in International Law: Being a Treatise on the Law and Practice Relating to Colonial Expansion* (Longmans, Green & Co., 1926)

Lugard, FD, *The Dual Mandate in British Tropical Africa* (3rd edn, Blackwood, 1926)

Wright, Q, *Mandates Under the League of Nations* (University of Chicago Press, 1930), ch. 1

Lenin, VI, *Imperialism: The Highest Stage of Capitalism* (International Publishers, 1939)

Furnivall, JS, *Colonial Policy and Practice: A Comparative Study of Burma and Netherlands India* (CUP, 1948)

Hobson, JA, *Imperialism: A Study* (4th edn, Allen & Unwin, 1948)

Mellor, GR, *British Imperial Trusteeship 1783–1750* (Faber & Faber, 1951)

Chowdhuri, RN, *International Mandates and Trusteeship Systems: A Comparative Study* (Martinus Nijhoff, 1955), ch. 1

Lauterpacht, H/Jennings, RY, 'International Law and Colonial Questions, 1870–1914' (1959), reprinted in E Lauterpacht (ed.), *Hersch Lauterpacht, International Law, Collected Papers* (1975), vol. 2, 95

Various Authors, *The Cambridge History of the British Empire* (8 vols, CUP, 1929–1963)

Robinson, KE, *The Dilemmas of Trusteeship: Aspects of British Colonial Policy Between the Wars* (OUP, 1965)

Thornton, AP, *Doctrines of Imperialism* (Wiley & Sons, 1965)

Anstey, R, *King Leopold's Legacy: The Congo under Belgian Rule, 1908–1960* (OUP, 1966)

Fieldhouse, DK, *The Colonial Empires: A Comparative Survey from the Eighteenth Century* (Weidenfeld and Nicolson, 1966)

Alexandrowicz, CH, *An Introduction to the History of the Law of Nations in the East Indies* (Clarendon Press, 1967)

Gann, LH/Duignan, P, *The Burden of Empire: An Appraisal of Western Colonialism in Africa South of the Sahara* (Pall Mall Press, 1967)

Rodney, W, *How Europe Underdeveloped Africa* (Bogle-L'Ouverture Publications, 1972)

Alexandrowicz, CH, *The European-African Confrontation: A Study in Treaty-Making* (Sijthoff, 1973)

Fetter, B (ed.), *Colonial Rule in Africa: Readings from Primary Sources* (University of Wisconsin Press, 1979)

Fieldhouse, DK, *Colonialism 1870–1945: An Introduction* (Palgrave Macmillan, 1981)

Kamoche, JG, *Imperial Trusteeship and Political Evolution in Kenya 1923–1963: A Study of the Official Views and the Road to Decolonization* (University Press of America, 1981)

Gong, GW, *The Standard of 'Civilization' in International Society* (Clarendon Press, 1984)

Doyle, MW, *Empires* (Cornell University Press, 1986)

Jackson, RH, *Quasi-States: Sovereignty, International Relations and the Third World* (CUP, 1990), 71–108

Pakenham, T, *The Scramble for Africa* (Random House, 1991)

Jennings, R/Watts, A (eds), *Oppenheim's International Law, vol. 1, Peace* (9th edn, Longman, 1992), §§ 84–5

Osterhammel, J, *Colonialism: A Theoretical Overview* (1995) (SL Frisch, transl., Markus Wiener Publishers, 1997 edn.)

Ferro, M, *Colonization: A Global History* (Routledge, 1997)

Burkholder, MA (ed.), *Administrators of Empires* (Ashgate, 1998)

Hochschild, A, *King Leopold's Ghost* (Houghton Mifflin, 1999)

Russell-Wood, AJR (ed.), *Government and Governance of European Empires: 1450–1800* (Ashgate, 2000)

Christie, C, *Ideology and Revolution in Southeast Asia 1900–1975* (Routledge/Curzon, 2001)

Simpson, AWB, *Human Rights and the End of Empire: Britain and the Genesis of the European Convention* (OUP, 2001), ch. 6

Crawford, N, *Argument and Change in World Politics: Ethics, Decolonization, and Humanitarian Intervention* (CUP, 2002), chs 7 and 8

Hyam, R, *Britain's Imperial Century, 1815–1914* (3rd edn, Palgrave Macmillan, 2002)

Koskenniemi, M, *The Gentle Civilizer of Nations* (CUP, 2002), 116–78

Dimier, V, *Le gouvernement des colonies, regards croisés franco-britanniques* (Editions de l'Université de Bruxelles, 2004)

Anderson, D, *Histories of the Hanged: Britain's Dirty War in Kenya and the End of Empire* (Weidenfeld & Nicolson, 2005)

Kerr, PH, 'Political Relations between Advanced and Backward Peoples', in AJ Grant, A Greenwood, JDI Hughes, PH Kerr and FF Urquhart, *An Introduction to the Study of International Relations* (Macmillan, 1916), 141

Brown, PM, 'Editorial Comment: Imperialism', 39 (1945) *AJIL* 84

Alexandrowicz, CH, 'The Juridical Expression of the Sacred Trust of Civilization', 65 (1971) *AJIL* 149

Sanderson, GN, 'The European Partition of Africa: Origins and Dynamics', ch. 2 in R Oliver and GN Sanderson (eds), *The Cambridge History of Africa – Vol. 6: From 1870 to 1905* (CUP, 1985)

Burroughs, P, 'Imperial Institutions and the Government of Empire', in *The Oxford History of the British Empire – Vol. III: The 19th Century* (OUP, 1999), 170

Higgins, R, 'Colonial law and the clarity of drafting: the International Court of Justice and William Dale's two abiding interests', Inaugural Sir William Dale Memorial Lecture, Chancellor Hall, Senate House, University of London, 2 July 2001, reprinted in *Amicus Curiae*, issue 37 (September/October 2001), 16

Dimier, V, 'On Good Colonial Government: Lessons from the League of Nations', 18 (2004) *Global Society* 279

5.3.3 Post-colonial studies

Sartre, J-P, *Colonialism and Neocolonialism* (1956) (Haddour, Brewer and McWilliams transl., Routledge, 2001 edn.)

Fanon, F, *The Wretched of the Earth* (1961) (R Philcox transl., Grove Press, 2004 edn.)

Fanon, F, *Toward the African Revolution: Political Essays* (1964) (H Chevalier transl., Monthly Review Press, 1967 edn.)

Nkrumah, K, *Neo-Colonialism: The Last Stage of Imperialism* (Panaf, 1965)

Chakravorty Spivak, G, *In Other Worlds: Essays in Cultural Politics* (Routledge, 1988)

Chakravorty Spivak, G, *The Post-Colonial Critic* (Routledge, 1990)

Said, EW, *Culture and Imperialism* (Vintage, 1993)

Bhabha, H, *The Location of Culture* (Routledge, 1994)

Ashcroft, B/Griffiths, G/Tiffin, H (eds), *The Post-Colonial Studies Reader* (Routledge, 1995)

Ribeiro, D, *The Brazilian People: The Formation and Meaning of Brazil* (G Rabassa transl., University Press of Florida, 2000), ch. 3

Said, EW, *Orientalism. Western Conceptions of the Orient* (reissue with new afterword, Penguin Books, 1995)

Guha, R (ed.), *A Subaltern Studies Reader, 1986–1995* (University of Minnesota Press, 1997)

Moore-Gilbert, B, *Postcolonial Theory: Context, Practices, Politics* (Verso, 1997)

Loomba, A, *Colonialism/Postcolonialism* (Routledge, 1998)

Chakravorty Spivak, G, *A Critique of Postcolonial Reason: Toward a History of the Vanishing Present* (Harvard University Press, 1999)

Chandra, B, *Essays on Colonialism* (Sangam Books, 1999)

Scott, D, *Refashioning Futures: Criticism after Postcoloniality* (Princeton University Press, 1999)

Ashcroft, B/Griffiths, G/Tiffin, H, *Post-Colonial Studies: The Key Concepts* (Routledge, 2000)

Young, RJC, *Postcolonialism – An Historical Introduction* (Blackwell, 2001)

Gregory, D, *The Colonial Present: Afghanistan, Palestine, Iraq* (Blackwell, 2004)

Ibhawoh, B, *Imperialism and Human Rights: Colonial Discourses of Rights and Liberties in African History* (SUNY Press, 2006)

Chakrabarty, D, 'Postcoloniality and the Artifice of History: Who Speaks for "Indian" Pasts?', 37 (Winter 1992) *Representations* 1

Chakravorty Spivak, G, '"Woman" as Theatre: United Nations Conference on Women, Beijing 1995', 75 (1996) *Radical Philosophy* 2

Tharoor, S, 'The Messy Afterlife of Colonialism', 8 (2002) *Global Governance* 1

5.3.4 Post-colonial and third world approaches to international law

Chimni, BS, *International Law and World Order: A Critique of Contemporary Approaches* (Sage, 1993)

Grovogui, SN, *Sovereigns, Quasi Sovereigns and Africans: Race and Self-Determination in International Law* (University of Minnesota Press, 1996)

Okafor, OC, *Re-Defining Legitimate Statehood: International Law and State Fragmentation in Africa* (Martinus Nijhoff, 2000)

Anghie, A/Chimni, BS/Mickelson, K/Okafor, OC (eds), *The Third World and International Order: Law, Politics and Globalization* (Brill, 2003)

Rajagopal, B, *International Law from Below: Development, Social Movements and Third World Resistance* (CUP, 2003)

Anghie, A, *Imperialism, Sovereignty and the Making of International Law* (CUP, 2005)

Amos, V/Parmar, P, 'Challenging Imperial Feminism', 17 (July 1984) *Feminist Review* 3

Sathirathai, S, 'An Understanding of the Relationship between International Legal Discourse and Third World Countries', 25 (1984) *Harvard International Law Journal* 395

Berman, N, '"But the Alternative is Despair", European Nationalism and the Modernist Renewal of International Law', 106 (1992–93) *Harvard Law Review* 1792

Anghie, A, 'The Heart of My Home: Colonialism, Environmental Damage, and the Nauru case', 34 (1993) *Harvard International Law Journal* 445

Nesiah, V, 'Towards a Feminist Internationality: A Critique of US Feminist Legal Scholarship', 16 (1993) *Harvard Women's Law Journal* 189

Gordon, RE, 'Some Legal Problems with Trusteeship', 28 (1995) *Cornell International Law Journal* 301

Mutua, MW, 'Why Redraw the Map of Africa: A Legal and Moral Inquiry', 16 (1995) *Michigan Journal of International Law* 1113

Mutua, MW, 'Putting Humpty Dumpty Back Together Again: the Dilemmas of the African Post-Colonial State', 21 (1995) *Brooklyn Journal of International Law* 505

Anghie, A, 'Francisco de Vitoria and the Colonial Origins of International Law', 5 (1996) *Social & Legal Studies* 321

Otto, D, 'Subalternity and International Law: the Problems of Global Community and the Incommensurability of Difference', 5 (1996) *Social & Legal Studies* 337

Richardson, HJ, '"Failed States", Self-Determination, and Preventative Diplomacy: Colonialist Nostalgia and Democratic Expectations', 10 (1996) *Temple International & Comparative Law Journal* 1

Gordon, RE, 'Saving Failed States: Sometimes a Neocolonialist Notion', 12 (1997) *American University Journal of International Law & Policy* 903

Gathii, J, 'International Law and Eurocentricity', 9 (1998) *EJIL* 184

Mickelson, K, 'Rhetoric or Rage: Third World Voices in International Legal Discourse', 16 (1998) *Wisconsin International Law Journal* 353

Anghie, A, 'Finding the Peripheries: Sovereignty and Colonialism in Nineteenth-Century International Law', 40 (1999) *Harvard International Law Journal* 1

Berman, N, 'In the Wake of Empire', 14 (1998–99) *American University International Law Review* 1521

Gathii, J, 'Good Governance as a Counter Insurgency Agenda to Oppositional and Transformative Social Projects in International Law', 5 (1999) *Buffalo Human Rights Law Review* 107

Rajagopal, B, 'Locating the Third World in Cultural Geography', (1998–99) *Third World Legal Studies* 1

Berman, N, 'Imperial Rivalry and the Genealogy of Human Rights: The Nationality Decrees Case', 94 (2000) *ASIL Proc.* 53

Gathii, J, 'Symposium Issue Foreword: Alternative and Critical: The Contribution of Research and Scholarship on Developing Countries to International Legal Theory', 41 (2000) *Harvard International Law Journal* 263

Mutua, MW, 'What is TWAIL?', 94 (2000) *ASIL Proc.* 39

Okafor, OC, 'After Martyrdom: International Law, Sub-State Groups, and Construction of Legitimate Statehood in Africa', 41 (2000) *Harvard International Law Journal* 503

Rajagopal, B, 'From Resistance to Renewal: The Third World, Social Movements, and the Expansion of International Institutions', 41 (2000) *Harvard International Law Journal* 529

Shalakany, A, 'Arbitration and the Third World: Bias under the Scepter of Neo-Liberalism', 41 (2000) *Harvard International Law Journal* 419

Anghie, A, 'Time Present and Time Past: Globalization, International Financial Institutions, and the Third World', 32 (2000) *NYU Journal of International Law & Politics* 24

Anghie, A, 'Colonialism and the Birth of International Institutions: Sovereignty, Economy, and the Mandate System of the League of Nations', 34 (2002) *NYU Journal of International Law & Politics* 513

Kapur, R, 'The Tragedy of Victimization Rhetoric: Resurrecting the "Native" Subject in International/Post-Colonial Feminist Legal Politics', 15 (2002) *Harvard Human Rights Journal* 1

Nesiah, V, 'Placing International Law: White Spaces on a Map', 16 (2003) *LJIL* 1

Nesiah, V, 'The Ground Beneath Her Feet: TWAIL Feminisms', in A Anghie, BS Chimni, K Mickelson, and OC Okafor (eds), *The Third World and International Order: Law, Politics and Globalization* (Brill, 2003), 133

Anghie, A/Chimni, BS, 'Third World Approaches to International Law and Individual Responsibility in Internal Conflicts' in SR Ratner and A-M Slaughter (eds), *The Methods of International Law* (ASIL, 2004), 185

Gathii, J, 'Foreign and Other Economic Rights upon Conquest and under Occupation: Iraq in Comparative and Historical Context', 25 (2004) *University of Pennsylvania Journal of International Economic Law* 491

Berman, N, 'Intervention in a "Divided World": Axes of Legitimacy', 17 (2006) *EJIL* 769

Chimni, BS, 'Third World Approaches to International Law: A Manifesto', 8 (2006) *International Community Law Review* 3

Gupta, J, 'Broadening Third World Legal Scholarship to Include Introspection and Interdisciplinarity', 8 (2006) *International Community Law Review* 65

Yasuaki, O, 'A Transcivilizational Perspective on Global Legal Order in the Twenty-first Century: A Way to Overcome West-centric and Judiciary-centric Deficits in International Legal Thoughts', 8 (2006) *International Community Law Review* 29

Tomuschat, C, 'World Order Models: A Disputation with B.S. Chimni and Yasuaki Onuma', 8 (2006) *International Community Law Review* 71

Berman, N, 'Les Ambivalences Impériales', in E Jouannet (ed.), *Impéralisme et Droit International en Europe et en Amérique* (2007)

5.4 Self-Determination

Sureda, AR, *The Evolution of the Right of Self-Determination* (Sijthoff, 1973)

Ofuatey-Kodjoe, W, *The Principle of Self-Determination in International Law* (Nellen Publishing Co., 1977)

Pomerance, M, *Self-Determination in Law and Practice* (Martinus Nijhoff, 1982)

Shaw, MN, *Title to Territory in Africa. International Legal Issues* (OUP, 1986), chs 2 and 3

Crawford, J (ed.), *The Rights of Peoples* (OUP, 1992)

Jennings, RY/Watts, A (eds), *Oppenheim's International Law, Vol. 1, Peace* (9th edn, Longman, 1992), 285–95

Cassese, A, *Self-Determination of Peoples: A Legal Reappraisal* (CUP, 1995)

Grovogui, SN, *Sovereigns, Quasi Sovereigns and Africans: Race and Self-Determination in International Law* (University of Minnesota Press, 1996)

Hannum, H, *Autonomy, Sovereignty, and Self-Determination: The Accommodation of Conflicting Rights* (rev. edn, University of Pennsylvania Press, 1996)

Talmon, S, *Recognition of Governments in International Law with Particular Reference to Governments in Exile* (OUP, 1998), ch. 6

Bayefsky, A (ed.), *Self-Determination in International Law: Quebec and Lessons Learned* (Kluwer, 2000)

Jackson, RH, *The Global Covenant: Human Conduct in a World of States* (OUP, 2000), 74–8

Okafor, OC, *Re-Defining Legitimate Statehood: International Law and State Fragmentation in Africa* (Martinus Nijhoff, 2000)

Roth, BR, *Governmental Illegitimacy in International Law* (OUP, 2001), ch. 6

Crawford, N, *Argument and Change in World Politics: Ethics, Decolonization, and Humanitarian Intervention* (CUP, 2002), ch. 7

Knop, K, *Diversity and Self-Determination in International Law* (CUP, 2002)

Crawford, J, *The Creation of States in International Law* (2nd edn, OUP, 2006), 108–28

Kohen, MG (ed.), *Secession: International Law Perspectives* (CUP, 2006)

McWhinney, E, *Self-Determination of Peoples and Plural-ethnic States in Contemporary International Law: Failed States, Nation-building and the Alternative, Federal Option* (Martinus Nijhoff, 2007)

Summers, J, *Peoples and International Law: How Nationalism and Self-Determination Shape a Contemporary Law of Nations* (Martinus Nijhoff, 2007)

Xanthaki, A, *Indigenous Rights and United Nations Standards: Self-Determination, Culture and Land* (CUP, 2007)

Kay, DA, 'The Politics of Decolonization: The New Nations and the United Nations Political Process', 21 (1967) *International Organizations* 786

Kay, DA, 'The United Nations and Decolonization', in J Barros (ed.), *The United Nations: Past, Present and Future* (Free Press, 1972), 143

Pomerance, M, 'Methods of Self-Determination and the Argument of "Primitiveness"', 12 (1974) *Canadian Yearbook of International Law* 38

Cassese, A, 'The Self-Determination of Peoples', in L Henkin (ed.), *The International Bill of Human Rights: The Covenant on Civil and Political Rights* (Columbia University Press, 1981), 92

Berman, N, 'Sovereignty in Abeyance: Self-Determination and International Law', 7 (1988) *Wisconsin International Law Journal* 51

Thornberry, P, 'Self-determination, Minorities, Human Rights: A Review of International Instruments', 38 (1989) *ICLQ* 867

Cass, DZ, 'Re-Thinking Self-Determination: A Critical Analysis of Current International Law Theories', 18 (1992) *Syracuse Journal of International Law and Commerce* 21

Franck, TM, 'The Emerging Right to Democratic Governance', 86 (1992) *AJIL* 46

Binder, G, 'The Case for Self-Determination', 29 (1993) *Stanford Journal of International Law* 223

Franck, TM, 'Postmodern Tribalism and the Right to Secession', in C Brolmann, R Lefebrer and M Ziek (eds), *People and Minorities in International Law* (Martinus Nijhoff, 1993), 2

Kimminich, O, 'A "Federal" Right of Self-Determination', in C Tomuschat (ed.), *Modern Law of Self-Determination* (Martinus Nijhoff, 1993), 83

Rosas, A, 'Internal Self-Determination', in C Tomuschat (ed.), *Modern Law of Self-Determination* (Martinus Nijhoff, 1993), 225

Salmon, J, 'Internal Aspects of the Right to Self-Determination: Towards a Democratic Legitimacy Principle?', in C Tomuschat (ed.), *Modern Law of Self-Determination* (Martinus Nijhoff, 1993), 253

Thornberry, P, 'The Democratic or Internal Aspect of Self-Determination with some Remarks on Federalism', in C Tomuschat (ed.), *Modern Law of Self-Determination* (Martinus Nijhoff, 1993), 101

Tomuschat, C, 'Self-Determination in a Post-Colonial World', in C Tomuschat (ed.), *Modern Law of Self-Determination* (Martinus Nijhoff, 1993), 1

Hannum, H, 'Rethinking Self-Determination', 34 (1993–94) *Virginia Journal of International Law*, 1

Kirgis, FL, 'The Degrees of Self-Determination in the United Nations Era', 88 (1994) *AJIL* 304

Koskenniemi, M, 'National Self-Determination Today: Problems of Legal Theory and Practice', 43 (1994) *ICLQ* 241

McCorquodale, R, 'Self-Determination: A Human Rights Approach', 43 (1994) *ICLQ* 857

Simpson, GJ, 'Judging the East Timor Dispute: Self-Determination at the International Court of Justice', 17 (1994) *Hastings International & Comparative Law Review* 323

Brietzke, PH, 'Self-Determination or Jurisprudential Confusion: Exacerbating Political Conflict', 14 (1995–6) *Wisconsin International Law Journal* 69

Chinkin, C, '*The East Timor Case (Portugal v Australia)*', 45 (1996) *ICLQ* 712

Simpson, GJ, 'Diffusion of Sovereignty: Self-Determination in the Post-Colonial Age', 32 (1996) *Stanford Journal of International Law* 255

Drew, C, 'The East Timor Popular Consultation: Self-Determination Denied', 4:2 (1999) *Human Rights Law Review* 3

Crawford, J, 'The Right of Self-Determination in International Law: Its Development and Future', in P Alston (ed.), *Peoples' Rights* (OUP, 2001), 7

Drew, C, 'The East Timor Story: International Law on Trial', 12 (2001) *EJIL* 651

Doehring, K, 'Self-determination', in B Simma (ed.), *The Charter of the United Nations. A Commentary* (2nd edn, OUP, 2002), vol. 1, 47

Nesiah, V, 'Placing International Law: White Spaces on a Map', 16 (2003) *LJIL* 1

Drew, C, 'Population Transfer: The Untold Story of the International Law of Self-Determination, unpublished doctoral thesis, LSE 2006 (on file at Senate House Library, University of London)

Drew, C, 'The Meaning of Self-determination: The "Stealing of the Sahara" Redux?', in K Arts and P Pinto Leite (eds), *International Law and the Question of Western Sahara* (International Platform of Jurists for East Timor, 2007)

5.5 Miscellaneous

Abbott, KW, 'Modern International Relations Theory: A Prospectus for International Lawyers', 14 (1989) *Yale Journal of International Law* 335

Abbott, KW, 'International Relations Theory, International Law, and the Regime Governing Atrocities in Internal Conflicts', 93 (1999) *AJIL* 361

Abbott, KW/Keohane, RO/Moravcsik, A/Slaughter, A-M/Snidal, D, 'The Concept of Legalization', 54 (2000) *International Organization* 401

Abi-Saab, G, *The United Nations Operation in the Congo 1960–1964* (OUP, 1979)

Abramowitz, M/Hurlburt, H, 'Can the EU Hack the Balkans?: A Proving Ground for Brussels', 81:5 (Sept/Oct 2002) *Foreign Affairs* 2

Acemoglu, D/Johnson, S/Robinson, J, 'Institutions as a Fundamental Cause of Long-Run Growth', ch. 6 in P Aghion and S Durlauf (eds), *Handbook of Economic Growth* (Elsevier, 2005)

Ackerly, BA/Stern, M/True, J (eds), *Feminist Methodologies for International Relations* (CUP, 2006)

Afsah, E/Guhr, AH, 'Afghanistan: Building a State to Keep the Peace', 9 (2005) *Max Planck Yearbook of United Nations Law* 373

Ahmed, S, 'No Size Fits All', 84:1 (Jan/Feb 2005) *Foreign Affairs* 162

Akehurst, M, 'Custom as a Source of International Law', 47 (1974–75) *BYIL* 1

Alexander, A, 'Refugee Status Determination Conducted by the UNHCR', 11 (1999) *International Journal of Refugee Law* 251

Allin, DH, 'NATO's Balkan Interventions', *Adelphi Paper No. 347*, July 2002

Allott, P, *Eunomia: New Order for a New World* (OUP, 1990)

Allott, P, *Eunomia: New Order for a New World* (2nd edn, OUP, 2001)

Amerasinghe, CF, *Principles of the Institutional Law of International Institutions* (CUP, 1996)

Amerasinghe, CF, *Principles of the Institutional Law of International Institutions* (2nd edn, CUP, 2005)

Anderson, CP, 'International Executives', 13 (1919) *AJIL* 85

Anderson, CP, 'United States Congressional Peace Resolution', 14 (1920) *AJIL* 384

Anderson, CP, 'The Peace Treaties', 15 (1921) *AJIL* 552

Archer, C, *International Organizations* (3rd edn, Routledge, 2001)

Aristotle, *Politics* (TA Sinclair transl., revised by TJ Saunders, Penguin Books, 1992)

Armstrong, D/Farrell, T/Lambert, H, *International Law and International Relations* (CUP, 2007)

Arnull, A/Dashwood, A/Ross, M/Wyatt, D, *Wyatt & Dashwood's European Union Law* (4th edn, Sweet and Maxwell, 2000)

Ashdown, P, 'What I Learned in Bosnia', *New York Times*, 28 October 2002, A25, column 2

Auerswald, PE/Auerswald, DP (eds), *The Kosovo Conflict: A Diplomatic History Through Documents* (Kluwer Law International, 2000)

Badinter, R, 'L'Europe du droit', 3 (1993) *EJIL* 15

Bailey, SD, 'Peaceful Settlement of International Disputes', in KV Raman (ed.), *Dispute Settlement through the United Nations* (Oceana Publications, 1977), 73

Bailey, SD/Daws, S, *The United Nations, A Concise Political Guide* (3rd edn, Macmillan, 1995)

Bain, W, 'The Idea of Trusteeship in International Society', 386 (2003) *The Round Table* 67

Baldwin, G, 'Iraq – Managing the Peace', 3 (2003) *Conflict, Security and Development* 431

Banerjee, D, 'Current Trends in UN Peacekeeping: A Perspective from Asia', 12:1 (2005) *International Peacekeeping* 18

Baros, M, 'The Arbitral Tribunal's Award for the Dispute over the Inter-entity Boundary in the Brčko Area', 3 (1998) *Journal of Armed Conflict Law* 233

Barros, J (ed.), *The United Nations: Past, Present and Future* (Free Press, 1972)

Bathurst, M, 'Legal Aspects of the Berlin Problem', 38 (1962) *BYIL* 255

Bathurst, M/Simpson, JL, *Germany and the North Atlantic Community: A Legal Survey* (Stevens & Sons, 1956)

Baty, T, 'Can Anarchy Be a State?', 28 (1934) *AJIL* 444

Bearden, M, 'Afghanistan, Graveyard of Empires', 80:6 (Nov/Dec 2001) *Foreign Affairs* 17

Beck, RJ/Arend, AC/Vander Lugt, RD (eds), *International Rules: Approaches from International Law and International Relations* (OUP, 1996)

Bekker, P, *The Legal Position of Intergovernmental Organizations – A Functional Necessity Analysis of Their Legal Status and Immunities* (Martinus Nijhoff, 1994)

Bellamy, AJ, 'Lessons Unlearned: Why Coercive Diplomacy Failed at Rambouillet', 7:2 (2000) *International Peacekeeping* 95

Bellamy, AJ, 'The "Next Stage" in Peace Operations Theory?', 11 (2004) *International Peacekeeping* 17

Bellamy, AJ/Williams, PR, 'Thinking Anew about Peace Operations', 11 (2004) *International Peacekeeping* 1

Bellamy, AJ/Williams, PR, 'What Future for Peace Operations? Brahimi and Beyond', 11 (2004) *International Peacekeeping* 183

Bellamy, AJ/Williams, PR/Griffin, S, *Understanding Peacekeeping* (Polity Press, 2004)

Belloni, R, 'Peacebuilding and Consociational Electoral Engineering in Bosnia and Herzegovina', 11 (2004) *International Peacekeeping* 334

Benard, A, 'Lessons from Iraq and Bosnia on the Theory and Practice of No-fly Zones' 27 (2004) *Journal of Strategic Studies* 454

Ben-Naftali, O/Gross, A/Michaeli, K, 'Illegal Occupation: Framing the Occupied Palestinian Territory', 23 (2005) *Berkeley Journal of International Law* 551

Benvenisti, E, 'The Security Council and the Law on Occupation: Resolution 1483 on Iraq in Historical Perspective', 1 (2003) *Israel Defense Forces Law Review* 19

Benvenisti, E, *The International Law of Occupation* (paperback edn, Princeton University Press, 2004)

Berdal, M/Leifer, M, 'Cambodia', ch. 2 in M Berdal and S Economides (eds), *United Nations Interventionism, 1991–2004* (OUP, 2007)

Bernard, A, 'Lessons from Iraq and Bosnia on the Theory and Practice of No-fly Zones', 27 (2004) *Journal of Strategic Studies* 454

Bernhardt, R, 'Customary International Law', in R Bernhardt (ed.), *Encyclopedia of Public International Law*, vol. 1 (1992), 898

Besson, Y, 'UNRWA and its Role in Lebanon', 10 (1997) *Journal of Refugee Studies* 335

Bethlehem, D/Weller, M (eds), *The 'Yugoslav' Crisis in International Law: General Issues, Part I* (CUP, 1997)

Bhavnani, KK, *Feminism and 'Race'* (OUP, 2001)

Bhuta, N, 'The Antinomies of Transformative Occupation', 16 (2005) *EJIL* 721

Biersteker, TJ/Weber, C (eds), *State Sovereignty as Social Construct* (CUP, 1996)

Biersteker, T/Spiro, P/Sriram, CL/Raffo, V (eds), *International Law and International Relations: Bridging Theory and Practice* (Routledge, 2006)

Bildt, C, *Peace Journey: The Struggle for Peace in Bosnia* (Weidenfeld & Nicolson, 1998)

Bildt, C, 'A Second Chance in the Balkans', 80:6 (Jan/Feb 2001) *Foreign Affairs* 148

Bina, M, 'Private Military Contractor Liability and Accountability after Abu Ghraib', 39 (2005) *Marshall Law Review* 1237

Bishop, JW, 'The "Contractual Agreements" with the Federal Republic of Germany', 49 (1955) *AJIL* 125

Bisschop, WR, *The Saar Controversy* (Sweet & Maxwell, 1924)

Bleimaier, JK, 'The Legal Status of the Free City of Danzig 1920–1939: Lessons to Be Derived from the Experience of a Non-State Entity in the International Community', 2 (1989) *Hague Yearbook of International Law* 69

Bloed, A/Wessel, RA (eds), *The Changing Functions of the Western European Union (WEU): Introduction and Basic Documents* (Martinus Nijhoff, 1994)

Blum, Y, 'UN Membership of the "New" Yugoslavia: Continuity or Break?', 86 (1993) *AJIL* 830

Blum, Y, 'Correspondents' Agora: UN Membership of the Former Yugoslavia', 87 (1993) *AJIL* 248

Boisson de Chazournes, L, 'The United Nations on Shifting Sands: About the Rebuilding of Iraq', 5 (2003) *International Law Forum* 254

Bonvin, B, 'Training and Non-security Aspects of the Police Democratisation in Bosnia and Herzegovina', 3 (2003) *Conflict, Security and Development* 417

Boothby, D, 'The Political Challenges of Administering Eastern Slavonia', 10 (2004) *Global Governance* 37

Bose, S, 'The Bosnian State a Decade after Dayton', 12 (2005) *International Peacekeeping* 322

Bothe, M, 'The Peace Process in Eastern Slavonia', 3 (1996) *International Peacekeeping* 6

Bothe, M/Ronzitti, N/Rosas, A (eds), *The OSCE in the Maintenance of Peace and Security: Conflict Prevention, Crisis Management, and Peaceful Settlement of Disputes* (Kluwer Law International, 1997)

Bothe, M, 'Peacekeeping' in B Simma (ed.), *The Charter of the United Nations. A Commentary* (2nd edn, OUP, 2002), 648

Bowen, S (ed.), *Human Rights, Self-Determination and Political Change in the Occupied Palestinian Territories* (Martinus Nijhoff, 1997)

Bowett, D, *United Nations Forces: A Legal Study of United Nations Practice* (Stevens, 1964)

Boyd, SM, 'The Applicability of International Law to the Occupied Territories', 1 (1971) *Israel Yearbook on Human Rights* 258

Boyle, FA, 'The Creation of the State of Palestine', 1 (1990) *EJIL* 301

Braillard, P/Djalili, M-R, *The Third World and International Relations* (Continuum, 1986)

British War Office, *The Law of War on Land, Being Part III of the Manual of Military Law* (HMSO, 1958)

Broms, B, *The United Nations* (Suomalainen Tiedeakatemia, 1990)

Bronson, R, 'When Soldiers Become Cops', 81:6 (Nov/Dec 2002) *Foreign Affairs* 122

Brown, BS, 'Human Rights, Sovereignty and the Final Status of Kosovo', 80 (2005) *Chicago-Kent Law Review* 235

Brownlie, I, 'The United Nations as a Form of Government' in JES Fawcett and R Higgins (eds), *International Organization: Law in Movement* (OUP, 1974)

Brownlie, I, *African Boundaries: A Legal and Diplomatic Encyclopedia* (University of California Press, 1979)

Brus, M, *Third Party Dispute Settlement in an Interdependent World* (Martinus Nijhoff, 1995)

Bull, H, *The Anarchical Society – A Study of Order in World Politics* (Macmillan, 1977)

Burg, SL/Shoup, PS, *The War in Bosnia-Herzegovina: Ethnic Conflict and International Intervention* (M E Sharpe, 1999)

Buss, D, 'Robes, Relics and Rights: The Vatican and the Beijing Conference on Women', 7 (1998) *Social and Legal Studies* 339

Buss, D/Manji, A (eds), *International Law: Modern Feminist Approaches* (Hart Publishing, 2005)

Butler, G, *A Handbook to the League of Nations* (2nd edn, reprint, 1928)

Buzan, B, *From International to World Society? English School Theory and the Social Structure of Globalisation* (CUP, 2004)

Byers, M, *Custom, Power and the Power of Rules* (CUP, 1999)

Byers, M (ed.), *The Role of Law in International Politics: Essays in International Relations and International Law* (OUP, 2001)

Byman, D, 'Five Bad Options for Iraq', 47:1 (2005) *Survival* 7

Caplan, R, 'International Authority and State Building: The Case of Bosnia and Herzegovina', 10 (2004) *Global Governance* 53

Caplan, R, *Europe and the Recognition of New States in Yugoslavia* (CUP, 2005)

Carment, D, 'Anticipating State Failure', in D Carment and A Schnabel (eds), *Conflict Prevention from Rhetoric to Reality – Volume 2: Opportunities and Innovation* (Lexington Books, 2004), 79

Carver, N, 'Is Iraq/Kurdistan a State Such That It Can Be Said to Operate State Systems and Thereby Offer Protection to its "Citizens"?', 14 (2002) *International Journal of Refugee Law* 57

Cassese, A, *International Law* (2nd edn, OUP, 2005)

Cerna, C, 'Universal Democracy: An International Legal Right or a Pipe Dream of the West?', 27 (1995) *NYU Journal of International Law & Politics* 289

Chalmers, D/Hadjiemmanuil, C/Monti, G/Tomkins, A, *European Union Law: Text and Materials* (CUP, 2006)

Chandler, D, 'The People-Centred Approach to Peace Operations: The New UN Agenda', 8:1 (2001) *International Peacekeeping* 1

Chandler, D, 'Imperialism may be out, but aggressive wars and colonial protectorates are back', *The Observer*, 14 April 2002, available at <http://observer.guardian.co.uk/worldview/story/0,,684308,00.html>

Chandler, D, 'Bosnia's new colonial governor', *The Guardian*, 9 July 2002, Comment & Analysis, 16

Chandler, D, 'From Dayton to Europe', 12 (2005) *International Peacekeeping* 336

Charlesworth, H/Chinkin, C/Wright, S, 'Feminist Approaches to International Law', 85 (1991) *AJIL* 613

Charlesworth, H, 'Women as Sherpas: Are Global Summits Useful for Women?', 22 (1996) *Feminist Studies* 537

Charlesworth, H, 'Feminist Methods in International Law', 93 (1999) *AJIL* 379

Charlesworth, H/Chinkin, C, *The Boundaries of International Law: A Feminist Analysis* (Manchester University Press, 2000)

Charlesworth, H, 'International Law: A Discipline of Crisis', 65 (2002) *Modern Law Review* 377

Charlesworth, H/Chinkin, C, 'Editorial Comment: Sex, Gender and September 11', 96 (2002) *AJIL* 600

Chaudhuri, N/Strobel, M (eds), Western *Women and Imperialism: Complicity and Resistance* (Indiana University Press, 1992)

Chaulia, SS, 'UNHCR's Relief, Rehabilitation and Repatriation of Rwandan Refugees in Zaire (1994–1997)', *Journal of Humanitarian Assistance* (8 April 2002), available at <http://www.jha.ac/articles/a086.htm>

Chayes, A/Handler Chayes, A, *The New Sovereignty: Compliance with International Regulatory Agreements* (Harvard University Press, 1995)

Chesterman, S, *Just War or Just Peace?: Humanitarian Intervention and International Law* (OUP, 2001)

Chesterman, S, 'Walking Softly in Afghanistan: the Future of UN State-Building', 44:3 (2002) *Survival* 37

Chesterman, S, 'Tiptoeing through Afghanistan: The Future of UN State-Building', International Peace Academy Report, September 2002, obtainable from <http://www.ipacademy.org/publications>

Chesterman, S, 'Occupation as Liberation: International Humanitarian Law and Regime Change', 18 (2004) *Ethics & International Affairs* 51

Chinkin, C, 'A Gendered Perspective to the Use of Force', 12 (1988–89) *Australian Yearbook of International Law* 279

Chinkin, C, *Third Parties in International Law* (Clarendon Press, 1993)

Chong, D, 'UNTAC in Cambodia: A New Model for Humanitarian Aid in Failed States?', 33 (2002) *Development & Change* 957

Chopra, J, *United Nations Authority in Cambodia* (Thomas J Watson Jr Institute for International Studies, Occasional Paper No. 15, 1994)

Chopra, J/Hohe, T, 'Participatory Intervention', 10 (2004) *Global Governance* 289

Clapham, A, 'State Responsibility, Corporate Responsibility, and Complicity in Human Rights Violations', in L Bomann-Larsen and O Wiggen (eds), *Responsibility in World Business: Managing Harmful Side-Effects of Corporate Activity* (UN University Press, 2004), 50

Clark, RS, 'The "Decolonization" of East Timor and United Nations Norms on Self-Determination and Aggression', 7 (1980) *Yale Journal of World Public Order* 2, reprinted as RS Clark, 'The "Decolonization' of East Timor and United Nations Norms on Self-Determination and Aggression', in *International Law and the Question of East Timor* (Catholic Institute for International Relations/International Platform of Jurists for East Timor, 1995), 65

Classen, CD, ' "Failed States" and the Prohibition of the Use of Force', in Société française pour le droit international (ed.), *Les nouvelles menaces contre la paix et la sécurité internationales – New Threats to International Peace and Security* (Pedone, 2004), 129

Claude, IL, *Swords into Ploughshares – The Problems and Progress of International Organization* (4th edn, Random House, 1971)

Claude, IL, 'The Management of Power in Changing United Nations', in RA Falk, SS Kim, and SH Mendlovitz (eds), *The United Nations and a Just World Order* (Westview, 1991), 143

Cliffe, L, *The Transition to Independence in Namibia* (Lynne Rienner, 1994)

Coicaud, J-M/Heiskanen, V (eds), *The Legitimacy of International Organizations* (UN University Press, 2001)

Colandrea, V, 'On the Power of the European Court of Human Rights to Order Specific Non-monetary Measures: Some Remarks in Light of the *Assanidze, Broniowski* and *Sejdovic Cases*', 7 (2007) *Human Rights Law Review* 396

Collantes Celador, G, 'Police Reform: Peacebuilding Through "Democratic Policing"?', 12 (2005) *International Peacekeeping* 364

Collier, J/Lowe, V, *The Settlement of Disputes in International Law* (OUP, 1999)

Conforti, B, *The Law and Practice of the United Nations* (Kluwer Law International, 1998)

Cook, M/Woollacott, A (eds), *Gendering War Talk* (Princeton University Press, 1993)

Cook, R (ed.), *Human Rights of Women: National and International Perspective* (University of Pennsylvania Press, 1994)

Cooper, R, 'Why we still need empires', *The Observer*, 7 April 2002, available at <http://observer.guardian.co.uk/worldview/story/0,,680117,00.html>

Cooper, SA, 'Air Power and the Coercive Use of Force', 24 (2001) *Washington Quarterly* 81

Corbett, PE, 'What is the League of Nations?', 5 (1924) *BYIL* 119

Cordone, C, 'Bosnia and Herzegovina: The Creeping Protectorate', in Henkin, AH (ed.), *Honoring Human Rights under International Mandates: Lessons from Bosnia, Kosovo and East Timor* (Aspen Institute, 2003), 21

Corten, O/Klein, P, *Droit d'ingérence ou obligation de réaction?* (2nd edn, Bruylant, 1996)

Cousens, EM, 'Making Peace in Bosnia Work', 30 (1997) *Cornell International Law Journal* 789

Cox, M, 'The Dayton Agreement in Bosnia and Herzegovina: A Study in Implementation Strategies', 69 (1999) *BYIL* 201

Craig, P/de Búrca, G (eds), *The Evolution of EU Law* (OUP, 1999)

Craig, P/de Búrca, G, *EU Law, Text, Cases & Materials* (3rd edn, OUP, 2002)

Cramer, C/Goodhand, J, 'Try again, Fail again, Fail better? War, the State, and the Post-Conflict Challenge in Afghanistan', 33 (2002) *Development & Change* 885

Craven, M, 'The European Community Arbitration Commission on Yugoslavia', 66 (1995) *BYIL* 333

Craven, M, 'The Genocide Case, the Law of Treaties and State Succession', 68 (1997) *BYIL* 127

Crawford, J, *The Creation of States in International Law* (OUP, 1979)

Crawford, J, 'The Creation of the State of Palestine: Too Much Too Soon?', 1 (1990) *EJIL* 307

Crawford, J, 'Democracy in International Law', 64 (1993) *BYIL* 113

Crawford, J, 'State Practice and International Law in Relation to Unilateral Secession', Report for the Attorney General of Canada, 19 February 1997, reproduced in A Bayefsky (ed.), *Self-determination in International Law: Quebec and Lessons Learned* (Kluwer, 2000), 31

Crawford, J, *The International Law Commission's Articles on State Responsibility. Introduction, Text and Commentaries* (CUP, 2002)

Crawford, J/Olleson, S, 'The Nature and Forms of International Responsibility', in M Evans (ed.), *International Law* (2nd edn, OUP, 2006), 451

Crawford, J, 'Holding International Organisations and Their Members to Account', Fifth Steinkraus-Cohen International Law Lecture, SOAS, 15 March 2007, lecture notes available at <http://www.lcil.cam.ac.uk/news/article.php?section=25&article=425>

Crawford, TW, 'Pivotal Deterrence and the Kosovo War: Why the Holbrooke Agreement Failed', 116:4 (2001–02) *Political Science Quarterly* 499

Cremona, M, 'The Common Foreign and Security Policy of the European Union and the External Relations Powers of the European Community', ch. 16 in D O'Keeffe and P Twomey (eds), *Legal Issues of the Maastricht Treaty* (Wiley Chancery Law, 1994)

Cremona, M, 'External Relations and External Competence, the Emergence of an Integrated Policy', ch 4 in P Craig and G de Búrca (eds), *The Evolution of EU Law* (OUP, 1999)

Crisp, J, 'A State of Insecurity: The Political Economy of Violence in Refugee-Populated Areas of Kenya', *New Issues in Refugee Research*, Working Paper No. 16, December 1999, available at <http://www.unhcr.org/publ/RESEARCH/3ae6a0c44.pdf>

Crocker, C/Hampson, FO/Aall, P (eds), *Turbulent Peace: The Challenges of Managing International Conflict* (USIP Press, 2001)

Crocker, C, 'Engaging Failing States', 82:5 (Sept/Oct 2003) *Foreign Affairs* 32

Crook, J, 'The 2001 Judicial Activity of the International Court of Justice' (2002) 96 *AJIL* 397

Cross, S/Komnenich, P, 'Ethnonational Identity, Security and the Implosion of Yugoslavia: The Case of Montenegro and the Relationship with Serbia', 33 (2005) *Nationality Papers* 1

Curtin, D/Dekker, I, 'The EU as a 'Layered' International Organization: Institutional Unity in Disguise', in P Craig, P/G de Búrca, *EU Law, Text, Cases & Materials* (2nd edn, OUP, 1998), 83

D'Amato, A, *The Concept of Custom in International Law* (Cornell University Press, 1971)

Daalder, I/Froman, M, 'Dayton's Incomplete Peace', 78:6 (Nov/Dec 1999) *Foreign Affairs* 106

Daalder, I, *Getting to Dayton: The Making of America's Bosnia Policy* (Brookings Institution Press, 2000)

Dallmeyer, DG (ed.), *Reconceiving Reality: Women and International Law* (ASIL, 1993)

Danchin, PG, 'Transitional Justice in Afghanistan: Confronting Violations of International Humanitarian and Human Rights Law', 4 (2001) *Yearbook of International Humanitarian Law* 3

Danilenko, GM, *Law-Making in the International Community* (Martinus Nijhoff, 1993)

Darmanović, S, 'Montenegro: Dilemmas of a Small Republic', 14 (2003) *Journal of Democracy* 145

Das, SM, 'Process Issues: An Argument for Inclusion of Grass-Roots Communities in the Formulation of National and International Initiatives in Rebuilding Afghanistan', *Journal of Humanitarian Assistance* (2 February 2002), 1

Dashwood, A, 'External Relations Provisions of the Amsterdam Treaty', (1998) 35 *Common Market Law Review* 1032

Dashwood, A, 'Implied External Competence of the EC', ch 8 in Koskenniemi, M (ed.), *International Law Aspects of the European Union* (Martinus Nijhoff, 1998)

Dashwood, A, 'States in the European Union', 23 (1998) *European Law Review* 201

Dashwood, A/Hillion, C (eds), *General Law of EC External Relations* (Sweet & Maxwell, 2000)

David Davies Memorial Institute, *International Disputes: The Legal Aspects* (1972)

Dawisha, AI/Dawisha, K, 'How to Build a Democratic Iraq', 82:3 (May/June 2003) *Foreign Affairs* 32

Daws, S/Weiss, T (eds), *The Oxford Handbook on the United Nations* (OUP, 2007)

Day, G/Freeman, G, 'Policekeeping is the Key: Rebuilding the Internal Security Architecture of Postwar Iraq', 79 (2003) *International Affairs* 299

de Nooy, G, (ed.), *Cooperative Security, the OSCE, and its Code of Conduct* (Martinus Nijhoff, 1996)

de Quadros, F, 'Decolonisation of Portuguese Territories', in R Bernhardt (ed.), *Encyclopedia of Public International Law*, vol. 10 (1987), 93

de Reuck, A/Knight, J (eds), *Conflict in Society* (Little, Brown, 1966)

de Rossanet, B, *War and Peace in the Former Yugoslavia* (Kluwer Law International, 1997)

Deiwert B, 'A New Trusteeship for World Peace and Security: Can an Old League of Nations Idea Be Applied to a Twenty-First Century Iraq', 14 (2003–2004) *Indiana International & Comparative Law Review* 771

Denza, E, *The Intergovernmental Pillars of the EU* (OUP, 2002)

Diamond, L, 'Building Democracy After Conflict: Lessons from Iraq', 16 (2005) *Journal of Democracy* 9

Diamond, L, 'Lessons from Iraq', 16 (2005) *Journal of Democracy* 9

Diehl, P, *International Peacekeeping* (Johns Hopkins University Press, 1993)

Dinstein, Y, 'The International Legal Status of the West Bank and the Gaza Strip', 28 (1998) *Israel Yearbook on Human Rights* 37

DiPrizio, RC, *Armed Humanitarians: U.S. Interventions from Northern Iraq to Kosovo* (Johns Hopkins University Press, 2002)

Dobbins, JF/Jones, SG/Crane, K/Rathmell, A/Steele, B/Teltschik, R/Timilsina, A, *The UN's Role in Nation-Building: from the Congo to Iraq* (2003), available at <http://www.rand.org/pubs/monographs/2005/RAND_MG304.pdf>

Dobbins, JF, 'Iraq: Winning the Unwinnable War', 84:1 (Jan/Feb 2005) *Foreign Affairs* 16

Dodge, T, 'A Sovereign Iraq?', 46:3 (2004) *Survival* 39

Dodge, T, 'Iraq's Future: The Aftermath of Regime Change', *Adelphi Paper 372*, April 2005

Donelan, MD/Grieve, MJ, *International Disputes: Case Histories 1945–1970* (Palgrave Macmillan, 1973)

Donini, A/Norah Niland, N/Wermester, K, *Nation-Building Unraveled? Aid, Peace and Justice in Afghanistan* (Kumarian Press, 2004)

Donlon, F, 'The Court of Bosnia and Herzegovina, War Crimes and Organized Crime Chambers and the Registry for War Crimes and Organized Crime', in A Fijalkowski (ed.), *International Institutional Reform, 2005 Hague Joint Conference on Contemporary Issues of International Law* (T.M.C. Asser Press, 2007), 84

Donnelly, J, 'Human Rights: A New Standard of Civilization?', 74:1 (1998) *International Affairs* 1

Dore, I, *The International Mandate System and Namibia* (Westview Press, 1985)

Douglas-Scott, S, *Constitutional Law of the European Union* (Pearson/Longman, 2002)

Doyle, MW, 'Kant, Liberal Legacies and Foreign Affairs', 12 (1983) *Philosophy and Public Affairs* 205 and 323

Doyle, MW, 'Remarks', 89 (1995) *ASIL Proc.* 275

Ducasse-Rogier, M, 'The Operational Role of the OSCE in the Field of Peace-Building: The Case of Bosnia and Herzegovina', in V-Y Ghebali and D Warner (eds), *The Operational Role of the OSCE in Southeastern Europe: Contributing to Regional Stability in the Balkans* (Ashgate Publishing, 2001), 24

Ducasse-Rogier, M, 'Recovering from Dayton: From "Peace-Building" to "State-Building" in Bosnia and Herzegovina', 15 (2004) *Helsinki Monitor* 76

Dugard, J, *The South West Africa/Namibia Dispute: Documents and Scholarly Writings on the Controversy between South Africa and the United Nations* (University of California Press, 1973)

Dugard, J, 'The Revocation of the Mandate for Namibia Revisited', 1 (1985) *South African Journal on Human Rights* 154

Dugard, J, *Recognition and the United Nations* (Grotius Publications, 1987)

Dulles, AW, 'That Was Then: Allen W. Dulles on the Occupation of Germany', 82:6 (Nov/Dec 2003) *Foreign Affairs* 2

Dunlap, B, 'State Failure and the Use of Force in the Age of Global Terror', 27 (2005) *Boston College International & Comparative Law Review* 453

Dupuy, R-J (ed.), *A Handbook on International Organizations* (2nd edn, Kluwer Law International, 1998)

Durch, WJ, 'UN Temporary Executive Authority', in WJ Durch (ed.), *The Evolution of UN Peacekeeping* (St. Martin's Press, 1994), 285

Durch, WJ, 'The UN Operation in the Congo: 1960–1964', in WJ Durch (ed.), *The Evolution of UN Peacekeeping* (St. Martin's Press, 1994), 315

Durch, WJ, 'United Nations Mission for the Referendum in Western Sahara', in WJ Durch (ed.), *The Evolution of UN Peacekeeping* (St. Martin's Press, 1994), 406

Duyvesteyn, I, 'The Concept of Conventional War and Armed Conflict in Collapsed States', in J Angstrom and I Duyvesteyn (eds), *Clausewitz and his Critics Revisited* (Swedish National Defence College, 2003)

Dworkin, G, 'Paternalism', in RA Wasserstrom (ed.), *Morality and the Law* (Wadsworth Publishing Company, 1971), 107

Dzinesa, GA, 'A Comparative Perspective of UN Peacekeeping in Angola and Namibia', 11 (2004) *International Peacekeeping* 644

Eagleton, C, 'International Organization and the Law of Responsibility', 76 (1950) *Recueil des Cours*, vol. I, 319

Eagleton, T, *Ideology: An Introduction* (Verso, 1991)

Eaton, MR, 'Common Foreign and Security Policy', ch. 14 in D O'Keeffe/P Twomey (eds), *Legal Issues of the Maastricht Treaty* (Wiley Chancery Law, 1994)

Economides, S/Taylor, P, 'Former Yugoslavia', ch. 3 in M Berdal/S Economides (eds), *United Nations Interventionism, 1991–2004* (OUP, 2007)

Edwards, G, 'Common Foreign and Security Policy: Incrementalism in Action?' in M Koskenniemi (ed.), *International Law Aspects of the European Union* (Martinus Nijhoff, 1998), 3

Eichelberger, CM, *UN: The First Twenty Years* (Harper & Row, 1965)

Elias, T, *The Modern Law of Treaties* (Oceana Publications, 1974)

Elkins, C, *Imperial Reckoning. The Untold Story of Britain's Gulag in Kenya* (Henry Holt, 2005)

Elliott, PD, 'The East Timor Dispute', 27 (1978) *ICLQ* 238

Emerson, P, 'How a Quota Borda System of Elections may Facilitate Reconciliation', in D Sokolović/F Bieber (eds), *Reconstructing Multiethnic Societies: The Case of Bosnia and Herzegovina* (Ashgate, 2001), 147

Engers, JF, 'The United Nations Travel and Identity Document for Namibians', 65 (1971) *AJIL* 571

Engle, K, 'International Human Rights and Feminism: When Discourses Meet', 13 (1992) *Michigan Journal of International Law* 517

Engle, K, 'Feminism and Its (Dis)contents: Criminalizing War-Time Rape in Bosnia', 99 (2005) *AJIL* 778

Falk, RA/Kim, SS/Mendlovitz, SH (eds), *The United Nations and a Just World Order* (Westview, 1991)

Farmer, A, 'Refugee Responses, State-like Behavior, and Accountability for Human Rights Violations: A Case Study of Sexual Violence in Guinea's Refugee Camps', 9 (2006) *Yale Human Rights and Development Law Journal* 44 (available at http://islandia.law.yale.edu/yhrdlj/)

Farrand, PC, 'Lessons from Brcko: Necessary Components for Future Internationally Supervised Territories', 15 (2001) *Emory International Law Review* 529

Fastenrath, U, 'Article 73', in B Simma (ed.), *The Charter of the United Nations. A Commentary* (2nd edn, OUP, 2002), vol. 2, 1089

Fastenrath, U, 'Article 74', in B Simma (ed.), *The Charter of the United Nations. A Commentary* (2nd edn, OUP, 2002), vol. 2, 1097

Feldman, N, *What We Owe Iraq: War and the Ethics of Nation Building* (Princeton University Press, 2004)

Ferguson, N, *Empire, How Britain Made the Modern World* (Allen Lane, 2003)

Ferguson, N, *Colossus: The Price of America's Empire* (Penguin, 2004)

Finch, GA, 'The Peace Conference of Paris, 1919', 13 (1919) *AJIL* 159

Finch, GA, 'The Treaty of Peace with Germany in the United States Senate', 14 (1920) *AJIL* 155

Findlay, T, *Cambodia: The Legacy and Lessons of UNTAC* (OUP, 1995)

Finnemore, M/Sikkink, K 'International Norm Dynamics and Political Change', 52 (1998) *International Organization* 887

Finnemore, M, 'New Directions, New Collaborations for International Law and International Relations', ch. 17 in T Biersteker, P Spiro, CL Sriram, and V Raffo (eds), *International Law and International Relations: Bridging Theory and Practice* (Routledge, 2006)

Fischer Williams, J, 'The Status of the League of Nations in International Law', in J Fischer Williams (ed.), *Chapters on Current International Law and the League of Nations* (Longmans, Green & Co., 1929), 477

Fitzmaurice, G, 'The Law and Procedure of the International Court of Justice, 1951–4: General Principles and Sources of Law', 30 (1953) *BYIL* 1

Forage, PC, 'Bombs for Peace: A Comparative Study of the Use of Air Power in the Balkans', 28 (2002) *Armed Forces & Society* 211

Forsythe, DP, 'Humanitarian protection: The International Committee of the Red Cross and the United Nations High Commissioner for Refugees', (2001) *IRRC*, vol. 83, issue 843, 675

Fox, G, 'The Right to Political Participation in International Law', 17 (1992) *Yale Journal of International Law* 539

Fox, G/Nolte, G, 'Intolerant Democracies', 36 (1995) *Harvard International Law Journal* 1

Fox, G/Roth, B (eds), *Democratic Governance and International Law* (CUP, 2000)

Fox, G, 'International Law and the Entitlement to Democracy after War', 9 (2003) *Global Governance* 179

Fox, G, 'The Occupation of Iraq', 36 (2005) *Georgetown Journal of International Law* 195

Franck, TM, 'The Stealing of the Sahara', 70 (1976) *AJIL* 694

Franck, TM, *Nation Against Nation: What Happened to the UN Dream and What the US Can Do About It* (OUP, 1985)

Franck, TM, *The Power of Legitimacy among Nations* (OUP, 1990)

Franck, TM, 'Democracy as a Human Right', in L Henkin and J Hargrove (eds), *Human Rights: An Agenda for the Next Century* (ASIL, 1994), 73

Franck, TM, *Recourse to Force, State Action against Threats and Armed Attacks* (CUP, 2002)

Friedman, TL, 'A Way Out of the Middle East Impasse', *New York Times*, 24 August 2001, A19, column 1

Friedman, TL, 'How About Sending NATO Somewhere Important?', *New York Times*, 4 September 2001, A23, column 1

Friedman, TL, 'Pull Up a Chair', *New York Times*, 20 March 2002, A29, column 5

Fukuyama, F, 'The End of History?', 16 (1989) *The National Interest* 3

Fukuyama, F, *The End of History and the Last Man* (Free Press, 1992)

Füredi, F, *The New Ideology of Imperialism: Renewing the Moral Imperative* (Pluto Press, 1994)

Gaeta, P, 'The Dayton Agreements and International Law', 7 (1996) *EJIL* 147

Gaeta, P, 'Is NATO Authorized or Obliged to Arrest Persons Indicted by the International Criminal Tribunal for the Former Yugoslavia?', 9 (1998) *EJIL* 174

Gagnon, G/Macklin, A/Simons, P, *Deconstructing Engagement: Corporate Self-Regulation in Conflict Zones – Implications for Human Rights and Canadian Public Policy*, University of Toronto Public Law Research Paper No. 04–07 (2003), available at <http://ssrn.com/abstract=557002>

Galbraith, P, 'Washington, Erdut and Dayton: Negotiating and Implementing Peace in Croatia and Bosnia and Herzegovina', 30 (1997) *Cornell International Law Journal* 643

Gallagher, T, 'Identity in Flux, Destination Uncertain: Montenegro During and After the Yugoslav Wars', 17 (2003) *International Journal of Politics, Culture and Society* 53

Gannon, K, 'Afghanistan Unbound', 83:3 (May/June 2004) *Foreign Affairs* 35

Gardam, J/Jarvis, M, 'Women and Armed Conflict: The International Response to the Beijing PFA', 32 (2000) *Columbia Human Rights Law Review* 1

Gasser, H-P, 'Protection of the Civilian Population', ch. 5 in D Fleck (ed.), *The Handbook of Humanitarian Law in Armed Conflicts* (OUP, 1995)

Geiger, R, 'The Trusteeship Council', in B Simma (ed.), *The Charter of the United Nations. A Commentary* (2nd edn, OUP, 2002), vol. 2, 1129

Geiss, R, 'Failed States: Legal Aspects and Security Implications', 47 (2005) *German Yearbook of International Law* 457

Gerson, A, 'Trustee Occupant: The Legal Status of Israel's Presence in the West Bank', 14 (1973) *Harvard International Law Journal* 1

Gerson, A, *Israel, the West Bank and International Law* (Frank Cass & Co., 1978)

Ghebali, V-Y/Warner, D (eds), *The Operational Role of the OSCE in Southeastern Europe: Contributing to Regional Stability in the Balkans* (Ashgate, 2001)

Gibson, S, 'Lack of Extraterritorial Jurisdiction over Civilians: A New Look at an Old Problem', 148 (1995) *Military Law Review* 114

Gisvold, G/O'Flaherty, M (eds), *Post-War Protection of Human Rights in Bosnia and Herzegovina* (Brill, 1998)

Glenny, M, *The Fall of Yugoslavia: The Third Balkan War* (3rd edn, Penguin Books, 1996)

Goldmann, M, 'Sierra Leone: African Solutions to African Problems?', 9 (2005) *Max Planck Yearbook of United Nations Law* 457

Goldstein, J/Kahler, M/Keohane, RO/Slaughter, A-M (eds), 'Legalization and World Politics', special issue of *International Organization* (vol. 54 (2000), issue 3), reprinted as, Kahler, M, Keohane, RO, and Slaughter, A-M (eds), *Legalization and World Politics* (MIT Press, 2001)

Goodson, L, 'Afghanistan's Long Road to Reconstruction', 14:1 (2003) *Journal of Democracy* 82

Goodson, L, 'Bullets, Ballots, and Poppies in Afghanistan', 16:1 (2005) *Journal of Democracy* 24

Goodwin-Gill, G/McAdam, J, *The Refugee in International Law* (3rd edn, OUP, 2007)

Gourevitch, A, 'The Unfailing of the State', 58:1 (2004) *Journal of International Affairs* 255

Grant, TD, 'Internationally Guaranteed Constitutive Order: Cyprus and Bosnia as Predicates for a New Nontraditional Actor in the Society of States', 8 (1998) *Journal of Transnational Law & Policy* 1

Grant, TD, 'The Security Council and Iraq: An Incremental Practice', 97 (2003) *AJIL* 823

Gray, C, *Judicial Remedies in International Law* (OUP, 1987)

Gray, C, 'Application of the Convention on the Prevention and Punishment of the Crime of Genocide (Bosnia and Herzegovina v Yugoslavia (Serbia and Montenegro))*, Orders of Provisional Measures of 8 April 1993 and 13 September 1993', 43 (1994) *ICLQ* 704

Gray, C, 'Peacekeeping After the Brahimi Report: Is There a Crisis of Credibility for the UN?', 6 (2001) *Journal of Conflict & Security Law* 267

Gray, C, *International Law and the Use of Force* (2nd edn, OUP, 2004)

Groom, A, 'The Trusteeship Council: A Successful Demise', in P Taylor and A Groom (eds), *The United Nations at the Millennium: The Principal Organs* (Continuum, 2000), 142

Gros, J-G, 'Towards a taxonomy of failed states in the New World Order: Decaying Somalia, Liberia, Rwanda and Haiti', 17 (1996) *Third World Quarterly* 455

Gruss, D, 'UNTEA and West New Guinea', 9 (2005) *Max Planck Yearbook of United Nations Law* 97

Guéhenno, J-M, 'On the Challenges and Achievements of Reforming UN Peace Operations, 9 (2002) *International Peacekeeping* 69

Guillaume, M/Marhic, G/Etienne, G, 'Le cadre juridique de l'action de la KFOR au Kosovo', 1999 *Annuaire Français de Droit International* 308

Gunn, GC, *Timor Loro Sae: 500 Years* (Livros do Oriente, 1999)

Hadzic, M, 'Kosovo and the Security Stabilization of South-East Europe', 7:2 (2000) *International Peacekeeping* 83

Haggenmacher, P, 'La doctrine des deux éléments du droit coutumier dans la pratique de la cour internationale', 90 (1986) *Revue Générale de Droit International Public* 5

Halchin, LE, 'The Coalition Provisional Authority (CPA): Origin, Characteristics, and Institutional Authorities', United States Congressional Research Service Report, 6 June 2005, available at <http://fpc.state.gov/documents/organization/48620.pdf>

Hales, JC, 'The Creation and Application of the Mandate System. (A Study in International Colonial Supervision.)', 25 (1939) *Transactions of the Grotius Society* 185

Hales, JC, 'The Reform and Extension of the Mandate System', 26 (1940) *Transactions of the Grotius Society* 153

Hall, HD, 'The Trusteeship System', 24 (1947) *BYIL* 33

Hall, HD, *Mandates, Dependencies and Trusteeship* (Stevens & Sons, 1948)

Hannikainen, L, 'The Case of East Timor from the perspective of *jus cogens*' in *International Law and the Question of East Timor* (Catholic Institute for International Relations/International Platform of Jurists for East Timor, 1995), 103

Hanset, W, 'A Success Story: The United Nations Transitional Authority for Eastern Slavonia', in Ghebali, V-Y and Warner, D (eds), *The Operational Role of the OSCE in Southeastern Europe: Contributing to Regional Stability in the Balkans* (Ashgate, 2001), 3

Hardt, M/Negri, A, *Empire* (Harvard University Press, 2000)

Harris, DJ/O'Boyle, M/Warbrick, C, *Law of the European Convention of Human Rights* (Butterworths, 1995)

Harris, DJ, *Cases and Materials on International Law* (6th edn, Sweet & Maxwell, 2004)

Harris, JP, 'Kosovo: An Application of the Principle of Self-Determination', 3 (1999) *Human Rights Brief* 28, available at <http://www.wcl.american.edu/hrbrief/v6i3/kosovo.htm>

Harvey, D, *The New Imperialism* (OUP, 2005)

Hathaway, JC, *The Rights of Refugees under International Law* (CUP, 2005)

Heininger, JE, *Peacekeeping in Transition: The United Nations in Cambodia* (Twentieth Century Fund Press, 1994)

Helander, B, 'Who Needs a State? Civilians, Security & Social Services in North-East Somalia', in P Richards (ed.), *No Peace, No War: An Anthropology of Contemporary Armed Conflicts: in Memoriam Bernhard Helander* (Ohio University Press, 2005)

Helton, AC, 'Rescuing the Refugees', 81:2 (March/April 2002) *Foreign Affairs* 71

Helwa, MA/Birch, B, 'The Demography and Housing Conditions of Palestinian Refugees in and Around the Camps in Amman, Jordan', 6 (1993) *Journal of Refugee Studies* 403

Hendry, ID/Wood, MC, *The Legal Status of Berlin* (CUP, 1987)

Herbst, J, 'Responding to State Failure in Africa', 21:3 (1996–97) *International Security* 120

Herman, LL, 'The Legal Status of Namibia and of the United Nations Council for Namibia', 13 (1975) *Canadian Yearbook of International Law* 306

Higgins, R, *The Development of International Law through the Political Organs of the United Nations* (OUP, 1963)

Higgins, R, *United Nations Peacekeeping, Vol. 1, The Middle East 1946–1967* (OUP, 1969)

Higgins, R, *United Nations Peacekeeping, Vol. 2, Asia 1946–1967* (OUP, 1970)

Higgins, R, 'Derogations under Human Rights Treaties', 48 (1976–77) *BYIL* 281

Higgins, R, *United Nations Peacekeeping, Vol. 3, Africa 1946–1967* (OUP, 1980)

Higgins, R, *United Nations Peacekeeping, Vol. 4, Europe 1946–1979* (OUP, 1981)

Higgins, R, 'The New United Nations and former Yugoslavia', 69:3 (1993) *International Affairs* 465

Higgins, R, *Problems and Process: International Law and How We Use It* (OUP, 1994)

Higgins, R, 'Peaceful Settlement of Disputes', 89 (1995) *ASIL Proc.* 293

Higgins, R, 'Second Generation Peacekeeping', 89 (1995) *ASIL Proc.* 275

Hill, N, *International Organization* (Harper, 1952)

Hill, SM/Malik, P, *Peacekeeping and the United Nations* (Ashgate, 1996)

Hille, S, 'Mutual Recognition of Croatia and Serbia (+ Montenegro)', 6 (1995) *EJIL* 598

Hillgruber, C, 'The Admission of New States to the International Community', 9 (1998) *EJIL* 491

Hirsch, M/Housen-Couriel, D/Lapidoth, R, *Whither Jerusalem? Proposals and Petitions Concerning the Future Status of Jerusalem* (Martinus Nijhoff, 1995)

Holbrooke, RC, *To End a War* (Random House, 1998)

Holsti, KJ, 'The Institutions of International Politics: Continuity, Change and Transformation', paper presented at the *Annual General Meeting of the International Studies Association*, New Orleans, 23 – 27 March 2002, available at <www.leeds.ac.uk/polis/englishschool/holsti02.doc>

House, A, *The UN in the Congo: The Political and Civilian Efforts* (University Press of America, 1978)

Howard, LM, 'UN Peace Implementation in Namibia: The Causes of Success', 9 (2002) *International Peacekeeping* 99

Human Rights Watch, 'Looking for Justice: The War Crimes Chamber in Bosnia and Herzegovina', Report, February 2006, available at <http://hrw.org/reports/2006/ij0206/>

Hylton, JS, 'Security Sector Reform: BiH Federation Ministry of the Interior', 9 (2002) *International Peacekeeping* 153

Hyndman, J/Nylund, BV, 'UNHCR and the Status of Prima Facie Refugees in Kenya', 10 (1998) *International Journal of Refugee Law* 21

Hyndman, J, *Managing Displacement: Refugees and the Politics of Humanitarianism* (University of Minnesota Press, 2000)

Ignatieff, M, 'State Failure and Nation-Building', ch. 9 in JL Holzgrefe and RO Keohane (eds), *Humanitarian Intervention: Ethical, Legal and Political Dilemmas* (CUP, 2003)

Imseis, A, 'On the Fourth Geneva Convention and the Occupied Palestinian Territory', 44 (2003) *Harvard International Law Journal* 89

Indyk, M, 'A US-Led Trusteeship for Palestine', *Washington Post*, 29 June 2002, A23

Indyk, M, 'A Trusteeship for Palestine?', 82:3 (May/June 2003) *Foreign Affairs* 51

International Crisis Group, 'Aid and Accountability: Dayton Implementation', ICG Bosnia Report No. 17, 24 November 1996, obtainable from <http://www.crisisgroup.org>

International Crisis Group, 'Is Dayton Failing?: Bosnia Four Years After the Peace Agreement', ICG Europe Report No. 80, 28 October 1999, obtainable from <http://www.crisisgroup.org>

International Crisis Group, 'Reunifying Mostar: Opportunities for Progress', ICG Balkans Report No. 90, 19 April 2000, obtainable from <http://www.crisisgroup.org>

International Crisis Group, 'Building Bridges in Mostar', Europe Report No. 150, 20 November 2003, obtainable from <http://www.crisisgroup.org>

International Law Association, Committee on Formation of Customary (General) International Law, 'Statement of Principles Applicable to the Formation of General Customary International Law', London, 2000, obtainable from <http://www.ila-hq.org/>

International Mission for Iraqi Elections (IMIE), website: <http://www.imie.ca>

International Mission for Iraqi Elections (IMIE), 'Final Report on the December 15, 2005, Iraqi Council of Representatives Elections', 12 April 2006, available at <http://www.imie.ca/pdf/final_report.pdf>

Jackson, JH, 'Sovereignty-Modern: A New Approach to an Outdated Concept', 97 (2003) *AJIL* 782

Jackson, RH/Sørensen, G, *Introduction to International Relations. Theories and Approaches* (3rd edn, OUP, 2006)

Jenkins, S, 'To say we must stay in Iraq to save it from chaos is a lie', *The Guardian*, 21 September 2005, 33

Jennings, RS, 'The Road Ahead: Lessons in Nation Building from Japan, Germany, and Afghanistan for Postwar Iraq', United States Institute of Peace, *Peaceworks No. 49*, April 2003

Jennings, RY, 'Government in Commission', (1946) *BYIL* 112

Johnson, L, 'Remarks' in 'Yugoslavia' Panel, 90 (1996) *ASIL Proc.* 471, 474

Jovanovic, V, 'The Status of the Federal Republic of Yugoslavia in the United Nations', 21 (1998) 21 *Fordham International Law Journal* 1719

Joyner, CC, *The United Nations and International Law* (CUP, 1997)

Judah, T, 'In Iraqi Kurdistan', 44:4 (2002) *Survival* 39

Juma'a Awad, H, 'Leave our country now', *The Guardian*, 18 February 2005, 26

Kaela, LCW, *The Question of Namibia* (Macmillan Press, 1996)

Kaikobad, KH, 'Problems of Belligerent Occupation: The Scope of Powers Exercised by the Coalition Provisional Authority in Iraq, April/May 2003–June 2004', 54 (2003) *ICLQ* 253

Kaldor, M, *New & Old Wars* (2nd edn, Polity Press, 2006)

Kamto, M, 'Le cadre juridique des opérations de maintien de la paix des Nations Unies', 3 (2001) *International Law Forum* 95

Kant, I, 'On the Relationship of Theory to Practice in Political Right' (1792), reproduced in *Kant – Political Writings* (HS Reiss ed., CUP, 1970), 74

Kant, I, *Perpetual Peace: A Philosophical Sketch* (1795), reproduced in *Kant – Political Writings* (HS Reiss ed., CUP, 1970), 93

Karnavas, MG, 'Creating the legal Framework of the Brčko District of Bosnia and Herzegovina, a Model for the Region and other Postconflict Countries', 97 (2003) *AJIL* 111

Karns, MP/Mingst, KA, 'Peacekeeping and the changing role of the United Nations: Four dilemmas', in R Thakur and A Schnabel (eds), *United Nations Peacekeeping Operations: Ad Hoc Missions, Permanent Engagement* (UN University Press, 2001), 215

Kassinger, TW/Williams, DJ, 'Commercial Law Reform Issues in the Reconstruction of Iraq', 33 (2004) *Georgia Journal of International & Comparative Law* 217

Keller, L, 'UNTAC in Cambodia – from Occupation, Civil War and Genocide to Peace', 9 (2005) *Max Planck Yearbook of United Nations Law* 127

Kelly, MJ, 'Transitional Justice in Peace Operations: Shaping the Twilight Zone in Somalia and East Timor', 4 (2001) *Yearbook of International Humanitarian Law* 213

Kelsen, H, 'The Legal Status of Germany According to the Declaration of Berlin', 39 (1945) *AJIL* 518

Kemp, W, *The OSCE in a New Context: European Security towards the Twenty-First Century* (Royal Institute of International Affairs, 1996)

Kennedy, D, 'The Move to Institutions', 8 (1986–7) *Cardozo Law Review* 841

Kennedy, D, 'When Renewal Repeats: Thinking Against the Box', 32 (2000) *NYU Journal of International Law & Politics* 335

Keohane, RO, 'International Institutions: Two Approaches', 32 (1988) *International Studies Quarterly* 379

Kim, J, 'Serbia and Montenegro Union: Prospects and Policy Implications', CRS Report for Congress, updated 2 February 2005

Kinloch-Pichat, S, *A UN Legion: Between Utopia and Reality* (Taylor & Francis, 2004)

Kirgis, F, *International Organizations in their Legal Setting* (2nd edn, West Publishing Co., 1993)

Klabbers, J, *The Concept of Treaty in International Law* (Kluwer Law International, 1996)

Klabbers, J, 'Presumptive Personality: The European Union in International Law', ch. 14 in M Koskenniemi (ed.), *International Law Aspects of the European Union* (Martinus Nijhoff, 1998)

Klabbers, J/Koskenniemi, M/Ribbelink, O/Zimmerman, A (eds), *State Practice Regarding State Succession and Issues of Recognition* (Kluwer Law International, 1999)

Klabbers, J, *An Introduction to International Institutional Law* (CUP, 2002)

Klein, J-P, 'The UN Transitional Administration in Eastern Slavonia (UNTAES)', 97 (2003) *ASIL Proc.* 205

Klug, T, 'An International Protectorate for the West Bank and the Gaza Strip?', May 2003, available at <http://www.opendemocracy.net/content/articles/PDF/1207.pdf>

Knaus, G/Cox, M, 'The "Helsinki Moment" in Southeastern Europe', 16:1 (2005) *Journal of Democracy* 39

Knaus, G/Martin, F, 'Travails of the European Raj', 14:3 (2003) *Journal of Democracy* 60

Knipping, F, (ed.), *The United Nations System and its Predecessors* (2 vols, OUP, 1997)

Kofman, D, 'Self-Determination in a Multiethnic State: Bosnians, Bosniaks, Croats and Serbs', in D Sokolović and F Bieber (eds), *Reconstructing Multiethnic Societies: The Case of Bosnia and Herzegovina* (Ashgate, 2001), 31

Koskenmäki, R, 'Legal Implications Resulting from State Failure in Light of the Case of Somalia', 73 (2004) *Nordic Journal of International Law* 1

Koskenniemi, M (ed.), *International Law Aspects of the European Union* (Martinus Nijhoff, 1998)

Koskenniemi, M, 'International Law Aspects of the Common Foreign and Security Policy', ch. 3 in M Koskenniemi (ed.), *International Law Aspects of the European Union* (Martinus Nijhoff, 1998)

Koutrakos, P, *EU International Relations Law* (Hart, 2006)

Kouvo, S, 'The United Nations and Gender Mainstreaming: Limits and Possibilities', ch. 11 in D Buss and A Manji (eds), *International Law: Modern Feminist Approaches* (Hart Publishing, 2005)

Krasner, S, *Sovereignty: Organized Hypocrisy* (Princeton University Press, 1999)

Krasner, S, 'Problematic Sovereignty', ch. 1 in S Krasner (ed.), *Problematic Sovereignty: Contested Rules and Political Possibilities* (Columbia University Press, 2001)

Krasner, S, 'Governance Failures and Alternatives to Sovereignty', CDDRL Working Paper No. 1 (November 2004), available at <http://iis-db.stanford.edu/pubs/20667/enhanced_sov_krasner_Aug_1_04.pdf>

Krauthammer, C, 'Trusteeship for Somalia; an old colonial idea whose time has come again', *Washington Post*, 9 October 1992

Kreijen, G (ed.), *State, Sovereignty, and International Governance* (OUP, 2002)

Kreijen, G, State Failure, Sovereignty and Effectiveness: Legal Lessons from the Decolonization of Sub-Saharan Africa (Brill, 2004)

Kretzmer, D, *The Occupation of Justice: The Supreme Court of Israel and the Occupied Territories* (SUNY Press, 2002)

Krieger, H (ed.), *The Kosovo Conflict and International Law: An Analytical Documentation 1974–1999* (CUP, 2001)

Kühn, W, 'Zukunft der UN – Friedenseinsätze Lehren aus dem Brahimi Report', (2000) *Bläütter für deutsche und internationale Politik* 1355

Kunz, JL, 'Ending the War with Germany', 46 (1952) *AJIL* 114

Kunz, JL, 'Identity of States under International Law', 48 (1955) *AJIL* 68

Kurtz, S, 'Democratic Imperialism: A Blueprint', Policy Review No. 118 (2003), obtainable from <http://www.policyreview.org>

Kuttner, S, 'Israel and the West Bank: Aspects of the Law of Belligerent Occupation', 7 (1977) *Israel Yearbook on Human Rights* 166

Lacey, M, 'Dadaab Journal – Where Showing Skin Doesn't Sell, a New Style Is a Hit', *New York Times*, 20 March 2006

Langenkamp, RD/Zedalis, RJ, 'What Happens to the Iraqi Oil?: Thoughts on Some Significant, Unexamined International Legal Questions Regarding Occupation of Oil Fields', 14 (2003) *EJIL* 417

Lansing, L, 'Some Legal Questions of the Peace Conference', 13 (1919) *AJIL* 631

Lauterpacht, H, *Recognition in International Law* (CUP, 1947)

Lauterpacht, H, 'The Mandate under International Law in the Covenant of the League of Nations', in H Lauterpacht and E Lauterpacht (eds), *International Law* (CUP, 1970), vol. III, 29

Lawrence, P, 'East Timor', in R Bernhardt, *Encyclopedia of Public International Law*, vol. 12 (1990), 3

Lawson, C, 'How Best to Build Democracy: Laying a Foundation for the New Iraq', 82:4 (July/August 2003) *Foreign Affairs* 206

Lee, R, 'United Nations Peacekeeping: Developments and Prospects' (1995) 28 *Cornell International Law Journal* 619

LeMarquand, DG, *International Rivers: The Politics of Cooperation* (Westwater Research Centre, University of British Columbia, 1977)

Letsas, G, *A Theory of Interpretation of the European Convention of Human Rights* (OUP, 2007)

Lewis, M, 'The Free City of Danzig', 5 (1924) *BYIL* 89

Lijnzaad, L, 'How Not to Be an Occupying Power: Some Reflections on UN Security Council Resolution 1483 and the Contemporary Law of Occupation', in L Lijnzaad, J van Sambeek and B Tahzib-Lie (eds), *Making the Voice of Humanity Heard* (Martinus Nijhoff, 2003), 298

Lischer, SK, *Dangerous Sanctuaries: Refugee Camps, Civil War, and the Dilemmas of Humanitarian Aid* (Cornell University Press, 2005)

Loescher, G/Milner, J, 'The Long Road Home: Protracted Refugee Situations in Africa', 47:2 (2005) *Survival* 153

Lorentzen, LA/Turpin, J (eds), *The Women and War Reader* (NYU Press, 1998)

Ludwig, R, *Letting the People Decide: The Evolution of United Nations Electoral Assistance* (ACUNS, 2001)

Lyon, P, 'The Rise and Fall and Possible Revival of International Trusteeship', 31 (1993) *Journal of Commonwealth & Comparative Politics* 96

Lyons, T/Samatar, AI, *Somalia: State Collapse, Multilateral Intervention, and Strategies for Political Reconstruction* (Brookings Institution, 1995)

Lyons, T, 'Post-conflict Elections and the Process of Demilitarizing Politics: The Role of Electoral Administration', 11:3 (2004) *Democratization* 36

MacGinty, R/Robinson, G, 'Peacekeeping and the Violence in Ethnic Conflict', in R Thakur and A Schnabel (eds), *United Nations Peacekeeping Operations: Ad Hoc Missions, Permanent Engagement* (UN University Press, 2001), 26

Machover, D, 'International Humanitarian Law and the Indonesian Occupation of East Timor', in *International Law and the Question of East Timor* (Catholic Institute for International Relations/International Platform of Jurists for East Timor, 1995), 205

Macleod, I/Hendry, ID/Hyett, S, *The External Relations of the European Communities* (OUP, 1996)

Malanczuk, P, 'Israel: Status, Territory and Occupied Territories', in R Bernhardt (ed.), *Encyclopedia of Public International Law*, vol. II (1995), 1468

Malanczuk, P, 'Some Basic Aspects of the Agreements between Israel and the PLO from the Perspective of International Law', 7 (1996) *EJIL* 485

Malanczuk, P (ed.), *Akehurst's Modern Introduction to International Law* (7th rev. edn, Routledge, 1997)

Mallaby, S, 'The Reluctant Imperialist: Terrorism, Failed States and the Case for American Empire', 81:2 (March/April 2002) *Foreign Affairs* 2

Malone, K, 'Comment: The Rights of Newly Emerging Democratic States Prior to International Recognition and the Serbo-Croatian Conflict', 6 (1992) *Temple International & Comparative Law Journal* 81

Mancini, F, 'Europe: the Case for Statehood', 4:1 (1998) *European Law Journal* 29

Mangone, G, A Short History of International Organization (McGraw-Hill, 1954)

Mann, FA, 'The Present Legal Status of Germany', 1 (1947) *ICLQ* 314, reproduced in FA Mann, *Studies in International Law* (OUP, 1973), 634

Mann, FA, 'Germany's Present Legal Status Revisited', 16 (1967) *ICLQ* 760, reproduced in FA Mann, *Studies in International Law* (OUP, 1973), 660

Manuell, J/Kontić, A, 'Transitional Justice: The Prosecution of War Crimes in Bosnia and Herzegovina under the "Rules of the Road"', 5 (2002) *Yearbook of International Humanitarian Law* 331

March, A/Sil, R, *The 'Republic of Kosova' (1989–1998) and the Resolution of Ethno-separatist Conflict: Rethinking 'Sovereignty' in the Post-Cold War Era* (University of Pennsylvania – Browne Center for International Politics, 1999)

Marek, K, *The Identity and Continuity of States in Public International Law* (2nd edn, Droz, 1968)

Margalith, AM, *The International Mandates* (OUP, 1930)

Marks, S, 'Civil Liberties at the Margin: the UK Derogation and the European Court of Human Rights', 15 (1995) *Oxford Journal of Legal Studies* 69

Marks, S, 'The European Convention on Human Rights and its "Democratic Society"', 66 (1995) *BYIL* 209

Marks, S, 'The End of History? Reflections on Some International Legal Theses', 8 (1997) *EJIL* 449

Marks, S, *The Riddle of All Constitutions: International Law, Democracy and the Critique of Ideology* (OUP, 2000)

Marks, S, 'Big Brother is Bleeping Us – With the Message that Ideology Doesn't Matter', 12 (2001) *EJIL* 109

Marshall, D/Inglis, S, 'The Disempowerment of Human Rights-Based Justice in the United Nations Mission in Kosovo', 16 (2003) *Harvard Human Rights Journal* 95

Marshall Brown, P, 'Editorial Comment: Imperialism', 39 (1945) *AJIL* 84

Marston, G, 'UK Materials on International Law 1982', 53 (1982) *BYIL* 391

Mason, JB, *The Danzig Dilemma* (Stanford University Press, 1946)

Matz, N, 'Civilization and the Mandate System under the League of Nations as Origin of Trusteeship', 9 (2005) *Max Planck Yearbook of United Nations Law* 47

Mazrui, AA, 'Decaying Parts of Africa Need Benign Colonization', International Herald Tribune, 4 August 1994

McBeth, A, 'Privatising Human Rights: What Happens to the State's Human Rights Duties when Services are Privatised?', 5 (2004) *Melbourne Journal of International Law* 133

McCarthy, C, 'The Paradox of the International Law of Military Occupation: Sovereignty and the Reformation of Iraq', 10 (2005) *Journal of Conflict & Security Law* 43

McCoubrey, H/Morris, J, *Regional Peacekeeping in the Post-Cold War Era* (Kluwer Law International, 2000)

McGoldrick, D, *The Human Rights Committee* (Clarendon Press, 1994)

McGoldrick, D, *International Relations Law of the European Union* (Longman, 1997)

McNair, A, *The Law of Treaties* (OUP, 1961)

Médecins Sans Frontières, 'HIV/AIDS & home-based care in western Kenya', August 2004, available at <http://www.msf.org.au/stories/twfeature/2004/053twf.shtml>

Mentan, T, *Dilemmas of Weak States: Africa and Transnational Terrorism in the Twenty-first Century* (Ashgate, 2004)

Meron, T, 'Remarks' in 'Yugoslavia' Panel, 90 (1996) *ASIL Proc.* 471, 483

Merrills, JG, *International Dispute Settlement* (4th edn, CUP, 2005)

Mertus, J/Goldberg, P, 'A Perspective on Women and International Human Rights After the Vienna Declaration: The Inside/Outside Construct', 26 (1994) *International Law and Politics* 201

Michalchuk, DJ, *Minority Rights as Preventive Diplomacy: OSCE-Sponsored Legal Reform and the Prevention of Ethnic Conflict in Post-Communist Countries* (unpublished dissertation, 2000)

Migration, Asylum, Refugees Regional Initiative (MARRI) Project, *Legal and Actual Status of Refugees, Displaced Persons and Returnees to Bosnia and Herzegovina to Access Their Basic Rights* (July 2005), available at <http://www.lex-ngo.org/dokumenti/access_to_rights_en.pdf>

Milano, E, 'Security Council Action in the Balkans: Reviewing the Legality of Kosovo's Territorial Status', 14 (2003) *EJIL* 999

Mill, JS, *On Liberty* (1859) (E Rapaport ed., Hackett, 1978)

Mill, JS, *Considerations on Representative Government* (Parker, Son and Bourn, 1861), 331

Miller, DH, 'The International Regime of Ports, Railways and Waterways' (1919) 13 *AJIL* 669

Mills, G, 'Better with the UN? Searching for Peace and Governance in Iraq', 10 (2004) *Global Governance* 281

Mitrany, D, 'The Functional Approach to World Organization', in RA Falk, SS Kim, and SH Mendlovitz (eds), *The United Nations and a Just World Order* (Westview Press, 1991)

Mohanty, CT/Russo, A/Torres, L (eds), *Third World Women and the Politics of Feminism* (Indiana University Press, 1991)

Monar, J, 'Mostar: Three Lessons for the European Union', 2 (1997) *European Foreign Affairs Review* 1

Morgenstern, F, *Legal Problems of International Organizations* (Grotius Publications, 1986)

Morphet, S, 'UN Peacekeeping and Election Monitoring', in A Roberts and B Kingsbury (eds), *United Nations, Divided World: The UN's Roles in International Relations* (2nd edn, Clarendon Press, 1993)

Morrow, I, 'The International Status of the Free City of Danzig', 18 (1937) *BYIL* 114

Mueller, J, *The Remnants of War* (Cornell University Press, 2004)

Mullerson, R, 'New Developments in the Former USSR and Yugoslavia', 33 (1993) *Virginia Journal of International Law* 299

Mullerson, R, 'The Continuity and Succession of States, by reference to the former USSR and Yugoslavia', 42 (1993) *ICLQ* 473

Murphy, SD, *Humanitarian Intervention: The United Nations in an Evolving World Order* (University of Pennsylvania Press, 1996)

Murray, A, 'Hostages of the empire', *The Guardian*, 1 July 2003, 19

Nakaya, S, 'Women and Gender Equality in Peace Processes: From Women at the Negotiating Table to Postwar Structural Reforms in Guatemala and Somalia', 9 (2003) *Global Governance* 459

Naldi, GJ, 'The Organization of African Unity and the Saharan Arab Democratic Republic', 26 (1982) *Journal of African Law* 152

Narayan U/Harding, S (eds), *Decentering the Center: Philosophy for a Multicultural, Postcolonial and Feminist World* (Indiana University Press, 2000)

Narayan, CVL, *United Nations' trusteeship of non-self-governing-territories* (Imprimeries populaires, 1951)

Naumann, K, 'NATO, Kosovo, and Military Intervention', 8 (2002) *Global Governance* 13

Ni Aolain, F, 'The Fractured Soul of the Dayton Peace Agreement: A Legal Analysis', 19 (1997–8) *Michigan Journal of International Law* 957, reprinted as Ni Aolain, F, 'The Fractured Soul of the Dayton Peace Agreement: A Legal Analysis' in D Sokolović and

F Bieber (eds), *Reconstructing Multiethnic Societies: The Case of Bosnia and Herzegovina* (Ashgate, 2001), 63

North, DC, *Institutions, Institutional Change, and Economic Performance* (CUP, 1990)

Northedge, FS/Donelan, MD, *International Disputes: The Political Aspects* (Europa, 1971)

Norwegian Nobel Committee, Press Release, 'The Nobel Peace Prize 2001', 12 October 2001, obtainable from <http://www.nobel.se/peace/laureates/2001/press.html>

O'Connell, DP, *The Law of State Succession* (CUP, 1956)

O'Connell, DP, 'The Status of Formosa and the Chinese Recognition Problem', 50 (1956) *AJIL* 405

OED Online, at <http://www.oed.com>

O'Keeffe, D/Twomey, P (eds), *Legal Issues of the Maastricht Treaty* (Wiley Chancery Law, 1994)

Oellers-Frahm, K, 'Restructuring Bosnia-Herzegovina: A Model with Pit-Falls', 9 (2005) *Max Planck Yearbook of United Nations Law* 179

Oeter, S, 'Yugoslavia, Dissolution' in R Bernhardt (ed.), *Encyclopedia of Public International Law*, vol. 4 (2000), 1599

Okuizumi, K, 'Peacebuilding Mission: Lessons from the UN Mission in Bosnia and Herzegovina', 24 (2002) *Human Rights Quarterly* 721

Okun, H, 'Introductory Remarks', in 'Yugoslavia' Panel, 90 (1996) *ASIL Proc.* 471

Olivier, S, *The League of Nations and Primitive Peoples* (OUP, 1918)

Oppenheim, L, *International Law*, vol. 1 (3rd edn, Longmans, Green & Co., 1921)

Orakhelashvili, A, 'The Post-War Settlement in Iraq: The UN Security Council Resolution 1483 (2003) and General International Law', 8 (2003) *Journal of Conflict & Security Law* 307

Orford, A, 'Contesting Globalization: A Feminist Perspective on the Future of Human Rights', in BH Weston and SP Marks (eds), *The Future of International Human Rights* (Transnational Publishers, 1999)

Orford, A, 'Muscular Humanitarianism: Reading the Narratives of the New Interventionism', 10 (1999) *EJIL* 679

Orford, A, 'Feminism, Imperialism and the Mission of International Law', 71 (2002) *Nordic Journal of International Law* 275

Osland, KM, 'The EU Police Mission in Bosnia and Herzegovina', 11 (2004) *International Peacekeeping* 544

Österdahl, I, 'Relatively Failed: Troubled Statehood and International Law', 14 (2005) *Finnish Yearbook of International Law* 49

Oswald, B, 'The Creation and Control of Places of Protection during United Nations Peace Operations', (2001) *IRRC*, vol. 83, issue 844, 1031

Otto, D, 'Holding Up Half the Sky, But for Whose Benefit? A Critical Analysis of the Fourth World Conference on Women', 6 (1996) *Australian Feminist Law Journal* 7

Otto, D, 'A Post-Beijing Reflection on the Limitations and Potential of Human Rights Discourse for Women', in KD Askin and DM Koenig (eds), *International Human Rights Law* (Transnational Publishers, 1999), vol. 1, 115

Otto, D, 'A Sign of "Weakness"? Disrupting Gender certainties in the Implementation of Security Council Resolution 1325', 13 (2006) *Michigan Journal of Gender and Law* 113

Ottolenghi, M, 'The Stars and Stripes in Al-Fardos Square: The Implications for the International Law of Belligerent Occupation', 72 (2003–4) *Fordham Law Review* 2177

Owen, D, *Balkan Odyssey* (Victor Gollancz, 1995)

Page Fortna, V, 'United Nations Transition Assistance Group in Namibia', in WJ Durch (ed.), *The Evolution of UN Peacekeeping* (St Martin's Press, 1994), 353

Palwankar, U, 'Applicability of International Humanitarian Law to United Nations Peace-Keeping Forces', (1993) *IRRC*, vol. 30, issue 294, 227

Parker, T, *The Ultimate Intervention: Revitalising the UN Trusteeship Council for the 21st Century* (Sandvika: Norwegian School of Management, 2003)

PeaceWomen – Women's International League for Peace and Freedom, 'Security Council 1325 Monitor', available at <http://www.peacewomen.org/un/sc/1325_Monitor/index.htm>

Pechota, V, *Complementary Structures of Third-Party Settlement of International Disputes* (UNITAR, 1971)

Peck, C, *The United Nations as a Dispute Settlement System: Improving Mechanisms for the Prevention and Resolution of Conflict* (Kluwer Law International, 1996)

Pellet, A, 'The Opinions of the Badinter Arbitration Committee: A Second Breath for the Self-Determination of Peoples', 3 (1992) *EJIL* 178

Pellet, A, 'Can a State Commit a Crime? Definitely, Yes!', 10 (1999) *EJIL* 425

Peou, S, 'Collaborative Human Security? The UN and Other Actors in Cambodia', 12:1 (2005) *International Peacekeeping* 105

Perouse de Montclos, M-A/Mwangi Kagwanja, P, 'Refugee Camps or Cities? The Socio-economic Dynamics of the Dadaab and Kakuma Camps in Northern Kenya', 13:2 (2000) *Journal of Refugees Studies* 205

Pettman, JJ, *Worlding Women: A Feminist International Politics* (Routledge, 1996)

Pfaff, W, 'A New Colonialism? Europe Must Go Back Into Africa', 74:1 (January/February 1995) *Foreign Affairs* 2

Pham, J-P, *Liberia: Portrait of a Failed State* (Reed, 2004)

Philipp, CE, 'Somalia – A Very Special Case', 9 (2005) *Max Planck Yearbook of United Nations Law* 517

Philpott, D, 'Sovereignty: An Introduction and Brief History', 48 (1995) *Journal of International Affairs* 353

Phuong, C, *The International Protection of Internally Displaced Persons* (CUP, 2005)

Pictet, JS (ed.), *The Geneva Conventions of 12 August 1949, Commentary to the IV Geneva Convention Relative to the Protection of Civilian Persons in Time of War* (International Committee of the Red Cross, 1958)

Pilger, J, 'The truths they never tell us', *New Statesman*, 26 November 2001

Playfair, E (ed.), *International Law and the Administration of Occupied Territories* (OUP, 1992)

Plunkett, M, 'Re-Establishing the Rule of Law in Peace Operation: The East Timor Experience', paper delivered at the *15th International Conference of the International Society for the Reform of the Criminal Law*, Canberra, 26–30 August 2001, available at <http://www.jsmp.minihub.org/Reports/Re-Establishing-Plunkett10203.pdf>

Poehlman-Doumbouya, S, 'Women and Peace in United Nations Documents: An Analysis', available at <http://www.peacewomen.org/un/UN1325/analysis.html>

Porter, B, *Empire and Superempire: Britain, America and the World* (Yale University Press, 2006)

Poulton, H, *The Balkans – Minorities and States in Conflict* (Minority Rights Publications, 1994)

Pugh, M, 'Postwar Political Economy in Bosnia and Herzegovina: The Spoils of Peace', 8 (2002) *Global Governance* 467

Pugh, M/Cooper, N (with J Goodhand), *War Economies in a Regional Context: Challenges of Transformation* (IPA/Lynne Rienner, 2004)

Quane, H, 'The UN and the Evolving Right to Self-Determination', 47 (1998) *ICLQ* 537

Quane, H, 'A Right to Self-Determination for the Kosovo Albanians?', 13 (2000) *LJIL* 219

Ragazzi, M, *The Concept of International Obligations Erga Omnes* (OUP, 1997)

Rama Mani, R, 'Beyond Retribution: Seeking Justice in the Shadows of War' (Polity Press, 2002)

Raman, KV (ed.), *Dispute Settlement through the United Nations* (Oceana Publications, 1977)

Ramcharan, B (ed.), *The International Conference on the Former Yugoslavia: Official Papers* (2 vols, Kluwer Law International, 1997)

Ratner, SR, 'The Cambodian Settlement Agreements', 87 (1993) *AJIL* 1

Rauschning, D, 'International Trusteeship System', in B Simma (ed.), *The Charter of the United Nations. A Commentary* (2nd edn, OUP, 2002), vol. 2, 1099

Redgwell, C, *Intergenerational Trusts and Environmental Protection* (Manchester University Press, 1999)

Rehn, E/Johnson Sirleaf, E, *Women, War and Peace: The Independent Experts' Assessment on the Impact of Armed Conflict on Women and Women's Role in Peace-building* (UNIFEM, 2002)

Reilly, B, 'Elections in Post-Conflict Scenarios: Constraints and Dangers', 9 (2002) *International Peacekeeping* 118

Reinisch, A, *International Organizations Before National Courts* (CUP, 2000)

Reisman, WM, *Puerto Rico and the International Process: New Roles in Association* (ASIL/ West Publishing Company, 1974)

Reisman, WM, 'Reflections on State Responsibility for Violations of Explicit Protectorate, Mandate, and Trusteeship Obligations', 10 (1989) *Michigan Journal of International Law* 231

Reisman, WM, 'Sovereignty and Human Rights in Contemporary International Law', 84 (1990) *AJIL* 866

Remacle, E, 'The Co-operation between International Organizations in the Management of the Third Yugoslav War', in V-Y Ghebali and D Warner (eds), *The Operational Role of the OSCE in Southeastern Europe: Contributing to Regional Stability in the Balkans* (Ashgate, 2001), 69

Reus-Smit, C (ed.), *The Politics of International Law* (CUP, 2004)

Reuter, P, *International Institutions* (JM Chapman transl., Allen & Unwin, 1958)

Rich, PB, 'Theories of Globalisation and Sub-state Conflict', in J Angstrom and I Duyvesteyn (eds), *Clausewitz and His Critics Revisited* (Swedish National Defence College, 2003)

Rich, R, 'Recognition of States: The Collapse of Yugoslavia and the Soviet Union', 4 (1993) *EJIL* 36

Richards Hope, J/Griffin, EN, 'The New Iraq: Revising Iraq's Commercial Law is a Necessity for Foreign Direct Investment and the Reconstruction of Iraq's Decimated Economy', 11 (2003–2004) *Cardozo Journal of International & Comparative Law* 876

Ringelheim, J, 'Considerations on the International Reaction to the Kosovo Crisis', (1999) *Revue belge de droit international* 475

Ringelheim, J, 'Lo status giuridico del Kosovo', in F Strazzari, L Rodriguez, G Arcadu, and B Carrai (eds), *La pace intrattabile, Kosovo 1999–2000, una radiografia del dopo bombe* (Asterios, 2000), 120

Ripley, T, *Operation Deliberate Force: The UN and NATO Campaign in Bosnia* (Centre for Defence and International Security Studies (CDISS), 1999)

Roberts, A, 'What is Military Occupation?', 55 (1984) *BYIL* 249

Roberts, A, 'Decline of Illusions: The Status of the Israeli-Occupied Territories over 21 Years', 64 (1988) *International Affairs* 345

Roberts, A, 'Prolonged Military Occupation: The Israeli-Occupied Territories since 1967', 84 (1990) *AJIL* 83

Roberts, A, and Kingsbury, B (eds), *United Nations, Divided World: The UN's Roles in International Relations* (2nd edn, Clarendon Press, 1993)

Roberts, A, 'The End of Occupation: Iraq 2004', 54 (2005) *ICLQ* 27

Roberts, S, *Order and Dispute: An Introduction to Legal Anthropology* (Penguin, 1979)

Roling, BVA, *International Law in an Expanded World* (Djambatan, 1960)

Rosenne, S, *The Law of Treaties: A Guide to the Legislative History of the Vienna Convention* (Oceana, 1970)

Rotberg, RI, 'Failed States in a World of Terror', 81:4 (July/Aug 2002) *Foreign Affairs* 127, reproduced in K Mingst, and J Snyder (eds), *Essential Readings in World Politics* (2nd edn, Norton & Co., 2004)

Rotberg, RI, *State Failure and State Weakness in a Time of Terror* (World Peace Foundation, 2003)

Rotberg, RI (ed.), *When States Fail: Causes and Consequences* (Princeton University Press, 2004)

Roth, BR, *Governmental Illegitimacy in International Law* (OUP, 2001)

Roy, O, 'Development and Political Legitimacy: the Cases of Iraq and Afghanistan', 4 (2004) *Conflict, Security and Development* 167

Rudden, B/Wyatt, D, *Basic Community Laws* (8th edn, OUP, 2002)

Russell, FM, *The International Government of the Saar* (University of California Press, 1926)

Sanderson, J, 'The Cambodian Experience: A Success Story Still?', in R Thakur and A Schnabel (eds), *United Nations Peacekeeping Operations: Ad Hoc Missions, Permanent Engagement* (UN University Press, 2001), 155

Sandoz, Y, 'The Application of Humanitarian Law by the Armed Forces of the United Nations Organization', (1978) *IRRC*, vol. 18, issue 206, 274

Sands, P/Mackenzie, R/Shany, Y (eds), *Manual on International Courts and Tribunals* (Butterworths, 1999)

Sands, P/Klein, P, *Bowett's Law of International Institutions* (5th edn, Sweet & Maxwell, 2001)

Sari, A, 'Status of Forces and Status of Mission Agreements under the ESDP: The EU's Emerging Practice' (*EJIL*, forthcoming 2007/2008, draft on file with the author)

Sarooshi, D, 'Conferrals by States of Powers on International Organizations: The Case of Agency', 74 (2003) *BYIL* 291

Sarooshi, D, *International Organizations and Their Exercise of Sovereign Powers* (OUP, 2005)

Saunders, C/LeRoy, K (eds), *The Rule of Law* (Federation Press, 2003)

Sawyer, A, 'Violent Conflicts and Governance Challenges in West Africa: the Case of the Mano River Basin Area', 42 (2004) *Journal of Modern African Studies* 437

Sayre, F, 'Legal Problems Arising from the United Nations Trusteeship System', 42 (1948) *AJIL* 267

Schachter, O, 'The Development of International Law through the Legal Opinions of the United Nations Secretariat', 25 (1948) *BYIL* 91

Schachter, O, 'State Succession: The Once and Future Law', 33 (1993) *Virginia Journal of International Law* 253

Schama, S, *A History of Britain, Volume 3: The Fate of Empire 1776 – 2000* (Miramax Books, 2002)

Scharf, MP, 'Musical Chairs: The Dissolution of States and Membership of the United Nations', 28 (1995) *Cornell International Law Journal* 29

Scharf, MP, and Williams, PR, 'Report of the Committee of Experts on Nation Rebuilding in Afghanistan', 10 December 2001, 36 (2002) *New England Law Review* 709

Scharf, MP, 'Earned Sovereignty: Juridical Underpinnings', 31 (2002–2003) *Denver Journal of International Law & Policy* 373

Schear, JA, 'Riding the Tiger: the United Nations and Cambodia's Struggle for Peace', in W Durch (ed.), *UN Peacebuilding, American Politics, and the Uncivil Wars of the 1990s* (St. Martin's Press, 1996), 135

Schermers, H/Blokker, N, *International Institutional Law* (3rd edn, Martinus Nijhoff, 1995)

Schiavone, G, *International Organizations: A Dictionary* (4th edn, Palgrave, 1997)

Schindler, D, 'United Nations Forces and International Humanitarian Law', in C Swinarski (ed.), *Studies and Essays on International Humanitarian Law and Red Cross Principles in Honour of Jean Pictet* (ICRC/Martinus Nijhoff, 1984), 521

Schmitt, M, 'Humanitarian Law and Direct Participation in Hostilities by Private Contractors or Civilian Employees', 5 (2005) *Chicago Journal of International Law* 511

Schnabel, A/Thakur, R (eds), *Kosovo and the Challenge of Humanitarian Intervention: Selective Indignation, Collective Action, and International Citizenship* (UN University Press, 2000)

Schnabel, A, 'Post-Conflict Peacebuilding and Second-Generation Preventive Action', 9 (2002) *International Peacekeeping* 7

Schreuer, C, 'The Brčko Final Award of 5 March 1999', 12 (1999) *LJIL* 575

Schreuer, C/Ebner, C, 'Article 100', in B Simma (ed.), *The Charter of the United Nations. A Commentary* (2nd edn, OUP, 2002), vol. 2, 1230

Schwarzenberger, G, 'The Standard of Civilization in International Law', 17 (1955) *Current Legal Problems* 212

Schweisfurth, T, 'Germany, Occupation after World War II', in R Bernhardt (ed.), *Encyclopedia of Public International Law*, vol. 3 (1982), 198

Seibert-Fohr, A, 'Reconstruction through Accountability', 9 (2005) *Max Planck Yearbook of United Nations Law* 555

Sereni, AP, 'Agency in International Law', 34 (1940) *AJIL* 638

Seyersted, F, 'Objective International Personality of Intergovernmental Organizations: Do Their Capacities Really Depend upon the Conventions Establishing Them?', 34 (1964) *Nordisk Tidsskrift for International Ret* 3

Seyersted, F, *United Nations Forces in the Law of Peace and War* (Sijthoff, 1966)

Shamgar, M, 'The Observance of International Law in the Administered Territories', 1 (1971) *Israel Yearbook on Human Rights* 262

Shaw, MN, *International Law* (5th edn, CUP, 2003)

Shehadi, N/Wilmshurst, E, 'The Special Tribunal for Lebanon: The UN on Trial?' (Chatham House Middle East/International Law Briefing Paper, July 2007), available at <http://www.chathamhouse.org.uk/research/international_law/papers/view/-/id/ 512/>

Shelton, D, *Remedies in International Human Rights Law* (2nd edn, OUP, 2005)

Shraga, D, 'The Second Generation UN-based Tribunals: A Diversity of Mixed Jurisdictions', in C Romano, A Nollkaemper, and JK Kleffner (eds), *Internationalized Criminal Courts: Sierra Leone, East Timor, Kosovo, and Cambodia* (OUP, 2004), 15

Siegel, AB, 'Associating Development Projects with Military Operations: Lessons from NATO's First Year in BiH', 8 (2001) *International Peacekeeping* 99

Silber, L/Little, A, *The Death of Yugoslavia* (2nd edn, Penguin and BBC Books, 1996)

Simma, B (ed.), *The Charter of the United Nations. A Commentary* (OUP, 1994)

Simma, B (ed.), *The Charter of the United Nations. A Commentary* (2nd edn, OUP, 2002)

Simmonds, R, *Legal Problems Arising from the United Nations Military Operations in the Congo* (Martinus Nijhoff, 1968)

Simmons, BA/Martin, LL, 'International Organizations and Institutions', ch. 9 in W Carlsnaes, T Risse, and BA Simmons (eds), *Handbook of International Relations* (Sage Publications, 2002)

Simmons, BA/Steinberg, RH (eds), *International Law and International Relations: An International Organization Reader* (OUP, 2007)

Simpson, G, *Great Powers and Outlaw States: Unequal Sovereigns in the International Legal Order* (CUP, 2004)

Sinclair, I, *The Vienna Convention on the Law of Treaties* (2nd edn, Manchester University Press, 1984)

Singer, PW, 'War, Profits, and the Vacuum of Law: Privatized Military Firms and International Law', 45 (2004) *Columbia Journal of Transnational Law* 521

Skubiszewski, K, 'Gdansk and the Dissolution of the Free City' in E Menzel, J Delbrück, K Ipsen, and D Rauschning (eds), *Recht im Dienst des Friedens: Festschrift für Eberhard Menzel zum 65 Geburtstag am 21 Jan 1976* (1975), 470

Slaughter Burley, A-M, 'International Law and International Relations Theory: A Dual Agenda', 87 (1993) *AJIL* 205

Slaughter, A-M/ Tulumello, A/Wood, S, 'International Law and International Relations Theory: A New Generation of Interdisciplinary Scholarship', 92 (1998) *AJIL* 367

Slaughter, A-M, 'International Law and International Relations', 285 (2000) *Recueil des Cours* 9

Slye, R, 'The Dayton Peace Agreement: Constitutionalism and Ethnicity', 21 (1996) *Yale Journal of International Law* 459

Smoljan, J, 'Socio-economic Aspects of Peacebuilding: UNTAES and the Organisation of Employment in Eastern Slavonia', 10 (2003) *International Peacekeeping* 27

Sokolović, D, 'Social Reconstruction and Moral Restoration', in D Sokolović and F Bieber (eds), *Reconstructing Multiethnic Societies: The Case of Bosnia and Herzegovina* (Ashgate, 2001)

Solana, J, 'NATO's Success in Kosovo', 78:6 (Nov/Dec 1999) *Foreign Affairs* 114

Sorel, J-M, 'La responsabilité des Nations Unies dans les opérations de maintien de la paix', 3 (2001) *International Law Forum* 127

Stahn, C, 'The Agreement on Succession Issues of the Former Socialist Federal Republic of Yugoslavia', 96 (2002) *AJIL* 379

Stansfield, GRV, *Iraqi Kurdistan: Political Development and Emergent Democracy* (Routledge, 2003)

Stavrapoulos, C, 'Current Legal Problems of the United Nations', 7 (1973) *International Lawyer* 70

Stedman/S, Rothchild, D/Cousens, EM (eds), *Ending Civil Wars: The Implementation of Peace Agreements* (IPA/Lynne Rienner, 2002)

Steele, J, 'Read the small print', *The Guardian*, 31 March 2003, 18

Steiner, C/Ademovic, N, 'Kompetenzstreitigkeiten im Gefüge von Dayton', in W Vitzthum and I Winkelmann (eds), *Bosnien-Herzegowina im Horizont Europas, Demokratische und föderale Elemente der Staatswerdung in Südosteuropa* (Duncker & Humblot, 2003)

Steiner, H, 'Political Participation as a Human Right', 1 (1988) *Harvard Human Rights Yearbook* 77

Steiner, J/Woods, L/Twigg-Flesner, C, *EU Law* (9th edn, OUP, 2006)

Straw, J, 'Failed and Failing States', speech given at the European Research Institute, University of Birmingham, 6 September 2002, available at <http://www.eri.bham.ac.uk/events/jstraw060902.pdf>

Synnott, H, 'State-Building in Southern Iraq', 47:2 (2005) *Survival* 33

Szasz, P, 'Introductory Note' [to the Dayton Peace Agreements], 35 (1996) *ILM* 75

Szasz, P, 'The Bosnian Constitution: the Road to Dayton and Beyond', 90 (1996) *ASIL Proc* 479

Szasz, P, 'The Dayton Accord: The Balkan Peace Agreement', (1997) *Cornell International Law Journal* 759

Takkenberg, L, 'The Protection of Palestine Refugees in the Territories Occupied by Israel', 3 (1991) *International Journal of Refugee Law* 414

Talmon, S, *Recognition of Governments in International Law with Particular Reference to Governments in Exile* (Clarendon Press, 1998)

Tardy, T, 'The United Nations and Iraq: A Role beyond Expectations, 11 (2004) *International Peacekeeping* 591

Terrett, S, *The Dissolution of Yugoslavia and the Badinter Arbitration Commission: A Contextual Study of Peace-Making Efforts in the Post-Cold War World* (Ashgate, 2000)

Tesón, F, 'The Kantian Theory of International Law', 92 (1992) *Columbia Law Review* 53

Tesón, FR, *Humanitarian Intervention: An Inquiry into Law and Morality* (2nd edn, Transnational Publishers, 1997)

Tesón, F, 'Kantian International Liberalism', in T Nardin and D Mapel (eds), *International Society: Diverse Ethical Perspectives* (Princeton University Press, 1998)

Thakur, R/Newman, E (eds), *New Millennium, New Perspectives: The United Nations, Security, and Governance* (UN University Press, 2000)

Thier, A/Chopra, J, 'Considerations for Political and Institutional Reconstruction in Afghanistan', *Journal of Humanitarian Assistance* (January 2002), available at <http://www.jha.ac/>

Thirlway, H, 'The Sources of International Law', in MD Evans (ed.), *International Law* (2nd edn, OUP, 2006), 115

Thompson, JB, *Ideology and Modern Culture: Critical Social Theory in the Era of Mass Communication* (Stanford University Press, 1990)

Thouvenin, J-M, 'Le statut juridique des forces de maintien de la paix des Nations Unies', 3 (2001) *International Law Forum* 105

Thürer, D, 'The "Failed State" and International Law', (1999) *IRRC*, vol. 81, issue 863, 731

Thürer, D, 'Current challenges to the law of occupation', speech delivered at the *6th Bruges Colloquium*, 20–21 October 2005, available at <http://www.icrc.org/web/eng/siteeng0.nsf/html/occupation-statement-211105?opendocument>

Tomuschat, C, 'The Two Germanies', ch. 13 in Bathurst, ME/Simmonds, KR/March Hunnings, N and Welch, J (eds), *Legal Problems of an Enlarged European Community* (Stevens & Sons, 1972)

Trefon, T, 'The Social Cost of Conflict in the Democratic Republic of Congo', in P Chabal, U Engel, and AM Gentili (eds), *Is Violence Inevitable in Africa?: Theories of Conflict and Approaches to Conflict Prevention* (Brill, 2005)

Trifunovska, S, *Yugoslavia through Documents: From its Creation to its Dissolution* (Martinus Nijhoff, 1994)

Trifunovska, S, *Yugoslavia through Documents: From its Dissolution to the Peace Settlement* (Martinus Nijhoff, 1999)

Turack, D, 'Passports Issued by Some Non-State Entities, 43 (1968–69) *BYIL* 209

Türk, D, 'Recognition of States: A Comment', 4 (1993) *EJIL* 66

Türk, D, 'The Dangers of Failed States and a Failed Peace in the Post Cold War Era', 27 (1995) *NYU Journal of International Law & Politics* 625

UNDP, *United Nations Development Programme Human Development Report – Kosovo 2004. The Rise of the Citizen: Challenges and Choices*, available at <http://hdr.undp.org/docs/reports/national/KOS_Kosovo/Kosovo_2004_en.pdf>

UNIFEM, 'Security Council Resolution 1325 – A Tool Box', available at <http://www.womenwarpeace.org/toolbox/toolbox.htm>

UNIFEM, *Women at the Peace Table: Making a Difference* (United Nations Development Fund for Women, 2000)

UNITAR, *The United Nations and the Maintenance of Peace and Security* (Kluwer, 1987)

United Kingdom Ministry of Defence, *Manual of the Law of Armed Conflict* (OUP, 2004)

United Nations Department of Public Information, *The United Nations and Cambodia 1991–1995* (United Nations Blue Book Series, 1995)

United Nations Department of Public Information, *The Blue Helmets: A Review of United Nations Peacekeeping* (3rd edn, 1996)

United Nations, 'Origin of the United Nations' (undated), available at <http://www.un.org/Overview/origin.html>

United States Department of the Army, *The Law of Land Warfare*, US Army Field Manual, FM 27–10 (US Government Printing Office, 1956)

Unnamed author, 'The New UN Mission in Eastern Slavonia', 3:1 (1996) *International Peacekeeping* 11

Unnamed author, 'Kosovo and Macedonia – Better and Worse', *The Economist*, 17 November 2001, 46

Unnamed author, 'Tony Blair cannot really want to invade Africa', *Sunday Telegraph*, 10 October 2004, 27

US Committee for Refugees, 'Statement Calling for Solutions to End the Warehousing of Refugees', undated (rolling process of endorsement), available at <http://www.refugees.org/uploadedFiles/Investigate/Anti_Warehousing/statement.pdf>

van Aduard, EJL, *Japan, from Surrender to Peace* (Martinus Nijhoff, 1953)

van der Veur, P, 'The UN in West Irian: A Critique', 18 (1963) *International Organization* 53

van Leeuwen, M, 'The Threat of Terrorism: How Do Nations Respond?', in A van Staden, J Rood, and H Labohm (eds), *Cannons and Canons: Clingendael Views of Global and Regional Politics* (Royal van Gorcum, 2003)

Vance, RT, 'Recognition as an Affirmative Step in the Decolonization Process: The Case of Western Sahara', 7 (1980) *Yale Journal of World Public Order* 45

Vandiver, M, 'Reclaiming Kozarac: Accompanying Returning Refugees', in D Sokolović and F Bieber (eds), *Reconstructing Multiethnic Societies: The Case of Bosnia and Herzegovina* (Ashgate, 2001), 167

Various Authors, 'Correspondents' Agora: UN Membership of the Former Yugoslavia', 87 (1993) *AJIL* 240

Various Authors, 'UN Peacekeeping: An Early Reckoning of the Second Generation', 89 (1995) *ASIL Proc.* 275

Various Authors, 'Yugoslavia' Panel, 90 (1996) *ASIL Proc.* 471

Verdirame, G, 'Field Report, Human Rights and Refugees: The Case of Kenya', 12 (1999) *Journal of Refugees Studies* 54

Vincent, J, 'The Factor of Culture in the Global International Order', in *Yearbook of World Affairs 1980*, 34

Vincent, J, 'Race in International Relations', 58 (1982) *International Affairs* 658

Vincent, J 'Racial Equality', in H Bull and A Watson (eds), *The Expansion of International Society* (Clarendon Press, 1984), 239

Vinjamuri, L, 'Order and Justice in Iraq', 45:4 (2003) *Survival* 135

Vité, S, 'L'applicabilité du droit international de l'occupation militaire aux activités des organisations internationales', (2004) *IRRC*, vol. 86, issue 853, 9

von Glahn, G, *Law Among Nations* (5th edn, University of Minnesota Press, 1981)

Vu, NT, 'The Holding of Free and Fair Elections in Cambodia: The Achievement of the United Nations' Impossible Mission', 16 (1995) *Michigan Journal of International Law* 1177

Wambaugh, S, *Plebiscites since the World War* (2 vols, Carnegie Endowment for International Peace, 1933)

Warbrick, C, 'The Recognition of States Part 1', 41 (1992) *ICLQ* 473

Warbrick, C, 'The Recognition of States Part 2', 42 (1993) *ICLQ* 433

Ward, M, 'The Case for International Trusteeship in Haiti', 7 (2006) *Canadian Military Journal* 25, available at <www.journal.forces.gc.ca/engraph/Vol7/no3/PDF/04-ward_e.pdf>

Waters, TW, 'Contemplating Failure and Creating Alternatives in the Balkans: Bosnia's Peoples, Democracy, and the Shape of Self-Determination', 29 (2004) *Yale Journal of International Law* 423

Weeramantry, C, *Nauru: Environmental Damage under International Trusteeship* (OUP, 1992)

Weiler, J, 'Europe: The Case against Statehood', 4 (1998) *European Law Journal* 43

Weiss, TG/Hoffman, PJ, 'Making Humanitarianism Work', in S Chesterman, M Ignatieff, and R Thakur (eds), *Making States Work: State Failure and the Crisis of Governance* (UN University Press, 2005), 296

Weller, M, 'The International Response to the Dissolution of the Socialist Federal Republic of Yugoslavia', 86 (1992) *AJIL* 569

Weller, M, 'International Law and Chaos', 52:1 (1993) *Cambridge Law Journal* 6

Weller, M, 'The Rambouillet Conference on Kosovo', 75:2 (1999) *International Affairs* 211

Weller, M (ed.), *The Crisis in Kosovo 1989–1999: From the Dissolution of Yugoslavia to Rambouillet and the Outbreak of Hostilities* (CUP, 1999)

Wells, HG, '42 to '44: A Contemporary Memoir upon Human Behaviour during the Crisis of the World Revolution* (Secker & Warburg, 1944)

Wetzel, RG/Rauschning, D, *The Vienna Convention on the Law of Treaties: Travaux Préparatoires* (Metzner, 1978)

White, F, *Mandates* (Jonathan Cape, 1926)

White, ND, *Keeping the Peace: The United Nations and the Maintenance of International Peace and Security* (2nd edn, Manchester University Press, 1997)

White, ND, 'Commentary on the Report of the Panel on United Nations Peace Operations (The Brahimi Report)', 6 (2001) *Journal of Conflict & Security Law* 127

White, ND, *The Law of International Organizations* (2nd edn, Manchester University Press, 2005)

Whiteman, M, *Digest of International Law* (US Department of State, 15 vols, 1963–1973)

Wickremasinghe, C, 'Immunities Enjoyed by Officials of States and International Organizations', ch. 13 in MD Evans (ed.), *International Law* (2nd edn, OUP, 2006)

Wilde, R, 'The Skewed Responsibility Narrative of the "Failed States" Concept', 9 (2003) *ILSA Journal of International & Comparative Law* 425

Wilde, R, 'Self-Determination in International Law and the Position of Montenegro', in S Elezovic (ed.), *Legal Aspects for Referendum in Montenegro in the Context of International Law and Practice* (Foundation Open Society Institute, Representative Office Montenegro, 2005), 25, obtainable from <http://www.osim.cg.yu>

Wilde, R, 'The Applicability of International Human Rights Law to the Coalition Provisional Authority (CPA) and Foreign Military Presence in Iraq', 11 (2005) *ILSA Journal of International & Comparative Law* 485

Wilde, R, 'The Trusteeship Council', ch. 8 in S Daws and T Weiss (eds), *The Oxford Handbook on the United Nations* (OUP, 2007)

Williamson, E/Osborn, J, 'A US Perspective on Treaty Succession and Related Issues in the Wake of the Breakup of the USSR and Yugoslavia', 33 (1993) *Virginia Journal of International Law* 261

Williamson, JC, 'Establishing Rule of Law in Post-War Iraq: Rebuilding the Justice System', 33 (2004) *Georgia Journal of International & Comparative Law* 229

Wills, S, 'Military Interventions on Behalf of Vulnerable Populations: The Legal Responsibilities of States and International Organisations Engaged in Peace Support Operations', 9 (2004) *Journal of Conflict & Security Law* 387

Wilson, A, 'The Laws of War in Occupied Territory', 18 (1932) *Transactions of the Grotius Society* 17

Wolf, DL (ed.), *Feminist Dilemmas in Fieldwork* (Westview Press, 1996)

Wolfrum, R, 'Iraq – from Belligerent Occupation to Iraqi Exercise of Sovereignty: Foreign Power versus International Community Interference', 9 (2005) *Max Planck Yearbook of United Nations Law* 1

Wood, M, 'Participation of Former Yugoslav States in the United Nations and in Multilateral Treaties', (1997) *Max Planck Yearbook of United Nations Law* 231

Woodhouse, T/Ramsbotham, O, 'Cosmopolitan Peacekeeping and the Globalization of Security', 12 (2005) *International Peacekeeping* 139

Woodward, S, *Balkan Tragedy: Chaos and Dissolution after the Cold War* (Brookings Institution, 1995)

Woodward, S, 'Remarks' in 'Yugoslavia' Panel, 90 (1996) *ASIL Proc.* 471

Woodward, S, 'Kosovo and the Region: Consequences of the Waiting Game', (2000) *The International Spectator*, No. 1, 35

Woolsey, LH, 'The Leticia Dispute Between Colombia and Peru', 27 (1933) *AJIL* 317

Woolsey, LH, 'The Leticia Dispute Between Colombia and Peru', 29 (1935) *AJIL* 94

Woolsey, TS, 'Peace Conference and Delegates at Paris', 13 (1919) 13 *AJIL* 79

Woolsey, TS, 'Reconstruction and International Law', 13 (1919) *AJIL* 187

Wright, Q, 'The Status of Germany and the Peace Proclamation', 46 (1952) *AJIL* 299

Yannis, A, 'State Collapse and Prospects for Political Reconstruction and Democratic Governance in Somalia', 5 (1997) *African Yearbook of International Law* 23

Yee, S, 'The New Constitution of Bosnia-Hercegovina', 7 (1996) *EJIL* 176

Yoo, J, 'Iraqi Reconstruction and the Law of Occupation', 11 (2004) *UC Davis Journal of International Law &Policy* 7

Young, K, 'UNHCR and ICRC in the former Yugoslavia: Bosnia-Herzegovina', (2001) *IRRC* vol. 83, issue 843, 781

Yusuf, AA, 'Government Collapse and State Continuity: the Case of Somalia', 13 (2003) *Italian Yearbook of International Law* 11

Yuval-Davis, N, *Gender & Nation* (SAGE Publications, 1997)

Zaagman, R, *Conflict prevention in the Baltic States: The OSCE High Commissioner on national minorities in Estonia, Latvia and Lithuania* (European Center for Minority Issues, 1999), available at <http://www.ecmi.de/download/monograph_1.pdf>

Zacarias, A, *The United Nations and International Peacekeeping* (Tauris Academic Studies, 1996)

Zartman, WI, *Collapsed States: The Disintegration and Restoration of Legitimate Authority* (Lynne Reiner, 1995)

Zieck, MYA, *UNHCR's Worldwide Presence in the Field* (Wolf Legal Publishers, 2006)

Zisk Marten, K, 'Defending against Anarchy: From War to Peacekeeping in Afghanistan', 26:1 (2003) *Washington Quarterly* 35

Žižek, S (ed.), *Mapping Ideology* (Verso, 1994)

Zwanenburg, M, 'Existentialism in Iraq: Security Council Resolution 1483 and the Law of Occupation', (2004) *IRRC*, vol. 86, issue 856, 745

Index